Microsoft® Office 2013 IN PRACTICE

word COMPLETE

Randy Nordell
AMERICAN RIVER COLLEGE

Microsoft® Office 2013 IN PRACTICE

word COMPLETE

Nordell

MICROSOFT OFFICE Word 2013 Complete: IN PRACTICE
Published by McGraw-Hill/Irwin, a business unit of The McGraw-Hill Companies, Inc., 1221 Avenue of the Americas, New York, NY, 10020.

Some ancillaries, including electronic and print components, may not be available to customers outside the United States.

This book is printed on acid-free paper.

1 2 3 4 5 6 7 8 9 0 QVS/QVS 1 0 9 8 7 6 5 4 3

ISBN 978-0-07-748690-7
MHID 0-07-748690-0

Senior Vice President, Products & Markets: *Kurt L. Strand*
Vice President, Content Production & Technology Services: *Kimberly Meriwether David*
Director: *Scott Davidson*
Senior Brand Manager: *Wyatt Morris*
Executive Director of Development: *Ann Torbert*
Development Editor II: *Alan Palmer*
Freelance Development Editor: *Erin Mulligan*
Digital Development Editor II: *Kevin White*
Senior Marketing Manager: *Tiffany Russell*
Lead Project Manager: *Rick Hecker*
Buyer II: *Debra R. Sylvester*
Designer: *Jana Singer*
Interior Designer: *Jesi Lazar*
Cover Image: *Corbis Images*
Content Licensing Specialist: *Joanne Mennemeier*
Manager, Digital Production: *Janean A. Utley*
Media Project Manager: *Cathy L. Tepper*
Typeface: *11/13.2 Adobe Caslon Pro*
Compositor: *Laserwords Private Limited*
Printer: *Quad/Graphics*

Library of Congress Cataloging-in-Publication Data

2013002531

www.mhhe.com

dedication

To Kelly. Thank you for your love, support, and encouragement during the seemingly endless hours of writing and editing throughout this project. Your feedback on the content and proofreading were immensely valuable. I could not have done this without you! I'm looking forward to a summer with you without deadlines.

—Randy Nordell

brief contents

contents

OFFICE

WORD

about the author

RANDY NORDELL, Ed.D.

Randy Nordell is a Professor of Business Technology at American River College in Sacramento, California. He has been an educator for over 20 years and has taught at the high school, community college, and university levels. He holds a bachelor's degree in Business Administration from California State University, Stanislaus, a single subject teaching credential from Fresno State University, a master's degree in Education from Fresno Pacific University, and a doctorate in Education from Argosy University. Randy is the author of *Microsoft Office 2013: In Practice* and *Microsoft Outlook 2010*, and he speaks regularly at conferences on the integration of technology into the curriculum. When he is not teaching, he enjoys spending time with his family, cycling, skiing, swimming, and enjoying the California weather and terrain.

preface

What We're About

We wrote *Microsoft Office Word 2013 Complete: In Practice* to meet the diverse needs of both students and instructors. Our approach focuses on presenting Office topics in a logical and structured manner, teaching concepts in a way that reinforces learning with practice projects that are transferrable, relevant, and engaging. Our pedagogy and content are based on the following beliefs.

Students Need to Learn and Practice Transferable Skills

Students must be able to transfer the concepts and skills learned in the text to a variety of projects, not simply follow steps in a textbook. Our material goes beyond the instruction of many texts. In our content, students practice the concepts in a variety of current and relevant projects *and* are able to transfer skills and concepts learned to different projects in the real world. To further increase the transferability of skills learned, this text is integrated with SIMnet so students also practice skills and complete projects in an online environment.

Your Curriculum Drives the Content

The curriculum in the classroom should drive the content of the text, not the other way around. This book is designed to allow instructors and students to cover all the material they need to in order to meet the curriculum requirements of their courses no matter how the courses are structured. *Microsoft Office Word 2013 Complete: In Practice* teaches the marketable skills that are key to student success. McGraw-Hill's Custom Publishing site, **Create**, can further tailor the content material to meet the unique educational needs of any school.

Integrated with Technology

Our text provides a fresh and new approach to an Office applications course. Topics integrate seamlessly with SIMnet with 1:1 content to help students practice and master concepts and skills using SIMnet's interactive learning philosophy. Projects in SIMnet allow students to practice their skills and receive immediate feedback. This integration with SIMnet meets the diverse needs of students and accommodates individual learning styles. Additional textbook resources found on the text's Online Learning Center (**www.mhhe.com/office2013inpractice**) integrate with the learning management systems that are widely used in many online and onsite courses.

Reference Text

In addition to providing students with an abundance of real-life examples and practice projects, we designed this text to be used as a Microsoft Office 2013 reference source. The core material, uncluttered with exercises, focuses on real-world use and application. Our text provides clear step-by-step instructions on how readers can apply the various features available in Microsoft Office in a variety of contexts. At the same time, users have access to a variety of both online (SIMnet) and textbook practice projects to reinforce skills and concepts.

instructor walkthrough

Textbook Learning Approach

Microsoft Office Word 2013 Complete: In Practice uses the *T.I.P.* approach:

- **T**opic
- **I**nstruction
- **P**ractice

Topics

- Each Office application section begins with foundational skills and builds to more complex topics as the text progresses.
- Topics are logically sequenced and grouped by topics.
- Student Learning Outcomes (SLOs) are thoroughly integrated with and mapped to chapter content, projects, end-of-chapter review, and test banks.
- Reports are available within SIMnet for displaying how students have met these Student Learning Outcomes.

Instruction (How To)

- How To guided instructions about chapter topics provide transferable and adaptable instructions.
- Because How To instructions are not locked into single projects, this textbook functions as a reference text, not just a point-and-click textbook.
- Chapter content is aligned 1:1 with SIMnet.

Practice (Pause & Practice and End-of-Chapter Projects)

- Within each chapter, integrated Pause & Practice projects (three to five per chapter) reinforce learning and provide hands-on guided practice.
- In addition to Pause & Practice projects, each chapter has 10 comprehensive and practical practice projects: Guided Projects (three per chapter), Independent Projects (three per chapter), Improve It Project (one per chapter), and Challenge Projects (three per chapter). Additional projects can also be found on **www.mhhe.com/office2013inpractice**.
- Pause & Practice and end-of-chapter projects are complete content-rich projects, not small examples lacking context.
- Select auto-graded projects are available in SIMnet.

Chapter Features

All chapters follow a consistent theme and instructional methodology. Below is an example of chapter structure.

Main headings are organized according to the ***Student Learning Outcomes (SLOs)***.

SLO 1.1 **Creating, Saving, and Opening Documents**

Microsoft Word allows you to create a variety of document types. Your cre edge of Word allow you to create, edit, and customize high-quality and pr documents.

You can create Word documents from a new blank document, from e plates, or from existing documents. Word allows you to save documents in a

Creating and Editing Documents

CHAPTER OVERVIEW

Microsoft Word (Word) has been and continues to be the leading word processing both the personal and business markets. Word improves with each new version and creating and editing personal, business, and educational documents. Word allows ate letters, memos, reports, flyers, brochures, and mailings without a vast amount o knowledge. This chapter covers the basics of creating and editing a Word documen

STUDENT LEARNING OUTCOMES (SLOs)

After completing this chapter, you will be able to:

SLO 1.1 Create, save, and open a Word document (p. W1-3).

SLO 1.2 Customize a document by entering and selecting text, using word wra and using *AutoComplete*, *AutoCorrect*, and *AutoFormat* features (p. W

SLO 1.3 Enhance a document using paragraph breaks, line breaks, spaces, ar non-breaking spaces (p. W1-10).

SLO 1.4 Edit a document using cut, copy, paste, the *Clipboard*, and the undo, and repeat features. (p. W1-14).

SLO 1.5 Customize a document using different fonts, font sizes, and attributes (p. W1-17).

SLO 1.6 Enhance a document using text alignment and line and paragraph spa (p. W1-27).

SLO 1.7 Finalize a document using Word's proofing tools (p. W1-31).

SLO 1.8 Apply custom document properties to a document (p. W1-35).

A list of Student Learning Outcomes begins each chapter. All chapter content, examples, and practice projects are organized according to the chapter SLOs.

CASE STUDY

Throughout this book you have the opportunity to put into practice the application features that you are learning. Each chapter begins with a case study that introduces you to the ***Pause & Practice*** *projects in the chapter. These Pause & Practice projects give you a chance to apply and practice key skills. Each chapter contains three to five Pause & Practice projects.*

Placer Hills Real Estate (PHRE) is a real estate company with regional offices throughout central California. In the Pause & Practice projects in this chapter, you create a business document related to the real estate business. PHRE encourages agents to use standard formats for their business documents. This ensures consistency in document appearance while also allowing agents to personalize their correspondence to customers and colleagues.

The *Case Study* for each chapter is a scenario that establishes the theme for the entire chapter. Chapter content, examples, figures, Pause & Practice projects, SIMnet skills, and projects throughout the chapter are closely related to this case study content. The three to five Pause & Practice projects in each chapter build upon each other and address key case study themes.

How To instructions enhance transferability of skills with concise steps and screen shots.

HOW TO: Open a Document

1. Click the **File** tab to open the *Backstage* view.
2. Click the **Open** button to display the *Open* area on the *Backstage* view.
3. In the *Places* area, select the location where the document is stored.
   - You can click **Recent Documents** and select a document at the right to open it.
   - You can also open a document from *SkyDrive* or *Computer.*
4. Select a folder or click **Browse** to open the *Open* dialog box (Figure 1-5).
5. Select the file and click the **Open** button.

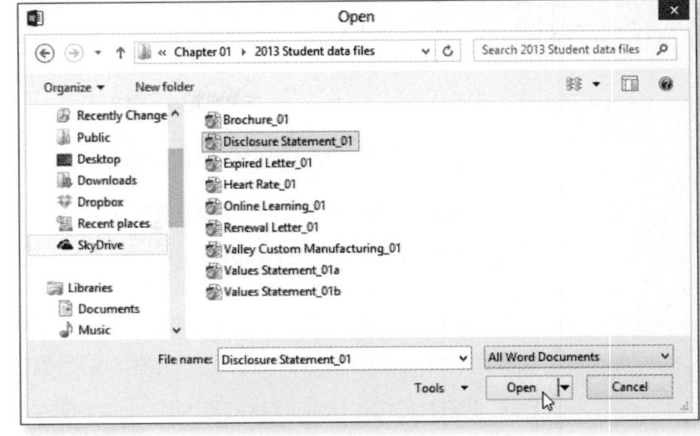

1-5 *Open* dialog box

How To instructions are easy-to-follow concise steps. Screen shots and other figures fully illustrate How To topics.

Students can complete hands-on exercises in either the Office application or in SIMnet.

simbook
1.5 — Changing Fonts, Font Sizes, And Attributes
Word has many features that you can use to customize the appearance of the text within a document. You can change the font and size of font; add styles such as bold, italics, and underlining; change the case of the text; add font and text effects; adjust the scale, spacing, and position of text; and change the default font settings. You can use buttons in the Font group on the Home tab, the Font dialog box, and the mini toolbar to apply formatting to text.
Font and Font Size
There are two main categories of fonts: serif and sans serif. Serif fonts have structural details (flair) at the top and bottom of most of the letters. Some commonly used serif fonts are Cambria, Times New Roman, and Courier New. Sans serif fonts have no structural details on the letters. Commonly used sans serif fonts are Calibri, Arial, and Century Gothic.
Font size is measured in points (pt.); the larger the point, the larger the font. Most documents use between 10 and 12 pt. font sizes. Titles and headings generally are larger font sizes.
another way
show me
guide me
let me try
HOW TO: CHANGE FONT AND FONT SIZE
1. Select the text you want to change.
2. Click the Font drop-down list to display the list of available fonts (Figure 1-27).

Pause & Practice 1-1: Create a business letter in block format with mixed punctuation.

Pause & Practice 1-2: Edit the business letter using copy, paste, and *Format Painter.* Modify the font size, color, style, and effects of selected text

Pause & Practice 1-3: Finalize the business letter by modifying line spacing and paragraph spacing, changing paragraph alignment, translating text, using proofing tools, and adding document properties.

Pause & Practice projects, which each cover two to three of the student learning outcomes in the chapter, provide students with the opportunity to review and practice skills and concepts. Every chapter contains three to five Pause & Practice projects.

MORE INFO

Avoid saving too many different versions of the same document. Rename only when you have a good reason to have multiple versions of a document.

More Info provides readers with additional information about chapter content.

Another Way notations teach alternative methods of accomplishing the same task or feature such as keyboard shortcuts.

Marginal Notations present additional information and alternative methods.

End-of-Chapter Projects

Ten learning projects at the end of each chapter provide additional reinforcement and practice for students. Many of these projects are available in SIMnet for completion and automatic grading.

- ***Guided Projects (three per chapter):*** Guided Projects provide guided step-by-step instructions to apply Office features, skills, and concepts from the chapter. Screen shots guide students through the more challenging tasks. End-of-project screen shots provide a visual of the completed project.
- ***Independent Projects (three per chapter):*** Independent Projects provide students further opportunities to practice and apply skills, instructing students what to do, but not how to do it. These projects allow students to apply previously learned content in a different context.
- ***Improve It Project (one per chapter):*** In these projects, students apply their knowledge and skills to enhance and improve an existing document. Improve It projects are open-ended and allow students to use their critical thinking and creativity to produce attractive professional documents.
- ***Challenge Projects (three per chapter):*** Challenge Projects encourage creativity and critical thinking by integrating Office concepts and features into relevant and engaging projects.

Appendix

- ***Office 2013 Shortcuts:*** Appendix A covers the shortcuts available in Microsoft Office and within each of the specific Office applications. Information is in table format for easy access and reference.

Online Learning Center: www.mhhe.com/office2013inpractice

Students and instructors can find the following resources at the Online Learning Center, **www.mhhe.com/office2013inpractice**

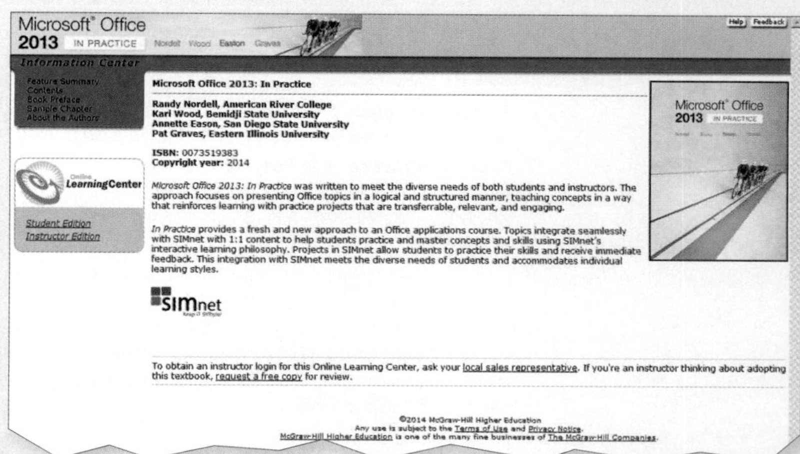

Student Resources

- ***Data Files:*** Files contain start files for all Pause & Practice, Integration, and end-of-chapter projects.
- ***SIMnet Resources:*** Resources provide getting started and informational handouts for instructors and students.
- ***Check for Understanding:*** A combination of multiple choice, fill-in, matching, and short answer questions are available online to assist students in their review of the skills and concepts covered in the chapter.

Integration Projects

- ***Integrating Applications:*** Projects provide students with the opportunity to learn, practice, and transfer skills using multiple Office applications.
- ***Integrating Skills:*** Projects provide students with a comprehensive and integrated review of all of the topics covered in each application (Word, Excel, Access, and PowerPoint). Available in individual application texts.

Appendices

- ***SIMnet User Guide:*** Appendix B introduces students to the SIMnet user interface; content demonstrates how to use SIMnet to complete lessons and projects, take quizzes, and search for specific topics as well as how to create practice exercises.
- ***Office 2013 for Mac Users:*** Appendix C presents instructions for Mac users on how to partition their computer drive to use the PC version of Microsoft Office 2013.
- ***Business Document Formats:*** Appendix D is a guide to regularly used business document formatting and includes numerous examples and detailed instructions.

Instructor Resources

- ***Instructor's Manual:*** An Instructor's Manual provides teaching tips and lecture notes aligned with the PowerPoint presentations for each chapter. The Manual also includes the solutions for online ***Check for Understanding*** questions.
- ***Test Bank:*** The extensive test bank integrates with learning management systems (LMSs) such as Blackboard, WebCT, Desire2Learn, and Moodle.
- ***PowerPoint Presentations:*** PowerPoint presentations for each chapter can be used in onsite course formats for lectures or can be uploaded to LMSs.
- ***SIMnet Resources:*** These resources provide getting started and informational handouts for instructors.
- ***Solution Files:*** Files contain solutions for all Pause & Practice, Integration, Check for Understanding, and End-of-Chapter projects.

acknowledgments

REVIEWERS

We would like to thank the following instructors, whose invaluable insights shaped the development of this series.

Frank Abnet
Baker College

Sven Aelterman
Troy University

Nisheeth Agrawal
Calhoun Community College

Jack Alanen
California State University

Doug Albert
Finger Lakes Community College

Lancie Anthony Alfonso
College of Charleston

Farha Ali
Lander University

Beverly Amer
Northern Arizona University

Penny Amici
Harrisburg Area Community College

Leon Amstutz
Taylor University

Chris Anderson
North Central Michigan College

Wilma Andrews
Virginia Commonwealth University

Mazhar Anik
Owens Community College

M. Hashem Anwari
Nova Community College

Ralph Argiento
Guilford Technical Community College

Karen M. Arlien
Bismarck State College

Gary Armstrong
Shippensburg University

Tom Ashby
Oklahoma City Community College

Laura Atkins
James Madison University

William Ayen
University of Colorado

Abida Awan
Savannah State University

Ijaz Awan
Savannah State University

Tahir Aziz
J. Sargeant Reynolds Community College

Mark Bagley
Northwestern Oklahoma State University

Greg Ballinger
Miami Dade College

David Barnes
Penn State Altoona

Emily Battaglia
United Education Institute

Terry Beachy
Garrett College

Michael Beard
Lamar University—Beaumont

Anita Beecroft
Kwantlen Polytechnic University

Julia Bell
Walters State Community College

Paula Bell
Lock Haven University of Pennsylvania

David Benjamin
Pace University

Shantanu Bhagoji
Monroe College

Sai Bhatia
Riverside City College

Cindy Hauki Blair
West Hills College

Scott Blanchard
Rockford Career College

Ann Blackman
Parkland College

Jessica Blackwelder
Wilmington University

James Boardman
Alfred State College

John Bodden
Trident Technical College

Gary Bond
New Mexico State University

Abigail Bornstein
City College of San Francisco

Gina Bowers
Harrisburg Area Community College

Craig Bradley
Shawnee Community College

Gerlinde Brady
Cabrillo College

Gerald Braun
Xavier University

Janet Bringhurst
Utah State University

Brenda Britt
Fayetteville Technical Community College

Annie Brown
Hawaii Community College

Judith Brown
University of Memphis

Menka Brown
Piedmont Technical College

Shawn Brown
Kentucky Community & Technical College

Sylvia Brown
Midland College

Cliff Brozo
Monroe College

Barbara Buckner
Lee University

Sheryl Starkey Bulloch
Columbia Southern University

Rebecca Bullough
College of Sequoias

Kate Burkes
Northwest Arkansas Community College

Sharon Buss
Hawkeye Community College

Angela Butler
Mississippi Gulf Coast Community College

Lynn Byrd
Delta State University

Carolyn Calicutt
Saint Louis Community College

Anthony Cameron
Fayetteville Technical Community College

Eric Cameron
Passaic County Community College

Michael Carrington
Nova Community College

Debby Carter
Los Angeles Pierce College

Cesar Augustus Casas
St. Thomas Aquinas College

Sharon Casseday
Weatherford College

Mary Ann Cassidy
Westchester Community College

Terri Castillo
New Mexico Military Institute

Diane Caudill
Kentucky Community & Technical College

Emre Celebi
Louisiana State University

Jim Chaffee
The University of Iowa Tippie College of Business

Jayalaxmi Chakravarthy
Monroe Community College

Bob Chambers
Endicott College

Debra Chapman
University of South Alabama

Marg Chauvin
Palm Beach Community College

Stephen Cheskiewicz
Keystone College

Mark Choman
Luzerne County Community College

Kungwen Chu
Purdue University

Carin Chuang
Purdue University—North Central

Tina Cipriano
Gateway Technical College

Angela Clark
University of South Alabama

James Clark
University of Tennessee

Steve Clements
Eastern Oregon University

Sandra Cobb
Kaplan University

Paulette Comet
Community College of Baltimore County

Marc Condos
American River College

Ronald Conway
Bowling Green State University

Margaret Cooksey
Tallahassee Community College

Lennie Cooper
Miami Dade College—North

Michael Copper
Palm Beach State College—Lake Worth

Terri Cossey
University of Arkansas

Shannon Cotnam
Pitt Community College

Missie Cotton
North Central Missouri College

Charles Cowell
Tyler Junior College

Elaine Crable
Xavier University

Grace Credico
Lethbridge Community College

Doug Cross
Clackamas Community College

Kelli Cross
Harrisburg Area Community College

Geoffrey Crosslin
Kalamazoo Valley Community College

Christy Culver
Marion Technical College

Urska Cvek
Louisiana State University

Penny Cypert
Tarrant County College

Janet Czarnecki
Brown Mackie College

Don Danner
San Francisco State University

Michael Danos
Central Virginia Community College

Louise Darcy
Texas A&M University

Tamara Dawson
Southern Nazarene University

JD Davis
Southwestern College

Elaine Day
Johnson & Wales University

Jennifer Day
Sinclair Community College

Ralph De Arazoza
Miami Dade College

Lucy Decaro
College of Sequoias

Chuck Decker
College of the Desert

Corey DeLaplain
Keiser University East Campus

Edward Delean
Nova Community College Alexandria

Darren Denenberg
University of Nevada—Las Vegas

Joy DePover
Minneapolis Community & Technical College

Charles DeSassure
Tarrant County Community College

John Detmer
Del Mar College

Michael Discello
Pittsburgh Technical College

Sallie Dodson
Radford University

Veronica Dooly
Asheville-Buncombe Technical Community College

Gretchen Douglas
State University of New York College—Cortland

Debra Duke
Cleveland State University

Michael Dumdei
Texarkana College

Michael Dunklebarger
Alamance Community College

Maureen Dunn
Penn State University

Robert Dusek
Nova Community College

Barbara Edington
St. Francis College

Margaret Edmunds
Mount Allison University

Annette Edwards
Tennessee Technology Center

Sue Ehrfurth
Aims Community College

Donna Ehrhart
Genesee Community College

Roland Eichelberger
Baylor University

Issam El-Achkar
Hudson County Community College

Glenda Elser
New Mexico State University

Emanuel Emanouilidis
Kean University

Bernice Eng
Brookdale Community College

Joanne Eskola
Brookdale Community College

Mohammed Eyadat
California State University—Dominguez Hills

Nancy Jo Evans
Indiana University—Purdue University Indianapolis

Phil Feinberg
Palomar College

Deb Fells
Mesa Community College

Patrick Fenton
West Valley College

Jean Finley
Asheville-Buncombe Technical Community College

George Fiori
Tri-County Technical College Pendleton

Richard Flores
Citrus College

Kent Foster
Winthrop University

Penny Foster
Anne Arundel Community College

Brian Fox
Santa Fe College

Deborah Franklin
Bryant & Stratton College

Judith Fredrickson
Truckee Meadows Community College

Dan Frise
East Los Angeles College

Michael Fujita
Leeward Community College

Susan Fuschetto
Cerritos College

Janos Fustos
Metropolitan State College—Denver

Samuel Gabay
Zarem Golde Ort Technical Institute

Brian Gall
Berks Technical Institute

Lois Galloway
Danville Community College

Saiid Ganjalizadeh
The Catholic University of America

Lynnette Garetz
Heald College Corporate Office

Kurt Garner
Pitt Community College

Randolph Garvin
Tyler Junior College

Deborah Gaspard
Southeast Community College

Marilyn Gastineau
University of Louisiana

Bob Gehling
Auburn University—Montgomery

Amy Giddens
Central Alabama Community College

Tim Gill
Tyler Junior College

Sheila Gionfriddo
Luzerne County Community College

Mostafa Golbaba
Langston University Tulsa

Kemit Grafton
Oklahoma State University—Oklahoma City

Deb Gross
Ohio State University

Judy Grotefendt
Kilgore College

Debra Giblin
Mitchell Technical Institute

Robin Greene
Walla Walla Community College

Nancy Gromen
Eastern Oregon University

Lewis Hall
Riverside City College

Linnea Hall
Northwest Mississippi Community College

Kevin Halvorson
Ridgewater College

Peggy Hammer
Chemeketa Community College

Patti Hammerle
Indiana University—Purdue University Indianapolis

Dr. Bill Hammerschlag
Brookhaven College

Danielle Hammoud
West Coast University Corporate Office

John Haney
Snead State Community College

Ashley Harrier
Hillsborough Community College

Ranida Harris
Indiana University Southeast

Dorothy Harman
Tarrant County College

Marie Hartlein
Montgomery County Community College

Shohreh Hashemi
University of Houston Downtown

Michael Haugrud
Minnesota State University

Rebecca Hayes
American River College

Terri Helfand
Chaffey College

Julie Heithecker
College of Southern Idaho

Gerry Hensel
University of Central Florida—Orlando

Cindy Herbert
Metropolitan Community College

Jenny Herron
Paris Junior College

Marilyn Hibbert
Salt Lake Community College

Will Hilliker
Monroe County Community College

Ray Hinds
Florida College

Rachel Hinton
Broome Community College

Emily Holliday
Campbell University

Mary-Carole Hollingsworth
Georgia Perimeter College

Terri Holly
Indian River State College

Timothy Holston
Mississippi Valley State University

David Hood
East Central College

Kim Hopkins
Weatherford College

Wayne Horn
Pensacola Junior College

Christine Hovey
Lincoln Land Community College

Derrick Huang
Florida Atlantic University

Susan Hudgins
East Central University

Jeff Huff
Missouri State University—West Plains

Debbie Huffman
North Central Texas College

Michelle Hulett
Missouri State University

Laura Hunt
Tulsa Community College

Bobbie Hyndman
Amarillo College

Jennifer Ivey
Central Carolina Community College

Bill Jaber
Lee University

Sherry Jacob
Jefferson Community College

Yelena Jaffe
Suffolk University

Rhoda James
Citrus Community College

Ted Janicki
Mount Olive College

Jon Jasperson
Texas A&M University

Denise Jefferson
Pitt Community College

John Jemison
Dallas Baptist University

Joe Jernigan
Tarrant County College—NE

Mary Johnson
Mt. San Antonio College

Mary Johnson
Lone Star College

Linda Johnsonius
Murray State University

Robert Johnston
Heald College

Irene Joos
La Roche College

Yih-Yaw Jou
University of Houston—Downtown

Jan Kamholtz
Bryant & Stratton College

Valerie Kasay
Georgia Southern University

James Kasum
University of Wisconsin

Nancy Keane
NHTI Concord Community College

Michael Keele
Three Rivers Community College

Debby Keen
University of Kentucky

Judith Keenan
Salve Regina University

Jan Kehm
Spartanburg Community College

Rick Kendrick
Antonelli College

Annette Kerwin
College of DuPage

Manzurul Khan
College of the Mainland

Julia Khan-Nomee
Pace University

Karen Kidder
Tri-State Business Institute

Hak Joon Kim
Southern Connecticut State University

James Kirby
Community College of Rhode Island

Chuck Kise
Brevard Community College

Paul Koester
Tarrant County College

Kurt Kominek
Northeast State Tech Community College

Diane Kosharek
Madison Area Technical College

Carolyn Kuehne
Utah Valley University

Ruth Kurlandsky
Cazenovia College

John Karnik
Saint Petersburg College

Lana LaBruyere
Mineral Area College

Anita Laird
Schoolcraft College

Charles Lake
Faulkner State Community College

Marjean Lake
LDS Business College

Kin Lam
Medgar Evers College

Jeanette Landin
Empire College

Richard Lanigan
Centura College Online

Nanette Lareau
University of Arkansas Community College Morrilton

David Lee Largent
Ball State University

Linda Lannuzzo
LaGuardia Community College

Robert La Rocca
Keiser University

Dawn D. Laux
Purdue University

Deborah Layton
Eastern Oklahoma State College

Art Lee
Lord Fairfax Community College

Ingyu Lee
Troy University Troy

Kevin Lee
Guilford Technical Community College

Leesa Lee
Western Wyoming College

Thomas Lee
University of Pennsylvania

Jamie Lemley
City College of San Francisco

Linda Lemley
Pensacola State College

Diane Lending
James Madison University

Sherry Lenhart
Terra Community College

Julie Lewis
Baker College—Flint

Sue Lewis
Tarleton State University

Jane Liefert
Middlesex Community College

Renee Lightner
Florida State College

Nancy Lilly
Central Alabama Community College

Mary Locke
Greenville Technical College

Maurie Lockley
University of North Carolina

Haibing Lu
San Diego Mesa College

Frank Lucente
Westmoreland County Community College

Clem Lundie
San Jose City College

Alicia Lundstrom
Drake College of Business

Linda Lynam
Central Missouri State University

Lynne Lyon
Durham Technical Community College

Matthew Macarty
University of New Hampshire

Sherri Mack
Butler County Community College

Heather Madden
Delaware Technical Community College

Susan Mahon
Collin College Plano

Nicki Maines
Mesa Community College

Lynn Mancini
Delaware Technical Community College

Amelia Maretka
Wharton County Junior College

Suzanne Marks
Bellevue Community College

Juan Marquez
Mesa Community College

Carlos Martinez
California State University—Dominguez Hills

Santiago Martinez
Fast Train College

Lindalee Massoud
Mott Community College

Joan Mast
John Wood Community College

Deborah Mathews
J. Sargeant Reynolds Community College

Becky McAfee
Hillsborough Community College

Roberta Mcclure
Lee College

Martha McCreery
Rend Lake College

Sue McCrory
Missouri State University

Brian Mcdaniel
Palo Alto College

Rosie Mcghee
Baton Rouge Community College

Jacob McGinnis
Park University

Mike Mcguire
Triton College

Bruce McLaren
Indiana State University

Bill McMillan
Madonna University

David Mcnair
Mount Wachusett Community College

Gloria Mcteer
Ozarks Technical Community College

Dawn Medlin
Appalachian State University

Peter Meggison
Massasoit Community College

Barbara Meguro
University of Hawaii

Linda Mehlinger
Morgan State University

Gabriele Meiselwitz
Towson University

Joni Meisner
Portland Community College

Dixie Mercer
Kirkwood Community College

Donna Meyer
Antelope Valley College

Mike Michaelson
Palomar College

Michael Mick
Purdue University

Debby Midkiff
Huntington Jr. College of Business

Jenna Miley
Bainbridge College

Dave Miller
Monroe County Community College

Pam Milstead
Bossier Parish Community College

Shayan Mirabi
American Intercontinental University

Johnette Moody
Arkansas Tech University

Christine Moore
College of Charleston

Carmen Morrison
North Central State College

Gary Mosley
Southern Wesleyan University

Tamar Mosley
Meridian Community College

Ed Mulhern
Southwestern College

Carol Mull
Greenville Technical College

Melissa Munoz
Dorsey Business School

Marianne Murphy
North Carolina Central University

Karen Musick
Indiana University—Purdue University Indianapolis

Warner Myntti
Ferris State University

Brent Nabors
Reedley College

Shirley Nagg
Everest Institute

Anozie Nebolisa
Shaw University

Barbara Neequaye
Central Piedmont Community College

Patrick Nedry
Monroe County Community College

Melissa Nemeth
Indiana University—Purdue University Indianapolis

Eloise Newsome
Northern Virginia Community College

Yu-Pa Ng
San Antonio College

Fidelis Ngang
Houston Community College

Doreen Nicholls
Mohawk Valley Community College

Brenda Nickel
Moraine Park Technical College

Brenda Nielsen
Mesa Community College

Phil Nielson
Salt Lake Community College

Suzanne Nordhaus
Lee College

Ronald Norman
Grossmont College

Karen Nunam
Northeast State Technical Community College

Mitchell Ober
Tulsa Community College

Teri Odegard
Edmonds Community College

Michael Brian Ogawa
University of Hawaii

Lois Ann O'Neal
Rogers State University

Stephanie Oprandi
Stark State College of Technology

Marianne Ostrowksky
Luzerne County Community College

Shelley Ota
Leeward Community College

Youcef Oubraham
Hudson County Community College

Paul Overstreet
University of South Alabama

John Panzica
Community College of Rhode Island

Donald Paquet
Community College of Rhode Island

Lucy Parker
California State University—Northridge

Patricia Partyka
Schoolcraft College

James Gordon Patterson
Paradise Valley Community College

Laurie Patterson
University of North Carolina

Joanne Patti
Community College of Philadelphia

Kevin Pauli
University of Nebraska

Kendall Payne
Coffeyville Community College

Deb Peairs
Clark State Community College

Charlene Perez
South Plains College

Lisa Perez
San Joaquin Delta College

Diane Perreault
Tusculum College

Michael Picerno
Baker College

Janet Pickard
Chattanooga State Technical Community College

Walter Pistone
Palomar College

Jeremy Pittman
Coahoma Community College

Morris Pondfield
Towson University

James Powers
University of Southern Indiana

Kathleen Proietti
Northern Essex Community College

Ram Raghuraman
Joliet Jr. College

Patricia Rahmlow
Montgomery County Community College

Robert Renda
Fulton Montgomery Community College
Margaret Reynolds
Mississippi Valley State University
David Richwine
Indian River State College—Central
Terry Rigsby
Hill College
Laura Ringer
Piedmont Technical College
Gwen Rodgers
Southern Nazarene University
Stefan Robila
Montclair State University
Terry Rooker
Germanna Community College
Seyed Roosta
Albany State University
Sandra Roy
Mississippi Gulf Coast Community College—Gautier
Antoon Rufi
Ecpi College of Technology
Wendy Rader
Greenville Technical College
Harold Ramcharan
Shaw University
James Reneau
Shawnee State University
Robert Robertson
Southern Utah University
Cathy Rogers
Laramie County Community College
Harry Reif
James Madison University
Shaunda Roach
Oakwood University
Ruth Robbins
University of Houston—Downtown
Randy Rose
Pensacola State College
Kathy Ruggieri
Lansdale School of Business
Cynthia Rumney
Middle Georgia Technical College
Paige Rutner
Georgia Southern University
Candice Ryder
Colorado State University
Russell Sabadosa
Manchester Community College
Gloria Sabatelli
Butler County Community College
Glenn Sagers
Illinois State University
Phyllis Salsedo
Scottsdale Community College
Dolly Samson
Hawaii Pacific University
Yashu Sanghvi
Cape Fear Community College
Ramona Santamaria
Buffalo State College
Diane Santurri
Johnson & Wales University
Kellie Sartor
Lee College
Allyson Saunders
Weber State University
Theresa Savarese
San Diego City College
Cem Saydam
University of North Carolina
Jill Schaumloeffel
Garrett College
William Schlick
Schoolcraft College
Rory Schlueter
Glendale College
Art Schneider
Portland Community College
Helen Schneider
University of Findlay
Cheryl Schroeder-Thomas
Towson University
Paul Schwager
East Carolina University
Kay Scow
North Hennepin Community College
Karen Sarratt Scott
University of Texas—Arlington
Michael Scroggins
Missouri State University
Janet Sebesy
Cuyahoga Community College Western
Vicky Seehusen
Metropolitan State College Denver
Paul Seibert
North Greenville University
Pat Serrano
Scottsdale Community College
Patricia Sessions
Chemeketa Community College
Judy Settle
Central Georgia Technical College
Vivek Shah
Texas State University
Abul Sheikh
Abraham Baldwin Agricultural College
Lal Shimpi
Saint Augustine's College
Lana Shryock
Monroe County Community College
Joanne Shurbert
NHTI Concord Community College
Sheila Sicilia
Onondaga Community College
Pam Silvers
Asheville-Buncombe Technical Community College
Eithel Simpson
Southwestern Oklahoma State University
Beth Sindt
Hawkeye Community College
Mary Jo Slater
College of Beaver County
Diane Smith
Henry Ford College
Kristi Smith
Allegany College of Maryland
Nadine Smith
Keiser University
Thomas Michael Smith
Austin Community College
Anita Soliz
Palo Alto College
Don Southwell
Delta College
Mimi Spain
Southern Maine Community College
Sri' V. Sridharan
Clemson University
Diane Stark
Phoenix College
Jason Steagall
Bryant & Stratton College
Linda Stoudemayer
Lamar Institute of Technology
Nate Stout
University of Oklahoma
Lynne Stuhr
Trident Technical College
Song Su
East Los Angeles College
Bala Subramanian
Kean University
Liang Sui
Daytona State College
Denise Sullivan
Westchester Community College
Frank Sun
Lamar University
Beverly Swisshelm
Cumberland University
Cheryl Sypniewski
Macomb Community College
Martin Schedlbauer
Suffolk University
Lo-An Tabar-Gaul
Mesa Community College
Kathleen Tamerlano
Cuyahoga Community College
Margaret Taylor
College of Southern Nevada
Sandra Thomas
Troy University
Joyce Thompson
Lehigh Carbon Community College
Jay Tidwell
Blue Ridge Community and Technical College
Astrid Todd
Guilford Technical Community College
Byron Todd
Tallahassee Community College
Kim Tollett
Eastern Oklahoma State College
Joe Torok
Bryant & Stratton College
Tom Trevethan
Ecpi College of Technology
David Trimble
Park University
Charulata Trivedi
Quinsigamond Community College
Alicia Tyson-Sherwood
Post University
Angela Unruh
Central Washington University
Patricia Vacca
El Camino College
Sue van Boven
Paradise Valley Community College
Scott Van Selow
Edison College—Fort Myers
Linda Kavanaugh Varga
Robert Morris University
Kathleen Villarreal
Apollo University of Phoenix
Asteria Villegas
Monroe Community College
Michelle Vlaich-Lee
Greenville Technical College
Carol Walden
Mississippi Delta Community College
Dennis Walpole
University of South Florida
Merrill Warkentin
Mississippi State University
Jerry Waxman
The City University of New York, Queens College
Sharon Wavle
Tompkins Cortland Community College
Rebecca Webb
Northwest Arkansas Community College
Sandy Weber
Gateway Technical College
Robin Weitz
Ocean County College
Karen Welch
Tennessee Technology Center
Marcia Welch
Highline Community College
Lynne Weldon
Aiken Tech College
Jerry Wendling
Iowa Western Community College
Bradley West
Sinclair Community College
Stu Westin
University of Rhode Island
Billie Jo Whary
McCann School of Business & Technology
Charles Whealton
Delaware Technical Community College
Melinda White
Seminole State College
Reginald White
Black Hawk College
Lissa Whyte-Morazan
Brookline College
Sophia Wilberscheid
Indian River State College
Casey Wilhelm
North Idaho College
Amy Williams
Abraham Baldwin Agricultural College
Jackie Williams
University of North Alabama
Melanie Williamson
Bluegrass Community & Technical College
Jan Wilms
Union University
Rhonda Wilson
Connors State College
Diana Wolfe
Oklahoma State University—Oklahoma City
Veryl Wolfe
Clarion University of Pennsylvania
Paula Worthington
Northern Virginia Community College
Dezhi Wu
Southern Utah University
Judy Wynekoop
Florida Gulf Coast University
Kevin Wyzkiewicz
Delta College
Catherine Yager
Pima Community College
Paul Yaroslaski
Dodge City Community College
Annette Yauney
Herkimer County Community College
Yuqiu You
Morehead State University
Bahram Zartoshty
California State University—Northridge
Suzann Zeger
William Rainey Harper College
Steven Zeltmann
University of Central Arkansas
Cherie Zieleniewski
University of Cincinnati—Batavia
Mary Ann Zlotow
College of DuPage
Laurie Zouharis
Suffolk College
Matthew Zullo
Wake Technical Community College

TECHNICAL EDITORS

Chris Anderson
North Central Michigan College
Susan Fuschetto
Cerritos College
Mary Carole Hollingsworth
Georgia Perimeter College
Sandy Keeter
Seminole State College of Florida
Melinda White
Seminole State College of Florida
Rhoda James
Citrus College
Vicky Seehusen
Metropolitan State College Denver
Beverly Swisshelm
Cumberland University

Thank you to the wonderful team at McGraw-Hill for your confidence in me and support on this first edition. Paul, Alan, Erin, Wyatt, Tiffany, Rick, and Julianna, I thoroughly enjoy working with you all! Thank you also to Debbie Hinkle, Michael-Brian Ogawa, Laurie Zouharis, Amie Mayhall, Sarah Clifford, Jeanne Reed, Lyn Belisle, and all of the reviewers and technical editors for your expertise and invaluable insight, which helped shape this book.

—Randy

CHAPTER 1

Windows 8 and Office 2013 Overview

OFFICE 2013

CHAPTER OVERVIEW

Microsoft Office 2013 and Windows 8 introduce many new features including cloud storage for your files, Office file sharing, and enhanced online content. The integration of Office 2013 and Windows 8 means that files are more portable and accessible than ever when you use *SkyDrive*, Microsoft's free online cloud storage. The new user interface on Office 2013 and Windows 8 allows you to work on tablet computers and smart phones in a working environment that resembles that of your desktop or laptop computer.

STUDENT LEARNING OUTCOMES (SLOs)

After completing this chapter, you will be able to:

- SLO 1.1 Use the basic features of Windows 8 and Microsoft Office 2013 products (p. O1-2).
- SLO 1.2 Create, save, close, and open Office files (p. O1-12).
- SLO 1.3 Print, share, and customize Office files (p. O1-20).
- SLO 1.4 Use the *Ribbon*, tabs, groups, dialog boxes, task panes, galleries, and the *Quick Access* toolbar (p. O1-23).
- SLO 1.5 Use context menus, mini toolbars, and keyboard shortcuts in Office applications (p. O1-27).
- SLO 1.6 Customize the view and display size in Office applications and work with multiple Office files (p. O1-31).
- SLO 1.7 Organize and customize Office files and Windows folders (p. O1-34).

CASE STUDY

American River Cycling Club (ARCC) is a community cycling club that promotes fitness. ARCC members include recreational cyclists who enjoy the exercise and camaraderie and competitive cyclists who compete in road, mountain, and cyclocross races throughout the cycling season.

In the Pause & Practice projects, you incorporate many of the topics covered in the chapter to create, save, customize, and share Office 2013 files.

Pause & Practice 1-1: Log into Windows using your Microsoft account, customize the Windows *Start* page, open Office files, create a new file, open and rename an existing file, and share a file.

Pause & Practice 1-2: Modify an existing document, add document properties, customize the *Quick Access* toolbar, export a file as a PDF file, and share a document by sending a link.

Pause & Practice 1-3: Modify the working environment in Office and organize files and folders.

SLO 1.1

Using Windows 8 and Office 2013

Windows 8 is the ***operating system*** that makes your computer function and controls the working environment. The Office 2013 software provides you with common application programs such as Word, Excel, Access, and PowerPoint. These applications give you the ability to work with word processing documents, spreadsheets, presentations, and databases in your personal and business projects. Although the Windows 8 operating system and the Office software products work together, they have different functions on your computer.

Windows 8

The operating system on your computer makes all of the other software programs, including Office 2013, function. ***Windows 8*** has a new user interface—the new ***Start page***—where you can select and open a program. Alternatively you can go to the ***Windows desktop***, which has the familiar look of previous versions of Windows. You also have the option with Windows 8 to log in to your computer using a Windows account that synchronizes your Windows, Office, and ***SkyDrive*** cloud storage between computers.

Microsoft Account

In Windows 8 and Office 2013, your files and account settings are portable. In other words, your Office settings and files can travel with you and be accessed from different computers. You are not restricted to a single computer. When you create a free ***Microsoft account*** (Live, Hotmail, MSN, Messenger, or other Microsoft service account), you are given a free email account, a *SkyDrive* account, and access to Office Web Apps. If you do not yet have a Microsoft account, you can create one at www.live.com (Figure 1-1).

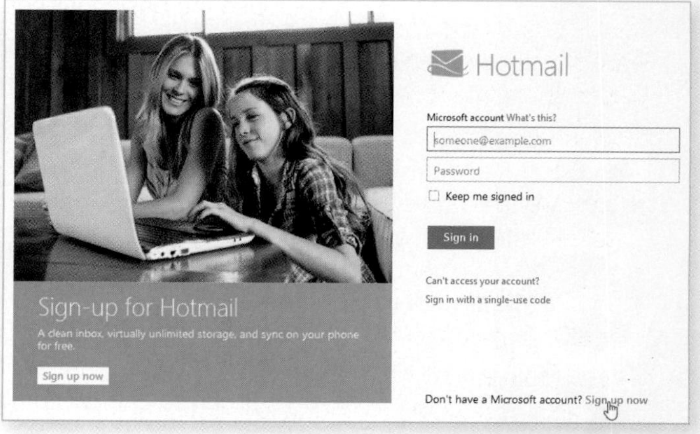

1-1 Create a Microsoft account

> **MORE INFO**
>
> You will use your Microsoft account for projects in this text.

When you sign in to your computer using Windows 8, you can log in with your Microsoft username and password. Windows uses this information to transfer your Office 2013 settings to the computer you are using and connects you to your ***SkyDrive*** folder.

Start Page

After logging in to Windows 8 using your Microsoft account (see *Pause & Practice: Office 1-1*, Step 1 on page 01–17), you are taken to the ***Start page*** (Figure 1-2), which is new to Windows 8. The *Start* page displays different ***apps*** (applications) as tiles (large and small buttons). Click an app tile to launch a program or task.

Windows 8 uses the term *apps* generically to refer to applications and programs. Apps include the Windows 8 Weather app, Microsoft Excel program, Control Panel, Google Chrome, or File Explorer.

When you start using Windows 8, you can customize your *Start* page. Include the apps you most regularly use, remove the apps you don't want displayed on the *Start* page, and rearrange apps tiles to your preference.

1-2 Windows *Start* page

HOW TO: Customize the Start Page

1. To move an app tile, click and drag the app tile to a new location on the *Start* page. The other app tiles shuffle to accommodate the placement of the app tile.
2. To remove an app tile from the *Start* page, right-click the app tile you want to remove to select it and display your options, and then select **Unpin from Start** (Figure 1-3).
   - When an app tile is selected, a check mark appears in the upper right corner.
   - The app tile is removed from the *Start* page, but the program or task is not removed from your computer.
   - Your options differ depending on the app tile you select.
   - You can right-click multiple app tiles, one after the other, to select and apply an option to all of them.
3. To add an app tile to the *Start* page, right-click a blank area of the *Start* page and click **All Apps** at the bottom right (Figure 1-4).
4. Right-click the app you want to add to select it and click **Pin to Start** (Figure 1-5).
5. To resize an app tile, right-click the app tile to select it and click **Larger** or **Smaller**.
   - All options do not apply to all apps.
6. To uninstall an app, right-click the app you want to uninstall to select it and click **Uninstall**.
   - Unlike the unpin option, this option uninstalls the program from your computer, not just your *Start* page.

1-3 App options

1-4 Display all apps

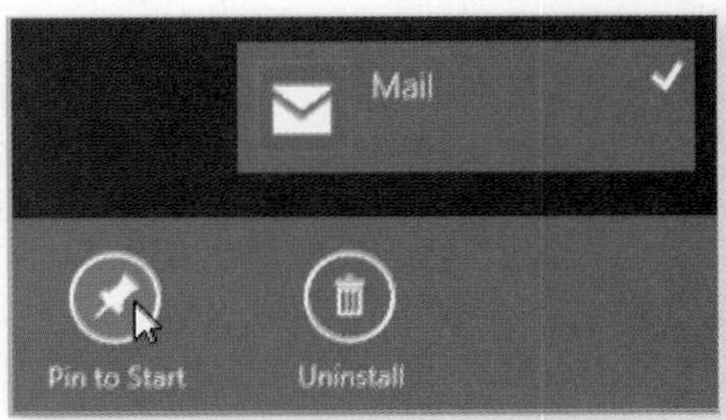

1-5 Pin selected app to *Start* page

Windows 8 Navigation Options

You can access the Windows 8 options and navigate quickly to other areas from the *Start* page, the Windows desktop, or anywhere on your computer. The ***Windows 8 navigation area*** and options appear on the right side of your computer monitor when you place your pointer on the small horizontal line at the bottom right corner (Figure 1-6). The following list describes the different options available from the navigation area:

- ***Search:*** Displays all of the apps available on your computer and opens a search area at the right of your screen.
- ***Share:*** Displays options for sharing selected apps with other users.
- ***Start:*** Displays the *Start* page.
- ***Devices:*** Displays the devices available on your computer.
- ***Settings:*** Displays options for customizing computer settings; displays power options (Figure 1-7).

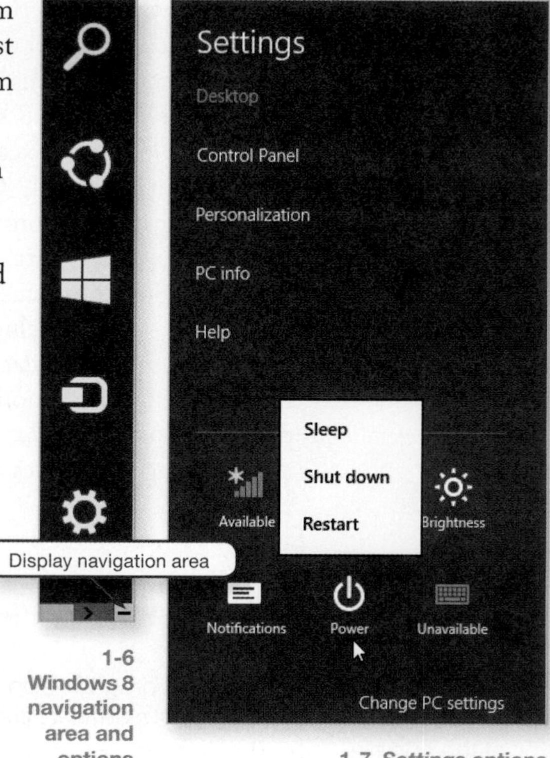

1-6 Windows 8 navigation area and options

1-7 *Settings* options

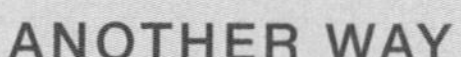

ANOTHER WAY

Click the bottom left corner of your computer screen to toggle between the *Start* page and the desktop.

Desktop and Taskbar

The **Windows desktop** is the working area of Windows and is similar to previous versions of Windows. Click the **Desktop** app tile on the *Start* page to go to the desktop (Figure 1-8). When you install a program on your computer, typically a shortcut to the program is added to the desktop. When you open a program from the *Start* page, such as Microsoft Word, the desktop displays and the program opens.

The ***Taskbar*** displays at the bottom of the desktop. You can open programs and folders from the *Taskbar* by clicking on an icon on the *Taskbar* (Figure 1-9). You can pin programs and other Windows items, such as the Control Panel or File Explorer, to the *Taskbar*.

1-8 Windows *Desktop* tile on the *Start* page

1-9 *Taskbar* at the bottom of the desktop

HOW TO: Pin a Program to the Taskbar

1. Go to the *Start* page if it is not already displayed.
   - Put your pointer in the bottom right corner of your computer monitor and select **Start** in the navigation area.
   - If you are on the desktop, you can also click the **Start page** icon that appears when you place your pointer in the bottom left corner of your monitor.

2. Right-click a program or Windows item to select it (Figure 1-10).
    - A check appears in the upper right of a selected item.
    - Options display at the bottom of the *Start* page.
3. Click **Pin to taskbar**.

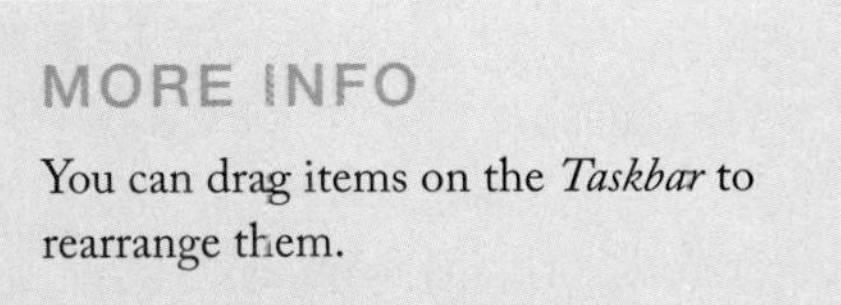

MORE INFO
You can drag items on the *Taskbar* to rearrange them.

1-10 Pin selected item to the *Taskbar*

File Explorer

The **File Explorer** is a window that opens on your desktop where you can browse for files stored on your computer (Figure 1-11). This window displays the libraries and folders on your computer on the left. When you select a library or folder on the left, the contents of the selection are displayed on the right. Double-click a file or folder on the right to open it.

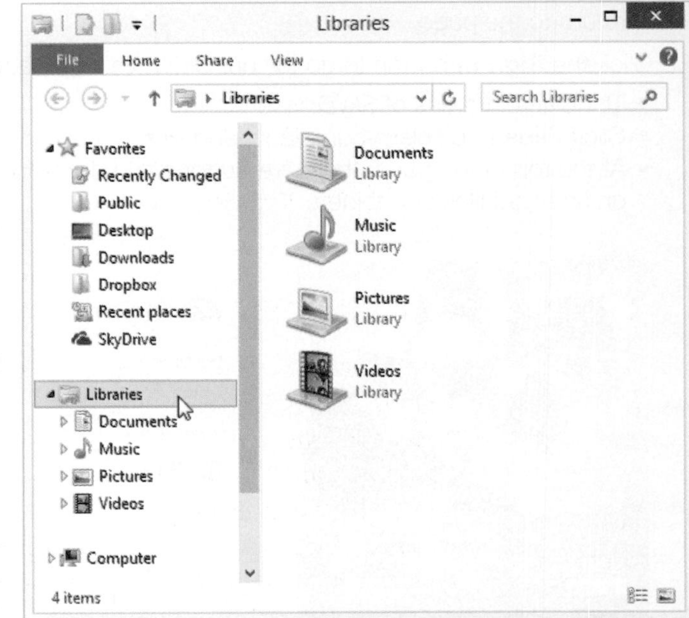

1-11 *File Explorer* window

SkyDrive

SkyDrive is a cloud storage area where you can store files in a private and secure online location that you can access from any computer. With cloud storage you don't have to be tied to one computer, and you don't have to carry your files with you on a portable storage device. When you store your files on *SkyDrive,* the files are actually saved on both your computer and on the cloud. *SkyDrive* synchronizes your files so when you change a file it is automatically updated on the *SkyDrive* cloud.

With Windows 8, the ***SkyDrive folder*** is one of your storage location folder options, similar to your *Documents* or *Pictures* folders (Figure 1-12). You can

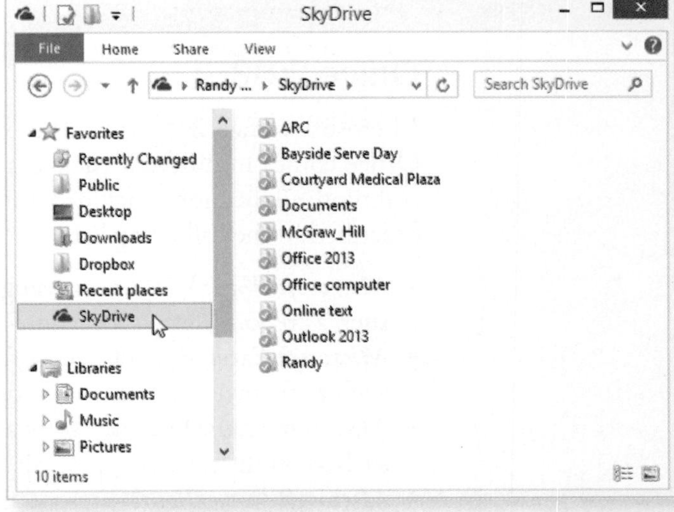

1-12 *SkyDrive* folder

save, open, and edit your *SkyDrive* files from a Windows folder. Your *SkyDrive* folder looks and functions similar to other Windows folders.

In addition to the *SkyDrive* folder on your computer, you can also access your *SkyDrive* files online using an Internet browser such as Internet Explorer, Google Chrome, or Mozilla Firefox. When you access *SkyDrive* online using a web browser, you can upload files, create folders, move and copy files and folders, and create Office files using Office Web Apps (see *Office Web Apps* later in this section).

HOW TO: Use SkyDrive Online

1. Open an Internet browser Window and navigate to the *SkyDrive* website (www.skydrive.com), which takes you to the *SkyDrive* sign in page (Figure 1-13).
   - You can use any Internet browser to access *SkyDrive* (e.g., Internet Explorer, Google Chrome, Mozilla Firefox).
2. Type in your Microsoft account email address and password.
   - If you are on your own computer, check the **Keep me signed in** box to stay signed in to *SkyDrive* when you return to the page.
3. Click the **Sign In** button to go to your *SkyDrive* web page.
   - The different areas of *SkyDrive* are listed under the *SkyDrive* heading on the left (Figure 1-14).
   - Click **Files** to display your folders and files in the folder area.
   - At the top of the page, there are buttons and drop-down menus that list the different actions you can perform on selected files and folders.

1-13 Log in to *SkyDrive* online

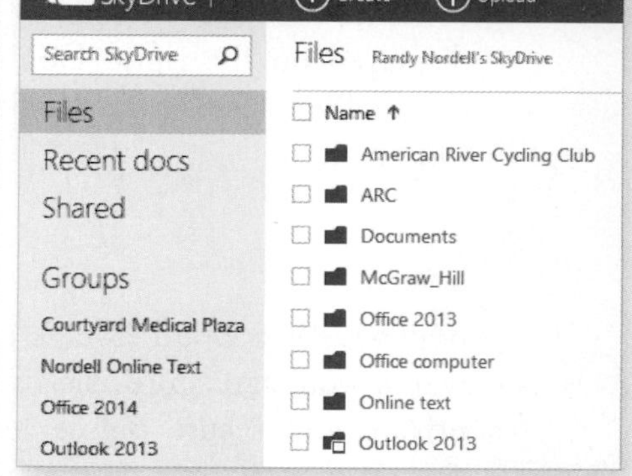

1-14 *SkyDrive* online

Office 2013

Microsoft Office 2013 is a suite of personal and business software applications. Microsoft Office comes in different packages and the applications included in each package vary. The common applications included in Microsoft Office and the primary purpose of each are described in the following list:

- ***Microsoft Word:*** Word processing software used to create, format, and edit documents such as reports, letters, brochures, and resumes.
- ***Microsoft Excel:*** Spreadsheet software used to perform calculations on numerical data such as financial statements, budgets, and expense reports.
- ***Microsoft Access:*** Database software used to store, organize, compile, and report information such as product information, sales data, client information, and employee records.
- ***Microsoft PowerPoint:*** Presentation software used to graphically present information in slides such as a presentation on a new product or sales trends.

- ***Microsoft Outlook:*** Email and personal management software used to create and send email and create and store calendar items, contacts, and tasks.
- ***Microsoft OneNote:*** Note-taking software used to take and organize notes, which can be shared with other Office applications.
- ***Microsoft Publisher:*** Desktop publishing software used to create professional-looking documents containing text, pictures, and graphics such as catalogs, brochures, and flyers.

Office Web Apps

Office Web Apps is free online software from Microsoft that works in conjunction with your online *SkyDrive* account (Figure 1-15). With Office Web Apps, you can work with Office files online, even on computers that do not have Office 2013 installed. This is a useful option when you use a computer at a computer lab or use a friend's computer that does not have Office 2013 installed.

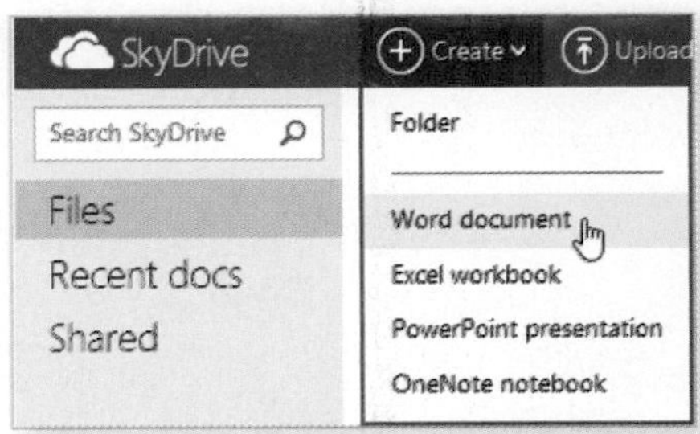

1-15 Office Web Apps

You can access Office Web Apps from your *SkyDrive* web page and create and edit Word documents, Excel workbooks, PowerPoint presentations, and OneNote notebooks. Office Web Apps is a scaled-down version of Office 2013 and not as robust in terms of features, but you can use it to create, edit, print, share, and insert comments on files. If you need more advanced features, you can open Office Web Apps files in Office 2013.

In *SkyDrive,* you can share files with others. When you share files or folders with others, you establish the access they have to the items you share. You can choose whether other users can only view files or view and edit files. To share a file or folder in your *SkyDrive,* send an email with a link to the shared items or generate a hyperlink that gives access to the shared files to others.

HOW TO: Share an Office Web Apps File

1. Log in to your *SkyDrive* account.
2. Click an Office file to open the file in Office Web Apps.
3. In read-only mode, click the **Share** button above the file. A sharing window opens with different options (Figure 1-16).
   - You can also click the **File** tab and select **Share** on the left.
4. To send an email, click **Send email**, type the recipient's email address, and type a brief message.

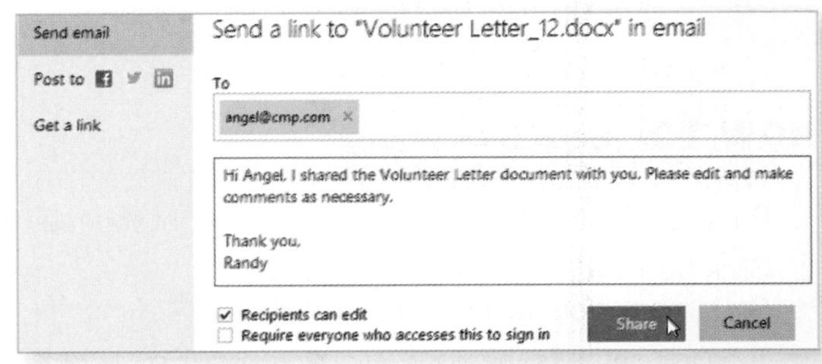

1-16 Share an Office Web Apps file

   - Enter a space after typing an email address to add another recipient.
   - Alternatively, you can click **Get a link** to generate a link to send to recipients.
5. Check the **Recipients can edit** box if you want the recipient to be able to edit the file.
   - Deselect this check box if you want recipients to only view the file.
   - You can also require recipients to sign in to *SkyDrive* in order to view or edit the file by checking the **Require everyone who accesses this to sign in** box.
6. Click the **Send** button.
   - Recipients receive an email containing a link to the shared file or folder.
   - A window may open, prompting you to enter a displayed code to prevent unauthorized sharing. Enter the displayed code to return to the sharing window and click **Send**.
7. Click the **X** in the upper right corner or the browser window to exit *SkyDrive.*

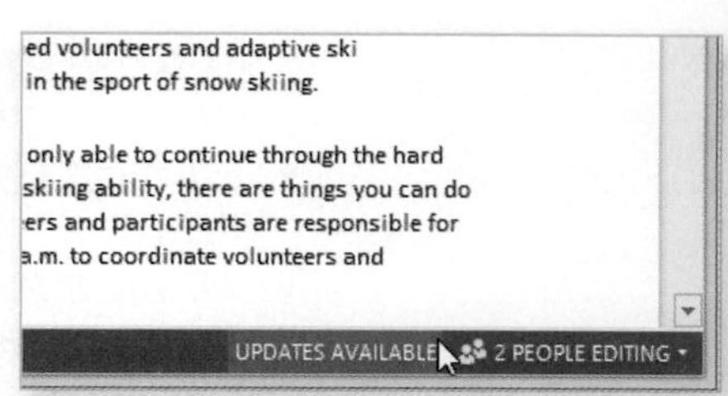

1-17 Collaboration information displayed in the *Status* bar

Office Web Apps let you synchronously (i.e., at the same time) or asynchronously (i.e., not at the same time) collaborate on an Office file with others who have access to the shared file. If two or more users are working on the same file in Office Web Apps, collaboration information is displayed at the bottom of the Office Web Apps window (Figure 1-17). You are alerted to available updates and told how many people are editing the file.

Click **Updates Available** in the *Status* bar to apply updates to your file. Click **People Editing** to view the names of users who are currently editing the file.

> **MORE INFO**
>
> The *Status* bar is displayed at the bottom of the application window and is available on all Office applications.

Open an Office Application

When using Windows 8, you click an app tile to open an Office application. If your *Start* page has the Office applications displayed, you can click the **Word 2013, Excel 2013, Access 2013**, or **PowerPoint 2013** tile to launch the application (Figure 1-18).

If the Office application apps are not on the *Start* page, you can search for the app.

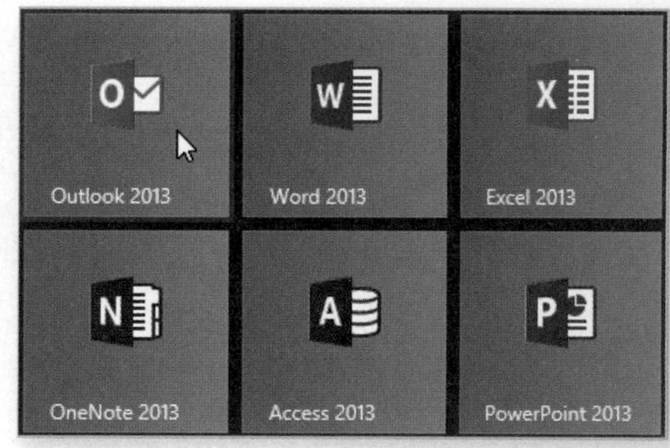

1-18 Launch an Office 2013 application

HOW TO: Search for an App

1. Put your pointer at the bottom right corner of your computer screen to display the Windows 8 navigation options.
2. Click **Search** to display all apps and the *Search* pane on the right (Figure 1-19).
3. Type the name of the application to open (e.g., Access). Windows displays the apps matching the search text.
4. Click the app to launch it.
    - Alternatively, you can click a blank area away from the *Search* pane to close the *Search* pane, scroll through the available apps on your computer, and click an app to launch it.

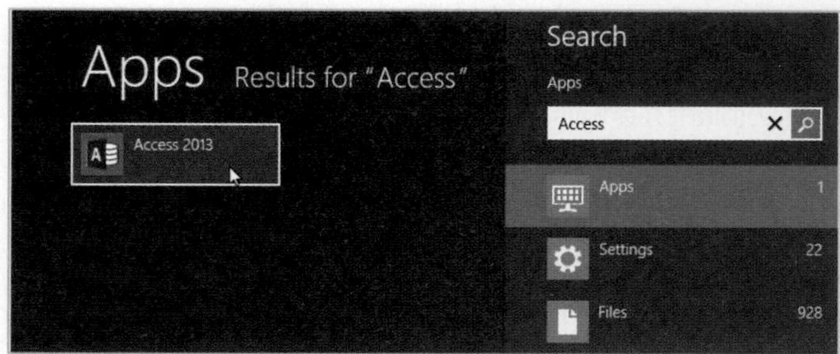

1-19 Search for an app

> **MORE INFO**
>
> Add commonly used apps to your Windows *Start* page to save you time.

Office Start Page

In addition to the new *Start* page in Windows 8, most of the Office applications (except Outlook and OneNote) have a new ***Start page*** that displays when you launch the application (Figure 1-20). From this *Start* page, you can create a new blank file (e.g., a Word document, an Excel workbook, an Access database, or a PowerPoint presentation), create a file from an online template, search for an online template, open a recently used file, or open another file. These options vary depending on the Office application.

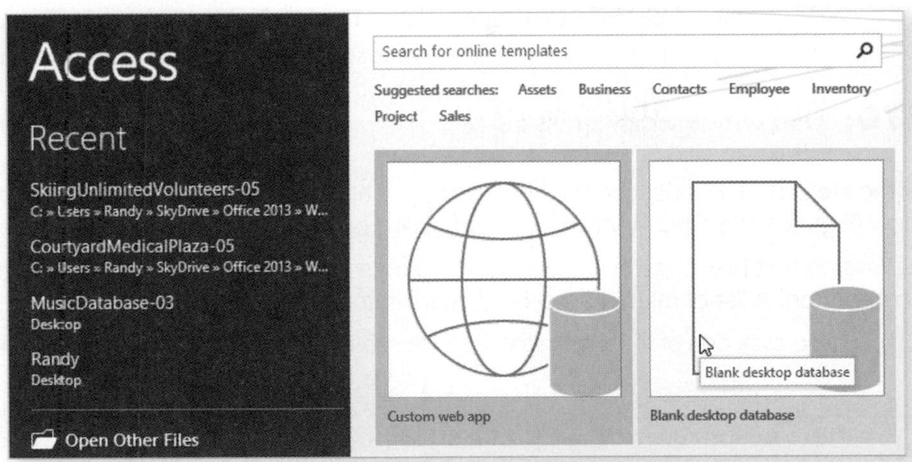

1-20 Access *Start* page

Press the **Esc** key to exit the *Start* page and enter the program. In Access, you have to open an existing database or create a new one to enter the program.

Backstage View

Office 2013 incorporates the ***Backstage view*** into all Office applications. Click the **File** tab on the *Ribbon* to open the *Backstage* view (Figure 1-21). *Backstage* options vary depending on the Office application. The following list describes some of the common tasks you can perform from the *Backstage* view:

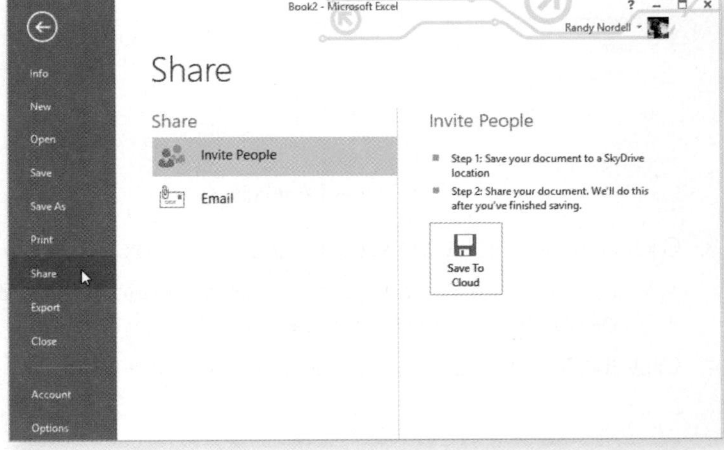

1-21 *Backstage* view in Excel

- ***Info:*** Displays document properties and other protection, inspection, and version options.
- ***New:*** Creates a new blank file or a new file from a template or theme.
- ***Open:*** Opens an existing file from a designated location or a recently opened file.
- ***Save:*** Saves a file. If the file has not been named, the *Save As* dialog box opens when you select this option.
- ***Save As:*** Opens the *Save As* dialog box.
- ***Print:*** Prints a file, displays a preview of the file, or displays print options.
- ***Share:*** Invites people to share a file or email a file.

- ***Export:*** Creates a PDF file from a file or saves as a different file type.
- ***Close:*** Closes an open file.
- ***Account:*** Displays your Microsoft account information.
- ***Options:*** Opens the *[Application] Options* dialog box (e.g., Excel Options).

Office 2013 Help

In each of the Office applications, a help feature is available where you can search for a topic and view help information related to that topic. Using the *[Application] Help* dialog box (e.g., *Access Help*), type in key words for your search. Links to online help resources display in the dialog box.

HOW TO: Use Office Help

1. Click the **Help** button (question mark) in the upper right corner of the Office application window (Figure 1-22). The *[Application] Help* dialog box opens (Figure 1-23).

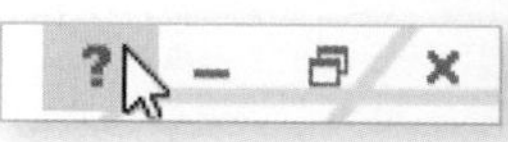

1-22 *Help* button

2. In the *Search* text box, type in key words for your search and press **Enter** or click the **Search** button. A list of related articles appears in the dialog box (Figure 1-24).
   - You can also click one of the links in the *Popular searches* and *Basics and beyond* areas to view related help articles.

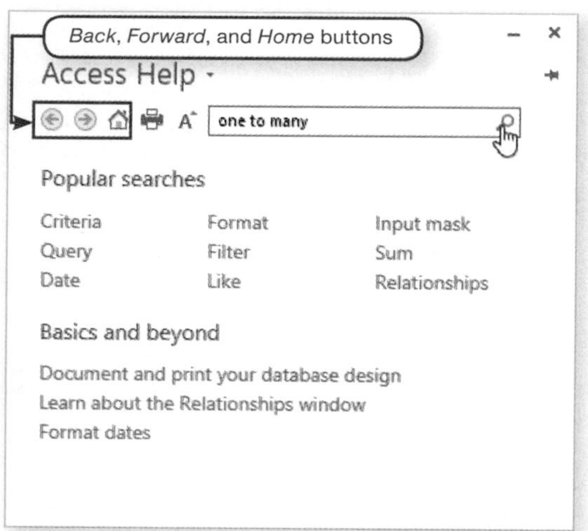

1-23 *Access Help* dialog box

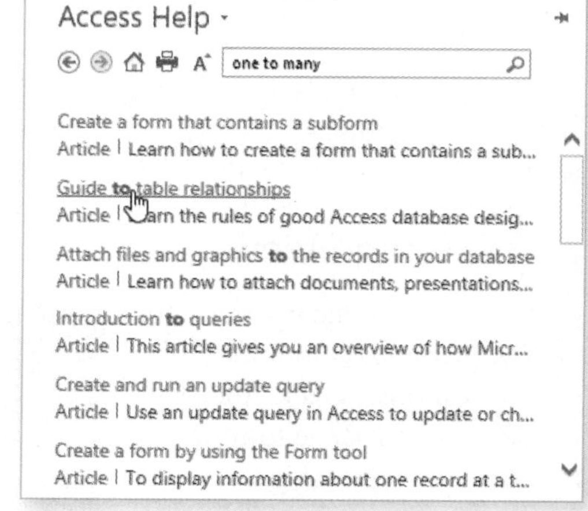

Access Help
one to many
Create a form that contains a subform
Article | Learn how to create a form that contains a sub...
Guide to table relationships
Attach files and graphics to the records in your database
Article | Learn how to attach documents, presentations...
Introduction to queries
Article | This article gives you an overview of how Micr...
Create and run an update query
Article | Use an update query in Access to update or ch...
Create a form by using the Form tool
Article | To display information about one record at a t...

1-24 Related articles displayed in the dialog box

3. Click a link to display the article in the dialog box.
   - You can use the *Back*, *Forward*, or *Home* buttons to navigate in the *Help* dialog box.
   - Scroll down to the bottom of the list of articles to use the *Next* and *Previous* buttons to view more articles.
4. Click the **X** in the upper right corner to close the *Help* dialog box.

> **ANOTHER WAY**
>
> **F1** opens the *Help* dialog box.

Mouse and Pointers

If you are using Office on a desktop or laptop computer, use your mouse (or touch pad) to navigate around files, click tabs and buttons, select text and objects, move text and objects, and resize objects. The following table lists mouse and pointer terminology used in Office.

Mouse and Pointer Terminology

Term	Description
Pointer	When you move your mouse, the pointer moves on your screen. There are a variety of pointers that are used in different contexts in Office applications. The following pointers are available in most of the Office applications (the appearance of these pointers varies depending on the application and the context used): • ***Selection pointer:*** Select text or an object. • ***Move pointer:*** Move text or an object. • ***Copy pointer:*** Copy text or an object. • ***Resize pointer:*** Resize objects or table column or row. • ***Crosshair:*** Draw a shape.
Insertion point	The vertical flashing line where text is inserted in a file or text box. Click the left mouse button to position the insertion point.
Click	Click the left mouse button. Used to select an object or button or to place the insertion point in the selected location.
Double-click	Click the left mouse button twice. Used to select text.
Right-click	Click the right mouse button. Used to display the context menu and the mini toolbar.
Scroll	Use the scroll wheel on the mouse to scroll up and down through your file. You can also use the horizontal or vertical scroll bars at the bottom and right of an Office file window to move around in a file.

Office 2013 on a Tablet

The new user interface in Windows 8 and Office 2013 is designed to facilitate use of Windows and the Office applications on a tablet computer or smart phone. With tablets and smart phones, you use a touch screen rather than using a mouse, so the process of selecting text and objects and navigating around a file is different from when you select and navigate on a desktop or laptop computer. The following table lists some of the gestures used when working on a tablet or smart phone (some of these gestures vary depending on the application used and the context).

Tablet Gestures

Gesture	Used To	How To
Tap	Make a selection or place the insertion point. Double tap to edit text in an object or cell.	
Pinch	Zoom in or resize an object.	
Stretch	Zoom out or resize an object.	
Slide	Move an object or selected text.	
Swipe	Select text or multiple objects.	

SLO 1.2

Creating, Saving, Closing, and Opening Files

Creating, saving, and opening files is primarily done from the *Start* page or *Backstage* view. These areas provide you with many options and a central location to perform these tasks. You can also use shortcut commands to create, save, and open files.

Create a New File

When you create a new file in an Office application, you can create a new blank file or a new file based on a template (in PowerPoint, you can also create a presentation based on a theme). On the *Start* page, click **Blank [file type]** to create a new blank file in the application you are using (in Word, you begin with a blank document; in Excel, a blank workbook; in Access, a blank desktop database; and in PowerPoint, a blank presentation). From the *Backstage* view, the new file options are available in the *New* area.

HOW TO: Create a New File from the Start Page

1. Open the Office application you want to use. The *Start* page displays when the application opens.
2. From the *Start* page, click **Blank [file type]** or select a template or theme to use for your new blank file. A new file opens in the application you are using.
   - The new file is given a generic file name (e.g., *Document1*, *Book1*, or *Presentation1*). You can name and save this file later.
   - When creating a new Access database, you are prompted to name the new file when you create it.
   - Some templates and themes (in PowerPoint only) are displayed on the *Start* page, but you can search for other online templates and themes using the *Search* text box at the top of the *Start* page.

MORE INFO

Esc closes the *Start* page and takes you into the Office application (except in Access).

If you have been using an application already and want to create a new file, you create it from the *Backstage* view.

HOW TO: Create a New File from the Backstage View

1. Click the **File** tab to display the *Backstage* view.
2. Select **New** on the left to display the *New* area (Figure 1-25).
3. Click **Blank [file type]** or select a template or theme to use in your new blank file. A new file opens in the application.
   - The new file is given a generic file name (e.g., *Document1*, *Book1*, or *Presentation1*). You can name and save this file later.
   - When you are creating a new Access database, you are prompted to name the new file when you create it.
   - Some templates and themes (in PowerPoint only) are displayed on the *Start* page, but you can search for other online templates and themes using the *Search* text box at the top of the *Start* page.

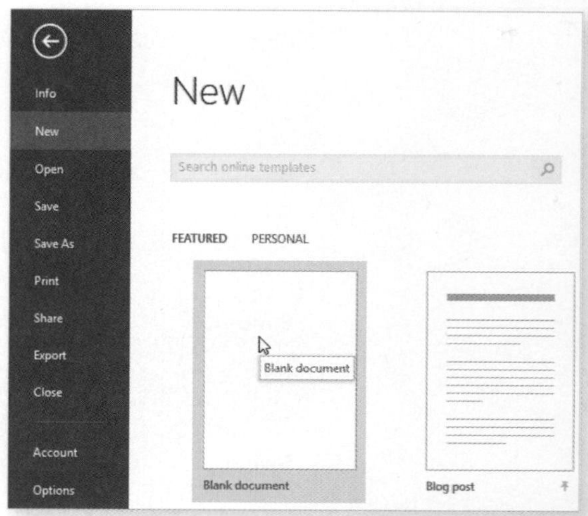

1-25 ***New* area in Word**

> **ANOTHER WAY**
>
> **Ctrl+N** opens a new file from within an Office application. In Access, **Ctrl+N** opens the *New* area in the *Backstage* view.

Save a File

In Access, you name a file as you create it, but in Word, Excel, and PowerPoint, you name a file after you have created it. When you save a file, you type a name for the file and select the location where the file is saved.

HOW TO: Save a File

1. Click the **File** tab to display the *Backstage* view.
2. Select **Save** or **Save As** on the left to display the *Save As* area (Figure 1-26).
   - If the file has not already been saved, clicking *Save* or *Save As* takes you to the *Save As* area on the *Backstage* view.
3. Select a place to save your file in the *Places* area.
4. On the right, click a folder in the *Recent Folders* area or click the **Browse** button to open the *Save As* dialog box (Figure 1-27).
5. In the *Folder* list on the left, select a location to save the file.
6. In the *File name* area, type a name for the file.
7. In the *Save as type*, select the file type to save.
   - By default, Office selects the file type, but you can change the file type in this area.
8. Click **Save** to close the dialog box and save the file.

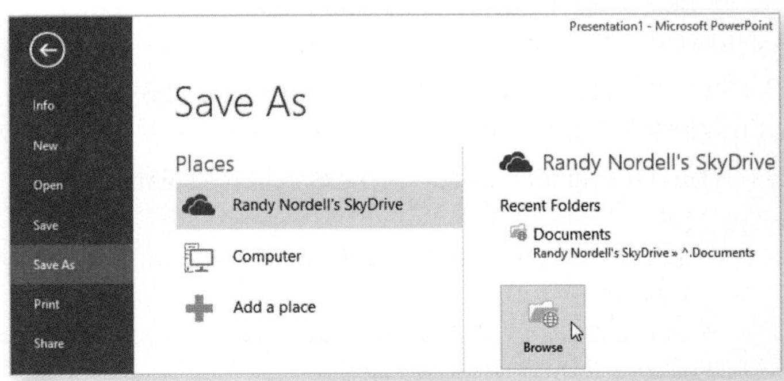

1-26 ***Save As* area in PowerPoint**

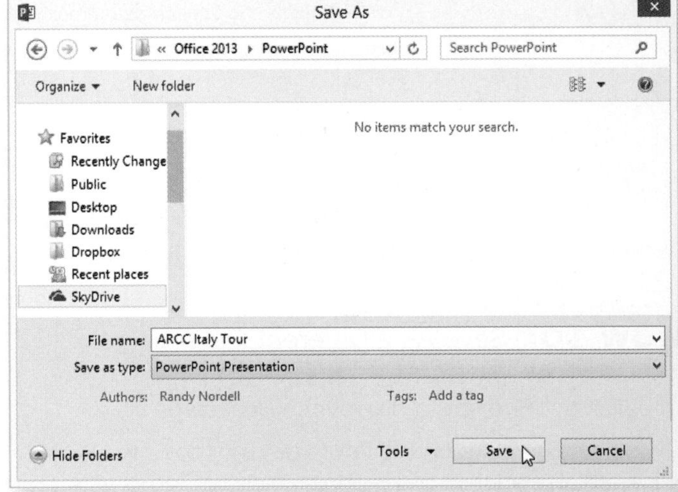

1-27 ***Save As* dialog box**

> **ANOTHER WAY**
>
> **Ctrl+S** opens the *Save As* area on the *Backstage* view when a file does not have a name. If a file has already been named, **Ctrl+S** saves the file without opening the *Backstage* view.

Create a Folder

When saving files, it is a good idea to create folders to organize your files. Organizing your files in folders makes it easier to find your files and saves you time when you are searching for a specific file (see *SLO 1.7: Organizing and Customizing Folders and Files* for more information on this topic). When you save an Office file, you can also create a folder in which to store that file.

HOW TO: Create a Folder

1. Click the **File** tab to display the *Backstage* view.
2. Select **Save As** on the left to display the *Save As* area.
3. Select a place to save your file in the *Places* area.
4. On the right, click a folder in the *Recent Folders* area or the **Browse** button to open the *Save As* dialog box.
5. In the *Folder* list at the left, select a location to save the file.
6. Click the **New Folder** button to create a new folder (Figure 1-28).
7. Type a name for the new folder and press **Enter**.

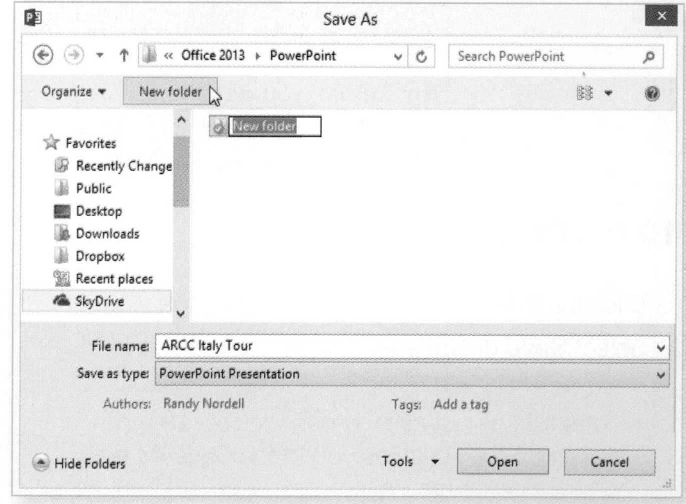

1-28 Create a new folder

> **ANOTHER WAY**
>
> **F12** opens the *Save As* dialog box (except in Access).

Save As a Different File Name

After you have saved a file, you can save it again with a different file name. If you do this, you have preserved the original file and you can continue to revise the second file for a different purpose. For example, you might want to save a different version of a file with a different file name.

HOW TO: Save As a Different File Name

1. Click the **File** tab to display the *Backstage* view.
2. Select **Save As** on the left to display the *Save As* area.
3. Select the location where you want to save your file in the *Places* area.
4. On the right, click a folder in the *Recent Folders* area or the **Browse** button to open the *Save As* dialog box.
5. In the *Folder* list on the left, select a location to save the file.
6. In the *File name* area, type a name for the file.
7. Click **Save** to close the dialog box and save the file.

Office 2013 File Types

When you save an Office file, by default Office saves the file in the most recent file format for that application. You also have the option of saving files in older versions of the Office application you are using. For example, you can save a Word document as an older version to share with or send to someone who uses an older version of Word. Each file has an extension at the end of the file name that determines the file type. The ***file name extension*** is automatically added to a file when you save it.

The following table lists some of the common file types used in the different Office applications.

Office File Types

File Type	Extension
Word Document	.docx
Word Template	.dotx
Word 97-2003 Document	.doc
Rich Text Format	.rtf
Excel Workbook	.xlsx
Excel Template	.xltx
Excel 97-2003 Workbook	.xls
Comma Separated Values (CSV)	.csv
Access Database	.accdb
Access Template	.accdt
Access Database (2000-2003 format)	.mdb
PowerPoint Presentation	.pptx
PowerPoint Template	.potx
PowerPoint 97-2003 Presentation	.ppt
Portable Document Format (PDF)	.pdf

Close a File

There are a few different methods you can use to close a file.

- Click the **File** tab and select **Close** on the left.
- Press **Ctrl+W**.
- Click the **X** in the upper right corner of the file window. This method closes the file and the program.

When you close a file, you are prompted to save the file if it has not been named or if changes were made after the file was last saved (Figure 1-29). Click **Save** to save and close the file or click **Don't Save** to close the file without saving. Click **Cancel** to return to the file.

1-29 Prompt to save a document before closing

Open an Existing File

You can open an existing file from the *Start* page when you open an Office application or you can open an existing file while you are working on another Office file.

HOW TO: Open a File from the Start Page

1. Open an Office application to display the *Start* page (Figure 1-30).
2. Select a file to open in the *Recent* area on the left.
   - If you select a file in the *Recent* area, the file must be located on the computer or an attached storage device in order to open. If the file has been renamed, moved, or on a storage device not connected to the computer, you received an error message.
3. Alternatively, click the **Open Other [file type]** (e.g., Documents, Workbooks, Files, or Presentations) link to open the *Open* area of the *Backstage* view (Figure 1-31).
4. Select a location in the *Places* area.
5. Select a folder in the *Recent Folders* area or click the **Browse** button to open the *Open* dialog box (Figure 1-32).
6. Select a location from the *Folder* list on the left.
7. Select the file to open and click the **Open** button.

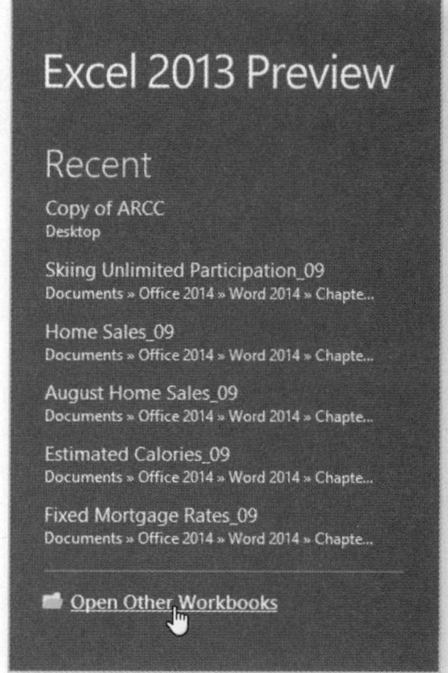

1-30 Open a file from the *Start* page

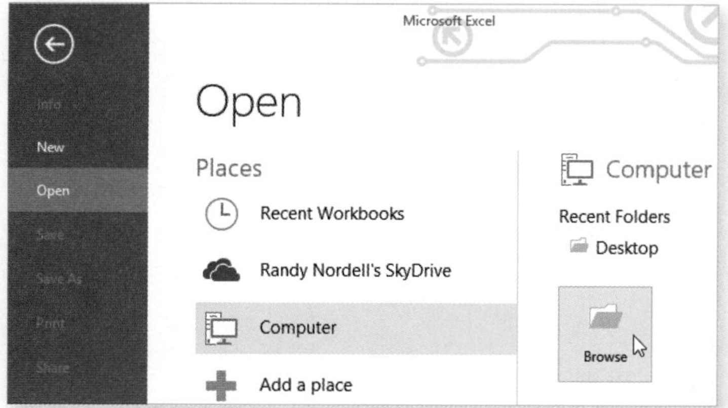

1-31 *Open* area in the *Backstage* view

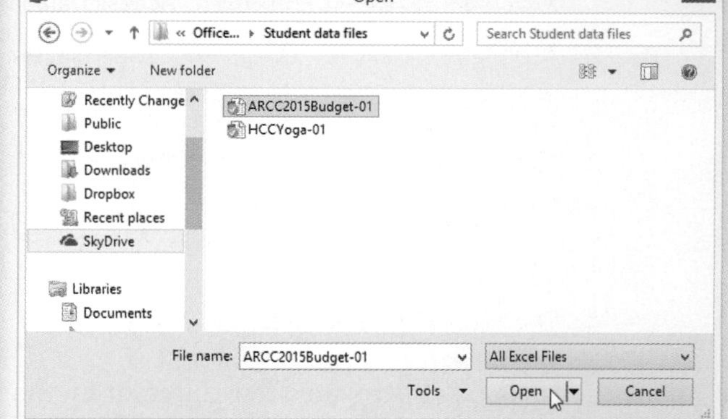

1-32 *Open* dialog box

To open a file from within an Office application, click the **File** tab to open the *Backstage* view and select **Open** on the left to display the *Open* area. Follow steps 4–7 above to open a file.

You can also open a file from a Windows folder. When you double-click a file in a Windows folder, the file opens in the appropriate Office application. Windows recognizes the file name extension and launches the correct program.

ANOTHER WAY

Ctrl+F12 opens the *Open* dialog box when you are in the working area of an Office application (except in Access).

PAUSE & PRACTICE: OFFICE 1-1

For this project, you log in to Windows using your Microsoft account, customize the Windows *Start* page, create and save a PowerPoint presentation, create a folder, open and rename an Excel workbook, use *Help*, and share a file in *SkyDrive*.

Note to Students and Instructor:

Students: *For this project, you share an Office Web App file with your instructor. You also create a Microsoft account if you don't already have one.*

Instructor: *In order to complete this project, your students need your Microsoft email address. You can create a new Live or Hotmail account for projects in this chapter.*

File Needed: ***ARCC2015Budget-01.xlsx***

Completed Project File Names: ***[your initials] PP O1-1a.pptx*** and ***[your initials] PP O1-1b.xlsx***

1. Log in to Windows using your Microsoft account if you are not already logged in.
   a. If you are not logged in to Windows using your Microsoft account, you might need to log out or restart to display the log in page. When Windows opens, type in your Windows account username and password.
   b. If you have not yet created a Microsoft account, open a browser Window and go to www.live.com and click the **Sign up now** link. Enter the required information to create your free Windows account.
2. After logging in to Windows, customize the *Start* page to include Office 2013 apps. If these apps tiles are already on the *Start* page, skip steps 2a–e.
   a. Right-click a blank area of the *Start* page.
   b. Click **All apps** on the bottom right to display the *Apps* area of Windows.
   c. Locate and right-click **Word 2013** to select it (Figure 1-33).
   d. Click **Pin to Start** on the bottom left to add this app to the *Start* page.
   e. Repeat steps 2a–d to pin *Excel 2013*, *Access 2013*, and *PowerPoint 2013* to the *Start* page.

Word 2013

1-33 Word 2013 selected

3. Return to the *Start* page and arrange apps.
   a. Place your pointer on the bottom right of your screen and select **Start** from the Windows navigation options.

> **ANOTHER WAY**
>
> Click the bottom left corner of your screen to return to the *Start* page.

   b. Drag the app tiles you added to the *Start* page to your preferred locations.
4. Create a PowerPoint presentation and save in a new folder.
   a. Click the **PowerPoint 2013** app tile on your *Start* page to open the application.
   b. On the PowerPoint *Start* page, click **Blank presentation** to create a new blank presentation (Figure 1-34). A new blank presentation opens.

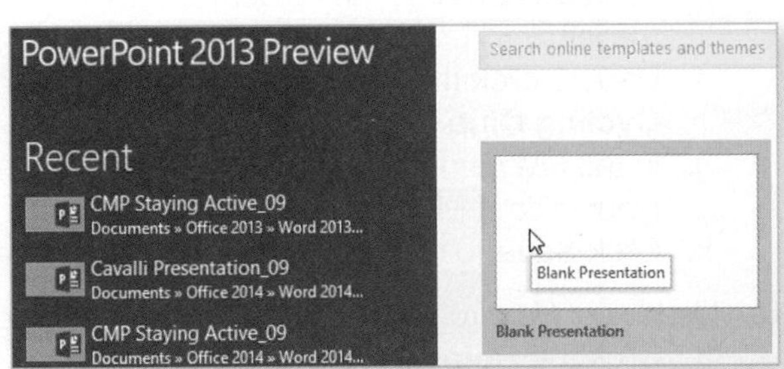

1-34 Create a new blank PowerPoint presentation

c. Click in the **Click to add title** area and type American River Cycling Club.
d. Click the **File** tab to open the *Backstage* view and click **Save As** on the left to display the *Save As* area.
e. Click ***[your name's]* SkyDrive** in the *Places* area and click **Browse** to open the *Save As* dialog box (Figure 1-35).
f. Click the **New Folder** button to create a new folder in your *SkyDrive* folder.
g. Type American River Cycling Club and press **Enter**.
h. Double-click the folder you created to open it.
i. In the *File name* area, type [your initials] PP O1-1a (Figure 1-36).
j. Click **Save** to close the dialog box and save the presentation.
k. Click the **X** in the upper right corner of the window to close the file and PowerPoint.

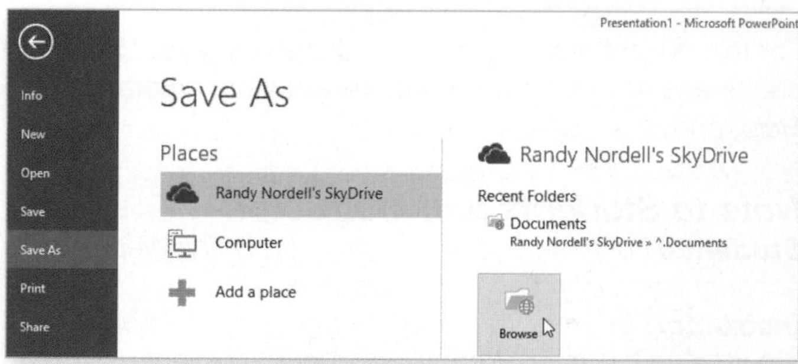

1-35 Save the file in *SkyDrive*

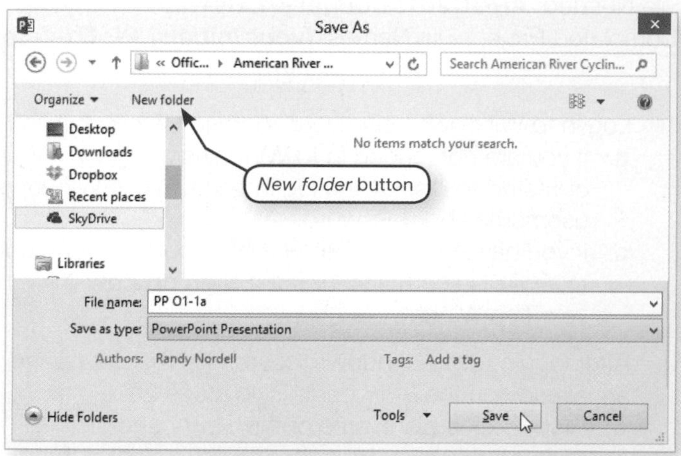

1-36 *Save As* dialog box

5. Open an Excel file and save as a different file name.
   a. Return to the Windows *Start* page.
   b. Click the **Excel 2013** app tile to open it.
   c. From the Excel *Start* page, click the **Open Other Workbooks** link on the bottom left to display the *Open* area of the *Backstage* view.
   d. Click **Computer** in the *Places* area and click **Browse** to open the *Open* dialog box (Figure 1-37).
   e. Browse to your student data files and select the ***ARCC2015Budget-01*** file.
   f. Click **Open** to open the workbook.
   g. Press **F12** to open the *Save As* dialog box.
   h. Click **SkyDrive** in the *Folder* list on the left.
   i. Double-click the **American River Cycling Club** folder to open it.
   j. In the *File name* area type [your initials] PP O1-1b.
   k. Click **Save** to close the dialog box and save the workbook.

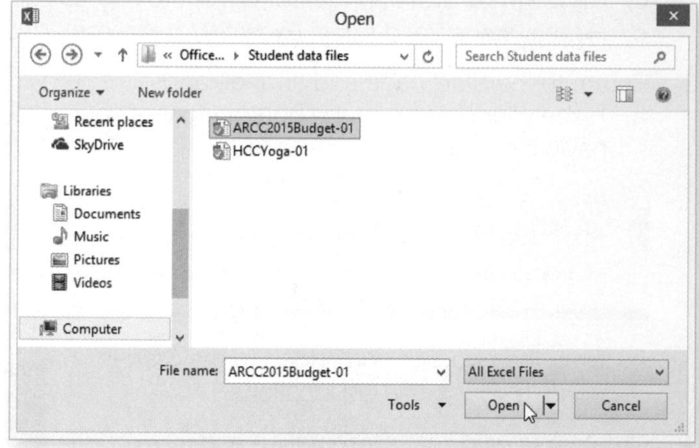

1-37 *Open* dialog box

6. Use *Excel Help* to find articles about selected topics.
   a. Click the **Help** button in the upper right corner of the Excel window. The *Excel Help* dialog box opens.

b. Type pivot table in the *Search* text box and press **Enter**.
c. Click one of the displayed articles and quickly read about pivot tables.
d. Click the **Home** button to return to the home page of Excel help.
e. Type sum function in the *Search* text box and press **Enter**.
f. Click one of the displayed articles and quickly read about sum functions.
g. Click the **X** in the upper right corner to close the *Excel Help* dialog box.
h. Press **Ctrl+W** to close the Excel workbook.
i. Click the **X** in the upper right corner of the Excel window to close Excel.

7. Share an Office Web Apps file on *SkyDrive* with your instructor.
   a. Return to the Windows *Start* page.
   b. Open an Internet browser window and go to the *SkyDrive* (www.skydrive.com) sign-in page (Figure 1-38).
   c. Type in your Microsoft account email address and password and click the **Sign In** button to go to your *SkyDrive* web page.
   d. Click the navigation button on the upper left and select **SkyDrive** (if your *SkyDrive* is not already displayed) (Figure 1-39).
   e. Click the **American River Cycling Club** folder to open it.
   f. Click the **PP O1-1b** Excel workbook to open it in Office Web Apps (Figure 1-40).
   g. Click the **File** tab to open the *Backstage* view.
   h. Click **Share** on the left and select **Share with People**. A sharing window opens with different options (Figure 1-41). Sharing requires the recipient to have a Microsoft account. Also, you might be directed to complete an online form for security purposes the first time you share a file.
   i. Click **Send email**, type your instructor's email address, and type a brief message.
   j. Check the **Recipients can edit** check box.
   k. Click the **Share** button.
8. Select **[your name]** on the upper right of the *SkyDrive* window and select the **Sign out** from the *Account* drop-down list.

1-38 Log in to *SkyDrive* online

1-39 Go to your *SkyDrive*

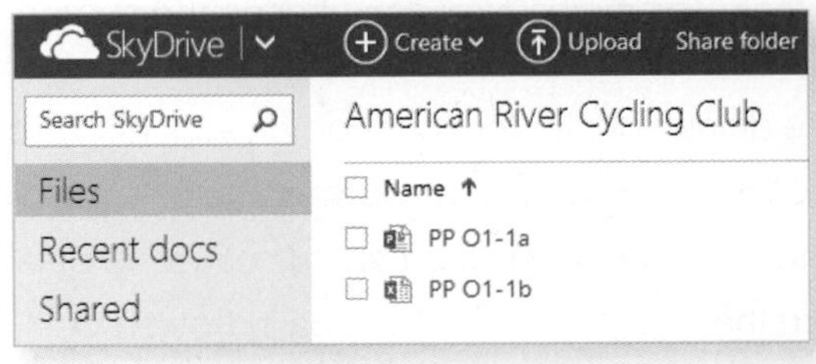

1-40 Open a file in Office Web Apps

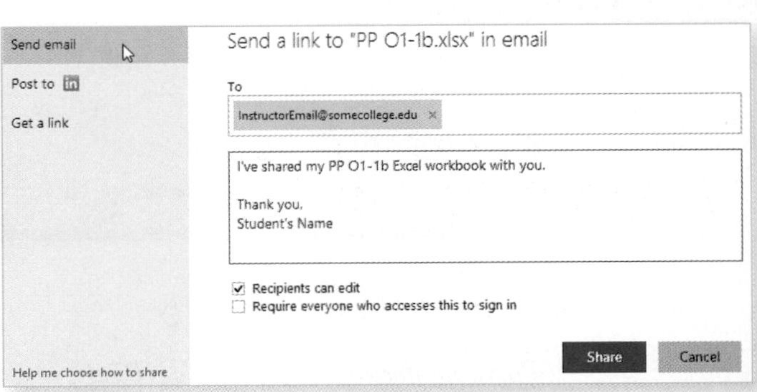

1-41 Share an Office Web App file

SLO 1.3

Printing, Sharing, and Customizing Files

On the *Backstage* view of any of the Office applications, you can print a file and customize how a file is printed. You can also export an Office file as a PDF file in most of the Office applications. In addition, you can add and customize document properties for an Office file and share a file in a variety of formats.

Print a File

You can print an Office file if you need a paper copy of it. The *Print* area on the *Backstage* view displays a preview of the open file and many print options. For example, you can choose which page or pages to print and change the margins of the file in the *Print* area. Some of the print settings vary depending on the Office application you are using and what you are printing.

HOW TO: Print a File

1. Open the file you want to print from a Windows folder or within an Office program.
2. Click the **File** tab to open the *Backstage* view.
3. Click **Print** on the left to display the *Print* area (Figure 1-42).
   - A preview of the file displays on the right. Click the **Show Margins** button to adjust margins or **Zoom to Page** button to change the view in the *Preview* area. The *Show Margins* button is only available in Word and Excel.
   - On the left a variety of options are listed in the *Settings* area.
   - The *Settings* options vary depending on the Office application you are using and what you are printing.
4. In the *Copies* area, you can change the number of copies to print.
5. The default printer for your computer is displayed in the *Printer* drop-down list.
   - Click the **Printer** drop-down list to select a different printer.
6. In the *Settings* area, you can customize what is printed and how it is printed.
   - In the *Pages* area (*Slides* area in PowerPoint), you can select a page or range of pages (slides) to print.
   - By default all pages (slides) are printed when you print a file.
7. Click the **Print** button to print your file.

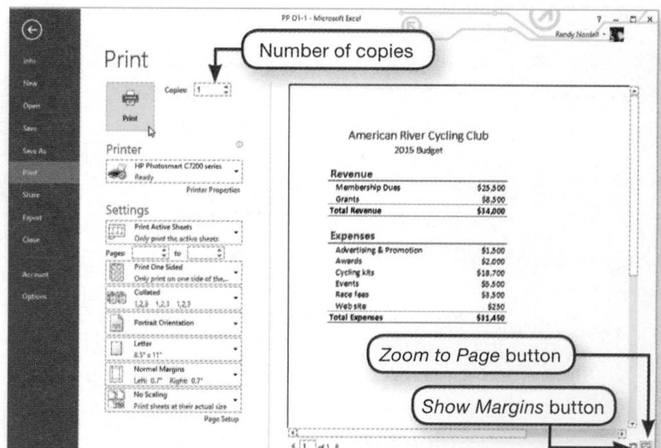

1-42 ***Print* area on the *Backstage* view**

> **ANOTHER WAY**
>
> **Ctrl+P** opens the *Print* area on the *Backstage* view.

Export as a PDF File

Portable document format, or ***PDF***, is a specific file format that is often used to share files that are not to be changed or to post files on a web site. When you create a PDF file from an Office application file, you are actually exporting a static image of the original file, similar to taking a picture of the file.

The advantage of working with a PDF file is that the format of the file is retained no matter who opens the file. PDF files open in Adobe Reader, which is free software that is installed on most computers, or Adobe Acrobat, which is software users have to buy. Because a PDF file is a static image of a file, it is not easy for other people to edit your files. When you want people to be able to view a file but not make changes, PDF files are a good choice.

> **MORE INFO**
>
> Word 2013 allows you to open PDF files and edit the file as a Word document.

When you export an Office application file as a PDF file, Office creates a static image of your file and prompts you to save the file. The file is saved as a PDF file.

HOW TO: Export a File as a PDF File

1. Open the file you want to export to a PDF file.
2. Click the **File** tab and click **Export** to display the *Export* area on the Backstage view (Figure 1-43).
3. Select **Create PDF/XPS Document** and click the **Create PDF/XPS**. The *Publish as PDF or XPS* dialog box opens.
4. Select a location to save the file.
5. In the *File name* area, type a name for the file.
6. Click **Publish** to close the dialog box and save the PDF file.
   - A PDF version of your file may open. You can view the file and then close it.

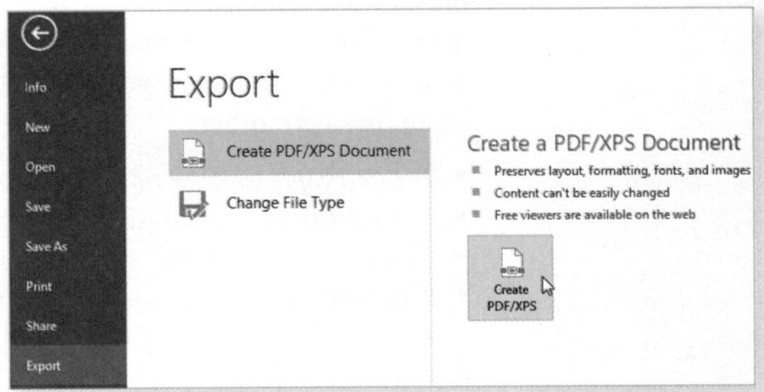

1-43 Export a file as a PDF file

Document Properties

Document properties are hidden codes in a file that contain identifying information about that file. Each piece of document property information is called a ***field***. You can view and modify document properties in the *Info* area of the *Backstage* view.

Some document properties fields are automatically generated when you work on a file, such as *Size, Total Editing Time, Created,* and *Last Modified.* But you can modify other document properties fields, such as *Title, Comments, Subject, Company,* and *Author.* You can use document property fields in different ways such as inserting the *Company* field in a document footer.

HOW TO: View and Modify Document Properties

1. Click the **File** tab and click **Info**. The document properties display on the right (Figure 1-44).
2. Click in the text box area of a field that can be edited (e.g., *Add a title* or *Add a tag*) and type your custom document property information.
3. Click the **Show All Properties** link at the bottom to display additional document properties.
   - When all properties are displayed, click **Show Fewer Properties** to display fewer properties.
   - This link toggles between *Show All Properties* and *Show Fewer Properties*.
4. Click the **File** tab to return to the file.

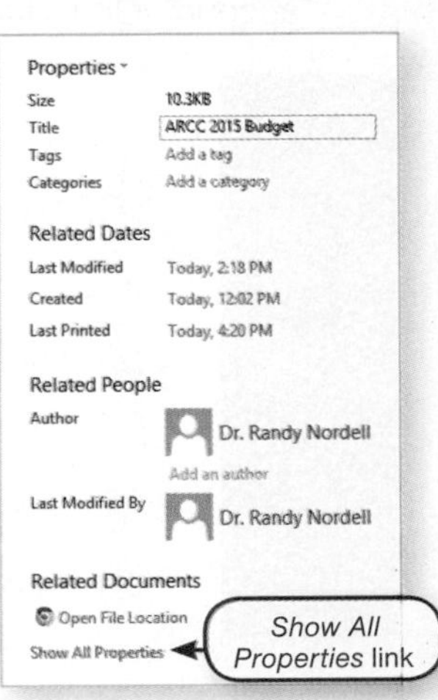

1-44 Document properties

Share a File

Windows 8 and Office 2013 have been developed to help you share and collaborate effectively. The *Share* area on the *Backstage* view provides different options for sharing files from within an Office application. When you save a file to your *SkyDrive*, Office gives you a variety of options to share your file (Figure 1-45). Your sharing options vary depending on the Office application you are using. The following list describes some common ways you can share files with others:

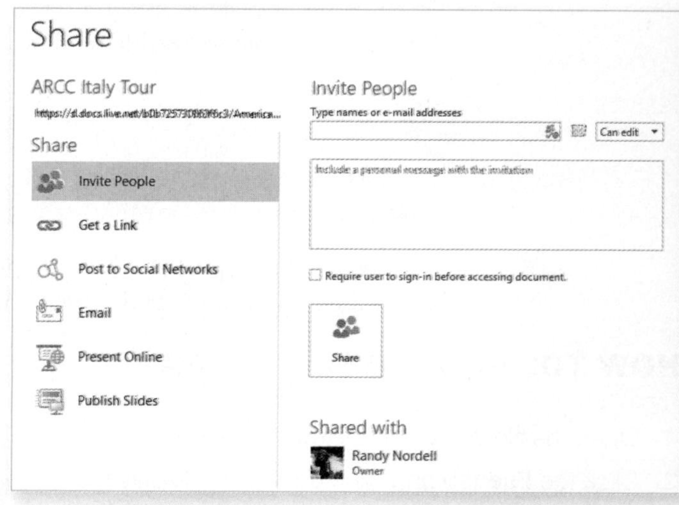

1-45 Share an Office file

- *Invite People* to view or edit your file.
- *Get a Link* to the online file that you can send to others or post online.
- *Post to Social Networks* such as LinkedIn or Facebook.
- *Email* the file as an attachment, link, or PDF file.

> **MORE INFO**
>
> There is not a *Sharing* area on the *Backstage* view in Access.

HOW TO: Share a File

1. Click the **File** tab and select **Share**.
   - If your file is not saved on *SkyDrive*, select **Invite People** and click **Save to Cloud** (Figure 1-46).
   - Save your file to your *SkyDrive* folder.
   - If your file is not saved to *SkyDrive*, you will not have all of the sharing options.
2. Select one of the *Share* options on the left. Additional information is displayed on the right (Figure 1-47).
   - In most of the *Share* options, you can set the permission level to **Can view** or **Can edit**, which controls what others can do with your file.
   - In order to post a file to a social network site, you must connect your social network site to your Microsoft account. Go to the *Account* area of the *Backstage* view to connect to social network sites.

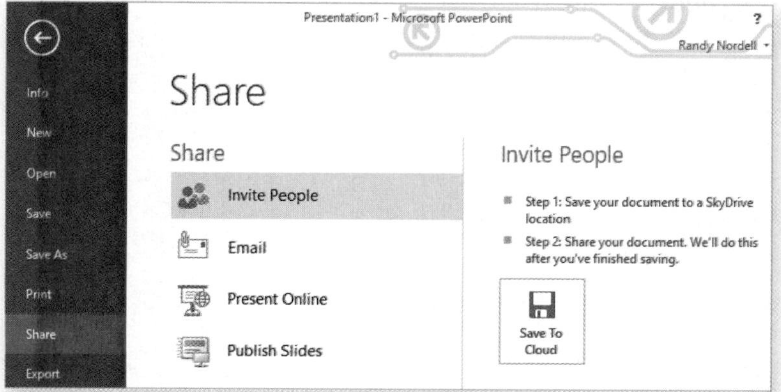

1-46 Save a file to the cloud before sharing

1-47 Share a file on a social network site

Program Options

Using the program options, you can make changes that apply globally to the Office program. For example, you can change the default save location to your *SkyDrive* folder or you can turn off the *Start* page that opens when you open an Office application.

Click the **File** tab and select **Options** on the left to open the **[Program] Options** dialog box (e.g., Word Options, Excel Options, etc.) (Figure 1-48). Click one of the categories on the left to display the category options on the right. The categories and options vary depending on the Office application you are using.

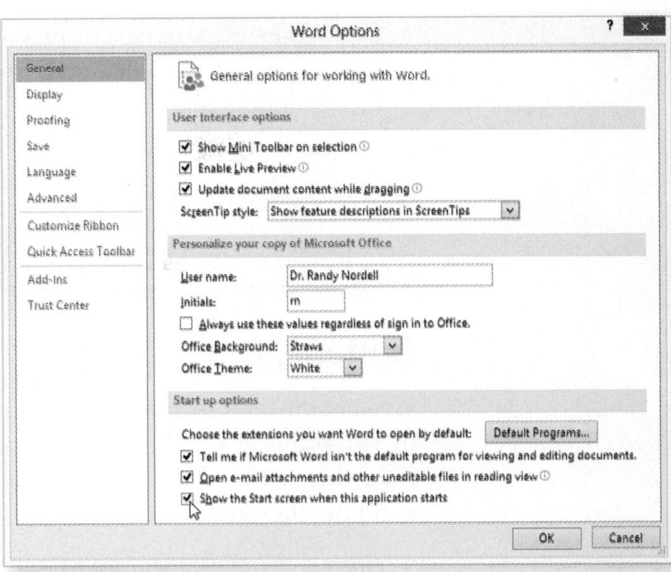

1-48 *Word Options* dialog box

Using the Ribbon, Tabs, and Quick Access Toolbar

SLO 1.4

You can use the *Ribbon,* tabs, groups, buttons, drop-down lists, dialog boxes, task panes, galleries, and the *Quick Access* toolbar to modify your Office files. This section describes the different tools you can use to customize your files.

The Ribbon, Tabs, and Groups

The ***Ribbon***, which appears at the top of an Office file window, displays the many features available to use on your files. The *Ribbon* is a collection of **tabs**. On each tab are ***groups*** of features. The tabs and groups that are available on each Office application vary. Click a tab to display the groups and features available on that tab.

Some tabs are always displayed on the *Ribbon* (e.g., *File* tab and *Home* tab). Other tabs are ***context-sensitive***, which means that they only appear on the *Ribbon* when a specific object is selected in your file. Figure 1-49 displays the context-sensitive *Table Tools Table* tab that displays in Access when you open a table.

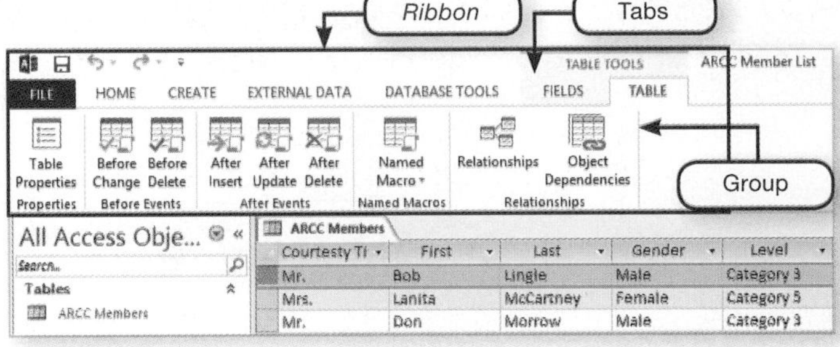

1-49 Context-sensitive *Table Tools Table* tab displayed

Ribbon Display Options

The *Ribbon* is by default displayed when an Office application is open, but you can customize how the *Ribbon* displays. The ***Ribbon Display Options*** button is in the upper right corner of an Office application window (Figure 1-50). Click the **Ribbon Display Options** button to select one of the three options.

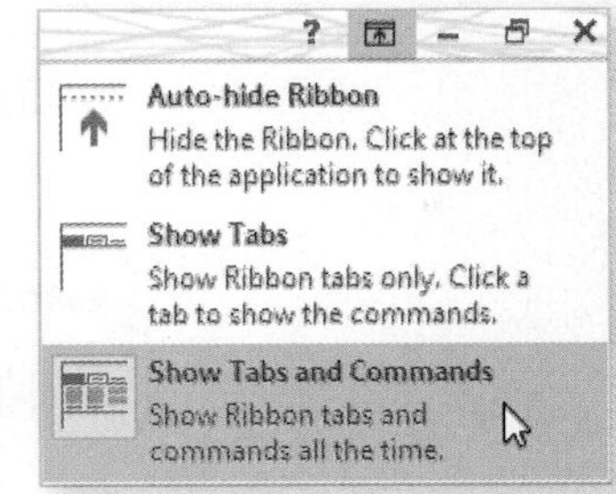

Auto-hide Ribbon
Hide the Ribbon. Click at the top of the application to show it.
Show Tabs
Show Ribbon tabs only. Click a tab to show the commands.
Show Tabs and Commands
Show Ribbon tabs and commands all the time.

1-50 *Ribbon Display Options*

- ***Auto-Hide Ribbon:*** Hides the *Ribbon*. Click at the top of the application to display the *Ribbon*.
- ***Show Tabs:*** *Ribbon* tabs display. Click a tab to open the *Ribbon* and display the tab.
- ***Show Tabs and Commands:*** Displays the *Ribbon* and tabs, which is the default setting in Office applications.

> MORE INFO
>
> **Ctrl+F1** collapses or expands the *Ribbon* to display only tabs.

Buttons, Drop-Down Lists, and Galleries

Groups on each of the tabs contain a variety of ***buttons***, ***drop-down lists***, and ***galleries***. The following list describes each of these features and how they are used:

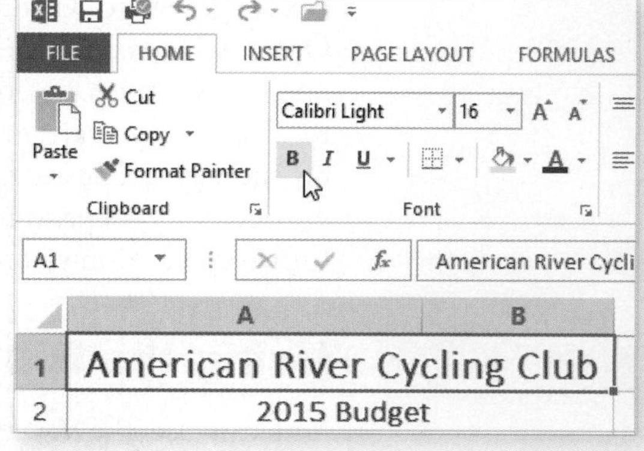

1-51 *Bold* button in the *Font* group on the *Home* tab

- ***Button:*** Applies a feature to selected text or object. Click a button to apply the feature (Figure 1-51).
- ***Drop-Down List:*** Displays the various options available for a feature. Some buttons are drop-down lists only, which means when you click one of these buttons the drop-down list of options appears (Figure 1-52). Other buttons are ***split buttons***, which have both a button you click to apply a feature and an arrow you click to display a drop-down list of options (Figure 1-53).

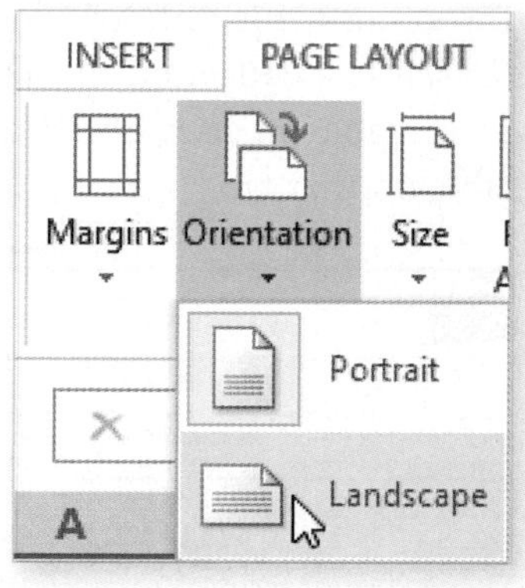

1-52 Drop-down list

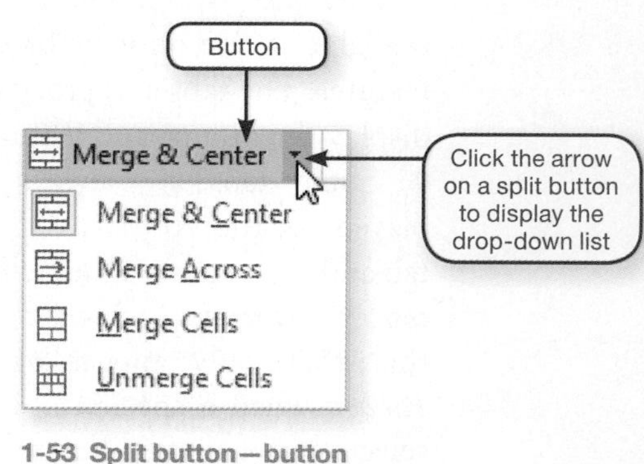

1-53 Split button—button and drop-down list

- ***Gallery:*** Displays a collection of option buttons. Click an option in a gallery to apply the feature. Figure 1-54 is the *Styles* gallery. You can click the **More** button to display the entire gallery of options or click the **Up** or **Down** arrow to display a different row of options.

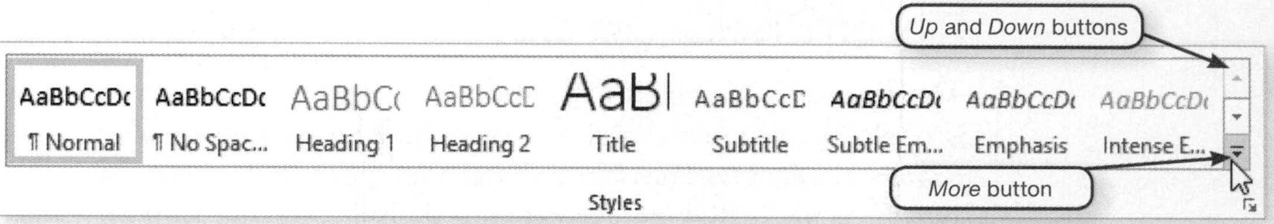

1-54 *Styles* gallery in Word

Dialog Boxes, Task Panes, and Launchers

Not all of the features that are available in an Office application are displayed in the groups on the tabs. Additional options for some groups are displayed in a ***dialog box*** or ***task pane***. A ***launcher***, which is a small square in the bottom right of some groups, opens a dialog box or displays a task pane when you click it (see Figure 1-56).

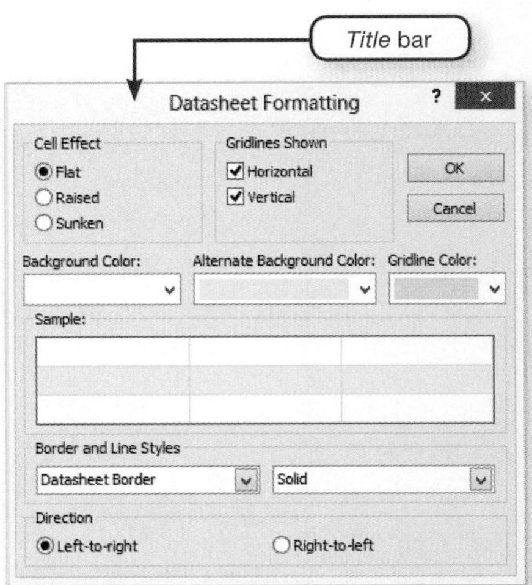

1-55 *Datasheet Formatting* dialog box

- ***Dialog box:*** A new window that opens to display additional features. You can move a dialog box by clicking and dragging on the title bar, which is the top of the dialog box where the title is displayed. Figure 1-55 is the *Datasheet Formatting* dialog box that opens when you click the *Text Formatting* launcher in Access.
- ***Task pane:*** Opens on the left or right of the Office application window. Figure 1-56 is the *Clipboard* pane, which is available in all Office applications. Task panes are named according to their feature (e.g., *Clipboard* pane or *Navigation* pane). You can resize a task pane by clicking and dragging on its left or right border. Click the **X** in the upper right corner to close a task pane.

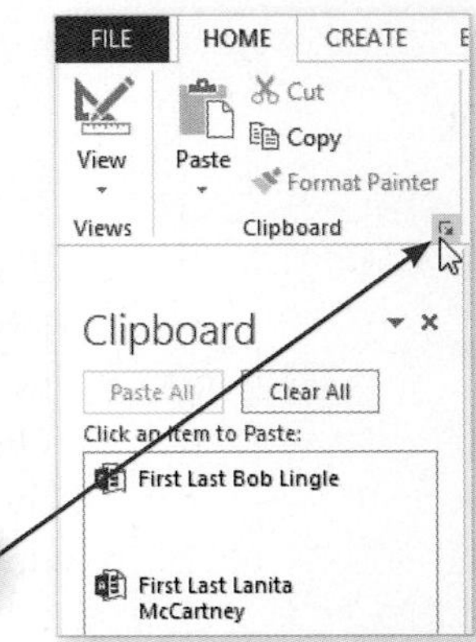

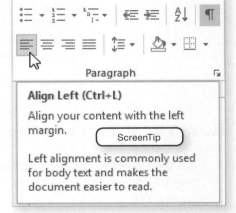

1-56 *Clipboard* pane

ScreenTips

ScreenTips display descriptive information about a button, drop-down list, launcher, or gallery selection in the groups on the *Ribbon*. When you put your pointer on an item on the *Ribbon*, a ScreenTip displays information about the selection (Figure 1-57). The ScreenTip appears temporarily and displays the command name, keyboard shortcut (if available), and a description of the command.

1-57 ScreenTip

Radio Buttons, Check Boxes, and Text Boxes

Within dialog boxes and task panes there are a variety of features you can apply using radio buttons, check boxes, text boxes, drop-down lists, and other buttons. A ***radio button*** is a round button that you click to select one option from a list of options. A selected radio button has a solid dot inside the round button. When you see a ***check box***, you can use it to select one or more options. A check appears in a check box you have selected. A ***text box*** is an area where you can type text.

A task pane or dialog box may also include drop-down lists or other buttons that open additional dialog boxes. Figure 1-58 shows the *Page Setup* dialog box in Excel, which includes a variety of radio buttons, check boxes, text boxes, drop-down lists, and other buttons that open additional dialog boxes.

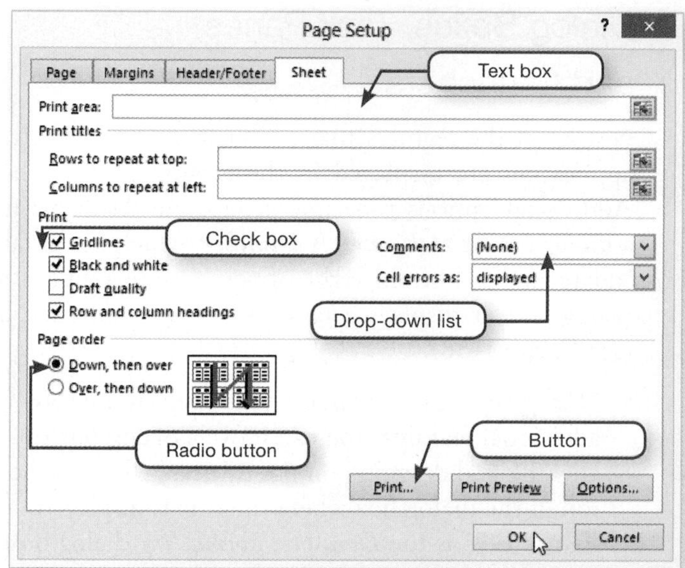

1-58 ***Page Setup*** **dialog box in Excel**

Quick Access Toolbar

The ***Quick Access toolbar*** is located above the *Ribbon* on the upper left of each Office application window. It contains buttons you can use to apply commonly used features such as *Save, Undo, Redo,* and *Open* (Figure 1-59). The *Undo* button is a split button. You can click the button to undo the last action performed or you can click the drop-down arrow to display and undo multiple previous actions.

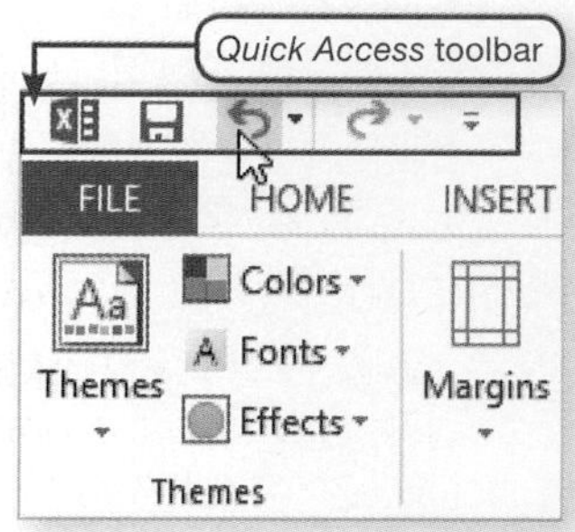

1-59 ***Quick Access*** **toolbar**

Customize the Quick Access Toolbar

You can customize the *Quick Access* toolbar to include features you regularly use, such as *Quick Print, New,* and *Spelling & Grammar.* The following steps show how to customize the *Quick Access* toolbar in Word. The customization process is similar for the *Quick Access* toolbar in the other Office applications.

HOW TO: Customize the Quick Access Toolbar

1. Click the **Customize Quick Access Toolbar** drop-down list on the right edge of the *Quick Access* toolbar (Figure 1-60).
2. Select a command to add to the *Quick Access* toolbar. The command appears on the *Quick Access* toolbar.
   - Items on the *Customize Quick Access Toolbar* drop-down list with a check mark are displayed on the *Quick Access* toolbar.
   - Deselect a checked item to remove it from the *Quick Access* toolbar.
3. To add a command that is not listed on the *Customize Quick Access Toolbar,* click the **Customize Quick Access Toolbar** drop-down list and select **More Commands**.

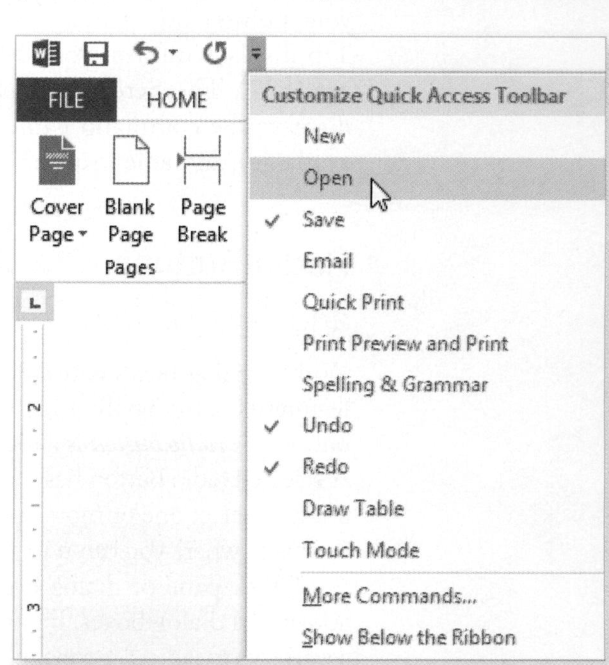

1-60 **Customize the *Quick Access* toolbar**

The *Word Options* dialog box opens with the *Quick Access Toolbar* area displayed (Figure 1-61).

4. Click the **Customize Quick Access Toolbar** drop-down list on the right and select **For all documents** or the current document.
   - If you select *For all documents*, the change is made to the *Quick Access* toolbar for all documents you open in Word.
   - If you select the current document, the change is made to the *Quick Access* toolbar in that document only.
5. On the left, select the command you want to add.
   - If you can't find the command you're looking for, click the **Choose commands from** drop-down list and select **All Commands**.
6. Click the **Add** button and the command name appears in the list on the right.
7. Add other commands as desired.
8. To rearrange commands on the *Quick Access* toolbar, select the command to move and click the **Move Up** or **Move Down** button.
9. Click **OK** to close the *Word Options* dialog box.

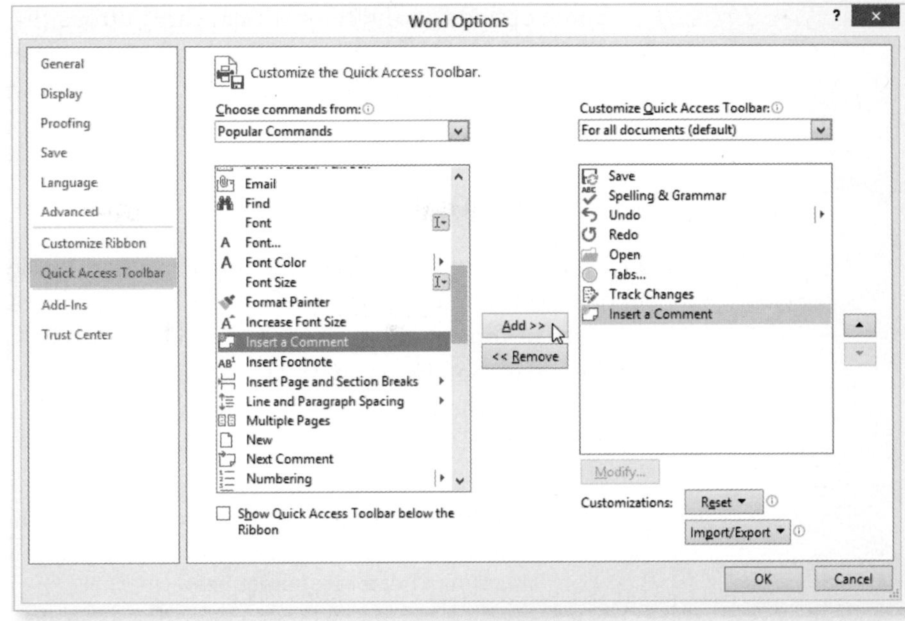

1-61 Customize the *Quick Access* toolbar in the *Word Options* dialog box

---

MORE INFO

To remove an item from the *Quick Access* toolbar, right-click an item and select **Remove from Quick Access Toolbar**.

SLO 1.5

Using a Context Menu, Mini Toolbar, and Keyboard Shortcuts

Most of the formatting and other features you will want to apply to text are available in groups on the different tabs. But many of these features are also available using content menus, mini toolbars, and keyboard shortcuts. You can use these tools to quickly apply formatting or other options to text or objects.

Context Menu

A ***context menu*** is displayed when you right-click text, a cell, or an object such as a picture, drawing object, chart, or *SmartArt* (Figure 1-62). The context menu is a vertical rectangle menu that lists a variety of options. These options are context-sensitive, which means they vary depending on what you right-click.

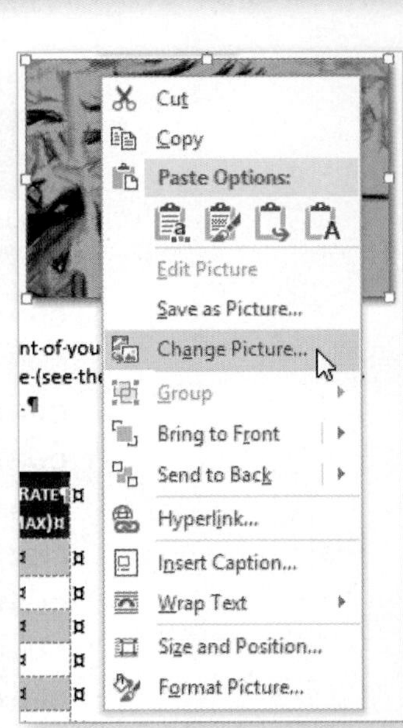

1-62 Context menu

Some options on the context menu are buttons that perform an action (e.g., *Cut* or *Copy*), some are buttons that open a dialog box or task pane (e.g., *Save as Picture* or *Size and Position*), and some are selections that display a drop-down list of selections (e.g., *Bring to Front* or *Wrap Text*).

Mini Toolbar

The ***mini toolbar*** is another context menu that displays when you right-click text, a cell, or an object in your file (Figure 1-63). The mini toolbar is a horizontal rectangle menu that lists a variety of formatting options. These options vary depending on what you right-click. The mini toolbar contains a variety of buttons and drop-down lists. Some mini toolbars automatically display when you select text or an object, such as when you select a row of a table in Word or PowerPoint.

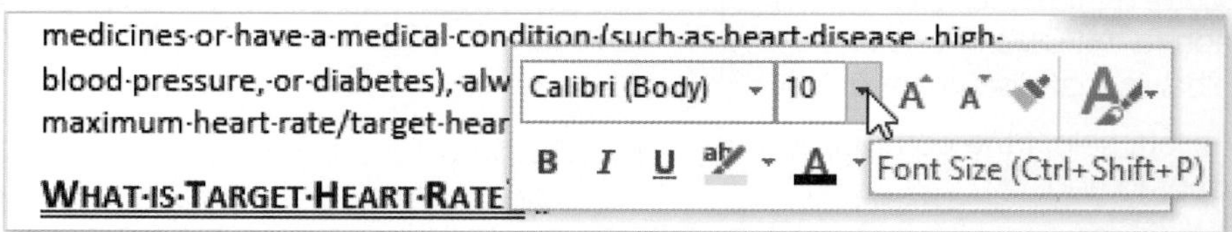

1-63 Mini toolbar

Keyboard Shortcuts

You can also use a ***keyboard shortcut*** to quickly apply formatting or perform actions. A keyboard shortcut is a keyboard key or combination of keyboard keys that you press at the same time. These can include the *Ctrl, Shift, Alt,* letter, number, and function keys (e.g., *F1* or *F7*). The following table lists some common Office keyboard shortcuts.

> **MORE INFO**
>
> See Appendix A for more Office 2013 keyboard shortcuts.

Common Office Keyboard Shortcuts

Keyboard Shortcut	Action or Displays	Keyboard Shortcut	Action or Displays
Ctrl+S	Save	**Ctrl+Z**	Undo
F12	*Save As* dialog box	**Ctrl+Y**	Redo or Repeat
Ctrl+O	*Open* area on the *Backstage* view	**Ctrl+1**	Single space
Shift+F12	*Open* dialog box	**Ctrl+2**	Double space
Ctrl+N	New blank file	**Ctrl+L**	Align left
Ctrl+P	*Print* area on the *Backstage* view	**Ctrl+E**	Align center
Ctrl+C	Copy	**Ctrl+R**	Align right
Ctrl+X	Cut	**F1**	*Help* dialog box
Ctrl+V	Paste	**F7**	*Spelling* pane
Ctrl+B	Bold	**Ctrl+A**	Select All
Ctrl+I	Italic	**Ctrl+Home**	Move to the beginning
Ctrl+U	Underline	**Ctrl+End**	Move to the end

PAUSE & PRACTICE: OFFICE 1-2

For this project, you work with a document for the American River Cycling Club. You modify the existing document, add document properties, customize the *Quick Access* toolbar, export the document as a PDF file, and share a link to the document.

Note to Instructor:
Students: *For this project, you share an Office Web App file with your instructor.*
Instructor: *In order to complete this project, your students need your Microsoft email address. You can create a new Live or Hotmail account for projects in this chapter.*

File Needed: ***ARCCTraining-01.docx***
Completed Project File Names: ***[your initials] PP O1-2.docx*** and ***[your initials] PP O1-2.pdf***

1. Open Word 2013 and open the ***ARCCTraining-01*** file from your student data files.
2. Save this document as ***[your initials] PP O1-2*** in the *American River Cycling Club* folder in your *SkyDrive* folder.
3. Use a button, drop-down list, and dialog box to modify the document.
   a. Select the first heading, "**What is Maximum Heart Rate?**"
   b. Click the **Bold** button [*Home* tab, *Font* group].
   c. Click the **Underline** drop-down arrow and select **Double underline** (Figure 1-64).
   d. Click the **launcher** in the *Font* group [*Home* tab] to open the *Font* dialog box (Figure 1-65).
   e. In the *Size* area, select **12** from the list or type 12 in the text box.
   f. In the *Effects* area, click the **Small caps** check box to select it.
   g. Click **OK** to close the dialog box and apply the formatting changes.
   h. Select the next heading, "**What is Target Heart Rate?**"
   i. Repeat steps 3b–g to apply formatting to selected text.

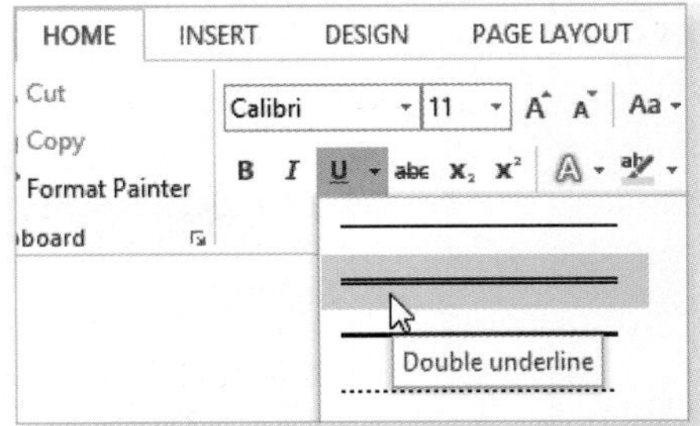

1-64 Apply *Double underline* to selected text

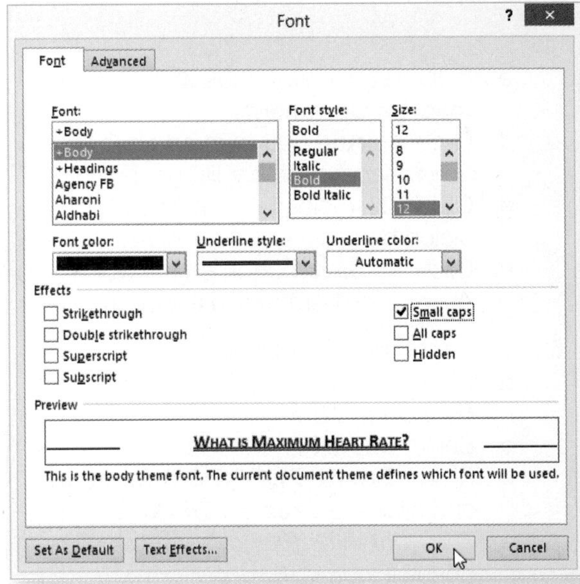

1-65 *Font* dialog box

4. Add document properties.
   a. Click the **File** tab to display the *Backstage* view.
   b. Select **Info** on the left. The document properties are displayed on the right.
   c. Click in the **Add a title** text box and type ARCC Training.
   d. Click the **Show All Properties** link near the bottom to display more document properties.
   e. Click in the **Specify the subject** text box and type Heart rate training.
   f. Click in the **Specify the company** text box and type American River Cycling Club.
   g. Click the **Show Fewer Properties** link to display fewer document properties.
   h. Click the **Back** arrow on the upper left to close the *Backstage* view and return to the document.

5. Customize the *Quick Access* toolbar.
   a. Click the **Customize Quick Access Toolbar** drop-down arrow and select **Open** (Figure 1-66).
   b. Click the **Customize Quick Access Toolbar** drop-down arrow again and select **Spelling & Grammar**.
   c. Click the **Customize Quick Access Toolbar** drop-down arrow and select **More Commands**. The *Word Options* dialog box opens (Figure 1-67).
   d. Click the **Customize Quick Access Toolbar** drop-down list on the right and select **For all documents**.

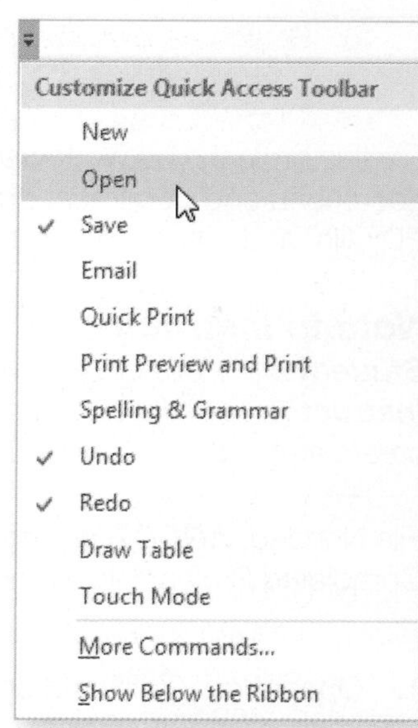

1-66 *Customize Quick Access Toolbar* drop-down list

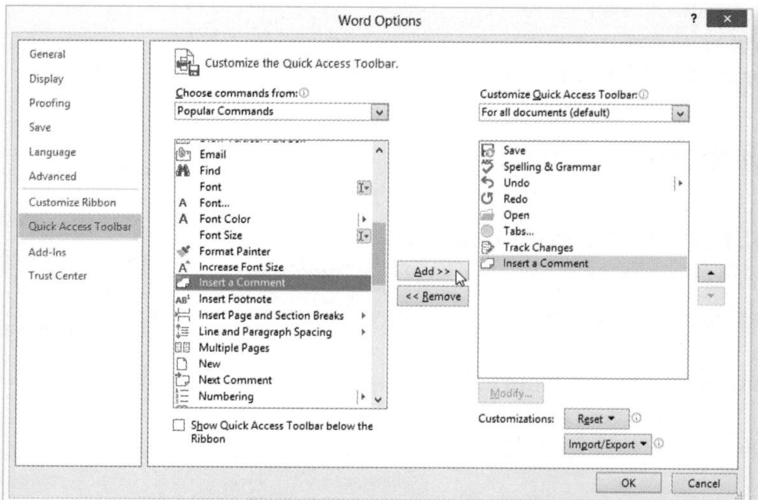

1-67 Customize the *Quick Access* toolbar in the *Word Options* dialog box

   e. In the list of commands at the left, click **Insert a Comment**.
   f. Click the **Add** button to add it to your *Quick Access* toolbar list on the right.
   g. Click **OK** to close the *Word Options* dialog box.
   h. Click the **Save** button on the *Quick Access* toolbar to save the document.

6. Export the file as a PDF file.
   a. Click the **File** tab to go to the *Backstage* view.
   b. Select **Export** on the left.
   c. Select **Create PDF/XPS Document** and click the **Create PDF/XPS** button. The *Publish as PDF or XPS* dialog box opens (Figure 1-68).
   d. Select the **American River Cycling Club** folder in your *SkyDrive* folder as the location to save the file.
   e. In the *File name* area, type [your initials] PP O1-2 if it is not already there.
   f. Deselect the **Open file after publishing** check box if it is checked.

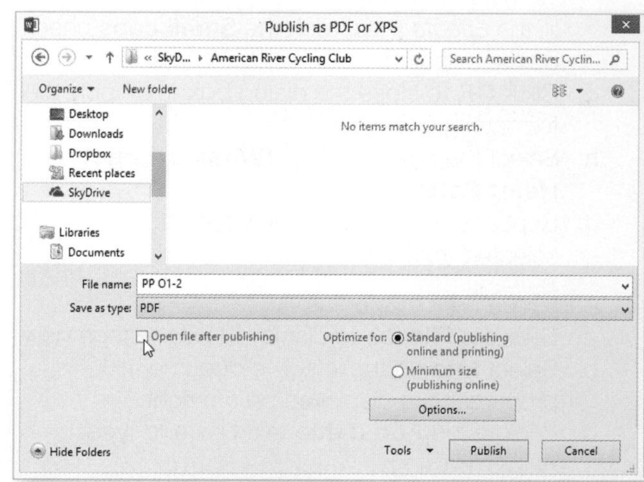

1-68 *Publish as PDF or XPS* dialog box

g. Select the **Standard** (publishing online and printing) radio button.
h. Click **Publish** to close the dialog box and create a PDF version of your file.

7. Get a link to share a document with your instructor.
   a. Click the **File** tab to open the *Backstage* view.
   b. Select **Share** at the left. Your file is already saved to *SkyDrive* so all of the *Share* options are available.
   c. Select **Get a Sharing Link** on the left (Figure 1-69).
   d. In the *View Link* area, click the **Create Link** button. A link for the document is created and displayed on the right of the button.
   e. Select this link and press **Ctrl+C** to copy the link.
   f. Click the **Back** arrow to close the *Backstage* view and return to your document.
8. Save and close the document (Figure 1-70).
9. Email the sharing link to your instructor.
   a. Using your email account, create a new email to send to your instructor.
   b. Include an appropriate subject line and a brief message in the body.
   c. Press **Ctrl+V** to paste the link to your document in the body of the email.
   d. Send the email message.

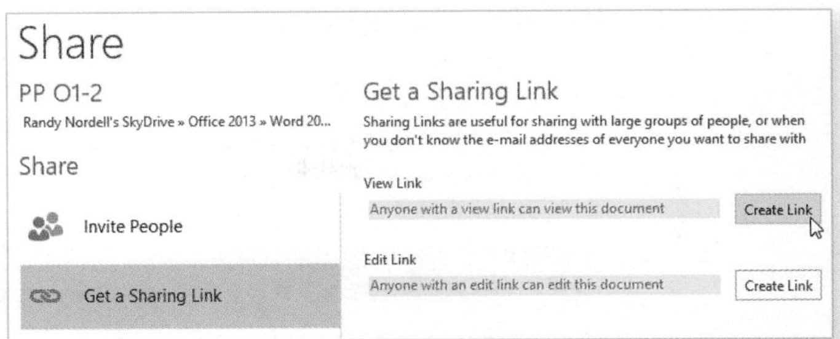

1-69 *Get a Link* to share a file

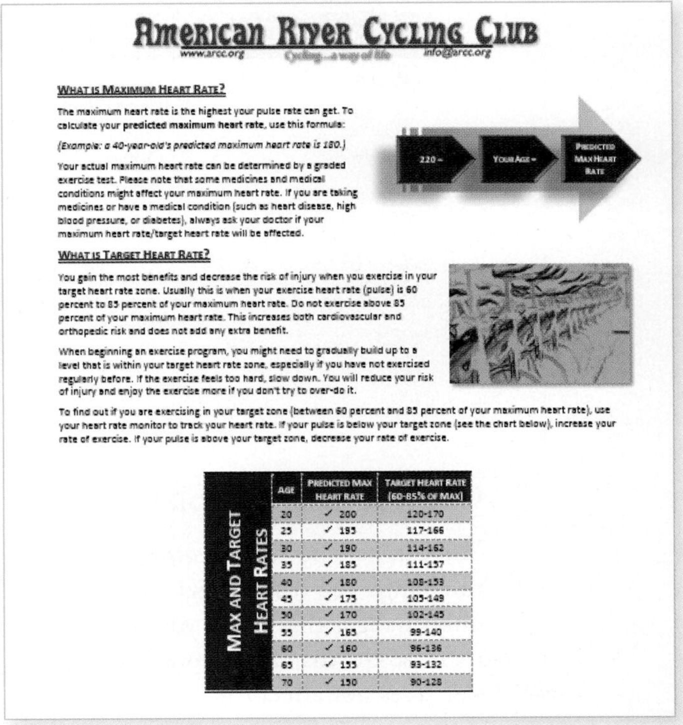

AMERICAN RIVER CYCLING CLUB

www.arcc.org Cycling...a way of life info@arcc.org

WHAT IS MAXIMUM HEART RATE?

The maximum heart rate is the highest your pulse rate can get. To calculate your **predicted maximum heart rate**, use this formula:

220 – Your Age = Predicted Max Heart Rate

(Example: a 40-year-old's predicted maximum heart rate is 180.)

Your actual maximum heart rate can be determined by a graded exercise test. Please note that some medicines and medical conditions might affect your maximum heart rate. If you are taking medicines or have a medical condition (such as heart disease, high blood pressure, or diabetes), always ask your doctor if your maximum heart rate/target heart rate will be affected.

WHAT IS TARGET HEART RATE?

You gain the most benefits and decrease the risk of injury when you exercise in your target heart rate zone. Usually this is when your exercise heart rate (pulse) is 60 percent to 85 percent of your maximum heart rate. Do not exercise above 85 percent of your maximum heart rate. This increases both cardiovascular and orthopedic risk and does not add any extra benefit.

When beginning an exercise program, you might need to gradually build up to a level that is within your target heart rate zone, especially if you have not exercised regularly before. If the exercise feels too hard, slow down. You will reduce your risk of injury and enjoy the exercise more if you don't try to over-do it.

To find out if you are exercising in your target zone (between 60 percent and 85 percent of your maximum heart rate), use your heart rate monitor to track your heart rate. If your pulse is below your target zone (see the chart below), increase your rate of exercise. If your pulse is above your target zone, decrease your rate of exercise.

MAX AND TARGET HEART RATES

AGE	PREDICTED MAX HEART RATE	TARGET HEART RATE (60-85% OF MAX)
20	✓ 200	120-170
25	✓ 195	117-166
30	✓ 190	114-162
35	✓ 185	111-157
40	✓ 180	108-153
45	✓ 175	105-149
50	✓ 170	102-145
55	✓ 165	99-140
60	✓ 160	96-136
65	✓ 155	93-132
70	✓ 150	90-128

1-70 PP O1-2 completed

SLO 1.6

Working with Files

When you work with Office files, there are a variety of views to display your file. You can change how a file is displayed, adjust the display size, work with multiple files, and arrange the windows to view multiple files. Because most people work with multiple files at the same time, Office makes it intuitive to move from one file to another or display multiple document windows at the same time.

File Views

Each of the different Office applications provides you with a variety of ways to view your document. In Word, Excel, and PowerPoint, the different views are available on the *View* tab

(Figure 1-71). You can also change views using the buttons on the right side of the *Status* bar at the bottom of the file window (Figure 1-72). In Access, the different views for each object are available in the *Views* group on the *Home* tab.

The following table lists the views that are available in each of the different Office applications.

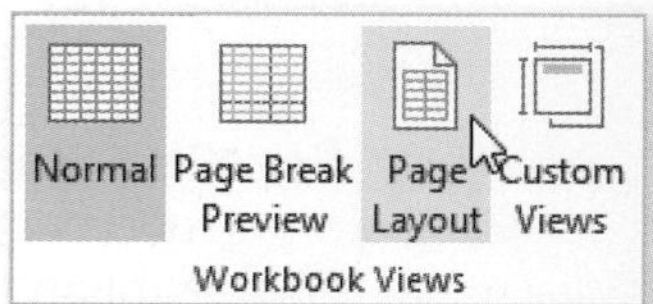

1-71 *Workbook Views* group on the *View* tab in Excel

1-72 PowerPoint views on the *Status* bar

File Views

Office Application	Views	Office Application	Views
Word	Read Mode Print Layout Web Layout Outline Draft	**Access** *(Access views vary depending on active object)*	Layout View Design View Datasheet View Form View SQL View Report View Print Preview
Excel	Normal Page Break View Page Layout View Custom Views	**PowerPoint**	Normal Outline View Slide Sorter Notes Page Reading View Presenter View

Change Display Size

You can use the ***Zoom feature*** to increase or decrease the display size of your file. Using *Zoom* to change the display size does not change the actual size of text or objects in your file; it only changes the size of your display. For example, if you change the *Zoom* level to 120%, you increase the display of your file to 120% of its normal size (100%), but changing the display size does not affect the actual size of text and objects in your file. You could also decrease the *Zoom* level to 80% to display more of your file on the screen.

There are a few different ways you can increase or decrease the *Zoom* level on your file. Your *Zoom* options vary depending on the Office application you are using.

- ***Zoom level on the* Status *bar*** (Figure 1-73): Click the + or – buttons to increase or decrease *Zoom* level.

1-73 *Zoom* level area on the *Status* bar in PowerPoint

- ***Zoom group on the View tab*** (Figure 1-74): There are a variety of *Zoom* options in the *Zoom* group. These vary depending on application.

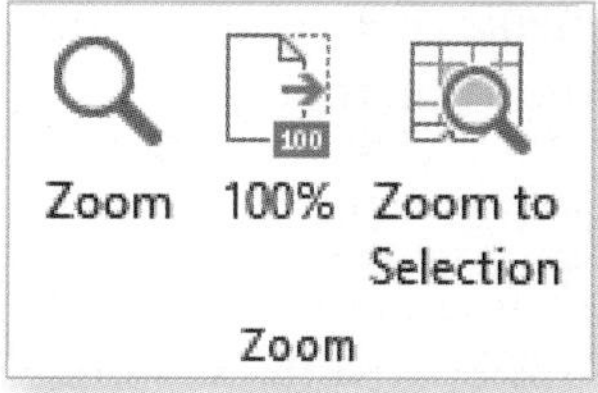

1-74 *Zoom* group in Excel

- ***Zoom dialog box*** (Figure 1-75): Click the **Zoom** button in the *Zoom* group on *View* tab or click **Zoom level** on the *Status* bar to open the *Zoom* dialog box.

> **MORE INFO**
>
> The *Zoom* feature is only available in Access in *Print Preview* view when you are working with reports.

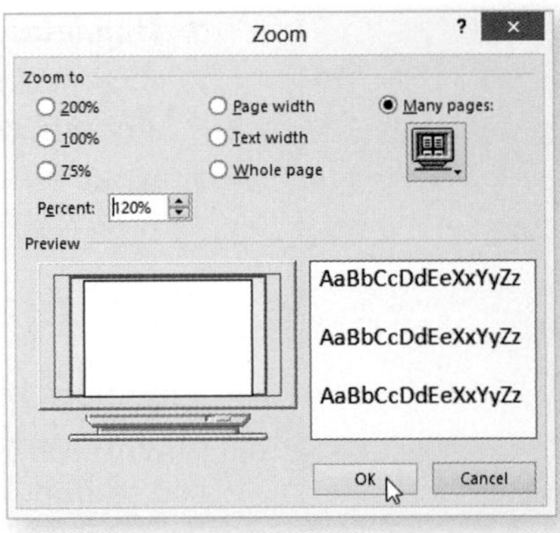

1-75 *Zoom* dialog box in Word

Manage Multiple Open Files and Windows

When you are working on multiple files in an Office application, each file is opened in a new window. You can ***minimize*** an open window to place the file on the Windows *Taskbar* (the bar at the bottom of the Windows desktop), ***restore down*** an open window so it does not fill the entire computer screen, or ***maximize*** a window so it fills the entire computer screen. The *Minimize, Restore Down/Maximize,* and *Close* buttons are in the upper right of a file window (Figure 1-76).

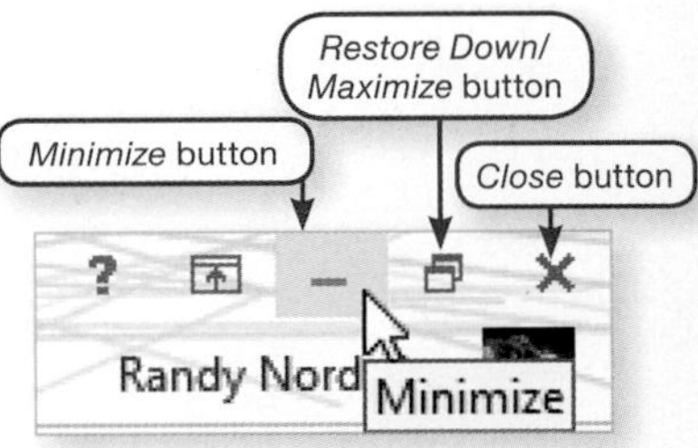

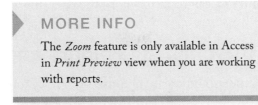

1-76 Window options buttons

> **MORE INFO**
>
> You can open only one Access file at a time. If you open another Access file, the first one closes.

- ***Minimize:*** Click the **Minimize** button to hide this window. When a document is minimized, it is not closed. It is collapsed so the window is not displayed on your screen. Click the application icon on the Windows *Taskbar* at the bottom to display thumbnails of open files. You can click an open file thumbnail to display the file (Figure 1-77).

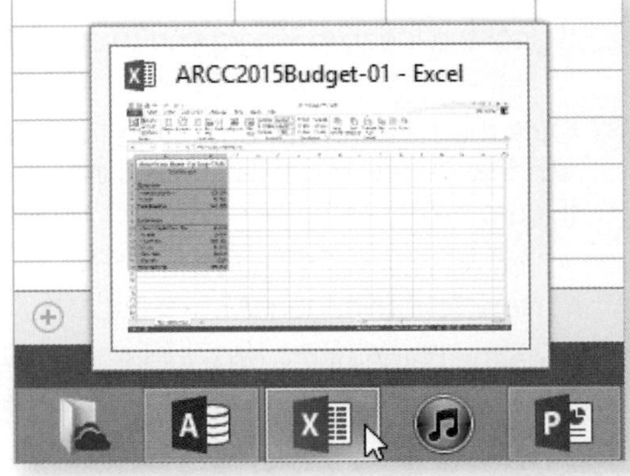

1-77 Display open files on the Windows *Taskbar*

- ***Restore Down/Maximize:*** Click the **Restore Down/Maximize** button to decrease the size of an open window or maximize the window to fill the entire screen. This button toggles between *Restore Down* and *Maximize.* When a window is restored down, you can change the size of a window by clicking and dragging on a border of the window. You can also move the window by clicking and dragging on the title bar at the top of the window.
- ***Close:*** Click the **Close** button to close the window. If there is only one open file, the Office application also closes when you click the *Close* button on the file.

You can switch between open files or arrange the open files to display more than one window at the same time. There are a few ways to do this.

- ***Switch Windows button:*** Click the **Switch Windows** button [*View* tab, *Window* group] (not available in Access) to display a drop-down list of open files. Click a file from the drop-down list to display the file.

- ***Windows Taskbar:*** Click an Office application icon on the Windows *Taskbar* to display the open files in that application. Click an open file to display it (see Figure 1-77).
- ***Arrange All button:*** Click the **Arrange All** button [*View* tab, *Window* group] to display all windows in an application. You can resize or move the open file windows.

Organizing and Customizing Folders and Files

The more you use your computer and create and use files, the more important it is to stay organized. You can do this by using folders to store related files, which makes it easier for you to find, edit, and share your files. For example, you can create a folder for the college you attend. Inside the college folder, you can create a folder for each of your courses. Inside each of the course folders you might create a folder for student data files, solution files, and group projects. Folders can store any type of files, and you are not limited to Office files.

Create a Folder

You can create folders inside of other folders. In *SLO 1.2: Creating, Saving, Closing, and Opening Files,* you learned how to create a new folder when saving an Office file in the *Save As* dialog box. You can also create a folder using a Windows folder.

HOW TO: Create a Windows Folder

1. Open a Windows folder.
   - From the Windows *Start* page, click **File Explorer**, **Computer**, or **Documents** to open a Windows window.
   - Your folders and computer locations are listed on the left.
2. Select the location where you want to create a new folder.
3. Click the **New folder** button on the top left of the window. A new folder is created in the folders area (Figure 1-78).
   - You can also click the **Home** tab and click the **New folder** button [*New* group].
4. Type the name of the new folder and press **Enter**.

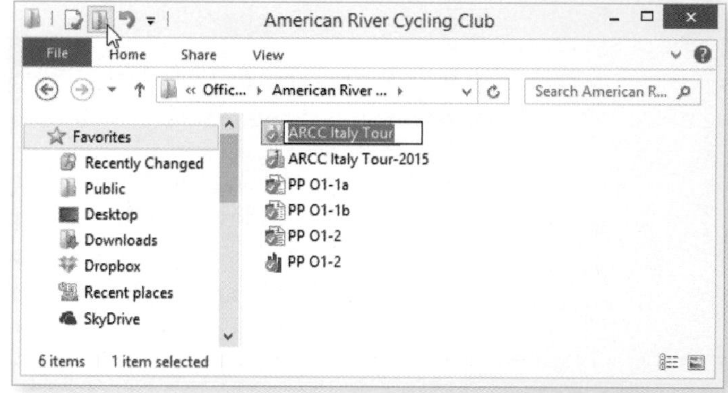

1-78 Create a new Windows folder

> **ANOTHER WAY**
>
> **Ctrl+Shift+N** creates a new folder in a Windows folder.

Move and Copy Files and Folders

You can move or copy files and folders using the *Move to* or *Copy to* buttons on the *Home* tab of a Windows folder. You can also use the move or copy keyboard shortcuts (**Ctrl+X, Ctrl+C, Ctrl+V**) or the drag and drop method. When you move a file or folder, you cut it from one location and paste it in another location. When you copy a file or folder, you create a copy of it and paste it in another location so the file or folder is in two or more locations. If there are files in a folder you move or copy, the files in the folder are moved or copied with the folder.

To move or copy multiple folders or files at the same time, press the **Ctrl** key and select multiple items to move or copy. Use the *Ctrl* key to select or deselect multiple non-adjacent files or folders. You can also use the *Shift* key to select a range of files or folders. Click the first file or folder in a range, press the **Shift** key, and select the last file or folder in the range to select all of the items in the range.

HOW TO: Move or Copy a File or Folder

1. In a Windows folder, select a file or folder to move or copy.
2. Click the **Home** tab to display the tab in the open window.
3. Click the **Move to** or **Copy to** button [*Organize* group] and select the location where you want to move or copy the file or folder (Figure 1-79).
   - If the folder you want is not available, select **Choose location** to open the *Move Items* or *Copy Items* dialog box.
   - To use the keyboard shortcuts, press **Ctrl+X** to cut the file or folder or **Ctrl+C** to copy the file or folder from its original location, go to the desired new location, and press **Ctrl+V** to paste it.
   - To use the drag and drop method to move a file or folder, select the file or folder and drag and drop on the new location.
   - To use the drag and drop method to copy a file or folder, press the **Ctrl** key, select the file or folder, and drag and drop on the new location.

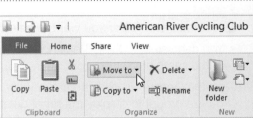

1-79 Move or copy a selected file or folder

> **ANOTHER WAY**
>
> Right-click a file or folder to display the context menu where you can select **Cut, Copy,** or **Paste.**

Rename Files and Folders

When you need to change the name of a file or folder, you can rename these in a Windows folder.

HOW TO: Rename a File or Folder

1. In a Windows folder, select the file or folder you want to rename.
2. Click the **Rename** button [*Home* tab, *Organize* group].
3. Type the new name of the file or folder and press **Enter**.

> **ANOTHER WAY**
>
> Select a file or folder to rename, press **F2**, type the new name, and press **Enter**. You can also right-click a file or folder and select **Rename** from the context menu.

Delete Files and Folders

You can also easily delete files and folders. When you delete a file or folder, it is moved from its current location to the ***Recycle Bin*** on your computer, which is the location where deleted items are stored. If a file or folder is in the *Recycle Bin,* you can restore this item to its original location or move it to a different location. You also have the option to permanently delete a file or folder; the item is deleted and not moved to the *Recycle Bin.* If an item is permanently deleted, you do not have the restore option.

There are several ways to delete a file or folder. To ensure that you don't delete anything by mistake, when you delete a file or folder, a confirmation dialog box opens, prompting you to confirm whether or not you want to delete the selected file or folder.

HOW TO: Delete Files and Folders

1. Select the file or folder you want to delete.
   - You can select multiple files and folders to delete at the same time.
2. Click the **Delete** drop-down arrow [*Home* tab, *Organize* group] to display the list of delete options (Figure 1-80).
3. Click **Recycle** or **Permanently delete**. A confirmation dialog box opens.
   - *Recycle* deletes the selected item(s) and moves them to the *Recycle Bin.*
   - *Permanently delete* deletes the item(s) from your computer.
   - The default action when you click the *Delete* button (not the drop-down arrow) is *Recycle*.
4. Click **Yes** to delete.

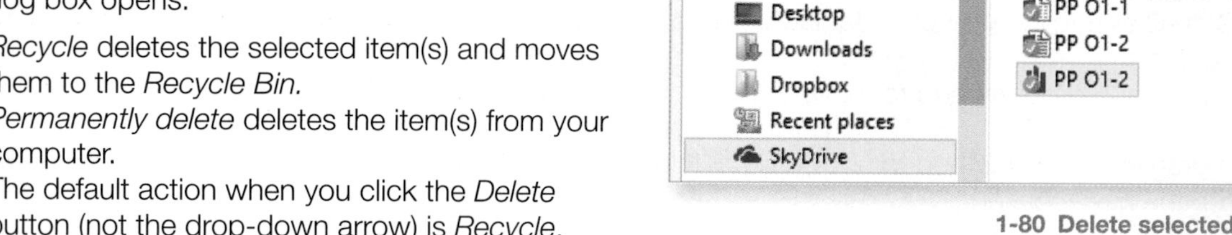

1-80 Delete selected files and folders

> **ANOTHER WAY**
>
> Press **Ctrl+D** or the **Delete** key on your keyboard to recycle selected item(s).
> Press **Shift+Delete** to permanently delete selected item(s).

Compressed and Zipped Folders

If you want to share multiple files or a folder of files with classmates, coworkers, friends, or family, you can ***zip*** the files into a ***zipped folder*** (also called a ***compressed folder***). For example, you can't attach an entire folder to an email message, but you can attach a zipped folder to an email message. Compressing files and folders decreases their size. You can zip a group of selected files, a folder, or a combination of files and folders, and then share the zipped folder with others through email or in a cloud storage location such as *SkyDrive.*

HOW TO: Create a Zipped Folder

1. Select the file(s) and/or folder(s) you want to compress and send.
2. Click the **Zip** button [*Share* tab, *Send* group] (Figure 1-81). A zipped folder is created.
   - The name of the zipped folder is the name of the first item you selected to zip. You can rename this folder.
   - The icon for a zipped folder looks similar to the icon for a folder except it has a vertical zipper down the middle of the folder.

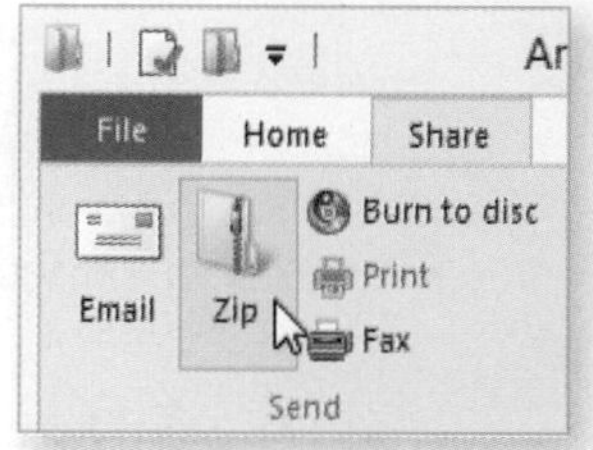

1-81 Create a zipped folder

> **ANOTHER WAY**
>
> Right-click a selected file(s) and/or folder(s), click **Send to,** and select **Compressed (zipped) folder.**

If you receive a zipped folder from someone via email, save the zipped folder and then you can ***extract*** its contents. Extracting a zipped folder creates a regular Window folder from the zipped folder.

HOW TO: Extract a Zipped Folder

1. After saving the zipped folder to a location on your computer, select the folder (Figure 1-82).
2. Click the **Extract all** button [*Compress Folder Tools Extract* tab]. The *Extract Compressed (Zipped) Folders* dialog box opens (Figure 1-83).
3. Click **Extract** to extract the folder.
   - Both the extracted folder and the zipped folder display in the folder where they are located.
   - If you check the **Show extracted files when complete** check box, the extracted folder will open after extracting.

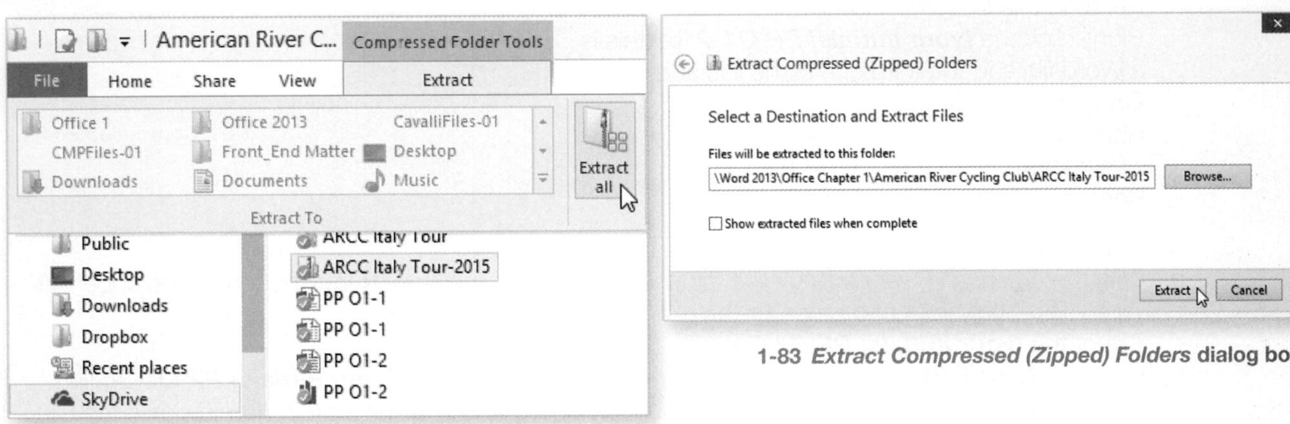

1-82 Extract files from a zipped folder

1-83 *Extract Compressed (Zipped) Folders* dialog box

PAUSE & PRACTICE: OFFICE 1-3

For this project, you copy and rename files in your *SkyDrive* folder on your computer, create a folder, move and copy files, create a zipped folder, and rename a zipped folder.

Files Needed: ***[your initials] PP O1-1a.pptx***, ***[your initials] PP O1-1b.xlsx***, and ***[your initials] PP O1-2.docx***
Completed Project File Names: ***[your initials] PP O1-3a.pptx***, ***[your initials] PP O1-3b.xlsx***, ***[your initials] PP O1-3c.docx***, and ***ARCC Italy Tour-[current year]*** (zipped folder)

1. Open your *SkyDrive* folder.
   a. From the Windows *Start* page, click the **File Explorer** or **Computer** tile to open a Windows folder. If these options are not available on the *Start* page, use *Search* to find and open the *File Explorer* or *Computer* window.

   b. Click the **SkyDrive** folder on the left to display the folders in your *SkyDrive* folder.
   c. Double click the **American River Cycling Club** folder to open it.

2. Copy and rename files.
   a. Select the ***[your initials] PP O1-1a*** file (this is a PowerPoint file).
   b. Click the **Copy to** button [*Home* tab, *Organize* group] and select **Choose Location** to open the *Copy Items* dialog box (Figure 1-84).
   c. Select the **American River Cycling Club** folder in your *SkyDrive* folder and click **Copy**.
   d. Select the copy of the file (***[your initials] PP O1-1a – Copy***) and click the **Rename** button [*Home* tab, *Organize* group].
   e. Type [your initials] PP O1-3a and press **Enter**.
   f. Select the ***[your initials] PP O1-1b*** file (this is an Excel file).
   g. Press **Ctrl+C** to copy the file and then press **Ctrl+V** to paste a copy of the file.
   h. Rename this file [your initials] PP O1-3b.
   i. Right-click the ***[your initials] PP O1-2*** file (this is a Word file and the third one in the list) and select **Copy** from the context menu.
   j. Right-click a blank area of the open window and select **Paste** from the context menu.
   k. Rename this file [your initials] PP O1-3c.

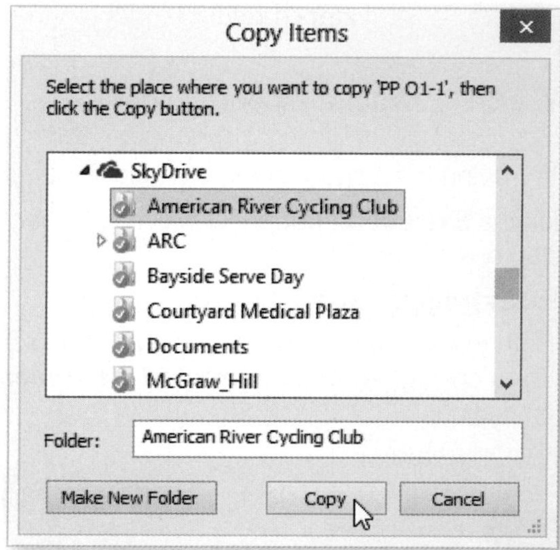

1-84 Copy selected file

3. Create a new folder and move files.
   a. With the *American River Cycling Club* folder still open, click the **New folder** button on the upper left.
   b. Type ARCC Italy Tour and press **Enter**.
   c. Select the ***[your initials] PP O1-3a*** file.
   d. Hold down the **Ctrl** key, select the ***[your initials] PP O1-3b*** and ***[your initials] PP O1-3c*** files.
   e. Click the selected files and drag and drop on the *ARCC Italy Tour* folder (don't hold down the *Ctrl* key while dragging). The files are moved to the *ARCC Italy Tour* folder.
   f. Double-click the **ARCC Italy Tour** folder to open it and confirm the files are moved.
   g. Click the **Up** or **Back** arrow to return to the *American River Cycling Club* folder.

4. Create a zipped folder.
   a. Select the **ARCC Italy Tour** folder.
   b. Click the **Zip** button [*Share* tab, *Send* group]. A zipped (compressed) folder is created.
   c. Right-click the zipped folder and select **Rename** from the context menu.
   d. At the end of the folder name, type - (a hyphen), type the current year, and press **Enter** (Figure 1-85).

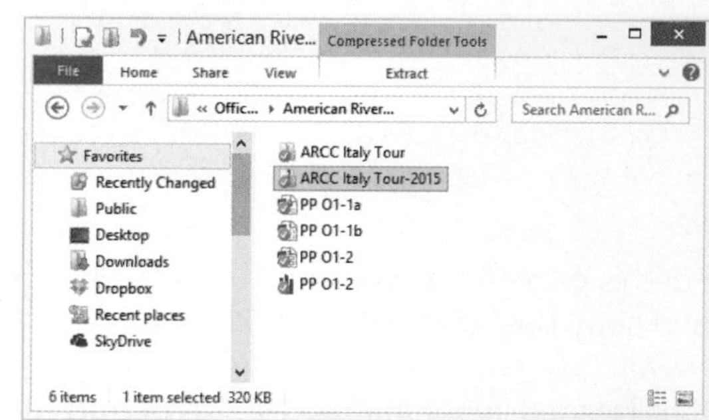

1-85 PP O1-3 completed

5. Email the zipped folder to your instructor.
   a. Using your email account, create a new email to send to your instructor.
   b. Include an appropriate subject line and a brief message in the body.
   c. Attach the ***ARCC Italy Tour-[current year]*** zipped folder to the email message.
   d. Send the email message.

Chapter Summary

1.1 Use the basic features of Windows 8 and Microsoft Office 2013 products (p. O1-2).

- ***Windows 8*** is the operating system on your computer.
- A ***Microsoft account*** is a free account you create. When you create a Microsoft account, you are given an email address, a ***SkyDrive*** account, and access to ***Office Web Apps***.
- ***SkyDrive*** is the ***cloud storage*** area where you can store files in a private and secure online location.
- In Windows 8, the ***SkyDrive folder*** is one of your file storage location options.
- The ***Start page*** in Windows 8 is where you select what you want to do on your computer.
- The ***Windows desktop*** is the working area of Windows and the ***Taskbar*** is at the bottom of the desktop. You can pin applications to the *Taskbar.*
- The ***File Explorer*** is a window that displays libraries, files, and folders on your computer.
- You can access your *SkyDrive* folders and files using an Internet browser window.
- ***Apps*** are the applications or programs on your computer. App buttons are arranged in tiles on the Windows 8 *Start* page.
- You can customize the *Start* page to add, remove, or arrange apps.
- ***Navigation options*** display on the right side of your computer monitor when you put your pointer in the bottom right corner.
- ***Office 2013*** is application software that contains ***Word***, ***Excel***, ***Access***, ***PowerPoint***, ***Outlook***, ***OneNote***, and ***Publisher***.
- ***Office Web Apps*** is free online software that works in conjunction with your online *SkyDrive* account.
- In *SkyDrive*, you can share Office files with others.
- When you open each of the Office applications, a ***Start page*** is displayed where you can open an existing file or create a new file.
- In the ***Backstage view*** in each of the Office applications, you can perform many common tasks such as saving, opening an existing file, creating a new file, printing, and sharing.
- ***Office Help*** contains searchable articles related to specific topics.
- Use the mouse (or touch pad) on your computer to navigate the pointer on your computer screen. Use the pointer or click buttons to select text or objects.
- When using Office 2013 on a tablet, use the touch screen to perform actions.

1.2 Create, save, close, and open Office files (p. O1-12).

- You can create a new Office file from the *Start* page or *Backstage* view of the Office application you are using.
- When you ***save a file*** for the first time, you give it a ***file name***.
- You can create ***folders*** to organize saved files, and you can save a file as a different file name.
- A variety of different ***file types*** are used in each of the Office applications.
- You can close an Office file when you are finished working on it. If the file has not been saved or changes have been made to the file, you are prompted to save the file before closing.
- In each of the Office applications, you can open an existing file from the *Start* page or from the *Backstage* view.

1.3 Print, share, and customize Office files (p. O1-20).

- You can print a file in a variety of formats. The *Print* area on the *Backstage* view lists your print options and displays a preview of your file.
- You can export a file as a ***PDF file*** and save the PDF file to post to a web site or share with others.
- ***Document properties*** contain information about a file.
- You can ***share*** Office files in a variety of ways and allow others to view or edit shared files.
- ***Program options*** are available on the *Backstage* view. You can use the program options to make global changes to an Office application.

1.4 Use the Ribbon, tabs, groups, dialog boxes, task panes, galleries, and the Quick Access toolbar (p. O1-23).

- The ***Ribbon*** appears at the top of an Office window. It contains ***tabs*** and ***groups*** that allow you to access features you regularly use.

- The ***Ribbon Display Options*** provides different ways the *Ribbon* can be displayed in Office applications.
- Within groups on each tab are a variety of ***buttons***, ***drop-down lists***, and ***galleries***.
- ***Dialog boxes*** contain additional features not always displayed on the *Ribbon*.
- Click the ***launcher*** in the bottom right corner of some groups to open a dialog box for that group.
- A ***ScreenTip*** displays information about commands on the *Ribbon*.
- Dialog boxes contain ***radio buttons***, ***check boxes***, ***drop-down lists***, and ***text boxes*** you can use to apply features.
- The ***Quick Access toolbar***, which contains buttons that allow you to perform commands, is displayed in all Office applications on the upper left.
- You can add or remove commands on the *Quick Access* toolbar.

1.5 Use context menus, mini toolbars, and keyboard shortcuts in Office applications (p. O1-27).

- A ***context menu*** displays when you right-click text or an object. The context menu contains different features depending on what you right-click.
- The ***mini toolbar*** is another context menu that displays formatting options.
- You can use ***keyboard shortcuts*** to apply features or commands.

1.6 Customize the view and display size in Office applications and work with multiple Office files (p. O1-31).

- In each of the Office applications, there are a variety of ***views***.
- The ***Zoom feature*** changes the display size of your file.
- You can work with multiple Office files at the same time and switch between open files.

1.7 Organize and customize Office files and Windows folders (p. O1-34).

- ***Folders*** store and organize your files.
- You can create, move, or copy files and folders. Files stored in a folder are moved or copied with that folder.
- You can rename a file to change the file name.
- When you delete a file or folder, it is moved to the ***Recycle Bin*** on your computer by default. Alternatively, you can permanently delete files and folders.
- A ***zipped (compressed) folder*** makes it easier and faster to email or share multiple files. You can zip files and/or folders into a zipped folder.
- When you receive a zipped folder, you can ***extract*** the zipped folder to create a regular Windows folder and access its contents.

Check for Understanding

In the ***Online Learning Center*** for this text (**www.mhhe.com/office2013inpractice**), there are a variety of resources that can be used to review the concepts covered in this chapter.

The following Online Learning Resources are available in the Online Learning Center:

- Multiple choice questions
- Short answer questions
- Matching exercises

In these projects, you use your *SkyDrive* to store files. If you don't have a Microsoft account, see *SLO 1.1: Using Windows 8 and Office 2013* for information about obtaining a free personal Microsoft account.

Guided Project 1-1

For this project, you organize and edit files for Emma Cavalli at Placer Hills Real Estate. You extract a zipped folder, rename files, manage multiple documents, and apply formatting.
[Student Learning Outcomes 1.1, 1.2, 1.4, 1.5, 1.6, 1.7]

Files Needed: ***CavalliFiles-01*** (zipped folder)
Completed Project File Names: ***[your initials] Office 1-1a.docx***, ***[your initials] Office 1-1b.docx***, ***[your initials] Office 1-1c.xlsx***, and ***[your initials] Office 1-1d.pptx***

Skills Covered in This Project

- Copy and paste a zipped folder.
- Create a new folder in your *SkyDrive* folder.
- Extract a zipped folder.
- Move a file.
- Rename a file.
- Open a Word document.
- Switch between two open Word documents.
- Save a Word document with a different file name.
- Change display size.
- Use a mini toolbar, keyboard shortcut, context menu, and dialog box to apply formatting to selected text.
- Close a Word document.

1. Copy a zipped folder and create a new *SkyDrive* folder.
   a. From the Windows *Start* page, click **File Explorer** or **Computer** to open a Windows folder. If these options are not available on the *Start* page, use *Search* to find and open a Windows folder.
   b. Browse to the location on your computer where you store your student data files.
   c. Select the ***CavalliFiles-01*** zipped folder and press **Ctrl+C** to copy the folder.
   d. Select your **SkyDrive** folder at the left and click the **New folder** button to create a new folder.
   e. Type PHRE and press **Enter**.
   f. Press **Enter** again to open the *PHRE* folder.
   g. Press **Ctrl+V** to paste the copied ***CavalliFiles-01*** zipped folder in the *PHRE* folder.
2. Extract a zipped folder.
   a. Select the ***CavalliFiles-01*** zipped folder.
   b. Click the **Compressed Folder Tools Extract** tab and click the **Extract all** button. The *Extract Compressed (Zipped) Folders* dialog box opens.
   c. Deselect the **Show extracted files when complete** check box.
   d. Click the **Extract** button. The zipped folder is extracted and there are now two *CavalliFiles-01* folders. One folder is zipped and the other is a regular folder.
   e. Select the zipped ***CavalliFiles-01*** folder and press **Delete** to delete the zipped folder.
3. Move and rename files.
   a. With the *PHRE* folder still open, double-click the **CavalliFiles-01** folder to open it.
   b. Click the first file, press and hold the **Shift** key, and click the last file to select all four files.
   c. Press **Ctr+X** to cut the files from the current location.

d. Click the **Up** button to move up to the *PHRE* folder (Figure 1-86).
e. Press **Ctrl+V** to paste and move the files.
f. Select the ***Cavalli files-01*** folder and press **Delete** to delete the folder.
g. Select the ***CavalliPHRE-01*** file, click the **File** tab, and click the **Rename** button [*Organize* group].
h. Type [your initials] Office 1-1a and press **Enter**.
i. Right-click the ***FixedMortgageRates-01*** file and select the **Rename** from the context menu.
j. Type [your initials] Office 1-1b and press **Enter**.

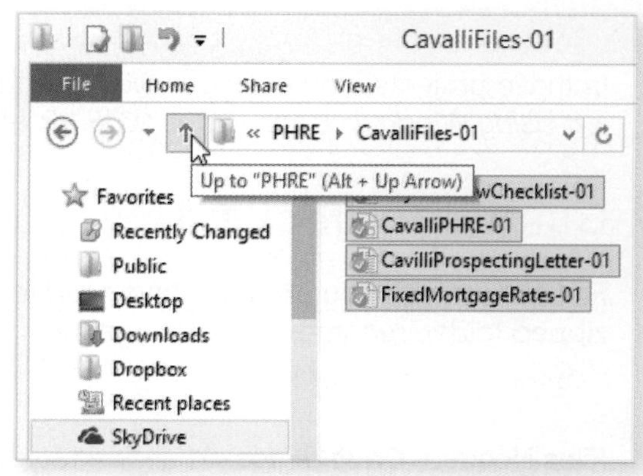

1-86 Go up to the *PHRE* folder

4. Open two Word documents and rename a Word document.

a. Press the **Ctrl** key and click the ***BuyerEscrowChecklist-01*** and ***CavalliProspectingLetter-01*** files to select both files.
b. Press the **Enter** key to open both files in Word.
c. If the *BuyerEscrowChecklist-01* document is not displayed, click the **Switch Documents** button [*View* tab, *Window* group] and select ***BuyerEscrowChecklist-01***. You can also switch documents by selecting the document on the *Taskbar*.
d. Click the **File** tab and select **Save As** at the left.
e. Select **[your name's] SkyDrive** in the *Places* area and select the **PHRE** folder or click **Browse** and select the **PHRE** folder. The *Save As* dialog box opens.
f. Type [your initials] Office 1-1c in the *File name* text box and click **Save**.
g. Press **Ctrl+W** to close the document. The *Cavalli Prospecting Letter_01* remains open.

5. Change display size and edit and rename a Word document.
a. Click the **Zoom In** or **Zoom Out** button at the bottom right of the document window to change the display size to 120% (Figure 1-87). This will vary depending on the current display size.
b. Select "**Placer Hills Real Estate**" in the first body paragraph of the letter and the mini toolbar is displayed (Figure 1-88).
c. Click the **Bold** button on the mini toolbar to apply bold formatting to the selected text.
d. Select the first sentence in the second body paragraph ("**I am also a Whitney Hills** . . . ") and press **Ctrl+I** to apply italic formatting to the selected sentence.
e. Select the text that reads "**Emma Cavalli**," below "Best regards."
f. Right-click the selected text and select **Font** from the context menu to open the *Font* dialog box.
g. Check the **Small Caps** check box in the *Effects* area and click **OK** to close the *Font* dialog box.
h. With "**Emma Cavalli**" still selected, click the **Bold** button [*Home* tab, *Font* group].
i. Press **F12** to open the *Save As* dialog box.
j. Type [your initials] Office 1-1d in the *File name* text box and click **Save**.
k. Click the **X** in the upper right corner of the document window to close the document and close Word.

120%

1-87 Use *Zoom* to increase or decrease the display size

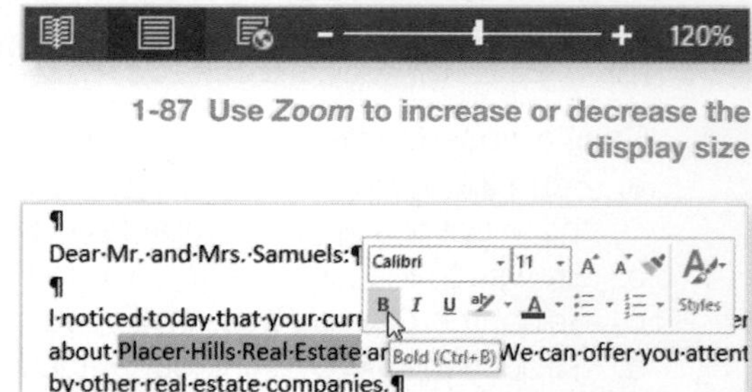

1-88 Use the mini toolbar to apply formatting

6. Your *PHRE* folder should contain the files shown in Figure 1-89.

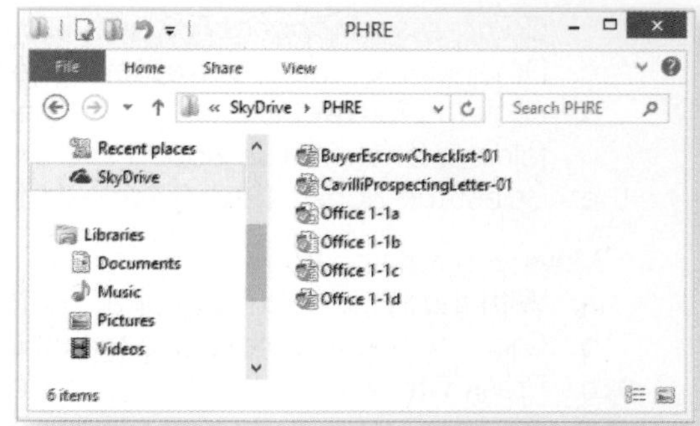

1-89 Office 1-1 completed

Guided Project 1-2

For this project, you modify an Excel file for Hamilton Civic Center. You rename a file, add document properties, use *Help* to search a topic, share the file, and export a file as a PDF file.
[Student Learning Outcomes 1.1, 1.2, 1.3, 1.4]

Note to Students and Instructor:
Students: *For this project, you share an Office file with your instructor.*
Instructor: *In order to complete this project, your students need your Microsoft email address. You can create a new Live or Hotmail account for projects in this chapter.*

File Needed: ***HCCYoga-01.xlsx***
Completed Project File Names: ***[your initials] Office 1-2.xlsx*** and ***[your initials] Office 1-2.pdf***

Skills Covered in This Project

- Open Excel and an Excel workbook.
- Create a new *SkyDrive* folder.
- Save an Excel workbook with a different file name.
- Add document properties to a file.
- Use *Microsoft Excel Help* to search for a topic.
- Open a Word document.
- Share a file.
- Export a file as a PDF file.

---

1. Open Excel 2013 and open an Excel workbook.
   a. From the Windows *Start* page, click **Excel 2013** to open this application. If Excel 2013 is not available on the *Start* page, use *Search* to find and open it.
   b. From the Excel *Start* page, click **Open Other Workbooks** to display the *Open* area of the *Backstage* view.
   c. In the *Places* area, select where your student data files are stored and click the **Browse** button to open the *Open* dialog box.
   d. Browse to the location where your student data files are stored, select the ***HCCYoga-01*** file, and click **Open** to open the Excel workbook.
2. Save a file as a different file name in your *SkyDrive* folder.
   a. Click the **File** tab to open the *Backstage* view and select **Save As** at the left.
   b. In the *Places* area, select **[your name's] SkyDrive**.
   c. Click the **Browse** button to open the *Save As* dialog box.
   d. Select the **SkyDrive** folder on the left and click the **New folder** button to create a new folder.
   e. Type HCC and press **Enter**.
   f. Double-click the **HCC** folder to open it.
   g. In the *File name* area, type [your initials] Office 1-2 and click **Save** to close the dialog box and save the file.
3. Add document properties to the Excel workbook.
   a. Click the **File** button to open the *Backstage* view and select **Info** on the left. The document properties are displayed on the right.
   b. Put your insertion point in the *Title* text box ("Add a title") and type Yoga Classes.
   c. Click the **Show All Properties** link to display more properties.

d. Put your insertion point in the *Company* text box and type Hamilton Civic Center.
e. Click the **back arrow** in the upper left of the *Backstage* window to return to the Excel workbook.

4. Use *Help* to learn about a topic.
   a. Click **Microsoft Excel Help** button (question mark) in the upper right corner of the Excel window or press **F1** to open the *Excel Help* dialog box.
   b. Put your insertion point in the *Search help* text box, type AutoSum, and press **Enter**.
   c. Click the first link and read about *AutoSum*.
   d. Click the **Back** button to return to the search list of articles and click the second link.
   e. Read about *AutoSum* and then click the **X** in the upper right corner to close the *Excel Help* dialog box.
5. Share an Excel workbook with your instructor.
   a. Click the **File** tab and select **Share** at the left.
   b. In the *Share* area, select **Invite People** (Figure 1-90).
   c. Type your instructor's email address in the *Type names or email addresses* area.
   d. In the drop-down list to the right of the email address, select **Can edit**.
   e. In the body, type a brief message.
   f. Click the **Share** button.
   g. Click the **Save** button to save and return to the workbook.

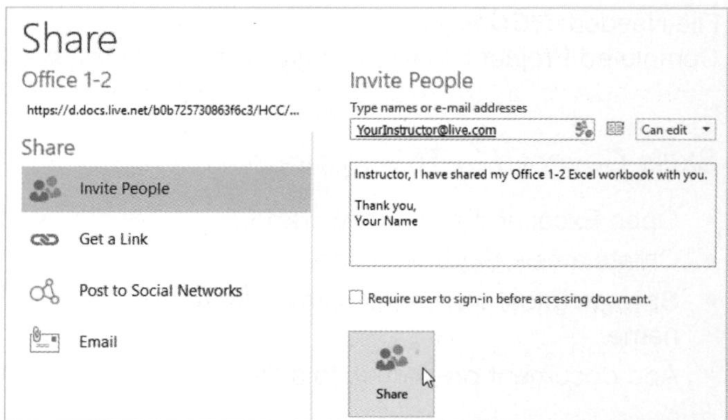

1-90 Invite people to share a file

6. Export the Excel workbook as a PDF file.
   a. Click the **File** button and select **Export** at the left.
   b. In the *Export* area, select **Create PDF/XPS Document** and click the **Create PDF/XPS** button. The *Publish as PDF or XPS* dialog box opens.
   c. Check the **Open file after publishing** check box. The publish location and file name are the same as the Excel file; don't change these.
   d. Click **Publish** to create and open the PDF file (Figure 1-91). The PDF file opens in an Internet browser window in *SkyDrive*.
   e. Close the Internet browser window.
7. Save and close the Excel file.
   a. Click the **Excel** icon on the Windows *Taskbar* to display the Excel file.
   b. Press **Ctrl+S** to save the file.
   c. Click the **X** in the upper right corner of the Excel window to close the file and Excel.

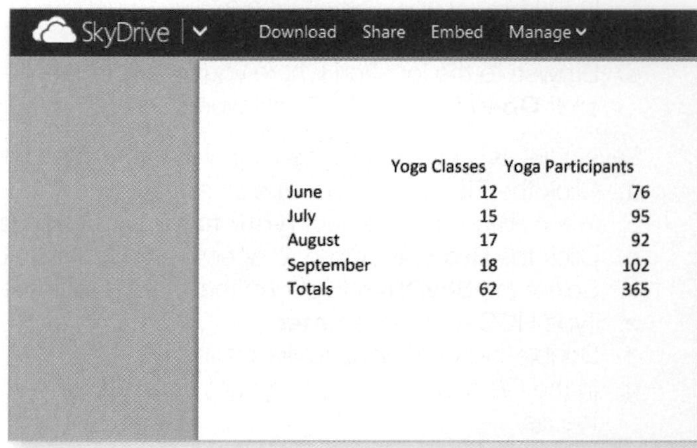

	Yoga Classes	Yoga Participants
June	12	76
July	15	95
August	17	92
September	18	102
Totals	62	365

1-91 PDF file displayed in *SkyDrive*

Independent Project 1-3

For this project, you organize and edit files for Courtyard Medical Plaza. You extract a zipped folder, rename files, export a file as a PDF file, and share a file in *SkyDrive*.
[Student Learning Outcomes 1.1, 1.3, 1.6, 1.7]

Note to Students and Instructor:

Students: *For this project, you share an* Office Web App *file with your instructor.*
Instructor: *In order to complete this project, your students need your Microsoft email address. You can create a new Live or Hotmail account for projects in this chapter.*

Files Needed: ***CMPFiles-01*** (zipped folder)
Completed Project File Names: ***[your initials] Office 1-3a.pptx***, ***[your initials] Office 1-3a-pdf.pdf***, ***[your initials] Office 1-3b.accdb***, ***[your initials] Office 1-3c.xlsx***, and ***[your initials] Office 1-3d.docx***

Skills Covered in This Project

- Copy and paste a zipped folder.
- Create a new folder in your *SkyDrive* folder.
- Extract a zipped folder.
- Move a file.
- Rename a file.
- Open a PowerPoint presentation.
- Export a file as a PDF file.
- Use *SkyDrive* to share a file.

1. Copy a zipped folder and create a new *SkyDrive* folder.
   a. Using a Windows folder, browse to locate the ***CMPFiles-01*** zipped folder in your student data files and copy the zipped folder.
   b. Go to your *SkyDrive* folder and create a new folder named Courtyard Medical Plaza within the *SkyDrive* folder.
2. Copy and extract the zipped folder and move files.
   a. Paste the zipped folder in the *Courtyard Medical Plaza* folder.
   b. Extract the zipped folder and then delete the zipped folder.
   c. Open the ***CMPFiles-01*** folder and move all of the files to the *Courtyard Medical Plaza* folder.
   d. Delete the ***CMPFiles-01*** folder.
3. Rename files in the *Courtyard Medical Plaza* folder.
   a. Rename the ***CMPStayingActive-01*** PowerPoint file to [your initials] Office 1-3a.
   b. Rename the ***CourtyardMedicalPlaza-01*** Access file to [your initials] Office 1-3b.
   c. Rename the ***EstimatedCalories-01*** Excel file to [your initials] Office 1-3c.
   d. Rename the ***StayingActive-01*** Word file to [your initials] Office 1-3d.
4. Export a PowerPoint file as a PDF file.
   a. From the *Courtyard Medical Plaza* folder, open the ***[your initials] Office 1-3a*** file. The file opens in PowerPoint.
   b. Export this file as a PDF file. Don't have the PDF file open after publishing.
   c. Save the file as [your initials] Office 1-3a-pdf and save in the *Courtyard Medical Plaza* folder.
   d. Close the PowerPoint file and exit PowerPoint.

5. Use *SkyDrive* to share a file with your instructor.
   a. Open an Internet browser window and log in to your *SkyDrive* (www.skydrive.com) using your Microsoft account.
   b. Go to your *SkyDrive* files and open the **Courtyard Medical Plaza** folder.
   c. Open the ***[your initials] Office 1-3a*** file in PowerPoint Web App.
   d. Share this file with your instructor.
   e. Send an email to share the file and include your instructor's email address and a brief message. Allow your instructor to edit the file.
   f. Sign out of *SkyDrive*.
6. Close the Windows folder containing the files for this project (Figure 1-92).

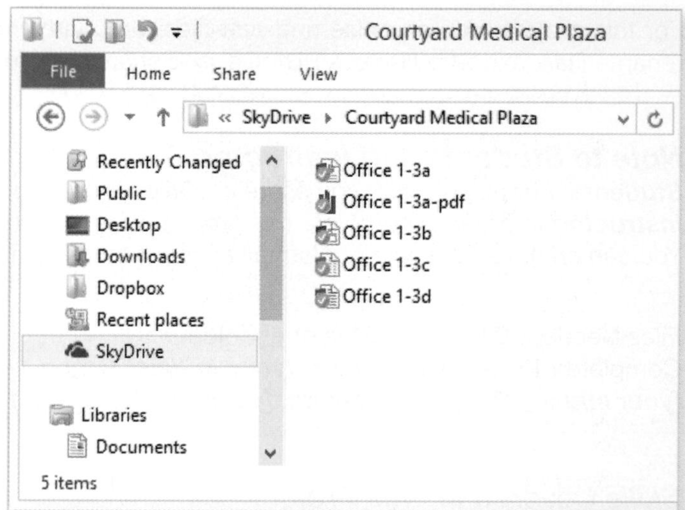

1-92 Office 1-3 completed

Independent Project 1-4

For this project, you modify a Word file for Life's Animal Shelter. You rename the document, add document properties, modify the document, share a link to the document, export a document as a PDF file, and create a zipped folder.
[Student Learning Outcomes 1.1, 1.2, 1.3, 1.4, 1.5, 1.6, 1.7]

Note to Students and Instructor:

Students: *For this project, you share an Office file with your instructor.*
Instructor: *In order to complete this project, your students need your Microsoft email address. You can create a new Live or Hotmail account for projects in this chapter.*

File Needed: ***LASSupportLetter-01.docx***
Completed Project File Names: ***[your initials] Office 1-4.docx***, ***[your initials] Office 1-4.pdf***, and ***LAS files*** (zipped folder)

Skills Covered in This Project

- Open Excel and an Excel file.
- Create a new *SkyDrive* folder.
- Save a file with a different file name.
- Apply formatting to selected text.
- Add document properties to the file.
- Use *Microsoft Excel Help* to search for a topic.
- Open a Word document.
- Share a file.
- Export a file as a PDF file.

1. Open Word 2013 and open a Word document.
   a. From the Windows *Start* page, open Word 2013.
   b. From the Word *Start* page, open the ***LASSupportLetter-01*** document from your student data files.
2. Create a new folder and save the document with a different file name.
   a. Open the **Save As** dialog box and create a new folder named LAS in your *SkyDrive* folder.
   b. Save this document as [your initials] Office 1-4.
3. Apply formatting changes to the document using a dialog box, keyboard shortcut, and mini toolbar.
   a. Select "**To**" and use the **launcher** to open the *Font* dialog box.
   b. Apply **Bold** and **All caps** to the selected text.
   c. Repeat the formatting on the other three memo guide words: "**From**," "**Date**," and "**Subject**."
   d. Select "**Life's Animal Shelter**" in the first sentence of the first body paragraph and use the keyboard shortcut to apply **bold** formatting.
   e. Select the first sentence in the second body paragraph ("**Would you again consider** . . . ") and use the mini toolbar to apply **italic** formatting.
4. Add the following document properties to the document:
   Title: Support Letter
   Company: Life's Animal Shelter
5. Get a link to share this document with your instructor.
   a. Create and copy an **Edit Link** you can email to your instructor.
   b. Create a new email to send to your professor using the email you use for this course.
   c. Include an appropriate subject line and a brief message in the body.
   d. Paste the link in the body of the email message and send the message.
6. Use the keyboard shortcut to **save** the file before continuing.
7. Export this document as a PDF file.
   a. Save the file in the same location and use the same file name.
   b. Close the PDF file if it opens after publishing.
8. Save and close the Word file and exit Word (Figure 1-93).
9. Create a zipped folder.
   a. Using a Windows folder, open the ***LAS*** folder in your *SkyDrive* folder.
   b. Select the two files and create a zipped folder.
   c. Rename the zipped folder LAS files (Figure 1-94).
10. Close the open Windows folder.

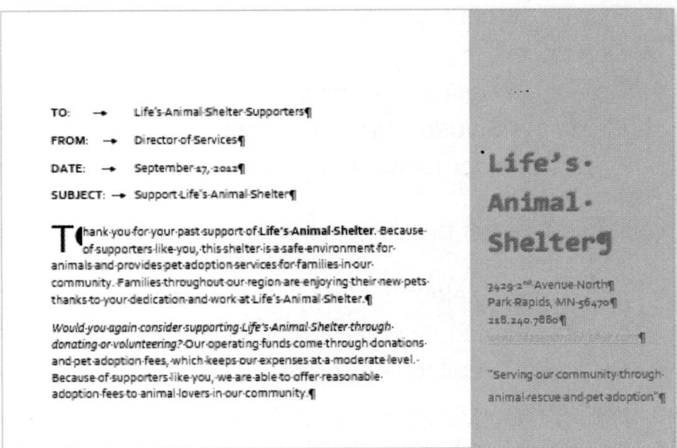

1-93 Office 1-4 completed

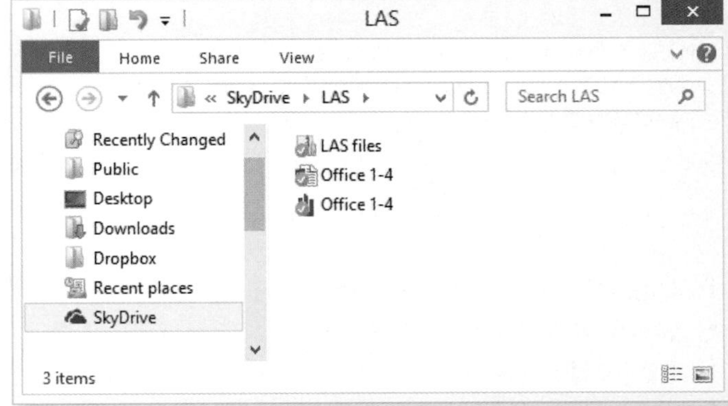

1-94 Office 1-4 completed

Challenge Project 1-5

For this project, you create folders to organize your files for this class and use *SkyDrive* to share a link with your professor.
[Student Learning Outcomes 1.1, 1.7]

Note to Students and Instructor:

Students: *For this project, you share an Office file with your instructor.*
Instructor: *In order to complete this project, your students need your Microsoft email address. You can create a new Live or Hotmail account for projects in this chapter.*

File Needed: None
Completed Project File Name: Email link to shared folder to your instructor

Using a Windows folder, create *SkyDrive* folders to contain all of the files for this class. Organize your files and folders according to the following guidelines:

- Create a *SkyDrive* folder for this class.
- Create a *Student data files* folder inside the class folder.
- Extract student data files if you have not already done so. Make sure they are in the *Student data files* folder.
- Create a *Solution files* folder inside the class folder.
- Inside the *Solution files* folder, create a folder for each chapter.
- Create a folder to store miscellaneous class files such as the syllabus and other course handouts.

Using an Internet browser, log in to your *SkyDrive* and share your class folder with your instructor.

- In *SkyDrive*, select the check box to the right of your class folder and click the **Share** button.
- Create a link to *View only* the folder.
- Create an email to your professor and include an appropriate subject line and a brief message in the body.
- Paste the link to your *SkyDrive* class folder in the body of the email message and send the email.

Challenge Project 1-6

For this project, you save a file as a different file name, customize the *Quick Access* toolbar, share a file with your professor, and export a file as a PDF file.
[Student Learning Outcomes 1.1, 1.2, 1.3, 1.4]

Note to Students and Instructor:

Students: *For this project, you share an Office file with your instructor.*
Instructor: *In order to complete this project, your students need your Microsoft email address. You can create a new Live or Hotmail account for projects in this chapter.*

File Needed: Use an existing Office file
Completed Project File Name: ***[your initials] Office 1-6***

Open an existing Word, Excel, or PowerPoint file. Save this file in a *SkyDrive* folder and name it ***[your initials] Office 1-6***. If you don't have any of these files, use one from your Pause & Practice projects or select a file from your student data files.

With your file open, perform the following actions:

- Customize the *Quick Access* toolbar to add command buttons. Add commands such as *New*, *Open*, *Quick Print*, and *Spelling* that you use regularly in the Office application.
- Share your file with your instructor. Use *Invite People* and include your instructor's email, an appropriate subject line, and a brief message in the body. Allow your instructor to edit the file.
- Export the document as a PDF file. Use the same file name and save it in the same *SkyDrive* folder as your open file.

Microsoft® Office

IN PRACTICE

word

Creating and Editing Documents

CHAPTER OVERVIEW

Microsoft Word (Word) has been and continues to be the leading word processing software in both the personal and business markets. Word improves with each new version and is used for creating and editing personal, business, and educational documents. Word allows you to create letters, memos, reports, flyers, brochures, and mailings without a vast amount of computer knowledge. This chapter covers the basics of creating and editing a Word document.

STUDENT LEARNING OUTCOMES (SLOs)

After completing this chapter, you will be able to:

SLO 1.1 Create, save, and open a Word document (p. W1-3).

SLO 1.2 Customize a document by entering and selecting text, using word wrap, and using *AutoComplete*, *AutoCorrect*, and *AutoFormat* features (p. W1-6).

SLO 1.3 Enhance a document using paragraph breaks, line breaks, spaces, and non-breaking spaces (p. W1-10).

SLO 1.4 Edit a document using cut, copy, paste, the *Clipboard*, and the undo, redo, and repeat features. (p. W1-14).

SLO 1.5 Customize a document using different fonts, font sizes, and attributes (p. W1-17).

SLO 1.6 Enhance a document using text alignment and line and paragraph spacing (p. W1-27).

SLO 1.7 Finalize a document using Word's proofing tools (p. W1-31).

SLO 1.8 Apply custom document properties to a document (p. W1-35).

CASE STUDY

Throughout this book you have the opportunity to put into practice the application features that you are learning. Each chapter begins with a case study that introduces you to the ***Pause & Practice*** *projects in the chapter. These Pause & Practice projects give you a chance to apply and practice key skills. Each chapter contains three to five Pause & Practice projects.*

Placer Hills Real Estate (PHRE) is a real estate company with regional offices throughout central California. In the Pause & Practice projects in this chapter, you create a business document related to the real estate business. PHRE encourages agents to use standard formats for their business documents. This ensures consistency in document appearance while also allowing agents to personalize their correspondence to customers and colleagues.

WORD

Pause & Practice 1-1: Create a business letter in block format with mixed punctuation.

Pause & Practice 1-2: Edit the business letter using copy, paste, and *Format Painter*. Modify the font size, color, style, and effects of selected text.

Pause & Practice 1-3: Finalize the business letter by modifying line spacing and paragraph spacing, changing paragraph alignment, translating text, using proofing tools, and adding document properties.

> **MORE INFO**
>
> *Appendix D* (online resource) contains examples of business documents.

SLO 1.1

Creating, Saving, and Opening Documents

Microsoft Word allows you to create a variety of document types. Your creativity and knowledge of Word allow you to create, edit, and customize high-quality and professional-looking documents.

You can create Word documents from a new blank document, from existing Word templates, or from existing documents. Word allows you to save documents in a variety of formats.

Create a New Document

All new documents are based on the ***Normal template*** (*Normal.dotx*). When you open Word, a blank document is displayed in the Word window. This document has default fonts, font sizes, line and paragraph spacing, and margins, all of which are controlled by the *Normal* template.

HOW TO: Create a New Document

1. Click the **File** tab to open the *Backstage* view (Figure 1-1).
2. Click the **New** button.
3. Select **Blank document**. A new blank document opens in Word.

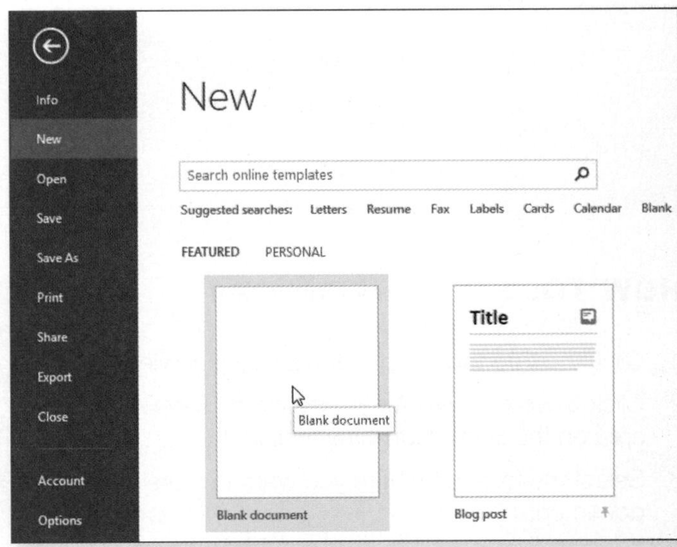

1-1 Open a blank document

> **ANOTHER WAY**
>
> **Ctrl+N** opens a new blank document.

Save a Document

When you create a blank document, Word automatically assigns a generic file name to this document, such as *Document1*. Save all your new documents using the ***Save As dialog box.***

You can save a Word document in a variety of formats. By default, a Word document is saved as a ***.docx*** file. If you are sharing a document with someone who is using an older version of Word, you might want to save your file as an older version of Word. To change the type of document format, select the format of your choice from the *Save as type* area of the *Save As* dialog box. The following table lists some of the more commonly used available formats.

Save Formats

Type of Document	File Extension	Uses
Word Document	.docx	Standard Word 2013 document
Word Macro-Enabled Document	.docm	Word document with embedded macros
Word 97-2003 Document	.doc	Word document that is compatible with previous versions of Microsoft Word
Word Template	.dotx	Creates a new document based upon a template
Word Macro-Enabled Template	.dotm	Creates a new document based upon a template with embedded macros
Portable Document Format (PDF)	.pdf	PDF files, which are more like pictures of a document, are used to preserve the formatting of a document
Rich Text Format (RTF)	.rtf	RTF files are in a more generic file format and can be read by many different types of word processors while retaining the basic format of the document
Plain Text	.txt	Plain text files contain only text with no special formatting and can be opened with most word processing programs
Open Document Text	.odt	This format is used in the Open Office word processing program

HOW TO: Save a New Document

1. Click the **File** tab to open the *Backstage* view.
2. Click **Save** or **Save As** to display the *Save As* area on the *Backstage* view (Figure 1-2).
3. Select the location where you want to store your document.
   - You can save to your *SkyDrive*, computer, or storage device.

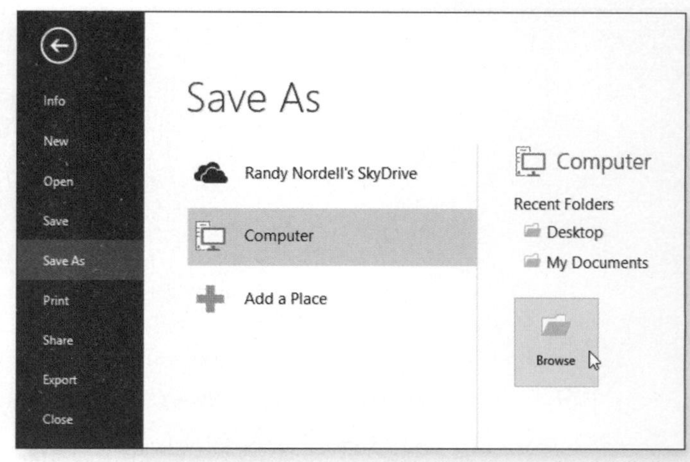

1-2 ***Save As*** **area of the** ***Backstage*** **view**

4. Select a folder in the *Recent Folders* area or click the **Browse** button to open the *Save As* dialog box (Figure 1-3).
5. Browse to the location on your *SkyDrive*, computer, or USB drive to save the file.
6. Type the file name in the *File name* area.
7. Click the **Save** button.

ANOTHER WAY

F12 opens the *Save As* dialog box.

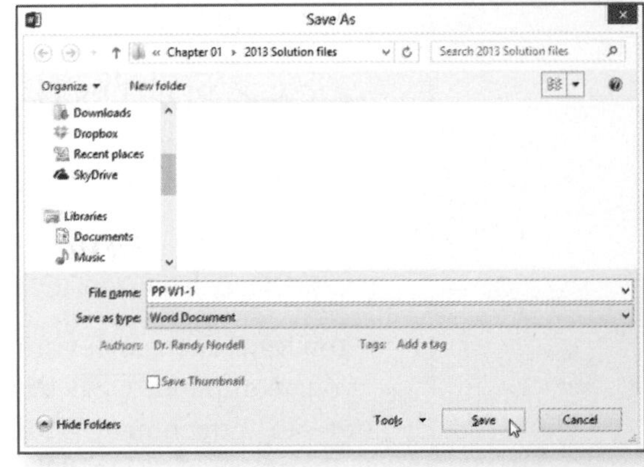

1-3 *Save As dialog box*

After you have saved a document once, you can save the document again by pressing **Ctrl+S** or clicking the **Save** button on the *Quick Access* toolbar. Word saves changes to an existing document without opening the *Save As* dialog box.

Save As a Different File Name

You can save a document as a different name by opening the *Save As* dialog box and giving the document a different file name. When you save as a different file name, the original document is not changed and is still available. Saving as a different file name creates a new version of the original document, but the new document has a different file name.

HOW TO: Save As a Different File Name

1. Click the **File** tab to open the *Backstage* view.
2. Click the **Save As** button to display the *Save As* area.
3. Select a recent folder or click the **Browse** button. The *Save As* dialog box opens (see Figure 1-3).
   - From within Word (not the Backstage view), you can also press **F12** to open the *Save As* dialog box.
4. Browse to the location on your computer or USB drive to save the file.
5. Type the file name in the *File name* area.
6. Click the **Save** button.

MORE INFO

Avoid saving too many different versions of the same document. Rename only when you have a good reason to have multiple versions of a document.

Share and Export Options

Word 2013 provides you with other sharing and export options. From the ***Share*** and ***Export*** area of the *Backstage* view, you have the options of saving a document to the cloud (*SkyDrive*), emailing a document, or saving it as a PDF document. Here are the *Share* and *Export* options, also seen in Figure 1-4.

- Invite People [*Share* area]
- Email [*Share* area]

- Present Online [*Share* area]
- Publish as Blog Post [*Share* area]
- Create PDF/XPS Document [*Export* area]
- Change File Type [*Export* area]

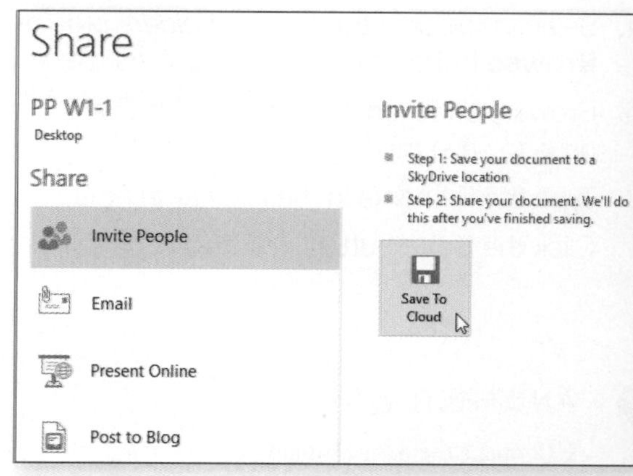

1-4 *Share* area of the *Backstage* view

Open a Document

You can open an existing document from your computer, USB drive, SkyDrive drive, or an attachment from an email. One advantage of using Microsoft Word is the program's ability to open different types of file formats and to save documents as different types of files.

HOW TO: Open a Document

1. Click the **File** tab to open the *Backstage* view.
2. Click the **Open** button to display the *Open* area on the *Backstage* view.
3. In the *Places* area, select the location where the document is stored.
   - You can click **Recent Documents** and select a document at the right to open it.
   - You can also open a document from *SkyDrive* or *Computer.*
4. Select a folder or click **Browse** to open the *Open* dialog box (Figure 1-5).
5. Select the file and click the **Open** button.

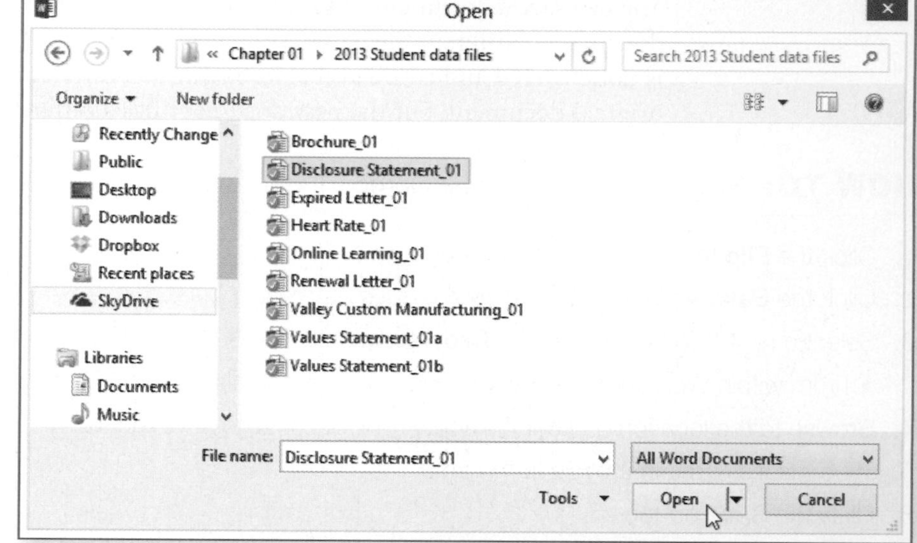

1-5 *Open* dialog box

> **ANOTHER WAY**
>
> **Ctrl+F12** opens the *Open* dialog box.

SLO 1.2

Entering and Selecting Text

When creating or editing a document, you can type new text, insert text from another document, or copy text from a web page or another document. It is important to understand how to enter text, use word wrap, and select text to create clean and professional-looking documents. Word provides you with options to automatically insert and correct text as well as the ability to control which words are automatically corrected by Word.

Type Text and Word Wrap

Word inserts text at the point in the document where the insertion point is flashing. By default, text is aligned at the left margin and the text wraps to the next line when it reaches the right margin, which is called ***word wrap.***

Show/Hide Formatting Symbols

You can turn on or off the display of formatting symbols. When the ***Show/Hide*** feature is turned on, the formatting symbols are visible in the document. You are able to see paragraph breaks, line breaks, spaces, tabs, and other formatting symbols that help you create clean documents and edit existing documents (Figure 1-6).

Click the **Show/Hide** button in the *Paragraph* group on the *Home* tab to toggle on and off *Show/Hide.* These symbols do not print, but they allow you to see the formatting that is in the document when you view it on your screen.

> **ANOTHER WAY**
>
> **Ctrl+Shift+8** turns on/off *Show/Hide.*

> **MORE INFO**
>
> When editing a document that has inconsistent formatting, begin by turning on **Show/Hide**.

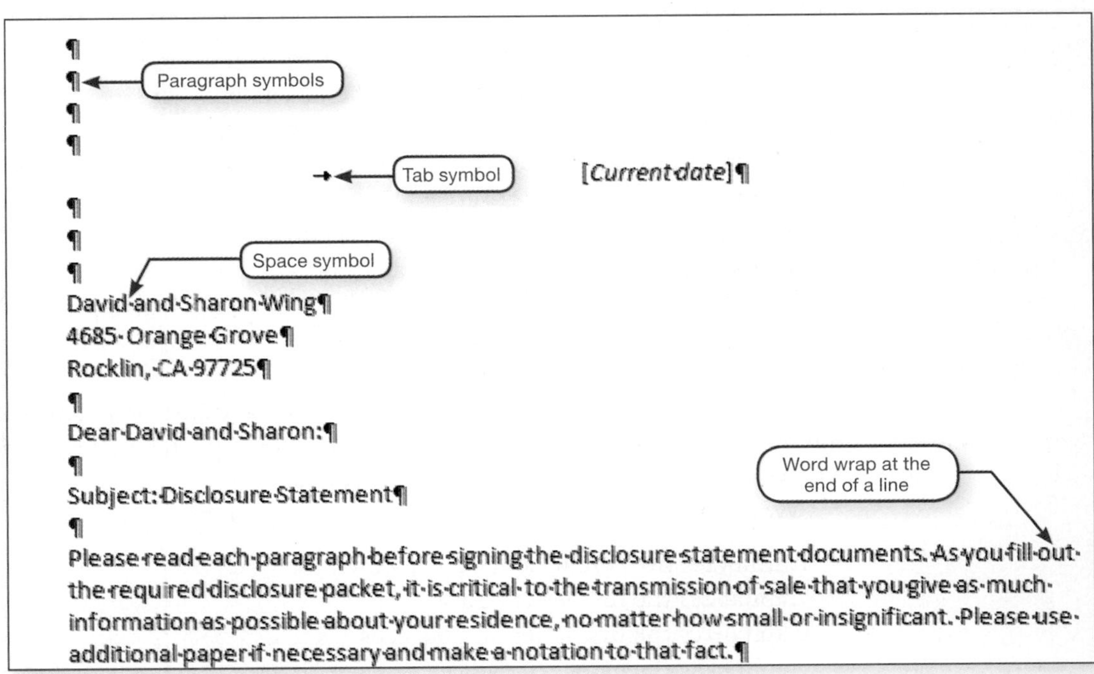

1-6 Document with *Show/Hide* turned on

Select Text

Word allows you select words, lines, sentences, paragraphs, or the entire document. You do this by clicking and dragging the pointer over the desired text, but there are a variety of additional quick methods to select text. The following table lists ways to select text.

> **ANOTHER WAY**
>
> **F8** is the selection function key.
>
> Press once—use the arrow keys to select text.
> Press twice—select word.
> Press three times—select sentence.
> Press four times—select paragraph.
> Press five times—select entire document.
>
> Press **Esc** to turn off **F8** selection.

Selecting Text

Select	Method
Word	Double-click the word.
Line	Click in the *Selection* area, which is to the left of the left margin. Your pointer becomes a right-pointing arrow.
Multiple lines of text	Click in the *Selection* area and drag up or down.
Sentence	Press **Ctrl+Click**. Hold down the **Ctrl** key and click the sentence.
Paragraph	Double-click in the *Selection* area to the left of the paragraph.
Multiple paragraphs	Click in the *Selection* area to the left of the first line of the paragraph and drag down.
Entire document	Press **Ctrl+A** or **Ctrl+Click** in the *Selection* area. You can also click the **Select** button [*Home* tab, *Editing* group] and choose **Select All**.
Non-adjacent text	Select text, press and hold the **Ctrl** key, and select non-adjacent text.

AutoComplete

When you type a day, month, or date, Word uses the ***AutoComplete*** feature to automatically complete typing the day, month, or date for you, which saves you a few key strokes and allows you to be more efficient and accurate when entering dates. As you begin to type the date, Word displays the information in an *AutoComplete* tag (Figure 1-7). Press **Enter** to accept the *AutoComplete* entry. If you do not want this *AutoComplete* entry, keep typing and the *AutoComplete* entry disappears.

1-7 *AutoComplete*

AutoCorrect and AutoFormat

When you're typing, do you ever misspell a word by transposing letters or omitting a letter or adding a letter? Because we all regularly make typing mistakes, the ***AutoCorrect*** feature recognizes and corrects commonly misspelled words.

Word automatically makes the following corrections:

- Eliminates two initial capitals in a word
- Capitalizes the first letter of a sentence
- Capitalizes the first letter of table cells
- Capitalizes the names of days
- Resolves accidental usage of the Caps Lock key

Word's ***AutoFormat*** controls the formatting of items such as numbered and bulleted lists, fractions, ordinal numbers, hyphens and dashes, quotes, indents, and hyperlinks. For example, when you type 3/4 followed by a space, *AutoFormat* automatically changes the format of the fraction to ¾.

AutoCorrect Options

When Word automatically makes a correction or formatting change, you have the option to accept the change, undo the change, stop Word from making the change, or open the *AutoCorrect Options* dialog box. If you keep typing, the change is accepted. Often when Word automatically corrects a word, you don't even recognize a change has been made.

AutoCorrect Smart Tag

If you do not want to accept a change, you can click the ***AutoCorrect Options smart tag*** on the changed word to open the *AutoCorrect Options* menu (Figure 1-8). For example, when you type reference initials at the end of a business letter, Word automatically capitalizes the first letter. You can undo this automatic capitalization by clicking on the *AutoCorrect Options* smart tag and selecting **Undo Automatic Capitalization**.

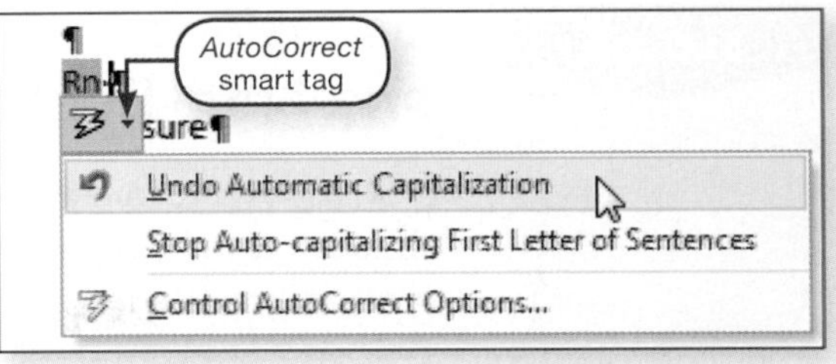

1-8 *AutoCorrect Options*

> **ANOTHER WAY**
>
> **Ctrl+Z** is *undo*. Press **Ctrl+Z** to reverse an automatic correction made by Word.

Add Custom AutoCorrect Entry

The *AutoCorrect* dialog box allows you to customize how Word automatically corrects and formats items in a document. In this dialog box, you can also add custom items to the *AutoCorrect* menu. For example, you can add a custom entry to the *AutoCorrect* menu to type your name every time you type your initials.

HOW TO: Add a Custom AutoCorrect Entry

1. Click the **File** tab to open the *Backstage* view.
2. Choose the **Options** button to open the *Word Options* dialog box.
3. Click the **Proofing** button on the left.
4. Select the **AutoCorrect Options** button. The *AutoCorrect* dialog box opens (Figure 1-9).
5. Type in the text you want to replace in the *Replace* box.
6. Type in the word(s) to replace the original text in the *With* box.
7. Choose **Add** to add this custom *AutoCorrect* entry.
8. Click **OK** to close the *AutoCorrect* dialog box.
9. Click **OK** to close the *Word Options* dialog box.

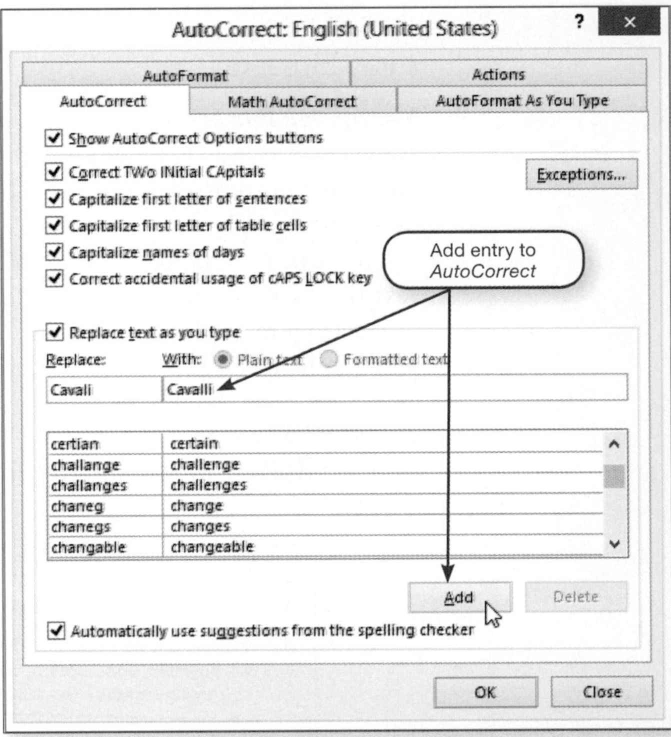

1-9 *AutoCorrect* dialog box

You can delete *AutoCorrect* entries in the *AutoCorrect* dialog box by selecting the entry and pressing **Delete**. You can also add exceptions to *AutoCorrect* by clicking the **Exceptions** button.

SLO 1.3

Using Paragraph Breaks, Line Breaks, and Non-Breaking Spaces

It is important to create attractive and readable documents. Using paragraph and line breaks allows you to break up a document into more readable chunks of information. The different types of breaks can be used for different purposes when you are formatting documents.

Paragraph Breaks

The ***Enter*** key inserts a ***paragraph break*** and is marked by a ***paragraph symbol*** that displays at the end of each paragraph when *Show/Hide* is turned on (Figure 1-10). Use paragraph breaks to control the amount of white space between paragraphs of text within a document.

Many formatting features, such as indents, numbering, bullets, text alignment, line spacing, and paragraph spacing, are applied to an entire paragraph. For example, if your insertion point is within a paragraph and you change the line spacing to double space, double spacing is applied to that paragraph only. It is not applied to the entire document or just the line where the insertion point is located.

¶
Paragraph symbols
David·and·Sharon·Wing¶
4685·Orange·Grove¶
Rocklin,·CA·97725¶
¶
Dear·David·and·Sharon:¶
¶
Subject:·Disclosure·Statement¶
¶
Please·read·each·paragraph·before·

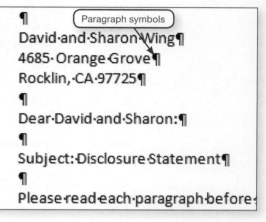

1-10 Paragraph breaks after and between lines

Line Breaks

You can use ***line breaks*** to control breaks between lines or sentences of text. They function similar to the way a paragraph break functions. The distinction between a paragraph break and a line break is that when line breaks are used, the text separated by line breaks is treated as one paragraph.

You can use line breaks within a numbered or bulleted list to allow for multiple lines of text on separate lines and blank lines between the text without creating a new number or bullet (Figure 1-11). You can also use line breaks to control the amount of space between paragraphs when you are using before and after spacing for paragraphs. For more on before and after paragraph spacing, see *SLO 1.6: Changing Text Alignment, Line Spacing, and Paragraph Spacing.*

Press **Shift+Enter** to insert a line break.

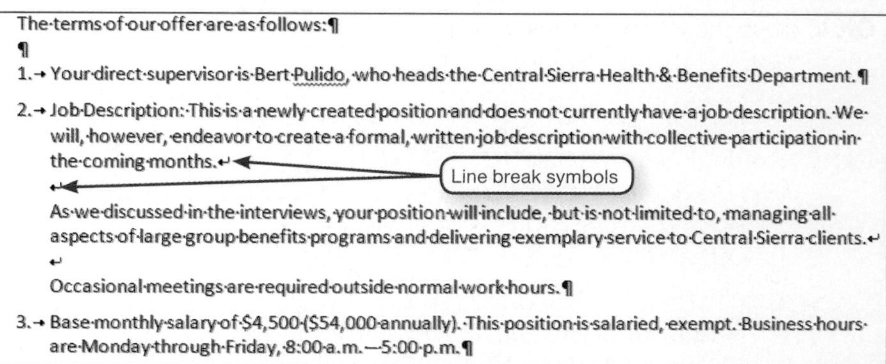

The·terms·of·our·offer·are·as·follows:¶
¶
1.→ Your·direct·supervisor·is·Bert·Pulido,·who·heads·the·Central·Sierra·Health·&·Benefits·Department.¶
2.→ Job·Description:·This·is·a·newly·created·position·and·does·not·currently·have·a·job·description.·We·will,·however,·endeavor·to·create·a·formal,·written·job·description·with·collective·participation·in·the·coming·months.↵
↵
As·we·discussed·in·the·interviews,·your·position·will·include,·but·is·not·limited·to,·managing·all·aspects·of·large·group·benefits·programs·and·delivering·exemplary·service·to·Central·Sierra·clients.↵
↵
Occasional·meetings·are·required·outside·normal·work·hours.¶
3.→ Base·monthly·salary·of·$4,500·($54,000·annually).·This·position·is·salaried,·exempt.·Business·hours·are·Monday·through·Friday,·8:00·a.m.—5:00·p.m.¶

1-11 Line breaks used in a numbered list

Spaces and Non-Breaking Spaces

Spaces are included between words. Use the **spacebar** to insert a space. Add just one space after most punctuation marks, including periods, commas, semicolons, and ending quotation marks. Do not use spaces after a beginning quotation mark, before or after a hyphen in a hyphenated word, or when using a dash.

There might be times when you are typing a document and word wrap breaks up words that you want to keep together. For example, you might want to keep a person's first and last name or a date together on the same line, but you don't want to add a line break or paragraph break at that point in your document. In this case, you can use a ***non-breaking space*** to keep these words together. In Figure 1-12, there is a non-breaking space between 8:00 and a.m., which keeps this information together.

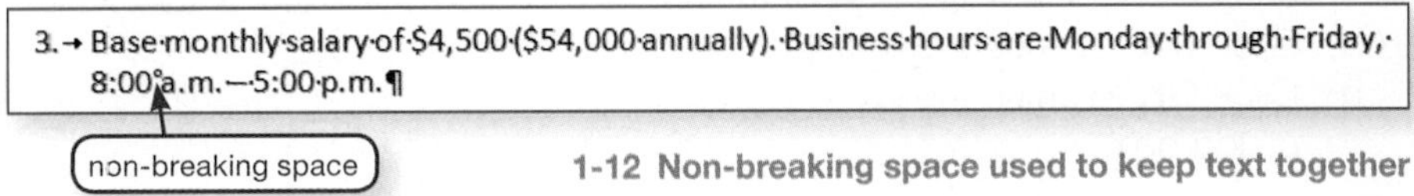

1-12 Non-breaking space used to keep text together

Press **Ctrl+Shift+Spacebar** to insert a non-breaking space between words. Don't insert an additional regular space between words when using a non-breaking space.

PAUSE & PRACTICE: WORD 1-1

In this project, you create a block format business letter for Emma Cavalli, a realtor consultant for Placer Hills Real Estate. In a block format business letter, all lines begin at the left margin. This document uses mixed punctuation, which means there is a colon after the salutation and a comma after the complimentary close (e.g., Best regards,). For more examples of business documents, see *Appendix D* (online resource).

File Needed: None
Completed Project File Name: ***[your initials] PP W1-1.docx***

1. Open a new document.
   a. Press **Ctrl+N** or click the **File** tab, click **New**, and click **Blank Document**.
2. Save the document.
   a. Press **F12** to open the *Save As* dialog box (Figure 1-13). You can also use **Save** or **Save As** in the *Backstage* view.
   b. Browse to the location on your computer or storage device to save the document.
   c. Type [your initials] PP W1-1 in the *File name* area.
   d. Click **Save** to close the dialog box and save the document.

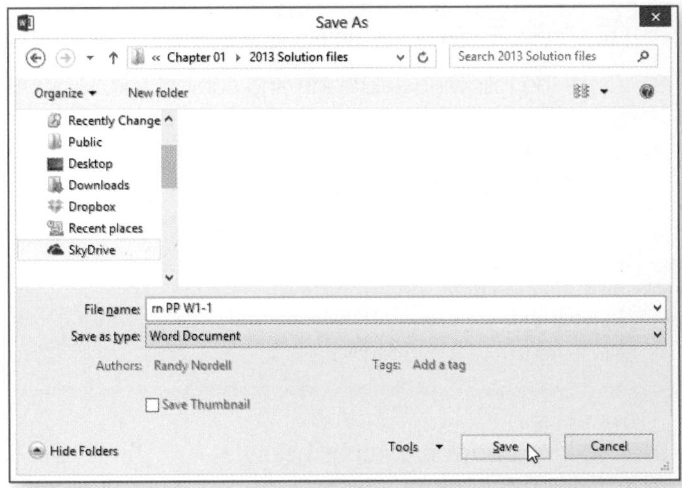

1-13 *Save As* dialog box

3. Create an *AutoCorrect* entry.
   a. Click the **File** tab to open the *Backstage* view and select **Options** to open the *Word Options* dialog box.
   b. Click the **Proofing** button on the left and select **AutoCorrect Options** to open the *AutoCorrect* dialog box (Figure 1-14).
   c. Click the **AutoCorrect** tab.
   d. Type Cavali in the *Replace* area and Cavalli in the *With* area.
   e. Click the **Add** button to add the *AutoCorrect* entry.
   f. Click **OK** to close the *AutoCorrect* dialog box.
   g. Click **OK** to close the *Word Options* dialog box.

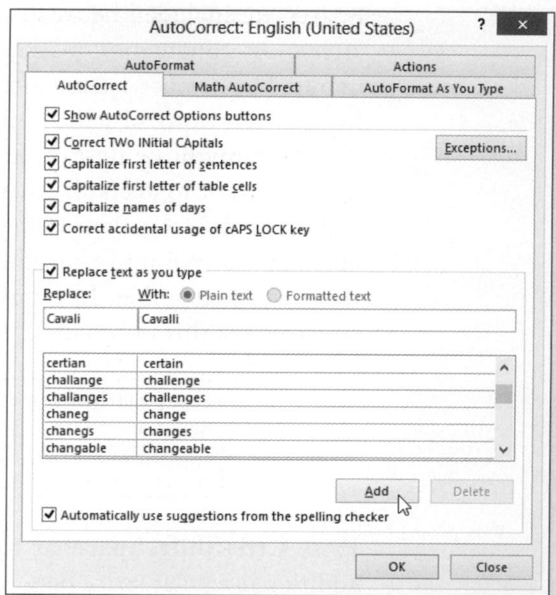

1-14 Add an *AutoCorrect* entry

4. Click the **Show/Hide** button [*Home* tab, *Paragraph* group] to turn on the *Show/Hide* feature.
5. Type the current date on the first line of the document. Type the date in month, day, year format (e.g., September 1, 2015).
   a. If the *AutoComplete* tag appears, press **Enter**, and the month is automatically inserted (Figure 1-15).
   b. Continue typing the rest of the date; press **Enter** if the *AutoCorrect* tag displays the current date.

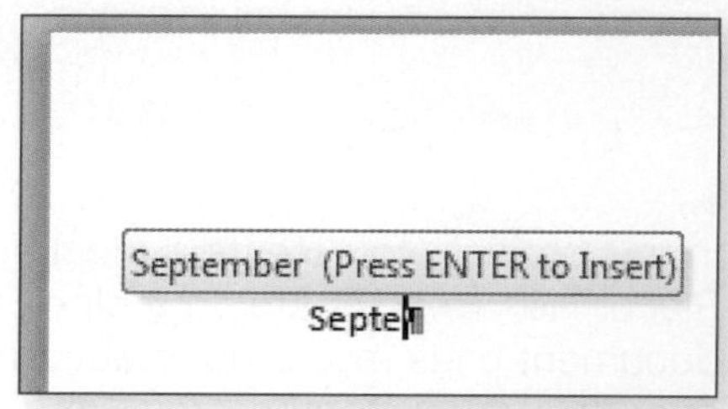

1-15 *AutoComplete* tag

6. Press **Enter** two times after typing the date.
7. Type the following information as the inside address of the letter (the recipient of the letter).
   a. Press **Shift+Enter** to insert a line break after the first and second lines to keep the lines together.

David and Sharon Wing
4685 Orange Grove Road
Rocklin, CA 97725

   b. Press **Enter** after the last line of the inside address.
8. Type the following salutation and subject line. Press **Enter** after typing each line.

Dear Mr. and Mrs. Wing:
Subject: Disclosure Statement

MORE INFO

In a business letter, use "Dear" followed by a courtesy title (such as Mr., Mrs., Ms., Miss, or Dr.) and the person's last name.

9. Type the body paragraphs below.
   a. Use word wrap for line endings. Do not press Enter at the end of each line.
   b. Press **Enter** at the end of each paragraph.

c. Press **Ctrl+Shift+Spacebar** to insert a non-breaking space between the words "Real" and "Estate" in the second paragraph. Use only a single non-breaking space; do not include a regular space.

Please read each paragraph before signing the disclosure statement documents. As you fill out the required disclosure packet, it is critical to the transmission of sale that you give as much information as possible about your residence, no matter how small or insignificant. Please use additional paper if necessary and make a notation to that fact.

If there is information about the neighborhood or neighbors that you as a buyer would want to know about, be sure to reveal that information. Be sure to address those types of questions on the Real Estate Transfer Disclosure Statement, item #11 on page 2.

10. Type Best regards, as the complimentary close and press **Enter** two times after. Be sure to include the comma after the complimentary close.
11. Type the letter writer's name, title, and company name.
    a. Insert a line break (**Shift+Enter**) at the end of the first two lines.

    Emma Cavalli
    Realtor Consultant
    Placer Hills Real Estate

    b. Press **Enter** after the company name.
12. Type your initials in lower case letters and press **Shift+Enter** to insert a line break.
    a. Word automatically capitalizes the first letter because it is the first word in a new paragraph.
    b. Click the **AutoCorrect** smart tag and select **Undo Automatic Capitalization** (Figure 1-16) or press **Ctrl+Z** to undo automatic capitalization.

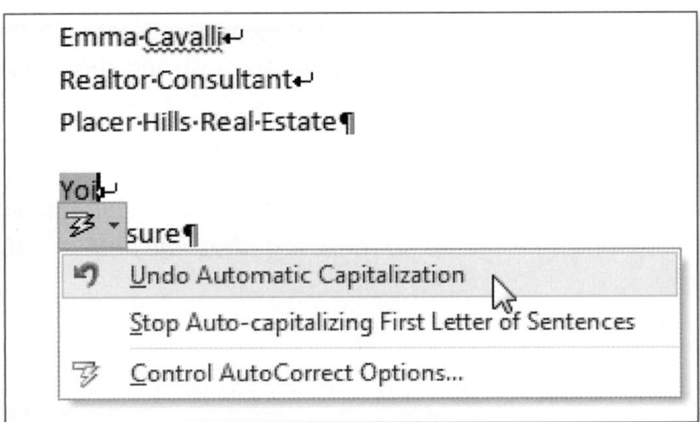

1-16 ***AutoCorrect*** **smart tag**

13. On the next line below the reference initials, type Enclosure. An enclosure notation indicates to the reader that something is enclosed with the letter.
14. Press **Ctrl+S** to save the document (Figure 1-17). You can also save the document by clicking on the **Save** button on the *Quick Access* toolbar or in the *Backstage* view.
15. Click the **File** tab and select **Close** (or press **Ctrl+W**) to close the document.

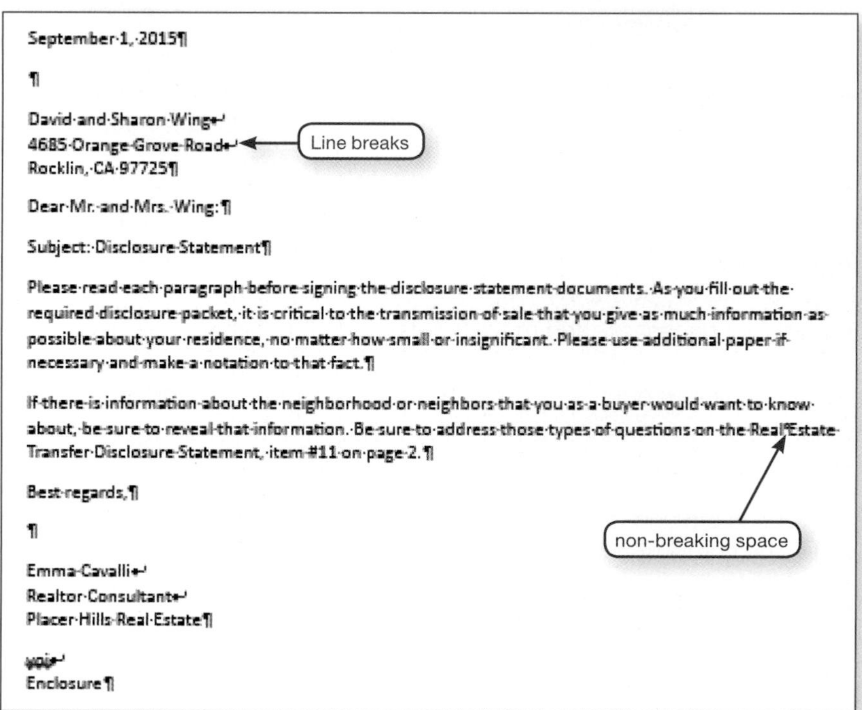

September 1, 2015

David and Sharon Wing
4685 Orange Grove Road
Rocklin, CA 97725

Dear Mr. and Mrs. Wing:

Subject: Disclosure Statement

Please read each paragraph before signing the disclosure statement documents. As you fill out the required disclosure packet, it is critical to the transmission of sale that you give as much information as possible about your residence, no matter how small or insignificant. Please use additional paper if necessary and make a notation to that fact.

If there is information about the neighborhood or neighbors that you as a buyer would want to know about, be sure to reveal that information. Be sure to address those types of questions on the Real Estate Transfer Disclosure Statement, item #11 on page 2.

Best regards,

Emma Cavalli
Realtor Consultant
Placer Hills Real Estate

yoi
Enclosure

1-17 PP W1-1 completed

SLO 1.4

Moving and Copying Text

Editing is an important phase in document creation. Editing involves not only proofreading and correcting grammar and spelling mistakes but also arranging text within a document, which can include cutting, copying, and pasting. Word makes it easy to move and copy information within a document or between multiple documents.

> **ANOTHER WAY**
> **Ctrl+C** to copy
> **Ctrl+X** to cut
> **Ctrl+V** to paste

Move Text

Moving is actually removing text from one location (cutting) and placing it in another location (pasting). There are two methods you can use to move text: ***drag and drop*** or ***cut*** and ***paste.***

HOW TO: Move Text Using Drag and Drop

1. Select the text you want to move.
2. Click and hold the selected text with your pointer.
3. Drag the text to the desired new location and release the pointer (Figure 1-18).

Drag pointer

If there is information about the neighborhood or neighbors that you as a buyer would want to know about, be sure to reveal that information. Be sure to address those types of questions on the Real Estate Transfer Disclosure Statement, item #11 on page 2.

Make note on the disclosure statement if you have had any work done with or without permits. Some examples include a gas spa, a new water heater, or a wholehouse fan where a trus may have been cut. If you had granate counters installed, that does not require a permit.

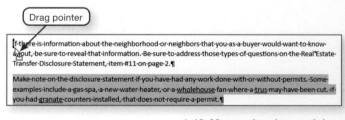

1-18 Move using drag and drop

There are a variety of ways to move text using cut and paste.

- ***Cut and Paste buttons:*** These buttons are in the *Clipboard* group on the *Home* tab.
- ***Shortcut commands:*** Press **Ctrl+X** to cut and **Ctrl+V** to paste.
- ***Context menu:*** Right-click the selected text to display this menu.

HOW TO: Move Text Using Cut and Paste

1. Select the text you want to move.
2. Click the **Cut** button [*Home* tab, *Clipboard* group].
   - You can also press **Ctrl+X** or right-click the selected text and choose **Cut** from the context menu.
3. Place your insertion point in the desired location.
4. Click the **Paste** button [*Home* tab, *Clipboard* group].
   - You can also press **Ctrl+V** or right-click the selected text and click the first **Paste** icon. *Note: See the **Paste Text and Paste Options** section below for the different paste options available.*

Copy Text

An efficient method of inserting text into a document is to copy it from another location, such as a web page or a different document, and paste it into your document. Copying text leaves the text in its original location and places a copy of the text in a new location.

You can ***copy*** text by using the ***drag and drop*** method or the ***Copy and Paste*** buttons. Use the drag and drop method when copying text within the same document. The drag and drop method for copying is similar to the method for moving, except that you hold the **Ctrl** key when dragging the text to be copied to an additional location. A + (plus sign) appears next to your pointer, indicating this text is being copied.

HOW TO: Copy Text Using Drag and Drop

1. Select the text you want to copy.
2. Hold the **Ctrl** key and click and hold the selected text with your pointer.
3. Drag to the desired new location and release the pointer (Figure 1-19).

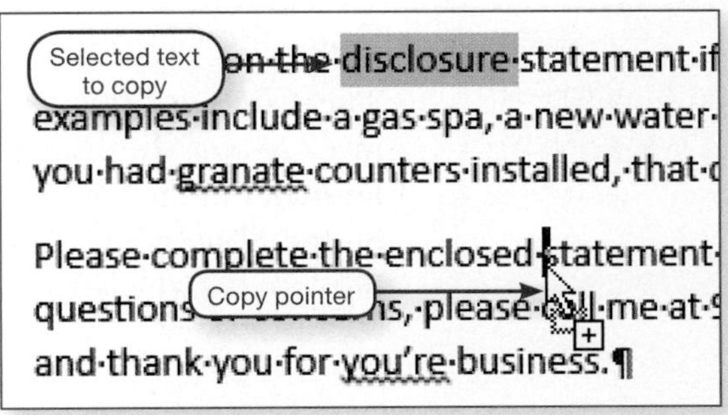

1-19 Copy using drag and drop

Copying text using the following copy and paste method is similar to moving text using the cut and paste method.

- ***Copy and Paste buttons:*** These buttons are in the *Clipboard* group on the *Home* tab.
- ***Shortcut commands:*** Press **Ctrl+C** to copy and **Ctrl+V** to paste.
- ***Context menu:*** Right-click the selected text to display this menu.

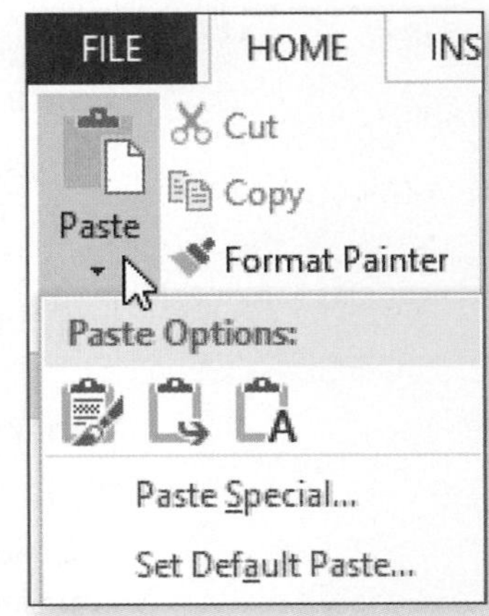

1-20 *Paste* options

Paste Text and Paste Options

You might want to paste text into a document and only want the plain text, or you might want to merge the format from the source document into the new document. Word provides multiple paste options.

You have three primary paste options when you use the *Paste* button in the *Clipboard* group (Figure 1-20) or from the context menu.

- ***Keep Source Formatting****—retains formatting from source document (the document where the text was copied)*
- ***Merge Formatting****—merges formatting from source document and current document*
- ***Keep Text Only****—pastes only unformatted text*

The default paste option is *Keep Source Formatting.* In addition to these paste options, there are other context-specific paste options that are available when you paste information from lists or paste text with a style applied.

MORE INFO

If you're having trouble with the format of pasted text, try pasting the text as plain text and formatting the text *after* you have pasted it into the document.

The Clipboard

When you copy or cut an item from a document, Word stores this information in the ***Clipboard.*** From the *Clipboard,* you can select a previously copied item and paste it into a document. When Word is open, the *Clipboard* stores multiple items copied from Word documents and also items from web pages or other documents. The *Clipboard* stores text, pictures, tables, lists, and graphics.

Open the Clipboard Task Pane

The ***Clipboard task pane*** displays all of the items stored in *Clipboard.* To display the *Clipboard* task pane, click the **launcher** in the bottom right corner of the *Clipboard* group on the *Home* tab (Figure 1-21). The *Clipboard* task pane is displayed on the left side of the Word window.

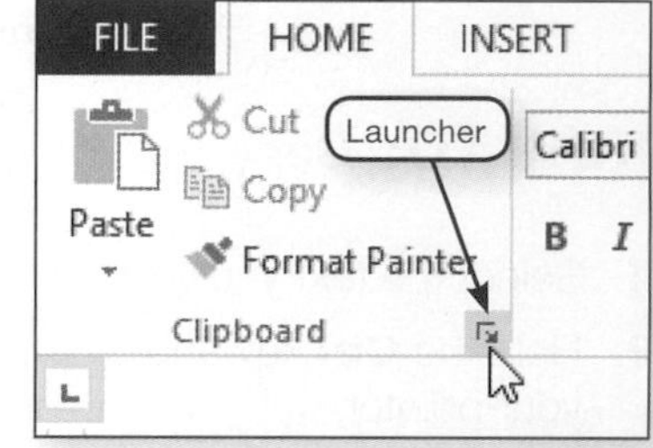

1-21 *Clipboard* launcher

MORE INFO

The ***launcher*** (also referred to as the ***dialog box launcher***) is referred to throughout this text. Click the **launcher** in the bottom right corner of a group to open a dialog box or pane to give you additional options.

Paste from the Clipboard

To paste an item from the *Clipboard* into a document at the insertion point in the document, select the item or click the drop-down arrow to the right of the item and choose **Paste** (Figure 1-22).

Other Clipboard Options

Paste All pastes all of the items in the *Clipboard* at the insertion point in the document. Selecting **Clear All** empties the content of the *Clipboard.* When you exit Word, the contents of the *Clipboard* are removed.

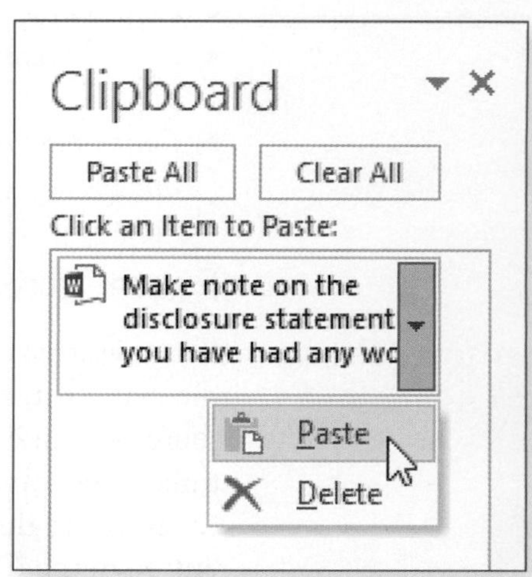

1-22 *Clipboard* task pane

At the bottom of the *Clipboard* task pane, there are a variety of display options. Choose from these by clicking on the **Options** button (Figure 1-23). Click the **X** in the upper right corner of the pane to close it.

Show Office Clipboard Automatically
Show Office Clipboard When Ctrl+C Pressed Twice
Collect Without Showing Office Clipboard
Show Office Clipboard Icon on Taskbar
Show Status Near Taskbar When Copying

1-23 ***Clipboard*** **options**

Undo, Redo, and Repeat Changes

You can undo, redo, or repeat previous actions. All of these buttons are available on the ***Quick Access toolbar.***

Undo

When you click the ***Undo*** button, the last action you performed is undone. You can undo multiple actions by clicking on the **Undo** drop-down arrow to the right of the button and selecting the items to undo (Figure 1-24).

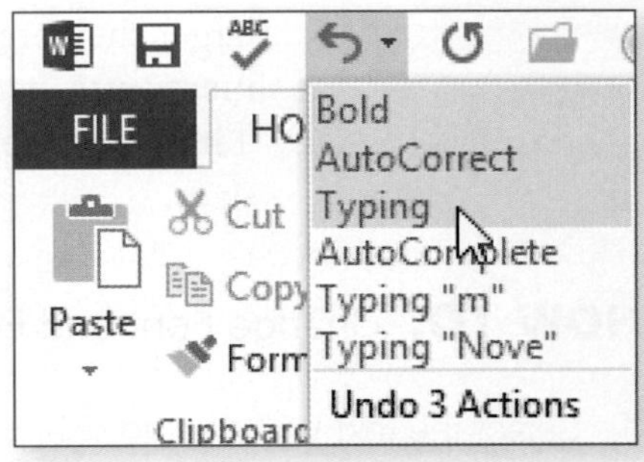

1-24 ***Undo*** **button on the** ***Quick Access*** **toolbar**

Redo and Repeat

The ***Redo*** and ***Repeat*** features are similar to the undo feature. The same button is used for both of these features, and it is context sensitive. Depending on the previous action performed, the button is either *Redo* or *Repeat.*

When you use the *Undo* button, the *Redo* button is activated so you can redo the previous change (Figure 1-25).

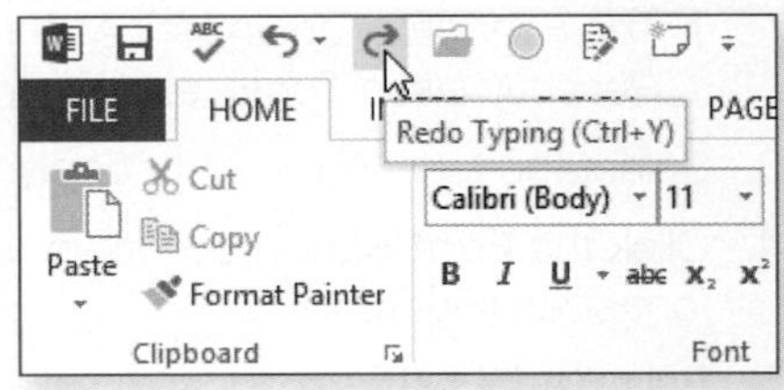

1-25 ***Redo*** **button on the** ***Quick Access*** **toolbar**

When you perform an action or apply formatting in a document, the *Repeat* button is activated so you can repeat the previous action or formatting (Figure 1-26). For example, if you need to copy the date or a name into a document in multiple places, you can use the *Repeat* feature to accomplish this task quickly and accurately.

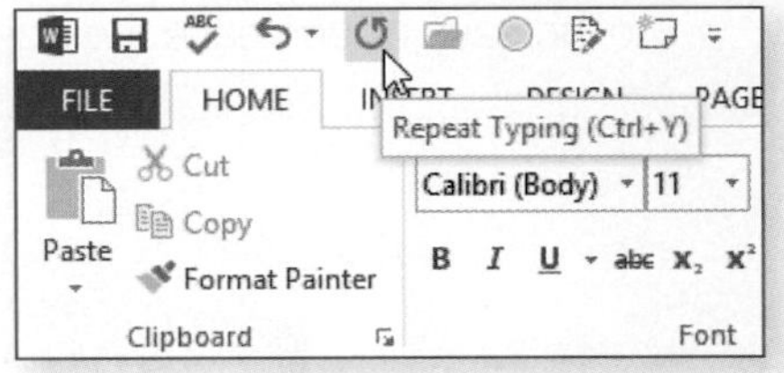

1-26 ***Repeat*** **button on the** ***Quick Access*** **toolbar**

> **ANOTHER WAY**
>
> **Ctrl+Z** is undo.
> **Ctrl+Y** is redo and repeat.

SLO 1.5

Changing Fonts, Font Sizes, and Attributes

Word has many features that you can use to customize the appearance of the text within a document. You can change the font and size of font; add styles such as bold, italics, and underlining; change the case of the text; add font and text effects; adjust the scale, spacing, and position of text; and change the default font settings. You can use buttons in the *Font* group on the *Home* tab, the *Font* dialog box, and the mini toolbar to apply formatting to text.

Font and Font Size

There are two main categories of fonts: serif and sans serif. ***Serif fonts*** have structural details (flair) at the top and bottom of most of the letters. Some commonly used serif fonts are Cambria, Times New Roman, and Courier New. ***Sans serif fonts*** have no structural details on the letters. Commonly used sans serif fonts are Calibri, Arial, and Century Gothic.

Font size is measured in ***points*** (pt.); the larger the point, the larger the font. Most documents use between 10 and 12 pt. font sizes. Titles and headings generally are larger font sizes.

> **MORE INFO**
>
> The default font and font size in Microsoft Word are *Calibri* and *11 pt.*, respectively.
>
> Font size of 72 pt. is approximately 1" in height.

HOW TO: Change Font and Font Size

1. Select the text you want to change.
2. Click the **Font** drop-down list to display the list of available fonts (Figure 1-27).
   - The *Font* drop-down list has three sections: *Theme Fonts*, *Recently Used Fonts*, and *All Fonts.*
3. Select the font you want to apply to the selected text.
4. Click the **Font Size** drop-down list to display the list of available font sizes (Figure 1-28).
5. Select a font size to apply to selected text.
   - You can also click in the **Font Size** area and type a size.
   - Use the **Increase Font Size** and **Decrease Font Size** buttons to increase or decrease the size of the font in small increments.

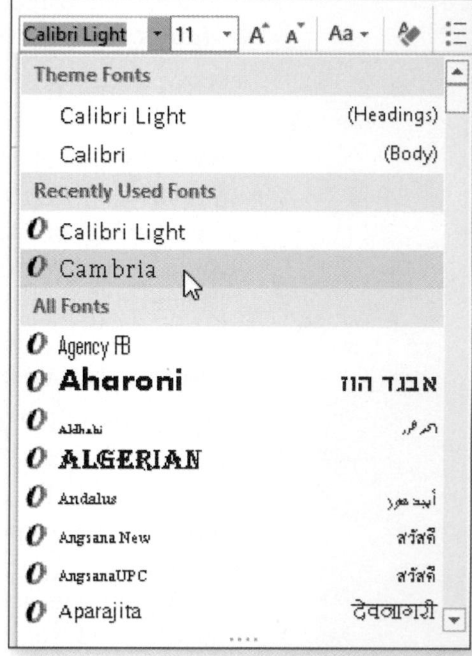

1-27 *Font* drop-down list

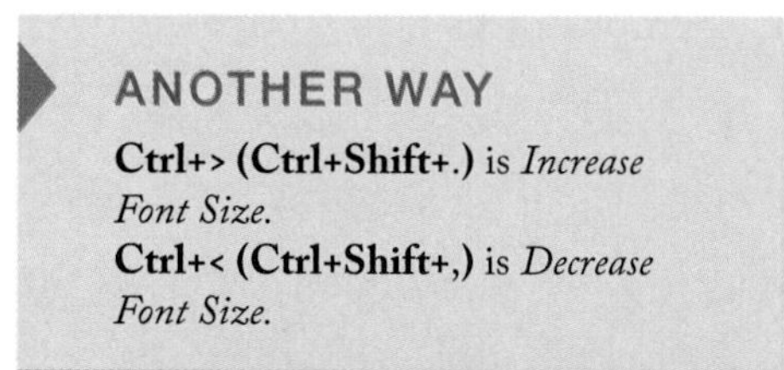

> **ANOTHER WAY**
>
> **Ctrl+> (Ctrl+Shift+.)** is *Increase Font Size.*
> **Ctrl+< (Ctrl+Shift+,)** is *Decrease Font Size.*

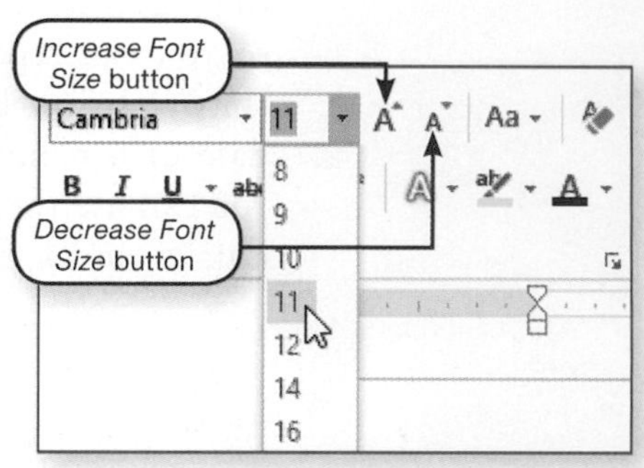

1-28 *Font Size* drop-down list

When creating a new document, you can choose a font and it applies to the entire document. If you want to change the font of an existing document, you must first select the text before applying the change.

Font Styles

You can add styles such as ***Bold, Italic,*** and ***Underline*** to fonts to improve their appearance or call attention to specific text. The font style buttons for *Bold, Italic,* and *Underline* are available in the *Font* group on the *Home* tab.

Bold, Italic, and Underline

To apply a font style, select the desired text and click the **Bold**, **Italic**, or **Underline** button in the *Font* group on the *Home* tab (Figure 1-29). You can also click one or more of the font style buttons to turn on a style. Type the text and click the font style button(s) again to turn off the style.

The ***mini toolbar*** displays when you select or right-click text (Figure 1-30). You can use the mini toolbar to apply text formatting. Like the content menu, the mini toolbar is context-sensitive and displays different options depending on the selection you right-click.

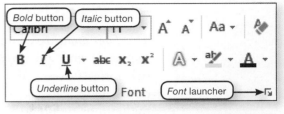

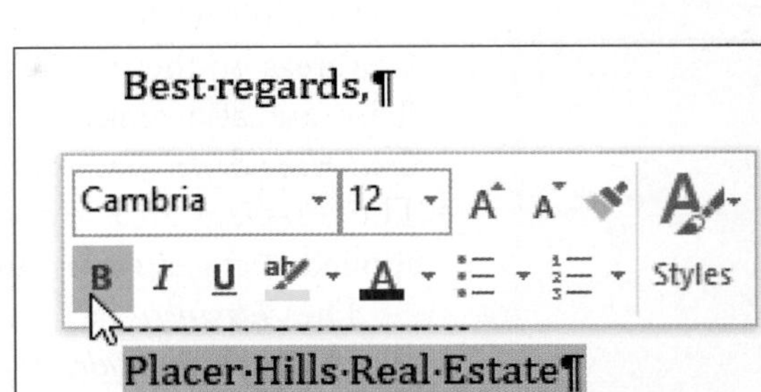

1-29 ***Font*** **group on the** ***Home*** **tab**

1-30 Select or right-click text to display the mini toolbar

> **ANOTHER WAY**
>
> **Ctrl+B** is *Bold.*
> **Ctrl+I** is *Italic.*
> **Ctrl+U** is *Underline.*

Other Font Style Buttons

There are other styles and effects in the *Font* group on the *Home* tab and on the mini toolbar.

- *Strikethrough*
- *Subscript*
- *Superscript*
- *Text Effects and Typography,* which includes *Outline, Shadow, Reflection, Glow, Number Styles, Ligatures, and Style Sets*
- *Text Highlight Color*
- *Font Color*

Change Case

The ***Change Case*** feature is a quick and easy way to change the case of a single word or group of words. The *Change Case* button is in the *Font* group on the *Home* tab (Figure 1-31).

Your different case options are:

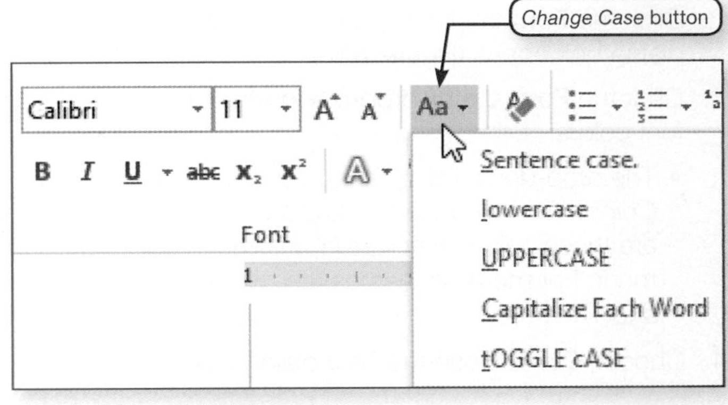

1-31 ***Change Case*** **options**

- *Sentence case* (capitalizes the first letter of the sentence)
- *lowercase*
- *UPPERCASE*
- *Capitalize Each Word*
- *tOGGLE cASE* (changes letters that are uppercase to lowercase and lowercase letters to uppercase)

Font Dialog Box

The ***Font dialog box*** combines many of the font style and ***effect options*** in one location for easy access. You can open the *Font* dialog by clicking the **Font** launcher in the bottom right corner of the *Font* group (Figure 1-32).

In addition to the *Font, Font Style,* and *Size* areas on the *Font* tab in this dialog box, there are also areas to change *Font Color, Underline Style, Underline Color,* and *Effects.* The *Preview* area gives you a preview of applied changes, styles, and effects.

The *Advanced* tab lists *Character Spacing* options such as *Scale, Spacing, Position,* and *Kerning.* From this tab, you can also open the *Format Text Effects* dialog box.

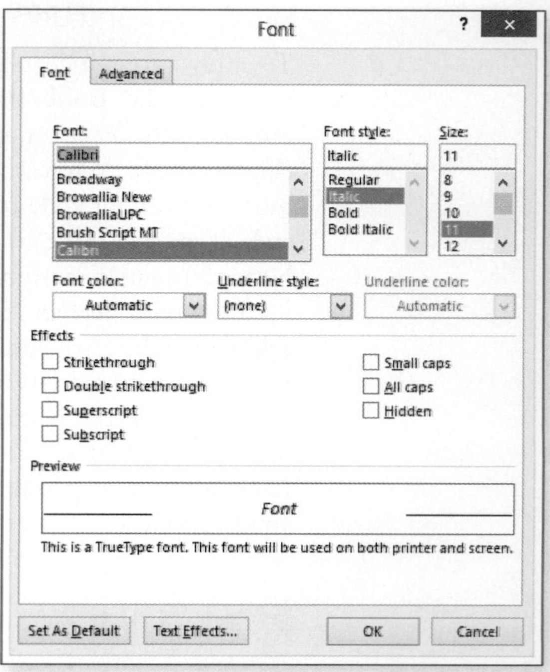

1-32 ***Font* dialog box**

> **ANOTHER WAY**
>
> **Ctrl+D** opens the *Font* dialog box.

Font Color

By default, the font color in a Word document is black. You can change the font color of selected text to add emphasis. The ***Font Color*** drop-down list in the *Font* dialog box displays a list of available font colors.

HOW TO: Change Font Color

1. Select the text you want to be a different color.
2. Click the **Font** launcher [*Home* tab, *Font* group]. The *Font* dialog box opens (Figure 1-33).
3. Click the **Font Color** drop-down arrow to display the list of font colors.
   - The drop-down list of font color options includes *Theme Colors*, *Standard Colors*, and *More Colors.* Theme colors are those colors associated with the theme of the document. For more on themes, see *Section 2.7: Using Styles and Themes.*
4. Choose **OK** to close the *Font* dialog box.

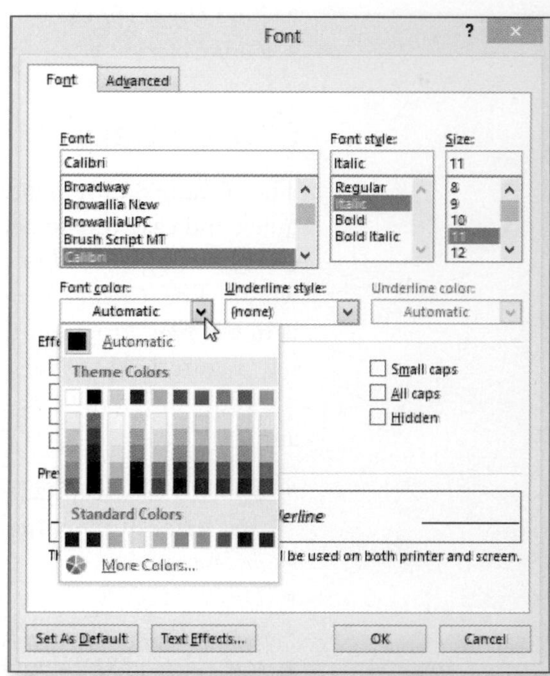

1-33 **Change font color in the *Font* dialog box**

> **ANOTHER WAY**
>
> Change the font color by clicking on the **Font Color** button [*Home* tab, *Font* group].

Underline Style and Color

When you underline selected text, the default underline style is a solid black underline. Word provides a variety of additional underline styles. You can also change the color of the underline.

The ***Underline Style*** and ***Underline Color*** drop-down lists are available in the *Font* dialog box (Figure 1-34). A preview of how the formatted text will appear in your document is displayed in the *Preview* area of the *Font* dialog box.

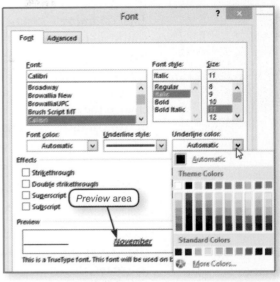

1-34 Change *Underline* style and color

Font Effects

In the *Font* dialog box you can choose a variety of font effects from the ***Effects*** section. Some of these font effects are available in the *Font* group on the *Home* tab. The following table lists the different font styles and effects.

Font Styles and Effects

Style/Effect	Example
Bold	This **word** is in bold.
Italic	This *word* is in italic.
Bold and Italic	This ***word*** is in bold and italic.
Underline	This sentence is underlined.
Double Underline	This word is double underlined.
Underline Words Only	This sentence is words only underlined.
Thick Underline with Color	This word has a thick, colored underline.
Strikethrough	This ~~word~~ has a strikethrough.
Double Strikethrough	~~This sentence has a double strikethrough.~~
Subscript	H_2O uses a subscript number.
Superscript	Footnotes and endnotes use superscript numbers or letters.[1]
Small Caps	MICROSOFT WORD 2013 is in small caps.
All Caps	THIS SENTENCE IS IN ALL CAPS.
Hidden	
Text Highlight Color	This word has a highlight color.
Font Color	This sentence has a font color applied.

> **MORE INFO**
>
> *Hidden* text appears in your on-screen document, but it does not print or display in print preview.

Character Spacing

The ***Character Spacing*** options allow you to add more or less space between letters and words. You can also raise and lower letters and words (Figure 1-35).

The ***Scale*** option allows you to change the spacing of a word or group of words by a percentage. You can choose from preset percentages, or you can type in a custom percentage for scaling.

Spacing has three options: *Normal, Expanded,* and *Condensed.* For *Expanded* and *Condensed,* you can choose the amount of points by which to expand the selected text.

The ***Position*** option raises or lowers text by a selected number of points.

Kerning adjusts the space between letters in a proportional font.

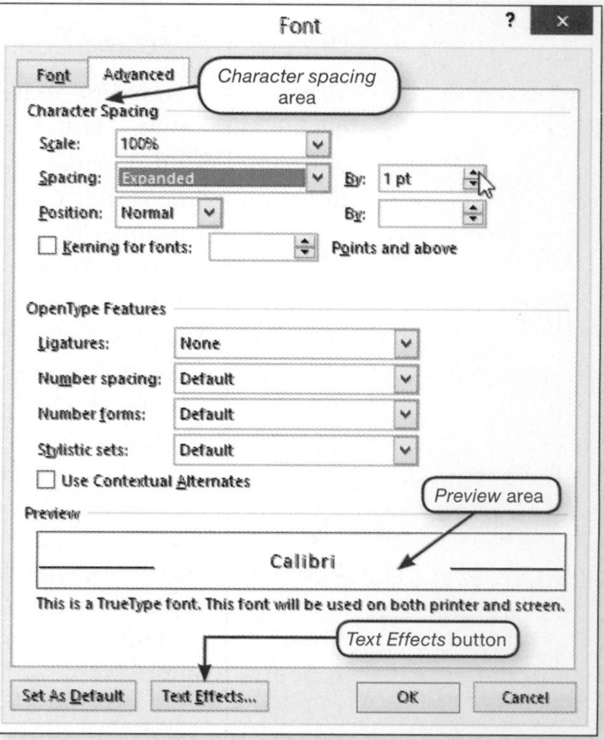

1-35 *Font* dialog box *Advanced* tab

Text Effects

With ***Text Effects,*** you can add special formatting features to selected text, such as *Outline, Shadow, Reflection,* and *Glow* (Figure 1-36).

The *Text Effects* button is located in the *Font* group on the *Home* tab. There are many preset options for each of the different text effects, and there are more custom text effect options available in the *Format Text Effects* dialog box.

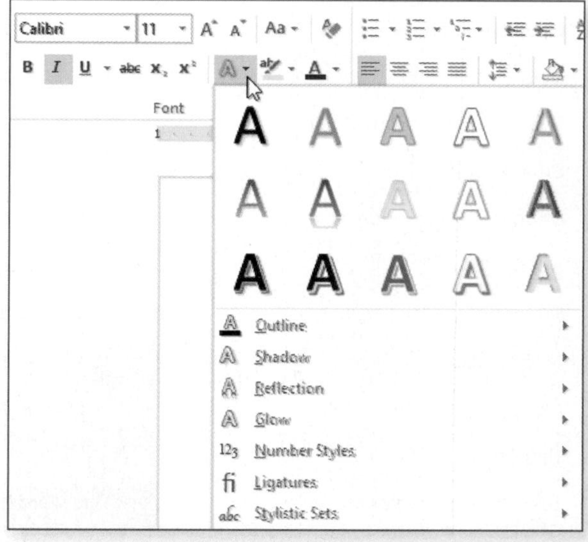

1-36 *Text Effects* button in the *Font* group

HOW TO: Use the Format Text Effects Dialog Box

1. Select the text you want to format.
2. Click the **Font** launcher [*Home* tab, *Font* group]. The *Font* dialog box opens.
3. Click the **Text Effects** button at the bottom. The *Format Text Effects* dialog box opens (Figure 1-37).
4. Click the **Text Fill & Outline** button to display fill and outline options.
   - Select **Text Fill** or **Text Outline** to expand and display options.
5. Click the **Text Effects** button to display text effect options.
   - Select **Shadow**, **Reflection**, **Glow**, **Soft Edges**, or **3-D Format** to expand and display options.
   - Each of these categories has *Presets* you can choose or you can customize the effect.
6. Select the text effect of your choice on the left.
7. To the right of each option you can choose a preset option from the drop-down list or customize the text effect as desired.
8. Click **OK** to close the *Format Text Effects* dialog box and click **OK** to close the *Font* dialog box.

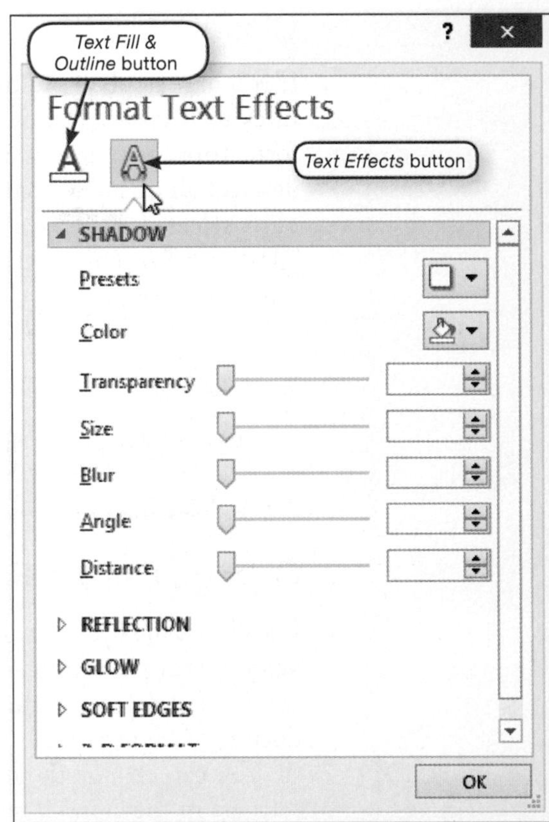

1-37 ***Format Text Effects* dialog box**

Format Painter

The ***Format Painter*** copies font, font size, line spacing, indents, bullets, numbering, styles, and many other features in Word and applies the formatting to a word, phrase, or entire paragraph. This feature saves time in applying formats and keeps your document consistent in format.

HOW TO: Use the Format Painter

1. Select the text that has the formatting you want to copy.
2. Click the **Format Painter** button [*Home* tab, *Clipboard* group (Figure 1-38). The *Format Painter* icon appears as your pointer (Figure 1-39).
3. Click the word or select the paragraph you want to format and Word applies the formatting to the selected text.
   - Double-click the **Format Painter** button to apply formatting to multiple non-adjacent selections.
   - Click the **Format Painter** button again to turn off the *Format Painter.*

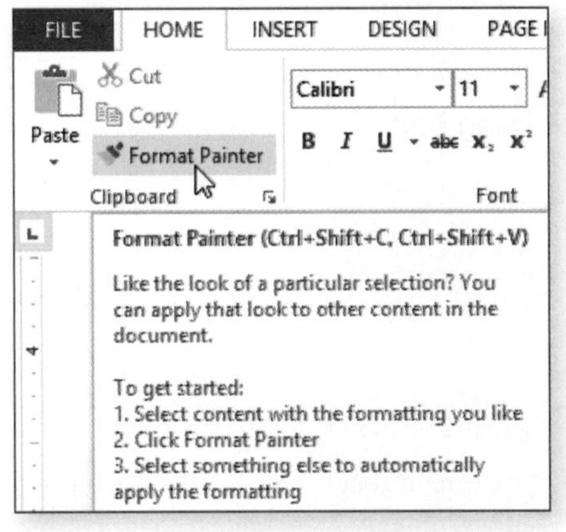

1-38 ***Format Painter* button**

1-39 ***Format Painter* icon**

Clear Formatting

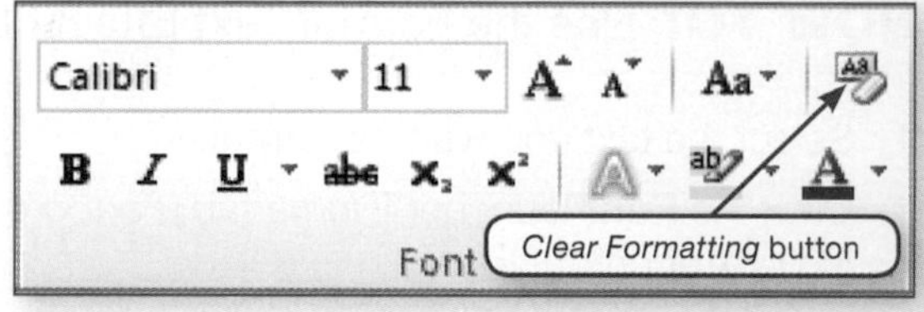

1-40 ***Clear Formatting*** **button in the** ***Font*** **group**

If you have applied multiple formatting features to text and you decide to remove the formatting, you don't have to individually deselect all of the formatting options previously selected. The ***Clear Formatting*** feature allows you to remove all formatting for the selected text and change it back to plain text (Figure 1-40).

> **MORE INFO**
>
> Be careful when using the *Clear Formatting* feature. It not only clears all text formatting but also clears line and paragraph spacing, numbering, bullets, and style formatting.

Change Default Font and Font Size

Recall that the default font in Microsoft Word is *Calibri,* and the default font size is *11 pt.* This ***default*** setting is used on each new blank document you create. Each new document is based on the *Normal.dotx* template. This template stores the default settings for documents and controls document elements such as font, font size, line spacing, paragraph spacing, alignment, and styles.

You can change the default settings on the current document only or change the default settings in the *Normal* template. If you change the default settings for the *Normal* template, each new blank document you create uses this new default font and font size.

HOW TO: Change the Default Font and Font Size

1. Select the text you want to format.
2. Click the **Font** launcher [*Home* tab, *Font* group]. The *Font* dialog box opens (Figure 1-41).
3. Click the **Font** tab if it is not already selected.
4. Select the font and font size to set as the default.
5. Click the **Set As Default** button at the bottom left. A confirmation dialog box opens giving you two options: *This document only?* or *All documents based on the Normal template?* (Figure 1-42).
6. Select an option.
7. Click **OK** to close the dialog box.

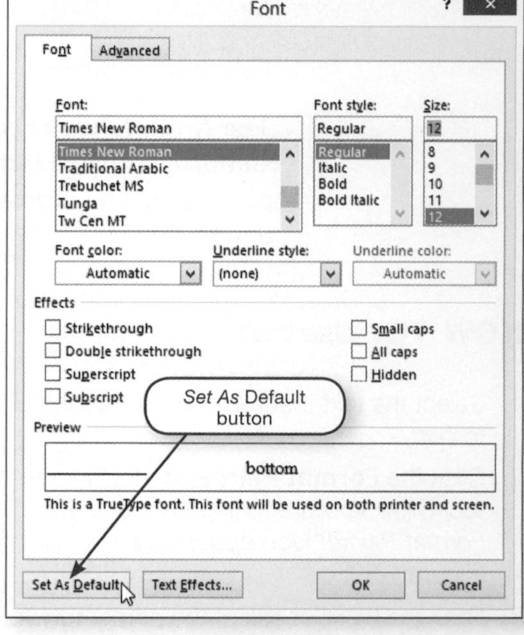

1-41 ***Set As Default*** **button in the** ***Font*** **dialog box**

> **MORE INFO**
>
> Be careful about changing the default settings in the *Normal* template. Do this only when you are sure you want to make this global default settings change.

Microsoft Word

Do you want to set the default font to Times New Roman, 12 pt for:

This document only?

All documents based on the Normal template?

OK Cancel

1-42 Change default setting confirmation options

PAUSE & PRACTICE: WORD 1-2

In this Pause & Practice project, you customize the content of your block format letter using cut, copy, paste, and the *Clipboard.* You also enhance your document by changing the font and applying font attributes.

Files Needed: ***[your initials] PP W1-1.docx***, ***DisclosureStatement-01.docx***
Completed Project File Name: ***[your initials] PP W1-2.docx***

---

1. Open the ***[your initials] PP W1-1*** document.
2. Save this document as ***[your initials] PP W1-2***.
   a. Press **F12** to open the *Save As* dialog box.
   b. Change the file name to [your initials] PP W1-2.
   c. Click **Save** to rename the document and close the *Save As* dialog box.
3. Open the ***DisclosureStatement-01*** document. Ignore any spelling and grammar errors in this document; you will fix these in Pause & Practice 1-3.
4. In the ***DisclosureStatement-01*** document, copy both paragraphs of text to the *Clipboard.*
   a. Press **Ctrl+A** to select the text.
   b. Press **Ctrl+C** or click the **Copy** button [*Home* tab, *Clipboard* group].
   c. Close the document without saving.
5. Paste the contents of the *Clipboard* into the document.
   a. In the ***[your initials] PP W1-2*** document, place your insertion point to the left of "Best regards,".
   b. Click the **Clipboard** launcher [*Home* tab, *Clipboard* group] to display the *Clipboard* pane.
   c. Click the **drop-down arrow** to the right of the copied text in the *Clipboard* (Figure 1-43).
   d. Select **Paste**. The paragraphs of text are pasted in the document at the insertion point.
   e. Close the *Clipboard* by clicking on the **X** in the upper right corner.

1-43 Paste text from the *Clipboard*

6. Copy the formatting of the first paragraph to the two new paragraphs.
   a. Place your insertion point in the first body paragraph of the letter.
   b. Click the **Format Painter** button [*Home* tab, *Clipboard* group].
   c. Select the last two paragraphs in the body of the letter. Be sure to include the paragraph mark at the end of the last body paragraph (Figure 1-44).

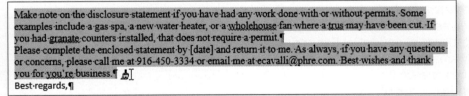

Make·note·on·the·disclosure·statement·if·you·have·had·any·work·done·with·or·without·permits.·Some·examples·include·a·gas·spa,·a·new·water·heater,·or·a·wholehouse·fan·where·a·trus·may·have·been·cut.·If·you·had·granate·counters·installed,·that·does·not·require·a·permit.¶
Please·complete·the·enclosed·statement·by·[date]·and·return·it·to·me.·As·always,·if·you·have·any·questions·or·concerns,·please·call·me·at·916-450-3334·or·email·me·at·ecavalli@phre.com.·Best·wishes·and·thank·you·for·you're·business.¶
Best·regards,¶

1-44 Apply the *Format Painter* to selected text

7. Copy text using the drag and drop method.
   a. Select the word "**disclosure**" in the first sentence of the third body paragraph.
   b. Hold down the **Ctrl** key and drag and drop the text between the words "enclosed" and "statement" (Figure 1-45).

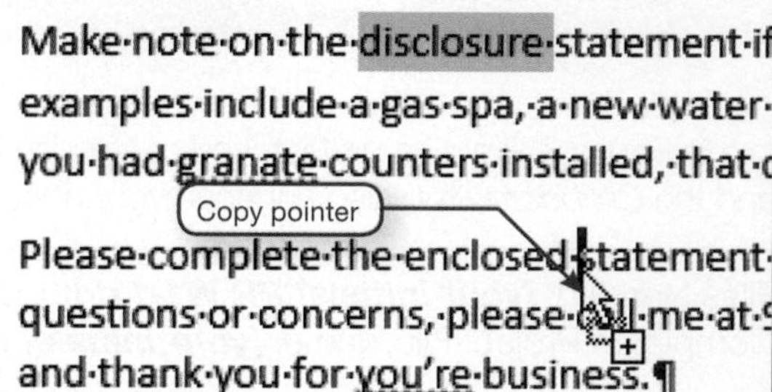

1-45 Copy text using drag and drop

8. Move the third body paragraph ("Make note . . .") so it becomes the second body paragraph.
   a. Select the third paragraph in the body of the letter, including the paragraph mark at the end of the paragraph.
   b. Click the **Cut** button [*Home* tab, *Clipboard* group] or press **Ctrl+X**. The selected paragraph is cut from the document and stored in the *Clipboard.*
   c. Place your insertion point at the beginning of the second body paragraph.
   d. Click the **Paste** button [*Home* tab, *Clipboard* group] or press **Ctrl+V**.

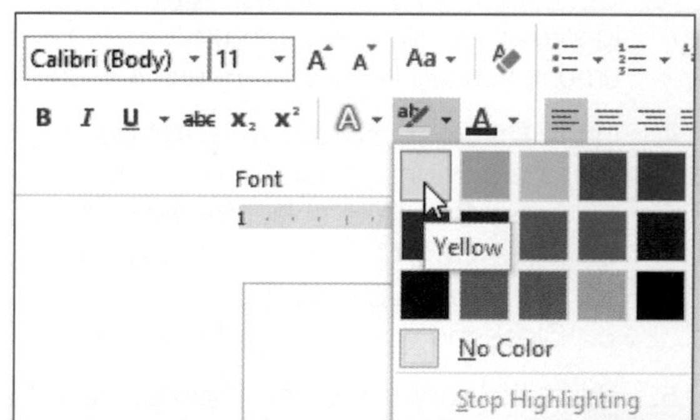

1-46 Apply text highlight color

9. Insert and format a date.
   a. Replace the placeholder "[date]" in the last paragraph with the date one week from today.
   b. Use month, day, year format (e.g., September 8, 2015).
   c. Select the date.
   d. On the **Text Highlight Color** drop-down list button [*Home* tab, *Font* group], choose **yellow** text highlight color (Figure 1-46).

10. Change the font and font size of the entire document.
   a. Press **Ctrl+A** to select all of the text in the document.
   b. Click the **Font** drop-down list button [*Home* tab, *Font* group] and select **Cambria**.
   c. Click the **Font Size** drop-down list button [*Home* tab, *Font* group] and select **12**.

11. Change the case and spacing of selected text.
   a. Select the word "**Subject**" in the subject line of the document.
   b. Click the **Change Case** button [*Home* tab, *Font* group] and select **UPPERCASE**.
   c. Select the entire subject line.
   d. Click the **Font** launcher [*Home* tab, *Font* group] to open the *Font* dialog box. **Ctrl+D** also opens the *Font* dialog box (Figure 1-47).
   e. Click the **Advanced** tab.
   f. In the *Character Spacing* area, click the **Spacing** drop-down list and select **Expanded**.
   g. In the *By* area to the right of *Spacing*, click the up arrow to change the character spacing to be expanded by **1.5 pt**.
   h. Click **OK** to close the *Font* dialog box.

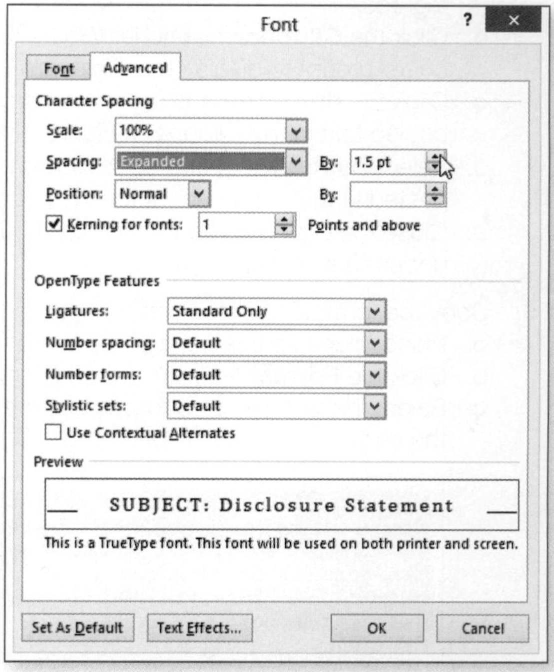

1-47 Change character spacing

12. Apply font styles to selected text.
    a. Select the email address "**ecavalli@phre.com**" in the last body paragraph.
    b. Click the **Font Color** drop-down list button [*Home* tab, *Font* group] and select **Dark Blue** in the *Standard Colors* area.
    c. Click the **Underline** button or press **Ctrl+U** to apply an underline to the selected email address.
    d. Select the writer's name "**Emma Cavalli**" (below "Best regards,") and open the *Font* dialog box.
    e. In the *Effects* area on the *Font* tab, check the **Small caps** box.
    f. Click **OK** to close the *Font* dialog box.
    g. Select the writer's title "**Realtor Consultant**" and click the **Italic** button or press **Ctrl+I**.
    h. Select the company name "**Placer Hills Real Estate**" and click the **Bold** button or press **Ctrl+B**.
13. Save and close the document (Figure 1-48).

September 1, 2015

David and Sharon Wing
4685 Orange Grove Road
Rocklin, CA 97725

Dear Mr. and Mrs. Wing:

SUBJECT: Disclosure Statement

Please read each paragraph before signing the disclosure statement documents. As you fill out the required disclosure packet, it is critical to the transmission of sale that you give as much information as possible about your residence, no matter how small or insignificant. Please use additional paper if necessary and make a notation to that fact.

Make note on the disclosure statement if you have had any work done with or without permits. Some examples include a gas spa, a new water heater, or a wholehouse fan where a trus may have been cut. If you had granate counters installed, that does not require a permit.

If there is information about the neighborhood or neighbors that you as a buyer would want to know about, be sure to reveal that information. Be sure to address those types of questions on the Real Estate Transfer Disclosure Statement, item #11 on page 2.

Please complete the enclosed disclosure statement by September 8, 2015 and return it to me. As always, if you have any questions or concerns, please call me at 916-450-3334 or email me at ecavalli@phre.com. Best wishes and thank you for you're business.

Best regards,

EMMA CAVALLI
Realtor Consultant
Placer Hills Real Estate

yoi
Enclosure

1-48 PP W1-2 completed

SLO 1.6

Changing Text Alignment, Line Spacing, and Paragraph Spacing

In addition to word wrap, line breaks, and paragraphs breaks, you can use text alignment, line spacing, and paragraph spacing to control the layout and the white space between parts of your document.

Understand Default Settings

Just as there are default settings for font and font size, there are default settings for paragraph alignment, line spacing, and paragraph spacing. These default settings are stored in the *Normal* template on which all new blank documents are based. The following table summarizes these default settings:

Normal Template Default Settings

Setting	Default Setting
Font	Calibri
Font Size	11 pt.
Horizontal Paragraph Alignment	Left
Line Spacing	1.08 lines
Paragraph Spacing—Before	0 pt.
Paragraph Spacing—After	8 pt.

Paragraph Alignment

Paragraph alignment controls how a paragraph is aligned horizontally on the page. A paragraph can be a single word, a group of words, a sentence, or multiple sentences. Paragraphs are separated by paragraph breaks. A group of words using word wrap and line breaks is considered one paragraph.

The four different paragraph alignment options are:

- ***Left*** (default): The paragraph is aligned at the left margin.
- ***Center:*** The paragraph is centered between the left and right margins.
- ***Right:*** The paragraph begins and is aligned at the right margin.
- ***Justify:*** The paragraph is aligned flush with both the left and right margins.

ANOTHER WAY

Ctrl+L is *Align Text Left.*
Ctrl+E is *Center* text.
Ctrl+R is *Align Text Right.*
Ctrl+J is *Justify* text.

Change the alignment of a paragraph by clicking a paragraph alignment button in the *Paragraph* group on the *Home* tab (Figure 1-49). When changing the alignment of a paragraph, the entire paragraph need not be selected; the insertion point only needs to be within the paragraph for the alignment to be applied. Text alignment can also be changed in the *Paragraph* dialog box, which we discuss later.

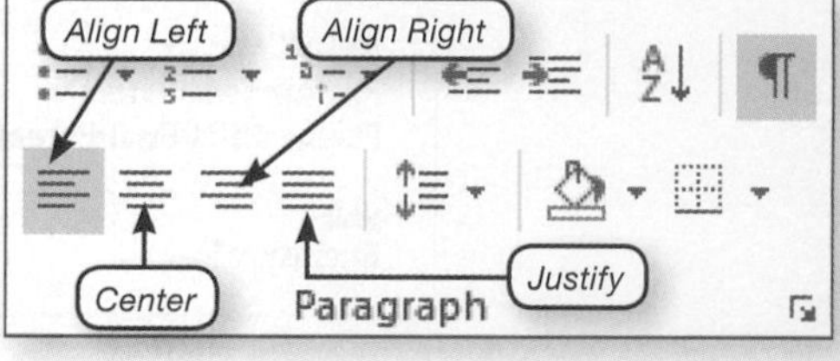

1-49 Paragraph alignment options in the *Paragraph* group

Line Spacing

Line spacing refers to the amount of blank space between lines of text within a paragraph. The default setting in Word is 1.08 lines, which is slightly more than single spaced. Most documents you type are single spaced or 1.08 line spacing, but there are times you may want to use double spacing (2 lines), such as when typing an academic report.

As with paragraph alignment, you can apply line spacing to an individual paragraph, multiple paragraphs, or an entire document.

You can change the line spacing using the **Line and Paragraph Spacing** button in the *Paragraph* group on the *Home* tab (Figure 1-50). You can choose from the preset line spacing options, or you can select **Line Spacing Options** and set custom line spacing in the *Paragraph* dialog box.

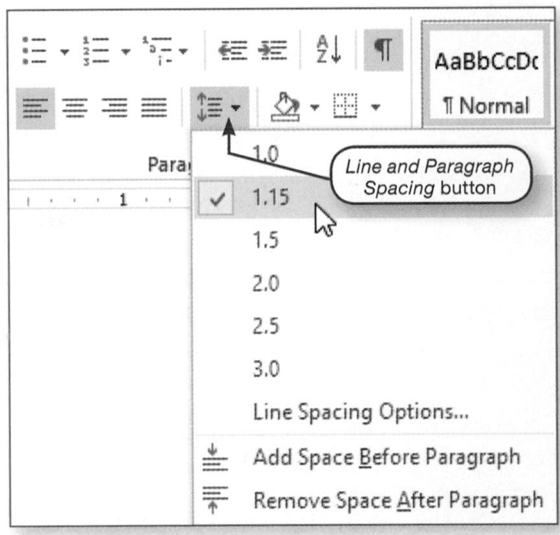

1-50 *Line and Paragraph Spacing* button in the *Paragraph* group

> **ANOTHER WAY**
>
> **Ctrl+1** is single space (1 line).
> **Ctrl+5** is 1.5 line spacing.
> **Ctrl+2** is double space (2 lines).

When you select **Line Spacing Options,** the *Paragraph* dialog box opens. In the box, you see different line spacing options (Figure 1-51).

The *At Least* and *Exactly* options allow you to specify points of spacing, rather than lines of spacing, between lines of text. The *Multiple* option allows you to set a line spacing option that is not a whole number, such as 1.3 or 2.25 line spacing.

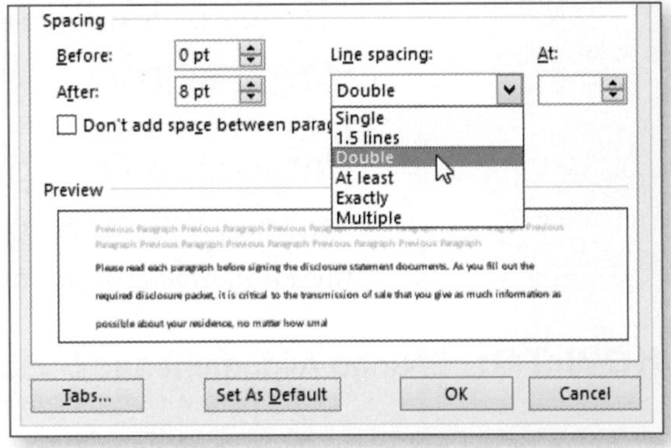

1-51 Line spacing options in the *Paragraph* dialog box

> **MORE INFO**
>
> If a document has inconsistent line spacing, it looks messy and unprofessional. Select the entire document and set the line spacing to enhance consistency. Consistent line spacing also improves readability.

Paragraph Spacing

While line spacing controls the amount of space between lines of text in a paragraph, ***paragraph spacing*** controls the amount of spacing before and after paragraphs (before and after a paragraph break). For example, you might want the text of a document to be single spaced, but you prefer to have more blank space between paragraphs. You can use paragraph spacing to accomplish this task. You can also do this by inserting multiple paragraph breaks—pressing *Enter* more than once.

Before and *After* paragraph spacing is set in points. The default after paragraph spacing in Word is 8 pt., which is a little less than one blank line.

Change before and after paragraph spacing from the *Paragraph* group on the *Page Layout* tab (Figure 1-52). You can also change before and after paragraph spacing in the *Paragraph* dialog box and from the *Line and Paragraph Spacing* button in the *Paragraph* group on the *Home* tab.

From the *Line and Paragraph Spacing* button in the *Paragraph* group on the *Home* tab, you can **Add/Remove Space Before Paragraph** or **Add/ Remove Space After Paragraph** (Figure 1-53). These options are context sensitive, depending on whether there is already *Before* or *After* paragraph spacing.

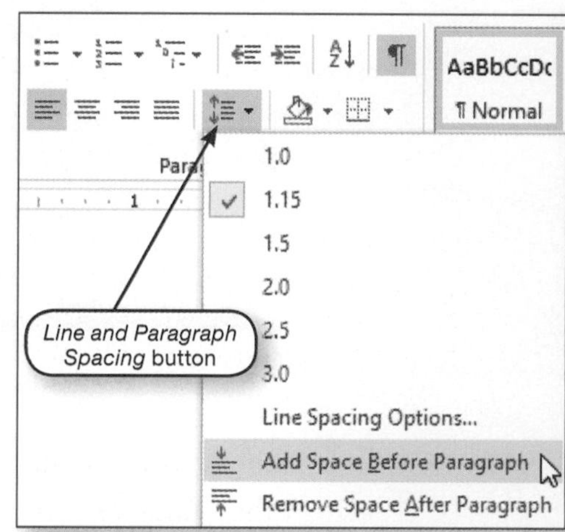

1-52 ***Paragraph* group on the *Page Layout* tab**

MORE INFO

Use line breaks to keep lines of text together. *Before* and *After* paragraph spacing is not applied to lines of text where line breaks are used.

1-53 Add/Remove paragraph spacing options

Paragraph Dialog Box

The ***Paragraph dialog box*** combines many of the alignment and spacing options included in the *Paragraph* groups on the *Home* and *Page Layout* tabs.

HOW TO: Change Alignment and Spacing in the Paragraph Dialog Box

1. Select the text you want to format.
2. Click the **Paragraph** launcher [*Home* or *Page Layout* tab, *Paragraph* group] to open the *Paragraph* dialog box (Figure 1-54).
3. Click the **Alignment** drop-down list in the *General* area and select **Left**, **Centered**, **Right**, or **Justified**.
4. The *Indentation* section of this dialog box lets you control indents. (For more on indents, see Chapter 2.)
5. In the *Spacing* section, you can change paragraph spacing and line spacing.
   - Type the number of points for spacing or use the up and down arrows.
   - The *Don't add space between paragraphs of the same style* check box controls paragraph spacing between paragraphs of the same style, which is primarily used with numbered and bulleted lists and outlines.
6. Click the **Line spacing** drop-down list to select line spacing.
   - You can select **Multiple** and type in a specific line spacing in the *At* area.
7. The *Preview* area displays how your document will look with changes.
8. Click **OK** to close the *Paragraph* dialog box.

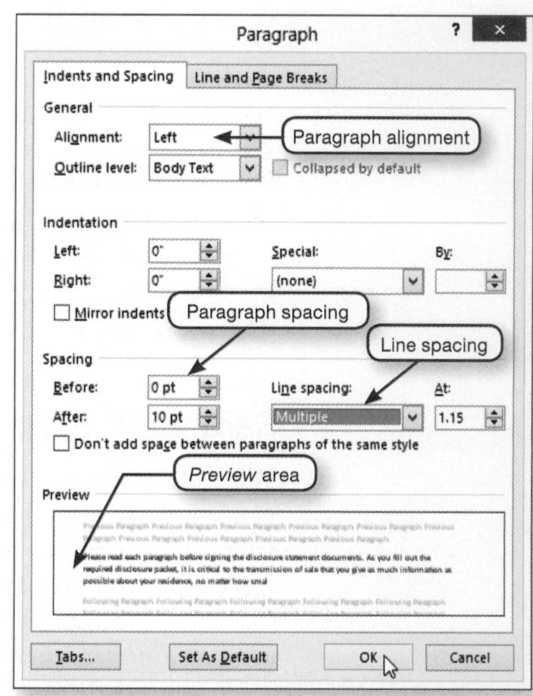

1-54 ***Paragraph* dialog box**

Change Default Line and Paragraph Spacing

You can set default paragraph alignment and spacing settings in the *Paragraph* dialog box. This process is similar to changing the font and font size default settings.

HOW TO: Change the Default Paragraph Alignment and Spacing

1. Click the **Paragraph** launcher [*Home* or *Page Layout* tab, *Paragraph* group] to open the *Paragraph* dialog box.
2. Click the **Indents and Spacing** tab if it is not already selected.
3. Make the desired changes to paragraph and line spacing.
4. Click the **Set As Default** button on the bottom left. Select one of the two options in the confirmation dialog box that opens: *This document only* or *All documents based on the Normal template* (Figure 1-55).
5. Click **OK**.

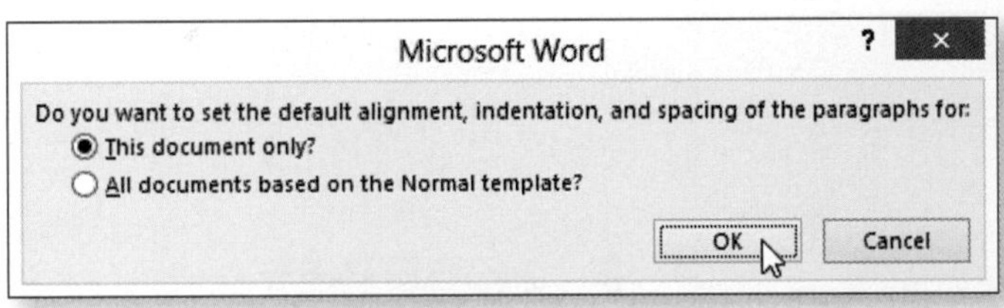

1-55 Change default setting confirmation options

SLO 1.7

Checking Spelling and Grammar and Using the Thesaurus

The words and grammar you use in a document reflect your professionalism and the reputation of your organization. Word provides you with many proofing and editing tools to improve the quality of the documents you produce. The spelling, grammar, thesaurus, and research features help you to produce high-quality and professional-looking documents.

Automatic Spelling and Grammar Notifications

Recall that Word uses *AutoCorrect* to automatically correct many commonly misspelled words. But there are many ***spelling errors*** that Word does not automatically correct. When you are typing a document, Word is constantly checking the words you type against the words in its dictionary. When Word doesn't recognize a word, it marks it with a ***red wavy underline***.

Word also checks the grammar of what you are typing and marks potential word choice or ***grammatical errors*** with a ***blue wavy underline***.

> **MORE INFO**
>
> Just because Word marks a word as a possible spelling or grammatical error, it does not necessarily mean that the word is misspelled. Many proper nouns are not included in the dictionary.

HOW TO: Correct Spelling and Grammatical Errors

1. Right-click a word that has a red or blue wavy underline. A context menu opens (Figure 1-56).
2. This menu provides different editing options.
   - Select the correct word from the list to replace the misspelled word.

- Select **Ignore All** to ignore all instances of this spelling throughout the document. Select **Ignore Once** to ignore a potential grammar error.
- Select **Add to Dictionary** to add the word to the Word dictionary.

3. When you select an option, the context menu closes.
4. Right-click the next item with a wavy red or blue underline to repeat the editing process.

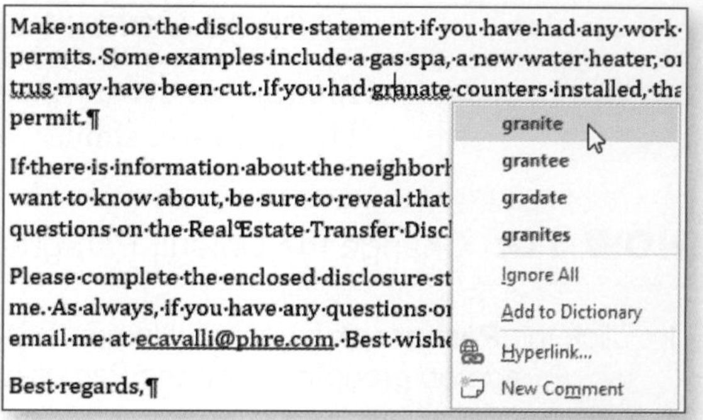

Make·note·on·the·disclosure·statement·if·you·have·had·any·work·
permits.·Some·examples·include·a·gas·spa,·a·new·water·heater,·o
trus·may·have·been·cut.·If·you·had·granate·counters·installed,·th
permit.¶
If·there·is·information·about·the·neighbor
want·to·know·about,·be·sure·to·reveal·that
questions·on·the·Real·Estate·Transfer·Disc
Please·complete·the·enclosed·disclosure·st
me.·As·always,·if·you·have·any·questions·o
email·me·at·ecavalli@phre.com.·Best·wish
Best·regards,¶
granite
1. a very hard natural igneous rock formation of visibly crystalline texture formed essentially of quartz and orthoclase or microcline and used especially for building and for monuments
2. unyielding firmness or endurance
grantee
gradate
granites
Ignore All
Add to Dictionary
Hyperlink...
New Comment

1-56 Correct a spelling error

> **MORE INFO**
>
> Don't rely solely on Word's spelling and grammar checkers to proofread your document. These helpful features cannot replace the proofreading and editing that you should do on every document you produce.

Spelling and Grammar Checking

When finalizing a document, it is important to proofread it one last time and give it one last spelling and grammar check. This is especially true with longer documents. You can use the ***Spelling and Grammar pane*** to check your entire document for potential spelling and grammatical errors.

The *Spelling and Grammar* pane is context-sensitive. The name of the pane (*Spelling* or *Grammar*) and the available options change depending on whether a potential spelling or grammatical error is detected.

HOW TO: Use the Spelling and Grammar Pane

1. Click the **Spelling & Grammar** button [*Review* tab, *Proofing* group] to open the *Spelling* pane (Figure 1-57).
   - The first potential spelling or grammatical error is displayed in the *Spelling* or *Grammar* pane.
2. If the word does not need to be changed, select **Ignore**, **Ignore All**, or **Add**.
   - If you select *Add*, the selected word is added to the dictionary so it is not detected as a potential error in the future.
3. If the word needs to be changed, select the correct word and select **Change** or **Change All**.
   - *Change* changes the word and *Change All* changes all instances of the misspelled word.
   - A definition of the selected word is displayed below the list of word options.
   - If no word options are available, retype the word in the body of the document.
4. When the spell and grammar check is complete, a dialog box opens.
5. Click **OK** to finish.

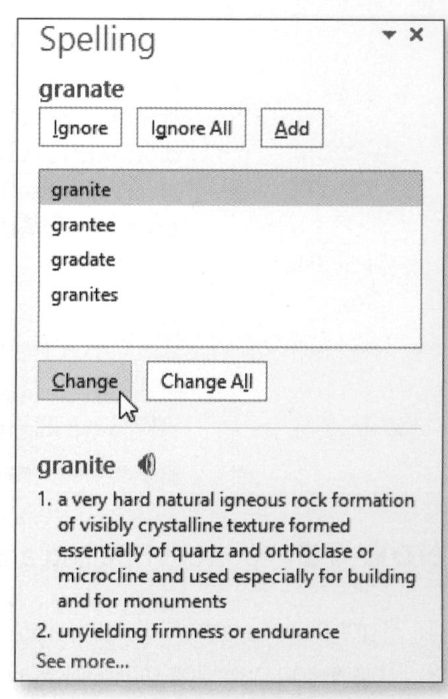

1-57 *Spelling and Grammar* pane

> **ANOTHER WAY**
>
> **F7** opens the *Spelling and Grammar* pane.

Customize the Dictionary

When you are spell checking a document, you can easily add a word to the ***Word dictionary.*** When you add a word to the dictionary, Word actually creates a custom dictionary for you. You can manually add or delete words from the custom dictionary.

HOW TO: Add Words to the Custom Dictionary

1. Click the **File** tab to open the *Backstage* view.
2. Click the **Options** button to open the *Word Options* dialog box.
3. Click the **Proofing** button.
4. Click the **Custom Dictionaries** button. The *Custom Dictionaries* dialog box opens (Figure 1-58).
5. Select the dictionary to edit in the *Dictionary List.*
   - The *RoamingCustom.dic* is the default dictionary.
6. Click the **Edit Word List** button. Your custom dictionary dialog box opens (Figure 1-59). The words that have been previously added to your dictionary are displayed in the *Dictionary* area.
7. Click in the **Word(s)** area, type a word to add to your dictionary, and click the **Add** button to add the word to your dictionary.
   - Words can be deleted from the dictionary by clicking the **Delete** button.
8. Click **OK** when finished to close the *RoamingCustom.dic* dialog box.
9. Click **OK** to close the *Custom Dictionaries* dialog box.
10. Click **OK** to close the *Word Options* dialog box.

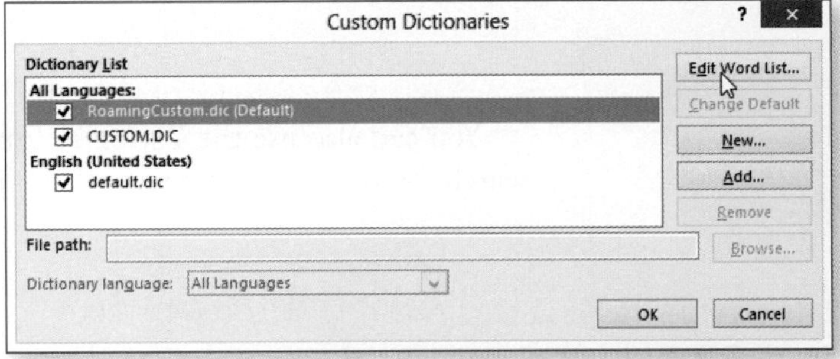

1-58 *Custom Dictionaries* dialog box

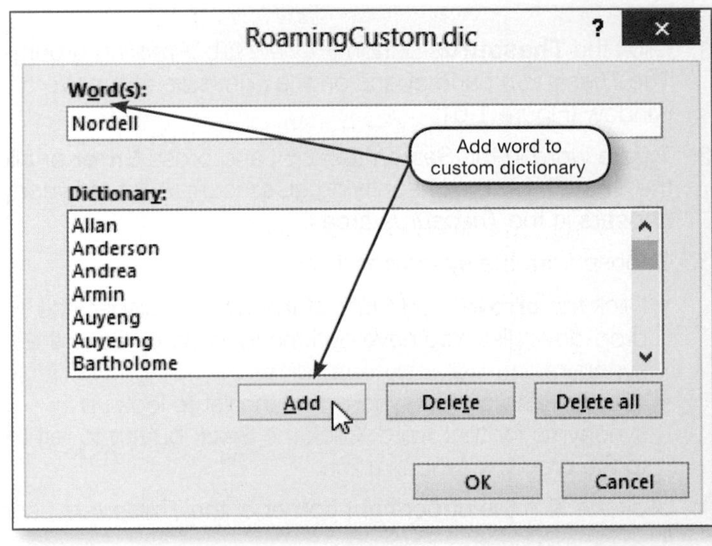

1-59 Add word to custom dictionary

The Thesaurus

Word provides a ***Thesaurus*** that you can use to find ***synonyms*** of words to add variety to your writing. A varied vocabulary makes you appear more educated and professional.

There are two ways to use the *Thesaurus* to find synonyms. The first and quickest way is to select a word in the document and use the context menu (right-click) to replace a selected word with an appropriate synonym.

HOW TO: Find Synonyms Using the Context Menu

1. **Select** the word you want to replace with an appropriate synonym.
2. Right-click the selected word to display the context menu (Figure 1-60).
3. Put your pointer on **Synonyms**. Another context menu appears with a list of synonym choices.
4. Select the synonym you prefer. The selected synonym replaces the selected word in the text and the menus close.

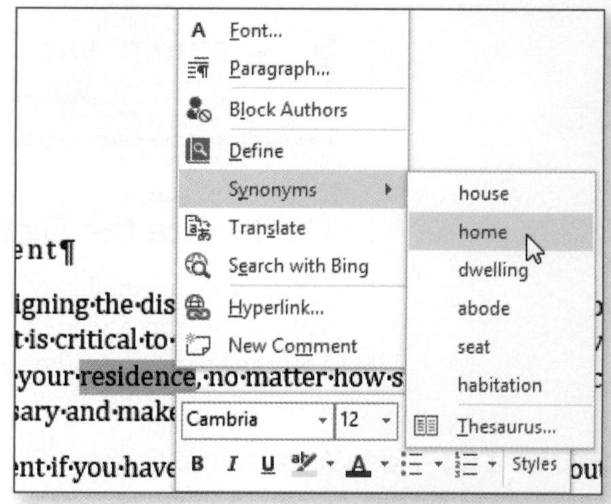

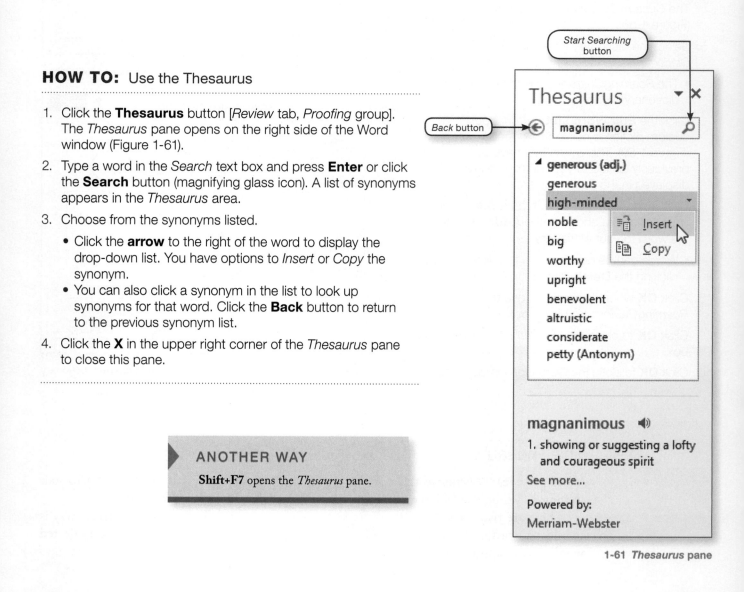

1-60 Use *Thesaurus* to find synonyms

You can also use the *Thesaurus* feature in the *Thesaurus* pane. This method allows you to search for synonyms of any word, not just a selected word in your document.

HOW TO: Use the Thesaurus

1. Click the **Thesaurus** button [*Review* tab, *Proofing* group]. The *Thesaurus* pane opens on the right side of the Word window (Figure 1-61).
2. Type a word in the *Search* text box and press **Enter** or click the **Search** button (magnifying glass icon). A list of synonyms appears in the *Thesaurus* area.
3. Choose from the synonyms listed.
   - Click the **arrow** to the right of the word to display the drop-down list. You have options to *Insert* or *Copy* the synonym.
   - You can also click a synonym in the list to look up synonyms for that word. Click the **Back** button to return to the previous synonym list.
4. Click the **X** in the upper right corner of the *Thesaurus* pane to close this pane.

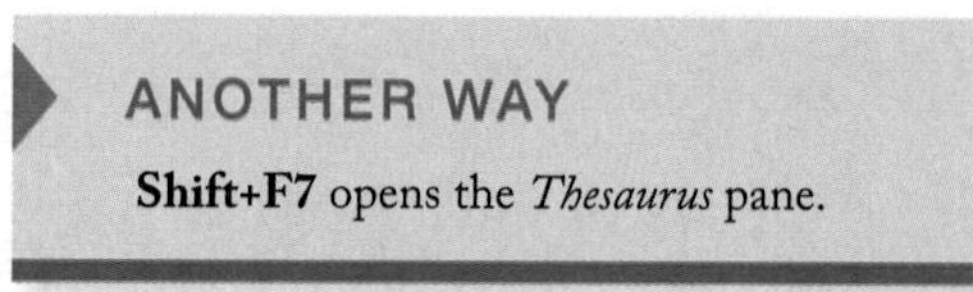

ANOTHER WAY

Shift+F7 opens the *Thesaurus* pane.

1-61 *Thesaurus* pane

Word Count

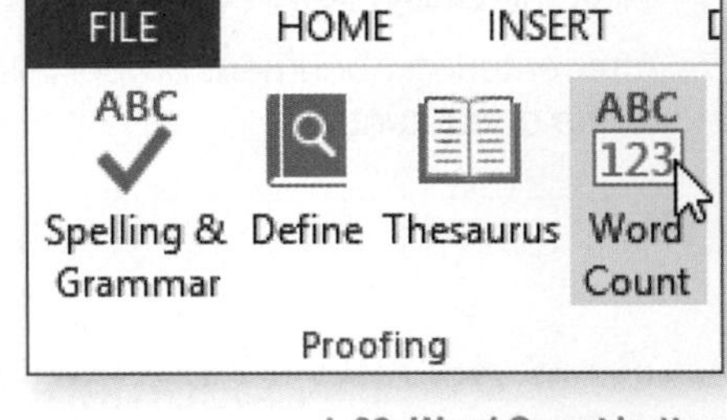

1-62 *Word Count* button

Word also provides you with a ***word count*** option. Click the **Word Count** button in the *Proofing* group on the *Review* tab (Figure 1-62) to get the following information: number of pages, words, characters (no spaces), characters (with spaces), paragraphs, and lines (Figure 1-63). You can also choose to have Word count words in text boxes, footnotes, and endnotes, which are not by default included in the word count.

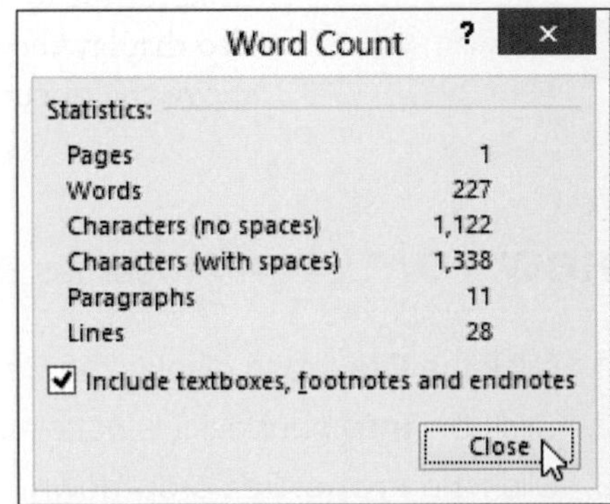

1-63 *Word Count* dialog box

> **ANOTHER WAY**
>
> Click **WORDS** at the bottom left of the *Status* bar to open the *Word Count* dialog box.

SLO 1.8

Customizing Document Properties

Word allows you to include details about a document, which are called ***document properties.*** These details are not visible in the text of the document but are included as hidden information within the document. These include fields such as *Title, Author, Comments, Subject, Company, Created,* and *Last Modified.* Some of the document properties are automatically generated, such as *Words, Total Editing Time,* and *Last Modified,* whereas other document property details can be edited individually.

Document Properties

The document properties can be viewed and edited in the *Info* area on the *Backstage* view. Document properties are saved within the document and can be viewed by others who view or use the document.

HOW TO: Add Document Properties

1. Click the **File** tab to display the *Backstage* view.
2. Click the **Info** button if it is not already selected.
3. The document properties are displayed on the right side of the window (Figure 1-64).
4. Document property field names are listed on the left, and the information in these fields is listed on the right.
5. Click in a field and type information to edit the document property.
    - Some properties cannot be changed. These properties are automatically generated by Word.

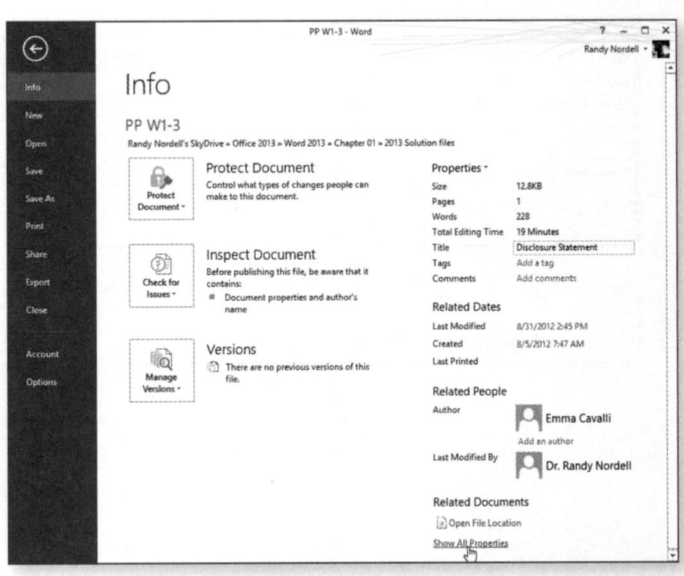

1-64 Document properties on the *Backstage* view

6. Click the **Show All/Fewer Properties** link at the bottom to display more or fewer document property fields.
7. After entering document properties, click the **Back** arrow in the upper left corner of the Backstage view to return to the document.

Document Panel

In addition to viewing and editing the document properties on the *Backstage* view, you can also display the properties in the ***Document panel***, which appears in the regular Word window above the document and below the tab.

HOW TO: Use the Properties Panel

1. Click the **File** tab to display the *Backstage* view.
2. Click the **Info** button if it is not already selected.
3. Click the **Properties** drop-down list at the top of the *Properties* area (Figure 1-65).
4. Select **Show Document Panel**. The *Backstage* view closes and the *Document* panel is displayed above the document in the Word window (Figure 1-66).
5. Edit or add text in the *Document Properties* fields as desired.
6. Click the **X** in the upper right corner of the *Document* panel (not the Word window) to close the panel.

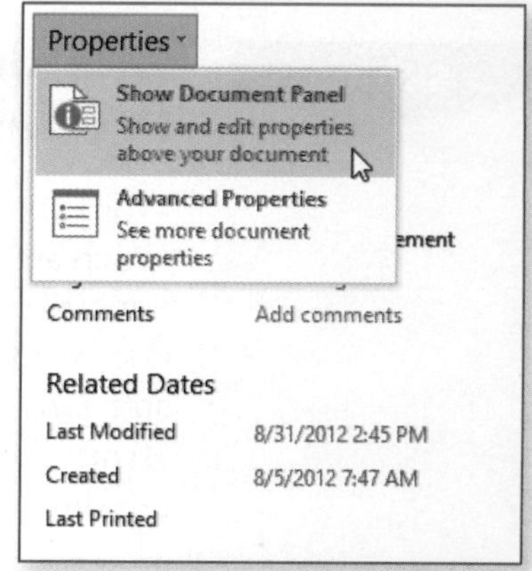

1-65 ***Show Document Panel***

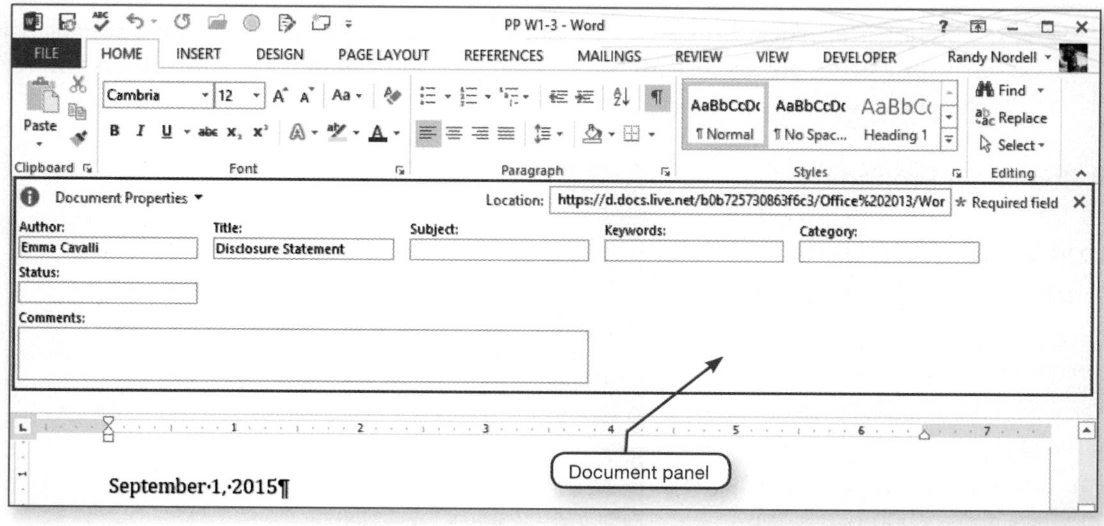

1-66 ***Document*** **panel**

PAUSE & PRACTICE: WORD 1-3

In the final Pause & Practice project in this chapter, you put the finishing touches on a document. You customize paragraph and line spacing, change paragraph alignment, and use spelling and grammar checkers to produce an error-free document. You also modify the document properties.

File Needed: ***[your initials] PP W1-2.docx***
Completed Project File Name: ***[your initials] PP W1-3.docx***

1. Open the ***[your initials] PP W1-2*** document.
2. Save this document as ***[your initials] PP W1-3***.
   a. Press **F12** to open the *Save As* dialog box.
   b. Change the file name to [your initials] PP W1-3.
   c. Click **Save** to rename the document and close the *Save As* dialog box.
3. Change the line and paragraph spacing on the entire document and set as the default for this document only.
   a. Press **Ctrl+A** to select the entire document.
   b. Click the **Paragraph** launcher [*Home* or *Page Layout* tab, *Paragraph* group] to open the *Paragraph* dialog box (Figure 1-67).
   c. Change the *Line spacing* to **Single**.
   d. Change the *After* spacing to **12 pt.**, using the up arrow or typing in the amount of spacing.
   e. Click the **Set As Default** button. A dialog box opens.
   f. Click the **This document only?** radio button and click **OK** to close the dialog box.

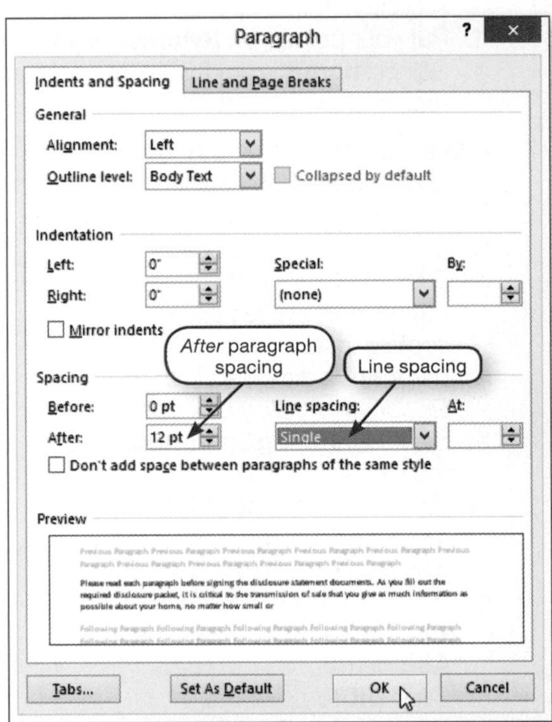

1-67 Change line and paragraph spacing in the *Paragraph* dialog box

> **ANOTHER WAY**
>
> Change line spacing in the *Paragraph* group on the *Home* tab. Change *Before* and *After* paragraph spacing in the *Paragraph* group on the *Page Layout* tab.

4. Add paragraph spacing before the date line of the business letter.
   a. Select or place your insertion point in the first line (date line) of the business letter.
   b. Click the **Page Layout** tab.
   c. Change the *Before* spacing to **72 pt**. Note: 72 pt. is approximately 1", which is commonly used as the spacing before the date line on business letters (Figure 1-68).

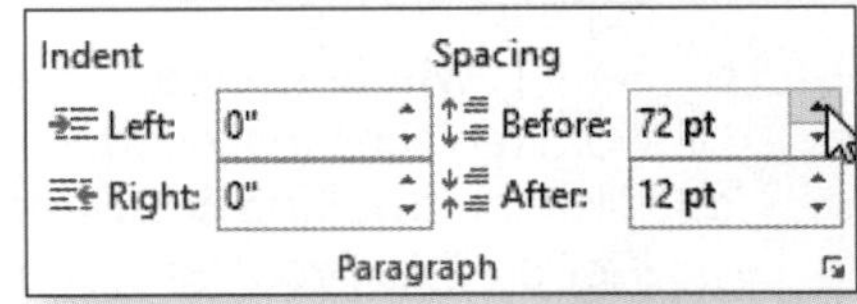

1-68 Change paragraph spacing in the *Paragraph* group

5. Change the paragraph alignment of selected text.
   a. Select or place your insertion point in the subject line of the business letter.
   b. Click the **Center** button [*Home* tab, *Paragraph* group] or press **Ctrl+E**.

6. Use the *Thesaurus* to find synonyms for selected words.
   a. Select the word "**reveal**" in the third body paragraph.
   b. Click the **Thesaurus** button [*Review* tab, *Proofing* group]. The *Thesaurus* pane opens on the right side of the Word window with a list of synonyms for the selected word (Figure 1-69).
   c. Click the **drop-down arrow** to the right of the word "divulge" and choose **Insert**. The word "reveal" is replaced with "divulge."
   d. Click the **X** in the upper right corner of the *Thesaurus* pane to close the pane.
   e. Right-click the word "**residence**" in the first body paragraph. A context menu opens.
   f. Put your pointer on **Synonyms** and a list of synonyms appears.
   g. Select "**home**" from the list of synonyms. The word "residence" is replaced with "home."

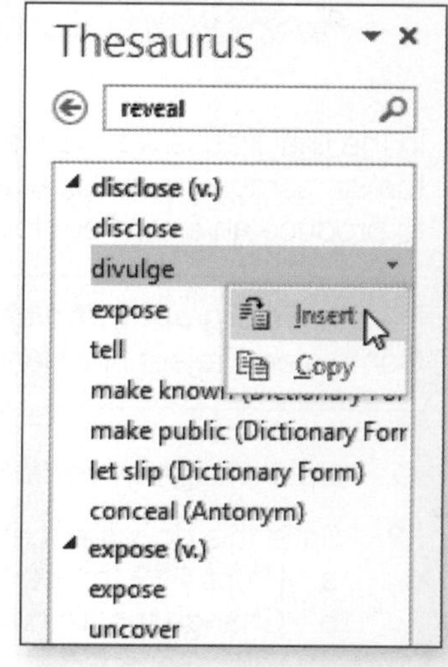

1-69 Insert a synonym from the *Thesaurus* pane

7. Add a word to the custom dictionary.
   a. Click the **File** tab to open the *Backstage* view.
   b. Click the **Options** button to open the *Word Options* dialog box.
   c. Click the **Proofing** button.
   d. Click the **Custom Dictionaries** button in the *When correcting spelling in Microsoft Office programs* area. The *Custom Dictionaries* dialog box opens.
   e. Select **RoamingCustom.dic** in the *Dictionary List.*
   f. Click the **Edit Word List** button. The *RoamingCustom.dic* dialog box opens (Figure 1-70).
   g. Type your last name in the *Word(s)* area and click the **Add** button.
   h. Click **OK** to close the *RoamingCustom.dic* dialog box.
   i. Click **OK** to close the *Custom Dictionaries* dialog box.
   j. Click **OK** to close the *Word Options* dialog box.

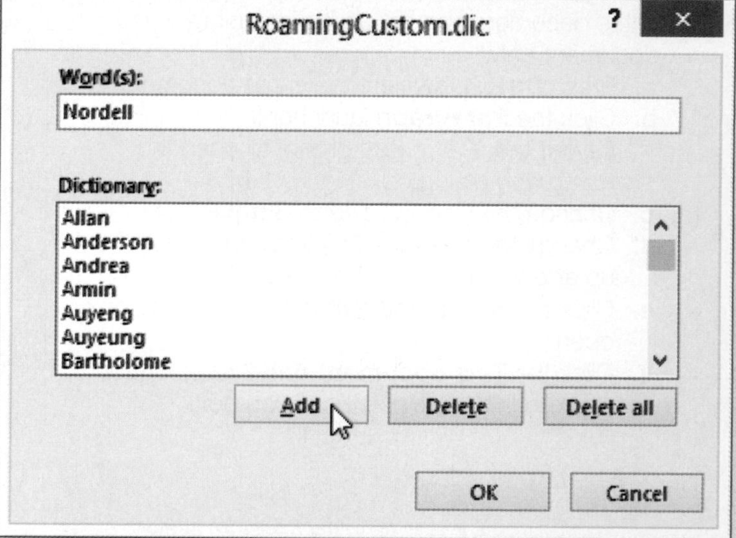

1-70 Add a word to the custom dictionary

8. Spell and grammar check the document.
   a. Right-click the word "**whole house**" in the second paragraph. A context list of words appears (Figure 1-71).
   b. Select "**whole house**." The correctly spelled word replaces the incorrectly spelled word.
   c. Click the **Spelling & Grammar** button [*Review* tab, *Proofing* group] or press **F7** to open the *Spelling* pane on the right (Figure 1-72).
   d. Select "**truss**" and click **Change**.
   e. Continue spell checking the remainder of the document. Change "granate" to "granite" and "you're" to "your."
   f. Click **Add** for "Cavalli."

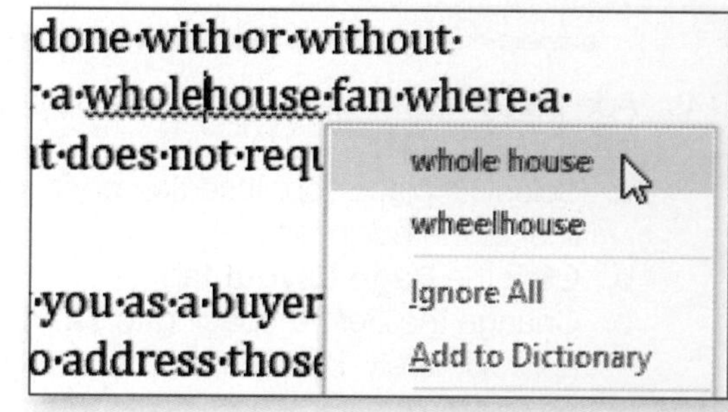

1-71 Correct spelling using the context menu

g. Click **Ignore** for your reference initials (if it is marked as incorrect).
h. Click **Ignore** for the capitalization grammar error (lower case reference initials).
i. Click **OK** to close the dialog box that opens and informs you that the spelling and grammar check is complete. The *Spelling and Grammar* pane closes.

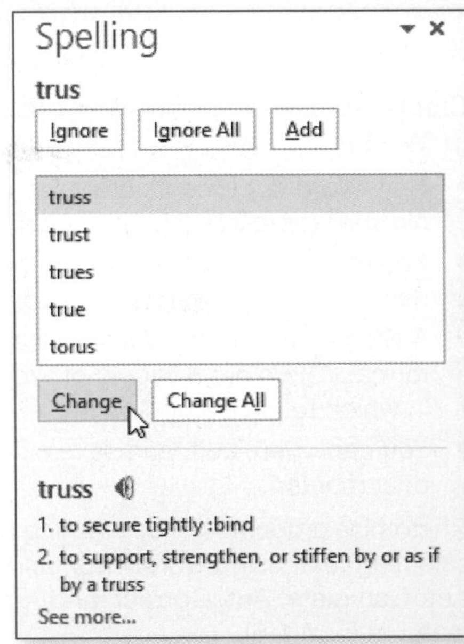

1-72 *Spelling and Grammar* pane

9. Add document properties to your letter.
   a. Click the **File** tab to open the *Backstage* view.
   b. Click the **Info** button on the left if it is not already selected. The document properties are displayed on the right side of the *Backstage* view (Figure 1-73).
   c. Click in the *Title* field and type Disclosure Statement.
   d. In the *Author* area, right-click the existing author and select **Remove Person**.
   e. In the *Author* area, click **Add an author**, type Emma Cavalli, and press **Tab**.
   f. Click the **Show All Properties** link at the bottom. More document properties are displayed.
   g. Click in the *Company* area and type Placer Hills Real Estate.
   h. Click the **Properties** drop-down list at the top of the *Properties* area and choose **Show Document Panel**. The document properties are displayed in the *Document* panel.
   i. Click the **X** in the upper right corner of the *Document* panel to close it.

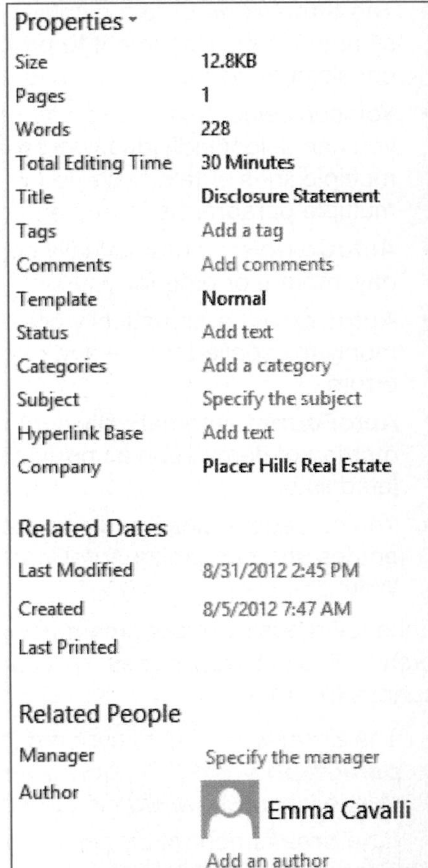

1-73 Document properties on the *Backstage* view

10. Save and close the document (Figure 1-74).

September 1, 2015

David and Sharon Wing
4685 Orange Grove Road
Rocklin, CA 97725

Dear Mr. and Mrs. Wing:

SUBJECT: Disclosure Statement

Please read each paragraph before signing the disclosure statement documents. As you fill out the required disclosure packet, it is critical to the transmission of sale that you give as much information as possible about your home, no matter how small or insignificant. Please use additional paper if necessary and make a notation to that fact.

Make note on the disclosure statement if you have had any work done with or without permits. Some examples include a gas spa, a new water heater, or a whole house fan where a truss may have been cut. If you had granite counters installed, that does not require a permit.

If there is information about the neighborhood or neighbors that you as a buyer would want to know about, be sure to divulge that information. Be sure to address those types of questions on the Real Estate Transfer Disclosure Statement, item #11 on page 2.

Please complete the enclosed disclosure statement by September 8, 2015 and return it to me. As always, if you have any questions or concerns, please call me at 916-450-3334 or email me at ecavalli@phre.com. Best wishes and thank you for your business.

Best regards,

EMMA CAVALLI
Realtor Consultant
Placer Hills Real Estate

yoi
Enclosure

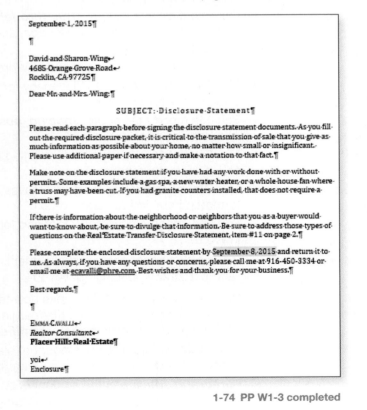

1-74 PP W1-3 completed

Chapter Summary

1.1 Create, save, and open a Word document (p. W1-3).

- New Word documents are based on the ***Normal template*** (*Normal.dotx*).
- You can save documents with the existing file name or with a different file name.
- A ***Word document*** (***.docx***) is the standard file format. There are a variety of Word file formats in which to save a document.
- You can open, edit, and save existing Word documents.

1.2 Customize a document by entering and selecting text, using word wrap, and using AutoComplete, AutoCorrect, and AutoFormat features (p. W1-6).

- ***Word wrap*** automatically wraps text to the next line as you reach the right margin of the document.
- The ***Show/Hide*** button displays formatting symbols in the document to properly and consistently format documents.
- You can select text in a variety of ways, and you can select individual words, an entire line, multiple lines of text, a sentence, a paragraph, multiple paragraphs, or the entire document.
- ***AutoComplete*** automatically completes a day, month, or date for you.
- ***AutoCorrect*** automatically corrects commonly misspelled words and capitalization errors.
- ***AutoFormat*** automatically controls the formatting of items such as numbered and bulleted lists.
- You can add, delete, and edit *AutoCorrect* entries and customize *AutoCorrect* options in Word.

1.3 Enhance a business document using paragraph breaks, line breaks, spaces, and non-breaking spaces (p. W1-10).

- The ***Enter*** key on the keyboard inserts a ***paragraph break***. The ***paragraph symbol*** is visible when Show/*Hide* is turned on.
- ***Line breaks*** control breaks between lines or sentences to retain paragraph formatting between lines.
- ***Non-breaking spaces*** keep related words together.

1.4 Edit a business document using cut, copy, paste, the Clipboard, and the undo, redo, and repeat features (p. W1-14).

- You can move or copy selected text within a document. There are a variety of methods to ***cut***, ***copy***, and ***paste*** text in a document.
- The ***Clipboard*** stores text that you have cut or copied. You can use the *Clipboard* to paste text into your document.
- You can ***Undo***, ***Redo***, and ***Repeat*** previous actions when working on a document. These features are available on the ***Quick Access*** toolbar.

1.5 Customize a business document using different fonts, font sizes, and attributes (p. W1-17).

- ***Serif*** and ***sans serif*** are the two main categories of ***fonts***.
- Fonts are measured in ***points*** (pt.). Most documents use between 10 and 12 pt. font size.
- You can change fonts and font size for specific text or the entire document.
- ***Bold***, ***italic***, and ***underline*** are font styles that you can apply quickly to text.
- Other font effects include ***strikethrough***, ***subscript***, ***superscript***, ***small caps***, and ***all caps***.
- You can change the case of text in Word.
- The ***Font dialog box*** provides many font, size, style, and ***effect*** options.
- You can modify the ***scale***, ***spacing***, ***position***, and ***kerning*** of selected text.
- The ***Format Painter*** applies formatting from selected text to other text.
- The ***Clear Formatting*** feature removes all formatting applied to selected text.
- You can change the ***default*** font and font size in Word.

1.6 Enhance a document using text alignment and line and paragraph spacing. (p. W1-27).

- ***Paragraph alignment*** describes how text is aligned horizontally between the margins of a document: ***left***, ***center***, ***right***, or ***justified***.
- ***Line spacing*** refers to the amount of blank space between lines of text in a paragraph.
- ***Paragraph spacing*** is the amount of space between paragraphs. Paragraph spacing is measured in points.

- You can modify alignment, line spacing, and paragraph spacing on the *Home* or *Page Layout* tab or in the ***Paragraph dialog box***.
- You can change the default line and paragraph spacing in Word.

1.7 Finalize a document using Word's proofing tools (p. W1-31).

- By default, Word automatically checks documents for ***spelling*** and ***grammatical errors***.
- Word marks potential spelling, incorrect word, or grammatical errors with a colored wavy line under the words. You can correct errors by selecting from options in the context menu.
- You can manually spell and grammar check a document using the *Spelling and Grammar* pane.
- You can customize the ***Word dictionary*** by adding, deleting, or modifying words in the word list.
- The ***Thesaurus*** finds synonyms for words in your document.
- Word also provides you with ***Word Count***.

1.8 Apply custom document properties to a document (p. W1-35).

- *You can add* ***document properties***, such as *Title*, *Author*, *Company*, *Subject*, *Created*, and *Last Modified*, into a document.
- You can add document properties on the *Backstage* view or in the ***Document panel***.

Check for Understanding

In the ***Online Learning Center*** for this text (**www.mhhe.com/office2013inpractice**), there are a variety of resources that can be used to review the concepts covered in this chapter.

The following Online Learning Resources are available in the Online Learning Center.

- Multiple choice questions
- Short answer questions
- Matching exercises

Guided Project 1-1

In this project, Jennie Owings at Central Sierra Insurance is writing a business letter to Hartford Specialty regarding the renewal of the insurance policy for Valley Custom Manufacturing. This business letter is typed in block format and uses open punctuation. See *Appendix D* (online reference) for an example of a block format business letter and open and mixed punctuation.
[Student Learning Outcomes 1.1, 1.2, 1.3, 1.4, 1.5, 1.6, 1.7]

File Needed: ***ValleyCustomManufacturing-1.docx***
Completed Project File Name: ***[your initials] Word 1-1.docx***

Skills Covered in This Project

- Use business letter format.
- Change line spacing.
- Change paragraph spacing.
- Use *AutoComplete*.
- Use paragraph breaks for proper spacing between the parts of a business letter.
- Copy and paste using the *Clipboard*.
- Use *Show/Hide*.
- Undo automatic capitalization.
- Change font size.
- Apply font styles.
- Use spelling and grammar checker.
- Add words to dictionary.

1. Open a new Word document and save it as ***[your initials] Word 1-1***.
2. Change the line and paragraph spacing of the document.
   a. Click the **Paragraph** launcher [*Home* or *Page Layout* tab, *Paragraph* group]. (Figure 1-75).
   b. Change the *Line spacing* to **Single**.
   c. Change the *After* paragraph spacing to **0 pt**.
   d. Choose **OK** and close the *Paragraph* dialog box.
3. Type the current date on the first line of the document.
   a. Use month, day, year format (e.g., September 1, 2015).
   b. As you begin typing the date, press **Enter** as *AutoComplete* completes the month and current date.
   c. Press **Enter** four times (quadruple space, QS) after the date.
4. Type the inside address.
   a. Press **Enter** once (single space, SS) at the end of each of the first three lines.

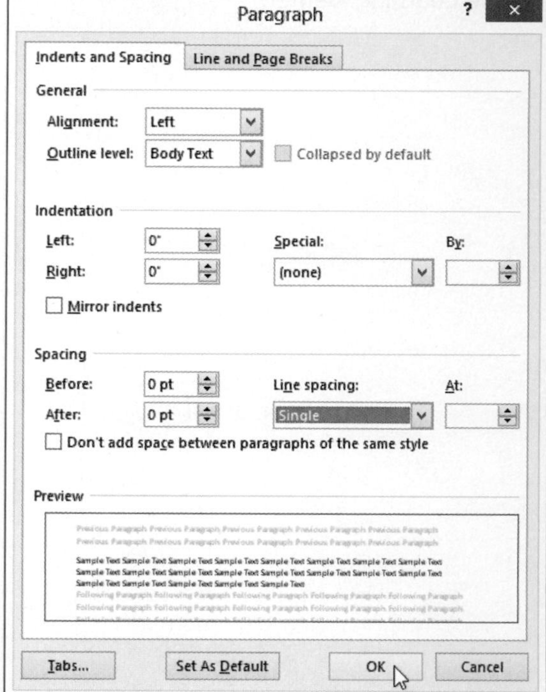

1-75 *Paragraph* dialog box

b. Press **Enter** twice (double space, DS) after the last line of the inside address.

Mrs. Cammie Speckler
Hartford Specialty
4788 Market Street, Suite A205
San Francisco, CA 95644

5. Type Dear Mrs. Speckler as the salutation. No colon is used after the salutation when using open punctuation.
6. Press **Enter** two times.
7. Type RE: Valley Custom Manufacturing as the subject line.
8. Press **Enter** two times.
9. Copy text from another document and paste it into the current document.
   a. Open the ***ValleyCustomManufacturing-01*** document from your student data files.
   b. Press **Ctrl+A** to select the entire document.
   c. Click the **Copy** button [*Home* tab, *Clipboard* group] or press **Ctrl+C**.
   d. Close ***ValleyCustomManufacturing-01*** without saving the document.
   e. In the ***[your initials] Word 1-1*** document, place your insertion point at the end of the document (a DS below the subject line).
   f. Click the **Clipboard** launcher [*Home* tab, *Clipboard* group] to open the *Clipboard* pane (Figure 1-76).

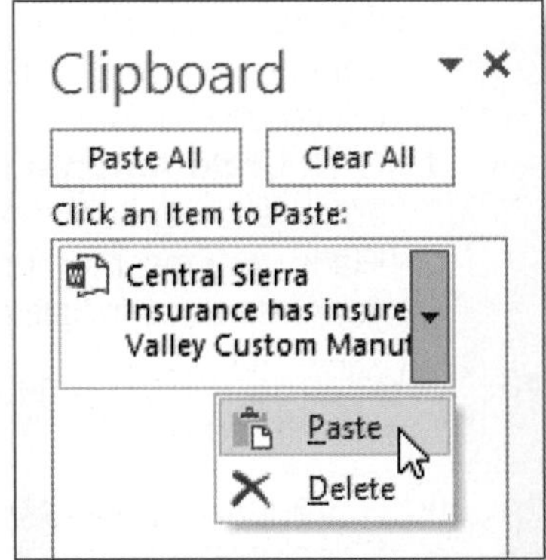

1-76 Paste from the *Clipboard*

   g. Select the **drop-down arrow** to the right of the copied text in the *Clipboard* and click **Paste**. The paragraphs of text are pasted in the body of the document.
   h. Click the **X** in the upper left corner of the *Clipboard* pane to close it.
10. Use the *Format Painter* to format the inserted paragraphs.
    a. Place your insertion point in the first line of the document.
    b. Click the **Format Painter** button [*Home* tab, *Clipboard* group].
    c. Select the body paragraphs of the letter to apply the formatting (Figure 1-77).

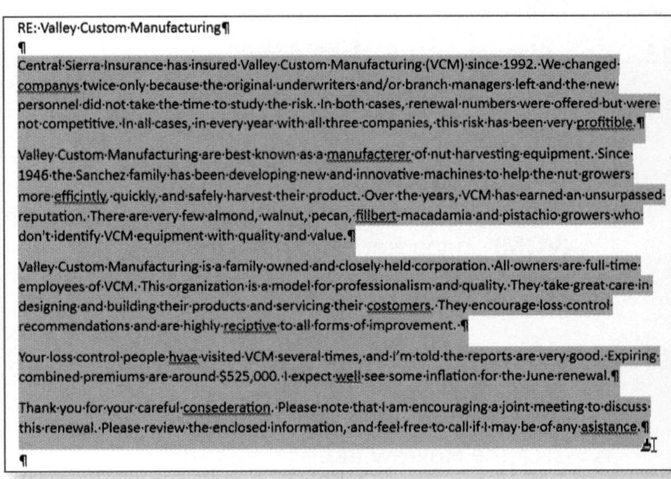

RE: Valley Custom Manufacturing

Central Sierra Insurance has insured Valley Custom Manufacturing (VCM) since 1992. We changed companys twice only because the original underwriters and/or branch managers left and the new personnel did not take the time to study the risk. In both cases, renewal numbers were offered but were not competitive. In all cases, in every year with all three companies, this risk has been very profitible.

Valley Custom Manufacturing are best known as a manufacterer of nut harvesting equipment. Since 1946 the Sanchez family has been developing new and innovative machines to help the nut growers more efficintly, quickly, and safely harvest their product. Over the years, VCM has earned an unsurpassed reputation. There are very few almond, walnut, pecan, fillbert-macadamia and pistachio growers who don't identify VCM equipment with quality and value.

Valley Custom Manufacturing is a family owned and closely held corporation. All owners are full-time employees of VCM. This organization is a model for professionalism and quality. They take great care in designing and building their products and servicing their costomers. They encourage loss control recommendations and are highly reciptive to all forms of improvement.

Your loss control people hvae visited VCM several times, and I'm told the reports are very good. Expiring combined premiums are around $525,000. I expect well see some inflation for the June renewal.

Thank you for your careful consederation. Please note that I am encouraging a joint meeting to discuss this renewal. Please review the enclosed information, and feel free to call if I may be of any asistance.

1-77 Use the *Format Painter* to copy formatting

11. Insert a blank line between each of the body paragraphs so there is a double space after each body paragraph (one blank line between paragraphs).
    a. Turn on **Show/Hide** [*Home* tab, *Paragraph* group] if it is not already turned on.
    b. Place your insertion point at the end of the first body paragraph and press **Enter**.
    c. Repeat for each of the body paragraphs.

12. Enter the closing lines of the document.
    a. Place your insertion point on the blank line below the body of the letter, press **Enter**, and type Sincerely. No comma is used after the salutation when using open punctuation.
    b. Press **Enter** four times and type the writer's name, title, and company.

        Jennie Owings, Vice President
        Central Sierra Insurance

    c. Press **Enter** two times and type your reference initials (your first and last initials in lower case letters).
    d. Press **Enter**. *AutoCorrect* automatically capitalizes the first letter of your reference initials.
    e. Click the **AutoCorrect Options** smart tag (Figure 1-78). The *AutoCorrect Options* smart tag appears when you place your pointer below your reference initials.
    f. Click **Undo Automatic Capitalization** to undo the automatic capitalization of your reference initials.
    g. Place your insertion point on the blank line below your reference initials and type Enclosure.

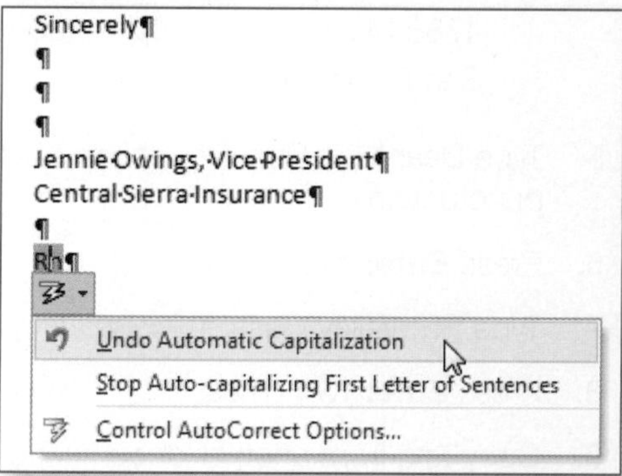

1-78 *AutoCorrect* smart tag

13. Select the entire document (**Ctrl+A**) and change the font size to **10 pt**.
14. Add paragraph spacing before the date line.
    a. Select or place your insertion point in the date line.
    b. Click the **Page Layout** tab.
    c. Change the *Before* spacing to **72 pt**. [*Paragraph* group] (Figure 1-79).

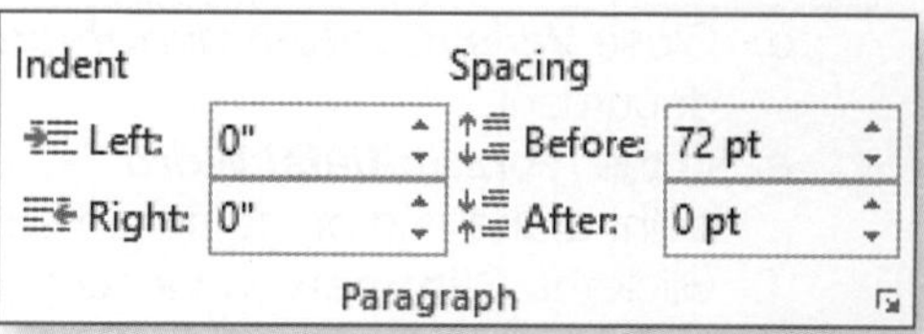

1-79 Change *Before* paragraph spacing on the date line

15. Apply font styles to selected text.
    a. Select the words "**Central Sierra Insurance**" in the first paragraph.
    b. Click the **Underline** button [*Home* tab, *Font* group] or press **Ctrl+U**.
    c. Select the words "**Valley Custom Manufacturing (VCM)**" in the first paragraph.
    d. Click the **Bold** button [*Home* tab, *Font* group] or press **Ctrl+B**.
16. Spell and grammar check the entire document.
    a. Press **Ctrl+Home** to move to the top of the document.
    b. Click the **Review** tab.
    c. Click the **Spelling & Grammar** button [*Proofing* group]. The *Spelling* pane opens (Figure 1-80).
    d. Click **Add** to add "Cammie" and "Speckler" to the dictionary.

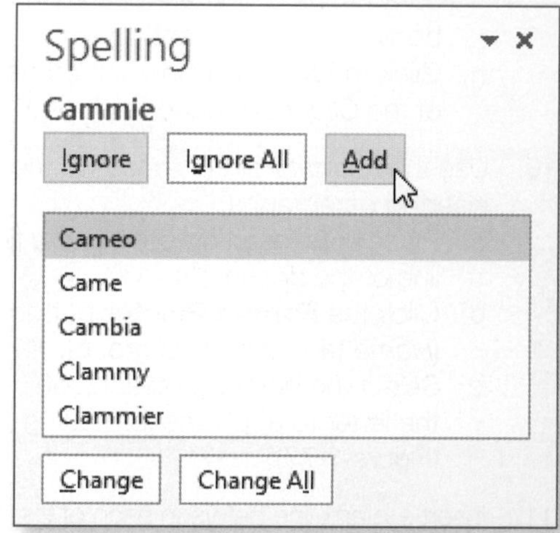

1-80 Add word to the dictionary

e. Change other words as necessary to correct spelling, incorrect word usage, and grammatical errors. If prompted tc continue checking the document from the beginning, choose **Yes**.

f. Click **Ignore Once** if your reference initials are marked as a potential spelling or grammatical error.

17. Save and close the document (Figure 1-81).

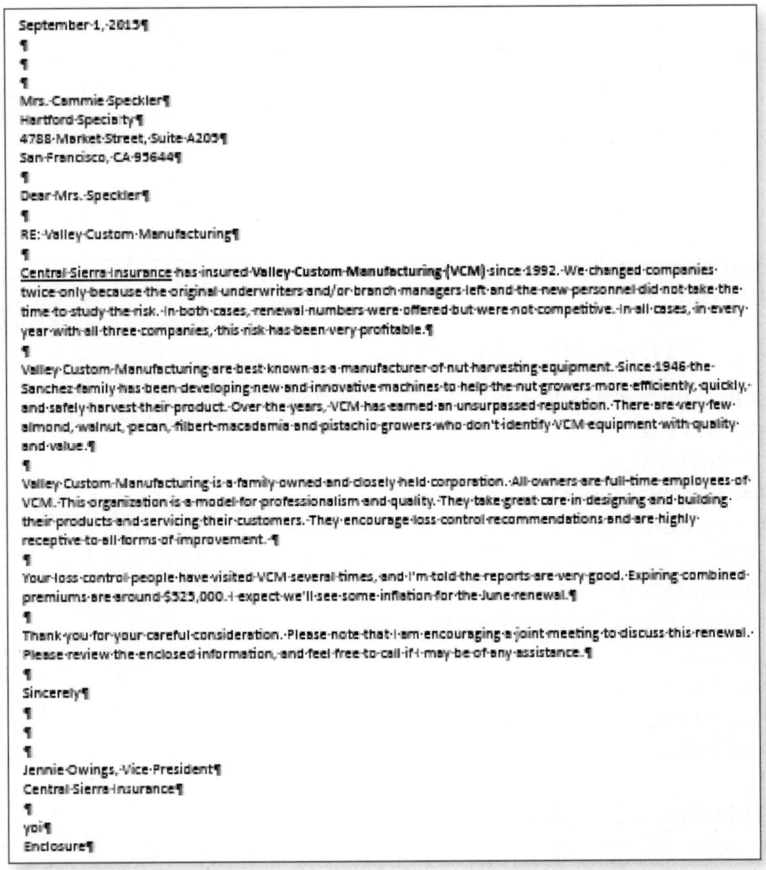

September 1, 2015

Mrs. Cammie Speckler
Hartford Specialty
4788 Market Street, Suite A205
San Francisco, CA 93644

Dear Mrs. Speckler

RE: Valley Custom Manufacturing

Central Sierra Insurance has insured **Valley Custom Manufacturing (VCM)** since 1992. We changed companies twice only because the original underwriters and/or branch managers left and the new personnel did not take the time to study the risk. In both cases, renewal numbers were offered but were not competitive. In all cases, in every year with all three companies, this risk has been very profitable.

Valley Custom Manufacturing are best known as a manufacturer of nut harvesting equipment. Since 1946 the Sanchez family has been developing new and innovative machines to help the nut growers more efficiently, quickly, and safely harvest their product. Over the years, VCM has earned an unsurpassed reputation. There are very few almond, walnut, pecan, filbert macadamia and pistachio growers who don't identify VCM equipment with quality and value.

Valley Custom Manufacturing is a family owned and closely held corporation. All owners are full-time employees of VCM. This organization is a model for professionalism and quality. They take great care in designing and building their products and servicing their customers. They encourage loss control recommendations and are highly receptive to all forms of improvement.

Your loss control people have visited VCM several times, and I'm told the reports are very good. Expiring combined premiums are around $325,000. I expect we'll see some inflation for the June renewal.

Thank you for your careful consideration. Please note that I am encouraging a joint meeting to discuss this renewal. Please review the enclosed information, and feel free to call if I may be of any assistance.

Sincerely

Jennie Owings, Vice President
Central Sierra Insurance

yoi
Enclosure

1-81 Word 1-1 completed

Guided Project 1-2

Sierra Pacific Community College District is a multi-campus community college district. In this project, you format an informational handout regarding online learning.
[Student Learning Outcomes 1.1, 1.3, 1.4, 1.5, 1.6, 1.7, 1.8]

File Needed: ***OnlineLearning-01.docx***
Completed Project File Name: ***[your initials] Word 1-2.docx***

Skills Covered in This Project

- Open and edit an existing document.
- Change line spacing.
- Change paragraph spacing.
- Change default paragraph settings in your current document.
- Use *Show/Hide*.
- Change font size and apply color, styles, and effects.
- Cut and paste to move a paragraph.
- Use drag and drop to move a paragraph.
- Apply a shadow text effect.
- Use the *Format Painter*.
- Use spelling and grammar checker.
- Add document properties.

---

1. Open the ***OnlineLearning-01*** document from your student data files.
2. Save this document as ***[your initials] Word 1-2***.
3. Change the line and paragraph spacing of the entire document, and use these settings as the default for this document.
   a. Press **Ctrl+A** to select the entire document.
   b. Click the **Paragraph** launcher [*Home* or *Page Layout* tab, *Paragraph* group] to open the *Paragraph* dialog box (Figure 1-82).
   c. In the *Line spacing* area, select **Multiple** from the drop-down list.
   d. In the *At* area, type 1.2.
   e. Change the paragraph spacing *After* to **12 pt**.
   f. Click **Set As Default**. A dialog box opens (Figure 1-83).
   g. Select the **This Document Only?** radio button.
   h. Click **OK** to close the *Paragraph* dialog box.
4. Turn on **Show/Hide** [*Home* tab, *Paragraph* group] and **delete** the one extra blank line between each paragraph including the title.
5. Change the font and font size of the entire document.
   a. Select the entire document (**Ctrl+A**).
   b. Change the font to **Cambria** and the size to **11 pt**. [*Home* tab, *Font* group].
6. Change the paragraph spacing, alignment, font size, styles, effects, and color of the title.
   a. Select the title of the document (**Online Learning Information**).
   b. Click the **Page Layout** tab.
   c. Change the *Before* spacing to **36 pt**. and the *After* spacing to **18 pt**. [*Paragraph* group].
   d. Click the **Center** button [*Home* tab, *Paragraph* group].
   e. Click the **launcher** [*Font* group]. The *Font* dialog box opens (Figure 1-84).
   f. Change the *Font* style to **Bold**.

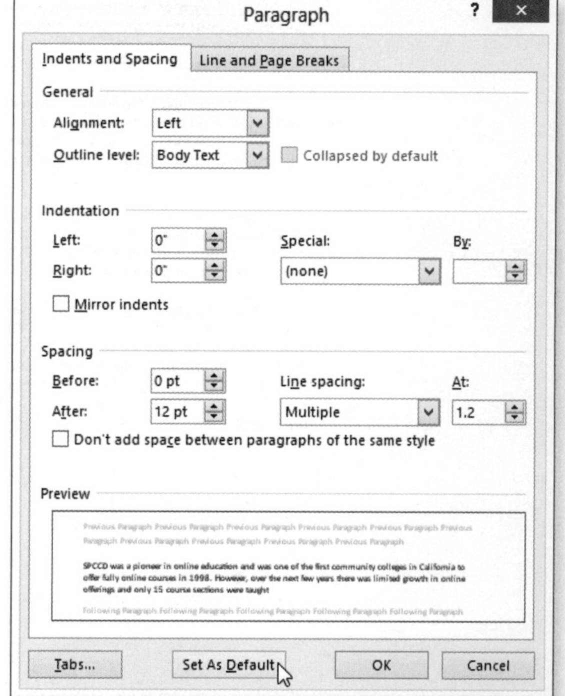

1-82 Change line and *After* paragraph spacing

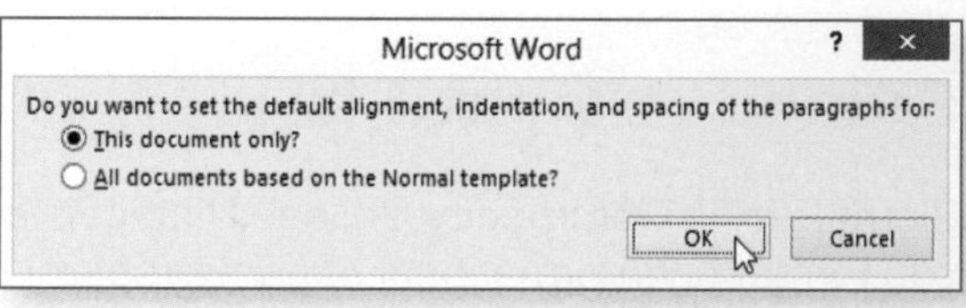

1-83 Set as default for this document only

g. Change the *Size* to **24**.
h. In the *Effects* area, click the **Small caps** check box.
i. On the **Font color** drop-down list [*Font* group], choose **Blue-Gray**, **Text 2** from the *Theme Colors.*
j. Click the **Advanced** tab.
k. Click the **Spacing** drop-down list and select **Expanded**. Change the *By* to **1.2**.
l. Click **OK** to close the *Font* dialog box.

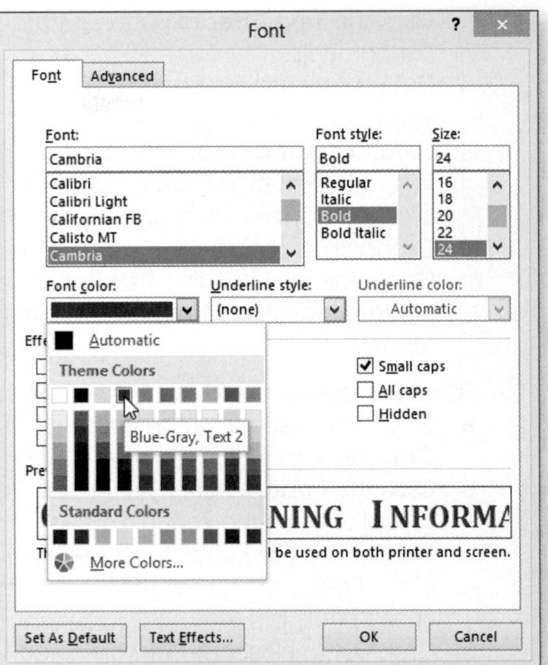

1-84 Change font style, size, effects, and color

7. Move paragraphs in the document and insert a heading.
   a. Select the last paragraph in the document, including the paragraph mark at the end of the document.
   b. Click the **Cut** button [*Home* tab, *Clipboard* group] or press **Ctrl+X**.
   c. Place your insertion point before the second line of the document ("Definition of Online Learning Modalities").
   d. Click the **Paste** button [*Home* tab, *Clipboard* group] or press **Ctrl+V**.
   e. Click at the beginning of the pasted paragraph and type Where are we now with Online Learning?
   f. Press **Enter**.
   g. Select the paragraph that begins "Hybrid Course:", including the paragraph mark at the end of the paragraph.
   h. Move this paragraph using the drag and drop method so it appears before the paragraph that begins with "Television or Tele-Web Course:" (Figure 1-85).

Television·or·Tele-Web·Course:·This·type·of·course·uses·cable·TV·to·deliver·some·or·all·of·the·course·content.·A·tele-web·course·merges·online·and·TV·delivery.·Typically,·only·a·limited·number·of·face-to-face·meetings·are·held·and·the·remainder·of·the·course·is·conducted·using·television·delivery·of·content·and·web-based·activities,·communication·and·discussion.¶

Hybrid·Course:·A·hybrid·course·is·a·course·that·is·taught·online·using·similar·web-based·tools·and·activities·as·an·online·class.·Some·potion·of·the·course·meeting·time·is·conducted·online,·and·the·remaining·percentage·of·the·class·is·conducted·in·a·traditional·classroom·manner.¶

1-85 Move paragraph using drag and drop

8. Format section headings in the document.
   a. Select the first section heading ("**Where are we now with online learning?**").
   b. Click the **Font** launcher [*Home* tab, *Font* group] to open the *Font* dialog box (Figure 1-86).
   c. Change the font *Size* to **12 pt**.
   d. Change the *Font color* to **Blue-Gray**, **Text 2**.
   e. Change the *Underline style* to **Double Underline**.
   f. Change the *Underline color* to **Blue-Gray**, **Text 2**.
   g. In the *Effects* area, click the **All caps** check box.
   h. Click **OK** to close the *Font* dialog box.

i. Click the **Text Effects** button [*Home* tab, *Font* group].
j. Put your pointer on **Shadow;** a list of shadow options is displayed (Figure 1-87).
k. Select **Offset Diagonal Bottom Right**.
l. With the formatted heading still selected, click the **Format Painter** button [*Home* tab, *Clipboard* group].
m. Select the next heading (**"Definition of Online Learning Modalities"**) to apply formatting.

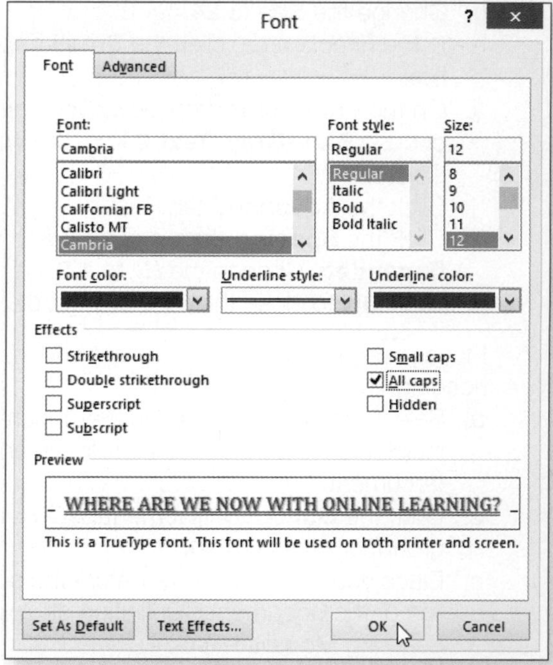

1-86 Format heading using *Font* dialog box

9. Format paragraph headings in the document.
   a. Select the first paragraph heading ("**Online Course:"**), including the colon.
   b. Click the **Font** launcher [*Home* tab, *Font* group] to open the *Font* dialog box.
   c. Change the *Font color* to **Blue-Gray**, **Text 2**.
   d. In the *Effects* area, click the **Small caps** check box.
   e. Click **OK** to close the *Font* dialog box.
   f. Use the **Format Painter** to copy this format to the other paragraph headings ("Hybrid Course:", "Television or Tele-Web Course:", "Web-Enhanced Course:"). Double-click the **Format Painter** button to apply this formatting to multiple selections. Click the **Format Painter** button again to turn off the *Format Painter.*

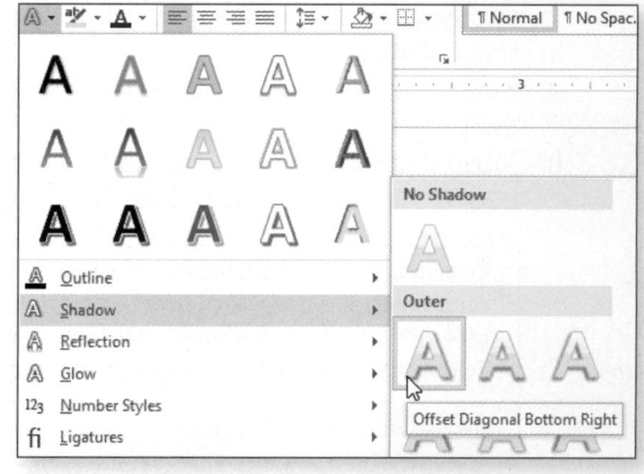

1-87 Apply *Shadow* text effect

10. Correct spelling and grammar in the document using the context menu.
    a. Right-click the first misspelled word ("**management**") and choose the correct spelling from the list of options.
    b. Repeat this process for "**potion**".
    c. Click **Ignore All** or **Ignore Once** on the other words that are marked as potentially incorrect.
11. Select the sentence in parentheses at the end of the document, including the parentheses, and click the **Italic** button [*Home* tab, *Font* group] or press **Ctrl+I**.
12. Add document properties using the *Document* panel.
    a. Click the **File** tab to open the *Backstage* view.
    b. Click the **Info** button if it is not already selected.
    c. Click the **Properties** button on the right and choose **Show Document Panel**. The *Document* panel is displayed above the document.
    d. In the *Author* area, delete the existing author name and type Tanesha Morris.
    e. In the *Title* area, type Online Learning Information.
    f. In the *Subject* area, type Online Learning.
    g. In the *Status* area, type Draft.
    h. Click the **X** in the upper right of the *Document* panel to close it.

13. Save and close the document (Figure 1-88).

ONLINE LEARNING INFORMATION

WHERE ARE WE NOW WITH ONLINE LEARNING?

SPCCD was a pioneer in online education and was one of the first community colleges in California to offer fully online courses in 1998. However, over the next few years there was limited growth in online offerings and only 15 course sections were taught online during Fall 2000. The adoption of a learning management system in Spring 2001, and the availability of training to teach online, and recruitment of new faculty interested in teaching online resulted in a rapid increase in online offerings.

DEFINITION OF ONLINE LEARNING MODALITIES

All online learning modes offered at SPCCD will be considered in the plan. Currently, these include the following: online, hybrid, television, and tele-web.

ONLINE COURSE: An online course is a course that is offered over the Internet. Typically, content is presented through web pages and class discussions using a combination of email, mailing lists, bulletin boards, chat rooms, or newsgroups. All class meetings, assignments, lectures, and assessments are online (with the exception of orientation meetings or other face-to-face examinations as determined by the professor).

HYBRID COURSE: A hybrid course is a course that is taught online using similar web-based tools and activities as an online class. Some portion of the course meeting time is conducted online, and the remaining percentage of the class is conducted in a traditional classroom manner.

TELEVISION OR TELE-WEB COURSE: This type of course uses cable TV to deliver some or all of the course content. A tele-web course merges online and TV delivery. Typically, only a limited number of face-to-face meetings are held and the remainder of the course is conducted using television delivery of content and web-based activities, communication, and discussion.

WEB-ENHANCED COURSE: This type of course is taught face-to-face for 100% of the course meeting time, but classroom assignments and materials are supplemented with web-based activities. Examples are: online projects, hand outs and materials, online discussion, or online testing *(Note: this is a definition of a non-online learning course which uses online learning tools).*

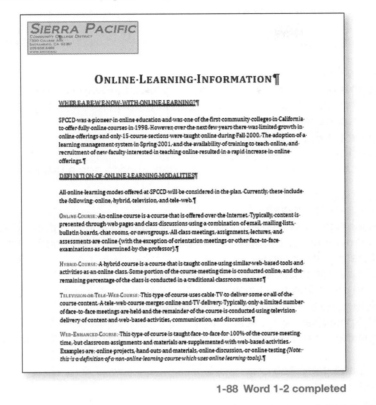

1-88 Word 1-2 completed

Guided Project 1-3

In this project, you create a memo about using heart rate to increase the effectiveness of training to send out to American River Cycling Club members.
[Student Learning Outcomes 1.1, 1.2, 1.3, 1.5, 1.6, 1.7, 1.8]

File Needed: ***HeartRate-01.docx***
Completed Project File Name: ***[your initials] Word 1-3.docx***

Skills Covered in This Project

- Open and edit an existing document.
- Change line spacing.
- Change paragraph spacing.
- Use *Show/Hide*.
- Add a memo heading to a document.
- Change paragraph alignment.
- Change font size and apply styles and effects.
- Use the *Format Painter*.
- Add text highlight color.
- Use non-breaking space.
- Use *Thesaurus*.
- Add words to the dictionary.
- Add document properties.

1. Open the ***HeartRate-01*** document from your student data files.
2. Save the document as ***[your initials] Word 1-3***.
3. Change line and paragraph spacing of the entire document and insert a paragraph break between each paragraph.
   a. Press **Ctrl+A** to select the entire document.
   b. Click the **Paragraph** launcher [*Home* or *Page Layout* tab, *Paragraph* group].
   c. In the *Line spacing* area, select **Single** from the drop-down list.
   d. Change the *After* paragraph spacing to **0 pt**.
   e. Click **OK** to close the *Paragraph* dialog box.
   f. Turn on **Show/Hide** [*Home* tab, *Paragraph* group].
   g. Click at the end of each paragraph and press **Enter** once to add a blank line between each of the paragraphs.
4. Add a memo heading to the document.
   a. Place your insertion point at the beginning of the first paragraph and press **Enter**.
   b. Press the **up arrow** key on keyboard to move to the blank line above the first paragraph.
   c. Type TO: and press **Tab** two times.
   d. Type All ARCC Club Members and press **Enter** two times.
   e. Type FROM: and press **Tab** two times.
   f. Type Taylor Mathos, ARCC Coach and press **Enter** two times.
   g. Type DATE: and press **Tab** two times.
   h. Type the current date in month, day, year format (e.g., September 1, 2015) and press **Enter** two times.
   i. Type SUBJECT: and press **Tab** once.
   j. Type Heart Rate Training and press **Enter** two times.
5. Change paragraph alignment and font styles of selected text.
   a. Select the second and third paragraphs in the body of the memo (beginning with "**220 – Your Age. . .**" and ending with "**. . .heart rate is 180.)**"), including the paragraph mark at the end of the third paragraph.
   b. Click the **Center** button [*Home* tab, *Paragraph* group] or press **Ctrl+E**.
   c. Select the paragraph beginning "220 – Your Age . . . " and click the **Bold** button [*Home* tab, *Font* group] or press **Ctrl+B**.
   d. Select the next paragraph and click the **Italic** button [*Home* tab, *Font* group] or press **Ctrl+I**.
   e. Delete the blank line between the second and third paragraphs (Figure 1-89).

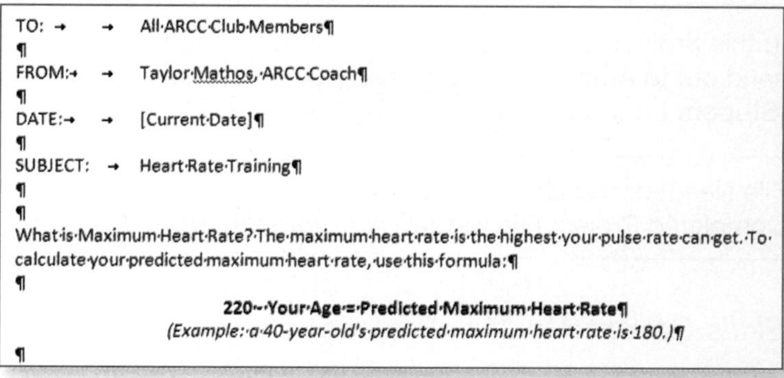

TO: → → All·ARCC·Club·Members¶
¶
FROM:→ → Taylor·Mathos,·ARCC·Coach¶
¶
DATE:→ → [Current·Date]¶
¶
SUBJECT: → Heart·Rate·Training¶
¶
¶
What·is·Maximum·Heart·Rate?·The·maximum·heart·rate·is·the·highest·your·pulse·rate·can·get.·To·calculate·your·predicted·maximum·heart·rate,·use·this·formula:¶
¶
220·–·Your·Age·=·Predicted·Maximum·Heart·Rate¶
(Example:·a·40-year-old's·predicted·maximum·heart·rate·is·180.)¶
¶

1-89 Memo heading added and paragraphs formatted

6. Change the font and style of selected text.
   a. Press **Ctrl+A** to select the entire document.
   b. Click the **Increase Font Size** button [*Home* tab, *Font* group] to increase the font size to 12 pt. (Figure 1-90).
   c. In the first sentence of the first body paragraph, select the words "**Maximum Heart Rate**".

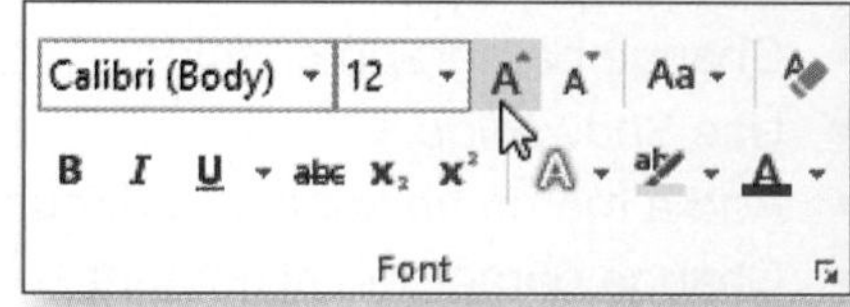

1-90 *Increase Font Size* button

d. Click the **Font** launcher [*Home* tab, *Font* group] to open the *Font* dialog box (Figure 1-91).
e. Change the *Font style* to **Bold**.
f. Change the *Underline style* to **Words only**.
g. Change the *Underline color* to **Green, Accent 6**.
h. In the *Effects* area, select the **Small caps** check box.
i. Click **OK** to close the *Font* dialog box.
j. With the words still selected, click the **Format Painter** button [*Home* tab, *Clipboard* group].
k. Select the words "**Target Heart Rate Zone**" in the first sentence of the fifth paragraph in the body ("You gain the most benefits . . ."). The *Format Painter* applies the formatting to the selected words.
l. Select the last two sentences of the fifth paragraph ("Do not exercise above 85 percent . . .").
m. Click the **Text Highlight Color** drop-down arrow [*Home* tab, *Font* group] (Figure 1-92).
n. Select **Gray-25%** text highlighting.

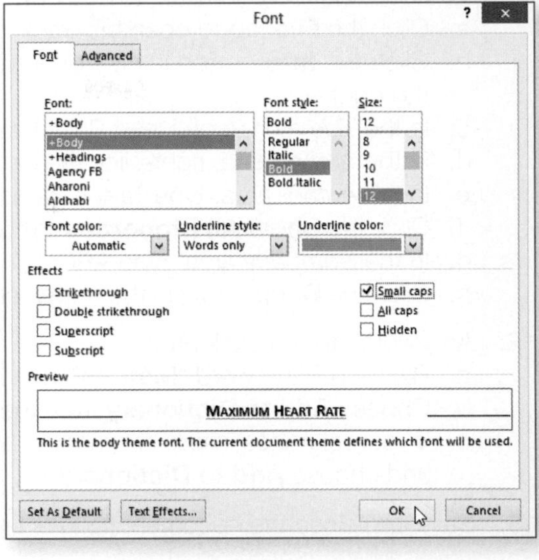

1-91 Change font style and effects

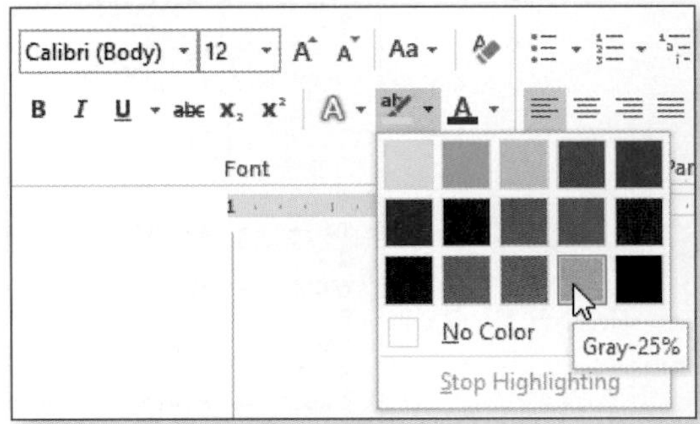

1-92 *Text Highlight Color* button and drop-down list

7. Use a non-breaking space to keep words together.
   a. In the first sentence of the fifth paragraph in the body ("You gain the most benefits . . ."), delete the space between the words "Target" and "Heart."
   b. Place your insertion point between these two words and press **Ctrl+Shift+Spacebar** to insert a non-breaking space. "Target" is wrapped to the next line so the words do not break between lines.
8. Add paragraph spacing before the first line of the document.
   a. Select the first line of the document.
   b. Change the *Before* spacing to **72 pt**. [*Page Layout* tab, *Paragraph* group].
9. Use the thesaurus to find synonyms for selected words.
   a. Right-click the word "**medicines**" in the third sentence of the first body paragraph.
   b. Put your pointer on **Synonyms** to display a list of synonyms (Figure 1-93).
   c. Select **"medications"** as the synonym.
   d. In the last sentence of the fifth paragraph ("You gain the most benefits . . ."), right-click the word "**added**."
   e. Put your pointer on **Synonyms** and select "**additional**."
10. Add reference initials to the document.
   a. Click at the end of the last paragraph and press **Enter** two times.
   b. Type your reference initials in lower case letters.

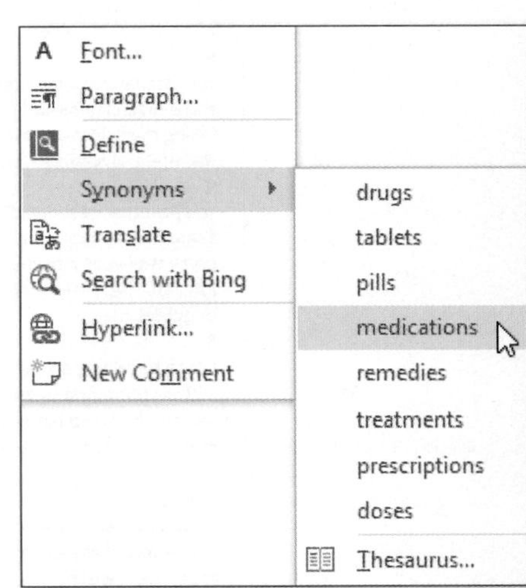

1-93 Select synonym from context menu

11. Add document properties.
    a. Click the **File** tab to open the *Backstage* view.
    b. Click the **Info** button if it is not already selected to display the document properties at the right.
    c. In the *Title* area, type Heart Rate Training.
    d. In the *Author* area, right-click the existing author and select **Remove Person**.
    e. In the *Author* area, type Taylor Mathos.
    f. Click the **Show All Properties** link at the bottom of the document properties.
    g. In the *Company* area, type ARCC.
    h. Click the **Back** arrow in the upper left of the *Backstage* view to the document.
12. Add words to the dictionary.
    a. Right-click the word "**Mathos**" in the second line of the memo heading.
    b. Choose **Add to Dictionary** from the context menu.
    c. If your reference initials are marked as incorrectly spelled (red wavy underline), right-click them and choose **Add to Dictionary**.
13. Save and close the document (Figure 1-94).

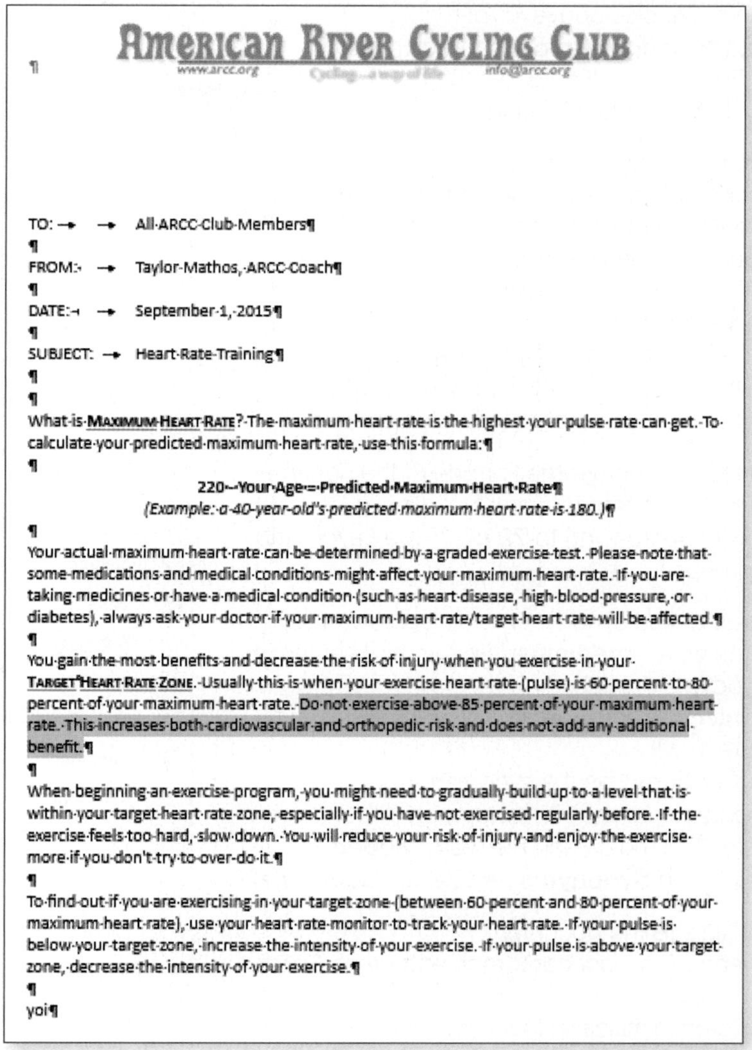

American River Cycling Club

www.arcc.org Cycling...a way of life info@arcc.org

TO: All ARCC Club Members

FROM: Taylor Mathos, ARCC Coach

DATE: September 1, 2015

SUBJECT: Heart Rate Training

What is MAXIMUM HEART RATE? The maximum heart rate is the highest your pulse rate can get. To calculate your predicted maximum heart rate, use this formula:

220 – Your Age = Predicted Maximum Heart Rate

(Example: a 40-year-old's predicted maximum heart rate is 180.)

Your actual maximum heart rate can be determined by a graded exercise test. Please note that some medications and medical conditions might affect your maximum heart rate. If you are taking medicines or have a medical condition (such as heart disease, high blood pressure, or diabetes), always ask your doctor if your maximum heart rate/target heart rate will be affected.

You gain the most benefits and decrease the risk of injury when you exercise in your TARGET HEART RATE ZONE. Usually this is when your exercise heart rate (pulse) is 60 percent to 80 percent of your maximum heart rate. Do not exercise above 85 percent of your maximum heart rate. This increases both cardiovascular and orthopedic risk and does not add any additional benefit.

When beginning an exercise program, you might need to gradually build up to a level that is within your target heart rate zone, especially if you have not exercised regularly before. If the exercise feels too hard, slow down. You will reduce your risk of injury and enjoy the exercise more if you don't try to over-do it.

To find out if you are exercising in your target zone (between 60 percent and 80 percent of your maximum heart rate), use your heart rate monitor to track your heart rate. If your pulse is below your target zone, increase the intensity of your exercise. If your pulse is above your target zone, decrease the intensity of your exercise.

yoi

1-94 Word 1-3 completed

Independent Project 1-4

In this project, you format a business letter for Emma Cavalli to send to clients whose current home listings are expiring.
[Student Learning Outcomes 1.1, 1.2, 1.3, 1.4, 1.5, 1.6, 1.7, 1.8]

File Needed: ***ExpiredLetter-01.docx***
Completed Project File Name: ***[your initials] Word 1-4.docx***

Skills Covered in This Project

- Open and edit an existing document.
- Change line spacing.
- Change paragraph alignment and spacing.
- Change font and font size.
- Use *Show/Hide*.
- Format document as a block format business letter with mixed punctuation.
- Use *AutoCorrect*.
- Move text.
- Change font styles and effects.
- Use spelling and grammar checker.
- Add document properties.

1. Open the ***ExpiredLetter-01*** document from your student data files.
2. Save this document as ***[your initials] Word 1-4***.
3. Select the entire document and make the following formatting changes:
   a. Change the before and after paragraph spacing to **0 pt**.
   b. Change the line spacing to **Single**.
   c. Change the paragraph alignment to **Left**.
   d. Change the font and font size to **Calibri** and **11 pt**.
4. Turn on **Show/Hide** and press **Enter** to add an extra space between each paragraph.
5. Add the following information to the top of the business letter:
   a. Press **Ctrl+Home** to move your insertion point to the top of the document.
   b. Type the current date and press **Enter** four times.
   c. Type the following inside address and press **Enter** two times after the last line.

      Mr. Rick Hermann
      9035 Masi Drive
      Fair Oaks, CA 95528

   d. Supply an appropriate salutation and use mixed punctuation.
   e. Press **Enter** two times after the salutation; there should be one blank line between the salutation and the body of the letter.
   f. Add **72 pt**. *Before* paragraph spacing on the date line.
6. Press **Enter** two times after the last paragraph and type in the closing lines.
   a. Type Best regards, and press **Enter** four times.
   b. Type the following closing lines.

      Emma Cavalli
      Realtor Consultant
      Placer Hills Real Estate

   c. Press **Enter** two times after the company name and type your reference initials in lower case letters.

7. Move the third body paragraph so it appears before the second body paragraph. Make sure there is one blank line between each of the body paragraphs.
8. In the second body paragraph ("There was a lot of detail . . ."), move the last two sentences to the beginning of the paragraph. Make sure there is proper spacing between sentences.
9. Select "**Placer Hills Real Estate**" in the first body paragraph and make the company name **Bold**, **Underline**, and **Small caps**.
10. Select the first sentence in the third paragraph ("The service and experience . . .") and make it **Italic**.
11. Apply formatting to the closing lines of the business letter.
    a. Select the writer's name at the bottom and make it **Small caps**.
    b. Select the writer's title and make it **Italic**.
    c. Select the company name below the writer's title and make it **Bold**.
12. Add the following document properties:
    a. *Title*: Expired Letter
    b. *Company*: Placer Hills Real Estate
    c. *Manager*: Kelsey Kroll
    d. *Author*: Emma Cavalli
13. Spell and grammar check the entire document, ignoring proper nouns.
14. Save and close the document (Figure 1-95).

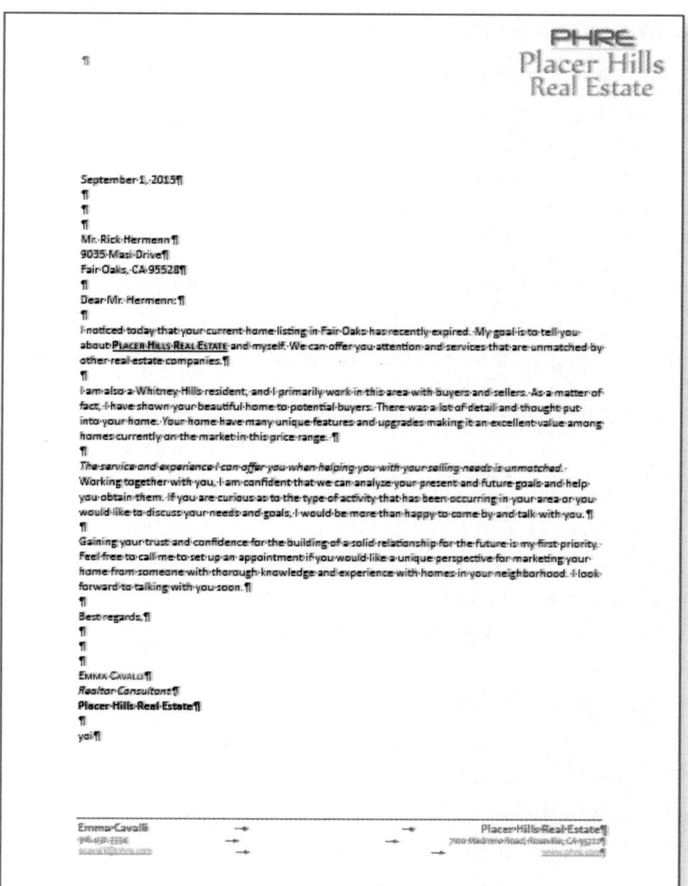

PHRE
Placer Hills
Real Estate

September 1, 2015

Mr. Rick Hermenn
9035 Masi Drive
Fair Oaks, CA 95528

Dear Mr. Hermenn:

I noticed today that your current home listing in Fair Oaks has recently expired. My goal is to tell you about <u>**PLACER HILLS REAL ESTATE**</u> and myself. We can offer you attention and services that are unmatched by other real estate companies.

I am also a Whitney Hills resident, and I primarily work in this area with buyers and sellers. As a matter of fact, I have shown your beautiful home to potential buyers. There was a lot of detail and thought put into your home. Your home have many unique features and upgrades making it an excellent value among homes currently on the market in this price range.

The service and experience I can offer you when helping you with your selling needs is unmatched. Working together with you, I am confident that we can analyze your present and future goals and help you obtain them. If you are curious as to the type of activity that has been occurring in your area or you would like to discuss your needs and goals, I would be more than happy to come by and talk with you.

Gaining your trust and confidence for the building of a solid relationship for the future is my first priority. Feel free to call me to set up an appointment if you would like a unique perspective for marketing your home from someone with thorough knowledge and experience with homes in your neighborhood. I look forward to talking with you soon.

Best regards,

EMMA CAVALLI
Realtor Consultant
Placer Hills Real Estate

yoi

Emma Cavalli — Placer Hills Real Estate

1-95 Word 1-4 completed

Independent Project 1-5

In this project, you combine information from different documents to create a memo for Sierra Pacific Community College District. This memo is a draft of the values statement for the district. **[Student Learning Outcomes 1.1, 1.3, 1.4, 1.5, 1.6, 1.8]**

File Needed: ***ValuesStatement-01a.docx***, ***ValuesStatement-01b.docx***
Completed Project File Name: ***[your initials] Word 1-5.docx***

Skills Covered in This Project

- Open and edit an existing document.
- Change line spacing.
- Change paragraph spacing.
- Change font and font size.
- Format document as a memo.
- Use spelling and grammar checker.
- Add words to the dictionary.
- Change font styles and effects.
- Use the *Format Painter*.
- Move text.
- Add document properties.

---

1. Open the ***ValuesStatement-01a*** document from your student data files.
2. Save this document as ***[your initials] Word 1-5***.
3. Open the ***ValuesStatement-01b*** document from your student data files.
4. Select all of the text in this document and copy to the *Clipboard*.
5. Close the ***ValuesStatement-01b*** document without saving.
6. In the ***[your initials] Word 1-5*** document, press **Enter** at the end of the document and paste the copied text from the *Clipboard*.
7. **Delete** the extra paragraph breaks between the first four paragraphs and at the end of the document.
8. Select the entire document and make the following formatting changes:
   a. Change after paragraph spacing to **12 pt**.
   b. Change the line spacing to **1.15**.
   c. Change the font and font size to **Calibri** and **10 pt**.
9. Press **Enter** at the top of the document and add the memo information above the existing text.
   a. Press **Tab** (once or twice) after the guidewords to line up information at 1".
   b. Press **Enter** once at the end of the first three lines of the memo heading.

   TO: All SPCCD faculty, staff, and managers
   FROM: Lanita Morrow, Chancellor
   DATE: [Current Date]
   SUBJECT: Draft of SPCCD Values Statement
10. Select the first line of the memo heading and change the before paragraph spacing to **24 pt**.
11. Select the last line of the memo heading and change the after paragraph spacing to **18 pt**.
12. Spell and grammar check the entire document.
13. Add the chancellor's first and last names to the dictionary if they are marked as potential spelling errors.

14. Select the first paragraph heading (**“Access”**) in the body of the memo and apply the following style changes:
    a. *Font style*: **Bold**
    b. *Font color*: **Blue-Gray**, **Text 2**
    c. *Underline*: **Double Underline**
    d. *Underline color*: **Blue-Gray**, **Text 2**
    e. *Effects*: **Small caps**
15. Use the *Format Painter* to apply these styles to each of the other paragraph headings in the body of the memo.
16. Use cut and paste or drag and drop to move the body paragraphs so they are ordered alphabetically by paragraph heading. Exclude the first body paragraph. Be sure to include the paragraph symbol at the end of each paragraph when cutting or dragging.
17. Delete any extra blank lines at the end of the document so this document fits on one page.
18. Add the following document properties:
    a. *Title*: SPCCD Values Statement
    b. *Company*: Sierra Pacific Community College District
    c. *Author*: Yoon Soo Park
19. Save and close the document (Figure 1-96).

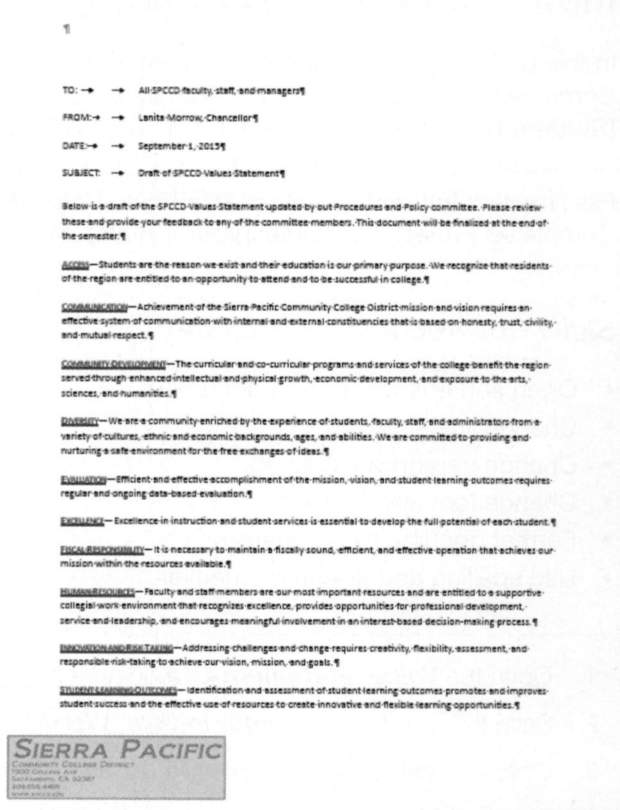

TO: All SPCCD faculty, staff, and managers

FROM: Lanita Morrow, Chancellor

DATE: September 1, 2015

SUBJECT: Draft of SPCCD Values Statement

Below is a draft of the SPCCD Values Statement updated by out Procedures and Policy committee. Please review these and provide your feedback to any of the committee members. This document will be finalized at the end of the semester.

ACCESS—Students are the reason we exist and their education is our primary purpose. We recognize that residents of the region are entitled to an opportunity to attend and to be successful in college.

COMMUNICATION—Achievement of the Sierra Pacific Community College District mission and vision requires an effective system of communication with internal and external constituencies that is based on honesty, trust, civility, and mutual respect.

COMMUNITY DEVELOPMENT—The curricular and co-curricular programs and services of the college benefit the region served through enhanced intellectual and physical growth, economic development, and exposure to the arts, sciences, and humanities.

DIVERSITY—We are a community enriched by the experience of students, faculty, staff, and administrators from a variety of cultures, ethnic and economic backgrounds, ages, and abilities. We are committed to providing and nurturing a safe environment for the free exchanges of ideas.

EVALUATION—Efficient and effective accomplishment of the mission, vision, and student learning outcomes requires regular and ongoing data-based evaluation.

EXCELLENCE—Excellence in instruction and student services is essential to develop the full potential of each student.

FISCAL RESPONSIBILITY—It is necessary to maintain a fiscally sound, efficient, and effective operation that achieves our mission within the resources available.

HUMAN RESOURCES—Faculty and staff members are our most important resources and are entitled to a supportive collegial work environment that recognizes excellence, provides opportunities for professional development, service and leadership, and encourages meaningful involvement in an interest-based decision-making process.

INNOVATION AND RISK TAKING—Addressing challenges and change requires creativity, flexibility, assessment, and responsible risk-taking to achieve our vision, mission, and goals.

STUDENT LEARNING OUTCOMES—Identification and assessment of student learning outcomes promotes and improves student success and the effective use of resources to create innovative and flexible learning opportunities.

SIERRA PACIFIC
COMMUNITY COLLEGE DISTRICT

1-96 Word 1-5 completed

Independent Project 1-6

In this project, you use formatting features in Word to create a professional and appealing brochure for Emma Cavalli at Placer Hills Real Estate.
[Student Learning Outcomes 1.1, 1.2, 1.3, 1.4, 1.5, 1.6, 1.7, 1.8]

File Needed: ***Brochure-01.docx***
Completed Project File Name: ***[your initials] Word 1-6.docx***

Skills Covered in This Project

- Open and edit an existing document.
- Change font and font size.
- Change paragraph spacing.
- Change line spacing.
- Use line breaks.
- Change paragraph alignment.
- Change font styles and effects.
- Use the *Format Painter.*
- Move text.
- Use the thesaurus to find synonyms.
- Add document properties.

1. Open the ***Brochure-01*** dccument from your student data files.
2. Save this document as ***[your initials] Word 1-6***.
3. Select the entire document and make the following formatting changes:
   a. Change the font and font size to **Candara** and **10 pt**.
   b. Change the after-paragraph spacing to **6 pt**.
   c. Change the line spacing to **Single**.
4. On the first five lines of the document ("Emma Cavalli to E-mail . . ."), delete the paragraph symbols at the end of each line and insert a line break (**Shift+Enter**).
5. **Center** the first six lines of the document ("Emma Cavalli to Web . . .").
6. Select the first line of the document and make the following changes:
   a. *Font style*: **Bold**
   b. *Size*: **12 pt**.
   c. *Font color*: **Green**, **Accent 6**, **Darker 50%**
   d. *Underline style*: **Thick Underline**
   e. *Underline color*: **Green**, **Accent 6**, **Darker 50%**
7. Select the second line of the document and make it **Bold**.
8. Select the third line of the document and make it **Italic**.
9. Select the first section heading, "**Personal Statement**," and apply **Bold**, **Underline**, and **Small Caps** formatting. Change the before paragraph spacing to **12 pt**. and the after paragraph spacing to **3 pt**.
10. Use the *Format Painter* to copy this formatting to the other section headings ("Real Estate Experience," "Why I am a Real Estate Agent," "What Clients are Saying," "Professional Credentials," and "Education & Training").
11. In the "Why I am a Real Estate Agent" section, combine the four sentences into one paragraph, deleting paragraph marks and inserting spaces as needed.
12. In the "What Clients are Saying" section, make the following changes:
    a. Select the first quote (don't include the names of the individuals who said the quote), make it **Italic**, and change the after spacing to **0 pt**.
    b. Select the source of the quote ("**-Rod & Luisa Ellisor**, **Rocklin**, **CA**") and right-align this text.
    c. Repeat the above two steps for the second quote in this section.
13. Move the third section heading and the paragraph below it ("Why I am a Real Estate Agent") so it appears before the second section ("Real Estate Experience").
14. Select the lines of text in the "Professional Credentials" section (don't include the heading) and change the after-paragraph spacing to **3 pt**.
15. Use the *Format Painter* to repeat the above formatting to the lines of text (excluding the heading) in the "Education & Training" section.
16. Use the thesaurus to find an appropriate synonym for the following words:
    a. Replace "surpass" (in the "Personal Statement" section) with "**exceed**."
    b. Replace "emotions" (in the "Why I am a Real Estate Agent" section) with "**sentiments**."
17. Add the following document properties:
    a. *Title*: Brochure
    b. *Company*: Placer Hills Real Estate
    c. *Author*: Emma Cavalli

18. Save and close the document (Figure 1-97).

PHRE
Placer Hills
Real Estate
2100 Madrone Road | Roseville, CA 95722
www.phre.com | 916.450.3300

Emma Cavalli
Realtor Consultant
"Putting Your Needs First"
Phone: 916.450.3334
E-mail: ecavalli@phre.com
Web: www.phre.com/ecavalli

PERSONAL STATEMENT
I am dedicated to listening to your needs as a buyer or seller and providing you with prompt and excellent service to exceed your expectations.

WHY I AM A REAL ESTATE AGENT
I enjoy working with people and negotiating on their behalf. Communication, organization, and availability are skills I possess that make me a client focused real estate agent. I am extremely conscientious of the sentiments involved in both the buying and selling process. Customer service and satisfaction are important to me, and I pride myself in giving you the best service possible.

REAL ESTATE EXPERIENCE
I have had the pleasure of working with buyers, sellers, and investors for over 15 years. Each transaction is new and exciting.

WHAT CLIENTS ARE SAYING
Here is what others have said about me:

"It was a pleasure working with Emma Cavalli. She was very responsive and listened to all of our needs. Her marketing plan sold our home in just 3 days!"

-Rod & Luisa Ellisor, Rocklin, CA

"Emma is conscientious, personable, and professional. Her dedication and commitment to meeting our needs has been apparent from the beginning. Emma can be counted on to do what she says. I would not hesitate to refer Emma to my friends and family."

-Jon & Robin Anderson, Roseville, CA

PROFESSIONAL CREDENTIALS
Licensed California Real Estate Salesperson
Member of National Association of Realtors
Member California Association of Realtors
Member of Realtor.com
Distinguished Realtor Award from peers
Community Service Board position for Distinguished Schools for the Roseville Unified School District
Elected Parent/Teacher Club President for Winchester Elementary School 2013-2014, 2014-2015

EDUCATION & TRAINING
University of Nevada, Reno—Business Administration B.A.
Real Estate Code of Ethics
Certified Contract Consultant
Certified Maximum Productivity Consultant

1-97 Word 1-6 completed

Improve It Project 1-7

In this project, you create a block format business letter for Margaret Jepson, an insurance agent at Central Sierra Insurance. You fix the formatting and text in this document and add opening and closing lines to create a properly formatted business letter. For more information on creating a correctly formatted block format business letter, see *Appendix D* (online reference).
[Student Learning Outcomes 1.1, 1.2, 1.3, 1.5, 1.6, 1.8]

File Needed: ***RenewalLetter-01.docx***
Completed Project File Name: ***[your initials] Word 1-7.docx***

Skills Covered in This Project

- Open and edit an existing document.
- Change font and font size.
- Change paragraph spacing.
- Change line spacing.
- Use spelling and grammar checker.
- Format a business letter.
- Change paragraph alignment.
- Change font styles and effects.
- Use the *Format Painter*.
- Add document properties.

1. Open the ***RenewalLetter-01*** document from your student data files.
2. Save this document as ***[your initials] Word 1-7***.
3. Use **Single** line spacing and **0 pt**. before- and after-paragraph spacing on the entire document.
4. Use **Calibri** font and **11 pt**. font size.
5. Correct spelling and grammar as needed.
6. Type the current date at the top of the document.
7. Type the inside address.

    Mr. Rick DePonte
    8364 Marshall Street
    Granite Bay, CA 95863

8. Include an appropriate salutation. Use mixed punctuation.
9. Include the insurance policy information in the subject line.

    Policy HO-2887-5546-B

10. At the end of the document, supply an appropriate complimentary close. Use mixed punctuation.
11. Type the information below as the writer's name, title, and company.

    Margaret Jepson, ARM, CIC, CRM
    Insurance Agent
    Central Sierra Insurance

12. Include your reference initials and an enclosure notation at the end of the business letter.
13. **Center** the four lines of renewal premium information in the body of the letter.
14. Apply **Bold** and **Small caps** formatting to the headings for each of these four lines of renewal premium information.
15. Format the "Total Premium" amount as **Bold**, **Italic**, and **Double Underline**.
16. Replace *[Company Name]* with Hartford Specialty.
17. Replace *[First Name]* with the appropriate information.
18. Use **72 pt**. before paragraph spacing on the date line.
19. Add *Title* (Renewal Letter), *Company*, and *Author* document properties to the letter.
20. Proofread and edit the document carefully. Make sure there is proper spacing between each of the parts of the block format business letter. This document fits on one page.
21. Save and close the letter (Figure 1-98).

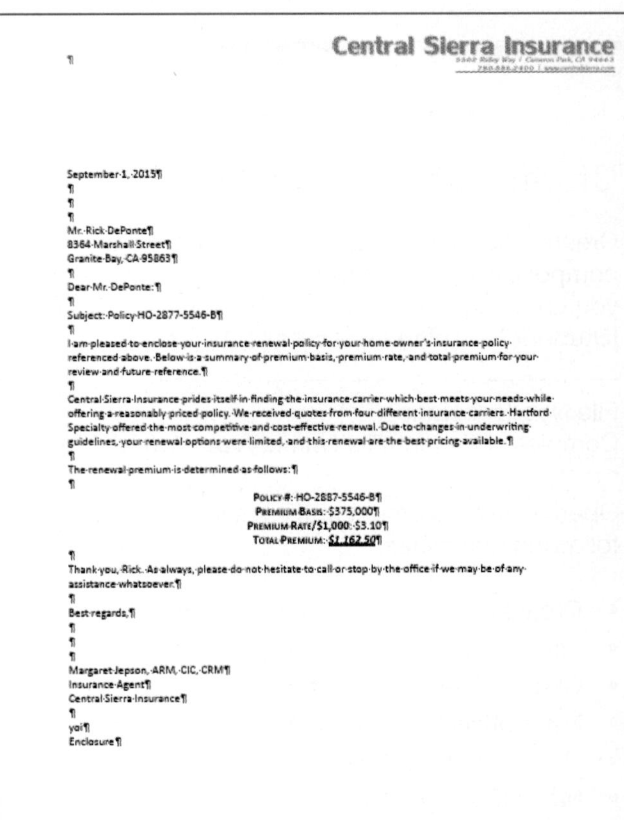

Central Sierra Insurance

September 1, 2015

Mr. Rick DePonte
8364 Marshall Street
Granite Bay, CA 95863

Dear Mr. DePonte:

Subject: Policy HO-2877-5546-B

I am pleased to enclose your insurance renewal policy for your home owner's insurance policy referenced above. Below is a summary of premium basis, premium rate, and total premium for your review and future reference.

Central Sierra Insurance prides itself in finding the insurance carrier which best meets your needs while offering a reasonably priced policy. We received quotes from four different insurance carriers. Hartford Specialty offered the most competitive and cost-effective renewal. Due to changes in underwriting guidelines, your renewal options were limited, and this renewal are the best pricing available.

The renewal premium is determined as follows:

POLICY #: HO-2887-5546-B
PREMIUM BASIS: $375,000
PREMIUM RATE/$1,000: $3.10
TOTAL PREMIUM: ***$1,162.50***

Thank you, Rick. As always, please do not hesitate to call or stop by the office if we may be of any assistance whatsoever.

Best regards,

Margaret Jepson, ARM, CIC, CRM
Insurance Agent
Central Sierra Insurance

yoi
Enclosure

1-98 Word 1-7 completed

Challenge Project 1-8

Create a cover letter for a job application. A cover letter typically accompanies a resume to introduce an applicant to a prospective employer. You can use and modify an existing cover letter, or you can create a new one. It is important to customize each cover letter for each job for which you are applying.

There are many online resources available to help you with both content and format. One of the best online resources for writing is the Online Writing Lab (OWL) from Purdue University (**http://owl.english.purdue.edu/owl/**). You can search this site for helpful information about cover letters. **[Student Learning Outcomes 1.1, 1.2, 1.3, 1.4, 1.5, 1.6, 1.7, 1.8]**

File Needed: None
Completed Project File Name: ***[your initials] Word 1-8.docx***

Open a new document and save this document as ***[your initials] Word 1-8***.

Type this document as a personal business letter in block format. For more information on formatting a personal business letter see *Appendix D* (online reference). Modify your document according to the following guidelines:

- Move sentences and paragraphs as needed to produce a well-organized cover letter.
- Add words to the dictionary as needed.
- Use the thesaurus to find synonyms as needed.
- Include document properties and spell and grammar check the document.

Challenge Project 1-9

Create a list of five places you would like to visit in the next five years. For each of the places you list, compose a short paragraph about that place and why it is interesting to you. Research each of the places you choose on the Internet. Use your own words when composing the paragraphs about each place. **[Student Learning Outcomes 1.1, 1.2, 1.3, 1.4, 1.5, 1.6, 1.7, 1.8]**

File Needed: None
Completed Project File Name: ***[your initials] Word 1-9.docx***

Open a new document and save it as ***[your initials] Word 1-9***. Modify your document according to the following guidelines:

- Create and format a title for the document.
- Format each of the headings by modifying the font, style, and attributes.
- Change line and paragraph spacing as needed to create an attractive and readable document.
- Use consistent line and paragraph spacing throughout the document.
- Use the *Format Painter* to keep formatting consistent throughout the document.
- Move the paragraphs so the places are listed in order of your preference.
- Include document properties and spell and grammar check the document.

Challenge Project 1-10

Create a flyer for an upcoming event for an organization to which you belong. Be sure to include all the relevant information for this event and arrange it attractively and professionally on the page. **[Student Learning Outcomes 1.1, 1.2, 1.3, 1.5, 1.6, 1.7, 1.8]**

File Needed: None
Completed Project File Name: ***[your initials] Word 1-10.docx***

Open a new document and save it as ***[your initials] Word 1-10***. Modify your document according to the following guidelines:

- Create and format a title for the document.
- Format the information by modifying the fonts, styles, and attributes.
- Change line and paragraph spacing as needed to create an attractive and readable document.
- Change the text alignment as desired.
- Use the *Format Painter* to keep formatting consistent throughout the document.
- Include document properties and spell and grammar check the document.

CHAPTER 2

Formatting and Customizing Documents

CHAPTER OVERVIEW

In addition to giving you the ability to create basic business documents, Microsoft Word 2013 provides formatting and editing tools you can use to customize a variety of documents. Formatting features such as custom margins, tab stops, indents, page numbering, headers, footers, breaks, lists, styles, themes, borders, and shading help you to produce readable and attractive professional and personal documents.

STUDENT LEARNING OUTCOMES (SLOs)

After completing this chapter, you will be able to:

SLO 2.1 Format a document by customizing margins, page orientation, paper size, and vertical alignment (p. W2-63).

SLO 2.2 Improve alignment and white-space usage by setting, using, and editing tab stops in a document (p. W2-66).

SLO 2.3 Understand and apply indents to control text alignment (p. W2-71).

SLO 2.4 Enhance document layout by effectively using page numbers, headers, and footers (p. W2-76).

SLO 2.5 Control pagination with page and section breaks (p. W2-83).

SLO 2.6 Present information using customized bulleted and numbered lists (p. W2-85).

SLO 2.7 Increase document consistency and format with styles and themes (p. W2-89).

SLO 2.8 Effectively edit a document using find and replace (p. W2-93).

SLO 2.9 Improve overall document design and format with borders, shading, horizontal lines, and hyperlinks (p. W2-96).

CASE STUDY

Courtyard Medical Plaza has a preschool for its employees' children. The preschool is currently looking for qualified applicants to fill a vacant teacher position.

In the Pause & Practice projects, you are modifying a resume for Richelle Wilkinson. You use features covered in this chapter to create an attractive and informative resume.

Pause & Practice 2-1: Edit the resume to change margins and include tab stops and indents.

Pause & Practice 2-2: Modify the resume to include a header with text and a page number.

Pause & Practice 2-3: Enhance the resume by using bulleted lists, a page break, and a theme.

Pause & Practice 2-4: Finalize the resume by using find and replace, borders, shading, and hyperlinks.

WORD

SLO 2.1

Customizing Margins and Page Layout

You can use margins to create ***white space*** around the edges of a document. White space improves the readability of a document and prevents the document from appearing cluttered. The document type and content influence the margins you choose for the document. You can also customize a document by changing the orientation, page size, or vertical alignment.

Page Layout Settings

When you open a new Word document, the default settings control margins, page orientation, paper size, and vertical alignment. The default settings for a new document are as follows:

Default Page Layout Settings

Page Layout Option	Default Setting
Margins	1" top, bottom, left, and right
Page Orientation	Portrait
Paper Size	8.5"×11" (Letter)
Vertical Alignment	Top

These settings are applied to the entire Word document, and you can easily change all of these settings in Word.

Margin Settings

Margin settings are measured in inches; the default margin settings for a new Word document are 1". Word provides you with a variety of ***preset margins settings.*** You can choose and change margins on the *Page Layout* tab.

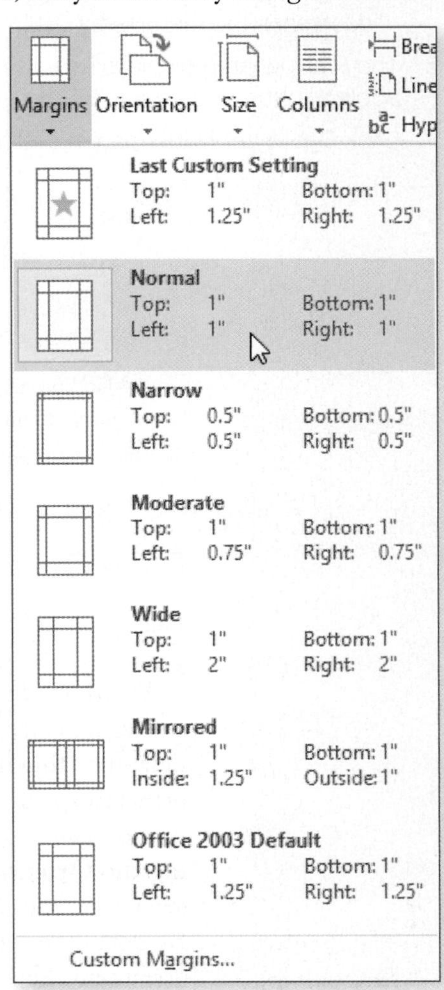

2-1 Preset margin settings drop-down list

HOW TO: Change Margin Settings

1. Click the **Page Layout** tab.
2. Click the **Margins** button [*Page Setup* group]. Preset margin options appear in the *Margins* drop-down list (Figure 2-1).
3. Select the desired margin settings from the drop-down list of options.

The *Margins* drop-down list provides preset margin options. You are not limited to these preset options; you can also create your own custom margin settings.

> **MORE INFO**
>
> At the top of this *Margins* list, the ***Last Custom Setting*** option displays the most recent custom margin settings you have used.

Page Setup Dialog Box

If you want margin settings that are not listed in the preset margin settings in the *Margins* drop-down list, use the ***Page Setup dialog box*** (Figure 2-2) to change one or more of the margin settings and create custom margins.

HOW TO: Set Custom Margins

1. Click the **Page Layout** tab.
2. Click the **Margins** button [*Page Setup* group]. The *Margins* drop-down list opens.
3. Click **Custom Margins**. The *Page Setup* dialog box opens (Figure 2-2).
4. Click the **Margins** tab if it is not already selected.
5. Change the *Top, Bottom, Left,* and *Right* margin settings as desired. You can do this in two different ways.
   - Click in the **Top**, **Bottom**, **Left**, or **Right** margin box, and type in your desired margin setting.
   - Click the **up** or **down arrow** to increase or decrease the margin size. Each click of the *up* or *down arrow* increases or decreases the margins by 0.1".
6. The *Preview* area displays how the margin settings appear when applied to the document.
7. Click **OK** to apply the margin settings.

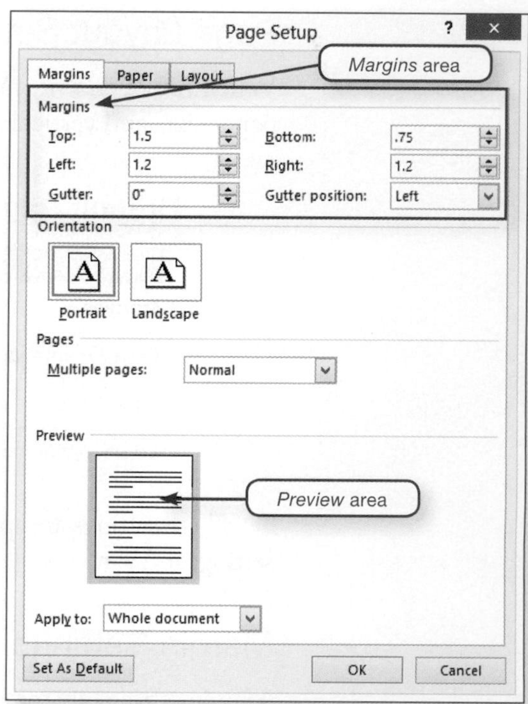

2-2 *Page Setup* dialog box

> **MORE INFO**
>
> Margin settings are applied to the entire document by default. However, you can apply different margin settings to different sections of a document. Sections and section breaks are covered later in this chapter.

Page Orientation

Page orientation refers to the direction of the page. The two different orientation options in Word are ***Portrait*** and ***Landscape.*** Portrait is the tall orientation (8.5"×11") which is the default setting in Word. Landscape is the wide orientation (11"×8.5").

You can change page orientation by clicking the **Orientation** button in the *Page Setup* group on the *Page Layout* tab (Figure 2-3). By default, orientation is applied to the entire document. You can also change page orientation in the *Page Setup* dialog box.

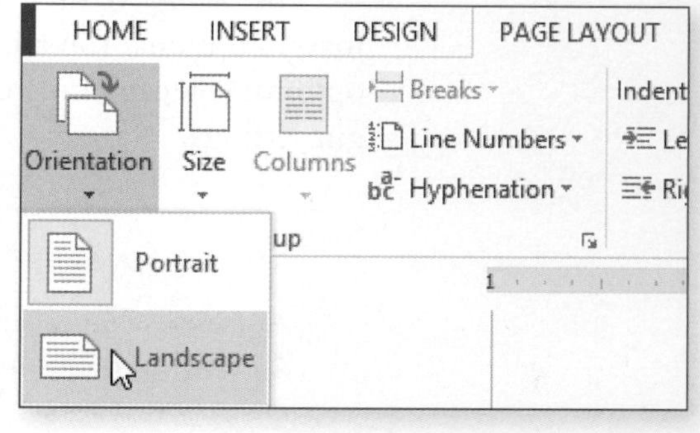

2-3 Page orientation settings

Paper Size

Paper size refers to the actual size of the paper of your final printed document. A new document in Word is letter size, which is 8.5"×11" by default. Word also provides other preset paper size settings, some of which are displayed in Figure 2-4.

You can change paper size by clicking the **Size** button in the *Page Setup* group on the *Page Layout* tab. You can also set a custom paper size in the *Page Setup* dialog box. When a different paper size is set, the margins of the document remain the same. You can change the margins if necessary.

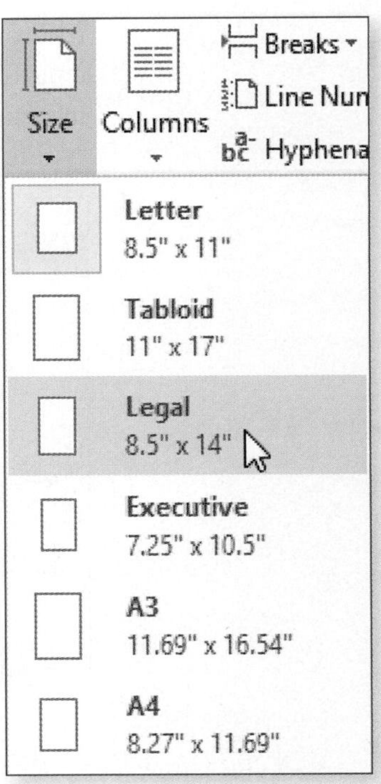

2-4 Paper size preset setting options

Vertical Alignment

If you are creating a flyer or a title page for a report, you might want to balance or center the information vertically on the page. Changing the ***vertical alignment*** of a page, section, or document is a much more effective method than using paragraph breaks (pressing *Enter* multiple times) to align information vertically.

Word gives you four different vertical alignment options.

- ***Top***—The text begins at the top of the document.
- ***Center***—Information is centered vertically between the margins.
- ***Justified***—Space is automatically added between lines to fill up the entire vertical space between the top and bottom margins.
- ***Bottom***—The text begins at the bottom of the document.

HOW TO: Change Vertical Alignment

1. Click the **Page Layout** tab.
2. Click the **Page Setup** launcher [*Page Setup* group]. The *Page Setup* dialog box opens.
3. Click the **Layout** tab.
4. In the *Page* area, click the **Vertical alignment** drop-down list (Figure 2-5).
5. Select the vertical alignment option of your choice.

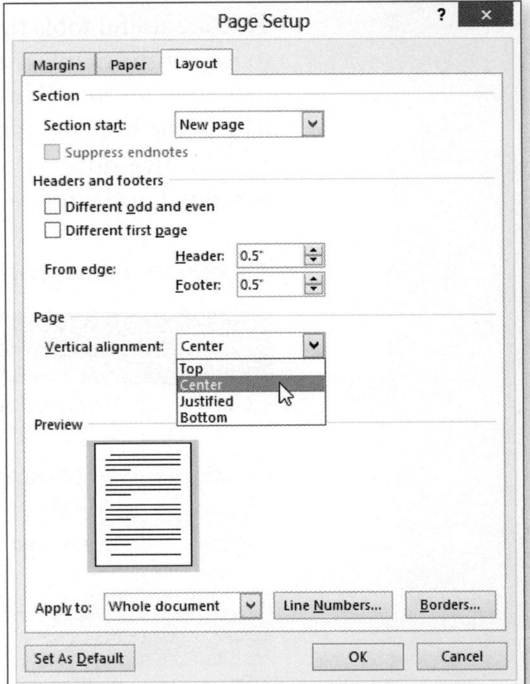

2-5 Change vertical alignment

Use the Ruler

Microsoft Word provides horizontal and vertical rulers that displays both the typing line length and the vertical typing space available in a document. The rulers are broken into 1/8" increments. Half-inch markers are longer vertical lines and inch markers are numerical. The typing area on the rulers is displayed in white, while the margin area is shaded (Figure 2-6).

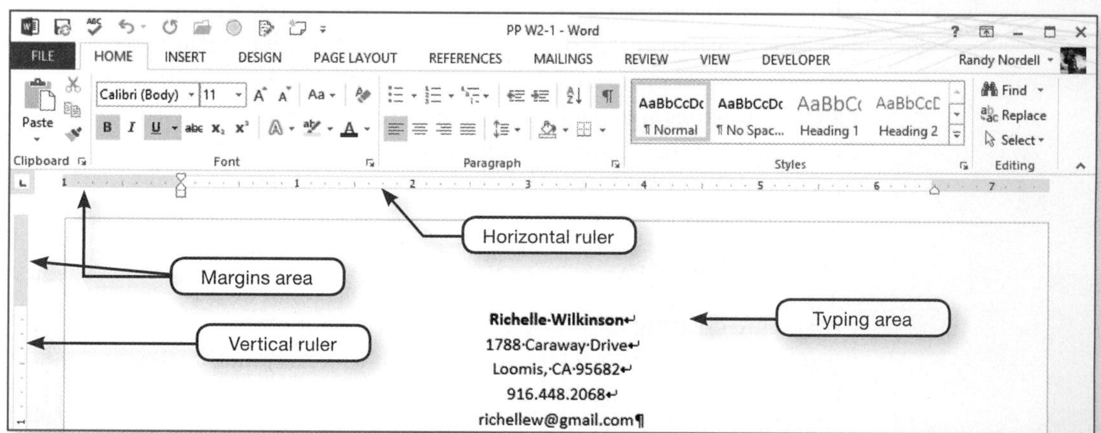

2-6 Horizontal and vertical rulers displayed

To display the rulers, select the **Ruler** check box on the *View* tab in the *Show* group. This check box toggles on and off the display of the rulers.

MORE INFO

The rulers are increasingly important and useful as you begin using tab stops, indents, columns, tables, and section breaks.

SLO 2.2

Setting, Using, and Editing Tab Stops

Tabs are useful tools that you can employ to control the alignment of text. A tab is often used to indent the first line of a paragraph. A ***tab stop*** is where your insertion point stops when you press the *Tab* key. Tabs can also be used, for example, to align text in columns, or to begin the date at the horizontal midpoint on a modified block business letter.

The five different types of tabs stops that you can set and use in your documents are described in the following table.

Types of Tab Stops

Type of Tab Stop	Description	Tab Stop Indicator	Tab Stop in Use
Left	Text is left aligned at the tab stop		Left tab
Center	Text is centered on the tab stop		Center tab
Right	Text is right aligned at the tab stop		Right tab
Decimal	Decimal point is aligned at the tab stop		Decimal tab 620.50 8.375
Bar	A vertical bar (line) is inserted at the tab stop		There is a bar | tab between these words

Set Tabs Stops

Tabs are different from margins because tab stops apply to a paragraph or selected paragraphs rather than an entire document or sections of a document. This is important to keep in mind when setting, using, and editing tab stops.

You can set tab stops before text is typed, or you can set tab stops on existing text. If you open a *new* document and set a left tab stop at 3.25", that tab stop is set on the first line of the document and is set on each subsequent line and paragraph in the document.

On the other hand, if you open an *existing* document and set a tab stop on the first line, the tab stop is only set for that paragraph. When setting a tab stop on existing documents or text, remember to select all the text or paragraphs where you want the tab settings to apply.

There are two ways to set a tab stop in Word.

- *Tabs* dialog box
- Ruler

Use the Tabs Dialog Box to Set Tab Stops

The ***Tabs dialog box*** is an effective and easy method to set single or multiple tab stops. The *Tabs* dialog box is available from the *Paragraph* dialog box, which you can open from the *Paragraph* group on either the *Home* or *Page Layout* tabs.

EXPERIENCE¶

HEAD·TEACHER,·LOOMIS·LEARNING·CENTER¶

Loomis,·CA → October·2010-Present¶

Develop·and·implement·a·developmentally·appropriate·preschool the·ages·of·two·and·four·years.¶

2-7 Select text before setting tab stops

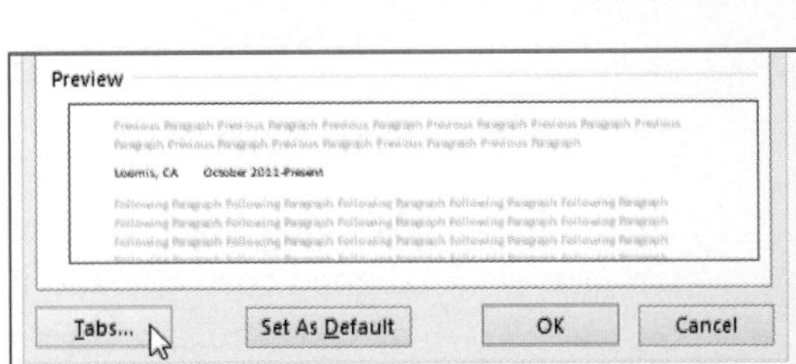

2-8 *Tabs* button in the *Paragraph* dialog box

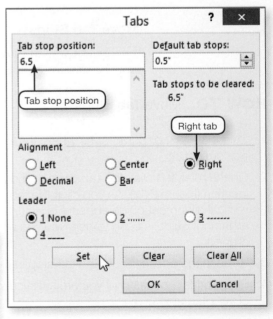

HOW TO: Set Tab Stops Using the Tabs Dialog Box

1. Select the text where you want to set a tab stop (Figure 2-7).
2. Click the **Home** tab.
3. Click the **Paragraph** launcher to open the *Paragraph* dialog box.
4. Click the **Tabs** button (Figure 2-8). The *Tabs* dialog box opens.
5. Click in the **Tab stop position** area and type the desired tab stop position.
6. In the *Alignment* area, select the type of tab stop radio button you want.
7. Click the **Set** button. The tab stop appears in the list of tab stops below the *Tab stop position* area (Figure 2-9).
8. Click **OK** to close the *Tabs* dialog box.
    - The tab stop is applied to the selected text.
    - The tab stop is visible on the ruler.

Tabs

Tab stop position: 6.5

Default tab stops: 0.5"

Tab stops to be cleared: 6.5"

Tab stop position

Right tab

Alignment: Left, Center, Right, Decimal, Bar

Leader: 1 None, 2 ...., 3 -------, 4 ____

Set, Clear, Clear All, OK, Cancel

2-9 Set 6.5" right tab stop in the *Tabs* dialog box

MORE INFO

Set and use tab stops to line up and balance columns of text rather than pressing *Tab* multiple times between columns.

Use the Ruler to Set Tab Stops

Using the ruler to set tab stops is a quick way to add them to a document. You can also easily move or remove tab stops using the ruler. Use the ***tab selector*** to select the type of tab stop you want. The tab selector is located at the top of the vertical ruler on the left side of the Word window. When setting tab stops on an existing document, it is very important to select the text or paragraphs where you want the tab stop to apply before setting the tab stop.

HOW TO: Set Tab Stops Using the Ruler

1. Select the text where you want the new tab stop(s) to appear.
2. Click the **tab selector** to select the type of tab stop to apply (Figure 2-10).
3. Click the ruler to set a tab stop.
   - When setting tab stops using the ruler, click the bottom edge of the ruler to set a tab stop (Figure 2-11).

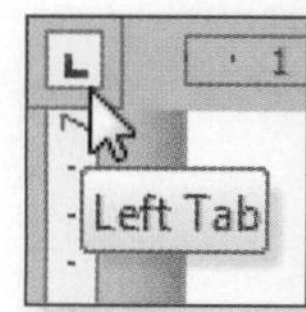

2-10 ***Tab Selector*** **button**

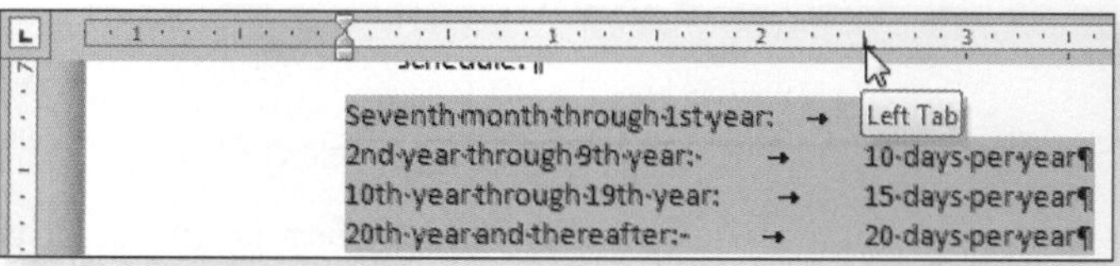

2-11 Set left tab stop at 2.5" on the ruler

> **MORE INFO**
>
> Use the ***Format Painter*** to copy tab stops from one area of your document to other areas.

Edit Tab Stops

Aligning text using tab stops can sometimes be tedious. It can be challenging to get text aligned correctly and balanced between columns. But as you set and use tab stop more regularly, you become more comfortable selecting the correct type of tab stop to use, adjusting the settings of existing tab stops, and removing tab stops. When using multiple columns, adjust tab stops so you have about the same amount of white space between columns.

Move Tab Stops

The easiest way to move tab stops is by using the ruler. When using the ruler to adjust a tab stop, be sure to select the appropriate text before moving a tab stop.

HOW TO: Move Tab Stops

1. Select the text or paragraphs where the tab stops you want to edit are set.
2. On the ruler, left click the **tab stop** and drag it to the new location (Figure 2-12). As you click the tab stop to be moved, a vertical alignment guide appears on your document. This alignment guide is used to help you see where your text is aligned.
3. Release the pointer to set the tab stop in the new location.
4. Repeat this process until you are satisfied with the placement of your tab stops.

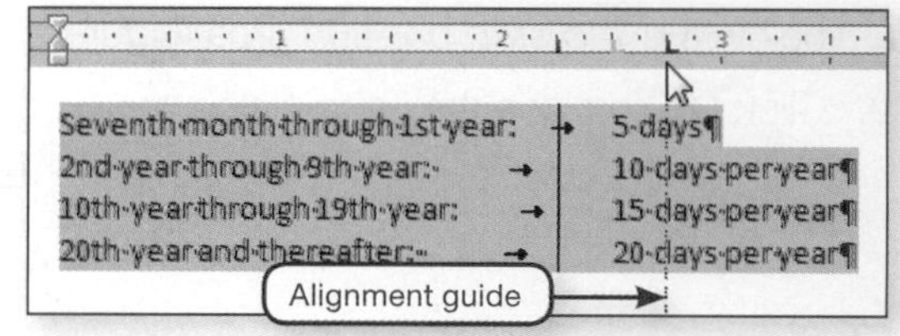

2-12 Move a tab stop using the ruler

> **ANOTHER WAY**
>
> Adjust tab stops in the *Tabs* dialog box by clearing an existing tab stop and setting a new tab stop.

If you hold down the **Alt** key when you are moving a tab stop, a different ruler appears that allows you to place the tab stop at a specific measurement (Figure 2-13).

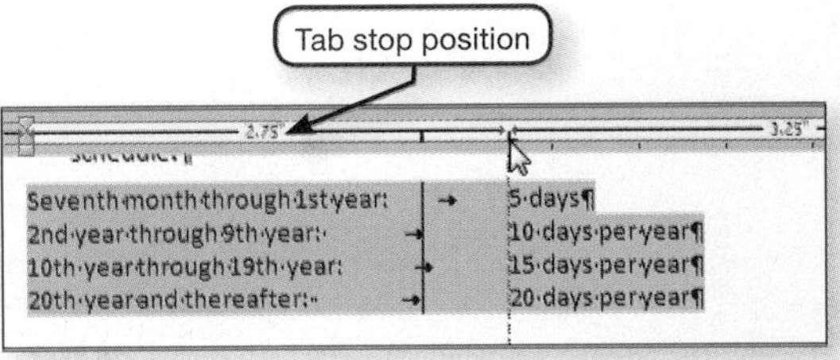

2-13 Use the *Alt* key to adjust a tab stop

Remove Tab Stops

Occasionally, when setting tab stops using the ruler, you unintentionally add unwanted tab stops. Or sometimes you might just want to remove unwanted tab stops to clean up an existing document. It is very important to select the text or paragraphs where the tab stops you want to remove are before performing these actions. Following are three different ways to remove tab stops.

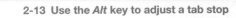

- Drag a tab stop off the ruler.
- Clear a single tab stop in the *Tabs* dialog box.
- Clear all tab stops in the *Tabs* dialog box.

To clear a single tab stop using the ruler, select the text or paragraphs, select the tab stop you want to remove, drag down below the ruler, and release the pointer.

When using the *Tabs* dialog box to remove tab stops, you can clear a single tab stop or clear all existing tab stops on the selected text or paragraphs.

HOW TO: Clear Tab Stops Using the Tabs Dialog Box

1. Select the text or paragraphs that contain the tab stops you want to remove.
2. Click the **Paragraph** launcher [*Home* or *Page Layout* tab] to open the *Paragraph* dialog box.
3. Click the **Tabs** button to open the *Tabs* dialog box.
4. To clear a single tab stop, select the tab stop to be cleared in the list of existing tab stops and click the **Clear** button (Figure 2-14). Repeat on any other tab stops you want to remove.
   - To clear all tab stops, click the **Clear All** button.
5. Click **OK** to close the *Tabs* dialog box.

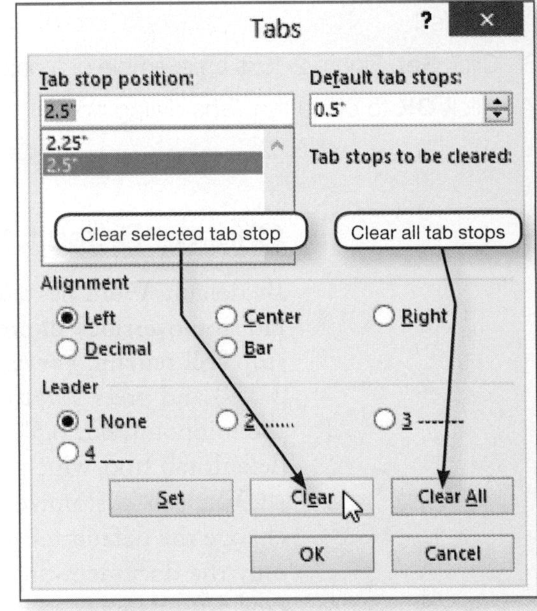

2-14 Clear tab stops in the *Tabs* dialog box

Tab Leaders

You can use ***leaders*** to insert dots or a line between information when using tab stops. The most common type of leader is the dot leader, which is regularly used in a table of contents. In a table of contents, a dot leader is inserted between the text and the right aligned page number. Leaders make it easier for readers to read across a line where there is a gap on the same line. Leaders can also be used to insert a dashed line in the blank space between columns or to create a solid underline when creating a printed form.

Word has three different types of leaders. Examples of each of these are in the following table.

Types of Leaders

Leader	Example of Use
Dot	Chapter 1 4
Dash	Vacation Days ------- 10 days per year
Solid Underline	Name ____________________

You can add leaders to existing or new tab stops, but they can only be added in the *Tabs* dialog box.

HOW TO: Add a Tab Leader

1. Select the text or paragraphs where you want to add a tab leader.
2. Click the **Paragraph** launcher [*Home* or *Page Layout* tab] to open the *Paragraph* dialog box.
3. Click the **Tabs** button to open the *Tabs* dialog box.
4. Select an existing tab stop or type in the *Tab stop position* text box for a new tab stop.
5. In the *Leader* area, select the type of leader to be applied.
6. Click **Set**. Figure 2-15 is an example of a dash leader.
7. Click **OK** to close the *Tabs* dialog box.

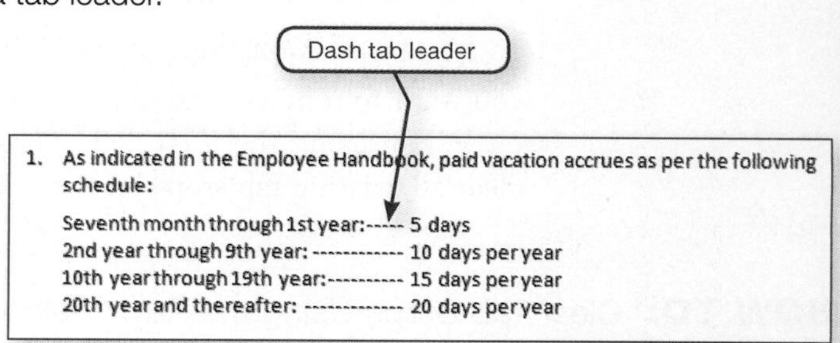

Dash tab leader
1. As indicated in the Employee Handbook, paid vacation accrues as per the following schedule:
Seventh month through 1st year:----- 5 days
2nd year through 9th year: ------------ 10 days per year
10th year through 19th year:---------- 15 days per year
20th year and thereafter: ------------- 20 days per year

2-15 Tab stop with a dash leader

Change Default Tab Stops

By default, Word has a left tab stop every 0.5". When you set a tab stop in Word, this custom tab stop overrides all preceding default tab stops. The default tab stops after your custom tab stop still remain. For example, if you set a left tab stop at the horizontal midpoint (typically 3.25") and press *Tab* to move to the horizontal midpoint, your insertion point will move to the midpoint, not 0.5". But if you press *Tab* again, your insertion point will stop at the next default tab stop, which would be 3.5".

You can customize the default tab stops. If you change the default tab stop setting, this change affects only the document on which you are working, not all new documents.

HOW TO: Change Default Tab Stops

1. Click the **Paragraph** launcher [*Home* or *Page Layout* tab] to open the *Paragraph* dialog box.
2. Click the **Tabs** button to open the *Tabs* dialog box.
3. In the *Default tab stops* area, use the up or down arrow to change the default tab stops (Figure 2-16).
4. Click **OK** to close the *Tabs* dialog box.

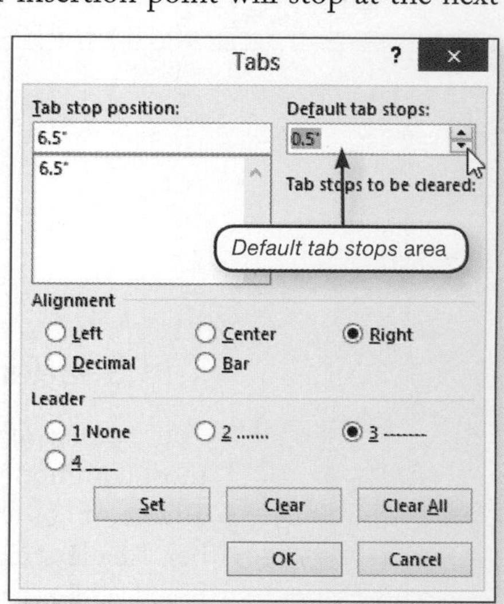

2-16 Change default tab stops

Using Indents

SLO 2.3

Indents are another powerful tool to help you control how text is arranged between the left and right margins. Indents can be thought of as temporary margins. You can use indents to indent the first line of each paragraph, set off a long quote in a report, or indent the carry-over lines when creating bulleted or numbered lists.

The four different types of indents that you can set and use in your document are described in the following table.

Types of Indents

Indent	Example of Use	Ruler Indent Marker
Left Indent	This line has a ***left indent***.	Left Indent
Right Indent	This line has a ***right indent***.	Right Indent
First Line Indent	This line has a ***first line indent***.	First Line Indent
Hanging Indent	This line has a ***hanging indent***.	Hanging Indent

Similar to setting tab stops, it is important to select the text where you want to apply the indent settings before applying the new settings. You can set indents using the ruler, the *Paragraph* group on the *Page Layout* tab, or the *Paragraph* dialog box.

Left and Right Indents

Indents are applied to paragraphs, not just lines of text within a paragraph. When setting an indent, select the text or paragraphs on which to apply the indent. If your insertion point is in a paragraph, the indent you set is applied to that paragraph only.

HOW TO: Set a Left and Right Indent

1. Select the text or paragraph where you want to apply the indent. If it is just one paragraph, place your insertion point in that paragraph.
2. Click the **Page Layout** tab.
3. Change the *Left* and *Right* indent settings [*Paragraph* group]. This change is applied to the selected text (Figure 2-17).

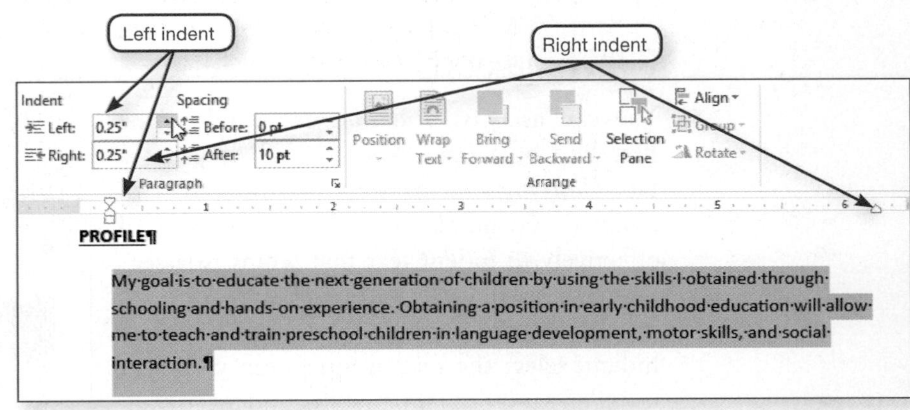

2-17 Change left and right indents

When an indent is set on a paragraph and you press *Enter* at the end of the paragraph, the indent carries over to the next paragraph.

Indents can also be set using the ruler by dragging the indent marker to the desired location after you select the text you want to indent. As you drag the indent marker, an alignment guide appears to display where your text aligns.

HOW TO: Use the Ruler to Set Indents

1. Select the text or paragraph you want to indent. If it is just one paragraph, place your insertion point in that paragraph.
2. Left click the **left indent marker**, drag to the desired location, and release the pointer. The left indent is applied to the text (Figure 2-18).
3. Left click the **right indent marker**, drag to the desired location, and release the pointer. The right indent is applied to the text (Figure 2-19).

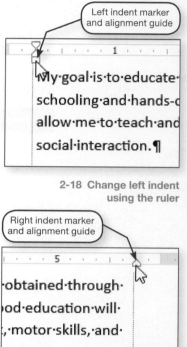

2-18 Change left indent using the ruler

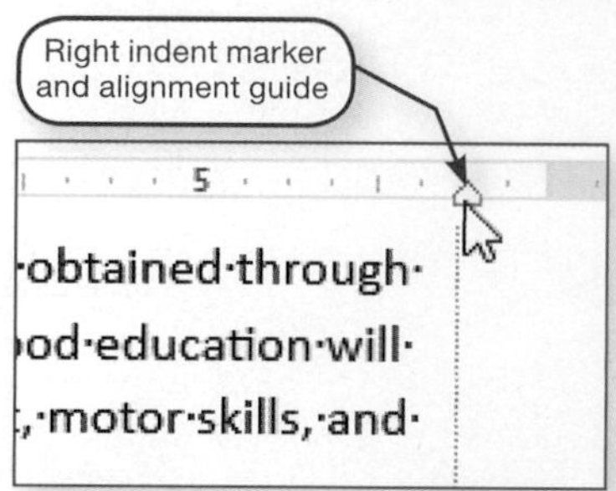

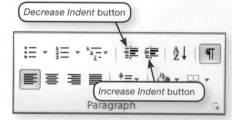

2-19 Change right indent using the ruler

> **ANOTHER WAY**
>
> Set left and right indents using the *Paragraph* dialog box. Click the **Paragraph** launcher to open the *Paragraph* dialog box.

The ***Decrease Indent*** and ***Increase Indent*** buttons in the *Paragraph* group on the *Home* tab increase or decrease the left indent in increments of 0.5" (Figure 2-20). Remove a left indent by clicking at the beginning of the paragraph and pressing **Backspace**.

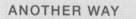

2-20 *Decrease Indent* and *Increase Indent* buttons

First Line and Hanging Indents

You can use ***first line indents*** to indent the first line of a paragraph instead of using a tab. ***Hanging indents*** are typically used with bulleted and numbered lists but can be used effectively to indent text that wraps to a second or more lines.

When using the ruler to set a first line indent, select the text or paragraph you want to indent and drag the first line indent marker to the desired location (Figure 2-21). The alignment guide displays where the first line of each paragraph will align.

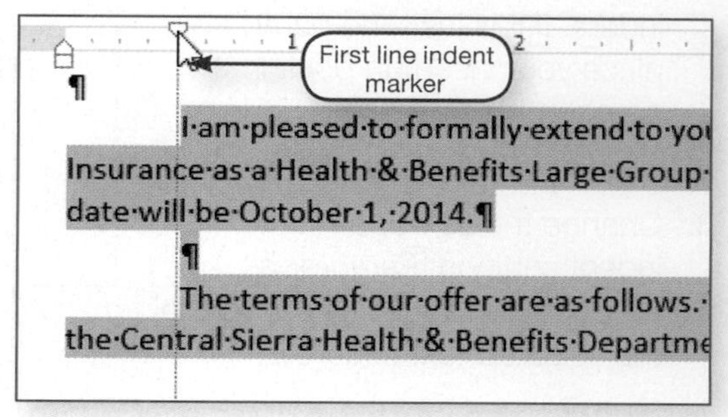

2-21 Set a first line indent using the ruler

To set a hanging indent, select the text or paragraph on which to apply the indent and drag the hanging indent marker to the desired location (Figure 2-22). The alignment guide displays where the carryover lines of the paragraph will align.

You can use the *Paragraph* dialog box to set either a first line or a hanging indent.

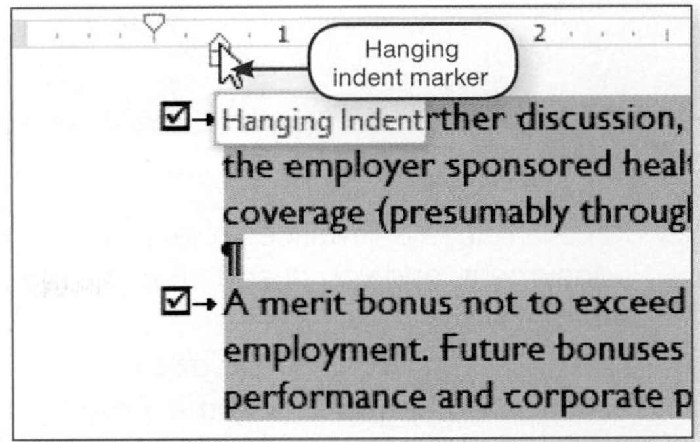

2-22 Set a hanging indent using the ruler

HOW TO: Set a First Line or a Hanging Indent Using the Paragraph Dialog Box

1. Select the text or paragraph you want to indent.
2. Click the **Paragraph** launcher [*Home* or *Page Layout* tab] to open the *Paragraph* dialog box.
3. Click the **Special** drop-down list in the *Indentation* area and choose the type of indent (Figure 2-23).
4. In the *By* area, either type the indent amount or use the up or down buttons to increase or decrease the amount of the indent.
   - The *Preview* area displays how the text will look with the indent applied.
5. Click **OK** to close the *Paragraph* dialog box.

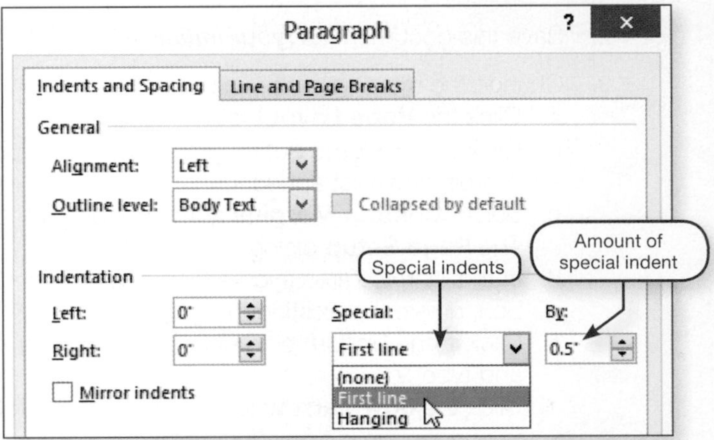

2-23 Set first line or hanging indent using the *Paragraph* dialog box

An ***outdent*** can be used to line up information outside the left or right margins. Outdents are sometimes used to set off section headings so they are slightly to the left of the left margin. You can do this by setting a ***negative value*** (–0.25") in the indents area in the *Paragraph* dialog box or *Paragraph* group on the *Page Layout* tab or by dragging the indent marker outside of the left or right margins.

Remove Indents

Removing indents moves the indent markers back to either the left or right margin, so the margins control the alignment of text rather than the indents. Remember to select the paragraph or paragraphs before removing the indents. You can remove indents using the *Paragraph* dialog box or the *Paragraph* group on the *Page Layout* tab. When using either of these methods, set the indents value to 0" (Figure 2-24).

The ruler can also be used to remove indents. When using this method, select the text or paragraphs on which to remove the indents, and drag the indent marker(s) to the margin.

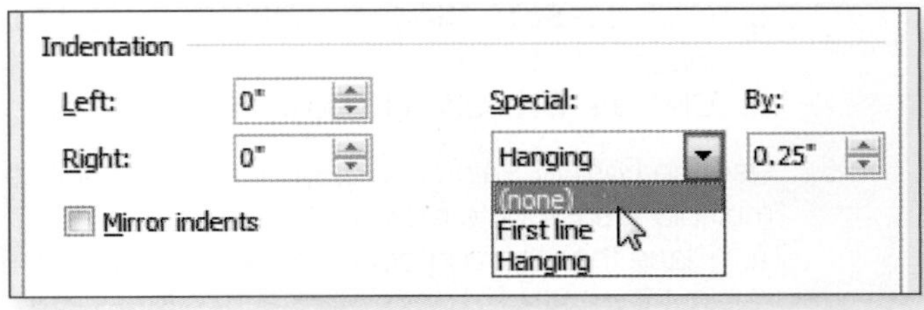

2-24 Remove indents using the *Paragraph* dialog box

PAUSE & PRACTICE: WORD 2-1

In this Pause & Practice project, you format a resume for Richelle Wilkinson. This resume is a two-page document, and you change the margins, set tab stops and leaders, and use indents.

File Needed: ***Resume-02.docx***
Completed Project File Name: ***[your initials] PP W2-1.docx***

1. Open the ***Resume-02*** document in your student data files.
2. Save this document as ***[your initials] PP W2-1.***
3. Change the margins of the resume.
   a. Click the **Page Layout** tab.
   b. Click the **Margins** button [*Page Setup* group]. A drop-down list appears.
   c. Select **Custom Margins** at the bottom of the list. The **Page Setup** dialog box opens.
   d. In the *Margins* area (Figure 2-25), click in the *Top* box, delete the existing margin, and type .75.
   e. Click in the *Bottom* box, delete the existing margin, and type .75.
   f. Click the **down arrow** to the right of the *Left* box to change the left margin to **1"**.
   g. Click the **down arrow** to the right of the *Right* box to change the right margin to **1"**.
   h. Click the **Apply to** drop-down list at the bottom of the dialog box and select **Whole document**.
   i. Click **OK** to apply the new margin settings and close the dialog box.

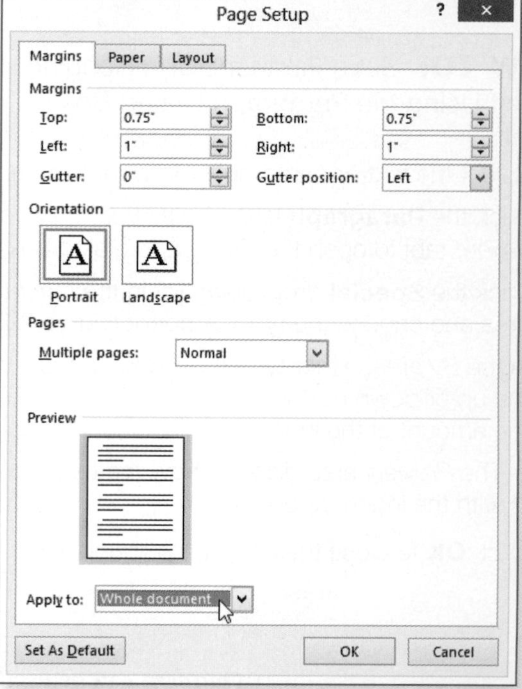

2-25 Change margins in the ***Page Setup*** dialog box

4. Set a right tab stop with a dash leader.
   a. Select **"Loomis, CA October 2011Present"** below *"Head Teacher, Loomis Learning Center."*
   b. Click the **Paragraph** launcher [*Page Layout* or *Home* tab]. The *Paragraph* dialog box opens.
   c. Click the **Tabs** button in the bottom left of the *Paragraph* dialog box. The *Tabs* dialog box opens (Figure 2-26).
   d. In the *Tab stop position* area, type 6.5.
   e. In the *Alignment* area, click the **Right** radio button.
   f. In the *Leader* area, click the **3** (dash leader) radio button.
   g. Click the **Set** button to set this tab stop and leader.
   h. Click the **OK** button to close the dialog box.
5. Use the *Format Painter* to apply the tab setting to multiple areas of the resume.
   a. Place the insertion point somewhere in the line you just formatted.
   b. Double-click the **Format Painter** button [*Home* tab, *Clipboard* group].

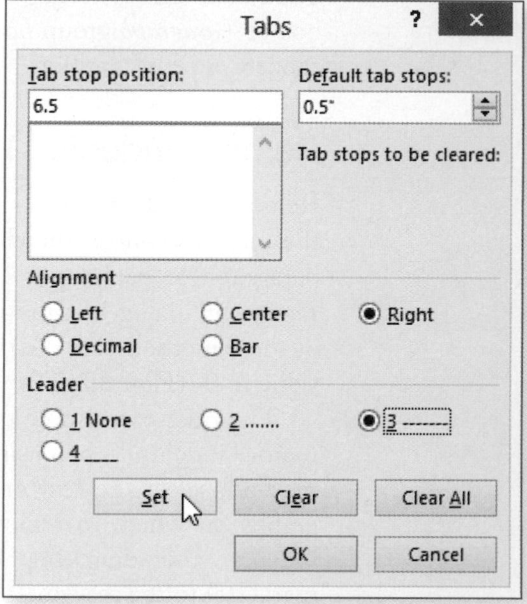

2-26 Set a right tab stop with a dash leader

c. Click each of the city/date lines in the "Experience" and "Education" sections to apply the tab settings to these lines as shown in Figure 2-27.
d. Click the **Format Painter** button to turn it off.

6. Remove an existing tab stop and set a left tab stop.
   a. On the second page, select the lines of text below the "References" heading.
   b. Click the **Paragraph** launcher [*Page Layout* or *Home* tab] to open the *Paragraph* dialog box.
   c. Click the **Tabs** button in the bottom left of the *Paragraph* dialog box. The *Tabs* dialog box opens (Figure 2-28).
   d. In the *Tab stop position* area, select the existing tab stop and click the **Clear** button to remove the existing tab.
   e. In the *Tab stop position* area, type 3.75.
   f. In the *Alignment* area, click the **Left** radio button.
   g. In the *Leader* area, click the **1 None** radio button.
   h. Click the **Set** button to set this left tab stop.
   i. Click the **OK** button to close the dialog box.

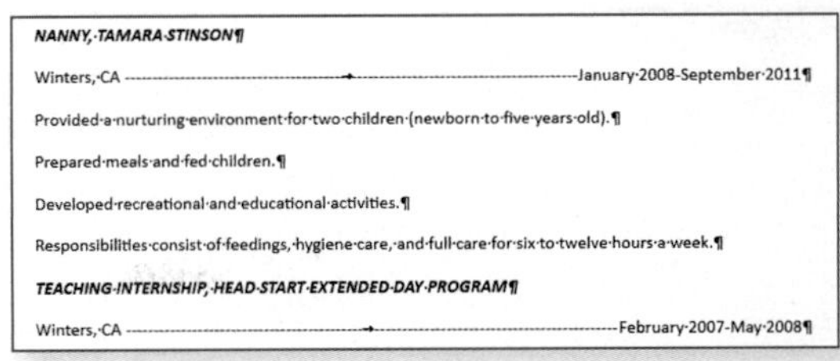

NANNY, TAMARA STINSON
Winters, CA ---------- January 2008-September 2011
Provided a nurturing environment for two children (newborn to five years old).
Prepared meals and fed children.
Developed recreational and educational activities.
Responsibilities consist of feedings, hygiene care, and full care for six to twelve hours a week.
TEACHING INTERNSHIP, HEAD START EXTENDED DAY PROGRAM
Winters, CA ---------- February 2007-May 2008

2-27 Use the *Format Painter* to apply tab settings

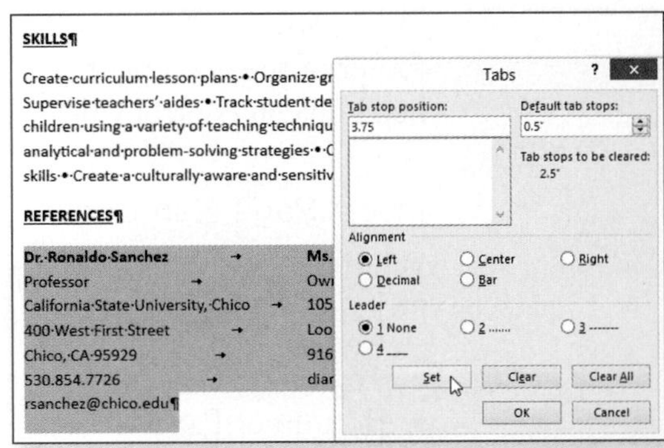

2-28 Set a left tab stop on selected text

7. Apply a left and right indent to selected text.
   a. Place the insertion point in the paragraph below the "Profile" heading on the first page.
   b. Click the **Page Layout** tab.
   c. Click in the **Left** indent area [*Paragraph* group], type .25, and press **Enter**.
   d. Click in the **Right** indent area, type .25, and press **Enter**.

8. Save and close this document (Figure 2-29).

Richelle Wilkinson
1788 Caraway Drive
Loomis, CA 95682
916.448.2068
richellew@gmail.com

PROFILE

My goal is to educate the next generation of children by using the skills I obtained through schooling and hands-on experience. Obtaining a position in early childhood education will allow me to teach and train preschool children in language development, motor skills, and social interaction.

EXPERIENCE

HEAD TEACHER, LOOMIS LEARNING CENTER
Loomis, CA ---------- October 2011-Present
Develop and implement a developmentally appropriate preschool program for children between the ages of two and four years.
Develop curriculum and activities for the students.
Educate the child as a whole focusing on language skills and social development.
Facilitate parent/teacher conferences and oversee teachers' aides.

NANNY, TAMARA STINSON
Winters, CA ---------- January 2008-September 2011
Provided a nurturing environment for two children (newborn to five years old).
Prepared meals and fed children.
Developed recreational and educational activities.
Responsibilities consist of feedings, hygiene care, and full care for six to twelve hours a week.

TEACHING INTERNSHIP, HEAD START EXTENDED DAY PROGRAM
Winters, CA ---------- February 2007-May 2008
Developed age-appropriate activities for preschool children.
Conducted meetings with parents.
Prepared and implemented curriculum at the preschool level.
Cared for children with special needs.

EDUCATION

CALIFORNIA STATE UNIVERSITY CHICO, BACHELOR OF ARTS IN CHILD DEVELOPMENT
Chico, CA ---------- September 2006-May 2009
Minor in Psychology
Child Development Honors Program
Dean's List: Spring 2006-Spring 2009
Supervised Practicum in CSU Chico Child Development Center

SKILLS

Create curriculum lesson plans • Organize group projects • Conduct parent teacher meetings • Supervise teachers' aides • Track student development through objective evaluations • Instruct children using a variety of teaching techniques including Montessori and Vygotsky • Incorporate analytical and problem-solving strategies • Communicate using effective verbal and listening skills • Create a culturally aware and sensitive environment

REFERENCES

Dr. Ronaldo Sanchez	Ms. Diana Samuels
Professor	Owner, Loomis Learning Center
California State University, Chico	105 McRosen Avenue
400 West First Street	Loomis, CA 95682
Chico, CA 95929	916.228.4557
530.854.7726	diana.samuels@loomislearning.com
rsanchez@chico.edu	

2-29 PP W2-1 completed

SLO 2.4

Inserting Page Numbers, Headers, and Footers

Page numbering, headers, and ***footers*** are regularly used in multiple-page documents. You can set the header and footer information to appear on each page of the document, which means you only have to type the information once, and Word repeats that information on each of the subsequent pages. The header area of a document is above the top margin, and the footer is below the bottom margin.

Page Numbering

When you use Word to insert page numbers, a ***page number field*** is inserted in the header or footer of the document. This page number field automatically displays the current page number. You can control where the page number is placed and the page number format.

Insert Page Number

Word gives you a variety of page number locations, horizontal alignment options, and number format options. The following is a list of the basic page number placement options.

- Top of Page
- Bottom of Page
- Page Margins
- Current Position

Page numbers at the top or bottom of the document can be aligned at the left, center, or right.

HOW TO: Insert a Page Number

1. Click the **Insert** tab.
2. Click the **Page Number** button [*Header & Footer* group]. A drop-down list of options appears (Figure 2-30).
3. Click either **Top of Page** or **Bottom of Page**. Another drop-down list of page number options appears.
   - The top three options in this list are simple page numbers aligned at the left, center, or right.
   - Further down this list there are custom page number options.
4. Click one of the page number options to insert the current page number. The header and footer open with the page number inserted, and the *Headers & Footer Tools Design* tab opens (Figure 2-31).
5. Click the **Close Header and Footer** button [*Close* group].

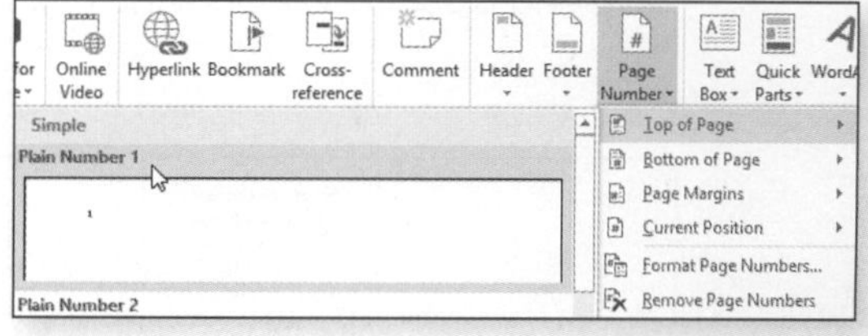

2-30 Insert page number

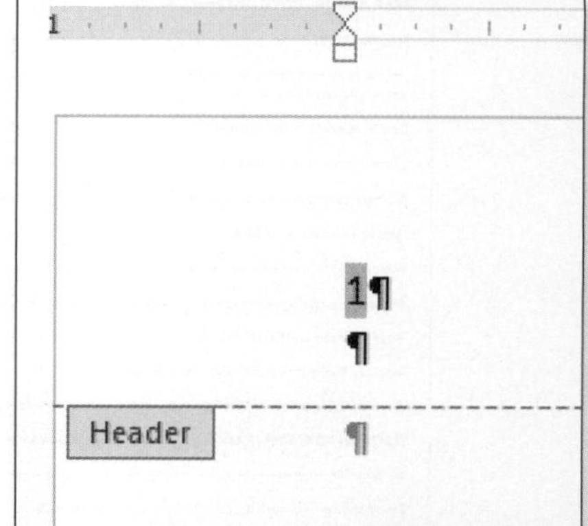

2-31 Page number inserted in the header on the left

ANOTHER WAY

Close the header and footer by **double-clicking** in the body of the document.

When you close the header and footer, the page number appears in gray rather than black like the text of the document. The header and footer are outside the boundaries of the margins. If you want to edit the page number or contents of the header and footer, you have to open the header and footer. There are three ways to do this.

- Double-click in the header or footer area of the document.
- Click the **Insert** tab, click the **Header** or **Footer** button in the *Header & Footer* group, and choose **Edit Header** or **Edit Footer**.
- Right-click the header or footer and select **Edit Header** or **Edit Footer**.

Different First Page

There are times when you might not want the page number and header or footer to print on the first page, but you want it to appear on the second and continuing pages. For example on both multiple-page business letters and reports, the page number is typically not on the first page but is on the second and subsequent pages. Word gives you the option to set a ***different first page.***

HOW TO: Set a Different First Page Header and Footer

1. After inserting a page number in the header or footer, open the header and footer if it is not already open.
2. Click the **Different First Page** check box [*Options* group] (Figure 2-32).
3. Click the **Close Header and Footer** button [*Close* group]. The page number, header, and footer no longer appear on the first page but do appear on the second and continuing pages.

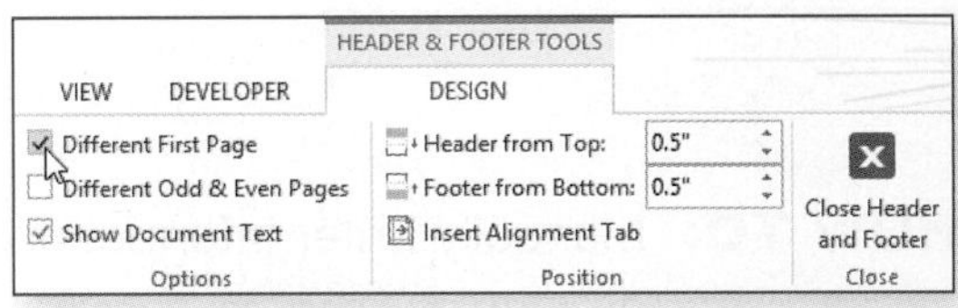

2-32 *Different First Page* option check box

> **MORE INFO**
>
> When inserting a page number, header, or footer, it is best to insert it on the first page of the document. This becomes increasingly important as you add section breaks to a document.

Page Number Format

When using page numbering, you might want a different type of page number format, numbering to begin with a different page number, or a chapter number before the page number. The *Page Number Format* dialog box provides you with page numbering options (Figure 2-33).

HOW TO: Format Page Numbers

1. After inserting a page number, click the **Page Number** button [*Insert* tab, *Header & Footer* group].
2. From the drop-down list, select **Format Page Numbers**. The *Page Number Format* dialog box opens (Figure 2-33).
3. In the *Number format* area, click the **drop-down list** and select a page number format. There are six preset page numbering options from which to choose.
4. In the *Page numbering* section, you have the option to *Continue from previous section* (default setting) or *Start at* a different page number.
5. Click the **Start at** radio button to set a different starting page number.
6. Type in the starting page number or use the up or down arrow to set the starting page number.
7. Click **OK** to close the *Page Number Format* dialog box.

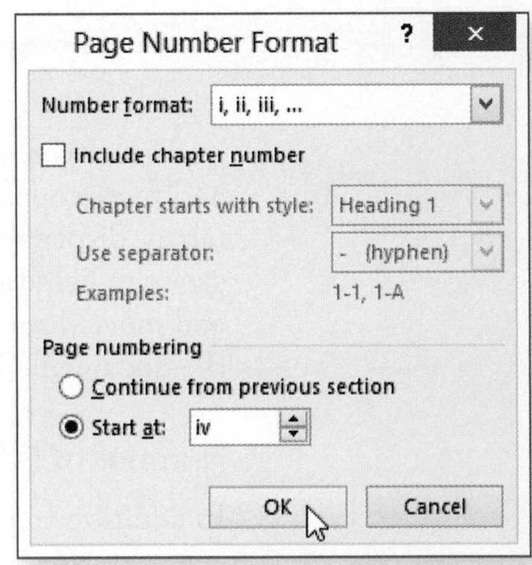

2-33 Page numbering options

Remove Page Number

If you want to remove the page numbering from a document, there are two different ways to do this.

- Open the header and footer and manually delete the page number.
- Select **Remove Page Numbers** from the *Page Numbers* drop-down list (Figure 2-34).

2-34 Remove page numbers

Insert Header and Footer Content

In addition to inserting page numbers into the header or footer of a document, you might want to include the number of pages in the document, date or time, title of the document, or company name. You can enter information manually into the header or footer, or you can have Word insert document property fields.

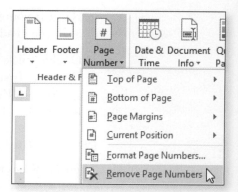

HOW TO: Manually Enter Information in the Header or Footer

1. Click the **Insert** tab.
2. Click the **Header** button and choose **Edit Header** in the drop-down list, or double-click in the *Header* area of the document (above the top margin). The header of the document opens and the *Header & Footer Tools Design* tab is displayed.
3. In the *Header* area, type in your information (Figure 2-35).
   - You can change the formatting and alignment as desired.
   - You can insert a page number with the header or footer open.
4. Close the header.

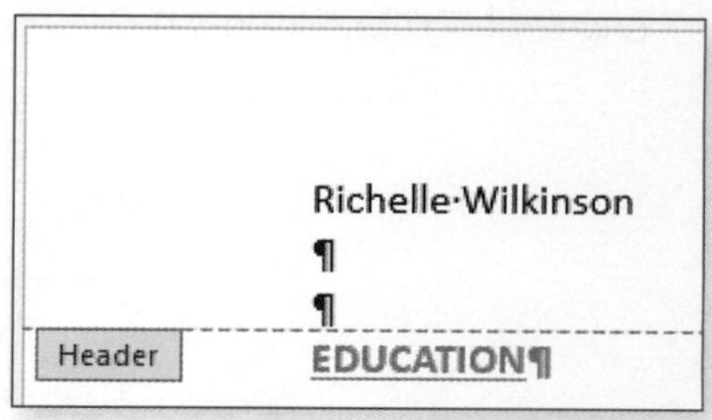

2-35 Manually enter information in the header

MORE INFO

In the header and footer, there is a center tab stop at the horizontal midpoint and a right tab stop at the right margin. You can move these tab stops, remove them, or add additional tab stops.

When you edit a header or footer, both the header and footer open and the *Header & Footer Tools Design* tab is displayed. On this tab, there is a *Navigation* group to help you move between the header and footer and move through the different headers and footers in the document (Figure 2-36).

2-36 *Navigation* group in the *Header & Footer Tools Design* tab

Number of Pages Field

In addition to inserting the current page number in a document, you can add a field code to automatically insert the total number of pages in a document (*NumPages* field).

HOW TO: Insert the Number of Pages Field

1. Open the header or footer. The page number should already be inserted in the document.
2. Click before the page number, type Page, and press **spacebar**.
3. Click after the page number and press **spacebar**, type of, and press **spacebar**.
4. Click the **Quick Parts** button [*Header & Footer Tools Design* tab, *Insert* group] (Figure 2-37).
5. Select **Field** from the drop-down list. The *Field* dialog box opens (Figure 2-38).
6. In the *Field names* area, scroll down and select **NumPages**. The description of the field is displayed in the *Description* area.
7. In the *Format* area, click **1, 2, 3**. This is the format of the page number.
8. Click **OK** to close the *Field* dialog box. The number of pages in the document is inserted (Figure 2-39).
9. Close the header or footer.

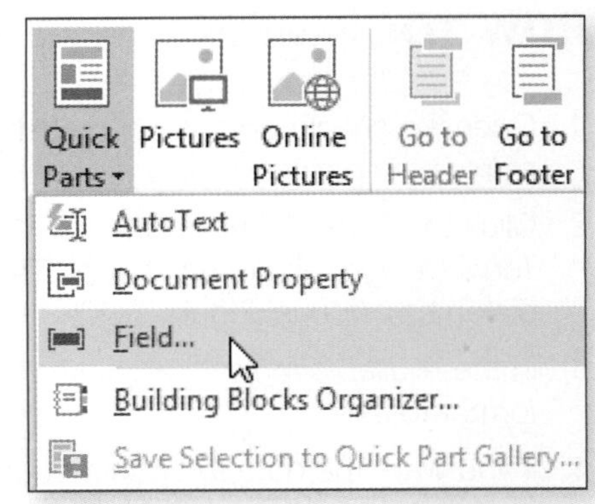

2-37 Insert field code

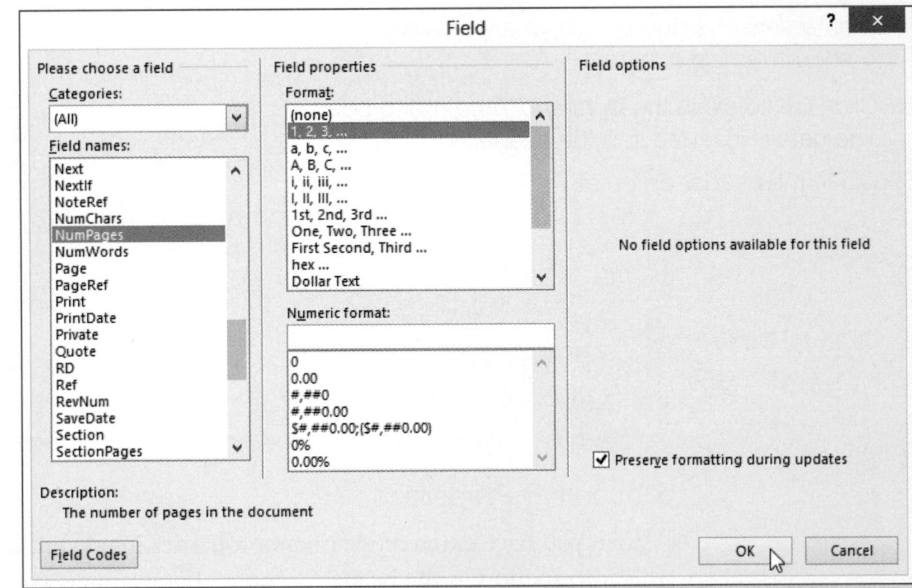

2-38 Insert *NumPages* field from the *Field* dialog box

MORE INFO

When inserting text before or after a page number, be sure to include a space between the word and the page number. Word does not automatically do this for you.

2-39 Page number and number of pages fields inserted into the header

Date and Time

You can type a date or the time in the header or footer of a document, or you can have Word insert this information. The advantages of inserting the date and time are that you have a variety of date and time formats from which to choose, and you can choose to have the date and time update automatically.

HOW TO: Insert the Date and Time

1. Open the header or footer and position the insertion point at the position where you want the date inserted.
2. Click the **Date & Time** button [*Header & Footer Tools Design* tab, *Insert* group]. The *Date and Time* dialog box opens (Figure 2-40).
3. In the *Available formats* area, select the date or time format to use
4. If you want the date to update automatically, check the **Update automatically** check box.
   - Don't use the *Update automatically* on time-sensitive documents where the date should remain constant.
5. Click **OK** to close the *Date and Time* dialog box. The date is inserted into the header.
6. Close the header or footer.

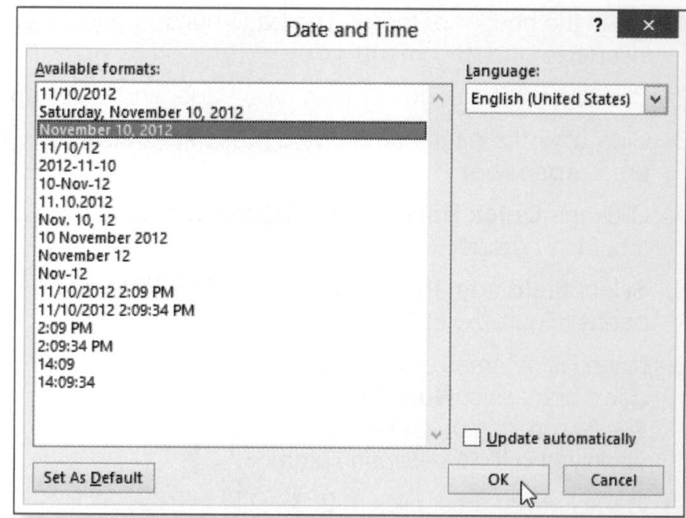

2-40 *Date and Time* dialog box

> **MORE INFO**
>
> Inserting a date or time is not limited to headers and footers. You can insert the date or time in the body of a document by clicking **Date & Time** [*Insert* tab, *Text* group].

Document Properties

When you have entered document properties in a Word document, you can automatically insert this information in the header or footer. For example, you might want to include the title of the document, name of the author, or date last modified. One of the advantages of inserting document properties rather than typing this information is that when you update the document properties, these fields are automatically updated in the header or footer and throughout the document.

HOW TO: Insert Document Properties

1. Open the header or footer and place the insertion point at the location where you want the document property inserted.
2. Click the **Document Info** button [*Header & Footer Tools Design* tab, *Insert* group] (Figure 2-41).
3. Select the document property field or click **Document Property** and select the document property field of your choice from the drop-down list. The document property field is inserted in the document.
   - You can also click the **Quick Parts** button [*Header & Footer Tools Design* tab, *Insert* group] and select **Document Property**.
4. Close the header or footer.

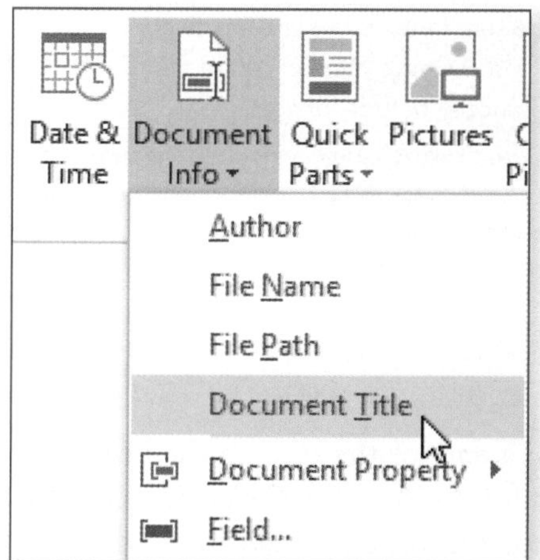

2-41 Insert document property field

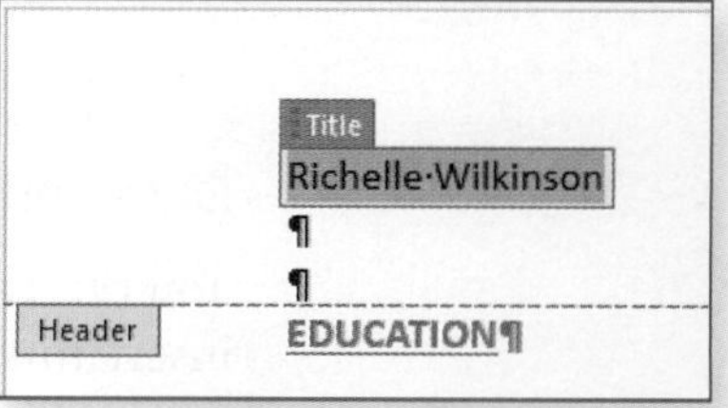

2-42 *Title* document property field inserted in the header

> **MORE INFO**
>
> Inserting document properties is not limited to headers and footers. Click the **Quick Parts** button [*Insert* tab, *Text* group] to insert this information in the body of a document.
>
> Press the **right arrow** key to deselect a field code.

Built-In Headers, Footers, and Page Numbers

In addition to inserting basic page numbers, manually adding header or footer content, and inserting date and time, Word provides you with a variety of built-in custom header, footer, and page number format options. Many of the header and footer options include document properties that are automatically inserted and updated.

HOW TO: Insert a Built-In Header

1. Click the **Insert** tab.
2. Click the **Header** button [*Header & Footer* group] and select a built-in header from the choices in the drop-down list. (Figure 2-43) The selected header is inserted into the document.
   - Document property fields are automatically updated with the document information.
   - Some fields, such as *Pick the date,* require you to input or select information.
3. Close the header.

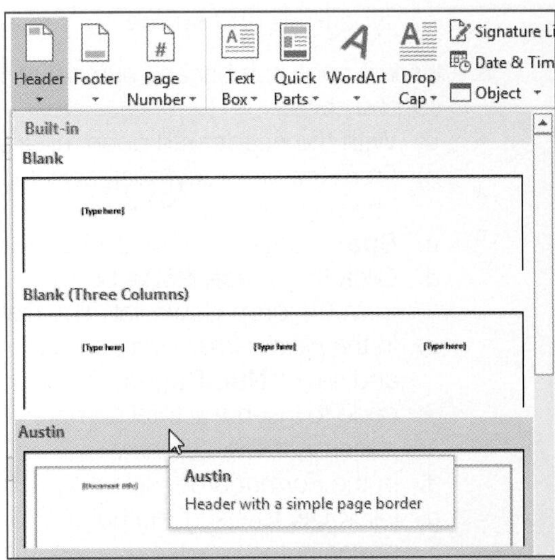

2-43 List of built-in headers

Keep in mind when you are using built-in headers, footers, and page numbers that many of these use tables, graphics, and advanced formatting, which makes editing more challenging without a thorough understanding of this type of content.

PAUSE & PRACTICE: WORD 2-2

In this Pause & Practice project, you modify the resume from *Pause & Practice 2-1*. You add a header that appears only on the second page of this document and insert a document property field, page number, and Word field into the header.

File Needed: ***[your initials] PP W2-1.docx***
Completed Project File Name: ***[your initials] PP W2-2.docx***

1. Open the ***[your initials] PP W2-1*** document created in *Pause & Practice 2-1*.
2. Save this document as ***[your initials] PP W2-2***.

3. Edit the document properties.
   a. Click the **File** tab to open the *Backstage* view.
   b. In the *Info* area, click in the *Title* document property text box and type Richelle Wilkinson.
   c. Click the **Back** arrow to return to the resume.
4. Insert a document property field in the header of the resume.
   a. Place the insertion point at the beginning of the first page.
   b. Click the **Insert** tab.
   c. Click the **Header** button [*Header & Footer* group], and select **Edit Header** from the drop-down list. The header on the first page opens.
   d. Click the **Quick Parts** button [*Header & Footer Tools Design* tab, *Insert* group], select **Document Property**, and select **Title** from the drop-down list.
   e. Press the **right arrow** key once to deselect the document property field you just inserted.
   f. Press **Tab** two times to move to the right margin.
   g. Type Page and **space** once. Leave the header open.
5. Insert a page number and number of pages field to the header and make it display only on the second page.
   a. With the header still open, click the **Page Number** button [*Header & Footer* group].
   b. From the drop-down list, select **Current Position**, and then select **Plain Number**. The page number is inserted.
   c. **Space** once, type of, and **space** once.
   d. Click the **Quick Parts** button [*Header & Footer Tools Design* tab, *Insert* group] and select **Field** from the drop-down list. The *Field* dialog box opens (Figure 2-44).
   e. In the *Field names* area, scroll down and select **NumPages**. This is a field code to insert the total number of pages in the document.
   f. In the *Format* area, select **1**, **2**, **3**.
   g. Click **OK** to insert the number of pages in the header.
   h. Press **Enter** two times to insert two blank lines after the header.
   i. Check to ensure that there are spaces between each of the words and page numbers.
   j. Check the **Different First Page** check box [*Options* group]. This removes the page number from the first page; the page number is still displayed on the second and subsequent pages (Figure 2-45).

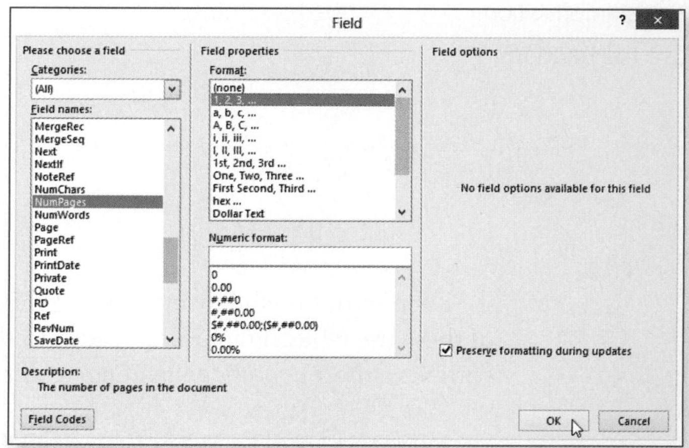

2-44 Insert *NumPages* field

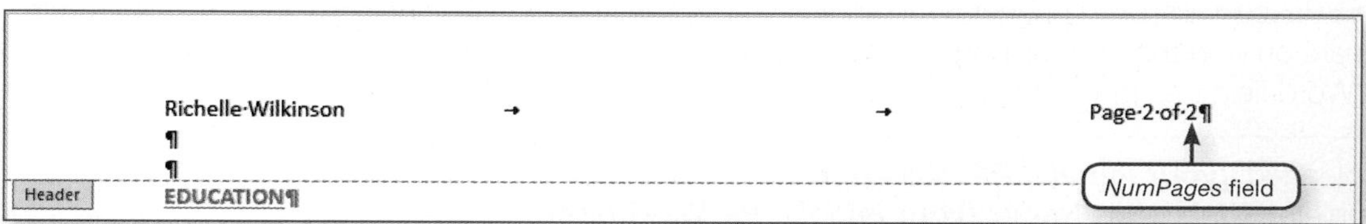

2-45 Header with custom text, page number, and number of pages

   k. Click the **Close Header and Footer** button [*Close* group] to close the header and return to the document.

6. Save and close the document (Figure 2-46).

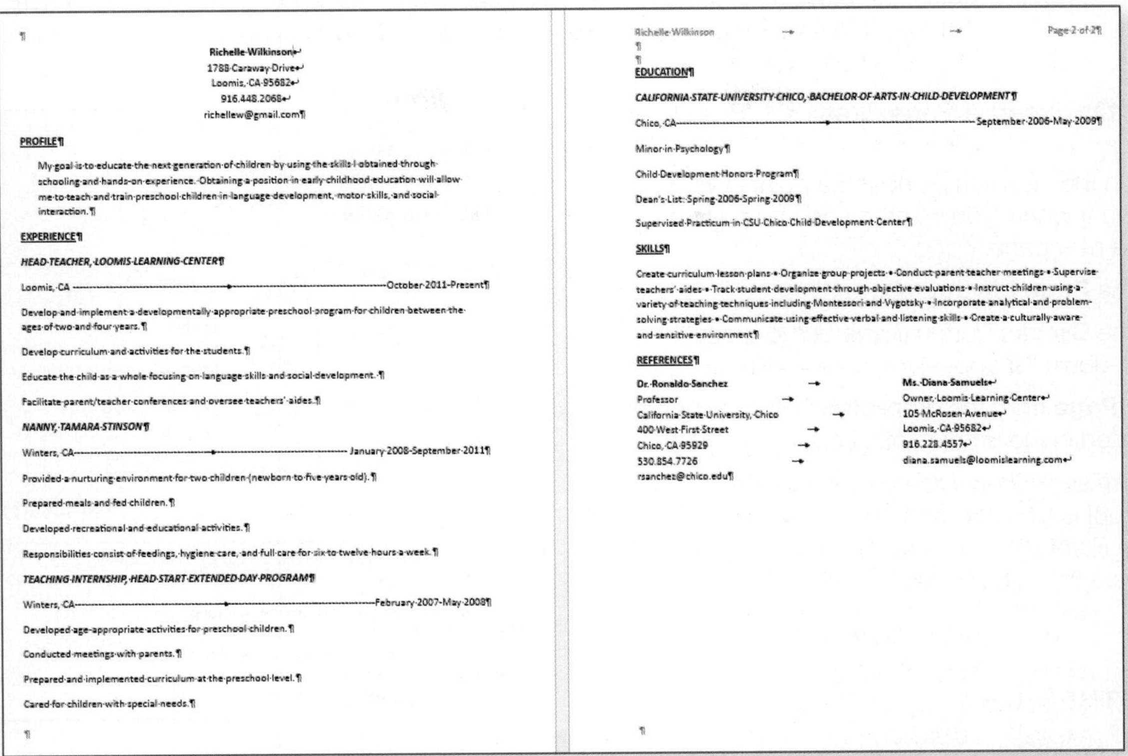

Richelle Wilkinson
1788 Caraway Drive
Loomis, CA 95682
916.448.2068
richellew@gmail.com

PROFILE

My goal is to educate the next generation of children by using the skills I obtained through schooling and hands-on experience. Obtaining a position in early childhood education will allow me to teach and train preschool children in language development, motor skills, and social interaction.

EXPERIENCE

HEAD TEACHER, LOOMIS LEARNING CENTER

Loomis, CA ---------- October 2011-Present

Develop and implement a developmentally appropriate preschool program for children between the ages of two and four years.

Develop curriculum and activities for the students.

Educate the child as a whole focusing on language skills and social development.

Facilitate parent/teacher conferences and oversee teachers' aides.

NANNY, TAMARA STINSON

Winters, CA ---------- January 2008-September 2011

Provided a nurturing environment for two children (newborn to five years old).

Prepared meals and fed children.

Developed recreational and educational activities.

Responsibilities consist of feedings, hygiene care, and full care for six to twelve hours a week.

TEACHING INTERNSHIP, HEAD START EXTENDED DAY PROGRAM

Winters, CA ---------- February 2007-May 2008

Developed age-appropriate activities for preschool children.

Conducted meetings with parents.

Prepared and implemented curriculum at the preschool level.

Cared for children with special needs.

Richelle Wilkinson Page 2 of 2

EDUCATION

CALIFORNIA STATE UNIVERSITY CHICO, BACHELOR OF ARTS IN CHILD DEVELOPMENT

Chico, CA ---------- September 2006-May 2009

Minor in Psychology

Child Development Honors Program

Dean's List: Spring 2006-Spring 2009

Supervised Practicum in CSU Chico Child Development Center

SKILLS

Create curriculum lesson plans • Organize group projects • Conduct parent teacher meetings • Supervise teachers' aides • Track student development through objective evaluations • Instruct children using a variety of teaching techniques including Montessori and Vygotsky • Incorporate analytical and problem-solving strategies • Communicate using effective verbal and listening skills • Create a culturally aware and sensitive environment

REFERENCES

Dr. Ronaldo Sanchez	Ms. Diana Samuels
Professor	Owner, Loomis Learning Center
California State University, Chico	105 McRosen Avenue
400 West First Street	Loomis, CA 95682
Chico, CA 95929	916.228.4557
530.854.7726	diana.samuels@loomislearning.com
rsanchez@chico.edu	

2-46 PP W2-2 completed

SLO 2.5

Using Page and Section Breaks

As you're typing a document and you get to the bottom of the page, Word automatically moves to the top of the next page so you can continue typing; this is referred to as a ***soft page break.*** The document's content and margins determine how much information fits on a page and what information flows to a new page.

There may be times when you want to start a new page before you get to the bottom margin or you might want different margins or page orientation in a different section of your document. When this happens, Word provides options for page and section breaks (Figure 2-47).

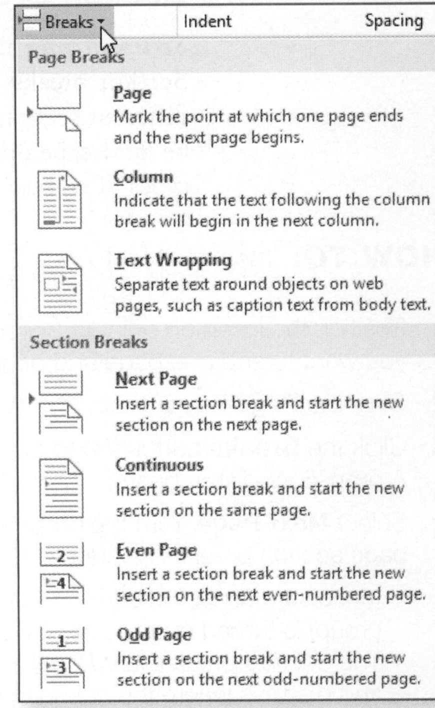

Breaks
Indent
Spacing
Page Breaks
Page
Mark the point at which one page ends and the next page begins.
Column
Indicate that the text following the column break will begin in the next column.
Text Wrapping
Separate text around objects on web pages, such as caption text from body text.
Section Breaks
Next Page
Insert a section break and start the new section on the next page.
Continuous
Insert a section break and start the new section on the same page.
Even Page
Insert a section break and start the new section on the next even-numbered page.
Odd Page
Insert a section break and start the new section on the next odd-numbered page.

2-47 Page and section breaks

MORE INFO

Turn **Show/Hide** [*Home* tab, *Paragraph* group] on when working with page and section breaks, so you can view the placement of these breaks.

Page Breaks

Page breaks end one page and begin a new page. When you insert page breaks, you, rather than the margins, control where one page ends and a new page begins. There are three different types of page breaks: *Page*, *Column*, and *Text Wrapping*.

HOW TO: Insert a Page Break

1. Position the insertion point at the point in your document where you want to end one page and begin a new page.
2. Click the **Page Layout** tab.
3. Click the **Breaks** button [*Page Setup* group]. A drop-down list appears (Figure 2-48).
4. Select **Page** from the drop-down list. A page break is inserted in the document.
   - Make sure *Show/Hide* [*Home* tab, *Paragraph* group] is turned on.
   - The *Page Break* indicator is visible and displays where the page breaks (Figure 2-49).

INSERT DESIGN PAGE LAYOUT REFERENCES MAILI
Size Columns Breaks Indent Spacing
Page Setup
Page Breaks
Page
Mark the point at which one page ends and the next page begins.
Column
Indicate that the text following the column break will begin in the next column.
Text Wrapping
Separate text around objects on web pages, such as caption text from body text.

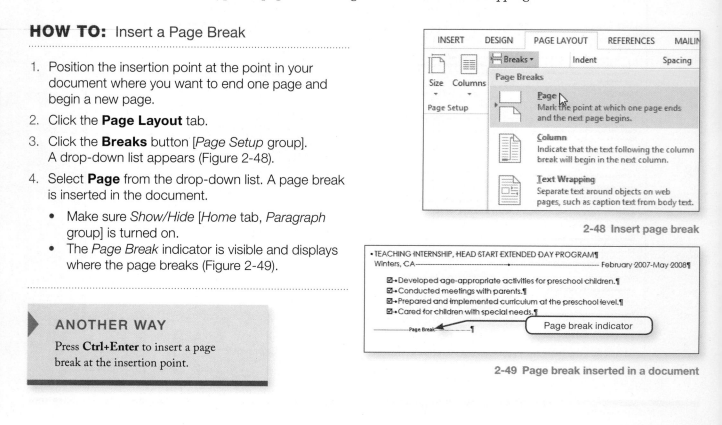

2-48 Insert page break

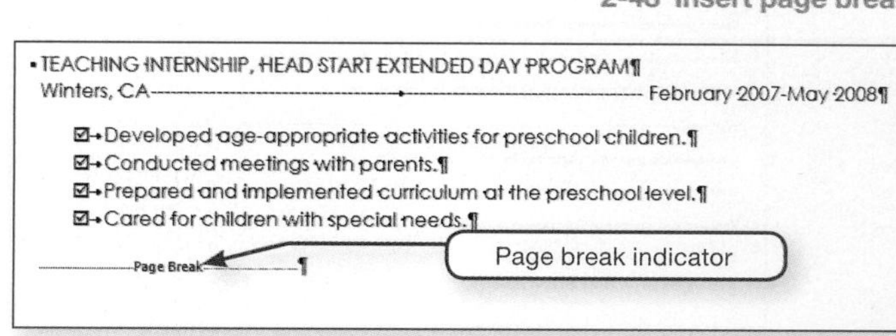

2-49 Page break inserted in a document

ANOTHER WAY

Press **Ctrl+Enter** to insert a page break at the insertion point.

Section Breaks

Section breaks allow you even more formatting control over your document than page breaks. Section breaks can be used to format different headers, footers, and page numbering in different sections of your document. For example, if you want one page in your document to be landscape orientation, you can use a section break to control this. There are four different types of section breaks: *Next Page*, *Continuous*, *Even Page*, and *Odd Page*.

HOW TO: Insert a Next Page Section Break

1. Position the insertion point at the point in your document where you want to end one page and begin a new page.
2. Click the **Page Layout** tab.
3. Click the **Breaks** button [*Page Setup* group]. A drop-down list appears.
4. Select **Next Page** from the drop-down list. A next page section break is inserted in the document.
   - Make sure *Show/Hide* [*Home* tab, *Paragraph* group] is turned on.
   - The *Section Break (Next Page)* indicator is visible and displays where the next page section break occurs (Figure 2-50).

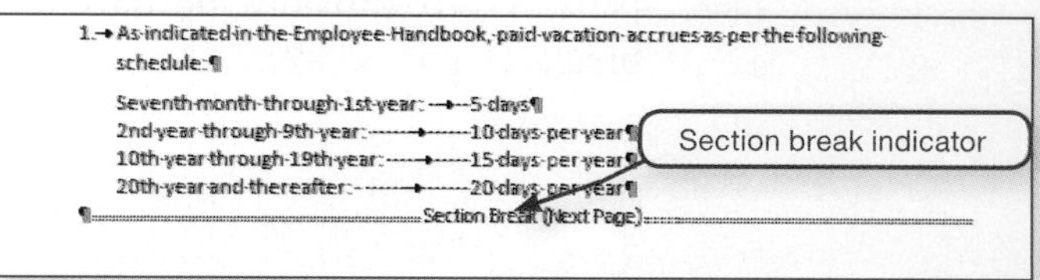

2-50 *Next Page* section break inserted in a document

Edit Page and Section Breaks

When finalizing a document, you might need to change the placement of a page or section break or remove one or more of these from the document. You can move and delete breaks in the same way you move or delete text from a document.

There are two different ways to move a section or page break to a new location. First select the **Page Break** or **Section Break**, and then use one of the move options below.

- Cut and paste
- Drag and drop (Figure 2-51)

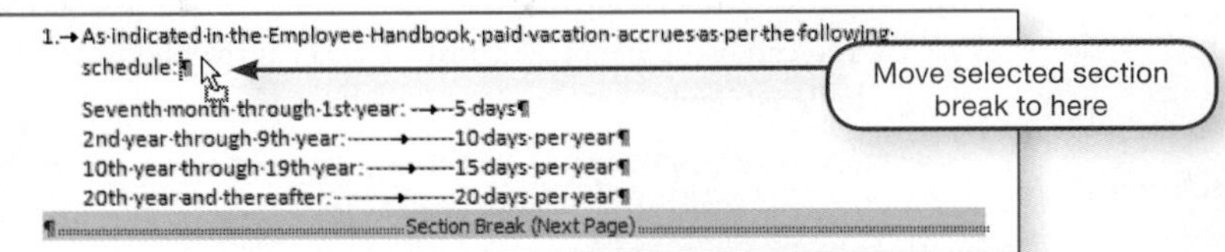

2.51 Move section break using drag and drop

To delete a page or section break, select the break and press **Delete**.

SLO 2.6

Using Bulleted and Numbered Lists

Bulleted and ***numbered lists*** highlight important information. Generally, bulleted lists are used when the order of information is not important, while numbered lists are used for sequential information. Word provides you with automatic bulleted and numbered lists, but you can also customize how your list information is displayed and aligned.

> **MORE INFO**
>
> When using bulleted and numbered lists, do not use a period at the end of lists containing only words or short phrases. If you are using complete sentences in your list, use a period at the end of each sentence.

Create Bulleted Lists

You can create a bulleted list from existing text or you can create a new bulleted list. When you turn on bullets, you choose the type of bullet to use from a library of bullet options.

HOW TO: Create a Bulleted List

1. Select the text to be converted to a bulleted list, or, if you are beginning a new bulleted list, place the insertion point at the location where you want to begin the list.
2. Click the **Home** tab.
3. Click the **Bullets** drop-down arrow [*Paragraph* group] to open the library of bullet options (Figure 2-52).
   - If you click the *Bullets* button, the most recently used bullet will be applied.
4. Select the bullet to be used from the list of options.
5. Type your information after the bullet.
6. Press **Enter** to add another bullet.
7. Click the **Bullet** button to turn off bullets or press **Enter** two times after the last bullet.

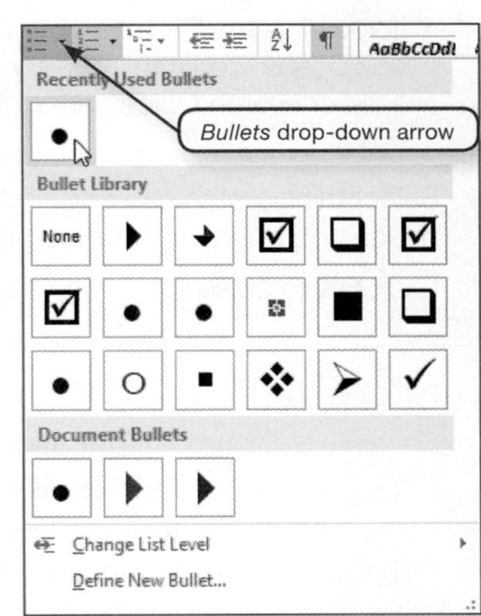

2-52 *Bullets* drop-down list

By default, bulleted lists are formatted using a hanging indent. The first line is indented 0.25" and the hanging indent is set at 0.5". You can adjust the indent using the *Decrease Indent* or *Increase Indent* buttons, ruler, or *Paragraph* dialog box.

You can add new bulleted items in the middle or at the end of the list by pressing **Enter** in front of or at the end of an existing bulleted item. To add a bulleted item before the first item in the list, click at the beginning of the first item and press **Enter**.

> **MORE INFO**
>
> You can use a line break (**Shift+Enter**) at the end of a bulleted sentence to add a blank line between bulleted items.

Customize Bullets

In addition to using the bullets listed in the bullets library, you can select and use a custom bullet. You have the option of using a symbol from one of the font groups or you can use a picture. If you are using a picture, you can select one from the picture library or import a graphic of your own to use as a bullet.

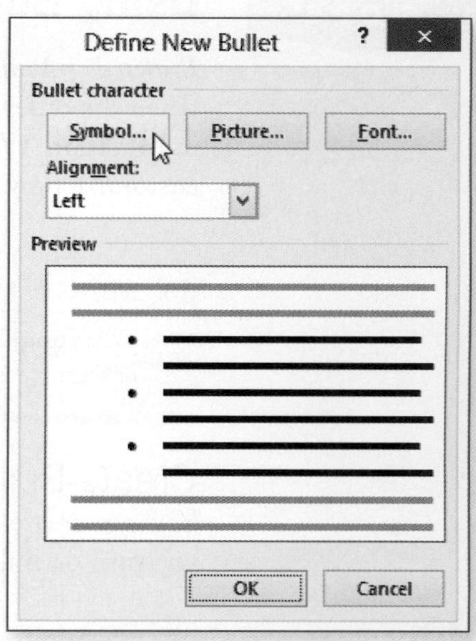

2-53 ***Define New Bullet*** **dialog box**

HOW TO: Use Custom Bullets

1. Click the **Bullets** drop-down arrow [*Home* tab, *Paragraph* group] and select **Define New Bullet**. The *Define New Bullet* dialog box opens (Figure 2-53).
2. Click the **Symbol** or **Picture** button to open the *Symbol* or *Picture Bullet* dialog box.
   - If you click the **Symbol** button, the *Symbol* dialog box opens (Figure 2-54). You can select a symbol from any of the font sets (the most common are *Symbol, Wingdings,* and *Webdings*) or from *Recently used symbols*.
   - If you click the **Picture** button, the *Insert Pictures* dialog box opens. You can import your own picture bullet from a file or search Office.com or Bing for a picture to use as a bullet.
3. Select the bullet to use and click **OK** (or **Insert** or **Open** depending on the open dialog box) to close the dialog box.
4. Click **OK** to close the *Define New Bullet* dialog box.

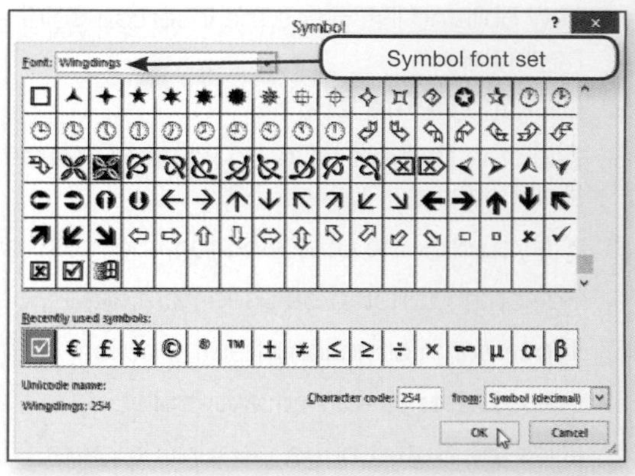

2-54 ***Symbol*** **dialog box**

You also have the option of having multiple levels of bullets with a different bullet for each level. Each subsequent level of bullet is indented to distinguish it from the previous level. There are a few ways to increase or decrease the bullet level.

- Click the **Bullets** drop-down arrow [*Home* tab, *Paragraph* group], and select a bullet list level from the **Change List Level** drop-down list (Figure 2-55).
- Select or click at the beginning of a bulleted item, and press **Tab** to increase bullet level.
- Select or click at the beginning of a bulleted item and click the **Increase Indent** button [*Home* tab, *Paragraph* group] to increase bullet level.

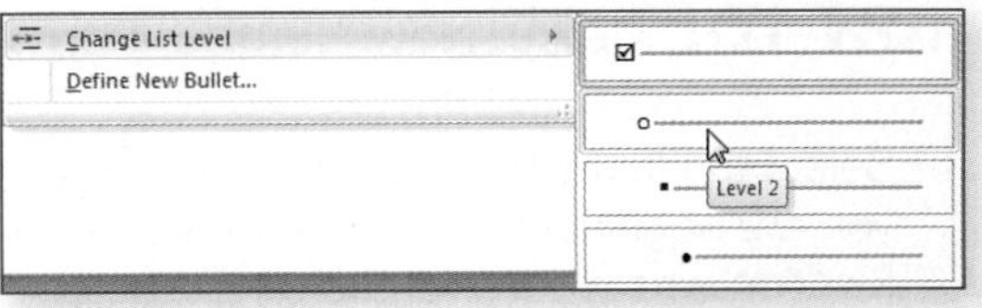

2-55 Change bulleted list level

> **MORE INFO**
>
> **Shift+Tab** or **Decrease Indent** decreases the bullet level.

Create Numbered Lists

Creating a numbered list is similar to creating a bulleted list. There is a ***Numbering Library*** that contains number format options.

HOW TO: Create a Numbered List

1. Select the text you want to convert to a numbered list, or, if you are beginning a new numbered list, place the insertion point at the location where you want to begin the list.
2. Click the **Home** tab.
3. Click the **Numbering** drop-down arrow [*Paragraph* group] to open the *Numbering Library* of number format options (Figure 2-56).
   - If you click the *Numbering* button, the most recently used number format is applied.
4. Select the number format to be used from the list of options. The number format is applied to selected text.

2-56 Number format options

> **ANOTHER WAY**
>
> Both the *Numbering* and *Bullets* drop-down lists are available from the context menu.

Customize Numbering

In addition to being able to select a format from the *Numbering Library*, you also have the options to *Change List Level*, *Define New Number Format*, and *Set Numbering Value*.

The *Change List Level* option in the *Numbering* drop-down list allows you to select the level of the list. The numbering of each subsequent level of the list is dependent upon the number format you select.

You are not limited to the numbering formats available in the *Numbering* drop-down list. The *Define New Number Format* option allows you to customize how the numbered list is displayed.

HOW TO: Define New Number Format

1. Select the text where you want to change the number format, or, if you are beginning a new numbered list, place the insertion point at the location where you want to begin the list.
2. Click the **Numbering** drop-down arrow [*Home* tab, *Paragraph* group], and select **Define New Number Format**. The *Define New Number Format* dialog box opens (Figure 2-57).
3. In the *Number style* area, you can select from a list of number format options. You can also change the font of the numbering.
4. In the *Number format* area, you can customize how the numbers are displayed. Typically, a period follows the numbers, but you can change this to an ending parenthesis, hyphen, other character, or nothing.
5. Numbers are aligned at the left by default, but you can change the number alignment to center or right in the *Alignment* area.
6. The *Preview* area displays how your number format will appear in your document.
7. Click **OK** to apply the number format and close the dialog box.

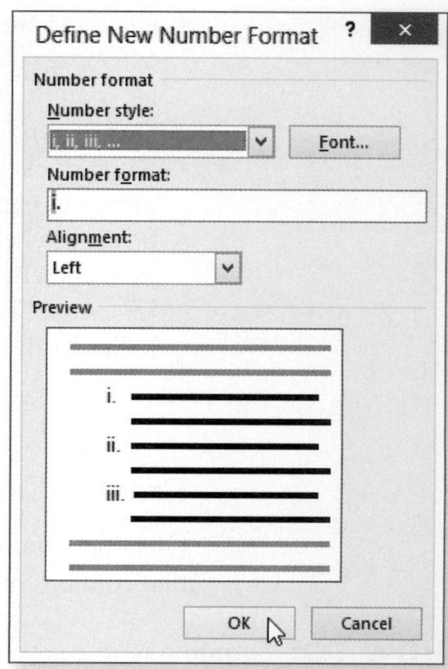

2-57 *Define New Number Format* dialog box

The *Set Numbering Value* option allows you to *Start new list* or *Continue from previous list*. You can also set the number value to begin a new list. The *Set Numbering Value* dialog box can be opened from the *Numbering* drop-down list or from the context menu (Figure 2-58).

When using numbering, the context menu gives you the options to *Adjust List Indents*, *Restart at 1*, *Continue Numbering*, and *Set Numbering Value* (Figure 2-59).

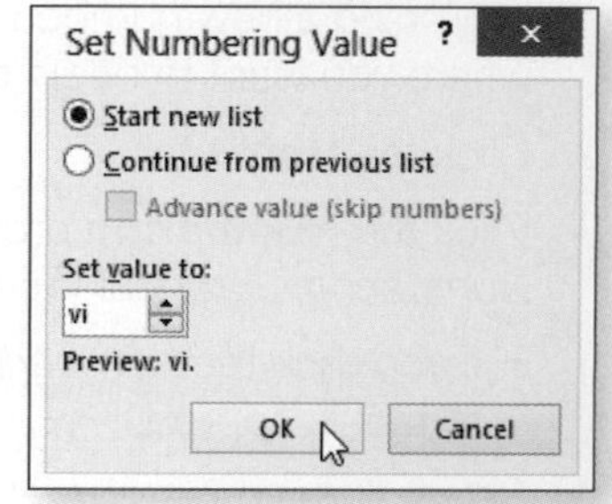

2-58 *Set Numbering Value* dialog box

> **MORE INFO**
>
> Use the *Format Painter* to copy numbered or bulleted list formatting to other areas in a document.

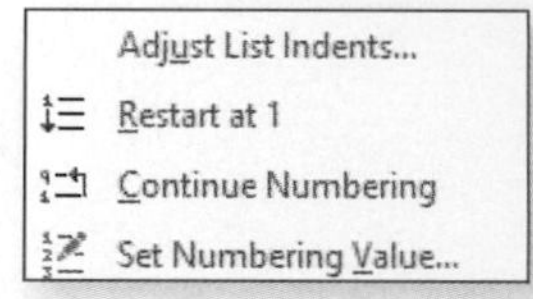

2-59 Context menu numbering options

Multilevel Lists

Multilevel lists allow you to customize a list using a combination of numbers, letters, or bullets. Word provides you with a *List Library* from which to select a multilevel list. You can customize an existing multilevel list or you can define your own.

As you define a new multilevel list, you have the option to make the following customizations on each level of the list.

- Number format including font and starting number
- Number style, which can be a number, letter, Roman numeral, or bullet
- Position of the number and the text that follows

HOW TO: Define a New Multilevel List

1. Select the text or the beginning point on which to apply a multilevel list.
2. Click the **Multilevel List** button [*Home* tab, *Paragraph* group].

3. From the drop-down list, select **Define new Multilevel list**. The *Define new Multilevel list* dialog box opens (Figure 2-60).
4. Click the **More** button at the bottom left of the dialog box to display all formatting options.
5. In the *Click level to modify* area, select the level you want to modify.
6. In the *Number format* area, select the number format, starting number, and number style for the selected level.
7. In the *Position* area, set the number alignment, the position at which the number is aligned, and the position of the text indent (which is a hanging indent).
8. The **Set for All Levels** button opens a dialog box that allows you to set the indents for all levels.
9. Click **OK** to apply the multilevel list settings.

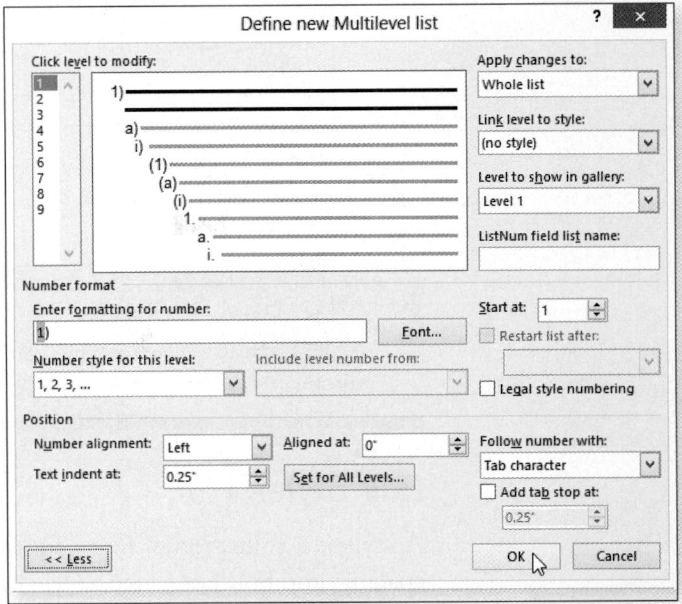

2-60 ***Define New Multilevel List*** **dialog box**

SLO 2.7

Using Styles and Themes

Styles are a collection of preset formatting that you can apply to selected text. You can use styles to apply preset formatting to titles, section headings, paragraph headings, text, lists, and tables. ***Themes*** are a collection of fonts, colors, and effects that you can apply to an entire document. Both styles and themes keep the formatting consistent throughout a single document or multiple documents.

Style Gallery

The ***Style gallery*** in the *Styles* group on the *Home* tab provides you with numerous built-in styles to apply to selected text in a document (Figure 2-61). The *Style* gallery does not display all of the available styles but rather a list of the more commonly used styles.

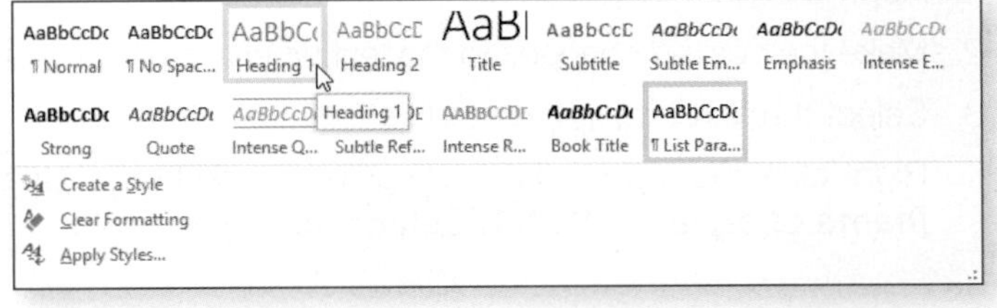

2-61 ***Style*** **gallery**

Apply Built-In Styles

You can quickly preview or apply styles to selected text or paragraphs. To preview a style, put the pointer on a style in the *Style* gallery. A live preview of the style is displayed on the selected text or paragraph. You can apply a style to the text by clicking a style.

HOW TO: Use the Style Gallery

1. Select the text or paragraph where you want to apply the style.
2. From the *Style* gallery [*Home* tab, *Styles* group], select a style to apply to the text.
   - To see the second row of styles available in the *Style* gallery, click the **down arrow** at the right side of the gallery (Figure 2-62).
   - To see all of the styles in the *Style* gallery, click the **More** button.

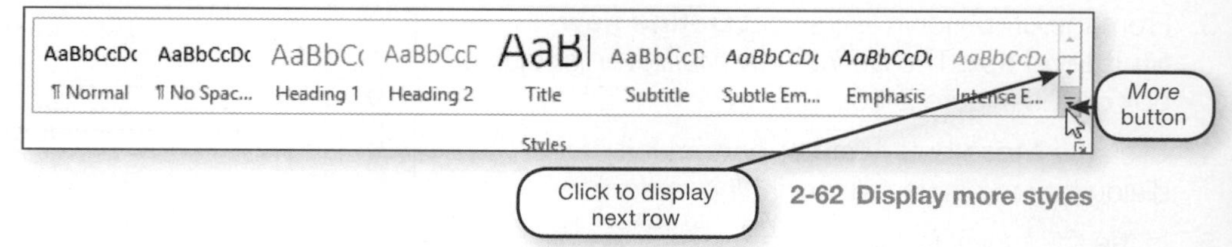

2-62 Display more styles

> **ANOTHER WAY**
>
> Apply a style to selected text by **right-clicking** the text, choosing **Styles** from the mini toolbar, and selecting the desired style to apply.

Edit Styles

A style is a collection of fonts, font sizes, styles, color, effects, indents, line spacing, paragraph spacing, and borders. Once a style has been applied to the text, you can change the formatting of this text. One way to do this is to make changes to font, font size, color, style, effects, etc. to the selected text without actually changing the style. The other option you have is to modify the style. The advantage of modifying a style when you make a change is that the style will be consistent when applied to text in a document. When a style is modified, existing text with that style applied is automatically updated to match the modified style.

There are two ways to modify a style.

- Update style to match selection
- Modify style

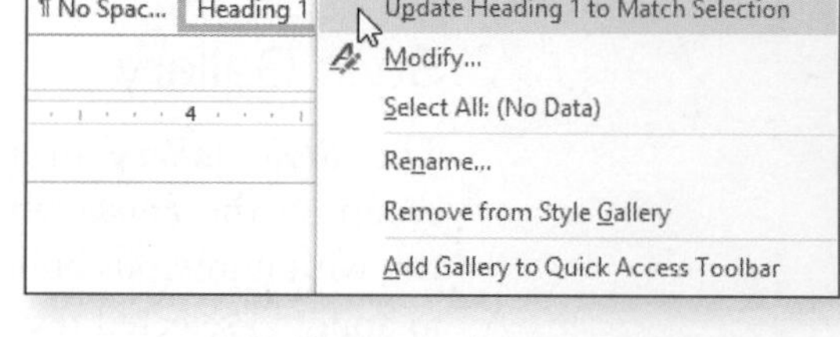

2-63 Update style from the *Style* gallery

HOW TO: Update Style to Match Selection

1. Apply a style to selected text.
2. Make the desired changes to the text where the style was applied.
3. Select the text that you changed.
4. Right-click the style in the *Style* gallery and choose **Update *[name of style]* to Match Selection** (Figure 2-63).

You can also modify a style using the *Modify Style* dialog box.

HOW TO: Modify an Existing Style

1. Right-click the style to modify in the *Style* gallery and select **Modify**. The *Modify Style* dialog box opens (Figure 2-64).
2. Make desired changes to the style. You can make basic formatting changes from this dialog box.
   - Click the **Format** button to open other dialog boxes, such as *Font, Paragraph, Tabs, Borders,* etc.
   - Click **OK** to apply changes from another dialog box.
   - The formatting changes are shown and described in the *Preview* area.
3. Click **OK** to apply the style change and close the *Modify Style* dialog box.

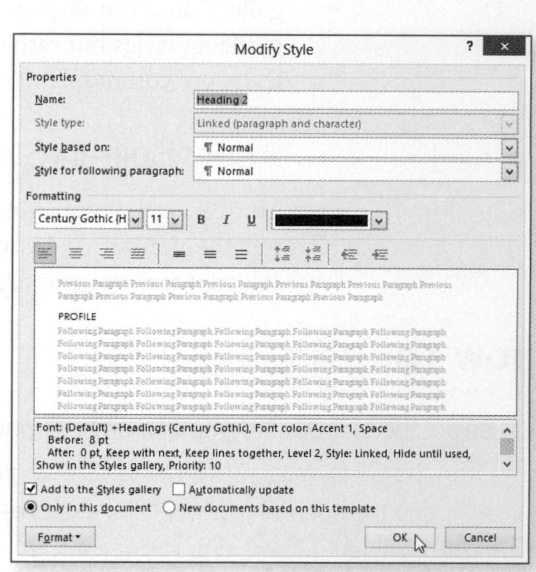

2-64 *Modify Style* dialog box

Apply Themes

A theme is a collection of fonts, colors, and effects. Themes are similar to styles, but instead of applying to just selected text, themes apply to an entire document. All documents have a theme; the default theme for a new document is *Office*. You can change the theme of a document or you can individually change the colors, fonts, or effects set in a document.

HOW TO: Change the Document Theme

1. Click the **Design** tab.
2. Click the **Themes** button [*Document Formatting* group].
3. From the *Themes* gallery, select the theme to be applied (Figure 2-65).
4. You can also click the **Colors**, **Fonts**, or **Effects** buttons to change each of these individually within the existing theme.

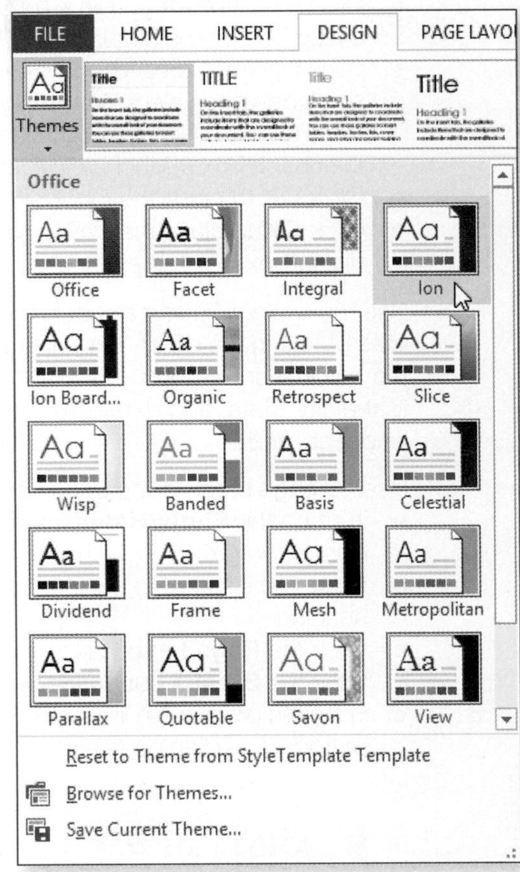

2-65 Change the theme of a document

PAUSE & PRACTICE: WORD 2-3

In this Pause & Practice project, you modify the resume you edited in *Pause & Practice 2-2*. You add a bulleted list, customize the bulleted list, insert a page break, apply and modify styles, and apply a document theme.

File Needed: ***[your initials] PP W2-2.docx***
Completed Project File Name: ***[your initials] PP W2-3.docx***

1. Open the ***[your initials] PP W2-2*** document created in *Pause & Practice 2-2*.
2. Save this document as ***[your initials] PP W2-3***.
3. Convert text to bulleted list and customize the bullet.
   a. Select the four paragraphs of text below the "Experience" heading and the city, state, and date line.
   b. Click the **Bullets** button [*Home* tab, *Paragraph* group]. The selected text is converted to a bulleted list (Figure 2-66).

c. With the bulleted paragraphs still selected, click the **Bullets** drop-down arrow, and select **Define New Bullet**. The *Define New Bullet* dialog box opens.
d. Click the **Symbol** button. The *Symbol* dialog box opens (Figure 2-67).
e. Click the **Font** drop-down list and scroll down to select **Wingdings**.
f. In the list of symbols, scroll down and select the **check box** symbol (*Character code 254*).
g. Click **OK** to close the *Symbol* dialog box.
h. Click **OK** to close the *Define New Bullet* dialog box.

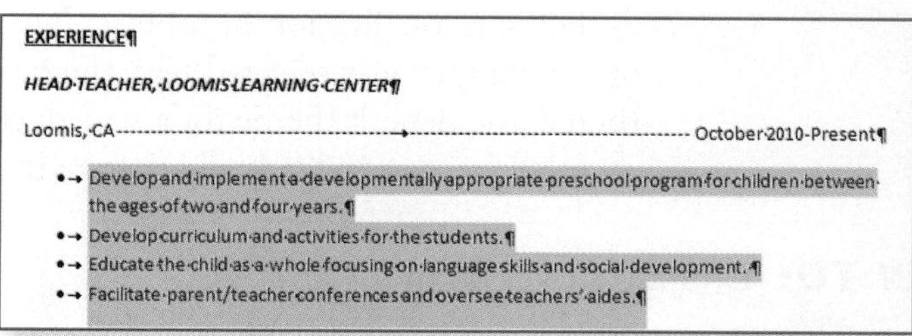

2-66 Apply bullets to selected text

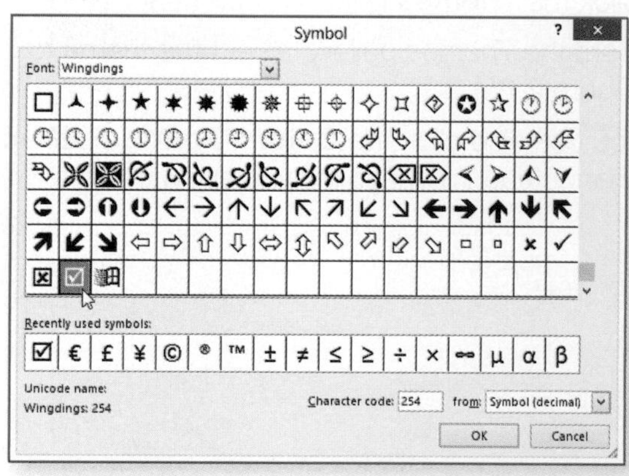

2-67 *Symbol* dialog box

4. Use the *Format Painter* to apply this bullet format to lines of text in the other "Experience" sections and the "Education" section. Don't apply bullet formatting to the city, state, and date lines with the tab stop and leader applied.
5. Insert a page break in the document.
   a. Turn on the **Show/Hide** feature [*Home* tab, *Paragraph* group].
   b. Place the insertion point in front of the "Education" heading.
   c. Click the **Page Layout** tab.
   d. Click the **Breaks** button [*Page Setup* group].
   e. From the drop-down list select **Page** in the *Page Breaks* section. A page break is inserted at the bottom of the first page and the "Education" section is pushed to the next page.

> **ANOTHER WAY**
>
> **Ctrl+Enter** inserts a page break.

6. Change the theme of the document.
   a. Click the **Design** tab.
   b. Click the **Themes** button [*Document Formatting* group].
   c. Scroll down the list of themes and select **Ion**.
7. Apply styles from the *Style* gallery to text.
   a. On the first page of the letter, select **"Richelle Wilkinson"** and click the **Title** style from the *Style* gallery [*Home* tab].
   b. With this text still selected, change the font size to **20 pt**.
   c. Apply the **Heading 1** style to each of the main headings ("Profile," "Experience," "Education," "Skills," and "References").
   d. Apply the **Heading 2** style to each of the bold and italicized subheadings in the "Experience" and "Education" sections.
8. Modify a style.
   a. Select the **"Profile"** heading.
   b. Change the *Before* paragraph spacing to **16 pt**.

c. Right-click the **Heading 1** style in the *Style* gallery and select **Update Heading 1 to Match Selection** (Figure 2-68). This style change is applied to all text with *Heading 1* style.
d. On the second page, select **"CALIFORNIA STATE UNIVERSITY CHICO, BACHELOR OF ARTS IN CHILD DEVELOPMENT"** and change the font size to **11 pt**.
e. Right-click the **Heading 2** style in the *Style* gallery and select **Update Heading 2 to Match Selection**.

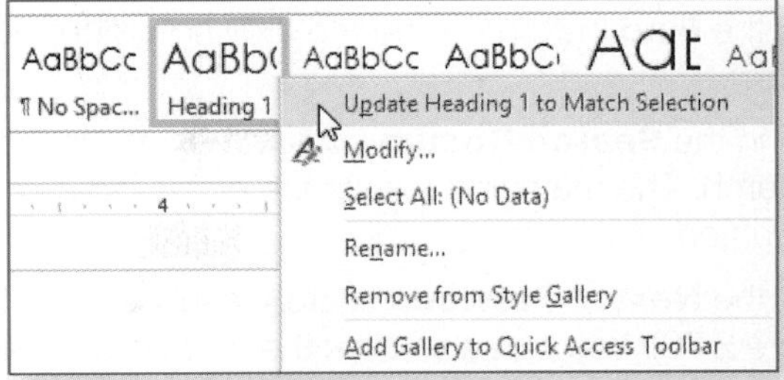

2-68 Update style to match selection

9. Save and close the document (Figure 2-69).

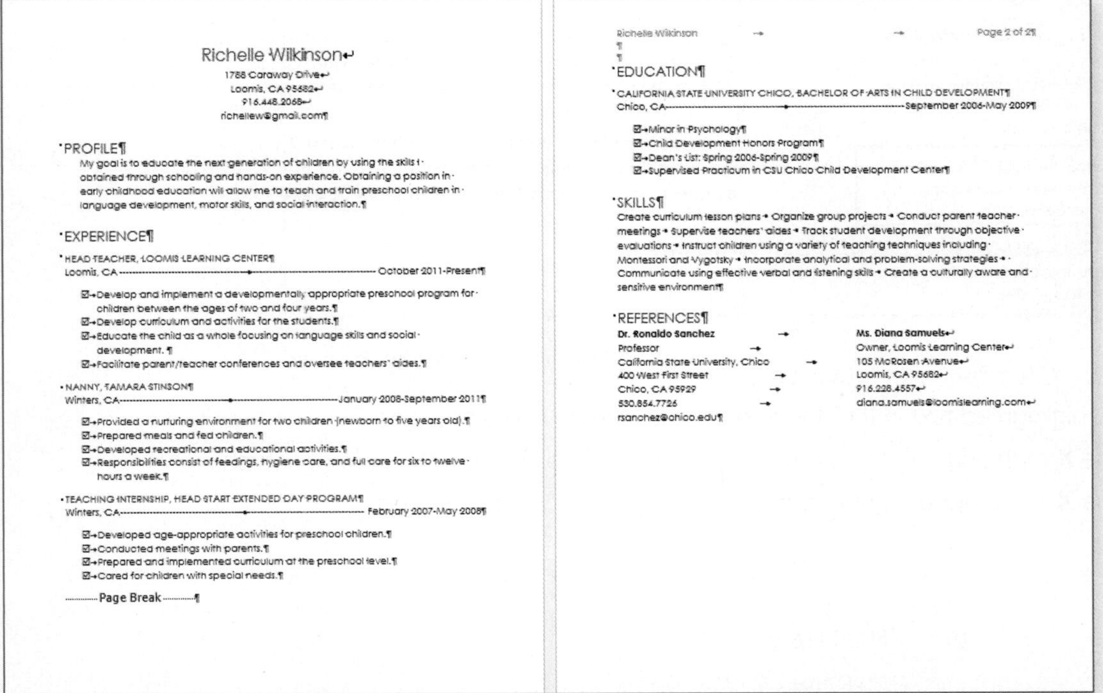

Richelle Wilkinson
1788 Caraway Drive
Loomis, CA 95682
916.448.2068
richellew@gmail.com

PROFILE
My goal is to educate the next generation of children by using the skills I obtained through schooling and hands-on experience. Obtaining a position in early childhood education will allow me to teach and train preschool children in language development, motor skills, and social interaction.

EXPERIENCE

HEAD TEACHER, LOOMIS LEARNING CENTER
Loomis, CA — October 2011-Present

- Develop and implement a developmentally appropriate preschool program for children between the ages of two and four years.
- Develop curriculum and activities for the students.
- Educate the child as a whole focusing on language skills and social development.
- Facilitate parent/teacher conferences and oversee teachers' aides.

NANNY, TAMARA STINSON
Winters, CA — January 2008-September 2011

- Provided a nurturing environment for two children (newborn to five years old).
- Prepared meals and fed children.
- Developed recreational and educational activities.
- Responsibilities consist of feedings, hygiene care, and full care for six to twelve hours a week.

TEACHING INTERNSHIP, HEAD START EXTENDED DAY PROGRAM
Winters, CA — February 2007-May 2008

- Developed age-appropriate activities for preschool children.
- Conducted meetings with parents.
- Prepared and implemented curriculum at the preschool level.
- Cared for children with special needs.

Page Break

Richelle Wilkinson — Page 2 of 2

EDUCATION

CALIFORNIA STATE UNIVERSITY CHICO, BACHELOR OF ARTS IN CHILD DEVELOPMENT
Chico, CA — September 2006-May 2009

- Minor in Psychology
- Child Development Honors Program
- Dean's List: Spring 2006-Spring 2009
- Supervised Practicum in CSU Chico Child Development Center

SKILLS
Create curriculum lesson plans • Organize group projects • Conduct parent teacher meetings • Supervise teachers' aides • Track student development through objective evaluations • Instruct children using a variety of teaching techniques including Montessori and Vygotsky • Incorporate analytical and problem-solving strategies • Communicate using effective verbal and listening skills • Create a culturally aware and sensitive environment

REFERENCES

Dr. Ronaldo Sanchez
Professor
California State University, Chico
400 West First Street
Chico, CA 95929
530.854.7726
rsanchez@chico.edu

Ms. Diana Samuels
Owner, Loomis Learning Center
105 McRosen Avenue
Loomis, CA 95682
916.228.4557
diana.samuels@loomislearning.com

2-69 PP W2-3 completed

SLO 2.8

Using Find and Replace

Find and ***Replace*** are two extremely useful and powerful tools in Word. The *Find* feature allows you to search for and locate words and phrases in a document. The *Replace* feature allows you to search for a word or phrase and replace it with other text. You can also use *Find* and *Replace* to search for a specific type of formatting in a document and replace it with different formatting. These features are particularly useful in longer documents.

Find

You can use the *Navigation* pane in Word to search for text and display all instances of the matching text. Word highlights in yellow each instance of the matching text in the document. You are able to navigate through the document, see each instance, and make edits as desired.

HOW TO: Use Find in the Navigation Pane

1. Click the **Find** button [*Home* tab, *Editing* group]. The *Navigation* pane is displayed at the left side of the Word window.
2. Click in the **Search Document** text box at the top of the *Navigation* pane and type in the text you want to search. The matching results are displayed below the text box and the matching text in the document is highlighted.
3. Click the **Next** or **Previous** search result buttons to move through each matching instance in the document (Figure 2-70). You can also click the matching instances below the *Search Document* text box to go to a specific occurrence of the matching text.

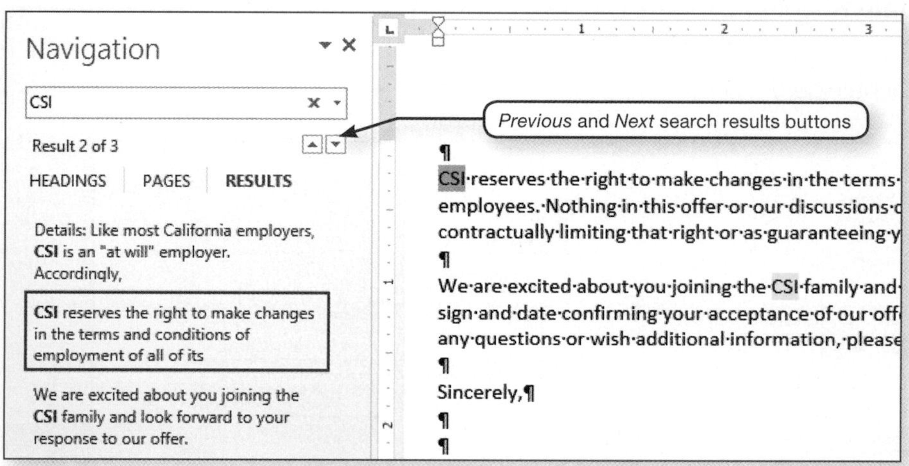

2-70 Use *Find* in the *Navigation* pane

4. Edit the highlighted text in the document if you want to make changes.
5. Click the **X** to the right of the *Search Document* text box to clear the current search.
6. Click the **X** in the upper right of the *Navigation* pane to close the pane.

> **ANOTHER WAY**
>
> **Ctrl+F** opens the *Find* feature in the *Navigation* pane.

Find and Replace

The ***Find and Replace*** dialog box gives you three different advanced options for searching your document.

- Find
- Replace
- Go To

The *Find* tab of the *Find and Replace* dialog box not only searches for text in your document but also searches for specific formatting (such as font styles, line spacing, or paragraph spacing). For example, you can search for all text that is bold or italic, or that has 6 pt. after paragraph spacing.

Using the *Replace* feature you can search for text, formatting, or a combination of text and formatting and replace the matching text with other text, formatting, or formatted text. This feature is a quick and efficient way to find and replace information in a document.

HOW TO: Use Replace

1. Click the **Replace** button [*Home* tab, *Editing* group] or press **Ctrl+H**. The *Find and Replace* dialog box opens with the *Replace* tab displayed (Figure 2-71).
2. Click in the **Find what** text box and type the text for which you are searching.
3. Click in the **Replace with** text box and type the text you want to replace the found text.
4. Click the **More** button to display advanced find options. The *Less* button hides the advanced find options.
5. Click the **Format** or **Special** button to add formatting options or special characters to either the text for which you are searching or the replacement text.
6. When the first occurrence is found you have the options to *Replace* (this occurrence), *Replace All* (all occurrences), or *Find Next* (skip this occurrence without replacing and move on to the next).
7. Click the **Find Next** button to move to the next occurrence of the matching text and formatting.
8. When you finish finding and replacing text in the document, a dialog box opens informing you that Word has finished searching the document. Click **OK** to close this dialog box.
9. Click the **X** in the upper right corner to close the *Find and Replace* dialog box.

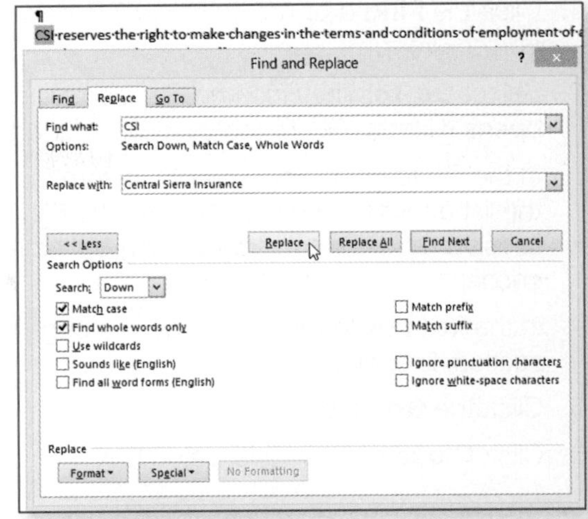

2-71 Replace text

When using *Find* or *Replace*, wildcards can be used to help find information. You can use wildcards before, after, or between words.

- Use the question mark (?) as a wildcard for a single character. For example, ***w???*** finds any words that begins with "w" and contains four letters (e.g., when, with, or wish).
- Use an asterisk (*) as a wildcard for a string of characters. For example, **search*** finds any form of the word "search" (e.g., searches, searching, or searched).

ANOTHER WAY

Ctrl+H opens the *Find and Replace* dialog box.

MORE INFO

It is a good idea to use **Match Case** when replacing acronyms (capital letters) with words so the replaced words will not be all upper case. Also, use **Find whole words only** to refine your search.

Go To

The ***Go To*** feature allows you to go quickly to specific items in your document. This feature is available in the *Find and Replace* dialog box. This feature is different from *Find* in that *Go To* moves you to specific objects in your document such as a page, section, or bookmark.

HOW TO: Use the Go To Feature

1. Click the **Find** drop-down arrow [*Home* tab, *Editing* group].
2. Select **Go To**. The *Find and Replace* dialog box opens with the *Go To* tab displayed (Figure 2-72).
3. In the *Go to what* area, select the item to go to from the list of options. The text box to the right is context sensitive and changes depending on the item chosen.
4. In the text box to the right, type in a page number, section, line, etc.
5. Click the **Go To** button.
6. Click **Close** to close this dialog box.

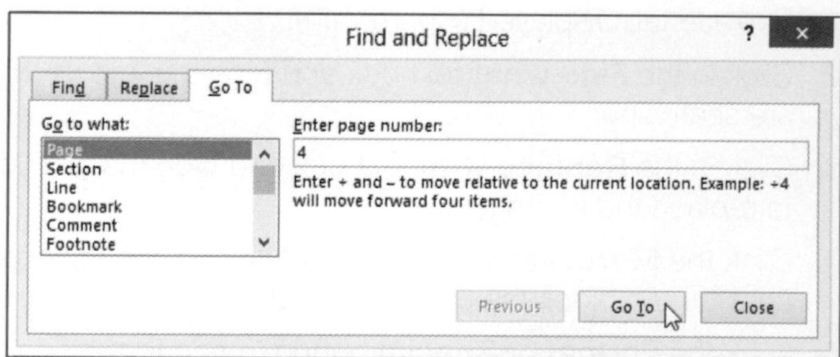

2-72 *Go To* in the *Find and Replace* dialog box

> **ANOTHER WAY**
>
> **Ctrl+G** or **F5** opens the *Find and Replace* dialog box with the *Go To* tab selected.

SLO 2.9

Using Borders, Shading, and Hyperlinks

Borders and ***shading*** are excellent ways to set off or emphasize important information in a document. In Word, there are many different border and shading options including many preset border options. You also have the option of applying custom borders and shading to selected text or areas of your document.

A ***hyperlink*** functions like a button and can be used to take a reader to a web page, open an existing or new document, open an email message, or take a reader to another location in the current document. You can add a hyperlink to text or a graphic in a document.

Apply Built-In Borders

You can use the built-in border options to quickly apply borders to selected text. Borders are typically applied to paragraphs, but they can also be applied to other selected text. Borders are, by default, applied to the paragraph where your insertion point is unless specific text is selected.

The built-in borders are available from the *Borders* button in the *Paragraph* group on the *Home* tab. Figure 2-73 shows the different types of built-in borders.

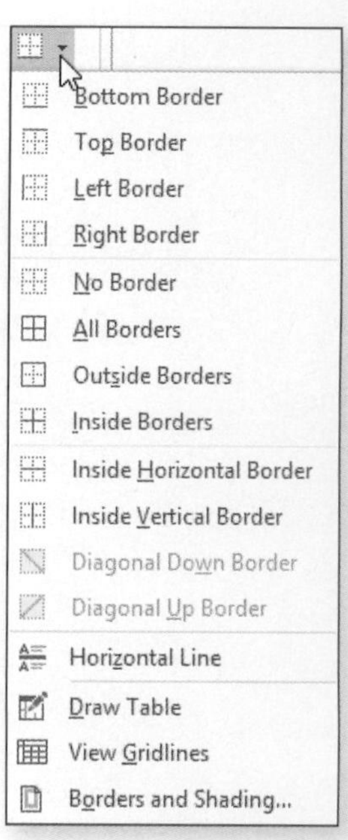

2-73 *Borders* drop-down list

HOW TO: Apply Built-In Borders

1. Select the paragraph or place the insertion point in the paragraph where you want to apply the border.
2. Click the **Home** tab.
3. Click the **Borders** drop-down arrow [*Paragraph* group] (Figure 2-73).
4. Click the border option to apply to the paragraph.

MORE INFO

You can remove borders by selecting the paragraph or text on which the border is applied and clicking the **No Border** option in the *Borders* drop-down list.

Customize Borders

The ***Borders and Shading*** dialog box gives you many more options to customize the type of border you use. Not only can you customize the style, width, and color of border line, but also you can customize where the border is placed in relation to the selected text. The *Borders and Shading* dialog box is available from the *Borders* drop-down list in the *Paragraph* group on the *Home* tab.

HOW TO: Apply Custom Borders

1. Select the paragraph(s) you want to border.
2. Click the **Borders** drop-down arrow [*Home* tab, *Paragraph* group] and choose the **Borders and Shading** option at the bottom of the list. The *Borders and Shading* dialog box opens (Figure 2-74).
3. In the *Setting* area, select the type of border to use. Your options are *None, Box, Shadow, 3-D,* and *Custom*.
4. In the *Style* area, select a style of the line from the list of options.
5. In the *Color* area, select line color.
6. In the *Width* area, select the width of the border line. The width of the line is measured in points.
7. The *Preview* area shows you how the border will appear in your document.
   - You can turn on or off a specific border by either clicking any of the border buttons in the *Preview* area or clicking the border itself.
8. Click the **Options** button to open the *Borders and Shading Options* dialog box (Figure 2-75). This dialog box gives you the option to add in additional space (padding) between the border and the text at the *Top, Bottom, Left,* and *Right*. The spacing is measured in points.
9. Click **OK** to close the *Borders and Shading Options* dialog box.
10. Click **OK** to close the *Borders and Shading* dialog box.

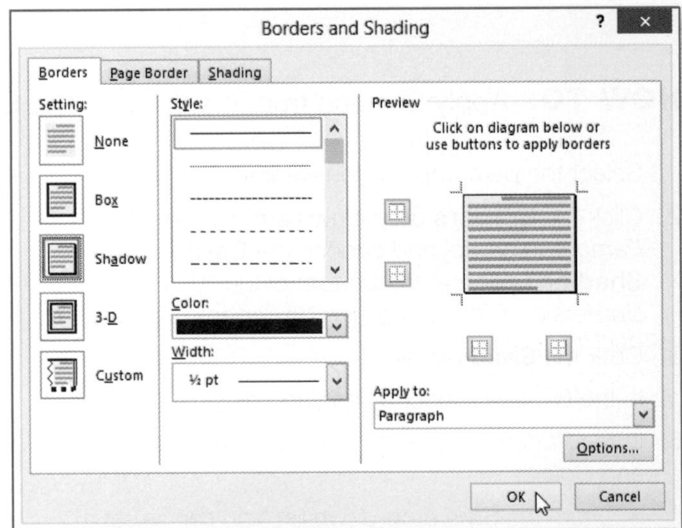

2-74 ***Borders and Shading* dialog box**

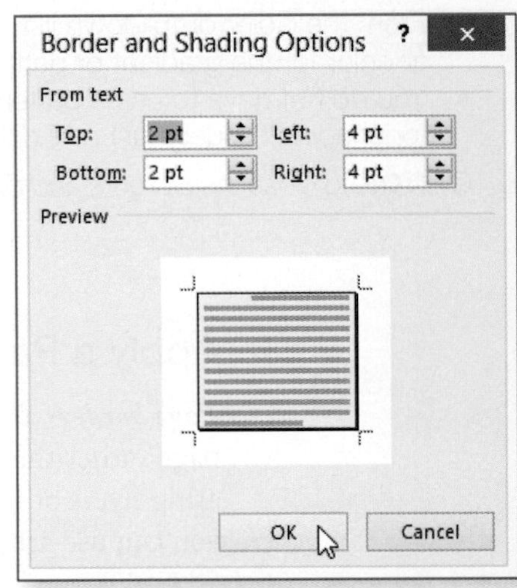

2-75 ***Border and Shading Options* dialog box**

MORE INFO

When you use the *Borders* button [*Paragraph* group], the last border you choose becomes the function of the *Borders* button. For example, if you last applied a bottom border, you can apply a bottom border again by clicking the **Borders** button.

Apply Shading

Applying shading to a paragraph or text is very similar to applying borders. The *Shading* option is available from the *Shading* button in the *Paragraph* group on the *Home* tab or in the *Borders and Shading* dialog box on the *Shading* tab.

The shading colors available are dependent upon the theme of the document. In the *Shading* drop-down list, you can select from *Theme Colors* or *Standard Colors* (Figure 2-76). If you want a color that is not available in the menu, you can click *More Colors* to select from a color palette.

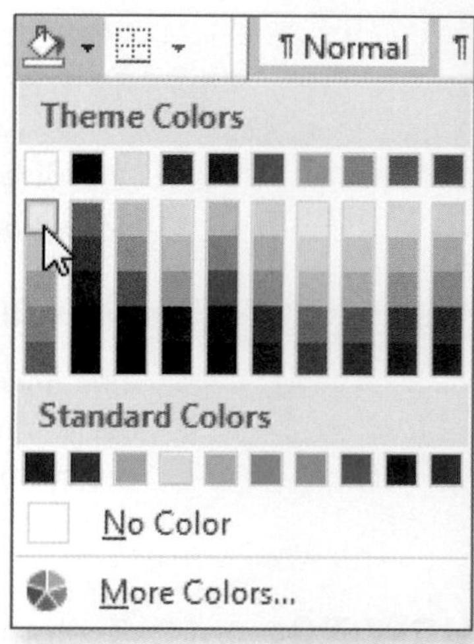

2-76 Shading color options from the *Shading* drop-down list

HOW TO: Apply Shading from the Borders and Shading Dialog Box

1. Select the paragraph(s) you want to shade.
2. Click the **Borders** drop-down arrow [*Home* tab, *Paragraph* group] and choose the **Borders and Shading** option at the bottom of the list. The *Borders and Shading* dialog box opens (Figure 2-77).
3. Click the **Shading** tab.
4. In the *Fill* area, select a shading color.
5. In the *Patterns* area, you can select a shading *Style* and *Color*.
   - From the *Style* drop-down list, you can select a gradient percent or a fill pattern as the shading style.
   - From the *Color* drop-down list, you can select a fill color for the gradient or pattern you selected.
   - You do not have to use a pattern style or color for shading. Usually just a fill color is sufficient.
6. Click **OK** to close the *Borders and Shading* dialog box.

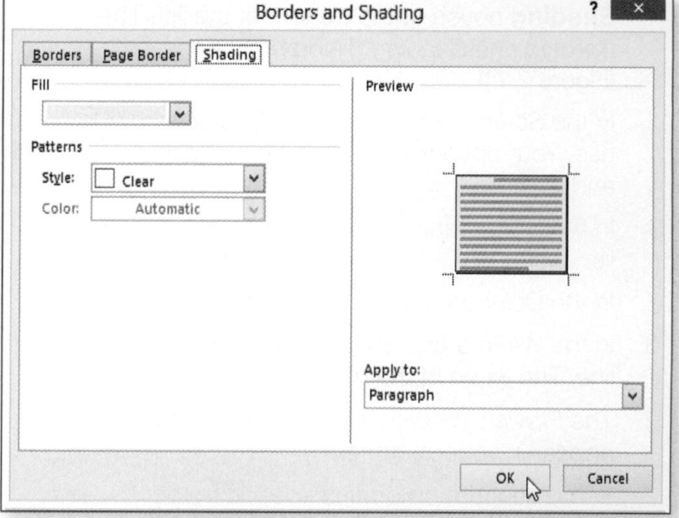

2-77 Shading options in the *Borders and Shading* dialog box

Apply a Page Border

Page borders are different from paragraph or text borders; a page border is around the entire page rather than selected paragraphs or text. Page borders are useful and attractive when creating flyers or handouts. A page border can be a line with varying styles, widths, and colors, or you can use art graphics as a page border.

HOW TO: Apply a Page Border

1. Click the **Design** tab.
2. Click the **Page Borders** button [*Page Background* group]. The *Borders and Shading* dialog box opens with the *Page Border* tab displayed (Figure 2-78).
3. In the *Setting* area, select the type of page border you want to apply.

4. You can select either a page border *Style* or *Art* from the drop-down lists.
5. You can change the *Color* and *Width* as desired.
6. In the *Preview* area, you can customize how the page border appears by turning on or off top, bottom, left, or right borders.
7. In the *Apply to* area, you can select the page(s) where you want to apply the page border. Your options are:
   - *Whole document*
   - *This section*
   - *This section – First page only*
   - *This section – All except first page*
8. Click **OK** to close the *Borders and Shading* dialog box.

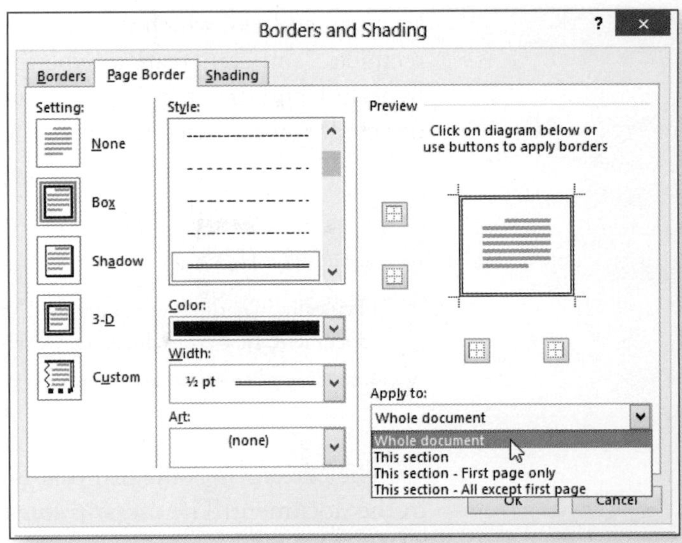

2-78 Apply a page border

> **MORE INFO**
>
> When you apply a page border, the text in the document is not affected because the page border is placed outside the margin boundaries.

Insert a Horizontal Line

In addition to being able to insert top and bottom borders on selected text, you can also insert a ***horizontal line*** to use as a border to separate information on a page. A horizontal line is actually a graphic that is inserted into the document. When you insert a horizontal line, the line is the width of the page. More information about using and customizing graphics is covered in *SLO 4.5: Working with Graphics.*

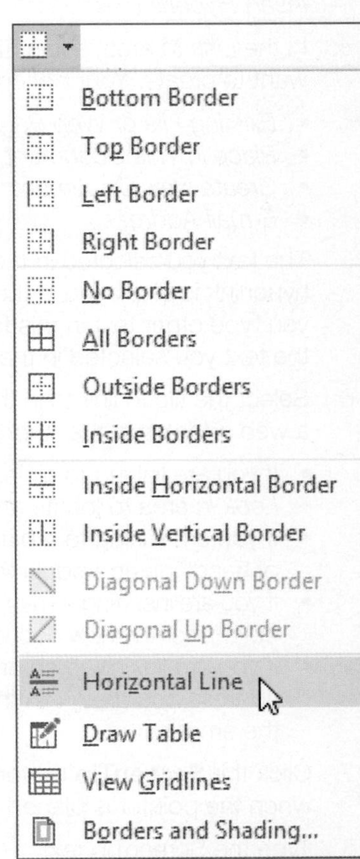

2-79 Insert a horizontal line

HOW TO: Insert a Horizontal Line

1. Place your insertion point in the document where you want a horizontal line.
2. Click the **Borders** drop-down arrow *[Home* tab, *Paragraph* group].
3. Select **Horizontal Line** from the drop-down list (Figure 2-79).
   - The horizontal line is treated as a separate paragraph and has a paragraph mark to the right.

Create a Hyperlink

A hyperlink is an excellent way to direct users to information on a web site, another document, or a location in the same document. You can also create a hyperlink for an email address, which automatically opens a new Outlook email message addressed to the recipient. You can create a hyperlink by selecting the text or figure you want to turn into a hyperlink and then providing the information about the online location where the user will be directed. You can also customize the ScreenTip and the target frame.

> **MORE INFO**
>
> Typically, hyperlinks are underlined and a different color to distinguish them from regular text in a document. In a Word document, **Ctrl+Click** opens a hyperlink.

The ***ScreenTip*** is the text that is displayed when you place your pointer over the hyperlink in the document. The ***target frame*** is the window where the hyperlink document or web site opens. There are many different target frame options from which to choose. Usually it is best to choose **New window** if the link is to a different document or a web page. An email message always opens in a new window.

HOW TO: Create a Hyperlink

1. Select the text or graphic where you want to create a hyperlink.
2. Click the **Insert** tab.
3. Click the **Hyperlink** button [*Links* group]. The *Insert Hyperlink* dialog box opens (*Figure 2-80*).
4. In the *Link to* area, select the type of hyperlink you want to create. Your options are:
   - *Existing File or Web Page*
   - *Place in This Document*
   - *Create New Document*
   - *E-mail Address*
5. The text you selected in the document as the hyperlink is displayed in the *Text to display* area. If you type other text in this text box, it will replace the text you selected in the document.

2-80 ***Insert Hyperlink*** **dialog box**

6. Select the file to link to in the *Look in* area, or type a web address in the *Address* area.
   - If you are linking to a file, you can browse your computer in the *Look in* area to locate and select the file.
   - If you are linking to a place in the document, you are given a list of headings and bookmarks from which to choose.
   - If you are inserting a link to create a new document, you are given options for the new document.
   - If you are linking to an email address, you type in the email address and are given the option to create a subject line for the email.
7. Click the **ScreenTip** button to insert text that will be displayed when the pointer is placed over the hyperlink (Figure 2-81).
8. Type the ScreenTip text.
9. Click **OK** to close the *Set Hyperlink ScreenTip* dialog box.

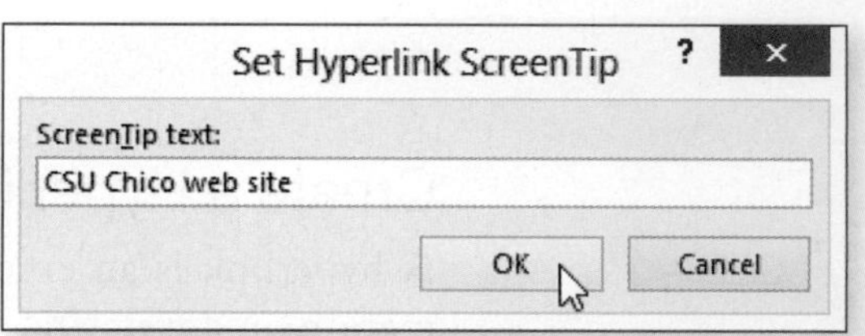

2-81 ***Set Hyperlink ScreenTip*** **dialog box**

10. Click the **Target Frame** button to open the *Set Target Frame* dialog box (Figure 2-82)
    - From the drop-down list of options, select where the hyperlink destination will be opened .
    - The *Set as default for all hyperlinks* check box allows you to make your target frame selection the default for all hyperlinks in your document.
11. Click **OK** to close the *Set Target Frame* dialog box.
12. Click **OK** to insert the hyperlink and close the *Insert Hyperlink* dialog box.

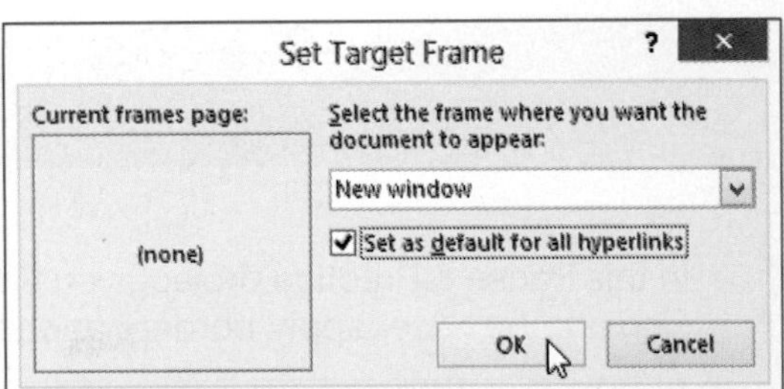

2-82 *Set Target Frame* dialog box

ANOTHER WAY

Ctrl+K opens the *Insert Hyperlink* dialog box.

Edit or Remove a Hyperlink

There might be times when you have incorporated text from a web site or another document that includes hyperlinks to a document, or you might want to edit a hyperlink in an existing document. Word allows you to quickly edit hyperlinks to change hyperlink information, add a ScreenTip, or change the target frame.

HOW TO: Edit a Hyperlink

1. Select or click the hyperlink to be edited.
2. Click the **Hyperlink** button [*Insert* tab, *Links* group]. You can also press **Ctrl+K** or right-click the selected hyperlink and select **Edit Hyperlink**. The *Edit Hyperlink* dialog box opens.
3. Make the desired changes to the hyperlink information or options.
4. Click **OK** to close the *Edit Hyperlink* dialog box.

You can quickly remove a hyperlink from a document without deleting the text in the document. When you remove a hyperlink from existing text, the text is not deleted. Only the hyperlink attached to the text is deleted.

HOW TO: Remove a Hyperlink

1. Select or click the hyperlink to be removed.
2. Click the **Hyperlink** button [*Insert* tab, *Links* group] or press **Ctrl+K** to open the *Edit Hyperlink* dialog box (Figure 2-83).
3. Click the **Remove Link** button.
4. Click **OK** to close the *Edit Hyperlink* button.

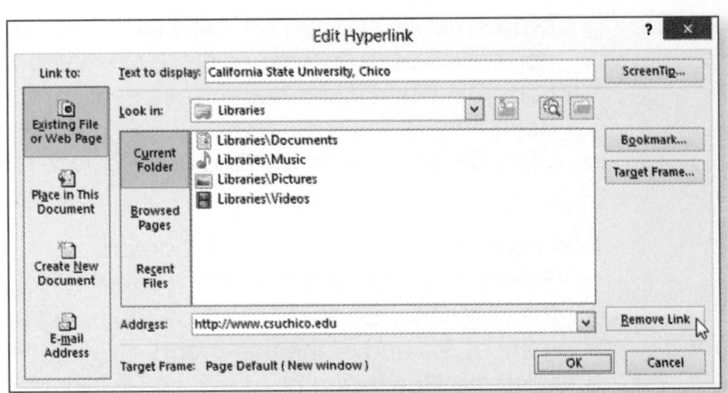

2-83 Remove hyperlink

ANOTHER WAY

Right-click a hyperlink and select **Remove Hyperlink**.

PAUSE & PRACTICE: WORD 2-4

In this Pause & Practice project, you finalize the resume you worked on in *Pause & Practice 2-3*. You use *Find and Replace,* apply borders and shading to selected text, and add hyperlinks to the document.

File Needed: ***[your initials] PP W2-3.docx***
Completed Project File Name: ***[your initials] PP W2-4.docx***

1. Open the ***[your initials] PP W2-3*** document created in *Pause & Practice 2-3*.
2. Save this document as ***[your initials] PP W2-4.***
3. Use *Find and Replace* to replace the hyphen between dates with an en dash.
   a. Press **Ctrl+Home** to move to the top of the document.
   b. Click the **Replace** button [*Home* tab, *Editing* group] or press **Ctrl+H** to open the *Find and Replace* dialog box (Figure 2-84).

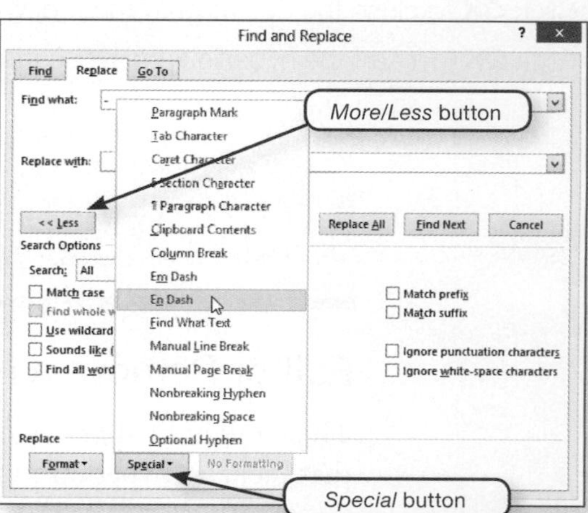

2-84 Use Find and Replace

   c. Type - (hyphen) in the *Find what* text box.
   d. Place the insertion point in the *Replace with* text box.
   e. Click the **More** button if the *Search Options* are not already displayed.
   f. Click the **Special** button and select **En Dash**.
   g. Click the **Less** button to make the **Find and Replace** dialog box smaller.
   h. Click the **Find Next** button to locate the first instance of the text for which you are searching.

> **MORE INFO**
>
> Word highlights each found occurrence. If you need to, you can move the *Find and Replace* dialog box to view highlighted text.

   i. Choose **Find Next** to skip the hyphenated word in the first paragraph.
   j. Click the **Replace** button to replace the hyphen between the dates with an en dash.
   k. Choose **Replace** to replace each occurrence of a hyphen between dates; choose **Find Next** to skip and not replace each occurrence of a hyphenated word.
   l. Click **OK** when Word has finished searching the document.
   m. Click **Close** to close the *Find and Replace* dialog box.
4. Add borders and shading to a paragraph.
   a. Select the paragraph after the "Profile" heading on the first page. Be sure to include the paragraph mark at the end of the paragraph.
   b. Click the **Borders** drop-down arrow [*Home* tab, *Paragraph* group] and select **Borders and Shading** to open the *Borders and Shading* dialog box (Figure 2-85).

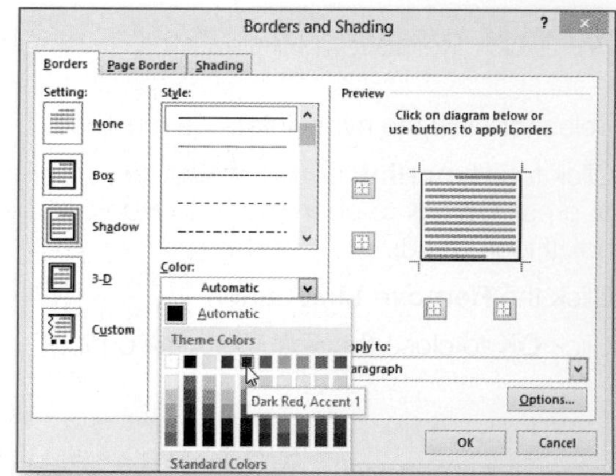

2-85 Select border color in the *Borders and Shading* dialog box

c. Select **Shadow** in the *Setting* area.
d. Select the **solid line** in the *Style* area.
e. Click the **Color** drop-down list and select **Dark Red**, **Accent 1**.
f. Select **½ pt** in the *Width* area.
g. Select **Paragraph** in the *Apply to* area.
h. Click the **Options** button to open the *Borders and Shading Options* dialog box.
i. Change *Top* and *Bottom* to **2 pt**.
j. Click **OK** to close the *Borders and Shading Options* dialog box.
k. Click the **Shading** tab (Figure 2-86).
l. Click the **Fill** drop-down list and choose **White**, **Background 1**, **Darker 5%**.
m. Click **OK** to close the *Borders and Shading* dialog box.

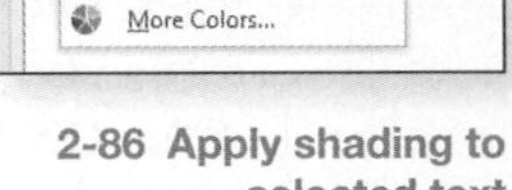

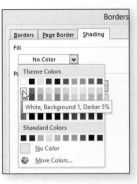

2-86 Apply shading to selected text

5. Add bottom border to the header.
   a. Double-click the header on the second page of the resume to open the second-page header.
   b. Place the insertion point in the first line of the header.
   c. Click the **Borders** drop-down arrow [*Home* tab, *Paragraph* group].
   d. Select **Bottom Border**. A bottom border is applied below the header text.
   e. Click the **Close Header and Footer** button [*Header & Footer Tools Design* tab, *Close* group].
6. Insert a hyperlink to an email address.
   a. Select the email address in the heading information on the first page.
   b. Click the **Hyperlink** button [*Insert* tab, *Links* group] or press **Ctrl+K** to open the *Insert Hyperlink* dialog box (Figure 2-87).
   c. Click the **E-mail Address** button in the *Link to* area.
   d. Type richellew@gmail.com in the *Text to display* area.
   e. Type richellew@gmail.com in the *E-mail address* area. Word automatically inserts "mailto:" before the email address.
   f. Click **OK** to close the *Insert Hyperlink* dialog box.

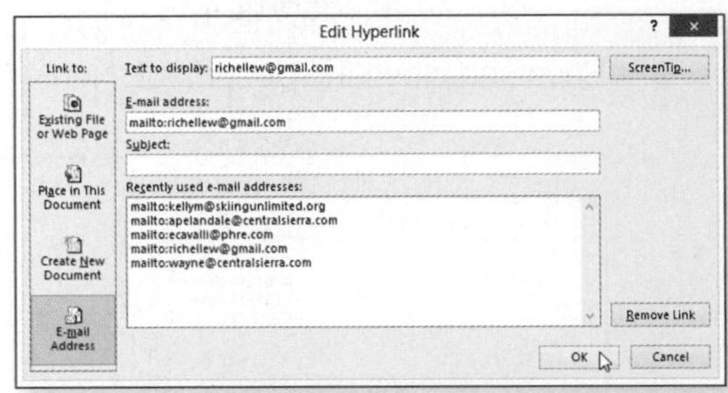

2-87 Insert hyperlink to an email address

7. Insert a hyperlink to a web site.
   a. Select **"California State University, Chico"** in the "References" section on the second page.
   b. Click the **Hyperlink** button or press **Ctrl+K** to open the *Insert Hyperlink* dialog box (Figure 2-88).
   c. Select **Existing File or Web Page** in the *Link to* area. The *Text to display* area has *California State University, Chico* already filled in.
   d. In the *Address* area, type www.csuchico.edu. Word automatically inserts "*http://*" before the web address.
   e. Click the **ScreenTip** button. The *Set Hyperlink ScreenTip* dialog box opens (Figure 2-89).
   f. Type CSU Chico web site in the *ScreenTip text* area.

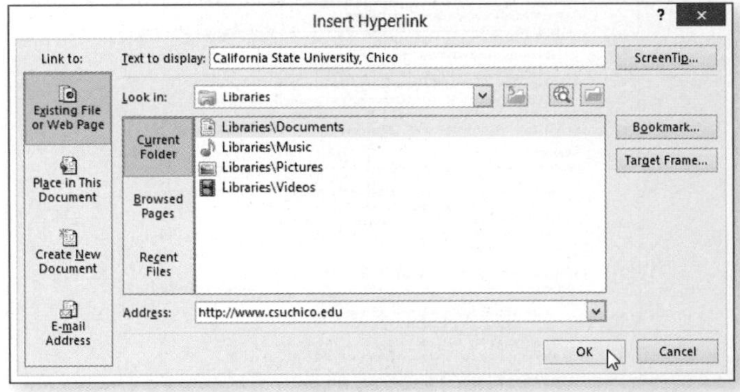

2-88 Insert hyperlink to a web page

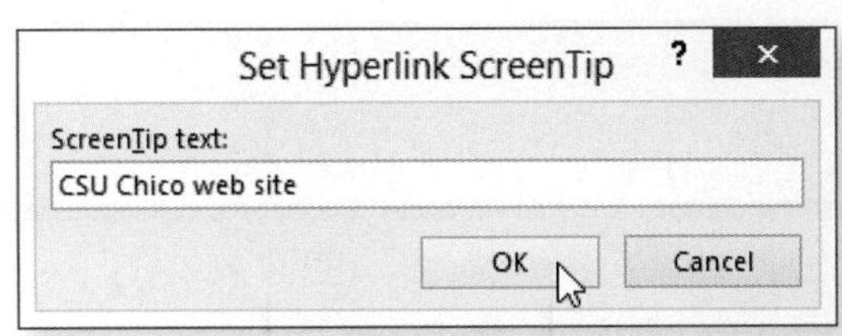

2-89 *Set Hyperlink ScreenTip* dialog box

g. Click **OK** to close the *Set Hyperlink ScreenTip* dialog box.
h. Click the **Target Frame** button in the *Insert Hyperlink* dialog box to open the *Set Target Frame* dialog box (Figure 2-90).
i. Select **New window** from the drop-down list.
j. Check the **Set as default for all hyperlinks** check box.
k. Click **OK** to close the *Set Target Frame* dialog box.
l. Click **OK** to close the *Insert Hyperlink* dialog box.

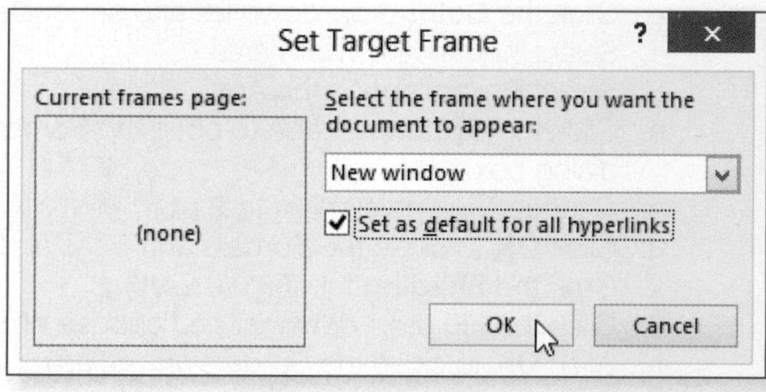

2-90 *Set Target Frame* dialog box

8. Automatically add hyperlinks to email addresses.
   a. Place the insertion point after "rsanchez@chico.edu" in the "References" section on the second page.
   b. Press the **spacebar** once to automatically add a hyperlink to the email address.
   c. Repeat the above steps to automatically add a hyperlink to the "diana.samuels@loomislearning.com" email address.
9. Save and close the document (Figure 2-91).

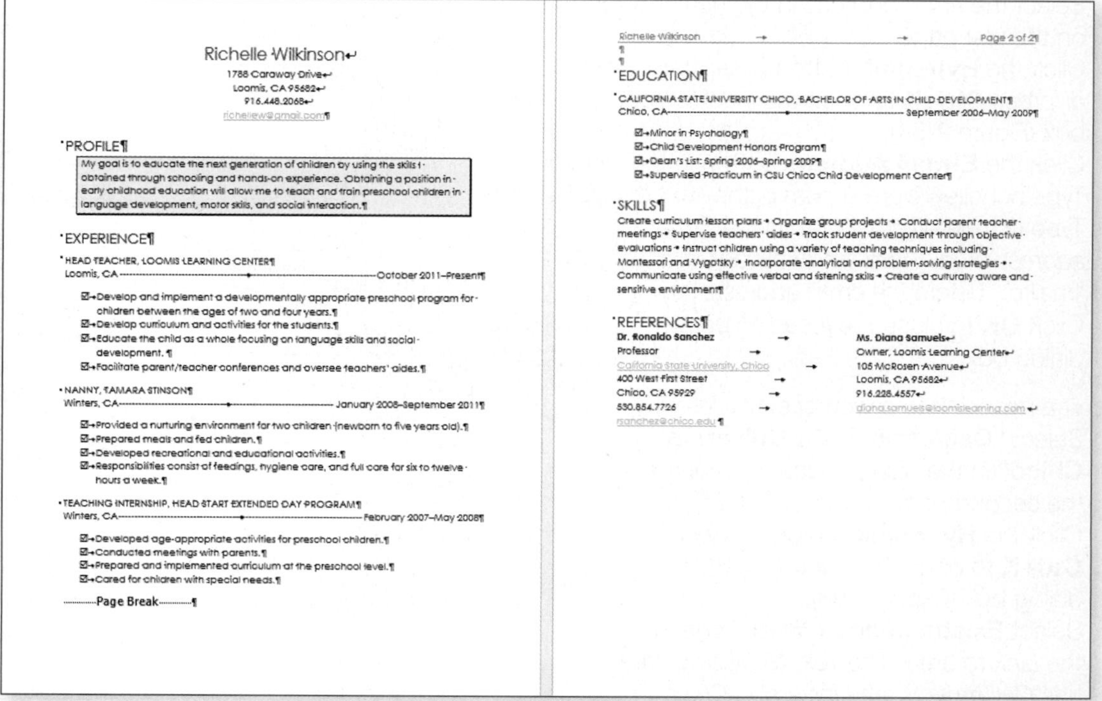

Richelle Wilkinson
1788 Caraway Drive
Loomis, CA 95682
916.448.2068
richellew@gmail.com

PROFILE

My goal is to educate the next generation of children by using the skills I obtained through schooling and hands-on experience. Obtaining a position in early childhood education will allow me to teach and train preschool children in language development, motor skills, and social interaction.

EXPERIENCE

HEAD TEACHER, LOOMIS LEARNING CENTER
Loomis, CA — October 2011–Present

- Develop and implement a developmentally appropriate preschool program for children between the ages of two and four years.
- Develop curriculum and activities for the students.
- Educate the child as a whole focusing on language skills and social development.
- Facilitate parent/teacher conferences and oversee teachers' aides.

NANNY, TAMARA STINSON
Winters, CA — January 2008–September 2011

- Provided a nurturing environment for two children (newborn to five years old).
- Prepared meals and fed children.
- Developed recreational and educational activities.
- Responsibilities consist of feedings, hygiene care, and full care for six to twelve hours a week.

TEACHING INTERNSHIP, HEAD START EXTENDED DAY PROGRAM
Winters, CA — February 2007–May 2008

- Developed age-appropriate activities for preschool children.
- Conducted meetings with parents.
- Prepared and implemented curriculum at the preschool level.
- Cared for children with special needs.

Page Break

Richelle Wilkinson — Page 2 of 2

EDUCATION

CALIFORNIA STATE UNIVERSITY CHICO, BACHELOR OF ARTS IN CHILD DEVELOPMENT
Chico, CA — September 2006–May 2009

- Minor in Psychology
- Child Development Honors Program
- Dean's List: Spring 2006–Spring 2009
- Supervised Practicum in CSU Chico Child Development Center

SKILLS

Create curriculum lesson plans • Organize group projects • Conduct parent teacher meetings • Supervise teachers' aides • Track student development through objective evaluations • Instruct children using a variety of teaching techniques including Montessori and Vygotsky • Incorporate analytical and problem-solving strategies • Communicate using effective verbal and listening skills • Create a culturally aware and sensitive environment

REFERENCES

Dr. Ronaldo Sanchez	**Ms. Diana Samuels**
Professor	Owner, Loomis Learning Center
California State University, Chico	105 McRosen Avenue
400 West First Street	Loomis, CA 95682
Chico, CA 95929	916.228.4557
530.854.7726	diana.samuels@loomislearning.com
rsanchez@chico.edu	

2-91 PP W 2-4 completed

Chapter Summary

2.1 Format a document by customizing margins, page orientation, paper size, and vertical alignment (p. W2-63).

- Adjust the ***margins*** of a document to increase or decrease the ***white space*** surrounding the text. You can adjust the top, bottom, left, and right margins of a document.
- ***Landscape*** and ***portrait*** are the two ***page orientation*** options.
- A standard sheet of paper is 8½"×11". Select other paper sizes or create a custom paper size.
- By default, text is aligned vertically at the top of the document. You can also ***vertically align*** text center, justified, or bottom.
- Use horizontal and vertical ***rulers*** to display the typing area on a document.
- You can change default page settings in the *Page Setup* dialog box.

2.2 Improve alignment and white-space usage by setting, using, and editing tab stops in a document (p. W2-66).

- There are five different types of tab stops: ***left***, ***center***, ***right***, ***decimal***, and ***bar***.
- Set, modify, or remove tab stops using the ruler or the *Tabs* dialog box.
- Leaders can be used with tab stops. There are three different types of leaders: ***dot***, ***dash***, and ***solid underline***.
- In a Word document, default tab stops are set every 0.5". You can change the default tab stops.

2.3 Understand and apply indents to control text alignment (p. W2-71).

- ***Indents*** can function as temporary margins and allow you to arrange paragraphs horizontally between the margins.
- There are four different types of indents: ***left***, ***right***, ***first line***, and ***hanging***.
- You can apply, modify, and remove indents with the ruler, *Page Layout* tab, or *Paragraph* dialog box.

2.4 Enhance document layout by effectively using page numbers, headers, and footers (p. W2-76).

- You can insert a ***page number*** into the header or footer in various locations.
- The ***Different First Page*** option allows you to remove a page number from the first page or have a header and footer.
- ***Headers*** and ***footers*** are areas above and below a document's top and bottom margins.
- You type header and footer content once and it appears on subsequent pages.
- You can customize headers and footers with text, page numbers, the date, and other document property fields.
- You have a variety of built-in header, footer, and page numbering options.

2.5 Control pagination with page and section breaks (p. W2-83).

- *Use* ***page breaks*** to control the ending and beginning of pages in a document.
- *Use* ***section breaks*** to allow for different page setup formatting on different sections of a document.
- There are four different types of section breaks: ***next page***, ***continuous***, ***even page***, and ***odd page***.
- Section breaks are visible in a document when the *Show/Hide* feature is turned on.

2.6 Present information using customized bulleted and numbered lists (p. W2-85).

- *Use* ***bulleted*** and ***numbered lists*** to emphasize important information.
- You can customize lists by using different symbols or pictures as bullets.
- Use numbering to display an ordered list.
- You can customize number format and levels.
- ***Multilevel lists*** allow you to customize a list using a combination of numbers, letters, or bullets.

2.7 Increase document consistency and format with styles and themes (p. W2-89).

- A ***style*** is a collection of preset formatting that you can apply to selected text.
- The ***Style gallery*** is a collection of built-in styles available in a document.
- You can modify existing styles.
- A ***theme*** is a collection of fonts, colors, and effects that you can apply to a document.

2.8 Effectively edit a document using find and replace (p. W2-93).

- The ***Find*** feature in Word allows you to search for specific information in a document.
- The ***Navigation pane*** displays all occurrences of the text for which you are searching.
- The ***Replace*** feature allows you to search for specific information in a document and replace it with other information.
- Both *Find* and *Replace* allow you to search for and replace formatting in a document.
- Use the ***Go To*** feature to go directly to a page, section, line, or other area in your document.

2.9 Improve overall document design and format by using borders, shading, horizontal lines, and hyperlinks (p. W2-96).

- *You can apply* ***borders*** and ***shading*** to text and paragraphs in a document.
- Word provides a variety of built-in border and shading options that you can apply to text, or you can customize borders and shading using the *Borders and Shading* dialog box.
- You can apply ***page borders*** to an individual page or all pages in a document.
- A ***horizontal line*** is a graphic that you can insert into a document.
- A ***hyperlink*** takes readers to a web page, a different document, or a different location in a document.

Check for Understanding

On the ***Online Learning Center*** for this text (**www.mhhe.com/office2013inpractice**), there are a variety of resources that can be used to review the concepts covered in this chapter.

The following Online Learning Resources are available on the Online Learning Center.

- Multiple choice questions
- Short answer questions
- Matching exercises

Guided Project 2-1

In this project, you create a form for contractors seeking insurance coverage at Central Sierra Insurance. You use a theme, styles, a multilevel list, tab stops, leaders, indents, borders and shading, a page break, and page numbering.
[Student Learning Outcomes 2.1, 2.2, 2.3, 2.4, 2.5, 2.6, 2.7, 2.9]

File Needed: ***InsuranceQuestionnaire-02.docx***
Completed Project File Name: ***[your initials] Word 2-1.docx***

Skills Covered in This Project

- Modify an existing document.
- Change margins.
- Apply a document theme.
- Change font size, line spacing, and paragraph spacing.
- Apply a style to selected text.
- Modify an existing style.
- Apply borders and shading to selected text.
- Set and use a tab stop with an underline leader.
- Apply and modify a multilevel list.
- Insert a page break.
- Insert a page number in the footer.

---

1. Open the ***InsuranceQuestionnaire-02*** document from your student data files.
2. Save this document as ***[your initials] Word 2-1***.
3. Change the margins of the document.
   a. Click the **Margins** button [*Page Layout* tab, *Page Setup* group] and select **Custom Margins**. The *Page Setup* dialog box opens.
   b. Change the *Left* and *Right* margins to **0.75"**.
   c. Click **OK** to close the *Page Setup* dialog box.
4. Change the theme and color set of the document.
   a. Click the **Themes** button [*Design* tab, *Document Formatting* group].
   b. Select **Integral** from the drop-down list.
   c. Click the **Colors** button [*Document Formatting* group] (Figure 2-92).
   d. Select **Aspect** from the drop-down list.
5. Change the font size, paragraph spacing, and line spacing on the entire document.
   a. Press **Ctrl+A** to select the entire document.
   b. Change the font size to **11 pt**.
   c. Change the line spacing to **Single** (1.0).
   d. Change the *After* paragraph spacing to **6 pt**.

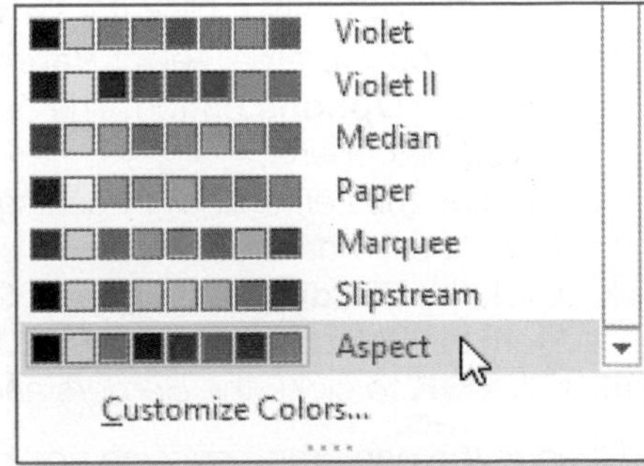

2-92 Select color set

6. Apply styles to selected text.
   a. Place the insertion point in the first line of text ("Contractor's Insurance Questionnaire").
   b. Click the **Title** style [*Home* tab, *Styles* group] in the *Style* gallery.
   c. Select the second line of the document (**"Please carefully . . . "**).
   d. Right-click the selected text and click **Styles** on the mini toolbar. The *Style* gallery list appears.
   e. Select **Book Title** from the *Style* gallery.
   f. With this text still selected, click the **Change Case** button in the *Font* group, and select **UPPERCASE**.
   g. Select **"Applicant's Instructions"** and apply the **Intense Quote** style from the *Style* gallery.
   h. In the next paragraph ("Please answer ALL questions . . ."), apply the **Strong** style to the three words in all caps ("ALL," "NONE," and "NONE").
   i. On the second page of the document, select **"Insurance Application Disclaimer"** and apply the **Intense Quote** style.

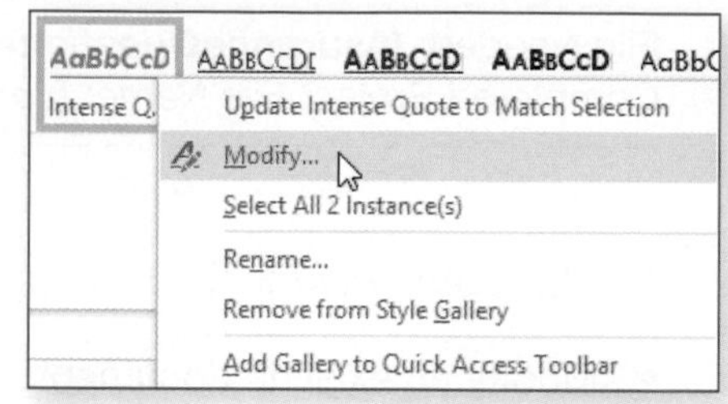

2-93 Modify an existing style

7. Modify an existing style.
   a. Click the **More** button [*Home* tab, *Styles* group] to display the *Style* gallery.
   b. Right-click the **Intense Quote** style in the *Style* gallery and select **Modify** (Figure 2-93). The *Modify Style* dialog box opens.
   c. In the *Formatting* area, change the font size to **12 pt**.
   d. Click the **Format** button on the bottom left and select **Paragraph**. The *Paragraph* dialog box opens.
   e. Change the *Left* and *Right* indent to **0**.
   f. Click **OK** to close the *Paragraph* dialog box.
   g. Click the **Only in this document** radio button to apply the style changes to only this document.
   h. Click **OK** to close the *Modify Style* dialog box. The change should be applied to all text formatted with the *Intense Reference* style on both the first and second pages.

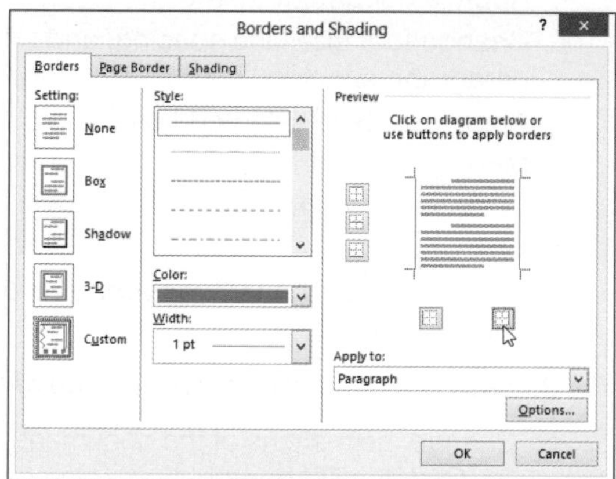

2-94 Border option settings

8. Add borders and shading to selected text.
   a. On the second page, select the three paragraphs below "Insurance Application Disclaimer."
   b. Click the **Borders** drop-down arrow [*Home* tab, *Paragraph* group] and select **Borders and Shading**. The *Borders and Shading* dialog box opens (Figure 2-94).
   c. In the *Setting* area, select **Custom**.
   d. In the *Style* area, select the solid line border.
   e. In the *Color* area, select **Orange**, **Accent 1**.
   f. In the *Width* area, select **1 pt**.
   g. In the *Preview* area, click the **Left** and **Right** border buttons.
   h. In the *Apply to* area, select **Paragraph**.
   i. Click the **Options** button. The *Border and Shading Options* dialog box opens.
   j. Change the *Left* and *Right* settings to **5 pt**. and click **OK** to close the *Border and Shading Options* dialog box.
   k. Click the **Shading** tab (Figure 2-95).
   l. From the *Fill* drop-down list, select **Orange**, **Accent 1**, **Lighter 80%**.
   m. Click **OK** to close the *Borders and Shading* dialog box.

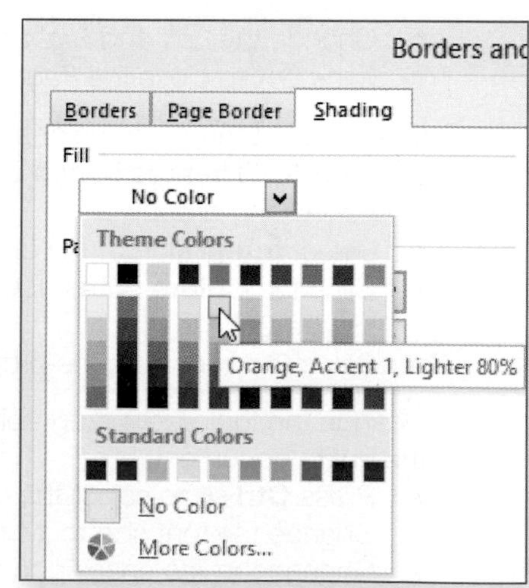

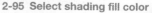

2-95 Select shading fill color

9. Change the paragraph spacing and add a tab stop with an underline leader to selected text.
   a. Select the last three lines of text on the second page.
   b. Click the **Paragraph** launcher [*Home* or *Page Layout* tab].

c. Change the *Before* paragraph spacing to **12 pt**.
d. Click the **Tabs** button to open the *Tabs* dialog box (Figure 2-96).
e. In the *Tab stop position* area, type 7.
f. Click the **Right** radio button in the *Alignment* area.
g. Click the **4** (solid underline) radio button in the *Leader* area.
h. Click the **Set** button to set this tab stop.
i. Click **OK** to close the *Tabs* dialog box.
j. Click at the end of the "Name and Title of the Insured" line and press **Tab**. A solid underline is inserted across the page to the right margin.
k. Repeat the above step (j.) on the next two lines.

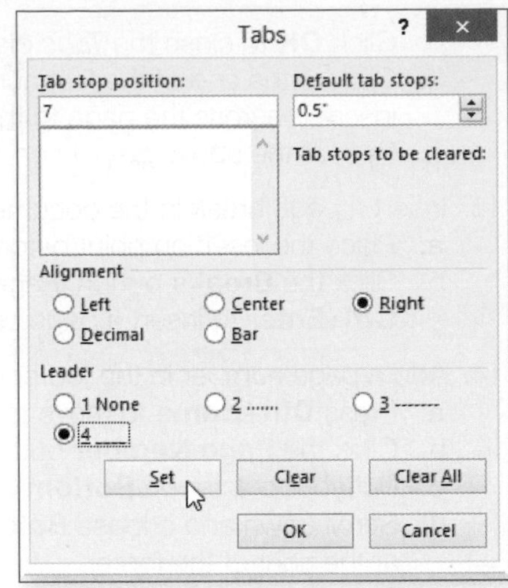

2-96 Set a right tab stop with an underline leader

10. Add a multilevel list to selected text and modify lists settings.
    a. Select the lines of text beginning with "Applicant" on the first page and ending with the last "If yes, please explain:" on the second page.
    b. Click the **Multilevel List** button [*Home* tab, *Paragraph* group] and select the **1)**, **a)**, **i)** option.
    c. With the text still selected, click the **Multilevel List** button and select **Define new Multilevel list**. The *Define new Multilevel list* dialog box opens (Figure 2-97).
    d. Click the **Set for All Levels** button. The *Set for All Levels* dialog box opens.
    e. Set the *Bullet/Number position for first level* to **0"**.
    f. Set the *Text position for first level* to **0.3"**.
    g. Set the *Additional indent for each level* to **0.3"**.
    h. Click **OK** to close the *Set for All Levels* dialog box.
    i. Click **OK** to close the *Define new Multilevel list* dialog box.

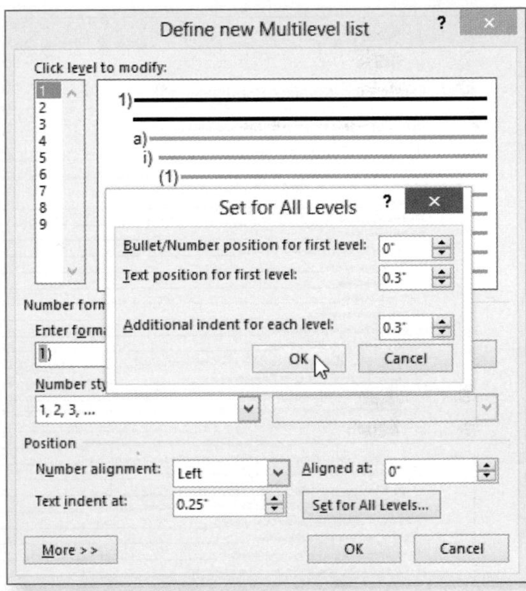

2-97 Change settings for a multilevel list

11. Increase indent on selected lines.
    a. Click anywhere on the list to deselect it.
    b. Place your insertion point in 13 in the numbered list ("If yes, . . .") and click **Increase Indent** [*Home* tab, *Paragraph* group]. This line is now letter *a)*.
    c. Repeat the above step (b.) on each of the lines in the list that begin with "If yes, . . .". There should be 28 numbered items in the list when you finish this process.
12. Change paragraph spacing to the multilevel list and add a right tab stop with an underline leader.
    a. Select the entire multilevel list.
    b. Click the **Paragraph** launcher [*Home* or *Page Layout* tab].
    c. Deselect the **Don't add space between paragraphs of the same style** check box (Figure 2-98).
    d. Click the **Tabs** button to open the *Tabs* dialog box.
    e. In the *Tab stop position* area, type 7.
    f. Click the **Right** radio button in the *Alignment* area.
    g. Click the **4** (solid underline) radio button in the *Leader* area.
    h. Click the **Set** button to set this tab stop.

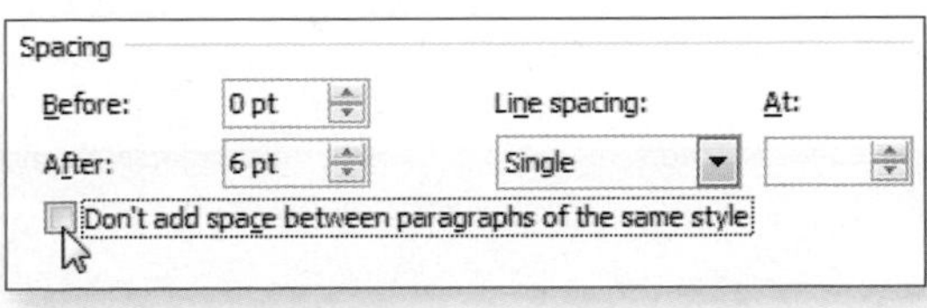

2-98 Add spacing between lines of text with the same style

   i. Click **OK** to close the *Tabs* dialog box.
   j. Click at the end of the first numbered item ("Applicant:") and press **Tab**. A solid underline will be inserted across the page to the right margin.
   k. Repeat the above step (j.) on each of the numbered and lettered paragraphs.

13. Insert a page break in the document.
   a. Place the insertion point before the text in number 22 in the multilevel list.
   b. Click the **Breaks** button [*Page Layout* tab, *Page Setup* group] and select **Page Break**, or press **Ctrl+Enter** to insert a page break.

14. Add a page number in the footer of the document.
   a. Press **Ctrl+Home** to move to the top of the document.
   b. Click the **Page Number** button [*Insert* tab, *Header & Footer* group].
   c. Put your pointer on **Bottom of Page** to display the drop-down list.
   d. Scroll down and choose **Bold Numbers 3** in the *Page X of Y* section. The page number is inserted at the right of the footer.
   e. Click the blank line below the page number in the footer and press **Backspace** to delete the blank line.
   f. Click the **Close Header and Footer** button [*Header & Footer Tools Design* tab, *Close* group].

15. Save and close the document (Figure 2-99).

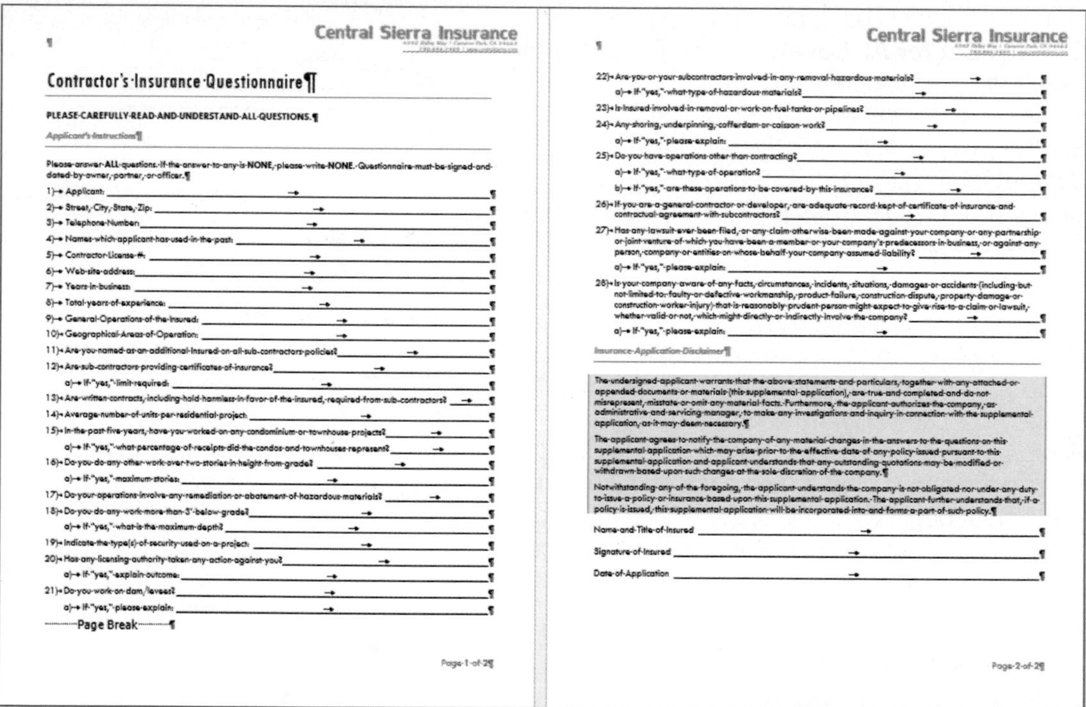

Central Sierra Insurance

Contractor's Insurance Questionnaire

PLEASE CAREFULLY READ AND UNDERSTAND ALL QUESTIONS.

Applicant's Instructions

Please answer **ALL** questions. If the answer to any is **NONE**, please write **NONE**. Questionnaire must be signed and dated by owner, partner, or officer.

1) Applicant: ________
2) Street, City, State, Zip: ________
3) Telephone Number: ________
4) Names which applicant has used in the past: ________
5) Contractor License #: ________
6) Web site address: ________
7) Years in business: ________
8) Total years of experience: ________
9) General Operations of the Insured: ________
10) Geographical Areas of Operation: ________
11) Are you named as an additional Insured on all sub-contractors policies? ________
12) Are sub-contractors providing certificates of insurance? ________
   a) If "yes," limit required: ________
13) Are written contracts, including hold harmless in favor of the insured, required from sub-contractors? ________
14) Average number of units per residential project: ________
15) In the past five years, have you worked on any condominium or townhouse projects? ________
   a) If "yes," what percentage of receipts did the condos and townhouses represent? ________
16) Do you do any other work over two stories in height from grade? ________
   a) If "yes," maximum stories: ________
17) Do your operations involve any remediation or abatement of hazardous materials? ________
18) Do you do any work more than 3' below grade? ________
   a) If "yes," what is the maximum depth? ________
19) Indicate the type(s) of security used on a project: ________
20) Has any licensing authority taken any action against you? ________
   a) If "yes," explain outcome: ________
21) Do you work on dam/levees? ________
   a) If "yes," please explain: ________

Page Break

Page 1 of 2

Central Sierra Insurance

22) Are you or your subcontractors involved in any removal hazardous materials? ________
   a) If "yes," what type of hazardous materials? ________
23) Is Insured involved in removal or work on fuel tanks or pipelines? ________
24) Any shoring, underpinning, cofferdam or caisson work? ________
   a) If "yes," please explain: ________
25) Do you have operations other than contracting? ________
   a) If "yes," what type of operation? ________
   b) If "yes," are these operations to be covered by this insurance? ________
26) If you are a general contractor or developer, are adequate record kept of certificate of insurance and contractual agreement with subcontractors? ________
27) Has any lawsuit ever been filed, or any claim otherwise been made against your company or any partnership or joint venture of which you have been a member or your company's predecessors in business, or against any person, company or entities on whose behalf your company assumed liability? ________
   a) If "yes," please explain: ________
28) Is your company aware of any facts, circumstances, incidents, situations, damages or accidents (including but not limited to: faulty or defective workmanship, product failure, construction dispute, property damage or construction worker injury) that is reasonably prudent person might expect to give rise to a claim or lawsuit, whether valid or not, which might directly or indirectly involve the company? ________
   a) If "yes," please explain: ________

Insurance Application Disclaimer

The undersigned applicant warrants that the above statements and particulars, together with any attached or appended documents or materials (this supplemental application), are true and completed and do not misrepresent, misstate or omit any material facts. Furthermore, the applicant authorizes the company, as administrative and servicing manager, to make any investigations and inquiry in connection with the supplemental application, as it may deem necessary.

The applicant agrees to notify the company of any material changes in the answers to the questions on this supplemental application which may arise prior to the effective date of any policy issued pursuant to this supplemental application and applicant understands that any outstanding quotations may be modified or withdrawn based upon such changes at the sole discretion of the company.

Notwithstanding any of the foregoing, the applicant understands the company is not obligated nor under any duty to issue a policy or insurance based upon this supplemental application. The applicant further understands that, if a policy is issued, this supplemental application will be incorporated into and forms a part of such policy.

Name and Title of Insured ________

Signature of Insured ________

Date of Application ________

Page 2 of 2

2-99 Word 2-1 completed

Guided Project 2-2

In this project, you create a checklist for employees at Placer Hills Real Estate to track the tasks they need to complete when a house enters escrow. You create a bulleted list, modify a bullet in a list, set and modify tab stops, apply and modify styles, and insert document properties in the footer. **[Student Learning Outcomes 2.1, 2.2, 2.3, 2.4, 2.6, 2.7, 2.9]**

File Needed: ***SellerEscrowChecklist-02.docx***
Completed Project File Name: ***[your initials] Word 2-2.docx***

Skills Covered in This Project

- Modify an existing document.
- Change margins, line spacing, font, and font size.
- Set a tab stop using the ruler.
- Set a tab stop with leader.
- Apply a style to selected text.
- Modify an existing style.
- Apply and customize a bulleted list.
- Use the *Format Painter*.
- Insert a document property field and date in the footer.
- Apply a border in the footer.

1. Open the ***SellerEscrowChecklist-02*** document from your student data files.
2. Save this document as ***[your initials] Word 2-2***.
3. Change margins, vertical alignment, line spacing, and font and font size, and delete blank lines.
   a. Click the **Margins** button [*Page Layout* tab, *Page Setup* group].
   b. Select **Normal** from the drop-down list.
   c. Click the **Page Setup** launcher to open the *Page Setup* dialog box.
   d. Click the **Layout** tab.
   e. In the *Page* area, change *Vertical alignment* to **Center**.
   f. Click **OK** to close the *Page Setup* dialog box.
   g. Press **Ctrl+A** to select the entire document.
   h. Change the font to **Calibri**.
   i. Change the font size to **12 pt**.
   j. Change the line spacing to **2.0** (Double).
   k. Turn on **Show/Hide** and delete all of the blank lines between the lines of text.
4. Add text to the document.
   a. Click after "Seller" in the second line of the document and press **Tab** once.
   b. Type Property Address.
   c. Click after "Escrow Company" and press **Tab** once.
   d. Type Escrow #.
   e. Click after "Tasks to be Completed" and press **Tab** once.
   f. Type Date Completed.
5. Set tab stops using the ruler to line up information.
   a. Select the second and third lines of text (beginning with "Seller").
   b. Ensure that the **Left Tab** is selected in the tab selector area to the left of the horizontal ruler.
   c. Click the ruler at **3.5"**. If you click the wrong location on the ruler, drag the tab stop to the correct location (Figure 2-100).
   d. Select the fourth line of text (beginning with "Tasks").
   e. Click to the **tab selector** to change to a center tab stop (Figure 2-101).
   f. Click the ruler at **5.5"**.

Tab selector
Left Tab

2-100 Set left tab stop using the ruler

2-101 Center tab stop

6. Set tab stops and add leaders to create lines for users to fill in information.
   a. Select the second and third lines of text (beginning with "Seller").
   b. Click the **Paragraph** launcher. The *Paragraph* dialog box opens.
   c. Click the **Tabs** button. The *Tabs* dialog box opens.
   d. In the *Tab stop position* area, type 3.
   e. Click the **Right** radio button in the *Alignment* area.
   f. Click the **4** (solid underline) radio button in the *Leader* area.
   g. Click the **Set** button to set this tab stop.
   h. In the *Tab stop position* area, type 6.5.
   i. Click the **Right** radio button in the *Alignment* area.
   j. Click the **4** (solid underline) radio button in the *Leader* area.
   k. Click the **Set** button to set this tab stop.
   l. Click **OK** to close the *Tabs* dialog box.
7. Use tab stops to align text.
   a. Place the insertion point before "Property Address" and press **Tab** once.
   b. Click after "Property Address" and press **Tab** once.
   c. Place the insertion point before "Escrow #" and press **Tab** once.
   d. Click after "Escrow #" and press **Tab** once.
8. Apply styles to selected text and modify a style.
   a. Place the insertion point in the first line of text ("Seller Escrow Checklist").
   b. Select **Title** style in the *Style* gallery [*Home* tab, *Styles* group].
   c. Change the *After* paragraph spacing to **24 pt**. [*Page Layout* tab, *Paragraph* group].
   d. Click the **Center** alignment button to center the title.
   e. Select **"Tasks to be Completed"**.
   f. Apply the **Book Title** style from the *Style* gallery.
   g. Change the font size of the selected text to **14 pt**. and apply a **Double underline**.
   h. Right-click the **Book Title** style in the *Style* gallery and select **Update Book Title to Match Selection**. The *Book Title* style is updated.
   i. Select **"Date Completed"** and apply the **Book Title** style.
9. Create a bulleted list to selected text and apply a custom bullet.
   a. Select the remaining lines of text beginning with "Open Escrow . . .".
   b. Click the **Bullets** drop-down arrow *[Home* tab, *Paragraph* group] and select **Define New Bullet**. The *Define New Bullet* dialog box opens.
   c. Click the **Symbol** button. The *Symbol* dialog box opens (Figure 2-102).
   d. Click the **Font** drop-down arrow and select **Wingdings**.
   e. Scroll down the list and select the **open square** bullet (Character code 113).
   f. Click **OK** to close the *Symbol* dialog box.
   g. Click the **Font** button in the *Define New Bullet* dialog box. The *Font* dialog box opens.
   h. Change the *Size* to **14 pt**.
   i. Click **OK** to close the *Font* dialog box.
   j. Click **OK** to close the *Define New Bullet* dialog box.
   k. With the bulleted list still selected, click the **Decrease Indent** button to align the bullet at the left margin.

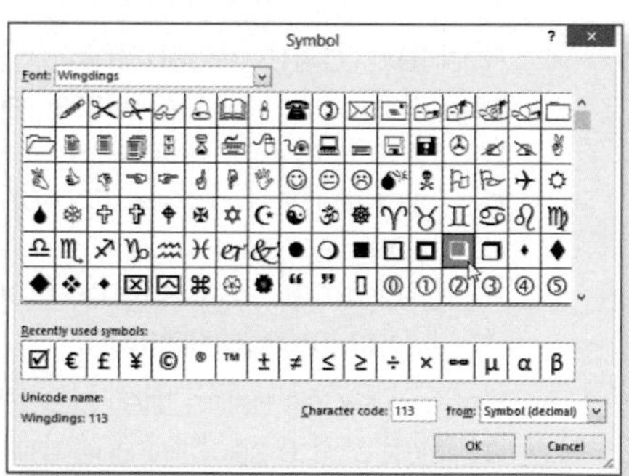

2-102 Select a symbol for a custom bullet

10. Change the hanging indent and add tab stops.
   a. Select the bulleted list.
   b. Click the **Paragraph** launcher to open the *Paragraph* dialog box.
   c. Change the hanging indent to **0.3"**.

d. Click the **Tabs** button. The *Tabs* dialog box opens (Figure 2-103).
e. In the *Tab stop position* area, type 4.5.
f. Click the **Left** radio button in the *Alignment* area.
g. Click the **1 None** radio button in the *Leader* area.
h. Click the **Set** button to set this tab stop.
i. In the *Tab stop position* area, type 6.5.
j. Click the **Right** radio button in the *Alignment* area.
k. Click the **4** (solid underline) radio button in the *Leader* area.
l. Click the **Set** button to set this tab stop.
m. Click **OK** to close the *Tabs* dialog box.
n. Place the insertion point after "Open Escrow with Escrow Company" and press **Tab** two times. A solid underline is inserted between 4.5" and 6.5".
o. Repeat the step above (n.) on the remaining lines in the bulleted list.

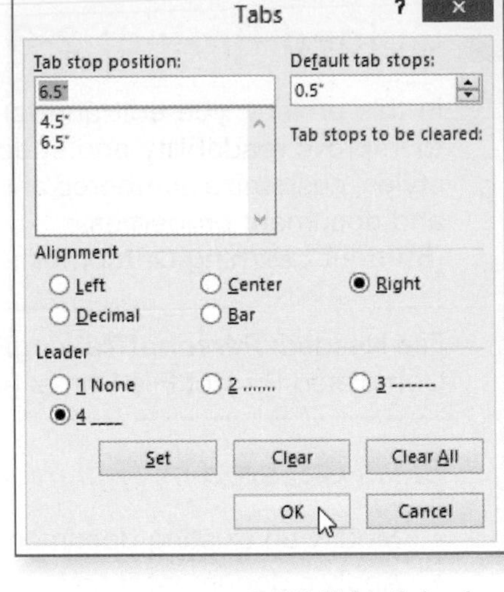

2-103 *Tabs* dialog box

11. Add text to the document.
    a. Press **Enter** after the last line of text in the document.
    b. Click the **Bullets** button [*Home* tab, *Paragraph* group] to turn off the bullet on this line.
    c. Type Fax/Email Clear Pest Report and press **Enter**.
    d. Type Title and press **Enter**.
    e. Type Lender and press **Enter**.
    f. Type Buyer's Agent.

12. Apply a style to selected text and use the *Format Painter*.
    a. Select **"Fax/Email Clear Pest Report"** and apply the **Subtle Reference** style.
    b. Click one of the bulleted items.
    c. Click the **Format Painter** button [*Home* tab, *Clipboard* group] to copy the formatting of this bulleted item.
    d. Select the last three lines of text (beginning with "Title . . ."). The *Format Painter* copies the bullet formatting and tab settings to these lines of text.
    e. Press **Tab** two times after each of these last three lines to insert the tab stops and leaders.

13. Insert a document property field, the date, and a border in the footer of the document.
    a. Click the **Footer** button [*Insert* tab, *Header & Footer* group].
    b. Select **Edit Footer** from the drop-down list. The footer opens.
    c. Click the **Quick Parts** button [*Header & Footer Tools Design* tab, *Insert* group].
    d. Click **Document Property** and select **Company**. The *Company* document property field is inserted.
    e. Press the **right arrow** key once to deselect the *Company* field.
    f. Press **Tab** two times, type Last Updated:, and **space** once. The text aligns at the right side of the footer.
    g. Click the **Date & Time** button [*Header & Footer Tools Design* tab, *Insert* group]. The *Date and Time* dialog box opens.
    h. Select the third option (month, day, year) and click the **Update automatically** check box.
    i. Click **OK** to close the dialog box.
    j. Select all of the text in the footer and change the font to **Calibri** and the font size to **10 pt**.
    k. Click the **Borders** drop-down arrow [*Home* tab, *Paragraph* group] and select **Top Border**.
    l. Click the **Close Header and Footer** button [*Header & Footer Tools Design* tab, *Close* group].

14. Save and close the document (Figure 2-104).

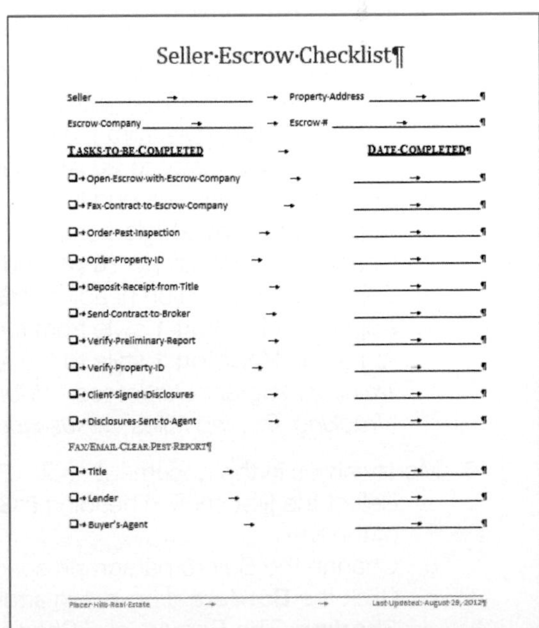
Seller·Escrow·Checklist¶

Seller → → Property·Address → ¶
Escrow·Company → → Escrow·# → ¶
TASKS·TO·BE·COMPLETED → DATE·COMPLETED¶
❑→Open·Escrow·with·Escrow·Company → → ¶
❑→Fax·Contract·to·Escrow·Company → → ¶
❑→Order·Pest·Inspection → → ¶
❑→Order·Property·ID → → ¶
❑→Deposit·Receipt·from·Title → → ¶
❑→Send·Contract·to·Broker → → ¶
❑→Verify·Preliminary·Report → → ¶
❑→Verify·Property·ID → → ¶
❑→Client·Signed·Disclosures → → ¶
❑→Disclosures·Sent·to·Agent → → ¶
FAX/EMAIL·CLEAR·PEST·REPORT¶
❑→Title → → ¶
❑→Lender → → ¶
❑→Buyer's·Agent → → ¶

Placer·Hills·Real·Estate → → Last·Updated:·August·29,·2012¶

2-104 Word 2-2 completed

Guided Project 2-3

In this project, you edit and format the personal training guide for the American River Cycling Club to improve readability and effectiveness. You use find and replace, apply a document theme, modify styles, customize numbered and bulleted lists, apply borders and shading, and insert headers, footers, and document properties.
[Student Learning Outcomes 2.3, 2.4, 2.6, 2.7, 2.8, 2.9]

File Needed: ***PersonalTrainingProgram-02.docx***
Completed Project File Name: ***[your initials] Word 2-3.docx***

Skills Covered in This Project

- Modify an existing document.
- Apply a document theme.
- Change line spacing and paragraph spacing.
- Apply a style to selected text.
- Modify an existing style.
- Apply borders and shading to selected text.
- Customize a multilevel bulleted list.
- Use *Find* and *Replace*.
- Insert a hyperlink.
- Insert header, footer, page number, and document properties.

1. Open the ***PersonalTrainingProgram-02*** document from your student data files.
2. Save this document as ***[your initials] Word 2-3***.
3. Apply a document theme and change the line and paragraph spacing.
   a. Click the **Themes** button [*Design* tab, *Document Formatting* group].
   b. Select **Slice** from the drop-down list of theme options.
   c. Select the entire document.
   d. Change the line spacing to **1.15**.
   e. Change the after paragraph spacing to **10 pt**.
   f. Turn on **Show/Hide** and delete any blank lines in the document.
4. Apply styles to the title, subtitle, and section headings.
   a. Select the title (first line) of the document.
   b. Apply the **Title** style from the *Style* gallery [*Home* tab, *Styles* group].
   c. Change the font size to **20 pt**., make it **bold**, and **center** it horizontally.
   d. Select the subtitle (second line) of the document.
   e. Apply the **Subtitle** style from the *Style* gallery.
   f. Change the font size to **16 pt**. and **center** horizontally.
   g. Select the first section heading **("General Guidelines")**.
   h. Apply the **Heading 1** style from the *Style* gallery.
   i. Apply the **Heading 1** style to the remaining section headings in the document *("Personal Training Program Guidelines," "More About Long Rides," "Training Intensity and Heart Rate," "Tracking Training Miles versus Hours,"* and *"Using a Training Log"*).
5. Modify styles in the document.
   a. Select the first section heading **("General Guidelines")** including the paragraph mark at the end of the line.
   b. Change the *Before* paragraph spacing to **12 pt**. and the *After* paragraph spacing to **6 pt**.
   c. Click the **Borders** drop-down arrow [*Home* tab, *Paragraph* group] and select **Borders and Shading**. The *Borders and Shading* dialog box opens.

d. In the *Setting* area, select **Shadow**.
e. In the *Style* area, select the solid line.
f. In the *Color* area, select **Dark Blue**, **Accent 1**, **Darker 50%** (Figure 2-105).
g. In the *Width* area, select **1 pt**.
h. In the *Apply to* area, make sure that **Paragraph** is selected.
i. Click the **Shading** tab and in the *Fill* area, select **Dark Blue**, **Accent 1**, **Lighter 80%**.
j. In the *Apply to* area, make sure that **Paragraph** is selected and click **OK** to close the *Borders and Shading* dialog box.
k. With the heading still selected, right-click the **Heading 1** style in the *Style gallery*.
l. Select **Update Heading 1 to Match Selection**. All of the headings with the *Heading 1* style applied are automatically updated in the document.

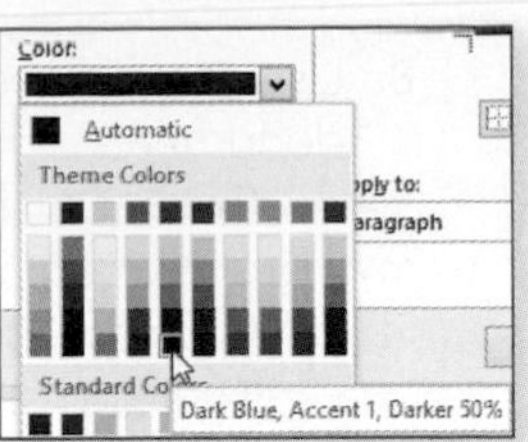

2-105 Select border line color

6. Customize the bullets and indents for the bulleted list.
   a. Right-click the first bulleted item on the first page and select **Adjust List Indents**. The *Define new Multilevel list* dialog box opens.
   b. Click **1** in the *Click level to modify* area.
   c. In the *Number style for this level* area, select **New Bullet** from the drop-down list (Figure 2-106). The *Symbol* dialog box opens.
   d. In the *Font* area, select **Webdings** from the drop-down list (Figure 2-107).
   e. Click the **right pointing triangle** (Character code 52) and click **OK** to close the *Symbol* dialog box.
   f. Click **2** in the *Click level to modify* area in the *Define new Multilevel list* dialog box.
   g. In the *Number style for this level* area, select **New Bullet** from the drop-down list. The *Symbol* dialog box opens.
   h. In the *Font* area, select **Webdings** from the drop-down list.
   i. Click the **double right pointing triangle** (Character code 56) and click **OK** to close the *Symbol* dialog box.
   j. Click the **Set for All Levels** button in the *Define new Multilevel list* dialog box. The *Set for All Levels* dialog box opens (Figure 2-108).
   k. Change the *Bullet/Number position for first level* to **0.25"**.
   l. Change the *Text position for first level* to **0.5"**.
   m. Change *Additional indent for each level* to **0.25"**.
   n. Click **OK** to close the *Set for All Levels* dialog box.
   o. Click **OK** to close the *Define new Multilevel list* dialog box. All of the first and second level bullets and indents in the entire document are changed.

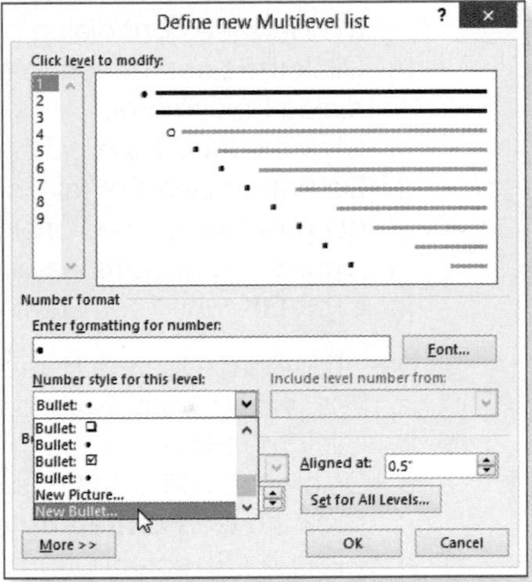

2-106 Customize bulleted list

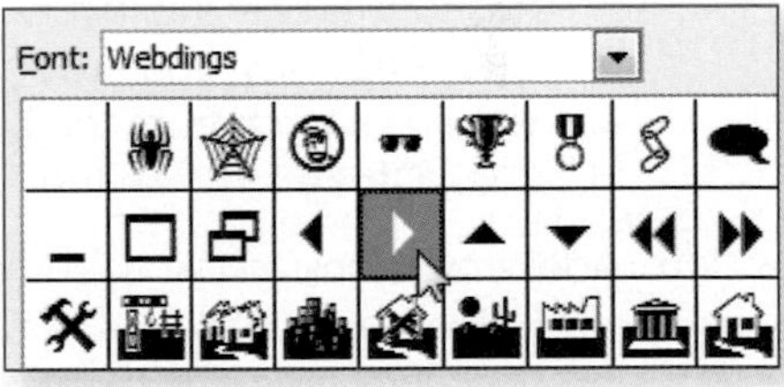

2-107 Select bullet from Webdings font set

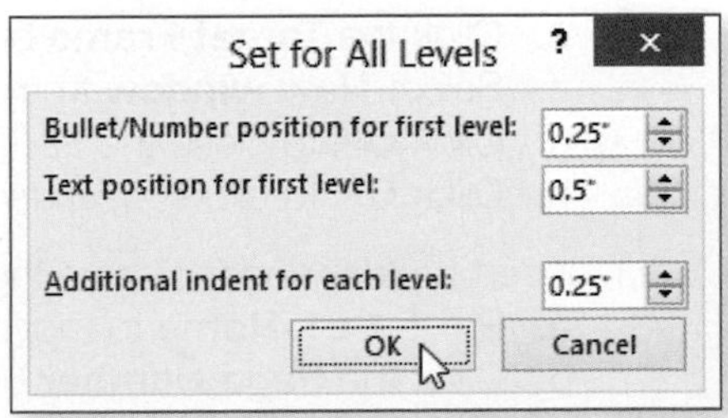

2-108 Set indents for all levels

7. Use the *Find* feature to find text in the document.
   a. Press **Ctrl+Home** to go to the beginning of the document.
   b. Press **Ctrl+F** to open *Find* in the *Navigation* pane.
   c. Type personal training program in the *Search Document* area. All instances of this text appear below in the *Navigation* pane.
   d. Click after "personal training program" in the first body paragraph on the first page and type (PTP). Make sure there is one space before and after the parentheses.
   e. Select **"PTP"** and make **italic**.
   f. Click the **X** in the upper right of the *Navigation* pane to close this pane.

8. Use the replace feature to find and replace text in the document.
   a. Press **Ctrl+Home** to go to the beginning of the document.
   b. Click the **Replace** button [*Home* tab, *Editing* group]. The *Find and Replace* dialog box opens with the *Replace* tab selected (Figure 2-109).
   c. In the *Find what* area, type personal training program.
   d. In the *Replace with* area, type PTP.
   e. Click the **More** button to display more search options.
   f. Click the **Format** button and select **Font**. The *Replace Font* dialog box opens.
   g. Click **Italic** in the *Font style* area and click **OK** to close the *Replace Font* dialog box.
   h. Click the **Less** button to make the *Find and Replace* dialog box smaller.
   i. Click the **Find Next** button to find the first occurrence of "personal training program" in the document.
   j. Do not replace this text in the title, first body paragraph, or section heading. Replace all other occurrences of "personal training program" with "*PTP*." Click the **Replace** button to replace the highlighted occurrence or click the **Find Next** button to skip and not replace an occurrence.
   k. Click **OK** when you are finished searching the document.

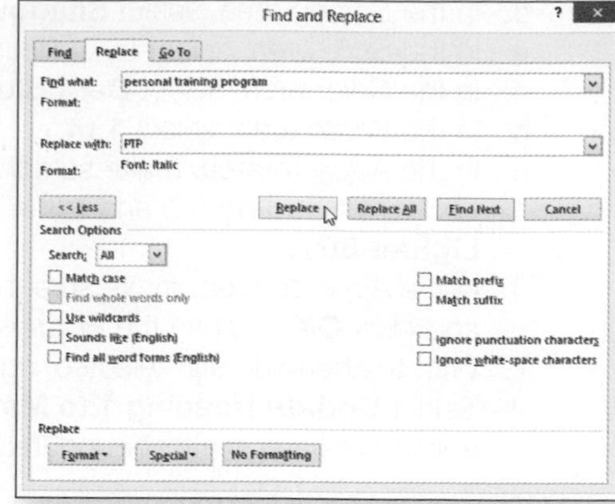

2-109 Replace text with text and formatting

9. Use the replace feature to replace some hyphens with an em dash.
   a. With the *Find and Replace* dialog box still open, delete the text in the *Find what* area and type - (hyphen).
   b. Click the **More** button.
   c. Delete the text in the *Replace with* area.
   d. Click the **No Formatting** button at the bottom of the dialog box to clear the *Replace with* formatting.
   e. Click the **Special** button and select **Em Dash**.
   f. Click the **Less** button.
   g. Click the **Find Next** button to find the first occurrence of the hyphen. Replace the hyphen with an em dash when a hyphen is used to set off part of a sentence; skip (click **Find Next**) when the hyphen is used in a hyphenated word.
   h. Click **OK** when you are finished searching the document (click **No** if a dialog box opens asking if you want to search from the beginning of the document).
   i. Click **Close** to close the *Find and Replace* dialog box.

10. Add a hyperlink to the document.
   a. Select the subtitle of the document **("American River Cycling Club")**.
   b. Click the **Hyperlink** button [*Insert* tab, *Links* group] or press **Ctrl+K**. The *Insert Hyperlink* dialog box opens.
   c. Click the **Existing File or Web Page** button in the *Link to* area.
   d. Type www.arcc.org in the *Address* area.
   e. Click the **Target Frame** button. The *Set Target Frame* dialog box opens.
   f. Select **New window** from the drop-down list.
   g. Click **OK** to close the *Set Target Frame* dialog box.
   h. Click **OK** to close the *Insert Hyperlink* dialog box.

11. Insert header and footer on the second and continuing pages.
   a. Press **Ctrl+Home** to move to the beginning of the document.
   b. Click the **Page Number** button [*Insert* tab, *Header & Footer* group].
   c. Click **Top of Page** and select **Accent Bar 2** from the drop-down list. The header is inserted and remains open with the *Header & Footer Tools Design* tab displayed.
   d. Check the **Different First Page** check box [*Options* group] to remove the header from the first page so it only displays on the second and continuing pages.

12. Insert document property fields in the footer.
    a. With the header still open, click the **Go to Footer** button [*Navigation* group].
    b. Click the **Next** button [*Navigation* group] to move to the footer on the second page.
    c. Click the **Quick Parts** button [*Insert* group] and select **Document Property**.
    d. Select **Company** to insert the company document property field.
    e. Press the **right arrow** key once to deselect the property field.
    f. Press **Tab** two times to move the insertion point to the right margin in the footer.
    g. Click the **Quick Parts** button [*Insert* group] and select **Document Property**.
    h. Select **Title** to insert the title document property field.
    i. Press **Ctrl+A** to select all of the text in the footer.
    j. Make this text **bold** and **italic**.
    k. Click the **Close Header and Footer** button [*Header & Footer Tools Design* tab, *Close* group]. The header and footer information should appear on the second and continuing pages in the document.
13. Save and close the document (Figure 2-110).

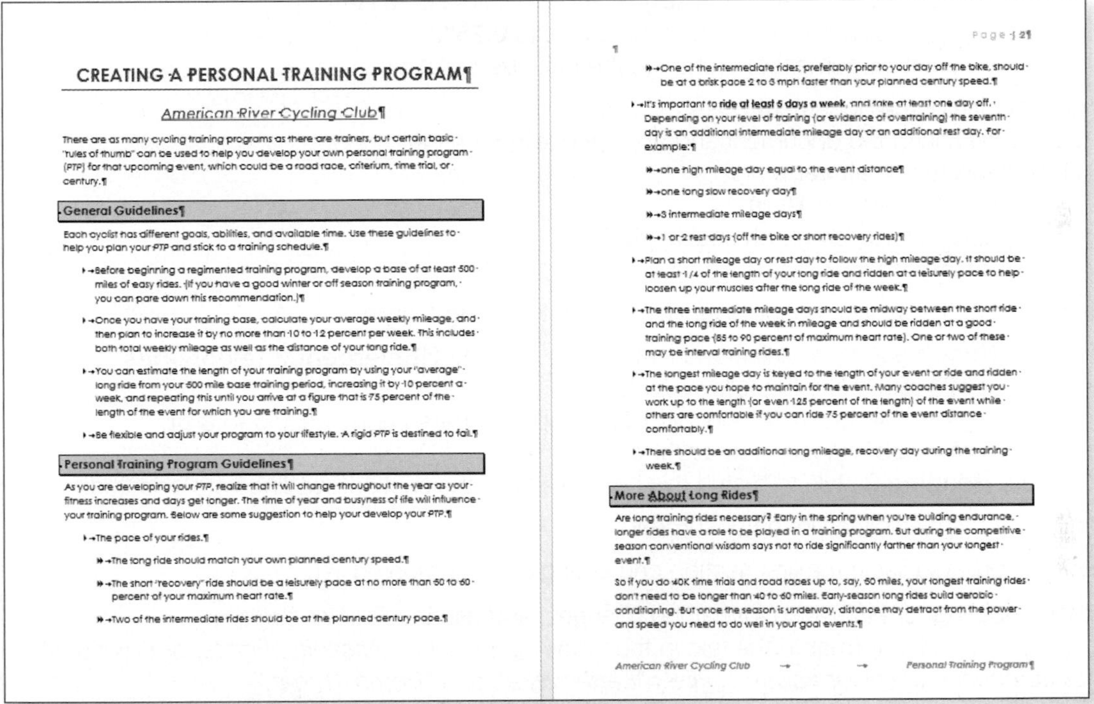

CREATING A PERSONAL TRAINING PROGRAM

American River Cycling Club

There are as many cycling training programs as there are trainers, but certain basic "rules of thumb" can be used to help you develop your own personal training program (PTP) for that upcoming event, which could be a road race, criterium, time trial, or century.

General Guidelines

Each cyclist has different goals, abilities, and available time. Use these guidelines to help you plan your *PTP* and stick to a training schedule.

- Before beginning a regimented training program, develop a base of at least 500 miles of easy rides. (If you have a good winter or off season training program, you can pare down this recommendation.)
- Once you have your training base, calculate your average weekly mileage, and then plan to increase it by no more than 10 to 12 percent per week. This includes both total weekly mileage as well as the distance of your long ride.
- You can estimate the length of your training program by using your "average" long ride from your 500 mile base training period, increasing it by 10 percent a week, and repeating this until you arrive at a figure that is 75 percent of the length of the event for which you are training.
- Be flexible and adjust your program to your lifestyle. A rigid *PTP* is destined to fail.

Personal Training Program Guidelines

As you are developing your *PTP*, realize that it will change throughout the year as your fitness increases and days get longer. The time of year and busyness of life will influence your training program. Below are some suggestion to help your develop your *PTP*.

- The pace of your rides.
  - The long ride should match your own planned century speed.
  - The short "recovery" ride should be a leisurely pace at no more than 50 to 60 percent of your maximum heart rate.
  - Two of the intermediate rides should be at the planned century pace.

Page | 2

  - One of the intermediate rides, preferably prior to your day off the bike, should be at a brisk pace 2 to 3 mph faster than your planned century speed.
- It's important to **ride at least 5 days a week**, and take at least one day off. Depending on your level of training (or evidence of overtraining) the seventh day is an additional intermediate mileage day or an additional rest day. For example:
  - one high mileage day equal to the event distance
  - one long slow recovery day
  - 3 intermediate mileage days
  - 1 or 2 rest days (off the bike or short recovery rides)
- Plan a short mileage day or rest day to follow the high mileage day. It should be at least 1/4 of the length of your long ride and ridden at a leisurely pace to help loosen up your muscles after the long ride of the week.
- The three intermediate mileage days should be midway between the short ride and the long ride of the week in mileage and should be ridden at a good training pace (85 to 90 percent of maximum heart rate). One or two of these may be interval training rides.
- The longest mileage day is keyed to the length of your event or ride and ridden at the pace you hope to maintain for the event. Many coaches suggest you work up to the length (or even 125 percent of the length) of the event while others are comfortable if you can ride 75 percent of the event distance comfortably.
- There should be an additional long mileage, recovery day during the training week.

More About Long Rides

Are long training rides necessary? Early in the spring when you're building endurance, longer rides have a role to be played in a training program. But during the competitive season conventional wisdom says not to ride significantly farther than your longest event.

So if you do 40K time trials and road races up to, say, 50 miles, your longest training rides don't need to be longer than 40 to 60 miles. Early-season long rides build aerobic conditioning. But once the season is underway, distance may detract from the power and speed you need to do well in your goal events.

American River Cycling Club *Personal Training Program*

2-110 Word 2-3 completed (pages 1 and 2 of 5)

Independent Project 2-4

In this project, you use styles, indents, lists, tab stops, the replace feature, footers, and document properties to customize the Emergency Procedures document for Sierra Pacific Community College District. **[Student Learning Outcomes 2.1, 2.2, 2.3, 2.4, 2.6, 2.7, 2.9]**

File Needed: ***EmergencyProcedures-02.docx***
Completed Project File Name: ***[your initials] Word 2-4.docx***

Skills Covered in This Project

- Modify an existing document.
- Apply a document theme.
- Change margins and font size.
- Apply and modify a style.
- Apply borders to selected text.
- Apply and customize a numbered and bulleted list.
- Use the *Format Painter.*
- Set and modify tab stops.
- Use *Replace.*
- Insert a footer with document properties and current date.
- Insert a page border.
- Center text vertically.

---

1. Open the ***EmergencyProcedures-02*** document from your student data files.
2. Save this document as ***[your initials] Word 2-4***.
3. Format the entire document.
   a. Change the document theme to **Integral** and the color set to **Red**.
   b. Change the top, bottom, left, and right margins to **0.75"**.
   c. Select the entire document and change the font size to **12 pt**.
4. Format the title of the document.
   a. Select the title of the document and apply **Heading 1** style.
   b. Format this text in **all caps**.
   c. Change the font size to **16 pt**.
   d. Change the before paragraph spacing to **0 pt**.
   e. Add a **bottom border** to the title.
5. Select each of the section headings and apply the **Heading 2** style.
6. Modify the **Heading 2** style. Select the first section heading **("Emergency Telephones [Blue Phones]")** and make the following changes.
   a. Change before paragraph spacing to **12 pt**. and after paragraph spacing to **3 pt**.
   b. Apply **small caps** effect and **underline**.
   c. Update **Heading 2** style to match this heading. All of the section headings are updated.
7. Delete all of the blank lines in the document.
8. Select the bulleted list in the first section and change to a numbered list.
9. Apply numbering format, make formatting changes, and use the *Format Painter*.
   a. Apply numbering format to the text in the following sections: "*Assaults, Fights, or Emotional Disturbances*"; "*Power Failure*"; "*Fire*"; "*Earthquake*"; and "*Bomb Threat*."
   b. With the numbered list in the "Bomb Threat" section selected, use the *Paragraph* dialog box to set before and after paragraph spacing to **2 pt**., and deselect the **Don't add space between paragraphs of the same style** check box.
   c. Use the **Format Painter** to copy this numbering format to each of the other numbered lists.
   d. Reset each numbered list so it begins with **1**.
10. Select the text in the "Accident or Medical Emergency" section and apply and customize a bulleted list.
   a. Use a **solid square bullet** (Wingdings, Character code 110).
   b. Set left indent at **0.25"** and hanging indent at **0.25"**.
   c. Set before and after paragraph spacing to **2 pt**.
   d. Deselect the **Don't add space between paragraphs of the same style** check box.
11. Use the *Format Painter* to apply this bulleted list format to the following text in the following sections: "*Tips to Professors and Staff*" and "*Response to Students*."
12. Select the text in the "Emergency Telephone Locations" section and change indent, paragraph spacing, and style.

a. Set a **0.25"** left indent.
b. Set before and after paragraph spacing to **2 pt**.
c. Deselect the **Don't add space between paragraphs of the same style** check box.
d. Apply **Book Title** style to each of the telephone locations. Select only the location, not the text in parentheses or following text.

13. Select the text in the "Emergency Phone Numbers" section, change left indent and paragraph spacing, and set a tab stop with a dot leader.
    a. Set a **0.25"** left indent for this text.
    b. Set before and after paragraph spacing to **2 pt**.
    c. Deselect the **Don't add space between paragraphs of the same style** check box.
    d. Set a **right tab stop** at the right margin and use a **dot leader (2)**.
    e. Press **Tab** before the phone number on each of these lines. The phone numbers align at the right margin with a dot leader between the text and phone number.
14. Apply the **Intense Reference** style to the paragraph headings in the "Accident or Medical Emergency" section ("*Life-Threating Emergencies*" and "*Minor Emergencies*").
15. Use the *Replace* feature to replace all instances of "Phone 911" with "PHONE 911" with **bold** font style.
16. Insert a footer with document property fields and the current date that appears on every page.
    a. Edit the footer and use the ruler to move the center tab stop to **3.5"** and the right tab stop to **7"**.
    b. Insert the **Title** document property field at the left.
    c. Insert the **Company** document property field at center. Use the center tab stop for alignment.
    d. Insert the **current date** (third date format) that is updated automatically at the right. Use the right tab stop for alignment.
    e. Change the font size of all the text in the footer to **10 pt**.
    f. Add a **top border** to the text in the footer.
17. Insert a page border on the entire document. Use **Shadow** setting, **solid line** style, **Dark Red**, **Accent 1** color, and **1 pt**. line width.
18. Center the entire document vertically.
19. Save and close the document (Figure 2-111).

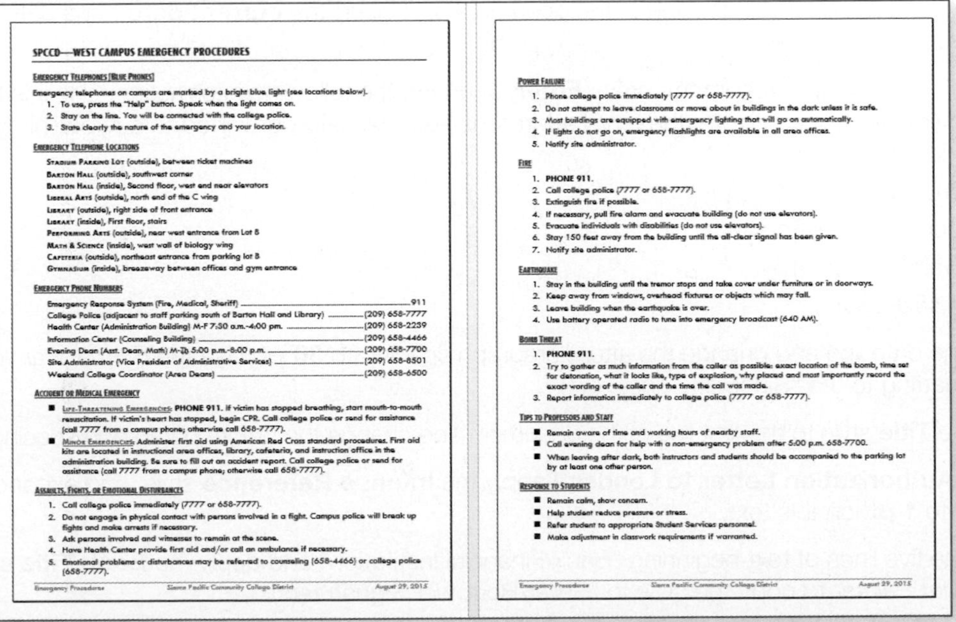

SPCCD—WEST CAMPUS EMERGENCY PROCEDURES

EMERGENCY TELEPHONES [BLUE PHONES]

Emergency telephones on campus are marked by a bright blue light (see locations below).
1. To use, press the "Help" button. Speak when the light comes on.
2. Stay on the line. You will be connected with the college police.
3. State clearly the nature of the emergency and your location.

EMERGENCY TELEPHONE LOCATIONS

STADIUM PARKING LOT (outside), between ticket machines
BARTON HALL (outside), southwest corner
BARTON HALL (inside), Second floor, west end near elevators
LIBERAL ARTS (outside), north end of the C wing
LIBRARY (outside), right side of front entrance
LIBRARY (inside), First floor, stairs
PERFORMING ARTS (outside), near west entrance from Lot 8
MATH & SCIENCE (inside), west wall of biology wing
CAFETERIA (outside), northeast entrance from parking lot B
GYMNASIUM (inside), breezeway between offices and gym entrance

EMERGENCY PHONE NUMBERS

Emergency Response System (Fire, Medical, Sheriff) 911
College Police (adjacent to staff parking south of Barton Hall and Library) .... (209) 658-7777
Health Center (Administration Building) M-F 7:30 a.m.-4:00 pm. .... (209) 658-2239
Information Center (Counseling Building) .... (209) 658-4466
Evening Dean (Asst. Dean, Math) M-Th 5:00 p.m.-8:00 p.m. .... (209) 658-7700
Site Administrator (Vice President of Administrative Services) .... (209) 658-8501
Weekend College Coordinator (Area Deans) .... (209) 658-6500

ACCIDENT OR MEDICAL EMERGENCY

- LIFE-THREATENING EMERGENCIES: **PHONE 911.** If victim has stopped breathing, start mouth-to-mouth resuscitation. If victim's heart has stopped, begin CPR. Call college police or send for assistance (call 7777 from a campus phone; otherwise call 658-7777).
- MINOR EMERGENCIES: Administer first aid using American Red Cross standard procedures. First aid kits are located in instructional area offices, library, cafeteria, and instruction office in the administration building. Be sure to fill out an accident report. Call college police or send for assistance (call 7777 from a campus phone; otherwise call 658-7777).

ASSAULTS, FIGHTS, OR EMOTIONAL DISTURBANCES

1. Call college police immediately (7777 or 658-7777).
2. Do not engage in physical contact with persons involved in a fight. Campus police will break up fights and make arrests if necessary.
3. Ask persons involved and witnesses to remain at the scene.
4. Have Health Center provide first aid and/or call an ambulance if necessary.
5. Emotional problems or disturbances may be referred to counseling (658-4466) or college police (658-7777).

Emergency Procedures | Sierra Pacific Community College District | August 29, 2015

POWER FAILURE

1. Phone college police immediately (7777 or 658-7777).
2. Do not attempt to leave classrooms or move about in buildings in the dark unless it is safe.
3. Most buildings are equipped with emergency lighting that will go on automatically.
4. If lights do not go on, emergency flashlights are available in all area offices.
5. Notify site administrator.

FIRE

1. **PHONE 911.**
2. Call college police (7777 or 658-7777).
3. Extinguish fire if possible.
4. If necessary, pull fire alarm and evacuate building (do not use elevators).
5. Evacuate individuals with disabilities (do not use elevators).
6. Stay 150 feet away from the building until the all-clear signal has been given.
7. Notify site administrator.

EARTHQUAKE

1. Stay in the building until the tremor stops and take cover under furniture or in doorways.
2. Keep away from windows, overhead fixtures or objects which may fall.
3. Leave building when the earthquake is over.
4. Use battery operated radio to tune into emergency broadcast (640 AM).

BOMB THREAT

1. **PHONE 911.**
2. Try to gather as much information from the caller as possible: exact location of the bomb, time set for detonation, what it looks like, type of explosion, why placed and most importantly record the exact wording of the caller and the time the call was made.
3. Report information immediately to college police (7777 or 658-7777).

TIPS TO PROFESSORS AND STAFF

- Remain aware of time and working hours of nearby staff.
- Call evening dean for help with a non-emergency problem after 5:00 p.m. 658-7700.
- When leaving after dark, both instructors and students should be accompanied to the parking lot by at least one other person.

RESPONSE TO STUDENTS

- Remain calm, show concern.
- Help student reduce pressure or stress.
- Refer student to appropriate Student Services personnel.
- Make adjustment in classwork requirements if warranted.

Emergency Procedures | Sierra Pacific Community College District | August 29, 2015

2-111 Word 2-4 completed

Independent Project 2-5

In this project, you format a bank authorization letter for Placer Hills Real Estate. You modify the formatting of an existing document, apply a theme, apply and modify styles, set tab stops, apply borders, and insert and edit hyperlinks.
[Student Learning Outcomes 2.1, 2.2, 2.7, 2.9]

File Needed: ***BankAuthorization-02.docx***
Completed Project File Name: ***[your initials] Word 2-5.docx***

Skills Covered in This Project

- Modify an existing document.
- Apply a document theme.
- Change margins.
- Insert automatically updated date.
- Apply and modify a style.
- Expand font spacing.
- Change paragraph spacing.
- Use the *Format Painter*.
- Set and use tab stops.
- Apply borders and shading to selected text.
- Insert a hyperlink.
- Edit a hyperlink.

---

1. Open the ***BankAuthorization-02*** document from your student data files.
2. Save this document as ***[your initials] Word 2-5***.
3. Format the document.
   a. Change the document theme to **Whisp**.
   b. Change the margins to **Normal**.
   c. Select the entire document and change the after paragraph spacing to **18 pt**.
4. Insert a blank line after the first line of the document and insert the **current date** (third date format) that is updated automatically.
5. Click at the end of the document, press **Enter**, and type the following information. Use line breaks after the first three lines. (Note: the email address is automatically converted to a hyperlink; you will edit this later).

   Emma Cavalli
   Placer Hills Real Estate
   ecavalli@phre.com
   916-450-3334
6. Select the date line and change the after paragraph spacing to **30 pt**. Use the *Format Painter* to copy this formatting to the "Sincerely," line.
7. Apply the **Title** style to the first line of the document and change the before paragraph spacing to **36 pt**.
8. Select **"Authorization Letter to Lender,"** apply the **Intense Reference** style, and expand the font spacing to **1 pt**. on this text.
9. Select the five lines of text beginning "Bank/Financial Institution" and apply the **Book Title** style. Use the *Format Painter* to copy the style to "Seller/Borrower Signature(s)".

10. Select the five lines of text beginning "Bank/Financial Institution" and set a **right tab stop** at the right margin with a **solid underline leader**. Press **Tab** after each of these lines to insert the solid underline leader to the right margin.
11. Select the paragraph beginning "Please consider . . ." and apply a border and shading to the paragraph.
    a. Use **Shadow** setting, **solid line** style, **Black**, **Text 1**, **Lighter 50%** color, and **1½ pt**. line width.
    b. Change the options so there is **4 pt**. padding from text on the top, bottom, left, and right.
    c. Set the shading fill color to **White**, **Background 1**, **Darker 5%**.
12. Select the **"Seller/Borrower Signature(s)"** line and apply a top border that is **solid line**, **black**, and **2¼ pt**. width.
13. Select **"Placer Hills Real Estate"** in the closing lines and insert a hyperlink.
    a. Type www.phre.com as the web page address.
    b. Set the target frame to **New window** and make this the default for all hyperlinks.
14. Edit the "ecavalli@phre.com" email hyperlink and type Email Emma Cavalli as the ScreenTip.
15. Save and close the document (Figure 2-112).

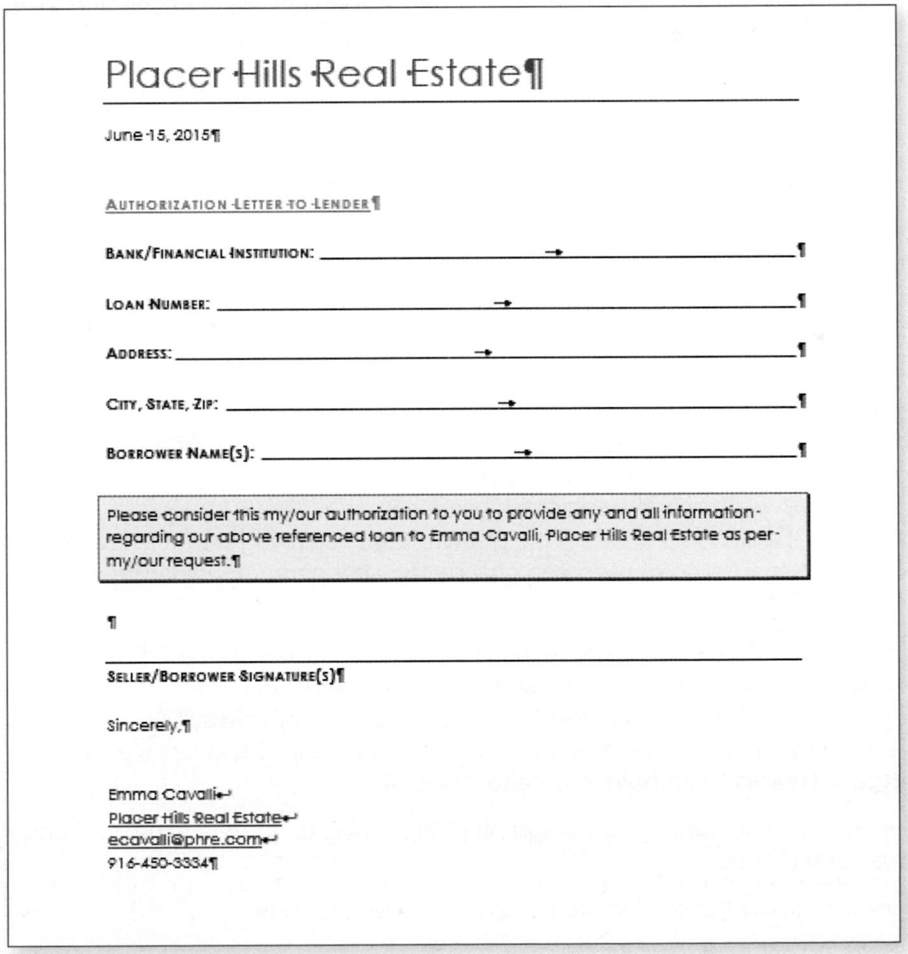

Placer Hills Real Estate¶

June 15, 2015¶

AUTHORIZATION LETTER TO LENDER¶

BANK/FINANCIAL INSTITUTION: ¶

LOAN NUMBER: ¶

ADDRESS: ¶

CITY, STATE, ZIP: ¶

BORROWER NAME(S): ¶

Please consider this my/our authorization to you to provide any and all information regarding our above referenced loan to Emma Cavalli, Placer Hills Real Estate as per my/our request.¶

¶

SELLER/BORROWER SIGNATURE(S)¶

Sincerely,¶

Emma Cavalli
Placer Hills Real Estate
ecavalli@phre.com
916-450-3334¶

2-112 Word 2-5 completed

Independent Project 2-6

In this project, you edit, format, and customize the conference registration form for Central Sierra Insurance's Agriculture Insurance Conference. You use a continuous section break, *Find and Replace*, tab stops and leaders, styles, bullets, indents, borders, shading, and hyperlinks.
[Student Learning Outcomes 2.1, 2.2, 2.3, 2.4, 2.5, 2.6, 2.7, 2.9]

File Needed: ***ConferenceRegistrationForm-02.docx***
Completed Project File Name: ***[your initials] Word 2-6.docx***

Skills Covered in This Project

- Modify an existing document.
- Change margins, font, font size, line spacing, and paragraph spacing.
- Insert a header.
- Apply a style.
- Use *Find and Replace*.
- Insert a continuous section break.
- Insert a horizontal line.
- Set different margins for different sections.
- Customize a bulleted list and indents.
- Set and use tab stops and leaders.
- Apply borders and shading to selected text.
- Insert hyperlinks.

---

1. Open the ***ConferenceRegistrationForm-02*** document from your student data files.
2. Save this document as ***[your initials] Word 2-6***.
3. Format the document.
   a. Change the top and bottom margins to **0.5"**.
   b. Select all of the text in the document and change the font size to **10 pt**., line spacing to **1** (SS), and after paragraph spacing to **6 pt**.
4. Apply styles to title and subtitle.
   a. Cut the first line of the document and paste it in the header. Apply **Title** style, align **center**, and change the after paragraph spacing to **6 pt**.
   b. Delete the blank line below the text in the header.
   c. In the body of the document, select the first two lines beginning with "Central Sierra Insurance," apply **Subtitle** style, align **center**, and change the after paragraph spacing to **6 pt**.
5. Use *Find* and *Replace*.
   a. Use *Find* to find all occurrences of "Agriculture Insurance Conference."
   b. Apply **italic** formatting to each occurrence except in the header.
   c. Use *Replace* to find all occurrences of "Oct." and replace with **"May"**.
   d. Use *Replace* to find all occurrences of "Westfield Hotel & Spa" and replace with **"Northgate Resort"** with **bold** and **italic** font style.
6. Click at the end of the second body paragraph ("Please help us to determine . . .") and insert a **continuous** section break.
7. On the blank line below the section break, insert a **horizontal line**.
8. Click in the document below the section break and change the left and right margins to **1.25"** and apply to **This section**.

9. Select the two lines of text below the horizontal line and set a **right tab stop** with a **solid underline leader** at the right margin. Press **Tab** after each of these lines to insert the **solid underline leader** to the right margin.
10. Customize bullets and indents for the different levels.
    a. Use the *Define new Multilevel list* dialog box (in the *Multilevel List* drop-down list).
    b. On the first, second, and third levels, change the bullet to an open square bullet and change the font size of the bullet to **12 pt**.
    c. Set the indents for all levels so that the first level begins at **0"**, the text for the first level begins at **0.25"**, and additional indent for each level is **0.25"**.
    d. Apply this formatting to all of the bulleted lists.
11. Set tab stops with a leader.
    a. Select the **"Flying—Arrival time:"** line and set a **right tab stop** at **3"** with a solid underline leader.
    b. Press **Tab** after this line to insert the leader.
    c. Select the **"I need directions to *Northgate Resort* from:"** line and set a **right tab stop** at **5"** with a **solid underline leader**.
    d. Press **Tab** after this line to insert the leader.
12. Change indents and apply custom borders and shading to selected text.
    a. Select the last two lines of the document, align **center**, and change the left and right indents to **1"**.
    b. With these two lines selected, apply a double border, **¾ pt.**, and **Dark Blue**, **Text 2** to the top and bottom border of the selected text.
    c. Apply **Dark Blue**, **Text 2**, **Lighter 80%** shading to the selected text.
13. Insert a hyperlink to an email address at each of the two occurrences of "apelandale@centralsierra.com."
    a. Make sure the *Text to display* area just displays the email address and not "mailto: . . ."
    b. Type Email Asia Pelandale as the ScreenTip for each of these hyperlinks.
14. Save and close the document (Figure 2-113).

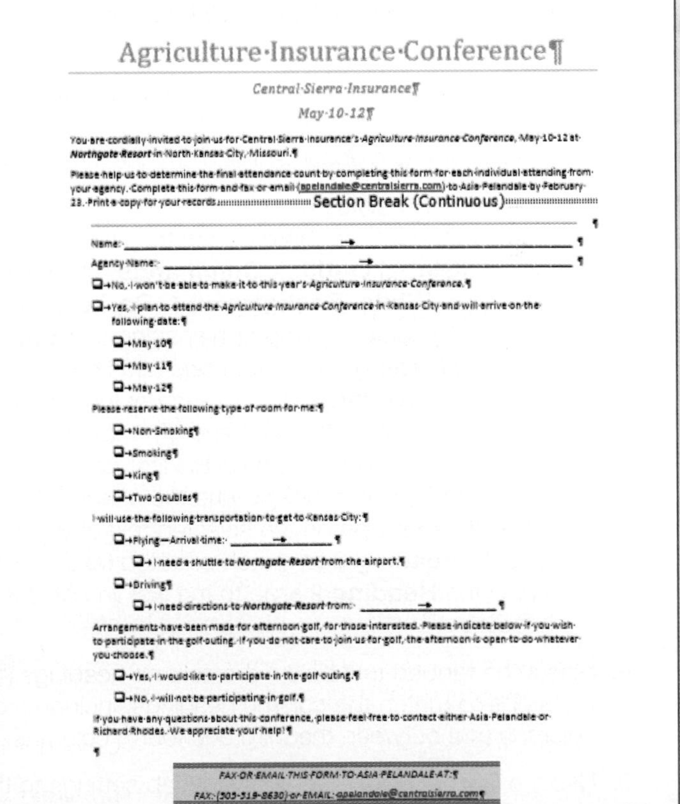

Agriculture Insurance Conference

Central Sierra Insurance

May 10-12

You are cordially invited to join us for Central Sierra Insurance's *Agriculture Insurance Conference*, May 10-12 at ***Northgate Resort*** in North Kansas City, Missouri.

Please help us to determine the final attendance count by completing this form for each individual attending from your agency. Complete this form and fax or email (apelandale@centralsierra.com) to Asia Pelandale by February 23. Print a copy for your records. Section Break (Continuous)

Name: ____________________

Agency Name: ____________________

- No, I won't be able to make it to this year's *Agriculture Insurance Conference*.
- Yes, I plan to attend the *Agriculture Insurance Conference* in Kansas City and will arrive on the following date:
    - May 10
    - May 11
    - May 12

Please reserve the following type of room for me:

- Non-Smoking
- Smoking
- King
- Two Doubles

I will use the following transportation to get to Kansas City:

- Flying—Arrival time: __________
    - I need a shuttle to ***Northgate Resort*** from the airport.
- Driving
    - I need directions to ***Northgate Resort*** from: __________

Arrangements have been made for afternoon golf, for those interested. Please indicate below if you wish to participate in the golf outing. If you do not care to join us for golf, the afternoon is open to do whatever you choose.

- Yes, I would like to participate in the golf outing.
- No, I will not be participating in golf.

If you have any questions about this conference, please feel free to contact either Asia Pelandale or Richard Rhodes. We appreciate your help!

FAX OR EMAIL THIS FORM TO ASIA PELANDALE AT:

FAX: (505-519-8630) or EMAIL: apelandale@centralsierra.com

2-113 Word 2-6 completed

Improve It Project 2-7

In this project, you clean up a document that contains shortcuts for Microsoft Outlook. Courtyard Medical Plaza wants to make this document available to all of its employees. You use tab stops, styles, and many other page layout features that you have learned in this chapter to create a professional and attractive reference document.
[Student Learning Outcomes 2.1, 2.2, 2.4, 2.5, 2.7, 2.9]

File Needed: ***OutlookShortcuts-02.docx***
Completed Project File Name: ***[your initials] Word 2-7.docx***

Skills Covered in This Project

- Modify an existing document.
- Change margins, line spacing, and paragraph spacing.
- Apply and modify a style.
- Apply borders and shading to selected text.
- Set and modify tab stops and leaders.
- Use the *Format Painter*.
- Insert a page break.
- Edit footer content and tab stops.

---

1. Open the ***OutlookShortcuts-02*** document from your student data files.
2. Save this document as ***[your initials] Word 2-7***.
3. Format the document.
   a. Change the page orientation to **Landscape**.
   b. Change the top margin to **0.5"** and the bottom, left, and right margins to **0.75"**.
   c. Select the entire document and change the line spacing to **1** and the after paragraph spacing to **4 pt**.
4. Modify and apply styles.
   a. Remove the bottom border from the title and change the after paragraph spacing to **0 pt**.
   b. Select **"Global Outlook Commands,"** add a **1 pt.**, **Dark Blue**, **Text 2** top and bottom border, and apply **White**, **Background 1**, **Darker 5%** shading.
   c. Change the before paragraph spacing to **12 pt**. and the after spacing to **0 pt**.
   d. Update **Heading 1** to match selected text.
   e. Apply the **Heading 1** style to each of the remaining headings (*"Mail," "Calendar," "Contacts," "Tasks," "Notes," "Journal,"* and *"Formatting"*).
   f. Select the third line of text on the first page ("Activity Shortcut . . .") and change the before paragraph spacing to **6 pt**. and the after spacing to **3 pt**.
   g. Set **left tab stops** on the selected text at **3"**, **5"**, and **8.25"**.
   h. Update **Heading 2** to match selected text.
   i. Apply the **Heading 2** style to the first line of text ("Activity Shortcut . . .") after each section heading.
5. Select the tabbed text below the column headings ("Activity Shortcut . . .") in the first section and set tab stops to match the column headings. Include a dot leader between the text in the first and second columns and between the third and fourth columns.
6. Use the *Format Painter* to apply the tab settings to the text in the other sections.
7. Delete any blank lines and extra tabs.

8. Remove the existing footer and insert a footer with **Courtyard Medical Plaza** at the left, **Outlook Shortcuts** aligned at the center tab stop, and **Page X of Y** aligned at the right tab stop.
   a. You need to adjust the tab stops on the ruler in the footer.
   b. For the page number, use *Page X of Y* format where *X* is the page number and *Y* is the number of pages in the document (Hint: for *Y*, insert *NumPages* field).
   c. Apply a **1 pt.**, **Dark Blue**, **Text 2** top border in the footer.
   d. Set the footer so it does not appear on the first page.
9. Insert page breaks where necessary to keep groupings together. This document fits on four pages.
10. Check the document for consistent formatting. Make any necessary changes.
11. Save and close the document (Figure 2-114).

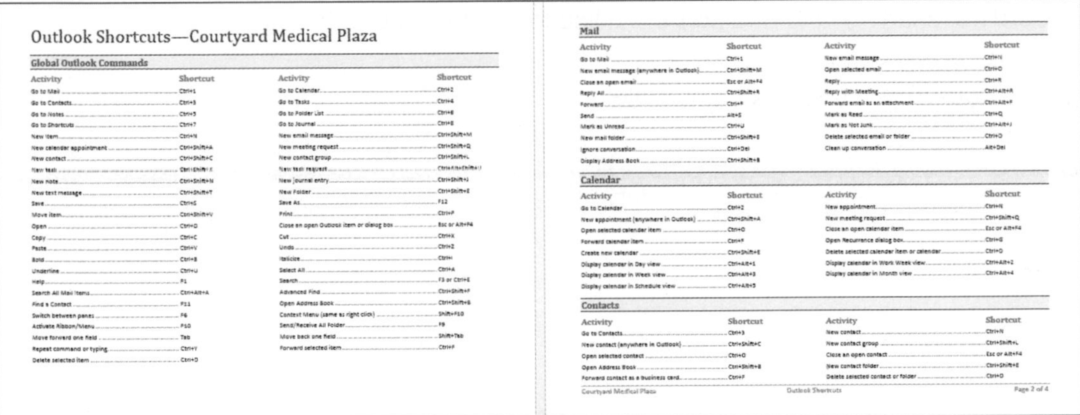

Outlook Shortcuts—Courtyard Medical Plaza

Global Outlook Commands

Activity	Shortcut	Activity	Shortcut
Go to Mail	Ctrl+1	Go to Calendar	Ctrl+2
Go to Contacts	Ctrl+3	Go to Tasks	Ctrl+4
Go to Notes	Ctrl+5	Go to Folder List	Ctrl+6
Go to Shortcuts	Ctrl+7	Go to Journal	Ctrl+8
New item	Ctrl+N	New email message	Ctrl+Shift+M
New calendar appointment	Ctrl+Shift+A	New meeting request	Ctrl+Shift+Q
New contact	Ctrl+Shift+C	New contact group	Ctrl+Shift+L
New task	Ctrl+Shift+K	New task request	Ctrl+Alt+Shift+U
New note	Ctrl+Shift+N	New journal entry	Ctrl+Shift+J
New text message	Ctrl+Shift+T	New Folder	Ctrl+Shift+E
Save	Ctrl+S	Save As	F12
Move item	Ctrl+Shift+V	Print	Ctrl+P
Open	Ctrl+O	Close an open Outlook item or dialog box	Esc or Alt+F4
Copy	Ctrl+C	Cut	Ctrl+X
Paste	Ctrl+V	Undo	Ctrl+Z
Bold	Ctrl+B	Italicize	Ctrl+I
Underline	Ctrl+U	Select All	Ctrl+A
Help	F1	Search	F3 or Ctrl+E
Search All Mail Items	Ctrl+Alt+A	Advanced Find	Ctrl+Shift+F
Find a Contact	F11	Open Address Book	Ctrl+Shift+B
Switch between panes	F6	Context Menu (same as right click)	Shift+F10
Activate Ribbon/Menu	F10	Send/Receive All Folder	F9
Move forward one field	Tab	Move back one field	Shift+Tab
Repeat command or typing	Ctrl+Y	Forward selected item	Ctrl+F
Delete selected item	Ctrl+D		

Mail

Activity	Shortcut	Activity	Shortcut
Go to Mail	Ctrl+1	New email message	Ctrl+N
New email message (anywhere in Outlook)	Ctrl+Shift+M	Open selected email	Ctrl+O
Close an open email	Esc or Alt+F4	Reply	Ctrl+R
Reply All	Ctrl+Shift+R	Reply with Meeting	Ctrl+Alt+R
Forward	Ctrl+F	Forward email as an attachment	Ctrl+Alt+F
Send	Alt+S	Mark as Read	Ctrl+Q
Mark as Unread	Ctrl+U	Mark as Not Junk	Ctrl+Alt+J
New mail folder	Ctrl+Shift+E	Delete selected email or folder	Ctrl+D
Ignore conversation	Ctrl+Del	Clean up conversation	Alt+Del
Display Address Book	Ctrl+Shift+B		

Calendar

Activity	Shortcut	Activity	Shortcut
Go to Calendar	Ctrl+2	New appointment	Ctrl+N
New appointment (anywhere in Outlook)	Ctrl+Shift+A	New meeting request	Ctrl+Shift+Q
Open selected calendar item	Ctrl+O	Close an open calendar item	Esc or Alt+F4
Forward calendar item	Ctrl+F	Open Recurrence dialog box	Ctrl+G
Create new calendar	Ctrl+Shift+E	Delete selected calendar item or calendar	Ctrl+D
Display calendar in Day view	Ctrl+Alt+1	Display calendar in Work Week view	Ctrl+Alt+2
Display calendar in Week view	Ctrl+Alt+3	Display calendar in Month view	Ctrl+Alt+4
Display calendar in Schedule view	Ctrl+Alt+5		

Contacts

Activity	Shortcut	Activity	Shortcut
Go to Contacts	Ctrl+3	New contact	Ctrl+N
New contact (anywhere in Outlook)	Ctrl+Shift+C	New contact group	Ctrl+Shift+L
Open selected contact	Ctrl+O	Close an open contact	Esc or Alt+F4
Open Address Book	Ctrl+Shift+B	New contact folder	Ctrl+Shift+E
Forward contact as a business card	Ctrl+F	Delete selected contact or folder	Ctrl+D

Courtyard Medical Plaza Outlook Shortcuts Page 2 of 4

2-114 Word 2-7 completed (pages 1 and 2 of 4)

Challenge Project 2-8

Create an agenda for an upcoming meeting for an organization you are a member of, such as a club, church, volunteer organization, student group, or neighborhood association. Do some online research to find out some of the common components of agendas. Robert's Rules of Order is a good source of information about meetings and guidelines for meeting protocol.
[Student Learning Outcomes 2.1, 2.2, 2.3, 2.6, 2.7, 2.9]

File Needed: None
Completed Project File Name: ***[your initials] Word 2-8.docx***

Create a new document and save it as ***[your initials] Word 2-8***. An agenda can include, but is not limited to, the following items:

- Organization name as the title
- Meeting date, start time, and end time

- Meeting location
- Meeting attendees
- Topic headings
- Topic subheadings—include details for each topic heading
- The time each topic is expected to last

Modify your document according to the following guidelines:

- Apply styles.
- Use a multilevel list for the agenda items and subheadings.
- Customize number or bullet format and indents as needed.
- Use a right tab stop with a leader to line up the amount of time to be spent on each main topic heading.
- Apply borders, shading, and/or a horizontal line to create an attractive agenda.
- Adjust margins as needed.
- Include an appropriate header and/or footer.

Challenge Project 2-9

Update your resume using some of the document formatting features learned in this chapter. Edit your resume so it is consistently formatted, easy to read, and professional looking. Do some online research on resumes to get ideas about formatting and content.
[Student Learning Outcomes 2.1, 2.2, 2.3, 2.4, 2.5, 2.6, 2.7, 2.8, 2.9]

File Needed: None
Completed Project File Name: ***[your initials] Word 2-9.docx***

Open your existing resume or create a new document and save it as ***[your initials] Word 2-9***. Modify your document according to the following guidelines:

- Apply a document theme.
- Apply styles to headings and subheadings to improve consistency in format.
- Adjust margins as needed.
- Use bulleted lists with customized bullets and indents to attractively arrange information.
- Set and use tab stops and indents as necessary to line up information.
- Apply borders, shading, and/or a horizontal line to set off information in your resume.
- Use page or section breaks as needed.
- Use *Find and Replace* as needed.
- Insert hyperlinks for appropriate information (e.g., email address and company names).
- If your resume is more than one page, include a header and/or footer on the second and continuing pages.

Challenge Project 2-10

Format your favorite recipe using some of the formatting features learned in this chapter. You can look up recipes online on the Food Network, Epicurious, Simply Recipes, or other food web sites. **[Student Learning Outcomes 2.1, 2.2, 2.3, 2.6, 2.7, 2.9]**

File Needed: None
Completed Project File Name: ***[your initials] Word 2-10.docx***

Create a new document and save it as ***[your initials] Word 2-10***. Your recipe should include, but is not limited to, the following:

- Recipe title
- Descriptive paragraph about the recipe
- Tab stops to arrange quantity and ingredients (and special instructions if needed)
- Numbered, step-by-step instructions
- Recipe source and/or additional information

Modify your document according to the following guidelines:

- Apply a document theme.
- Apply styles.
- Adjust margins as needed.
- Set and use a combination of tab stops (e.g., left, right, center, decimal, bar, and leaders) as necessary to attractively line up information.
- Use a numbered list for instructions.
- Use left, right, first line, and/or hanging indents as necessary.
- Apply borders, shading, page border, and/or a horizontal line to set off information in your recipe.
- Insert hyperlinks to appropriate information (e.g., link to online recipe).

CHAPTER 3

Working with Reports and Multipage Documents

CHAPTER OVERVIEW

Creating a long report with a table of contents, citations, footnotes or endnotes, a reference page, and headers and footers can be a challenging task. Word 2013 has numerous tools that automatically create these components in report or multipage document. Using these tools not only saves you time when you are working on this type of document, but also improves consistency within your documents.

STUDENT LEARNING OUTCOMES (SLOs)

After completing this chapter, you will be able to:

SLO 3.1 Insert and edit footnotes and endnotes in a document (p. W3-129).

SLO 3.2 Create a bibliography with properly formatted sources and insert citations into a document (p. W3-134).

SLO 3.3 Create and edit a table of contents based on headings (p. W3-144).

SLO 3.4 Insert a cover page and modify content and content control fields (p. W3-148).

SLO 3.5 Integrate bookmarks into a multipage document (p. W3-153).

SLO 3.6 Apply and customize headers and footers in a multipage document (p. W3-156).

Case Study

American River Cycling Club (ARCC) is a community cycling club that promotes fitness for the entire region. ARCC members include recreational cyclists who enjoy the exercise and camaraderie and competitive cyclists who compete in road, mountain, and cyclo-cross races throughout the cycling season.

For the Pause & Practice projects, you create a report for club members about how to develop a personal training program. In this report, you incorporate many of the report features covered in the chapter to produce a professional-looking and useful report.

Pause & Practice 3-1: Insert endnotes into the report, convert endnotes to footnotes, add reference sources, insert citations, and create a bibliography page.

Pause & Practice 3-2: Apply styles to headings in the report, create a table of contents based on the headings in the document, modify the table of contents, and insert a cover page.

Pause & Practice 3-3: Insert and view bookmarks, create hyperlinks and cross-references to bookmarks, and customize headers and footers in the report.

WORD

SLO 3.1

Using Footnotes and Endnotes

Footnotes and ***endnotes*** cite reference sources used in a document. You can also use them to include additional notational information that does not cleanly fit within the text of the document. Footnotes appear at the bottom of each page, while endnotes are listed at the end of the document.

As you insert footnotes and endnotes into your document, Word numbers them consecutively. If another footnote or endnote is inserted before or between existing notes, Word automatically reorders notes. You can also customize number format and convert footnotes to endnotes or endnotes to footnotes.

Insert Footnotes

When a footnote is inserted into a document, a ***reference marker***, which is a number or letter in superscript format (in a smaller font and slightly raised above the typed line), is inserted directly after the word. Word then places the insertion point at the bottom of the page to insert the text of the footnote. A thin top border above the note distinguishes it from the text in the body of the document.

Footnotes are placed in the body of the document at the bottom of the page, not in the footer, and the text on a page with a footnote is adjusted to allow space for the footnote.

HOW TO: Insert a Footnote

1. Position the insertion point directly after the word where the footnote is to be inserted.
2. Click the **References** tab.
3. Click the **Insert Footnote** button [*Footnotes* group] (Figure 3-1). A reference marker is inserted in the body of the document (Figure 3-2), and the insertion point is positioned after the corresponding reference marker in the footnote area of the page.

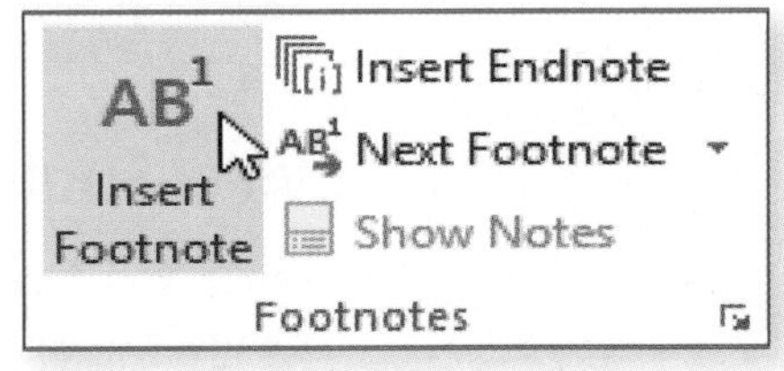

3-1 ***Insert Footnote* button**

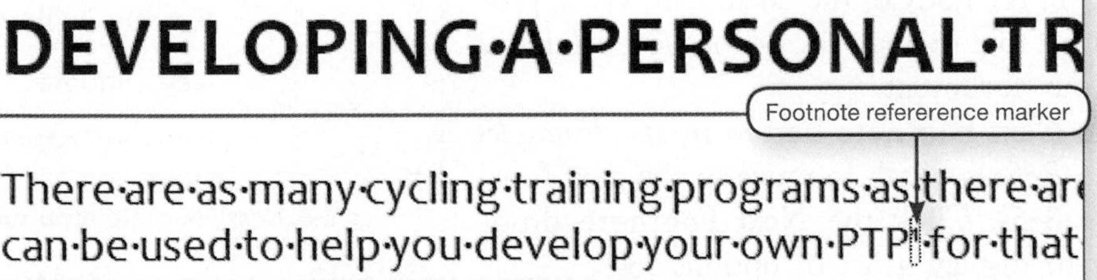

DEVELOPING·A·PERSONAL·TR
Footnote refererence marker
There·are·as·many·cycling·training·programs·as·there·ar
can·be·used·to·help·you·develop·your·own·PTP1·for·that
criterium,·time·trial,·or·century.¶

3-2 Footnote reference marker in the body of the document

4. Type the footnote text in the footnote area of the page (Figure 3-3).

3-3 Footnote text at the bottom of the page

Insert Endnotes

Inserting endnotes is similar to inserting footnotes. The main difference is the text for the endnote is placed after the text at the end of the document rather than at the bottom of the page where the note appears.

HOW TO: Insert an Endnote

1. Position the insertion point directly after the word where the endnote is to be inserted.
2. Click the **References** tab.
3. Click the **Insert Endnote** button [*Footnotes* group] (Figure 3-4). The reference marker is inserted in the body of the document and the insertion point is positioned after the corresponding reference marker at the end of the document.
4. Type the endnote text.

3-4 ***Insert Endnote*** **button**

> **ANOTHER WAY**
>
> **Alt+Ctrl+F** inserts a footnote.
> **Alt+Ctrl+D** inserts an endnote.

View Footnotes and Endnotes

Once you have footnotes or endnotes in your document, it is easy to see the footnote or endnote text at the bottom of a page or at the end of the document, but you might have a difficult time locating the reference markers in the body of the document. Word provides you with a tool to easily locate footnote reference markers in your document.

Click the **Next Footnote** button in the *Footnotes* group on the *References* tab to move to the next footnote (Figure 3-5). Click the **Next Footnote** drop-down arrow to display a list of options to move to next or previous footnotes or endnotes. Click the **Show Notes** button in the *Footnotes* group to toggle between the note reference markers and the note text.

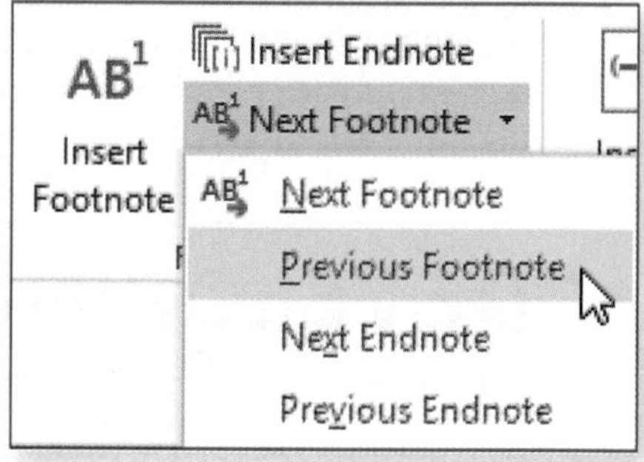

3-5 ***Next Footnote*** **drop-down list**

Word also displays the text of the footnote or endnote when you place your pointer over a reference marker (Figure 3-6).

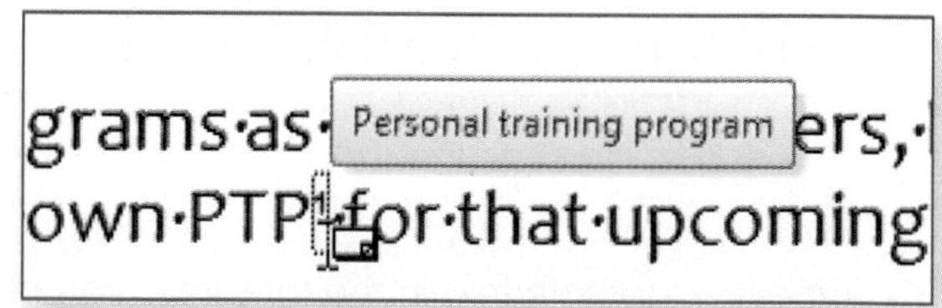

3-6 Footnote text displayed

Customize Footnotes and Endnotes

By default, footnotes are numbered consecutively with numbers (e.g., 1, 2, 3) and endnotes are numbered with lowercase Roman numerals (e.g., i, ii, iii). You might decide to use letters or symbols such as an asterisk (*), section mark (§), or number or pound symbol (#) as reference markers. You can customize how notes are numbered and where they are displayed in a document.

HOW TO: Customize Footnotes and Endnotes

1. Select the **References** tab.
2. Click the **Footnotes** launcher [*Footnotes* group] to open the *Footnote and Endnote* dialog box (Figure 3-7).
3. In the *Location* area, select either **Footnotes** or **Endnotes**.
   - In the drop-down list for *Footnotes,* you have the option to position the footnote text at the *Bottom of page* (default) or *Below text*.
   - In the drop-down list for *Endnotes,* you have the option to position the endnote text at the *End of document* (default) or *End of section*.
4. In the *Format* area, you can change any of the following: *Number format, Custom mark, Start at,* or *Numbering.*
5. In the *Apply changes* area, you can apply changes to the *Whole document* or *This section* (if there are sections in your document).
6. Click **Apply** to close the dialog box and apply the changes. Do not press *Insert,* which inserts a footnote or endnote in the document.

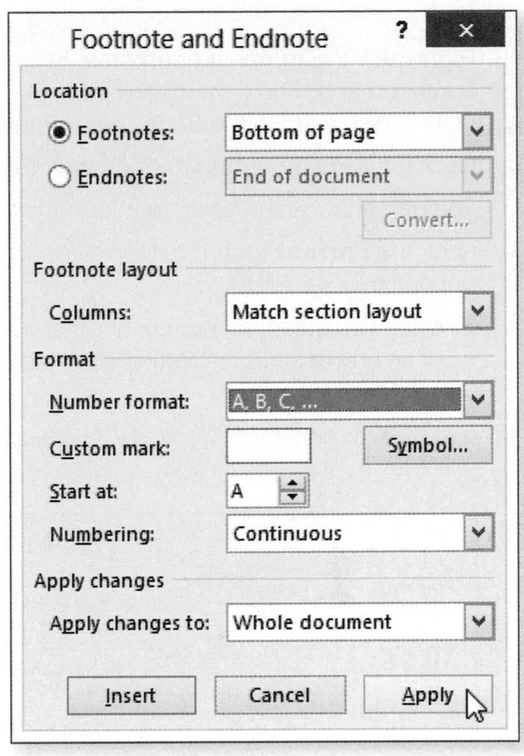

3-7 *Footnote and Endnote* dialog box

MORE INFO

You can also use the *Footnote and Endnote* dialog box to insert a footnote or endnote.

Modify Footnote and Endnote Format

In addition to customizing placement and note format, you can also change how the text of the footnotes and endnotes appears. You do this the same way you format regular text in the document.

Select the footnote or endnote text and apply any formatting changes such as font, font size, style, line or paragraph spacing, or text effects (Figure 3-8). You can apply changes using the buttons on the *Home* or *Page Layout* tab, the context menu (right-click selected text), the mini toolbar, or keyboard shortcuts.

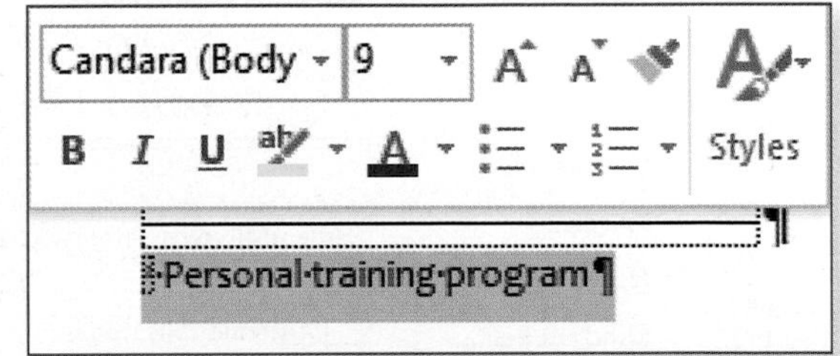

3-8 Apply formatting to footnote text

Modify Footnote and Endnote Styles

The appearance of the footnotes and endnotes in your document is determined by styles. Styles control the font, font size, text styles and effects, and paragraph formatting. When you insert a footnote in your document, Word applies the *Footnote Text* style; this style controls the formatting of all of the footnote text in your document.

You can modify the footnote or endnote style, which automatically updates all of your footnote or endnote text to reflect the changes you made to the style.

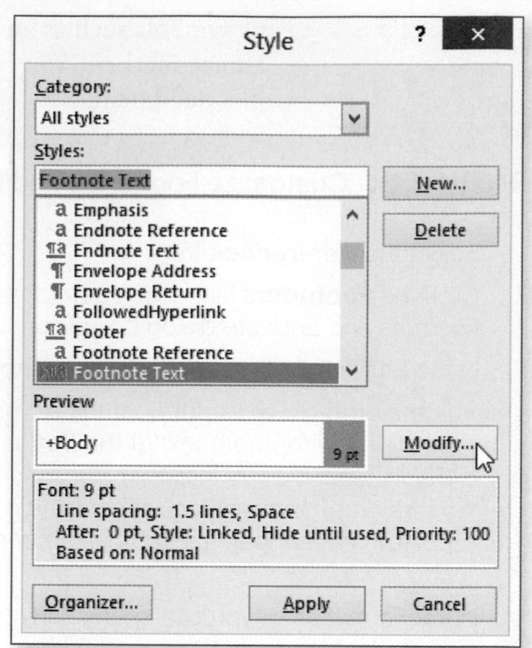

3-9 *Style* dialog box

HOW TO: Modify the Footnote or Endnote Style

1. Right-click the footnote or endnote text and select **Style** from the context menu. The *Style* dialog box opens and the name of the style is displayed in the *Styles* area (Figure 3-9).
2. Click the **Modify** button to open the *Modify Style* dialog box.
3. You can change the basic font formatting in the *Formatting* area.
4. Click the **Format** button to display a list of other formatting options (Figure 3-10).
   - When you select an option, another dialog box opens.
   - Make any desired formatting changes and click **OK** to close the dialog box.
5. Click **OK** to close the *Modify Style* dialog box.

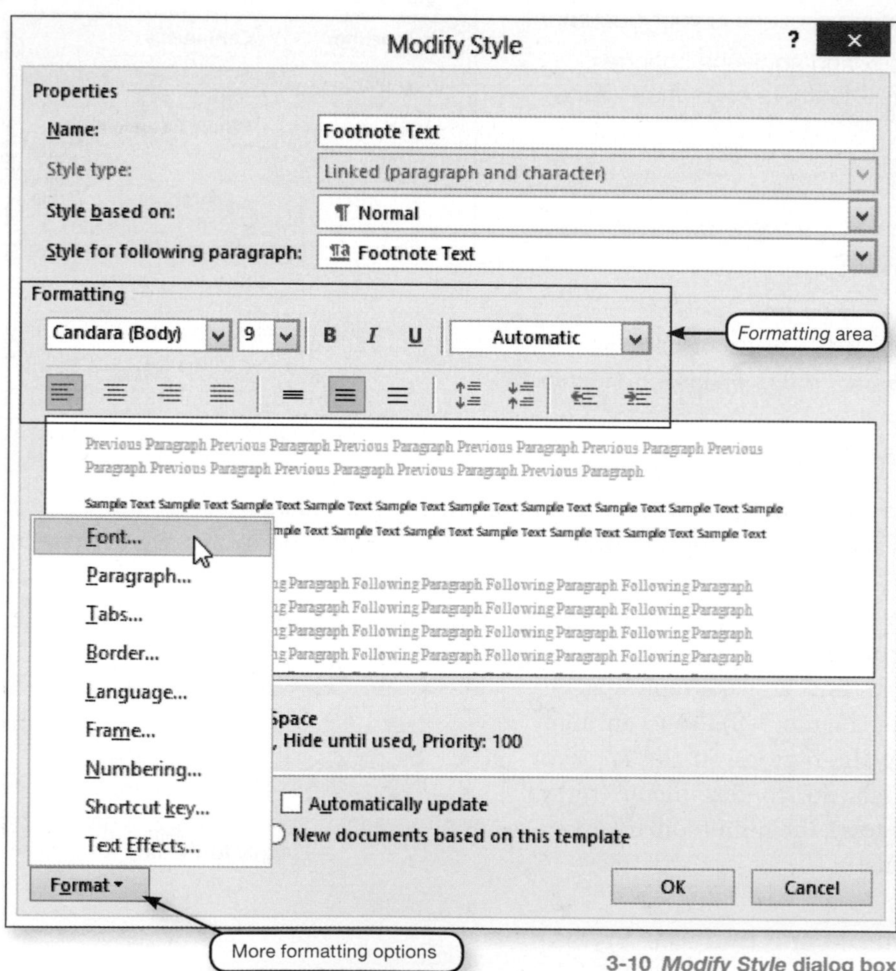

3-10 *Modify Style* dialog box

6. Click **Apply** to apply any changes to the style and close the *Style* dialog box.

Convert Footnotes and Endnotes

There might be times when you want to convert footnotes to endnotes or endnotes to footnotes. Rather than deleting and re-creating them, you can convert notes. When you convert notes, Word automatically renumbers the reference markers and moves the note text to the correct location in the document.

HOW TO: Convert All Notes

1. Click the **Footnotes** launcher [*References* tab, *Footnotes* group] to open the *Footnote and Endnote* dialog box.
2. In the *Location* area, click the **Convert** button. The *Convert Notes* dialog box opens (Figure 3-11).
3. Select from one of the three convert options.
4. Click **OK** to close the *Convert Notes* dialog box.
5. Click **Close** to close the *Footnote and Endnote* dialog box. Do not click *Insert* or Word will insert a footnote or endnote.

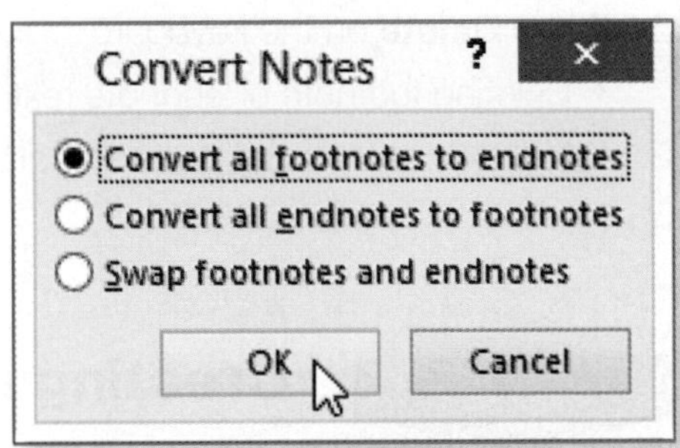

3-11 *Convert Notes* dialog box

> **MORE INFO**
>
> All three of the convert options are active *only* if you have both footnotes and endnotes in your document. Otherwise, only one option is active.

You can convert individual notes using the context menu. Right-click a footnote or endnote (*not* the reference marker in the text of the document) and select **Convert to Endnote** or **Convert to Footnote** (Figure 3-12).

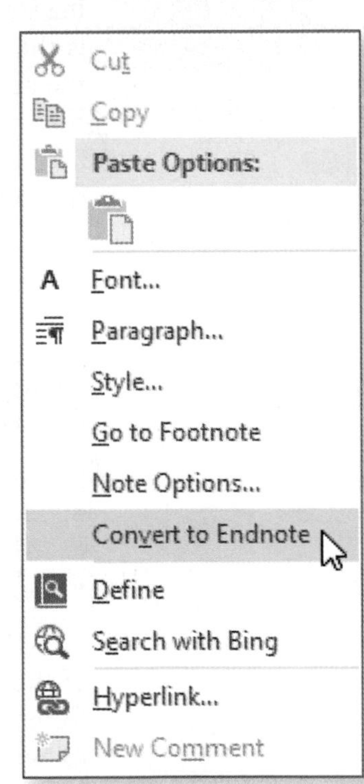

3-12 Convert individual notes

Move Footnotes and Endnotes

You can move footnotes and endnotes in the same way you move text in a document. To move a note, select the **reference marker** in the body of the document (Figure 3-13) and use one of the following methods:

- Drag and drop
- **Ctrl+X** to cut and **Ctrl+V** to paste
- **Cut** and **Paste** buttons [*Home* tab, *Clipboard* group]
- **Cut** and **Paste** options in the context menu

grams·as·there·are
own·PTP1·for·that·

3-13 Select note to move

> **MORE INFO**
>
> When moving a note, select the note carefully to ensure that you are only moving the note and not any spaces or text.

Delete Footnotes and Endnotes

When you delete a note, Word removes the reference marker and the text of the note. Your remaining notes are renumbered and remain in consecutive order.

HOW TO: Delete a Note

1. Select the **reference marker** in the body of the document (*not* the text of the footnote or endnote at the bottom of the page or end of the document).
2. Press **Delete** on the keyboard.
   - Deleting footnote or endnote text in footnote or endnote area will not delete note reference.
3. Check to ensure proper spacing around text where the note was deleted.

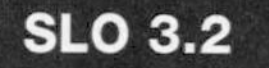

SLO 3.2

Creating a Bibliography and Inserting Citations

Typically, the most tedious and time-consuming aspect of writing a research paper is compiling sources, creating a bibliography page, and citing sources in the body of the report. A ***source*** is the complete bibliographic reference for a book, journal article, or web page. A ***citation*** is the abbreviated source information that you place in the body of the report to give credit to the source of the information you use. A ***bibliography*** or ***works cited*** page lists the sources used in the report. Word has tools to create sources, insert citations, and create a bibliography or works cited page at the end of your report.

Report Styles

There are a variety of report styles, and each differs not only in the overall format of the report but also in the format for sources and citations. The most common report styles are the following:

- APA (American Psychological Association)
- Chicago *(The Chicago Manual of Style)*
- MLA (Modern Language Association)
- Turabian

MLA and APA are the two most common report formats. The following table lists some of the general characteristics of each of these two report styles. Within each of these report formats, there can be much variance depending on the preference of your instructor. Always follow the formatting instructions your instructor provides.

Common Report Styles

Report Features	APA	MLA
Font	11 or 12 pt.	11 or 12 pt.
Line Spacing	Academic APA is double spaced and business APA is single spaced.	Double space.
Margins	For an unbound report use 1" for all margins. For a left bound report use 1.5" left margin and 1" top, bottom, and right margins.	Use 1" margins.

Heading Information	Heading information is typically typed on a title page.	Left align at the top of the first page and include author's name, instructor's name, class, and date on separate lines.
Title	The title is either on the title page or centered on the first page of the report.	Centered on the first page of the report.
Header	Include report title and page number on the right.	Include author's last name and page number on the right.
Uses	Typically use in social and behavioral sciences, business, and nursing.	Typically use in humanities.

Bibliography Styles

As you begin compiling your sources for your report, the first thing you need to do is select the ***bibliography style*** of the report. Most likely your instructor will tell you what style to use. You can then select this bibliography style in Word so Word correctly formats sources and citations.

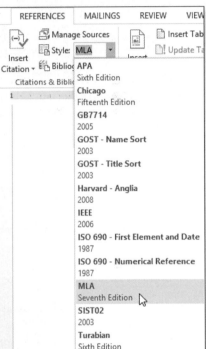

HOW TO: Set the Bibliography Style of the Report

1. Click the **Reference** tab.
2. Click the **Style** drop-down arrow [*Citations & Bibliography* group].
3. Select the style of the report from the drop-down list of report styles (Figure 3-14).

> **MORE INFO**
>
> The report style you select controls the formatting of sources and citations; it does not control the overall formatting of your report. To do that, you must apply the correct formatting to the body of your report.

3-14 Select bibliography style

Add a New Source

As you are writing a report, you should be gathering bibliographic information about sources used in your report (e.g., author; title of book, journal, or article; publication date and edition; publisher or online location). You need to add this information to your report in Word. Word inserts a citation in your report at the insertion point and stores this source information. You then can access these stored sources to insert additional citations and create a bibliography page.

HOW TO: Add a New Source

1. Position the insertion point in your document at the point where you want to insert a citation.
2. Click the **Insert Citation** button [*References* tab, *Citations & Bibliography* group].

3. Select **Add New Source**. The *Create Source* dialog box opens (see Figure 3-16).
4. Select the type of source in the *Type of Source* area.
   - The fields for the source change depending on the type of source you choose.
5. Click the **Edit** button to the right of the *Author* area. The *Edit Name* dialog box opens (Figure 3-15).
   - Type the author name in this box so you can specify first, middle, and last names.
   - Add additional authors if your source has more than one author.
   - If the source is an organization or company (e.g., USA Cycling or Velo News), click the **Corporate Author** check box instead of the *Edit* button in the *Create Source* dialog box (see Figure 3-16).
6. Type in the author information and click **OK** when finished (see Figure 3-15).
   - Click the **Add** button to add additional authors.
   - You can also reorder multiple authors by selecting an author in the *Names* area and clicking the **Up** or **Down** button.
7. Type in other source information as needed (Figure 3-16).
   - As you type in other source information, Word automatically creates a *Tag name* for your source.
   - You can edit the *Tag name* if desired.

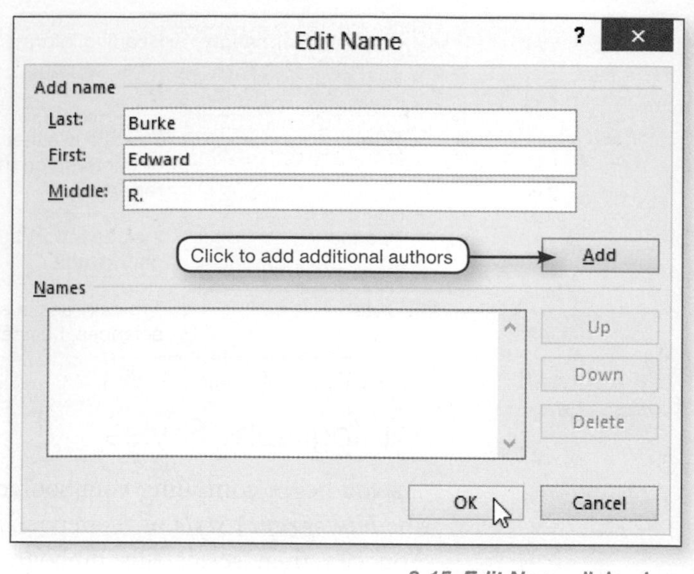

3-15 ***Edit Name*** **dialog box**

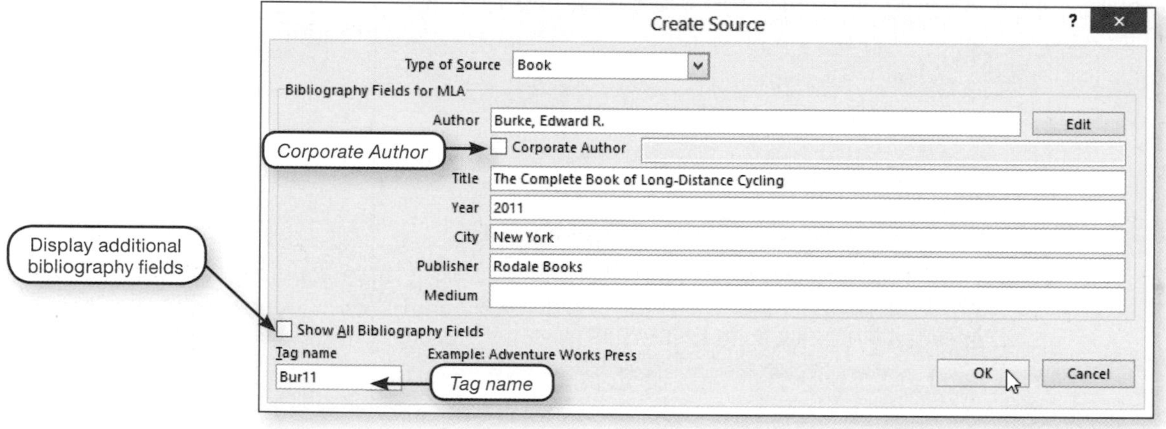

3-16 ***Create Source*** **dialog box**

8. Click the **Show All Bibliography Fields** check box to display more fields. For example, you might need to type in the edition of the book.
9. Click **OK** to close the *Create Source* dialog box.
10. The citation is inserted in the document in the report style you selected (Figure 3-17).

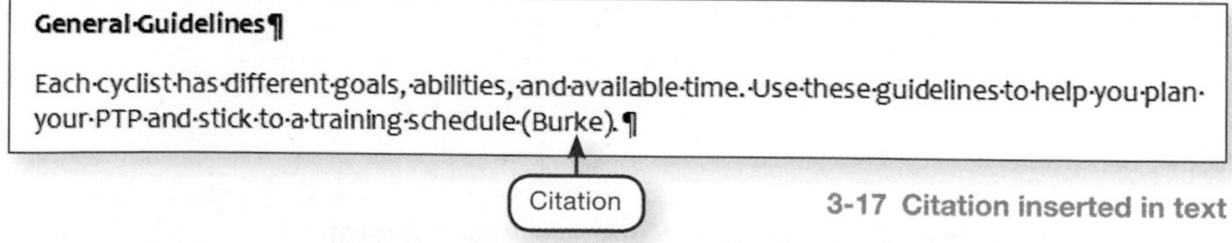

General·Guidelines¶
Each·cyclist·has·different·goals,·abilities,·and·available·time.·Use·these·guidelines·to·help·you·plan·your·PTP·and·stick·to·a·training·schedule·(Burke).¶
Citation

3-17 Citation inserted in text

Insert Citations

Many times you will cite a source more than once in a report. Once you have added a source to your document, you can insert this same citation again in your document without entering source information again. When inserting a citation, you can choose from citations you have previously created.

HOW TO: Insert a Citation

1. Position the insertion point in your document at the point where you want a citation inserted.
2. Click the **Insert Citation** button [*References* tab, *Citations & Bibliography* group].
   - A list of previously used or created sources is displayed in the drop-down list (Figure 3-18).
3. Select from your list of sources.
4. The citation is inserted in the document.
   - When a citation is inserted, Word automatically inserts a space between the citation and the preceding word.

Citations available in the document

REFERENCES | MAILINGS

Insert Citation ▾ | Manage Sources | Style: APA | Bibliography ▾

Burke, Edward R. The Complete Book of Long-Distance Cycling, (2011)

Chapple, Thomas Base Building for Cyclists, (2009)

Velo News Training Tips for Recreational Cyclists, (2012)

Add New Source...

Add New Placeholder...

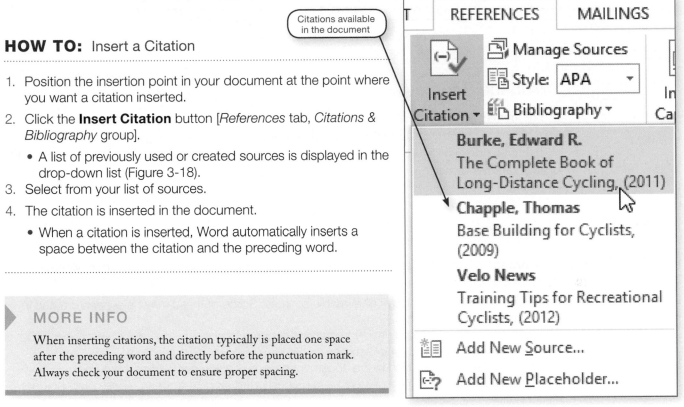

3-18 Insert citation from a previously created source

> **MORE INFO**
>
> When inserting citations, the citation typically is placed one space after the preceding word and directly before the punctuation mark. Always check your document to ensure proper spacing.

Insert a Placeholder

There might be times when you need to insert a citation but do not have all of the bibliographic information to create the source. You can insert a ***placeholder*** in the report to temporarily mark a spot where a citation needs to be completed. Later, you can go back in and add bibliographic source information for any placeholders inserted in the document.

HOW TO: Insert a Placeholder

1. Position the insertion point in your document at the point where you want a placeholder inserted.
2. Click the **Insert Citation** button [*References* tab, *Citations & Bibliography* group].
3. Select **Add New Placeholder**. The *Placeholder Name* dialog box opens (Figure 3-19).

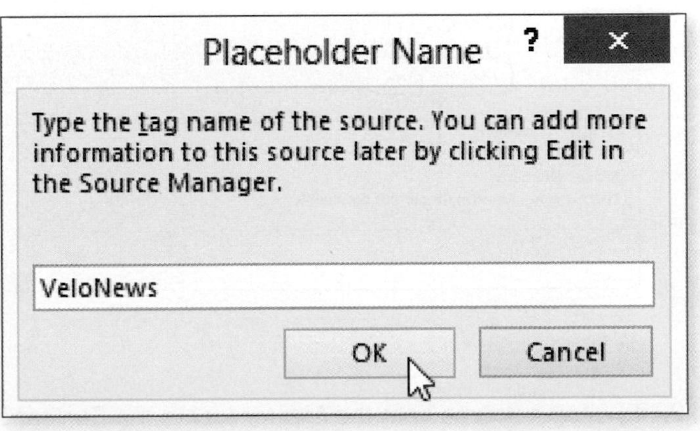

3-19 Insert a placeholder

4. Type in the name of the placeholder.
   - You can't use spaces between words in the placeholder text.
   - Use an underscore or merge words together when naming a placeholder.
5. Click **OK**. The placeholder is inserted into the document and looks similar to a citation (Figure 3-20).

3-20 Placeholder in the body of the document

Manage Sources

The ***Source Manager*** dialog box allows you to create sources, copy sources created and used in other documents, modify sources, and add bibliographic information to placeholders. This dialog box displays which sources are used in your report and the placeholders that need bibliographic information.

HOW TO: Manage Sources

1. Click the **Manage Sources** button [*References* tab, *Citations & Bibliography* group]. The *Source Manager* dialog box opens (Figure 3-21).
   - The *Master List* of sources on the left displays *all* available sources. Some of these may have been created in other Word documents.
   - The *Current List* displays the sources available in your current document.
   - The *Preview* area displays the contents of your source.
   - The sources in the *Current List* that are cited in the document have a check mark next to them.
   - The sources in the *Current List* that are placeholders have a question mark next to them. These placeholders need additional information.

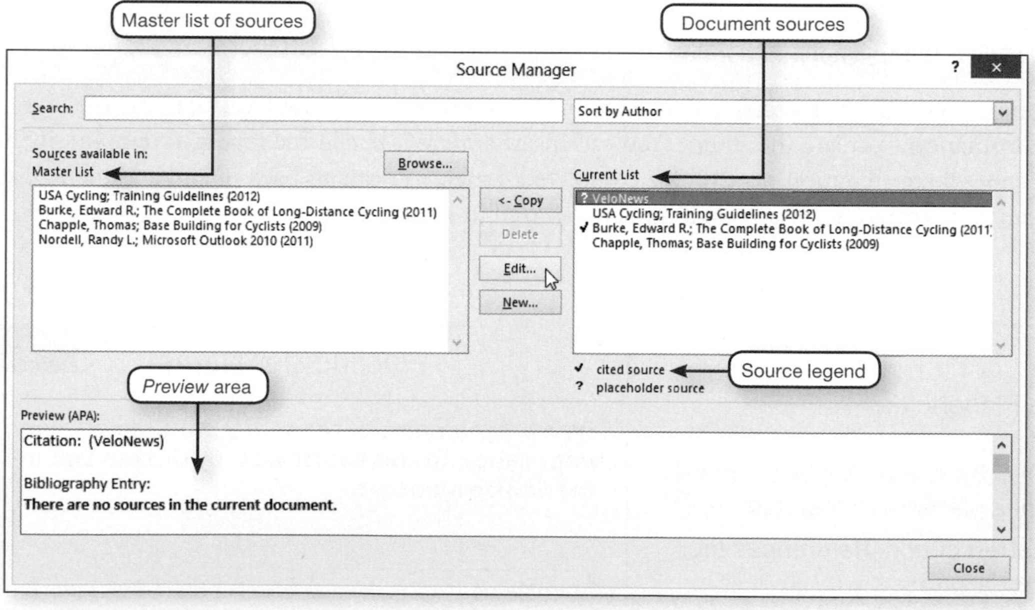

3-21 *Source Manager* dialog box

2. To copy a source from the *Master List* to the *Current List,* select the source and press the **Copy** button. The copied source remains on the *Master List.*

3. To edit a source from either list, select the source and click the **Edit** button. The *Edit Source* dialog box opens.
   - Make changes to the source and press **OK**.
   - Word automatically updates any citations in your document if you make changes to the source.
4. To add bibliographic information to a placeholder, select the placeholder and click the **Edit** button. The *Edit Source* dialog box opens.
   - Add bibliographic information to the placeholder and press **OK**.
   - When bibliographic information is added to a placeholder, it becomes a complete source and the question mark next to it changes to a check.
   - Word automatically replaces the placeholder with a citation in your document when you add bibliographic information to a placeholder.
5. Click the **New** button to create a new source. The *Create Source* dialog box opens.
   - Type in the bibliographic information and press **OK**.
   - This source is now available as a citation to insert in your document.
   - This source is also added to the *Master List*.
6. To delete a source from either list, select the source and click the **Delete** button.
   - You cannot delete a source from the *Current List* if it is cited in the document.
   - If a source is in both lists and you delete it from one list, it is not deleted from the other list.
7. Click **Close** to close the *Source Manager* dialog box and apply any changes made.

Edit Citations and Sources

After citations are inserted into the document, you can edit the citation or source without using the *Source Manager* dialog box. When you click a citation in your document, you see a drop-down list of editing options (Figure 3-22).

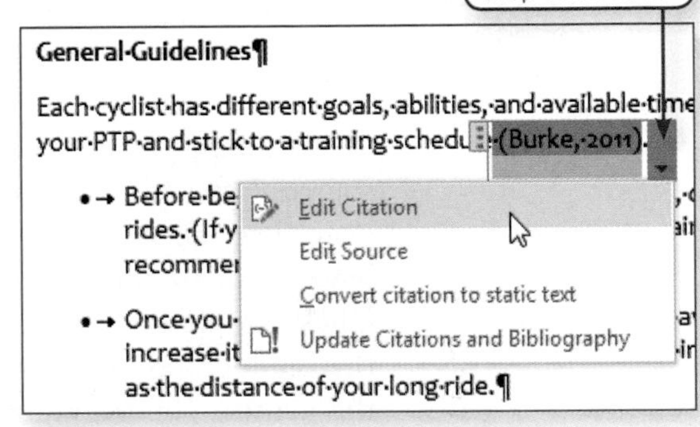

3-22 Edit citation options

- ***Edit Citation:*** Options in the *Edit Citation* dialog box allow you to add a page number to the citation or suppress any currently displayed information.
- ***Edit Source:*** Options in the *Edit Source* dialog box allow you to update source bibliographic information.
- ***Convert citation to static text:*** This option changes the citation from a Word field that is automatically generated and updated to static text that is not updated.
- ***Update Citations and Bibliography:*** This option updates your bibliography page to reflect any changes you have made to citations or sources.

MORE INFO

You can edit placeholders using either the drop-down list or context menu.

You can move or delete a citation or placeholder in the body of the text by clicking the citation or placeholder handle on the left and dragging to a new location (to move) or by pressing **Delete** (to delete) on your keyboard (Figure 3-23).

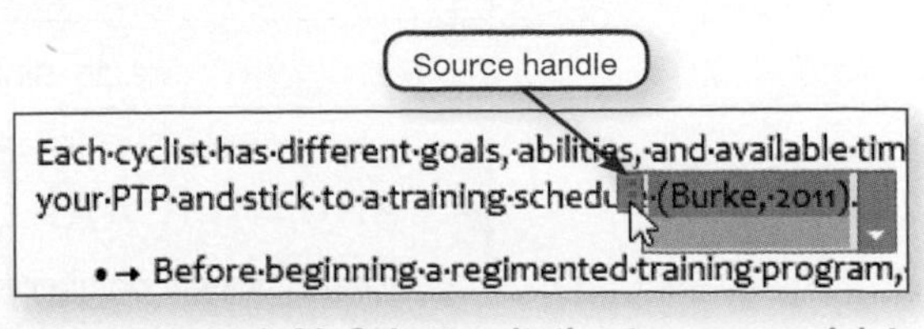

3-23 Select a citation to move or delete

Insert a Bibliography

Once you have created your sources and inserted citations in the body of the report, you are now ready to create a bibliography page. The bibliography page is automatically generated from the sources in your document and is formatted according to the style of report you selected. Word provides you with a few bibliography options.

The *Bibliography, References*, and *Works Cited* built-in options insert a title before the sources. The *Insert Bibliography* option just inserts the sources; you can add a title of your choice. If you are planning on using a table of contents in your report, it is best to use one of the built-in options because Word applies a style for the bibliography title, which allows the bibliography page to automatically be included in the table contents.

HOW TO: Insert a Bibliography

1. Position the insertion point in your document at the point where you want the bibliography to begin.
   - It is usually good to insert a page break (**Ctrl+Enter**) at the end of the document and begin the bibliography on a new page.
2. Click the **Bibliography** button [*References* tab, *Citations & Bibliography* group] to display the list of options (Figure 3-24).
3. Select your bibliography option. The bibliography is inserted in the document.

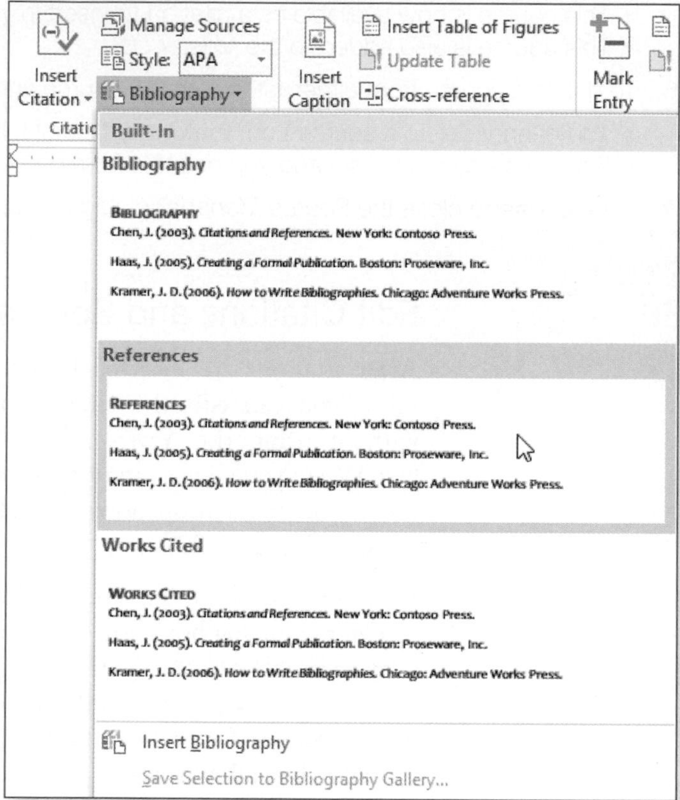

3-24 Insert bibliography

If changes are made to sources after the bibliography page has been inserted, you have to update the bibliography. Click one of the references on the bibliography page to select the entire bibliography and click the **Update Citations and Bibliography** (Figure 3-25).

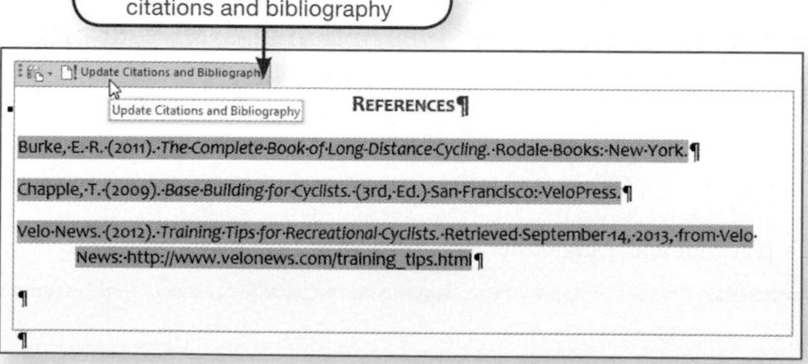

3-25 Bibliography inserted into the document

> **ANOTHER WAY**
>
> Right-click your bibliography and choose **Update Field** or press **F9** to update your bibliography.

PAUSE & PRACTICE: WORD 3-1

For this Pause & Practice project, you modify the *Developing a Personal Training Program* report for American River Cycling Club. You select the report style, add and modify notes, add sources and citations, and insert a bibliography page.

File Needed: ***PersonalTrainingProgram-03.docx***
Completed Project File Name: ***[your initials] PP W3-1.docx***

1. Open the ***PersonalTrainingProgram-03*** document from your student data files.
2. Save this document as ***[your initials] PP W3-1***.
3. Insert endnotes into the report.
   a. Position the insertion point after "PTP" (first page, first paragraph).
   b. Click **Insert Endnote** [*References* tab, *Footnotes* group]. Word moves the insertion point to the endnote area on the last page.
   c. Type Personal training program.
   d. Position the insertion point after the first instance of "Max VO2" (third page, "Training Intensity and Heart Rate" section).

> **MORE INFO**
> Use the *Find* feature in the *Navigation* pane to locate specific words.

   e. Click **Insert Endnote** [*References* tab, *Footnotes* group].
   f. Type The highest rate of oxygen consumption attainable during maximal or exhaustive exercise.
   g. Position the insertion point after "RPM" (third page, "Training Intensity and Heart Rate" section).
   h. Click **Insert Endnote** [*References* tab, *Footnotes* group].
   i. Type Revolutions per minute.
   j. Apply **bold** and **italic** formatting to the words "maximal" and "exhaustive" in the second endnote (Figure 3-26).

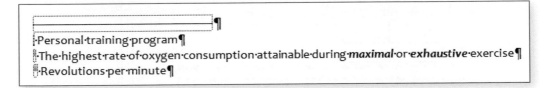

¶
·Personal·training·program¶
·The·highest·rate·of·oxygen·consumption·attainable·during·***maximal***·or·***exhaustive***·exercise¶
·Revolutions·per·minute¶

3-26 Endnotes added to report

4. Convert endnotes to footnotes and change numbering.
   a. Click the **Footnotes** launcher [*References* tab, *Footnotes* group]. The *Footnote and Endnote* dialog box opens.
   b. Click the **Convert** button to open the *Convert Notes* dialog box (Figure 3-27).
   c. Select **Convert all endnotes to footnotes** and click **OK**.

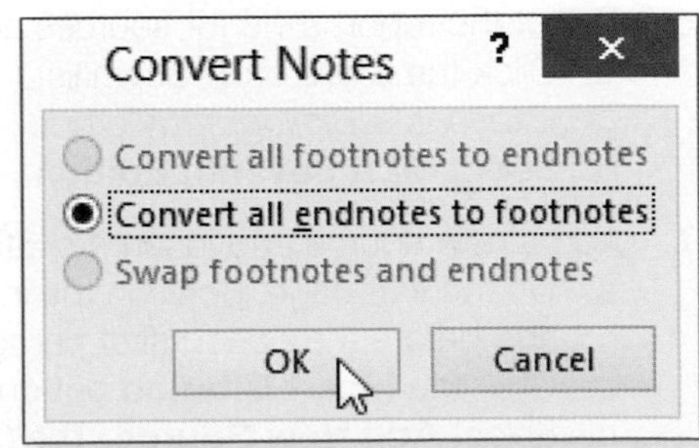

3-27 Convert endnotes to footnotes

d. Click **Close** to the close the *Footnote and Endnote* dialog box.
e. Click the **Footnotes** launcher again to open the *Footnote and Endnote* dialog box.
f. Click the **Footnotes** radio button.
g. Click the **Number format** drop-down arrow and select **a, b, c . . .** option (Figure 3-28). Don't change any of the other *Format* settings.
h. Choose **Apply** to close the *Footnote and Endnote* dialog box and apply the changes.
i. Check your document to confirm that endnotes have been converted to footnotes and that the number format has been changed.

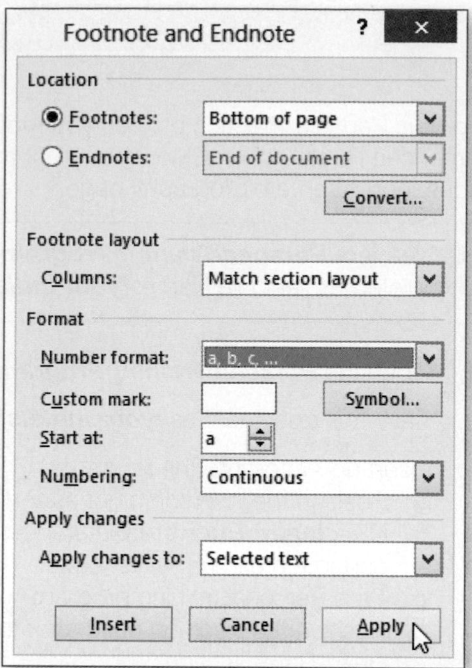

3-28 Change number format of footnotes

5. Change the style of the footnotes.
   a. Right-click the footnote text at the bottom of the first page.
   b. Select **Style** from the context menu. The *Style* dialog box opens.
   c. Click the **Modify** button to open the *Modify Style* dialog box (Figure 3-29).
   d. Change the font size to **9 pt**.
   e. Change line spacing to **1.5**.
   f. Click **OK** to close the *Modify Style* dialog box.
   g. Choose **Apply** to close the *Style* dialog box.

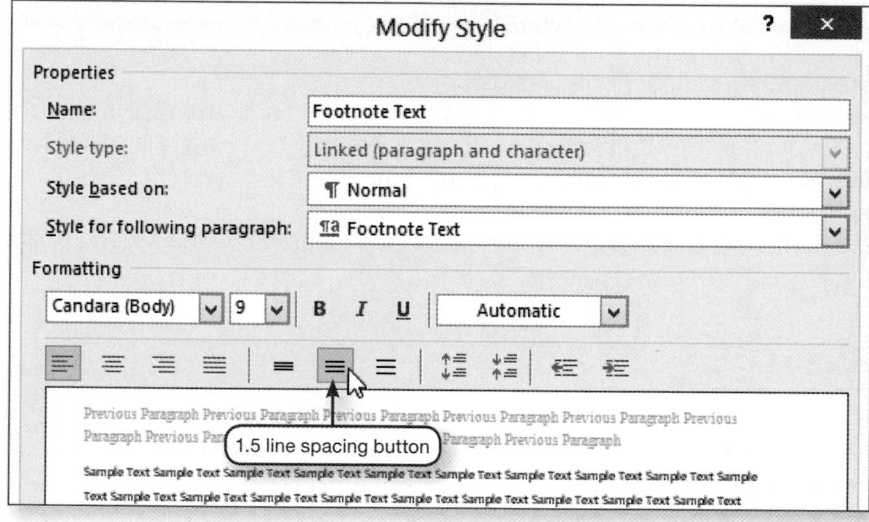

3-29 Modify *Footnote Text* style

6. Select the report style for sources and citations.
   a. Click the **Style** drop-down list [*References* tab, *Citations & Bibliography* group].
   b. Select **MLA Seventh Edition**.
7. Add a new source and insert a citation.
   a. On the first page, position the insertion point after the word "schedule" and before the period (first paragraph, "General Guidelines" section).
   b. Click the **Insert Citation** button [*References* tab, *Citations & Bibliography* group].
   c. Select **Add New Source**. The *Create Source* dialog box opens.
   d. Select **Book** as the type of source.

e. Click the **Edit** button to open the *Edit Name* dialog box.
f. In the *Author* area, type Burke for *Last,* Edward for *First,* and R. for *Middle*.
g. Click **OK** to close the dialog box.
h. Type the following in the *Create Source* dialog box:

Title: The Complete Book of Long-Distance Cycling

Year: 2011

City: New York

Publisher: Rodale Books

Tag name: Burke

i. Click **OK** to add the source, insert the citation, and close the dialog box.

8. Add a placeholder to the report.
   a. On the first page, position the insertion point after the word "speed" and before the period (last bulleted item, "Pace of Rides" section).
   b. Click the **Insert Citation** button [*References* tab, *Citations & Bibliography* group].
   c. Select **Add New Placeholder**. The *Placeholder Name* dialog box opens.
   d. Type VeloNews (no space between words) as the placeholder text.
   e. Press **OK** to insert the placeholder and close the dialog box.

9. Manage sources to add a new source and complete bibliographic information for the placeholder.
   a. Click the **Manage Sources** button [*References* tab, *Citations & Bibliography* group]. The *Source Manager* dialog box opens.
   b. Select **VeloNews** in the *Current List* area and click the **Edit** button.
   c. Type the following:

      Type of Source: **Document from Web Site**
      Corporate Author (check **Corporate Author** check box): Velo News
      Name of Web Page: Training Tips for Recreational Cyclists
      Name of Web Site: Velo News
      Year: 2012
      Year Accessed: 2013 (check **Show All Bibliography Fields** box)
      Month Accessed: September
      Day Accessed: 14
      URL: http://www.velonews.com/training_tips.html

   d. Click **OK** to close the *Edit Source* dialog box. The placeholder is updated as a complete source.
   e. Click the **New** button to create a new source.
   f. Type the following:

      Type of Source: **Book**
      Author: Thomas Chapple
      Title: Base Building for Cyclists
      Year: 2009
      City: San Francisco
      Publisher: VeloPress
      Edition (check **Show All Bibliography Fields** check box): 3rd
      Tag name: Chapple

   g. Click **OK** to close the *Create Source* dialog box.
   h. Click **Close** to close the *Source Manager* dialog box.

10. Insert citations into the report.
    a. On the second page, position the insertion point after "rest day" and before the period (first paragraph, "Number of Rides per Week" section).

b. Click the **Insert Citation** button [*References* tab, *Citations & Bibliography* group] (Figure 3-30).
c. Select the **Chapple**, **Thomas** source. The citation is inserted into the report.
d. Using the **Insert Citation** button, insert the following citations:

Burke, **Edward**, **R.**: after "training week" and before the period (page 2, last bulleted item in the "Duration of Rides" section).
Chapple, **Thomas:** after "maximum heart rate" and before the period (page 3, first paragraph in "Training Intensity and Heart Rate" section).
Velo News: after "overtraining" and before the period (page 3, at the end of "Other Heart Rate Factors" section).

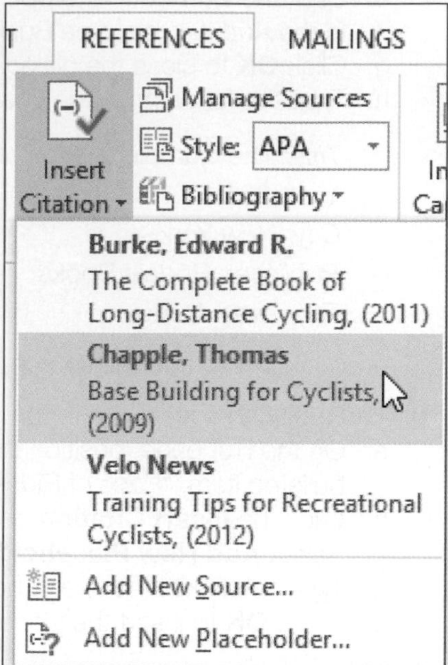

3-30 Insert a citation

11. Insert a bibliography and change report style.
    a. Position the insertion point on the blank line at the end of the document and press **Ctrl+Enter** to insert a page break.
    b. Click the **Bibliography** button [*References* tab, *Citations & Bibliography* group] and select **References** from the drop-down list. The *Reference* page is inserted on the blank page at the end of the document.
    c. **Center** the *References* title and apply **10 pt**. after paragraph spacing.
    d. Click the **Style** drop-down list [*References* tab, *Citations & Bibliography* group].
    e. Select **APA Sixth Edition**.
12. Save and close the document (Figure 3-31).

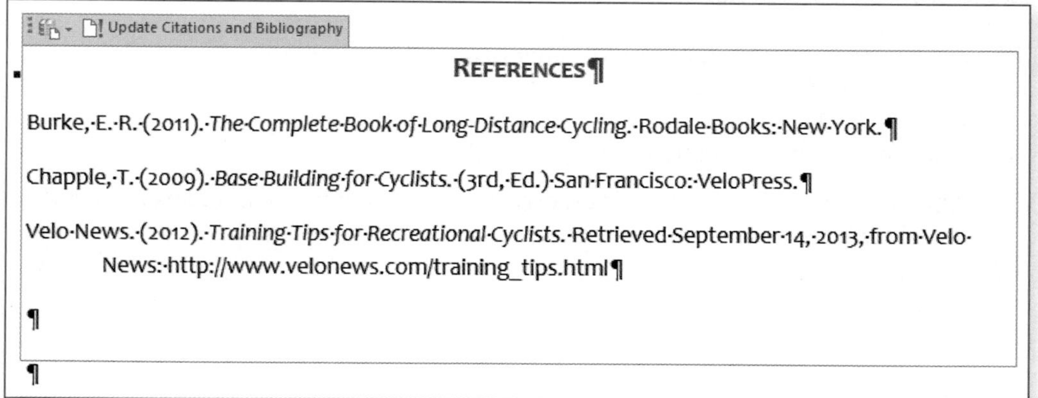

3-31 PP W3-1 References page

SLO 3.3

Inserting a Table of Contents

Most long reports have a ***table of contents*** to provide readers with an overview of the material covered in the report. The table of contents reflects the headings in the report; some tables of contents list only the main headings while others might list second- and third-level headings. Typically, a table of contents lists headings on the left and page numbers on the right with a dot leader separating them.

You can create a table of contents manually by typing in the headings, using a tab with a dot leader, and then typing the page number. But with Word you can automatically generate a table of contents based upon the headings in your report. This saves you time, and, if you generate your table of contents this way, it automatically updates if topics are moved or page numbering changes in the report.

Use Heading Styles for a Table of Contents

Word can automatically generate a table of contents listing the headings in your report if ***heading styles*** are applied to each heading. Styles control the appearance of text by applying a specific font, font size, color, font styles and effects, and spacing to the text on which a style is applied. The document ***theme*** determines the appearance of the styles. Many of the commonly used styles are displayed in the *Styles* gallery.

> **MORE INFO**
>
> Styles and themes were introduced in Chapter 2.

The first step in automatically generating a table of contents in a report is to apply a heading style to each heading in the document. Word provides you with multiple levels of heading styles (e.g., Heading 1, Heading 2, etc.).

HOW TO: Apply Heading Styles

1. Select the heading where you want to apply a style.
2. Click the heading style to apply [*Home* tab, *Styles* group] (Figure 3-32). The style is applied to the heading.
   - Apply *Heading 1* to main headings, *Heading 2* to second level headings, and other heading styles as needed.
   - When you place the insertion point on a style, Word displays a live preview of the style and temporarily applies the style to the selected text.
   - Click the **More** button to expand the *Style* gallery to display more styles.

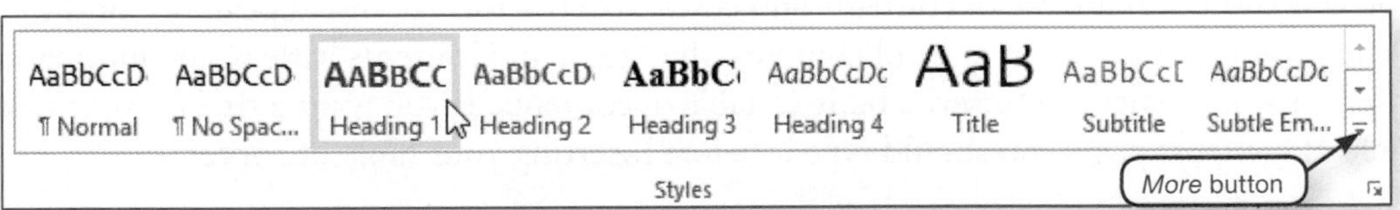

3-32 Document styles displayed in the *Style* gallery

3. Continue to select headings and apply styles. Every heading that you want to have in your table of contents must have a style.
   - When a heading style has been applied to text, there is an *Expand/Collapse* button to the left of the heading (Figure 3-33). Click the **Expand/ Collapse** button to expand or collapse the text below the heading.

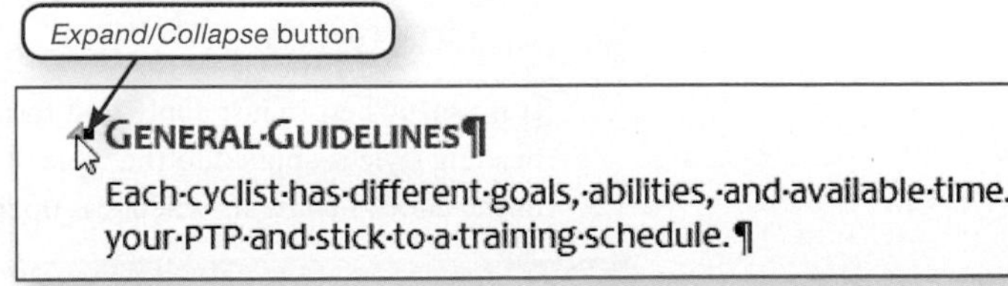

3-33 Expand or collapse text below heading

Insert a Built-In Table of Contents

You can insert a built-in table of contents that includes the headings in your document. Word inserts the table of contents at the point in your report where the insertion point is located. It is a good idea to insert a blank page before the first page of your report for your table of contents.

HOW TO: Insert a Built-In Table of Contents

1. Place the insertion point before the first line of the report and press **Ctrl+Enter** to insert a page break.
2. Position the insertion point at the top of the new first page.
3. Click the **References** tab.
4. Click the **Table of Contents** button [*Table of Contents* group] (Figure 3-34).
5. Select a built-in table of contents to insert. The table of contents is inserted into your report (Figure 3-35).

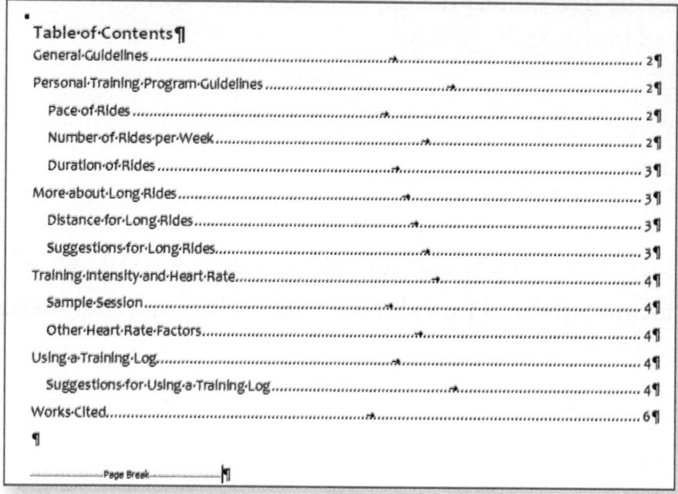

Table·of·Contents¶
General·Guidelines .... 2¶
Personal·Training·Program·Guidelines .... 2¶
Pace·of·Rides .... 2¶
Number·of·Rides·per·Week .... 2¶
Duration·of·Rides .... 3¶
More·about·Long·Rides .... 3¶
Distance·for·Long·Rides .... 3¶
Suggestions·for·Long·Rides .... 3¶
Training·Intensity·and·Heart·Rate .... 4¶
Sample·Session .... 4¶
Other·Heart·Rate·Factors .... 4¶
Using·a·Training·Log .... 4¶
Suggestions·for·Using·a·Training·Log .... 4¶
Works·Cited .... 6¶
¶
Page Break ¶

3-35 Table of contents inserted into the report

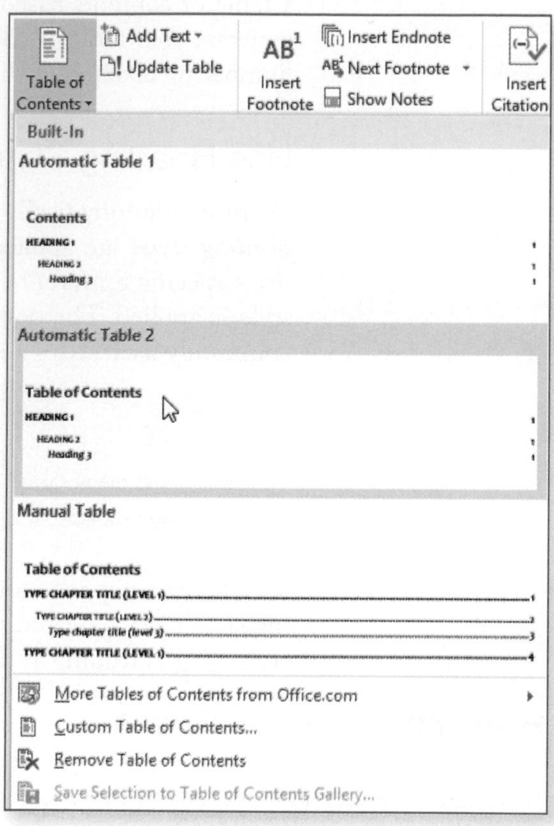

3-34 Insert built-in table of contents

Insert a Custom Table of Contents

You can also insert a table of contents and customize the format and appearance of the table. When you insert a custom table of contents, the "Table of Contents" title is not automatically inserted as it is when you insert a built-in table of contents. If you want a title on your custom table of contents page, you should type it before inserting your table of contents.

> **MORE INFO**
>
> It is usually best to just apply font formatting (not a heading style) to the table of contents title. If a heading style is applied to the table of contents title, the table of contents title is included as an item in the table of contents when it is updated.

HOW TO: Insert a Custom Table of Contents

1. Place the insertion point before the first line of your report and press **Ctrl+Enter** to insert a page break.
2. Position the insertion point at the top of the new first page.
   - If desired, type a title for the table of contents and press **Enter**. Do not apply a heading style to the title.
3. Click the **Table of Contents** button [*References* tab, *Table of Contents* group].

4. Select **Custom Table of Contents**. The *Table of Contents* dialog box opens (Figure 3-36).
   - A preview of the table of contents appears in the *Print Preview* area.
   - Below the *Print Preview* area, you can choose to not display page numbers or not have them aligned on the right and select the type of leader to use with right-aligned page numbers.
5. In the *General* area, select a table of contents format from the **Formats** drop-down list.
6. Select the number of heading levels to display in the *Show levels* area.
7. Click **OK** to insert the table of contents.

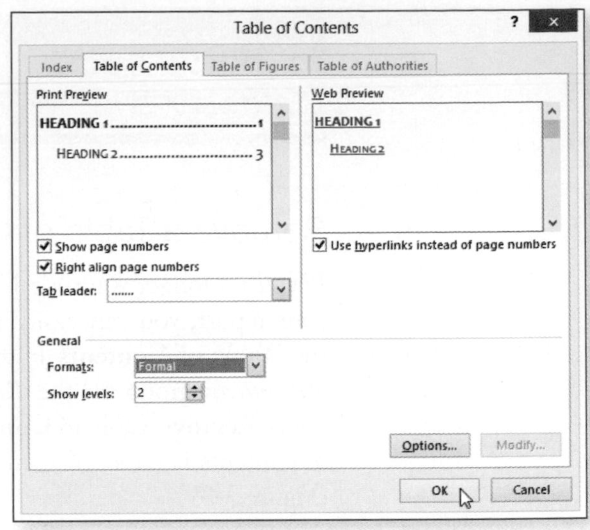

3-36 *Table of Contents* dialog box

Modify a Table of Contents

After inserting a table of contents, you might decide that you want a different format or to change the levels of headings that are displayed. When you update a table of contents, you are actually replacing the old table of contents with a new one.

HOW TO: Modify a Table of Contents

1. Click anywhere in the table of contents.
2. Click the **Table of Contents** button [*References* tab, *Table of Contents* group].
3. Select **Custom Table of Contents**. The *Table of Contents* dialog box opens.
4. Make changes to the table of contents.
5. Click **OK**. A dialog box opens, confirming you want to replace the existing table of contents (Figure 3-37).
6. Click **YES** to insert the new table of contents.

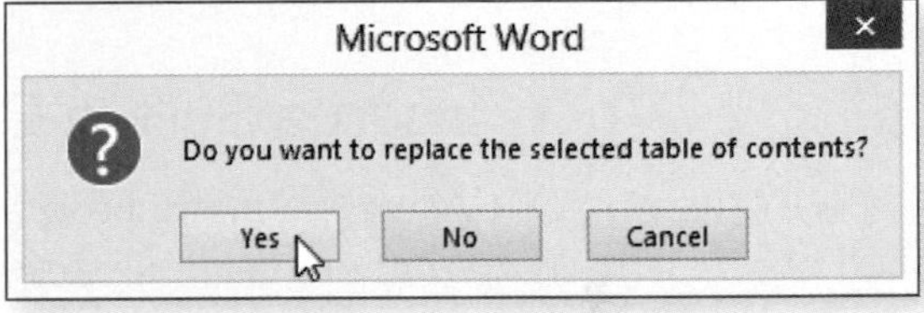

3-37 Replace existing table of contents

Update a Table of Contents

When you make changes to your report such as adding or modifying headings, content, or page breaks, the content and page numbers in the table of contents may no longer be accurate. You need to update the table of contents to reflect these changes. You have the option of updating only page numbers or updating the entire table of contents, which includes both content and page numbers.

HOW TO: Update a Table of Contents

1. Click anywhere in the table of contents.
2. Click the **Update Table** button [*References* tab, *Table of Contents* group]. The *Update Table of Contents* dialog box opens (Figure 3-38).
3. Select either **Update page numbers only** or **Update entire table**.
4. Click **OK** to update the table of contents.

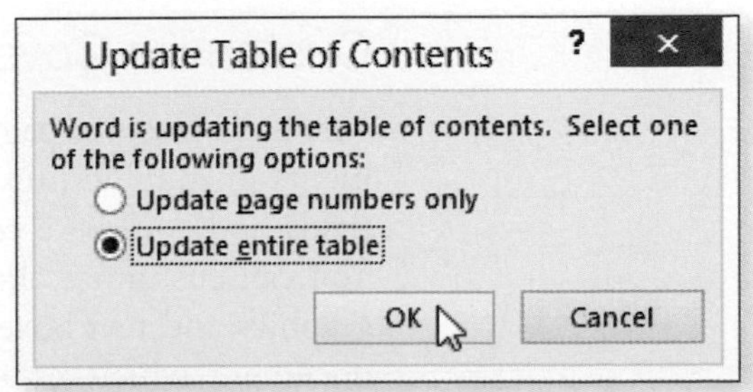

3-38 Update table of contents

> **ANOTHER WAY**
>
> Press **F9** or right-click the table of contents and select **Update Field** to update the table of contents.

Remove a Table of Contents

If you no longer want a table of contents in your report, you can easily remove it. Click the **Table of Contents** button in the *Table of Contents* group on the *References* tab and select **Remove Table of Contents.** The table of contents is removed from your document (Figure 3-39).

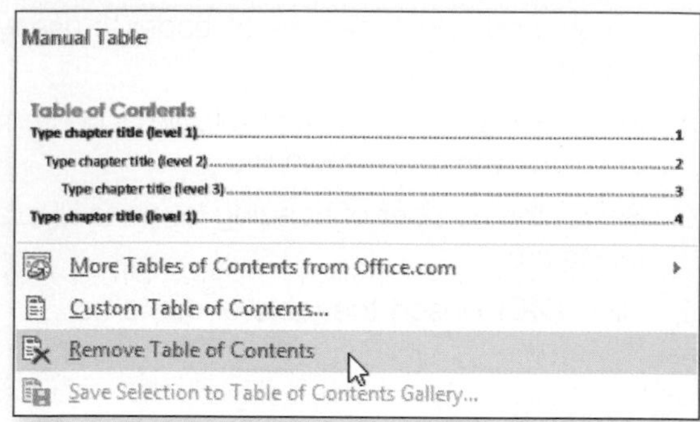

3-39 Remove table of contents

SLO 3.4

Inserting a Cover Page

Some reports have a title page as the cover or introduction. If you're writing a formal report in APA style, there is a specific way you must organize the title page. But if you're presenting a market analysis or product feasibility report at work, you might want a ***cover page*** to introduce the report with professional appeal. Word provides you with a variety of cover page options.

Insert a Built-In Cover Page

When you insert a cover page into a document, Word automatically inserts it at the beginning of the document and inserts a page break to push the existing first page content to the second page.

To insert a cover page, click the **Cover Page** button in the *Pages* group on the *Insert* tab and select one of the built-in cover pages from the drop-down list (Figure 3-40). More custom cover pages are available on Office.com. Select **More Cover Pages from Office.com** to display a list of additional cover pages.

3-40 Insert built-in cover page

Customize Cover Page Content

The built-in cover pages in Word are arrangements of graphics, text boxes, and Word fields. Some of the fields are document property fields and some are ***content control fields,*** fields where you can type custom information. You can customize the content of the fields, delete unwanted Word fields, and modify the graphics and text boxes on the cover page. Cover pages are controlled by the theme of your document, which means the colors and fonts change depending on the theme selected for the document.

Customize Document Property Content

If you have added information to the document properties of your document, Word automatically populates the document properties fields in the cover page. When you type information into a document property field on the cover page, Word adds this information to your document properties.

Properties ▾

Size	889KB
Pages	7
Words	1610
Total Editing Time	30 Minutes
Title	Developing a Personal Tra...
Tags	Add a tag
Comments	Add comments
Template	Normal
Status	Add text
Categories	Add a category
Subject	Specify the subject
Hyperlink Base	Add text
Company	American River Cycling Cl...

Related Dates

Last Modified	Today, 12:07 PM
Created	9/4/2012 11:21 AM
Last Printed	

Related People

Manager	Olesia Sokol
Author	Add an author
Last Modified By	Randy Nordell

Related Documents

Open File Location

Show Fewer Properties

3-41 Document properties on the *Backstage* view

HOW TO: Customize Document Properties

1. Click the **File** tab to open the *Backstage* view and select **Info** to display document properties (Figure 3-41).
2. Click the **Show All Properties** link at the bottom.
   - This link toggles between *Show All Properties* and *Show Fewer Properties*.
3. Add or modify document property content.
   - Some fields, such as *Last Modified* and *Created,* cannot be modified.
   - To remove the *Author,* right-click the author and select **Remove Person**.
4. Click the **Back** arrow to return to the document. Word updates the document property fields on the cover page.

Add or Remove Document Property Fields

You can also add document property fields to the cover page or remove them. When you add a document property field to a cover page, the content of this field is automatically populated with the information from your document properties.

HOW TO: Add Document Property Fields

1. Position the insertion point at the place where you want to insert the document property field.
2. Click the **Insert** tab.
3. Click the **Quick Parts** button [*Text* group] (Figure 3-42).
4. Choose **Document Property**.
5. Select a document property field from the drop-down list. The document property field is inserted into the document.

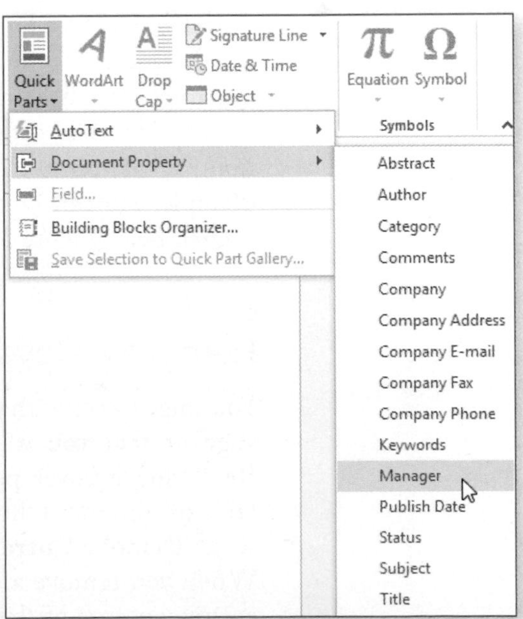

3-42 Insert document property field

> **MORE INFO**
>
> You can insert document property fields anywhere in a document.

To remove a document property field, click the **field handle** and press **Delete** (Figure 3-43). Make sure to check for proper spacing and paragraph breaks when you delete a document property field.

3-43 Delete document property field

Print Document Properties

After customizing document properties, you can print the document properties included in a document. When you print document properties, only a page listing the document properties prints, not the document itself.

HOW TO: Print Document Properties

1. Click the **File** tab to open the *Backstage* view.
2. Click **Print** on the left.
3. Click **Print All Pages** and select **Document Info** from the drop-down list (Figure 3-44).
4. Click the **Print** button to print the document properties.

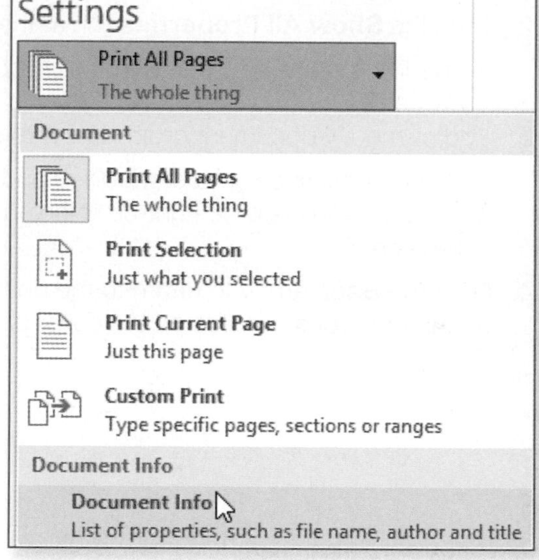

3-44 Print document properties

Customize Content Control Fields

When you insert a cover page into a document, many of the fields are content control fields, which are fields where you type or select custom content (Figure 3-45). You may want to add content to some of these fields and remove others. You can remove Word content control fields the same way you remove a document property field (see Figure 3-43).

To insert custom content into a content control field, click in the field and type the information. You can type whatever information you want into a content control field. For example, you can type a web address into the *Address* field (Figure 3-45).

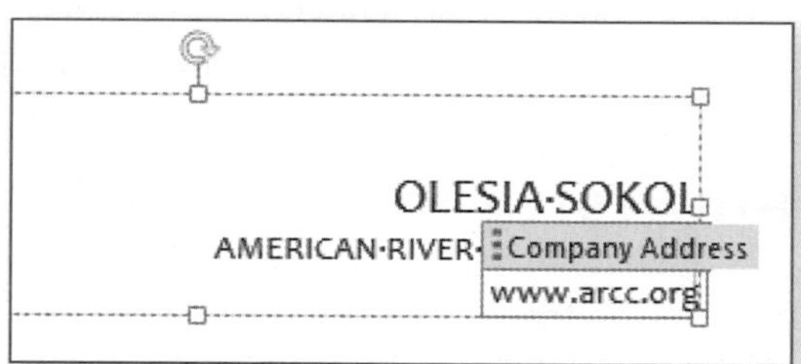

3-45 Insert text into a content control field

Remove a Cover Page

You might decide that you no longer want a cover page or that you want to insert a different one. Removing a cover page is similar to removing a table of contents. Click the **Cover Page** button and select **Remove Current Cover Page** (Figure 3-46). When you remove a cover page, Word deletes the entire contents of the cover page and removes the page break.

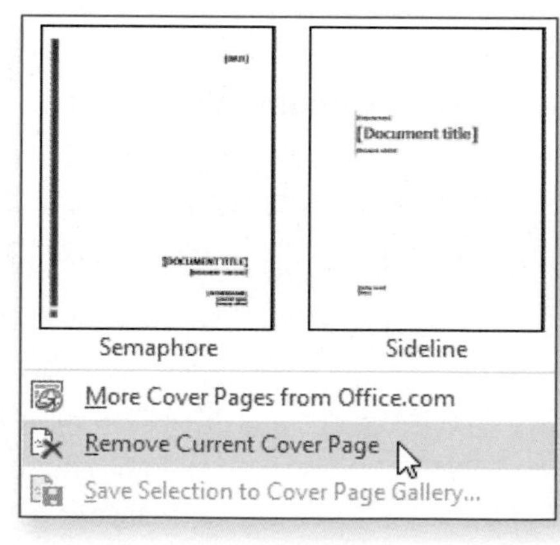

3-46 Remove cover page

PAUSE & PRACTICE: WORD 3-2

For the Pause & Practice project, you continue to modify the *Personal Training Program* report for American River Cycling Club. You apply styles to headings in the report, insert and modify a table of contents, and insert and modify a cover page.

File Needed: ***[your initials] PP W3-1.docx***
Completed Project File Name: ***[your initials] PP W3-2.docx***

1. Open the ***[your initials] PP W3-1*** document created in *Pause & Practice 3-1*.
2. Save this document as ***[your initials] PP W3-2***.
3. Apply styles to the headings in the report.
   a. Select the "**General Guidelines**" heading on the first page.
   b. Click the **Heading 1** style [*Home* tab, *Styles* group] to apply this style to the selected heading (Figure 3-47). If the *Heading 1* style is not visible, click the **More** button to display the entire *Styles* gallery.

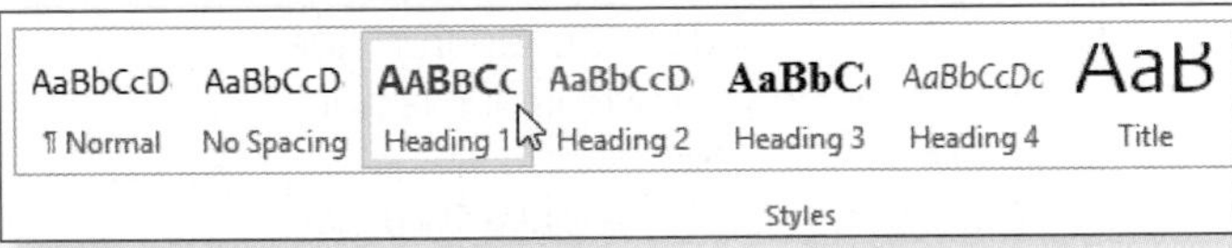

3-47 Apply *Heading 1* style

   c. Apply the **Heading 1** style to the following headings (bolded headings in the document):

      Personal Training Program Guidelines
      More about Long Rides
      Training Intensity and Heart Rate
      Using a Training Log

   d. Apply the **Heading 2** style to the following headings (underlined headings in the document):

      Pace of Rides
      Number of Rides per Week
      Duration of Rides
      Distance for Long Rides
      Suggestions for Long Rides
      Sample Session
      Other Heart Rate Factors
      Suggestions for Using a Training Log

4. Insert a page break and add a table of contents.
   a. Turn on **Show/Hide** [*Home* tab, *Paragraph* group].
   b. Position the insertion point at the beginning of the document before the title ("Developing a Personal Training Program") and press **Ctrl+Enter** to insert a page break.
   c. Position the insertion point before the page break on the new first page.
   d. Click the **Table of Contents** button [*References* tab, *Table of Contents* group] (Figure 3-48).
   e. Select **Automatic Table 2** from the drop-down list. The table of contents is inserted on the first page of the report.

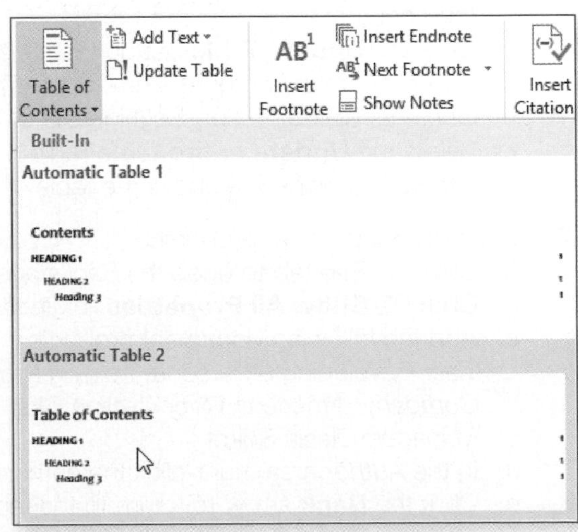

3-48 Insert table of contents

5. Customize the table of contents.
   a. Position the insertion point anywhere in the body of the table of contents.
   b. Click the **Table of Contents** button [*References* tab, *Table of Contents* group].
   c. Select **Custom Table of Contents** to open the *Table of Contents* dialog box (Figure 3-49).
   d. Click the **Formats** drop-down list and select **Formal**.
   e. In the *Show levels* area, set the number of levels at **2**.
   f. Check the **Right align page numbers** check box if it is not already checked.
   g. Select the dot leader option from the *Tab leader* drop-down list if it is not already selected.
   h. Click **OK** to close the dialog box. A dialog box opens, confirming you want to replace the existing table of contents (Figure 3-50).
   i. Click **YES** to replace the existing table of contents.

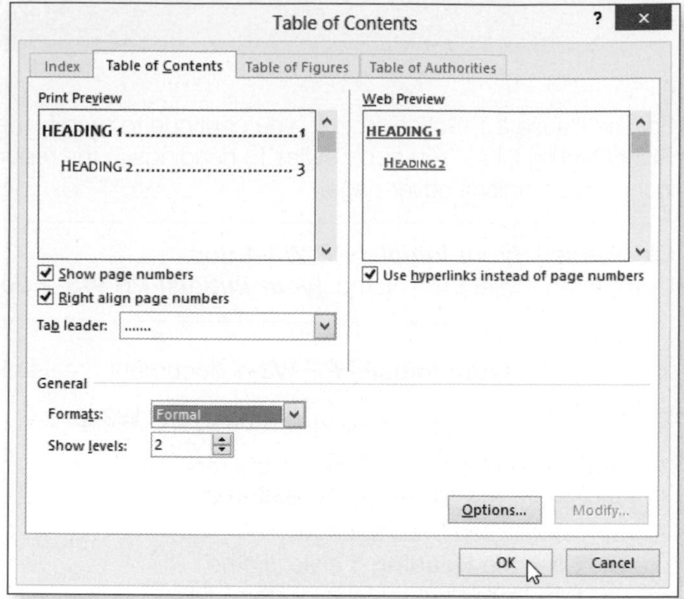

3-49 Customize table of contents

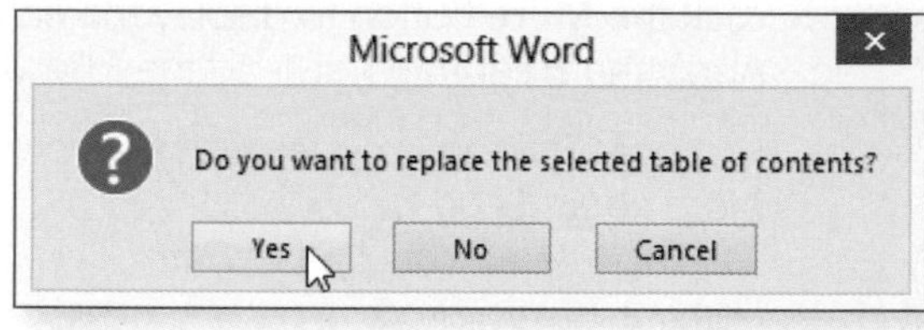

3-50 Replace existing table of contents

6. Insert page breaks and update table of contents.
   a. On the second page, position the insertion point in front of the "Number of Rides per Week" heading and press **Ctrl+Enter** to insert a page break and push this heading to the next page.
   b. Repeat this process on the following headings:

      Suggestions for Long Rides
      Using a Training Log
   c. Press **Ctrl+Home** to move to the beginning of the document.
   d. Click the **Update Table** button [*References* tab, *Table of Contents* group]. The *Update Table of Contents* dialog box opens (Figure 3-51).
   e. Select the **Update entire table** radio button and click **OK**.
   f. If there is a blank line above the table of contents, select it and press **Delete**.

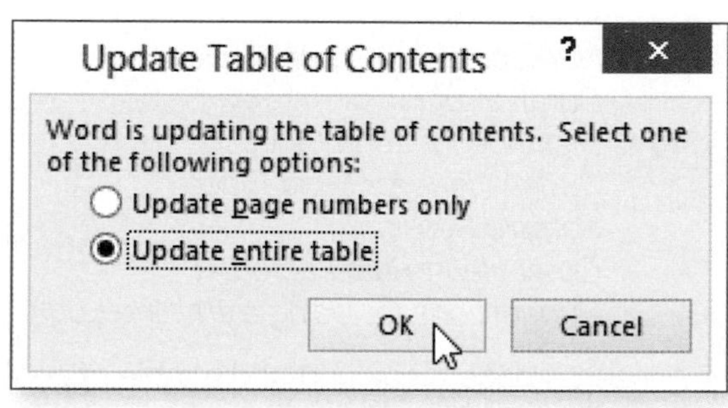

3-51 Update entire table of contents

7. Customize document properties.
   a. Click the **File** tab to open the *Backstage* view and select **Info** to display document properties.
   b. Click the **Show All Properties** link in the document properties area.
   c. Add the following document properties:
      Title: Developing a Personal Training Program
      Company: American River Cycling Club
      Manager: Olesia Sokol
   d. In the *Author* area, right-click the author's name and select **Remove Person**.
   e. Click the **Back** arrow to return to the report.

8. Add a cover page and customize fields.
   a. Click the **Cover Page** button [*Insert* tab, *Pages* group] and select **Semaphore**. The cover page is inserted on a page before the table of contents.
   b. Click the **Date** field drop-down arrow to display the calendar and select the current date.
   c. Click the **Author** document property field, select the field handle, and press **Delete** to delete the field (Figure 3-52). The insertion point is positioned on the blank line where the *Author* field was removed.

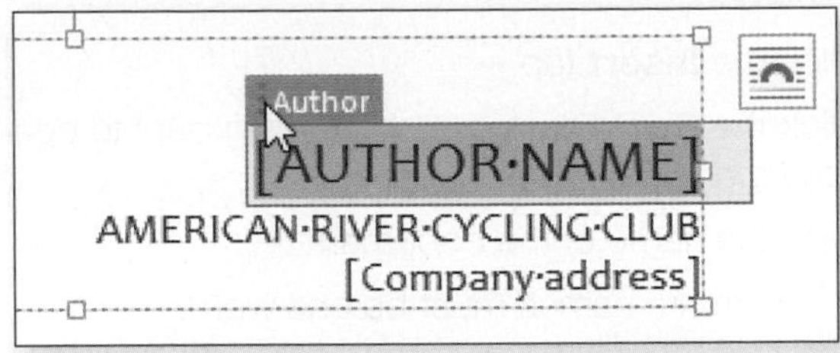

3-52 Delete document property field

   d. Click the **Quick Parts** button [*Insert* tab, *Text* group].
   e. Choose **Document Property** and select **Manager** from the drop-down list. The *Manager* document property field is inserted into the cover page.
   f. Click in the **Company Address** field and type: www.arcc.org.
   g. Select and delete the **Subject** field ("[Document Subtitle]").
   h. Click in the **Title** field and apply **bold** format. The bold formatting is applied to the entire title.

9. Save and close the document (Figure 3-53).

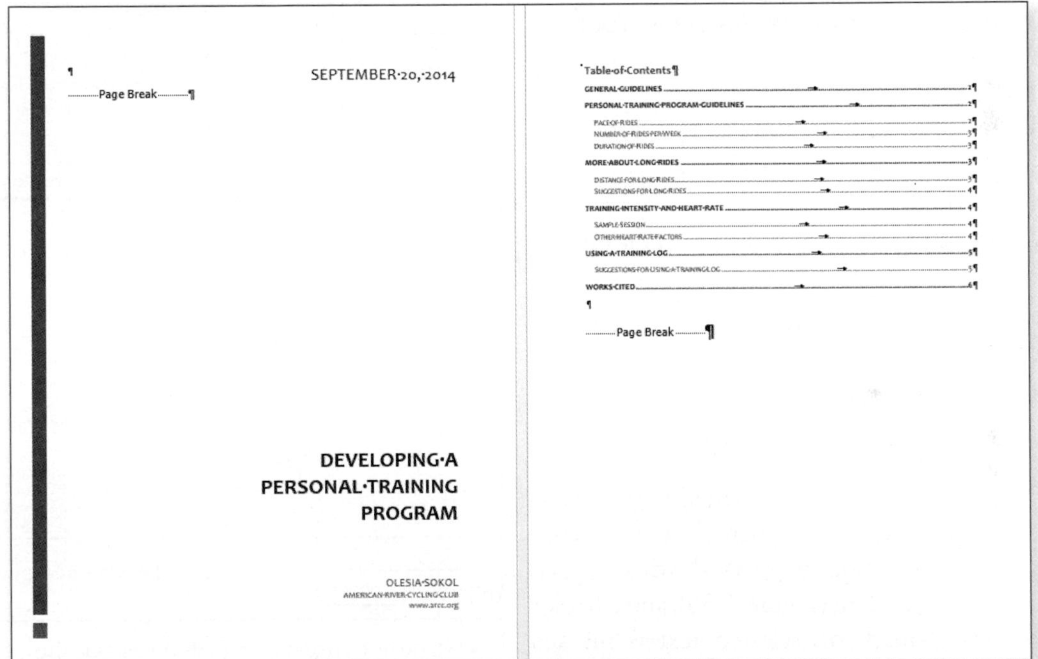

3-53 PP W3-2 cover page and table of contents

SLO 3.5 Using Bookmarks

When working with long documents, you can add a ***bookmark*** for a location or selected text in the document. Once you have inserted a bookmark, you can create a hyperlink to this location, create a cross-reference to this location, or index the bookmark to be included on an index page.

Add a Bookmark

Use bookmarks to mark a specific location, a word, or selected text, including a table.

HOW TO: Add a Bookmark

1. Position the insertion point or select the text you want to bookmark.
2. Click the **Insert** tab.
3. Click the **Bookmark** button [*Links* group] to open the *Bookmark* dialog box (Figure 3-54).
4. Type the name of the bookmark.
   - Bookmark names must be one word.
5. Click **Add** to add the bookmark and close the dialog box.

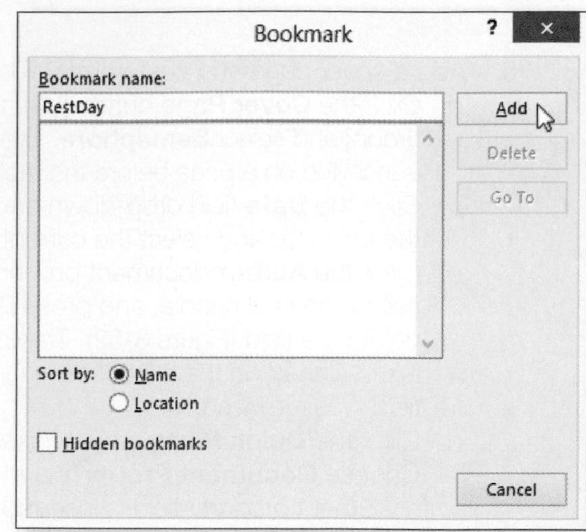

3-54 ***Bookmark*** **dialog box**

View Bookmarks in a Document

When a bookmark is added, by default it is not visible in your document. But you can make bookmarks visible in Word by changing a setting in the ***Word Options*** dialog box.

HOW TO: Make Bookmarks Visible in Your Document

1. Click the **File** tab to open the *Backstage* view.
2. Click the **Options** button to open the *Word Options* dialog box.
3. Select **Advanced** on the left of the *Word Options* dialog box (Figure 3-55).
4. Check the **Show bookmarks** check box in the *Show document content* area.
5. Click **OK** to close the dialog box.

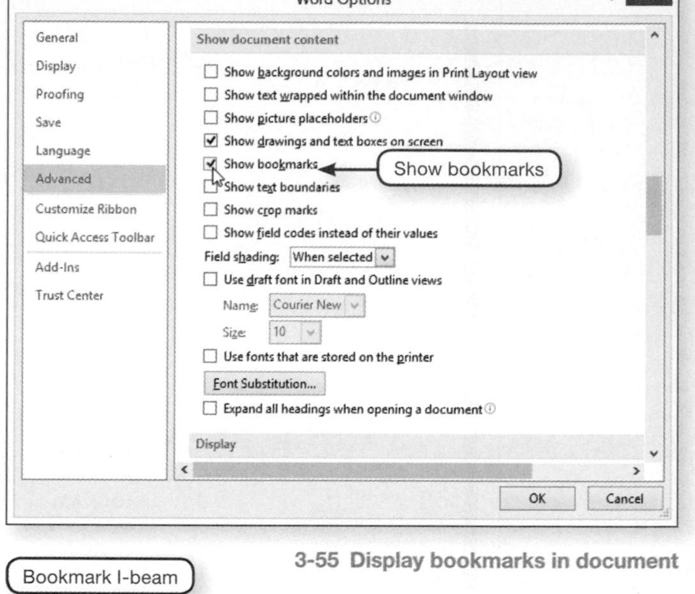

3-55 Display bookmarks in document

When bookmarks are made visible, a bookmark at a specific location is marked with a gray I-beam (Figure 3-56), and a bookmark on selected text is marked with gray brackets (Figure 3-57).

3-56 Bookmark at specific location in the document

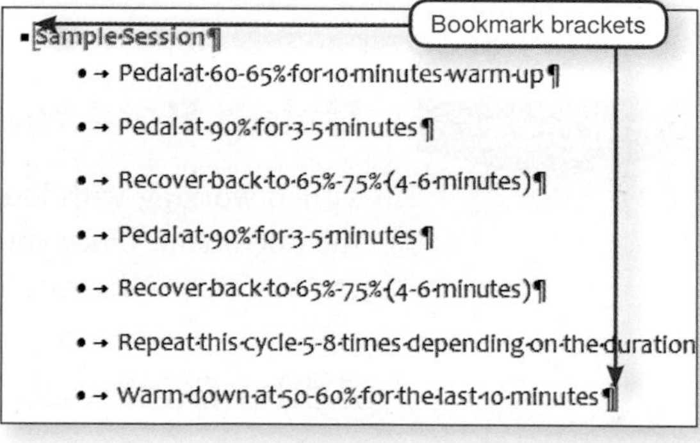

3-57 Bookmark on selected text

Go To a Bookmark

There are a couple of ways to quickly move to a bookmark in your document.

- **Insert Bookmark** button [*Insert* tab, *Links* group]: In the *Bookmark* dialog box, select the bookmark and click **Go To.**
- **Find and Replace** dialog box: Click the **Find** drop-down arrow [*Home* tab, *Editing* group] and select **Go To** (Figure 3-58). Select **Bookmark** in the *Go to what* area, select the bookmark, and click **OK.**

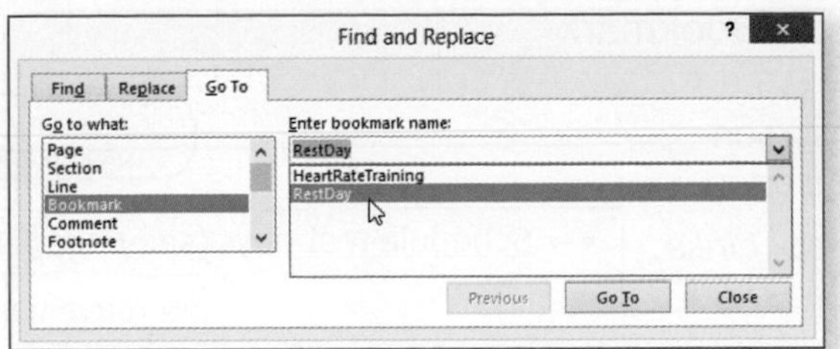

3-58 Go to selected bookmark

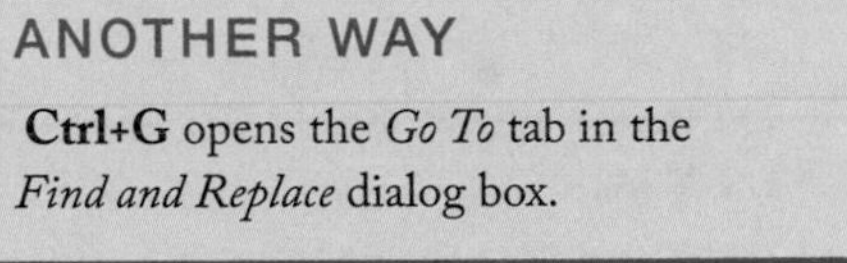

ANOTHER WAY

Ctrl+G opens the *Go To* tab in the *Find and Replace* dialog box.

Hyperlink to a Bookmark

You can create a ***hyperlink*** in your document that takes the reader to the bookmarked area.

HOW TO: Create a Hyperlink to a Bookmark

1. Select the text on which to create a hyperlink.
2. Click the **Hyperlink** button [*Insert* tab, *Links* group] or press **Ctrl+K**. The *Insert Hyperlink* dialog box opens (Figure 3-59).
3. Choose **Place in This Document** in the *Link to* area.

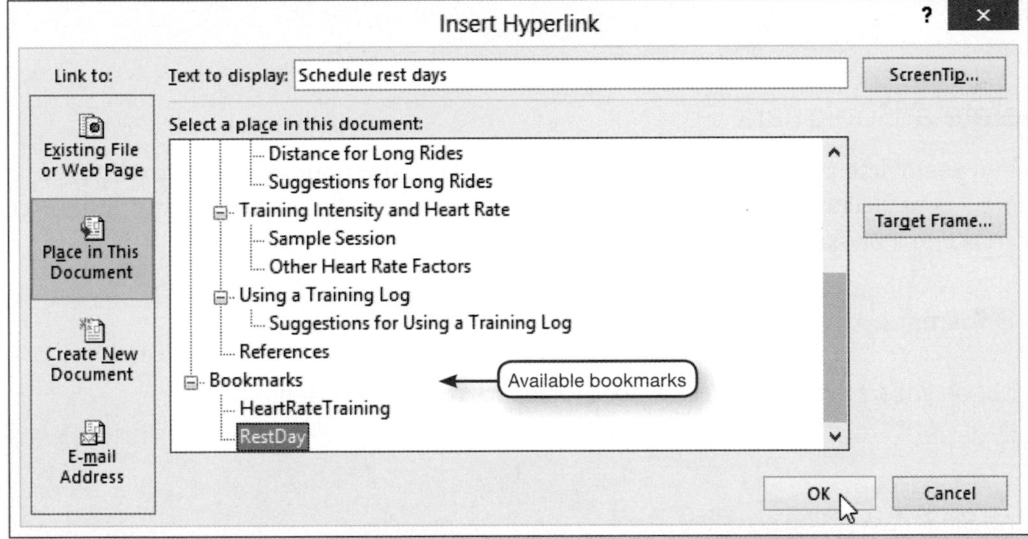

3-59 Insert hyperlink to a bookmark

4. Select from the available bookmarks.
5. Click **OK** to insert the hyperlink and close the dialog box.
   - The selected text is blue and underlined.
   - Press **Ctrl** and click the hyperlink to move to the bookmark.

Cross-Reference a Bookmark

You can also ***cross-reference*** a bookmark. For example, you can insert a page number that references a bookmark at another location in the document (e.g., "Schedule rest days (*see page 3*)"). When a cross-reference page number is linked to a bookmark, the page number is automatically updated if the bookmarked text moves to a different page.

HOW TO: Create a Cross-Reference to a Bookmark

1. Type any preceding text and position the insertion point where you want the cross-reference inserted.
2. Click the **Cross-reference** button [*Insert* tab, *Links* group]. The *Cross-reference* dialog box opens (Figure 3-60).
3. Select **Bookmark** in the *Reference type* area.
   - Check the **Insert as hyperlink** check box if you want the cross-reference to be a hyperlink to the bookmark.
4. In the *Insert reference to* area, select the type of reference from the drop-down list.
   - You can reference a page number, the bookmarked text, or the words "above" or "below."
   - If you choose *Page number,* you can also include the words "above" or "below" after the page number (e.g., "see page 3 above").
5. Select the bookmark in the *For which bookmark* area.
6. Click **Insert** to insert the cross-reference.
7. Click **Close** to close the dialog box.

3-60 Insert cross-reference to a bookmark

Delete a Bookmark

When you delete a bookmark from a document, Word does not remove hyperlinks or cross-references associated with this bookmark. You must manually remove a hyperlink or cross-reference to a bookmark.

HOW TO: Delete a Bookmark

1. Click the **Bookmark** button [*Insert* tab, *Links* group]. The *Bookmark* dialog box opens.
2. Select the bookmark to delete.
3. Click **Delete**.
4. Click **Close** to close the *Bookmark* dialog box.

SLO 3.6

Using Advanced Headers and Footers

You can use headers and footers to include page numbers and document information at the top or bottom of each page in a report or multipage document. Headers appear at the top of the page and footers appear at the bottom. You type headers and footers just once and then they are automatically displayed on subsequent pages. Page numbers can automatically be inserted in the header or footer. You can also add custom content such as text, document property fields, the date, or borders.

Page and Section Breaks

For multipage documents, it is a good idea to insert page or section breaks to control page endings or special formatting in different sections. A *Page* break controls where one page ends and another begins. Use a *Next Page* section break when special document layout formatting is applied to a whole page or multiple pages of a document, such as landscape orientation to one page of the document. Use a *Continuous* section break when special formatting is applied to a section of the document, such as two-column format to specific text on one page.

> **MORE INFO**
>
> Don't use a section break to control page endings where a page break will suffice.

HOW TO: Insert a Page or Section Break

1. Place the insertion point in the document at the point where you want the page or section break.
   - If you are inserting a continuous section break, it is best to select the text on which to apply the section break.
   - When you insert a continuous break on selected text, Word inserts a continuous section break before and after the selected text.
2. Click the **Breaks** button [*Page Layout* tab, *Page Setup* group] (Figure 3-61).
3. Select the type of break from the drop-down list.

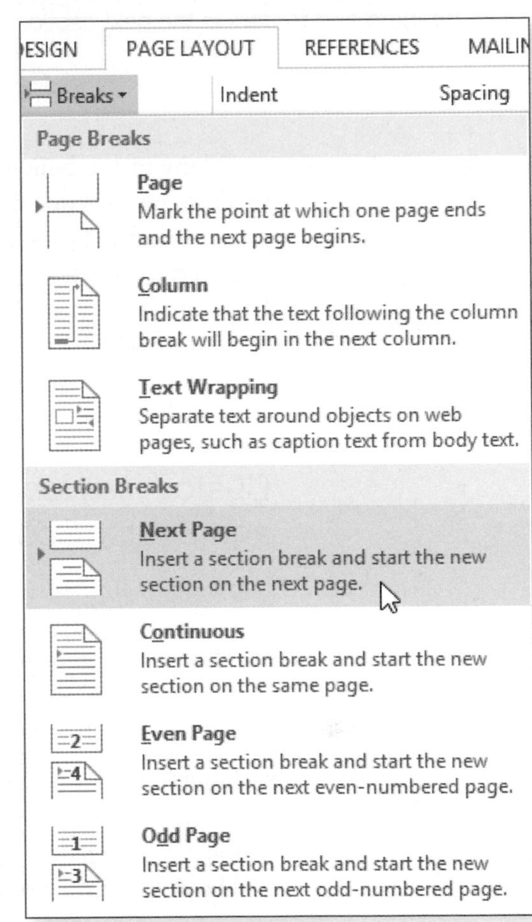
ESIGN
PAGE LAYOUT
REFERENCES
MAILIN
Breaks
Indent
Spacing
Page Breaks
Page
Mark the point at which one page ends and the next page begins.
Column
Indicate that the text following the column break will begin in the next column.
Text Wrapping
Separate text around objects on web pages, such as caption text from body text.
Section Breaks
Next Page
Insert a section break and start the new section on the next page.
Continuous
Insert a section break and start the new section on the same page.
Even Page
Insert a section break and start the new section on the next even-numbered page.
Odd Page
Insert a section break and start the new section on the next odd-numbered page.

3-61 Insert page or section break

> **ANOTHER WAY**
>
> **Ctrl+Enter** inserts a page break.

When working with page and section breaks, it is best to have the *Show/Hide* feature turned on so you can see where these breaks are located in a document. To delete a page or section break, select the break and press **Delete.**

Built-In Headers, Footers, and Page Numbers

Word provides you with a variety of built-in headers, footers, and page numbering options that you can insert into a document. You can also customize this built-in content. You can insert this content with the header or footer open or while you are in the main document.

HOW TO: Insert a Built-In Header or Footer

1. Click the **Insert** tab.
2. Click the **Header**, **Footer**, or **Page Number** button [*Header & Footer* group].

3. Select the built-in header, footer, or page number from the drop-down list (Figure 3-62). The content is inserted and the header or footer opens.
   - If you're inserting a page number, select the position (*Top of Page, Bottom of Page, Page Margins,* or *Current Position*) to insert the page number.
   - The colors and fonts of the built-in headers, footers, and page numbers are determined by the theme of your document.
   - More built-in headers, footers, and page numbers are displayed when you place your pointer on *More Headers (Footer* or *Page Numbers) from* Office.com.
   - You can insert odd and even headers, footers, and page numbering into a document. We discuss odd and even headers and footers in the next section.

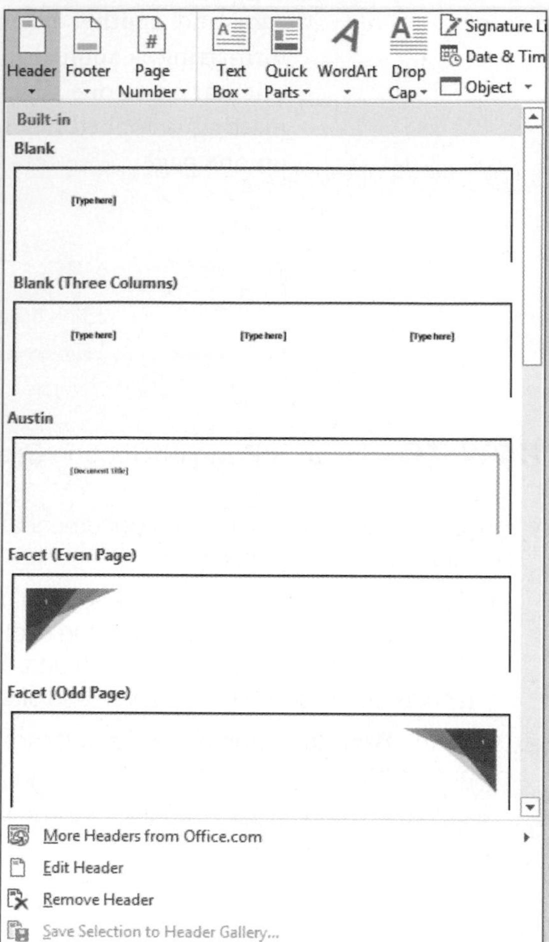

3-62 Insert built-in header

Many of the built-in headers and footers in Word contain document property fields or content control fields. You can enter information in the document property area and these fields are automatically populated. For content control fields such as *Date* or *Year,* you can select or type the content to be displayed in these fields (see Figure 3-62).

Customize Header and Footer Content

You are not limited to built-in content in the header and footer of your document. You can type text or insert content control fields. You can format header and footer text as you would other text in your document; you can apply font formatting and borders, insert graphics, and modify or set tabs for alignment.

You can open a header or footer in the following ways:

- Double-click on the header or footer area of the document.
- Right-click the header or footer area and select **Edit Header** or **Edit Footer.**
- Click the **Header** or **Footer** button [*Insert* tab, *Header & Footer* group] and select **Edit Header** or **Edit Footer.**

HOW TO: Insert Custom Content in the Header or Footer

1. Open the header or footer. See above for different ways to open the header or footer. The ***Header & Footer Tools Design*** tab open (Figure 3-63).
2. Insert content from the ***Header & Footer Tools Design*** tab.

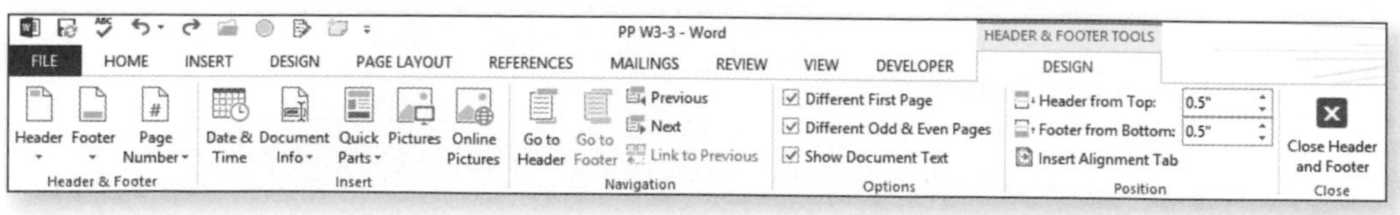

3-63 ***Header & Footer Tools Design*** **tab**

3. Type content to display in the header or footer.
4. Align information in the header or footer (Figure 3-64).
    - By default a center tab is set at the midpoint between the left and right margins and a right is set at the right margin.
    - You can insert a tab by clicking the **Insert Alignment Tab** button [*Position* group].
    - You can modify, add, or remove tabs on the ruler or in the *Tabs* dialog box [*Paragraph* dialog box, *Tabs* button].

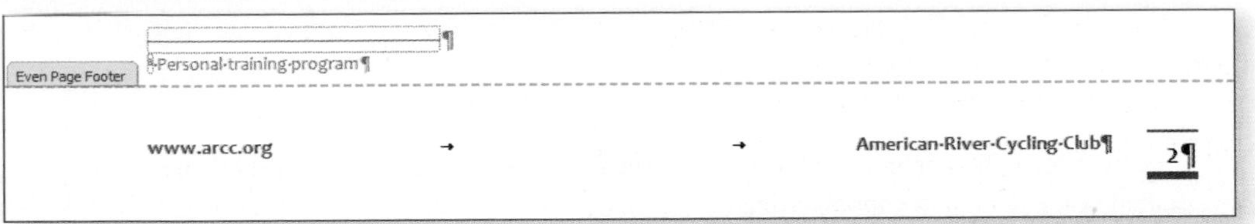

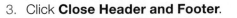

3-64 Built-in and custom content inserted in the footer

5. You can change the position of the header and footer in the ***Position*** group.
    - By default, the header and footer are positioned 0.5" from the top and bottom of the page.
    - The settings can also be changed in the *Page Setup* dialog box on the *Layout* tab.
6. Click **Close Header and Footer** to return to the main document.

Different Headers and Footers

It's common on long documents to have different header and footer content on different pages. Word options allow you to have a different first page header and footer as well as different headers and footers on odd and even pages.

Different First Page

On many reports, you don't include a page number or header and footer content on the first page, but this information is included on subsequent pages. When you select the ***Different First Page*** option, Word removes existing content from the header and footer on the first page. You can choose to leave the first page header and footer blank, or you can insert content that is different from the second and subsequent pages headers and footers.

HOW TO: Insert a Different First Page Header and Footer

1. Open the header or footer on the first page of the document.
2. Check the **Different First Page** check box [*Header & Footer Tools Design* tab, *Options* group] (Figure 3-65).
    - When the *Different First Page* check box is checked, the header (or footer) tab displays *First Page Header* (or *First Page Footer*) to distinguish it from other headers and footers in the document, which are labeled *Header* (or *Footer*) (Figure 3-66).
    - The header (or footer) tab label changes when you apply other header and footer formatting such as odd and even pages or have different headers for different sections of your document.
3. Click **Close Header and Footer**.

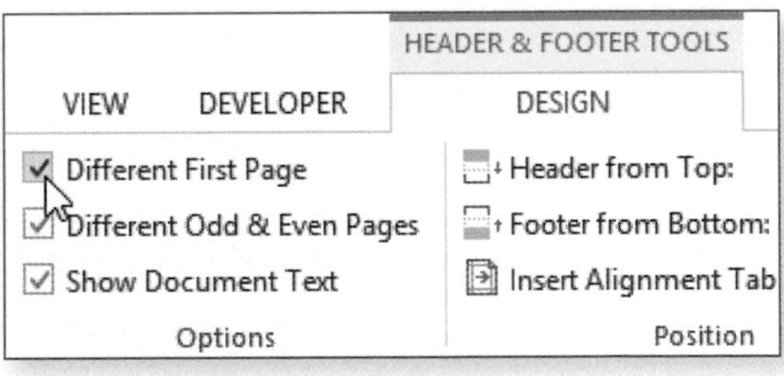

3-65 Set different first page header and footer

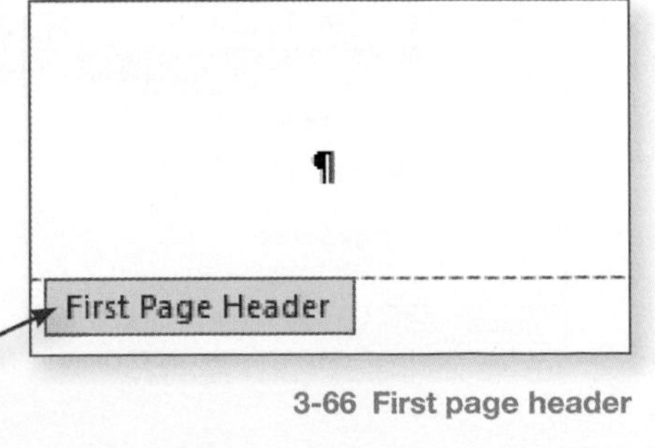

3-66 First page header

Different Odd and Even Pages

Just as you can have different header and footer content on the first page, Word provides you with the option of having ***different odd and even*** header and footer content on a multipage document. For example, you might want the title of the report to appear on all even pages in the footer and the page number and a company name to appear on odd pages.

MORE INFO

It's best to insert header and footer content on the first page of your document and then make any desired header and footer option changes.

HOW TO: Insert Different Odd and Even Headers and Footers

1. Open the header or footer on the first page of the document.
2. Check the **Different Odd & Even Pages** check box [*Header & Footer Tools Design* tab, *Options* group].
   - When the *Different Odd & Even Pages* check box is checked, the header (or footer) tab displays *Odd* (or *Even*) *Page Header* (or *Footer*) to distinguish it from other headers and footers in the document (Figure 3-67).
3. Click **Close Header and Footer**.

3-67 Odd page footer

Link to Previous

When you have different sections in your document, the headers and footers are by default linked to previous headers and footers. For example, a page number that appears in the footer of the first section of a document will also appear in the same position in the next section footer because it is linked to the previous footer. You can break this link to format header and footer content in one section independently of the header or footer in another section.

HOW TO: Link or Unlink Headers or Footers

1. Open the header or footer to be unlinked from the previous section (Figure 3-68).
   - By default the *Link to Previous* button is on (highlighted).
   - The *Same as Previous* label is displayed on the right of the header or footer.

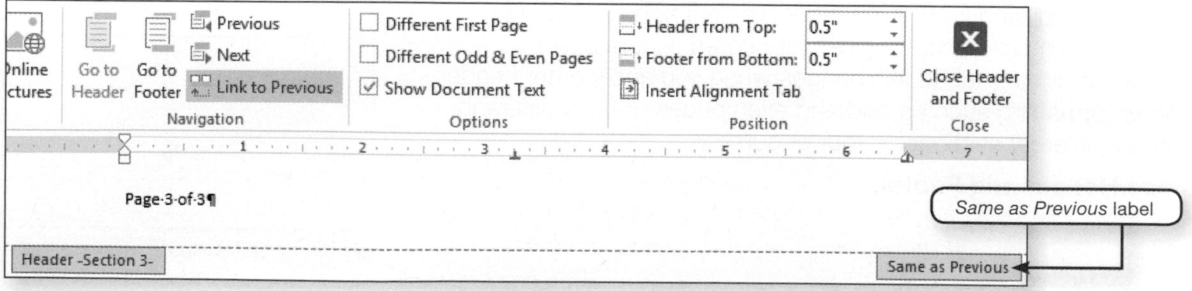

3-68 *Link to Previous* button

2. Click the **Link to Previous** button [*Header & Footer Tools Design* tab, *Navigation* group] to unlink it from the previous section.
   - The *Same as Previous* label is no longer displayed.
   - The header or footer content is still displayed, but you can now change it without it changing the header or footer content in the previous section.
   - The *Link to Previous* button is no longer highlighted.
3. If you want to link header or footer content to a previous section after it has been unlinked, click the **Link to Previous** button. A dialog box opens asking if you want to link the header or footer to the previous section (Figure 3-69).

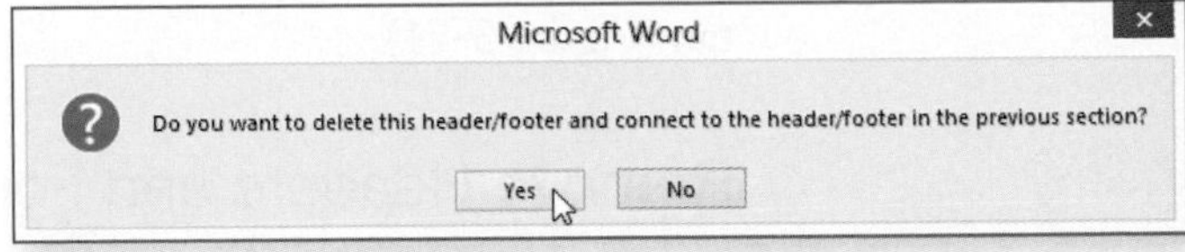

Microsoft Word
Do you want to delete this header/footer and connect to the header/footer in the previous section?
Yes
No

3-69 Link header or footer to previous section

4. Click **Yes**.
5. Click **Close Header and Footer**.

Format Page Numbers

When you number the pages in your document, you can change the page number format and starting page number. For example, on a report you might want to number the front matter pages (title page, table of contents, executive summary) with Roman numerals and number the body pages with regular numbers. If you are using different numbering for different sections of a document, you need to insert a next page section break between sections. This allows you to format the page numbering of each section differently.

HOW TO: Format Page Numbers

1. Select the page number to format in the header or footer.
2. Click the **Page Number** button [*Header & Footer Tools Design* tab, *Header & Footer* group].
3. Select **Format Page Numbers** from the drop-down list. The *Page Number Format* dialog box opens (Figure 3-70).
4. In the *Number format* area, select the number format from the drop-down list.
5. In the *Page numbering* area, select either the **Continue from previous section** or **Start at** radio button.
   - If you select *Continue from previous section,* the numbering continues consecutively from the previous section.
   - If you select *Start at,* you select the starting page number for the section.
6. Click **OK** to close the *Page Number Format* dialog box.

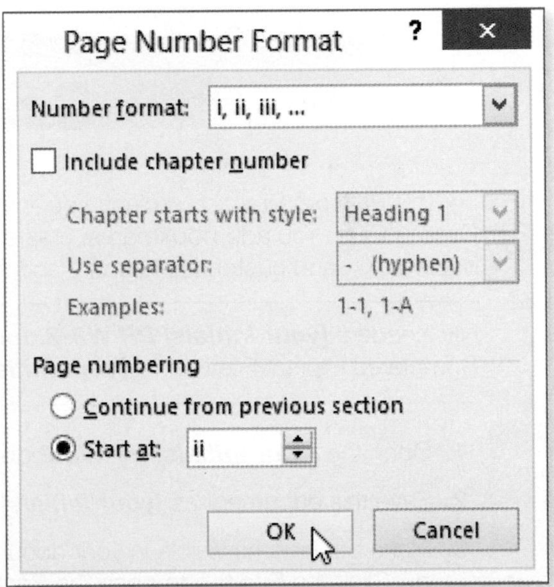

3-70 *Page Number Format* dialog box

When you include a Word cover page in a multipage document, the cover page is *not* considered the first page. Word considers the cover page as "page 0" when inserting page numbers in the header or footer, table of contents, or cross-reference links. For this reason, the page numbering in your document might be different from the page number displayed in the *Status* bar (bottom left of the Word window) of the document.

Navigate between Headers and Footers

When you are in a header or footer of a document, there are a variety of buttons you can use to move from the header to the footer or to the next or previous header or footer. These navigation buttons are in the *Navigation* group on the *Header & Footer Tools Design* tab (Figure 3-71).

3-71 Header and footer navigation buttons

Remove Headers and Footers

To remove a header or footer from a document, you can open the header or footer and manually delete the content. All linked header or footer content is also removed when you do this. Word can also automatically remove the header or footer from a document.

HOW TO: Remove a Header or Footer

1. Click the **Insert** button.
2. Click the **Header or Footer** button [*Header & Footer* group].
3. Select **Remove Header** or **Remove Footer** from the drop-down list (Figure 3-72). The header or footer content is removed.

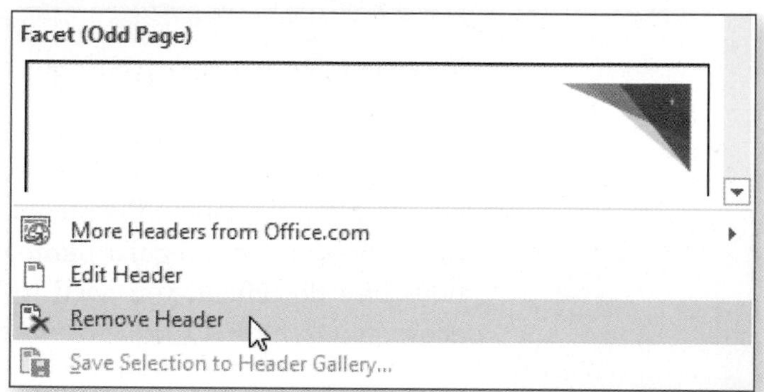

3-72 Remove header

PAUSE & PRACTICE: WORD 3-3

For this Pause & Practice project, you finalize the *Personal Training Program* report for American River Cycling Club. You add bookmarks, create hyperlinks to bookmarks, create cross-reference links to bookmarks, and customize headers and footers.

File Needed: ***[your initials] PP W3-2.docx***
Completed Project File Name: ***[your initials] PP W3-3.docx***

1. Open the ***[your initials] PP W3-2*** document created in *Pause & Practice 3-2*.
2. Save this document as ***[your initials] PP W3-3***.
3. Make bookmarks visible in your document.
   a. Click the **File** tab to open the *Backstage* view.
   b. Select **Options** to open the *Word Options* dialog box (Figure 3-73).
   c. Select **Advanced** on the left.
   d. Check the **Show bookmarks** check box in the *Show document content* area.
   e. Click **OK** to close the dialog box.

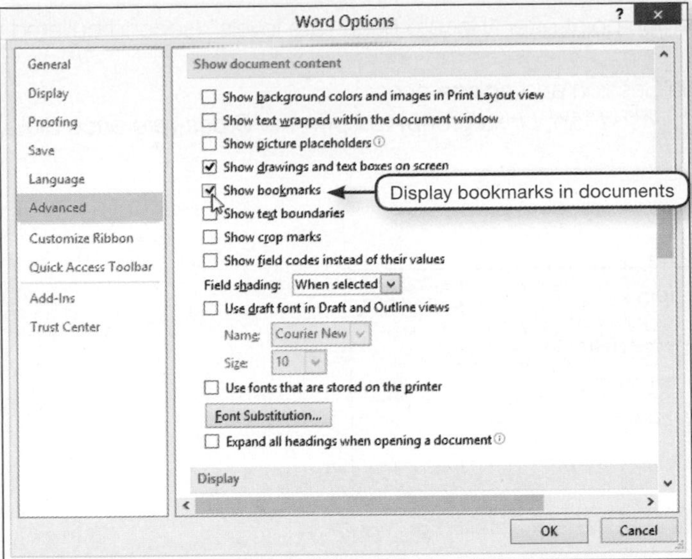

3-73 Display bookmarks in document

4. Insert bookmarks.
   a. Place the insertion point before "one or two rest days" (fourth page, fourth bullet).
   b. Click the **Bookmark** button [*Insert* tab, *Links* group]. The *Bookmark* dialog box opens (Figure 3-74).
   c. Type RestDay and click **Add** to add the bookmark and close the dialog box. An I-beam bookmark is displayed before the text.
   d. On the fifth page, select the text beginning with "**Sample Session**" and ending with the last bulleted item in that section.
   e. Click the **Bookmark** button.
   f. Type HeartRateTraining and click **Add** to add the bookmark and close the dialog box. Bookmark brackets are displayed around the selected text.

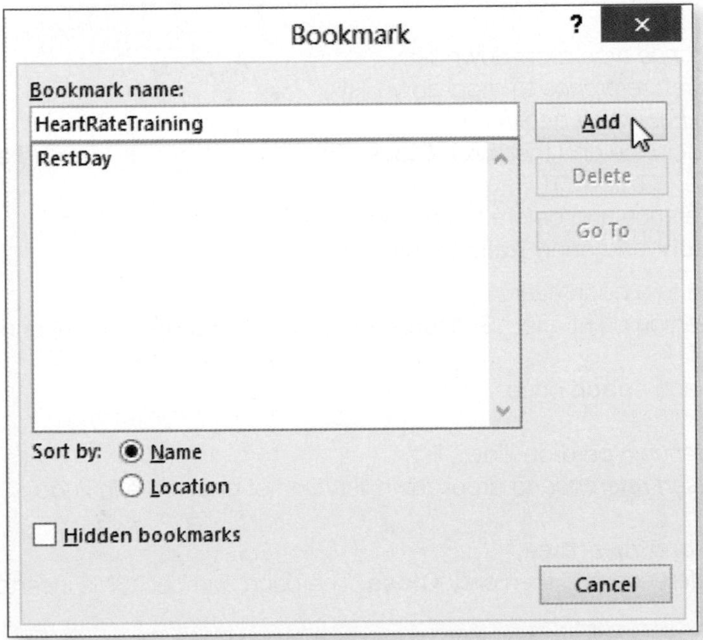

3-74 Insert bookmarks

5. Insert a cross-reference to a bookmark.
   a. On the sixth page, place your insertion point after "Record heart rate levels" (second bulleted item) and before the period.
   b. **Space** once and type (see Sample Session and **space** once.
   c. Click the **Cross-reference** button [*Insert* tab, *Links* group] to open *the Cross-reference* dialog box (Figure 3-75).

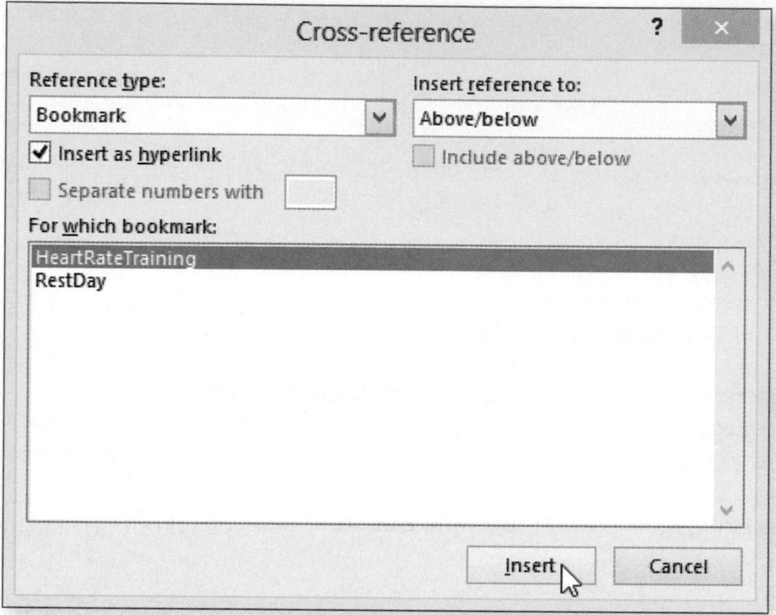

3-75 Insert cross-reference to a bookmark

   d. Select **Bookmark** from the *Reference type* drop-down list.
   e. Select **Above/below** from the *Insert reference to* drop-down list.
   f. Select **HeartRateTraining** in the *For which bookmark* area.
   g. Click **Insert** to insert the cross-reference and then click **Close**. The word "above" is inserted after the text.
   h. Type) after the inserted cross-reference and before the period.
   i. Select the words "**Sample Session**" and apply **italic** formatting.
6. Insert a page number cross-reference to a bookmark.
   a. On the sixth page, place your insertion point after "Schedule rest days" (fifth bulleted item) and before the period.
   b. **Space** once and type (see page and **space** once.
   c. Click the **Cross-reference** button.
   d. Select **Bookmark** from the *Reference type* drop-down list.
   e. Select **Page number** from the *Insert reference to* drop-down list. Do not check the *Include above/below* check box.
   f. Select **RestDay** in the *For which bookmark* area.
   g. Click **Insert** to insert the cross-reference and then click **Close**. The page number "3" is inserted after the text.
   h. Type) after the inserted cross-reference and before the period.
   i. Select the words "**page 3**" and apply **italic** formatting.

7. Insert hyperlinks to bookmarks.
   a. On the sixth page, select "**Record heart rate levels**" (second bulleted item).
   b. Click the **Hyperlink** button [*Insert* tab, *Links* group] to open *the Insert Hyperlink* dialog box (Figure 3-76).

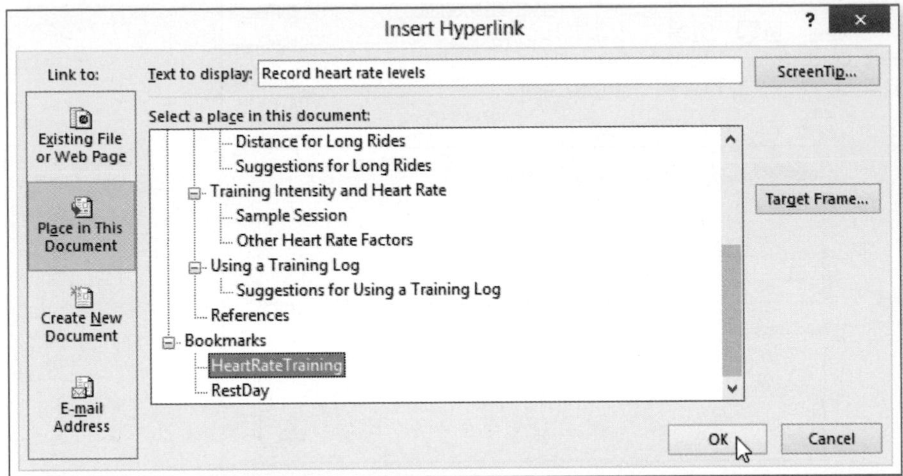

3-76 Insert hyperlink to a bookmark

   c. Select **Place in This Document** in the *Link to* area.
   d. Select **HeartRateTraining** in the *Bookmarks* list.
   e. Click **OK** to insert the hyperlink to the bookmark.
   f. On the sixth page, select "**Schedule rest days**" (fifth bulleted item).
   g. Click the **Hyperlink** button [*Insert* tab, *Links* group] to open *the Insert Hyperlink* dialog box.
   h. Select **Place in This Document** in the *Link to* area.
   i. Select **RestDay** in the *Bookmarks* list.
   j. Click **OK** to insert the hyperlink to the bookmark (Figure 3-77).

- → Record·heart·rate·levels·(see·*Sample·Session*·above). amount·of·time·spent·in·each·zone.·Lump-sum·hours near·or·above·lactate·threshold.·In·other·words,·qua
- → Keep·record·of·your·body·statistics.·Regularly·check mass,·and·muscle·mass,·and·body·water.·A·good·sca measurements.¶
- → Record·how·do·you·feel.·More·important·than·intens overall·well-being.·Mental·state·is·one·of·the·best·ind doing·too·much.·Do·you·feel·vigorous·or·flat?·Am·I·ea the·motions?·Do·rides·feel·so·good·that·I·extend·ther through·a·lackluster·hour·and·head·home?¶
- → Schedule·rest·days·(see·*page*·3).·Hard·training·doesn and·recovery·are·the·essential·catalysts.·If·you·don't Record·this·information·in·your·electronic·diary·(inclu

3-77 Cross-references and hyperlinks to bookmarks

8. Insert odd page and even page footers.
   a. Press **Ctrl+Home** to move to the top of the document.
   b. Click the **Footer** button [*Insert* tab, *Header & Footer* group] and select **Edit Footer** to open the footer.
   c. Check the **Different First Page** (if it is not already checked) and the **Different Odd & Even Pages** check boxes [*Header & Footer Tools Design* tab, *Options* group].
   d. Click the **Next** button [*Navigation* group] to move to the footer on the second page (Figure 3-78).

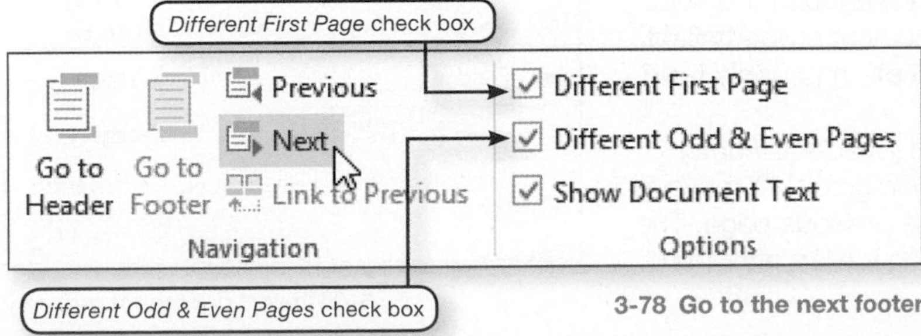

3-78 Go to the next footer

e. Click the **Page Number** button [*Header & Footer* group].
f. Select **Bottom of Page** and select **Two Bars 1** from the drop-down list of built-in page numbers (Figure 3-79). The page number "1" is inserted on the second page.

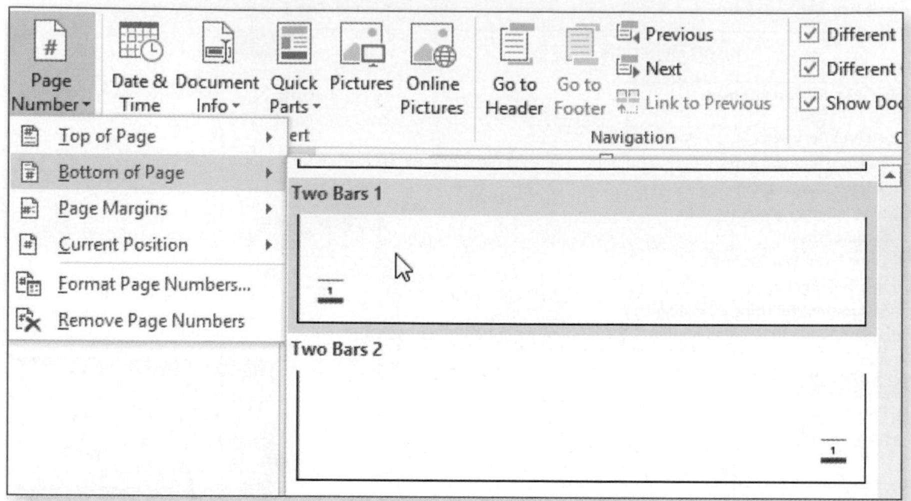

3-79 Select built-in page number

> **MORE INFO**
>
> Word considers the cover page as page 0. The table of contents page is page 1.

g. Click the **Next** button [*Navigation* group] to move to the footer on the next page.
h. Click the **Page Number** button [*Header & Footer* group].
i. Select **Bottom of Page** and select **Two Bars 2** from the drop-down list of built-in page numbers. The page number "2" is inserted on the right. Leave the footer open to add custom content in the next step.

9. Add custom content to the odd and even footers.
   a. The insertion point should be in the even page footer.
   b. Press **Ctrl+R** to align the insertion point on the right.
   c. Click the **Document Info** button [*Header & Footer Tools Design* tab, *Insert* group] (Figure 3-80).
   d. Select **Document Property** and choose **Company** from the drop-down list. The *Company* document property field is inserted with the company name displayed in this field.
   e. Select the **Company** document property field, change the font size to **10 pt.**, and apply **bold** formatting.
   f. Click the **Previous** button [*Header & Footer Tools Design* tab, *Navigation* group] to move to the odd page footer on the previous page. The insertion point should be on the left after the page number "1."

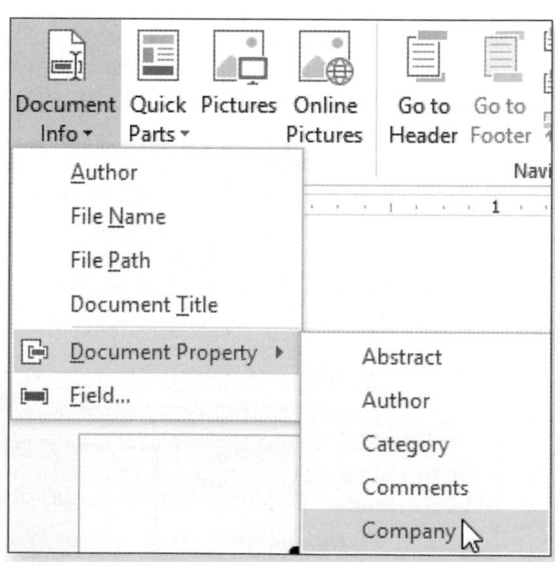

3-80 Insert document property field

g. Click the **Quick Parts** button [*Header & Footer Tools Design* tab, *Insert* group].
h. Select **Document Property** and choose **Title** from the drop-down list. The *Title* document property field is inserted with the document title displayed in this field.
i. Select the **Title** document property field, change the font size to **10 pt.**, and apply **bold** formatting.
j. Click the **Close Header and Footer** button [*Header & Footer Tools Design* tab, *Close* group].

10. Review the document to ensure correct page numbering.
    a. There should be no header or footer on the cover page of the document.
    b. The table of contents page should be numbered "1" in the footer on the left with the title of the report following the page number.
    c. The first body page of the report should be numbered "2" in the footer on the right with the company name preceding the page number.
    d. Each subsequent page should be numbered consecutively with odd and even footers.
11. Save and close the document (Figure 3-81).

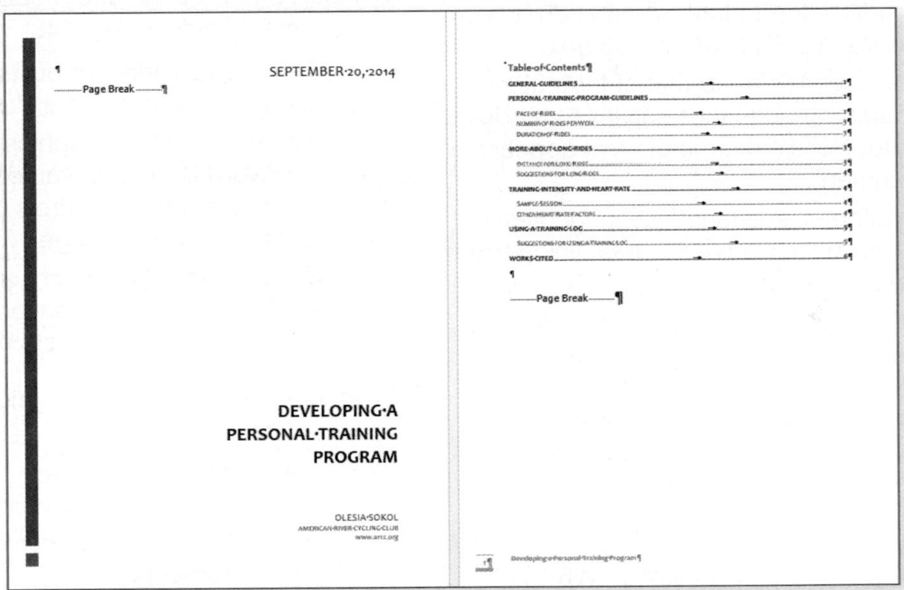

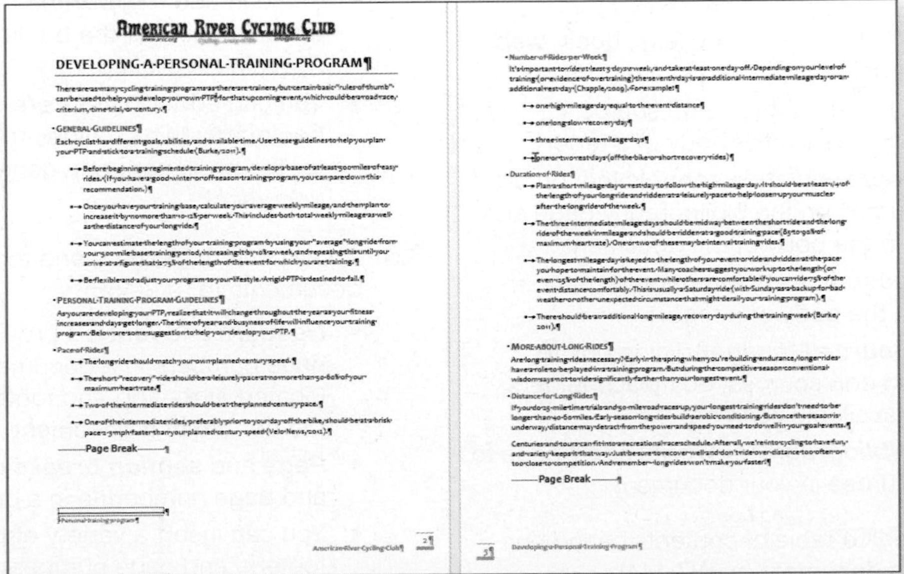

3-81 PP W3-3 completed (first four of seven pages)

Chapter Summary

3.1 Insert and edit footnotes and endnotes in a document (p. W3-129).

- *Use* ***Footnotes*** and ***endnotes*** to include additional information or reference sources.
- Footnotes appear at the bottom of the page and endnotes appear at the end of the document.
- A ***reference marker*** is a number, letter, or symbol that marks a footnote or endnote in the body of the document.
- Change the location, number format, and starting number for footnotes and endnotes in the ***Footnote and Endnote*** dialog box.
- Word styles control the format of footnotes and endnotes. Change these styles to modify how your footnote and endnote text appears in the document.
- Convert footnotes to endnotes or endnotes to footnotes using the ***Convert Notes*** dialog box.
- Move footnotes and endnotes using the drag and drop method or using cut and paste.
- When you delete a footnote or endnote reference marker, the associated footnote and endnote text is also deleted. Footnotes and endnotes are automatically renumbered if one is deleted or inserted.

3.2 Create a bibliography using proper source format and insert citations in a document (p. W3-134).

- A ***source*** is the complete bibliographic information for a reference (e.g., book, web page, journal article) used in a report.
- A ***citation*** is the abbreviated source information used in the body of a report.
- The ***bibliography style*** controls the format of the sources on the bibliography page and citations in the body of the document.
- Add a ***placeholder*** to temporarily mark a citation in the body of a report.
- Use the ***Source Manager*** dialog box to create and edit sources, edit placeholders, and view available sources.
- Insert a ***bibliography*** or ***works cited*** page to list the sources in your document.

3.3 Create and edit a table of contents based on headings in a document (p. W3-144).

- Word can automatically generate a ***table of contents*** for a document.
- ***Heading styles*** (e.g., Heading 1, Heading 2) determine the content for a table of contents.
- You can use built-in table of contents formats or customize the format of the table of contents.
- Use the ***Table of Contents*** dialog box to customize the format and levels displayed in the table of contents.
- When document heading or pagination is changed, the table of contents can be updated to reflect these changes.

3.4 Insert a cover page and modify content and document fields (p. W3-148).

- There are a variety of built-in ***cover pages*** available to use on your documents.
- A cover page has graphics, colors, text boxes, and Word fields that you can customize. The document theme controls the colors and fonts on the cover page.
- Use ***document property*** and ***content control fields*** to display information on the cover page. This content can be customized or deleted.

3.5 Integrate bookmarks into a multipage document (p. W3-153).

- Use a ***bookmark*** to mark a specific location or selected text in a document.
- In ***Word Options***, you can set bookmarks in your documents.
- You can add a ***hyperlink*** to a bookmark; this takes the user to the bookmark when the hyperlink is clicked.
- You can add a ***cross-reference*** to a bookmark; this provides the page number for the bookmark or a general location in the document.

3.6 Apply custom headers and footers in multipage documents (p. W3-156).

- ***Headers*** and ***footers*** provide information and page numbers in a document. Headers are located at the top and footers are located at the bottom of a document.
- ***Page*** and ***section breaks*** control pagination and page numbering in a document.
- You can insert a variety of built-in headers, footers, and page numbers into a document.
- You can customize content and page numbering in headers and footers.

- ***Different first page*** headers and footers allow you to include different information on the first page of a document.
- *Use* ***odd and even page*** headers and footers to display different information on odd and even pages in a document.
- Change the page number format and starting page number in the ***Page Number Format*** dialog box.

Check for Understanding

In the ***Online Learning Center*** for this text (www.mhhe.com/office2013inpractice), there are a variety of resources that can be used to review the concepts covered in this chapter.

The following Online Learning Resources are available in the Online Learning Center:

- Multiple-choice questions
- Short answer questions
- Matching exercises

Guided Project 3-1

For this project, you customize the *Online Learning Plan* for Sierra Pacific Community College District. You add a customized cover page, apply styles, create a table of contents, insert and modify footnotes, and insert headers and footers.
[Student Learning Outcomes 3.1, 3.3, 3.4, 3.6]

File Needed: ***OnlineLearningPlan-03.docx***
Completed Project File Name: ***[your initials] Word 3-1.docx***

Skills Covered in This Project

- Customize document properties.
- Insert a cover page and add content.
- Delete and add document property fields.
- Apply font formatting to text.
- Apply styles to selected text.
- Insert page breaks.
- Create a table of contents based on heading styles.
- Insert footnotes.
- Modify footnote number format.
- Insert built-in page numbers in the header.
- Insert document property fields and the date in the footer.
- Modify header and footer text formatting.
- Update a table of contents.

1. Open the ***OnlineLearningPlan-03*** document from your student data files.
2. Save this document as ***[your initials] Word 3-1***.
3. Add document properties.
   a. Click the **File** tab to open the *Backstage* view.
   b. Click **Show All Properties** in the *Properties* area.
   c. Add the following document properties:
      Title: Online Learning Plan
      Company: Sierra Pacific Community College District
      Manager: Hasmik Kumar
   d. Click the **Back** arrow to return to the document.
4. Insert a cover page and modify content control fields.
   a. Press **Ctrl+Home** to move to the top of the document.
   b. Click the **Cover Page** button [*Insert* tab, *Pages* group].
   c. Select the **Austin** built-in cover page from the drop-down list. The cover page is inserted before the first page of the document.
   d. Click the **Subtitle** content control field handle and press **Delete** (Figure 3-82).

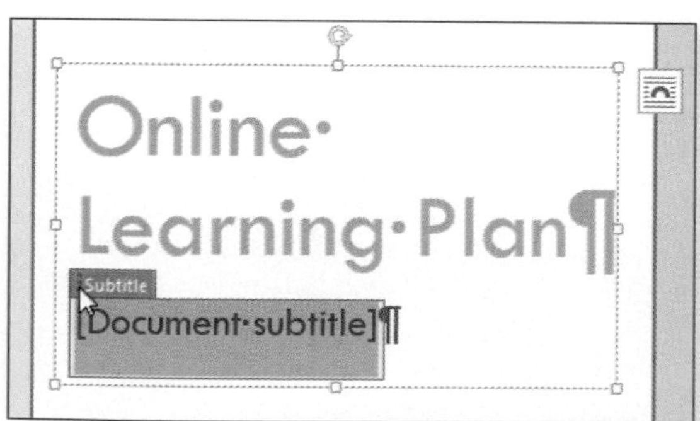

3-82 Delete content control field

e. Delete the blank line after the *Title* field.
f. Select the **Title** field and change the font size to **48 pt**.
g. Click the **Abstract** content control field and type This report was developed by the Online Learning Task Force at Sierra Pacific Community College District to review and update the district's strategic plan for online learning.
h. Select the **Abstract** field, change the text alignment to **left**, and apply **italic** formatting.
i. Click the **Author** content control field handle and press **Delete**.
j. With the insertion point on the blank line where the *Author* field was deleted, click the **Quick Parts** button [*Insert* tab, *Text* group] (Figure 3-83).
k. Select **Document Property** and select **Manager** from the drop-down list.
l. Apply **bold** formatting to the *Manager* document property field.

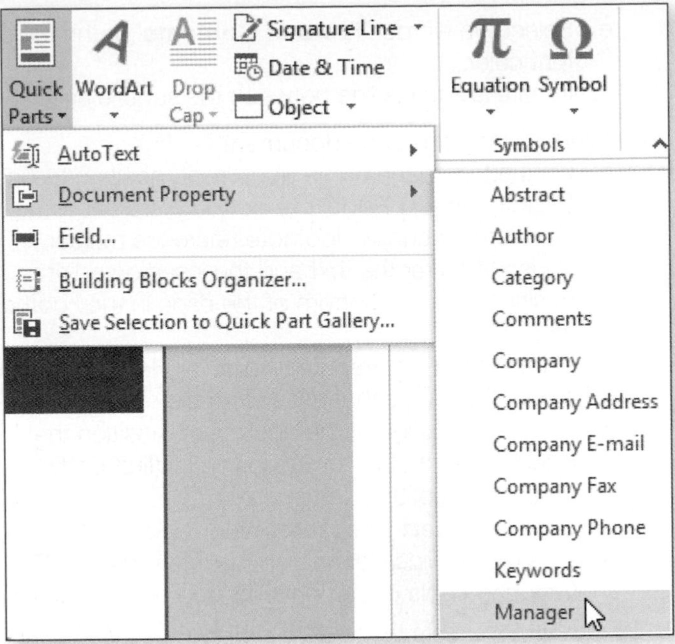

3-83 Insert document property field

5. Apply styles to the document.
   a. Apply the **Heading 1** style to all of the main headings (those in all caps and bold) in the document. Do not include information on the cover page.
   b. Apply the **Heading 2** style to all subheadings (those underlined) in the document.
   c. On the second page of the document, select the title ("**Online Learning Plan**") and apply the **Title** style.
   d. On the second page of the document, select the subtitle ("**Sierra Pacific Community College District**") and apply the **Subtitle** style.
6. Insert a table of contents into the report.
   a. Click in front of the first main heading in the document ("Purpose of this Plan") and insert a page break.
   b. On the second page of the document, click directly after the subtitle and press **Enter**.
   c. With the insertion point on the blank line below the subtitle, click the **Table of Contents** button [*References* tab, *Table of Contents* group] (Figure 3-84).
   d. Select **Automatic Table 2**. The table of contents is inserted below the subtitle.

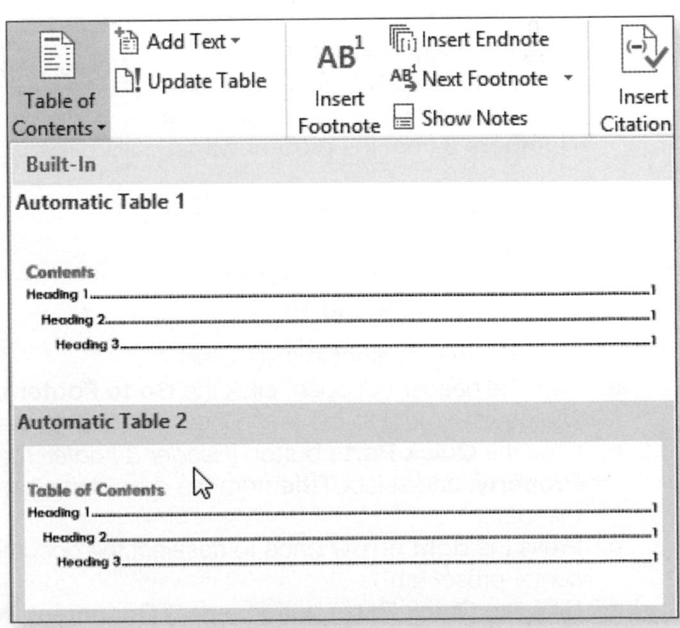

3-84 Insert table of contents

e. Select the words "**Table of Contents**" in the table of contents and apply **Black**, **Text 1** font color.
f. If there is a blank line between the subtitle and "Table of Contents," delete it.

7. Insert footnotes into the document.
   a. On the third page of the document, position the insertion point after "Web-Enhanced course."
   b. Click the **Insert Footnote** button [*References* tab, *Footnotes* group]. A footnote reference marker is inserted after the text and the insertion point is positioned at the bottom of the page in the *Footnotes* area.
   c. In the *Footnotes* area, type Just for clarification, this is a non-OL course that uses OL tools.
   d. On the third page of the document, position the insertion point after "online learning" (first body paragraph, second sentence).
   e. Click the **Insert Footnote** button and in the footnote area type Online learning will be referred to as OL throughout this document. This footnote becomes footnote 1 and the other footnote automatically becomes number 2.

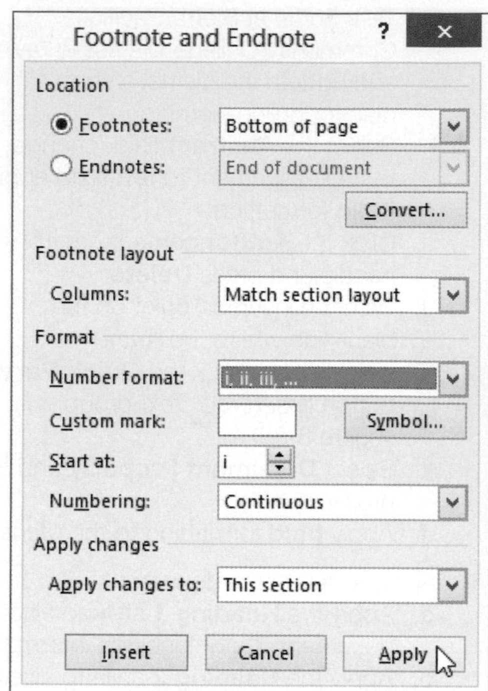

3-85 Modify footnote number format

8. Modify footnote number format.
   a. Click the **Footnotes** launcher to open the *Footnote and Endnote* dialog box (Figure 3-85).
   b. Select **i**, **ii**, **iii**, **. . .** from the *Number format* drop-down list.
   c. Click **Apply** to close the dialog box and apply the number format change.

9. Insert and modify content in the header.
   a. Position the insertion point at the top of the table of contents page.
   b. Click the **Page Number** button [*Insert* tab, *Header & Footer* group].
   c. Select **Top of Page** and select **Bold Numbers 3** from the drop-down list (Figure 3-86).
   d. Delete the blank line below the page number.
   e. Select the text in the header and change the font size to **10 pt**.

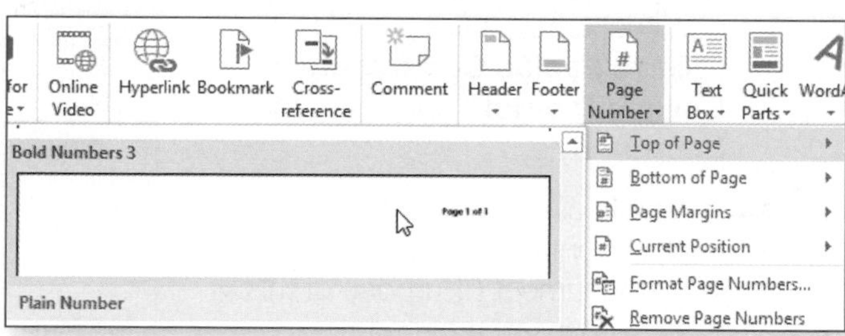

3-86 Insert page number

10. Insert and modify content in the footer.
    a. With the header still open, click the **Go to Footer** button [*Header & Footer Tools Design* tab, *Navigation* group] to move the insertion point to the footer.
    b. Click the **Quick Parts** button [*Header & Footer Tools Design* tab, *Insert* group], select **Document Property**, and select **Title** from the drop-down list to insert the *Title* document property field into the footer.
    c. Press the **right arrow** once to deselect the document property field and press **Tab** to move to the center preset tab.
    d. Click the **Quick Parts** button, select **Document Property**, and select **Company** from the drop-down list.

e. Press the **right arrow** once to deselect the document property field and press **Tab** to move to the right preset tab.
f. Type Last modified: and **space** once.
g. Click the **Date & Time** button [*Header & Footer Tools Design* tab, *Insert* group] to open the *Date and Time* dialog box.
h. Select the first date format (e.g., 1/31/2015) and deselect the **Update automatically** check box.
i. Click **OK** to close the dialog box and insert the date.
j. Select the text in the footer and change the font size to **10 pt**.
k. Click the **Close Header and Footer** button [*Header & Footer Tools Design* tab, *Close* group].

11. Insert a page break.
    a. Position the insertion point before the last subheading ("How are Courses and Programs Selected for Online Learning Delivery?") on the first body page of the report (the page after the table of contents).
    b. Press **Ctrl+Enter** to insert a page break.
12. Update the table of contents.
    a. Click in the table of contents.
    b. Click the **Update Table** button [*References* tab, *Table of Contents* group]. The *Update Table of Contents* dialog box opens (Figure 3-87).
    c. Select the **Update entire table** radio button.
    d. Click **OK** to close the dialog box and update the table.
13. Save and close the document (Figure 3-88).

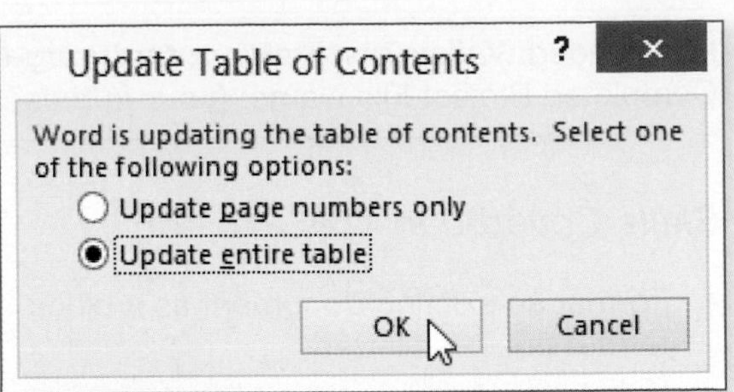

3-87 *Update Table of Contents* dialog box

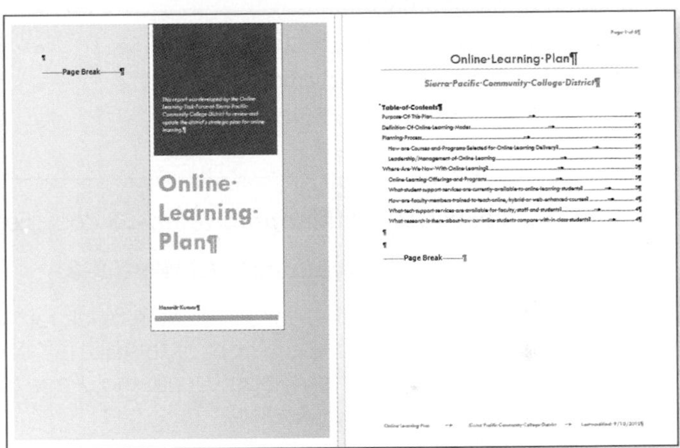

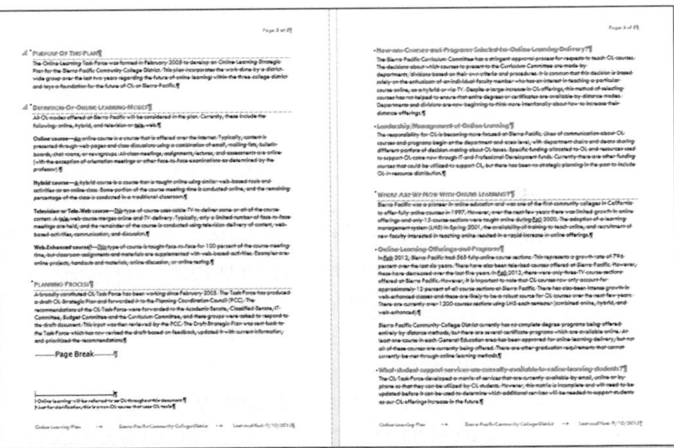

3-88 Word 3-1 completed (first four of six pages)

Guided Project 3-2

For this project, you create a multipage insurance renewal letter that Central Sierra Insurance will send on behalf of Valley Custom Manufacturing. You format this document as a business letter, insert and customize header content, use footnotes and endnotes, and insert a bookmark.
[Student Learning Outcomes 3.1, 3.5, 3.6]

File Needed: ***ValleyCustomManufacturing-03.docx***
Completed Project File Name: ***[your initials] Word 3-2.docx***

Skills Covered in This Project

- Format an existing document as a block format business letter.
- Insert a next page section break.
- Change margins and header location on a section of a document.
- Use a different first page header.
- Insert header content and page number.
- Format the page number in the header.
- Apply bottom border.
- Insert footnotes.
- Convert footnotes to endnotes and change number format.
- Insert a bookmark for selected text.
- Insert a cross-reference to a bookmark.
- Create a hyperlink to a bookmark.
- Insert a page break to control pagination.

1. Open the ***ValleyCustomManufacturing-03*** document from your student data files.
2. Save this document as ***[your initials] Word 3-2***.
3. Format the first page of the document as a block format business letter.
   a. Place your insertion point in front of "LIABILITY" on the first page.
   b. Click the **Breaks** button [*Page Layout* tab, *Page Setup* group] and select **Next Page** section break from the drop-down list.
   c. On the last blank line on the first page, type Sincerely, and press **Enter** four times.
   d. Type Jennie Owings, Vice President and press **Enter** once.
   e. Type Central Sierra Insurance and press **Enter** two times.
   f. Type your initials in lower case letters with no spaces or punctuation and press **Enter**. Word automatically capitalizes the first letter of your initials. Use the **smart tag** to undo automatic capitalization or press **Ctrl+Z** to undo the last action (Figure 3-89).

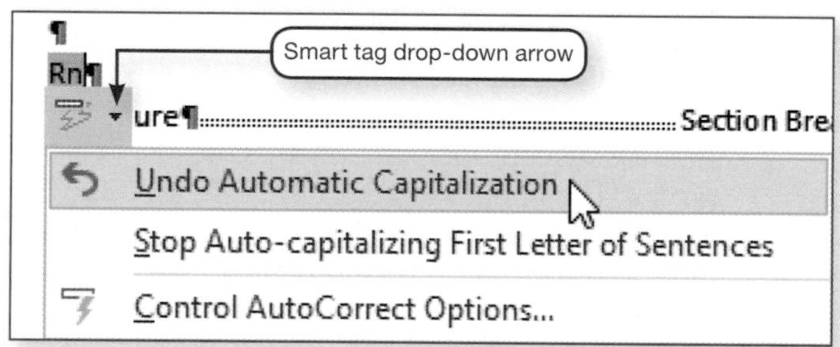

3-89 Use smart tag to undo automatic capitalization

   g. Type Enclosure on the line after your reference initials.
   h. Press **Ctrl+Home** to go to the top of the document and press **Enter** four times.
   i. Place the insertion point on the first blank line at the top and click the **Date & Time** button [*Insert* tab, *Text* group]. The *Date and Time* dialog box opens.
   j. Select the date in proper business letter format (e.g., April 12, 2014) and check the **Update automatically** check box.
   k. Click **OK** to close the dialog box and insert the date.
   l. On the dateline, apply **24 pt**. before paragraph spacing.
4. Modify the margins and header position in the second section of the document.
   a. Place your insertion point in the second section of the document (page 2 or 3).
   b. Click the **Margins** button [*Page Layout* tab, *Page Setup* group] and select **Custom Margins** from the drop-down list. The *Page Setup* dialog box opens.
   c. Change the *Top* margin to **1.5"** and the *Left* and *Right* margins to **1.25"**.

d. Click the **Layout** tab (Figure 3-90).
e. In the *Headers and footers* area, change the *From edge Header* setting to **1"**.
f. In the *Apply to* area, select **This section** from the drop-down list.
g. Click **OK** to close the dialog box and apply the settings.

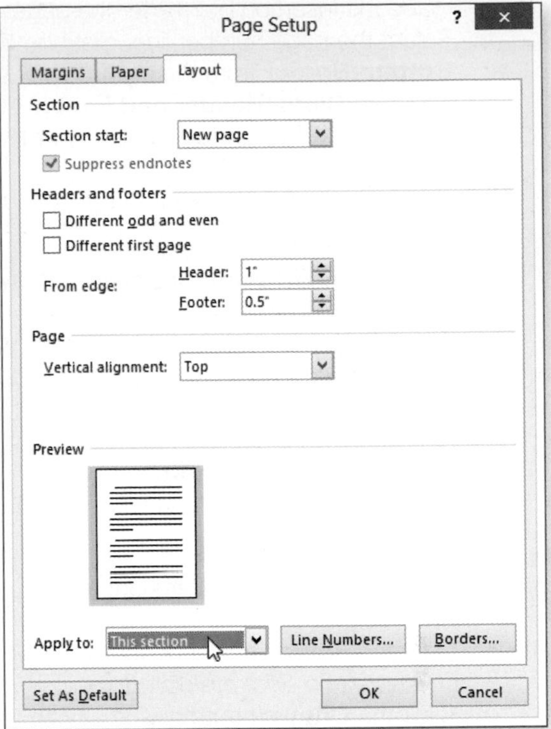

3-90 Change header position in this section of the document

5. Insert header content on the second and continuing pages.
   a. Press **Ctrl+Home** to move to the top of the document.
   b. Click the **Header** button [*Insert* tab, *Header & Footer* group].
   c. Select **Edit Header** from the drop-down list.
   d. Check the **Different First Page** check box [*Header & Footer Tools Design* tab, *Options* group].
   e. Click the **Next** button [*Header & Footer Tools Design* tab, *Navigation* group] to move to the header in section 2.
   f. Type Valley Custom Manufacturing and press **Enter**.
   g. Click the **Date & Time** button [*Header & Footer Tools Design* tab, *Insert* group]. The *Date and Time* dialog box opens.
   h. Select the date in proper business letter format (e.g., April 12, 2014) and check the **Update automatically** check box.
   i. Click **OK** to close the dialog box and insert the date.
6. Insert page number in the header and format page number.
   a. With the header still open, press **Enter** after the date.
   b. Type Page and **space** once.
   c. Click the **Page Number** button [*Header & Footer Tools Design* tab, *Header & Footer* group].
   d. Select **Current Position** and **Plain Number** from the drop-down list of page number options.
   e. Click the **Page Number** button and select **Format Page Numbers** to open the *Page Number Format* dialog box (Figure 3-91).
   f. In the *Page numbering* area, click the **Start at** radio button and change the page number to **2**.
   g. Click **OK** to close the dialog box.

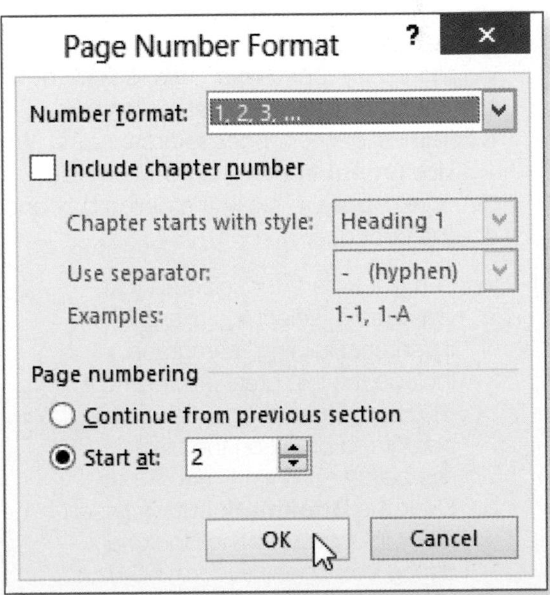

3-91 Format page number

h. Place the insertion point after the page number and press **Enter** two times.
i. Select the page number line, click the **Borders** button [*Home* tab, *Paragraph* group], and select **Bottom Border** from the drop-down list.
j. Click the **Close Header and Footer** button [*Header & Footer Tools Design* tab, *Close* group].

7. Insert footnotes.
   a. Place the insertion point after the period at the end of the last line of text on page 4.
   b. Click the **Insert Footnote** button [*References* tab, *Footnotes* group].
   c. In the footnotes area, type A list of drivers was faxed as a separate attachment.
   d. On the first page, place the insertion point at the end of the fourth body paragraph (after "2013 renewal.").
   e. Click the **Insert Footnote** button.
   f. In the footnotes area, type Inflation is anticipated to be 2 percent.

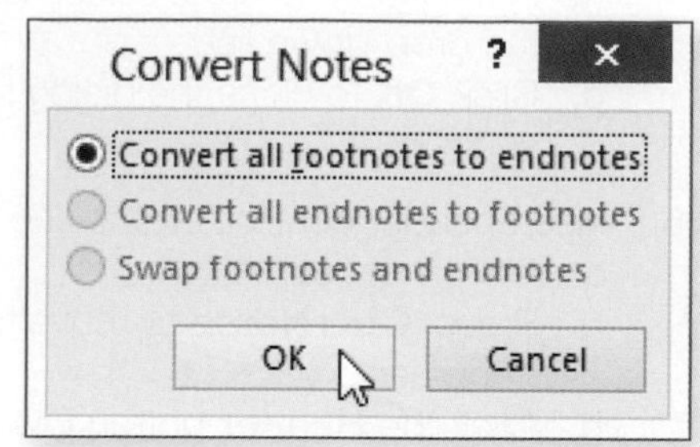

3-92 Convert footnotes to endnotes

8. Convert footnotes to endnotes and change number format.
   a. Click the **Footnotes** launcher to open the *Footnote and Endnote* dialog box.
   b. Click the **Convert** button. The *Convert Notes* dialog box opens (Figure 3-92).
   c. Select the **Convert all footnotes to endnotes** radio button and click **OK** to close the *Convert Notes* dialog box.
   d. Click **Close** to close the *Footnote and Endnote* dialog box.
   e. Click the **Footnotes** launcher to open the *Footnote and Endnote* dialog box (Figure 3-93).
   f. Select the **Endnotes** radio button if it is not selected.
   g. In the *Number format* area, select **a**, **b**, **c**, **. . .** from the drop-down list.
   h. In the *Apply changes to* area, select **Whole document** from the drop-down list.
   i. Click **Apply** to close the dialog box and apply the changes.

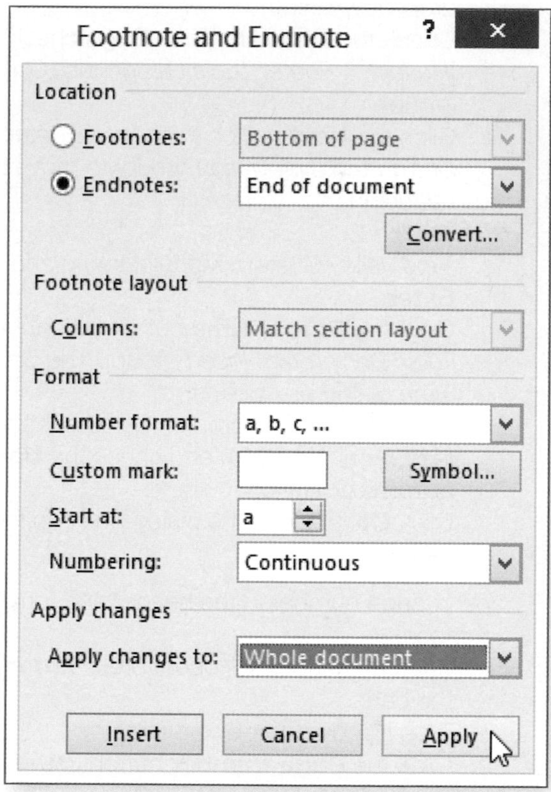

3-93 Change endnote number format

9. Insert a bookmark for selected text.
   a. On page 3, select the "Parts and Inventory Building" paragraph. Include the line break at the end of the paragraph, but do *not* include the paragraph break on the blank line below.
   b. Click the **Bookmark** button [*Insert* tab, *Links* group]. The *Bookmark* dialog box opens (Figure 3-94).

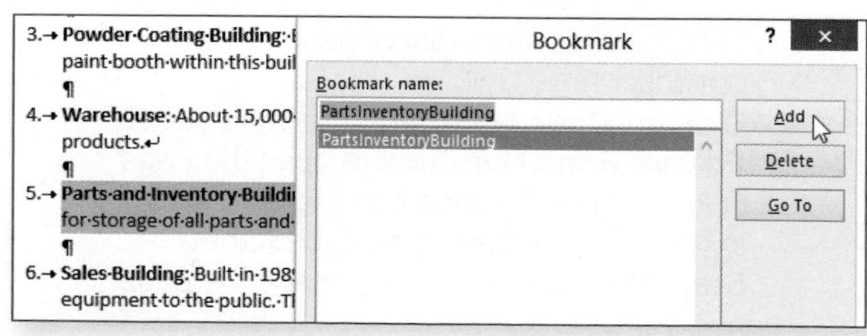

3-94 Insert bookmark on selected text

c. In the *Bookmark name* area, type PartsInventoryBuilding.
d. Click **Add** to close the dialog box and add the bookmark for selected text.

10. Insert a cross-reference link to a bookmark.
    a. On page 2 in the "Farm Equipment Dealers" section, place the insertion point after "2001" and before the period.
    b. **Space** once and type (see #5 on page and **space** once.
    c. Click the **Cross-reference** button [*Insert* tab, *Links* group] to open the *Cross-reference* dialog box (Figure 3-95).
    d. In the *Reference type* area, select **Bookmark**.
    e. In the *Insert reference to* area, select **Page number**.
    f. In the *For which bookmark* area, select **PartsInventoryBuilding**.
    g. Click **Insert** and then click **Close**.
    h. Type) after the inserted cross-reference page number.

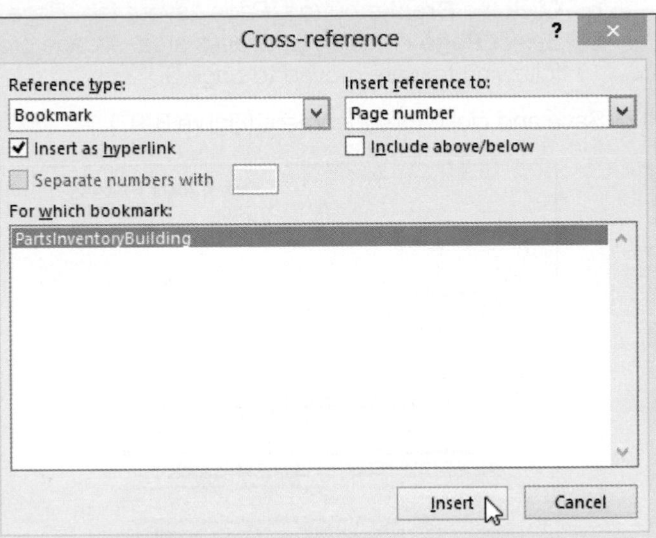

3-95 Insert cross-reference to a bookmark

11. Create a hyperlink to a bookmark.
    a. On page 2 in the "Farm Equipment Dealers" section, select "**new building completed in 2001**."
    b. Click the **Hyperlink** button [*Insert* tab, *Links* group] to open the *Insert Hyperlink* dialog box (Figure 3-96).
    c. In the *Link to* area, select **Place in This Document**.
    d. In the *Select a place in this document* area, select the **PartsInventoryBuilding** bookmark.
    e. Click **OK** to close the dialog box and insert the hyperlink.

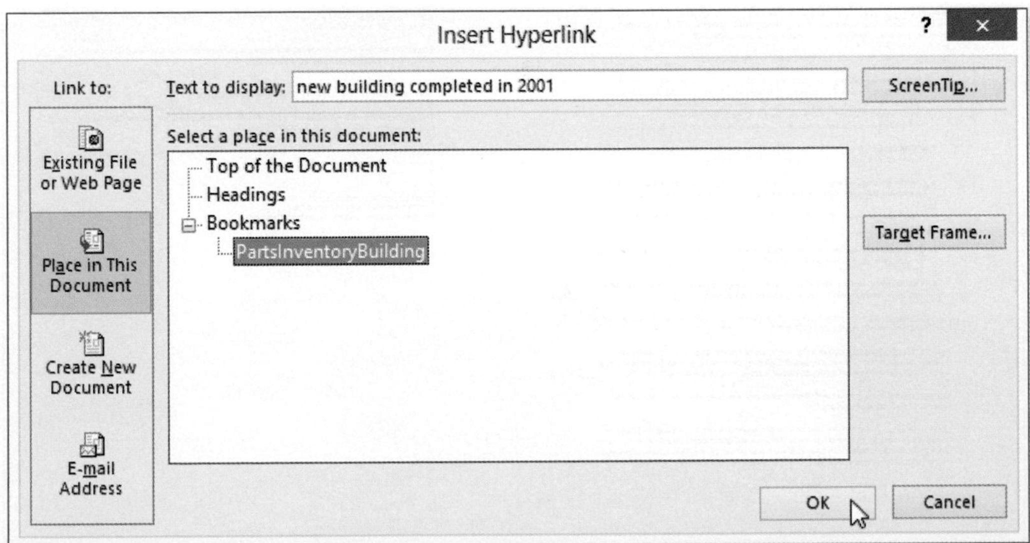

3-96 Insert hyperlink to a bookmark

12. Insert a page break to control pagination.
    a. On page 2, place the insertion point in front of the "PROPERTY" heading.
    b. Click the **Breaks** button [*Page Layout* tab, *Page Setup* group].
    c. Select **Page** in the *Page Breaks* area. A page break is inserted and the "PROPERTY" heading and following text are moved to page 3.
13. Save and close the document (Figure 3-97).

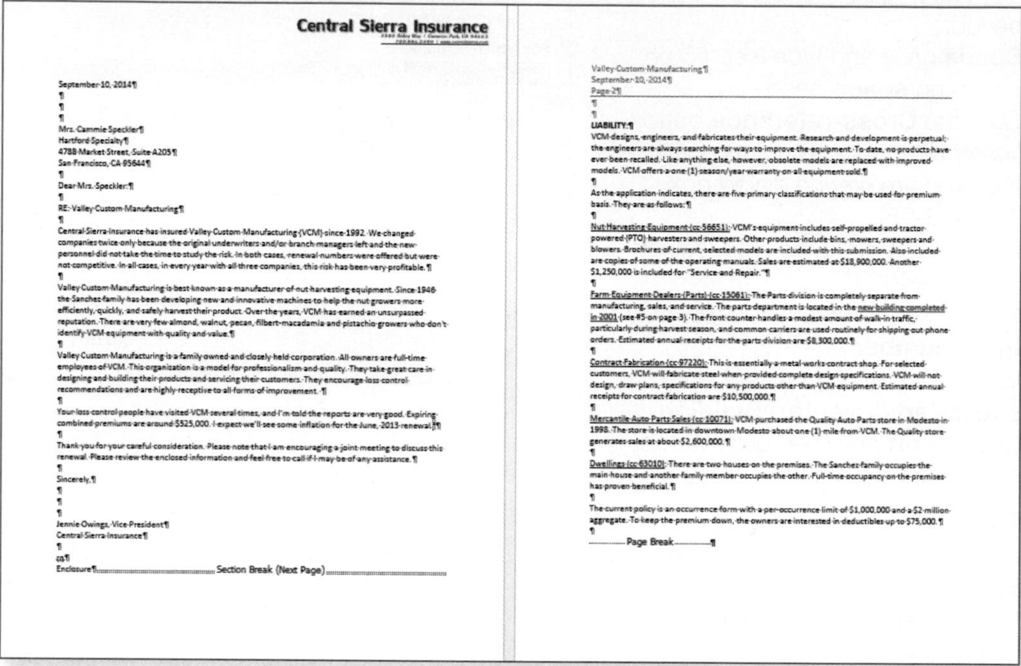

Central Sierra Insurance

September 10, 2014

Mrs. Cammie Speckler
Hartford Specialty
4788 Market Street, Suite A205
San Francisco, CA 95644

Dear Mrs. Speckler:

RE: Valley Custom Manufacturing

Central Sierra Insurance has insured Valley Custom Manufacturing (VCM) since 1992. We changed companies twice only because the original underwriters and/or branch managers left and the new personnel did not take the time to study the risk. In both cases, renewal numbers were offered but were not competitive. In all cases, in every year with all three companies, this risk has been very profitable.

Valley Custom Manufacturing is best known as a manufacturer of nut harvesting equipment. Since 1946 the Sanchez family has been developing new and innovative machines to help the nut growers more efficiently, quickly, and safely harvest their product. Over the years, VCM has earned an unsurpassed reputation. There are very few almond, walnut, pecan, filbert-macadamia and pistachio growers who don't identify VCM equipment with quality and value.

Valley Custom Manufacturing is a family owned and closely held corporation. All owners are full-time employees of VCM. This organization is a model for professionalism and quality. They take great care in designing and building their products and servicing their customers. They encourage loss control recommendations and are highly receptive to all forms of improvement.

Your loss control people have visited VCM several times, and I'm told the reports are very good. Expiring combined premiums are around $525,000. I expect we'll see some inflation for the June, 2013 renewal.[1]

Thank you for your careful consideration. Please note that I am encouraging a joint meeting to discuss this renewal. Please review the enclosed information and feel free to call if I may be of any assistance.

Sincerely,

Jennie Owings, Vice President
Central Sierra Insurance

cs
Enclosure .... Section Break (Next Page) ....

Valley Custom Manufacturing
September 10, 2014
Page 2

LIABILITY:
VCM designs, engineers, and fabricates their equipment. Research and development is perpetual; the engineers are always searching for ways to improve the equipment. To date, no products have ever been recalled. Like anything else, however, obsolete models are replaced with improved models. VCM offers a one (1) season/year warranty on all equipment sold.

As the application indicates, there are five primary classifications that may be used for premium basis. They are as follows:

Nut Harvesting Equipment (cc 56651): VCM's equipment includes self-propelled and tractor powered (PTO) harvesters and sweepers. Other products include bins, mowers, sweepers and blowers. Brochures of current, selected models are included with this submission. Also included are copies of some of the operating manuals. Sales are estimated at $18,900,000. Another $1,250,000 is included for "Service and Repair."

Farm Equipment Dealers (Parts) (cc 15061): The Parts division is completely separate from manufacturing, sales, and service. The parts department is located in the new building completed in 2001 (see #5 on page 3). The front counter handles a modest amount of walk-in traffic, particularly during harvest season, and common carriers are used routinely for shipping out phone orders. Estimated annual receipts for the parts division are $8,300,000.

Contract Fabrication (cc 97220): This is essentially a metal works contract shop. For selected customers, VCM will fabricate steel when provided complete design specifications. VCM will not design, draw plans, specifications for any products other than VCM equipment. Estimated annual receipts for contract fabrication are $10,500,000.

Mercantile Auto Parts Sales (cc 10071): VCM purchased the Quality Auto Parts store in Modesto in 1998. The store is located in downtown Modesto about one (1) mile from VCM. The Quality store generates sales at about $2,600,000.

Dwellings (cc 63010): There are two houses on the premises. The Sanchez family occupies the main house and another family member occupies the other. Full-time occupancy on the premises has proven beneficial.

The current policy is an occurrence form with a per occurrence limit of $1,000,000 and a $2 million aggregate. To keep the premium down, the owners are interested in deductibles up to $75,000.

.... Page Break ....

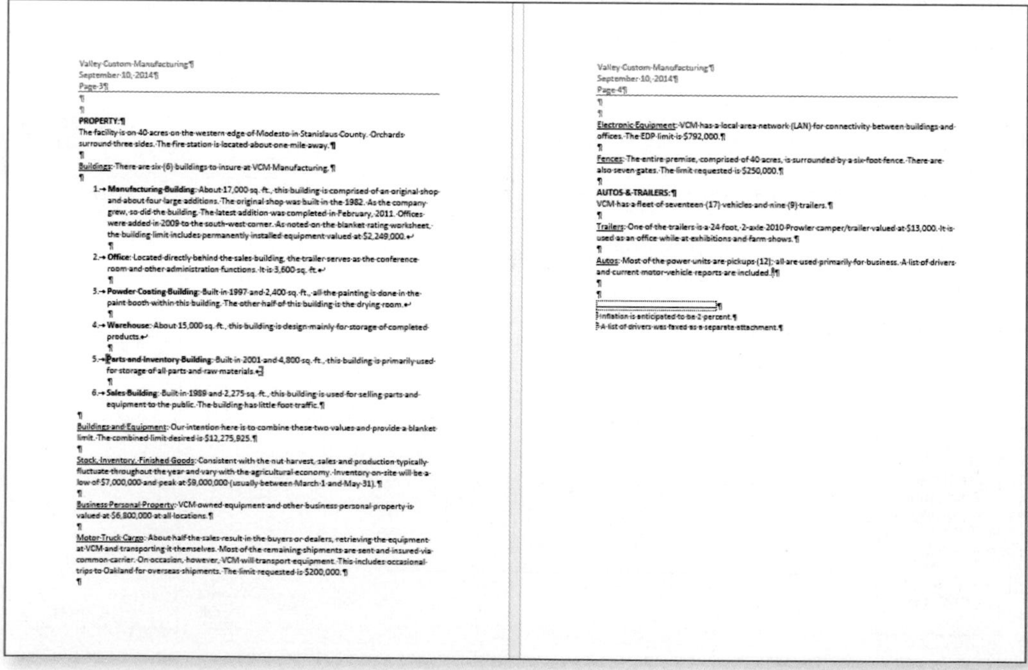

Valley Custom Manufacturing
September 10, 2014
Page 3

PROPERTY:
The facility is on 40 acres on the western edge of Modesto in Stanislaus County. Orchards surround three sides. The fire station is located about one mile away.

Buildings: There are six (6) buildings to insure at VCM Manufacturing.

1. **Manufacturing Building**: About 17,000 sq. ft., this building is comprised of an original shop and about four large additions. The original shop was built in the 1982. As the company grew, so did the building. The latest addition was completed in February, 2011. Offices were added in 2009 to the south-west corner. As noted on the blanket rating worksheet, the building limit includes permanently installed equipment valued at $2,249,000.
2. **Office**: Located directly behind the sales building, the trailer serves as the conference room and other administration functions. It is 3,600 sq. ft.
3. **Powder Coating Building**: Built in 1997 and 2,400 sq. ft., all the painting is done in the paint booth within this building. The other half of this building is the drying room.
4. **Warehouse**: About 15,000 sq. ft., this building is design mainly for storage of completed products.
5. **Parts and Inventory Building**: Built in 2001 and 4,800 sq. ft., this building is primarily used for storage of all parts and raw materials.
6. **Sales Building**: Built in 1989 and 2,275 sq. ft., this building is used for selling parts and equipment to the public. The building has little foot traffic.

Buildings and Equipment: Our intention here is to combine these two values and provide a blanket limit. The combined limit desired is $12,275,925.

Stock, Inventory, Finished Goods: Consistent with the nut harvest, sales and production typically fluctuate throughout the year and vary with the agricultural economy. Inventory on-site will be a low of $7,000,000 and peak at $9,000,000 (usually between March 1 and May 31).

Business Personal Property: VCM owned equipment and other business personal property is valued at $6,800,000 at all locations.

Motor Truck Cargo: About half the sales result in the buyers or dealers, retrieving the equipment at VCM and transporting it themselves. Most of the remaining shipments are sent and insured via common carrier. On occasion, however, VCM will transport equipment. This includes occasional trips to Oakland for overseas shipments. The limit requested is $200,000.

Valley Custom Manufacturing
September 10, 2014
Page 4

Electronic Equipment: VCM has a local area network (LAN) for connectivity between buildings and offices. The EDP limit is $792,000.

Fences: The entire premise, comprised of 40 acres, is surrounded by a six-foot fence. There are also seven gates. The limit requested is $250,000.

AUTOS & TRAILERS:
VCM has a fleet of seventeen (17) vehicles and nine (9) trailers.

Trailers: One of the trailers is a 24 foot, 2-axle 2010 Prowler camper/trailer valued at $13,000. It is used as an office while at exhibitions and farm shows.

Autos: Most of the power units are pickups (12); all are used primarily for business. A list of drivers and current motor vehicle reports are included.[2]

[1] Inflation is anticipated to be 2 percent.
[2] A list of drivers was faxed as a separate attachment.

3-97 Word 3-2 completed

Guided Project 3-3

For this project, you customize the *Teen Substance Abuse* report for Courtyard Medical Plaza. You insert citations and a placeholder, manage sources, create a bibliography, and use odd and even page headers and footers.
[Student Learning Outcomes 3.2, 3.3, 3.6]

File Needed: ***TeenSubstanceAbuse-03.docx***
Completed Project File Name: ***[your initials] Word 3-3.docx***

Skills Covered in This Project

- Set bibliography style.
- Insert a placeholder for a citation.
- Create a source and insert a citation.
- Use the *Source Manager* to edit a placeholder and create a new source.
- Insert a bibliography page.
- Use styles to format title and headings.
- Create a table of contents.
- Insert built-in odd and even headers and footers.
- Insert a document property field into a header.
- Update a table of contents.

---

1. Open the ***TeenSubstanceAbuse-03*** document from your student data files.
2. Save this document as ***[your initials] Word 3-3***.
3. Select the report style and insert placeholders for a citation.
   a. Click the **Style** drop-down list [*References* tab, *Citations & Bibliography* group].
   b. Select **Chicago Fifteenth Edition**.
   c. On the first page in the "What Problems Can Teen Substance Abuse Cause?" section, place the insertion point at the end of the last sentence in the second paragraph and before the period.
   d. Click the **Insert Citation** button [*References* tab, *Citations & Bibliography* group].
   e. Select **Add New Placeholder**. The *Placeholder Name* dialog box opens.
   f. Type Foundation and click **OK**. The placeholder for the citation is inserted into the report.
   g. On the second page in the "Can Teen Substance Use And Abuse Be Prevented?" section, place the insertion point at the end of the last sentence in the first paragraph and before the period.
   h. Click the **Insert Citation** button and select the **Foundation** placeholder from the drop-down list (Figure 3-98).

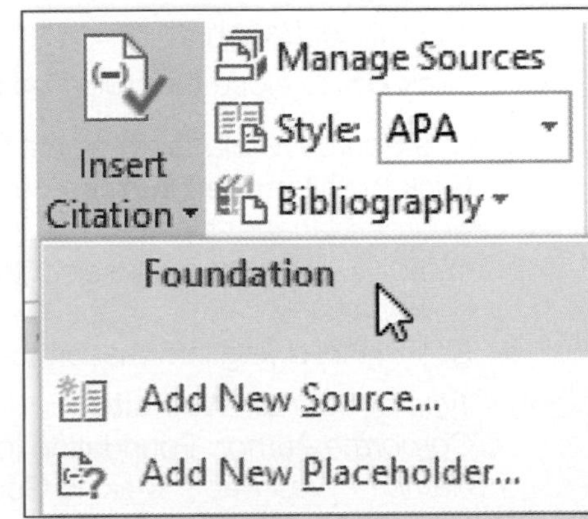

3-98 Insert placeholder for a citation

4. Insert a citation into the report.
   a. On the first page in the "What Is Teen Substance Abuse?" section, place the insertion point at the end of the last sentence in the second paragraph and before the period.

b. Click the **Insert Citation** button and select **Add New Source**. The *Create Source* dialog box opens (Figure 3-99).

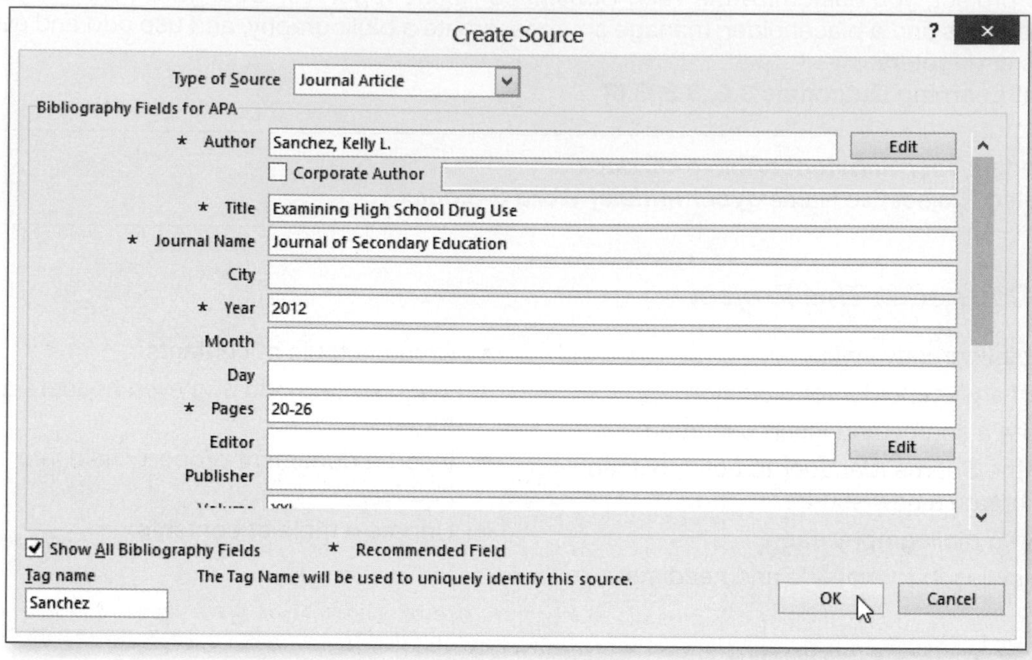

3-99 ***Create Source*** **dialog box**

c. Create a new source with the following information:

Type of Source: **Journal Article**
Author: Kelly L. Sanchez
Title: Examining High School Drug Use
Journal Name: Journal of Secondary Education
Year: 2012
Pages: 22-26
Volume: XXI (check the **Show All Bibliography Fields** check box to display these last two fields)
Issue: 2
Tag Name: Sanchez

d. Click **OK** to close the dialog box and insert the citation. The citation is inserted into the report.

5. Use the *Source Manager* to create a new source and provide source information for a placeholder.
   a. Click the **Manage Sources** button [*References* tab, *Citations & Bibliography* group] to open the *Source Manager* dialog box.
   b. In the *Current List* area, select the **Foundation** placeholder and click **Edit**. The *Edit Source* dialog box opens.
   c. Use the following information to edit the placeholder source:

   Type of Source: **Web site**
   Corporate Author: Foundation for Teen Health
   Name of Web Page: Making Good Choices
   Year: 2013
   Year Accessed: 2013
   Month Accessed: June
   Day Accessed: 25
   URL: http://foundationforteenhealth.org/choices.htm
   Tag Name: Foundation

d. Click **OK** to close the dialog box and update the placeholders. The placeholders in the report are updated with the proper citation from the source information.
e. With the *Source Manager* dialog box still open, click the **New** button. The *Create Source* dialog box opens.
f. Create a new source with the following information:

Type of Source: **Document From Web site**
Corporate Author: Courtyard Medical Plaza
Name of Web Page: Teen Mental Health
Name of Web Site: Courtyard Medical Plaza
Year: 2013
Month: March
Day: 6
URL: http://cmp.com/Teen_Mental_Health.pdf
Tag Name: CMP

g. Click **OK** to close the dialog box and click **Close** to close the *Source Manager* dialog box.

6. Insert citations into the report.
   a. On the first page in the "Why Do Teens Abuse Drugs and Alcohol?" section, place the insertion point at the end of the last sentence in the second paragraph and before the period.
   b. Click the **Insert Citation** button and select the **Courtyard Medical Plaza** citation from the drop-down list.
   c. On the second page in the "What You Should Do If You Find Out That Your Teen Is Using?" section, place the insertion point at the end of the last sentence in the second paragraph and before the period.
   d. Click the **Insert Citation** button and select the **Sanchez**, **Kelly L**. citation from the drop-down list.
7. Insert a bibliography page at the end of the document.
   a. Press **Ctrl+End** to move to the end of the document.
   b. Insert a **page break**.
   c. With the insertion point on the blank last page, click the **Bibliography** button [*References* tab, *Citations & Bibliography* group].
   d. Select **Bibliography** to insert a bibliography into the document.
8. Apply styles to the title and section headings and insert a table of contents.
   a. Apply the **Title** style to the title of the report on the first page.
   b. Apply the **Heading 1** style to each of the bold section headings in the report.
   c. Press **Ctrl+Home** to move the insertion point to the beginning of the report.
   d. Click the **Blank Page** button [*Insert* tab, *Pages* group] to insert a blank page before the first page of the report.
   e. Place your insertion point at the top of the new first page, type Teen Substance Abuse, and press **Enter**. The text should be formatted as *Title* style. If it's not, apply the **Title** style.
   f. Click the **Table of Contents** button [*References* tab, *Table of Contents* group] and select **Automatic Table 1** from the drop-down list. The table of contents is inserted below the title.
9. Insert odd and even page headers and customize content.
   a. With the insertion point still on the first page, click the **Header** button [*Insert* tab, *Header & Footer* group] and click **More Headers from Office.com**.
   b. Select **Origin (Odd Page)** from the drop-down list of built-in headers.
   c. In the header, click the **Title** document property handle and press **Delete**.
   d. Click the **Document Info** button, click **Document Property**, and select **Company** from the drop-down list.

e. Select the **Company** document property field and change the after paragraph spacing to **0 pt.** and line spacing to **1** (single).
f. Check the **Different Odd & Even Pages** check box [*Header & Footer Tools Design* tab, *Options* group and click the **Next** button to move to the *Even Page Header*.
g. Click the **Header** button [*Header & Footer Tools Design* tab, *Header & Footer* group].
h. Click **More Headers from Office.com** and select **Origin (Even Page)** from the drop-down list.
i. Delete the **Title** document property field and insert the **Company** document property field.
j. Select the **Company** document property field and change the after paragraph spacing to **0 pt.** and line spacing to **1**.

10. Insert odd and even page footers.
    a. With the header still open, click the **Go to Footer** button [*Header & Footer Tools Design* tab, *Navigation* group] to move to the *Even Page Footer*.
    b. Click the **Page Number** button [*Header & Footer* group], click **Bottom of Page**, and select **Brackets 2**.
    c. Click the **Previous** button [Navigation group] to move to the *Odd Page Footer*.
    d. Click the **Page Number** button [*Header & Footer* group], click **Bottom of Page**, and select **Brackets 2**.
    e. Click the **Close Header and Footer** button [*Close* group].
11. Insert page breaks to control pagination.
    a. On page 2, click before the last section heading and insert a **page break**.
    b. On page 3, click before the last section heading and insert a **page break**.
12. Update the table of contents.
    a. Click the table of contents on the first page.
    b. Click the **Update Table** button at the top of the content control field. The *Update Table of Contents* dialog box opens (Figure 3-100).

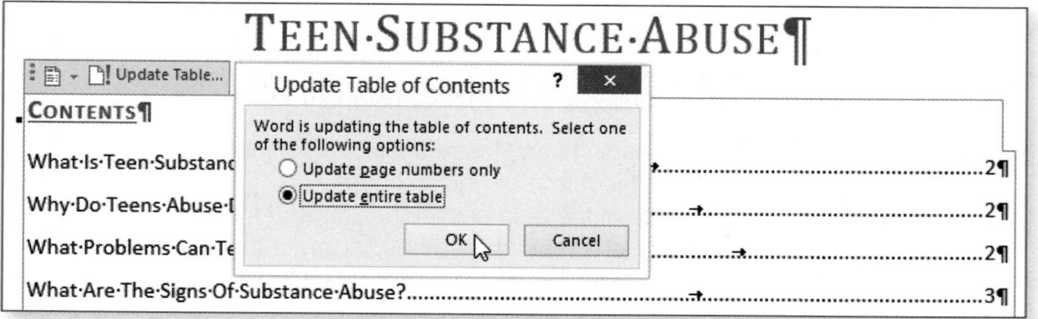

3-100 Update table of contents

    c. Select the **Update entire table** radio button and click **OK**.
13. Save and close the document (Figure 3-101).

Courtyard Medical Plaza

Teen Substance Abuse

Contents

Page Break

1

Courtyard Medical Plaza

Teen Substance Abuse

What Is Teen Substance Abuse?

Many teens try alcohol, tobacco, or drugs, but using these substances is not safe or legal. Some teens try these substances only a few times and stop. Others can't control their urges or cravings for them. This is substance abuse.

Teens may try a number of substances, including cigarettes, alcohol, household chemicals (inhalants), prescription and over-the-counter medicines, and illegal drugs. Marijuana is the illegal drug that teens use most often (Sanchez 2012).

Why Do Teens Abuse Drugs And Alcohol?

Teens use alcohol and other drugs for many reasons. They may do it because they want to fit in with friends or certain groups. They may also take a drug or drink alcohol because they like the way it makes them feel. Or they may believe that it makes them more grown up. Teens tend to try new things and take risks, and they may take drugs or drink alcohol because it seems exciting.

Teens with family members who have problems with alcohol or other drugs are more likely to have serious substance abuse problems. Also, teens who feel that they are not connected to or valued by their parents are at greater risk. Teens with poor self-esteem or emotional or mental health problems, such as depression, also are at increased risk (Courtyard Medical Plaza 2013).

What Problems Can Teen Substance Abuse Cause?

Substance abuse can lead to serious problems such as poor schoolwork, loss of friends, problems at home, and lasting legal problems. Alcohol and drug abuse is a leading cause of teen death or injury related to car accidents, suicides, violence, and drowning. Substance abuse can increase the risk of pregnancy and sexually transmitted diseases (STDs), including HIV, because of unprotected sex.

Even casual use of certain drugs can cause severe medical problems, such as an overdose or brain damage. Many illegal drugs today are made in home labs, so they can vary greatly in strength. These drugs also may contain bacteria, dangerous chemicals, and other unsafe substances (Foundation for Teen Health 2013).

Page Break

2

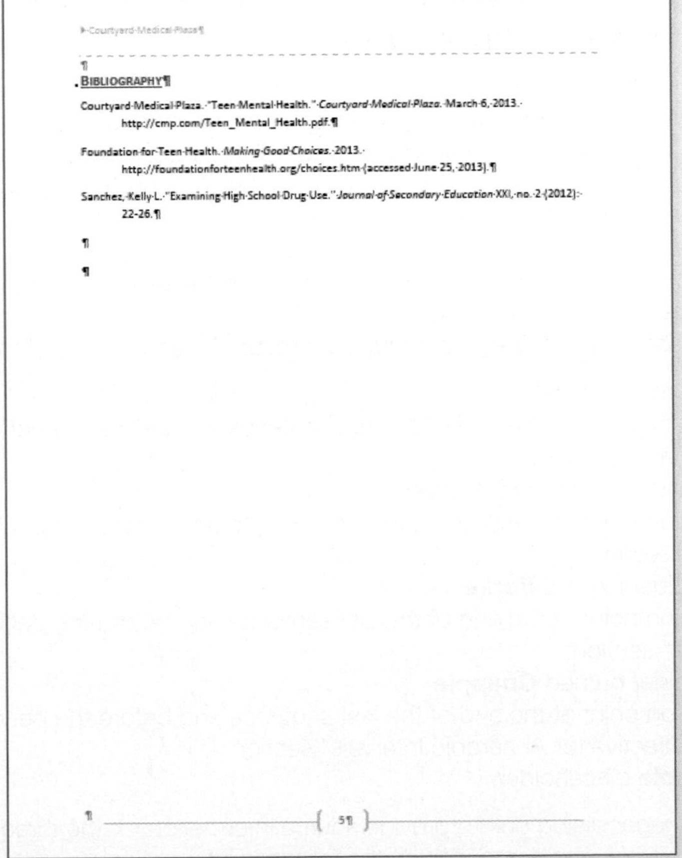

Courtyard Medical Plaza

Bibliography

Courtyard Medical Plaza. "Teen Mental Health." *Courtyard Medical Plaza.* March 6, 2013. http://cmp.com/Teen_Mental_Health.pdf.

Foundation for Teen Health. *Making Good Choices.* 2013. http://foundationforteenhealth.org/choices.htm (accessed June 25, 2013).

Sanchez, Kelly L. "Examining High School Drug Use." *Journal of Secondary Education* XXI, no. 2 (2012): 22-26.

5

3-101 Word 3-3 completed (pages 1, 2, and 5 displayed)

Independent Project 3-4

For this project, you modify the *Tips for Better Heart Rate Monitor Training* document from the American River Cycling Club. You insert and modify endnotes, insert placeholders, create sources, insert a bibliography page, bookmark selected text, and use custom headers and footers.
[Student Learning Outcomes 3.1, 3.2, 3.4, 3.5, 3.6]

File Needed: ***HeartRateMonitorTraining-03.docx***
Completed Project File Name: ***[your initials] Word 3-4.docx***

Skills Covered in This Project

- Insert endnotes.
- Insert a placeholder for a citation.
- Use the *Source Manager* to edit placeholders and create a new source.
- Change the bibliography style.
- Insert a bibliography page.
- Create a bookmark for selected text.
- Create a hyperlink to a bookmark.
- Add document properties.
- Insert and modify a cover page.
- Insert custom headers and footers.
- Insert page breaks.

---

1. Open the ***HeartRateMonitorTraining-03*** document from your student data files.
2. Save this document as ***[your initials] Word 3-4***.
3. Insert endnotes.
    a. Insert an endnote at the end of the first paragraph on the first page.
    b. In the endnote area, type See the bibliography for related books and articles.
    c. Insert an endnote at the end of the first sentence in the "Analyze Your Heart Rate Data" section.
    d. In the endnote area, type See the ARCC web site (www.arcc.org) for information about specific heart rate monitors.
    e. Insert an endnote at the end of the second sentence of the second paragraph in the "Comparing Heart Rate Values with Others" section.
    f. In the endnote area, type 220-age is a rough estimate of maximum heart rate.
4. Insert placeholders for citations.
    a. Place the insertion point at the end of the last sentence and before the period in the "Know Your Resting Heart Rate" section.
    b. Insert a placeholder named **VeloNews**.
    c. Place the insertion point at the end of the last sentence and before the period in the "Perform a Threshold Test" section.
    d. Insert a placeholder named **Burke**.
    e. Place the insertion point at the end of the last sentence and before the period in the "Analyze Your Heart Rate Data" section.
    f. Insert a placeholder named **Chapple**.
    g. Place the insertion point at the end of the last sentence and before the period in the "A Heart Rate Monitor Is Not Effective for Anaerobic Intervals" section.
    h. Insert the **Chapple** placeholder.
5. Use the *Source Manager* dialog box to provide source information for the three placeholders.
    a. Edit the *VeloNews* placeholder to include the following information:

Type of Source: **Web site**
Corporate Author: Velo News
Name of Web Page: Training Tips for Recreational Cyclists
Year: 2012
Year Accessed: 2013
Month Accessed: May
Day Accessed: 2
URL: http://velonews.com/training_tips.html

b. Edit the *Burke* placeholder to include the following information. When you save the edit, click **No** if a dialog box opens and asks if you want to update the source.

Type of Source: **Book**
Author: Edward R. Burke
Title: The Complete Book of Long-Distance Cycling
Year: 2011
City: New York
Publisher: Rodale Books

c. Edit the *Chapple* placeholder to include the following information. When you save the edit, click **No** if a dialog box opens and asks if you want to update the source.

Type of Source: **Book**
Author: Thomas Chapple
Title: Base Building for Cyclists
Year: 2009
City: San Francisco
Publisher: VeloPress

6. Change the style of the report to **APA Sixth Edition**.
7. Convert all endnotes to footnotes and change the footnote number format to **A**, **B**, **C**.
8. Insert a bibliography at the end of the document.
   a. Insert a page break at the end of the document.
   b. Insert the built-in **References** page on the last page.
   c. **Center** the *References* heading.
9. Insert a bookmark for selected text.
   a. Select the "**Perform a Threshold Test**" heading on the first page and insert a bookmark.
   b. Name the bookmark **LactateThreshold**.
10. Create a hyperlink to a bookmark.
   a. On the first page, select "**maximum heart rate**" in the first paragraph (third sentence).
   b. Insert a hyperlink to the **LactateThreshold** bookmark.
11. Add the following text to the document properties.

    Title: Tips for Better Heart Rate Training
    Company: American River Cycling Club
    Manager: Olesia Sokol
12. Insert a cover page.
   a. Insert the **Ion (Dark)** built-in cover page.
   b. In the *Year* field, select the current date.
   c. Delete the **Subtitle** and **Author** fields.
   d. In the *Company Address* field, type www.arcc.org.
   e. Select the **Title** field, change the font size to **40 pt**., apply **bold** formatting, and align **center**.

13. Insert a header and footer.
    a. In the header of the second page, type Page, **space** once, and insert a plain page number in the current position.
    b. **Right align** the header information.
    c. In the footer, type American River Cycling Club on the left and www.arcc.org on the right (use tabs to align the text on the right).
    d. Change the font size of the information in the header and footer to **10 pt**.
    e. Apply a **½ pt. top** and **bottom black border** to the information in the footer.
    f. No header or footer should appear on the cover page.
14. Insert **page breaks** where necessary to keep headings on the same page with the text that follows.
15. Save and close the document (Figure 3-102).

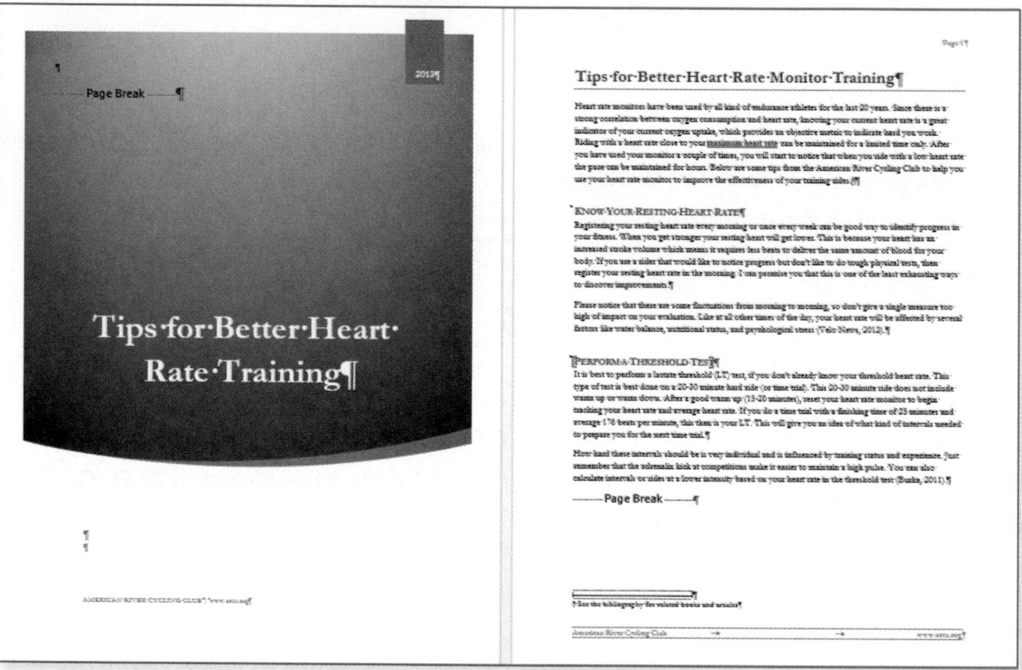

3-102 Word 3-4 completed (cover page and page 1 displayed)

Independent Project 3-5

Sierra Pacific Community College District gives incoming college students a *Student Success Tips* document. For this project, you modify the document to include heading styles, a table of contents, footnotes, and bookmarks.
[Student Learning Outcomes 3.1, 3.3, 3.5, 3.6]

File Needed: ***StudentSuccess-03.docx***
Completed Project File Name: ***[your initials] Word 3-5.docx***

Skills Covered in This Project

- Change margins.
- Apply title and heading styles.
- Insert a bookmark for selected text.
- Create a cross-reference and a hyperlink to a bookmark.
- Insert and modify footnotes.
- Insert a table of contents.
- Use a different first page footer.
- Insert page numbers and a document property field into the footer.
- Modify text format and right indent.
- Insert page breaks.
- Update a table of contents.

---

1. Open the ***StudentSuccess-03*** document from your student data files.
2. Save this document as ***[your initials] Word 3-5***.
3. Change the margins to **1"** top, bottom, left, and right on the entire document.
4. Apply styles to the title and headings.
   a. Apply the **Title** style to the title on the first page.
   b. Apply the **Heading 1** style to all the bold headings
   c. Apply the **Heading 2** style to all the underlined headings.
5. Insert a bookmark for selected text.
   a. Select the "**Procrastination**" heading and all of the text in that section.
   b. Insert a bookmark named **Procrastination** on the selected text.
   c. If bookmarks are not visible in your document, change the *Word Options* settings to make them visible.
6. Create a cross-reference to a bookmark.
   a. Find the word "Procrastination" in the "How to Reduce Test Anxiety" section.
   b. After "Procrastination," create a cross-reference to insert the page number of the *Procrastination* bookmark.
   c. Insert text so the cross-reference reads "(see page x)" where "x" is the inserted page number of the bookmark.
7. Create a hyperlink to a bookmark.
   a. Select the word "**Procrastination**" in the "How to Reduce Test Anxiety" section.
   b. Insert a hyperlink to the **Procrastination** bookmark on the selected text.
   c. Test the hyperlink to make sure it takes the reader to the *Procrastination* bookmark.
8. Insert footnotes and apply text formatting.
   a. Insert a footnote after "Weekly Schedules" in the "Schedule Your Time" section on the first page.
   b. For the footnote text, type Weekly Schedules are available from your counselor or in the college bookstore.
   c. In the "Schedule Your Time" section, insert a footnote at the end of "Be sure to schedule your time for all these in your 119 hours."
   d. For the footnote text, type Be sure to schedule recreational and down time in your 119 hours.
   e. Apply **italic** formatting to the text of the footnotes.
9. Move a footnote and modify footnote number format.
   a. Move the first footnote so it appears after "Weekly Schedule" in the "Track Your Time" section.
   b. Change the footnote number format to **a**, **b**, **c**.
10. Insert a table of contents.
   a. Insert a page break before the first page.
   b. Type Student Success Tips on the first line on the new first page and press **Enter**.

c. Apply the **Title** style to the title on the new first page.
d. On the blank line below the title, insert the **Automatic Table 1** table of contents.

11. Insert a footer on the second and continuing pages.
    a. Edit the footer on the first page of the document (table of contents).
    b. Set the first page footer to be different from the remaining footers.
    c. Go to the footer on the second page.
    d. Insert the **Vertical**, **Right** built-in page number format from the *Page Margins* page numbering options.
    e. In the footer, change the alignment to **right** and insert the **Company** document property field (Figure 3-103).
    f. Change the font size to **10 pt**. and apply **bold** formatting to the document property field.
    g. Change the right indent in the footer to **–.5"**.
    h. Close the footer.

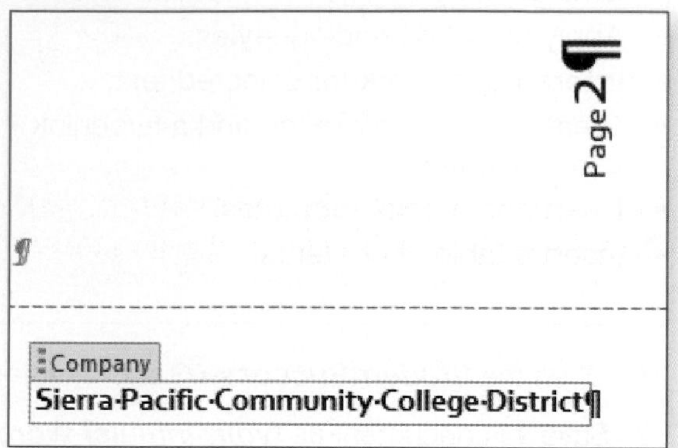

3-103 Footer on second and continuing pages

12. Insert page breaks to keep headings and text together.
13. Update the table of contents.
14. Save and close the document (Figure 3-104).

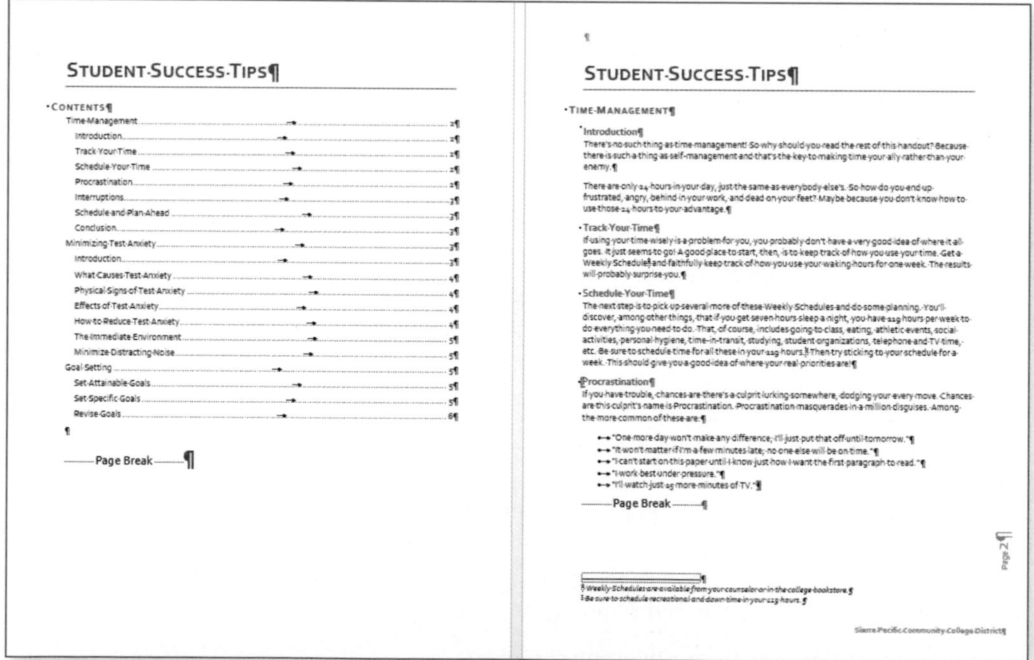

3-104 Word 3-5 completed (first two pages of six)

Independent Project 3-6

Courtyard Medical Plaza works closely with the Skiing Unlimited winter ski program. In this project, you modify the *Skiing Unlimited Training Guide* to include a table of contents, cover page, and odd and even headers.
[Student Learning Outcomes 3.3, 3.5, 3.6]

File Needed: ***SkiingUnlimitedTrainingGuide-03.docx***
Completed Project File Name: ***[your initials] Word 3-6.docx***

Skills Covered in This Project

- Change margins.
- Edit document properties.
- Apply title and heading styles.
- Insert a custom table of contents.
- Insert and customize odd and even headers.
- Insert a document property field into headers.
- Insert a cover page.
- Customize content and insert document property fields.
- Insert page breaks.
- Update a table of contents.

1. Open the ***SkiingUnlimitedTrainingGuide-03*** document from your student data files.
2. Save this document as ***[your initials] Word 3-6***.
3. Change the left and right margins to **1"**.
4. Edit the following document properties.
   Title: Skiing Unlimited Training Guide
   Company: Courtyard Medical Plaza
   Manager: Kallyn Nickols
5. Apply styles to the title and headings.
   a. Apply the **Title** style to the title on the first page.
   b. Apply the **Heading 1** style to all the bold headings.
   c. Apply the **Heading 2** style to all the underlined headings.
   d. Apply the **Heading 3** style to all the italicized headings.
6. Insert a custom table of contents.
   a. Insert a page break before the first page.
   b. Type Table of Contents on the first line on the new first page and press **Enter**.
   c. Apply the **Title** style to the title on the new first page.
   d. On the blank line below the title and before the page break, click the **Table of Contents** button and select **Custom Table of Contents** to insert a custom table of contents.
   e. Select **Fancy** format and show **2** levels of headings.
7. Insert header and footer.
   a. On the first page, insert the **Bold Numbers 3** built-in page number at the top of the page.
   b. Delete the extra **Enter** in the header.
   c. In the footer, insert the **Title** document property field on the left and the **Company** field on the right. Use tabs to align the field on the right.
   d. **Bold** the text in the footer.

8. Insert and modify a cover page.
   a. Insert the **Grid** cover page.
   b. Delete the **Subtitle** field and insert the **Company** document property field.
   c. Change the font size of the *Company* document property field to **20 pt**.
   d. In the *Abstract* field, type On behalf of the Skiing Unlimited winter ski program, Courtyard Medical Plaza has developed this training guide for Skiing Unlimited volunteers.
   e. On the Abstract field, apply **italic** formatting and change the text color to **Black**, **Text 1**.
9. Insert page breaks where necessary to keep headings with the text below.
   a. Insert a page break before the "Visual Impaired (VI)" heading.
   b. Insert other page breaks as necessary to keep headings with the text below.
10. Update the table of contents.
11. Save and close the document (Figure 3-105).

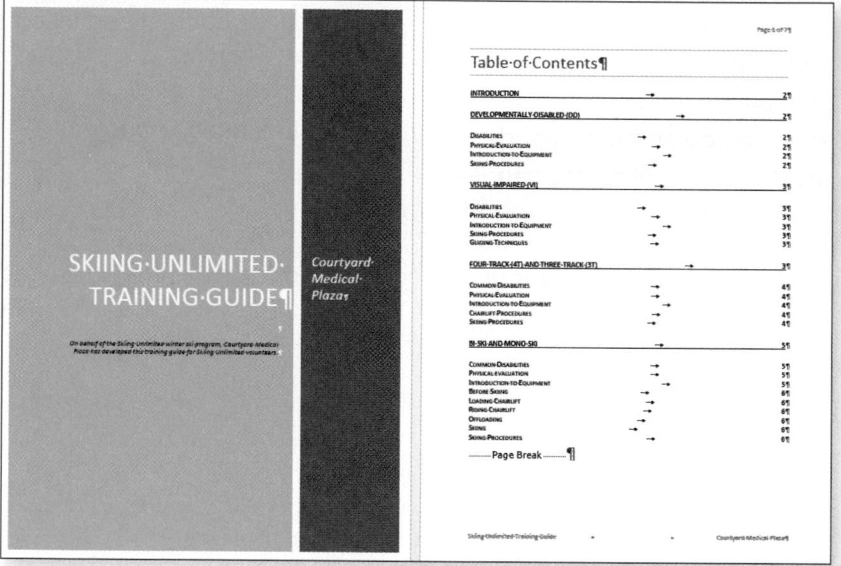

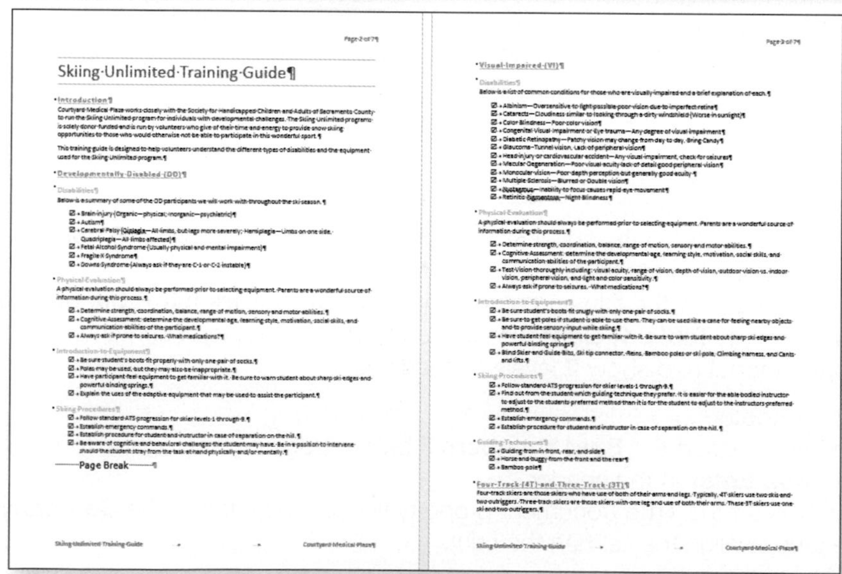

3-105 Word 3-6 completed (first four pages of eight)

Improve It Project 3-7

American River Cycling Club is working with a cycling tour company to set up a trip to cycle through the Tuscany region of Italy. The original document from the cycling tour company needs to be improved. Modify this document to remove some of the existing content and add a cover page, footnotes, bookmarks, and a footer.
[Student Learning Outcomes 3.1, 3.4, 3.5, 3.6]

File Needed: ***ItalyTourItinerary-03.docx***
Completed Project File Name: ***[your initials] Word 3-7.docx***

Skills Covered in This Project

- Change margins.
- Edit document properties.
- Apply a title and heading styles.
- Insert a custom table of contents.
- Insert and customize odd and even headers.
- Insert a document property field into headers.
- Insert a cover page.
- Customize content and insert document property fields.
- Insert and align pictures.
- Insert page breaks.
- Update a table of contents.

---

1. Open the ***ItalyTourItinerary-03*** document from your student data files.
2. Save this document as ***[your initials] Word 3-7***.
3. Remove existing content.
   a. Remove the existing cover page.
   b. Remove the existing table of contents.
   c. Remove the existing headers and footers on all pages of the itinerary.
   d. Delete the existing bookmark in the document.
4. Change the page orientation to **Landscape**.
5. Apply the **Day** style to each of the day headings in the itinerary.
6. Insert page breaks.
   a. Click in front of "Day 3" and insert a page break.
   b. Repeat this on each of the odd numbered days so only two days appear on each page.
7. Add text and apply style.
   a. Place your insertion point on the blank line after the text in the "Day 2" section.
   b. Press **Enter** and type Notes and Questions at the insertion point.
   c. Apply **Day** style to the text you just typed.
   d. Repeat steps b and c to insert this information at the end of the "Day 4," "Day 6," and "Day 8" sections.

8. Insert a bookmark for selected text.
   a. On the last page, select the text beginning with "**Kilometers to Miles Conversion**" to "**49.6 miles**."
   b. Insert a bookmark named **kmConversion** for the selected text.
9. Insert hyperlinks to a bookmark.
   a. On the first page in the "Day 2" section, select "**Distance: 83 km**" (don't select the paragraph mark) and insert a hyperlink to the **kmConversion** bookmark.
   b. Repeat this on each of the other riding days of the tour. Don't select the footnote after the "Day 3" distance.
   c. Test the hyperlink on page 1. It should take you to the bookmarked text on page 4.
10. Move and delete footnotes.
    a. Move the first footnote (after the distance on "Day 3") to appear after the distance on "Day 2."
    b. Change the footnote text to Day 2 is the longest day of the tour.
    c. Delete the second footnote reference marker after "Day 4." The footnote text is removed when you delete the footnote reference marker.
11. Insert footnotes.
    a. After the "Day 4" distance, insert a footnote and type Day 4 is an optional riding day.
    b. After the "Day 5" distance, insert a footnote and type Day 5 has two routes from which to choose.
    c. After the "Day 6" distance, insert a footnote and type Day 6 has three routes from which to choose. The 68 km route has a couple of substantial climbs.
12. Edit the following document properties.

    Title: Cycling Classic Tuscany: Tour Itinerary
    Company: American River Cycling Club
13. Insert and modify a cover page.
    a. Insert the **Semaphore** cover page.
    b. Select next **June 15** as the date.
    c. Change the font size of the *Title* field to **32 pt.**
    d. Delete the **Subject** (*Document Subtitle*) and **Author** fields.
    e. Change the font size of the *Company* field to **14 pt**.
    f. In the *Address* field, type www.arcc.org.
14. Insert footers on the second and continuing pages.
    a. On the second page of the document, edit the footer.
    b. Change the alignment to **right**, insert the **Company** document property field, deselect the field, and **space** once.
    c. Type | (horizontal line; **Shift+**) and **space** once.
    d. Type Page followed by a **space**.
    e. Insert a plain page number in the current position.
    f. **Bold** all of the text in the footer.

15. Save and close the document (Figure 3-106).

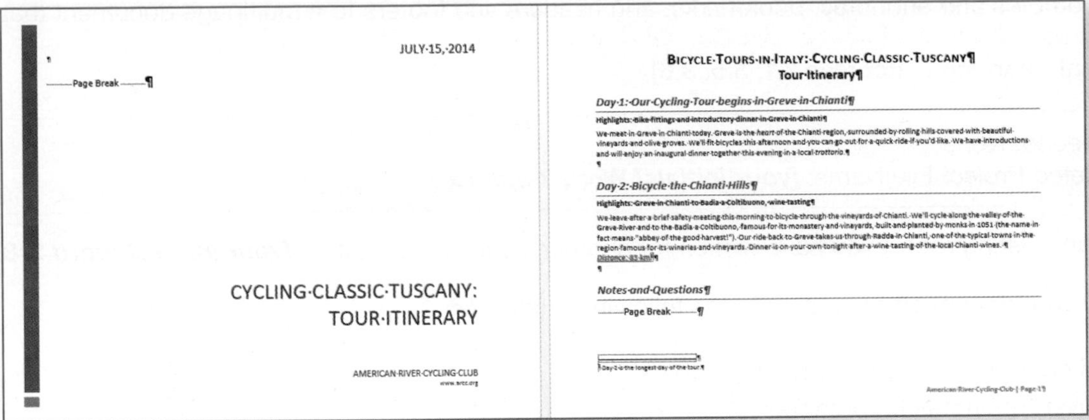

3-106 Word 3-5 completed (first two pages of five)

Challenge Project 3-8

Modify a report you have written for another class to include citations, a bibliography or works cited page, and headers and footers.
[Student Learning Outcomes 3.2, 3.6]

File Needed: None
Completed Project File Name: ***[your initials] Word 3-8.docx***

Open an existing report you have and save it as ***[your initials] Word 3-8***.

Modify your document according to the following guidelines:

- Select the citation style to use for your report (e.g., APA, MLA, Chicago).
- Add citations to the body of your report and create sources.
- Add placeholders for citations in the body of your report.
- Insert a bibliography or works cited page at the end of your report.
- Use the *Source Manager* dialog box to edit placeholders and sources and add new sources, if necessary.
- Insert other citations in the body as necessary.
- Update the bibliography page.
- Insert a header, footer, and page number from the built-in list of options.
- Use different first page headers and footers.
- Insert page breaks to control pagination as necessary.

Challenge Project 3-9

Add footnotes and endnotes, bookmarks, and headers and footers to a multipage document that you have written.
[Student Learning Outcomes 3.1, 3.5, 3.6]

File Needed: None
Completed Project File Name: ***[your initials] Word 3-9.docx***

Open an existing report you have written for another class and save it as ***[your initials] Word 3-9***.

Modify your document according to the following guidelines:

- Add endnotes to the document.
- Convert endnotes to footnotes.
- Change the number format for footnotes.
- Move a footnote to a new location.
- Delete a footnote.
- Add two bookmarks. Insert one at a specific location in your document and another one for selected text.
- Create a hyperlink to a bookmark.
- Create a cross-reference to a bookmark.
- Insert a custom header or footer in your document.
- Add a page number in the header or footer of the document.
- Insert page breaks to control pagination as necessary.

Challenge Project 3-10

Modify a report or multipage document you have written for another class to include a table of contents, a cover page, and headers and footers.
[Student Learning Outcomes 3.3, 3.4, 3.6]

File Needed: None
Completed Project File Name: ***[your initials] Word 3-10.docx***

Open an existing report or multipage document and save it as ***[your initials] Word 3-10***.

Modify your document according to the following guidelines:

- Apply *Heading 1* and *Heading 2* styles to the headings of your document. If the document does not have headings, add two levels of headings to the document.
- Insert a built-in or custom table of contents as the first page of your document.
- Include two levels of headings in the table of contents.
- Customize the title, company, and author document property fields.
- Insert a cover page of your choice.
- Customize the cover page by adding or removing a document property or content control fields.
- Add custom content to content control fields.
- Insert a header, footer, and page number from the built-in list of options.
- Use different first page headers and footers.
- Insert page breaks to control pagination as necessary.
- Update the table of contents.

CHAPTER 4

Using Tables, Columns, and Graphics

CHAPTER OVERVIEW

Tables, columns, and graphics enhance the appearance and readability of your Word documents. For example, you can use tables to attractively arrange and align information in column and row format. Columns improve readability and provide additional white space in a document. You can also insert and manipulate graphics to add attention-grabbing visual elements to your documents. This chapter introduces you to the Word tools that allow you to add and customize tables, columns, and graphics.

STUDENT LEARNING OUTCOMES (SLOs)

After completing this chapter, you will be able to:

SLO 4.1 Improve the design and readability of a document by using tables to present and arrange information (p. W4-197).

SLO 4.2 Modify a table by changing column and row size, aligning text, using the *Table Properties* dialog box, sorting data, and using *AutoFit* (p. W4-201).

SLO 4.3 Enhance the appearance and function of a table by using the *Table Tools* tabs, applying borders and shading, using table styles, inserting formulas, and converting text into a table (p. W4-207).

SLO 4.4 Modify the layout and design of a document using columns to present information (p. W4-214).

SLO 4.5 Enrich a document by adding and modifying visual elements such as pictures, shapes, *SmartArt,* and *WordArt* (p. W4-218).

Case Study

Placer Hills Real Estate (PHRE) is a real estate company with regional offices throughout central California. In the Pause & Practice projects in this chapter, you modify a brochure for Emma Cavalli, a realtor consultant with PHRE. In the past, Emma distributed brochures that were poorly laid out and designed and that negatively impacted the effectiveness of her message. You modify one of Emma's brochures to include tables, columns, and graphics. Your modifications will improve the overall layout and effectiveness of the document.

Pause & Practice 4-1: Modify an existing brochure to include a table that presents information attractively.

Pause & Practice 4-2: Enhance the table in the brochure by using borders, shading, and table styles.

Pause & Practice 4-3: Improve the readability of the brochure by arranging text in columns.

Pause & Practice 4-4: Add visual elements to the brochure to improve the overall design of the document.

WORD

SLO 4.1

Creating and Editing Tables

In Chapter 2 you learned about aligning information into column and row format using tab stops. ***Tables*** are another tool that you can use to organize information into column and row format. In addition to lining up information, tables allow you more formatting options than tabs do for alignment.

> **MORE INFO**
>
> On web pages, most of the information is organized into table and row format even though you might not see table borders or structure.

Tables

You can insert tables almost anywhere in a Word document. A table is made up of individual ***cells***. You enter information in the cells of a table. Cells are grouped into ***columns*** and ***rows***. When using tables, it is important to distinguish between cells, columns, and rows (Figure 4-1).

- ***Cell:*** The area where a column and row intersect
- ***Column:*** A vertical grouping of cells (think of vertical columns that support a building)
- ***Row:*** A horizontal grouping of cells (think of horizontal rows of seating in a stadium or auditorium)

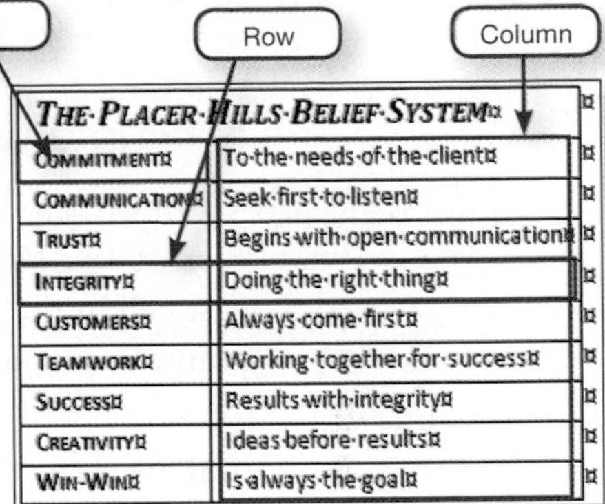

THE·PLACER·HILLS·BELIEF·SYSTEM¤	
COMMITMENT¤	To·the·needs·of·the·client¤
COMMUNICATION¤	Seek·first·to·listen¤
TRUST¤	Begins·with·open·communication¤
INTEGRITY¤	Doing·the·right·thing¤
CUSTOMERS¤	Always·come·first¤
TEAMWORK¤	Working·together·for·success¤
SUCCESS¤	Results·with·integrity¤
CREATIVITY¤	Ideas·before·results¤
WIN-WIN¤	Is·always·the·goal¤

4-1 Table

HOW TO: Insert a Table

1. Place your insertion point in your document where you want to insert a table.
2. Click the **Insert** tab.
3. Click the **Table** button [*Tables* group] to open the drop-down list.
4. Click and drag across the *Insert Table* grid to select the number of columns and rows you want to have in the table (Figure 4-2).
   - As you drag across the grid, the *Insert Table* label changes to display the size of the table (e.g., *3x2 Table*).
5. Select the desired table size to insert into the document. The table is inserted into your document.

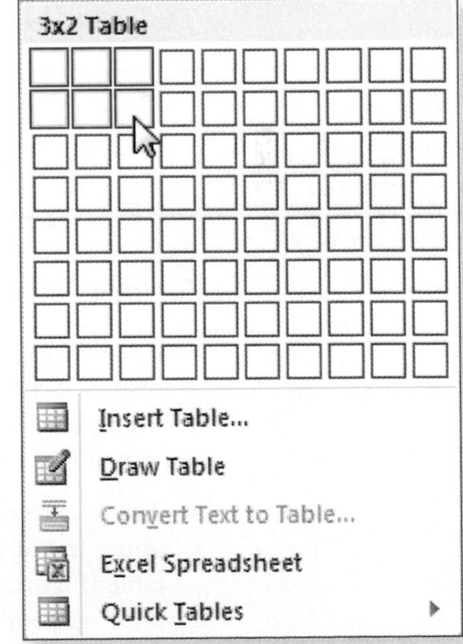

4-2 *Insert Table* drop-down list

> **MORE INFO**
>
> Word lists table dimensions in column and row format. For example, a three column and two row table is a 3x2 table.

When you insert a table using the *Insert Table* grid, the table size is limited depending on the size and resolution of your computer screen. You can also insert a table using the ***Insert Table*** dialog box.

HOW TO: Insert a Table Using the Insert Table Dialog Box

1. Click the **Insert** tab.
2. Click the **Table** button [*Tables* group] to open the drop-down list.
3. Select **Insert Table.** The *Insert Table* dialog box opens (Figure 4-3).
4. In the *Table size* area, select the desired number of columns and rows.
5. Choose **OK** to insert the table.

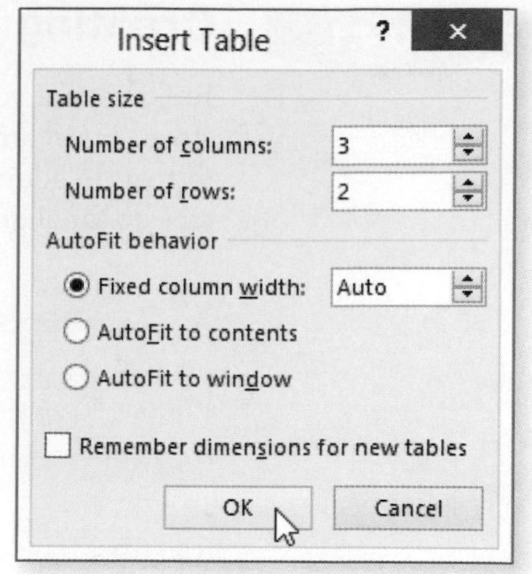

4-3 ***Insert Table*** **dialog box**

Navigate within a Table

To move the insertion point within a table, press **Tab** to move forward one cell in the current row. When you get to the end of a row and press *Tab,* the insertion point moves to the first cell in the next row. **Shift+Tab** moves you back one cell at a time. You can also use your pointer and click in a cell to insert the insertion point.

Table Tools Layout Tab

When a table is inserted into a document, the ***Table Tools tabs*** are displayed. There are two *Table Tools* tabs: ***Design*** and ***Layout***. These context-sensitive toolbars are activated whenever the insertion point is in the table or when a region of the table is selected. The *Table Tools Layout* tab lists a variety of formatting options (Figure 4-4). For more on the *Table Tools Design* tab, see *SLO 4.3: Formatting and Editing Tables.*

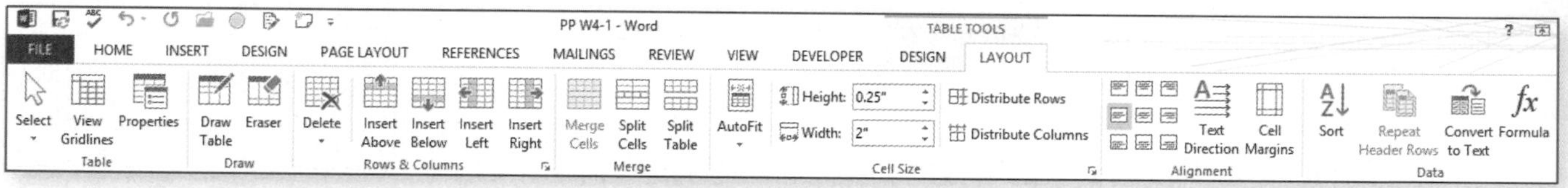

4-4 ***Table Tools Layout*** **tab**

Select Table and Text

When you are working with tables, at times you will want to select the entire table, a cell, column, or row, or multiple cells, columns, or rows. Word provides a variety of table selection tools.

- ***Table selector handle:*** This handle appears at the upper left of the table when the pointer is on the table (Figure 4-5). Click the **table selector** to select the entire table.
- ***Row selector:*** The row selector is the right-pointing arrow when your pointer is just to the left of the table row (Figure 4-6). When the pointer becomes the row selector, click to select a single row. To select multiple rows, click and drag up or down.

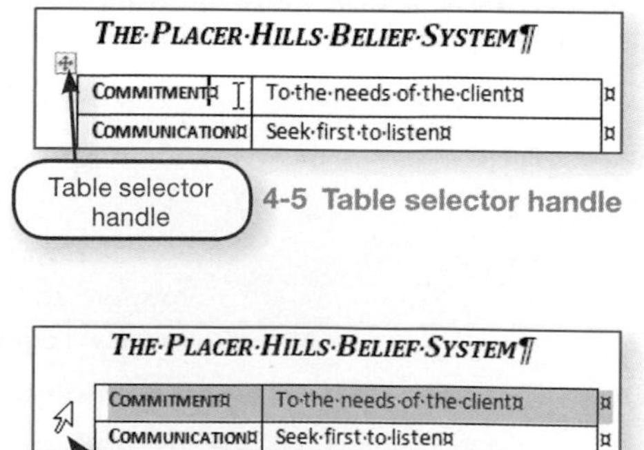

4-5 Table selector handle

4-6 Row selector

- ***Column selector:*** The column selector is the thick, black down arrow when your pointer is on the top of a column (Figure 4-7). When the pointer becomes the column selector, click to select a single column. To select multiple colums, click and drag left or right.
- ***Cell selector:*** The cell selector is the thick, black right-pointing arrow when your pointer is just inside the left border of a cell (Figure 4-8). When the pointer becomes the cell selector, click to select a single cell. To select multiple cells, click and drag left, right, up, or down. When the cell selector is displayed, double-click to select the entire row.
- ***Select button:*** The select button is on the *Table Tools Layout* tab in the *Table* group. Click the **Select** button to access a drop-down list of table selection options (Figure 4-9).

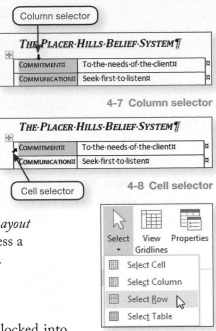

4-7 Column selector

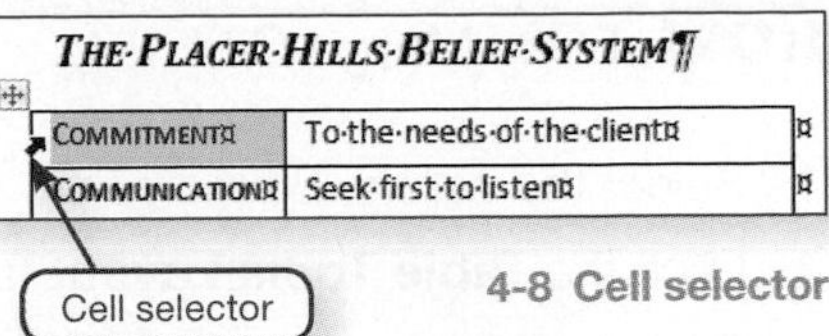

4-8 Cell selector

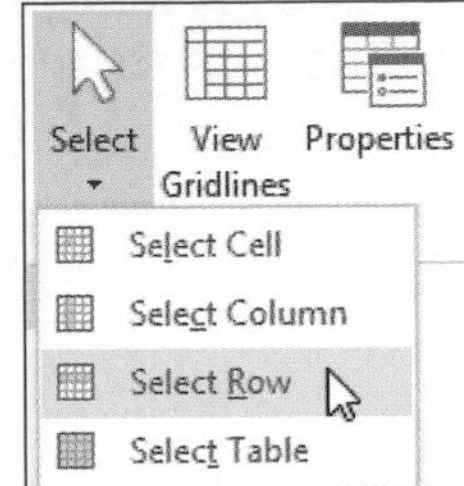

4-9 *Select* drop-down list

Add Rows and Columns

When you insert a table into a document, you are not locked into your original table dimensions; you can always add columns and rows to the table in a variety of ways.

- ***Insert Control:*** Place your pointer on the left outside edge of a row or top outside edge of a column to display the insert row or column control (plus sign). Click the **insert control** to add a row or column (Figure 4-10). Select multiple rows or columns and click the insert control to add the number or rows or columns selected.
- ***Table Tools Layout tab***—In the *Rows & Columns* group, you can insert a row above or below the current row or a column to the left or right of the current column (see Figure 4-4).
- ***Mini toolbar:*** Select a cell, row, column, or table to display the mini toolbar. You can also right-click the table to display the mini toolbar. Click the **Insert** button to display a list of insert options (Figure 4-11).
- ***Insert Cells dialog box:*** Open this dialog box by clicking the **Rows & Columns** launcher on the *Table Tools Layout* tab (Figure 4-12).
- ***Tab:*** When your insertion point is in the last cell in the last row, you can press **Tab** to insert a new row below the last row.

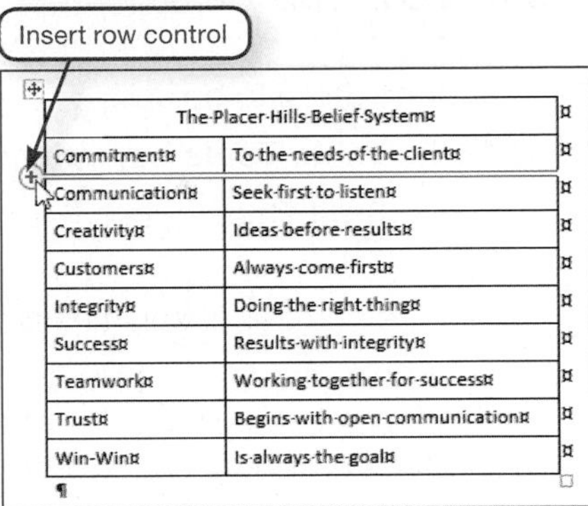

4-10 Insert row control

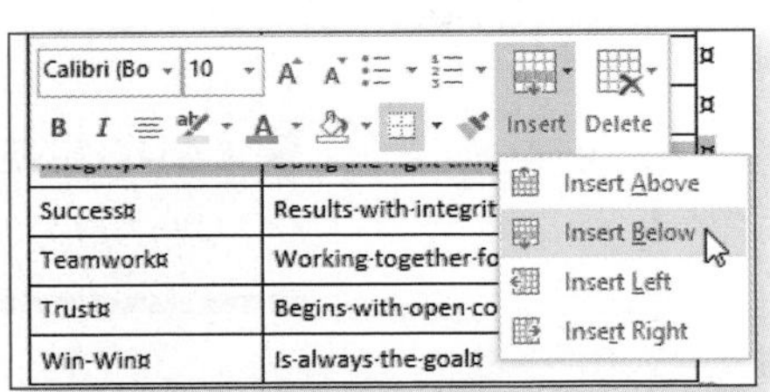

4-11 Use the mini toolbar to insert a row

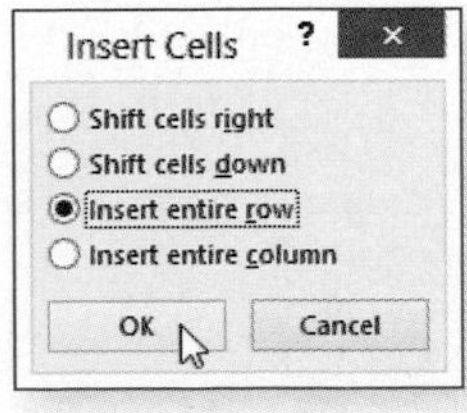

4-12 *Insert Cells* dialog box

> **MORE INFO**
>
> Be careful about *using Shift cells right* from the *Insert Cells* dialog box. This pushes cells to the right creating a new column in that one row, not the entire table.

Merge and Split Cells

Many times when you use tables you want to span information across multiple columns, such as when you are inserting a title or subtitle in a table. You can do this by merging columns, rows, and cells.

HOW TO: Merge Cells

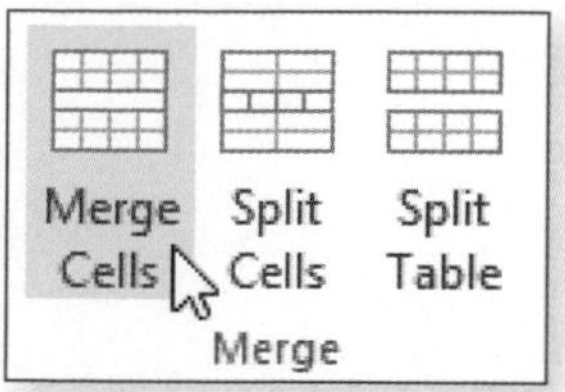

4-13 *Merge Cells* button

1. Select the cells to be merged.
2. Click the **Table Tools Layout** tab.
3. Click the **Merge Cells** button [*Merge* group] (Figure 4-13). The cells are merged into one cell.

Word also allows you to split a cell into multiple cells. You can split cells that have previously been merged or split a single cell into multiple columns and rows. When you are splitting cells, the *Split Cells* dialog box prompts you to specify the number of columns and rows.

HOW TO: Split Cells

1. Select the cell(s) to be split.
2. Click the **Table Tools Layout** tab.
3. Click the **Split Cells** button [*Merge* group]. The *Split Cells* dialog box opens (Figure 4-14).
4. Select the number of columns and rows that you want in the split cell.
   - By default, the *Merge cells before split* check box is selected. When this check box is selected, Word merges the selected cells before splitting them into the desired number of columns and rows.
5. Click **OK** to split the cells.

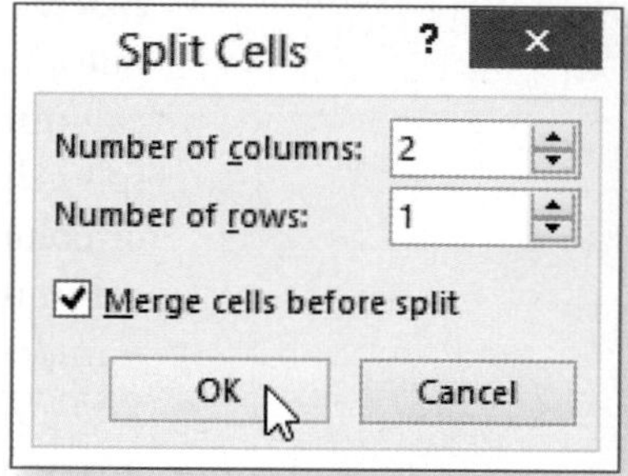

4-14 *Split Cells* dialog box

ANOTHER WAY

Both *Merge Cells* and *Split Cells* are available from the context menu.

Copy or Move Columns and Rows

You can copy or move columns and rows in a table similar to how you copy or move text in a document. Select the column or row to copy or move, and use one of the following methods:

- *Drag and drop:* Drag and drop the column or row in the new location to move it. Hold the **Ctrl** key while dragging and dropping to copy a column or row.
- *Keyboard Shortcuts:* **Ctrl+C** (copy), **Ctrl+X** (cut), and **Ctrl+V** (paste).
- *Context menu:* Right-click on the selected column or row and select **Cut**, **Copy**, or **Paste**.
- *Clipboard group on the Home tab:* Use the **Cut**, **Copy**, and **Paste** buttons in this group.

Remove Columns and Rows

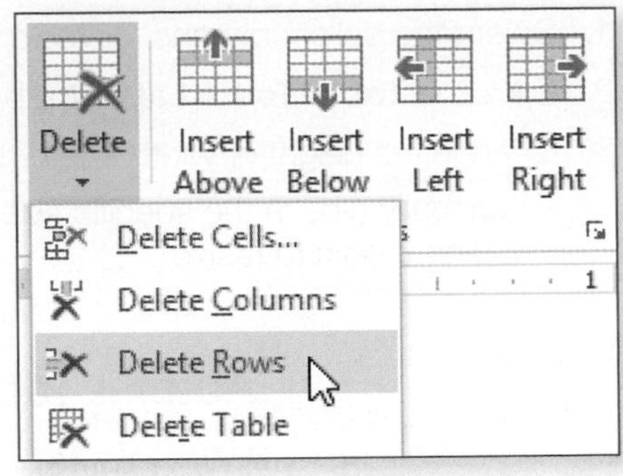

4-15 *Delete* options

At some point, you will need to remove columns or rows from your table. Removing columns and rows is very similar to inserting columns and rows. Use the *Delete* button in the *Rows & Columns* group on the *Table Tools Layout* tab or the mini toolbar to remove cells, columns, rows, or an entire table. You have the following options (Figure 4-15):

- *Delete Cells . . .*: This will open the *Delete Cells* dialog box.
- *Delete Columns*
- *Delete Rows*
- *Delete Table*

Delete a Table

If you select an entire table and press *Delete* on your keyboard, only the information in the table is deleted; the blank table remains in your document. To delete a table, you select the **Delete Table** option from the *Delete* button on the *Table Tool Layout* tab or mini toolbar (see Figure 4-15).

SLO 4.2

Arranging Text in Tables

You can adjust the width of columns and the height of rows and control how text is aligned within the cells of a table. Word provides you with a variety of table resizing and text alignment options. You also can sort information automatically within a table.

Resize Columns and Rows

Many times you need to adjust columns and rows to better fit the information in the table. When you insert a table into a document, the default size for the table is the width of the document. You can manually adjust the width of columns and height of rows in a couple of ways.

You can manually drag the column or row borders to increase or decrease the size of a column or row. When you put your pointer on the vertical border of a column, the pointer changes to a ***resizing pointer*** (Figure 4-16). You can drag the column border to the left or right to adjust the size of the column. You can use the same method to adjust the height of a row by dragging the top or bottom border of a row up or down.

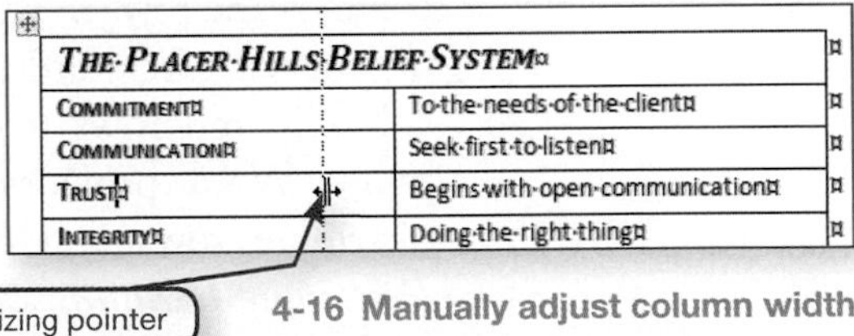

THE PLACER HILLS BELIEF SYSTEM	
COMMITMENT	To the needs of the client
COMMUNICATION	Seek first to listen
TRUST	Begins with open communication
INTEGRITY	Doing the right thing

4-16 Manually adjust column width

> **MORE INFO**
>
> When you manually adjust the height of a row, it adjusts the height of the selected row only. Normally, you want to keep the height of rows consistent.

Word also allows you to type in a specific size for columns and rows. It is difficult to adjust column and row sizes of a table with merged cells. It is best to adjust the size of columns and rows before merging cells. If you're adjusting the size of columns or rows after merging cells, be very specific about the cells you select.

HOW TO: Resize Columns and Rows

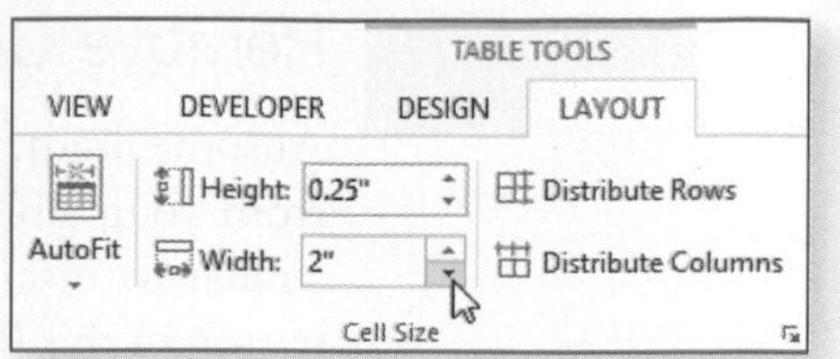

4-17 Set cell *Height* and *Width*

1. Select the cells, columns, or rows you want to resize.
2. Click the **Table Tools Layout** tab.
3. Change the height or width to the desired size [*Cell Size* group] (Figure 4-17).
   - Manually type in the specific size or use the up or down arrows (spinner box) to resize.

AutoFit Tables

When you insert a table into a document, the table is automatically set to the width of the document (inside the left and right margins). Word has three different ***AutoFit*** options to adjust the column width of the table. The *AutoFit* options are in the *Cell Size* group on the *Table Tools Layout* tab (Figure 4-18).

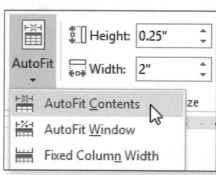

4-18 *AutoFit* options

- ***AutoFit Contents:*** Adjusts column widths to fit the contents of the table.
- ***AutoFit Window:*** Distributes the column widths so the table fits across the width of the page (this is the default setting when you insert a table into a document).
- ***Fixed Column Width:*** Adjusts columns to a fixed column width.

MORE INFO

When you insert a table, the table has the same formatting as the text in the document. If your rows seem too high, it might be because your document contains before or after paragraph spacing that is controlling the height of the rows in your table.

Distribute Rows and Columns

There might be times when you adjust the sizes of columns and rows in a table and the table seems cluttered or uneven afterwards, or you might just want your columns and rows to be the same size as a starting point. Word provides you with features to evenly distribute rows and columns. ***Distribute Rows*** and ***Distribute Columns*** are on the *Table Tools Layout* tab in the *Cell Size* group (Figure 4-19).

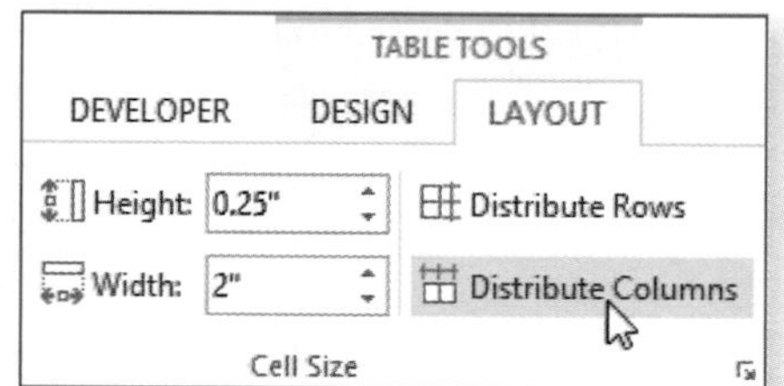

4-19 Distribute rows and columns

- ***Distribute Rows:*** This feature evenly distributes the rows based on the height of the existing table, making all rows a consistent height.
- ***Distribute Columns:*** This feature evenly distributes the columns based on the width of the existing table, making all columns the same width.

ANOTHER WAY

AutoFit and *Distribute* options are available from the context menu when a table is selected.

Text Alignment

In Chapter 1, you learned about paragraph alignment and how to left align, right align, center, or justify text. You learned how to change the vertical alignment of a page or section in Chapter 2. Similarly, when using tables, you have both horizontal and vertical alignment options. Text can be aligned vertically and horizontally within a cell and can be aligned independently of other cells. There are nine alignment options within the cell of a table. The following alignment options are in the *Alignment* group on the *Table Tools Layout* tab (Figure 4-20):

- *Align Top Left*
- *Align Top Center*
- *Align Top Right*
- *Align Center Left*
- *Align Center*
- *Align Center Right*
- *Align Bottom Left*
- *Align Bottom Center*
- *Align Bottom Right*

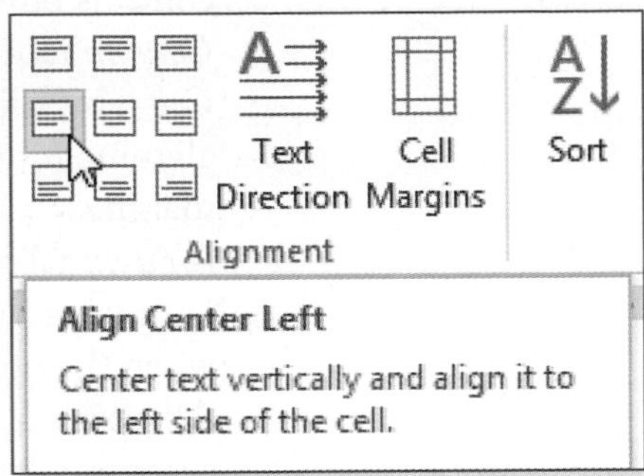

4-20 Text alignment options in a table

> **MORE INFO**
>
> For horizontal alignment, text in the table is usually aligned on the left and numbers are aligned on the right. If you increase row height, it's generally best to vertically center text within a cell.

Cell Margins

In addition to being able to change alignment in cells, you can also adjust ***cell margins***. Just like the margins on a Word document, the cells of a table have top, bottom, left, and right margins. The default cell margins are 0" top and bottom, and 0.08" left and right.

HOW TO: Change Cell Margins

1. To change the cell margins on the entire table, select the entire table. Cell margins can also be changed on individual cells.
2. Click the **Table Tools Layout** tab.
3. Click the **Cell Margins** button [*Alignment* group]. The *Table Options* dialog box opens (Figure 4-21).
4. Make the desired changes to the *Top, Bottom, Left,* and *Right* cell margins.
   - You can also add spacing between cells in the *Default cell spacing* area. This puts padding (space) around the outside of the cells.
   - If you don't want the size of your table to be automatically adjusted, deselect the **Automatically resize to fit contents** check box.
5. Click **OK** to apply the cell margin settings.

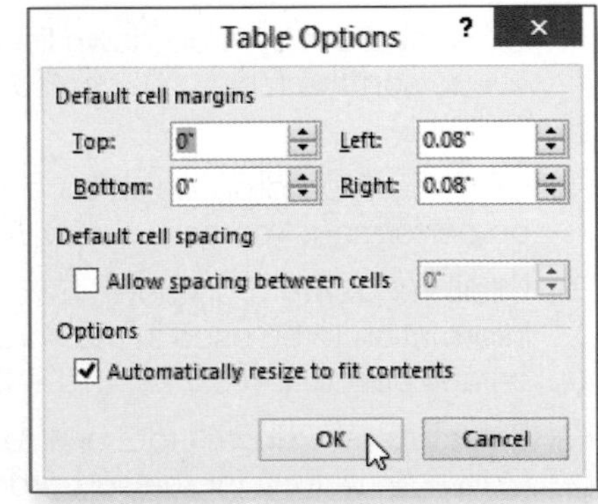

4-21 *Table Options* dialog box

Table Properties Dialog Box

The ***Table Properties*** dialog box consolidates some of table sizing and alignment options in one location. In the dialog box, there are separate tabs for *Table, Row, Column, Cell,* and *Alt Text.* To open the *Table Properties* dialog box, click the **Properties** button in the *Table* group on the *Table Tools Layout* tab (Figure 4-22). You can also open the *Table Properties* dialog box from the context menu.

- *Table* tab: Adjusts the size of the table, alignment, text wrapping, positioning, borders and shading, and cell margins.
- *Row* tab: Adjusts the height of rows and controls how rows break between pages.
- *Column* tab: Adjusts the width of columns.
- *Cell* tab: Adjusts the width of cells, vertical alignment of information in cells, and cell margins.
- *Alt Text* tab: Alternative text (Alt text) is an information tag that is displayed when the pointer is placed on the table. Alt text is also used with screen readers to accommodate those with visual impairments. Alt text is very common with web pages.

4-22 ***Table Properties*** **dialog box**

Sort Data in Tables

A very useful feature in Word is the ability to sort information within a table. You might want to arrange the text in the first column of a table alphabetically or sort numbers in descending order. When you use the ***Sort*** feature on a table, rows of information are rearranged according to how you specify the sort.

HOW TO: Sort Information in a Table

1. Place your insertion point somewhere in the table.
2. Select the **Table Tools Layout** tab.
3. Click the **Sort** button [*Data* group]. The entire table is selected and the *Sort* dialog box opens (Figure 4-23).
4. Click the **Sort by** drop-down list and select the column to use to sort the table. You can sort by any of the columns in the table.
5. Click the **Type** drop-down list and select the type of sort to be performed. You can sort by *Text, Number,* or *Date.*
6. Click the **Using** drop-down list and select the cell information to be used in the sort. *Paragraphs* is the default option and usually this is the only option available.
7. Select **Ascending** (A to Z or 1 to 10) or **Descending** (Z to A or 10 to 1) for the sort order.
8. If desired, you can add a second or third sort on different columns. Use the *Then by* options to add additional sorts.
9. If your table has a header row (title or column headings), click the **Header row** radio button to omit this row from the sort.
10. Click **OK** to perform the sort. Your table is sorted according to your settings.

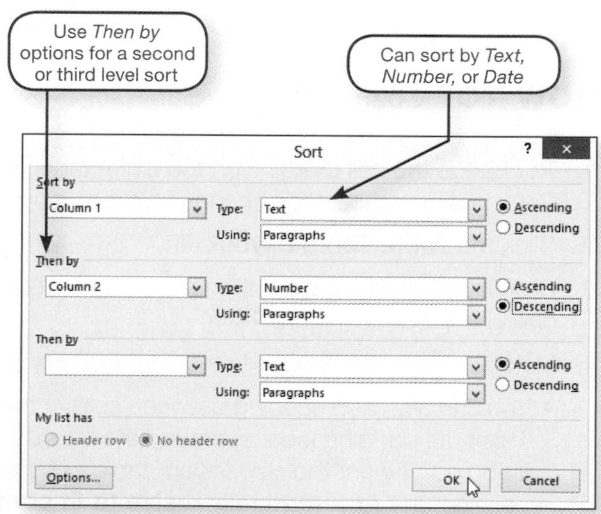

4-23 ***Sort*** **dialog box**

MORE INFO

If your table has both a title and column headings, select the rows of the table to be sorted before clicking the *Sort* button so that only the data in the table is sorted.

ANOTHER WAY

Manually sort rows using copy (**Ctrl+C**), cut (**Ctrl+X**), and paste (**Ctrl+V**), or the drag and drop method.

PAUSE & PRACTICE: WORD 4-1

For this Pause & Practice project, you begin modifying Emma Cavalli's brochure. You add a table to the end of this document and then modify the table.

File Needed: ***Brochure-04.docx***
Completed Project File Name: ***[your initials] PP W4-1.docx***

1. Open the ***Brochure-04*** document from your student data files.
2. Save this document as ***[your initials] PP W4-1***.
3. Move to the end of the document and insert a 3x7 table.
   a. Press **Ctrl+End** to move to the end of the document.
   b. Click the **Insert** tab.
   c. Click the **Table** button [*Tables* group] and select a 3x7 table using the table grid. The table is inserted into the document.
4. Type the information in the following table. Press **Tab** to move from one cell to the next cell in the row. Leave the third column blank.

Commitment	To the needs of the client	
Communication	Seek first to listen	
Integrity	Doing the right thing	
Customers	Always come first	
Teamwork	Work together for success	
Success	Results with integrity	
Creativity	Ideas before results	

5. Delete a column and insert rows.
   a. Place the insertion point in any cell in the last column and click the **Delete** button [*Table Tools Layout* tab, *Rows & Columns* group].
   b. Select **Delete Columns**.
   c. Place the insertion point in the second row and click the **Insert Below** button [*Table Tools Layout* tab, *Rows & Columns* group]. A blank row is inserted below the second row.

d. Type the following information in the third row:

Trust	Begins with communication

e. Click in the last cell of the table (bottom right cell) and press **Tab.** A new row is inserted at the bottom of the table.
f. Type the following information in the third row:

Win-Win	Is always the goal

6. *AutoFit* table and adjust column and row size.
   a. Place your insertion point somewhere in the table.
   b. Click the **AutoFit** button [*Table Tools Layout* tab, *Cell Size* group] and select **AutoFit Contents.** The column widths are adjusted to fit the contents of the table.
   c. Place the insertion point in the first column.
   d. Change the *Width* to **1.2"** [*Table Tool Layout* tab, *Cell Size* group]
   e. Place the insertion point in the second column.
   f. Change the *Width* to **2"**.
   g. Use the table selector handle to select the entire table.
   h. Click the **Properties** button [*Table Tool Layout* tab, *Table* group] to open the *Table Properties* dialog box (Figure 4-24).
   i. Click the **Row** tab and check the **Specify height** check box.
   j. Type .25 in the *Specify height* field and select **Exactly** in the *Row height is* drop-down list.
   k. Click **OK** to close the *Tables Properties* dialog box and apply these settings.

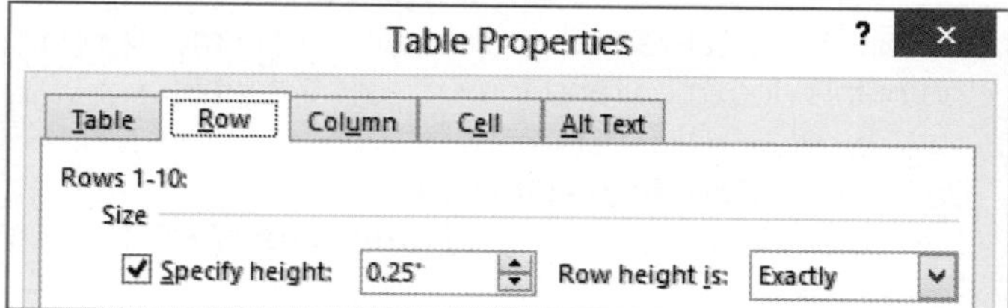

4-24 Change row height on the selected table

7. Insert a row and merge cells.
   a. Click anywhere in the table so the entire table is no longer selected.
   b. Select the first row of the table, select **Insert** on the mini toolbar, and click **Insert Above.** A new row is inserted at the top of the table.
   c. With the first row selected, click the **Merge Cells** button [*Table Tools Layout* tab, *Merge* group]. The cells in the first row are merged into one cell.
   d. Type The Placer Hills Belief System in the merged first row.

8. Sort the table by text in the first column.
   a. Select the **second through tenth (last) rows** of the table.
   b. Click the **Sort** button [*Table Tools Layout* tab, *Data* group]. The *Sort* dialog box opens (Figure 4-25).
   c. Sort by **Column 1** in **Ascending** order. Leave *Type* as **Text** and *Using* as **Paragraphs**.
   d. Click **OK** to perform the sort. The rows below the title are sorted in ascending order.

4-25 Sort the table by the first column in ascending order

9. Change cell margins and text alignment.
   a. Select the entire table.
   b. Click the **Cell Margins** button [*Table Tools Layout* tab, *Alignment* group]. The *Table Options* dialog box opens (Figure 4-26).
   c. In the *Left* and *Right* cell margins, type .05.
   d. Select the **Automatically resize to fit contents** check box and press **OK**.
   e. With the table still selected, click the **Align Center Left** button (first button in the second row) [*Table Tools Layout* tab, *Alignment* group].
   f. Click in the first row of the table to deselect the table.
   g. Right-click the first row of the table.
   h. Click the **Center** button on the mini toolbar. The title is centered horizontally.

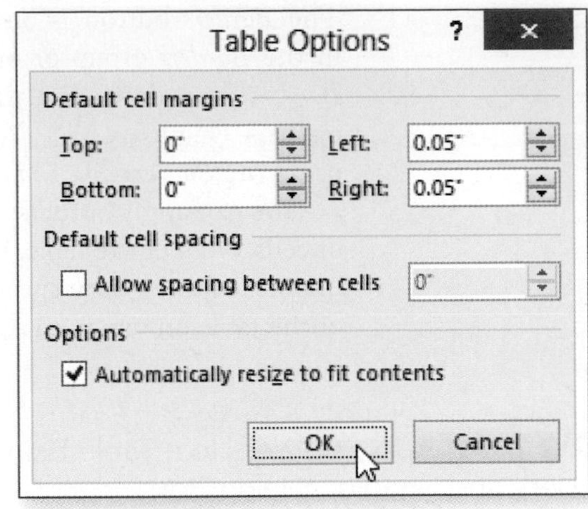

4-26 Change cell margins

10. Save and close this document (Figure 4-27).

The·Placer·Hills·Belief·System¤	
Commitment¤	To·the·needs·of·the·client¤
Communication¤	Seek·first·to·listen¤
Creativity¤	Ideas·before·results¤
Customers¤	Always·come·first¤
Integrity¤	Doing·the·right·thing¤
Success¤	Results·with·integrity¤
Teamwork¤	Work·together·for·success¤
Trust¤	Begins·with·communication¤
Win-Win¤	Is·always·the·goal¤

4-27 PP W4-1 completed (table only displayed)

SLO 4.3

Formatting and Editing Tables

In addition to the ability to adjust the structure of tables, Word provides you with many tools to enhance the overall appearance of tables. For example, you can add custom borders and shading and table styles to tables. You can also add formulas to tables and convert text into tables.

Table Tools Design Tab

Word provides you with two *Table Tools* tabs when you work with tables: *Design* and *Layout*. Both tabs are context-sensitive and are only displayed when the table or portion of the table is selected or when the insertion point is somewhere in the table. The ***Table Tools Design tab*** allows you to apply table styles and options (Figure 4-28). You can also draw tables using the tools on this tab.

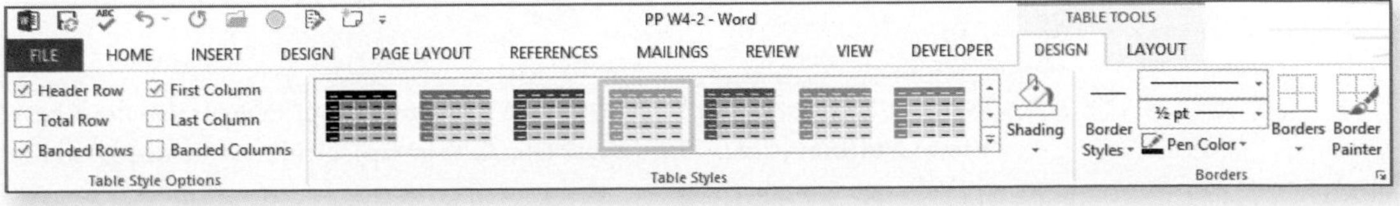

4-28 *Table Tools Design* tab

Table Borders

The *Borders* button is on the *Table Tools Design* tab in the *Borders* group or on the mini toolbar. On the *Borders* drop-down list, there are a variety of border options (Figure 4-29). You can also apply borders using the *Borders and Shading* dialog box.

You can apply borders to an individual cell, a group of cells, or an entire table. When applying borders, it is important to be very specific when selecting the area of the table on which to apply the borders.

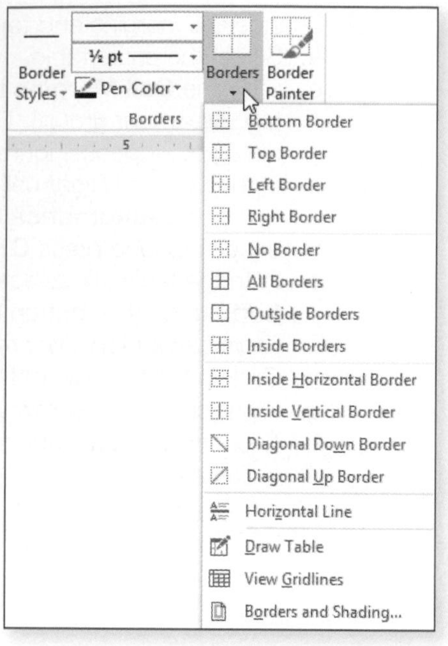

4-29 *Borders* drop-down list

HOW TO: Apply Borders to a Table Using the Borders and Shading Dialog Box

1. Select the entire table or the desired area of the table where you want borders.
2. Click the **Borders** button [*Table Tools Design* tab, *Borders* group].
3. Select **Borders and Shading** to open the *Borders and Shading* dialog box (Figure 4-30).
4. In the *Apply to* area, select the portion of the table where you want to apply the border settings.
5. In the *Setting* area, select the border from the list of options.
   - You can remove all borders by selecting **None**.
6. Select the *Style* of the border from the list of options.
7. Choose the color of the border from the *Color* drop-down list.
8. Change the width of the border with the *Width* drop-down list.
9. In the *Preview* area, you can see how your borders will be applied to your table.
   - In the *Preview* area, you can also apply or deselect borders on specific areas of your table.
   - You can click the buttons in the *Preview* area or click the displayed borders to turn borders on or off.
10. Click **OK** to apply the border settings and close the *Borders and Shading* dialog box.

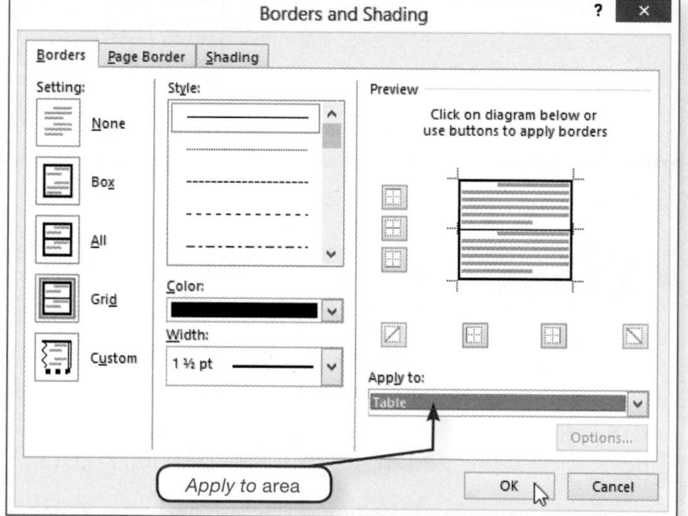

4-30 *Borders and Shading* dialog box

> **MORE INFO**
>
> Without borders, it is difficult to see the structure of your table. If you don't have borders, click **View Gridlines** [*Table Tools Layout* tab, *Table* group]. Gridlines are displayed in the document only; they do not print.

Table Shading

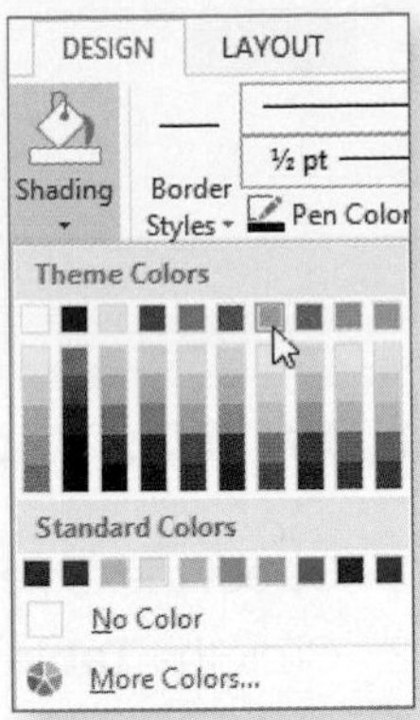

4-31 Table *Shading* options

Like table borders, you can apply shading to specific cells or to an entire table. In the *Shading* drop-down list in the *Table Styles* group on the *Table Tools Design* tab, you can choose from *Theme Colors* or *Standard Colors* (Figure 4-31). Theme colors change depending on the theme of your document. You can choose a custom color by selecting **More Colors**, which opens the *Colors* dialog box. You can also remove shading by selecting **No Color**.

You can also apply, change, or remove shading with the *Shading* tab in the *Borders and Shading* dialog box.

ANOTHER WAY

Apply borders and shading from the mini toolbar by right-clicking the table or a portion of the table.

Table Styles

Table Styles are built-in styles that you can apply to your tables. These table styles include a variety of borders, shading, alignment, and formatting options. Word provides a wide variety of built-in table styles in the *Table Styles* group on the *Table Tools Design* tab. Click the **More** button on the bottom right to display the *Table Styles* gallery (Figure 4-32).

After you have applied a table style to a table, you can still customize all aspects of the table. You can also remove all formatting of a table by selecting the **Clear** option at the bottom of the *Table Styles* gallery.

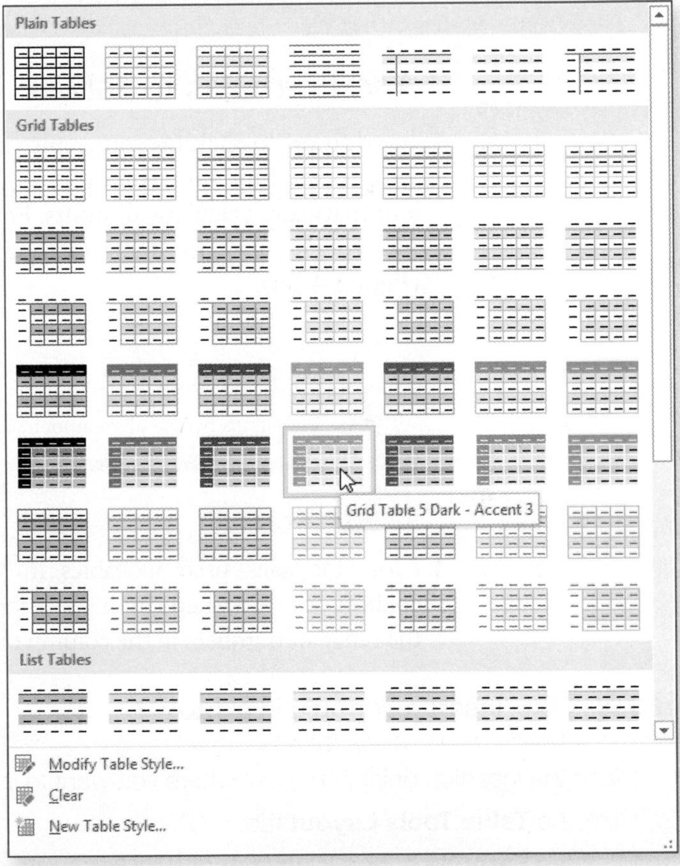

4-32 *Table Styles* gallery

Table Style Options

Word offers a variety of ***Table Style Options*** to customize tables (Figure 4-33). For example, many tables have a header row or column, or a total or last row, where you might want to apply special formatting for emphasis. When any of these options is selected, Word includes special formatting when a table style is applied. Select your table style options before applying a table style.

☑ Header Row ☑ First Column
☐ Total Row ☐ Last Column
☑ Banded Rows ☐ Banded Columns
Table Style Options

4-33 *Table Style Options* group

> **MORE INFO**
>
> With ***Banded Rows***, every other row is shaded. You can also apply ***Banded Columns*** in the *Table Style Options* group.

HOW TO: Apply a Table Style and Options

1. Select the table on which to apply a table style.
2. Click the **Table Tools Design** tab.
3. Select the options you want to apply to the table [*Table Style Options* group].
   - Consider the content of your table when deciding which table style options to choose.
   - When you select or deselect table style options, the thumbnails of the table styles in the *Table Styles* gallery change to reflect the options you have chosen.
4. Click the **More** button to display the *Table Styles* gallery.
   - You can scroll down in the *Table Styles* gallery to view more table styles.
5. Choose a table style. Word applies the style and options to your table.

Add Formulas to Tables

In addition to making your tables more attractive and easier to read with formatting and style options, you can add ***formulas*** to tables to automatically calculate amounts. For example, you can add a formula in a total row of the table to total the numbers in the rows above (Figure 4-34).

Formula that adds the numbers above

Placer·Hills·Real·Estate↵ Monthly·Home·Sales¤	
Week·1¤	15¤
Week·2¤	24¤
Week·3¤	19¤
Week·4¤	28¤
Total¤	86¤

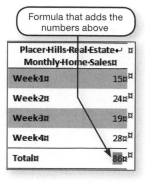

4-34 Formula in a table

> **MORE INFO**
>
> Remember, it's best to align amount figures on the right in a table.

Insert a Formula

Most formulas used in tables in Word are simple formulas that calculate numbers in a column or row. When you insert a formula, Word, by default, inserts the ***SUM*** formula and adds the range of numbers in the column or row. Word also allows you to insert more complex formulas.

HOW TO: Insert a Formula in a Table

1. Place the insertion point in the cell where you want to insert the formula.
2. Click the **Table Tools Layout** tab.
3. Click the **Formula** button [*Data* group]. The *Formula* dialog box opens (Figure 4-35).
4. The formula appears in the *Formula* box.
   - You can select different formula functions from the *Paste function* drop-down list.
5. In the *Number format* area, select number format from the drop-down list.
6. Click **OK** to insert the formula.

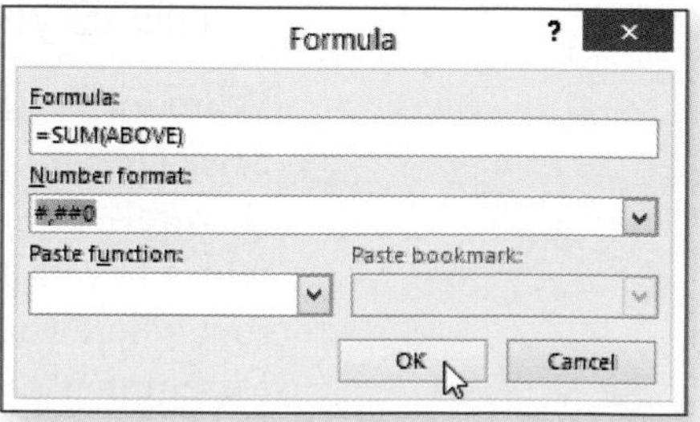

4-35 *Formula* dialog box

Update a Formula

A formula automatically adds values in a table, and you can automatically update it if any of the values change. There are two ways to update a formula:

- Right-click the formula and select **Update Field**.
- Select the formula and press the **F9** function key.

Convert Text into a Table

You will not always be creating a table from scratch. Many times you want to create a table from existing text. For example, you might want to convert information that is arranged into a table using tabs, or you might want to convert a table into text. Word provides you with options to ***convert text to a table*** or ***convert a table to text***.

When converting text into a table, the selected text must be separated by tabs, commas, paragraph breaks, or other characters. Word uses these characters to separate text into individual cells in the table.

HOW TO: Convert Text to a Table

1. Select the text to be converted to a table.
2. Click the **Insert** tab.
3. Click **Tables** [*Tables* group] and select **Convert Text to Table**. The *Convert Text to Table* dialog box opens (Figure 4-36).
4. In the *Table size* area, make desired changes to the number of columns or rows.
   - Word automatically detects the size of the table you need.
   - You might not be able to change one or both of the values, depending on the text you selected.
5. In the *AutoFit behavior* area, select an *AutoFit* option. The default setting is *Fixed column width.*
6. In the *Separate text at* area, select how you want Word to separate columns and rows.
   - Word automatically picks an option based on the text you have selected.
7. Click **OK** to convert the text to a table.

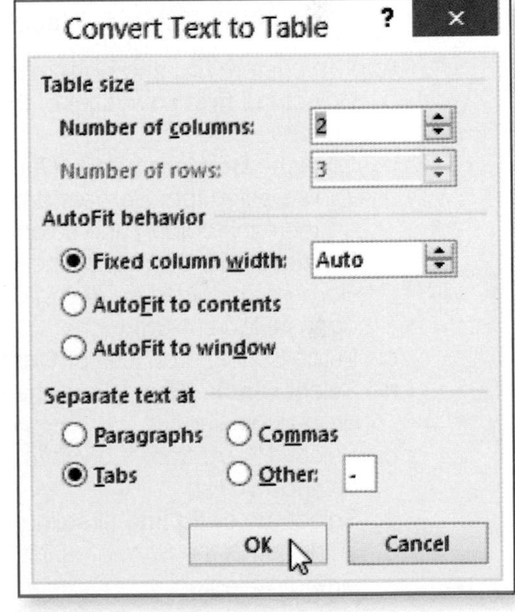

4-36 ***Convert Text to Table*** **dialog box**

> **MORE INFO**
>
> To convert a table to text, click the **Convert to Text** button [*Table Tool Layout* tab, *Data* group] to open the *Convert Table to Text* dialog box.

PAUSE & PRACTICE: WORD 4-2

For this Pause & Practice project, you continue to modify Emma's brochure. You apply a table style and table style options to the table you created in the previous Pause & Practice project. You also convert text to a table and apply borders and shading.

File Needed: ***[your initials] PP W4-1.docx***
Completed Project File Name: ***[your initials] PP W4-2.docx***

1. Open the ***[your initials] PP W4-1*** file you created in *Pause & Practice 4-1.*
2. Save this document as ***[your initials] PP W4-2***.
3. Apply table style options and a table style.
   a. Select the table at the end of the document.
   b. Click the **Table Tools Design** tab.
   c. Select **Header Row**, **Banded Rows**, and **First Column** [*Table Style Options* group] if they are not already selected. The other check boxes should not be selected.
   d. Click the **More** button in the *Table Styles* group to open the *Table Styles* gallery.
   e. Select the **Grid Table 5 Dark – Accent 3** style (Figure 4-37). The style is applied to the table.

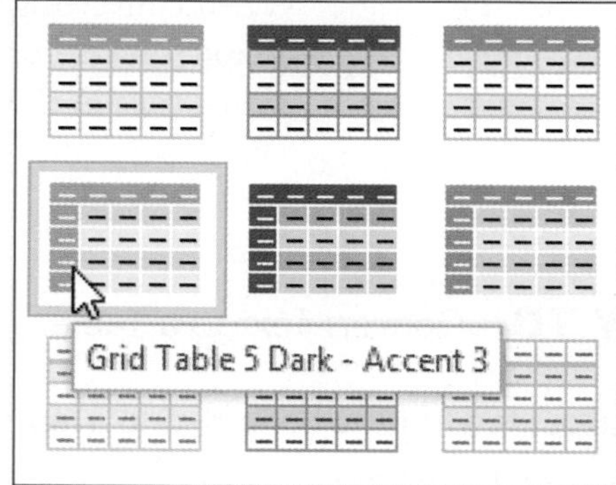

4-37 Select table style

4. Apply a custom top and bottom border to the table.
   a. Select the **first row** (title) of the table.
   b. Click the **Borders** button [*Table Tools Design* tab, *Borders* group or on the mini toolbar] and select **Borders and Shading.** The *Borders and Shading* dialog box opens (Figure 4-38).
   c. In the *Setting* area, select **Custom.**
   d. Select **Black**, **Text 1** from the *Color* drop-down list.
   e. Select **1½ pt.** from the *Width* drop-down list.
   f. Select the **solid line** (first line style in the list) in the *Style* area if it is not already selected.
   g. In the *Preview* area, click the **top boundary** of the cell to add a top border.

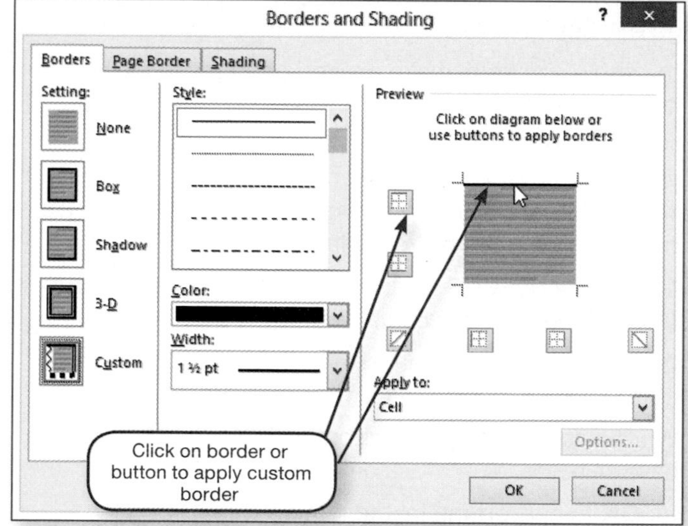

4-38 Apply custom borders

   h. Click **OK** to close the dialog box and add the border.
   i. Select the **bottom row** of the table.
   j. Open the *Borders and Shading* dialog box and apply the same custom border to the bottom of the selected row (**Black**, **1½ pt.**, **solid line**).
   k. Click **OK** to add the border and close the dialog box.
5. Vertically align text in cells.
   a. Select the entire table and click the **Properties** button [*Table Tools Layout* tab, *Table* group] to open the *Table Properties* dialog box.

b. Click the **Cell** tab and select **Center** in the *Vertical alignment* area.
c. Click **OK** to close the dialog box.

6. Make formatting changes to the text in the table.
   a. Select the first row.
   b. Open the *Font* dialog box, change *Size* to **12** and *Font color* to **Black**, **Text 1**, and check **All caps** in the *Effects* area.
   c. Click **OK** to close the *Font* dialog box.
   d. Select the first column, not including the title.
   e. Open the *Font* dialog box and check **Small caps** in the *Effects* area.
   f. Click **OK** to close the *Font* dialog box.

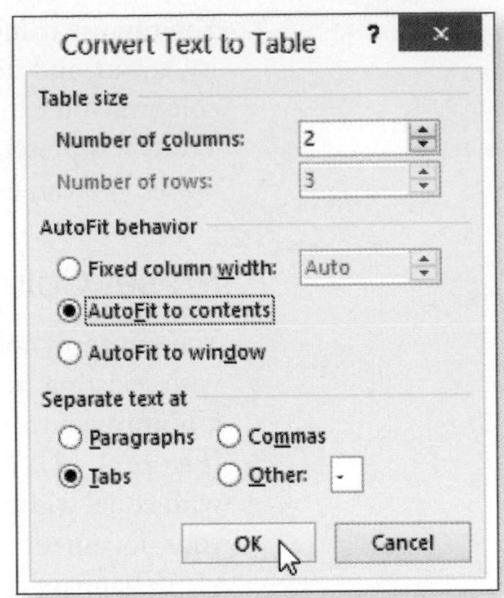

4-39 ***Convert Text to Table*** **dialog box**

7. Convert text to a table.
   a. On the first page, select the three lines of text after "Realtor Consultant" ("Phone" through "www.phre.com/ecavalli"). Be sure to include the paragraph mark at the end of the third line.
   b. Click the **Insert** tab.
   c. Click the **Table** button [*Tables* group] and select **Convert Text to Table**. The *Convert Text to Table* dialog box opens (Figure 4-39).
   d. Change the *AutoFit behavior* to **AutoFit to contents.**
   e. Click **OK** to convert selected text to a table.

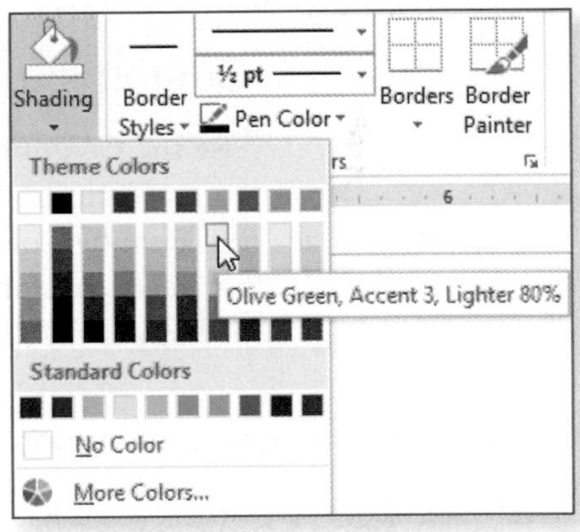

4-40 Select ***Shading*** **color**

8. Remove all borders and add custom borders and shading.
   a. With the table selected, click the **Borders** drop-down arrow [*Table Tools Design* tab, *Borders* group].
   b. Select **No Border** to remove all borders.
   c. With the table still selected, click the **Borders** drop-down arrow and select **Top Border.**
   d. With the table still selected, click the **Borders** drop-down arrow and select **Bottom Border**.
   e. With the table still selected, click the **Shading** drop-down arrow [*Table Tools Design* tab, *Table Styles* group] and select **Olive Green, Accent 3, Lighter 80%** (Figure 4-40).

9. Save and close the document (Figure 4-41).

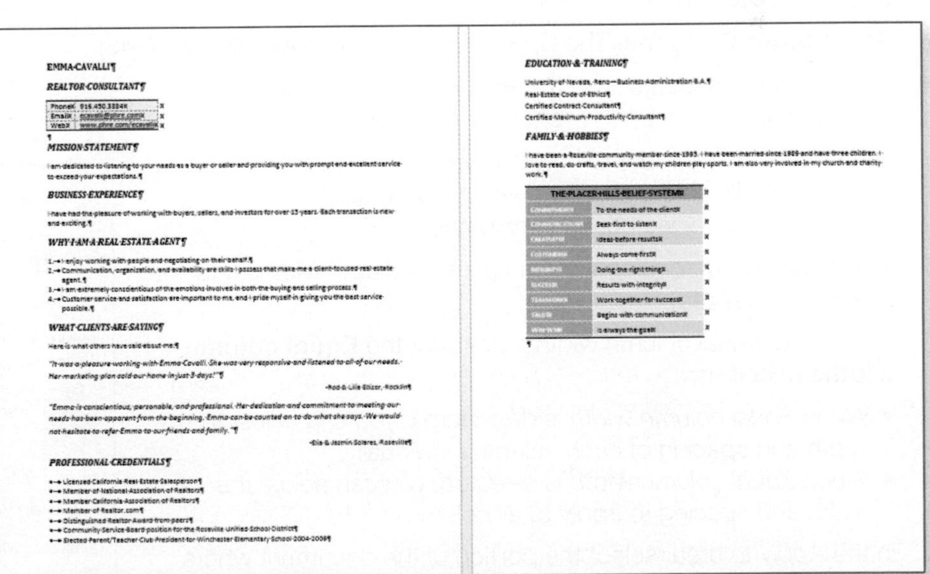

EMMA CAVALLI

REALTOR CONSULTANT

Phone	916.450.3334
Email	ecavalli@phre.com
Web	www.phre.com/ecavalli

MISSION STATEMENT

I am dedicated to listening to your needs as a buyer or seller and providing you with prompt and excellent service to exceed your expectations.

BUSINESS EXPERIENCE

I have had the pleasure of working with buyers, sellers, and investors for over 15 years. Each transaction is new and exciting.

WHY I AM A REAL ESTATE AGENT

1. I enjoy working with people and negotiating on their behalf.
2. Communication, organization, and availability are skills I possess that make me a client-focused real estate agent.
3. I am extremely conscientious of the emotions involved in both the buying and selling process.
4. Customer service and satisfaction are important to me, and I pride myself in giving you the best service possible.

WHAT CLIENTS ARE SAYING

Here is what others have said about me:

"It was a pleasure working with Emma Cavalli. She was very responsive and listened to all of our needs. Her marketing plan sold our home in just 3 days!"

–Rod & Lilia Ellisor, Rocklin

"Emma is conscientious, personable, and professional. Her dedication and commitment to meeting our needs has been apparent from the beginning. Emma can be counted on to do what she says. We would not hesitate to refer Emma to our friends and family."

–Elia & Jazmin Solares, Roseville

PROFESSIONAL CREDENTIALS

- Licensed California Real Estate Salesperson
- Member of National Association of Realtors
- Member California Association of Realtors
- Member of Realtor.com
- Distinguished Realtor Award from peers
- Community Service Board position for the Roseville Unified School District
- Elected Parent/Teacher Club President for Winchester Elementary School 2004-2006

EDUCATION & TRAINING

University of Nevada, Reno—Business Administration B.A.
Real Estate Code of Ethics
Certified Contract Consultant
Certified Maximum Productivity Consultant

FAMILY & HOBBIES

I have been a Roseville community member since 1995. I have been married since 1989 and have three children. I love to read, do crafts, travel, and watch my children play sports. I am also very involved in my church and charity work.

THE PLACER HILLS BELIEF SYSTEM	
[illegible]	To the needs of the client
[illegible]	Seek first to listen
[illegible]	Ideas before results
[illegible]	Always come first
[illegible]	Doing the right thing
[illegible]	Results with integrity
[illegible]	Work together for success
[illegible]	Begins with communication
[illegible]	Is always the goal

4-41 PP W4-2 completed

SLO 4.4

Using Columns

You can use columns to arrange text and tables into narrower widths and improve the readability, layout, and design of a document. In a normal Word document, text is arranged in a single column. You can apply columns to an entire document or to selected sections of a document. Word has preset column setting options or you can customize column settings to meet your needs. You can use column and section breaks to control column endings and balance columns.

Preset Column Settings

You can apply column settings to a new document or to a document with existing text. To apply preset column settings, click the **Columns** button on the *Page Layout* tab in the *Page Setup* group (Figure 4-42). The *Two* and *Three* column options set columns with equal width, while the *Left* and *Right* column options arrange your document in two columns of unequal width.

When you apply columns to a document, the column settings are applied only to that section of the document. If there are no section breaks, columns are applied to the entire document.

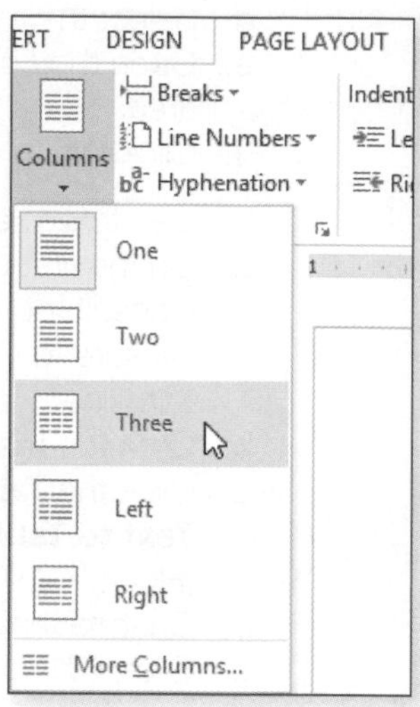

4-42 Preset column options

Customize Columns

Use the ***Columns dialog box*** to apply column settings or customize current column settings. In the *Columns* dialog box you can select the number of columns, adjust the column width and space between columns, insert a line between columns, and select the portion of the document where the column settings will be applied.

HOW TO: Customize Columns Using the Columns Dialog Box

1. Click the **Page Layout** tab.
2. Click the **Columns** button [*Page Setup* group].
3. Select **More Columns**. The *Columns* dialog box opens (Figure 4-43).
4. Select column settings from the *Presets* options or *Number of columns* box.
   - Based on the number of columns you choose, Word automatically sets the column width and spacing.
   - The default spacing between columns is 0.5".
5. In the *Width and spacing* area, adjust the column widths and spacing as desired.
6. To apply unequal column widths, deselect the **Equal column widths** check box.
   - When *Equal column width* is deselected, you can adjust the width and spacing of each column individually.
   - When *Equal column width* is selected, you can adjust the width and spacing to apply to all columns.
7. In the *Apply to* area, select the portion of the document where you want to apply column settings.
   - You can apply column settings to the *Whole document* or from *This point forward.*

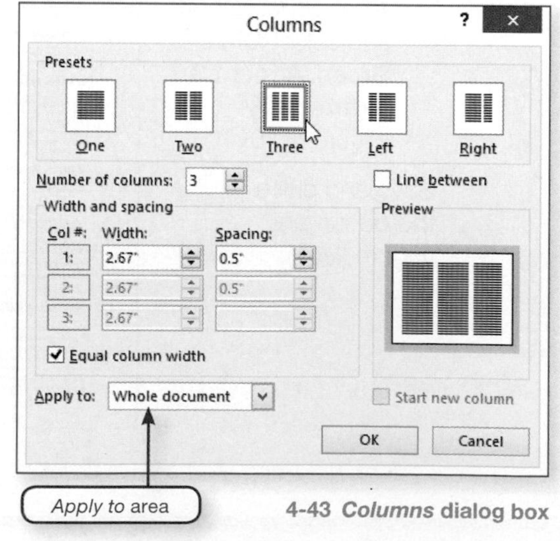

4-43 *Columns* dialog box

- When *This point forward* is selected, Word inserts a continuous section break at the insertion point in the document and applies column settings to the text after the continuous section break.
- If you select text, you will be given the option to apply column settings to *Selected text* in the *Apply to* area.

8. Check the **Line between** check box to insert a vertical line between columns.
9. The *Preview* area displays a thumbnail of how your columns will appear.
10. Click **OK** to apply column settings.

Convert Text to Columns

You can apply column settings to the *whole document*, from *this point forward*, or to *selected text*. Depending on the portion of the document where you are applying column settings, Word applies the column settings and inserts any needed section breaks. These options are in the *Columns* dialog box in the *Apply to* area. The following table describes how Word handles each of the options.

Apply to Column Options

Columns Applied to	Actions
Whole Document	Word applies column settings to the entire document. No section breaks are added.
This point forward	Word inserts a continuous section break before the insertion point in the document and applies the column setting beginning at the insertion point, which becomes a new section of the document.
Selected text	When text is selected and column settings are applied, Word inserts a continuous section break before and after the selected text. The column settings apply only to that section.

Use Column Breaks

Column widths control the horizontal text wrapping, while the top and bottom margins or section breaks control where a column ends and wraps to the next column. You can insert ***column breaks*** to end a column and push subsequent text to the next column.

HOW TO: Insert a Column Break

1. Place the insertion point where you want the column to end or the next column to begin.
2. Click the **Page Layout** tab.
3. Click the **Breaks** button [*Page Layout* group].
4. Select **Column** in the *Page Breaks* options (Figure 4-44).
   - You see a column break indicator when *Show/Hide* is turned on (Figure 4-45).

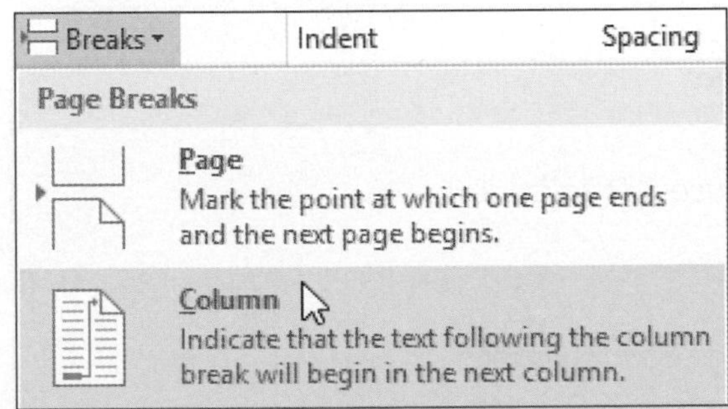

4-44 Insert column break

WHY·I·AM·A·REAL·ESTATE·AGENT¶

1.→ I·enjoy·working·with·people·and· negotiating·on·their·behalf.¶
2.→ Communication,·organization,·and· availability·are·skills·I·possess·that·make· me·a·client-focused·real·estate·agent.¶
3.→ I·am·extremely·conscientious·of·the· emotions·involved·in·both·the·buying·and· selling·process.¶
4.→ Customer·service·and·satisfaction·are· important·to·me,·and·I·pride·myself·in· giving·you·the·best·service·possible.¶

.......................Column Break.......................

4-45 Column break inserted

ANOTHER WAY

Ctrl+Shift+Enter inserts a column break.

MORE INFO

Always turn on *Show/Hide* (**Ctrl+Shift+8**) when using page, section, or column breaks to help you see these elements in your document.

Balance Columns

Column breaks are one way to balance columns on a page. Another way is to use a ***continuous section break***. To make columns approximately equal in length on a page, insert a continuous section break at the end of the last column on the page. Word automatically adjusts your columns so they are about the same length.

HOW TO: Balance Columns Using a Continuous Section Break

1. Place the insertion point at the end of the last column in your document.
2. Click the **Page Layout** tab.
3. Click the **Breaks** button [*Page Layout* group].
4. Select **Continuous** in the *Section Breaks* options.
   - You see a continuous section break indicator when *Show/Hide* is turned on.

MORE INFO

Balancing columns using a continuous section break works only if there are no other column breaks controlling column endings on that page.

PAUSE & PRACTICE: WORD 4-3

For this Pause & Practice project, you apply columns to Emma's brochure. With the use of columns and column breaks, you attractively arrange the columns and make the document fit on one page.

File Needed: ***[your initials] PP W4-2.docx***
Completed Project File Name: ***[your initials] PP W4-3.docx***

1. Open the ***[your initials] PP W4-2*** file you saved in *Pause & Practice 4-2.*
2. Save this document as ***[your initials] PP W4-3***.
3. Change the page orientation and margins.
   a. Click the **Orientation** button [*Page Layout* tab, *Page Setup* group].
   b. Select **Landscape**.

c. Click the **Margins** button and choose *Custom Margins*.
d. Change the *Top* margin to **1.2"**, and the *Bottom, Left,* and *Right* margins to **0.5"**.
e. Click **OK** to close the dialog box and apply the margin settings. If a dialog box opens informing you that the margins are outside the printable area, click **Ignore**.

4. Arrange the text in columns.
   a. Move to the top of the document.
   b. Click the **Columns** button [*Page Layout* tab, *Page Setup* group] and choose **Two**. The text is arranged into two columns.
5. Customize column settings using the *Columns* dialog box.
   a. Click the **Columns** button [*Page Layout* tab, *Page Setup* group] and choose **More Columns**. The *Columns* dialog box opens (Figure 4-46).
   b. In the *Presets* area, select **Three**.
   c. In the *Width and spacing* area, change the *Spacing* to **0.6"**.
   d. In the *Apply to* area, select **Whole document**.
   e. Click **OK** to apply custom column settings.

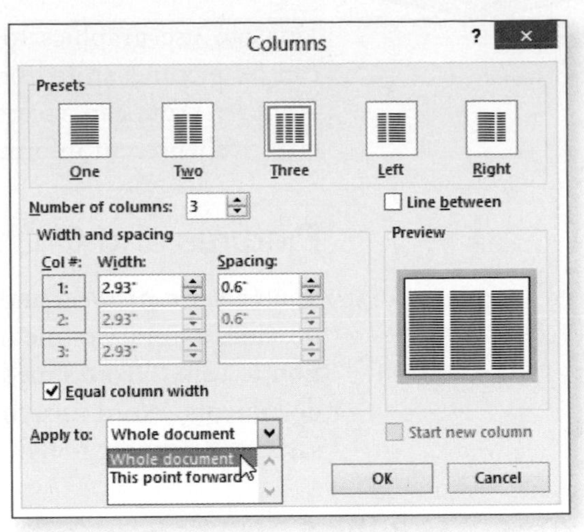

4-46 Customize column settings

6. Use column breaks to control column endings.
   a. Place the insertion point in front of "What Clients are Saying."
   b. Click the **Breaks** button [*Page Layout* tab, *Page Setup* group].
   c. Select **Column** in the *Page Breaks* options to insert a column break.
   d. Place the insertion point in front of "Education & Training."
   e. Press **Ctrl+Shift+Enter** to insert a column break.
7. Save and close the document (Figure 4-47).

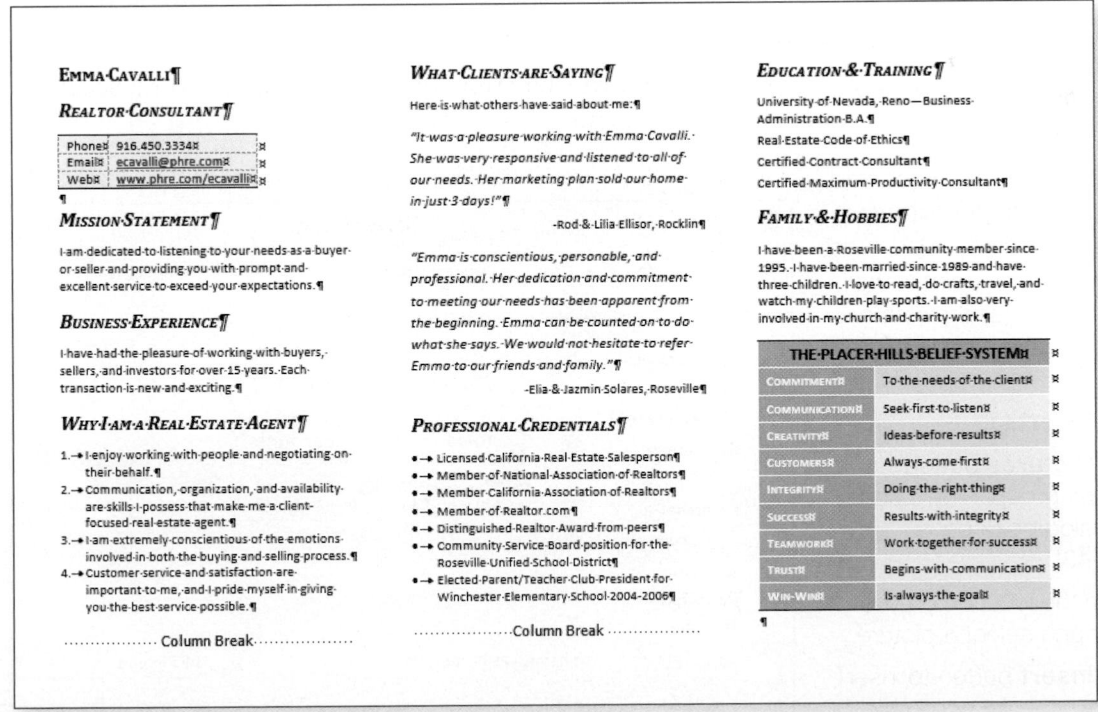

EMMA CAVALLI

REALTOR CONSULTANT

Phone	916.450.3334
Email	ecavalli@phre.com
Web	www.phre.com/ecavalli

MISSION STATEMENT

I am dedicated to listening to your needs as a buyer or seller and providing you with prompt and excellent service to exceed your expectations.

BUSINESS EXPERIENCE

I have had the pleasure of working with buyers, sellers, and investors for over 15 years. Each transaction is new and exciting.

WHY I AM A REAL ESTATE AGENT

1. I enjoy working with people and negotiating on their behalf.
2. Communication, organization, and availability are skills I possess that make me a client-focused real estate agent.
3. I am extremely conscientious of the emotions involved in both the buying and selling process.
4. Customer service and satisfaction are important to me, and I pride myself in giving you the best service possible.

.... Column Break ....

WHAT CLIENTS ARE SAYING

Here is what others have said about me:

"It was a pleasure working with Emma Cavalli. She was very responsive and listened to all of our needs. Her marketing plan sold our home in just 3 days!"

-Rod & Lilia Ellisor, Rocklin

"Emma is conscientious, personable, and professional. Her dedication and commitment to meeting our needs has been apparent from the beginning. Emma can be counted on to do what she says. We would not hesitate to refer Emma to our friends and family."

-Elia & Jazmin Solares, Roseville

PROFESSIONAL CREDENTIALS

- Licensed California Real Estate Salesperson
- Member of National Association of Realtors
- Member California Association of Realtors
- Member of Realtor.com
- Distinguished Realtor Award from peers
- Community Service Board position for the Roseville Unified School District
- Elected Parent/Teacher Club President for Winchester Elementary School 2004-2006

.... Column Break ....

EDUCATION & TRAINING

University of Nevada, Reno—Business Administration B.A.

Real Estate Code of Ethics

Certified Contract Consultant

Certified Maximum Productivity Consultant

FAMILY & HOBBIES

I have been a Roseville community member since 1995. I have been married since 1989 and have three children. I love to read, do crafts, travel, and watch my children play sports. I am also very involved in my church and charity work.

THE PLACER HILLS BELIEF SYSTEM	
COMMITMENT	To the needs of the client
COMMUNICATION	Seek first to listen
CREATIVITY	Ideas before results
CUSTOMERS	Always come first
INTEGRITY	Doing the right thing
SUCCESS	Results with integrity
TEAMWORK	Work together for success
TRUST	Begins with communication
WIN-WIN	Is always the goal

4-47 PP W4-3 completed

SLO 4.5

Working with Graphics

You can use graphics to visually present information and enhance a document. Graphics can be pictures stored on your computer, online pictures or clip art, shapes, *SmartArt,* and *WordArt.* You can insert and customize each of these to meet your specific needs and effectively present information visually.

Pictures and Online Pictures

You can use ***pictures*** and ***clip art*** to enhance your documents with a visual element. Word provides a library of media that includes illustrations, photographs, video, and audio. In addition to using Word's media library, you can also add your own pictures and graphics to Word documents. Word uses the term *picture* generically to refer to any type of visual image that is saved as a graphic file. Below is a table of common types of graphic formats.

Types of Graphics

Format	Full Name	Extension	Details
PNG	Portable Network Graphics	.png	Used with pictures and editing pictures. High-quality resolution.
JPEG	Joint Photographic Experts Group	.jpeg or .jpg	Relatively small file size. Many pictures are saved and distributed in JPEG format.
TIFF	Tagged Image File Format	.tiff	Used with high-quality digital photos and has a larger file size than JPEG or PNG.
GIF	Graphics Interchange Format	.gif	Used with graphics and clip art with fewer colors.
WMF	Windows Metafile	.wmf	Windows format used with many clip art and graphic images.
BMP	Windows Bitmap	.bmp	Proprietary Windows format used with many Microsoft clip art and graphic images.

Insert a Picture

You can use your own picture or a picture from the media library in Word. See the steps below to insert a picture into a document.

HOW TO: Insert a Picture

1. Place the insertion point in the document at the approximate area where you want the picture inserted.
2. Click the **Insert** tab.
3. Click the **Pictures** button [*Illustrations* group]. The *Insert Picture* dialog box opens (Figure 4-48).
4. Browse to the location on your computer and select a picture.
5. Click the **Insert** button to insert the picture and close the *Insert Picture* dialog box.

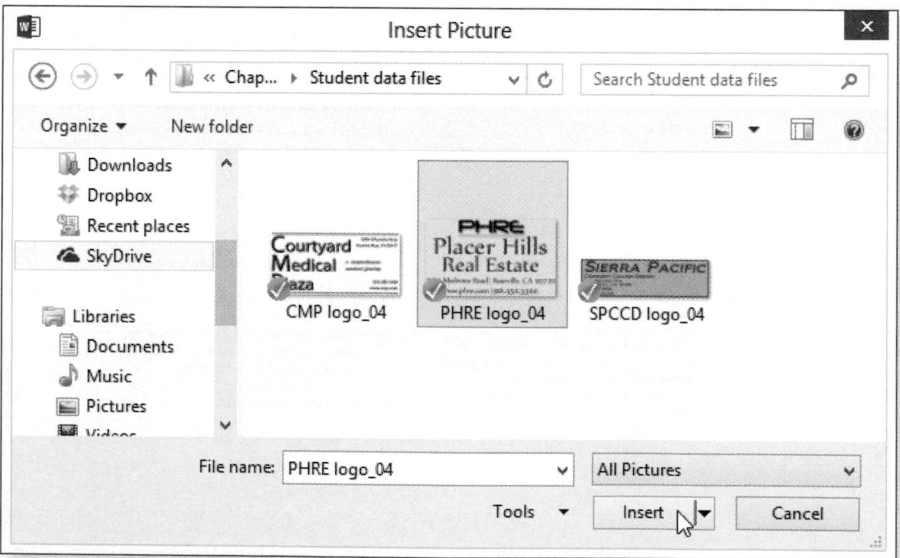

4-48 ***Insert Picture*** **dialog box**

You might find a picture on the Internet and want to use it in a document. You can either save the picture and insert it as explained above or copy the picture and paste it into your document. Press **Ctrl+C** to copy the picture and **Ctrl+V** to paste the picture.

Include pictures obtained from the web only if you have permission from the image owner to avoid copyright infringement. For academic purposes, you may include images if you reference their sources as you would any other research citation.

> **ANOTHER WAY**
>
> Use the context menu (right-click) to both copy the picture and paste it into a document.

Search for an Online Picture

Word provides a variety of clip art and picture choices in its royalty-free media library on Office.com. You can also search for images using ***Bing Image Search***. When using an image from *Bing Image Search*, make sure you have the permission of the image owner to avoid copyright infringement.

HOW TO: Search for and Insert Online Pictures

1. Place the insertion point in the document where you want the picture inserted.
2. Click the **Insert** tab.
3. Click the **Online Pictures** button [*Illustrations* group] to open the *Insert Pictures* dialog box.
4. Click in the *Office.com Clip Art* or *Bing Image Search* text box, type the keywords for the graphic you want to find, and press **Enter**. Thumbnails of the pictures appear in the list below (Figure 4-49).

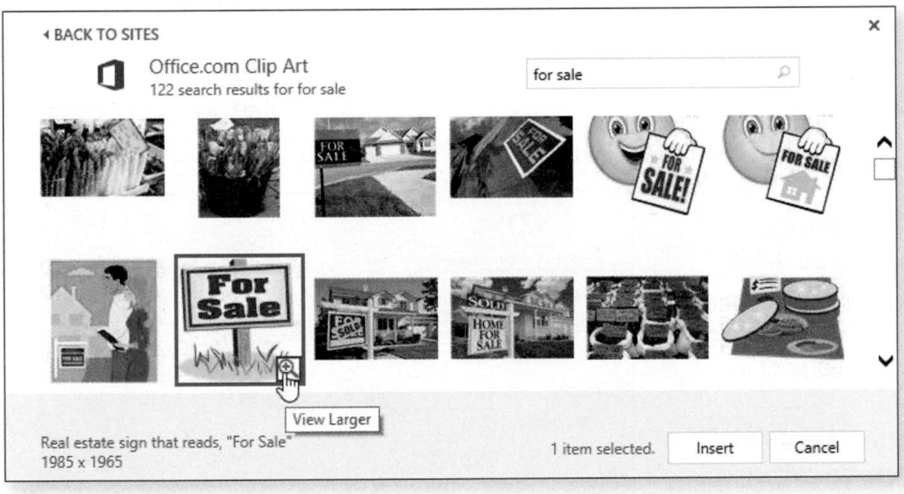

4-49 Insert graphic from the *Insert Pictures* dialog box

5. Select the picture to insert into your document.
   - Click the **View Larger** button in the bottom right corner of a graphic to view a larger picture.
   - Click the **X** in the upper right corner to close the larger image.
6. Click the **Insert** button to insert the picture into your document.

In the *Insert Pictures* dialog box, you are not limited to inserting clip art only. When you search for a picture, Word provides you with a list of pictures and clip art that match the keywords in your search.

Arrange Graphics within a Document

Once you have inserted an image into a document, you can adjust its size and arrange it in the document. Word provides you with a number of options to resize, align, and wrap text around graphics in your document.

Resize a Graphic

In most cases you will need to resize your graphic to fit properly in your document. You can do this a couple of different ways. You can drag the top, bottom, side, or corner handles to resize the graphic manually, or you can set a specific size for the graphic.

When you select (click) a graphic, ***sizing handles*** appear on each side and in each corner (Figure 4-50). To resize the graphic, click and hold one of the handles and drag in or out to decrease or increase the size of the graphic. Use the corner handles to keep the resized image proportional. If you use the side, top, or bottom handles to resize, the proportions of the image may become distorted. You can also resize the image to a specific size or to a percentage of its original size.

4-50 Resize graphic using the sizing handles

HOW TO: Resize an Image

1. Click the image to select it. The *Picture Tools Format* tab opens.
2. Click the **up** or **down** arrows in the *Height* or *Width* area [*Size* group] to increase or decrease the size (Figure 4-51). Resizing in this manner keeps the graphic proportional.
3. You can also resize the graphic in the *Layout* dialog box.
4. Click the **Size** launcher. The *Layout* dialog box opens with the *Size* tab displayed (Figure 4-52).
5. You can change the size of the graphic to a specific size in the *Height* and *Width* area. You can also scale the graphic to make it a percentage of its original size in the *Scale* area.
   - Keep the *Lock aspect ratio* box selected to prevent the graphic from becoming distorted in size.
   - In the *Original size* area, the original size of the graphic is displayed. You can reset the graphic to its original size by clicking the **Reset** button.
6. Click **OK** to resize the graphic and close the dialog box.

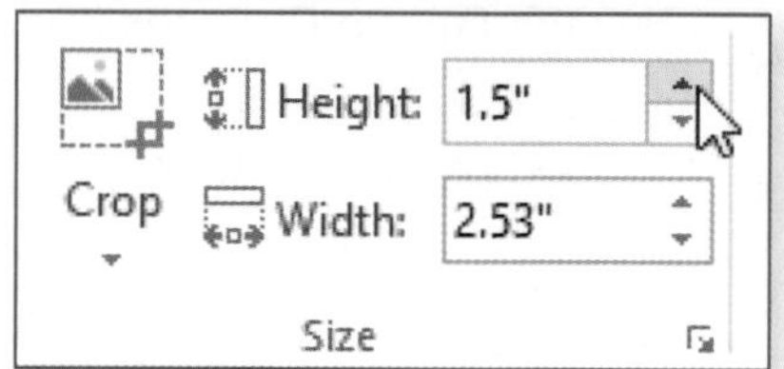

4-51 *Size* group on the *Picture Tools Format* tab

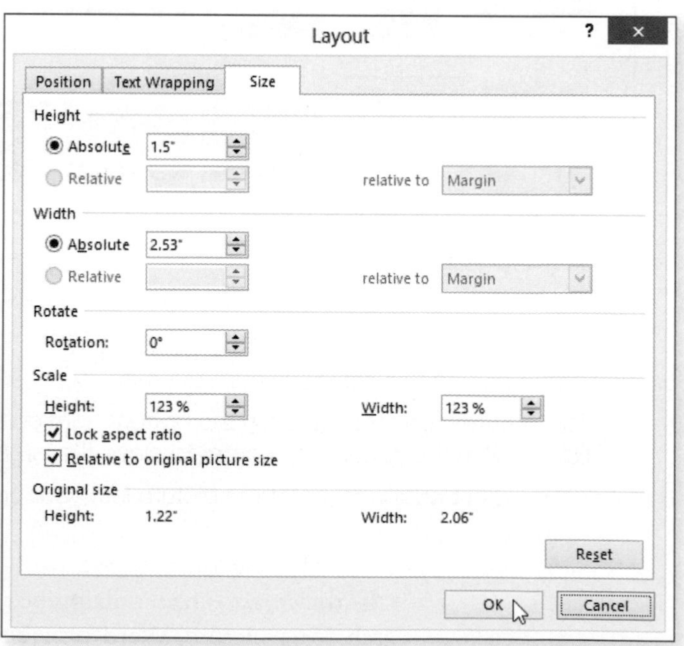

4-52 *Layout* dialog box

ANOTHER WAY

Open the *Layout* dialog box by right-clicking the graphic and selecting **Size and Position.**

Wrap Text around a Graphic

You can select how the text aligns or wraps around your graphic with a variety of ***text wrapping*** options. You can control how the text wraps around the graphic and choose to position the graphic in front of or behind the text.

HOW TO: Wrap Text

1. Click the graphic to select it.
2. Click the **Wrap Text** button [*Picture Tools Format* tab, *Arrange* group] (Figure 4-53).
3. Select a text wrapping option.
   - Select **More Layout Options** to open the *Layout* dialog box with the *Text Wrapping* tab displayed. Options in this dialog box allows you to customize text wrapping.
   - You can also click the **Layout Options** button to the right of a selected graphic and select a text wrapping option.

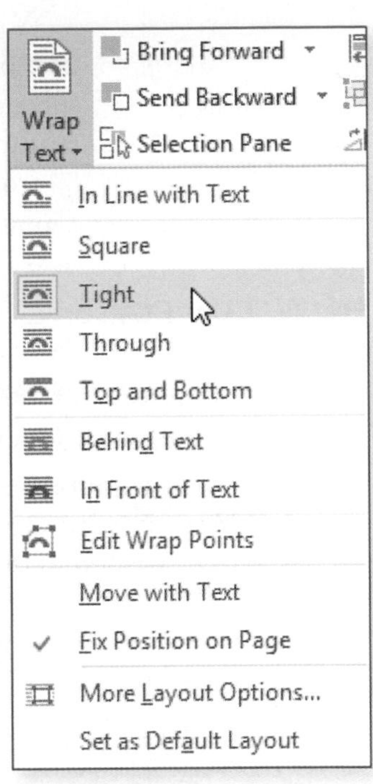

4-53 *Wrap Text* options

In the *Layout* dialog box on the *Text Wrapping* tab, there are additional options to control how text wraps around a graphic (Figure 4-54). In the ***Wrap text*** area, you can choose *Both sides, Left only, Right only,* or *Largest only.* In the ***Distance from text*** area, you can set a specific distance from the graphic to wrap text.

MORE INFO

In Line with Text is the default option when a graphic is inserted into a document.

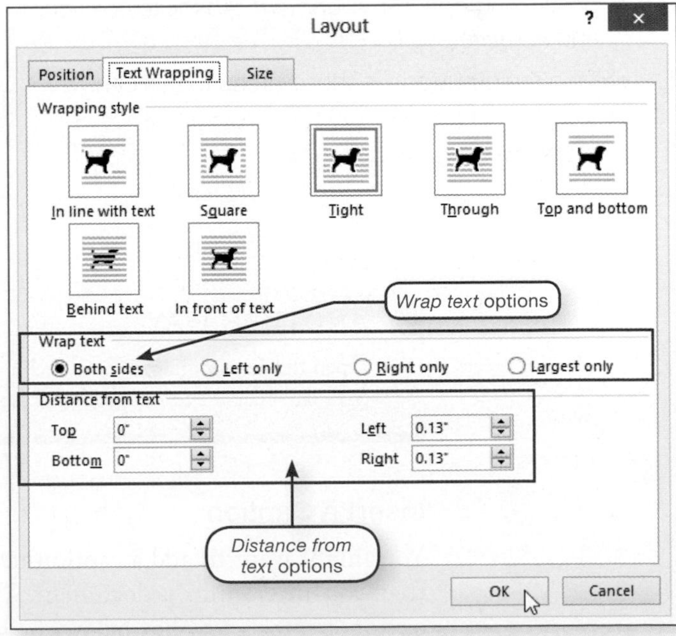

4-54 ***Text Wrapping*** **tab in the** ***Layout*** **dialog box**

Position a Graphic

In addition to adjusting the size of a graphic and specifying how text wraps around a graphic, you can also determine the position of the graphic in your document. You can align a graphic left, right, or center by selecting the graphic and clicking the **Align** button in the *Arrange* group on the *Picture Tools Format* tab (Figure 4-55).

> **ANOTHER WAY**
>
> The alignment buttons [*Home* tab, *Paragraph* group] also work to horizontally align a graphic, or you can use the following shortcuts:
>
> **Ctrl+L** to align left
> **Ctrl+E** to align center
> **Ctrl+R** to align right

Align ▾
Align Left
Align Center
Align Right
Align Top
Align Middle
Align Bottom
Distribute Horizontally
Distribute Vertically
Align to Page
✓ Align to Margin
Align Selected Objects
✓ Use Alignment Guides
View Gridlines
Grid Settings...

4-55 *Align* options

You can position a graphic in a document in a specific location by dragging the graphic to the desired location. You can also specify the location relative to the margins, page, or column. For example, you can position a graphic 5" from the left margin and 6" from the top margin of the document. The *Position* tab in the *Layout* dialog box offers customization options (see Figure 4-56).

HOW TO: Position a Graphic

1. Select the graphic to be positioned.
2. Click the **Picture Tools Format** tab.
3. Click the **Position** button [*Arrange* group] and select **More Layout Options**. The *Layout* dialog box opens with the *Position* tab selected (Figure 4-56).
4. In this dialog box, you can set both the horizontal and vertical alignment of the graphic.
   - In the *Horizontal* area, you have the following positioning options: *Alignment, Book layout, Absolute position,* and *Relative position.*
   - In the *Vertical* area, you have the following positioning options: *Alignment, Absolute position,* and *Relative position.*
5. Use the radio buttons in these areas to select how the graphic is aligned.
6. Click **OK** to close the dialog box.

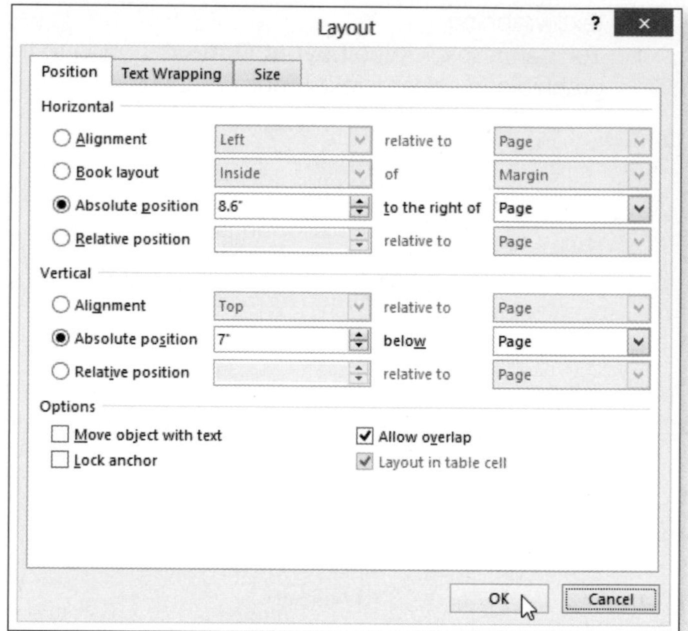

4-56 *Position* tab in the *Layout* dialog box

> **ANOTHER WAY**
>
> Open the *Layout* dialog box by clicking the **Size** launcher [*Picture Tools Format* tab].

Insert a Caption

You might want to add a caption to a picture or chart that you insert into a document. The *Insert Caption* option creates a text box below the graphic where you can enter a caption (Figure 4-57).

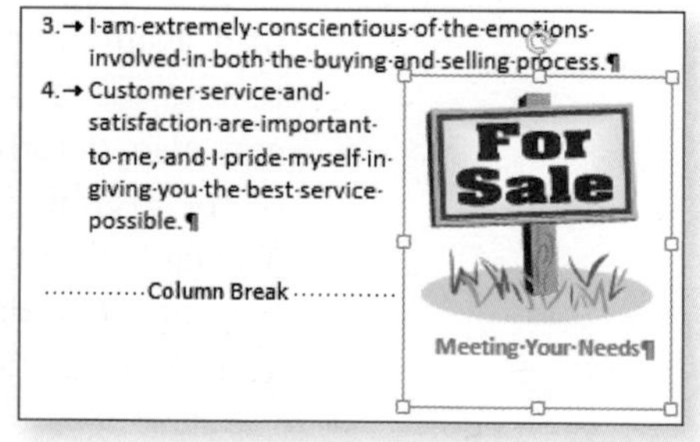

4-57 Graphic with caption below

HOW TO: Insert a Caption

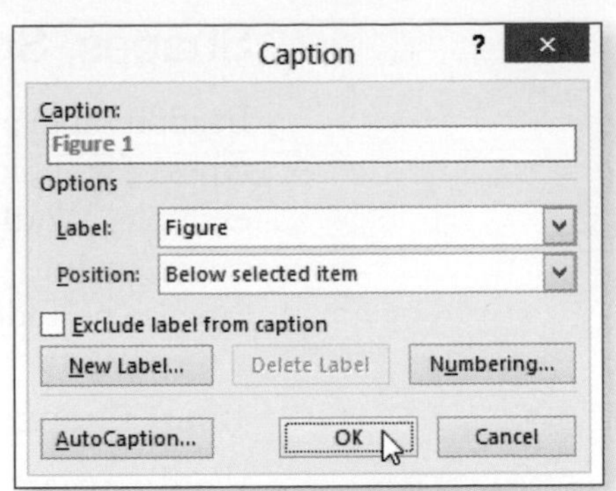

4-58 *Caption* dialog box

1. Select the graphic that needs a caption.
2. Right-click the graphic and select **Insert Caption** from the context menu. The *Caption* dialog box opens (Figure 4-58).
   - Word automatically creates a caption for the object you have selected.
   - In the *Caption* area, you can add a description after the label, but you cannot delete the label.
   - After a caption is added to a graphic, you can delete the label and number and customize the caption text.
3. In the *Label* area, choose *Equation, Figure,* or *Table.*
   - You can add a custom label by clicking the *New Label* button and typing a custom label.
   - You can remove the label (but not the number) by checking the *Exclude label from caption* option.
4. In the *Position* area, you can choose to place the caption below or above the selected item.
5. Click **OK** to insert the caption.
6. You can edit the caption in the text box after it is added to the graphic (Figure 4-59). You can also customize the size and color of the caption text and adjust the size and positioning of the text box.

4-59 Caption added to graphic

ANOTHER WAY

Insert a caption by clicking the **Insert Caption** button [*References* tab, *Captions* group].

Group Graphics Objects

When you work with graphics, you may want to ***group*** together related graphics and objects. For example, you might want to group a picture and caption. The advantage of doing this is that the grouped graphics become one object that can be resized and positioned together.

HOW TO: Group and Ungroup Graphics

1. Hold down the **Ctrl** key and click the graphics to be grouped (Figure 4-60).
2. Click the **Group** button [*Picture Tools Format* tab, *Arrange* group].
3. Select **Group**. The selected objects become one grouped object (Figure 4-61).
4. To ungroup grouped items, click the **Group** button in the *Arrange* group on the *Picture Tools Format* tab and select **Ungroup**.

4-60 Multiple objects selected

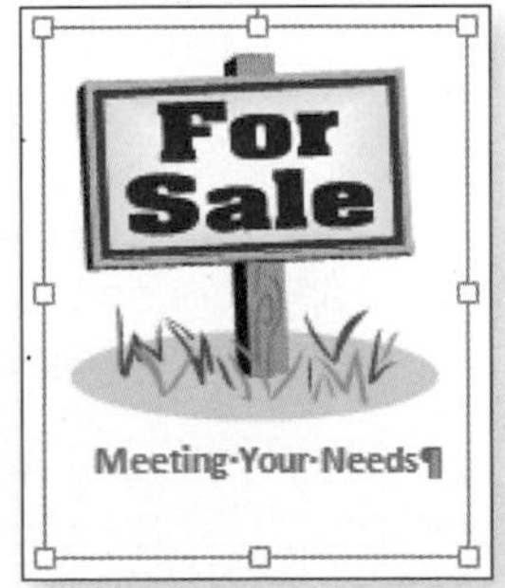

4-61 Grouped objects

ANOTHER WAY

Group and *Ungroup* options are available in the context menu by right-clicking a graphic.

Shapes, SmartArt, and WordArt

In addition to pictures and clip art, you can insert other types of graphic items into your Word documents. For example, Word provides a variety of ***shapes*** that you can insert into your document. ***SmartArt*** and ***WordArt*** can also be added to enhance documents.

Insert Shapes

Word's *Shapes* gallery groups shapes into categories (Figure 4-62). When you insert a shape or line into your document, you are actually drawing the object in your document. Once the object is drawn in your document, you can edit the size, position, alignment, and text wrapping of the object.

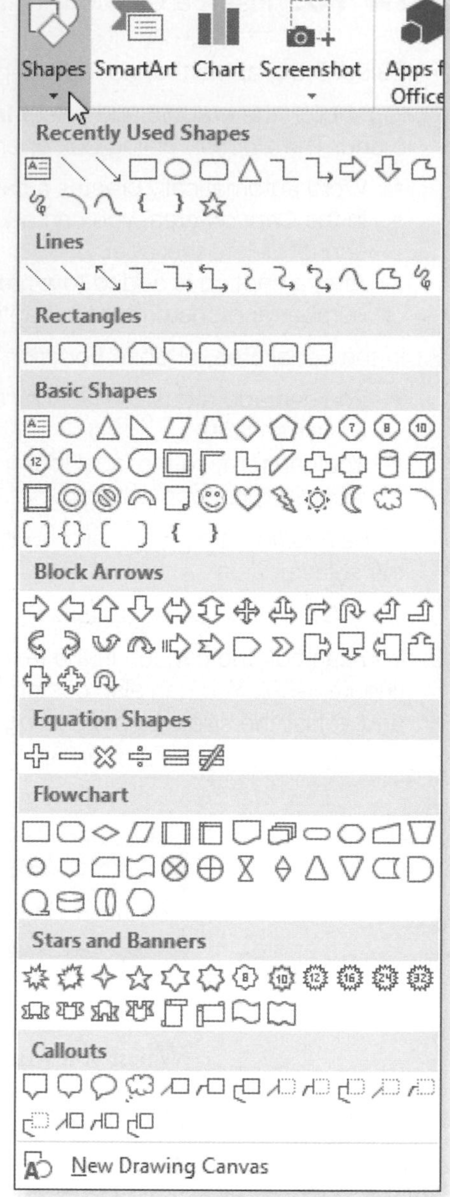

4-62 *Shapes* drop-down list

HOW TO: Insert a Shape

1. Click the **Insert** tab.
2. Click the **Shapes** button [*Illustrations* group] to display the gallery of shape options.
3. Select the shape you want to use. Your pointer becomes a drawing crosshair (large dark plus sign).
4. Click and drag to create the shape (Figure 4-63). When you release the pointer, the shape is inserted into the document.

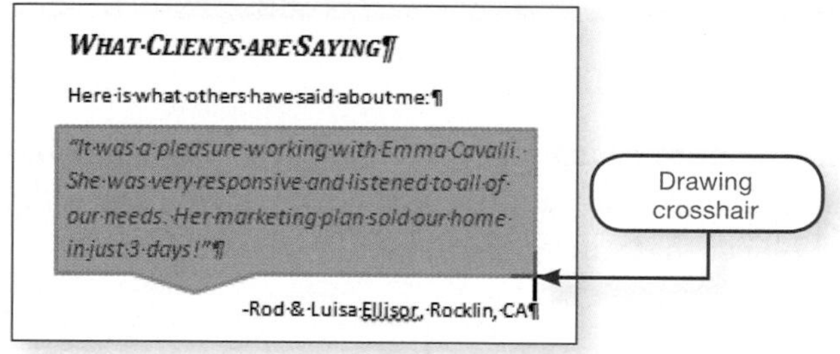

4-63 Draw a shape

- You don't have to be perfectly accurate when you create the shape because you can easily resize the shape after it is inserted.
- You can change the text wrapping on a shape so the shape appears on top of or behind the text, or you can have text wrap around a shape.

MORE INFO

If you want to create a perfect square or circle or to draw a straight line, hold down the **Shift** key while drawing.

Customize Shapes

Once a shape has been inserted into a document, you can move or resize it. Also, you can change the line size, color, and fill of the shapes. See Figure 4-64 and its callouts for examples of the available selection and sizing handles. The following is a list of those options:

Sizing handles
Rotational handle
Selection/ move pointer
WHAT CLIENTS ARE SAYING
Here is what others have said about me:
"It was a pleasure working with Emma Cavalli. She was very responsive and listened to all of our needs. Her marketing plan sold our home in just 3 days!"
Shape adjustment handle
-Rod & Lilia Ellisor, Rocklin

4-64 Shape selected with handles displayed

- ***Selection/move pointer:*** This pointer (four-pointed arrow) allows you to select and move objects. Select multiple objects by holding down the *Ctrl* key.
- ***Sizing handles:*** There are sizing handles in each corner and on each side of the shape. When you select one of these, the pointer becomes a sizing pointer (two-pointed arrow).
- ***Rotation handle:*** The rotation handle is the circle at the top of the selected shape. Rotate a shape by clicking and dragging this handle to the left or right.
- ***Shape Adjustment handle:*** This handle is the yellow diamond. You can use this handle to change the shape of an object (not all shapes have this handle available). You can also use this handle to change the size or location of a callout, corner roundness, and other shape elements.

You can change the ***Shape Fill***, ***Shape Outline***, and ***Shape Effects*** of a shape. Each of these areas includes many customization options to enhance shapes. When the shape is selected, the *Drawing Tools Format* tab is displayed (Figure 4-65).

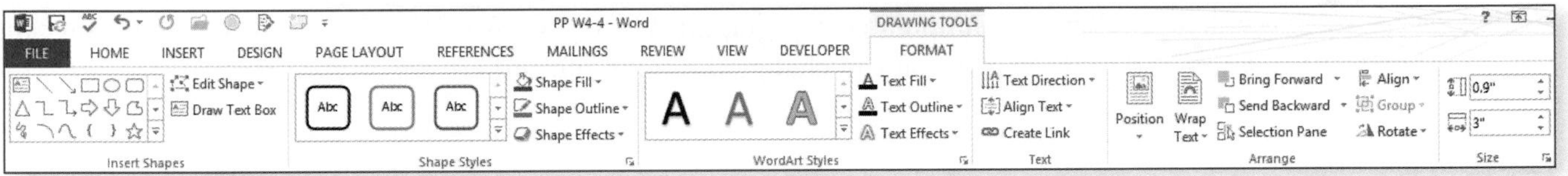

4-65 *Drawing Tools Format* tab

Insert SmartArt

SmartArt allows you to graphically present information in your document in a visually attractive way. There are a variety of categories of *SmartArt* and within each category there are numerous options available (Figure 4-66).

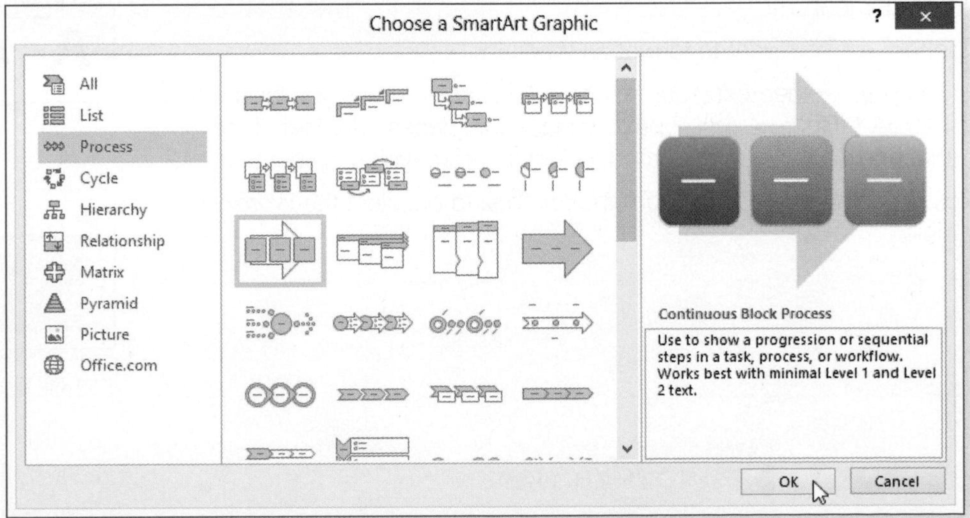

4-66 *Choose a SmartArt Graphic* dialog box

Customize SmartArt

SmartArt graphics are a combination of shapes and text boxes. Once you insert a *SmartArt* graphic into a document, you can use *SmartArt Tools Design* and *Format* tabs to customize the text content and the graphic's structure.

HOW TO: Insert and Customize SmartArt

1. Position your insertion point in your document where you want to insert the *SmartArt.*
2. Click the **Insert** tab.
3. Click the **SmartArt** button [*Illustrations* group]. The *Choose a SmartArt Graphic* dialog box opens (see Figure 4-66).
4. Select a *SmartArt* graphic. A preview and description of the *SmartArt* are displayed on the right of the dialog box.
5. Click **OK** to insert the *SmartArt* into the document.
6. Customize the graphic using the *SmartArt Tools Design* and *Format* tabs.
   - The *SmartArt Tools Design* tab controls the overall design and colors of the *SmartArt* objects.
   - The *SmartArt Tools Format* tab allows you to customize the shape of objects, colors, borders, fill, and effects.

Insert WordArt

WordArt can visually enhance a title of a document or add emphasis to certain text within a document. When you insert *WordArt,* you are actually inserting a text box in the document which can then be manipulated as a graphic. Once you insert *WordArt* in a document, you can resize and move it, and you can change the color, fill, and effects of this object.

HOW TO: Insert WordArt

1. Position your insertion point in your document where you want to insert the *WordArt.*
2. Click the **Insert** tab.
3. Click the **WordArt** button [*Text* group] and select a *WordArt* style from the gallery of options (Figure 4-67). The *WordArt* text box is inserted into your document.
4. Type the text you want to format as *WordArt.*
   - The placeholder text (*Your text here*) is selected when you insert the *WordArt* (Figure 4-68). Type to replace the placeholder text. If the placeholder text is deselected, select it before typing in your text.
5. Click your document away from the text box to deselect the *WordArt* graphic.

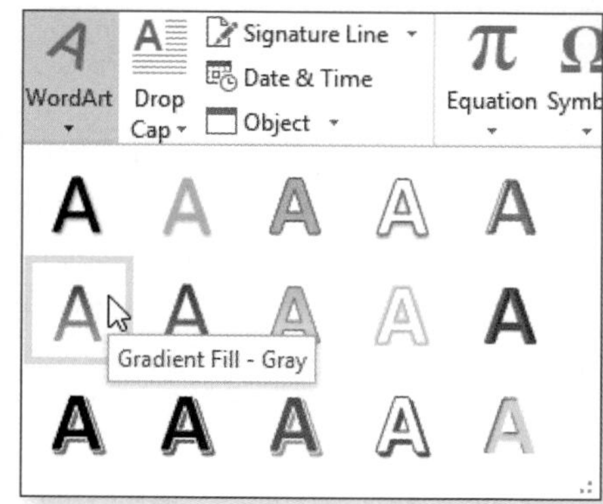

4-67 *WordArt* gallery

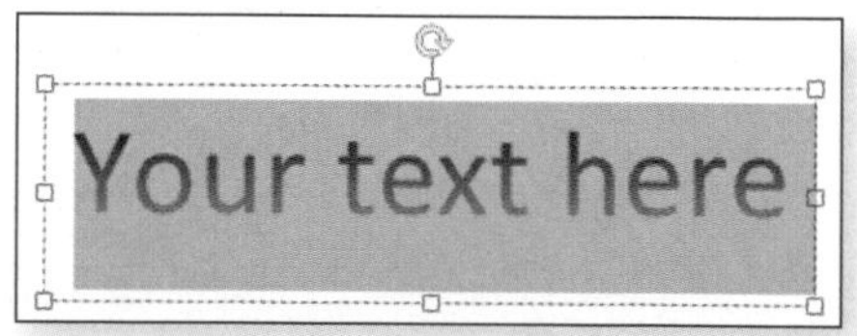

4-68 WordArt inserted into a document

> **ANOTHER WAY**
>
> To select text in your document to be converted to *WordArt,* first select the text and then select the *WordArt* format. The selected text is converted to *WordArt* and placed in a text box.

Customize WordArt

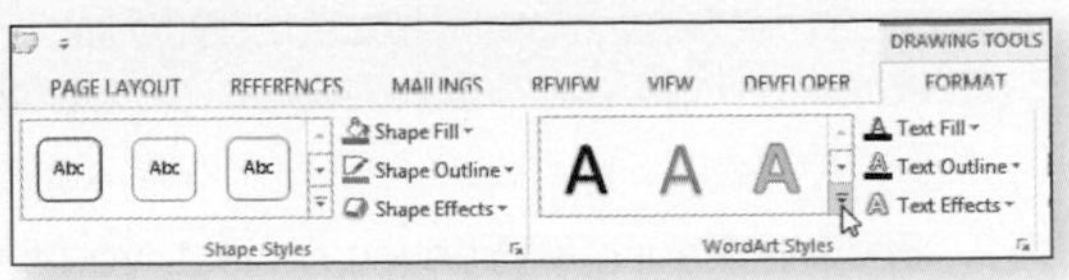

4-69 *Drawing Tools Format* tab

Customizing *WordArt* is similar to customizing other graphic objects in Word. When the *WordArt* text box is selected, the *Design Tools Format* tab is displayed (Figure 4-69). From this tab, you can change the style of the *WordArt*, add a border to the text box, and change the fill, outline, and effects of the *WordArt* text.

Resize *WordArt* by using the sizing handles on the corners and sides. Rotate the *WordArt* text box with the rotation handle. You can change the position and text wrapping of the *WordArt* in the same way you manipulate other graphics.

Enhance Graphics with Styles

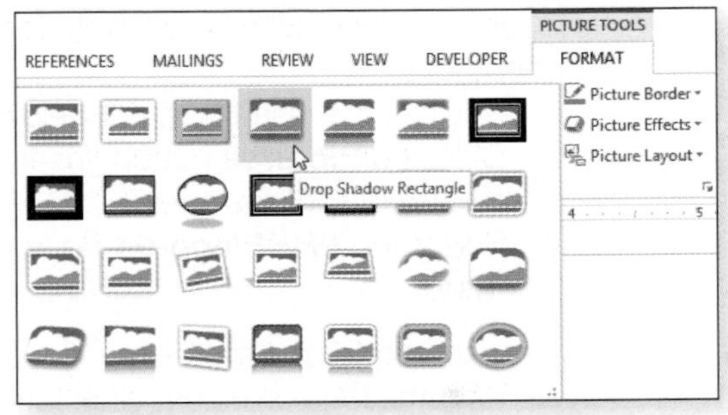

4-70 *Picture Styles* gallery

Each of the different types of graphics has a variety of styles, fills, outlines, and effects that you can apply. Context-sensitive tabs appear when you select a graphic object. On each of these context-sensitive tabs, there are a variety of ***styles galleries*** (Figure 4-70).

When applying styles to graphics, Word provides you with a ***live preview***. When you place your pointer on a style from one of the style galleries, Word temporarily applies the style to the selected graphic to preview how it will appear in the document.

Insert Symbols and Special Characters

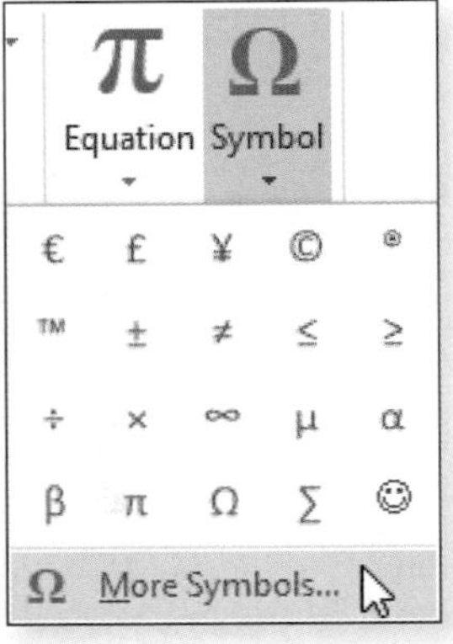

4-71 *Symbol* button on the *Insert* tab

In addition to pictures, Clip Art, *WordArt,* shapes, *SmartArt,* and other types of graphic objects, Word has a variety of symbols and other special characters that you can insert into a document (Figure 4-71). The *Symbols, Wingdings,* and *Webdings* font sets have an assortment of characters and symbols that can be inserted into a document. There are also additional special characters available, such as the em dash, en dash, and copyright and trademark symbols.

HOW TO: Insert a Symbol

1. Click the **Insert** tab.
2. Click the **Symbol** button [*Symbols* group]. A drop-down list of recently used symbols is displayed.
3. Select **More Symbols** (see Figure 4-71). The *Symbol* dialog box opens (Figure 4-72).
4. Click the **Font** drop-down list on the *Symbols* tab to select the font set.
   - Or click the **Special Character** tab to display the list of available special characters.
5. Click a symbol or special character to insert.
6. Click **Insert** to insert the symbol in the document.
7. Click **Close** to close the dialog box.

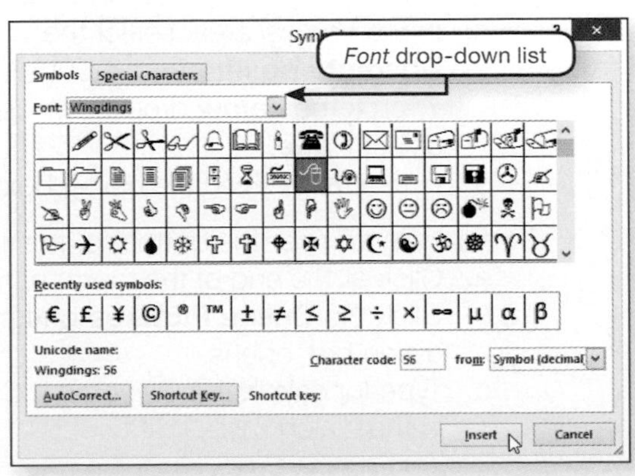

4-72 *Symbol* dialog box

PAUSE & PRACTICE: WORD 4-4

For this Pause & Practice project, you finalize Emma's brochure by inserting a picture, clip art, shapes, and *WordArt*. You format and arrange these graphic objects attractively in the document.

Files Needed: ***[your initials] PP W4-3.docx* and *PHRElogo-04.png***
Completed Project File Name: ***[your initials] PP W4-4.docx***

1. Open the ***[your initials] PP W4-3*** file you saved in *Pause & Practice 4-3.*
2. Save this document as ***[your initials] PP W4-4***.
3. Insert the Placer Hills Real Estate logo at the bottom right corner of the document.
   a. Position the insertion point below the table in the third column.
   b. Click the **Pictures** button [*Insert* tab, *Illustrations* group]. The *Insert Picture* dialog box opens.
   c. Select the ***PHRElogo-04*** file from the student data files and click **Insert.**

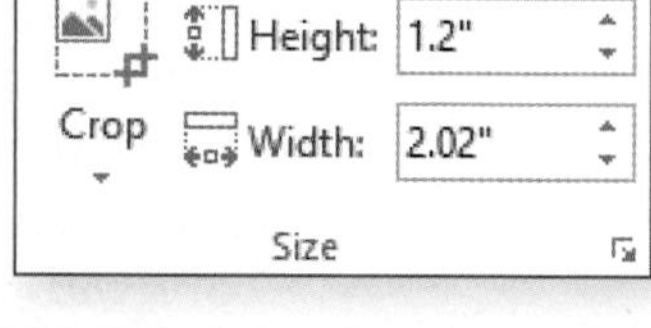

4-73 Adjust the size of a graphic

4. Arrange and format the logo.
   a. With the logo selected, click the **Wrap Text** button [*Picture Tools Format* tab, *Arrange* group] and choose **In Front of Text**.
   b. In the *Height* box [*Size* group] type 1.2 and press **Enter** (Figure 4-73). The width automatically adjusts to keep the graphic proportional.
   c. Click in the middle of the graphic and drag the graphic near the bottom right corner of the document.
   d. Click the **Picture Border** button [*Picture Styles* group] and select **Olive Green**, **Accent 3** (Figure 4-74).
   e. Click the **Picture Border** again, click **Weight**, and select **1½ pt**.
   f. Click the **Position** button [*Arrange* group] and select **More Layout Options.** The *Layout* dialog box opens with the *Position* tab displayed (Figure 4-75).
   g. In the *Horizontal* area, select the **Absolute position** radio button, type 8.6, click the ***to the right of*** drop-down list, and select **Page**.
   h. In the *Vertical* area, select the **Absolute position** radio button, type 7, click the ***below*** drop-down list, and select **Page**.
   i. Click **OK** to close the dialog box.

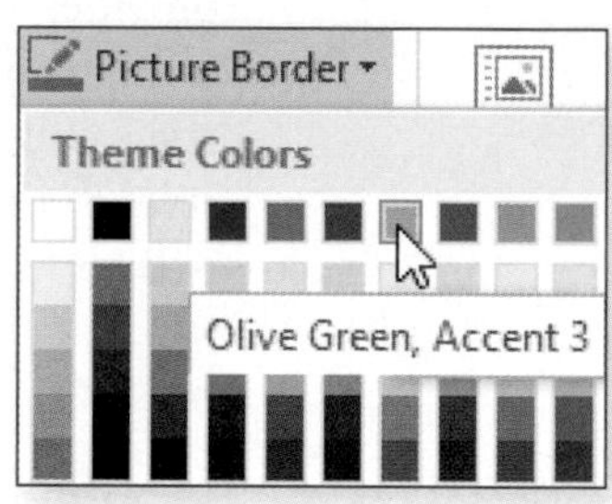

4-74 Select *Picture Border* color

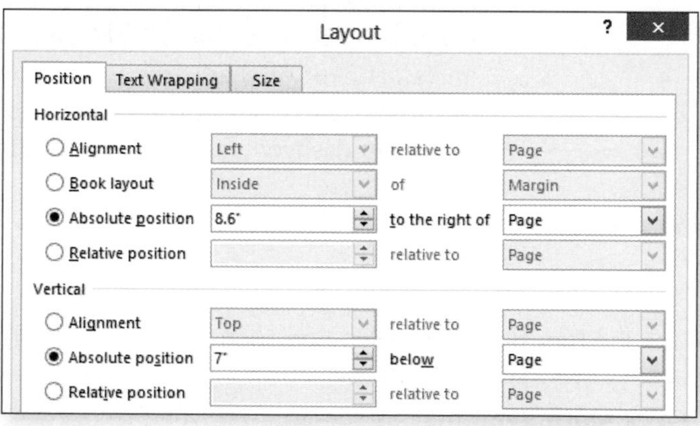

4-75 *Layout* dialog box

5. Add clip art near the bottom of the first column.
   a. Click at the end of the fourth numbered item in the first column.
   b. Click the **Online Pictures** button [*Insert* tab, *Illustrations* group]. The *Insert Pictures* dialog box opens.
   c. Type for sale in the *Office.com Clip Art* text box and press **Enter**. A list of clip art options appears in the dialog box.

d. Select the clip art shown in Figure 4-76 and click **Insert.** The clip art is inserted into the document. Don't be concerned about the clip art at this point. If this clip art is not available, you can insert the ***ForSale-04*** picture from your student data files.
e. With the clip art selected, change the *Height* [*Picture Tools Format* tab, *Size* group] to **1.2"** and press **Enter.**
f. Right-click the clip art, choose **Wrap Text**, and select **Square**.
g. Select the graphic and position it so it is to the right of the fourth numbered item in the first column.

4-76 Insert clip art

6. Insert a caption for the clip art.
   a. Right-click the clip art and choose **Insert Caption.** The *Caption* dialog box opens.
   b. Click **OK** to close the *Caption* dialog box and insert the caption.
   c. In the caption text box, delete the placeholder text and type Meeting Your Needs.
   d. Press **Ctrl+E** or click the **Center** button [*Home* tab, *Paragraph* group] to center the text in the caption.
   e. With the caption still selected, hold down the **Ctrl** key and click the clip art to select it also. Both the clip art and the caption should be selected.
   f. Click the **Group** button [*Picture Format Tools* tab, *Arrange* group] and choose **Group**. The two objects are grouped into one object (Figure 4-77).

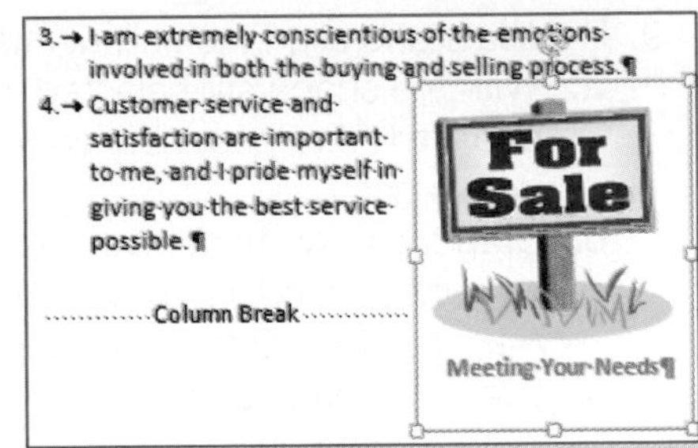

4-77 Clip art and captions grouped

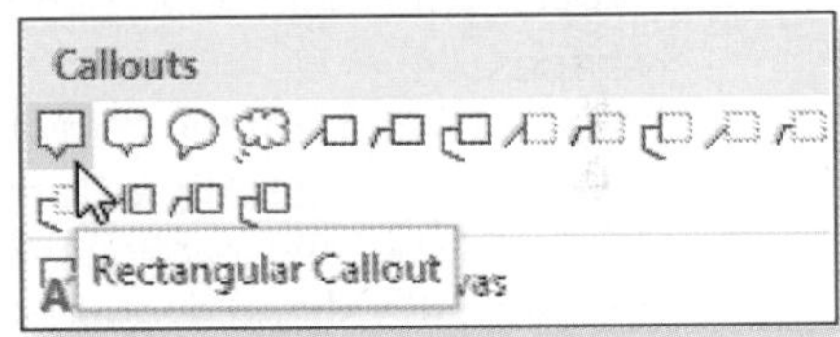

4-78 Select shape

7. Change the paragraph spacing on the two quotes in the second column.
   a. Click in the first quoted paragraph in the second column (beginning with "It was a pleasure . . .").
   b. Change the *After* paragraph spacing to **12 pt**.
   c. Click in the second quoted paragraph in the second column (beginning with "Emma is conscientious . . .").
   d. Change the *After* paragraph spacing to **12 pt**.

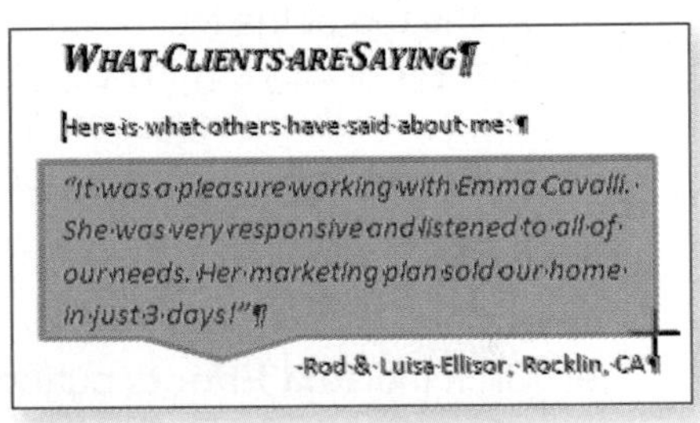

4-79 Draw rectangular shape

8. Add and format a shape to the quoted text.
   a. Click the **Shapes** button [*Insert* tab, *Illustration* group] and select **Rectangular Callout** (Figure 4-78). Your pointer changes to a crosshair (dark plus sign).
   b. On the first quote in the second column, drag from the upper left to the lower right to draw the shape over the quoted text (Figure 4-79).
   c. With the shape still selected, click the **Send Backward** drop-down arrow [*Drawing Tools Format* tab, *Arrange* group] and select **Send Behind Text** (Figure 4-80). The text is displayed over the shape.
   d. Click the **More** button [*Drawing Tools Format* tab, *Shape Styles* group] to display the gallery of shape styles.
   e. Select **Colored Outline – Olive Green**, **Accent 3** (Figure 4-81).
   f. Click the **Shape Fill** button [*Drawing Tools Format* tab, *Shape Styles* group] and select **Olive Green**, **Accent 3**, **Lighter 80%**.

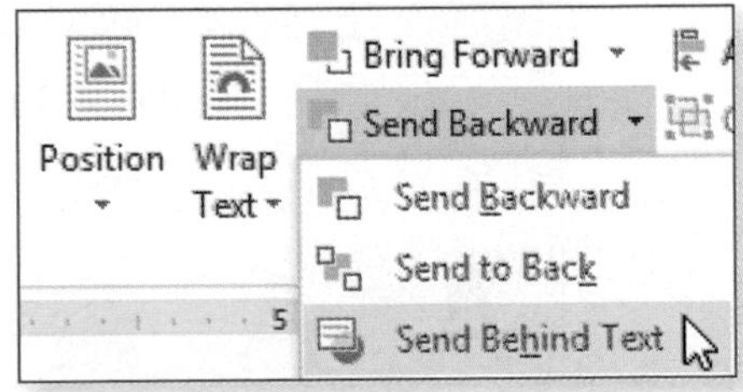

4-80 *Send Behind Text*

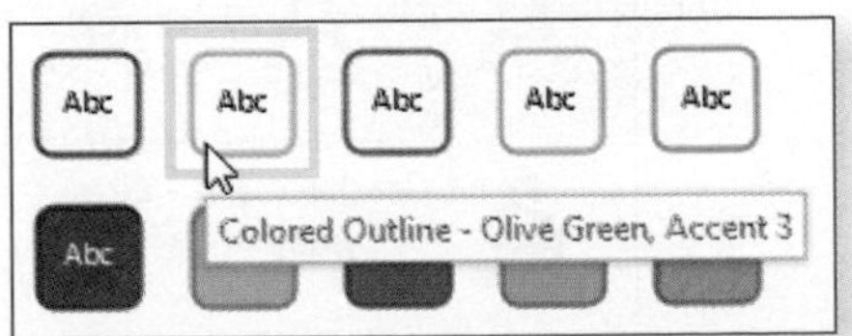

4-81 Apply shape style

g. Click the **Shape Effects** button [*Drawing Tools Format* tab, *Shape Styles* group], select **Shadow**, and choose **Offset Diagonal Bottom Right** (Figure 4-82).
h. With the shape still selected, change the *Shape Height* to **0.9"** and the *Shape Width* to **3"** [*Drawing Tools Format* tab, *Size* group].
i. Drag the shape so it is evenly positioned behind the text. You can also use the keyboard arrow keys to position a selected shape.

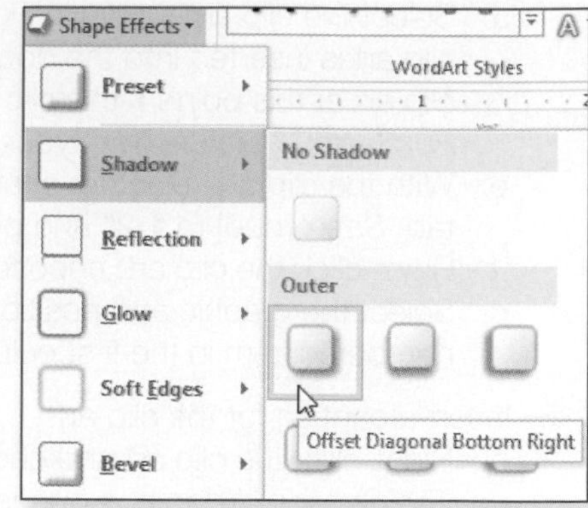

4-82 Select a shape *Shadow* option

9. Replicate and align the callout shape.
   a. With the shape still selected, press **Ctrl+C** to copy it and **Ctrl+V** to paste the copy of the shape into the document.
   b. Drag the new shape over the second quote.
   c. With the second shape still selected, change the *Shape Height* to **1.4"** [*Drawing Tools Format* tab, *Size* group].
   d. Drag the shape so it is evenly positioned behind the text (Figure 4-83).
   e. With the second shape selected, hold down the **Shift** key and click the right edge of the first shape to select both shapes.
   f. Click the **Align** button [*Drawing Tools Format* tab, *Arrange* group] and select **Align Center**.
   g. Make any necessary minor vertical position adjustments by selecting the shape and using the up or down arrow keys.

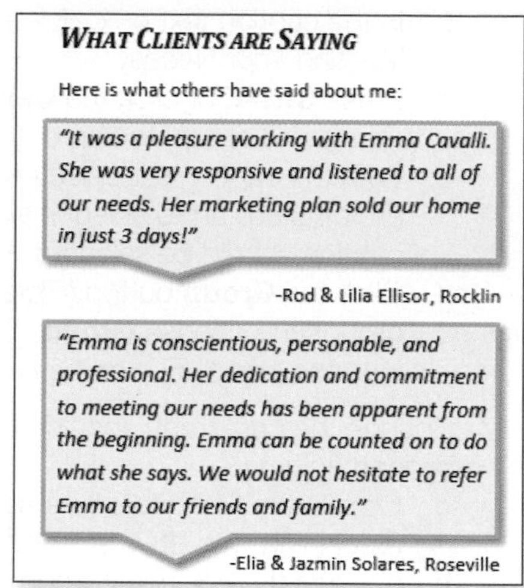

4-83 Shapes positioned behind text

10. Add *WordArt* to the brochure and customize it.
   a. At the top of the first column, select the text **"Emma Cavalli"** (including the paragraph mark).
   b. Click the **WordArt** button [*Insert* tab, *Text* group].
   c. In the *WordArt* gallery, select **Gradient Fill – Gray** (Figure 4-84). The selected text is converted to *WordArt.*
   d. With the *WordArt* selected, change the *Shape Height* to **0.8"** and the *Shape Width* to **3.6"** [*Drawing Tools Format* tab, *Size* group].
   e. Click the **Text Effects** button [*Drawing Tools Format* tab, *WordArt Styles* group], click **Reflection**, and select **Tight Reflection, touching** (Figure 4-85).

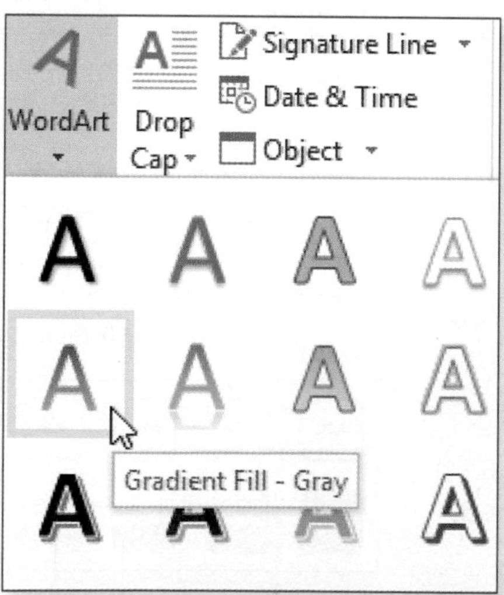

4-84 Select *WordArt* style

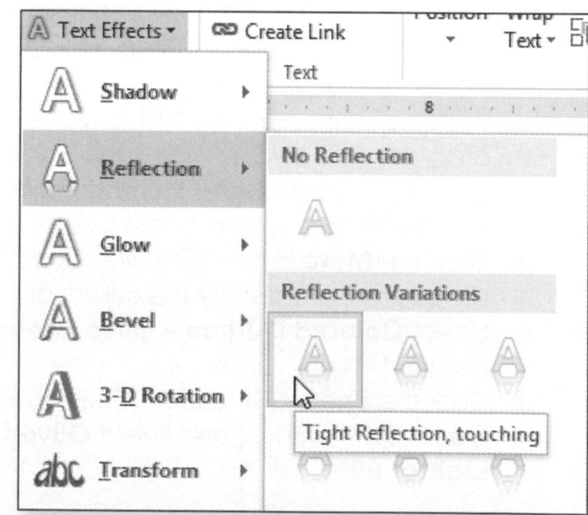

4-85 Apply a *Reflection* text effect

f. Click the **Position** button [*Drawing Tools Format* tab, *Arrange* group] and select **More Layout Options.** The *Layout* dialog box opens.
g. In the *Horizontal* area, change the *Absolute position* to **0.2"** *to the right of* **Page**.
h. In the *Vertical* area, change the *Absolute position* to **0.2"** *below* **Page**.
i. Click **OK** to close the *Layout* dialog box.

11. Save and close the document (Figure 4-86).

Emma Cavalli

Realtor Consultant

Phone	916.450.3334
Email	ecavalli@phre.com
Web	www.phre.com/ecavalli

Mission Statement

I am dedicated to listening to your needs as a buyer or seller and providing you with prompt and excellent service to exceed your expectations.

Business Experience

I have had the pleasure of working with buyers, sellers, and investors for over 15 years. Each transaction is new and exciting.

Why I Am a Real Estate Agent

1. I enjoy working with people and negotiating on their behalf.
2. Communication, organization, and availability are skills I possess that make me a client-focused real estate agent.
3. I am extremely conscientious of the emotions involved in both the buying and selling process.
4. Customer service and satisfaction are important to me, and I pride myself in giving you the best service possible.

Meeting Your Needs

What Clients are Saying

Here is what others have said about me:

"It was a pleasure working with Emma Cavalli. She was very responsive and listened to all of our needs. Her marketing plan sold our home in just 3 days!"

-Rod & Lilia Ellisor, Rocklin

"Emma is conscientious, personable, and professional. Her dedication and commitment to meeting our needs has been apparent from the beginning. Emma can be counted on to do what she says. We would not hesitate to refer Emma to our friends and family."

-Elia & Jazmin Solares, Roseville

Professional Credentials

- Licensed California Real Estate Salesperson
- Member of National Association of Realtors
- Member California Association of Realtors
- Member of Realtor.com
- Distinguished Realtor Award from peers
- Community Service Board position for the Roseville Unified School District
- Elected Parent/Teacher Club President for Winchester Elementary School 2004-2006

Education & Training

University of Nevada, Reno—Business Administration B.A.

Real Estate Code of Ethics

Certified Contract Consultant

Certified Maximum Productivity Consultant

Family & Hobbies

I have been a Roseville community member since 1995. I have been married since 1989 and have three children. I love to read, do crafts, travel, and watch my children play sports. I am also very involved in my church and charity work.

THE PLACER HILLS BELIEF SYSTEM	
Commitment	To the needs of the client
Communication	Seek first to listen
Creativity	Ideas before results
Customers	Always come first
Integrity	Doing the right thing
Success	Results with integrity
Teamwork	Work together for success
Trust	Begins with communication
Win-Win	Is always the goal

4-86 PP W4-4 completed

Chapter Summary

4.1 Improve the design and readability of a document by using tables to present and arrange information (p. W4-197).

- ***Tables*** organize information in column and row format. A ***column*** is a vertical grouping of cells, and a ***row*** is a horizontal grouping of cells.
- A ***cell*** is where a column and row intersect.
- *Use* ***Tab*** to move forward to the next cell and ***Shift+Tab*** to move to the previous cell.
- ***Table Tools Layout*** and ***Table Tools Design*** tabs provide you with many table formatting features.
- You can copy or move columns or rows in a table.
- You can add or delete columns and rows from existing tables.
- When working with tables, you can select individual cells, a range of cells, rows, columns, or an entire table.
- A group of cells can be ***merged*** to create one cell. Cells can also be ***split*** into multiple cells.

4.2 Modify a table by changing the column and row size, aligning text, using the *Table Properties* dialog box, sorting data in tables, and using *AutoFit* (p. W4-201).

- You can resize columns and rows in a table.
- The ***AutoFit*** feature allows you to automatically resize the table to fit the contents or window or change to a fixed width.
- Text in a cell can be ***aligned*** both horizontally and vertically.
- ***Cell margins*** control the amount of spacing around the text within a cell.
- The ***Table Properties*** dialog box provides size and alignment options for cells, rows, columns, or an entire table.
- You can sort table information in ascending or descending order.

4.3 Enhance the appearance and function of a table by using the *Table Tools* tabs, applying borders and shading, using table styles, inserting formulas, and converting text into a table (p. W4-207).

- You can apply ***borders*** and ***shading*** to parts of a table or to the entire table.
- ***Table Styles*** are collections of borders, shading, and formatting that you can apply to a table. Word provides a gallery of table styles.
- You can apply ***Table Style Options*** to a header row, total row, banded rows, first column, or last column.
- ***Formulas*** in a table perform mathematical calculations.
- You can convert existing text into a table in Word.

4.4 Modify the layout and design of a document by using columns to present information (p. W4-214).

- You can arrange text in a document in ***columns***.
- You can choose from preset column settings or you can customize column settings and space between columns using the ***Columns dialog box.***
- ***Column breaks*** control column endings.
- Balance columns with column breaks or a ***continuous section break***.

4.5 Enrich a document by adding and modifying visual elements such as pictures, shapes, *SmartArt,* and *WordArt* (p. W4-218).

- ***Pictures*** and ***clip art*** add visual appeal to a document. Word can insert a variety of graphic file types.
- You can ***resize*** and ***position*** graphics at specific locations in a document.
- ***Text wrapping*** controls how text wraps around graphics.
- The ***Layout dialog box*** has options to change the position, text wrapping, and size of graphic objects.
- You can insert customized ***captions*** for graphics.
- Graphic objects can be ***grouped*** together to create one graphic object, which makes resizing and positioning easier.
- ***Shapes*** can be inserted into a document and resized and customized. You can change fill color, outline color and width, and shape effects.
- ***SmartArt*** graphically presents information in a document.
- ***WordArt*** is special text formatting that you can insert into a document.
- Word provides a variety of formatting options and styles for *SmartArt, WordArt,* and other graphic objects.
- You can insert a variety of ***symbols*** and ***special characters*** into documents. Use the ***Symbols dialog box*** to select different symbols and characters.

Check for Understanding

In the ***Online Learning Center*** for this text (**www.mhhe.com/office2013inpractice**), there are a variety of resources that can be used to review the concepts covered in this chapter.

The following Online Learning Resources are available in the Online Learning Center:

- Multiple choice questions
- Short answer questions
- Matching exercises

Guided Project 4-1

For this project, you modify the values statement document for Sierra Pacific Community College District to arrange text in columns, insert the company logo, and use shapes.
[Student Learning Outcomes 4.4, 4.5]

Files Needed: ***ValuesStatement-04.docx* and *SPCCDlogo-04.png***
Completed Project File Name: ***[your initials] Word 4-1.docx***

Skills Covered in This Project

- Modify an existing document.
- Change page orientation.
- Change margins.
- Apply columns to text.
- Modify column settings.
- Insert a column break.
- Insert a picture.
- Change picture color.
- Modify picture size and position.
- Insert a shape.
- Modify shape size and position.
- Modify shape fill and outline.

1. Open the ***ValuesStatement-04*** document from your student data files.
2. Save this document as ***[your initials] Word 4-1.***
3. Change the orientation and change the margins of the document.
   a. Change the orientation of the document to **Landscape**.
   b. Change the top and bottom margins to **0.5"**.
   c. Change the left and right margins to **0.75"**.
4. Apply column formatting to the text in the body of the document.
   a. Place the insertion point in front of the first paragraph heading ("Access").
   b. Click the **Columns** button [*Page Layout* tab, *Page Setup* group] and select **More Columns**. The *Columns* dialog box opens (Figure 4-87).
   c. Select **Three** in the *Presets* area.
   d. In the *Width and spacing* area, change the *Spacing* to **0.4"**.
   e. In the *Apply to* area, select **This point forward** from the drop-down list.
   f. Click **OK** to close the *Columns* dialog box.
5. Insert a column break to balance the columns on the page.
   a. Place the insertion point in front of the "Student Learning Outcomes" paragraph heading.
   b. Click the **Breaks** button [*Page Layout* tab, *Page Setup* group] and select **Column**.

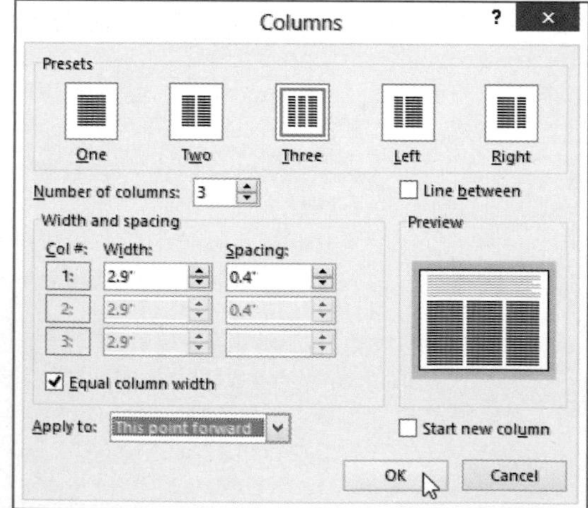

4-87 ***Columns* dialog box**

6. Insert the company logo on the bottom left of the document and resize and position it.
   a. Click at the end of the first column.
   b. Click the **Pictures** button [*Insert* tab, *Illustrations* group].
   c. Select the ***SPCCDlogo-04*** file from the student data files and click **Insert**.
   d. Click the **Wrap Text** button [*Picture Tools Format* tab, *Arrange* group] and select **Behind Text**.
   e. Right-click the logo and choose **Size and Position**. The *Layout* dialog box opens (Figure 4-88).
   f. In the *Scale* area, change the *Height* to **120%** and press **Tab**. The width automatically adjusts to keep the logo proportional.
   g. Click the **Position** tab.
   h. In the *Horizontal* area, change the *Absolute position* to **0.3"** *to the right of* **Page**.
   i. In the *Vertical* area, change the *Absolute position* to **7.2"** *below* **Page**.
   j. Click **OK** to close the *Layout* dialog box.

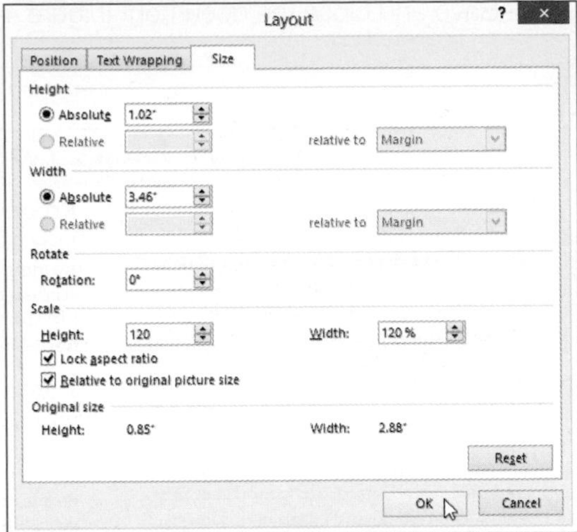

4-88 Resize logo as a percentage of its original size

7. Change the color of the logo.
   a. With the logo selected, click the **Color** button [*Picture Tools Format* tab, *Adjust* group].
   b. Select **Saturation**: **0%** in the *Color Saturation* area (Figure 4-89).

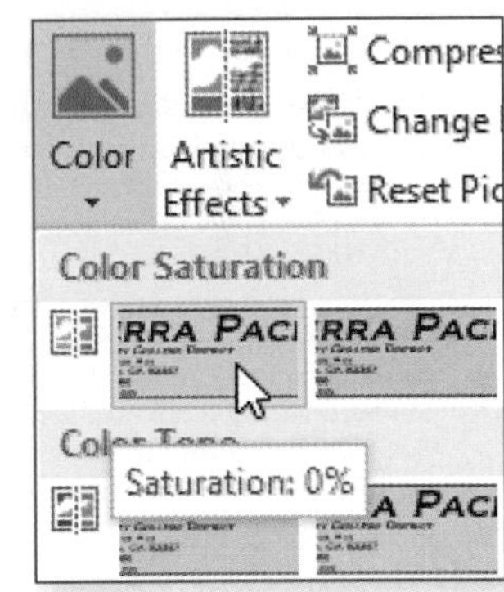

4-89 Change *Color Saturation*

8. Add a shape around the title, and then resize the shape and modify the outline and fill.
   a. Click the **Shapes** button [*Insert* tab, *Illustrations* group].
   b. Select **Snip Single Corner Rectangle** from the *Shapes* gallery. Your pointer becomes a crosshair (dark plus sign) (Figure 4-90).
   c. Click and drag the crosshair over the title and then release the pointer (Figure 4-91).
   d. Click the **Shape Fill** button [*Drawing Tools Format* tab, *Shape Styles* group] and select **White, Background 1, Darker 15%**.
   e. Click the **Shape Outline** button [*Drawing Tools Format* tab, *Shape Styles* group] and select **White, Background 1, Darker 50%**.
   f. Click the **Shape Outline** button again, select **Weight**, and select **1½ pt**.
   g. Click the **Send Backward** drop-down arrow [*Drawing Tools Format* tab, *Arrange* group] and select **Send Behind Text** from the drop-down list.
   h. Change the *Shape Height* [*Drawing Tools Format* tab, *Size* group] to **0.4"** and the *Shape Width* to **6.3"**.
   i. Click the **Align** button [*Drawing Tools Format* tab, *Arrange* group] and select **Align Center**.
   j. Use the up and down arrow keys on the keyboard to vertically center the shape behind the title.

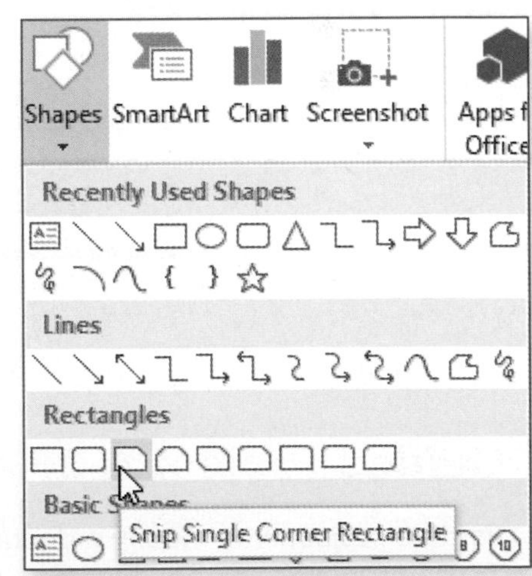

4-90 Select shape

4-91 Draw shape around the title

9. Save and close the document (Figure 4-92).

SIERRA·PACIFIC·COMMUNITY·COLLEGE·DISTRICT·VALUES¶

- ACCESS¶
  Students·are·the·reason·we·exist·and·their·education·is·our·primary·purpose.·We·recognize·that·residents·of·the·region·are·entitled·to·an·opportunity·to·attend·and·to·be·successful·in·college.¶
- BENEFITS·OF·EDUCATION¶
  Individuals·and·society·benefit·from·citizens·who·achieve·the·full·extent·of·their·personal,·intellectual,·and·physical·ability;·engage·in·critical·and·creative·thinking;·exhibit·responsible·citizenship;·succeed·in·a·competitive·global·work·environment;·and·participate·in·lifelong·learning.¶
- EXCELLENCE¶
  Excellence·in·instruction·and·student·services·is·essential·to·develop·the·full·potential·of·each·student.¶
- LEADERSHIP¶
  Responsible·leadership·and·service·among·all·Sierra·Pacific·Community·College·District·faculty,·staff,·and·students·are·nurtured·and·encouraged·so·the·college·will·be·a·leader·for·positive·change,·growth,·and·transformation·in·student-oriented·educational·practices.¶
- ....Column Break..................

SIERRA PACIFIC
COMMUNITY COLLEGE DISTRICT
7300 COLLEGE AVE
SACRAMENTO, CA 92387
209.658.4466
WWW.SPCCD.EDU

STUDENT·LEARNING·OUTCOMES¶
Identification·and·assessment·of·student·learning·outcomes·promotes·and·improves·student·success·and·the·effective·use·of·SPCCD·resources·to·create·innovative·and·flexible·learning·opportunities.¶

- DIVERSITY¶
  We·are·a·community·enriched·by·the·experience·of·students,·faculty,·staff,·and·administrators·from·a·variety·of·cultures,·ethnic·and·economic·backgrounds,·age·is·and·abilities.·We·are·committed·to·providing·and·nurturing·a·safe·environment·for·the·free·exchanges·of·ideas.¶
- COMMUNITY·DEVELOPMENT¶
  The·curricular·and·co-curricular·programs·and·services·of·the·college·benefit·the·region·served·through·enhanced·intellectual·and·physical·growth,·economic·development,·and·exposure·to·the·arts,·sciences,·and·humanities.¶
- HUMAN·RESOURCES¶
  Faculty·and·staff·members·are·our·most·important·resources·and·are·entitled·to·a·supportive,·collegial·work·environment·that·recognizes·excellence,·provides·opportunities·for·professional·development,·service·and·leadership,·and·encourages·meaningful·involvement·in·an·interest-based·decision-making·process.¶
- COMMUNICATION¶
  Achievement·of·the·Sierra·Pacific·Community·College·District·mission·and·vision·requires·an·effective·system·of·communication·with·internal·and·external·constituencies·that·is·based·on·honesty,·trust,·civility,·and·mutual·respect.¶
- INNOVATION·AND·RISK·TAKING¶
  Addressing·challenges·and·change·requires·creativity,·assessment,·flexibility,·and·responsible·risk-taking·to·achieve·our·vision,·mission·and·goals.¶
- FISCAL·RESPONSIBILITY¶
  It·is·necessary·to·maintain·a·fiscally·sound,·efficient,·and·effective·operation·that·achieves·our·mission·within·the·resources·available.¶
- EVALUATION¶
  Efficient·and·effective·accomplishment·of·the·ARC·mission,·vision,·and·student·learning·outcomes·requires·regular·and·ongoing·data-based·evaluation.¶

4-92 Word 4-1 completed

Guided Project 4-2

For this project, you modify a document about maximum and target heart rate for the American River Cycling Club. You arrange text in a table and insert and modify *SmartArt* and clip art.
[Student Learning Outcomes 4.1, 4.2, 4.3, 4.5]

File Needed: ***MaximumHeartRate-04.docx***
Completed Project File Name: ***[your initials] Word 4-2.docx***

Skills Covered in This Project

- Modify an existing document.
- Insert and resize *WordArt.*
- Position and modify *WordArt.*
- Convert text to a table.
- Apply a table style.
- Modify table and text alignment.
- Change cell margins in a table.
- Insert and add text to a *SmartArt* graphic.
- Resize, position, and format *SmartArt.*
- Insert, resize, and position a graphic.
- Insert a caption
- Align and group graphic objects.

---

1. Open the ***MaximumHeartRate-04*** document from your student data files.
2. Save this document as ***[your initials] Word 4-2.***
3. Insert *WordArt* as the title of the document and modify the *WordArt.*
   a. Select the title of the document, **"American River Cycling Club."**
   b. Click the **WordArt** button [*Insert* tab, *Text* group].
   c. Select **Fill – Red**, **Accent 2**, **Outline – Accent 2** from the *WordArt* gallery (Figure 4-93).
   d. Change the *Shape Width* [*Drawing Tools Format* tab, *Size* group] to **6.5"**.
   e. Click the **Position** button [*Drawing Tools Format* tab, *Arrange* group] and select **More Layout Options**. The *Layout* dialog box opens (Figure 4-94).
   f. In the *Horizontal* area select **Alignment** and **Centered** *relative to* **Margin**.
   g. In the *Vertical* area select **Absolute position** and enter **0.2"** *below* **Page**.
   h. Click **OK** to close the *Layout* dialog box.
   i. Click the **Text Effects** button [*Drawing Tools Format* tab, *WordArt Styles* group] and select **Reflection**.
   j. Select **Tight Reflection**, **touching** (Figure 4-95).

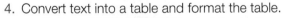

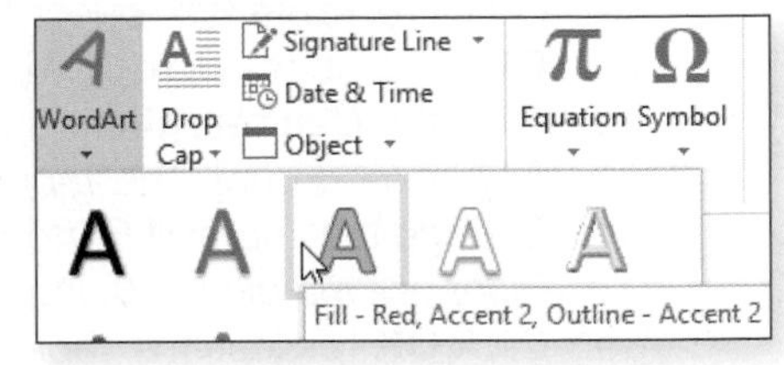

4-93 Insert *WordArt*

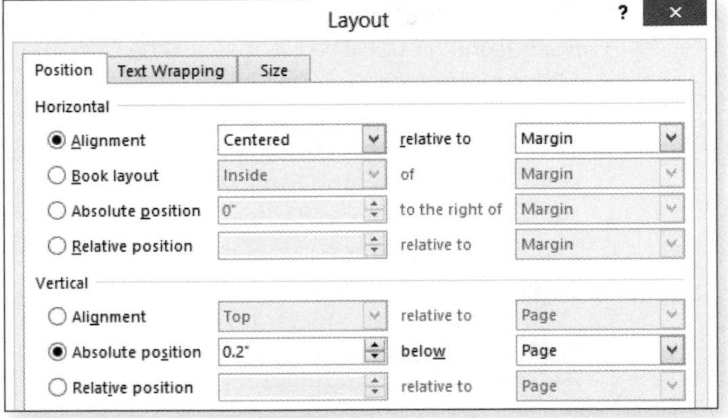

4-94 Adjust position of *WordArt*

4. Convert text into a table and format the table.
   a. Select all of the tabbed text at the bottom of the document.
   b. Click the **Table** button [*Insert* tab, *Tables* group] and select **Convert Text to Table**. The *Convert Text to Table* dialog box opens.
   c. In the *AutoFit behavior* area, click the **AutoFit to contents** radio button.
   d. Click **OK** to close the dialog box.
   e. Click the **Table Tools Design** tab.
   f. Select the **Header Row** and **Banded Rows** check boxes [*Table Style Options* group] and deselect the other check boxes.
   g. In the *Table Styles* group, click the **More** button to display the *Table Styles* gallery.

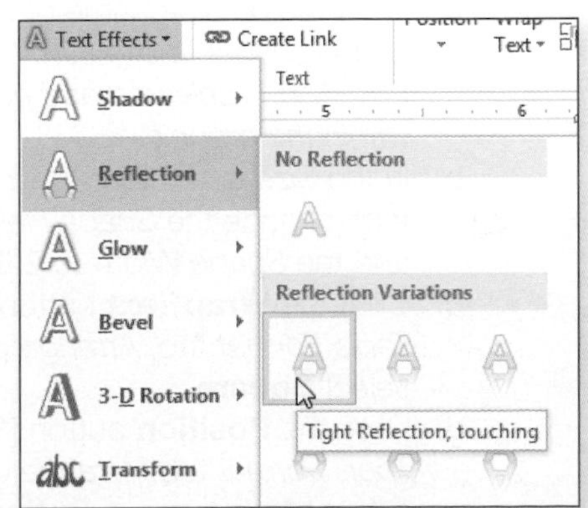

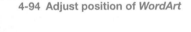

4-95 *Reflection* options

h. Select **Grid Table 4 – Accent 2** (Figure 4-96).

i. In the second column of the first row, place the insertion point before "Zone" and press **Enter**.

j. In the third column of the first row, place the insertion point before "Heart" and press **Enter**.

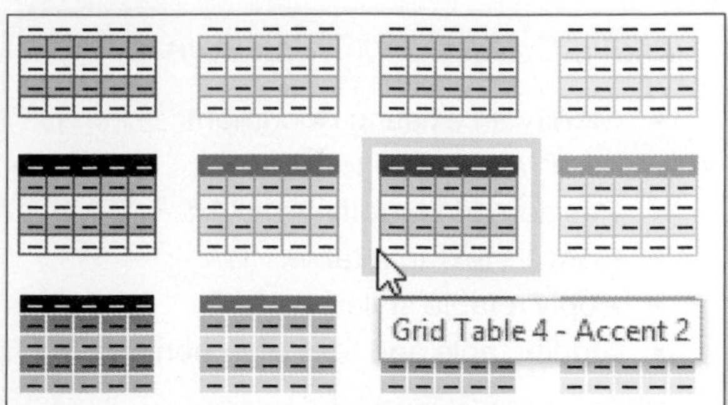

4-96 *Table Styles* gallery

5. Adjust the size and alignment of the table.
   a. Use the table selector handle to select the entire table.
   b. Click the **Align Center** button [*Table Tool Layout* tab, *Alignment* group] (Figure 4-97).
   c. With the table still selected, click the **Properties** button [*Table Tools Layout* tab, *Table* group].
   d. Click the **Table** tab, select **Center** in the *Alignment* area, and click **OK** to close the dialog box.
   e. Click the **Cell Margins** button [*Table Tools Layout* tab, *Alignment* group]. The *Table Options* dialog box opens.
   f. Change the *Top* and *Bottom* cell margins to **0.03"** and the *Left* and *Right* cell margins to **0.1"**.
   g. Click **OK** to close the *Table Options* dialog box.

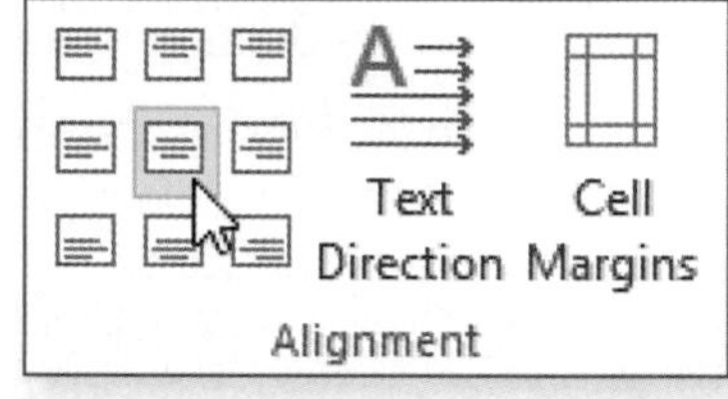

4-97 Text alignment options

6. Insert and modify a *SmartArt* graphic.
   a. Place the insertion point at the end of the "(Example: . . ." line near the top of the document.
   b. Click the **SmartArt** button [*Insert* tab, *Illustrations* group]. The *Choose a SmartArt Graphic* dialog box opens (Figure 4-98).
   c. Click **Process** in the list of *SmartArt* types.
   d. Select **Continuous Block Process** and press **OK** to insert the *SmartArt.*
   e. Click the first placeholder text (*[Text]*) and type 220, **space** once, and type – (hyphen or minus).
   f. Click the next placeholder text and type Your Age, **space** once, and type =.
   g. Click the last placeholder text and type Predicted Maximum Heart Rate.

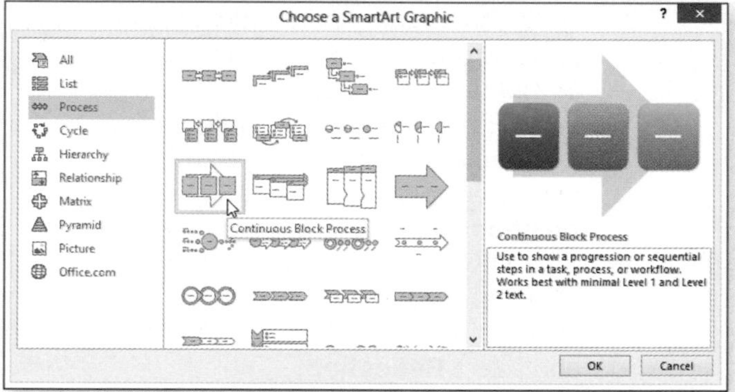

4-98 *Choose a SmartArt Graphic* dialog box

7. Format, resize, and position the *SmartArt.*
   a. Click the outside frame of the *SmartArt* graphic. *Note: make sure the entire* SmartArt *is selected and not an object within the graphic.*
   b. In the *Size* group [*SmartArt Tools Format* tab], change the *Shape Height* to **1.5"** and the *Shape Width* to **2.6"**.
   c. Click the **Wrap Text** button [*SmartArt Tools Format* tab, *Arrange* group] and select **Square**.
   d. Click the **Position** button [*SmartArt Tools Format* tab, *Arrange* group] and select **More Layout Options**. The *Layout* dialog box opens (Figure 4-99).

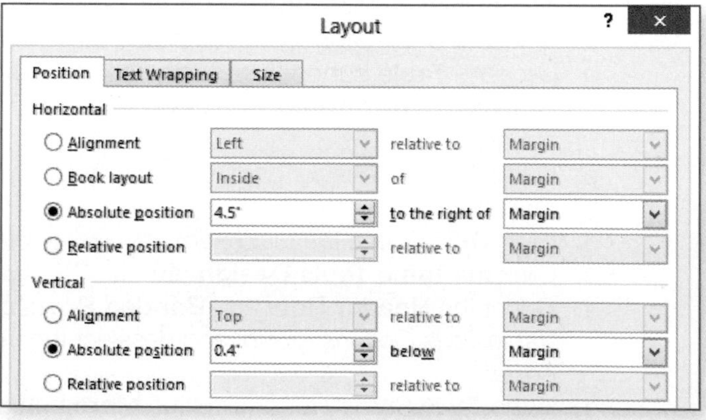

4-99 Adjust *SmartArt* position

e. In the *Horizontal* area select **Absolute position** and enter **4.5"** *to the right of* **Margin**.
f. In the *Vertical* area select **Absolute position** and enter **0.4"** *below* **Margin**.
g. Click **OK** to close the *Layout* dialog box.
h. With the *SmartArt* still selected, select **Intense Effect** as the *SmartArt* style [*SmartArt Tools Design* tab, *SmartArt Styles* group] (Figure 4-100).
i. Click the edge of the first text box to select it, and press **Ctrl+B** to make the text bold. Repeat this on the other two text boxes.
j. Select the last text box and click the **SmartArt Tools Format** tab.
k. Click the **Shape Fill** button and select **Red**, **Accent 2** as the fill color (Figure 4-101).

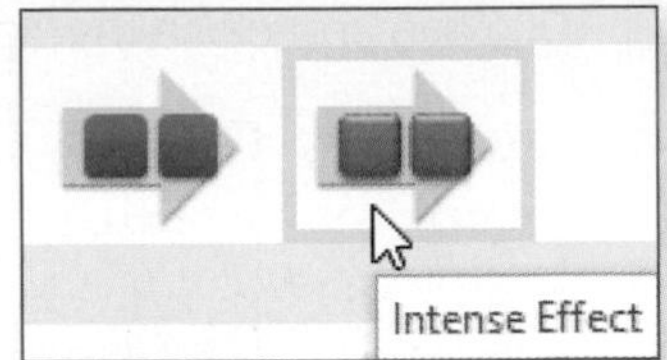

4-100 Apply *SmartArt* style

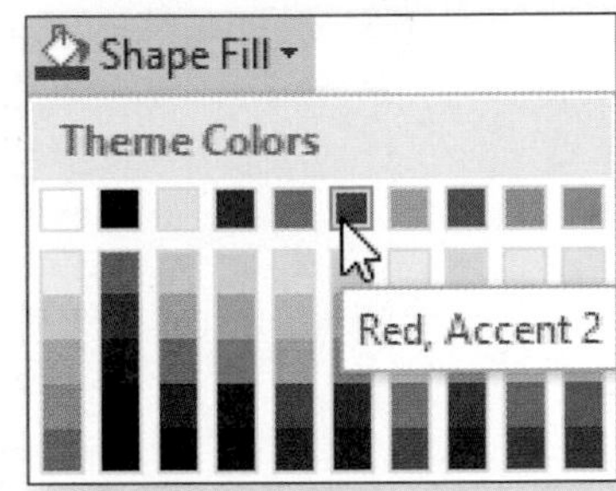

4-101 Change text box fill color

8. Insert clip art and resize and position the graphic.
   a. Place the insertion point at the end of the second paragraph heading ("Target Heart Rate").
   b. Click the **Online Pictures** button [*Insert* tab, *Illustrations* group] to open the *Insert Pictures* dialog box.
   c. Type heart rate in the *Office.com Clip Art* text box and press **Enter**.
   d. Select the **Heart cardiogram illustration** clip art and click **Insert** to insert it into the document (Figure 4-102). If this clip art is not available, insert the ***HeartRate-04*** picture from your student data files.
   e. Change the *Height* [*Picture Tools Format* tab, *Size* group] to **1"** and press **Enter**. The width automatically adjusts.
   f. Click the **Wrap Text** button [*Picture Tools Format* tab, *Arrange* group] and select **Tight**.
   g. Drag the clip art to the right of the heading and first paragraph in the "Target Heart Rate" section and place it approximately 0.5" from the right edge of the document.

4-102 Insert clip art

9. Format the clip art and insert a caption.
   a. With the clip art selected, click the **More** button in the *Pictures Styles* group [*Picture Tools Format* tab] to display the gallery of styles.
   b. Select the **Bevel Rectangle** picture style (Figure 4-103).
   c. Right-click the clip art and select **Insert Caption** from the context menu. The *Insert Caption* dialog box opens.
   d. Press **Enter** to insert the caption.
   e. Select the caption text, click the **Text Fill** button [*Drawing Tools Format* tab, *WordArt Styles* group], and select **Red**, **Accent 2** as the text color.
   f. With the caption text still selected, type Know your target heart rate to replace the caption placeholder text.
   g. In the *Size* group [*Drawing Tools Format* tab], change the *Height* to **0.2"** and the *Width* to **1.5"**.
   h. Press the **Ctrl** key and click the clip art. Both the caption and text box should be selected.
   i. Click the **Align** button [*Drawing Tools Format* tab, *Arrange* group] and select **Align Center**.
   j. Click the **Group** button [*Arrange* group] and select **Group**. The clip art and caption are grouped into one object.
   k. Drag the grouped clip art and caption so it is approximately 0.5" from the right edge of the document.

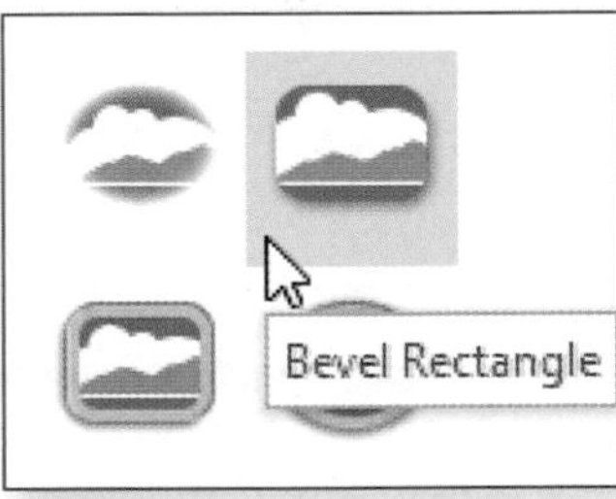

4-103 Apply *Picture Style* to clip art

10. Save and close the document (Figure 4-104).

American River Cycling Club

WHAT IS MAXIMUM HEART RATE?

The maximum heart rate is the highest your pulse rate can get. To calculate your **predicted maximum heart rate**, use this formula:

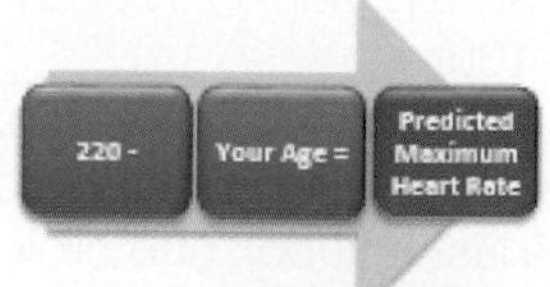

(Example: a 40-year-old's predicted maximum heart rate is 180.)

Your actual maximum heart rate can be determined by a graded exercise test. Please note that some medicines and medical conditions might affect your maximum heart rate. If you are taking medicines or have a medical condition (such as heart disease, high blood pressure, or diabetes), always ask your doctor if your maximum heart rate/target heart rate will be affected.

TARGET HEART RATE

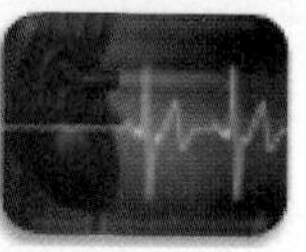

Know your target heart rate

You gain the most benefits and decrease the risk of injury when you exercise in your target heart rate zone. Usually this is when your exercise heart rate (pulse) is 60 percent to 80 percent of your maximum heart rate. Do not exercise above 85 percent of your maximum heart rate. This increases both cardiovascular and orthopedic risk and does not add any extra benefit.

When beginning an exercise program, you might need to gradually build up to a level that is within your target heart rate zone, especially if you have not exercised regularly before. If the exercise feels too hard, slow down. You will reduce your risk of injury and enjoy the exercise more if you don't try to over-do it.

To find out if you are exercising in your target zone (between 60 percent and 80 percent of your maximum heart rate), use your heart rate monitor to track your heart rate. If your pulse is below your target zone (see the chart below), increase your rate of exercise. If your pulse is above your target zone, decrease your rate of exercise.

Age	Target Heart Rate (HR) Zone (60-85%)	Predicted Maximum Heart Rate
20	120-170	200
25	117-166	195
30	114-162	190
35	111-157	185
40	108-153	180
45	105-149	175
50	102-145	170
55	99-140	165
60	96-136	160
65	93-132	155
70	90-128	150

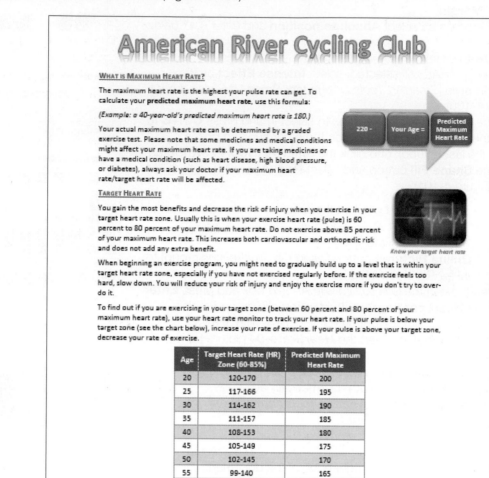

4-104 Word 4-2 completed

Guided Project 4-3

For this project, you format a buyer escrow checklist for Placer Hills Real Estate. You convert text to a table, format the table, and insert clip art and a picture.
[Student Learning Outcomes 4.1, 4.2, 4.3, 4.5]

Files Needed: ***BuyerEscrowChecklist-04.docx* and *PHRElogo-04.png***
Completed Project File Name: ***[your initials] Word 4-3.docx***

Skills Covered in This Project

- Modify an existing document.
- Convert text to a table.
- Add columns to a table.
- Apply bullets and modify alignment.
- Apply table styles and borders.
- Modify row width and column height.
- Center text vertically in a table.
- Insert and position clip art.
- Insert and resize a graphic.
- Use absolute position and text wrapping.
- Insert and resize a picture.
- Apply border and effects to a picture.

---

1. Open the ***BuyerEscrowChecklist-04*** document from your student data files.
2. Save this document as ***[your initials] Word 4-3***.
3. Convert text to a table.
   a. Select the text beginning with **"Task"** through **"Verify Preliminary Report with Lender**."
   b. Click the **Table** button [*Insert* tab, *Tables* group].
   c. Click the **Convert Text to Table** button. The *Convert Text to Table* dialog box opens.
   d. Click **OK** to accept the default settings. The text is converted to a table with 1 column and 14 rows.
4. Add columns and column headings to the table.
   a. With the table selected click the **Table Tools Layout** tab.
   b. Click the **Insert Right** button [*Rows & Columns* group]. A blank column is inserted to the right of the existing column.
   c. Click the **Insert Right** button two more times to insert two more columns. Your table should now have four columns.
   d. Type the following column headings in the first row:
      Column 2: Date Completed
      Column 3: Initials
      Column 4: Notes
   e. **Center** column headings.
5. Add bullets to selected text.
   a. Select all of the text in the first column below "Task."
   b. Apply an **open square bullet** to these items.
   c. Click the **Decrease Indent** button once so the first line indent is at 0" and the hanging indent is at 0.25".
6. Apply table style and apply formatting.
   a. Place your insertion point in the first cell in the first column.
   b. Click the **AutoFit** button [*Table Tools Layout* tab, *Cell Size* group] and select **AutoFit Contents**.
   c. Click the **Table Tools Design** tab.
   d. In the *Table Style Options* group, select **Header Row** and **Banded Rows**. The other options should be unchecked.
   e. Click the **More** button in the *Table Styles* group to open the gallery of table styles.
   f. Select **Grid Table 5 Dark** style (Figure 4-105).
   g. Select the column headings (first row of the table).
   h. **Bold** the column headings.

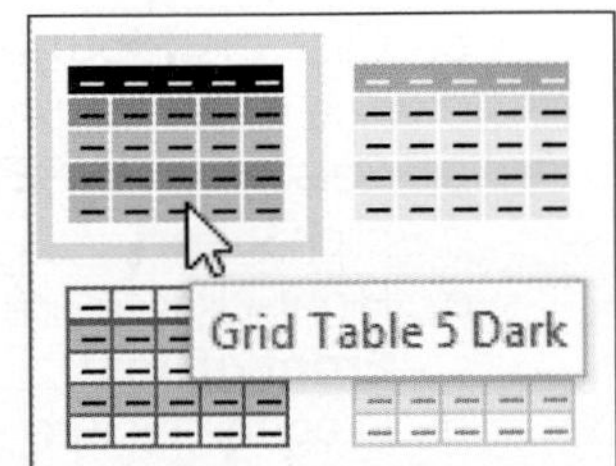

4-105 Apply table style

7. Modify cell size and alignment.
   a. Use the table selector handle to select the entire table, or use the **Select** button [*Table Tools Layout* tab, *Table* group] and click **Select Table**.

b. Change the *Height* [*Table Tools Layout* tab, *Cell Size* group] to **0.35"**. The row height changes on the entire table.
c. With the table still selected, click the **Properties** [*Table Tools Layout* tab, *Table* group] button. The *Table Properties* dialog box opens.
d. Click the **Cell** tab and select **Center** in the *Vertical alignment* area.
e. Click **OK** to close the *Table Properties* dialog box
f. Place your insertion point in the fourth column and change the *Width* [*Table Tools Layout* tab, *Cell Size* group] to **1.5"**.

8. Insert clip art and position it in the document.
   a. Place your insertion point at the end of the "Buyer(s):" line after the solid underline tab leader.
   b. Click the **Online Pictures** button [*Insert* tab, *Illustrations* group]. The *Insert Pictures* dialog box opens.
   c. In the *Office.com Clip Art* text box, type check and press **Enter**.
   d. Select the clip art shown in Figure 4-106 and click **Insert**. If this clip art is not available, insert the ***Check-04*** picture from your student data files.
   e. In the *Size* group [*Picture Tools Format* tab], change the *Height* to **1.5"** and press **Enter**. The width automatically adjusts to keep the clip art proportional.
   f. Click the **Wrap Text** button [*Picture Tools Format* tab, *Arrange* group] and select **Tight**.
   g. Click the **Position** button [*Picture Tools Format* tab, *Arrange* group] and select **More Layout Options** to open the *Layout* dialog box (Figure 4-107).
   h. In the *Horizontal* area, change the *Absolute position* to **5.2"** *to the right of* **Margin**.
   i. In the *Vertical* area, change the *Absolute position* to **0.8"** *below* **Margin**.
   j. Click **OK** to close the *Layout* dialog box.

4-106 Insert clip art

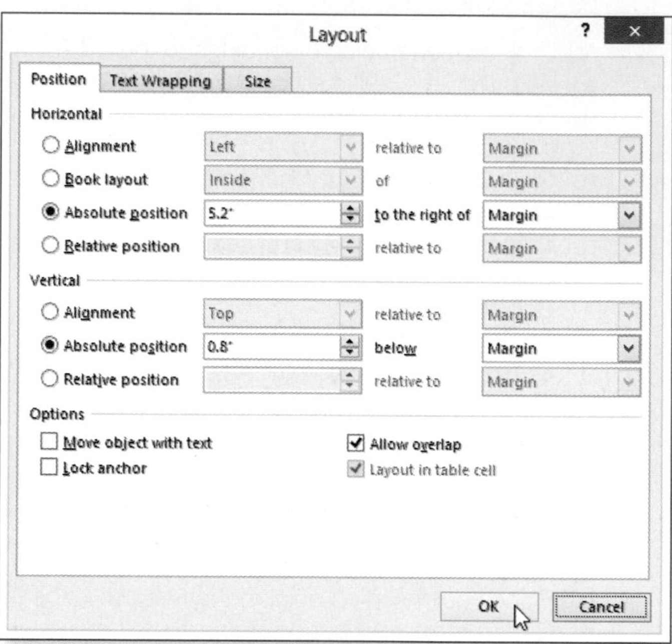

4-107 Position clip art

9. Insert a picture in the upper right of the document.
   a. Place your insertion point at the end of the title.
   b. Click the **Pictures** button [*Insert* tab, *Illustrations* group]. The *Insert Picture* dialog box opens.
   c. Select the ***PHRElogo-04*** file from the student data files and click **Insert**.
   d. Right-click the picture, select **Wrap Text**, and choose **In Front of Text**.
   e. Drag the picture so it is near the upper right corner of the document.
   f. Click the **Picture Border** button [*Picture Tools Format* tab, *Picture Styles* group] and select **Olive Green**, **Accent 2** (Figure 4-108).

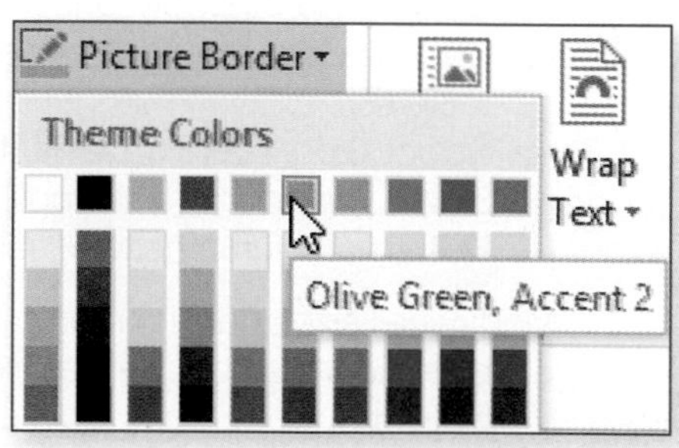

4-108 Apply *Picture Border* color

g. Click the **Picture Border** button, click **Weight**, and select **1½ pt**.
h. Click the **Picture Effects** button [*Picture Tools Format* tab, *Picture Styles* group], select **Shadow**, and select **Offset Bottom** (middle option in first row).

10. Save and close the document (Figure 4-109).

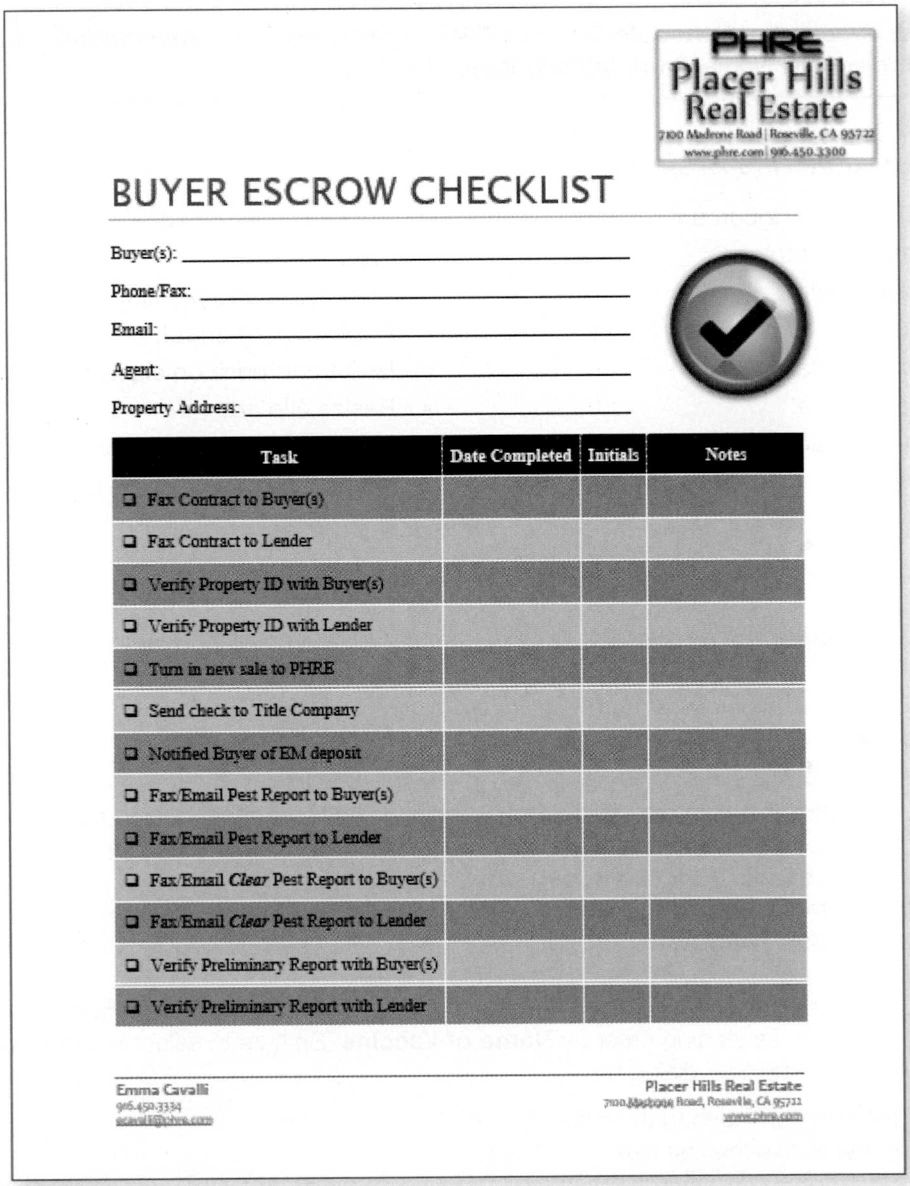

PHRE
Placer Hills Real Estate
7100 Madrone Road | Roseville, CA 95722
www.phre.com | 916.450.3300

BUYER ESCROW CHECKLIST

Buyer(s): ____________________

Phone/Fax: ____________________

Email: ____________________

Agent: ____________________

Property Address: ____________________

Task	Date Completed	Initials	Notes
❑ Fax Contract to Buyer(s)			
❑ Fax Contract to Lender			
❑ Verify Property ID with Buyer(s)			
❑ Verify Property ID with Lender			
❑ Turn in new sale to PHRE			
❑ Send check to Title Company			
❑ Notified Buyer of EM deposit			
❑ Fax/Email Pest Report to Buyer(s)			
❑ Fax/Email Pest Report to Lender			
❑ Fax/Email *Clear* Pest Report to Buyer(s)			
❑ Fax/Email *Clear* Pest Report to Lender			
❑ Verify Preliminary Report with Buyer(s)			
❑ Verify Preliminary Report with Lender			

Emma Cavalli
916.450.3334
ecavalli@phre.com

Placer Hills Real Estate
7100 Madrone Road, Roseville, CA 95722
www.phre.com

4-109 Word 4-3 completed

Independent Project 4-4

For this project, you format a vaccination schedule for Courtyard Medical Plaza by converting text to a table, formatting the table, and inserting a picture.
[Student Learning Outcomes 4.1, 4.2, 4.3, 4.5]

Files Needed: ***VaccinationSchedule-04.docx, CMPLogo-04.png,* and *Vaccination-04.png***
Completed Project File Name: ***[your initials] Word 4-4.docx***

Skills Covered in This Project

- Modify an existing document.
- Convert text to a table.
- Apply a table style.
- *AutoFit* table and change row height.
- Center text vertically.
- Sort text in a table.
- Insert rows and add information.
- Merge cells.
- Apply custom borders.
- Apply a style to text.
- Insert a picture.
- Adjust size and position.
- Apply picture effect.
- Insert and position clip art.
- Resize clip art.
- Add and format a caption.
- Align and group caption and clip art.

1. Open the ***VaccinationSchedule-04*** document from your student data files.
2. Save this document as ***[your initials] Word 4-4.***
3. Convert the tabbed text in the middle of the document to a table.
4. Select the entire table and make the following changes:
   a. Select **Banded Rows** in the *Table Style Options* group [*Table Tools Design* tab] and deselect all other check boxes.
   b. Apply the **List Table 1 Light – Accent 2** table style.
   c. Change the font size to **10 pt**.
   d. Choose **AutoFit Window**.
   e. Change row height to **0.25"**.
   f. Center all text vertically within each cell *(Hint: Use the* Cell *tab in the* Table Properties *dialog box).*
   g. Sort the table in ascending order by **Name of Vaccine**. Be sure to select **Header row** in the *My list has* area of the *Sort* dialog box.
5. Make the following changes to the table:
   a. Insert a row above the first row.
   b. Merge the three cells in the new first row and type **RECOMMENDED VACCINATION SCHEDULE**.
   c. **Bold** and **center** the first row.
   d. **Bold** and **italicize** the second row.
   e. On the first row, apply a **black**, **1½ pt**. top and bottom border.
   f. On the second row, apply a **black**, **1½ pt**. bottom border.
   g. On the last row, apply a **black**, **1½ pt**. bottom border.
   h. Horizontally center the column headings and the text in the third column.

6. Insert the following information alphabetically into the table. Insert rows where needed.

Meningococcal conjugate (MCV)	At 11-12 years	1
Hepatitis B (HepB)	At birth, 1-2 months, and 6 months	3

7. Modify the title of the document ("Vaccination Schedule").
   a. Apply **Title** style to the title of the document.
   b. Change the *After* paragraph spacing to **8 pt**.
   c. **Center** the title horizontally.
   d. Apply **small caps** and **bold** formatting to the title.

8. Insert the ***CMPLogo-04*** picture in the upper left of the document.
   a. Change text wrapping to **Top and Bottom**.
   b. Change the height of the logo to **1"**. Make sure that the logo remains proportional.
   c. Apply the **Offset Diagonal Bottom Right** shadow picture effect.
   d. Set the horizontal and vertical absolute position at **0.2"** to the right of and below page.

4-110 Insert clip art

9. Insert clip art and add a caption.
   a. Search for vaccination in *Office.com Clip Art.*
   b. Insert the clip art displayed in Figure 4-110. If this clip art is not available, insert the ***Vaccination-04*** picture from your student data files.
   c. Change the text wrapping to **Square**.
   d. Change the height of the clip art to **1.3"**. Make sure the graphic remains proportional.
   e. Position the clip art so it is to the right of the first and second paragraphs.
   f. Add Don't neglect your vaccinations! as the caption.
   g. **Center** the caption text, change the font color to **Red, Accent 2**, and turn off italics if it is applied to the text.
   h. Adjust the size of the caption text box as needed.
   i. Select the caption and the clip art and **Align Center**.
   j. **Group** the caption and the clip art.
   k. Position the grouped graphic to the right of the first and second paragraphs approximately 0.5" from the right edge of the document and adjust vertically so it does not interfere with the title alignment or the table.

VACCINATION SCHEDULE

Think of vaccines as a coat of armor for your child. To keep it shiny and strong, you have to make sure your child's immunizations are up to date. Timely vaccinations help to prevent disease and keep your family and the community healthy. Some immunizations are given in a single shot, while others require a series of shots over a period of time.

Don't neglect your vaccinations!

Vaccines for children and teenagers are listed alphabetically below with their routinely recommended ages. Missed doses will be assessed by your child's physician and given if necessary. Keep a personal record of all immunizations and bring it with you to each office visit.

RECOMMENDED VACCINATION SCHEDULE		
Name of Vaccine	*When It's Recommended*	*Total Doses*
Chickenpox (varicella)	At 12 months and 4-6 years	2
Diphtheria, tetanus, and pertussis (DTaP)	At 2, 4, 6 and 12-15 months, and 4-6 years	5
Haemophilus influenzae type b (Hib)	At 2, 4, 6, and 12 months	4
Hepatitis A (HepA)	At 12 and 18 months	3
Hepatitis B (HepB)	At birth, 1-2 months, and 6 months	3
Human papillomavirus (HPV)	3-dose series for girls at age 11-12 years	3
Inactivated influenza (flu shot)	Annually starting at age 6 months	Annually
Inactivated poliovirus (IPV)	At 2, 4, 6 months, and 4-6 years	4
Live intranasal influenza	Annually starting at age 2 years	Annually
Measles, mumps, and rubella (MMR)	At 12 months and 4-6 years	2
Meningococcal conjugate (MCV)	At 11-12 years	1
Pneumococcal conjugate (PCV)	At 2, 4, 6, and 12 months	4
Pneumococcal polysaccharide (PPSV)	At 2, 4, 6, and 12 months	4
Rotavirus (RV)	At 2, 4, and 6 months	3
Tetanus and diphtheria (Td)	At 11-12 years	1

These recommendations are for generally healthy children and teenagers and are for information only. If your child has ongoing health problems, special health needs or risks, or if certain conditions run in your family, talk with your child's physician. He or she may recommend additional vaccinations or schedules based on earlier immunizations and special health needs.

4-111 Word 4-4 completed

10. Save and close the document (Figure 4-111).

Independent Project 4-5

For this project, you create an emergency telephone information sheet for Sierra Pacific Community College District (SPCCD). You add and modify a *SmartArt* graphic, convert text to a table, insert a new table, format the tables, and insert the company logo.
[Student Learning Outcomes 4.1, 4.2, 4.3, 4.5]

Files Needed: ***EmergencyTelephones-04.docx* and *SPCCDlogo.png***
Completed Project File Name: ***[your initials] Word 4-5.docx***

Skills Covered in This Project

- Modify an existing document.
- Insert a *SmartArt* graphic.
- Add text to a *SmartArt* graphic.
- Resize, change color of, and apply style to *SmartArt.*
- Convert text to a table and *AutoFit.*
- Sort text in a table.
- Insert a row, merge cells, and add information.
- Apply a table style.
- Change cell margins and alignment.
- Apply a style to text.
- Insert a table and type text.
- Insert a picture.
- Adjust picture size and position.
- Insert a symbol and the current date.

---

1. Open the ***EmergencyTelephones-04*** document from your student data files.
2. Save this document as ***[your initials] Word 4-5.***
3. Insert a *SmartArt* graphic and add text.
   a. Place your insertion point in front of the second section heading ("Emergency Telephone Locations").
   b. Insert the **Vertical Chevron List** *SmartArt* graphic (Figure 4-112).
   c. Type 1 in the graphic text box in the upper left of the *SmartArt* graphic.
   d. Type 2 in the graphic text box below and type 3 in the third graphic text box in the first column of the graphic.
   e. Type the following text in the bulleted text boxes in the second column. You do not need to add bullets because bullets are already included in the *SmartArt.*

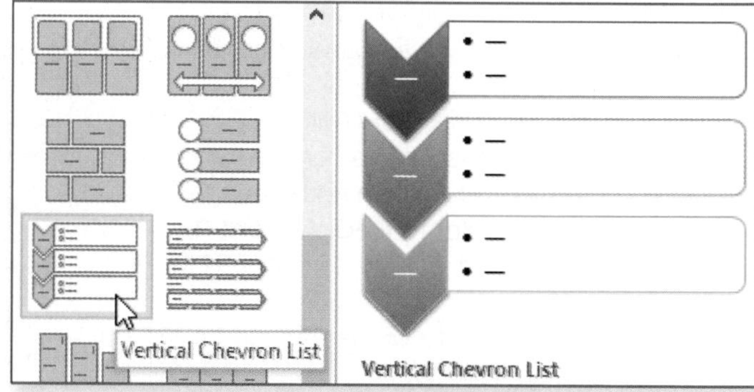

4-112 Insert *SmartArt* graphic

• Press the "Help" button • Speak when the light comes on
• Stay on the line • You will be connected with the college police
• State clearly the nature of the emergency and your location

   f. Delete the extra bullet in the last graphic in the second column.

4. Resize and format the *SmartArt* graphic.
   a. Change the size of the *SmartArt* to **70%** of its original size. Be sure to lock aspect ratio.
   b. Change the text wrapping to **Top and Bottom**.
   c. Change the color of the entire *SmartArt* graphic to **Dark 2 Fill** (Figure 4-113).
   d. Apply the **Intense Effect** *SmartArt* style.
5. Convert text to a table.
   a. Select the tabbed text below the second section heading ("Emergency Telephone Locations").
      Do not select the paragraph mark below the last row.
   b. Convert this text to a table and **AutoFit to contents**.
6. Sort the table text in ascending order by the first column.
7. Add a title row and insert text.
   a. Add a row above the first row.
   b. Merge the cells in this row.
   c. Type Blue Emergency Telephones in the merged first row.
8. Format the table.
   a. In the *Table Style Options* group, select **Header Row**, **First Column**, and **Banded Rows**.
   b. Apply the **List Table 2 – Accent 4** table style.
   c. Select the entire table and change the top and bottom cell margins to **0.04"** and the left and right cell margins to **0.1"**.
   d. Vertically **center** all text in the table *(Hint: use the* Cell *tab in the* Table Properties *dialog box)*.
   e. Horizontally **center** the text in the first row. This text should be centered vertically and horizontally.
9. Insert, resize, and position the SPCCD logo.
   a. Insert the ***SPCCDlogo_04*** picture at the top of the document.
   b. Change the width to **3"** and keep the size proportional.
   c. Change the text wrapping to **Top and Bottom** and drag the logo above the title.
   d. Set the horizontal and vertical absolute position at **0.3"** to the right of the page and below the page.
10. Modify the footer to include a symbol and the current date.
    a. Open the footer and **space** once at the end of the footer.
    b. Insert a **solid circle** from the *Symbol* font set (Character code 183) and **space** once after it.
    c. Type Revised: and **space** once.
    d. Insert the current date in MM/DD/YY format and set it so that it does not update automatically.
11. Save and close the document (Figure 4-114).

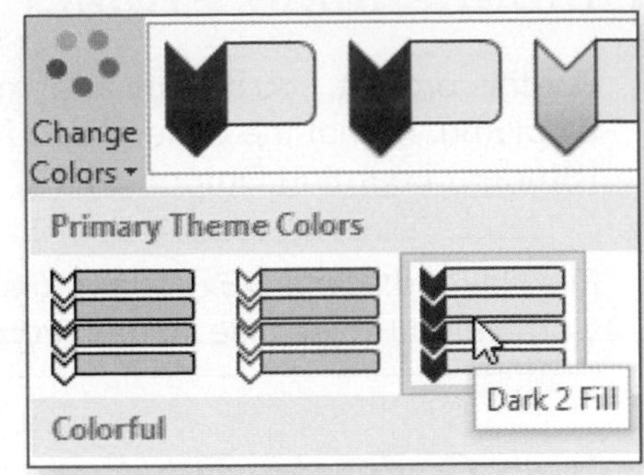

4-113 Change the *SmartArt* colors

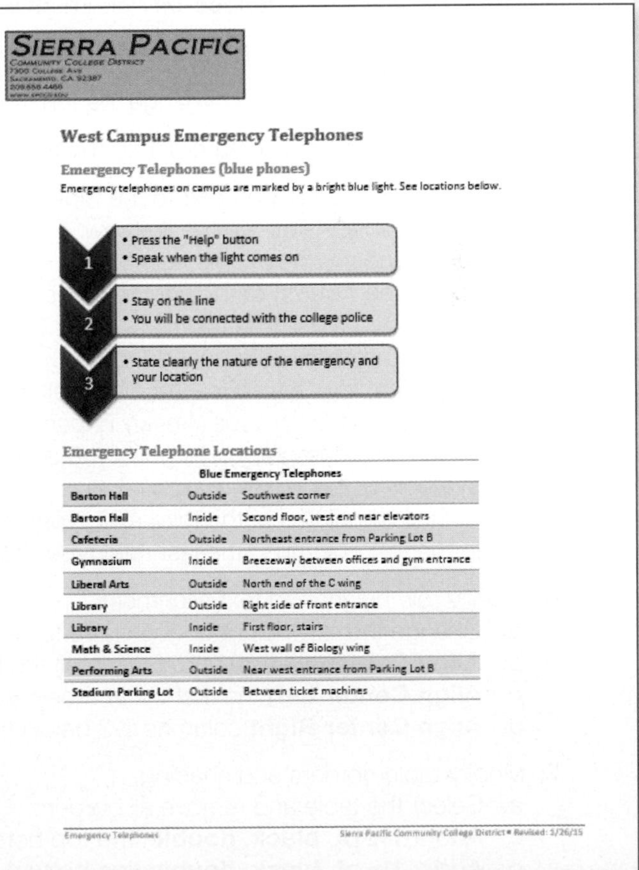

SIERRA PACIFIC

West Campus Emergency Telephones

Emergency Telephones (blue phones)

Emergency telephones on campus are marked by a bright blue light. See locations below.

1
• Press the "Help" button
• Speak when the light comes on

2
• Stay on the line
• You will be connected with the college police

3
• State clearly the nature of the emergency and your location

Emergency Telephone Locations

Blue Emergency Telephones		
Barton Hall	Outside	Southwest corner
Barton Hall	Inside	Second floor, west end near elevators
Cafeteria	Outside	Northeast entrance from Parking Lot B
Gymnasium	Inside	Breezeway between offices and gym entrance
Liberal Arts	Outside	North end of the C wing
Library	Outside	Right side of front entrance
Library	Inside	First floor, stairs
Math & Science	Inside	West wall of Biology wing
Performing Arts	Outside	Near west entrance from Parking Lot B
Stadium Parking Lot	Outside	Between ticket machines

Emergency Telephones   Sierra Pacific Community College District • Revised: 1/26/15

4-114 Word 4-5 completed

Independent Project 4-6

For this project, you modify a memo for Life's Animal Shelter. You edit an existing table, add rows and a column, format the table, insert formulas into the table, and insert and modify *WordArt*. **[Student Learning Outcomes 4.1, 4.2, 4.3]**

File Needed: ***WeeklyExpenses-04.docx***
Completed Project File Name: ***[your initials] Word 4-6.docx***

Skills Covered in This Project

- Modify an existing document.
- Modify a table row height.
- Change cell alignment.
- Add rows and a column to a table.
- Merge table rows.
- Modify borders and shading of the table.
- Insert formulas into a table.
- Set formula number format.
- Update formulas.
- Format selected text.
- Insert *WordArt.*
- Modify and position *WordArt.*
- Change paragraph spacing.
- Insert a date.

1. Open the ***WeeklyExpenses-04*** document from your student data files.
2. Save this document as ***[your initials] Word 4-6.***
3. Select the entire table and change the font size to **10 pt**.
4. Sort the table in ascending order by the first column excluding the header row.
5. Add rows, a column, and text to the table.
   a. Insert two rows above the first row.
   b. Insert one row below the last row.
   c. Insert one column to the right of the last column.
   d. Merge the cells in the first row.
   e. Merge the cells in the second row.
   f. In the first row, type Life's Animal Shelter.
   g. In the second row, type Weekly Expenses.
   h. If there is a paragraph symbol at the end of the title and subtitle text, delete the paragraph symbols in these two rows.
   i. In the last column in the third row, type Totals.
   j. In the first column in the last row, type Totals.
6. Modify row height and text alignment.
   a. Change the row height on the entire table to **0.3"**.
   b. **Align Center** (vertical and horizontal) the first two rows.
   c. **Align Center Left** the first column below the two merged rows.
   d. **Align Center Right** columns 2-9 below the two merged rows.
7. Modify table borders and shading.
   a. Select the table and remove all borders.
   b. Add a **1½ pt**, **black**, **double line** top border to the first row.
   c. Add a **1½ pt**, **black**, **double line** bottom border to the last row.
   d. Add a **½ pt**, **black**, **single line** top and bottom border to the third row.

e. Add a ½ **pt**, **black**, **single line** top border to the last row.
f. Add a ½ **pt**, **black**, **single line** right border to the first column. Don't include the first two rows (title and subtitle).
g. Add a ½ **pt**., **black**, **single line** left border to the last column. Don't include the first two rows (title and subtitle).
h. Apply **Orange**, **Accent 6**, **Lighter 60%** shading fill to the first two rows.
i. Apply **Orange**, **Accent 6**, **Lighter 60%** shading fill to the last row.
j. Apply **Orange**, **Accent 6**, **Lighter 60%** shading fill to the last column.

8. Insert formulas into the table.
   a. In the last row of the second column, insert a formula [*Table Tools Layout* tab, *Data* group] to add the figures above. The formula should be **=SUM(ABOVE)**. Use the **$#,##0.00;($#,##0.00)** number format (Figure 4-115).
   b. Insert the same formula and number format in remaining cells in the last row.
   c. In the last column of the fourth row, insert a formula to add the figures to the left. The formula should be **=SUM(LEFT)**. Use the **$#,##0.00;($#,##0.00)** number format.
   d. Insert the same formula and number format in remaining rows in the last column. Make sure to insert the correct formula in each of these cells **=SUM(LEFT)**. Replace "ABOVE" with "LEFT" in the formula, if needed.

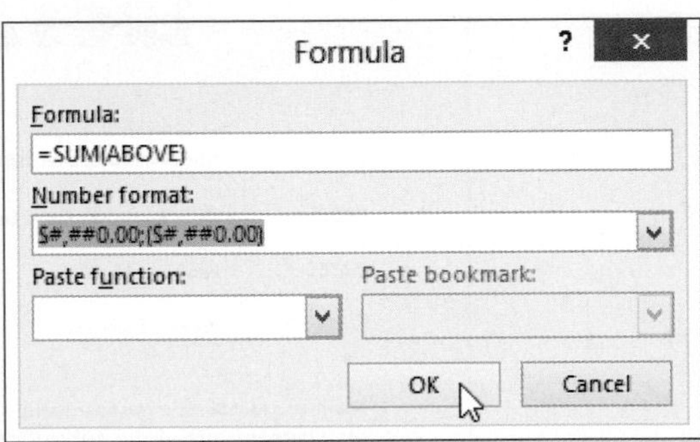

4-115 Insert a formula into the table

9. Change expense data and update formulas.
   a. Change the wages for Wednesday to 592.75.
   b. Select the total amounts in this column and row and press **F9** to update the formulas.
   c. Use **F9** to update the formulas for the wages total and grand total (bottom right cell).

10. Format text in the table.
   a. Apply **bold**, **small caps**, and **12 pt**. font size to the text in the first two rows.
   b. **Bold** and **italicize** text in the third and last rows.
   c. **Bold** and **italicize** text in the last column.
   d. **Italicize** the expense categories in the first column.
   e. Select the table and **AutoFit Contents**.

11. Insert *WordArt* for the company logo.
   a. At the top of the document, insert *WordArt* and use **Fill – Red**, **Accent 2**, **Outline – Accent 2** (Figure 4-116).
   b. Type Life's Animal Shelter as the text for the *WordArt*.

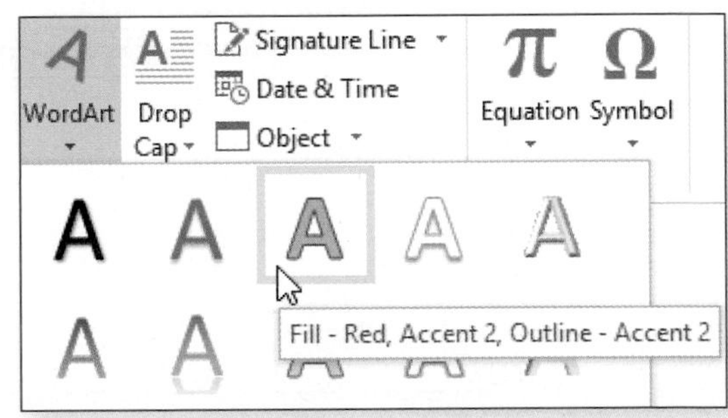

4-116 Insert *WordArt*

12. Modify and position *WordArt.*
   a. Change the text to **small caps** and **40 pt**.
   b. Change the text fill to **Orange**, **Accent 6**.
   c. Change the **Shadow** text effect to **Offset Right**.
   d. Using the *Layout* dialog box, change the horizontal **Alignment** to **Centered** relative to **Margin** and change vertical **Absolute position** to **0.2"** below **Page**.

13. Modify the heading lines of the memo.
    a. Add **36 pt**. before paragraph spacing on the first line ("TO: . . .") of the document.
    b. Insert the current date on the date line in the memo heading to replace the placeholder text and set it to update automatically.
14. Save and close the document (Figure 4-117).

LIFE'S ANIMAL SHELTER

TO: Life's Animal Shelter staff and volunteers

FROM: Kelly Sung, Director of Services

DATE: February 15, 2015

SUBJECT: Weekly Expenses

Thank you for the time you have spent volunteering at Life's Animal Shelter. Our staff and volunteers have contributed countless hours making this shelter a safe environment for animals and providing adoption services for families in our community. You have been a part of hundreds of animal rescues and adoptions over the past year. Families throughout our region are enjoying their new pets thanks to your dedication and work at Life's Animal Shelter.

I'm providing you with our expenses update for the last week. Our operating funds come through donations and pet adoption fees. Thank you for your help in keeping our expenses at a moderate level. Because of you, we are able to offer reasonable adoption fees to animal lovers in our community.

Again, thank you for all of your hard work. Because of you, Life's Animal Shelter valuably serves our community providing shelter and adoption services.

LIFE'S ANIMAL SHELTER WEEKLY EXPENSES								
Expenses	*Mon*	*Tue*	*Wed*	*Thurs*	*Fri*	*Sat*	*Sun*	*Totals*
Electricity	19.45	20.09	21.75	19.02	19.99	23.56	19.45	***$ 143.31***
Equipment	199.03	209.25	198.90	229.05	245.09	351.98	205.55	***$1,638.85***
Food	340.45	344.05	350.51	340.01	341.48	359.75	340.02	***$2,416.27***
Heat	25.75	26.01	28.05	25.03	25.99	31.04	24.99	***$ 186.86***
Medicine	525.33	529.31	535.25	524.59	527.99	543.39	540.01	***$3,725.87***
Wages	675.21	580.91	592.75	579.55	680.81	750.05	565.90	***$4,425.18***
Totals	***$1,785.22***	***$1,709.62***	***$1,727.21***	***$1,717.25***	***$1,841.35***	***$2,059.77***	***$1,695.92***	***$12,536.34***

Life's Animal Shelter Weekly Expenses

4-117 Word 4-6 completed

Improve It Project 4-7

For this project, you edit a document for Courtyard Medical Plaza. You arrange text in columns, position the company logo, and apply formatting to improve the overall layout of the document. [Student Learning Outcomes 4.4, 4.5]

Files Needed: ***StayingActive-04.docx* and *CMPlogo.png***
Completed Project File Name: ***[your initials] Word 4-7.docx***

Skills Covered in This Project

- Modify an existing document.
- Apply style formatting to the title and headings.
- Change font size and alignment.
- Change paragraph spacing.
- Arrange text in columns.
- Change spacing between columns.
- Use a column break to balance columns.
- Insert a picture.
- Update formulas.
- Format selected text.
- Insert *WordArt.*
- Modify and position *WordArt.*
- Change paragraph spacing.
- Insert a date.

1. Open the ***StayingActive-04*** document from your student data files.
2. Save this document as ***[your initials] Word 4-7***.
3. Modify the title of the document.
   a. Apply **Intense Reference** style.
   b. Change to **18 pt**. font size.
   c. Align **center**.
   d. Change paragraph spacing to **36 pt**. before and **12 pt**. after.
4. Modify section headings of the document ("Try Some of the Following Suggestions" and "To Keep Exercise Fun and Interesting").
   a. Apply **Subtle Reference** style.
   b. Change to **14 pt**. font size.
   c. Align **center**.
   d. Change paragraph spacing to **12 pt**. before and **6 pt**. after.
5. Format the last line of the document to make it part of the bulleted list that precedes it and format it consistently with the other bulleted items.
6. Apply column format to the multilevel list following the first section heading.
   a. Arrange the multilevel list in two-column format. Do not include the section heading. If the section break above the list has a number, turn off numbering on this line.
   b. Use **0.75"** space between columns.

7. Apply column format to the bulleted list following the second section heading.
   a. Arrange the bulleted list in two-column format. Do not include the section heading. If the section break above the list has a bullet, turn off bullets on this line.
   b. Use **0.75"** space between columns.
   c. Insert a **column break** before the third bulleted item to balance the columns.
8. Insert the ***CMPlogo-04*** picture at the top of the document.
9. Resize and position the logo.
   a. Change the width to **2.5"** and keep the size proportional.
   b. Change the text wrapping to **In Front of Text**.
   c. Set the horizontal and vertical absolute position at **0.2"** to the right of and below page.
10. Save and close the document (Figure 4-118).

TIPS FOR STAYING ACTIVE

Almost any activity that gets you moving and strengthens your muscles is good for your health and can help you meet your fitness and weight goal. If you haven't been exercising regularly, start out slowly and gradually increase duration, frequency, and intensity. If you have been exercising regularly, keep it up!

TRY SOME OF THE FOLLOWING SUGGESTIONS:

1) AIM FOR AT LEAST 30 TO 60 MINUTES OF MODERATE INTENSITY ACTIVITY ON MOST DAYS.
   a) You can get your exercise all at once, or spread it out during the day.
      i) For example, exercising for three 10-minute periods is just as effective as exercising for 30 minutes at a time.
   b) The more physical activity you do, the more calories you burn and the greater the health benefit.
2) IF YOU DON'T LIKE COUNTING CALORIES, TRY COUNTING YOUR STEPS! WALKING 10,000 STEPS A DAY CAN HELP YOU MANAGE YOUR WEIGHT.
   a) Use a pedometer (an easy-to-wear device that senses your body's motion) to count your steps and motivate you to increase your activity.
   b) Use a journal to track your walking.
3) USE BOTH AEROBIC AND STRENGTHENING ACTIVITIES ARE IMPORTANT TO LOSING WEIGHT AND KEEPING IT OFF.
   a) As you grow older, your body slows down and your metabolism—the rate at which your body burns calories—naturally decreases.
   b) Taking a brisk walk will boost your metabolism and keep you burning calories for hours afterward.
4) REMEMBER THAT ANY FORM OF EXERCISE IS GOOD FOR YOU.
   a) Household chores
      i) Cleaning windows
      ii) Vacuuming
      iii) Folding clothes
   b) Yard work and gardening
   c) Using stairs rather than an elevator
   d) Getting up and moving regularly at work

TO KEEP EXERCISE FUN AND INTERESTING:

- ✓ PICK ONE OR MORE ACTIVITIES YOU ENJOY. Regular exercise is more likely to become a healthy habit when it's fun as well as rewarding. Varying your activities can help prevent boredom.
- ✓ EXERCISE WITH A FRIEND. The support and companionship will help keep you going.
- ✓ THINK ABOUT THE PAYOFFS. Exercise not only helps control weight, it is beneficial to the body and mind in a number of ways. It improves health, boosts your immune system, helps control appetite, helps you feel more energetic and relaxed, and raises your self-confidence!
- ✓ SET REALISTIC EXERCISE GOALS. Reward yourself in healthy ways when you achieve them.

4-118 Word 4-7 completed

Challenge Project 4-8

It is always good to live within your means. A budget can help you track actual or anticipated spending and compare the amount you spend with your earnings. Using some of the skills you learned in this chapter, for this project you create a weekly or monthly budget.
[Student Learning Outcomes 4.1, 4.2, 4.3, 4.5]

File Needed: None
Completed Project File Name: ***[your initials] Word 4-8.docx***

Create a new document and save it as ***[your initials] Word 4-8.***

A budget can include, but is not limited to, the following elements:

- Document title
- Time frame of the budget
- Expenditure categories
- Days in the week or weeks in the month
- Row and column totals

Modify your document according to the following guidelines:

- Set up your budget in table format.
- Use column headings for days or weeks.
- Use row headings for expense categories.
- Use formulas to total rows and columns.
- Sort table by expenditure amounts.
- Apply table style formatting.
- Adjust shading and borders as needed.
- Adjust column width and row height.
- Modify cell margins.
- Format row and column totals.
- Insert a picture or clip art.
- Format, resize, and position clip art.
- Adjust document margins as needed.
- Include an appropriate header and/or footer.

Challenge Project 4-9

Most newspapers and magazines arrange text in column format to improve readability and overall attractiveness of the document. For this project, you arrange an existing document you have written (such as an essay, blog entry, article for a newspaper, or posting for Craigslist) in column format. **[Student Learning Outcomes 4.4, 4.5]**

File Needed: None
Completed Project File Name: ***[your initials] Word 4-9.docx***

Create a new document and save it as ***[your initials] Word 4-9.***

A document in column format can include, but is not limited to, the following elements:

- Document title
- Byline
- Section headings
- Graphics

Modify your document according to the following guidelines:

- Set up your article in column format. Don't include the title as part of the columns.
- Change space and/or add a line between columns.
- Use a column or continuous section break to balance the columns.
- Insert a graphic.
- Adjust size, wrapping, and position of the graphic.
- Add a caption to the graphic.
- Adjust margins as needed.
- Include an appropriate header and/or footer.

Challenge Project 4-10

A weekly schedule can help you get organized and manage work, school, family, and personal time more effectively. In this project, you use a table to create a weekly schedule and figure out the time you spend on each activity you engage in each day.
[Student Learning Outcomes 4.1, 4.2, 4.3, 4.5]

File Needed: None
Completed Project File Name: ***[your initials] Word 4-10.docx***

Create a new document and save it as ***[your initials] Word 4-10.***

A weekly schedule can include, but is not limited to, the following elements:

- Document title
- Days of the week
- Time commitment categories
- Row and column totals

Modify your document according to the following guidelines:

- Set up your weekly schedule in table format.
- Use column headings for days of the week.
- Use row headings for time commitment categories.
- Use formulas to total rows and columns.
- Apply table style formatting.
- Adjust shading and borders as needed.
- Adjust column width and row height.
- Adjust cell margins as needed.
- Format row and column totals.
- Insert a picture or clip art.
- Format, resize, and position clip art.
- Adjust document margins as needed.
- Include an appropriate header and/or footer.

CHAPTER 5

Using Templates and Mail Merge

CHAPTER OVERVIEW

Templates and mail merge are two valuable, time-saving features in Microsoft Word. ***Templates*** are documents on which other documents are based, such as memos, form letters, fax cover sheets, and many other useful business and personal documents. Using a template, you can create a new document based upon the template, which you can edit and customize, and which leaves the original template unchanged.

The ***Mail Merge*** features allow you to create form letters, labels, or envelopes without having to retype or create separate documents for each recipient. For example, you might want to create mailing labels for an annual holiday card list or send out a yearly letter to volunteers at an organization. Mail merge allows you to merge existing information, such as a letter, with addresses and other information from Access, Outlook, or Excel data files.

STUDENT LEARNING OUTCOMES (SLOs)

After completing this chapter, you will be able to:

SLO 5.1 Create and customize a template based on a Word sample template (p. W5-257).

SLO 5.2 Create and use a template from a blank document or an existing Word document (p. W5-262).

SLO 5.3 Use Word to create envelopes and mailing labels (p. W5-267).

SLO 5.4 Understand the types of merges and how to select or create a recipient list (p. W5-273).

SLO 5.5 Create a merged document using the *Mailings* tab (p. W5-274).

SLO 5.6 Use the *Mail Merge Wizard* to create a merged document (p. W5-286).

CASE STUDY

Courtyard Medical Plaza (CMP) is a full-service medical office complex providing customers with a variety of medical services in one plaza location. Kelly McFarland is the community services coordinator for CMP. She is also the director of volunteers for Skiing Unlimited, an adaptive snow ski program for disabled children and adults. CMP is a proud sponsor of the Skiing Unlimited program and encourages its employees to volunteer for this valuable community outreach program.

In the Pause & Practice projects in this chapter, you create a fax template, form letter template, mailing labels, and a merged form letter for Ms. McFarland.

Pause & Practice 5-1: Use a Word template to create a fax template.

Pause & Practice 5-2: Create a form letter template from an existing document.

Pause & Practice 5-3: Create mailing labels from a recipient list.

Pause & Practice 5-4: Use mail merge to create a form letter.

Pause & Practice 5-5: Use the *Mail Merge Wizard* to create mailing and return labels.

WORD

SLO 5.1

Using Templates

All documents created in Word are based upon a template. Template files contain default fonts, margins, line and paragraph spacing, styles, themes, and other preset formatting options. Templates create consistency in your documents. Another advantage of using a template is that the original document remains unchanged while you edit a new document based upon the template.

Word Normal Template

All new Word documents are based upon the ***Normal template***. A template file is a different type of file and has a different ***file name extension*** than a regular Word document. A file name extension follows the name of the file and typically consists of a period and three to five letters. A regular Word document has a ***.docx*** extension (for example, "*Document1.docx*"), while a template file has a ***.dotx*** extension (for example, "*Normal.dotx*"). See the following table for a list of file types and file name extensions.

Word File Types

File Name Extension	File Type	Sample File Name
.docx	Word Document	*Document1.docx*
.dotx	Word Template	*Normal.dotx*
.doc	Word 97-2003 Document	*Document1.doc*
.dot	Word 97-2003 Template	*Normal.dot*

MORE INFO

Although there are other types of files available in Word, most people typically use documents and templates when using Word.

Usually, you don't see the document extension for a Word file in the *Title* bar of Word or in a Windows folder, but the extension for each type of file is different in order to distinguish file types. By default, Windows does not display the file type and extension, but you can change the settings of Windows folders so the file name extension is displayed.

HOW TO: Display File Name Extensions in a Windows Folders (for Windows 8)

1. Open a Windows folder containing a variety of Word and other files.
2. Click the **View** tab.
3. Select the **File name extensions** check box [*Show/hide* group] (Figure 5-1).
   - The file name extension is displayed after the file name in the Windows folder (Figure 5-2).
   - In the *Layout* group [*View* tab], you can change how files are displayed in the folder (see Figure 5-1).

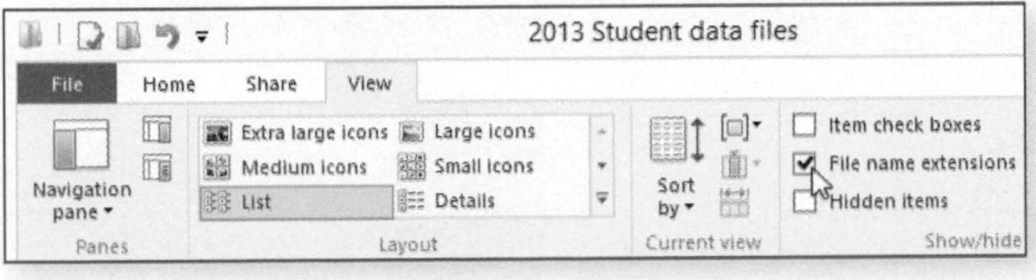

5-1 Display file name extensions in a Windows folder

5-2 Windows folder with file name extensions displayed

> **MORE INFO**
>
> If you are using a previous version of Windows, you can display file name extensions by deselecting the **Hide extensions for known file types** check box on the *View* tab in the *Folder Options* dialog box

In Chapter 1, we discussed changing default settings on a document such as font, size, margins, and line spacing or paragraph spacing. When you change the default settings for a document, you are actually making changes to the *Normal.dotx* template (Figure 5-3). All new blank Word documents are based upon the *Normal.dotx* template, and changes made to this template are applied to all new blank Word documents.

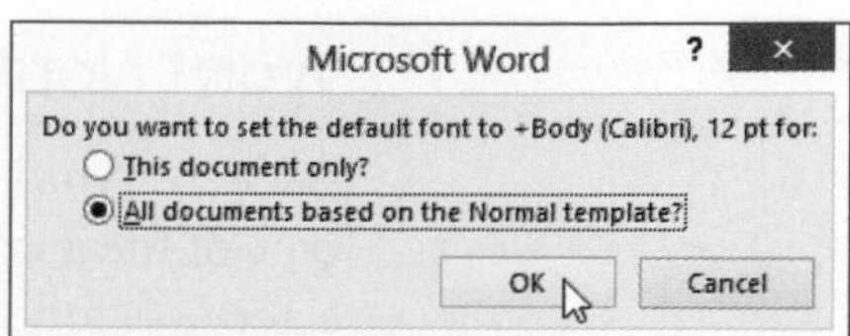

5-3 Options for changing default document settings

> **MORE INFO**
>
> Only make changes to the *Normal* template when you are absolutely sure you want these changes applied to all your new documents.

Online Templates

In addition to the *Normal.dotx* template, Word has a variety of online templates on Office.com. Some of these templates are displayed in the *New* area on the *Backstage* view. The online templates are grouped into categories, and each category has a variety of templates. You can click one of the *Suggested searches* links or *Search online templates.*

You can create a document based upon an online template. For example, you can create a new document based upon a fax, letter, agenda, or resume template. Templates provide the basic structure and formatting for the document, and you can customize them to meet your needs.

HOW TO: Open a Template in Word

1. From the working area in Word, click the **File** tab to display the *Backstage* view.
2. Click the **New** button on the left. Some sample templates are displayed on this page.
3. Click one of the template category links in the *Suggested searches* area, or type in key words to search for a template in the *Search for online templates* text box (Figure 5-4).
4. Click a template to open a window that contains information about the template (Figure 5-5).
5. Click the **Create** button. A document based on the Word template opens in a new Word window.

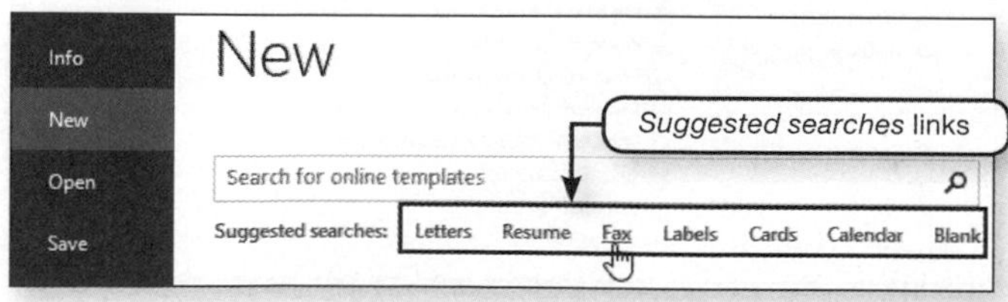

5-4 Search for online templates

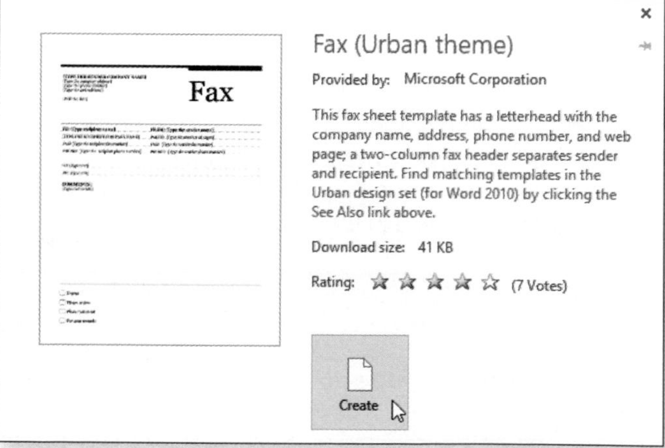

Fax
Fax (Urban theme)
Provided by: Microsoft Corporation
This fax sheet template has a letterhead with the company name, address, phone number, and web page; a two-column fax header separates sender and recipient. Find matching templates in the Urban design set (for Word 2010) by clicking the See Also link above.
Download size: 41 KB
Rating: (7 Votes)
Create

5-5 Create a document from an online template

> **MORE INFO**
>
> After creating a document based upon a template, you can save the document as a document (.docx) or a template (.dotx).

Customize a Template

After you have created a document based upon an online template, you can insert content, modify the format of the template, and remove any content fields that are not needed. In addition to a template that controls document aspects such as font, size, colors, styles, themes, and line and paragraph spacing, most templates include tables and content fields that control the arrangement and content of components in the template.

Insert Content

In an online template, there is a combination of text, tables, document property fields, and content control fields. The text functions as headings or content descriptions, while the document property and content control fields are areas where you enter your personalized text.

HOW TO: Insert Content in a Template

1. Click the **File** tab to open the *Backstage* view, and select **New** on the left.
2. Select an online template and click the **Create** button. A document based on the template opens in a new Word window.
3. Customize the text or formatting as desired.
4. Select a content control field and enter the desired text (Figure 5-6). Repeat this on the other control fields in the template.
   - If you have document properties such as *Author* or *Company* already in your document, the document property fields in the template are automatically populated with this information.
   - You can change document property information in the *Properties* area on the *Backstage* view or in the *Document Properties Panel*.

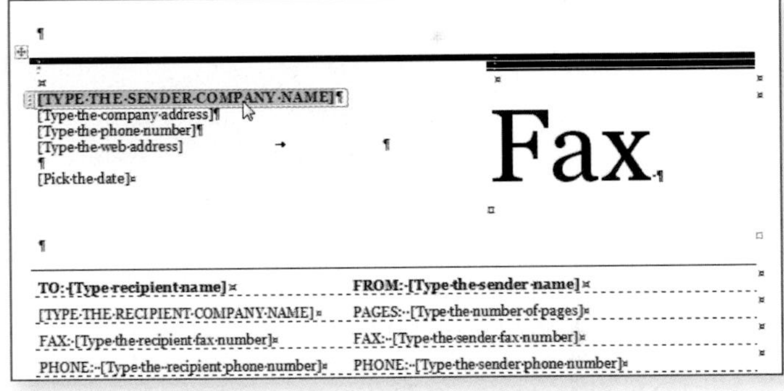

5-6 Insert content in a template

Remove Template Content

In most Word templates you use, there are more content control fields that you will want in your document. There are two ways to remove unneeded fields from your document.

- Click the content control field or content control handle to select the entire field and press **Delete** (Figure 5-7).
- Right-click the middle of the content control field and select **Remove Content Control** from the context menu (Figure 5-8).

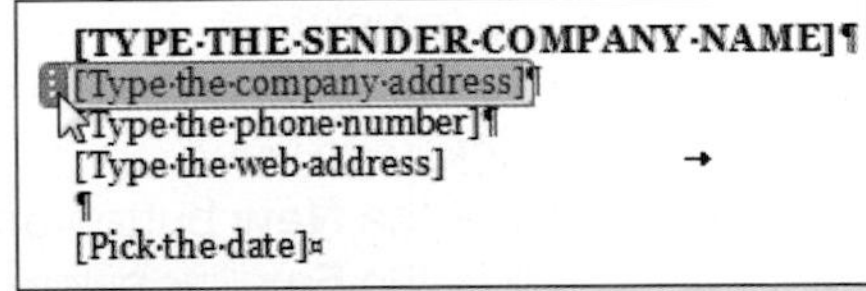

5-7 Select content control field

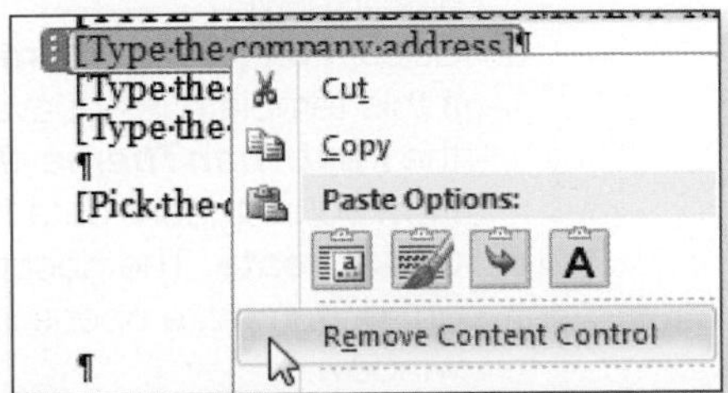

5-8 Remove content control field

MORE INFO

When removing a content control field using the context menu, click in the middle of the field. If you click the left edge of the field, the context menu is not displayed.

Modify Template Format

After creating a document based on an online template, you need to decide which fields you need and remove any unnecessary fields. In addition to removing fields, you can also change or remove any of the descriptive text used in the document. Knowledge of line and paragraph spacing, indents, tables, and borders and shading helps when you modify your template format.

Before modifying a template, ask yourself the following questions:

- Are there tables in my template? (Use the grabber handle to select each table in your template.)
- How many columns and rows are in each table? (Use the *View Gridlines* [*Table Tools Format* tab, *Table* group] to display gridlines to better view the table structure.)
- Are any of the cells merged?
- How is the text aligned within each cell?
- Are there borders and/or shading in the table or template?
- Are there tabs and indents in the template?
- What is the line and paragraph spacing?

If you take the time to ask yourself these questions, you will understand the structure and format of the template, which will help you modify the template to meet your needs.

PAUSE & PRACTICE: WORD 5-1

In this Pause & Practice project, you create a fax template for Kelly McFarland's Skiing Unlimited correspondence. You create a fax template from a sample template, edit the content and structure, and save the revised template.

File Needed: ***Urban Fax.dotx* (from Office.com templates)** or ***FaxUrbanTheme-05.docx***
Completed Project File Name: ***[your initials] PP W5-1.dotx***

1. Create a template based on a Word sample template.
   a. Click the **File** button to open the *Backstage* view.
   b. Click the **New** button on the left.
   c. Click the **Fax** link below *Search for online templates*. Online templates are displayed.
   d. Select **Fax (Urban theme)** (Figure 5-9). If this template is not available, open the ***FaxUrbanTheme-05*** document from your student data files.
   e. Click **Create**. The document based on the template opens in a new Word window.

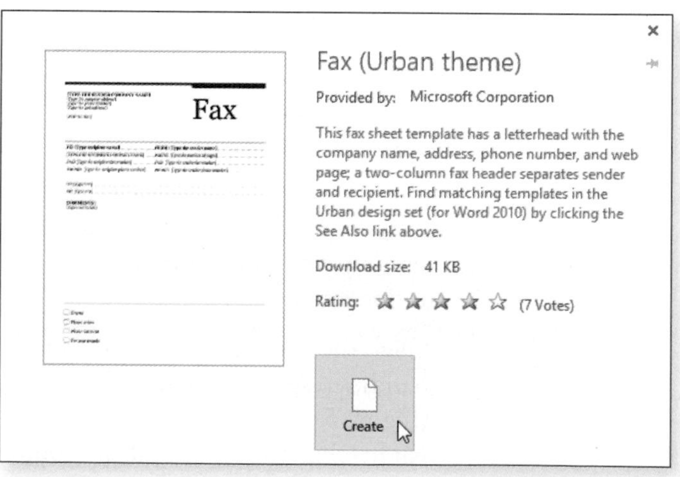

5-9 Create document based on Fax (Urban theme) template

2. Save the document as a *Word Template* file.
   a. Open the *Save As* dialog box from the *Backstage* view or press **F12**.
   b. Save the document as a template named ***[your initials] PP W5-1***.
   c. Click the **Save as type** drop-down list and select **Word Template**.
   d. Browse to the folder on your computer where you are saving your completed projects. Make sure you are very specific about the save location when saving Word template files.
   e. Click **Save** to save the template and close the dialog box. If a dialog box opens informing you the document will be upgraded to the newest file format, click **OK**.
3. Modify document property and type text in content control fields.
   a. Click the *File* tab to open the *Backstage* view.
   b. In the *Info* area, remove the existing author if there is one and type Kelly McFarland in the *Author* document property field.
   c. Click the **Back** button to return to the document.
   d. Fill in some of the content control fields with the following information:

Content Control Field	Enter Content
Type the sender company name.	SKIING UNLIMITED
Type the phone number.	916.854.2299
Type the web address.	www.skiingunlimited.org
Type the sender fax number.	916.854.2288
Type the sender phone number.	916.854.2299

4. Remove content control fields.
   a. Right-click the **Type the company address** field (Figure 5-10).
   b. Select **Remove Content Control**. The field is removed leaving a blank line between "SKIING UNLIMITED" and the phone number.
   c. Place your insertion point anywhere in the "*CC: [Type text]*" row.
   d. Click the **View Gridlines** button [*Table Tools Layout* tab, *Table* group].
   e. Click the **Delete** button [*Table Tools Layout* tab, *Rows & Columns* group] (Figure 5-11).
   f. Select **Delete Rows**. The content control field and the entire row are removed.

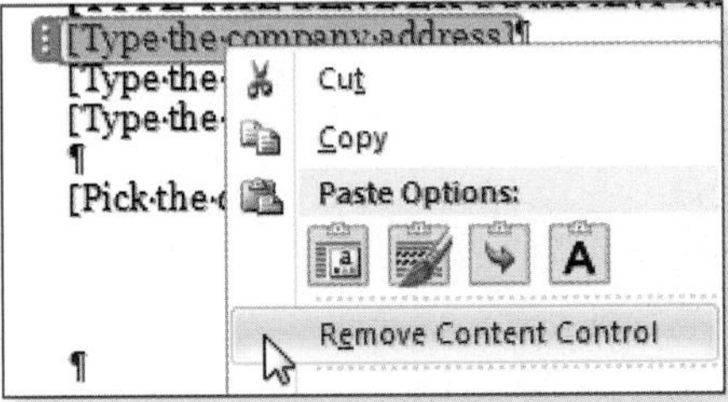

5-10 Remove content control field

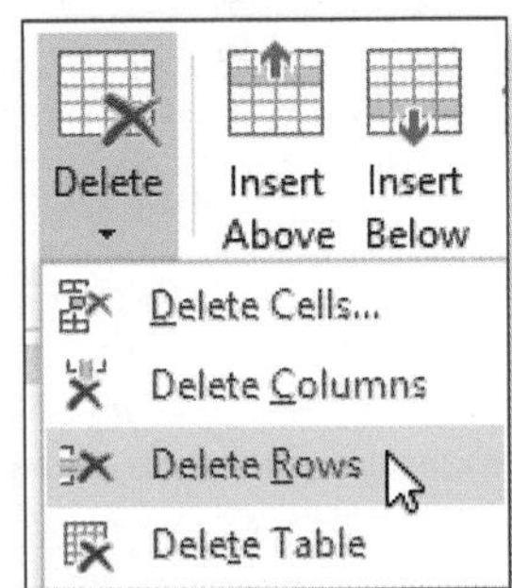

5-11 Delete row

5. Modify table format.
   a. Select the second table in the template (beginning "TO: [Type recipient name"]).
   b. Change the row height to **0.3"** [*Cell Size* group] (Figure 5-12).
   c. Change the alignment to **Align Center Left** [*Alignment* group].
6. Modify template content.
   a. Select the field containing "SKIING UNLIMITED" and change the font size to **16 pt**.
   b. Select "**Fax**" and apply **small caps**.
   c. In the third table at the bottom of the template, delete "**Please comment**" and type Please complete and return.

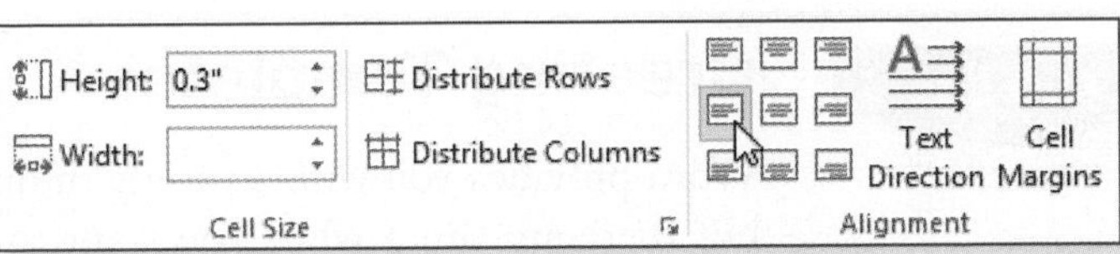

5-12 Modify row height and cell alignment

7. Save and close this template (Figure 5-13).

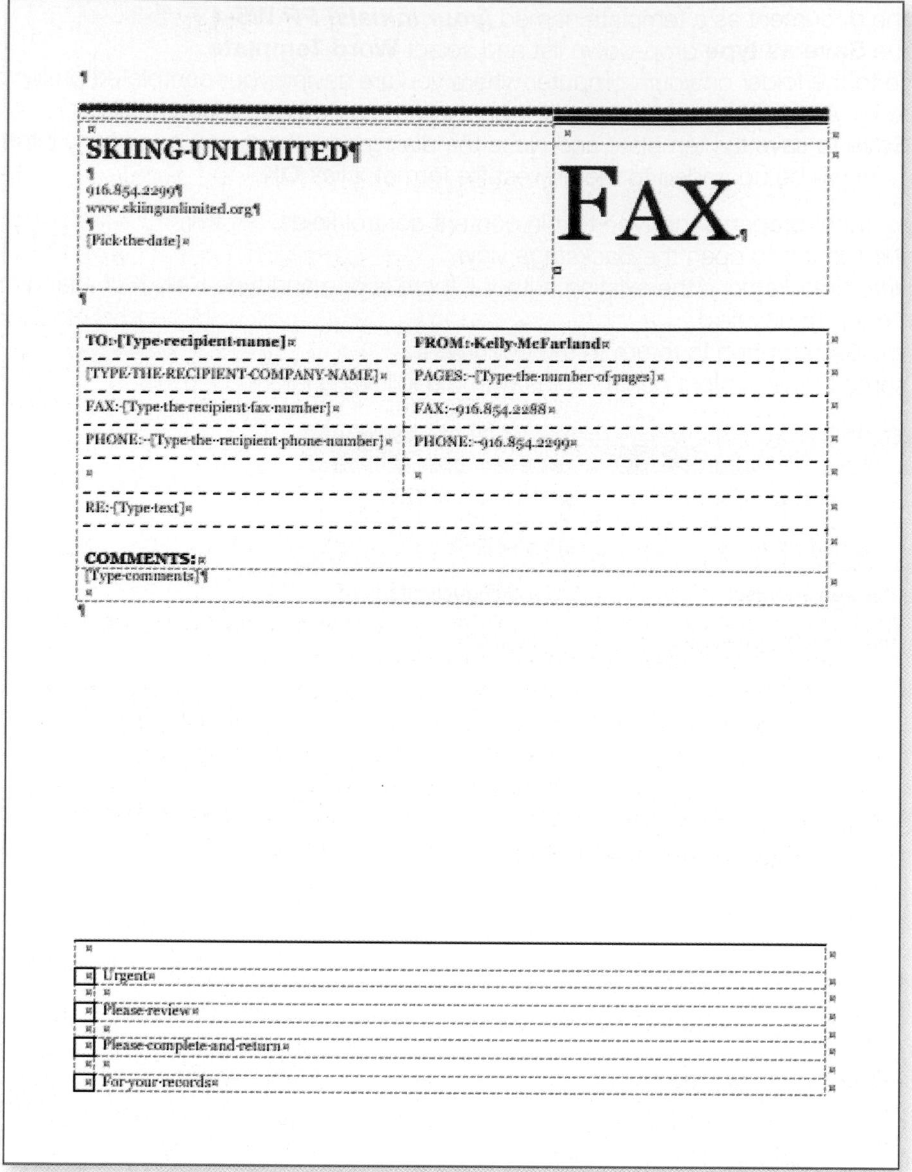

SKIING UNLIMITED
916.854.2299
www.skiingunlimited.org
[Pick the date]
FAX
TO: [Type recipient name]
FROM: Kelly McFarland
[TYPE THE RECIPIENT COMPANY NAME]
PAGES: [Type the number of pages]
FAX: [Type the recipient fax number]
FAX: 916.854.2288
PHONE: [Type the recipient phone number]
PHONE: 916.854.2299
RE: [Type text]
COMMENTS:
[Type comments]
Urgent
Please review
Please complete and return
For your records

5-13 PP W5-1 completed

SLO 5.2

Creating Templates

Word provides you with a variety of online templates you can customize to meet your needs, but there are times when you want to create your own template from a blank document or one of your existing documents. For example, you can create a template of a letter you use on a regular basis, or you can create a new template for an expense report that employees fill out monthly. The main advantage of using templates is that you can create a standardized document that you can use and customize without modifying the original template file.

Create a Template from a Blank Document

When you open a new document in Word, it is a Word document based upon the *Normal.dotx* template. You can convert a blank document into a template by saving it as a Word Template.

HOW TO: Create a Template from a Blank Document

1. Click the **File** tab to open the *Backstage* view (Figure 5-14).
2. Click the **New** button on the left.
3. Click the **Blank document** button. A new blank document opens in the Word window.
4. Press **F12** to open the *Save As* dialog box (Figure 5-15).
   - You can also open the *Save As* dialog box from the *Save As* area on the *Backstage* view.
5. Type the file name in the *File name* area.
6. Click the **Save as type** drop-down list and select **Word Template**.
   - When viewing files in a Windows folder, the document icon for a Word Template is different from a Word Document.
7. Browse to the location where you want to save the file.
8. Click **Save** to close the dialog box and save the template.

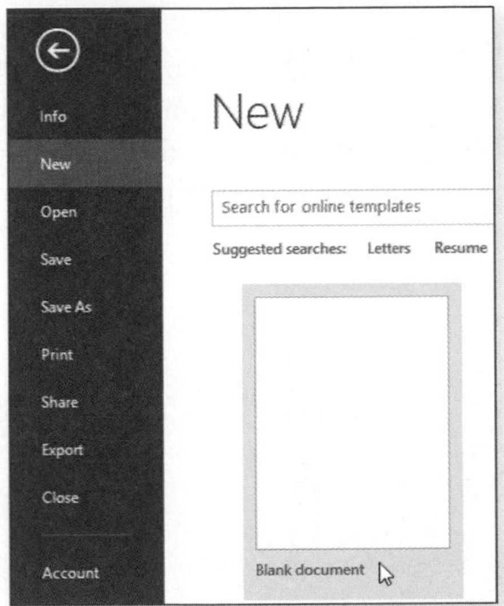

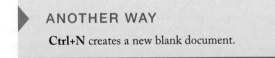

5-14 Create a new blank document

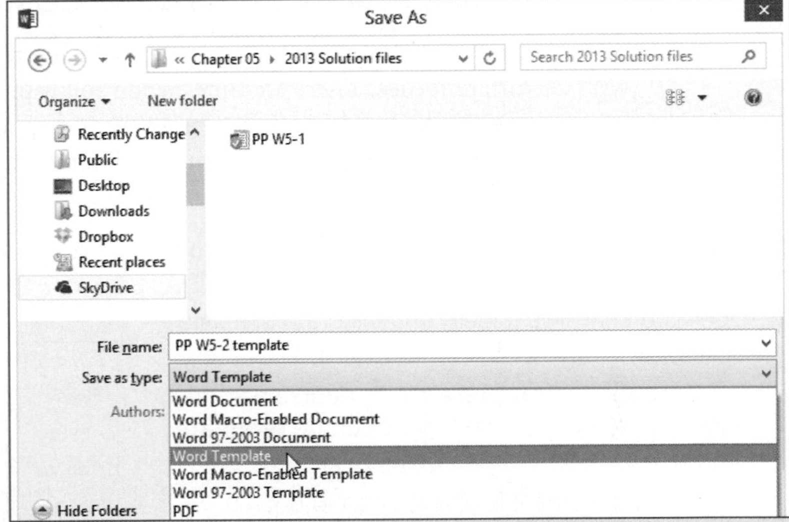

5-15 Save as a *Word Template*

> **ANOTHER WAY**
>
> **Ctrl+N** creates a new blank document.

Save an Existing Document as a Template

There are times when you want to save an existing file as a template. For example, you might save a course assignment sheet with your name, course title, and professor's name in the header as a template. Saving an existing document as a template is similar to saving a new document as a template.

HOW TO: Save an Existing Document as a Template

1. Open an existing Word document.
2. Press **F12** to open the *Save As* dialog box (see Figure 5-15).
   - You can also open the *Save As* dialog box from the *Save As* area on the *Backstage* view.
3. Type the file name in the *File name* area.
4. Click the **Save as type** drop-down list and select **Word Template**.
5. Browse to the location where you want to save the file.
6. Click **Save** to close the dialog box and save the template. The Word document is saved as a Word Template.

> **MORE INFO**
>
> When you save an existing document as a template, you will have two documents with the same name. The difference is the file type. To distinguish between them, refer to both the file icon and the file name extension.

Create a Document Based Upon a Template

One of the most confusing aspects of using templates is determining how to open each of the different files. There are times when you want to create a new Word document based upon an existing template, and there are times when you want to open and edit an existing template. When you create a document based upon a template, open the file from a Windows folder.

HOW TO: Create a Document Based Upon a Template

1. Open the Windows folder containing the template file (Figure 5-16).
2. Double-click the **template file** to open a document based upon that template, or select the **template file** (click once) and press **Enter**.
   - When a document is opened based upon a template file, Word gives the document a generic file name such as *Document1*, which is displayed in the title bar of the Word window.
3. Save the document.
   - When you save the document based upon a template, the *Save As* dialog box opens so you can give the document a unique name.
   - Notice that *Word Document* is already selected in the *Save as type* area of the *Save As* dialog box.

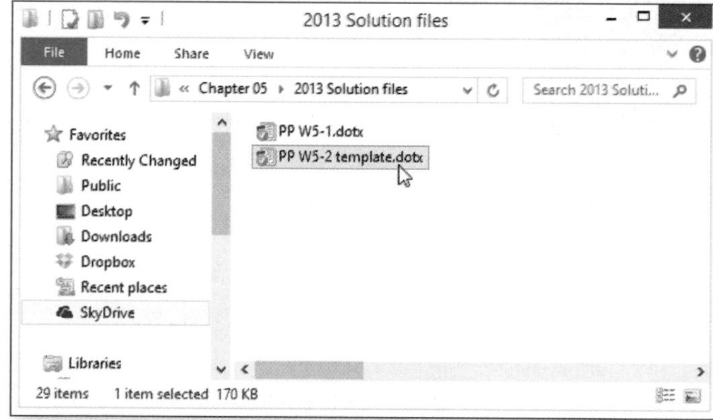

5-16 Open a document based upon a template

> **MORE INFO**
>
> Don't try to open a document based upon a template using the *Open* feature from within Word. This always opens the template, not a document based upon the template.

Edit a Template

There are times you need to edit the template document, not just the document based upon the template. Remember, opening a template so you can edit it is different from opening a document based upon a template.

There are two different ways to open a template to edit it.

- ***Open the template file from within Word.*** Press **Ctrl+F12** or click the **Browse** button in the *Open* area on the *Backstage view* to open the *Open* dialog box. Browse to find and select the **template file** and click **Open**.
- ***Open the template file from a Windows folder.*** Right-click the **template file** and select **Open** from the context menu.

When you open a template file to edit it, the file name displayed in the Word title bar is the name of the template rather than the generic document name (*Document1*) Word generates when you open a document based upon a template.

> **MORE INFO**
>
> Always open a template from within Word and open a document based upon a template from the Windows folder containing the template file.

PAUSE & PRACTICE: WORD 5-2

For this Pause & Practice project, you create a volunteer letter template file from an existing document for Kelly McFarland to send out to all the Skiing Unlimited program volunteers. You then make changes to the template and create a document based upon this template.

The document you create based upon this template is used in *Pause & Practice 5-4*. This document contains placeholder text that you will replace when you perform a mail merge in *Pause & Practice 5-4*.

File Needed: ***VolunteerLetter-05.docx***
Completed Project File Names: ***[your initials] PP W5-2 template.dotx*** and ***[your initials] PP W5-2.docx***

---

1. Open the ***VolunteerLetter-05*** document from your student data files.
2. Save the document as a *Word Template* file.
   a. Press **F12** to open the *Save As* dialog box or open the *Save As* dialog box from the *Backstage* view.
   b. Type [your initials] PP W5-2 template as the file name in the *File name* area.
   c. Click the **Save as type** drop-down list and select **Word Template**.
   d. Browse to the location on your computer where you save your solution files.
   e. Click **Save** to close the dialog box and save the template.
3. Make changes to the template.
   a. Place your insertion point at the beginning of the first paragraph, insert the current date [*Insert* tab, *Text* group], and set to update automatically. Use the proper date format for a letter (i.e., January 1, 2015).
   b. Press **Enter** four times and type [Address Block].
   c. Press **Enter** two times and type [Greeting Line].
   d. Press **Enter** two times.

e. Press **Ctrl+End** or place your insertion point at the end of the document (at the end of the last bulleted item) and press **Enter** three times. The bulleting is turned off.
f. Type Sincerely,.
g. Press **Enter** four times and type Kelly McFarland.
h. Press **Enter** once and type Community Services Coordinator.
i. On the date line, change the before paragraph spacing to **24 pt**.
j. Find "Courtyard Medical Plaza" and apply **bold** and **italic** formatting.
k. Find all occurrences of "Skiing Unlimited" and apply **italic** formatting.
l. Compare your document with Figure 5-18.

4. Save and close the template.
5. Open a document based upon the ***[your initials] PP W5-2 template*** file (Figure 5-17).
   a. Open the Windows folder containing the ***[your initials] PP W5-2 template*** file.
   b. Double-click the template file or select the template (click once) and press **Enter** to open a document based on the template.
6. Save the document as a Word document named ***[your initials] PP W5-2*** (Figure 5-18).
7. Close the document.

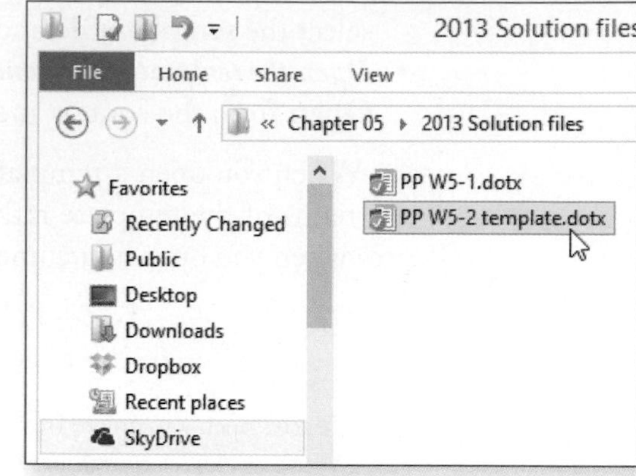

5-17 Open a document based upon a template

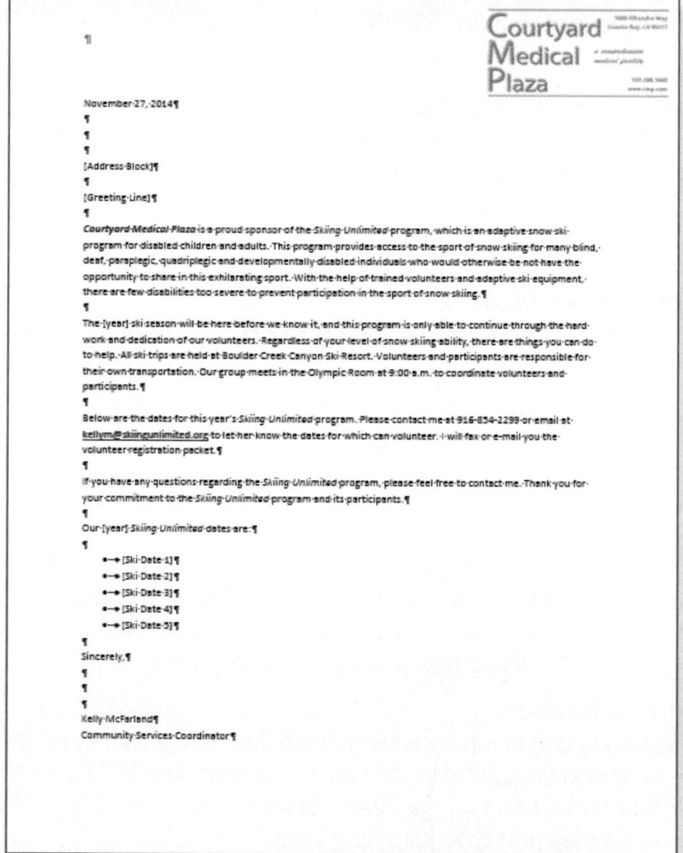

Courtyard Medical Plaza

November 27, 2014

[Address Block]

[Greeting Line]

Courtyard Medical Plaza is a proud sponsor of the *Skiing Unlimited* program, which is an adaptive snow ski program for disabled children and adults. This program provides access to the sport of snow skiing for many blind, deaf, paraplegic, quadriplegic and developmentally disabled individuals who would otherwise be not have the opportunity to share in this exhilarating sport. With the help of trained volunteers and adaptive ski equipment, there are few disabilities too severe to prevent participation in the sport of snow skiing.

The [year] ski season will be here before we know it, and this program is only able to continue through the hard work and dedication of our volunteers. Regardless of your level of snow skiing ability, there are things you can do to help. All ski trips are held at Boulder Creek Canyon Ski Resort. Volunteers and participants are responsible for their own transportation. Our group meets in the Olympic Room at 9:00 a.m. to coordinate volunteers and participants.

Below are the dates for this year's *Skiing Unlimited* program. Please contact me at 916-854-2299 or email at kellym@skiingunlimited.org to let her know the dates for which can volunteer. I will fax or e-mail you the volunteer registration packet.

If you have any questions regarding the *Skiing Unlimited* program, please feel free to contact me. Thank you for your commitment to the *Skiing Unlimited* program and its participants.

Our [year] *Skiing Unlimited* dates are:

- [Ski Date 1]
- [Ski Date 2]
- [Ski Date 3]
- [Ski Date 4]
- [Ski Date 5]

Sincerely,

Kelly McFarland
Community Services Coordinator

5-18 PP W5-2 completed

SLO 5.3

Creating Envelopes and Labels

In your professional or personal life, there might be times when you need to create ***envelopes*** or ***mailing labels*** for letters or cards. If you only have a couple to do, it's not a problem to write them by hand. But, if you are sending out invitations to 100 people for a grand opening of a new store or to 50 friends for a graduation party, it can be very time consuming to hand write all of these. Also, printed envelopes and labels look more professional. Word provides you with a mailing feature that allows you to quickly create envelopes and mailing labels.

Create an Envelope

Most inkjet and laser printers print envelopes. The *Envelopes and Labels* dialog box provides you with an area to type the delivery and return addresses. You can select the type of envelope or a specific size of envelope.

HOW TO: Create an Envelope

1. Open a new blank document.
2. Click the **Mailings** tab.
3. Click the **Envelopes** button [*Create* group] (Figure 5-19). The *Envelopes and Labels* dialog box opens and the *Envelopes* tab is selected (Figure 5-20).

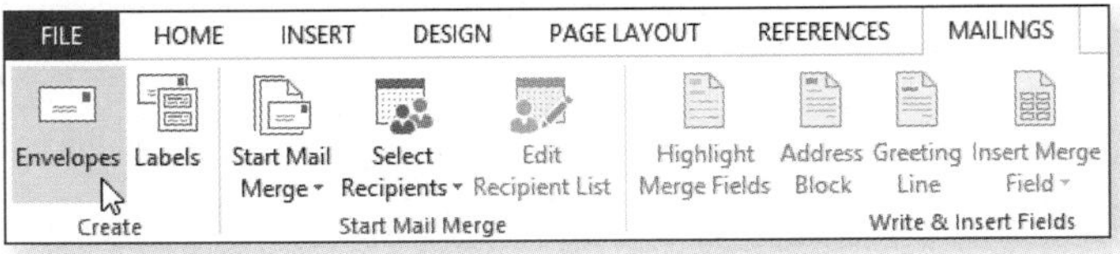

5-19 Create an envelope

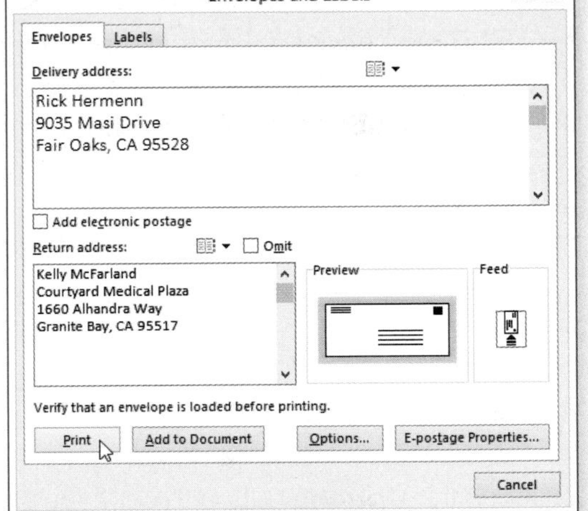

5-20 *Envelopes and Labels* dialog box

4. Click in the *Delivery address* area and type the mailing address.
5. Click in the *Return address* area and type the return address.
   - You can change the font, size, and style of the text for both the delivery and return addresses by selecting the text, right-clicking the selected text, and selecting **Font** from the context menu. The *Font* dialog box opens and you can make the desired changes.
6. Click the **Print** button.

Envelope Options

When creating and printing envelopes, you need to specify the type or size of envelope. Word provides you with an *Envelope Options* dialog box to select the type or size of the envelope, the font and size of the delivery and return address, and the position of the addresses on the envelope (Figure 5-21).

From the *Envelope and Labels* dialog box, click the **Options** button to open the *Envelope Options* dialog box. From the *Envelope size* drop-down list, select the envelope you will use. You can also make format and position adjustments for the addresses.

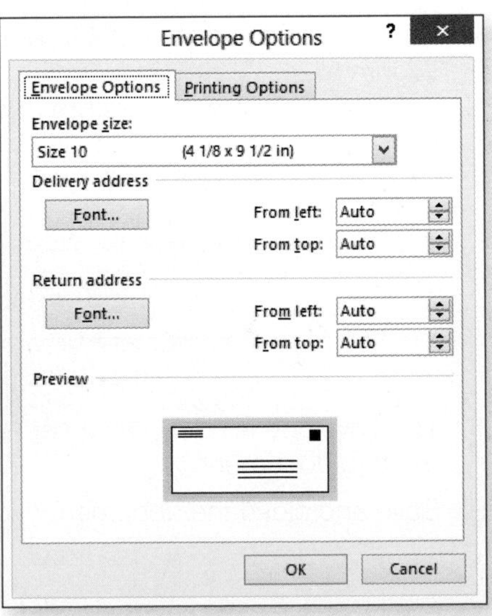

5-21 *Envelope Options* dialog box

Printing Options

A Printing Options tab is also available in the *Envelope Options* dialog box (Figure 5-22). This tab lets you specify how the envelope is fed into the printer. Word provides you with a recommended setting for printing, but you might need to select a different feed method depending on the printer you are using.

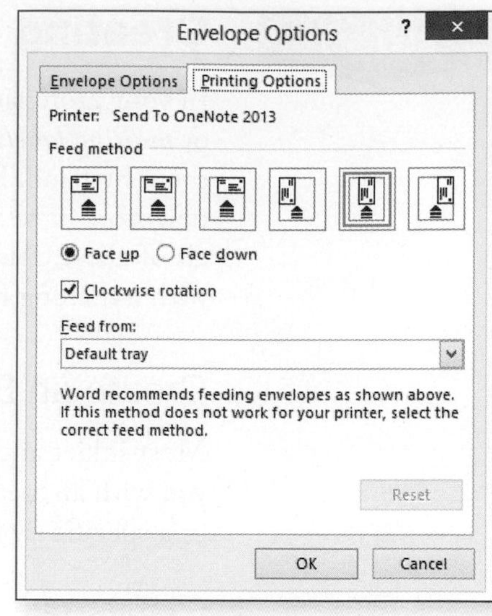

5-22 Envelope printing options

Add an Envelope to an Existing Document

Word also gives you the option of adding an envelope to an existing document. For example, Word can create an envelope based upon a letter you are sending to a potential client. Word uses the delivery address from the letter to automatically populate the *Delivery address* field in the envelope.

HOW TO: Add an Envelope to a Document

1. Open a letter document for which you need an envelope.
2. Click the **Envelopes** button [*Mailings* tab, *Create* group]. The *Envelopes and Labels* dialog box opens (Figure 5-23).
3. The *Delivery address* area is populated with the delivery address from the letter.
4. In the *Return address* area, type in the return address.
5. Click the **Options** button to set the envelope size and printing options and click **OK**.
6. Click the **Add to Document** button.
7. A dialog box opens asking if you want to set the return address as the default return address (Figure 5-24). Click **Yes** (or select **No** if you do not want this as the default return address).

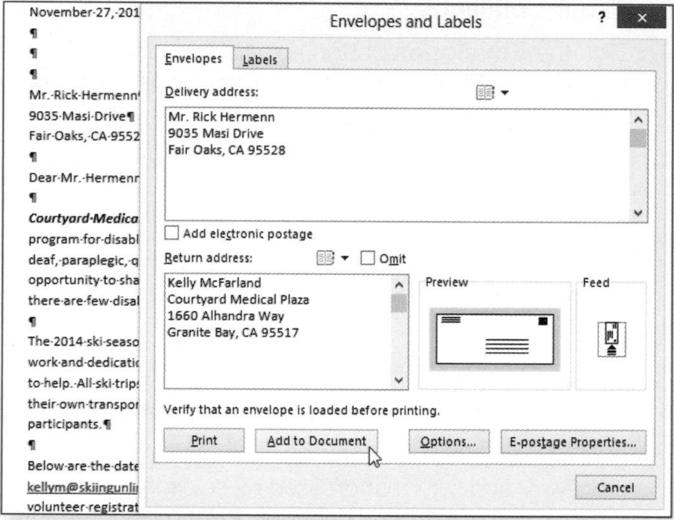

5-23 Add an envelope to an existing document

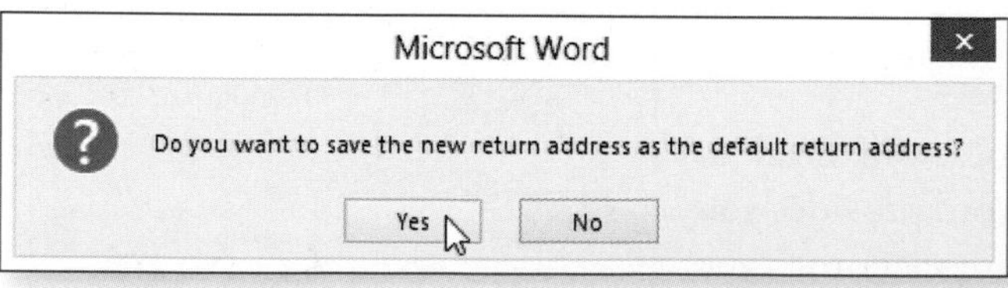

5-24 Set the default return address

8. The envelope is added as a separate page before the existing document.
9. Save and close the document (Figure 5-25).

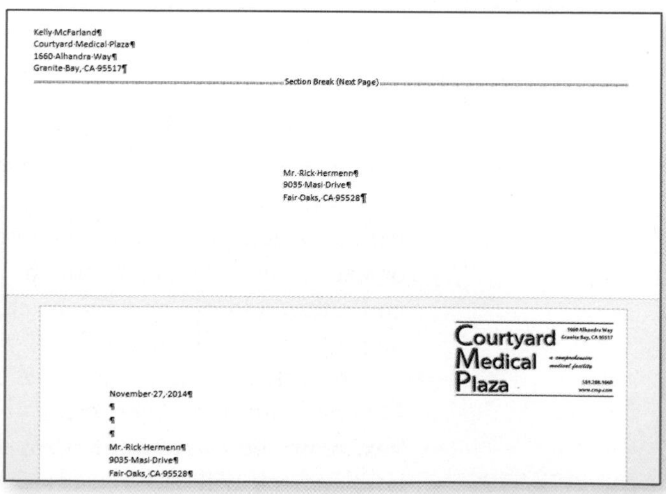

5-25 Envelope added to an existing document

Create Labels

Creating and printing labels is an excellent way to save time and produce professional-looking documents. You can purchase labels at most office supply stores; they come in a variety of sizes to meet your needs. You can create individual labels by typing the delivery address or other information for each label, or you can create a full page with the same information on every label (for example, a page of return address labels).

You are not limited to mailing labels only. You can use labels to print name badges for a conference, or you can print labels to identify project folders.

MORE INFO

Labels and envelopes can also be merged with a database or other data sources rather than typing each label or envelope individually. Merging is covered later in this chapter.

Label Options

Before creating and printing labels, it is important to decide what type of labels you are using and select the correct type and size of label in the *Label Options* dialog box.

HOW TO: Set Label Options

1. With a new document open, click the **Labels** button [*Mailings* tab, *Create* group]. The *Envelope and Labels* dialog box opens with the *Labels* tab selected.
2. Click the **Options** button to open the *Label Options* dialog box (Figure 5-26).
3. In the *Printer information* area, select the type of printer and the printer tray you are using.
4. In the *Label information* area, click the **Label vendors** drop-down list and select the vendor of the labels you are using.
5. In the *Product number* area, select the specific label product number.

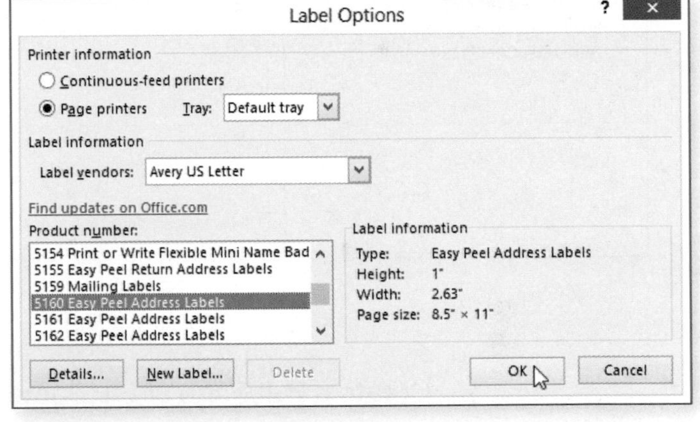

5-26 ***Label Options*** **dialog box**

- If you can't find your specific label, click the **Find updates on Office.com** link for an updated list of labels.
- You can make changes to a label by clicking the **Details** button, which shows dimensions.
- You can also create a custom label by clicking the **New Label** button.

6. Click **OK** to close the *Label Options* dialog box.

MORE INFO

Avery 5160 is one of the most common types of labels used for delivery and return address labels.

Create Individual Labels

When you are creating individual labels, Word opens a new document where you can type the information for each label. Based on the type of label you have selected, Word sets up a table in a new document. You type the information for each label in the cells of the table.

HOW TO: Create Individual Labels

1. With a new document open, click the **Labels** button [*Mailings* tab, *Create* group]. The *Envelope and Labels* dialog box opens with the *Labels* tab selected (Figure 5-27).
2. Click the **Options** button and select the type of label you want to use.
3. Click **OK** to close the *Label Options* dialog box.
4. Leave the *Address* area blank.
5. In the *Print* area, select the **Full page of the same label** radio button.
   - You are creating a full page of blank labels on which you will type the information for each label.
6. Click the **New Document** button. A new document opens with a preset table inserted in the document.
7. Type the information for each label.
   - Press **Enter** after each line of the label.
   - Press **Tab** twice to move to the next label. A blank column is added between each label to allow for spacing between labels.
8. After typing the labels, you can print and save and close the labels document (Figure 5-28).

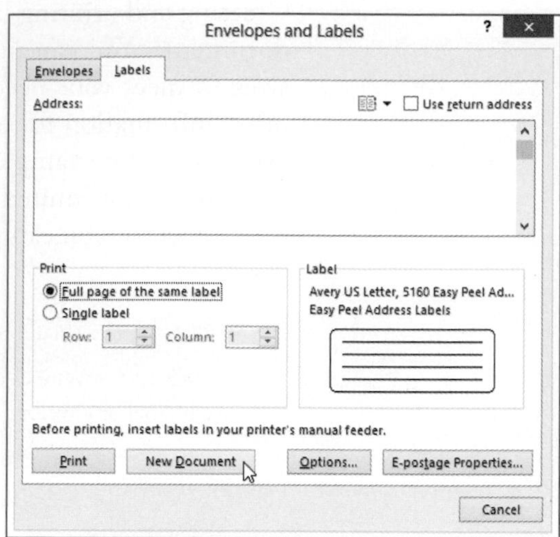

5-27 Create individual labels

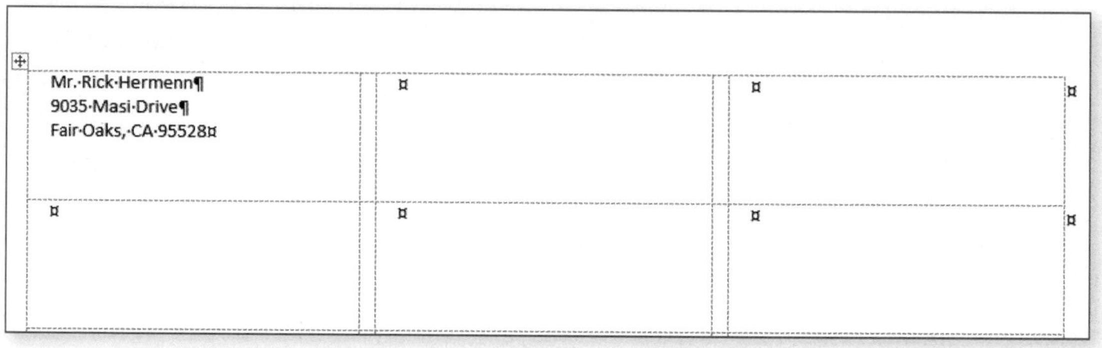

5-28 Type individual labels in the document

Create a Full Page of the Same Label

You can also print a full sheet of the same label. This saves you the time of typing the same label over and over or copying and pasting the same label information in each cell.

HOW TO: Create a Full Page of the Same Label

1. With a new document open, click the **Labels** button [*Mailings* tab, *Create* group]. The *Envelope and Labels* dialog box opens with the *Labels* tab selected (Figure 5-29).
2. Click the **Options** button and select the type of label you want to use.
3. Click **OK** to close the *Label Options* dialog box.
4. In the *Address* area, type the label information.
5. In the *Print* area, select the **Full page of the same label** radio button.
   - You are creating a full page of the same label, populated with the information you typed in the *Address* field.

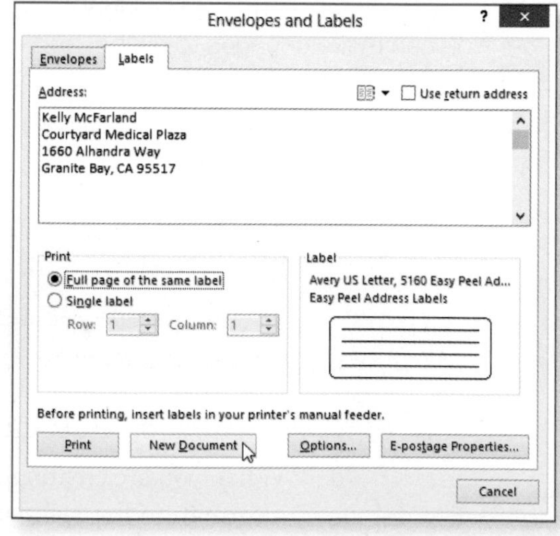

5-29 Create a full page of the same label

6. Click the **New Document** button. A new document opens containing a full page of the same label.
   - You can click the **Print** button to directly print the document without viewing it.
7. After reviewing the labels, you can print, save, and close the labels document (Figure 5-30).

5-30 Full page of the same label

> **MORE INFO**
>
> If you previously saved your return address, you can use this address for labels by checking the **Use return address** check box in the upper right corner of the *Envelopes and Labels* dialog box.

PAUSE & PRACTICE: WORD 5-3

In this Pause & Practice project, you create mailing labels for Kelly McFarland to use when sending out volunteer letters for the Skiing Unlimited program. You also create individual labels for delivery addresses and a full page of the same label for return addresses.

File Needed: None
Completed Project File Names: ***[your initials] PP W5-3a.docx*** and ***[your initials] PP W5-3b.docx***

1. Open a new Word document.
2. Set up the mailing labels.
   a. Click the **Labels** button [*Mailings* tab, *Create* group].
   b. Click the **Options** button. The *Label Options* dialog box opens (Figure 5-31).
   c. In the *Label Information* area, select **Avery US Letter** from the *Label vendors* drop-down list.
   d. In the *Product number* area, select **5160 Easy Peel Address Labels**.
   e. Click **OK** to close the *Label Options* dialog box.

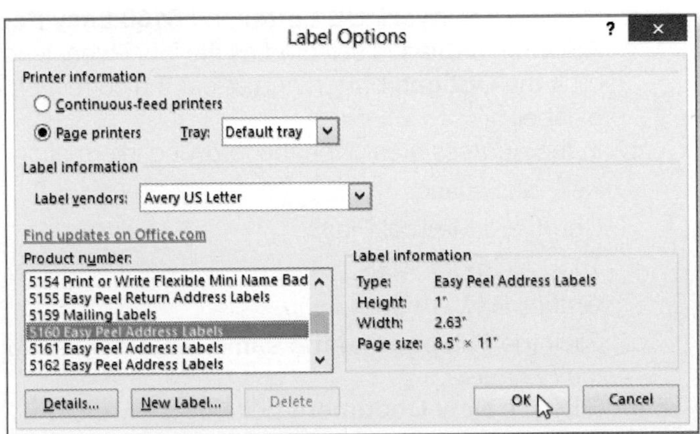

5-31 Select label type

3. Create individual mailing labels.
   a. With the *Envelopes and Labels* dialog box still open, leave the *Address* area blank (Figure 5-32).
   b. Click the **Full page of the same label** radio button in the *Print* area.
   c. Click the **New Document** button. A new Word document opens with the labels table inserted.
4. Save the document as ***[your initials] PP W5-3a***.
5. Type individual mailing labels.
   a. Use the following information to type six mailing labels.
   b. Press **Tab** two times after each label to move to the next label cell on the same row. At the end of the row, press **Tab** once to move to the label cell in the new row.

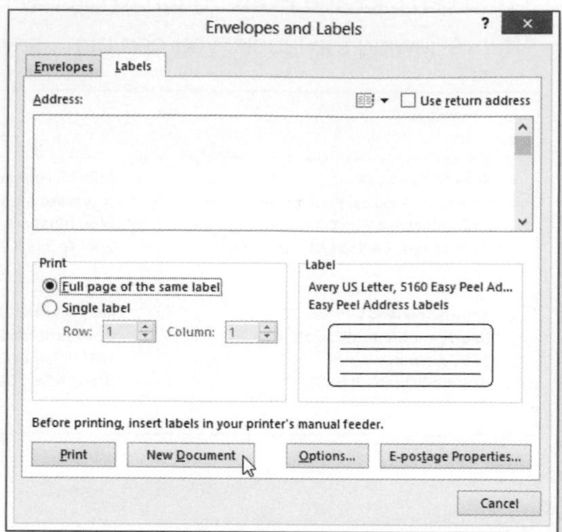

5-32 Create individual mailing labels

Mr. Rick Hermenn 9035 Masi Drive Fair Oaks, CA 95528	Dr. Karen Draper 784 Ehrlich Road Carmichael, CA 96774	Mr. Ty Han 1272 Eastwood Court Auburn, CA 95236
Dr. Seth Uribe 8263 Wales Avenue Roseville, CA 95722	Mr. Sawyer Petrosky 2741 Lake Road Granite Bay, CA 95517	Ms. Kallyn Nickols 7336 Ebony Way Auburn, CA 95236

6. Save and close this document (Figure 5-33).
7. Return to the open blank Word document.
8. Create a full page of the same label for return address labels.
   a. Click the **Labels** button [*Mailings* tab, *Create* group]. The *Envelopes and Labels* dialog box opens (Figure 5-34).
   b. Confirm that **Avery US Letter** and **5160 Easy Peel Address Labels** is selected as the label type. If not, click the **Options** button and select the correct type of label.
   c. In the *Address* area, type the following information:

      Kelly McFarland

      Courtyard Medical Plaza

      1660 Alhandra Way

      Granite Bay, CA 95517
   d. Click the **Full page of the same label** radio button in the *Print* area.
   e. Click the **New Document** button. A new Word document opens with a full page of the same label populated in the labels table.

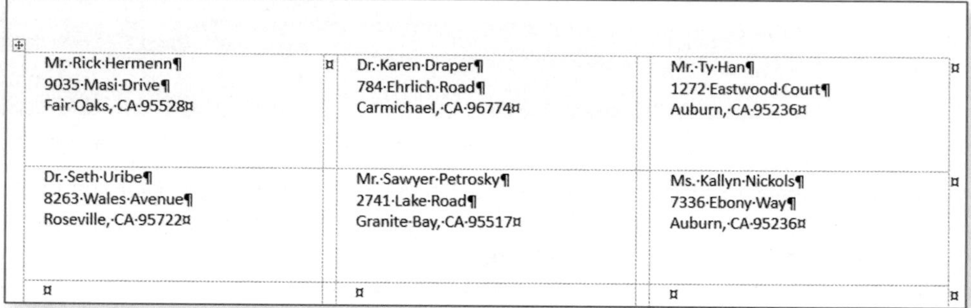

5-33 PP W5-3a completed

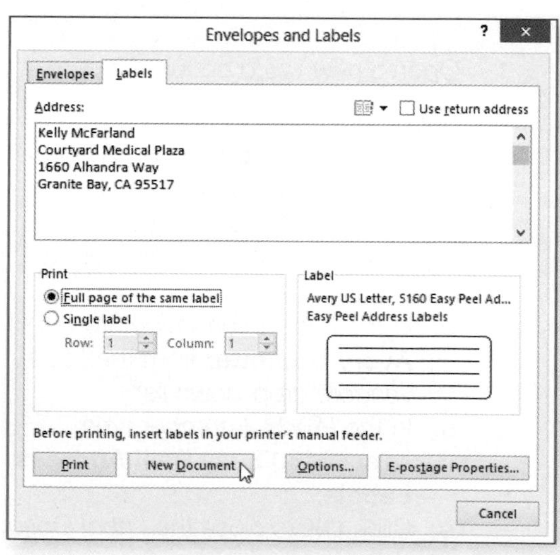

5-34 Create a full page of the same label

9. Save the document as ***[your initials] PP W5-3b*** and close the document (Figure 5-35).

Kelly·McFarland¶ Courtyard·Medical·Plaza¶ 1660·Alhandra·Way¶ Granite·Bay,·CA·95517¤	Kelly·McFarland¶ Courtyard·Medical·Plaza¶ 1660·Alhandra·Way¶ Granite·Bay,·CA·95517¤	Kelly·McFarland¶ Courtyard·Medical·Plaza¶ 1660·Alhandra·Way¶ Granite·Bay,·CA·95517¤
Kelly·McFarland¶ Courtyard·Medical·Plaza¶ 1660·Alhandra·Way¶ Granite·Bay,·CA·95517¤	Kelly·McFarland¶ Courtyard·Medical·Plaza¶ 1660·Alhandra·Way¶ Granite·Bay,·CA·95517¤	Kelly·McFarland¶ Courtyard·Medical·Plaza¶ 1660·Alhandra·Way¶ Granite·Bay,·CA·95517¤
Kelly·McFarland¶ Courtyard·Medical·Plaza¶ 1660·Alhandra·Way¶ Granite·Bay,·CA·95517¤	Kelly·McFarland¶ Courtyard·Medical·Plaza¶ 1660·Alhandra·Way¶ Granite·Bay,·CA·95517¤	Kelly·McFarland¶ Courtyard·Medical·Plaza¶ 1660·Alhandra·Way¶ Granite·Bay,·CA·95517¤

5-35 PP W5-3b completed

SLO 5.4

Understanding Mail Merge

Mail merge is one of Word's most helpful and time-saving features. Mail merge gives you the ability to merge a document, such as a form letter, labels, or envelopes, with a data source such as a database file or contact records from Microsoft Outlook. Merges can be very simple; for example, you can create a list of mailing labels from your Outlook contacts. Or they can be more complex; for example, you can merge address and account information for a client's insurance renewal letter. Before working with mail merge, it is important to understand the different components of a merge.

Types of Mail Merge

Word can perform a variety of different types of merges. The most common merges are letters, labels, and envelopes. The category of letters is somewhat misleading because you can merge into any type of document, not just a letter. For example, you can merge recipients into a report, memo, or form. When you start a mail merge, you select the type of merge to be performed (e.g., *Letters, Envelopes, Labels*).

Main Document

The ***main document*** is the Word document into which you merge recipient information from a secondary source. When you perform a letter mail merge, you can begin with an existing document, such as a business letter, or you can begin with a blank document. When you perform a labels or envelopes mail merge, you specify the type of label or envelope to use.

Recipients

The ***recipients*** come from data that is merged into the main document. For example, when you are using mail merge to send a letter to a group of people, recipients are the people who receive your letter (your main document). The recipients can be from an existing data source such as a Microsoft Access or Excel file. You can also create a new recipient list to merge into the main document, or you can use existing contact records from Microsoft Outlook.

The data source used for mail merge is essentially a database of information. It is important to understand some database terminology used in the mail merge process.

- ***Field:*** A field is an individual piece of information such as title, first name, last name, street address, etc.
- ***Record:*** A record is a collection of related fields; a record is all of the information about one recipient.
- ***File, Table, or Contacts Folder:*** A file, table, or *Microsoft Outlook Contacts* folder is a group of related records.

Figure 5-36 is a Microsoft Access table. The information in each cell is a ***field***. Each column heading is a ***field name***. A row of information is a ***record***. All of the information displayed is a ***table***.

Volunteers — Record — Address field

Title	First	Last	Address	City
Mr.	Ty	Han	1272 Eastwood Court	Auburn
Mr.	Rick	Hermenn	9035 Masi Drive	Fair Oaks
Dr.	Karen	Draper	784 Ehrlich Road	Carmichael
Dr.	Seth	Uribe	8263 Wales Avenue	Roseville
Mr.	Sawyer	Petrosky	2741 Lake Road	Granite Bay
Ms.	Kallyn	Nickols	7336 Ebony Way	Auburn

5-36 Microsoft Access database table

When you select recipients for a merge, you use a file, table, or *Contacts* folder as your data source of recipient information. You insert ***merge fields*** into the main document. Word then inserts fields from the data source into the main document according to the merge fields you have inserted in the main document.

SLO 5.5

Merging Using the Mailings Tab

There are two ways to perform a mail merge. You can use the *Mailings* tab or the *Mail Merge Wizard.* You can complete an entire merge using the buttons in the various groups on the *Mailings* tab. In this section we walk through the steps to perform a mail merge using the *Mailings* tab (Figure 5-37). The *Mail Merge Wizard* is covered in the next section.

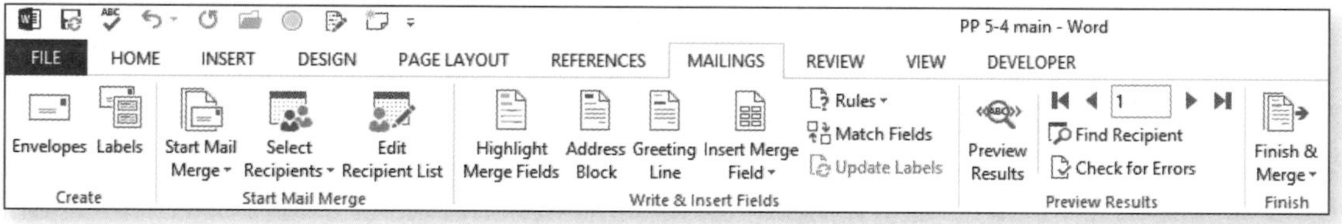

5-37 *Mailings* tab

Start the Mail Merge

The first step in performing a mail merge is to select the type of merge to be performed.

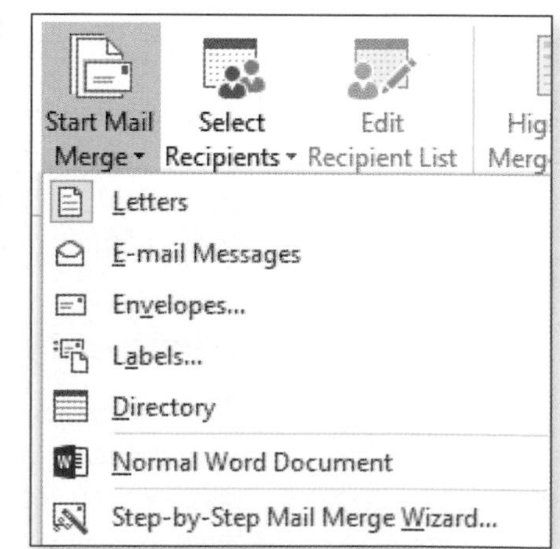

5-38 Types of mail merges

HOW TO: Start the Mail Merge

1. Click the **Mailings** tab.
2. Click the **Start Mail Merge** button [*Start Mail Merge* group] and select the type of merge to be performed (Figure 5-38).
   - If you are performing a mail merge using an existing document, make sure the document is open before clicking the *Start Mail Merge* button.
   - If you are performing a labels or envelopes mail merge, you are prompted to select the type of labels or envelopes in the *Labels Options* or *Envelope Options* dialog box.

Select Recipients

The next step in the mail merge process is to select the recipients, which is the data source to be merged into the main document. Word allows you to use a variety of database files, type a new list as the source data, or use Outlook Contacts.

Click the **Select Recipients** button [*Mailings* tab, *Start Mail Merge* group] and select the type of data source to be used as the recipients (Figure 5-39). A list of options with specific information about each type follows.

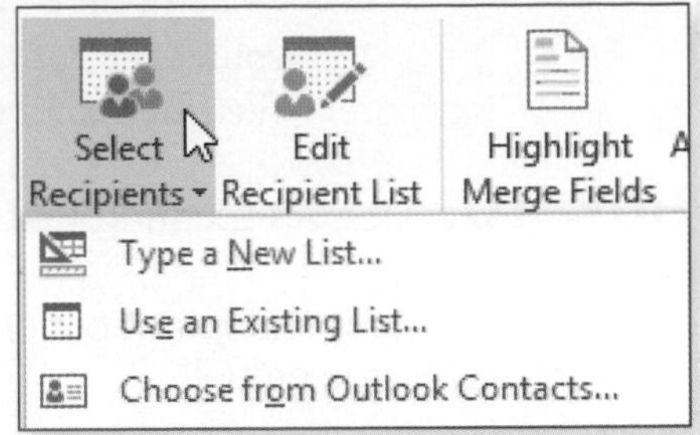

5-39 Types of recipient sources

MORE INFO

It is a good idea to proofread and edit your data source before beginning a mail merge.

Type a New List

The *Type a New List* option allows you to type in the recipients' information if you do not already have an existing data source. The data source is saved and you can edit it later and use it in other mail merges.

HOW TO: Type a New Recipient List for Mail Merge

1. Click the **Select Recipient** button [*Mailings* tab, *Start Mail Merge* group].
2. Select **Type a New List**. The *New Address List* dialog box opens (Figure 5-40).
   - Word provides you with default fields (e.g., *Title*, *First Name*, *Last Name*, etc.). These fields can be edited by clicking the **Customize Columns** button.
3. Type in recipients' information.
   - Press **Tab** to move from field to field.
   - You do not have to type information in every field.
   - You can begin a new record by pressing **Tab** after typing in the last field of information or by clicking the **New Entry** button.
4. Click **OK** when you have finished entering the recipient information. The *Save Address List* dialog box opens.
5. Type a name for the new address list, browse to the location where you want to save the file, and click **Save**.

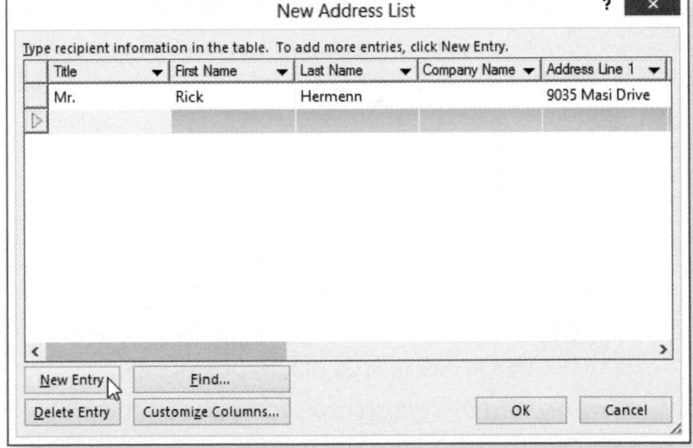

5-40 *New Address List* dialog box

MORE INFO

When creating a new address list for a mail merge, Word will save the document as a *Microsoft Office Address Lists* file (.mdb), which you can edit and use for other mail merges.

Use an Existing List

When you use an existing list for the recipients of a mail merge, you are prompted to open the source file containing the recipients' information. Word allows you to use a variety of database files for a mail merge.

HOW TO: Use an Existing List for Mail Merge

1. Click the **Select Recipient** button [*Mailings* tab, *Start Mail Merge* group].
2. Select **Use an Existing List**. The *Select Data Source* dialog box opens (Figure 5-41).
3. Browse to the location on your computer containing the data source file and click **Open**.
   - If you are using a database file with multiple tables, a dialog box opens prompting you to select the table to be used in the merge.

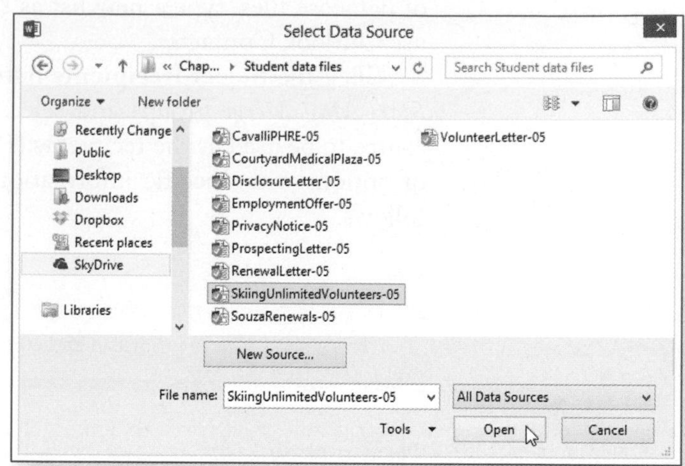

5-41 *Select Data Source* dialog box

Select from Outlook Contacts

If you are a regular Microsoft Outlook user, you probably have many contacts saved in Outlook. You can use information stored in an Outlook contacts folder to perform a mail merge.

HOW TO: Select from Outlook Contacts for Mail Merge

1. Click the **Select Recipient** button [*Mailings* tab, *Start Mail Merge* group].
2. Select **Choose from Outlook Contacts**.
   - If the *Choose Profile* dialog box opens (Figure 5-42), select the Outlook profile to use and click **OK**. The *Select Contacts* dialog box opens (Figure 5-43).
   - Typically, people only have one Outlook profile, but if you have more than one Outlook profile setup on your computer, choose the correct profile to use.

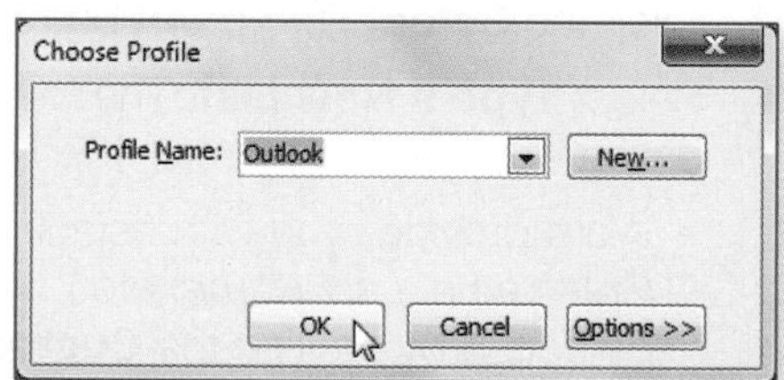

5-42 Select *Outlook* profile

3. In the *Select Contacts* dialog box, select the contacts folder to use for the mail merge.
4. Click **OK** to close the *Select Contacts* dialog box. The *Mail Merge Recipients* dialog box opens.
   - From within this dialog box, you can select the recipients to include in this merge, sort recipients, and filter recipients.
   - You can also perform these actions in the next step of the mail merge, which is to edit the recipient list.
5. Click **OK** to close the *Mail Merge Recipients* dialog box.

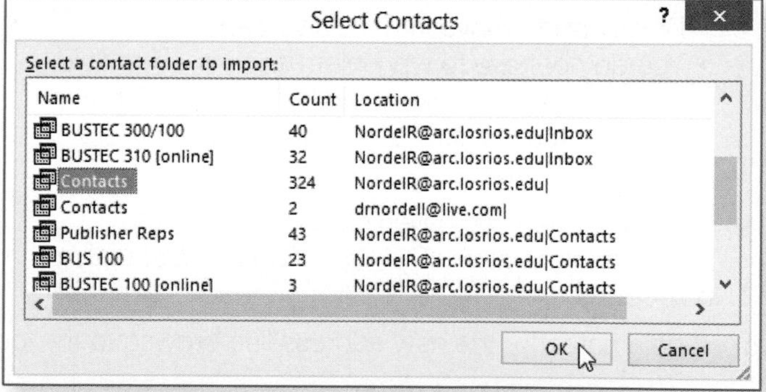

5-43 Select Outlook *Contacts* folder

Edit Recipients

After selecting or creating the recipient list, the next step in the mail merge process is to edit your recipient list. During this process you can select which records (recipients) to include in the merge, ***sort*** the records, and ***filter*** the records. Filtering is a powerful tool if you are working with a large number of records in your source data file. For example, you can filter for only those recipients from a specific town or zip code.

HOW TO: Edit Recipient List for Mail Merge

1. Click the **Edit Recipient List** button [*Mailings* tab, *Start Mail Merge* group]. The *Mail Merge Recipients* dialog box opens (Figure 5-44).
2. Use the check boxes in the second column to select or deselect recipients.
   - By default, all recipients in the data source file are included in the merge.
3. Sort the recipient list by clicking a column heading drop-down arrow and selecting **Sort Ascending** or **Sort Descending** (Figure 5-45).
   - You can also click the **Sort** link in the *Refine recipient list* area to sort recipients. A *Filter and Sort* dialog box opens.

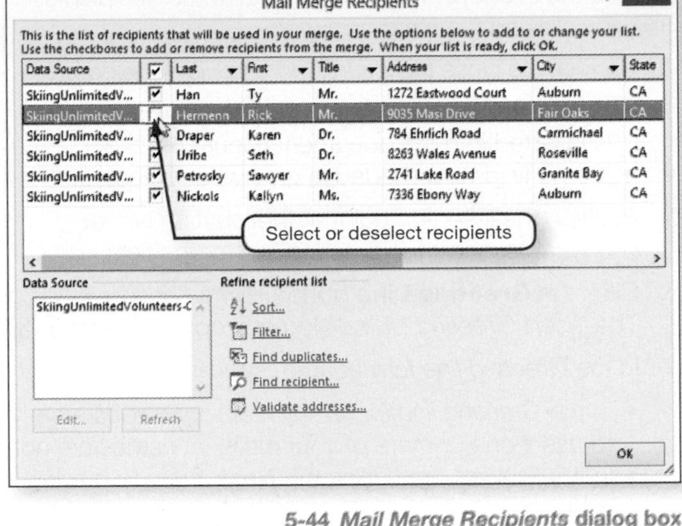

5-44 Mail Merge Recipients dialog box

4. Filter the recipient list by clicking a column heading drop-down arrow and selecting a criterion by which to filter the recipient list.
   - You can also click the **Filter** link in the *Refine recipient list* area to sort recipients. A *Filter and Sort* dialog box opens.
   - When you filter a data source, only those recipient records that match the criteria are displayed in the recipient list. To display all of the recipient records, select **(All)** from the column heading drop-down list.
5. Click **OK** to close the *Mail Merge Recipients* dialog box when you are finished editing the recipient list.

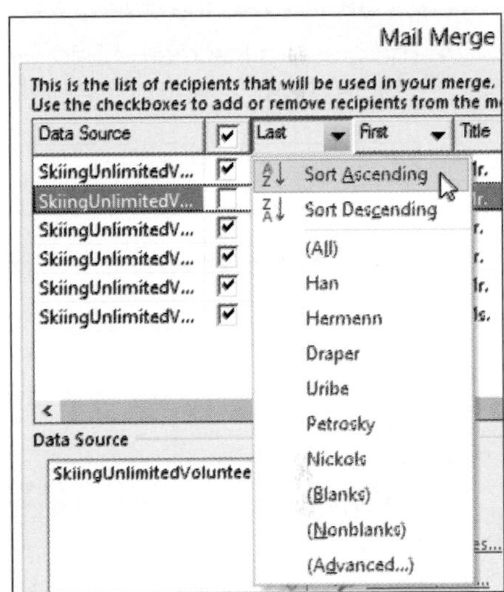

5-45 Sort or filter by field

> **MORE INFO**
>
> It's best to use the *Filter and Sort* dialog box if you're performing a sort or filter on more than one field. Click the **Sort** or **Filter** link in the *Mail Merge Recipients* dialog box to open the *Filter and Sort* dialog box.

Insert Merge Fields

After you edit the recipient list, you can insert merge fields into your main document, which might be a letter, labels, or envelopes. You can insert an ***address block***, ***greeting line***, or other ***merge fields*** from your data source into the main document. Both the *Address Block* and *Greeting Line* buttons in the *Write & Insert Fields* group combine individual fields to create an acceptable mailing address and greeting line.

HOW TO: Insert Merge Fields into the Main Document

1. With the main document for the mail merge open, position the insertion point at the location where you want to insert the address block merge field.
2. Click the **Address Block** button [*Write & Insert Fields* group]. The *Insert Address Block* dialog box opens (Figure 5-46).

3. In the *Specify address elements* area, select the format of how the recipient's name should appear.
    - A preview of the address block appears in the *Preview* area on the right.
    - In the *Preview* area, you can view other recipients by clicking the **Next** arrow.
4. Click **OK** to close the *Insert Address Block* dialog box.
    - The address block merge field (<<*AddressBlock*>>) is inserted into the document (Figure 5-47).
    - Merge fields are shaded in gray when selected.

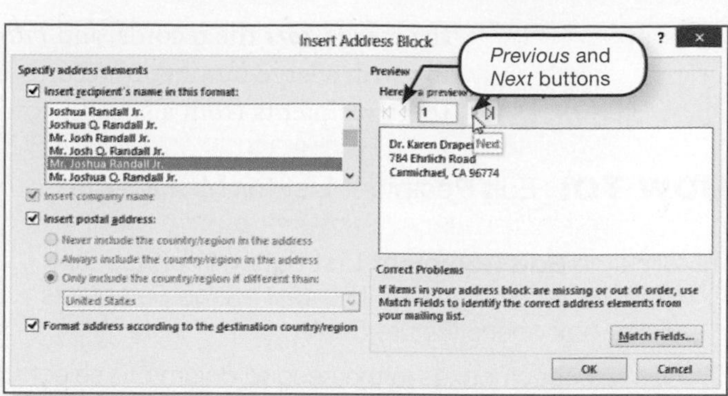

5-46 ***Insert Address Block*** **dialog box**

5. Position the insertion point at the location where you want to insert the greeting line merge field.
6. Click the **Greeting Line** button [*Write & Insert Fields* group]. The *Insert Greeting Line* dialog box opens (Figure 5-48).
7. In the *Greeting line format* area, specify how you want the greeting line to appear.
    - In the *Greeting line for invalid recipient names* area, you can specify a generic greeting to use if one or more of your recipient names are not valid.
    - In the *Preview* area, click the **Next** arrow to preview the greeting line for each of your recipients.
8. Click **OK** to close the *Insert Greeting Line* dialog box.
    - The greeting line merge field (<<*GreetingLine*>>) is inserted into the document (Figure 5-49).

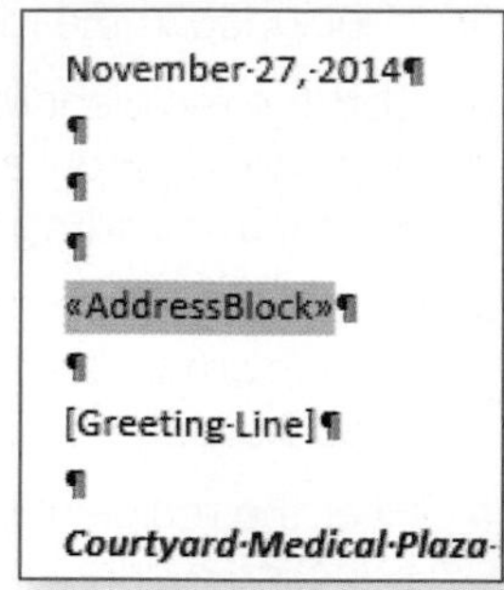

5-47 ***AddressBlock*** **merge field in the main document**

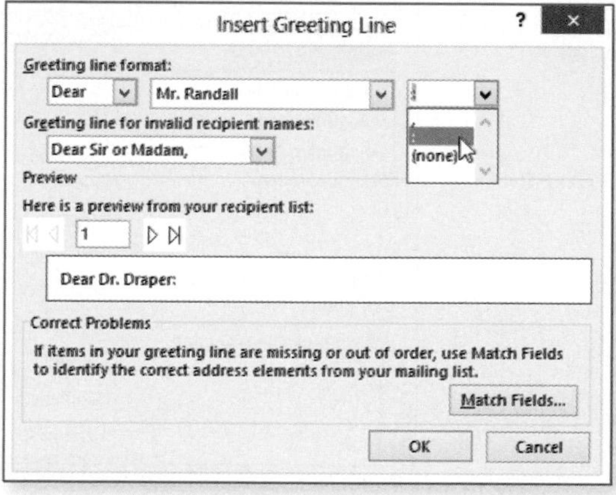

5-48 ***Insert Greeting Line*** **dialog box**

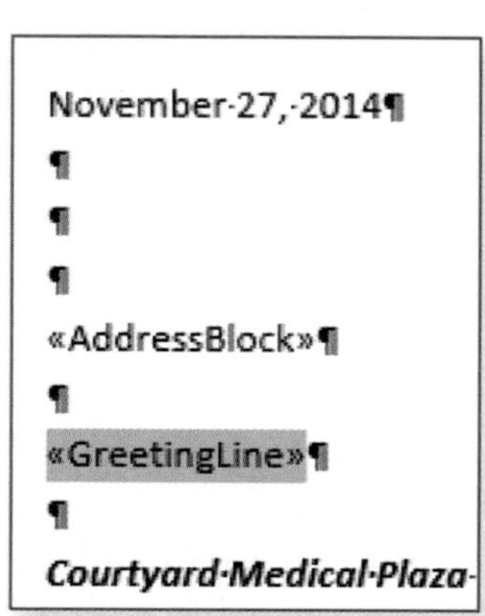

5-49 ***GreetingLine*** **merge field in the main document**

Match Fields

What if Word does not correctly build your address block or greeting line? If your data source uses field names that Word does not recognize or match with a corresponding Word field, you can use the ***match fields*** feature to manually match the field names from your data source to those field names recognized by Word.

HOW TO: Match Fields

1. Click the **Match Fields** button [*Mailings* tab, *Write & Insert Fields* group]. The *Match Fields* dialog box opens (Figure 5-50).
    - The fields on the left are Word merge fields.
    - The fields on the right are from your data source.

2. Select a field at the right to match the Word field at the left.
   - Not all of the fields at the right have to be matched. Word ignores fields that are not matched.
   - Each field drop-down list displays the available fields in your data source.
3. Click **OK** to close the *Match Fields* dialog box.

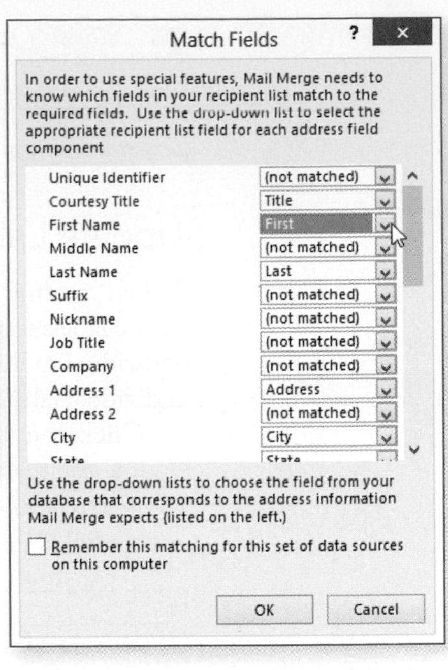

5-50 *Match Fields* dialog box

> **ANOTHER WAY**
>
> Click the **Match Fields** button in the *Insert Address Block* or *Insert Greeting Line* dialog box.

You can manually build your address block and greeting line by using individual merge fields from your data source. To build an address block, Word typically uses the following merge fields: *Courtesy Title, First Name, Last Name, Address 1, Address 2, City, State,* and *Postal Code.*

To build a greeting line, Word typically uses the following merge fields: *Courtesy Title* and *Last Name.* Be sure to include the word "Dear" or "To" before the recipient's name and ending punctuation if needed.

Insert Individual Merge Fields

You are not limited to inserting the address block and greeting line merge fields; you can also insert other fields from your data source into a main document. You can specify which merge fields are inserted into your document and the location of the merge code.

HOW TO: Insert Individual Merge Fields

1. Position the insertion point at the location where you want to insert the merge field (Figure 5-51).
2. Click the **Insert Merge Field** button [*Mailings* tab, *Write & Insert Fields* group].
   - If you click the *Insert Merge Field* drop-down arrow, a drop-down list of merge fields from your data source is displayed.
   - If you click the top half of the *Insert Mail Merge* button, the *Insert Merge Field* dialog box opens.
3. Select the merge field to be inserted into the main document. The merge field is inserted in the document (Figure 5-52).

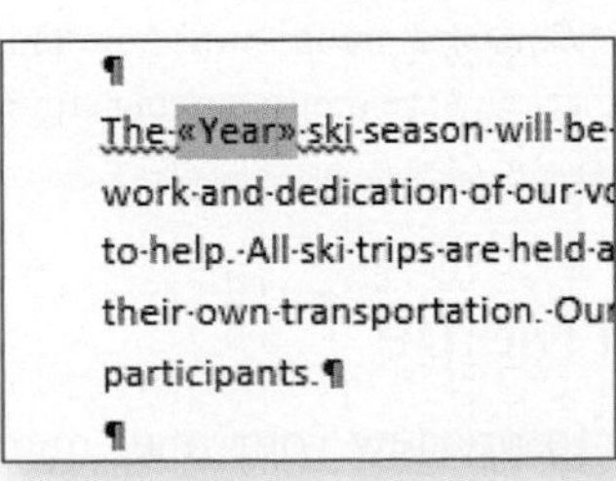

5-52 Individual merge field in the main document

Merge field is inserted at the insertion point

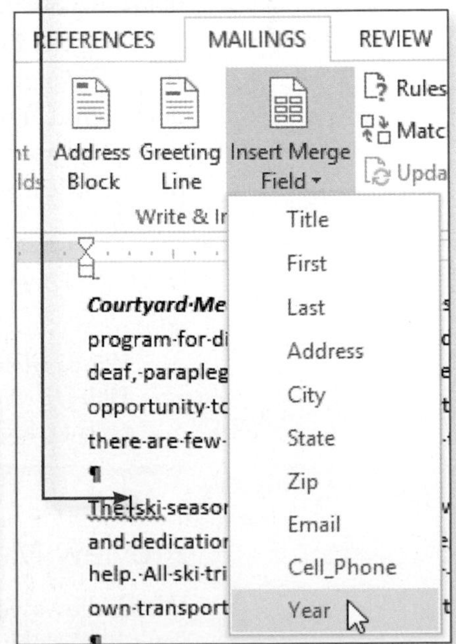

5-51 Insert individual merge field

> **MORE INFO**
>
> Make sure you include proper spacing and punctuation when inserting individual merge fields.

Update Labels

When creating a labels mail merge, Word inserts the address block only in the first cell (label) of the labels main document. You have to update the labels so the address block merge field or individual merge fields appear in each label. You don't need to insert the merge fields in each individual label. Word has a feature that automatically updates each label with the merge fields.

Click the **Update Labels** button in the *Write & Insert Fields* group to automatically update each label with the merge fields (Figure 5-53). On labels, Word inserts a next record (<<*NextRecord*>>) merge field code. When the mail merge is performed, Word inserts the merge fields into each subsequent label until all records are inserted into the labels.

«AddressBlock»¶	«Next·Record»«AddressBlock»¶	«Next·Record»«AddressBlock»¶
«Next·Record»«AddressBlock»¶	«Next·Record»«AddressBlock»¶	«Next·Record»«AddressBlock»¶

5-53 Labels updated in the main document

Highlight Merge Fields

When inserting merge fields into a main document, it can sometimes be difficult to see where the merge fields are unless they are selected. Word allows you to highlight merge fields in a document so you can easily locate each merge field.

Click the **Highlight Merge Fields** button in the *Write & Insert Fields* group to highlight each merge field in your main document (Figure 5-54). Doing this is helpful to ensure that there is proper spacing and punctuation around each merge field. You can toggle this feature on or off by clicking the *Highlight Merge Fields* button.

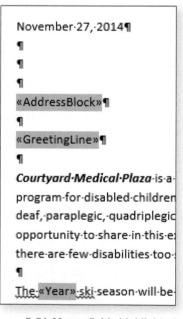

November·27,·2014¶
¶
¶
¶
«AddressBlock»¶
¶
«GreetingLine»¶
¶
Courtyard·Medical·Plaza·is·a·
program·for·disabled·children
deaf,·paraplegic,·quadriplegic
opportunity·to·share·in·this·e
there·are·few·disabilities·too·
¶
The·«Year»·ski·season·will·be·

5-54 Merge fields highlighted in main document

> **MORE INFO**
>
> When performing a mail merge, it is a good idea to have **Show/ Hide** [*Home* tab, *Paragraph* group] turned on. This makes it easier to check that you have proper spacing around merge fields.

Preview Mail Merge

Word allows you to preview your mail merge before finishing the merge. You can see how your final document will look and make any needed changes to the main document. Word can also automatically check your mail merge for errors.

HOW TO: Preview Mail Merge

1. Click the **Preview Results** button [*Mailings* tab, *Preview Results* group] (Figure 5-55). The merge fields from the first record of your data source are displayed in the main document.
2. Click the **Next Record** arrow to preview the next record from your data source.
3. Click the **Check for Errors** button [*Preview Results* group] to check for errors in the mail merge.
   - You are given three error checking options from which to choose (Figure 5-56).
   - The first option displays errors in a new document.
   - The second and third options complete the merge in a new document.
4. Select an error checking option and press **OK**.
   - Word displays any errors found and you can fix these in the data source before finalizing the merge.
5. If Word opened a new document, close this document.
6. Click the **Preview Results** button to turn off this feature. The merge fields are displayed in your main document.

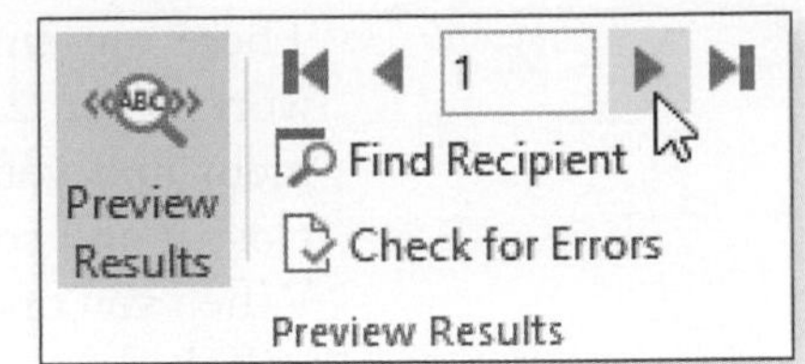

5-55 Preview next record in the main document

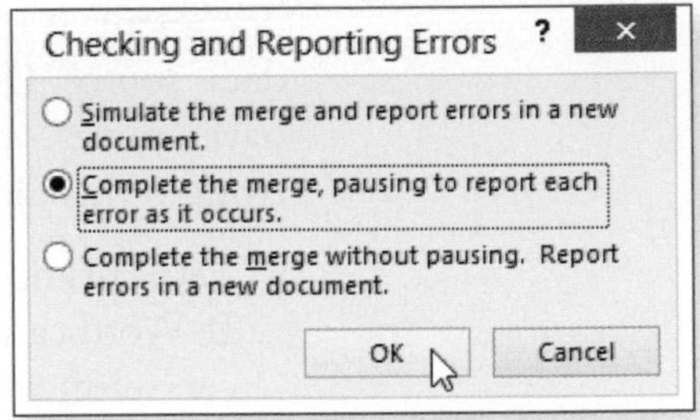

5-56 *Checking and Reporting Errors* dialog box

Finish and Merge

The final step in the mail merge process is merging your data source into the main document. You have two main options to choose from to finish your merge. You can merge into a new document where you can edit individual documents and save this file, or you can print the merged document.

HOW TO: Finish the Mail Merge

1. Save the main document before beginning the merge.
2. Click the **Finish & Merge** button [*Mailings* tab, *Finish* group].
3. Select either **Edit Individual Documents** or **Print Documents**. The *Merge to New Document* (Figure 5-57) or *Merge to Printer* dialog box opens.
   - Both of these dialog boxes allow you to choose which records to include in the merge.
4. Select a *Merge records* radio button and click **OK**.
   - If you selected *Edit Individual Documents*, your completed merge opens in a new window. You can edit, save, or print the completed merge.
   - If you selected *Print Document*, your completed merge is sent to your printer.
5. Save and close any open documents.

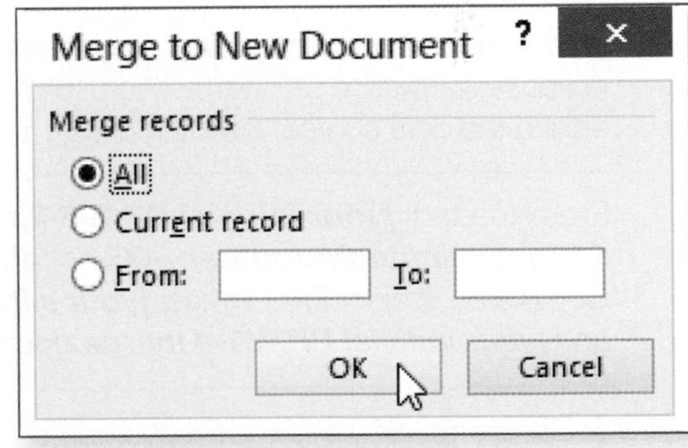

5-57 *Merge to New Document* dialog box

> **MORE INFO**
>
> The third *Finish & Merge* option is *Send Email Messages,* which requires the use of Microsoft Outlook. This option sends an email to each recipient.

Open an Existing Merge Document

There are times when you are working on a mail merge document and you have to save and close it and come back to it later. When you open a document that is linked to another data source file, Word alerts you with a dialog box informing you that your document is linked to another data source (Figure 5-58). You have three options to choose from in this dialog box.

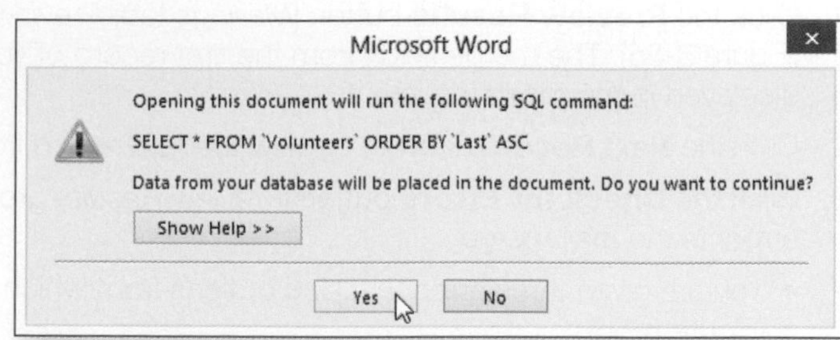

Microsoft Word
Opening this document will run the following SQL command:
SELECT * FROM `Volunteers` ORDER BY `Last` ASC
Data from your database will be placed in the document. Do you want to continue?
Show Help >>
Yes
No

5-58 Alert dialog box when opening a merge document

- ***Yes:*** This option opens your merge document and keeps it linked to the data source file. If Word cannot locate your data source, the *Select Data Source* dialog box opens where you can select your data source.
- ***No:*** This option opens your merge document; you can select the data source file by clicking the *Select Recipients* button.
- ***Show Help:*** This option displays the *Word Help* information in the dialog box.

> **MORE INFO**
>
> If the data source file linked to your merge main document was moved or deleted, you are prompted to select a data source for the main document.

PAUSE & PRACTICE: WORD 5-4

In this Pause & Practice project, you merge the Skiing Unlimited volunteer letter you created for Kelly McFarland in *Pause & Practice 5-2* with a Microsoft Access database to create a merged form letter. You are selecting and editing the data source, inserting merge fields into the main document, and finishing the merge.

Files Needed: ***[your initials] PP W5-2.docx*** and ***SkiingUnlimitedVolunteers-05.accdb***
Completed Project File Names: ***[your initials] PP W5-4 main.docx*** and ***[your initials] PP W5-4 merge.docx***

1. Open the ***[your initials] PP W5-2*** document you created in *Pause & Practice 5-2*. Don't open the ***[your initials] PP W5-2 template*** file.
2. Save the document as ***[your initials] PP W5-4 main***.
3. Begin the merge and select recipients.
   a. Click the **Mailings** tab.
   b. Click the **Start Mail Merge** button [*Start Mail Merge* group] and select **Letters** (Figure 5-59).

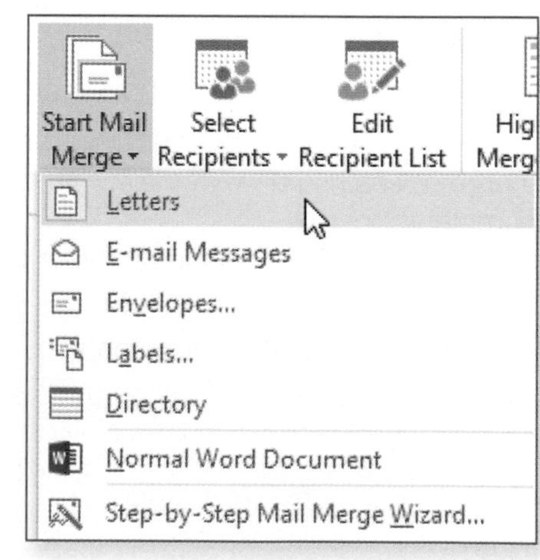

5-59 Select type of mail merge

c. Click the **Select Recipients** button [*Start Mail Merge* group] and select **Use an Existing List**. The *Select Data Source* dialog box opens.
d. Locate your student data files, select ***SkiingUnlimitedVolunteers-05*** (Access database file), and click **Open**.

4. Select recipients and sort the recipient list.
   a. Click the **Edit Recipient List** button [*Start Mail Merge* group]. The *Mail Merge Recipients* dialog box opens (Figure 5-60).
   b. Confirm that the check box for each recipient is checked.
   c. Click the **Last** column heading drop-down arrow and select **Sort Ascending**.
   d. Click **OK** to close the **Mail Merge Recipients** dialog box.

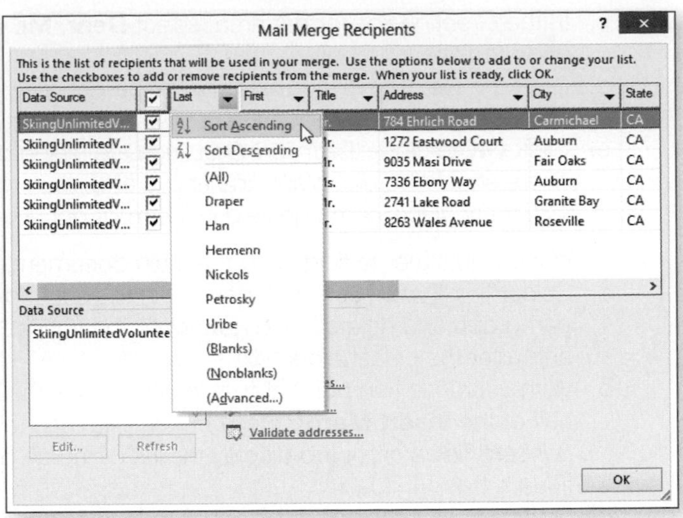

5-60 Select and sort the recipient list

5. Insert the address block merge field into the main document.
   a. Turn on **Show/Hide** [*Home* tab, *Paragraph* group].
   b. Select the "**[AddressBlock]**" placeholder text, not including the paragraph mark, and delete it.
   c. With your insertion point at that location, click the **Address Block** button [*Mailings* tab, *Write & Insert Fields* group]. The *Insert Address Block* dialog box opens (Figure 5-61).
   d. In the *Specify address elements* area, select **Mr. Joshua Randall Jr.** as the format for the recipient's name.
   e. Click the **Next** arrow in the *Preview* area to view the address block for each of the six recipients.
   f. Click **OK** to close the *Insert Address Block* dialog box. There should be three blank lines above and one blank line below the *<<AddressBlock>>* merge field in the main document.

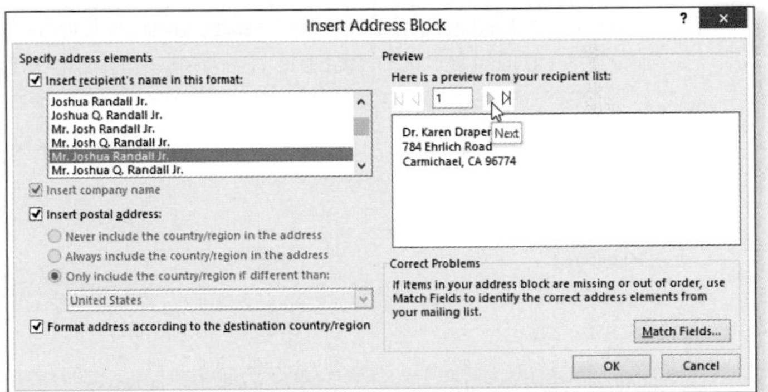

5-61 Insert address block into main document

6. Insert the greeting line merge field into the main document.
   a. Select the "**[GreetingLine]**" placeholder text, not including the paragraph mark, and delete it.
   b. With your insertion point at that location, click the **Greeting Line** button [*Mailings* tab, *Write & Insert Fields* group]. The *Insert Greeting Line* dialog box opens (Figure 5-62).

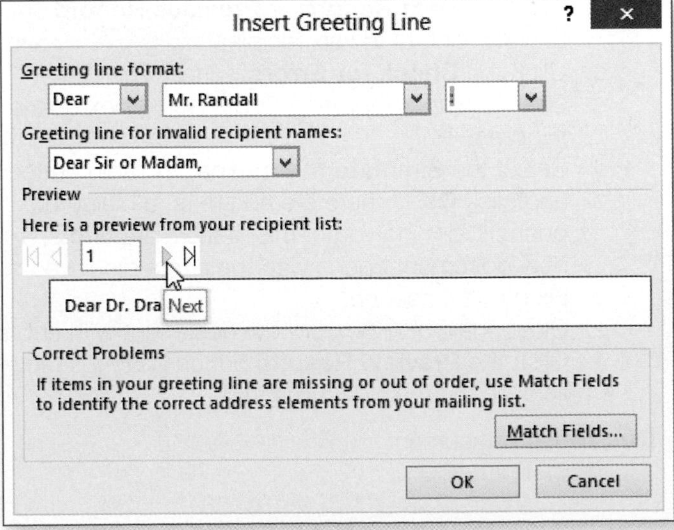

5-62 Insert greeting line into main document

c. In the *Greeting line format* area, select **Dear**, **Mr. Randall** and **:** (colon).
d. Click the **Next** or **Previous** arrow in the *Preview* area to view the greeting line for each of the six recipients.
e. Click **OK** to close the *Insert Greeting Line* dialog box. There should be one blank line above and below the *<<GreetingLine>>* merge field in the main document.

7. Insert individual merge fields into the main document.
   a. Select the "**[year]**" placeholder text in the second body paragraph and delete it. Do not delete the spaces before and after the placeholder text.
   b. With your insertion point at that location, click the bottom half of the **Insert Merge Field** button [*Mailings* tab, *Write & Insert Fields* group] to display the list of merge fields (Figure 5-63).
   c. Select **Year**. The *<<Year>>* merge field is inserted. There should be one space before and after the merge field
   d. Repeat this process to insert the *<<Year>>* merge field to replace the other "[year]" placeholder text before the bulleted list.
   e. Click the **Highlight Merge Fields** button [*Write & Insert Fields* group] to highlight the merge fields in the main document.
   f. Select the second occurrence of the **<<Year>>** merge field and **italicize** the field.

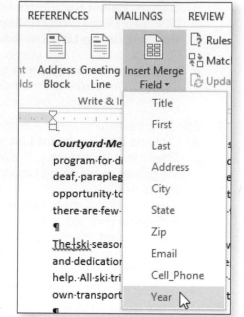

5-63 Insert individual merge field into main document

8. In the bulleted list, replace the placeholder text with the following dates:
   January 17
   January 24
   February 7
   February 21
   February 28

9. Preview the merge results and check for errors.
   a. Click the **Preview Results** button [*Mailings* tab, *Preview Results* group] to display the recipient information in the main document.
   b. Click the **Next Record** or **Previous Record** arrow to view each of the six recipients.
   c. Click the **Check for Errors** button. The *Checking and Reporting Errors* dialog box opens (Figure 5-64).
   d. Select the **Simulate the merge** . . . radio button and click **OK**. If there are no errors, a dialog box opens informing you of this. If there are errors, a new document opens with the errors displayed. Fix errors if needed.
   e. Close the dialog box or new document with errors displayed.
   f. Click the **Preview Results** button [*Mailings* tab, *Preview Results* group] to display the merge fields in the main document.

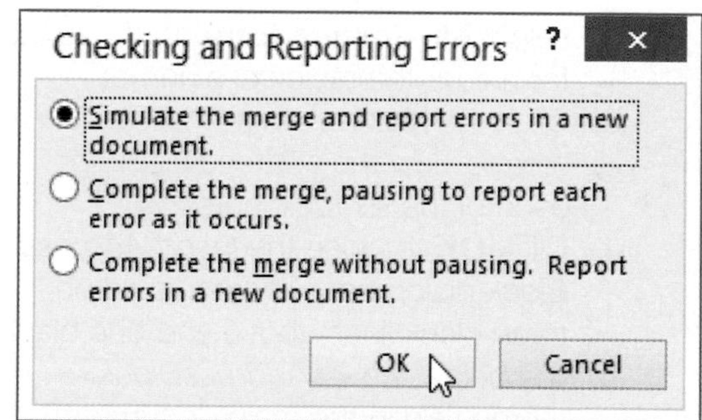

5-64 *Checking and Reporting Errors* dialog box

10. Save the document.

11. Finish the mail merge and save merged document.
    a. Click the **Finish & Merge** button [*Mailings* tab, *Finish* group] and select **Edit Individual Documents**. The *Merge to New Document* dialog box opens.
    b. Select the **All** radio button and click **OK**. The mail merge is opened in a new document.
    c. Scroll through the document to make sure each of the six letters are correct.
12. Save the merged document as ***[your initials] PP W5-4 merge*** and close the document (Figure 5-65).
13. Save and close the ***[your initials] PP W5-4 main*** document.

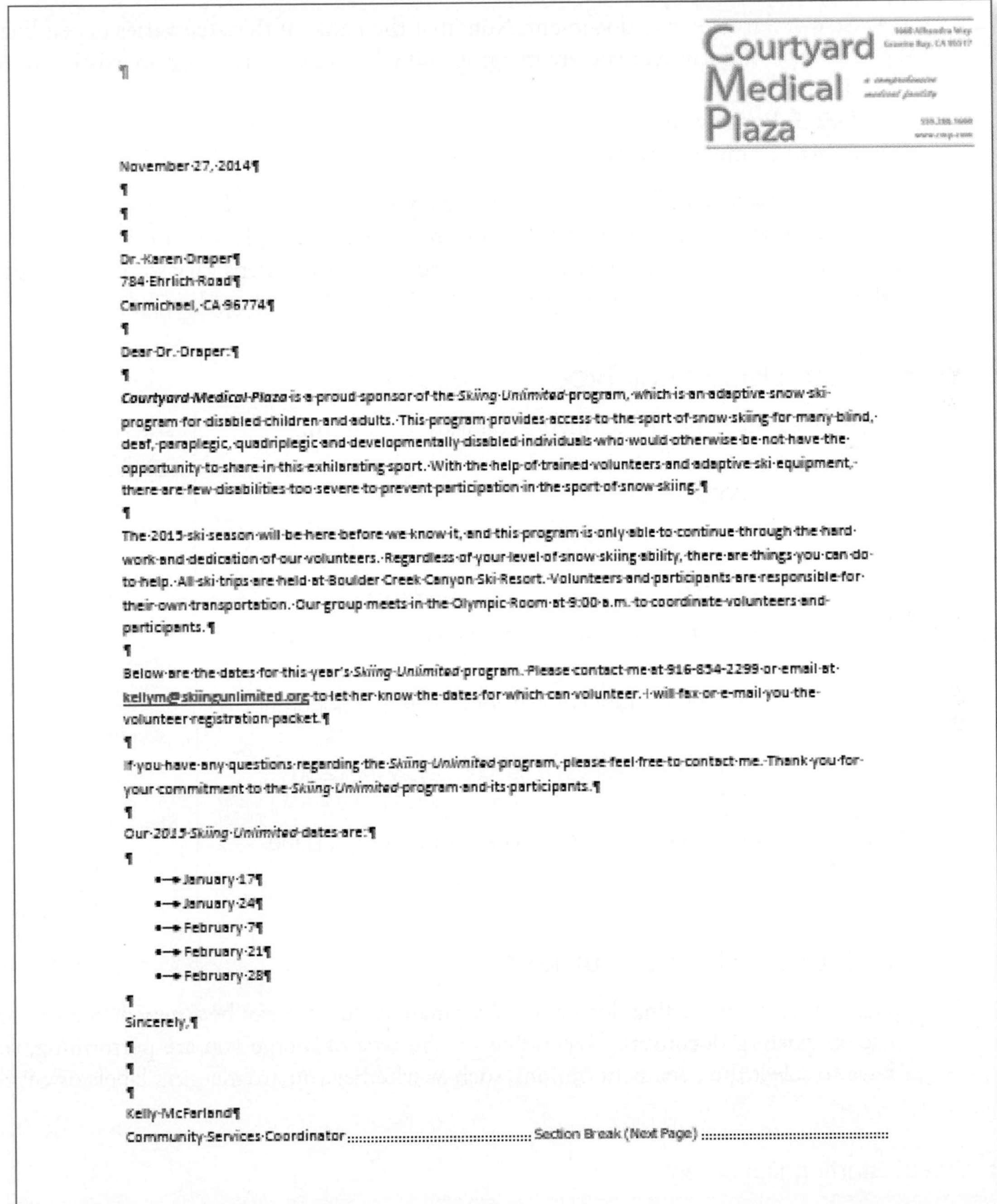

Courtyard Medical Plaza

November 27, 2014

Dr. Karen Draper
784 Ehrlich Road
Carmichael, CA 96774

Dear Dr. Draper:

Courtyard Medical Plaza is a proud sponsor of the *Skiing Unlimited* program, which is an adaptive snow ski program for disabled children and adults. This program provides access to the sport of snow skiing for many blind, deaf, paraplegic, quadriplegic and developmentally disabled individuals who would otherwise be not have the opportunity to share in this exhilarating sport. With the help of trained volunteers and adaptive ski equipment, there are few disabilities too severe to prevent participation in the sport of snow skiing.

The 2015 ski season will be here before we know it, and this program is only able to continue through the hard work and dedication of our volunteers. Regardless of your level of snow skiing ability, there are things you can do to help. All ski trips are held at Boulder Creek Canyon Ski Resort. Volunteers and participants are responsible for their own transportation. Our group meets in the Olympic Room at 9:00 a.m. to coordinate volunteers and participants.

Below are the dates for this year's *Skiing Unlimited* program. Please contact me at 916-854-2299 or email at kellym@skiingunlimited.org to let her know the dates for which can volunteer. I will fax or e-mail you the volunteer registration packet.

If you have any questions regarding the *Skiing Unlimited* program, please feel free to contact me. Thank you for your commitment to the *Skiing Unlimited* program and its participants.

Our *2015 Skiing Unlimited* dates are:

- January 17
- January 24
- February 7
- February 21
- February 28

Sincerely,

Kelly McFarland
Community Services Coordinator ::::::::::::: Section Break (Next Page) :::::::::::::

5-65 PP W5-4 merge completed (page 1 of 6 displayed)

SLO 5.6

Using the Mail Merge Wizard

Instead of using the *Mailings* tab to perform a mail merge, you can use the ***Mail Merge Wizard,*** which walks you through the mail merge process step by step. Using the *Mail Merge Wizard* is similar to using the *Mailings* tab. When you turn on the *Mail Merge Wizard,* a *Mail Merge* pane is displayed on the right side of the Word window. There are six main steps to performing a mail merge.

- ***Step 1:*** Select document type.
- ***Step 2:*** Select starting document.
- ***Step 3:*** Select recipients.
- ***Step 4:*** Arrange your document. Note that the name of this step varies depending on the type of document you are merging and whether you are using an existing or new document.
- ***Step 5:*** Preview your document.
- ***Step 6:*** Complete the merge.

The *How To* and figures that follow give you an example of using the *Mail Merge Wizard* to create mailing labels from a blank document. This example uses an Access database as the data source for the recipients. The options for each of the steps vary somewhat depending on the type of mail merge you are performing with the *Mail Merge Wizard.*

Select Document Type

First, select the type of mail merge you want to perform.

Mail Merge

Select document type

What type of document are you working on?

- Letters
- E-mail messages
- Envelopes
- Labels (selected)
- Directory

Labels

Print address labels for a group mailing.

Click Next to continue.

Step 1 of 6

→ Next: Starting document

Next wizard step

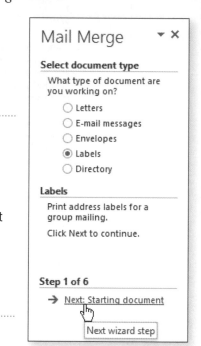

5-66 *Mail Merge Wizard:* Step 1

HOW TO: Select Document Type

1. Open a new Word document.
2. Click the **Start Mail Merge** button [*Mailings* tab, *Start Mail Merge* group].
3. Select **Step-by-Step Mail Merge Wizard**. The *Mail Merge* pane opens on the right (Figure 5-66).
4. In the *Select document type* area, click the radio button for the type of document to merge.
   - A description of the type of document appears in a section below the radio buttons.
5. Click the **Next: Starting document** link at the bottom of the *Mail Merge* pane.

Select Starting Document

Next, select your starting document. Your main document can be a new document or you can use an existing document. Depending on the type of merge you are performing, you might have to select the document options, such as whether you are merging labels or envelopes.

HOW TO: Select Starting Document

1. Click the **Change document layout** radio button in the *Select starting document* area if it is not already selected (Figure 5-67).
   - If you select *Start from existing document*, you are asked to select the document on which to perform the merge.

2. Click the **Label options** link in the *Change document layout* area. The *Label Options* dialog box opens.
3. Select the type of label to use.
4. Click **OK** to close the *Label Options* dialog box. The table of labels is displayed in the document.
5. Click the **Next: Select recipients** link to move to the next step in the *Mail Merge Wizard.*
   - You can click the **Previous** link in the *Mail Merge Wizard* to return to the previous step if necessary.

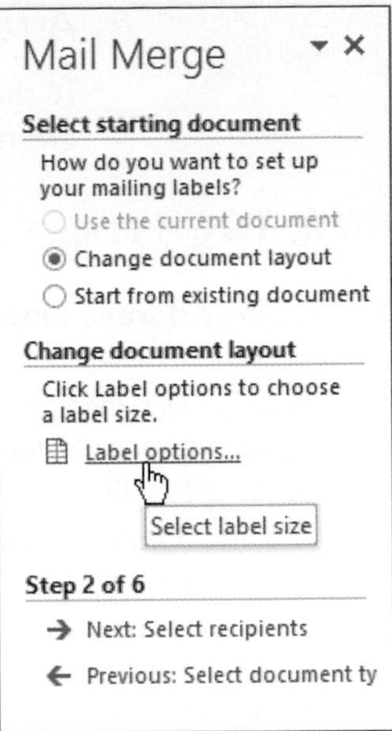

5-67 *Mail Merge Wizard:* Step 2

Select Recipients

Next, you select the recipients to merge into your main document. You can use an existing data source, use contacts from a Microsoft Outlook Contacts folder, or type a new recipient list.

HOW TO: Select Recipients

1. Click the **Use an existing list** radio button in the *Select recipients* area (Figure 5-68).
   - If you choose *Select from Outlook contacts*, you are asked to select the Outlook Contacts folder.
   - If you select *Type new list*, you click the *Create* link and type in the list of recipients.
2. Click the **Browse** link. The *Select Data Source* dialog box opens.
3. Select the data source file and click **Open**. The *Select Data Source* dialog box closes and the *Mail Merge Recipients* dialog box opens (Figure 5-69).

5-68 *Mail Merge Wizard:* Step 3

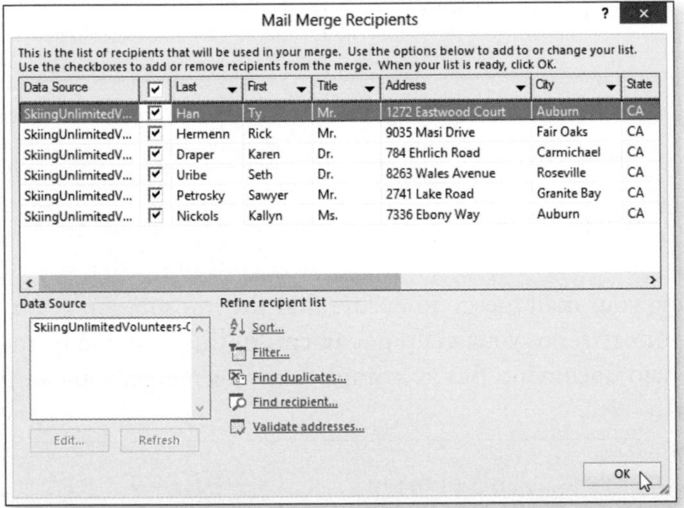

Data Source		Last	First	Title	Address	City	State
SkiingUnlimitedV...	☑	Han	Ty	Mr.	1272 Eastwood Court	Auburn	CA
SkiingUnlimitedV...	☑	Hermenn	Rick	Mr.	9035 Masi Drive	Fair Oaks	CA
SkiingUnlimitedV...	☑	Draper	Karen	Dr.	784 Ehrlich Road	Carmichael	CA
SkiingUnlimitedV...	☑	Uribe	Seth	Dr.	8263 Wales Avenue	Roseville	CA
SkiingUnlimitedV...	☑	Petrosky	Sawyer	Mr.	2741 Lake Road	Granite Bay	CA
SkiingUnlimitedV...	☑	Nickols	Kallyn	Ms.	7336 Ebony Way	Auburn	CA

5-69 Edit the mail merge recipients

4. In the *Mail Merge Recipients* dialog box, select the recipients to be included in the merge, sort by a field in the data source, or filter the data source by specific criteria.
5. Click **OK** to close the *Mail Merge Recipients* dialog box when you have finished editing the recipient list.
6. Click the **Next: Arrange your labels** link to move to the next step.

Arrange Your Document

In the next step, you insert merge fields into your document. You can insert an address block, greeting line, or other merge fields from your data source.

HOW TO: Arrange Your Document

1. Click the **Address block** link to insert the merge field into your main document. The *Insert Address Block* dialog box opens.
   - You can also insert individual merge fields into the label. Click the **More items** link in the *Arrange your labels* area to open the *Insert Merge Field* dialog box where you can add one or more merge fields to the label.
2. Select the address block format, confirm that the address block structure is correct, and preview the recipients in the *Preview* area.
   - If the address block is not displayed correctly, click the **Match Fields** button to match the fields from your data source with the Word merge fields used in the address block.
3. Click **OK** to close the *Insert Address Block* dialog box. The *<<AddressBlock>>* merge field is inserted into the first label in your document.
4. Click the **Update all Labels** button in the *Replicate* labels area (Figure 5-70). The *<<AddressBlock>>* merge field is inserted into each of the labels in your document (Figure 5-71).
5. Click the **Next: Preview your labels** link to move to the next step.

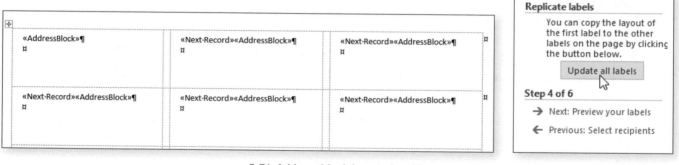

«AddressBlock»¶	«Next·Record»«AddressBlock»¶	«Next·Record»«AddressBlock»¶
«Next·Record»«AddressBlock»¶	«Next·Record»«AddressBlock»¶	«Next·Record»«AddressBlock»¶

5-71 Address block inserted and labels updated

Mail Merge

Arrange your labels

If you have not already done so, lay out your label using the first label on the sheet.

To add recipient information to your label, click a location in the first label, and then click one of the items below.

Address block...

Greeting line...

Electronic postage...

More items...

When you have finished arranging your label, click Next. Then you can preview each recipient's label and make any individual changes.

Replicate labels

You can copy the layout of the first label to the other labels on the page by clicking the button below.

Update all labels

Step 4 of 6

→ Next: Preview your labels

← Previous: Select recipients

5-70 *Mail Merge Wizard:* Step 4

Preview Your Document

The next to last step is previewing your mail merge to ensure that the information from the recipient data source is correctly merged into your main document. In this step, the recipient information is displayed in the main document. Before completing your merge, you can preview each of the recipients, find a specific recipient, or edit the recipient list (Figure 5-72). Click the **Next: Complete the merge** link in the *Mail Merge* pane to finish the mail merge.

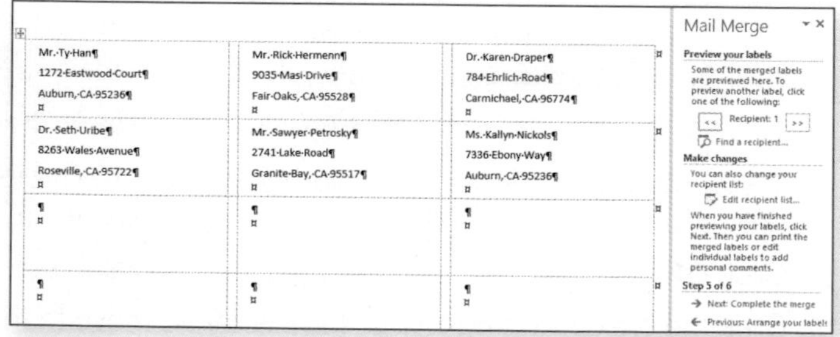

5-72 *Mail Merge Wizard:* Step 5

> **MORE INFO**
>
> When using the *Mail Merge Wizard*, you can click the **Previous** link at the bottom of the *Mail Merge* pane to go back to any of the previous steps.

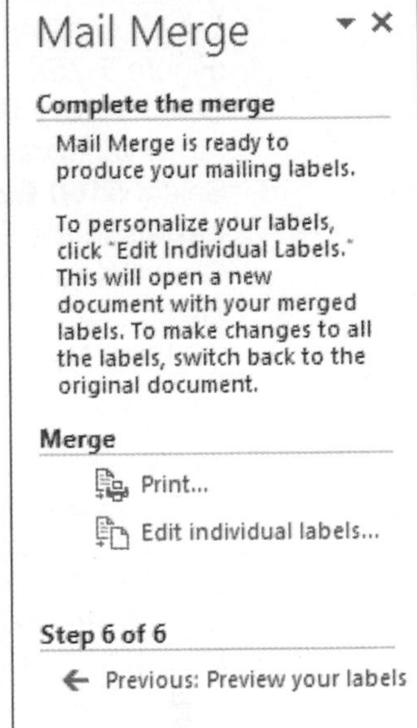

Mail Merge
Complete the merge
Mail Merge is ready to produce your mailing labels.
To personalize your labels, click "Edit Individual Labels." This will open a new document with your merged labels. To make changes to all the labels, switch back to the original document.
Merge
Print...
Edit individual labels...
Step 6 of 6
Previous: Preview your labels

5-73 *Mail Merge Wizard:* Step 6

Complete the Merge

You are given two options to complete the merge: *Print* or *Edit individual labels* (or *letters* or *envelopes)* (Figure 5-73). If you select *Print,* your merged main document is sent directly to the printer. If you select *Edit individual labels* (or *letters* or *envelopes*), Word opens a new document with the merge performed. You can then save and print this document.

> **MORE INFO**
>
> Be sure to save the mail merge main document so you can use the file for future mail merge jobs.

PAUSE & PRACTICE: WORD 5-5

In this Pause & Practice project, you create mailing labels for Kelly McFarland to use when she sends out volunteer letters for the Skiing Unlimited program. You create individual labels for delivery addresses using information from an Access database for the recipient list.

File Needed: ***SkiingUnlimitedVolunteers-05.accdb***
Completed Project File Names: ***[your initials] PP W5-5 labels.docx*** and ***[your initials] PP W5-5 labels merge.docx***

1. Open a new blank Word document.
2. Save the document as ***[your initials] PP W5-5 labels***.
3. Start the *Mail Merge Wizard* (Figure 5-74).
   a. Click the **Mailings** tab.
   b. Click the **Start Mail Merge** button [*Start Mail Merge* group] and select **Step-by-Step Mail Merge Wizard**. The *Mail Merge* pane opens on the right side of the Word window.
4. Select the document type and starting document.
   a. Click the **Labels** radio button in the *Select document type* area.
   b. Click the **Next: Starting document** link at the bottom of the *Mail Merge* pane to move to *Step 2 of 6*.

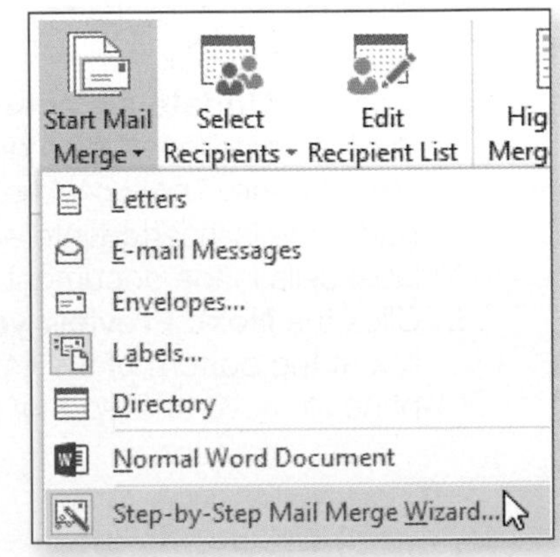

5-74 Open the *Mail Merge Wizard*

c. Click the **Change document layout** radio button in the *Select starting document* area.
d. Click the **Labels options** link in the *Change document layout* area. The *Labels Options* dialog box opens (Figure 5-75).
e. Select **Avery US Letter** from the *Label vendors* drop-down list.
f. Select **5160 Easy Peel Address Labels** in the *Product number* list.
g. Click **OK** to close the *Label Options* dialog box.
h. Click the **Next: Select recipients** link at the bottom of the *Mail Merge* pane to move to *Step 3 of 6*.

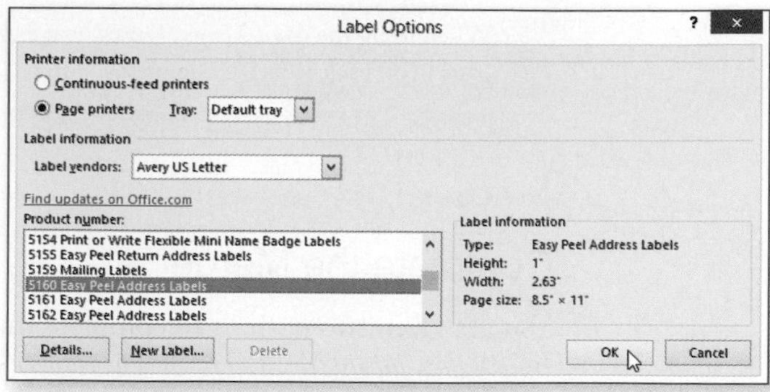

5-75 ***Label Options*** **dialog box**

5. Select recipients for the labels.
   a. Click the **Use an existing list** radio button in the *Select recipients* area.
   b. Click the **Browse** link in the *Use an existing list* area. The *Select Data Source* dialog box opens.
   c. Browse to the location on your computer containing your student data files.
   d. Select the ***SkiingUnlimitedVolunteers-05*** database and click **Open**. The *Mail Merge Recipients* dialog box opens (Figure 5-76).
   e. Click the **Last** column heading drop-down arrow and select **Sort Ascending** from the drop-down list.
   f. Click **OK** to close the *Mail Merge Recipients* dialog box.
   g. Click the **Next: Arrange your labels** link at the bottom of the *Mail Merge* pane to move to *Step 4 of 6*.

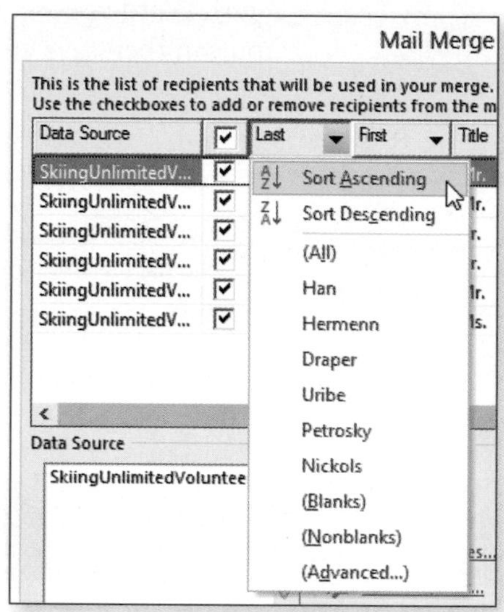

5-76 Sort mail merge recipients

6. Insert an address block to arrange labels.
   a. With your insertion point in the first label cell, click the **Address block** link in the *Arrange your labels* area. The *Insert Address Block* dialog box opens (Figure 5-77).
   b. Select the **Mr. Joshua Randall Jr.** option in the *Specify address elements* area.
   c. Confirm that the **Insert postal address** check box is checked.
   d. Click **OK** to close the *Insert Address Block* dialog box.
   e. Click the **Update all labels** button in the *Replicate labels* area of the *Mail Merge* pane. The *<<AddressBlock>>* field code is inserted into each of the label cells in the document.
   f. Click the **Next: Preview your labels** link at the bottom of the *Mail Merge* pane to move to *Step 5 of 6*.

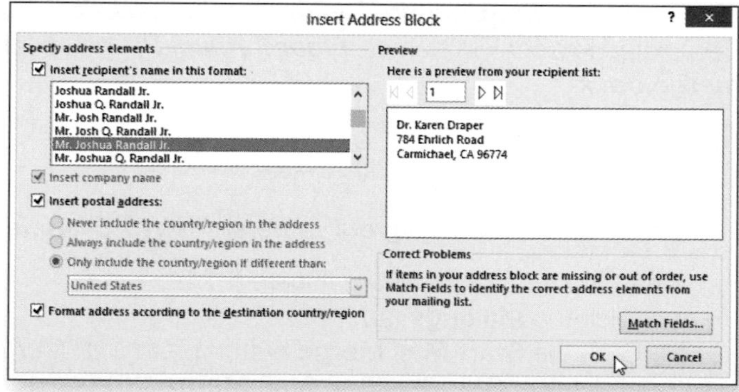

5-77 Insert address block into labels document

7. Preview labels and complete the merge.
   a. A preview of the labels is displayed in the labels document. Confirm that each label is displayed correctly.
   b. Click the **Next: Complete the merge** link at the bottom of the *Mail Merge* pane to move to *Step 6 of 6*.
   c. Click the **Edit individual labels** link in the *Merge* area. The *Merge to New Document* dialog box opens (Figure 5-78).
   d. Select the **All** radio button and click **OK**. A new document opens with the recipients merged into the labels.

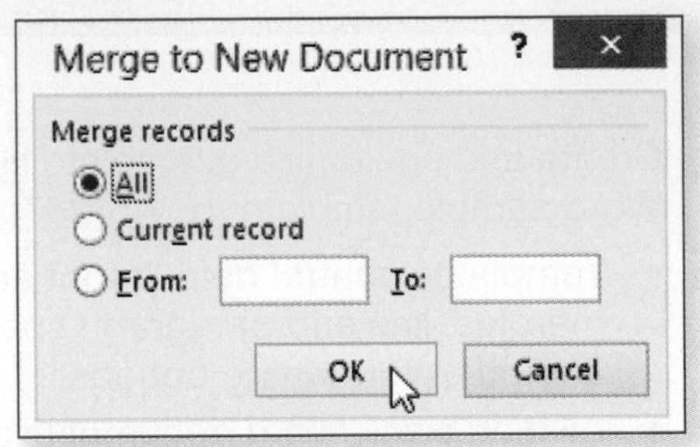

5-78 *Merge to New Document* dialog box

8. Save the completed merged document as ***[your initials] PP W5-5 labels merge*** and close the document (Figure 5-79).
9. Save and close the ***[your initials] PP W5-5 labels*** document.

Dr.·Karen·Draper¶ 784·Ehrlich·Road¶ Carmichael,·CA·96774¶	Mr.·Ty·Han¶ 1272·Eastwood·Court¶ Auburn,·CA·95236¶	Mr.·Rick·Hermenn¶ 9035·Masi·Drive¶ Fair·Oaks,·CA·95528¶
Ms.·Kallyn·Nickols¶ 7336·Ebony·Way¶ Auburn,·CA·95236¶	Mr.·Sawyer·Petrosky¶ 2741·Lake·Road¶ Granite·Bay,·CA·95517¶	Dr.·Seth·Uribe¶ 8263·Wales·Avenue¶ Roseville,·CA·95722¶

5-79 PP W5-5 labels merge completed

Chapter Summary

5.1 Create and customize a template file based on a Word sample template (p. W5-257).

- Templates control default font and size, margins, line and paragraph spacing, themes, and other formatting options.
- All new blank Word documents are based upon the ***Normal.dotx*** template.
- Word template files have a ***.dotx*** extension after the filename.
- You can change and save defaults in the Normal.dotx template; all new documents based upon this template incorporate these changes.
- Word also has a variety of templates from Office.com available in the *Backstage* view.
- Insert, delete, or customize template content to meet your needs.

5.2 Create and use a template from a blank document or an existing Word document (p. W5-262).

- Save a new Word document or an existing document (.docx) as a template (.dotx).
- You can open a new document based upon a template. You can edit this new document without affecting the content and format of the template.
- Templates can also be edited.

5.3 Use Word to create envelopes and mailing labels (p. W5-267).

- *Create **individual envelopes*** in Word or ***add an envelope*** to an existing document.
- Select the type or specific size of envelope to create and select how the envelope will print.
- Create ***mailing labels*** in Word by typing ***individual labels*** or creating a ***full sheet of the same label***.

5.4 Understand the types of merges and how to select or create a recipient list (p. W5-273).

- ***Mail merge*** allows you to merge a document with a ***data source*** such as an Access database or Outlook Contacts.
- The ***main document*** is the document into which information from a data source is merged.
- The data source consists of fields and records. A ***field*** is an individual piece of information, and a ***record*** is a group of related fields.

5.5 Create a merged document using the Mailings tab (p. W5-274).

- Use the ***Mailings tab*** to create and customize a mail merge job.
- Begin the mail merge by selecting the type of merge to perform.
- Select the recipients from an existing data source or type a new list of recipients.
- The recipient list can be ***sorted***, ***filtered***, or specific recipients selected.
- You can insert an ***address block*** or ***greeting line*** merge field into a document. These blocks combine individual fields from the data source to create a standard address block or greeting line for a letter or labels.
- You can insert individual ***merge fields*** from the data source into the main document.
- Preview the results of the merge in the main document before finalizing the merge.
- Send the finished merge results to the printer or to a new document where you can edit or save them.

5.6 Use the *Mail Merge Wizard* to create a merged document (p. W5-286).

- The ***Mail Merge Wizard*** gives you another option to create and customize a mail merge.
- The ***Mail Merge pane*** appears on the right side of the Word window.
- The *Mail Merge Wizard* walks you through each step of the merge process providing you with links and buttons to customize your merge.

Check for Understanding

In the ***Online Learning Center*** for this text (**www.mhhe.com/office2013inpractice**), there are a variety of resources that can be used to review the concepts covered in this chapter.

The following Online Learning Resources are available in the Online Learning Center:

- Multiple choice questions
- Short answer questions
- Matching exercises

Guided Project 5-1

For this project, you create a disclosure statement form letter for Emma Cavalli. You merge this letter with a Microsoft Access database containing a recipient list table. You also use the *Mail Merge Wizard* to create mailing labels.
[Student Learning Outcomes 5.3, 5.4, 5.5, 5.6]

Files Needed: ***DisclosureLetter-05.docx*** and ***CavalliPHRE-05.accdb***
Completed Project File Names: ***[your initials] Word 5-1 letter.docx***, ***[your initials] Word 5-1 letter merge.docx***, ***[your initials] Word 5-1 labels.docx***, and ***[your initials] Word 5-1 labels merge.docx***

Skills Covered in This Project

- Modify an existing document.
- Use the *Mailings* tab to create merged letters.
- Use an Access database table as the data source.
- Filter and sort a data source.
- Insert an address block and greeting line merge fields.
- Insert an individual merge field.
- Apply bold and italic formatting to a merge field.
- Highlight merge fields.
- Preview and complete a merge.
- Use the *Mail Merge Wizard* to create labels.
- Select label type and recipients.
- Filter and sort label recipients.
- Insert an address block and update labels.
- Preview and complete a label merge.

---

1. Open the ***DisclosureLetter-05*** document from your student data files.
2. Save the document as ***[your initials] Word 5-1 letter***.
3. Start the mail merge and select recipients.
   a. Click the **Mailings** tab.
   b. Click the **Start Mail Merge** button [*Start Mail Merge* group] and select **Letters**.
   c. Click the **Select Recipients** button [*Start Mail Merge* group] and select **Use an Existing List**. The *Select Data Source* dialog box opens.
   d. Browse to locate your student data files, select the ***CavalliPHRE-05*** database file, and click **Open**. The *Select Table* dialog box opens (Figure 5-80).
   e. Select **Current Clients** and click **OK**.

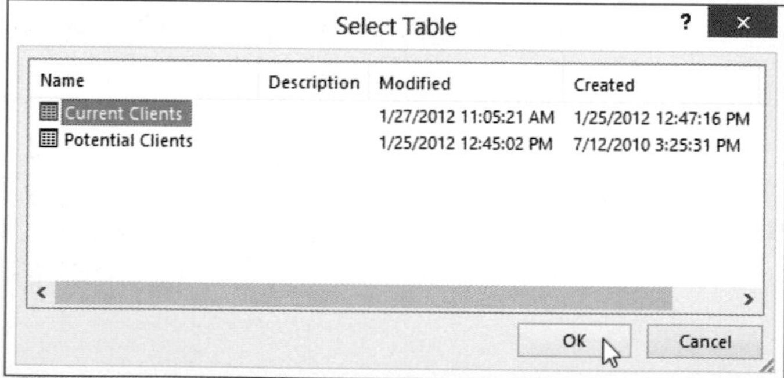

5-80 Select the database table to use as recipient list

4. Filter and sort the recipient list.
   a. Click the **Edit Recipient List** button [*Start Mail Merge* group]. The *Mail Merge Recipients* dialog box opens.
   b. Click the **City** column heading drop-down arrow and select **Roseville** (Figure 5-81). Only the records that match the filter (City=Roseville) are displayed.

c. Click the **Last** column heading drop-down arrow and select **Sort Ascending**. The filtered records are sorted by last name.
d. Click **OK** to close the *Mail Merge Recipients* dialog box.

5. Insert address block and greeting line merge fields.
   a. Turn on **Show/Hide** [*Home* tab, *Paragraph* group].
   b. Delete the "**[Address]**" placeholder text in the letter. Don't include the paragraph mark at the end of the line.
   c. Click the **Address Block** button [*Mailings* tab, *Write & Insert Fields* group]. The *Insert Address Block* dialog box opens (Figure 5-82).
   d. Select the **Mr. Joshua Randall Jr.** option in the *Specify address elements* area.
   e. Click **OK** to close the *Insert Address Block* dialog box. The *<<AddressBlock>>* merge field is inserted into the document.
   f. Delete the "**[Salutation]**" placeholder text in the letter. Don't include the paragraph mark at the end of the line.
   g. Click the **Greeting Line** button [*Write & Insert Fields* group]. The *Insert Greeting Line* dialog box opens (Figure 5-83).
   h. In the *Greeting line format* area, select **Dear**, **Mr. Randall**, and **(none)** from the three drop-down lists.
   i. Click **OK** to close the *Insert Greeting Line* dialog box. The *<<GreetingLine>>* merge field is inserted into the document.

6. Insert another merge field in the body of the document.
   a. In the first sentence of the fourth body paragraph, delete the "**[date]**" placeholder text. Don't delete the space before or after the placeholder text.
   b. Click the **Insert Merge Field** drop-down arrow [*Write & Insert Fields* group] and select **ReturnDate** from the drop-down list. The *<<ReturnDate>>* merge field is inserted.
   c. Make sure there is one space before and after the *<<ReturnDate>>* merge field.
   d. Select the **<<ReturnDate>>** merge field and apply **bold** and **italic** formatting.
   e. Click the **Highlight Merge Fields** button [*Write & Insert Fields* group]. The merge fields in the document are highlighted.

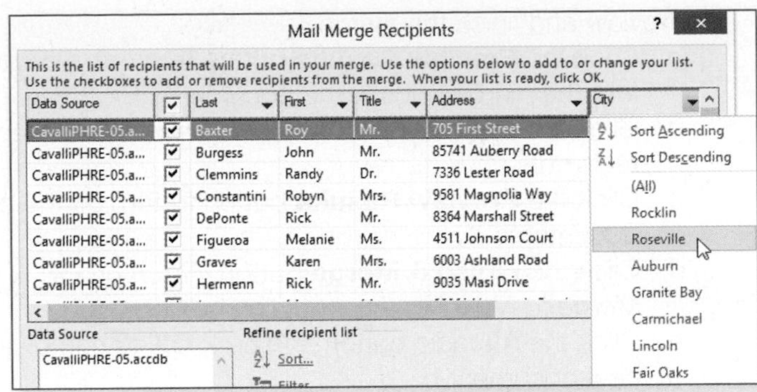

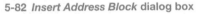

5-81 Filter recipient list

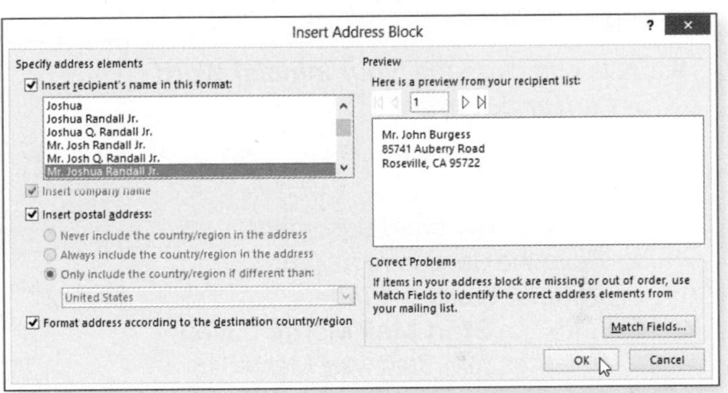

5-82 *Insert Address Block* dialog box

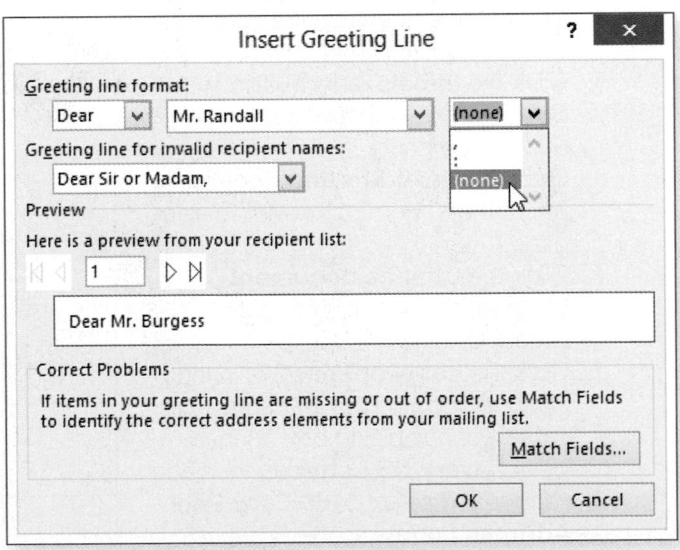

5-83 *Insert Greeting Line* dialog box

7. Preview and finish the merge.
   a. Click the **Preview Results** button [*Preview Results* group]. The recipient information is inserted into the merge fields in the document.
   b. Click the **Next Record** button to view the next recipient. Repeat this for each of the five recipients.
   c. Click the **Preview Results** button to turn off the previewing. The merge fields are displayed in the document.
   d. Click the **Finish & Merge** button [*Finish* group] and select **Edit Individual Documents**. The *Merge to New Document* dialog box opens.
   e. Click the **All** radio button and click **OK** to complete the merge. The completed merge opens in a new document.
8. Save the completed merge as ***[your initials] Word 5-1 letter merge*** and close this document (Figure 5-84).
9. Save and close the ***[your initials] Word 5-1 letter*** document.
10. Create mailing labels using the *Mail Merge Wizard*.
   a. Open a new Word document.
   b. Save the document as ***[your initials] Word 5-1 labels***.
   c. Click the **Start Mail Merge** button [*Mailings* tab, *Start Mail Merge* group] and select **Step-by-Step Mail Merge Wizard**. The *Mail Merge* pane opens on the right side of the Word window.
   d. Click the **Labels** radio button in the *Select document type* area of the *Mail Merge* pane.
   e. Click the **Next: Starting document** link at the bottom of the *Mail Merge* pane.
   f. Click the **Change document layout** radio button if it is not already selected.
   g. Click the **Label options** link in the *Change document layout* area. The *Label Options* dialog box opens.
   h. Select **Avery US Letter** as the *Label vendor* and select **5160 Easy Peel Address Labels** as the *Product number*.
   i. Click **OK** to close the *Label Options* dialog box.
   j. Click the **Next: Select Recipients** link at the bottom of the *Mail Merge* pane.
11. Select and edit recipient list.
   a. Click the **Use an existing list** radio button in the *Select recipients* area.
   b. Click the **Browse** button in the *Use an existing list* area. The *Select Data Source* dialog box opens.
   c. Browse to your student data files, select the **CavalliPHRE-05** database, and click **Open**. The *Select Table* dialog box opens.

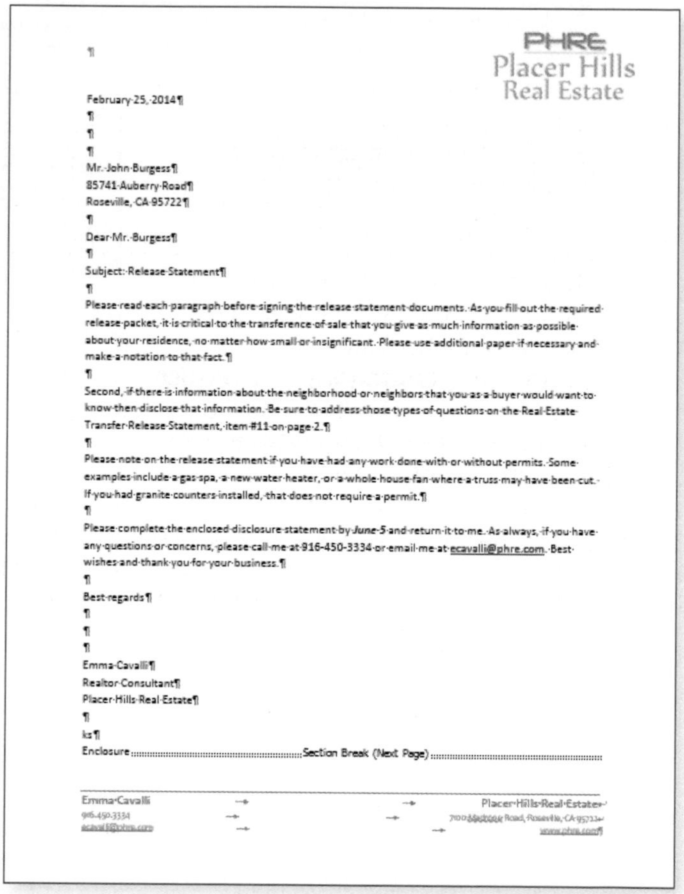

PHRE
Placer Hills
Real Estate

February 25, 2014

Mr. John Burgess
85741 Auberry Road
Roseville, CA 95722

Dear Mr. Burgess

Subject: Release Statement

Please read each paragraph before signing the release statement documents. As you fill out the required release packet, it is critical to the transference of sale that you give as much information as possible about your residence, no matter how small or insignificant. Please use additional paper if necessary and make a notation to that fact.

Second, if there is information about the neighborhood or neighbors that you as a buyer would want to know then disclose that information. Be sure to address those types of questions on the Real Estate Transfer Release Statement, item #11 on page 2.

Please note on the release statement if you have had any work done with or without permits. Some examples include a gas spa, a new water heater, or a whole house fan where a truss may have been cut. If you had granite counters installed, that does not require a permit.

Please complete the enclosed disclosure statement by *June 5* and return it to me. As always, if you have any questions or concerns, please call me at 916-450-3334 or email me at ecavalli@phre.com. Best wishes and thank you for your business.

Best regards

Emma Cavalli
Realtor Consultant
Placer Hills Real Estate

ks
Enclosure Section Break (Next Page)

Emma Cavalli Placer Hills Real Estate

5-84 Word 5-1 letter merge completed (page 1 of 5)

d. Select **Current Clients** and click **OK**. The *Mail Merge Recipients* dialog box opens.
e. Click the **Filter** link in the bottom half of the dialog box. The *Filter and Sort* dialog box opens (Figure 5-85).
f. On the *Filter Records* tab, click the **Field** drop-down arrow and select **City**.
g. Click the **Comparison** drop-down arrow and select **Equal to**.
h. In the *Compare to* field, type Roseville.
i. Click the **Sort Records** tab (Figure 5-86).
j. Click the **Sort by** drop-down arrow and select **Last**.
k. Click the **Ascending** radio button.
l. Click **OK** to close the *Filter and Sort* dialog box and click **OK** to close the *Mail Merge Recipients* dialog box.
m. Click the **Next: Arrange your labels** link at the bottom of the *Mail Merge* pane.

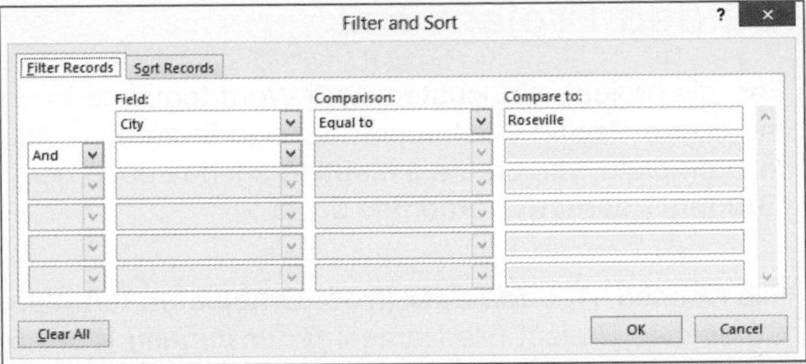

5-85 *Filter and Sort* dialog box

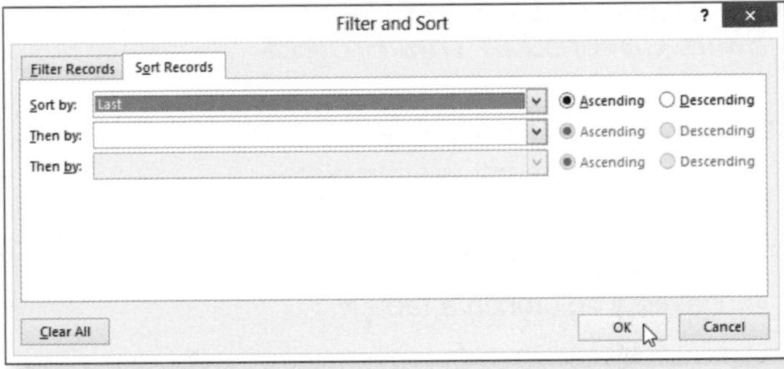

5-86 Sort records

12. Insert merge field and update labels.
    a. Click the **Address block** link in the *Arrange your labels* area. The **Insert Address Block** dialog box opens.
    b. Select the **Mr. Joshua Randall Jr.** option in the *Specify address elements* area.
    c. Click **OK** to close the *Insert Address Block* dialog box. The *<<AddressBlock>>* merge field is inserted into the labels document.
    d. Click the **Update all labels** button in the *Replicate labels* area. The *<<AddressBlock>>* merge field is inserted into each of the label cells in the document.
    e. Click the **Next: Preview your labels** link at the bottom of the *Mail Merge* pane.

13. Preview and finish the merge.
    a. Preview the recipients in the labels document.
    b. Click the **Next: Complete the merge** link at the bottom of the *Mail Merge* pane.
    c. Click the **Edit individual labels** link in the *Complete the merge* area. The *Merge to New Document* dialog box opens.
    d. Click the **All** radio button and click **OK** to complete the merge. The completed merge opens in a new document.

14. Save the completed merge as ***[your initials] Word 5-1 labels merge*** and close this document (Figure 5-87).

15. Save and close the ***[your initials] Word 5-1 labels*** document.

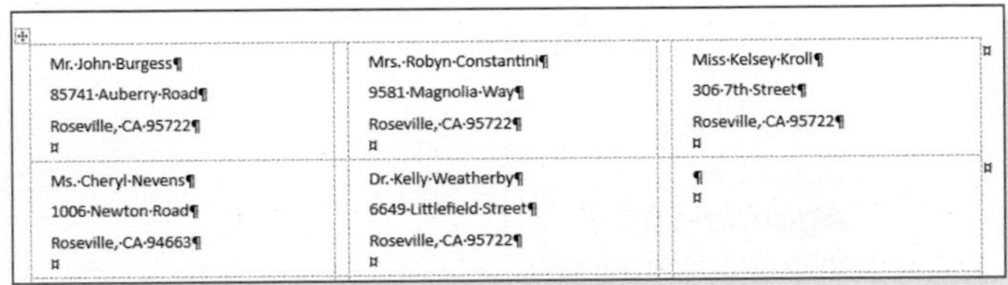

Mr. John Burgess¶ 85741 Auberry Road¶ Roseville, CA 95722¶	Mrs. Robyn Constantini¶ 9581 Magnolia Way¶ Roseville, CA 95722¶	Miss Kelsey Kroll¶ 306 7th Street¶ Roseville, CA 95722¶
Ms. Cheryl Nevens¶ 1006 Newton Road¶ Roseville, CA 94663¶	Dr. Kelly Weatherby¶ 6649 Littlefield Street¶ Roseville, CA 95722¶	¶

5-87 Word 5-1 labels merge completed

Guided Project 5-2

For this project, you customize a Word template to create a curriculum meeting agenda template for the Sierra Pacific Community College District Curriculum Committee. After customizing and saving this template, you create a meeting agenda document based upon this template.
[Student Learning Outcomes 5.1, 5.2]

File Needed: ***Agenda.dotx* (from Office.com templates)** or ***Agenda-05.docx***
Completed Project File Names: ***[your initials] Word 5-2 template.dotx*** and ***[your initials] Word 5-2 agenda.docx***

Skills Covered in This Project

- Download an online agenda template.
- Save a document as a template.
- Change margins.
- Modify template content.
- Delete a column in a table.
- *AutoFit* table contents.
- Open a document based upon a template.
- Add content to a document based upon a template.

---

1. Download an agenda template.
   a. Open Word and click the **File** tab to open the *Backstage* view (Figure 5-88).
   b. Click the **New** button.
   c. Click in the *Search for online templates* text box, type agenda, and press **Enter**. A list of agenda templates is displayed.
   d. Select **Agenda** and click **Create**. A document based upon this agenda template opens in the new Word window. If this template is not available, open the ***Agenda-05*** file from your student data files.

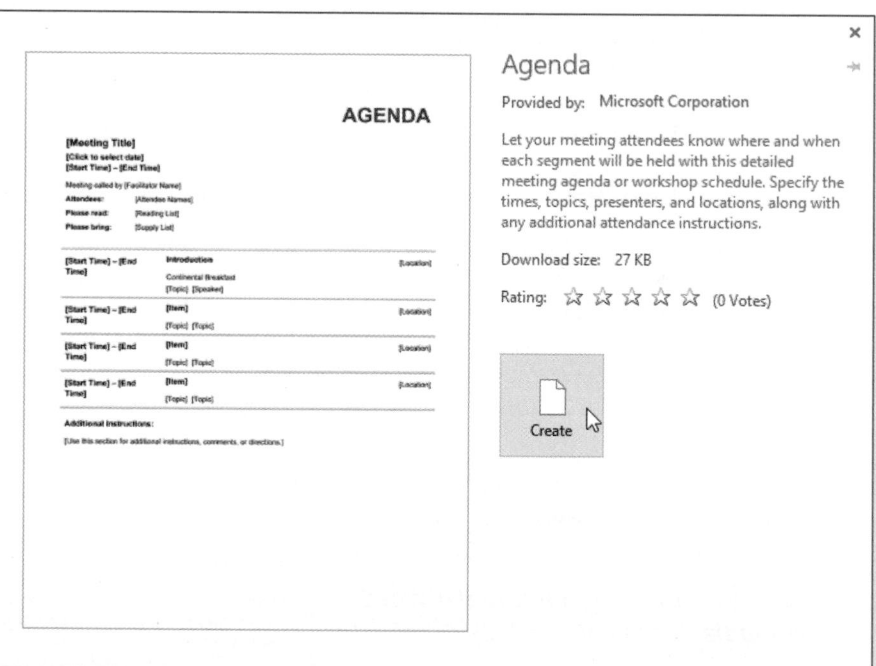

5-88 Create document based on online template

2. Save the document as a template.
   a. Open the *Save As* dialog box.
   b. In the *File name* area, type [your initials] Word 5-2 template.

c. In the *Save as type* area, select **Word Template** from the drop-down list.
d. Browse to the location on your computer to save this template.
e. Click **Save** to save the document as a Word template. If a dialog box opens informing you the document will be upgraded to the newest file format, click **OK**.

3. Customize the template content and format.
   a. Turn on **Show/Hide** [*Home* tab, *Paragraph* group].
   b. Change the top and bottom margins to **0.5"**.
   c. Place your insertion point before the title ("AGENDA"), type SPCCD CURRICULUM, **space** once, and **left** align this line.
   d. Change "Meeting Title" to Full Curriculum Committee Meeting.
   e. In the "Start Time" field, type 3.
   f. In the "End Time" field, type 5 p.m.
   g. In the "Facilitator Name" field, type Dr. Manuel Chavez.
   h. In the "Attendee Names" field, type Melissa Rogan, Roietta Jones, Tony Parsons, Ravi Singh, Rachel Salazar, Rebecca Frank, Kai Sung, and Heidi Anderson.
   i. In the "Reading List" field, type Curriculum printouts.
   j. Delete the third row of the first table ("Please bring").
   k. Replace "Additional Instructions:" near the bottom with Follow-up Notes:.

4. Customize the second table content and format.
   a. Delete the third column of the second table.
   b. Select the entire second table and **AutoFit Window**.
   c. Select and remove the **Continental Breakfast** field in the second column in the first row and delete the blank line above the *Topic* field.
   d. Select and remove the **Speaker** field in the second column in the first row and delete the tab after the *Topic* field.
   e. In the second through fourth rows, select and delete the second **Topic** fields and delete the tabs after the first *Topic* fields.
   f. In the *Start Time*, *End Time*, *Introduction*, and *Item* content control fields, type the following information. Don't remove or type any content in the *Topic* fields.

3:00 – 3:10	Preliminaries
3:10 – 4:00	1st Readings
4:00 – 4:15	2nd Readings
4:15 – 4:45	Degrees and Certificates

5. Save and close the template (Figure 5-89).

6. Open a document based upon the ***[your initials] Word 5-2 template***. *(Note: Do not open this template from within Word; open from a Windows folder.)*
   a. Browse to the Windows folder on your computer containing the ***[your initials] Word 5-2 template*** file.
   b. Double-click the ***[your initials] Word 5-2 template*** file to open a new document based upon this template.

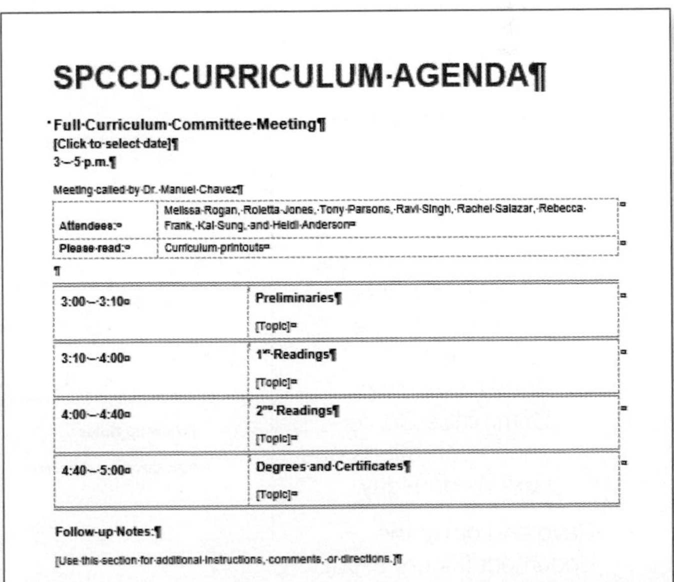

SPCCD CURRICULUM AGENDA

Full Curriculum Committee Meeting
[Click to select date]
3–5 p.m.

Meeting called by Dr. Manuel Chavez

Attendees:	Melissa Rogan, Roletta Jones, Tony Parsons, Ravi Singh, Rachel Salazar, Rebecca Frank, Kai Sung, and Heidi Anderson
Please read:	Curriculum printouts

3:00–3:10	Preliminaries [Topic]
3:10–4:00	1st Readings [Topic]
4:00–4:40	2nd Readings [Topic]
4:40–5:00	Degrees and Certificates [Topic]

Follow-up Notes:

[Use this section for additional instructions, comments, or directions.]

5-89 Word 5-2 template completed

7. Save this Word document as ***[your initials] Word 5-2 agenda***. Confirm that *Save as type* is **Word Document**; if it's not, change it.
8. Insert content into the agenda.
   a. In the "Click to select date" field, select the next Wednesday.
   b. In the "Topic" field below the "Preliminaries" heading, type the content below. Press **Enter** after the first line, but don't press *Enter* after the last item.
      Approve minutes
      State Curriculum Committee updates
   c. In the *Topic* field below the "1st Readings" heading, type the following and press **Enter** after each line except the last line:
      BIO 334
      BUS 300
      FITN 120
      PSCH 310
   d. In the *Topic* field below the "2nd Readings" heading, type the following and press **Enter** after each line except the last line:
      HUM 330
      HUM 335
      PSCH 315
      PSCH 320
   e. In the *Topic* field below the "Degrees and Certificates" field, type the following and press **Enter** after each line except the last line:
      ACCT Accounting Degree
      BUSTEC Office Professional Degree
      ARTNM Animation Certificate
   f. In the field below the "Follow-up Notes" heading, type the following:
      State Curriculum Committee Conference applications due next Wednesday.
9. Save and close the document (Figure 5-90).

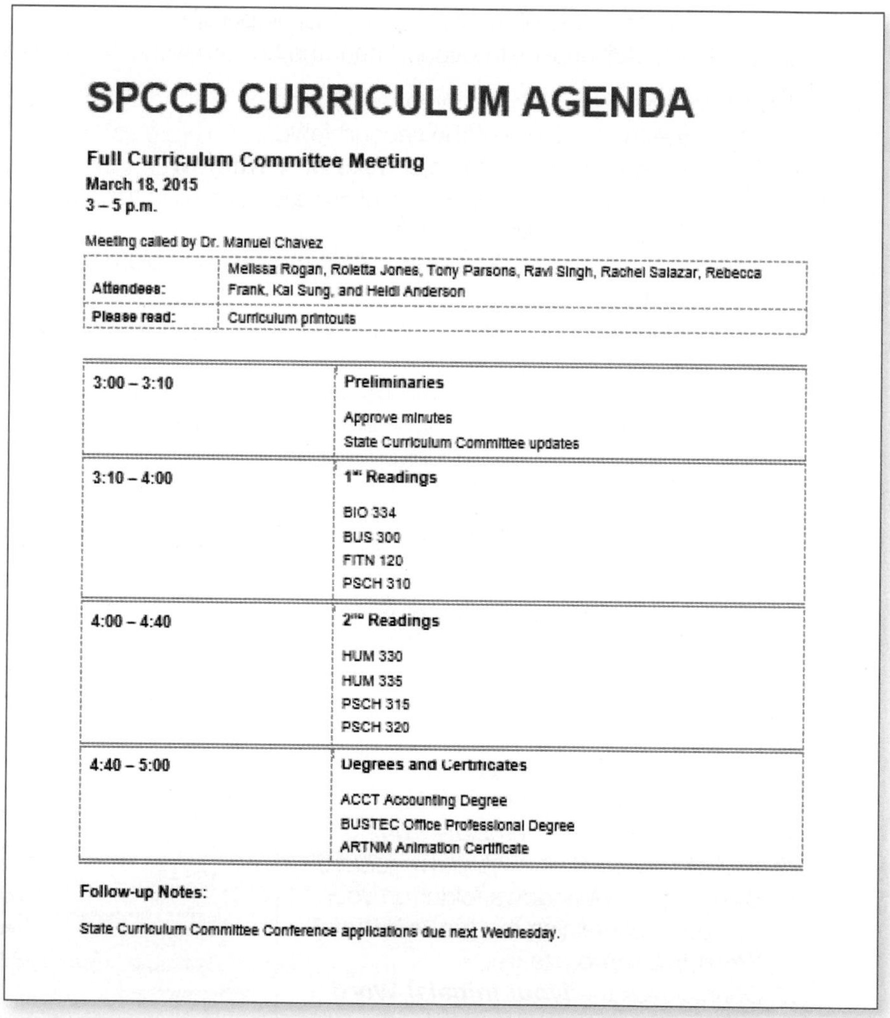

SPCCD CURRICULUM AGENDA

Full Curriculum Committee Meeting
March 18, 2015
3 – 5 p.m.

Meeting called by Dr. Manuel Chavez

Attendees:	Melissa Rogan, Roletta Jones, Tony Parsons, Ravi Singh, Rachel Salazar, Rebecca Frank, Kai Sung, and Heidi Anderson
Please read:	Curriculum printouts

3:00 – 3:10	**Preliminaries** Approve minutes State Curriculum Committee updates
3:10 – 4:00	**1st Readings** BIO 334 BUS 300 FITN 120 PSCH 310
4:00 – 4:40	**2nd Readings** HUM 330 HUM 335 PSCH 315 PSCH 320
4:40 – 5:00	**Degrees and Certificates** ACCT Accounting Degree BUSTEC Office Professional Degree ARTNM Animation Certificate

Follow-up Notes:

State Curriculum Committee Conference applications due next Wednesday.

5-90 Word 5-2 agenda completed

Guided Project 5-3

For this project, you create an insurance renewal letter template for Gretchen Souza at Central Sierra Insurance. You then create a renewal letter based upon the template and merge the letter with recipients and renewal information from an Access database.
[Student Learning Outcomes 5.1, 5.2, 5.4, 5.5]

Files Needed: ***RenewalLetter-05.docx*** and ***SouzaRenewals-05.accdb***
Completed Project File Names: ***[your initials] Word 5-3 template.dotx***, ***[your initials] Word 5-3 renewals.docx***, and ***[your initials] Word 5-3 renewals merge.docx***

Skills Covered in This Project

- Open an existing document and save as a template.
- Insert date and set date to update automatically.
- Open a new Word document based upon a template.
- Use the *Mailings* tab to create merged letters.
- Use an Access database table as a data source.
- Filter a data source.
- Deselect recipients.
- Insert address block and greeting line merge fields.
- Insert individual merge fields.
- Highlight merge fields.
- Preview a merge and check for errors.
- Complete a label merge.

---

1. Open the ***RenewalLetter-05*** document from your student data files.
2. Save the document as a template.
   a. Open the *Save As* dialog box.
   b. In the *File name* area, type [your initials] Word 5-3 template.
   c. In the *Save as type* area, select **Word Template** from the drop-down list.
   d. Browse to the location on your computer to save this template.
   e. Click **Save** to save the document as a Word template.
3. Insert current date field into the letter.
   a. Delete the "**[Insert current date]**" placeholder text. Don't delete the paragraph mark at the end.
   b. Click the **Date & Time** button [*Insert* tab, *Text* group]. The *Date and Time* dialog box opens.
   c. Select the third date option, check the **Update automatically** check box, and click **OK** to insert the current date and close the dialog box.
   d. Save and close the template.
4. Open a document based upon the ***[your initials] Word 5-3 template***. *(Note: Do not open this template from within Word; open from a Windows folder.)*
   a. Browse to the folder on your computer containing the ***[your initials] Word 5-3 template*** file.
   b. Double-click the ***[your initials] Word 5-3 template*** file to open a new Word document based upon this template.
5. Save this Word document as ***[your initials] Word 5-3 renewals***. Confirm that the *Save as type* is **Word Document**; if it's not, change it.
6. Start the mail merge and select the recipients.
   a. Click the **Start Mail Merge** button [*Mailings* tab, *Start Mail Merge* group] and select **Letters**.

b. Click the **Select Recipients** button [*Start Mail Merge* group] and select **Use an Existing List**. The *Select Data Source* dialog box opens.

c. Browse to locate your student data files, select the ***SouzaRenewals-05*** database file, and click **Open**.

d. Click the **Edit Recipient List** button [*Start Mail Merge* group]. The *Mail Merge Recipients* dialog box opens.

e. Click the **Last Name** column heading drop-down arrow and select **Sort Ascending**. The records are sorted by last name.

f. Deselect the check box on the last four recipients so they are not included in the merge (Figure 5-91).

g. Click **OK** to close the *Mail Merge Recipients* dialog box.

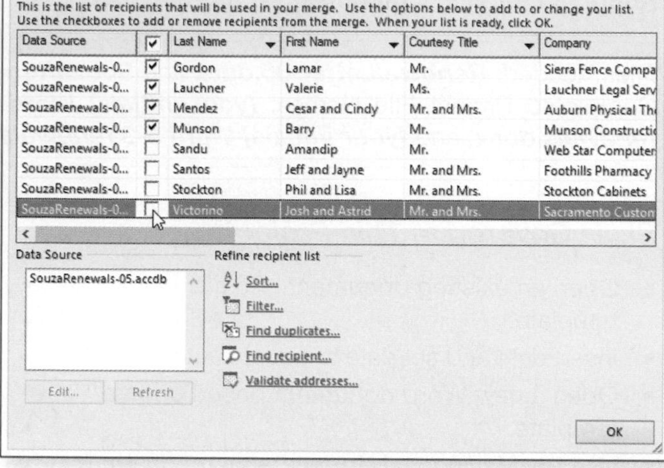

5-91 Sort and deselect recipients

7. Insert the address block and greeting line merge fields into the letter.

a. Turn on **Show/Hide** [*Home* tab, *Paragraph* group].

b. Delete the "**[Address]**" placeholder text in the letter. Don't include the paragraph mark at the end of the line.

c. Click the **Address Block** button [*Write & Insert Fields* group]. The *Insert Address Block* dialog box opens.

d. Select the **Mr. Joshua Randall Jr.** option in the *Specify address elements* area. Click through each of the four recipients in the *Preview* area.

e. Click **OK** to close the *Insert Address Block* dialog box. The *<<AddressBlock>>* merge field is inserted into the document.

f. Delete the "**[Greeting]**" placeholder text in the letter. Don't include the paragraph mark at the end of the line.

g. Click the **Greeting Line** button [*Write & Insert Fields* group]. The *Insert Greeting Line* dialog box opens (Figure 5-92).

h. In the *Greeting line format* area, select **Dear**, **Mr. and Mrs. Randall** and **:** (colon) from the three drop-down lists.

i. Click **OK** to close the *Insert Greeting Line* dialog box. The *<<GreetingLine>>* merge field is inserted into the document.

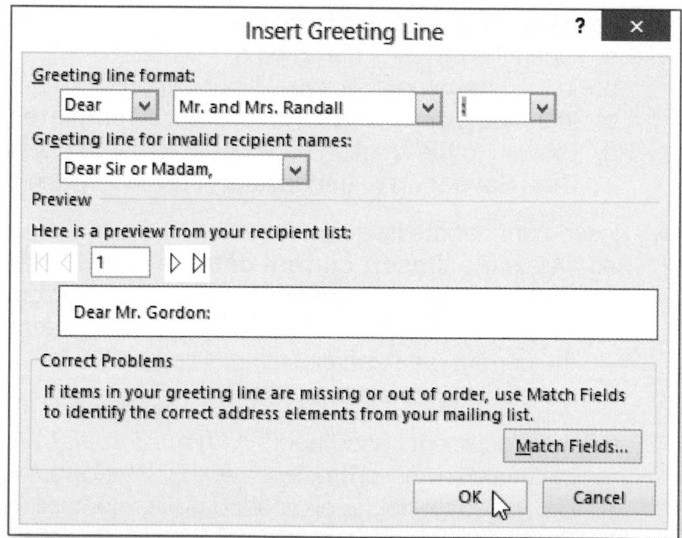

5-92 ***Insert Greeting Line*** **dialog box**

8. Insert other merge fields in the body and table of the document.

a. Click the **Highlight Merge Fields** button [*Write & Insert Fields* group]. The merge fields in the document are highlighted.

b. In the subject line, delete the "**[Policy Number]**" placeholder text. Don't delete the space before or after the placeholder text.

c. Click the **Insert Merge Field** drop-down arrow [*Write & Insert Fields* group] and select **Policy_Number** from the drop-down list. The *<<Policy_Number>>* merge field is inserted.

d. Make sure there is one space before and after the *<<Policy_Number>>* merge field.

e. Continue inserting merge fields in the document to replace the placeholder text using the information in the following table. Be sure to leave proper spacing and punctuation around merge fields (Figure 5-93).

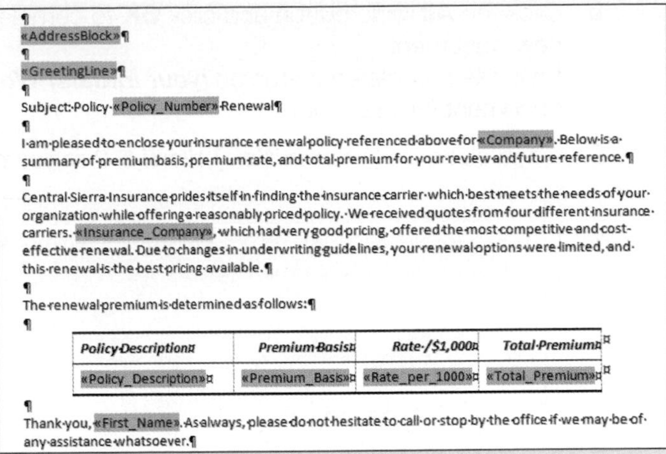

«AddressBlock»

«GreetingLine»

Subject: Policy «Policy_Number» Renewal

I am pleased to enclose your insurance renewal policy referenced above for «Company». Below is a summary of premium basis, premium rate, and total premium for your review and future reference.

Central Sierra Insurance prides itself in finding the insurance carrier which best meets the needs of your organization while offering a reasonably priced policy. We received quotes from four different insurance carriers. «Insurance_Company», which had very good pricing, offered the most competitive and cost-effective renewal. Due to changes in underwriting guidelines, your renewal options were limited, and this renewal is the best pricing available.

The renewal premium is determined as follows:

Policy Description	*Premium Basis*	*Rate /$1,000*	*Total Premium*
«Policy_Description»	«Premium_Basis»	«Rate_per_1000»	«Total_Premium»

Thank you, «First_Name». As always, please do not hesitate to call or stop by the office if we may be of any assistance whatsoever.

5-93 Merge fields inserted into the letter

Placeholder Text	Location	Merge Field
[Company]	First body paragraph	**Company**
[Insurance Company]	Second body paragraph	**Insurance_Company**
[Policy Description]	First column of table	**Policy_Description**
[Premium Basis]	Second column of table	**Premium_Basis**
[Rate per $1000]	Third column of table	**Rate_per_1000**
[Total Premium]	Fourth column of table	**Total_Premium**
[First Name]	Last body paragraph	**First_Name**

9. Preview and check for errors in the merge.
   a. Click the **Preview Results** button [*Preview Results* group]. The recipient information is inserted into the merge fields in the document.
   b. Click the **Next Record** or **Previous Record** button to preview all four recipients.
   c. Click the **Preview Results** button to turn off the previewing. The merge fields are displayed in the document.
   d. Click the **Check for Errors** button [*Preview Results* group]. The *Checking and Reporting Errors* dialog box opens (Figure 5-94).
   e. Click the **Simulate the merge** . . . radio button and click **OK**. A dialog box opens confirming that there are no errors (Figure 5-95). If there are errors, the errors are reported in a new document.
   f. Click **OK** to close the dialog box.

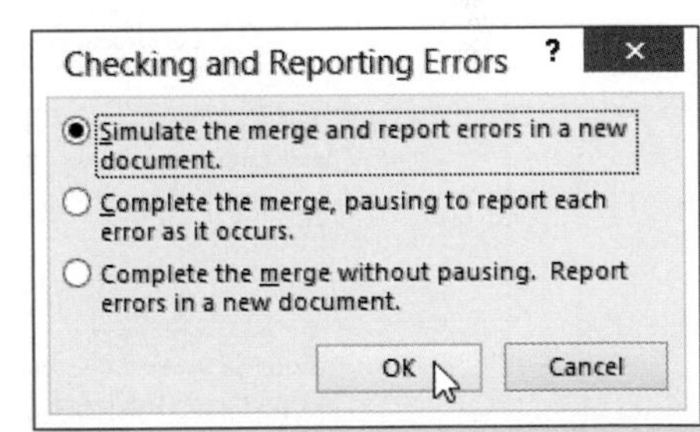

5-94 *Checking and Reporting Errors* dialog box

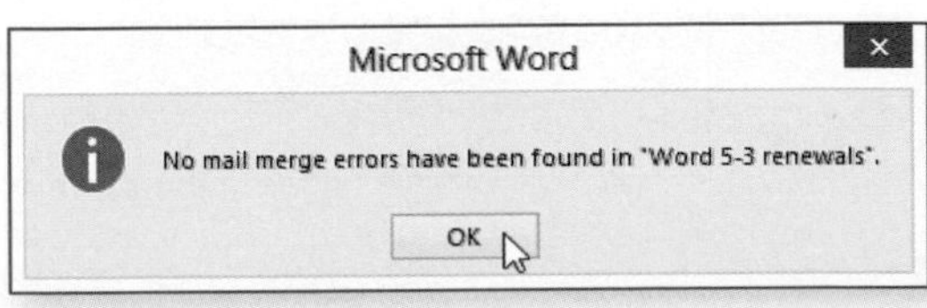

5-95 Dialog box confirming no errors in the merge

10. Finish and save the merge.
    a. Click the **Finish & Merge** button [*Finish* group] and select **Edit Individual Documents**. The *Merge to New Document* dialog box opens.

b. Click the **All** radio button and click **OK** to complete the merge. The completed merge opens in a new document.

c. Save the completed merge as ***[your initials] Word 5-3 renewals merge*** and close this document (Figure 5-96).

11. Save and close the ***[your initials] Word 5-3 renewals*** document.

Central Sierra Insurance
5502 Ridley Way / Cameron Park, CA 94663
780.886.2400 / www.centralsierra.com

March 6, 2015

Mr. Lamar Gordon
Sierra Fence Company
2405 Eureka Avenue
Fair Oaks, CA 95636

Dear Mr. Gordon:

Subject: Policy SF752284 Renewal

I am pleased to enclose your insurance renewal policy referenced above for Sierra Fence Company. Below is a summary of premium basis, premium rate, and total premium for your review and future reference.

Central Sierra Insurance prides itself in finding the insurance carrier which best meets the needs of your organization while offering a reasonably priced policy. We received quotes from four different insurance carriers. West Coast Insurance, which had very good pricing, offered the most competitive and cost-effective renewal. Due to changes in underwriting guidelines, your renewal options were limited, and this renewal is the best pricing available.

The renewal premium is determined as follows:

Policy Description	*Premium Basis*	*Rate /$1,000*	*Total Premium*
Construction	325000	21	6825

Thank you, Lamar. As always, please do not hesitate to call or stop by the office if we may be of any assistance whatsoever.

Sincerely,

Gretchen Souza, ARM, CIC, CRM
Central Sierra Insurance
gretchen@centralsierra.com

5-96 Word 5-3 renewals merge completed (page 1 of 4)

Independent Project 5-4

For this project, you create a letter for Emma Cavalli at Placer Hills Real Estate to send to prospective clients. You merge this letter with recipient information from an Access database and create mailing labels. **[Student Learning Outcomes 5.3, 5.4, 5.5, 5.6]**

Files Needed: ***ProspectingLetter-05.docx*** and ***CavalliPHRE-05.accdb***
Completed Project File Names: ***[your initials] Word 5-4 letter.docx***, ***[your initials] Word 5-4 letter merge.docx***, ***[your initials] Word 5-4 labels.docx***, and ***[your initials] Word 5-4 labels merge.docx***

Skills Covered in This Project

- Open an existing document and save as a template.
- Insert date and set to update automatically.
- Use the *Mailings* tab or *Mail Merge Wizard* to create merged letters and labels.
- Use an Access database table as the data source for the merged letters and labels.
- Filter and sort a recipient list.
- Insert address block and greeting line merge fields.
- Insert individual merge fields.
- Highlight merge fields.
- Add *Author* to document properties.
- Preview a merged document.
- Complete a letter and label merge.

1. Open the ***ProspectingLetter-05*** document from your student data files.
2. Save the document as ***[your initials] Word 5-4 letter***.
3. Insert the current date.
   a. Delete the **[Current date]** placeholder text (don't delete the paragraph mark).
   b. Insert the current date in proper letter format (i.e., January 1, 2015) and set the date to update automatically.
4. Using either the *Mailings* tab or the *Mail Merge Wizard*, start a letters mail merge.
5. Select the ***CavalliPHRE-05*** database as the existing recipient list.
   a. Use the **Potential Clients** table in this database.
   b. Edit the recipient list and filter for those recipients who live in the city of **Rocklin**.
   c. Sort the recipients in ascending order by last name.
6. Replace the "[Address]" placeholder text with an address block merge field.
   a. Be sure a courtesy title is included before the recipients' first and last names.
   b. Scroll through the recipients in the *Preview* area to make sure the address block is formatted correctly.
7. Replace the "[Salutation]" placeholder text with a greeting line merge field.
   a. Be sure a courtesy title is included before the recipients' last names.
   b. Include a colon after the greeting (mixed punctuation).
   c. Scroll through the recipients in the *Preview* area to make sure the greeting line is formatted correctly.
8. Insert merge fields in the body of the letter.
   a. Replace the "[City]" placeholder text with the **City** merge field.
   b. Replace the "[First name]" placeholder text with the **First** merge field.
   c. Turn on **Highlight Merge Fields**.

9. Replace "xx" with your reference initials at the end of the document.
10. Preview the merged letters.
11. Finish the merge to edit individual letters and save and close the documents.
    a. Save the merged letters as ***[your initials] Word 5-4 letter merge*** and close the document (Figure 5-97).
    b. Save and close the ***[your initials] Word 5-4 letter*** document.
12. Open a new blank Word document and save the document as ***[your initials] Word 5-4 labels***.
13. Using either the *Mailings* tab or the *Mail Merge Wizard*, start a labels merge.
    a. Use **Avery US Letter**, **5160 Easy Peel Address Labels** as the label type.
    b. Select the ***CavalliPHRE-05*** database as the existing recipient list.
    c. Use the **Potential Clients** table in this database.
    d. Edit the recipient list and filter for those recipients who live in the city of **Rocklin**.
    e. Sort the recipients in ascending order by last name.
    f. Insert address block merge field. Be sure a courtesy title is included before the recipients' first and last names.
    g. Update labels so the address block merge field appears in each of the label cells.

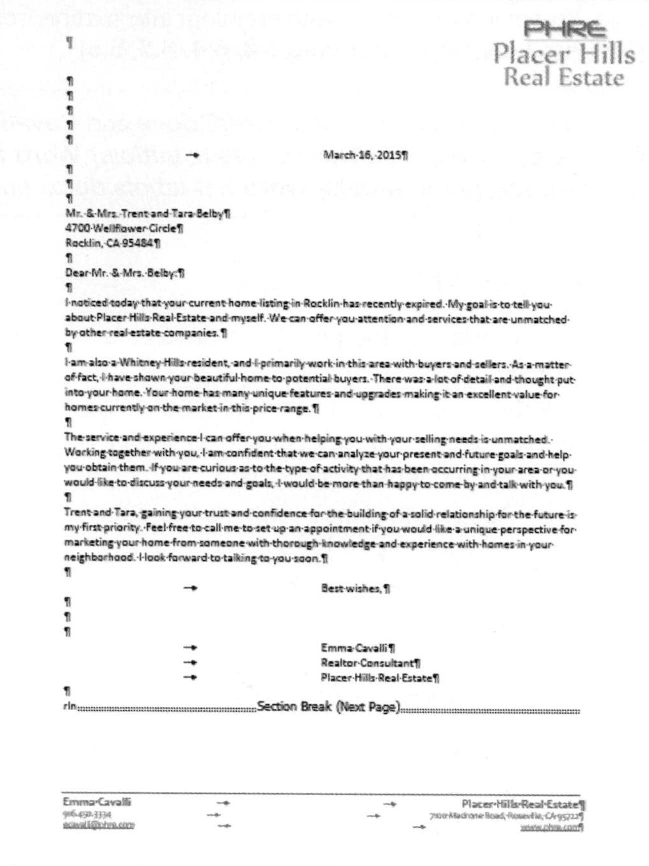

PHRE
Placer Hills
Real Estate

March 16, 2015

Mr. & Mrs. Trent and Tara Belby
4700 Wellflower Circle
Rocklin, CA 95484

Dear Mr. & Mrs. Belby:

I noticed today that your current home listing in Rocklin has recently expired. My goal is to tell you about Placer Hills Real Estate and myself. We can offer you attention and services that are unmatched by other real estate companies.

I am also a Whitney Hills resident, and I primarily work in this area with buyers and sellers. As a matter of fact, I have shown your beautiful home to potential buyers. There was a lot of detail and thought put into your home. Your home has many unique features and upgrades making it an excellent value for homes currently on the market in this price range.

The service and experience I can offer you when helping you with your selling needs is unmatched. Working together with you, I am confident that we can analyze your present and future goals and help you obtain them. If you are curious as to the type of activity that has been occurring in your area or you would like to discuss your needs and goals, I would be more than happy to come by and talk with you.

Trent and Tara, gaining your trust and confidence for the building of a solid relationship for the future is my first priority. Feel free to call me to set up an appointment if you would like a unique perspective for marketing your home from someone with thorough knowledge and experience with homes in your neighborhood. I look forward to talking to you soon.

Best wishes,

Emma Cavalli
Realtor Consultant
Placer Hills Real Estate

rln
Section Break (Next Page)

Emma Cavalli
Placer Hills Real Estate
www.phre.com

5-97 Word 5-4 letter merge completed (page 1 of 4)

14. Preview the merged labels.
15. Finish the merge to edit individual labels and save and close the documents.
    a. Save the merged document as ***[your initials] Word 5-4 labels merge*** and close the document.
    b. Save the close the ***[your initials] Word 5-4 labels*** document (Figure 5-98).

Mr. & Mrs. Trent and Tara Belby 4700 Wellflower Circle Rocklin, CA 95484	Dr. & Mrs. Paul and Song Choi 2993 Murietta Road Rocklin, CA 95484	Mr. & Mrs. Abel and Monica Solara 25663 Apen Drive Rocklin, CA 95428
Mr. Jason Waltz 5959 Quay Court Rocklin, CA 95428		

5-98 Word 5-4 labels merge completed

Independent Project 5-5

For this project, you create a business card template for the members of the American River Cycling Club. You use a business card template from Office.com, customize it, and save the document as a template. You then create a document based upon this template and customize the business cards for yourself. [Student Learning Outcomes 5.1, 5.2]

Files Needed: ***Business card (general format).dotx*** **(from Office.com templates)** or ***BusinessCards-05.docx***
Completed Project File Names: ***[your initials] Word 5-5 template.dotx*** and ***[your initials] Word 5-5 business cards.docx***

Skills Covered in This Project

- Download an Office.com business card template.
- Save a document as a template.
- Modify template content.
- Remove a content control field.
- Open a document based upon a template.
- Add content to a document based upon a template.

1. Create a document based on a business card template.
   a. In the *New* area on the *Backstage* view, search for business cards.
   b. Select the business card format shown in Figure 5-99.

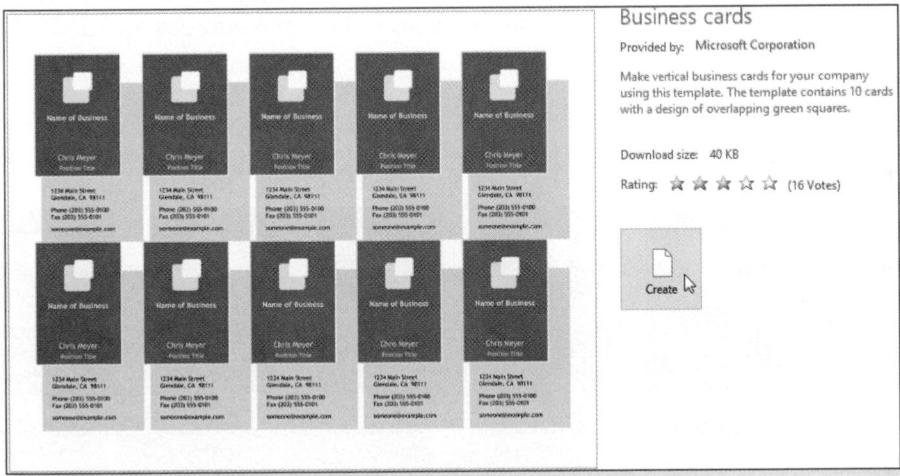

5-99 Create business cards from an online template

   c. Create a document based on this business card template. If this template is not available, open the ***BusinessCards-05*** document from your student data files.
2. Save the document as a Word template, name it ***[your initials] Word 5-5 template***, and make sure it is updated to the newest file format.
3. Customize template content.
   a. Turn on the **Show/Hide** feature.
   b. On the first business card (upper left) in the "Name of Business" field, type American River Cycling Club.

c. Change "American River Cycling Club" to **12 pt**. font size and **small caps**.
d. Remove the street address and the city, state, zip content control fields, including the paragraph marks at the end of each line.
e. Remove the fax number content control field, including the paragraph mark at the end of the line.
f. Repeat steps b–e on each of the other business cards. (*Note: You can copy and paste to replace the "Name of Business" field with "American River Cycling Club."*)

4. Save and close the template (Figure 5-100).

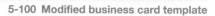

5-100 Modified business card template

5. Open a document based upon a template and save the document.
   a. Browse to the Windows folder containing the ***[your initials] Word 5-5 template*** file and double-click it to open a document based upon the template file. Do not open from within Word.
   b. Save the Word document as ***[your initials] Word 5-5 business cards***. Make sure you save the document as a Word document.
6. Customize the first business card (upper left).
   a. In the *Chris Meyer* field, type Kelsey Kroll.
   b. In the *Position Title* field, type ARCC Coach.
   c. In the *Phone (203) 555-0100 field*, type the following lines. Press **Enter** once after each of the first two lines. Undo automatic capitalization for the first word in the email address and undo automatic hyperlink of the email address.

      Cell/text 916.522.7741

      kelsey.kroll@arcc.org

      www.arcc.org
   d. Remove the ***someone@example.com*** content control field and delete the extra blank line.
7. Customize the remaining business cards using the information in 6a–d so all ten business cards have the same information.
8. Save and close the document (Figure 5-101).

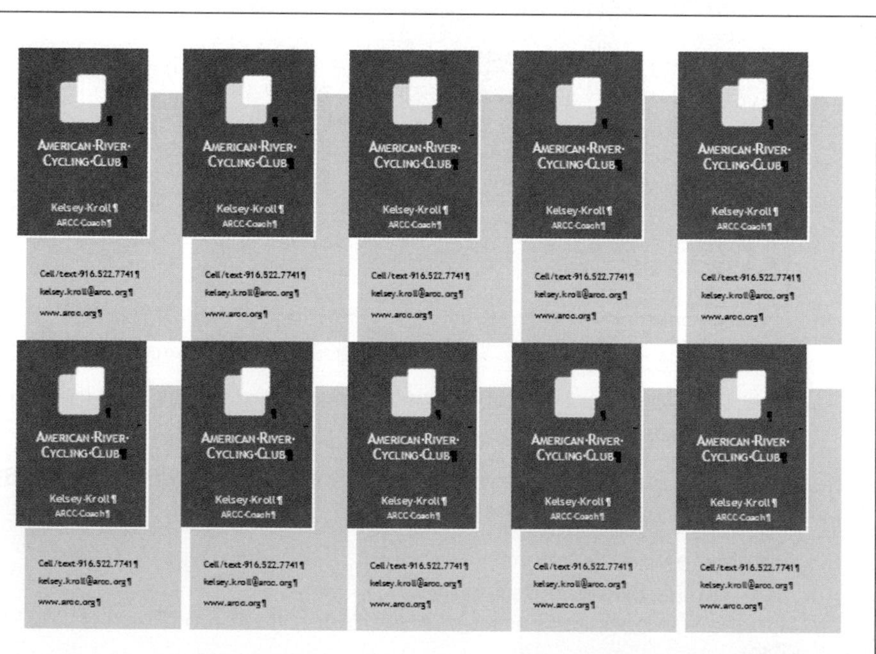

5-101 Word 5-5 business cards completed

Independent Project 5-6

For this project, you customize a privacy notice for Courtyard Medical Plaza that includes merge fields for recipients' names and employee information. You also create file folder labels for individual employees. **[Student Learning Outcomes 5.3, 5.4, 5.5, 5.6]**

Files Needed: ***PrivacyNotice-05.docx*** and ***CourtyardMedicalPlaza-05.accdb***
Completed Project File Names: ***[your initials] Word 5-6.docx***, ***[your initials] Word 5-6 merge.docx***, ***[your initials] Word 5-6 labels.docx***, and ***[your initials] Word 5-6 labels merge.docx***.

Skills Covered in This Project

- Edit an existing document.
- Set a left tab on selected lines.
- Use the *Mailings* tab or *Mail Merge Wizard* to create merged letters and labels.
- Use an Access database table as the data source for merged letters and labels.
- Filter and sort a recipient list.
- Insert individual merge fields.
- Apply formatting to merge fields.
- Insert date and set to update automatically.
- Preview merge documents.
- Complete a letter and label merge.

1. Open the ***PrivacyNotice-05*** document from your student data files.
2. Save the document as ***[your initials] Word 5-6***.
3. Using either the *Mailings* tab or the *Mail Merge Wizard*, start a letters mail merge.
4. Select the ***CourtyardMedicalPlaza-05*** database as the recipient list and select the **Employees** table in this database.
5. Edit the recipient list.
   a. Filter for those recipients who are in the **Accounting** or **Marketing** departments. *(Hint: Use the* Filter *and* Sort *dialog box.)*
   b. Sort the recipients in ascending order by last name.
6. Set a tab to line up merge fields.
   a. Select the four lines at the beginning of the document ("Name" through "Date") and set a **1.25"** left tab.
   b. Press **Tab** once at the end of each of these four lines.
7. Insert merge fields.
   a. Insert the **Title**, **First**, and **Last** merge fields after the tab after "Name." Make sure there is proper spacing between fields.
   b. **Bold** these three merge fields.
   c. Insert the **EmpNumber** merge field after the tab after "Employee Number."
   d. Insert the **Department** merge field after the tab after "Department."
8. Insert the current date after the tab after "Date."
   a. Use the "January 1, 2015" date format.
   b. Set the date so it does not update automatically.
9. Preview the results.
   a. Check to ensure proper spacing between names.
   b. There should be five recipients.

10. Complete the merge to edit individual documents.
11. Save the merged document as ***[your initials] Word 5-6 merge*** (Figure 5-102) and close the document.
12. Save and close the ***[your initials] Word 5-6*** document.

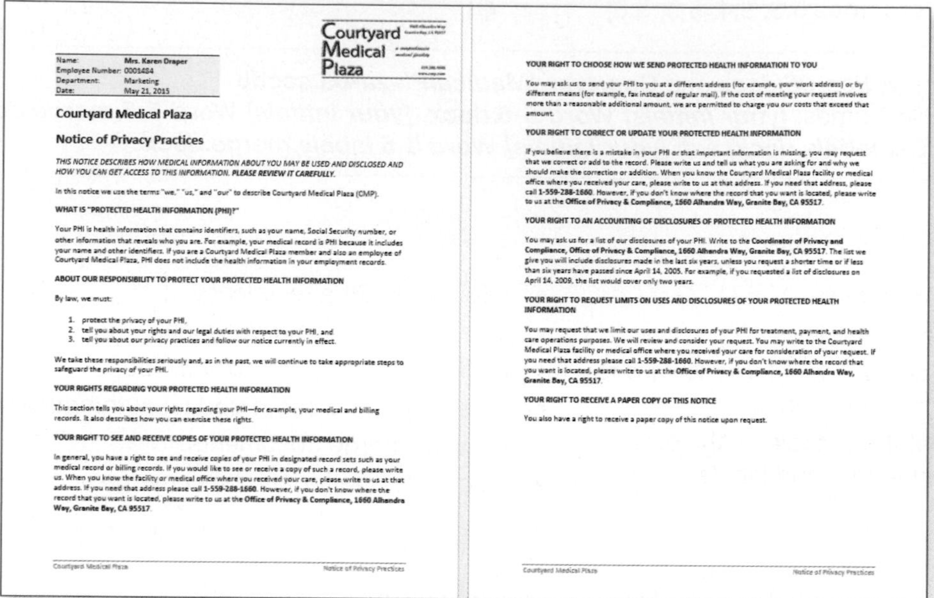

Name:	Mrs. Karen Draper
Employee Number:	0001484
Department:	Marketing
Date:	May 21, 2015

Courtyard Medical Plaza

Courtyard Medical Plaza

Notice of Privacy Practices

THIS NOTICE DESCRIBES HOW MEDICAL INFORMATION ABOUT YOU MAY BE USED AND DISCLOSED AND HOW YOU CAN GET ACCESS TO THIS INFORMATION. ***PLEASE REVIEW IT CAREFULLY.***

In this notice we use the terms "we," "us," and "our" to describe Courtyard Medical Plaza (CMP).

WHAT IS "PROTECTED HEALTH INFORMATION (PHI)?"

Your PHI is health information that contains identifiers, such as your name, Social Security number, or other information that reveals who you are. For example, your medical record is PHI because it includes your name and other identifiers. If you are a Courtyard Medical Plaza member and also an employee of Courtyard Medical Plaza, PHI does not include the health information in your employment records.

ABOUT OUR RESPONSIBILITY TO PROTECT YOUR PROTECTED HEALTH INFORMATION

By law, we must:

1. protect the privacy of your PHI,
2. tell you about your rights and our legal duties with respect to your PHI, and
3. tell you about our privacy practices and follow our notice currently in effect.

We take these responsibilities seriously and, as in the past, we will continue to take appropriate steps to safeguard the privacy of your PHI.

YOUR RIGHTS REGARDING YOUR PROTECTED HEALTH INFORMATION

This section tells you about your rights regarding your PHI—for example, your medical and billing records. It also describes how you can exercise these rights.

YOUR RIGHT TO SEE AND RECEIVE COPIES OF YOUR PROTECTED HEALTH INFORMATION

In general, you have a right to see and receive copies of your PHI in designated record sets such as your medical record or billing records. If you would like to see or receive a copy of such a record, please write us. When you know the facility or medical office where you received your care, please write to us at that address. If you need that address please call **1-559-288-1660**. However, if you don't know where the record that you want is located, please write to us at the **Office of Privacy & Compliance, 1660 Alhandra Way, Granite Bay, CA 95517**.

Courtyard Medical Plaza Notice of Privacy Practices

YOUR RIGHT TO CHOOSE HOW WE SEND PROTECTED HEALTH INFORMATION TO YOU

You may ask us to send your PHI to you at a different address (for example, your work address) or by different means (for example, fax instead of regular mail). If the cost of meeting your request involves more than a reasonable additional amount, we are permitted to charge you our costs that exceed that amount.

YOUR RIGHT TO CORRECT OR UPDATE YOUR PROTECTED HEALTH INFORMATION

If you believe there is a mistake in your PHI or that important information is missing, you may request that we correct or add to the record. Please write us and tell us what you are asking for and why we should make the correction or addition. When you know the Courtyard Medical Plaza facility or medical office where you received your care, please write to us at that address. If you need that address, please call **1-559-288-1660**. However, if you don't know where the record that you want is located, please write to us at the **Office of Privacy & Compliance, 1660 Alhandra Way, Granite Bay, CA 95517**.

YOUR RIGHT TO AN ACCOUNTING OF DISCLOSURES OF PROTECTED HEALTH INFORMATION

You may ask us for a list of our disclosures of your PHI. Write to the **Coordinator of Privacy and Compliance, Office of Privacy & Compliance, 1660 Alhandra Way, Granite Bay, CA 95517**. The list we give you will include disclosures made in the last six years, unless you request a shorter time or if less than six years have passed since April 14, 2005. For example, if you requested a list of disclosures on April 14, 2009, the list would cover only two years.

YOUR RIGHT TO REQUEST LIMITS ON USES AND DISCLOSURES OF YOUR PROTECTED HEALTH INFORMATION

You may request that we limit our uses and disclosures of your PHI for treatment, payment, and health care operations purposes. We will review and consider your request. You may write to the Courtyard Medical Plaza facility or medical office where you received your care for consideration of your request. If you need that address please call **1-559-288-1660**. However, if you don't know where the record that you want is located, please write to us at the **Office of Privacy & Compliance, 1660 Alhandra Way, Granite Bay, CA 95517**.

YOUR RIGHT TO RECEIVE A PAPER COPY OF THIS NOTICE

You also have a right to receive a paper copy of this notice upon request.

Courtyard Medical Plaza Notice of Privacy Practices

5-102 Word 5-6 merge completed (recipient 1 of 5)

13. Open a new Word document and save the document as ***[your initials] Word 5-6 labels***.
14. Using either the *Mailings* tab or the *Mail Merge Wizard*, start a labels mail merge.
    a. Select **Avery US Letter**, **45366 EcoFriendly Filing Labels**.
    b. Select the ***CourtyardMedicalPlaza-05*** database as the recipient list and select the **Employees** table in this database.
    c. Sort the recipients in ascending order by last name.
    d. Select the entire document and change the font to **Cambria** and the size to **10 pt**.
15. Insert merge fields and text in the labels.
    a. In the first cell (upper left) in the labels table, insert the **Last** and **First** fields. Be sure to separate the last and first name merge fields with a comma and space.
    b. Press **Enter** and type Employee Number:.
    c. Space once and insert the **EmpNumber** merge field.
    d. Press **Enter** and insert the **Department** merge field.
    e. Space once and type Department.
    f. Apply **bold**, **underline**, and **all caps** formatting to the merge fields on the first line of the label (<<Last>>, <<First>>).
16. Update labels and preview the merge.
17. Complete the merge to edit individual documents. There are ten labels with merged information.
18. Save the merged document as ***[your initials] Word 5-6 labels merge*** (Figure 5-103) and close the document.
19. Save and close the ***[your initials] Word 5-6 labels*** document.

DRAPER, KAREN¶ Employee Number: 0001484¶ Marketing Department¶	¤	**FALLON, TRISHA**¶ Employee Number: 0001736¶ Medicine Department¶
FAN, KAI¶ Employee Number: 0001984¶ Medicine Department¶	¤	**HAN, TY**¶ Employee Number: 0001325¶ Accounting Department¶
HERMENN, RICK¶ Employee Number: 0000552¶ Personnel Department¶	¤	**KIM, JAMIE**¶ Employee Number: 0000954¶ Accounting Department¶
NICKOLS, KALLYN¶ Employee Number: 0000746¶ Accounting Department¶	¤	**PETROSKY, SAWYER**¶ Employee Number: 0001080¶ Marketing Department¶
SOLARA, RAMON¶ Employee Number: 0000825¶ Personnel Department¶	¤	**URIBE, SETH**¶ Employee Number: 0006985¶ Medicine Department¶
Employee Number: ¶ Department¶ ¤	¤	Employee Number: ¶ Department¶ ¤

5-103 Word 5-6 labels merge completed

Improve It Project 5-7

For this project, you create an employment letter template from an existing employment letter from Central Sierra Insurance. You delete specific employment information, insert placeholder text, and modify the structure of the letter.
[Student Learning Outcomes 5.1, 5.2]

File Needed: ***EmploymentOffer-05.docx***
Completed Project File Name: ***[your initials] Word 5-7.dotx***

Skills Covered in This Project

- Save an existing document as a template.
- Delete numbered and lettered items from a document.
- Move numbered and lettered items.
- Change the level of an item in a multilevel list.
- Delete and insert a page break.
- Insert date.
- Delete text and insert placeholder text.
- Apply text highlight color.
- Modify header content.

---

1. Open the ***EmploymentOffer-05*** document from your student data files.
2. Save the document as a Word template named ***[your initials] Word 5-7***.
3. Delete text from the employment letter. Be sure to delete the paragraph mark at the end of the paragraphs being deleted and delete items in the order they are listed below.
   a. Delete item **16**.
   b. Delete item **11** including the three lettered items below the number.
   c. Delete items **7–9** including the lettered item on item **8**.
   d. Delete the page break at the end of the second page.
4. Move text from the employment letter. Be sure to include the paragraph mark at the end of the items being moved.
   a. Move item **5** so it appears before item 7.
   b. Move item **9** so it appears before item 8 and press **Increase Indent** to make this the third lettered item (c) of item 7.
5. Insert a **page break** at the beginning of item 7.
6. Delete the date, insert the current date in proper business letter format, and set the date so it updates automatically.
7. Delete text and insert placeholder text. Be sure to include appropriate spacing and punctuation around placeholder text.
   a. Delete all three lines of the inside address and type [Employee's name and address] as the placeholder text.
   b. Delete "**Mrs. Skaar**" in the salutation (do not delete the colon) and type [Employee].
   c. In the first body paragraph, delete "**Health & Benefits Large Group Specialist**" and type [Job title].
   d. In the first body paragraph, delete "**Cameron Park**" and type [Office location].
   e. In the first body paragraph, delete "**April 1, 2012**" and type [Start date].
   f. On item 1, delete "**Bert Pulido**" and type [Supervisor].
   g. On item 1, delete "**Central Sierra Health & Benefits**" and type [Department].

h. On item 2, delete all of the text after "Job Description" (don't delete the period or paragraph mark at the end of the paragraph) and type [Job description].
i. On item 3, delete "**$4,500**" and type [Salary]. Don't delete the period after "$4,500".

8. Apply yellow text highlight color (not text color) to all of the placeholder text. Highlight only the placeholder text and brackets, not the spaces or punctuation around the placeholder text.
9. In the header on the second page, delete the date, insert the current date in proper business letter format, and set the date so it updates automatically.
10. Proofread the document to check for proper business letter formatting, spacing between parts, and spacing and punctuation around placeholder text.
11. Save and close the template (Figure 5-104).

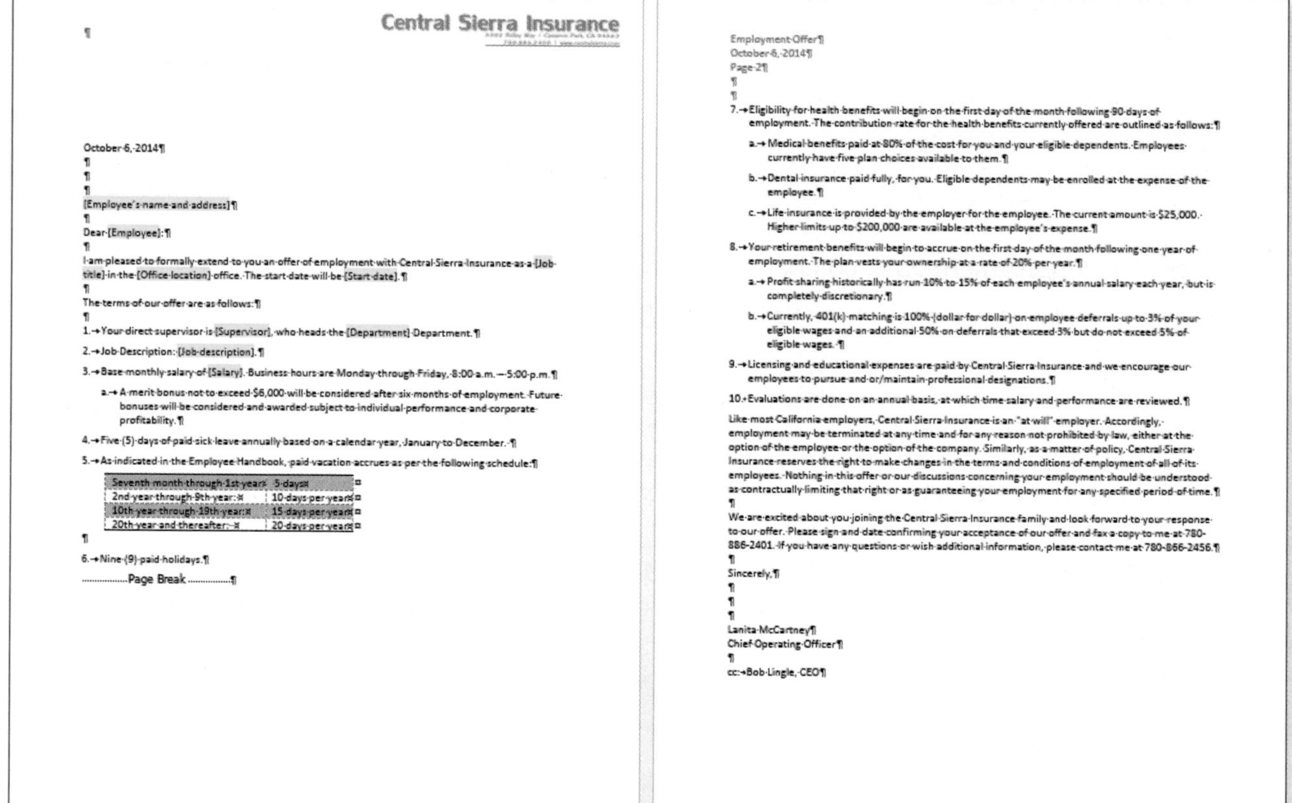

Central Sierra Insurance

October 6, 2014

[Employee's name and address]

Dear [Employee]:

I am pleased to formally extend to you an offer of employment with Central Sierra Insurance as a [Job title] in the [Office location] office. The start date will be [Start date].

The terms of our offer are as follows:

1. Your direct supervisor is [Supervisor], who heads the [Department] Department.
2. Job Description: [Job description].
3. Base monthly salary of [Salary]. Business hours are Monday through Friday, 8:00 a.m. — 5:00 p.m.
    a. A merit bonus not to exceed $6,000 will be considered after six months of employment. Future bonuses will be considered and awarded subject to individual performance and corporate profitability.
4. Five (5) days of paid sick leave annually based on a calendar year, January to December.
5. As indicated in the Employee Handbook, paid vacation accrues as per the following schedule:

Seventh month through 1st year:	5 days
2nd year through 9th year:	10 days per year
10th year through 19th year:	15 days per year
20th year and thereafter:	20 days per year

6. Nine (9) paid holidays.

Page Break

Employment Offer
October 6, 2014
Page 2

7. Eligibility for health benefits will begin on the first day of the month following 90 days of employment. The contribution rate for the health benefits currently offered are outlined as follows:
    a. Medical benefits paid at 80% of the cost for you and your eligible dependents. Employees currently have five plan choices available to them.
    b. Dental insurance paid fully, for you. Eligible dependents may be enrolled at the expense of the employee.
    c. Life insurance is provided by the employer for the employee. The current amount is $25,000. Higher limits up to $200,000 are available at the employee's expense.
8. Your retirement benefits will begin to accrue on the first day of the month following one year of employment. The plan vests your ownership at a rate of 20% per year.
    a. Profit sharing historically has run 10% to 15% of each employee's annual salary each year, but is completely discretionary.
    b. Currently, 401(k) matching is 100% (dollar for dollar) on employee deferrals up to 3% of your eligible wages and an additional 50% on deferrals that exceed 3% but do not exceed 5% of eligible wages.
9. Licensing and educational expenses are paid by Central Sierra Insurance and we encourage our employees to pursue and or/maintain professional designations.
10. Evaluations are done on an annual basis, at which time salary and performance are reviewed.

Like most California employers, Central Sierra Insurance is an "at will" employer. Accordingly, employment may be terminated at any time and for any reason not prohibited by law, either at the option of the employee or the option of the company. Similarly, as a matter of policy, Central Sierra Insurance reserves the right to make changes in the terms and conditions of employment of all of its employees. Nothing in this offer or our discussions concerning your employment should be understood as contractually limiting that right or as guaranteeing your employment for any specified period of time.

We are excited about you joining the Central Sierra Insurance family and look forward to your response to our offer. Please sign and date confirming your acceptance of our offer and fax a copy to me at 780-886-2401. If you have any questions or wish additional information, please contact me at 780-866-2456.

Sincerely,

Lanita McCartney
Chief Operating Officer

cc: Bob Lingle, CEO

5-104 Word 5-7 completed

Challenge Project 5-8

For this project, you create a form letter to use in a mail merge. You can merge information from a data source into any kind of document. The following is a list of examples for potential mail merge projects (you are not limited to these examples):

- A letter to your instructors informing them of an upcoming project and soliciting their input.
- A letter to family and friends inviting them to an upcoming event.
- A letter to solicit donations from your college's alumni.

You can use an existing database as your data source or you can type a new list with recipient information. Complete the merge to a new document to edit individual documents.
[Student Learning Outcomes 5.4, 5.5, 5.6]

File Needed: None
Completed Project File Names: ***[your initials] Word 5-8 main.docx***, ***[your initials] Word 5-8 data.accdb***, and ***[your initials] Word 5-8 merge.docx***

Create a new document and save it as ***[your initials] Word 5-8 main***. Modify your document according to the following guidelines:

- Use proper business letter formatting if applicable.
- Change line and paragraph spacing as needed to create an attractive and readable document. Use consistent line and paragraph spacing throughout the document.
- Insert placeholder text where the merge fields are inserted.
- Select recipients or create a new list for recipients. Save the data source as ***[your initials] Word 5-8 data***.
- Sort and/or filter the merge. Include at least five recipients in your merge.
- Insert merge fields as needed. Check for proper spacing and punctuation around merge fields.
- Highlight merge fields in the main document.
- Apply font formatting to at least one of the merge fields.
- Complete the mail merge to a new document and save as ***[your initials] Word 5-8 merge***.

Challenge Project 5-9

For this project, you create a Word template based upon one of the Word templates on Office.com. Choose from a brochure, business cards, an invitation, a schedule, or any of the other templates available from Office.com on the *Backstage* view.
[Student Learning Outcomes 5.1, 5.2]

File Needed: None
Completed Project File Names: ***[your initials] Word 5-9 template.dotx*** and ***[your initials] Word 5-9.docx***

Open a Word template of your choice and save the document as a Word template named ***[your initials] Word 5-9 template***. Modify your document according to the following guidelines:

- Customize the template to meet your needs adding text and placeholder text.
- Delete any placeholder text not needed.
- Apply formatting as needed.
- Save and close the template.
- Create a Word document based upon the template and save this document as ***[your initials] Word 5-9***.
- Replace placeholder text with custom content.
- Check for consistent and attractive formatting.

Challenge Project 5-10

For this project, you create a full sheet of return mailing labels and merged labels.
[Student Learning Outcomes 5.3, 5.4, 5.5, 5.6]

File Needed: None
Completed Project File Names: ***[your initials] Word 5-10 return labels.docx*** and ***[your initials] Word 5-10 mailing labels.docx***

Create a full sheet of return mailing labels.

- Select the types of labels to be used for your return labels. Look online to find specific label information.
- Type the information to be included on the return labels.
- Save the return labels as ***[your initials] Word 5-10 return labels***.

You can use an existing database as your data source or you can type a new list with recipient information. Complete the merge to a new document to edit individual labels. Modify your document according to the following guidelines:

- Select the types of labels to be used for your return labels.
- Select and sort recipients.
- Insert address block or individual merge fields.
- Change font and size as desired.
- Update all labels.
- Preview the labels and complete the merge.
- Save the merged mailing labels as ***[your initials] Word 5-10 mailing labels***.

CHAPTER 6

Using Custom Styles and Building Blocks

CHAPTER OVERVIEW

In Chapter 2, we introduced styles. In this chapter, you learn more about creating and managing custom styles. You also learn about building blocks, which allow you to save and use chunks of information. Building blocks, like styles, save you time and help you produce documents that are more consistent and easier to read and understand. This chapter also covers *Quick Parts* and *AutoText* building blocks and document property and Word fields.

STUDENT LEARNING OUTCOMES (SLOs)

After completing this chapter, you will be able to:

SLO 6.1 Create and modify a style using the *Style* gallery and *Styles* pane (p. W6-316).

SLO 6.2 Customize a document by managing styles and using a styles template (p. W6-325).

SLO 6.3 Use the *Building Blocks Organizer* to create and save information in a document (p. W6-335).

SLO 6.4 Create *AutoText* building blocks to save text and objects and insert them into documents (p. W6-338).

SLO 6.5 Use the *Quick Parts* gallery to store building blocks and insert them into documents (p. W6-344).

SLO 6.6 Customize and use document property and Word fields in a document (p. W6-346).

CASE STUDY

In the Pause & Practice projects in this chapter, you create a styles template and a document detailing flexibility exercises for the American River Cycling Club. In these documents, you use many of the features you learn about in the chapter to create, save, and insert information in a document.

Pause & Practice 6-1: Create, save, and modify styles in a new document.

Pause & Practice 6-2: Create a style template to create, save, and manage styles, and attach the styles template to a document.

Pause & Practice 6-3: Use the *Building Blocks Organizer* and *AutoText* entries to save information and insert it into a document.

Pause & Practice 6-4: Customize the *Quick Parts* gallery and use document properties fields in a document.

WORD

SLO 6.1

Creating and Using Custom Styles

You can use styles to apply formatting and keep formatting consistent in a document. A style is essentially a set of formatting commands that are grouped together so you can easily and quickly apply them to your text. Recall from *SLO 2.7: Using Styles and Themes* (p. W2-89) that ***styles*** are a collection of preset formatting that you can apply to selected text. You can use styles to apply preset formatting to titles, section headings, paragraph headings, text, lists, and tables. ***Themes*** are a collection of fonts, colors, and effects that you can apply to an entire document. Both styles and themes keep the formatting consistent throughout a single document or multiple documents.

A major benefit of using styles is that styles allow you to quickly modify formatting and update changes throughout a document. When you modify a style, Word automatically updates all text that has that style applied to it, creating a consistently formatted document and saving you time.

By default, each document you create in Word has a built-in style. The default style is *Normal* but you have many other options. You can apply or modify existing Word styles or create new styles. The text formatting in each of the styles is based upon the theme of the document. The default theme of a new document is *Office.* When the theme of a document changes, the font, size, color, and other attributes of each style change.

Style Gallery

The ***Style gallery*** is in the *Styles* group on the *Home* tab and contains some of the more commonly used styles. Click the **More** button in the *Style* gallery to display all of the styles in the gallery (Figure 6-1). Use the **Styles** down arrow to scroll through the styles in the *Style* gallery.

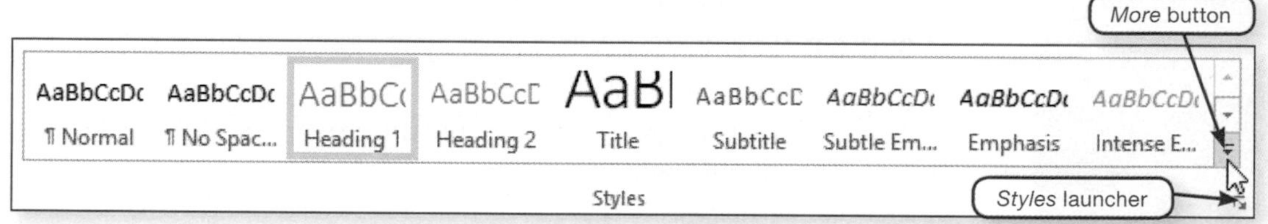

6-1 ***Style* gallery**

Apply a style to selected text or a paragraph by clicking on a style in the *Style* gallery. When you place your pointer on a style, Word temporarily applies the style to selected text so you can preview how the text will appear when the style is applied.

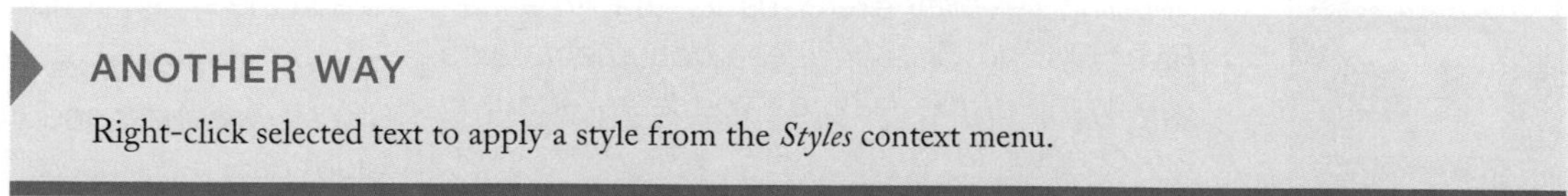

ANOTHER WAY

Right-click selected text to apply a style from the *Styles* context menu.

Styles Pane

The ***Styles pane*** lists the styles in the document and those displayed in the *Style* gallery. By default, this pane does not list all of the available styles in a document. You can apply a style, modify a style, or create a new style from the *Styles* pane.

HOW TO: Use the Styles Pane

1. Select the text where you want to apply a style.
2. Click the **Styles** launcher to open the *Styles* pane.
3. Place your pointer over a style to display the attributes of the style (Figure 6-2).
   - Check the **Show Preview** box to display a preview of styles in the *Styles* pane
4. Click a style to apply to selected text.
5. Resize the *Styles* pane by clicking and dragging the top, bottom, left, or right edge.
6. Move the *Styles* pane by clicking and dragging the top bar of the pane.
   - You can also click the **Styles** drop-down arrow to move, size, or close the *Styles* pane.
7. Click the **x** in the upper right corner to close the *Styles* pane.

6-2 ***Styles*** **pane**

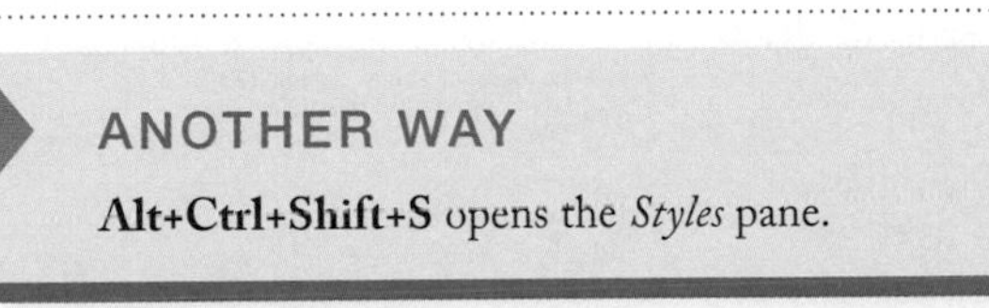

ANOTHER WAY

Alt+Ctrl+Shift+S opens the *Styles* pane.

Types of Styles

There are different types of styles available in Word documents. Some styles apply to selected text, while others apply to an entire paragraph. You can also create styles for lists and tables. The following table lists the different types of styles and a description of each type:

Types of Styles

Style Type	Description
Paragraph	Style applies to the entire paragraph.
Character	Style applies to selected text.
Linked	Style applies to selected text or an entire paragraph.
Table	Style applies to an entire table. Table styles are in the *Table Styles* gallery on the *Table Tools Design* tab.
List	Style applies to a paragraph or selected paragraphs.

An icon to the right of the style in the *Styles* pane indicates the type of style (Figure 6-3).

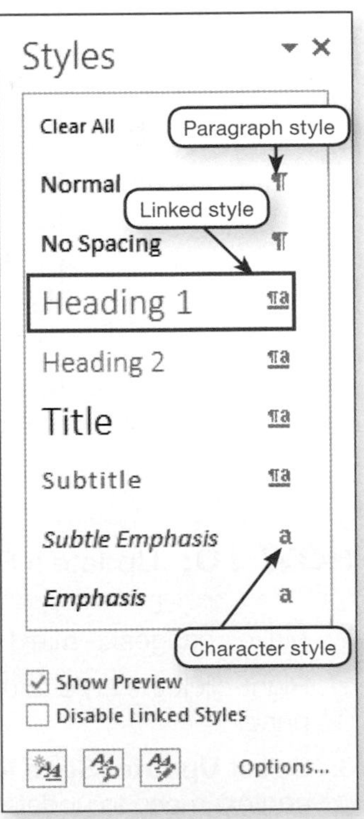

6-3 ***Styles*** **pane with preview turned on**

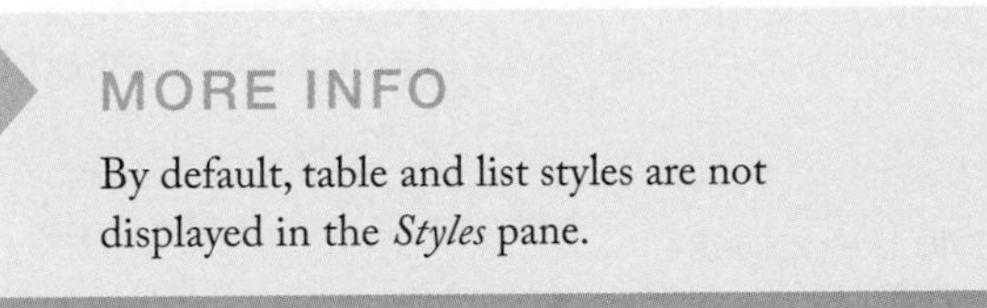

MORE INFO

By default, table and list styles are not displayed in the *Styles* pane.

Modify a Style

You can easily modify or update a style using the ***Modify Style*** dialog box. You can also update a style to match selected text that is already formatted.

HOW TO: Modify a Style

1. Right-click a style in the *Style* gallery or the *Styles* pane.
2. Select **Modify** from the context menu (Figure 6-4). The *Modify Style* dialog box opens (Figure 6-5).

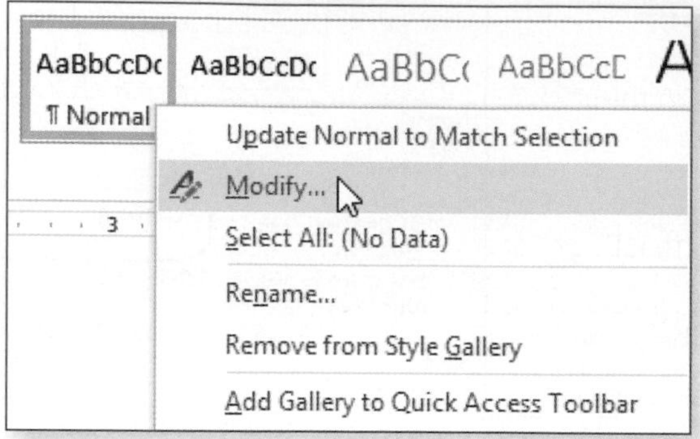

6-4 Modify a style

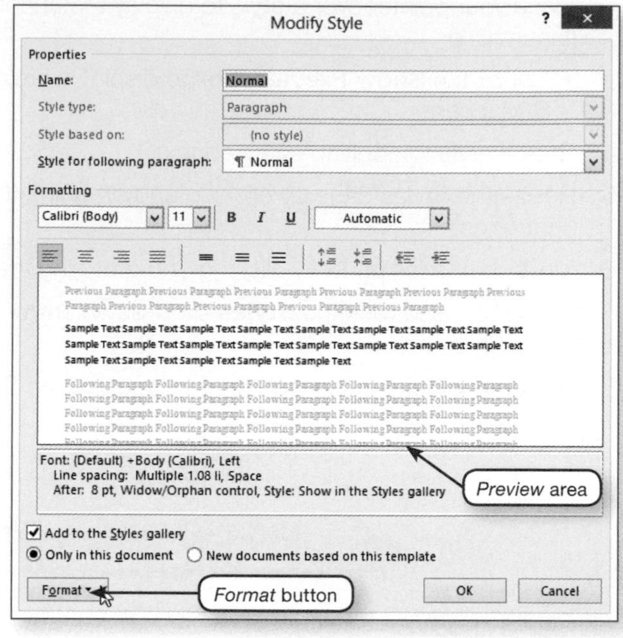

6-5 *Modify Style* dialog box

3. If you want to rename the style, type a new name for the style In the *Name* area.
4. In the *Formatting* area, you can change the font, size, color, style, alignment, and line spacing of the text as desired.
5. The *Preview* area displays how the text will appear in your document.
6. Choose the **Format** button to display a list of additional formatting options (Figure 6-6).
   - When you select one of the *Format* options, a dialog box opens where you can make additional changes to the style.
7. Click **OK** to close the *Modify Style* dialog box.

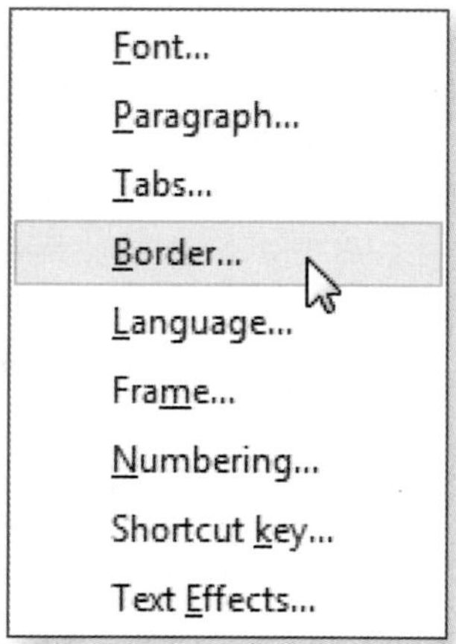

6-6 Style formatting options available from the *Format* button

Update a Style

When you update a style, the style is updated based on the formatting of the selected text. For example, if you change the font, size, color, and paragraph spacing of text that has the *Heading 1* style applied, you can update the *Heading 1* style to match the changes made. When you update or modify a style, all text in the document that has that style applied is automatically updated.

HOW TO: Update a Style

1. Make changes to a text selection where a style is applied.
2. Right-click the style to update in the *Style* gallery or the *Styles* pane.
3. Select **Update [Style Name] to Match Selection** from the context menu to update the style (Figure 6-7). The style is updated to match the selected text.

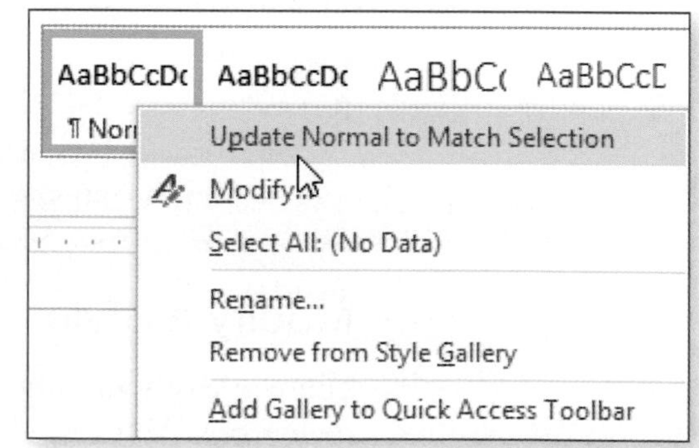

6-7 Update a style

> **ANOTHER WAY**
>
> Right-click selected text to update a style from the *Styles* context menu on the mini toolbar.

Create a New Style

You can create a new style from scratch or base a new style upon text that is already formatted. When you create a new style, you name the style and select a style type (*Paragraph*, *Character*, *Linked*, *Table*, or *List*). You have the option to base the new style on an existing style, which uses the formatting of the existing style as a starting point for the new style. You also set the style for the paragraph following text with a style applied. For example, when you press *Enter* after a *Heading 1* style, you can set *Normal* to be the style of the next paragraph.

HOW TO: Create a New Style

1. Click the **Styles** launcher to open the *Styles* pane.
2. Click the **New Style** button on the bottom left of the Styles pane (Figure 6-8). The *Create New Style from Formatting* dialog box opens (Figure 6-9).
3. In the *Name* area, type the name of the style.
4. In the *Style type* area, select the type of style.
5. From the *Style based on* drop-down list, select a style as the starting point for the new style.
6. From the *Style for following paragraph* drop-down list, select the style for the paragraph following the style.
   - When you press **Enter** after text, this option controls what style is applied to the next paragraph.

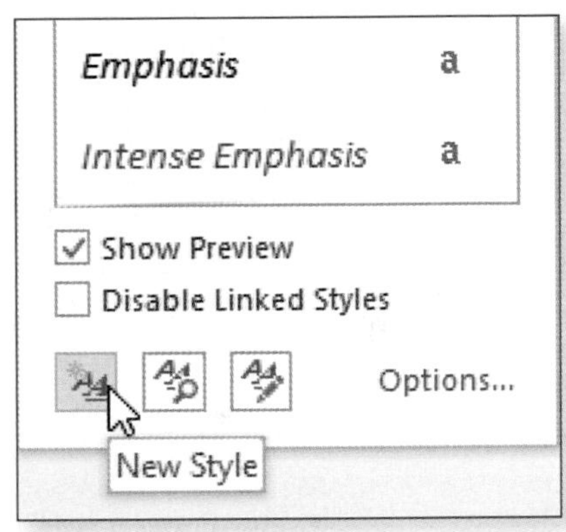

6-8 Create a new style

7. In the *Formatting* area, make changes to the font, size, style, color, and alignment as desired.
8. Click the **Format** button to select from other formatting options.
   - A new dialog box opens for each format option you choose.
   - Click **OK** to return to the *Create New Style from Formatting* dialog box.
9. Select the **Add to the Styles gallery** check box to add the new style to the *Style* gallery.
   - By default, this check box is selected when you create a new style.
10. Select the **Only in this document** radio button.
    - If you select **New documents based upon this template**, this style is added to the *Normal* template and is available on all new documents you create.
11. Click **OK** to close the dialog box.

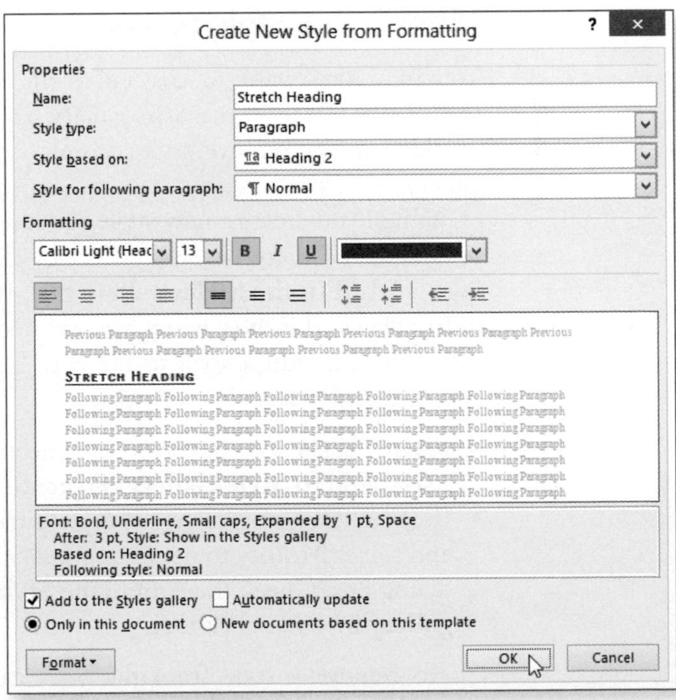

6-9 *Create New Style from Formatting* dialog box

> **MORE INFO**
>
> Recall from Chapter 1 that each new document is based on the *Normal.dotx* template. This template stores the default settings for documents and controls document elements such as font, size, line spacing, paragraph spacing, alignment, and styles.

Create a New Style from Selected Text

There will be times when you want to create a style based on text you have formatted in a document. When you do this, Word uses the existing formatting to create the new style, and you have the option to modify the settings of this style.

HOW TO: Create a New Style from Selected Text

1. Select the text to save as a new style.
2. Click the **More** button in the *Styles* group [*Home* tab].
3. Select **Create a Style**. The *Create New Style from Formatting* dialog box opens (Figure 6-10).
4. In the *Name* area, type the name of the new style.
5. Click **OK** to close the dialog box and create the new style. The new style is also added to the *Style* gallery.
   - You can also click the **Modify** button to open the *Create New Style from Formatting* dialog box that displays additional customization options (see Figure 6-9).

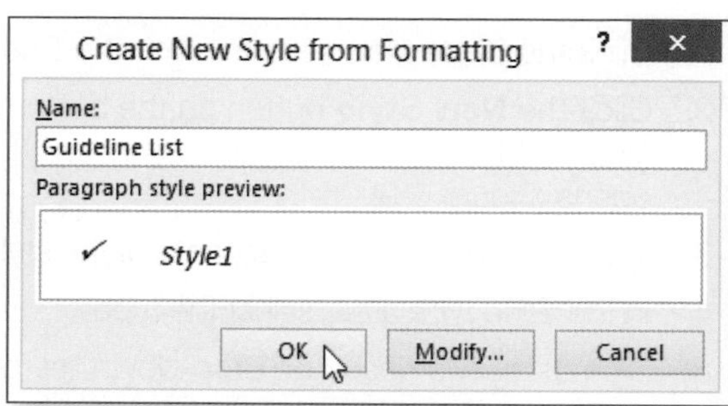

6-10 *Create New Style from Formatting* dialog box

Modify the Style Gallery

You may also want to customize the styles that are available in the *Style* gallery. You can quickly add or remove styles from the *Style* gallery.

When you create a new style, you have the option to add it to the *Style* gallery by checking the **Add to the Styles gallery** box. If you didn't check this box when you created the style, you can add a style to the *Style* gallery two different ways.

- Right-click a style in the *Styles* pane and select **Add to Style Gallery** (Figure 6-11).
- Right-click on a style in the *Styles* pane and select **Modify** to open the *Modify Style* dialog box. Check the **Add to the Styles gallery** box and click **OK**.

To remove a style from the *Style* gallery, right-click the style in the *Style* gallery or in the *Styles* pane and select **Remove from Style Gallery** (Figure 6-12).

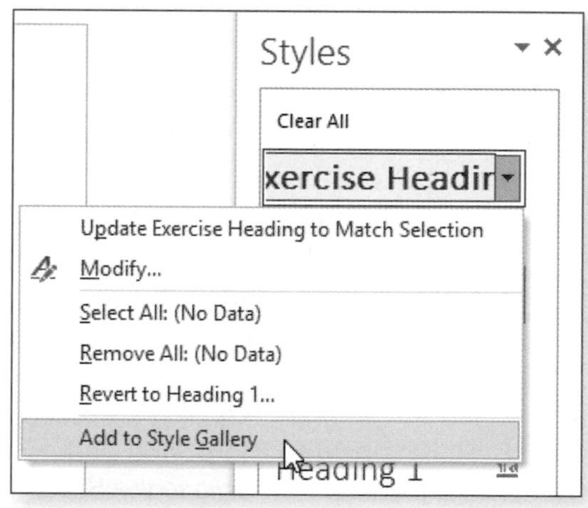

6-11 Add a style to *Style* gallery

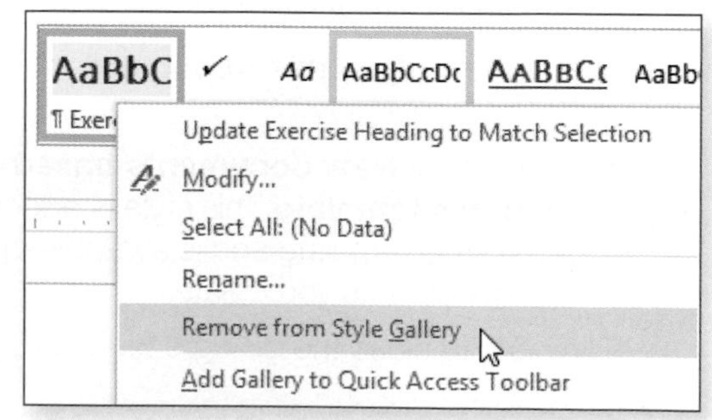

6-12 Remove a style from *Style* gallery

Clear Formatting

After you start creating, modifying, and applying styles, you might find that you need to remove the style formatting applied to text in your document. You could change or remove all of the specific formatting (font, size, style, color, borders, etc.), but this would take too much time. Word allows you to quickly clear formatting on selected text. When you clear formatting, *Normal* style is applied to the text.

Select the text where you want to remove formatting, and clear the formatting in one of the following ways:

- Click the **Clear All Formatting** button [*Home* tab, *Font* group] (Figure 6-13).
- Click the **More** button in the *Styles* group [*Home* tab] and select **Clear Formatting** (Figure 6-14).
- Click the **Clear All** option in the *Styles* pane (Figure 6-15).
- Select the formatted text, select **Styles** from the mini toolbar, and choose **Clear Formatting**.

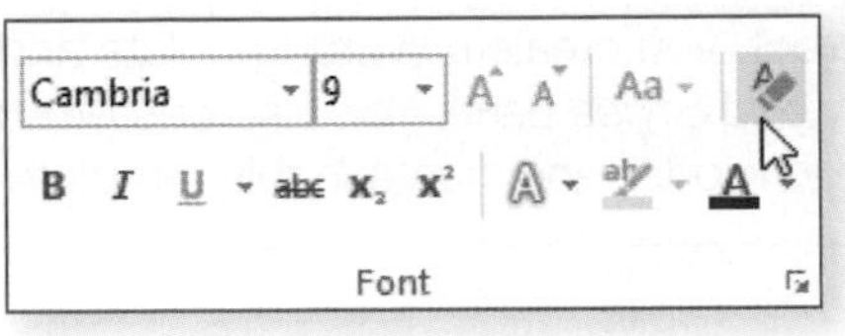

6-13 *Clear Formatting* button in the *Font* group

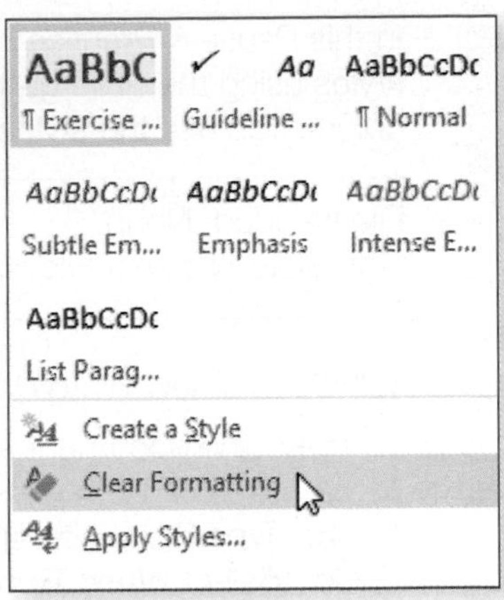

6-14 *Clear Formatting* from the *Style* gallery

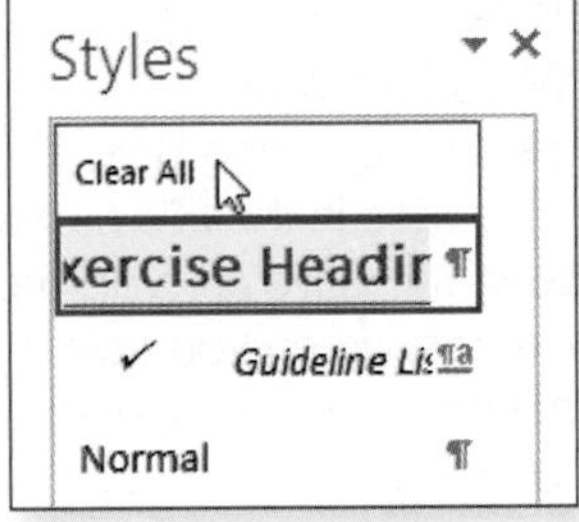

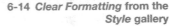

6-15 Clear formatting from the *Styles* pane

Change Document Style Set

In addition to individual styles, Word provides ***style sets***, which are groups of styles. When you change the style set of your document, the formatting of all the styles in your document changes based on the style set you select. The available style sets are in the *Style Sets* gallery in the *Document Formatting* group on the *Design* tab.

Style sets control the font, size, styles, colors, borders, and line and paragraph spacing of a document. By default, a new Word document uses the Word 2013 style set. You can change the style set to customize your document.

HOW TO: Change the Style Set

1. Select the **Design** tab.
2. Click the **More** button [*Document Formatting* group] to display the *Style Sets* gallery (Figure 6-16).

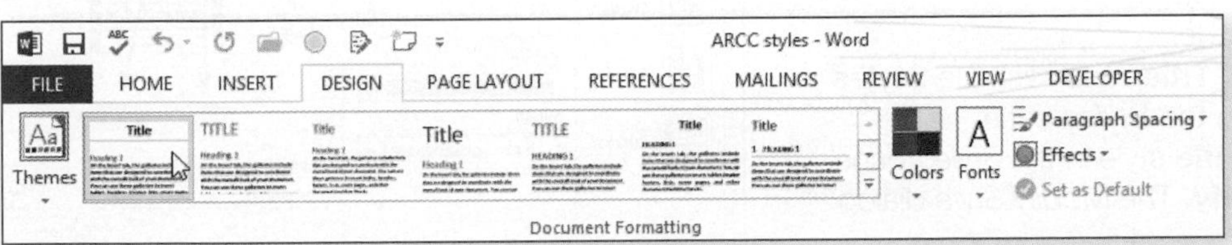

6-16 *Style Sets* in the *Document Formatting* group

3. Select a style set from the gallery. The formatting of all of the styles in your document changes based on the style set you choose.

You can also select different theme ***colors***, ***fonts***, and ***paragraph spacing*** to apply to your document. Click the **Colors, Fonts**, or **Paragraph Spacing** button in the *Document Formatting* group on the *Design* tab to display the drop-down lists. These settings override the existing theme settings in your document.

PAUSE & PRACTICE: WORD 6-1

In this Pause & Practice project, you create a Word template and modify existing styles and create new styles using the *Style* gallery and *Styles* pane. You also customize the *Style* gallery and change theme colors. You use the styles you modify and create in this template again in *Pause & Practice Word 6-2*.

File Needed: None
Completed Project File Name: ***[your initials] ARCC styles.dotx***

---

1. Open a new Word document.
2. Save the document as a Word template.
   a. Press **F12** to open the *Save As* dialog box.
   b. Type [your initials] ARCC styles in the *File name* text box.
   c. Select **Word Template** in the *Save as type* drop-down list. By default, Word changes the save location to a templates folder when you select *Word Template* as the file type.
   d. Browse to the location where you save your completed files.
   e. Click **Save** to close the dialog box and save the template.
3. Change the theme color of the document.
   a. Click **Colors** [*Design* tab, *Document Formatting* group].
   b. Select **Orange Red** from the drop-down list.
4. Type the following text, pressing **Enter** after each line:

   Title
   Normal
   Subtle Emphasis
   Exercise Heading
   Stretch Heading
   Guideline List

5. Apply styles to selected text.
   a. Select the word **"Title"** and click the **Title** style in the *Style* gallery [*Home* tab, *Styles* group].
   b. Select **"Subtle Emphasis**," click the **Styles** button on the mini toolbar, and select **Subtle Emphasis** from the drop-down list.
6. Modify an existing style.
   a. Select the word **"Title"** and click the **Styles** launcher to open the *Styles* pane.
   b. Right-click the **Title** style in the *Styles* pane and select **Modify**. The *Modify Style* dialog box opens.
   c. Click the **Format** button and select **Border** to open the *Borders and Shading* dialog box (Figure 6-17).

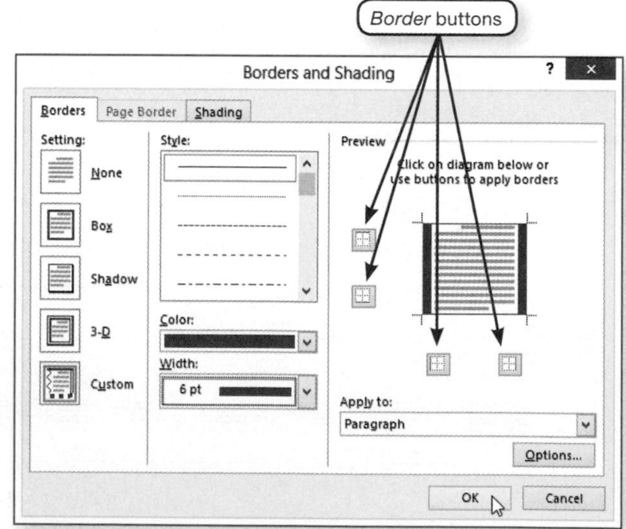

6-17 *Borders and Shading* dialog box

d. Click the **Color** drop-down list and select **Orange, Accent 1**.
e. Click the **Width** drop-down list and select **1 pt.**
f. Click the **Top Border** and **Bottom Border** buttons in the *Preview* area to apply a **1 pt.** top and bottom border.
g. Click the **Width** drop-down arrow and select **6 pt.**
h. Click the **Left Border** and **Right Border** buttons in the *Preview* area to apply a **6 pt.** left and right border.
i. Click **OK** to close the *Borders and Shading* dialog box and return to the *Modify Style* dialog box.
j. Click the **Format** button and select **Paragraph** to open the *Paragraph* dialog box.
k. Change the *After* paragraph spacing to **24 pt.** and click **OK** to close the *Paragraph* dialog box and return to the *Modify Style* dialog box (Figure 6-18).
l. In the *Formatting* area, click the **Bold** button and the **Center** alignment button.
m. Click **OK** to close the *Modify Style* dialog box.

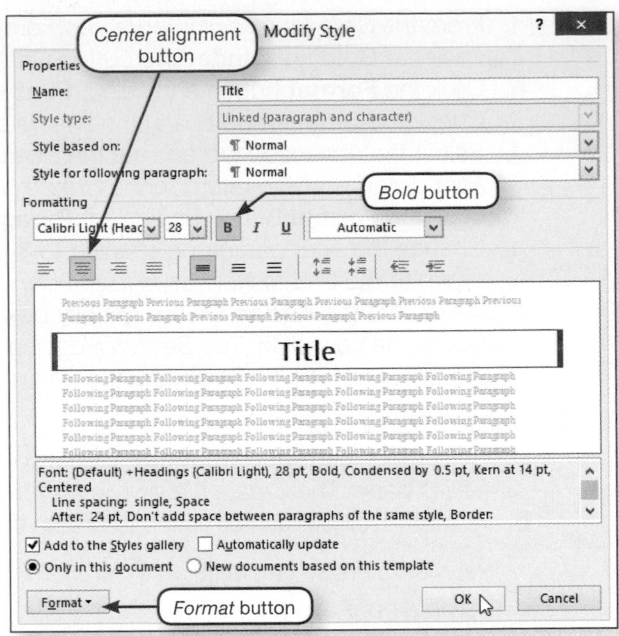

6-18 ***Modify Style* dialog box**

7. Modify text and update styles to match.
   a. Select the word "**Normal**" and change the line spacing to **single** and the *After* paragraph spacing to **10 pt.**
   b. Right-click the **Normal** style in the *Style* gallery and select **Update Normal to Match Selection** (Figure 6-19).
   c. Select the words "**Subtle Emphasis**" and apply **bold** formatting.
   d. Right-click the **Subtle Emphasis** style in the *Styles* pane and select **Update Subtle Emphasis to Match Selection**.

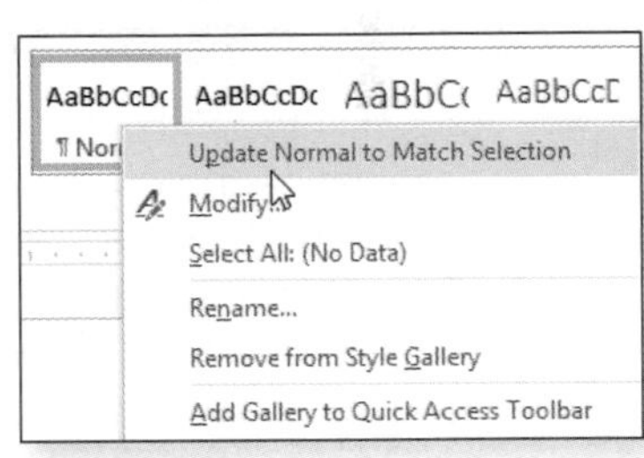

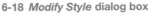

6-19 Update style to match selection

8. Create a new style.
   a. Select the "**Stretch Heading**" text in your document.
   b. Click the **New Style** button at the bottom left of the *Styles* pane (Figure 6-20) to open the *Create New Style from Formatting* dialog box (Figure 6-21).
   c. In the *Name* area, type Stretch Heading.
   d. From the *Style type* drop-down list, select **Paragraph**.
   e. From the *Style based on* drop-down list, select **Heading 2**.

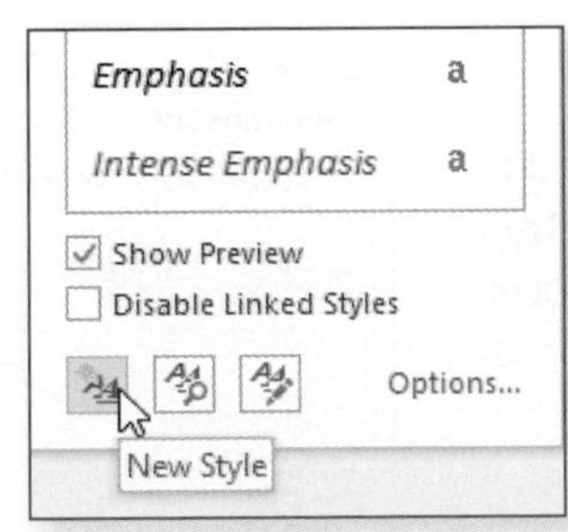

6-20 *New Style* button in the *Styles* pane

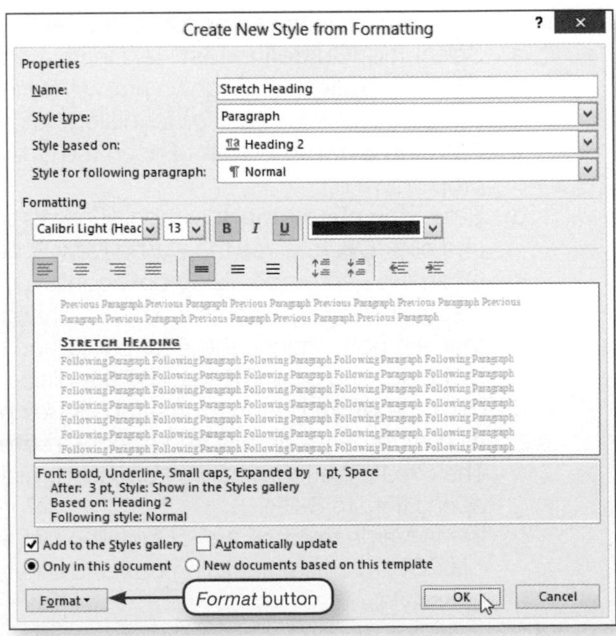

6-21 Create a new style

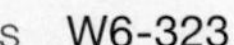

f. From the *Style for following paragraph* drop-down list, select **Normal**.
g. Click the **Bold** and **Underline** buttons in the *Formatting* area.
h. Click the **Format** button and select **Font** to open the *Font* dialog box.
i. Check the **Small caps** box in the *Effects* area.
j. Select the *Advanced* tab and set the *Spacing* to be **Expanded** by **1 pt.** and click **OK** to close the *Font* dialog box and return to the *Create New Style from Formatting* dialog box.
k. Click the **Format** button and select **Paragraph** to open the *Paragraph* dialog box.
l. Change the *After* paragraph spacing to **3 pt.** and click **OK** to close the *Paragraph* dialog box and return to the *Create New Style from Formatting* dialog box.
m. Make sure the **Add to Styles gallery** box is checked and click **OK** to close the dialog box and create the new style. The *Stretch Heading* style is applied to the selected text, and the style appears in the *Style* gallery and the *Styles* pane.

9. Create another new style.
   a. Select the "**Exercise Heading**" text in your document and click the **New Style** button in the *Styles* pane. The *Create New Style from Formatting* dialog box opens.
   b. Enter the following information to create the new style:

      Name: Exercise Heading

      Style type: **Paragraph**

      Style based on: **Heading 1**

      Style for following paragraph: **Stretch Heading**

      Formatting area: **Bold** and **Center** alignment
   c. Click the **Format** button and select **Border** to open the *Borders and Shading* dialog box.
   d. Change the border *Color* to **Orange**, **Accent 1**, the *Width* to **½ pt.,** and click the **Top Border** and **Bottom Border** buttons.
   e. Click the **Shading** tab, change the *Fill* to **White**, **Background 1**, **Darker 5%**, and click **OK** to close the *Borders and Shading* dialog box.
   f. Click the **Format** button and select **Paragraph** to open the *Paragraph* dialog box.
   g. Change the *After* paragraph spacing to **12 pt.** and click **OK** to close the *Paragraph* dialog box.
   h. Click **OK** to close the *Create New Style from Formatting* dialog box and create the new style.

10. Create a new style based on formatted text.
   a. Select the "**Guideline List**" text in your document and apply **italic** formatting.
   b. Click the **Bullets** drop-down arrow [*Home* tab, *Paragraph* group] and select **Define New Bullet** to open the *Define New bullet* dialog box.
   c. Click the **Symbol** button to open the *Symbol* dialog box and select **Wingdings** from the *Font* drop-down list.
   d. Select the **check mark** symbol (*Character code* 252), click **OK** to close the *Symbol* dialog box, and click **OK** to close the *Define New Bullet* dialog box.
   e. Open the *Paragraph* dialog box, confirm that the *Left* and *Hanging* indents are **0.25**" (change them if they are not), change the *After* paragraph spacing to **12 pt.,** and click **OK** to close the dialog box.
   f. Click the **More** button [*Home* tab, *Styles* group] to display the *Style* gallery, and select **Create a Style**. The *Create New Style from Formatting* dialog box opens (Figure 6-22).
   g. In the *Name* text box, type Guideline List and click **OK** to close the dialog box and create the new style.

6-22 *Create New Style from Formatting* dialog box

11. Remove styles from the *Style* gallery.
    a. Right-click the **Heading 1** style in the *Style* gallery.
    b. Select **Remove from Style Gallery** from the context menu (Figure 6-23).
    c. Right-click the **Heading 2** style in the *Styles* pane.
    d. Select **Remove from Style Gallery** from the context menu.
12. Save and close the document (Figure 6-24).

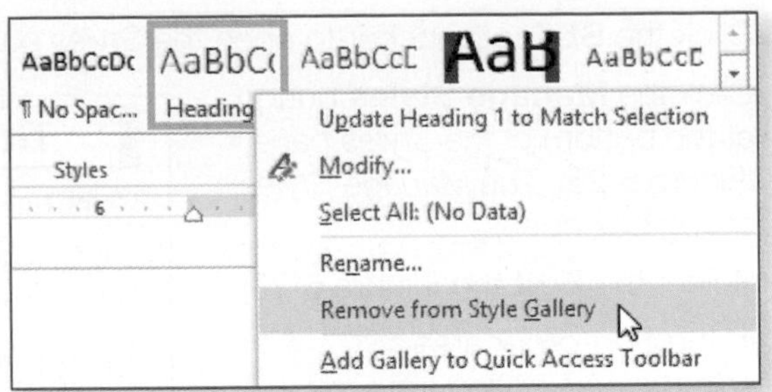

6-23 Remove a style from the *Style* gallery

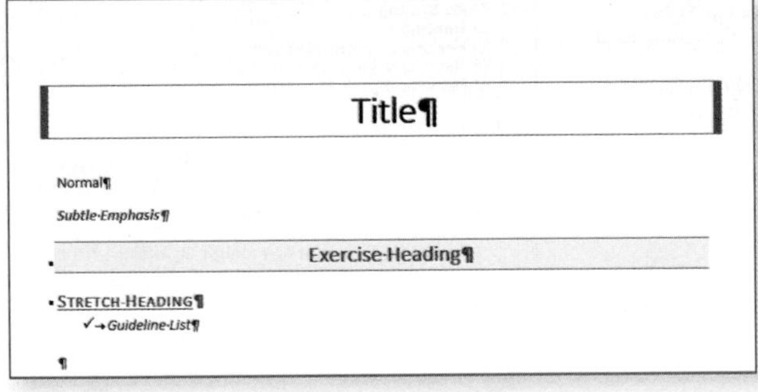

6-24 *ARCC styles* completed

SLO 6.2

Managing Styles

After you create and modify styles, you can use Word features to manage the styles in your documents. Manage your styles to determine which styles are displayed in the *Styles* pane, to delete styles from a document, to modify or rename styles, and to reorder styles in the *Styles* pane and *Style* gallery.

Styles can also be imported from or exported to another document. Recall from Chapter 5 that you can use templates to store styles you have created or modified and you can attach templates to other Word files.

Manage Styles Dialog Box

In the previous section of this chapter, you worked with the styles available in the *Style* gallery and *Styles* pane and added new styles. Word documents contain many styles that are not displayed in the *Style* gallery or *Styles* pane. The ***Manage Styles dialog box*** allows you to customize how styles are displayed and organized in a document.

Edit Style

The following options are available on the *Edit* tab in the *Manage Styles* dialog box:

- Change sort order.
- Edit a style.
- Preview a style.
- Modify or delete a style.
- Create a new style.
- Import and export styles.

HOW TO: Edit Styles in the Manage Styles Dialog Box

1. Click the **Styles** launcher to open the *Styles* pane.
2. Click the **Manage Styles** button at the bottom of the *Styles* pane (Figure 6-25). The *Manage Styles* dialog box opens.
3. Select the **Edit** tab (Figure 6-26).
4. In the *Sort order* area, select a sort option from the drop-down list.
   - The sort options are *Alphabetical*, *As Recommended*, *Font*, *Based on*, and *By type*.
   - To display more styles, deselect the *Show recommended styles only* check box.
   - On the *Recommend* tab, you can change which styles are recommended.
5. In the *Select a style to edit* area, select a style to modify or delete.
   - When you select a style, a preview and description of the style are displayed in the *Preview* area.
   - Click the **Modify** or **Delete** button to modify or delete the selected style.
6. Click the **New Style** button to create a new style.
7. The *Only in this document* and *New documents based on this template* radio buttons determine where these styles are available.
8. The *Import/Export* button opens the *Organizer* dialog box where you can import styles from or export styles to another Word document.
   - Importing and exporting styles is covered later in this section.
9. Click **OK** to close the *Manage Styles* dialog box.

6-25 ***Manage Styles* button in the *Styles* pane**

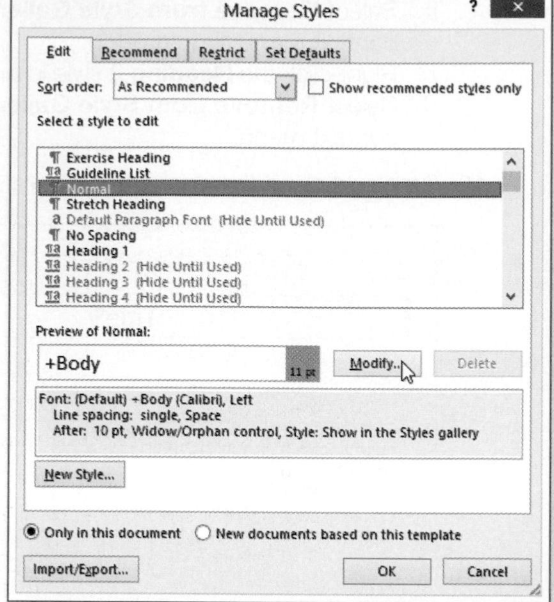

6-26 Edit styles in the *Manage Styles* dialog box

> **MORE INFO**
>
> The *Import/Export* button is available on all the tabs in the *Manage Styles* dialog box.

Recommended Styles

The recommended styles are those styles that are displayed in the *Style* gallery and *Styles* pane by default. You can modify the recommended styles list.

HOW TO: Modify the Recommended Styles List

1. Click the **Styles** launcher to open the *Styles* pane.
2. Click the **Manage Styles** button to open the *Manage Styles* dialog box.

3. Select the **Recommend** tab (Figure 6-27).
4. Deselect the **Show recommended styles only** check box to display all available styles.
5. Select a style and click the **Move Up** or **Move Down** button to reorder styles.
    - Sort order determines the order of styles displayed in the *Styles* gallery and *Styles* pane.
6. Select a style and click the **Show**, **Hide until used**, or **Hide** button to modify the recommended styles list.
    - When *Hide until used* is applied to a style, the style is hidden until the previous style is used. For example, the *Heading 3* style is not displayed until the *Heading 2* style is used in a document.
7. Click **OK** to close the *Manage Styles* dialog box.

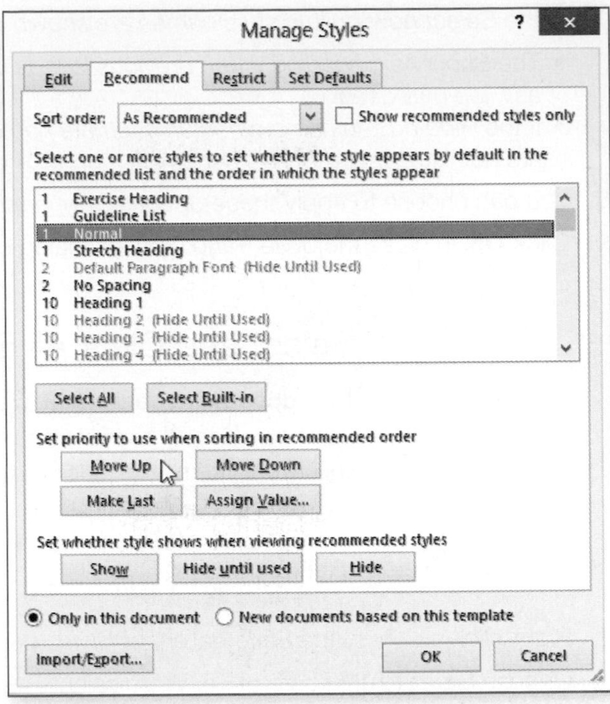

6-27 Recommended styles in the *Manage Styles* dialog box

Style Pane Options

You can use the ***Style Pane Options* dialog box** to control which styles are displayed and their order. The options in this dialog box control only the styles in the *Styles* pane, not those in the *Style* gallery. If you display additional styles in the *Styles* pane, you can always add a style to the *Style* gallery (see *SLO 6.1: Creating and Using Custom Styles, p. W6-316*).

HOW TO: Modify Style Pane Options

1. Click the **Styles** launcher to open the *Styles* pane.
2. Check the **Show Preview** box in the *Styles* pane to display a preview of the format of each style.
3. Click the **Options** link (Figure 6-28) to open the *Style Pane Options* dialog box (Figure 6-29).

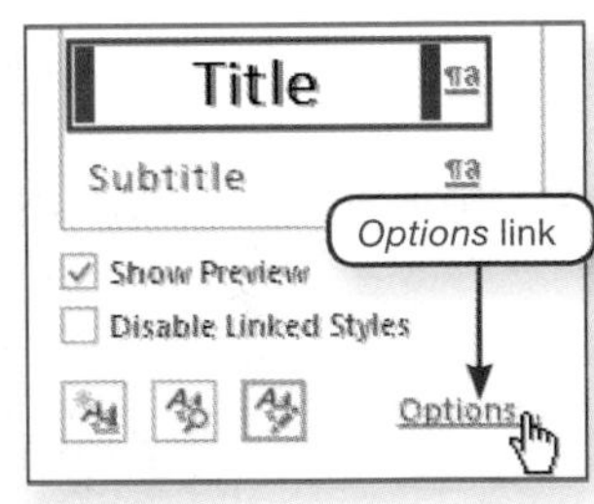

6-28 *Style Pane Options* button

4. In the *Select styles to show* area, select from the drop-down list which styles to display in the *Styles* pane.
    - The available options are *Recommended*, *In use*, *In current document*, and *All styles*.
5. In the *Select how list is sorted* area, select how to sort the styles in the *Styles* pane.
    - The sort options are *Alphabetical*, *As Recommended*, *Font*, *Based on*, and *By type*.
6. In the *Select formatting to show as styles* area, you can display paragraph, font, and list formatting applied to text in a document (Figure 6-30).
    - This option displays text formatting in a manner similar to how a style is displayed.
    - You can apply formatting to selected text as you would apply a style.

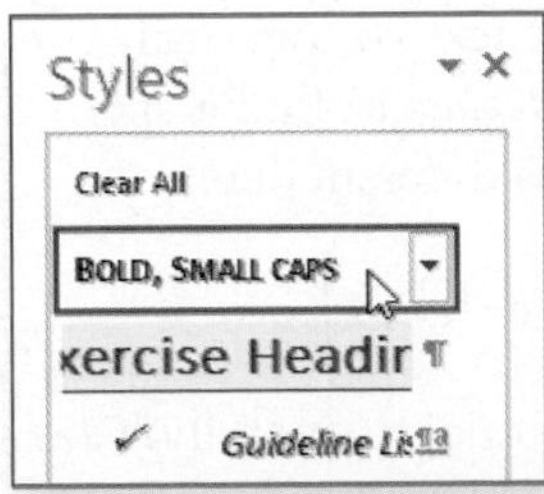

6-30 Formatting displayed as styles

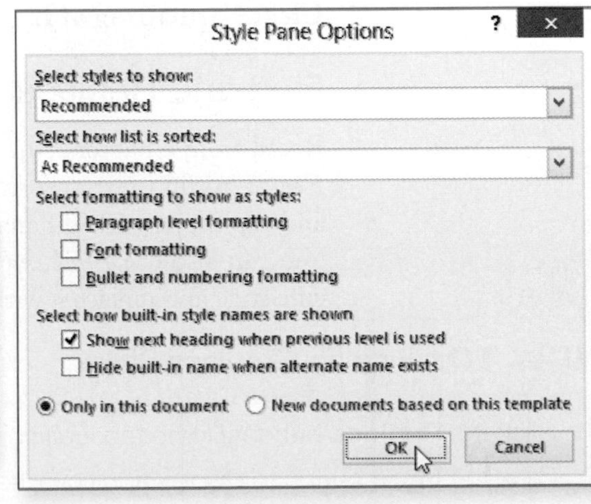

6-29 *Style Pane Options* dialog box

7. In the *Select how built-in style names are shown* area, you control which styles are displayed in the *Styles* pane.
    - The *Show next heading when previous level is used* check box controls the availability of styles that are marked as *Hide until used*.
    - If the *Hide built-in name when an alternate name exists* box is checked, built-in styles that have been renamed are not listed in the *Styles* pane.
8. You can choose to apply these options *Only in this document* or to *New documents based on this template*.
9. Click **OK** to close the *Style Pane Options* dialog box.

Select and Clear All Styles

In a document, you might want to replace all of one style with another style or you might want to clear all formatting of one style. Word allows you to select all of the instances of a specific style in your document. This is an excellent way to modify all the text with a specific style at one time rather than having to individually change each occurrence.

HOW TO: Select All Formatting

1. Right-click a style in the *Style* gallery or *Styles* pane.
2. Choose **Select All** (Figure 6-31). Word selects all instances of the style in the document.
    - After *Select All*, *(No Data)* or the number of instances of this style is displayed.
    - If the selected style is not used in the document, the *Select All* option is not active.
3. Once all of the instances of the style are selected, you can apply a different style, change formatting and update the style, or clear formatting.
    - The *Clear Formatting* option is available from the mini toolbar and *Styles* pane.
4. Click anywhere in the document to deselect all of the selected text.

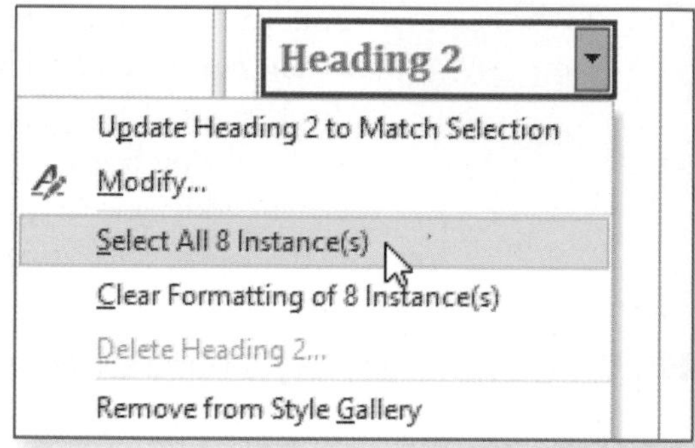

6-31 Select all instances of a style in a document

You can also remove all formatting on all instances of a specific style. This process is similar to selecting all instances. Right-click the style in the *Style* gallery or *Styles* pane and select **Clear Formatting of Instances** (Figure 6-32).

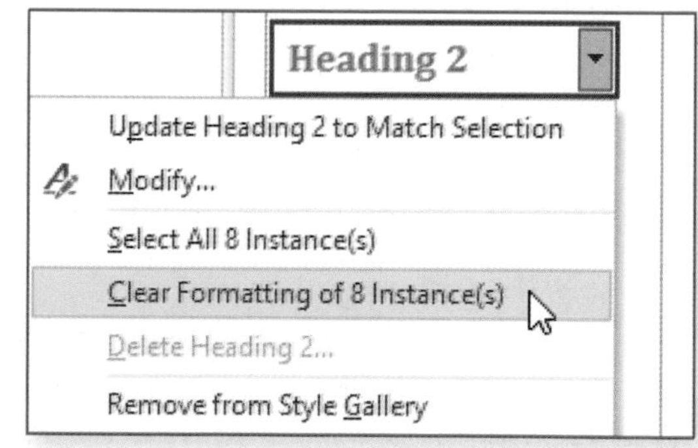

6-32 Clear formatting on all instances of a style

Find and Replace Styles

Recall from Chapter 2, that you can use *Find and Replace* to find text or formatting in a document and replace it with different text or formatting. You can also use *Find and Replace* to find a specific style and replace it with a different one.

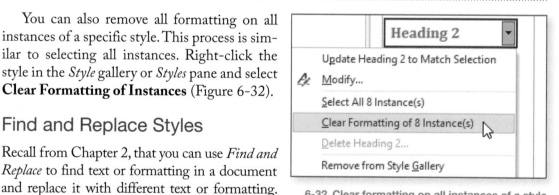

HOW TO: Find and Replace Styles

1. Click the **Replace** button [*Home* tab, *Editing* group] to open the *Find and Replace* dialog box.
2. Click the **More** button to display additional search options if they are not already displayed.
    - If the additional options are displayed, the *More* button changes to the *Less* button.

3. Click in the **Find what** text box.
4. Click the **Format** button and select **Styles**. The *Find Style* dialog box opens (Figure 6-33).
5. Select the style to find and click **OK** to close the *Find Style* dialog box.
6. Click in the **Replace with** text box.
7. Click the **Format** button and select **Styles**. The *Replace Style* dialog box opens.
8. Select the style you want to find and click **OK** to close the dialog box.
9. Click the **Find Next** button to highlight the first occurrence of the style in the document (Figure 6-34).

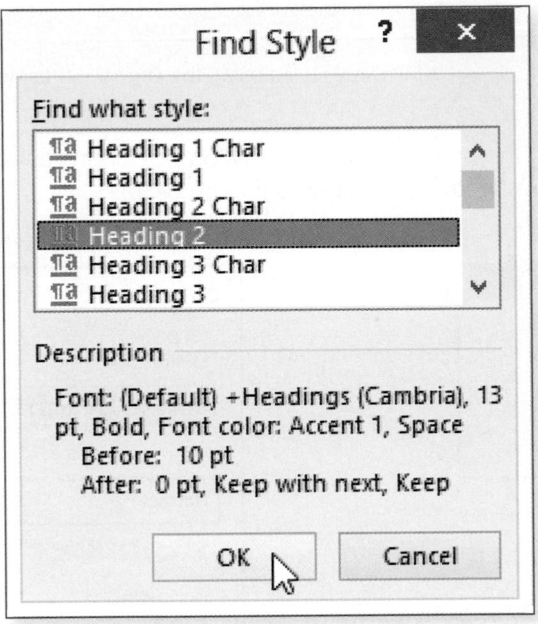

6-33 *Find Style* dialog box

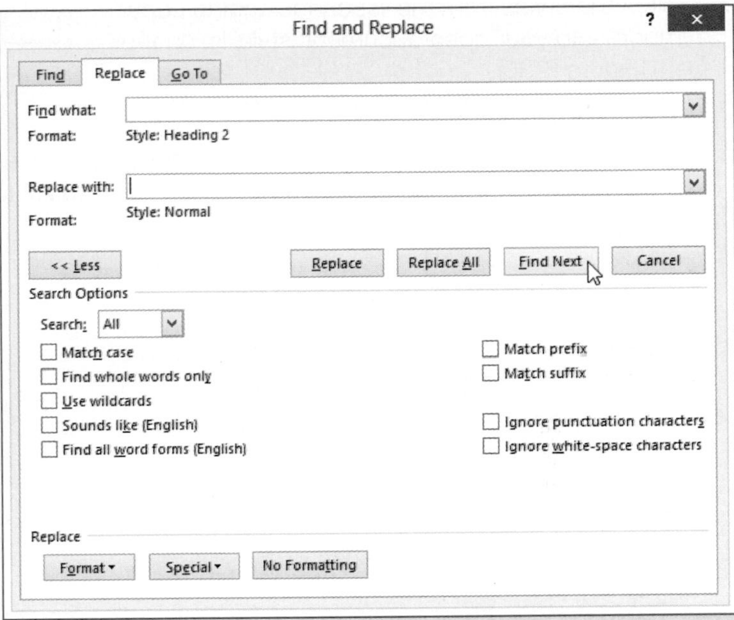

6-34 Find and replace styles

10. Click the **Replace** or **Replace All** button to replace an individual occurrence or all of the occurrences of a style with a different style.
11. Click **Cancel** (or the **X** in the upper right corner) when you are finished.

Import and Export Styles

In Word you can use styles from one document in other documents. This powerful and useful feature saves time and allows you to create consistent documents. Use the ***importing and exporting*** feature to import styles from or export styles to a different document.

Use the ***Organizer dialog box*** to copy styles from one document to another. You can copy all styles or just selected styles. When you copy built-in styles from one document to another, you are given the option to overwrite the existing built-in styles in the target document.

HOW TO: Import Styles from a Template

1. In the document where you are importing styles, click the **Manage Styles** button in the *Styles* pane.
2. Click the **Import/Export** button to open the *Organizer* dialog box.
   - The styles listed on the left are the styles in your open document.
   - The styles listed on the right are the styles in the *Normal* template.
3. Click the **Close File** button on the right to close the *Normal* template.

4. Click the **Open File** button to open the file containing the styles to import. The *Open* dialog box opens.
5. Browse to find the file containing the styles you want to import and click **Open**.
   - If you are importing from a regular Word document (.docx) or a file other than a template file, select the appropriate file type from the list of options available to the right of the *File name* text box.
6. Select the styles from the list on the right to copy (import) into your open document (style list on the left) (Figure 6-35).
7. Click the **Copy** button.
8. If you are importing styles with the same names as the styles in the open document, a dialog box opens asking if you want to overwrite the existing styles. Select **Yes to All** to overwrite existing styles (Figure 6-36).

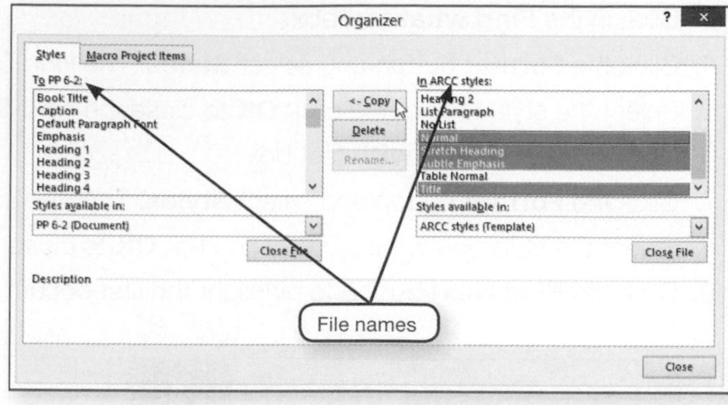

6-35 Copy styles using the *Organizer* dialog box

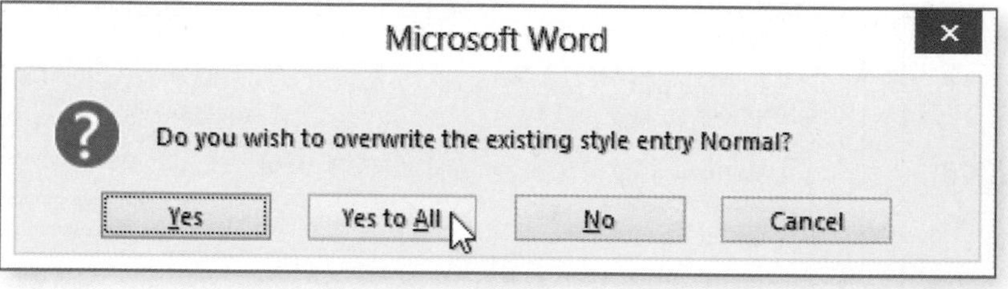

6-36 Overwrite styles

9. Click **Close** to close the *Organizer* dialog box.
   - The imported styles are available in the *Style* gallery and the *Styles* pane (Figure 6-37).

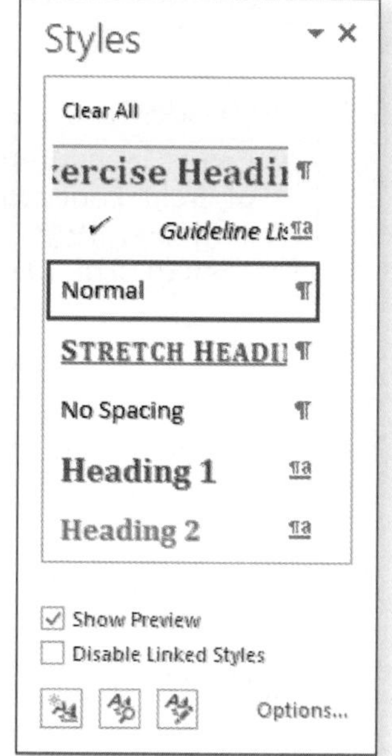

6-37 Imported styles displayed in the *Styles* pane

The process to export styles is the same as the importing process. When you are importing or exporting, make sure you pay attention to which files you are using to import and export styles. The name of the file is listed above each of the styles lists in the *Organize* dialog box as shown in Figure 6-35.

Styles Template

In *Pause & Practice 6-1*, you created a template containing new styles and modified styles. This is called a ***styles template***. You can attach a styles template to other documents and the styles in the template are available in any document where the styles template is attached. The advantage of using a styles template is that, when styles are updated in the styles template, these changes are automatically updated in all the documents that have the styles template attached.

Attach a Template to a Document

All new Word documents are, by default, based on the *Normal* template, which contains the theme and styles for the document. You can choose to attach a different template to a document or to multiple documents. You can set the styles from the template to update automatically in the document(s) where the template is attached.

HOW TO: Attach a Template to a Document

1. Open the document where you want to attach a template.
2. Click the **Document Template** button [*Developer* tab, *Templates* group] to open the *Templates and Add-ins* dialog box (Figure 6-38).
   - If the *Developer* tab is not available, click the **File** tab, select **Options**, click **Customize Ribbon**, and check the **Developer** box under *Main Tabs* in the *Customize the Ribbon* area.
3. Click the **Attach** button. The *Attach Template* dialog box opens.
4. Browse to find the template and click **Open**.
5. Check the **Automatically update document styles** check box.
   - If this box is not checked, styles in the document will not be updated from the template.
6. Click **OK** to close the *Templates and Add-ins* dialog box.

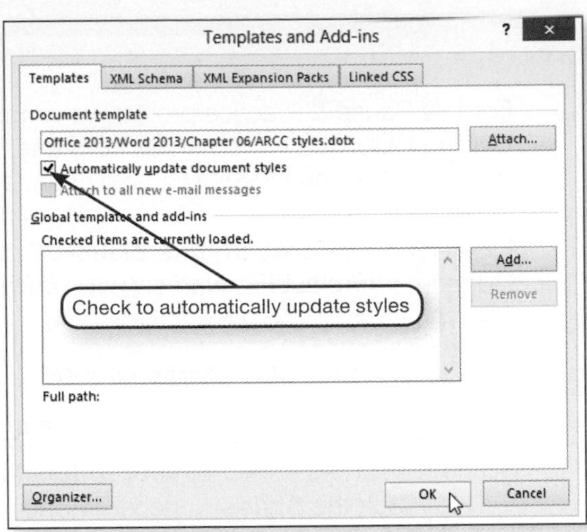

6-38 Attach a template to a document

When modifying styles in a template attached to other documents, make sure the other documents are closed. After modifying the styles in the template, save and close the template. When you open a document based on the modified template, the styles from the template are automatically updated and applied in the document.

Use the Organizer Dialog Box

You can use the *Organizer* dialog box to organize styles in documents that have a template attached. In a way similar to the method you use to import styles, you can use the *Organizer* dialog box to copy styles and to delete and rename styles.

HOW TO: Use the Organizer Dialog Box

1. Open the document that has a template attached.
2. Click the **Document Template** button [*Developer* tab, *Templates* group] to open the *Templates and Add-ins* dialog box (see Figure 6-38).
3. Click the **Organizer** button to open the *Organizer* dialog box.
4. Click the **Styles available in** drop-down arrow on the left to select from the available document and templates (Figure 6-39).
5. You can select a style from the style list and *Copy*, *Rename*, or *Delete* the style.
6. Click **Close** to close the *Organizer* dialog box.

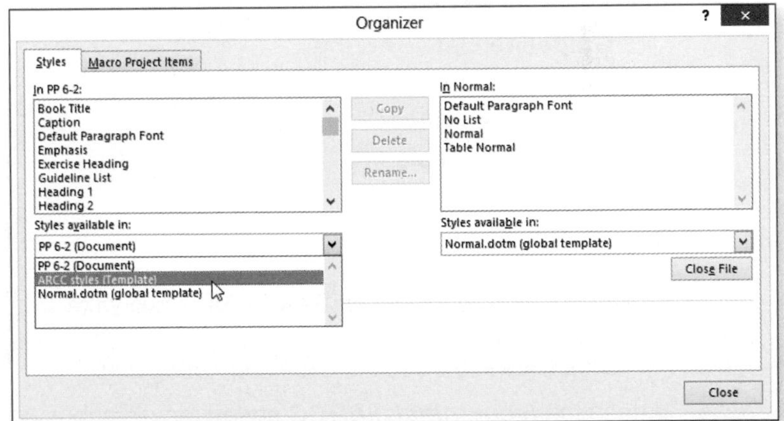

6-39 *Organizer* dialog box

> **MORE INFO**
>
> If you accidentally created a style and added it to the *Normal* template, you can delete the style in the *Organizer* dialog box.

PAUSE & PRACTICE: WORD 6-2

For this Pause & Practice project, you modify a document about flexibility exercises for the American River Cycling Club. You import styles from a template, attach a styles template to a document, replace and modify styles, manage styles, and change options in the *Styles* Pane.

Files Needed: ***FlexibilityExercises-06.docx*** and ***[your initials] ARCC styles.dotx***
Completed Project File Name: ***[your initials] PP W6-2.docx***

---

1. Open the ***FlexibilityExercises-06*** document from your student data files.
2. Save the document as ***[your initials] PP W6-2***.
3. Import styles from the ***[your initials] ARCC styles*** template you created in *Pause & Practice 6-1*.
   a. Click the **Styles** launcher to open the *Styles* pane.
   b. Click the **Manage Styles** button in the *Styles* pane to open the *Manage Styles* dialog box.
   c. Click the **Import/Export** button to open the *Organizer* dialog box.
   d. Click the **Close File** button at the right to close the *Normal* template.
   e. Click the **Open File** button to open *Open* dialog box.
   f. Browse to find the ***[your initials] ARCC Styles*** template and click **Open**.
   g. Select the styles from the following list to copy (import) into your document. Press the **Ctrl** key and select multiple, non-adjacent styles (Figure 6-40):

      Exercise Heading
      Guideline List
      Normal
      Stretch Heading
      Subtle Emphasis
      Title

   h. Click the **Copy** button.
   i. A dialog box opens asking if you want to overwrite the existing styles. Select **Yes to All** to overwrite existing files.
   j. Click **Close** to close the *Organizer* dialog box.

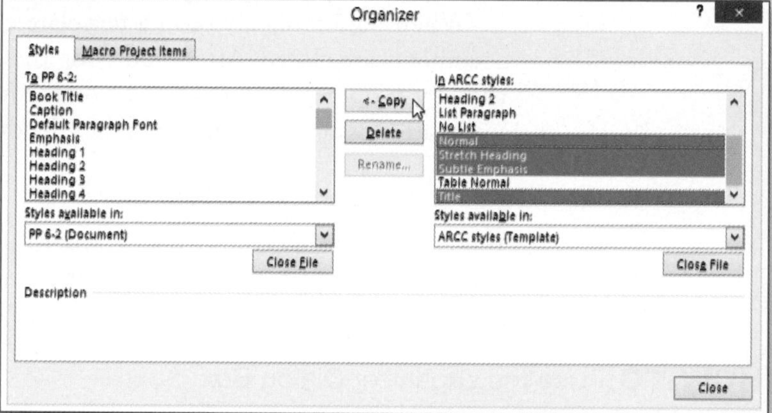

6-40 Copy styles using the *Organizer* dialog box

4. Attach the ***[your initials] ARCC styles*** template to your document.
   a. Click the **Document Template** button [*Developer* tab, *Templates* group] to open the *Templates and Add-ins* dialog box (Figure 6-41). If the *Developer* tab is not available, click the **File** tab, select **Options**, click **Customize Ribbon**, and check the **Developer** box under *Main Tabs* in the *Customize the Ribbon* area.

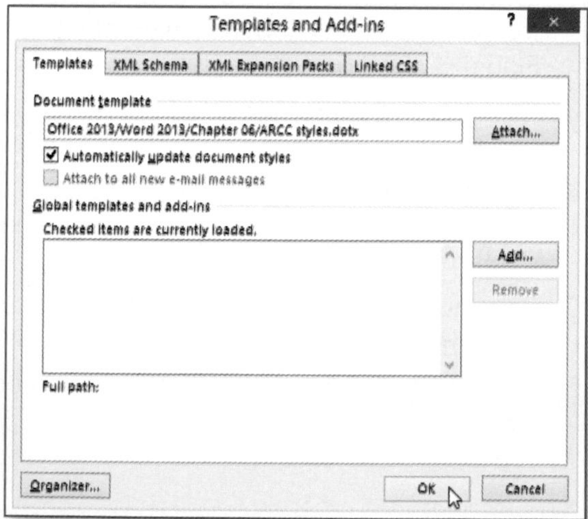

6-41 Attach the styles template to the document

b. Click the **Attach** button. The *Attach Template* dialog box opens.
c. Browse to find the ***[your initials] ARCC styles*** template and click **Open**.
d. Check the **Automatically update document styles** box.
e. Click **OK** to close the *Templates and Add-ins* dialog box.

5. Change the theme color and apply styles.
   a. Click the **Colors** button [*Design* tab, *Document Formatting* group] and choose **Orange Red**.
   b. Select "**static stretches**" in the second paragraph on the first page.
   c. Click the **Subtle Emphasis** style from the *Style* gallery or the *Styles* pane.
   d. On the first page, select the entire paragraph that begins "Here are some general guidelines . . ."
   e. Click the **Intense Reference** style from the *Style* gallery or the *Styles* pane.
   f. Select the list of guidelines below the "Here are some general guidelines . . ." paragraph.
   g. Click the **Guideline List** style from the *Style* gallery or the *Styles* pane.

6. Select instances of styles and replace with different styles.
   a. Right-click the **Heading 1** style in the *Styles* pane.
   b. Choose **Select All** (Figure 6-42). All of the text with *Heading 1* style is selected. Note: this selection might be displayed as "*Select All: (No Data)*."
   c. Click the **Exercise Heading** style in the *Style* gallery or the *Styles* pane to apply the *Exercise Heading* style to selected text.
   d. Select all instances of the *Heading 2* style.
   e. Apply the **Stretch Heading** to selected text.

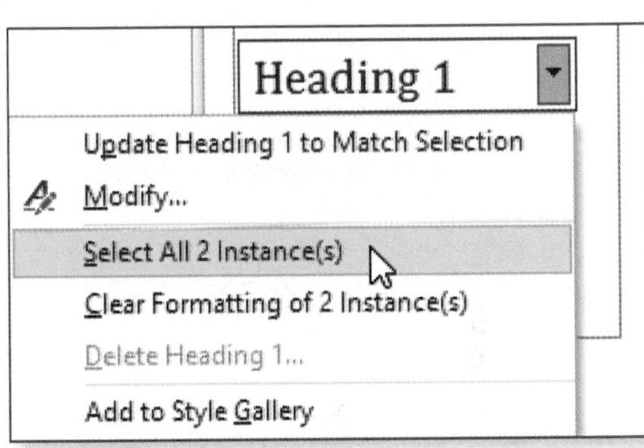

6-42 Select all instances of the *Heading 1* style

7. Save and close the document.
8. Modify a style in the styles template.
   a. Press **Ctrl + F12** to open the *Open* dialog box.
   b. Browse to find the ***[your initials] ARCC styles*** template and click **Open**.

> **MORE INFO**
>
> To edit a template, open it from Word. If you open a template from a Windows folder it will open as a document based on the template.

   c. Select the "**Guideline List**" text.
   d. Open the **Paragraph** dialog box.
   e. Deselect the **Don't add space between paragraphs of the same style** check box (Figure 6-43).
   f. Click **OK** to close the *Paragraph* dialog box.
   g. Right click the **Guideline List** style in the *Style* gallery (Figure 6-44).
   h. Select **Update Guideline List to Match Selection** to update the style.
   i. Save and close the template.

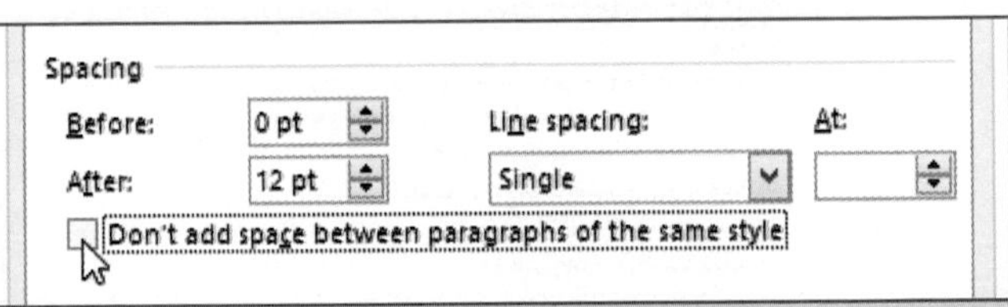

6-43 Make formatting changes to bulleted list

9. Open the document and change options in the *Styles* pane.
   a. Open the ***[your initials] PP W6-2*** document.

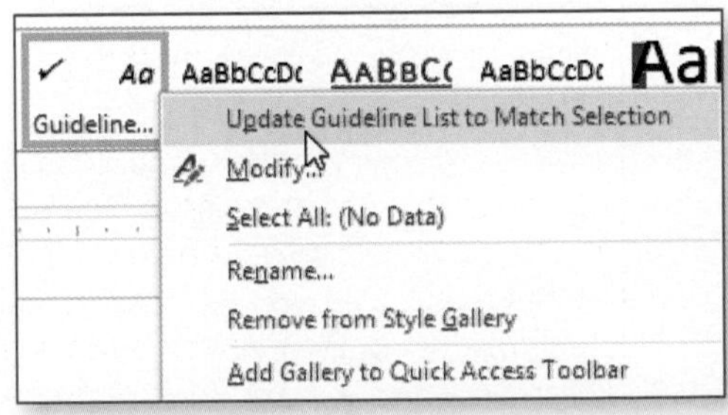

6-44 Update style to match selection

b. Open the *Styles* pane and click the **Options** link in the *Styles* pane to open the *Style Pane Options* dialog box (Figure 6-45).

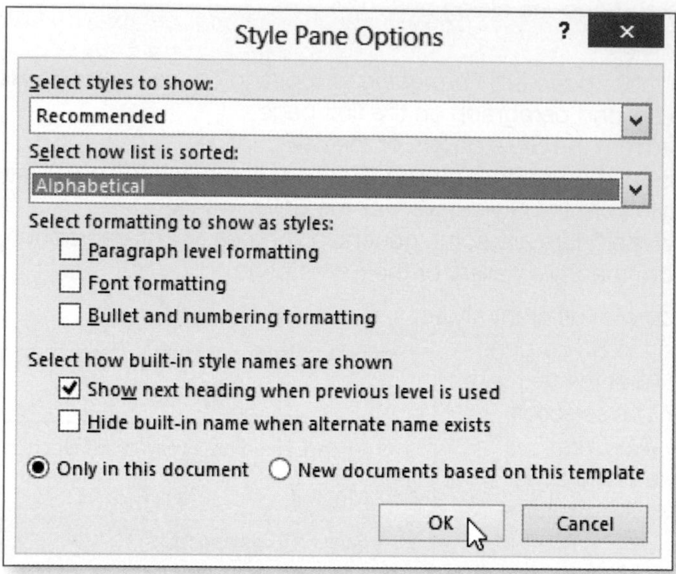

6-45 Change sort order in the ***Style Pane Options*** dialog box

c. Click the **Select how list is sorted** drop-down list and select **Alphabetical**.

d. Click **OK** to close the dialog box.

10. Save and close the document (Figure 6-46).

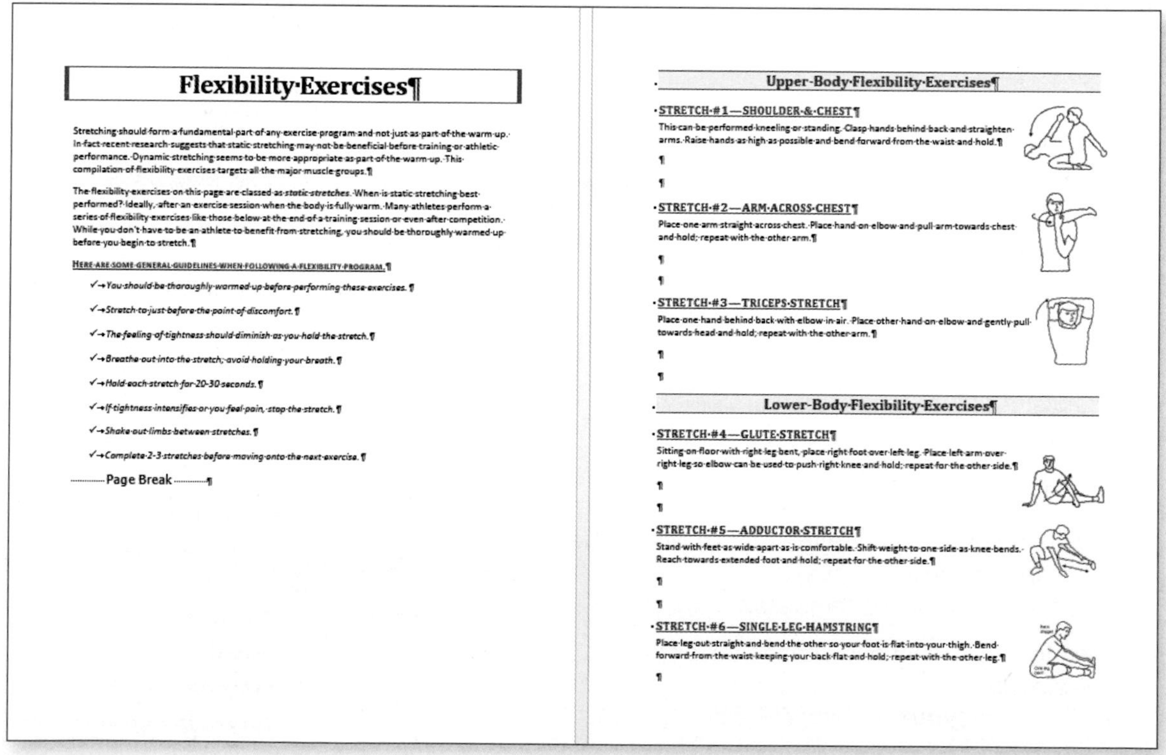

Flexibility Exercises

Stretching should form a fundamental part of any exercise program and not just as part of the warm up. In fact recent research suggests that static stretching may not be beneficial before training or athletic performance. Dynamic stretching seems to be more appropriate as part of the warm up. This compilation of flexibility exercises targets all the major muscle groups.

The flexibility exercises on this page are classed as *static stretches*. When is static stretching best performed? Ideally, after an exercise session when the body is fully warm. Many athletes perform a series of flexibility exercises like those below at the end of a training session or even after competition. While you don't have to be an athlete to benefit from stretching, you should be thoroughly warmed up before you begin to stretch.

HERE ARE SOME GENERAL GUIDELINES WHEN FOLLOWING A FLEXIBILITY PROGRAM.

- ✓ *You should be thoroughly warmed up before performing these exercises.*
- ✓ *Stretch to just before the point of discomfort.*
- ✓ *The feeling of tightness should diminish as you hold the stretch.*
- ✓ *Breathe out into the stretch; avoid holding your breath.*
- ✓ *Hold each stretch for 20-30 seconds.*
- ✓ *If tightness intensifies or you feel pain, stop the stretch.*
- ✓ *Shake out limbs between stretches.*
- ✓ *Complete 2-3 stretches before moving onto the next exercise.*

Page Break

Upper Body Flexibility Exercises

STRETCH #1—SHOULDER & CHEST

This can be performed kneeling or standing. Clasp hands behind back and straighten arms. Raise hands as high as possible and bend forward from the waist and hold.

STRETCH #2—ARM ACROSS CHEST

Place one arm straight across chest. Place hand on elbow and pull arm towards chest and hold; repeat with the other arm.

STRETCH #3—TRICEPS STRETCH

Place one hand behind back with elbow in air. Place other hand on elbow and gently pull towards head and hold; repeat with the other arm.

Lower Body Flexibility Exercises

STRETCH #4—GLUTE STRETCH

Sitting on floor with right leg bent, place right foot over left leg. Place left arm over right leg so elbow can be used to push right knee and hold; repeat for the other side.

STRETCH #5—ADDUCTOR STRETCH

Stand with feet as wide apart as is comfortable. Shift weight to one side as knee bends. Reach towards extended foot and hold; repeat for the other side.

STRETCH #6—SINGLE LEG HAMSTRING

Place leg out straight and bend the other so your foot is flat into your thigh. Bend forward from the waist keeping your back flat and hold; repeat with the other leg.

6-46 PP W6-2 completed (pages 1 and 2 of 3 pages)

Understanding and Using Building Blocks

Building blocks are stored pieces of information that you can use in your documents. The built-in headers and footers, page numbers, cover pages, tables of contents, and bibliographies that you have used in your projects are examples of building blocks. In addition to using Word's built-in building blocks, you can also create and save your own custom building blocks such as company logos, paragraphs of text, closing lines of a business letter, letterhead information, or footers.

Building Blocks Organizer

Building blocks are grouped into ***galleries***. The following are the different built-in building block galleries that are available in Word:

- *Bibliography* gallery
- *Cover Pages* gallery
- *Equations* gallery
- *Footers* gallery
- *Headers* gallery
- *Page Numbers* gallery
- *Table of Contents* gallery
- *Tables* gallery
- *Text Boxes* gallery
- *Watermarks* gallery

> **MORE INFO**
>
> *Quick Parts* and *AutoText* building block galleries are covered later in this chapter.

Within a gallery, building blocks are grouped by ***categories***. For example, in the *Page Numbers* gallery, each page number format (building block) is assigned to a category such as *Simple*, *Page X*, or *Page X of Y*.

The ***Building Blocks Organizer*** displays the available building blocks (Figure 6-47). Using the *Building Blocks Organizer*, you can preview, insert, delete, or change the properties of building blocks.

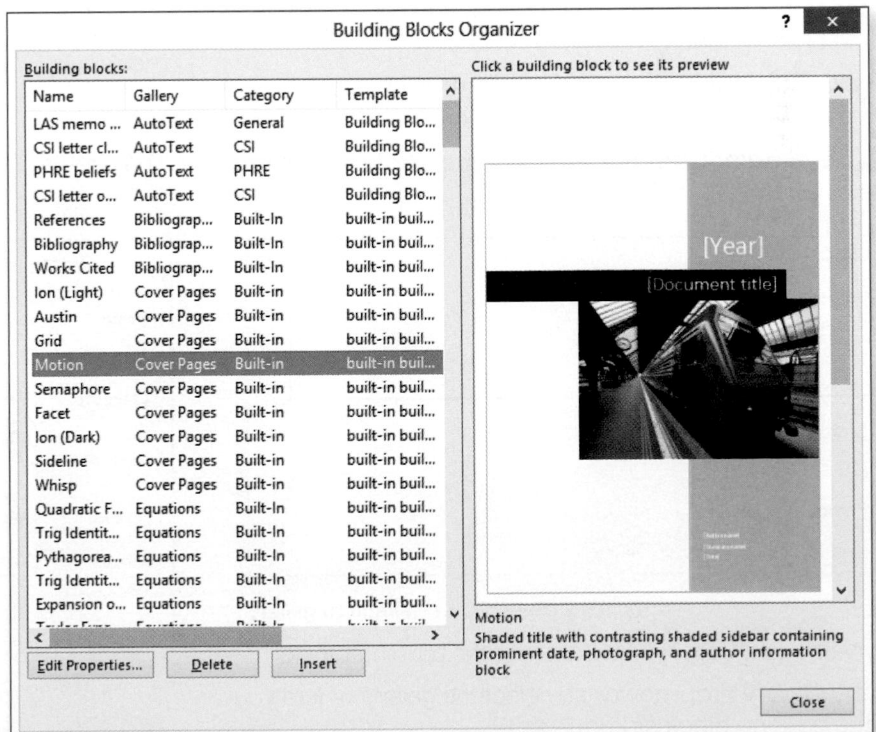

6-47 ***Building Blocks Organizer*** **dialog box**

HOW TO: Use the Building Blocks Organizer

1. Click the **Insert** tab.
2. Click the **Quick Parts** button [*Text* group].
3. Select **Building Blocks Organizer**. The *Building Blocks Organizer* dialog box opens (see Figure 6-47).
   - The *Name*, *Gallery*, *Category*, and *Template* of each building block are displayed.
   - By default, building blocks are listed in alphabetical order by gallery.
   - Click a column heading to change the sort order.
4. Click a building block to display it on the right side of the dialog box.
5. Click **Close** to close the *Building Blocks Organizer*.

Create a Building Block

By default, built-in building blocks are stored in the *Building Block* template. They are available in all new documents you create. You can create your own building blocks, add them to a gallery, assign them to a category, and select the template where you want to store them.

When you create a new building block, it is important to decide where you are going to store it. If you are using a styles template and attaching it to other documents, you can store your custom building blocks in this template. These building blocks are then available in all documents that have the styles template attached.

HOW TO: Create a Building Block

1. Select the information you want to save as a building block (Figure 6-48).
2. Click the button of the gallery where you want to save the building block.

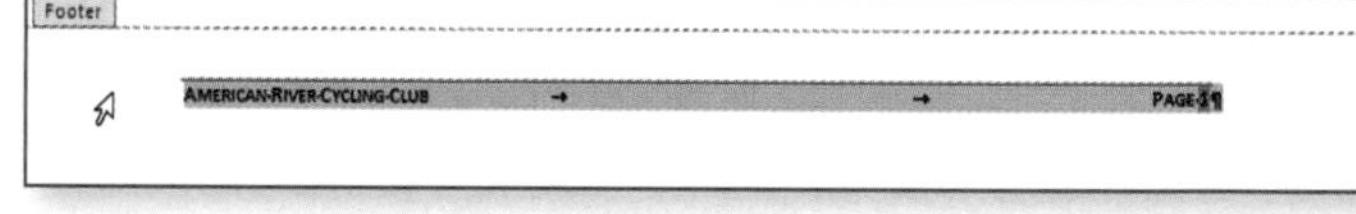

6-48 Select information to save as a building block

   - For example, if you are saving a footer building block to the *Footer* gallery, click the **Footer** button [*Header & Footer* group].
3. Select **Save Selection to [gallery name] Gallery** (Figure 6-49). The *Create New Building Block* dialog box opens (Figure 6-50).

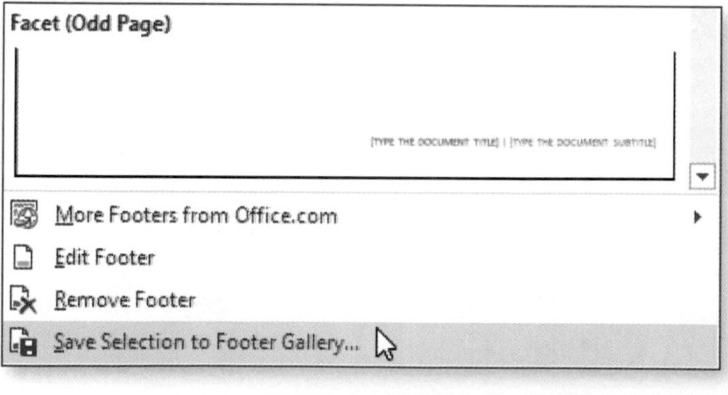

6-49 Save selection to gallery

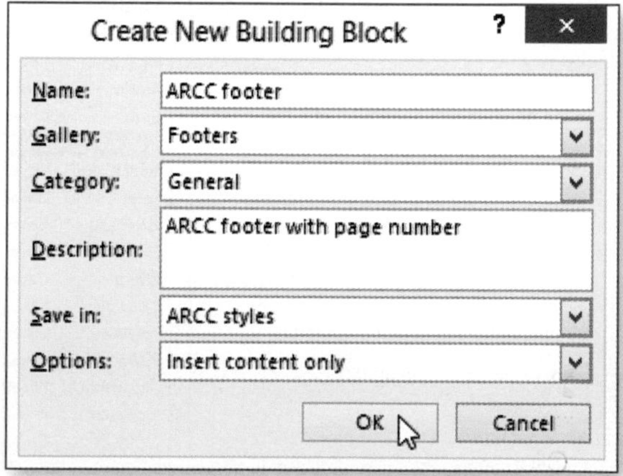

6-50 *Create New Building Block* dialog box

4. In the *Name* text box, type a name for the building block.
5. From the *Gallery* drop-down list, select the gallery where you want the building block stored.
   - This step is only necessary if you want to save the building block in a different gallery.

6. By default, new building blocks are saved in the *General* category. You can choose a different category or create a new category.
7. In the *Description* text box, you can type a description, but this is optional.
8. From the *Save in* drop-down list, choose where you want the building block stored.
   - Usually your options are *Building Blocks* or the *Normal* template.
   - If you are working on a document that has a template attached, this template is also a *Save in* option.
9. From the *Options* drop-down list, select how you want to insert content into a document.
   - The three options are: *Insert content only*, *Insert content in its own paragraph*, and *Insert content in its own page*.
10. Click **OK** to save the new building block.

Insert a Building Block

Once a building block is saved, you can insert it into a document. Use the *Building Blocks Organizer* or insert the building block from the list in the gallery where it was saved. For example, if you saved a *Footer* building block in the *Footers* gallery, it is available in the drop-down list of footers (Figure 6-51).

To insert a building block from the *Building Blocks Organizer*, place your insertion point in the document where you want to insert the building block, select the building block you want to insert, and click the **Insert** button. The building block is inserted into the document and the *Building Blocks Organizer* closes (Figure 6-52).

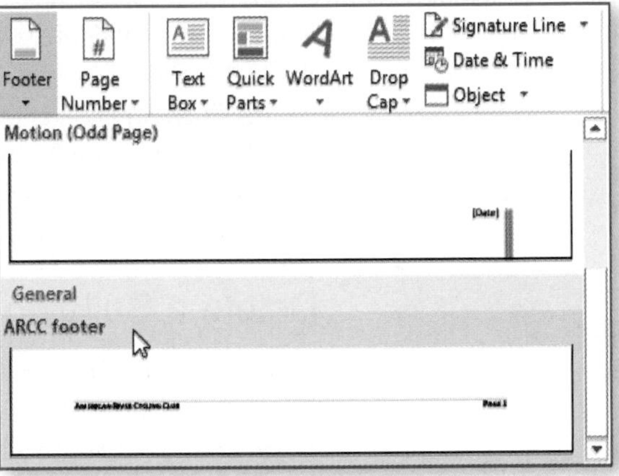

6-51 Insert *Footer* building block

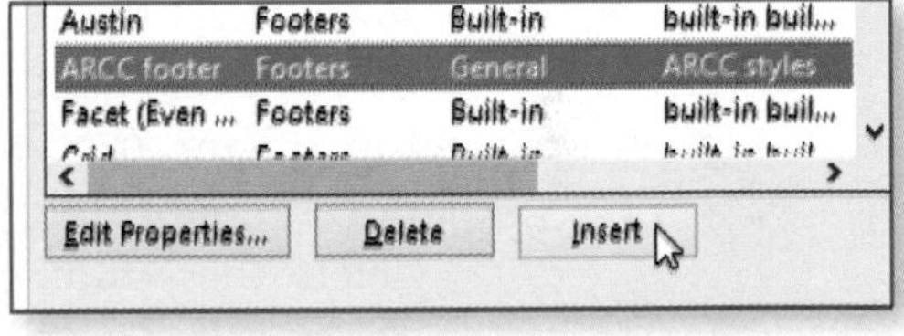

6-52 Insert building block from the *Building Blocks Organizer*

> **MORE INFO**
>
> When you exit Word after creating a building block, a dialog box might open asking if you want to save the building block. Click **Save** to save the building block.

Edit a Building Block

There might be times when you want to edit the properties of a building block to change the name, assign it to a different gallery or category, or store it in a different location. You can change building block properties in the *Building Blocks Organizer*. You can also create a new category within a gallery.

HOW TO: Edit Building Block Properties and Create a New Category

1. Click the **Quick Parts** button [*Insert* tab, *Text* group] and select **Building Blocks Organizer**.
2. Select the building block you want to edit.
3. Click the **Edit Properties** button to open the *Modify Building Block* dialog box.
4. Make desired changes to the building block properties.

5. Click the **Category** drop-down list (Figure 6-53).
6. Select **Create New Category**. The *Create New Category* dialog box opens (Figure 6-54).

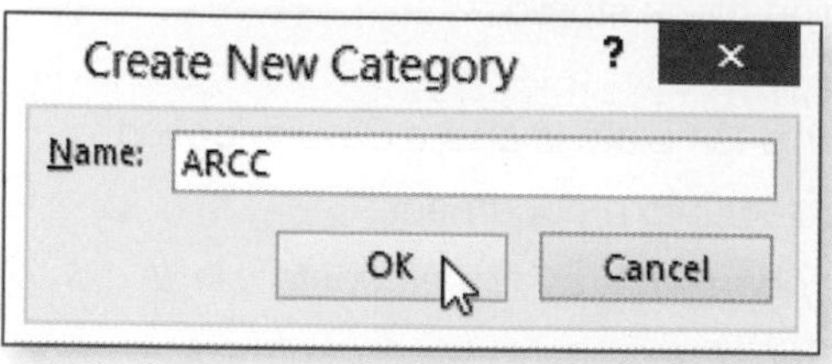

6-54 *Create New Category* dialog box

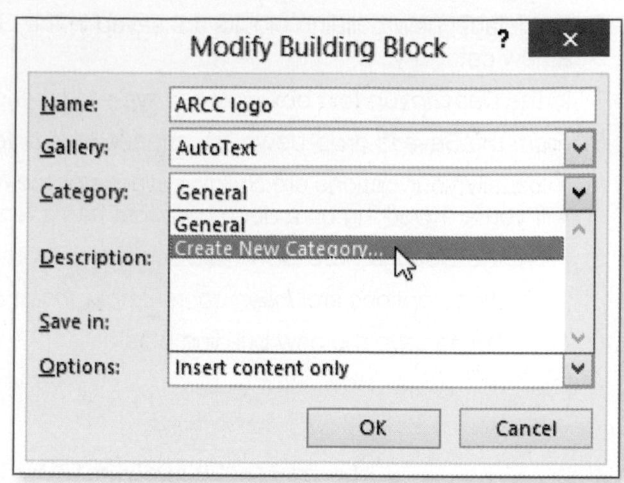

6-53 Create a new category

7. Type a name for the new category and click **OK**.
8. Click **OK** to close the *Modify Building Block* dialog box and save the changes to the building block.
9. Click **Yes** in the dialog box that asks if you want to redefine the building block (Figure 6-55).
10. Click **Close** to close the *Building Blocks Organizer*.

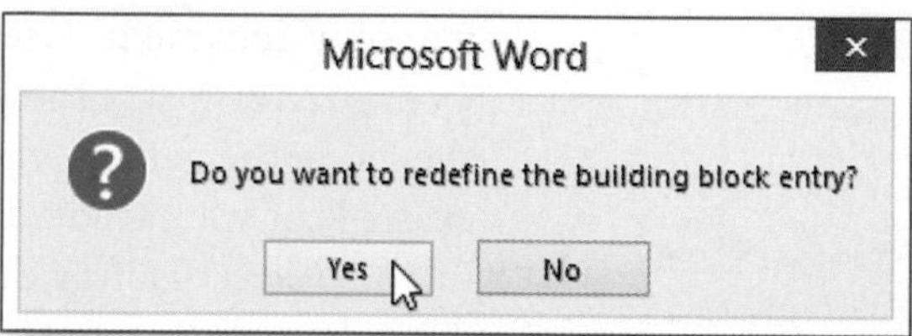

6-55 Redefine a building block

Delete a Building Block

You might find that you no longer need a building block that you created or you might want to change a building block. You can easily delete building blocks from the *Building Blocks Organizer*. To change a building block, you must delete the existing building block and recreate it as a new building block.

To delete a building block, open the *Building Blocks Organizer*, select the building block to delete, and click the **Delete** button (Figure 6-56). A dialog box opens confirming you want to delete the building block; select **Yes** to delete the building block.

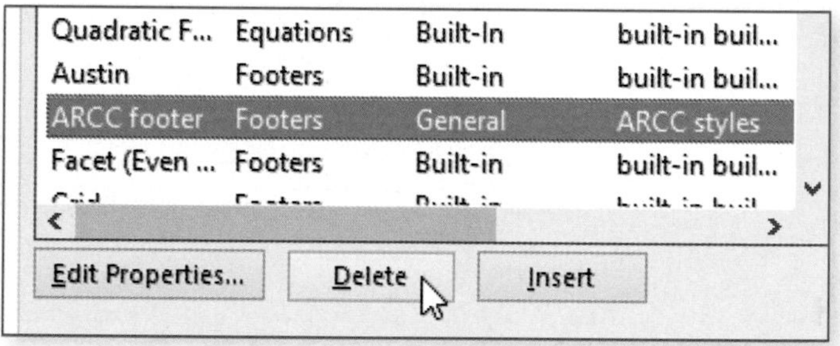

6-56 Delete a building block

SLO 6.4

Creating and Using AutoText Building Blocks

AutoText is another gallery where you can save building blocks you want to use in other documents. Use the *AutoText* gallery when the information you want to store does not fit into other building block galleries such as the *Footers* gallery or *Page Numbers* gallery. For example, you might want to save specific text that you know you will use in a number of documents, such as a company logo graphic, or text you know you will use again and again, such as the closing lines of a business letter, the opening lines of a memo, or a paragraph of text.

Create an AutoText Building Block

Similar to how you created building blocks, you select the text or object you want to save as *AutoText*. You then save this selection as an *AutoText* building block in the *AutoText* gallery.

HOW TO: Create an AutoText Building Block

1. Select the text or object to save as *AutoText*.
2. Click the **Quick Parts** button [*Insert* tab, *Text* group].
3. Click **AutoText** and select **Save Selection to AutoText Gallery** (Figure 6-57). The *Create New Building Block* dialog box opens (Figure 6-58).

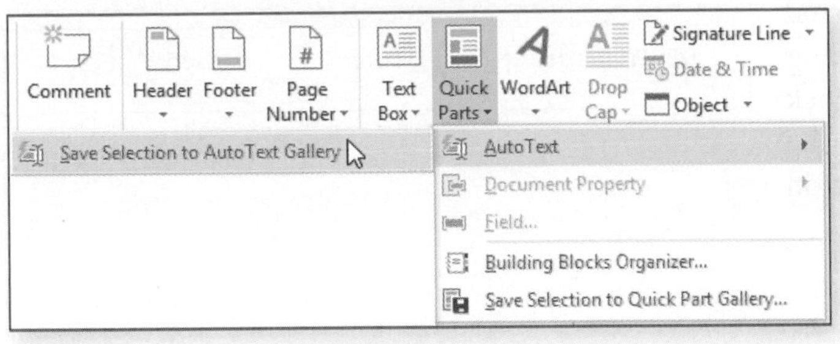

6-57 Save selection in the *AutoText* gallery

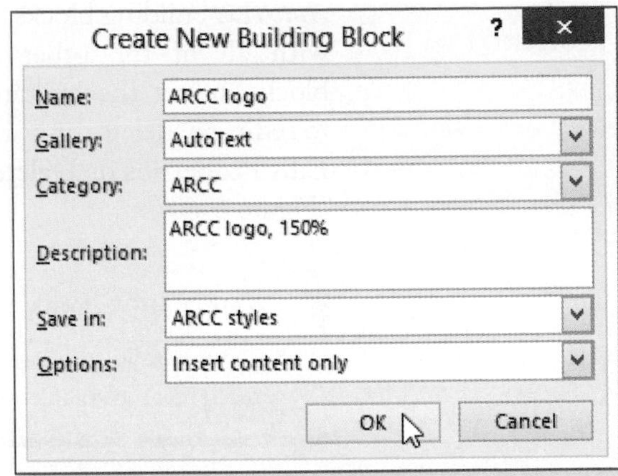

6-58 *Create New Building Block* dialog box

4. In the *Name* text box, type a name for the *AutoText*.
5. The selection is assigned to the *AutoText* gallery.
6. From the *Category* drop-down list, you can select the category or create a new category.
7. In the *Description* text box, type a description of the *AutoText*. A description is optional.
8. From the *Save in* drop-down list, select the location where you want to save the *AutoText*.
9. Click **OK** to close the dialog box and save the *AutoText*.

Insert an AutoText Building Block

AutoText building blocks are saved in the *AutoText* gallery, which is available from the *Quick Parts* drop-down list. You can also insert an *AutoText* building block from the *Building Blocks Organizer* dialog box.

HOW TO: Insert an AutoText Building Block

1. Place the insertion point in your document where you want the *AutoText* inserted.
2. Click the **Quick Parts** button and select **AutoText**. The *AutoText* gallery displays (Figure 6-59).
   - The category and name of the *AutoText* are listed above the *AutoText*.
   - Put your pointer on the *AutoText* building block to display its description.
3. Click the *AutoText* building block to insert it into the document.

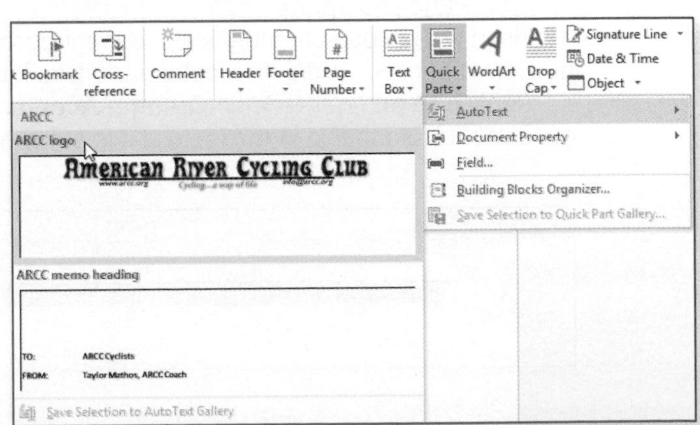

6-59 Insert *AutoText* building block from the *AutoText* gallery

Edit or Delete an AutoText Building Block

The process of editing or deleting an *AutoText* building block is similar to the process you use to edit other building blocks. Open the *Building Blocks Organizer*. The *AutoText* building blocks are listed with all of the other building blocks. Select the building block to edit or delete and click the **Edit Properties** or **Delete** button (Figure 6-60).

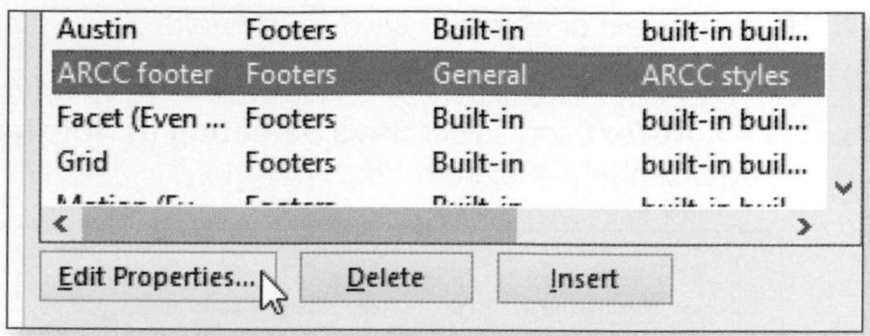

6-60 Edit *AutoText* building block properties

> **ANOTHER WAY**
>
> Right-click an *AutoText* building block and select **Edit Properties** to open the *Modify Building Block* dialog box or **Organize and Delete** to open the *Building Blocks Organizer*.

PAUSE & PRACTICE: WORD 6-3

For this Pause & Practice project, you modify the ***[your initials] ARCC styles*** template you created in *Pause & Practice 6-1* to include building blocks and *AutoText* building blocks. You also insert building blocks into the flexibility document you modified in *Pause & Practice 6-2*.

Files Needed: ***[your initials] ARCC styles.dotx***, ***[your initials] PP W6-2.docx***, and ***ARCC-logo-06.png***
Completed Project File Name: ***[your initials] PP W6-3.docx***

1. Open the ***[your initials] ARCC styles*** template you created in *Pause & Practice 6-1* and modified in *Pause & Practice 6-2*. Open the template from within Word, not from a Windows folder, so the template file opens, not a document based on the template.
2. Create a *Footer* building block.
   a. Edit the footer.
   b. Type American River Cycling Club at the left margin and press **Tab** two times.
   c. Type Page and **space** once.
   d. Insert a plain page number in the current position.
   e. Select all of the text in the footer and make it **bold**, **small caps**, and **10 pt.**
   f. Apply a **½ pt.** top border in **Orange**, **Accent 1** color.
   g. Select all of the text in the footer if it is not already selected (Figure 6-61).

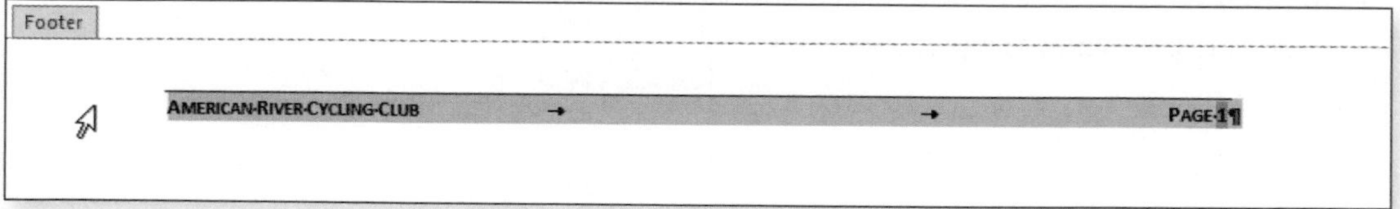

6-61 Select text to save as a *Footer* building block

h. Click the **Footer** button [*Header & Footer Tools Design* tab, *Header & Footer* group] and select **Save Selection to Footer Gallery**. The *Create New Building Block* dialog box opens.
i. Enter the following properties for the building block (Figure 6-62):

Name: ARCC footer
Gallery: **Footers**
Category: **General**
Description: ARCC footer with page number
Save in: ***[your initials]* ARCC styles**
Options: **Insert content only**

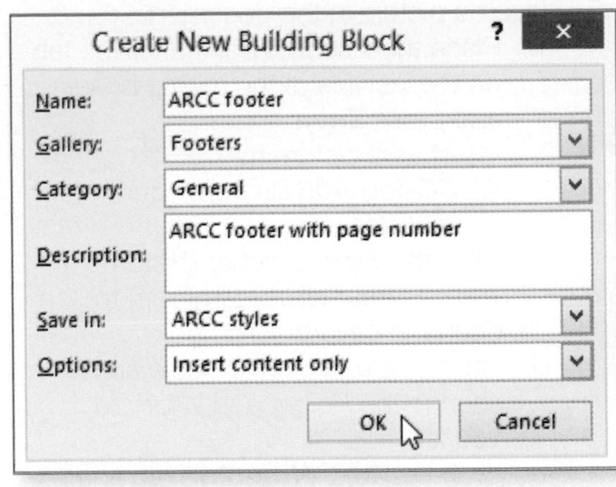

6-62 *Create New Building Block* dialog box

j. Click **OK** to close the dialog box and save the building block.
k. Close the footer.

3. Create a memo heading.
   a. Place the insertion point on the blank line after "Guideline List." If there is not a blank line after this line, press **Enter** after this line.
   b. Apply the **Normal** style to the blank line.
   c. Type TO:, press **Tab**, type ARCC Cyclists, and press **Enter**.
   d. Type FROM:, press **Tab**, type Taylor Mathos, ARCC Coach, and then press **Enter**.
   e. Type DATE:, press **Tab**, insert (don't type) current date (use January 1, 2014 format), and set to update automatically.
   f. Press **Enter** after the inserted date.
   g. Type SUBJECT: and press **Tab**.
   h. Select the first line of the memo heading and change the before paragraph spacing to **72 pt.**
   i. Select the last line of the memo heading and change the after paragraph spacing to **24 pt.**
   j. Select all of the lines of the memo heading and set a **1"** left tab.

4. Save a memo heading as an *AutoText* building block.
   a. Select all of the lines of the memo heading.
   b. Click the **Quick Parts** button [*Insert* tab, *Text* group], click **AutoText**, and select **Save Selection to AutoText Gallery**. The *Create New Building Block* dialog box opens (Figure 6-63).
   c. Enter the following properties for the building block:

      Name: ARCC memo heading
      Gallery: **AutoText**
      Category: **General**
      Description: ARCC memo heading
      Save in: ***[your initials]* ARCC styles**
      Options: **Insert content only**

   d. Click **OK** to close the dialog box and save the building block.

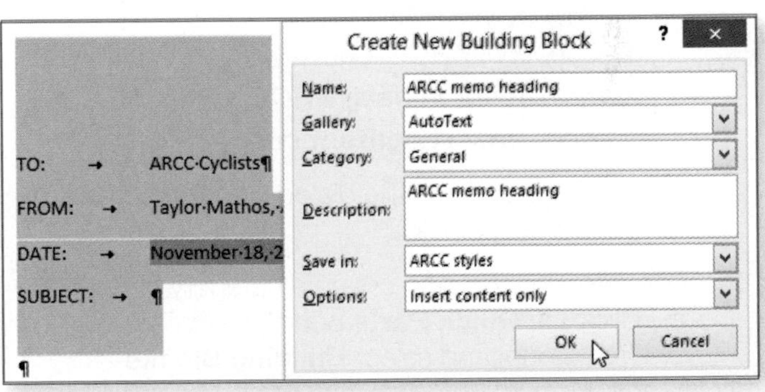

6-63 *Create New Building Block* dialog box

5. Insert a picture in the document.
   a. Place the insertion point after the tab on the last line of the memo heading and press **Enter**.
   b. Insert as a picture the ***ARCC-logo-06*** file from your student data files.
   c. Click the **Size** launcher [*Picture Tools Format* tab, *Size* group] to open the *Layout* dialog box.
   d. On the *Size* tab in the *Scale* area, change the *Height* and *Width* to **150%**.
   e. Click the **Text Wrapping** tab and change the *Wrapping style* to **Tight**.
   f. Click the **Position** tab (Figure 6-64) and change the *Horizontal* position to **Alignment**, **Centered** *relative to* **Page**.
   g. Change the *Vertical* position to **Absolute position**, **0.3** *below* **Page**.
   h. Click **OK** to close the *Layout* dialog box.

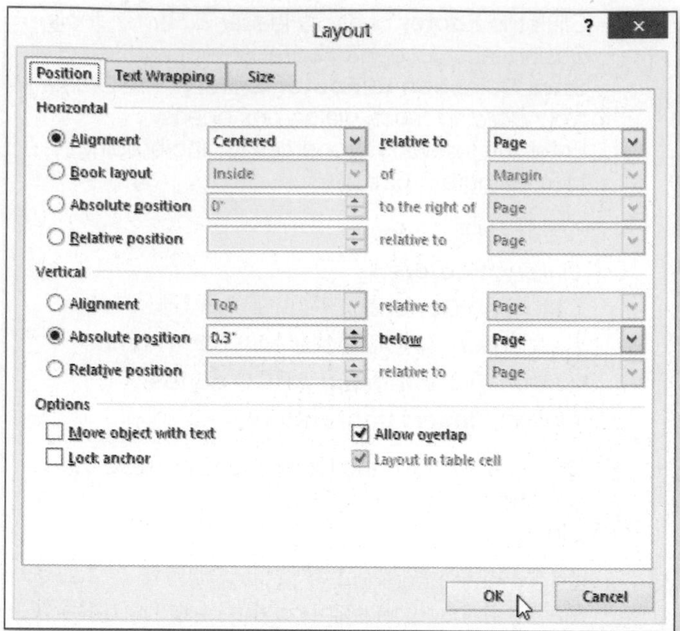

6-64 *Layout* dialog box

6. Save a graphic as an *AutoText* building block.
   a. With the graphic selected, click the **Quick Parts** button [*Insert* tab, *Text* group].
   b. Click **AutoText** and select **Save Selection to AutoText Gallery**. The *Create New Building Block* dialog box opens.
   c. Enter the following properties for the building block:

      Name: ARCC logo
      Gallery: **AutoText**
      Category: **General**
      Description: ARCC logo, 150%
      Save in: ***[your initials]* ARCC styles**
      Options: **Insert content only**

   d. Click **OK** to close the dialog box and save the building block.
7. Edit building blocks to create a category.
   a. Click the **Quick Parts** button [*Insert* tab, *Text* group] and select **Building Blocks Organizer**. The *Building Blocks Organizer* dialog box opens.
   b. Select the **ARCC logo** *AutoText* building block and click the **Edit Properties** button to open the *Modify Building Block* dialog box.
   c. Click the **Category** drop-down list and select **Create New Category** (Figure 6-65). The *Create New Category* dialog box opens.

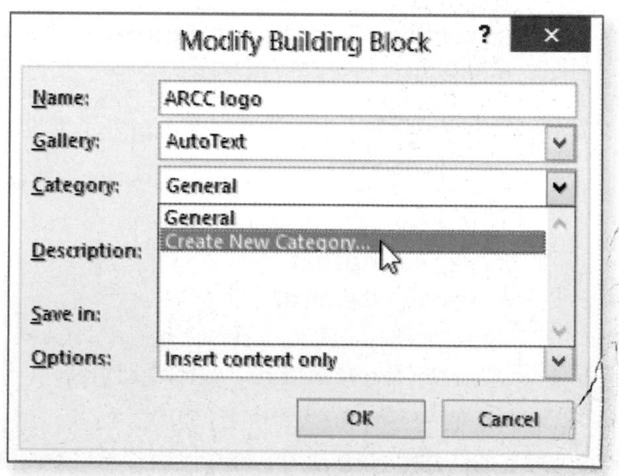

6-65 Create a new category

d. Type ARCC and press **OK** to close the *Create New Category* dialog box (Figure 6-66).
e. Click **OK** to close the *Modify Building Block* dialog box.
f. Click **Yes** when the dialog opens confirming you want to redefine the building block.
g. In the *Building Blocks Organizer*, select the **ARCC memo heading** *AutoText* building block and click the **Edit Properties** button.
h. Click the **Category** drop-down list and select **ARCC**.
i. Click **OK** to close the *Modify Building Block* dialog box.
j. Click **Yes** when the dialog box opens confirming you want to redefine the building block.
k. Click **Close** to close the *Building Blocks Organizer*.

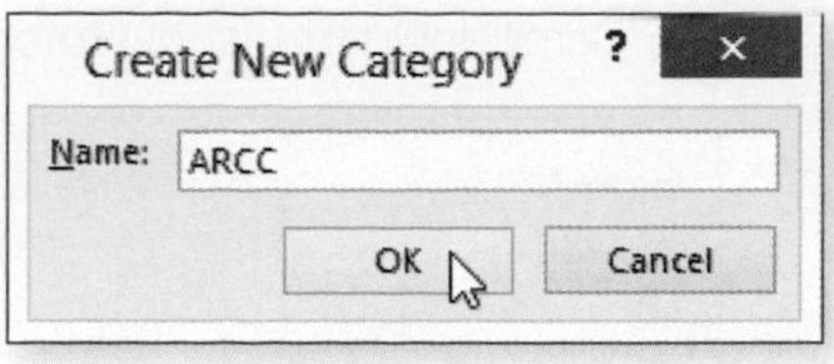

6-66 Name the new category

8. Save and close the ***[your initials] ARCC styles*** template.
9. Open the ***[your initials] PP W6-2*** file you created in *Pause & Practice 6-2*.
10. Save the document as ***[your initials] PP W6-3***.
11. Move the first page heading to the second page.
    a. Select "**Flexibility Exercises**" heading (including the paragraph mark) and cut (**Ctrl+X**) from the first page.
    b. Place the insertion point before "Upper-Body Flexibility Exercises" on the second page.
    c. Paste (**Ctrl+V**) the heading you cut from the first page.
12. Insert building blocks into the document.
    a. Place the insertion point at the beginning of the first page.
    b. Click the **Quick Parts** button [*Insert* tab, *Text* group] and select **AutoText**.
    c. Click the **ARCC memo heading** *AutoText* building block to insert it into the document (Figure 6-67). The memo heading is inserted at the top of the document.

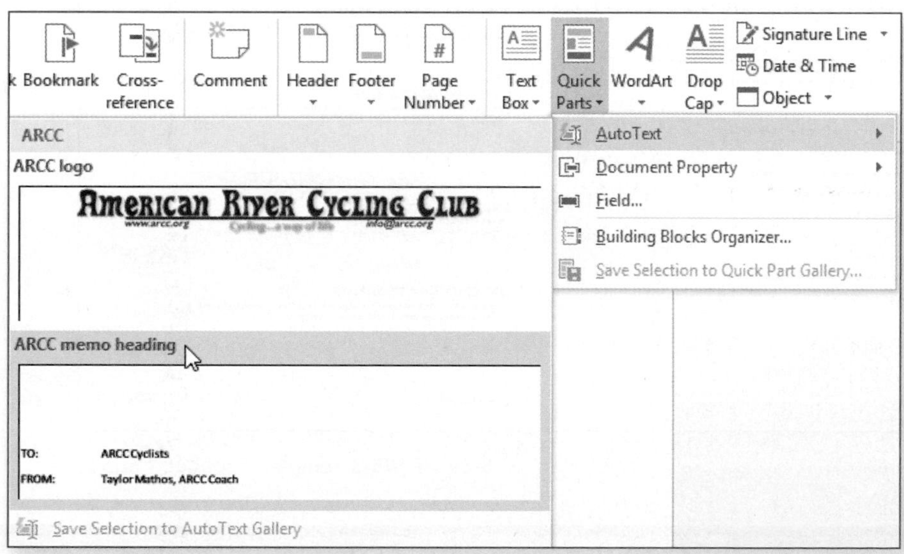

6-67 Insert *ARCC memo heading AutoText* building block

    d. Insert the **ARCC logo** *AutoText* building block into the document. The logo is inserted at the top of the document.
    e. Click the **Footer** button [*Insert* tab, *Header & Footer* group].

f. Scroll down the list of footers and select the **ARCC footer** building block (Figure 6-68).

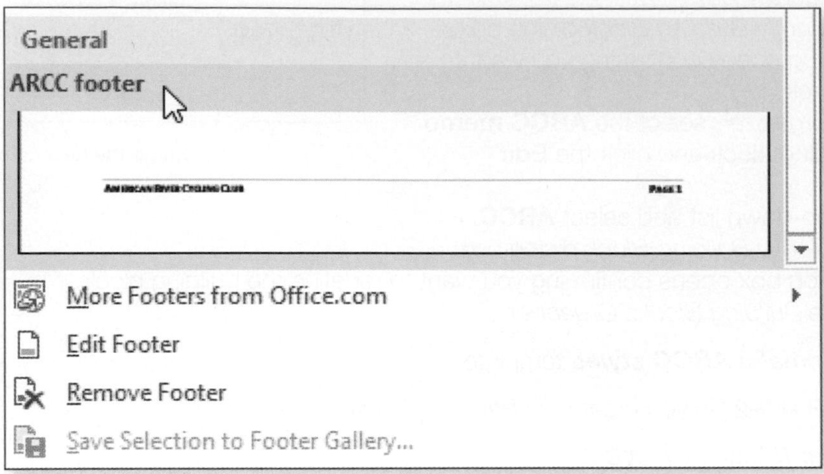

6-68 Insert *ARCC footer* building block

g. Delete the blank line in the footer and close the footer.

13. Save and close the document (Figure 6-69).

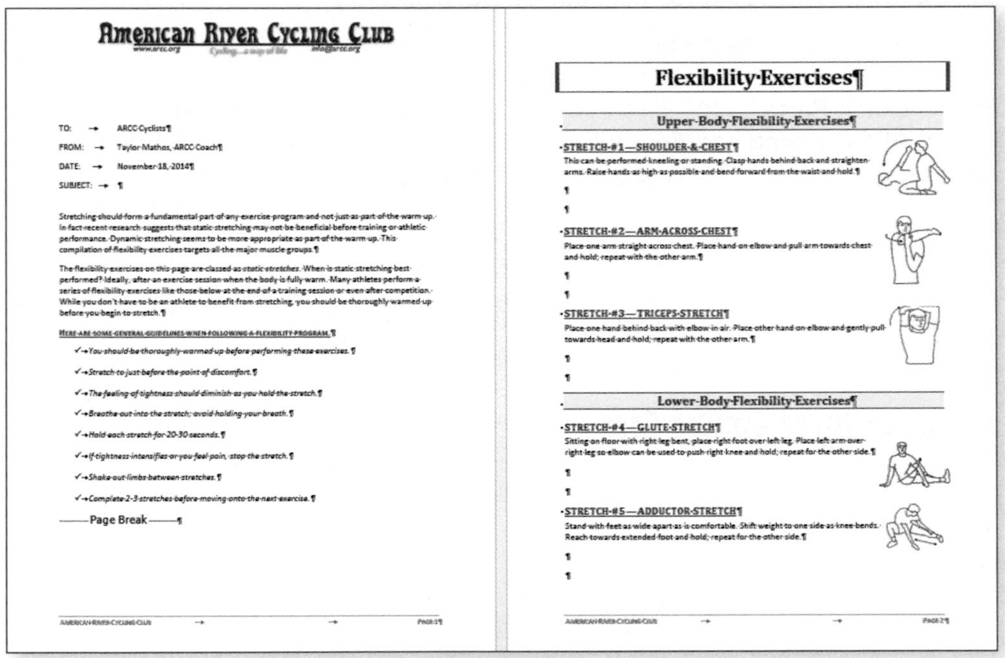

6-69 PP W6-3 completed (pages 1 and 2)

SLO 6.5 Using and Customizing Quick Parts Building Blocks

Quick Parts is an additional gallery of building blocks available in Word. You can use the *Quick Parts* gallery to store information you commonly use in documents. The advantage of saving a building block in the *Quick Parts* gallery is this gallery is very easy to access. *Quick Parts* building blocks are available from the *Quick Parts* drop-down list on the *Insert* tab.

Create a Quick Parts Building Block

Creating a *Quick Parts* building block is similar to creating other building blocks such as *AutoText*, *Footer*, or *Header* building blocks. When you create a *Quick Parts* building block, it is displayed in the *Quick Parts* drop-down list and listed in the *Building Blocks Organizer*.

HOW TO: Create a Quick Parts Building Block

1. Select the text or object you want to save as a *Quick Parts* building block.
2. Click the **Quick Parts** button [*Insert* tab, *Text* group].
3. Select **Save Selection to Quick Part Gallery** (Figure 6-70). The *Create New Building Block* dialog box opens (Figure 6-71).
4. In the *Name* text box, type a name for the *Quick Parts* building block.
5. The selection is assigned to the *Quick Parts* gallery.
6. From the *Category* drop-down list, you can select a category or create a new category.
7. In the *Description* text box, type a description of the *Quick Parts* building block.
8. From the *Save in* drop-down list, select the location to save the *Quick Parts* building block.
9. Click **OK** to close the dialog box and save the building block.

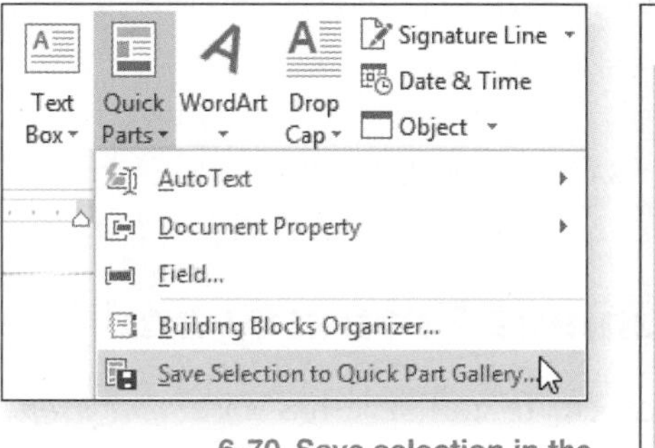

6-70 Save selection in the *Quick Parts* gallery

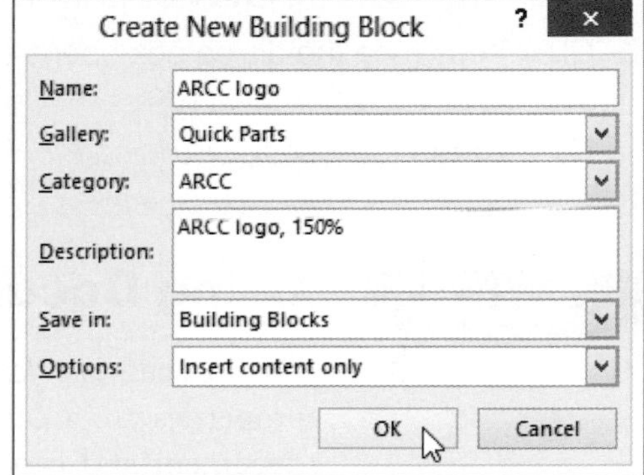

6-71 *Create New Building Block* dialog box

Insert a Quick Parts Building Block

Quick Parts building blocks are easily inserted into a document. Place the insertion point in the document at the position you want the building block inserted, click the **Quick Parts** button in the *Text* group on the *Insert* tab, and select the *Quick Parts* building block to insert (Figure 6-72).

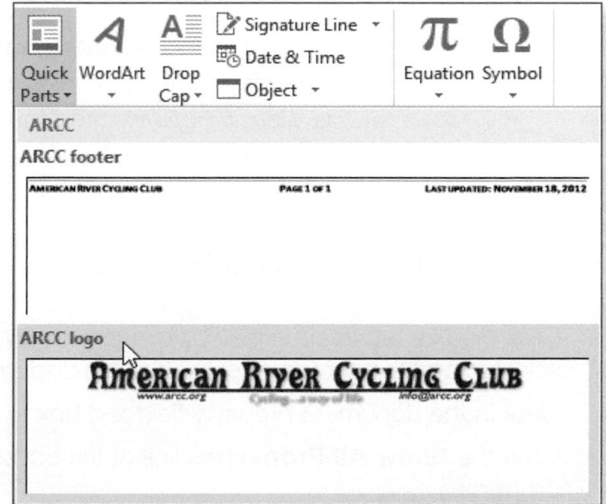

6-72 Insert *Quick Parts* building block from the *Quick Parts* gallery

Edit or Delete a Quick Parts Building Block

You edit and delete *Quick Parts* building blocks the same way you edit and delete other building blocks. You can also edit regularly used building blocks stored in other galleries to make them available in the *Quick Parts* gallery.

HOW TO: Add a Building Block to the Quick Parts Gallery

1. Click the **Quick Parts** button [*Insert* tab, *Text* group] and select **Building Blocks Organizer**. The *Building Blocks Organizer* dialog box opens.
2. Select the building block to add to the *Quick Parts* gallery.
3. Click the **Edit Properties** button to open the *Modify Building Block* dialog box (Figure 6-73).
4. Click the **Gallery** drop-down list and select **Quick Parts**.
5. Make any other desired changes to the building block.
   - You can create a new category for *Quick Parts*.
   - You can have multiple *Quick Parts* categories, and *Quick Parts* are grouped by the categories in the drop-down list.
6. Click **OK** to save the changes to the *Quick Parts* building block.
7. Click **Yes** when the dialog box opens asking you to confirm that you want to redefine the style.
8. Click **Close** to close the *Building Blocks Organizer* dialog box.

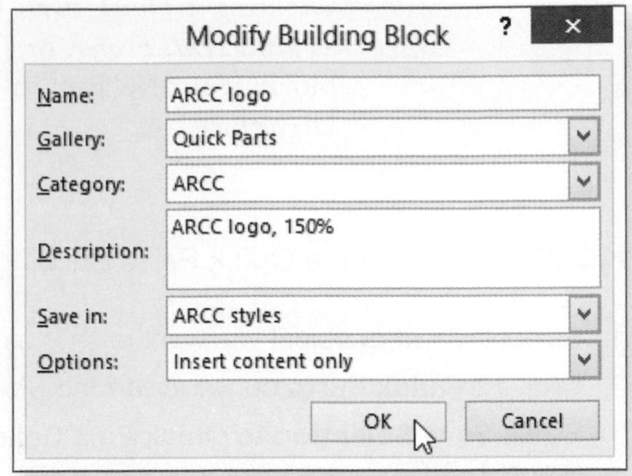

6-73 Add a building block to the *Quick Parts* gallery

SLO 6.6

Using Document Property and Word Fields

Each document you create and save has ***document properties*** associated with it. Document properties are a category of Word ***fields***. Word fields are special codes that are stored in a document and can be inserted into a document. Word fields automatically insert content, such as the *Company* document property field, the *NumPages* field (number of pages in the document), or a formula into a document.

> **MORE INFO**
>
> Inserting a custom formula field is covered in Chapter 7.

Document Properties

You can view and edit document properties on the *Backstage* view. You can edit some document properties such as *Title*, *Company*, and *Comments*, while others are automatically generated such as *Size*, *Pages*, *Words*, and *Last Modified*.

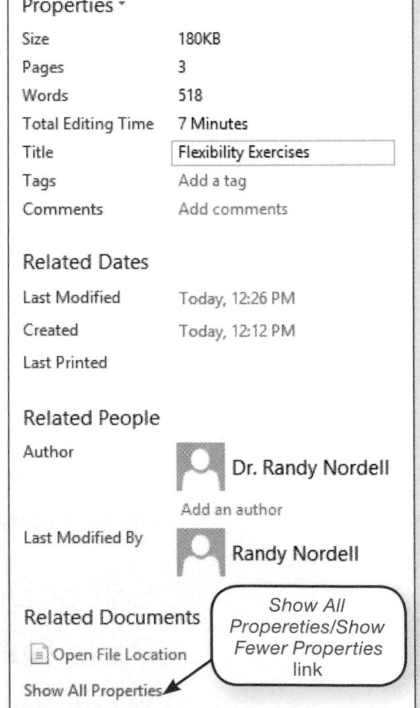

6-74 Document properties on the *Backstage* view

HOW TO: Edit Document Properties

1. Click the **File** tab to open the *Backstage* view. By default, the *Info* button is selected and the document properties are displayed on the right (Figure 6-74).
2. Click in the document property field text box to add or edit information.
3. Click the **Show All Properties** link at the bottom to display all document properties.
   - When all properties are displayed, the link changes to *Show Fewer Properties*.
4. Click the **Back** button or press **Esc** to return to the document.

ANOTHER WAY

You can also edit document properties in the *Document* panel. In the *Info* area on the *Backstage* view, click the **Properties** button and select **Show Document Panel**.

Advanced Document Properties

You can also view and edit document properties in the ***Properties dialog box***. This dialog box displays document information on four different tabs: *General*, *Summary*, *Statistics*, *Contents*, and *Custom*. The *General*, *Statistics*, and *Contents* tabs display document information. On the *Summary* tab, you can add or edit document properties.

On the *Custom* tab, you can add a custom document property field. For example, you might want to add a document property field that is not normally available in a document such as *Department*. You can then insert this field into a document.

HOW TO: Add a Custom Document Property Field

1. On the *Backstage* view in the *Info* area, click the **Properties** button and select **Advanced Properties**. The *[File name] Properties* dialog box opens.
2. Click the **Custom** tab (Figure 6-75).
3. In the *Name* area, select the custom document property field to add.
4. In the *Value* area, type the information you want to store in this field.
5. Click **Add** to add the custom document property field. The custom field appears in the *Properties* area.
6. Click **OK** to close the *[File name] Properties* dialog box.
7. Click the **Back** arrow to return to the document.

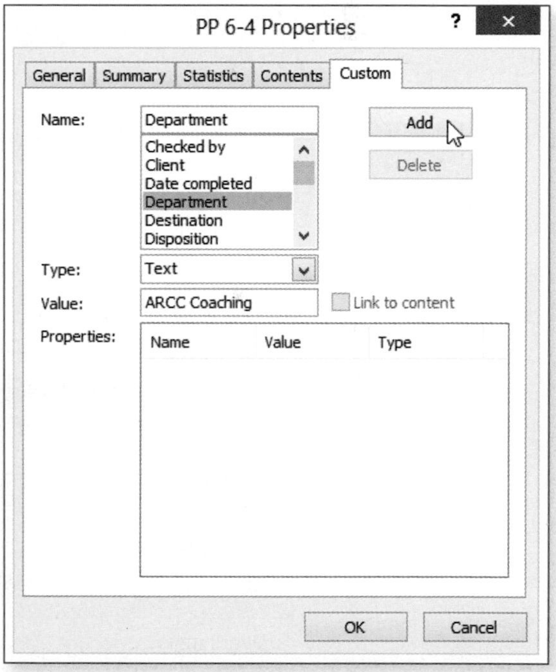

6-75 Add custom document properties in the *[File name] Properties* dialog box

MORE INFO

Insert custom document property fields using the *Field* dialog box, which is discussed in the *Insert a Word Field* section in this chapter.

Insert a Document Property Field

You can insert document property fields in the body of a document or in the header or footer. When you insert a document property field into your document, Word displays the content stored in that field in your document. If you edit the contents of a document property field on the *Backstage* view or in the *Document* panel, Word automatically updates the document property field in your document.

HOW TO: Insert a Document Property Field

1. Place the insertion point in your document where you want the document property field inserted.
2. Click the **Quick Parts** button [*Insert* tab, *Text* group].
3. Select **Document Property** (Figure 6-76).
4. Select the document property from the list of document properties. The document property field is inserted in the document at the insertion point (Figure 6-77).

6-76 Insert document property field

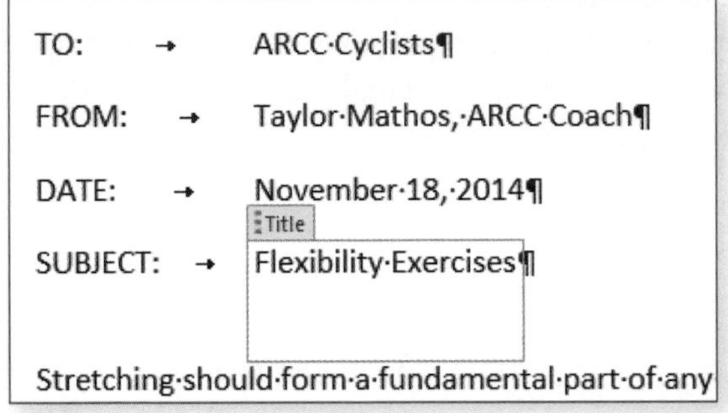

TO: → ARCC·Cyclists¶
FROM: → Taylor·Mathos,·ARCC·Coach¶
DATE: → November·18,·2014¶
Title
SUBJECT: → Flexibility·Exercises¶
Stretching·should·form·a·fundamental·part·of·any

6-77 Document property field inserted into document

Insert a Word Field

You can also insert Word fields into a document. There are a wide variety of fields that you can insert. You insert a Word field using the ***Field dialog box***. The following table lists some of the commonly used fields.

Commonly Used Fields

Field	Description
DocProperty	Inserts a document property or custom document property field.
FileName	Inserts the document file name.
NumPages	Inserts the number of pages in a document.
SaveDate	Inserts the dates the document was last saved.
UserInitials	Inserts your initials from your Office personalization options.
UserName	Inserts your name from your Office personalization options.

In the *Field* dialog box, the available fields are grouped in categories. Many of the fields have field properties, which determine how the content of the field is displayed in the document.

HOW TO: Insert a Word Field

1. Place the insertion point in your document where you want the field inserted.
2. Click the **Quick Parts** button [*Insert* tab, *Text* group].

3. Select **Field** to open the *Field* dialog box (Figure 6-78).
4. Select the field to insert from the list in the *Field names* area.
    - Fields are grouped into categories. Click the **Categories** drop-down list to view the available categories.
    - The fields in a category are displayed in the *Field names* area.
5. In the *Field properties* area, select the way you want the field to be displayed in the document.
6. Click **OK** to close the dialog box and insert the field into the document (Figure 6-79).

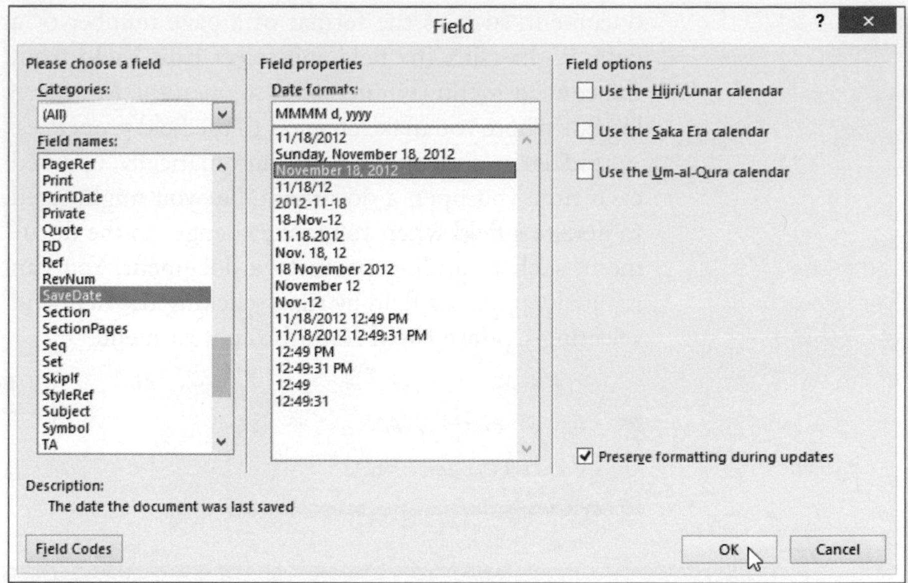

6-78 *Field* dialog box

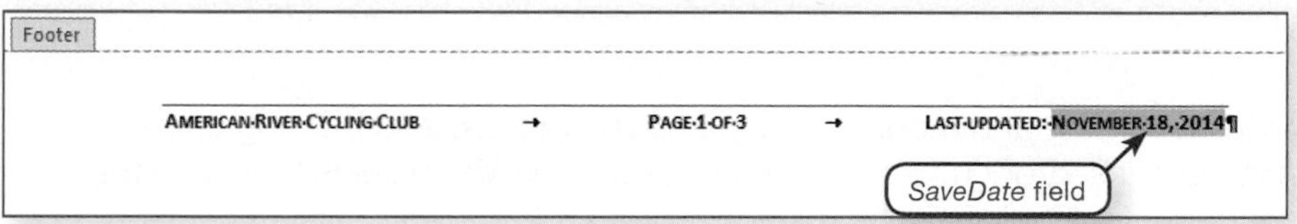

6-79 Field inserted into the footer

Personalize Microsoft Office

When you originally install and register Microsoft Office on your computer, you are prompted to provide your user name and initials to personalize Microsoft Office. These pieces of information are Word fields that can be used in your documents. You can change this personalization information after Microsoft Office has been installed on your computer.

HOW TO: Personalize Microsoft Office

1. Click the **File** tab to open the *Backstage* view.
2. Click the **Options** button to open the *Word Options* dialog box (Figure 6-80).
3. Click the **General** button.
4. In the *Personalize your copy of Microsoft Office*, type your information in the *User name* and *Initials* text boxes.
5. Click **OK** to close the *Word Options* dialog box.

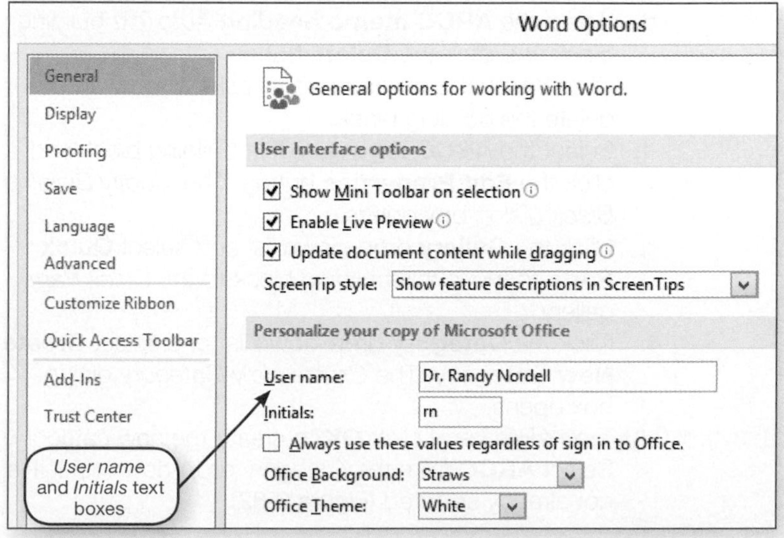

6-80 Personalize Microsoft Office

Edit and Update Fields

When you insert a field in your document, you select the field and set the field properties. There might be times when you want to edit a field to change how a field is displayed in your document, such as the format of a page number or a date. Right-click the field and select **Edit Field** from the context menu (Figure 6-81) to open the *Field* dialog box where you make changes to the field properties.

Fields in a document are automatically updated each time you open a document, but you might need to update a field when you make changes to the document, such as adding pages to a document. You can manually update a field by right-clicking the field and selecting **Update Field** from the context menu.

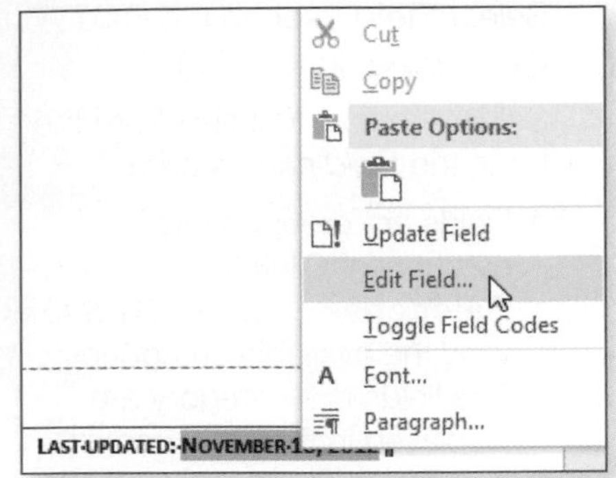

6-81 Select *Edit Field* from the context menu

> **ANOTHER WAY**
>
> Press **F9** to update a field.

PAUSE & PRACTICE: WORD 6-4

For this Pause & Practice project, you delete and modify existing building blocks, add building blocks to the *Quick Parts* gallery, customize and insert document properties, and insert Word fields to finalize the flexibility document for the American River Cycling Club.

File Needed: ***[your initials] PP W6-3.docx***
Completed Project File Name: ***[your initials] PP W6-4.docx***

---

1. Open the ***[your initials] PP W6-3*** document you modified in *Pause & Practice 6-3*.
2. Save the document as ***[your initials] PP W6-4***.
3. Delete and modify building blocks.
   a. Click the **Quick Parts** button [*Insert* tab, *Text* group] and select **Building Blocks Organizer** to open the *Building Blocks Organizer* dialog box.
   b. Select the **ARCC footer** *Footer* building block and click the **Delete** button.
   c. Click **Yes** when the dialog box opens asking if you want to delete the building block.
   d. Select the **ARCC memo heading** *AutoText* building block and click the **Delete** button.
   e. Click **Yes** in the dialog box that asks if you want to delete the building block.
   f. Select the **ARCC logo** *AutoText* building block and click the **Edit Properties** button. The *Modify Building Block* dialog box opens.
   g. Click the **Gallery** drop-down list and select **Quick Parts** to move this building block to the *Quick Parts* gallery.
   h. Click the **Category** drop-down list and select **Create New Category**. The *Create New Category* dialog box opens.
   i. Type ARCC and click **OK** to create the new category. Select **ARCC** from the *Category* drop-down list if it is not already selected (Figure 6-82).

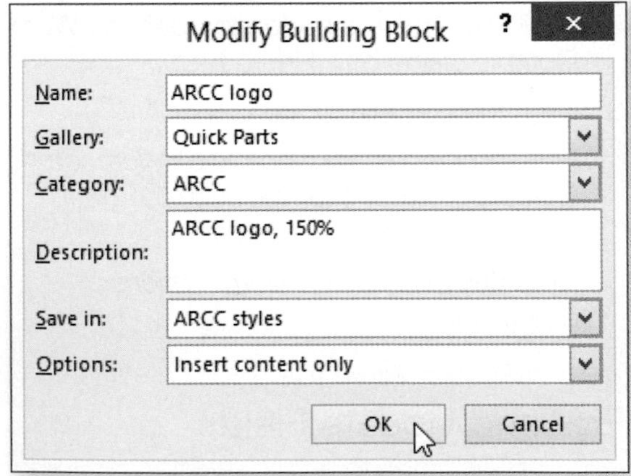

6-82 *Modify Building Block* dialog box

j. Click **OK** to close the dialog box and make the changes to the building block.
k. Click **Yes** when the dialog box opens asking if you want to redefine the building block.
l. Click **Close** to close the *Building Blocks Organizer* dialog box.

4. Customize and insert document properties.
   a. Click the **File** tab to open the *Backstage* view.
   b. In the *Title* area, type Flexibility Exercises.
   c. Click the **Show All Properties** link at the bottom of the document properties.
   d. In the *Company* area, type American River Cycling Club.
   e. Click the **Back** button to close the *Backstage* view and return to the document.
   f. Place the insertion point after the tab on the subject line of the memo heading.
   g. Click the **Quick Parts** button [*Insert* tab, *Text* group] and select **Document Property**.
   h. Select **Title** from the list of document properties. The *Title* document property field is inserted into the document (Figure 6-83).

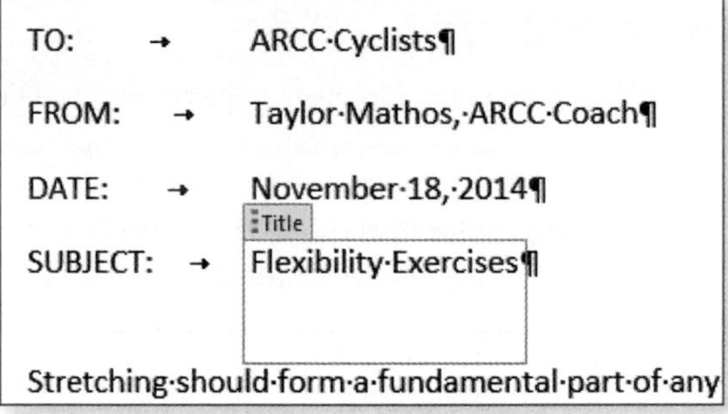

TO: → ARCC·Cyclists¶
FROM: → Taylor·Mathos,·ARCC·Coach¶
DATE: → November·18,·2014¶
Title
SUBJECT: → Flexibility·Exercises¶
Stretching·should·form·a·fundamental·part·of·any

6-83 ***Title*** **document property inserted**

5. Modify the footer to include document properties and Word fields.
   a. Open the footer on the first page of the document.
   b. Select "**American River Cycling Club**."
   c. Click the **Document Info** button [*Header & Footer Tools Design* tab, *Insert* group] and select **Document Property**.
   d. Select **Company** from the list of document properties. The *Company* document property field is inserted into the document.
   e. Place the insertion point directly before "*Page*" in the footer and press **Backspace** to remove one tab.
   f. Place the insertion point after the page number, **space** once, type of, and **space** once.
   g. Click the **Quick Parts** button and select **Field**. The *Field* dialog box opens (Figure 6-84).

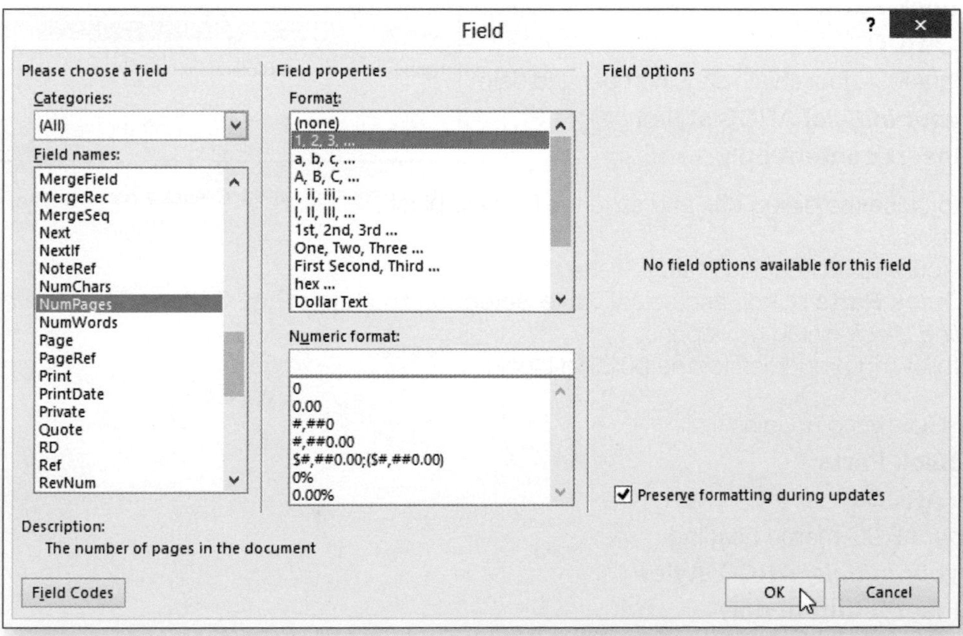

6-84 Insert *NumPages* field in the footer

h. In the *Field* names area, select **NumPages**.
i. In the *Format* area, select **1, 2, 3** and click **OK** to close the *Field* dialog box and insert the field.
j. Press **Tab** after the *NumPages* field, type Last updated:, and **space** once.
k. Click the **Quick Parts** button and select **Field**. The *Field* dialog box opens.
l. In the *Field* names area, select **SaveDate** and select the third date format (e.g., **May 26, 2014**) in the *Date formats* area.
m. Click **OK** to close the *Field* dialog box and insert the field.

> **MORE INFO**
>
> When you insert document property and Word fields, make sure you have proper spacing before and after the field.

6. Add the footer and memo heading to the *Quick Parts* gallery.
   a. Select the entire footer (Figure 6-85).

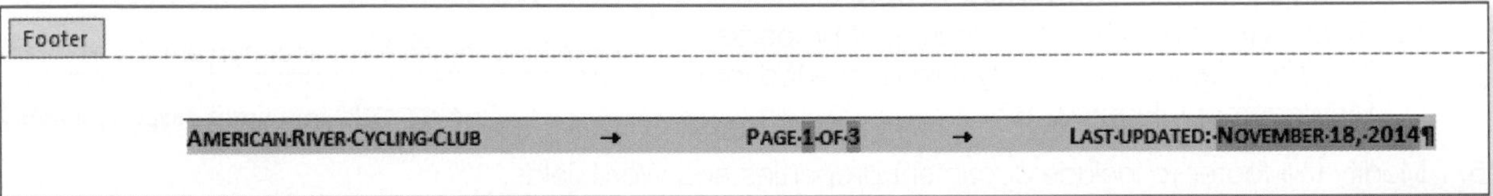

6-85 Select footer to save in the *Quick Parts* gallery

   b. Click the **Quick Parts** button and select **Save Selection to Quick Part Gallery**. The *Create New Building Block* dialog box opens.
   c. Enter the following properties for the building block (Figure 6-86):

      Name: ARCC footer
      Gallery: **Quick Parts**
      Category: **ARCC**
      Description: ARCC footer with page number and date
      Save in: ***[your initials]* ARCC styles**
      Options: **Insert content only**

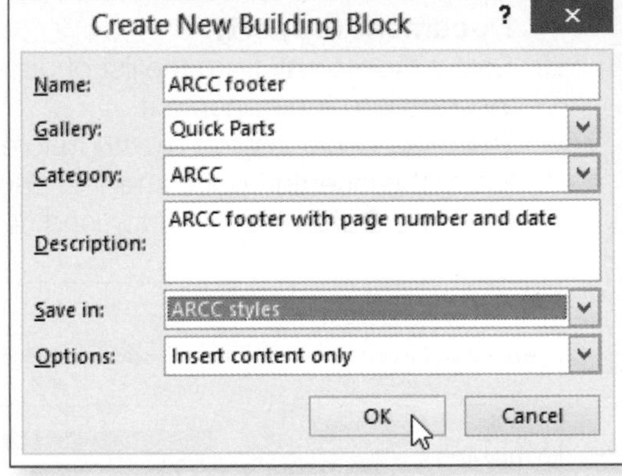

6-86 Create a new building block

   d. Click **OK** to close the dialog box and save the building block.
   e. Close the footer.
   f. Select the four memo heading lines.
   g. Click the **Quick Parts** button and select **Save Selection to Quick Part Gallery**. The *Create New Building Block* dialog box opens.
   h. Enter the following properties for the building block:

      Name: ARCC memo heading
      Gallery: **Quick Parts**
      Category: **ARCC**
      Description: ARCC memo heading
      Save in: ***[your initials]* ARCC styles**
      Options: **Insert content only**

   i. Click **OK** to close the dialog box and save the building block.

7. Save and close the document (Figure 6-87). Click **Yes** if a dialog box opens asking if you want to save changes to the ***ARCC styles*** template file (Figure 6-88).

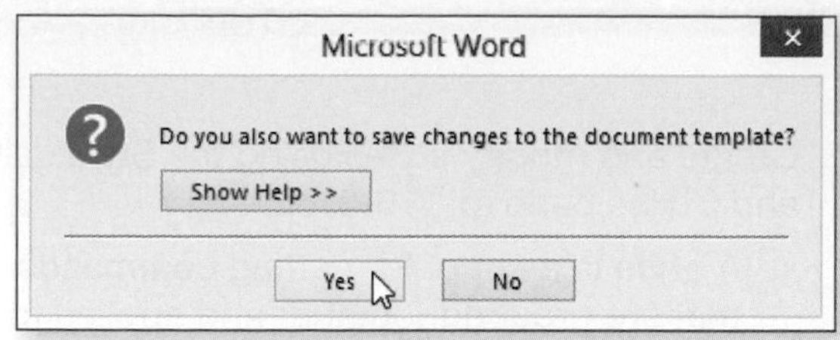

6-87 Save changes in template file

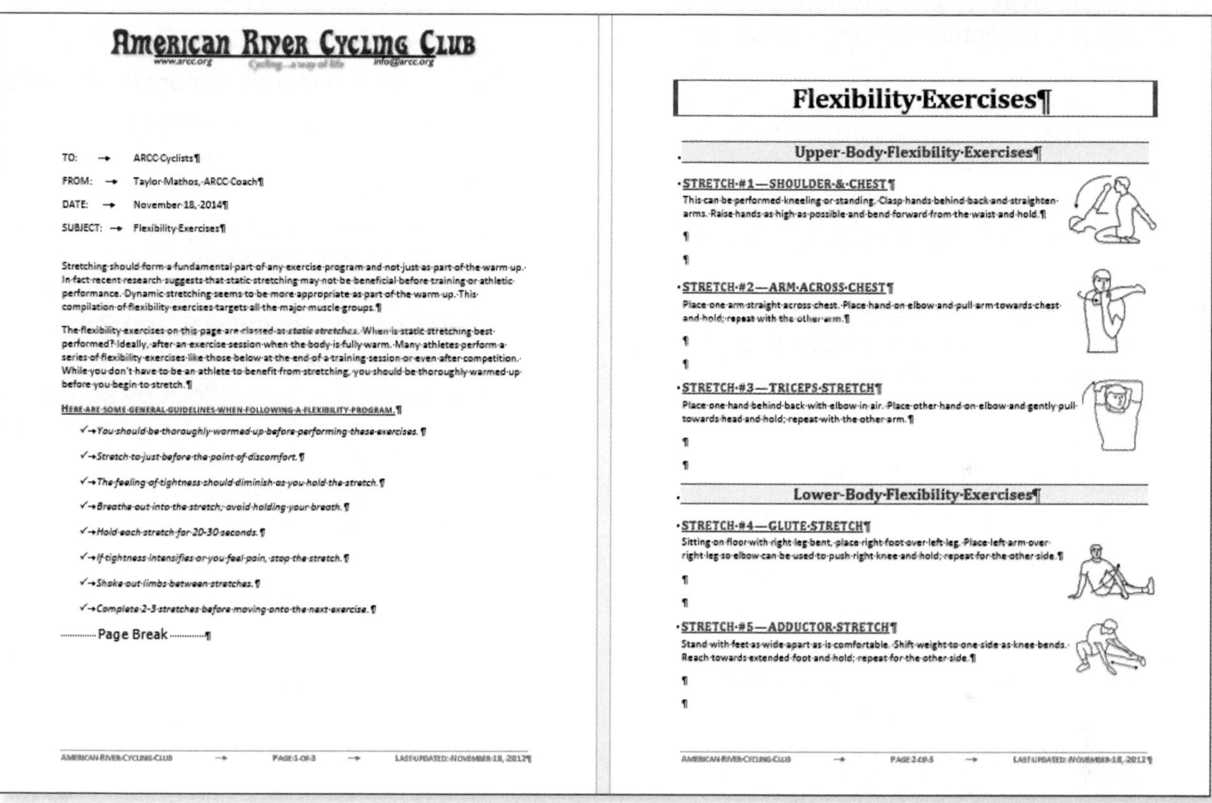

AMERICAN RIVER CYCLING CLUB

www.arcc.org   info@arcc.org

TO: ARCC Cyclists

FROM: Taylor Mathos, ARCC Coach

DATE: November 18, 2014

SUBJECT: Flexibility Exercises

Stretching should form a fundamental part of any exercise program and not just as part of the warm up. In fact recent research suggests that static stretching may not be beneficial before training or athletic performance. Dynamic stretching seems to be more appropriate as part of the warm up. This compilation of flexibility exercises targets all the major muscle groups.

The flexibility exercises on this page are classed as *static stretches*. When is static stretching best performed? Ideally, after an exercise session when the body is fully warm. Many athletes perform a series of flexibility exercises like those below at the end of a training session or even after competition. While you don't have to be an athlete to benefit from stretching, you should be thoroughly warmed up before you begin to stretch.

HERE ARE SOME GENERAL GUIDELINES WHEN FOLLOWING A FLEXIBILITY PROGRAM.

- ✓ *You should be thoroughly warmed up before performing these exercises.*
- ✓ *Stretch to just before the point of discomfort.*
- ✓ *The feeling of tightness should diminish as you hold the stretch.*
- ✓ *Breathe out into the stretch; avoid holding your breath.*
- ✓ *Hold each stretch for 20-30 seconds.*
- ✓ *If tightness intensifies or you feel pain, stop the stretch.*
- ✓ *Shake out limbs between stretches.*
- ✓ *Complete 2-3 stretches before moving onto the next exercise.*

.... Page Break ....

AMERICAN RIVER CYCLING CLUB → PAGE 1 OF 3 → LAST UPDATED: NOVEMBER 18, 2012

Flexibility Exercises

Upper-Body Flexibility Exercises

STRETCH #1—SHOULDER & CHEST

This can be performed kneeling or standing. Clasp hands behind back and straighten arms. Raise hands as high as possible and bend forward from the waist and hold.

STRETCH #2—ARM ACROSS CHEST

Place one arm straight across chest. Place hand on elbow and pull arm towards chest and hold; repeat with the other arm.

STRETCH #3—TRICEPS STRETCH

Place one hand behind back with elbow in air. Place other hand on elbow and gently pull towards head and hold; repeat with the other arm.

Lower-Body Flexibility Exercises

STRETCH #4—GLUTE STRETCH

Sitting on floor with right leg bent, place right foot over left leg. Place left arm over right leg so elbow can be used to push right knee and hold; repeat for the other side.

STRETCH #5—ADDUCTOR STRETCH

Stand with feet as wide apart as is comfortable. Shift weight to one side as knee bends. Reach towards extended foot and hold; repeat for the other side.

AMERICAN RIVER CYCLING CLUB → PAGE 2 OF 3 → LAST UPDATED: NOVEMBER 18, 2012

6-88 PP W6-4 completed (pages 1 and 2)

Chapter Summary

6.1 Create and modify styles using the Style gallery and Styles pane (p. W6-316).

- A ***style*** is a set of formatting commands that are grouped together and applied to text. Styles keep formatting consistent in documents.
- The ***Style gallery*** on the *Home* tab and the ***Styles pane*** contain the commonly used styles.
- The different types of styles available are ***Paragraph***, ***Character***, ***Linked***, ***Table***, and ***List***.
- You can apply styles to selected text using the *Style* gallery, *Styles* pane, or context menu.
- You can modify an existing style, create a new style, or update a style based on the formatting of selected text.
- Styles can be added to or removed from the *Style* gallery.
- You can clear all of the formatting on text by selecting the ***Clear Formatting*** button [*Home* tab, *Font* group] or select in the *Style* gallery or context menu. You can also apply the ***Clear All*** style from the *Styles* pane.
- You can change the ***Style Set*** or theme ***Fonts***, ***Colors***, and ***Paragraph Spacing*** to control the formatting of your document.

6.2 Customize documents by managing styles and using a styles template (p. W6-325).

- Use the ***Manage Styles dialog box*** to customize which styles are displayed, change the display order of styles, edit and create styles, and import and export styles.
- ***Recommended styles*** are displayed in the *Style* gallery and the *Styles* pane.
- The ***Style Pane Options dialog box*** also controls which styles are displayed and the order they are displayed in the *Styles* pane.
- You can ***select all instances*** or ***clear formatting of instances*** of styles in a document. When you select all instances of a style, you can apply formatting to these instances or replace each instance with another style.
- You can use the ***Find and Replace dialog box*** to find and replace styles in a document.
- You can ***import*** or ***export*** styles from a template or document to another template or document.
- A ***styles template*** contains styles that can be attached or imported to other documents.
- Use the ***Organizer dialog box*** to copy styles from one document to another.

6.3 Use the Building Blocks Organizer to create and save information in a document (p. W6-335).

- A ***building block*** is a piece of information that is saved and can be inserted into other documents.
- Building blocks are grouped into a variety of ***building block galleries***. Commonly used building block galleries include ***Footers gallery***, ***Headers gallery***, and ***Page Numbers gallery***.
- You create a building block by saving selected text or an object, such as a graphic or table, to a gallery.
- Use the ***Building Blocks Organizer*** to edit, insert, or delete building blocks.
- You can edit the properties of a building block and create a ***category*** to group building blocks.

6.4 Create AutoText building blocks to save text and objects and insert them into documents (p. W6-338).

- Use the ***AutoText gallery*** to store information that does not fit into one of the other galleries.
- *You can modify, insert, and delete* ***AutoText building blocks*** using the *Building Blocks Organizer.*
- The *AutoText* gallery is accessed by clicking the **Quick Parts** button [*Insert* tab, *Text* group] and selecting **AutoText**.

6.5 Use the Quick Parts gallery to store building blocks and insert them into documents (p. W6-344).

- The ***Quick Parts gallery*** is an easy access area to store building blocks.
- You can modify, insert, and delete ***Quick Parts building blocks*** using the *Building Blocks Organizer.*
- The *Quick Parts* gallery is accessed by clicking the **Quick Parts** button [*Insert* tab, *Text* group].

6.6 Customize and use document property and Word fields in a document (p. W6-346).

- ***Document property fields*** are included in each document you create.
- You can create ***custom document properties*** that can also be inserted into a document.
- View and customize document properties on the *Backstage* view and in the ***Document panel***.
- ***Word fields*** are special codes that are stored and can be used in a document.
- Use Word fields to insert a file name, user name, save date, and number of pages in a document.
- You insert Word fields using the ***Field dialog box***.
- The *Field* dialog box lists available fields. You can customize the properties of many fields, which determines how the field is displayed in the document.
- You can edit fields using the context menu and update them using the context menu or by pressing **F9**.

Check for Understanding

In the ***Online Learning Center*** for this text (**www.mhhe.com/office2013inpractice**), there are a variety of resources that can be used to review the concepts covered in this chapter.

The following Online Learning Resources are available in the Online Learning Center:

- Multiple choice questions
- Short answer questions
- Matching exercises

Guided Project 6-1

In this project, you modify the *Staying Active* document from Courtyard Medical Plaza to create new styles, modify existing styles, create a building block, and customize and insert document property and Word fields.
[Student Learning Outcomes 6.1, 6.2, 6.3, 6.5, 6.6]

Files Needed: ***StayingActive-06.docx*** and ***CMP-logo-06.png***
Completed Project File Name: ***[your initials] Word 6-1.docx***

Skills Covered in This Project

- Change the theme color set.
- Modify existing styles.
- Select all instances of a style.
- Replace an existing style with a different style.
- Create a new style based on selected text.
- Update styles to match a selection.
- Insert and position a picture.
- Save a picture as a *Quick Parts* building block.
- Insert a footer.
- Add a Word field to a footer.

---

1. Open the ***StayingActive-06*** document from your student data files.
2. Save the document as ***[your initials] Word 6-1***.
3. Change the color set of the document.
   a. Click the **Colors** button [*Design* tab, *Document Formatting* group].
   b. Select **Red** from the drop-down list of colors.
4. Modify existing styles.
   a. Right-click **Title** in the *Style* gallery [*Home* tab, *Styles* group] or *Styles* pane and select **Modify** to open the *Modify Style* dialog box (Figure 6-89).
   b. Click the **Center** alignment button.
   c. Click **Format** button and select **Font** to open the *Font* dialog box.
   d. Apply **Bold** font style, change the font size to **20 pt.**, and apply **All Caps** text effect.
   e. Click **OK** to close the *Font* dialog box.
   f. Click **OK** to close the *Modify Style* dialog box.
   g. Right-click **Heading 1** style in the *Style* gallery or *Styles* pane and select **Modify** to open the *Modify Style* dialog box.

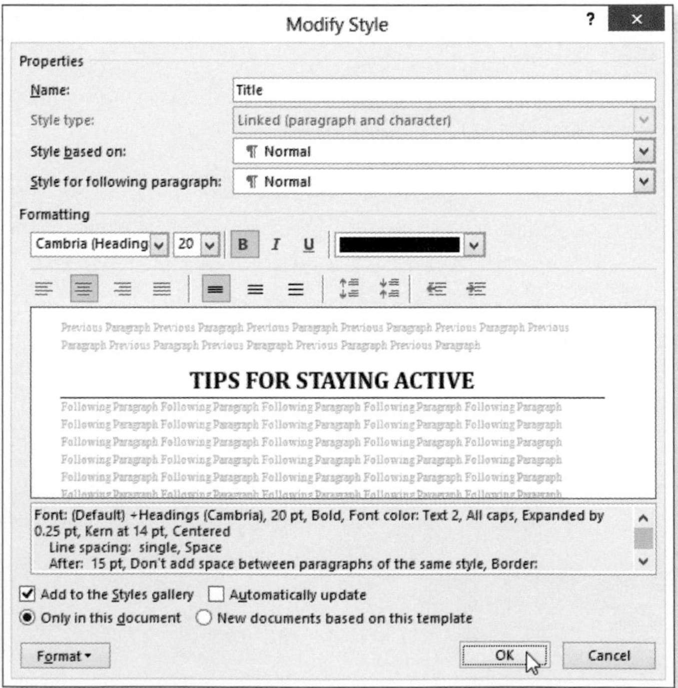

6-89 Modify *Title* style

h. Click the **Underline** button.
i. Open the *Font* dialog box, apply **Small Caps**, and close the *Font* dialog box.
j. Open the *Paragraph* dialog box, make the following changes, and click **OK** to close the *Paragraph* dialog box:

Before paragraph spacing: **12 pt.**
After paragraph spacing: **3 pt.**
Line spacing: **Single**

k. Click **OK** to close the *Modify Styles* dialog box.

5. Select all instances of a style and apply a different style.
   a. Click the **Styles** launcher [*Home* tab, *Styles* group] to open the *Styles* pane.
   b. In the *Styles* pane, right-click the **Heading 2** style and choose **Select All** (Figure 6-90). All of the text with *Heading 2* style applied is selected.
   c. Click the **Heading 1** style in the *Styles* panes or *Style* gallery to replace the *Heading 2* style with the *Heading 1* style.

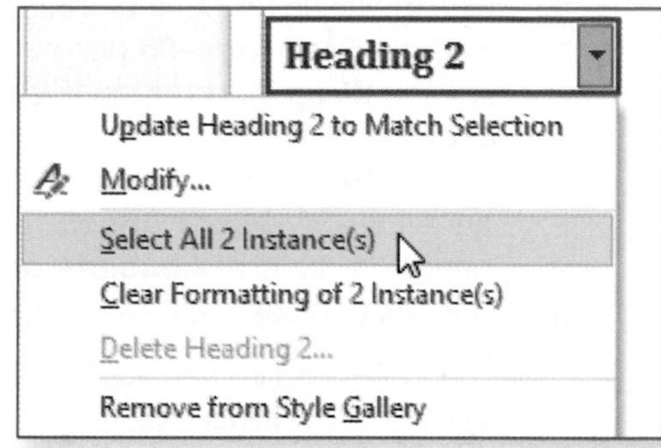

6-90 Select all instances of the *Heading 2* style

6. Create a new style based on selected text.
   a. Select all of the text after the "Keep Exercise Fun and Interesting" heading.
   b. Apply a **check mark bullet** to the selected text. If this bullet is not available from the *Bullet* drop-down list, define a new bullet, and select the check mark from the *Wingdings* font set (character code: 252).
   c. With the bulleted list still selected, click the **More** button in the *Styles* group [*Home* tab] and select **Create a Style**. The *Create New Style from Formatting* dialog box opens.
   d. Click the **Modify** button to view more formatting options.
   e. Make the following changes to the new style (Figure 6-91):

   Name: Bullet List
   Style type: **Paragraph**
   Style based on: **List Paragraph**
   Style for following paragraph: **Bullet List**

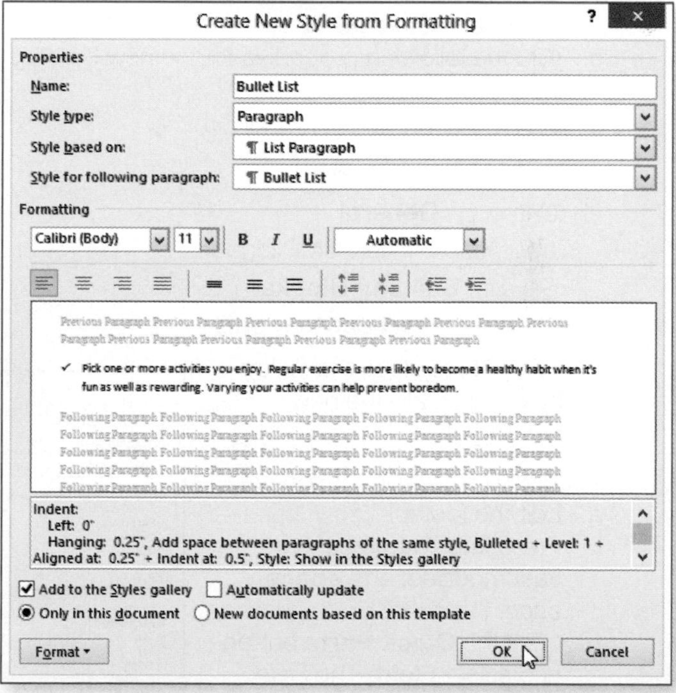

6-91 Create a new style from selected text

   f. Open the *Paragraph* dialog box, change the *Left* indent to **0"**, deselect the **Don't add space between paragraphs of the same style** check box, and click **OK** to close the *Paragraph* dialog box.
   g. Click **OK** to close the dialog box and create the new style.

7. Update styles to match a selection and apply a style.
   a. Select the paragraph after the title of the document.

b. Change the font size to **10 pt.**
c. With the paragraph still selected, right-click the **Normal** style in the *Style* gallery and choose **Update Normal to Match Selection**. All of the body text, including the numbered and bulleted lists, is changed to 10 pt.
d. Select the title and change the *Before* paragraph spacing to **48 pt.**
e. Right-click the **Title** style in the *Styles* pane and select **Update Title to Match Selection**.
f. Select the bulleted list at the bottom of the document and click the **Bullet List** style in the *Styles* pane.

8. Insert a picture and change text wrapping and position.
   a. Place the insertion point at the beginning of the document.
   b. Insert the ***CMP-logo-06*** picture from your student data files.
   c. Click the **Wrap Text** button [*Picture Tools Format* tab, *Arrange* group] and select **In Front of Text**.
   d. Click the **Position** button and select **More Layout Options** to open the *Layout* dialog box.
   e. Change the *Horizontal* **Absolute position** to **0.3"** to the right of **Page**.
   f. Change the *Vertical* **Absolute position** to **0.3"** below **Page**.
   g. Click **OK** to close the *Layout* dialog box.
9. Save the CMP logo in the *Quick Parts* gallery.
   a. Click the **CMP logo** picture to select it.
   b. Click the **Quick Parts** button [*Insert* tab, *Text* group] and select **Save Selection to Quick Part Gallery**. The *Create New Building Block* dialog box opens (Figure 6-92).
   c. Add the following properties for the new building block:

      Name: CMP logo
      Gallery: **Quick Parts**
      Category: **General**
      Description: Insert CMP logo
      Save in: **Building Blocks**
      Options: **Insert content only**

   d. Click **OK** to close the dialog box and create the new building block.

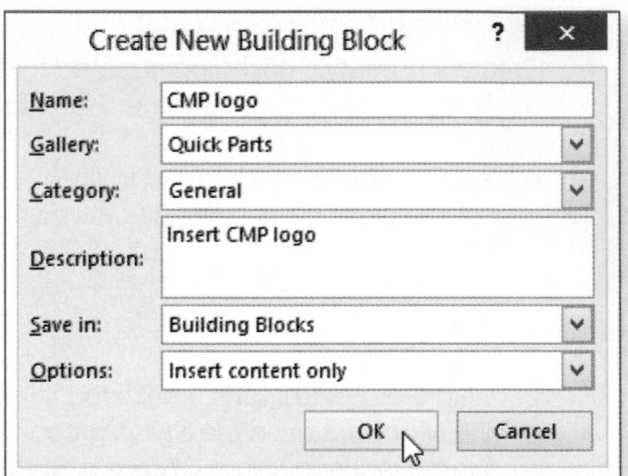

6-92 Save the CMP logo in the *Quick Parts* gallery

10. Insert a Word field in the footer.
    a. Edit the footer.
    b. Press **Tab** two times, type Last modified: and **space** once.
    c. Click the **Quick Parts** button and select **Field**. The *Field* dialog box opens.
    d. Select **SaveDate** in the *Field names* area and the short number date format (fourth option) in the *Date formats* area (Figure 6-93).

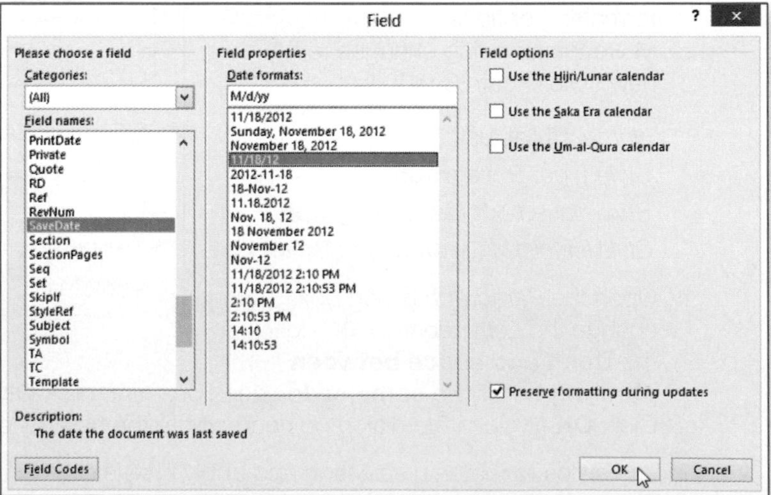

6-93 Insert the *SaveDate* field

e. Click **OK** to close the *Field* dialog box.
f. Select all of the text in the footer and apply **Italic** font style.
g. Close the footer.

11. Save and close the document (Figure 6-94). When you exit Word, a dialog box might open asking if you want to save the building block. Click **Save** to save the building block.

TIPS FOR STAYING ACTIVE

Almost any activity that gets you moving and strengthens your muscles is good for your health and can help you meet your fitness and weight goal. If you haven't been exercising regularly, start out slowly and gradually increase duration, frequency, and intensity. If you have been exercising regularly, keep it up!

STAYING ACTIVE

1) Aim for at least 30 to 60 minutes of moderate intensity activity on most days.
   a) You can get your exercise all at once, or spread it out during the day.
      i) For example, exercising for three 10-minute periods is just as effective as exercising for 30 minutes at a time.
   b) The more physical activity you do, the more calories you burn and the greater the health benefit.
2) If you don't like counting calories, try counting your steps!
   a) Walking 10,000 steps a day can help you manage your weight.
   b) Use a pedometer (an easy-to-wear device that senses your body's motion) to count your steps and motivate you to increase your activity.
   c) Use a journal to track your walking.
3) Use both aerobic and strengthening activities are important to losing weight and keeping it off.
   a) As you grow older, your body slows down and your metabolism—the rate at which your body burns calories—naturally decreases.
   b) Taking a brisk walk will boost your metabolism and keep you burning calories for hours afterward.
4) Remember that any form of exercise is good for you.
   a) Household chores
      i) Cleaning windows
      ii) Vacuuming
      iii) Folding clothes
   b) Yard work and gardening
   c) Using stairs rather than an elevator
   d) Getting up and moving regularly at work

KEEP EXERCISE FUN AND INTERESTING

✓ Pick one or more activities you enjoy. Regular exercise is more likely to become a healthy habit when it's fun as well as rewarding. Varying your activities can help prevent boredom.

✓ Exercise with a friend. The support and companionship will help keep you going.

✓ Think about the payoffs. Exercise not only helps control weight, it is beneficial to the body and mind in a number of ways. It improves health, boosts your immune system, helps control appetite, helps you feel more energetic and relaxed, and raises your self-confidence!

✓ Set realistic exercise goals. Reward yourself in healthy ways when you achieve them.

Last modified: 11/18/14

6-94 Word 6-1 completed

Guided Project 6-2

For this project, you create a styles template for Sierra Pacific Community College District. You modify existing styles, create new styles, and create building blocks. You attach this styles template to the *Emergency Procedures* document, import styles, apply styles to text, and insert building blocks. [Student Learning Outcomes 6.1, 6.2, 6.3, 6.5, 6.6]

Files Needed: ***SPCCDstyles-06.dotx*** and ***EmergencyProcedures-06.docx***
Completed Project File Names: ***[your initials] Word 6-2 styles.dotx*** and ***[your initials] Word 6-2.docx***

Skills Covered in This Project

- Edit a styles template.
- Modify text and update styles to match selected text.
- Create a new style based on selected text.
- Save a picture as a *Quick Parts* building block.
- Create a footer and insert document properties and a Word field.
- Create a *Footer* building block.
- Modify a document style set.
- Attach a template to a document.
- Insert a *Quick Parts* building block.
- Insert a footer from *Footer* gallery.
- Import styles from the styles template.
- Apply styles.
- Modify before and after paragraph spacing.

1. Open the ***SPCCDstyles-06*** template from your student data files. Open this template from within Word.
2. Save this template as ***[your initials] Word 6-2 styles***. Be sure to save as a template.
3. Modify text and update styles.
   a. Select the "**Heading 1**" text.
   b. Change the font size to **14 pt.** and apply **All caps** formatting.
   c. Right-click the **Heading 1** style in the *Style* gallery and select **Update Heading 1 to Match Selection**.
4. Create new styles.
   a. Select "**Text with Tab**" including the tab.
   b. Click the **New Style** button in the *Styles* pane (Figure 6-95). The *Create New Style from Formatting* dialog box opens.
   c. Enter the following properties for the new style (Figure 6-96):

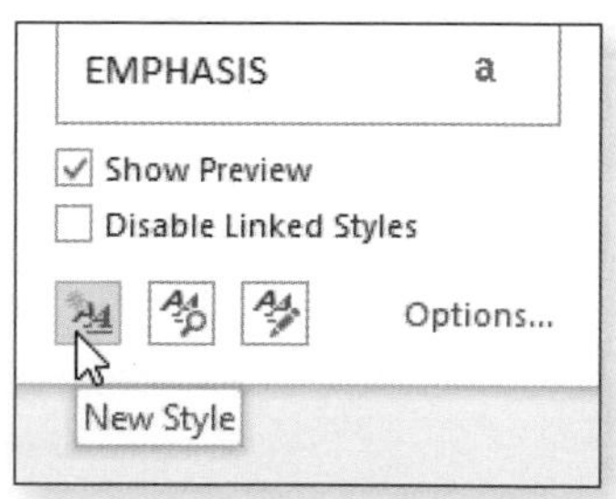

6-95 ***New Style*** **button in the** ***Styles*** **pane**

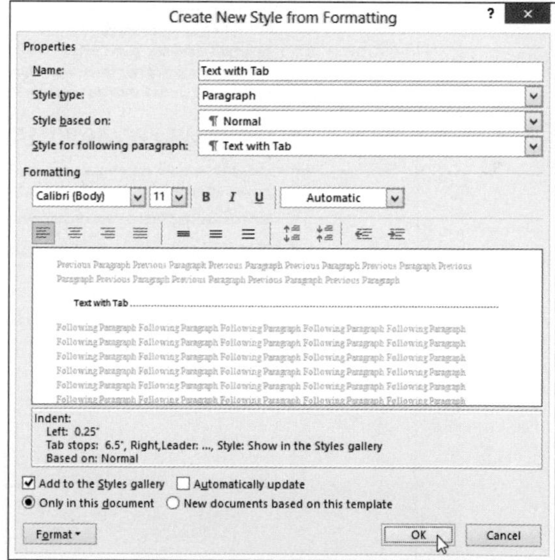

6-96 **Create a new style from selected text**

Name: Text with Tab
Style type: **Paragraph**
Style based on: **Normal**
Style for following paragraph: **Text with Tab**

d. Click the **Format** button and select **Tabs** to open the *Tabs* dialog box.
e. Set a **6.5" right** tab stop with a **dot leader** (2) and click **OK** to close the *Tabs* dialog box.
f. Click **OK** to close the *Create New Style from Formatting* dialog box and create the new style.
g. Select the "**Number List**" text.
h. Click the **More** button in the *Style* gallery [*Home* tab, *Styles* group] and select **Create a Style** to open the *Create New Style from Formatting* dialog box.
i. In the *Name* text box, type Number List.
j. Click **OK** to close the dialog box and create the new style.

5. Save the Sierra Pacific logo in the *Quick Parts* gallery.
   a. Click the **Sierra Pacific logo** picture to select it.
   b. Click the **Quick Parts** button [*Insert* tab, *Text* group] and select **Save Selection to Quick Part Gallery**. The *Create New Building Block* dialog box opens (Figure 6-97).
   c. Enter the following properties for the new building block:

      Name: SPCCD logo
      Gallery: **Quick Parts**
      Category: **General**
      Description: Insert SPCCD logo
      Save in: ***[your initials]*** **Word 6-2 styles**
      Options: **Insert content only**

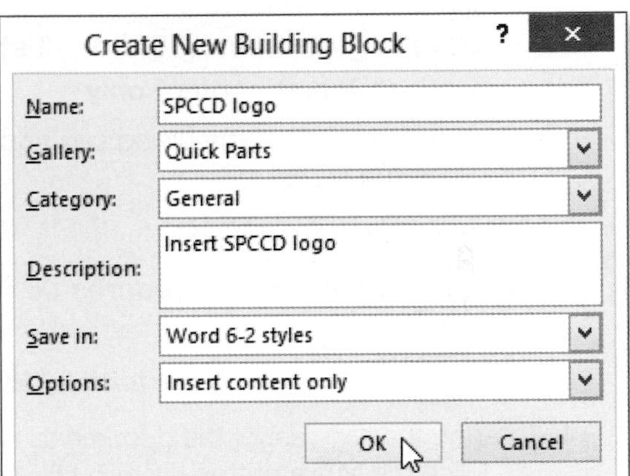

6-97 Save the SPCCD logo in the *Quick Parts* gallery

   d. Click **OK** to close the dialog box and create the new building block.

6. Create a footer and insert document property and Word fields.

   a. Edit the footer.
   b. Click the **Quick Parts** button [*Header & Footer Tools Design* tab, *Insert* group].
   c. Click **Document Property** and select **Title** from the list to insert it into the footer.
   d. Press the **right arrow** key once to deselect the document property field and press **Tab**.
   e. Insert the **Company** document property field.
   f. Press the **right arrow** key once to deselect the document property field and press **Tab**.
   g. Type Revised and **space** once.
   h. Click the **Quick Parts** button and select **Field** to open the *Field* dialog box.
   i. Select **SaveDate** in the *Field names* area and the third date format in the *Date formats* area.
   j. Click **OK** to close the *Field* dialog box.
   k. Select all of the text in the footer, change the font size to **10 pt.**, and apply a **Top Border** from the *Borders* drop-down list [*Home* tab, *Paragraph* group] (Figure 6-98).

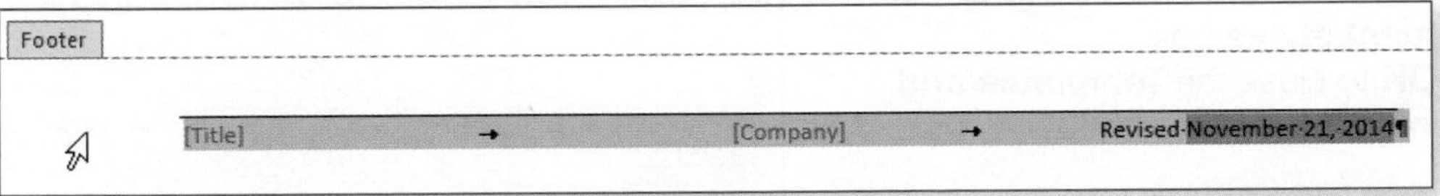

6-98 Footer with document property and Word fields

   l. Leave the footer open and text selected.

7. Create a *Footer* building block.
   a. With the footer selected, click the **Footer** button [*Header & Footer Tools Design* tab, *Header & Footer* group] and select **Save Selection to Footer Gallery**. The *Create New Building Block* dialog box opens.
   b. Click the **Category** drop-down list and select **Create New Category**. The *Create New Category* dialog box opens (Figure 6-99).
   c. Type SPCCD and click **OK** to create the new category.
   d. Enter the following properties for the new building block:

      Name: SPCCD footer

      Gallery: **Footers**

      Category: **SPCCD**

      Description: SPCCD footer

      Save in: ***[your initials]* Word 6-2 styles**

      Options: **Insert content only**
   e. Click **OK** to close the dialog box and create the new building block.
   f. Close the footer.

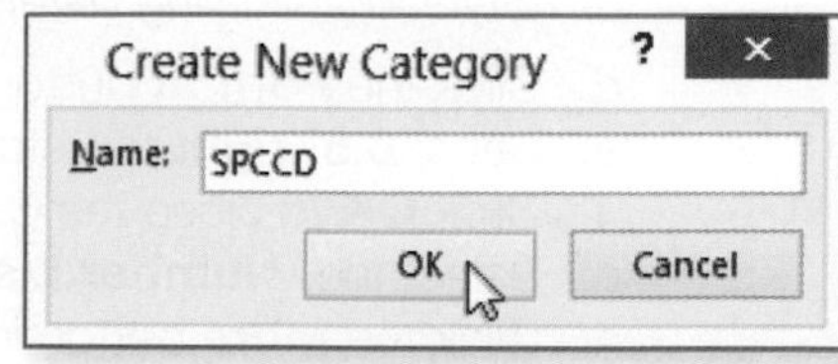

6-99 Create a new building block category

8. Save and close the template.
9. Open the ***EmergencyProcedures-06*** document from your student data files.
10. Save the document as ***[your initials] Word 6-2***.
11. Change the style set of the document.
    a. Click the **More** button [*Design* tab, *Document Formatting* group] to display *Style Set* gallery (Figure 6-100).
    b. Select **Shaded** from the list of options.

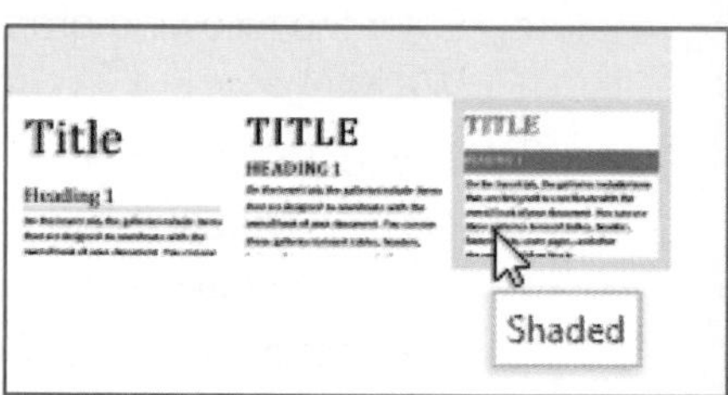

6-100 Select a style set

12. Customize the following document properties on the *Backstage* view:

    Title: Emergency Procedures

    Company: Sierra Pacific Community College District
13. Attach a template to the document.
    a. Click the **Document Template** button [*Developer* tab, *Templates* group]. The *Template and Add-ins* dialog box opens (Figure 6-101).
    b. Click the **Attach** button, browse to find the ***[your initials] Word 6-2 styles*** template, and click **Open** to attach the template.
    c. Check the **Automatically update document styles** box.
    d. Click **OK** to close the **Templates and Add-ins** dialog box.

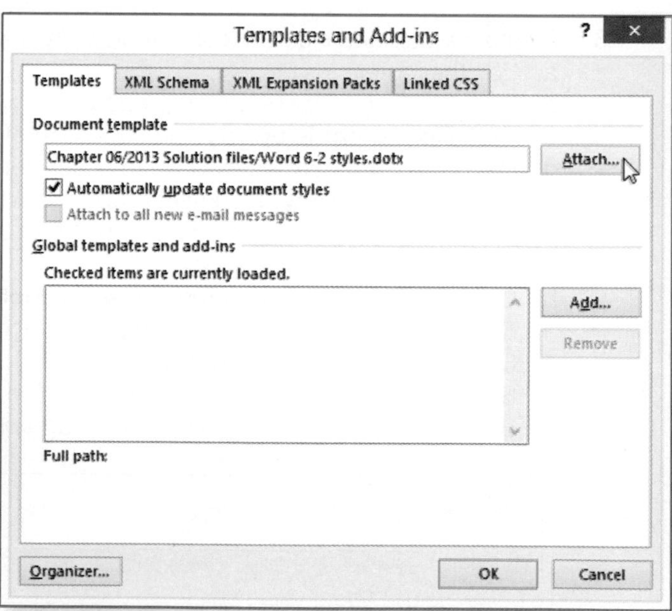

6-101 Attach styles template to document

14. Insert building blocks.
    a. Place the insertion point at the beginning of the document.

b. Click the **Quick Parts** button [*Insert* tab, *Text* group] and select the **SPCCD logo** to insert the picture at the top of the document.
c. Click the **Footer** button [*Header & Footer* group].
d. Select the **SPCCD footer** from the drop-down list. The footer will be inserted into the document with the document property fields inserted.
e. Delete the blank line after the footer.
f. Close the footer.

15. Import styles from a template.
    a. Click the **Manage Styles** button in the *Styles* pane to open the *Manage Styles* dialog box (Figure 6-102).
    b. Click the **Import/Export** button to open the *Organizer* dialog box.
    c. Click the **Close File** button at the right to close the *Normal* template.
    d. Click the **Open File** button, browse to find the ***[your initials] Word 6-2 styles*** template, and click **Open**.
    e. Copy the following styles from the ***[your initials] Word 6-2 styles*** template (list on the right), using the **Ctrl** key to select multiple non-adjacent styles (Figure 6-103):

Bullet List
Heading 1
Heading 2
Normal
Number List
Text with Tab

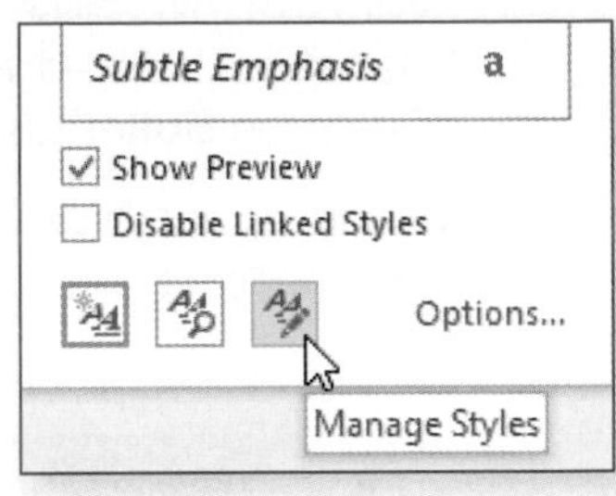

6-102 ***Manage Styles*** **button in the *Styles* pane**

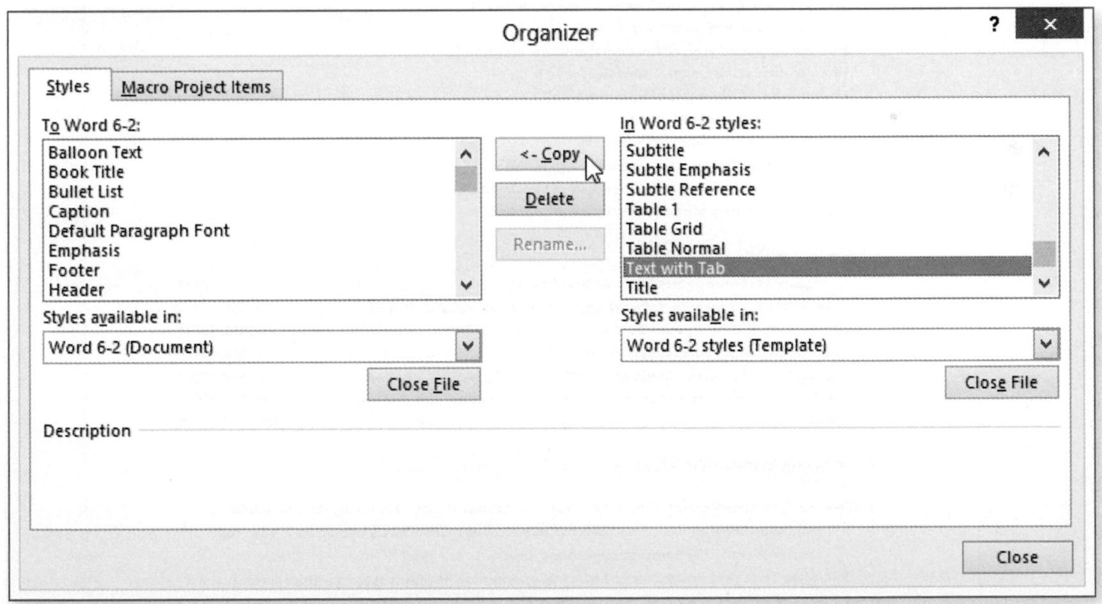

6-103 Import styles from styles template

f. Click the **Copy** button.
g. Click **Yes to All** in the dialog box that asks if you want to overwrite existing styles.
h. Click **Close** to close the *Organizer* dialog box.

16. Apply styles to selected text.
    a. Select the bulleted list in the "Emergency Telephones (Blue Phones)" section.
    b. Apply the **Number List** style.
    c. Select the lines of text below the "Emergency Telephone Locations" heading.
    d. Change the before and after paragraph spacing to **0 pt.**
    e. Select the lines of text below the "Emergency Phone Numbers" heading.
    f. Apply the **Text with Tab** style.
    g. With this text still selected, change the before and after paragraph spacing to **0 pt.**
    h. Select the bulleted list in the last section ("Accident or Medical Emergency").
    i. Apply the **Bullet List** style.
17. Save and close the document (Figure 6-104). If prompted to save changes in the template, select **Yes** to save changes.

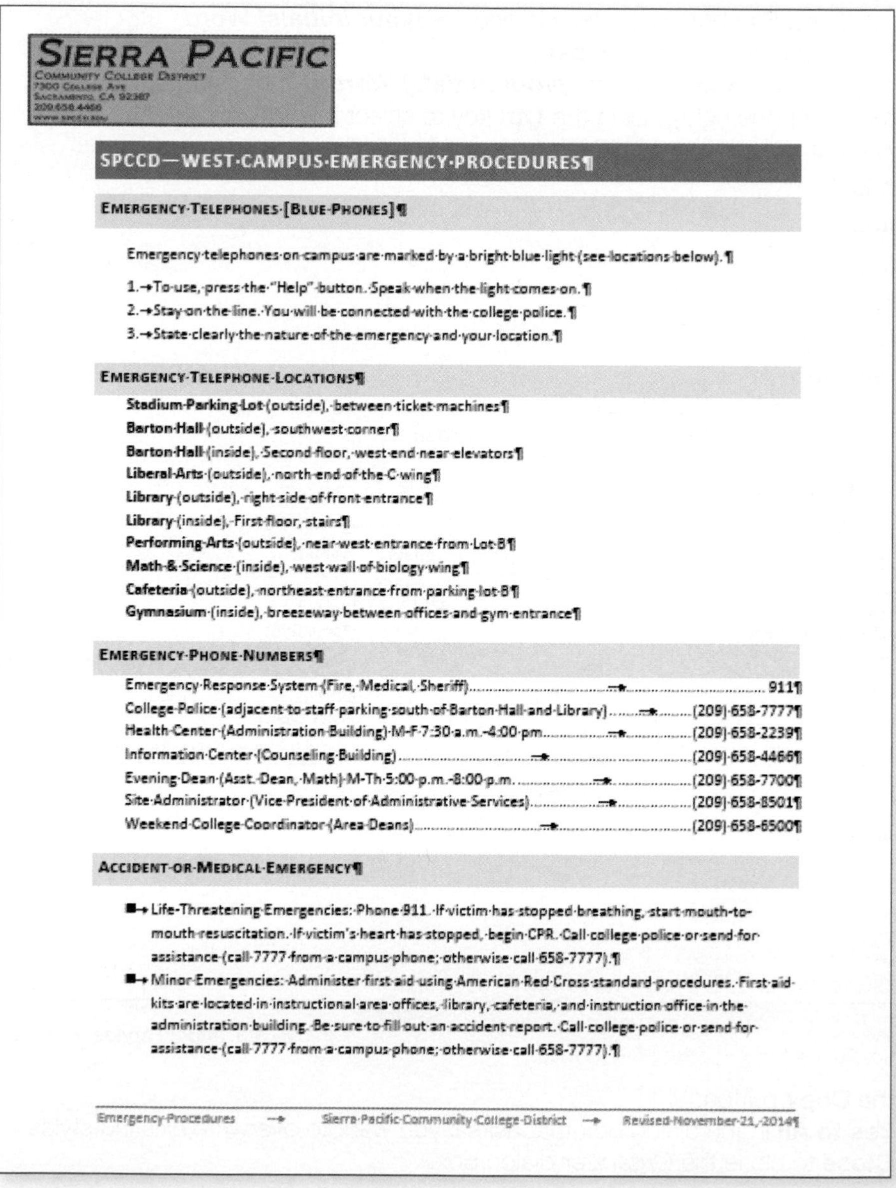

SIERRA PACIFIC
COMMUNITY COLLEGE DISTRICT

SPCCD—WEST CAMPUS EMERGENCY PROCEDURES

EMERGENCY TELEPHONES [BLUE PHONES]

Emergency telephones on campus are marked by a bright blue light (see locations below).

1. To use, press the "Help" button. Speak when the light comes on.
2. Stay on the line. You will be connected with the college police.
3. State clearly the nature of the emergency and your location.

EMERGENCY TELEPHONE LOCATIONS

Stadium Parking Lot (outside), between ticket machines
Barton Hall (outside), southwest corner
Barton Hall (inside), Second floor, west end near elevators
Liberal Arts (outside), north end of the C wing
Library (outside), right side of front entrance
Library (inside), First floor, stairs
Performing Arts (outside), near west entrance from Lot B
Math & Science (inside), west wall of biology wing
Cafeteria (outside), northeast entrance from parking lot B
Gymnasium (inside), breezeway between offices and gym entrance

EMERGENCY PHONE NUMBERS

Emergency Response System (Fire, Medical, Sheriff) 911
College Police (adjacent to staff parking south of Barton Hall and Library) .... (209) 658-7777
Health Center (Administration Building) M-F 7:30 a.m.-4:00 pm .... (209) 658-2239
Information Center (Counseling Building) .... (209) 658-4466
Evening Dean (Asst. Dean, Math) M-Th 5:00 p.m.-8:00 p.m. .... (209) 658-7700
Site Administrator (Vice President of Administrative Services) .... (209) 658-8501
Weekend College Coordinator (Area Deans) .... (209) 658-6500

ACCIDENT OR MEDICAL EMERGENCY

- Life-Threatening Emergencies: Phone 911. If victim has stopped breathing, start mouth-to-mouth resuscitation. If victim's heart has stopped, begin CPR. Call college police or send for assistance (call 7777 from a campus phone; otherwise call 658-7777).
- Minor Emergencies: Administer first aid using American Red Cross standard procedures. First aid kits are located in instructional area offices, library, cafeteria, and instruction office in the administration building. Be sure to fill out an accident report. Call college police or send for assistance (call 7777 from a campus phone; otherwise call 658-7777).

Emergency Procedures   Sierra Pacific Community College District   Revised November 21, 2014

6-104 Word 6-2 completed

Guided Project 6-3

For this project, you revise an insurance renewal form letter for Wayne Reza at Central Sierra Insurance. You modify existing styles, modify the *Styles* pane, create *AutoText* and *Quick Parts* building blocks, and insert document property and Word fields.
[Student Learning Outcomes 6.1, 6.2, 6.3, 6.4, 6.5, 6.6]

File Needed: ***RenewalLetter-06.docx***
Completed Project File Name: ***[your initials] Word 6-3.docx***

Skills Covered in This Project

- Change the *Styles* pane options.
- Add a style to the *Style* gallery.
- Modify a style.
- Update a style to match selected text.
- Customize the document properties.
- Insert a document property field into the letter.
- Create a footer and insert a Word field.
- Create a *Quick Parts* building block.
- Create *AutoText* building blocks.
- Create a new *AutoText* category.
- Assign *AutoText* building blocks to a category.

---

1. Open the ***RenewalLetter-06*** document from your student data files.
2. Save the document as ***[your initials] Word 6-3***.
3. Modify the *Styles* pane and *Style* gallery.
   a. Click the **Styles** launcher to open the *Styles* pane.
   b. Click the **Options** link in the *Styles* pane to open the *Style Pane Options* dialog box.
   c. Click the **Select styles to show** drop-down list and select **In use**.
   d. Click the **Only in this document** radio button if it is not already selected.
   e. Click **OK** to close the dialog box and apply the changes. Only styles in use are listed in the *Styles* pane.
   f. Right-click the **Footnote Text** style in the *Styles* pane and select **Add to Style Gallery**.
4. Modify and update styles.
   a. Right-click the **Normal** style in the *Style* gallery or *Styles* pane and select **Modify**. The *Modify Style* dialog box opens.
   b. Click the **Format** button and select **Paragraph** to open the *Paragraph* dialog box.
   c. Change the *Line spacing* to **Single** and click **OK** to close the *Paragraph* dialog box.
   d. Click **OK** to close the *Modify Style* dialog box.
   e. Select the footnote text at the bottom of the letter ("Note: the premium basis . . ."); don't select the footnote marker.
   f. Change the font to **Cambria** and apply **italic** formatting.
   g. Change the before and after paragraph spacing to **3 pt.**
   h. Right-click the **Footnote Text** style in the *Style* gallery and select **Update Footnote Text to Match Selection** to update this style.
5. Customize and insert document properties.
   a. Click the **File** tab to open the *Backstage* view.
   b. Customize the following document properties:

      Title: Renewal Letter
      Subject: type policy #
      Company: Central Sierra Insurance

c. Click the **Back** button to return to the letter.
d. Select "**Number**" in the subject line of the letter.
e. Click the **Quick Parts** button [*Insert* tab, *Text* group].
f. Click **Document Property** and select **Subject** to insert this field (Figure 6-105). Make sure there is one space before and after this document property field.

¶
Address¶
¶
Dear·First·Name¶
¶ Subject
Subject:·Policy·type·policy·#·Renewal¶
¶
I·am·pleased·to·enclose·your·insurance·renewal

6-105 Insert *Subject* document property field

6. Create a footer and insert a Word field.
   a. Open the footer.
   b. Click the **Align Right** button [*Home* tab, *Paragraph* group], type File name:, and **space** once.
   c. Click the **Quick Parts** button [*Header & Footer Tools Design* tab, *Insert* group] and select **Field** to open the *Field* dialog box (Figure 6-106).

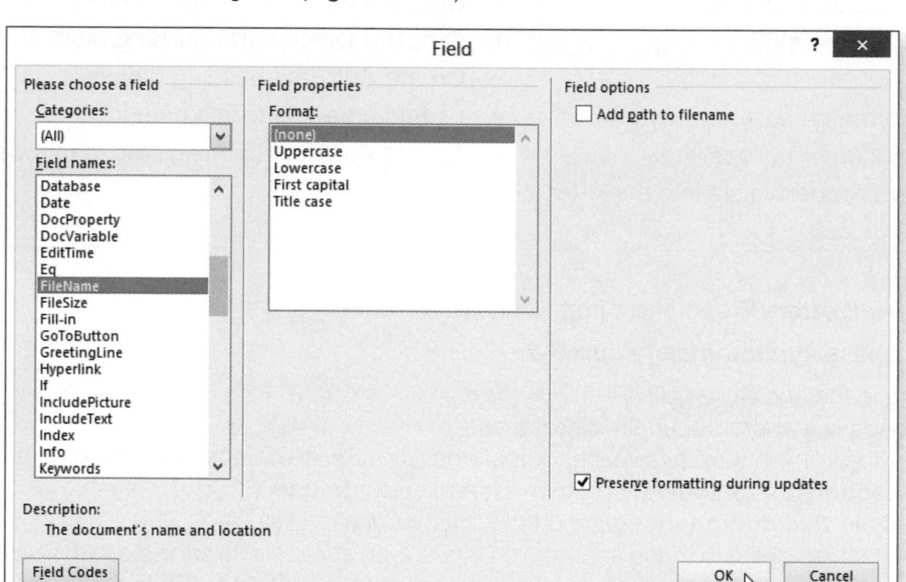

6-106 Insert *FileName* field in the footer

   d. Select **FileName** in the *Field* names area.
   e. Select **(none)** in the *Format* area.
   f. Click **OK** to close the dialog box and insert the field.
   g. Select all of the text in the footer and change the font size to **9 pt.**
   h. Close the footer.

7. Add the Central Sierra Insurance logo to the *Quick Part* gallery.
   a. Open the header and select the **Central Sierra Insurance logo**.
   b. Click the **Quick Parts** button and select **Save Selection to Quick Part Gallery**. The *Create New Building Block* dialog box opens (Figure 6-107).

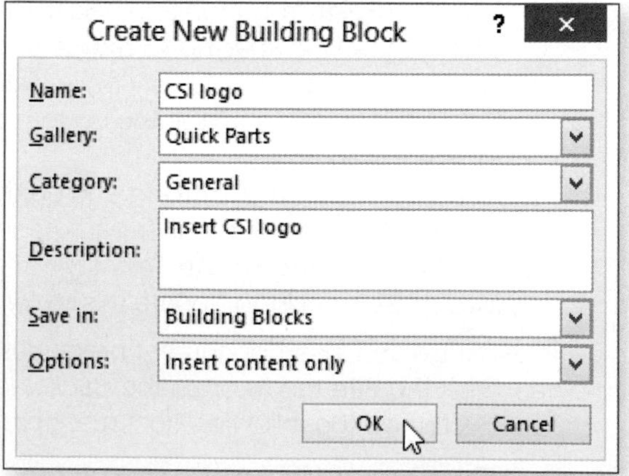

6-107 Save picture to *Quick Parts* gallery

c. Enter the following properties for the new building block:

Name: CSI logo
Gallery: **Quick Parts**
Category: **General**
Description: Insert CSI logo
Save in: **Building Blocks**
Options: **Insert content only**

d. Click **OK** to close the dialog box and save the *Quick Part* building block.
e. Close the header.

8. Create new *AutoText* building blocks.
    a. Select the opening lines of the letter beginning with the date and ending with the blank line after the subject line.
    b. Click the **Quick Parts** button, select **AutoText**, and choose **Save Selection to AutoText Gallery**. The *Create New Building Block* dialog box opens.
    c. Enter the following properties for the new building block:

    Name: CSI letter opening
    Gallery: **AutoText**
    Category: **General**
    Description: Insert opening lines of letter
    Save in: **Building Blocks**
    Options: **Insert content only**

    d. Click **OK** to close the dialog box and save the *AutoText* building block.
    e. Select the closing lines of the letter beginning with "**Sincerely**" and ending with the email address.
    f. Click the **Quick Parts** button, select **AutoText**, and choose **Save Selection to AutoText Gallery**. The *Create New Building Block* dialog box opens.
    g. Enter the following properties for the new building block:

    Name: CSI letter closing
    Gallery: **AutoText**
    Category: **General**
    Description: Insert closing lines of letter
    Save in: **Building Blocks**
    Options: **Insert content only**

    h. Click **OK** to close the dialog box and save the *AutoText* building block.

9. Create a new *AutoText* category and assign *AutoText* building blocks to this category.
    a. Click the **Quick Parts** button and select **Building Blocks Organizer** to open the *Building Blocks Organizer* dialog box.
    b. Select the **CSI letter closing** in the *Building blocks* area and click the **Edit Properties** button to open the *Modify Building Block* dialog box.
    c. Click the **Category** drop-down list and select **Create New Category**. The *Create New Category* dialog box opens (Figure 6-108).
    d. Type CSI and click **OK**. The new category is created and this category is selected for this *AutoText* building block.

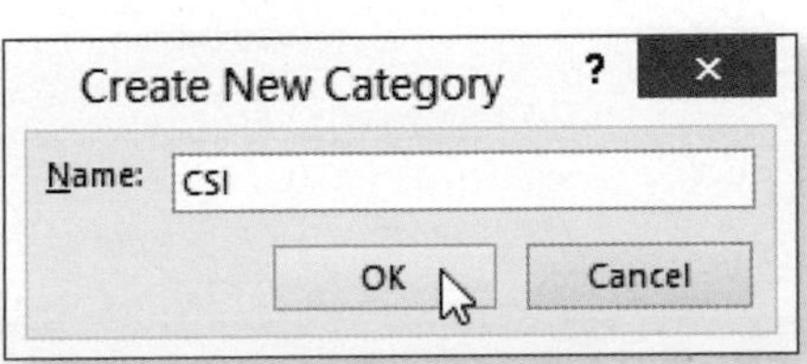

6-108 Create new *AutoText* category

e. Click **OK** to close the *Modify Building Block* dialog box and click **Yes** in the dialog box that opens asking if you want to redefine the building block.
f. With the *Building Blocks Organizer* still open, edit the properties of the **CSI letter opening** *AutoText* building block and assign this building block to the **CSI** category.
g. Close the *Building Blocks Organizer* dialog box.

10. Save and close the document (Figure 6-109). When you exit Word after creating and saving building blocks, you might be prompted to save these changes. Click **Yes** to save changes.

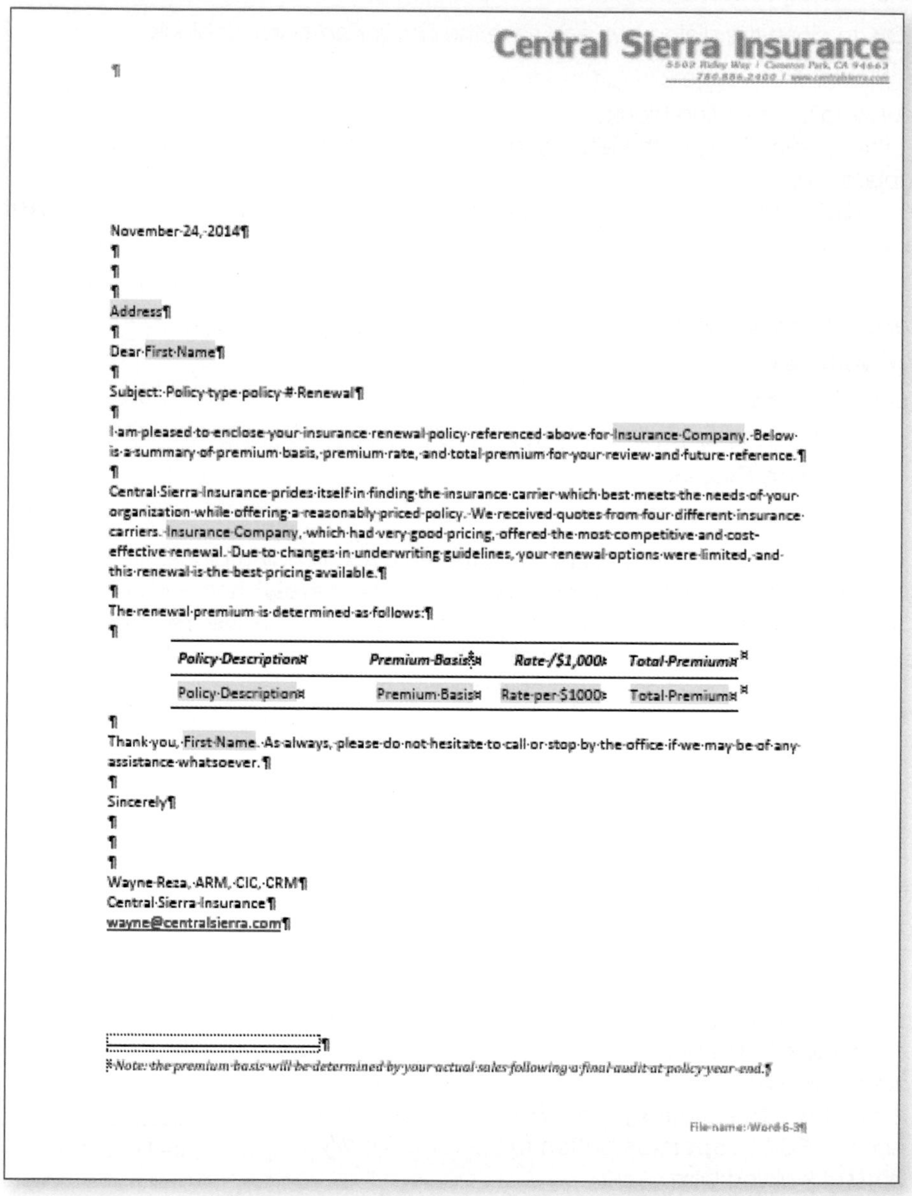

Central Sierra Insurance

November 24, 2014

Address

Dear First Name

Subject: Policy type policy # Renewal

I am pleased to enclose your insurance renewal policy referenced above for Insurance Company. Below is a summary of premium basis, premium rate, and total premium for your review and future reference.

Central Sierra Insurance prides itself in finding the insurance carrier which best meets the needs of your organization while offering a reasonably priced policy. We received quotes from four different insurance carriers. Insurance Company, which had very good pricing, offered the most competitive and cost-effective renewal. Due to changes in underwriting guidelines, your renewal options were limited, and this renewal is the best pricing available.

The renewal premium is determined as follows:

Policy Description	***Premium Basis****	***Rate /$1,000***	***Total Premium***
Policy Description	Premium Basis	Rate per $1000	Total Premium

Thank you, First Name. As always, please do not hesitate to call or stop by the office if we may be of any assistance whatsoever.

Sincerely

Wayne Reza, ARM, CIC, CRM
Central Sierra Insurance
wayne@centralsierra.com

**Note: the premium basis will be determined by your actual sales following a final audit at policy year-end.*

File name: Word 6-3

6-109 Word 6-3 completed

Independent Project 6-4

For this project, you revise the vaccination schedule for Courtyard Medical Plaza. You will update an existing style, create *AutoText* and *Quick Parts* building blocks, and insert document property and Word fields.
[Student Learning Outcomes 6.1, 6.3, 6.4, 6.5, 6.6]

Files Needed: ***VaccinationSchedule-06.docx*** and ***CMP-logo-06.png***
Completed Project File Name: ***[your initials] Word 6-4.docx***

Skills Covered in This Project

- Customize document properties.
- Insert a document property field.
- Modify text and update a style to match selected text.
- Insert and position a picture.
- Create a *Quick Parts* building block.
- Create an *AutoText* building block.
- Create a new *AutoText* category.
- Assign *AutoText* building blocks to a category.
- Create a footer and insert a Word field.

1. Open the ***VaccinationSchedule-06*** document from your student data files.
2. Save the document as ***[your initials] Word 6-4***.
3. Customize the following document properties:

   Title: Vaccination Schedule
   Company: Courtyard Medical Plaza

4. Insert a document property field and apply style.
   a. On the blank line at the beginning of the document, insert the **Title** document property field.
   b. Apply the **Title** style to the *Title* document property field.
5. Modify text and update a style.
   a. Make the following changes to the title of the document:

   Alignment: **Center**
   Font style: **Bold**
   Font effects: **Small Caps**
   Font color: **Red**, **Accent 2**
   Bottom border: **Black**, **Text 1** color, **2¼ pt.** width

   b. Update the *Title* style to match the formatted title text.
6. Insert a picture at the bottom left of the document.
   a. Place the insertion point at the end of the document.
   b. Insert the ***CMP-logo-06*** picture from your student data files.
   c. Change text wrapping to **Tight**.
   d. Change the *Horizontal* **Absolute position** to **0.3**" to the right of **Page**.
   e. Change the *Vertical* **Absolute position** to **9.6**" below **Page**.

7. Select the **CMP logo** and create a *Quick Part* building block using the following properties:
    Name: CMP logo bottom
    Gallery: **Quick Parts**
    Category: **General**
    Description: Insert CMP logo at the bottom left
    Save in: **Building Blocks**
    Options: **Insert content only**
8. Select the entire table and save it as an *AutoText* building block using the following properties:
    Name: Vaccination table
    Gallery: **AutoText**
    Category: **CMP** (create new category)
    Description: Insert Vaccination table
    Save in: **Building Blocks**
    Options: **Insert content only**
9. Insert a footer and a Word field.
    a. Type Last updated: right aligned in the footer.
    b. Insert the **SaveDate** field and use the third date format.
    c. Change the font size of all the information in the footer to **10 pt.** and apply **italics**.
10. Save and close the document (Figure 6-110).

VACCINATION SCHEDULE

Think of vaccines as a coat of armor for your child. To keep it shiny and strong, you have to make sure your child's immunizations are up to date. Timely vaccinations help to prevent disease and keep your family and the community healthy. Some immunizations are given in a single shot, while others require a series of shots over a period of time.

Don't neglect your vaccinations!

Vaccines for children and teenagers are listed alphabetically below with their routinely recommended ages. Missed doses will be assessed by your child's physician and given if necessary. Keep a personal record of all immunizations and bring it with you to each office visit.

RECOMMENED VACCINATION SCHEDULE		
Name of Vaccine	*When It's Recommended*	*Total Doses*
Chickenpox (varicella)	At 12 months and 4-6 years	2
Diphtheria, tetanus, and pertussis (DTaP)	At 2, 4, 6 and 12-15 months, and 4-6 years	5
Haemophilus influenzae type b (Hib)	At 2, 4, 6, and 12 months	4
Hepatitis A (HepA)	At 12 and 18 months	3
Hepatitis B (HepB)	At birth, 1-2 months, and 6 months	3
Human papillomavirus (HPV)	3-dose series for girls at age 11-12 years	3
Inactivated influenza (flu shot)	Annually starting at age 6 months	Annually
Inactivated poliovirus (IPV)	At 2, 4, 6 months, and 4-6 years	4
Live intranasal influenza	Annually starting at age 2 years	Annually
Measles, mumps, and rubella (MMR)	At 12 months and 4-6 years	2
Meningococcal conjugate (MCV)	At 11-12 years	1
Pneumococcal conjugate (PCV)	At 2, 4, 6, and 12 months	4
Pneumococcal polysaccharide (PPSV)	At 2, 4, 6, and 12 months	4
Rotavirus (RV)	At 2, 4, and 6 months	3
Tetanus and diphtheria (Td)	At 11-12 years	1

These recommendations are for generally healthy children and teenagers and are for information only. If your child has ongoing health problems, special health needs or risks, or if certain conditions run in your family, talk with your child's physician. He or she may recommend additional vaccinations or schedules based on earlier immunizations and special health needs.

Last updated: November 24, 2014

6-110 Word 6-4 completed

Independent Project 6-5

For this project, you create a styles template for Sierra Pacific Community College District, attach the styles template to a document, and import styles from a template into a document. You modify and update existing styles, create new styles, create *AutoText* and *Quick Parts* building blocks, and insert document property and Word fields.
[Student Learning Outcomes 6.1, 6.3, 6.4, 6.5, 6.6]

Files Needed: new template file, ***OnlineLearningPlan-06.docx***, and ***SPCCD-logo-06.png***
Completed Project File Names: ***[your initials] Word 6-5 styles.dotx*** and ***[your initials] Word 6-5.docx***

Skills Covered in This Project

- Create a styles template.
- Modify a style set and theme colors.
- Update styles to match selected text.
- Create new styles based on selected text.
- Save a picture as a *Quick Parts* building block.
- Create a footer and insert document properties and a Word field.
- Create a *Footer* building block.
- Attach a template to the document.
- Insert a *Quick Parts* building block.
- Insert footer from *Footer* gallery.
- Import styles from the styles template.
- Select all instances of a style and replace with a different style.

1. Open a new document and save it as a **Word Template** named ***[your initials] Word 6-5 styles***.
2. Change the *Style Set* to **Shaded** and the *Colors* to **Grayscale** [*Design* tab, *Document Formatting* group].
3. Type the following lines of text and press **Enter** after each line:

   Heading 1
   Heading 2
   Learning Mode
   Bullet List

4. Apply the **Heading 1** style to the "Heading 1" text and the **Heading 2** style to the "Heading 2" text.
5. Update styles.
   a. Select the "**Heading 1**" text and change the font size to **12 pt.** font size, font color to **Black, Text 1**, and apply **bold** formatting.
   b. Update the **Heading 1** style to match the selected text.
   c. Select the "**Heading 2**" text and change to **12 pt.** font size and **small caps**.
   d. Update the **Heading 2** style to match the selected text.
6. Modify the *Normal* style and set line spacing to **single**.
7. Create new styles.
   a. Select the "**Learning Mode**" text and make the following changes:

      Font style: **Bold** and **underline**
      Font effect: **Small caps**
      Font spacing: **Expanded** by **1pt**.

b. Select the "**Learning Mode**" text, create a new style, and name the new style Learning Mode. Select **Linked (paragraph and character)** as the *Style type* if it is not already selected.
c. Select the "**Bullet List**" text in the template and apply a **solid square bullet** (Wingdings, character code 110).
d. Select the "**Bullet List**" text, create a new style, and name the new style Bullet List. Select **Linked (paragraph and character)** as the *Style type* if it is not already selected.

8. Insert a picture, position it, and create a *Quick Parts* building block.
   a. Place the insertion point on the blank line below the bulleted list. If there is not a blank line below the bulleted list, position the insertion point at the end of the bulleted list, press **Enter** two times, and apply the **Normal** style.
   b. Insert the ***SPCCD-logo-06*** picture from your student data files.
   c. Change text wrapping to **Top and Bottom**.
   d. Change a *Horizontal* **Absolute position** to **0.3**" to the right of **Page**.
   e. Change a *Vertical* **Absolute position** to **0.3**" below **Page**.
   f. Select the logo and create a *Quick Parts* building block with the following properties:

      Name: SPCCD logo top
      Gallery: **Quick Parts**
      Category: **General**
      Description: Insert SPCCD logo
      Save in: ***[your initials]* Word 6-5 styles**
      Options: **Insert content only**

9. Edit the footer to include the following information and add to the *Footers* gallery:
   a. On the left, insert the **Title** document property field.
   b. In the center, insert the **Company** document property field. Use tabs to align information in the footer at the center and right.
   c. On the right, type Page, **space** once, insert a plain page number in the current position, **space** once, type of, **space** once, and insert **NumPages** field.
   d. Apply a **½ pt. black top border** to the footer.
   e. Select the entire footer and save it to the *Footers* gallery using the following information:

      Name: SPCCD footer
      Gallery: **Footers**
      Category: **General**
      Description: Footer with document properties
      Save in: ***[your initials]* Word 6-5 styles**
      Options: **Insert content only**

10. Save and close the template.
11. Open the ***OnlineLearningPlan-06*** document from your student data files.
12. Save the document as ***[your initials] Word 6-5***.
13. Customize the following document properties:

    Title: Online Learning Plan
    Company: Sierra Pacific Community College District

14. Change *Colors* [*Design* tab, *Document Formatting* group] to **Grayscale**.
15. Attach the ***[your initials] Word 6-5 styles*** template to the document and set it to automatically update styles.

16. Insert the following building blocks on the first page of the document:
    SPCCD logo top
    SPCCD footer (delete the blank line after the footer)
17. Import styles from the ***[your initials] Word 6-5 styles*** template and copy the following styles:
    Bullet List
    Heading 1
    Heading 2
    Learning Mode
    Normal
18. Select all instances of the **Intense Reference** style and apply the **Learning Mode** style.
19. Select the bulleted list on the last page and apply the **Bullet List** style.
20. Save and close the document (Figure 6-111).

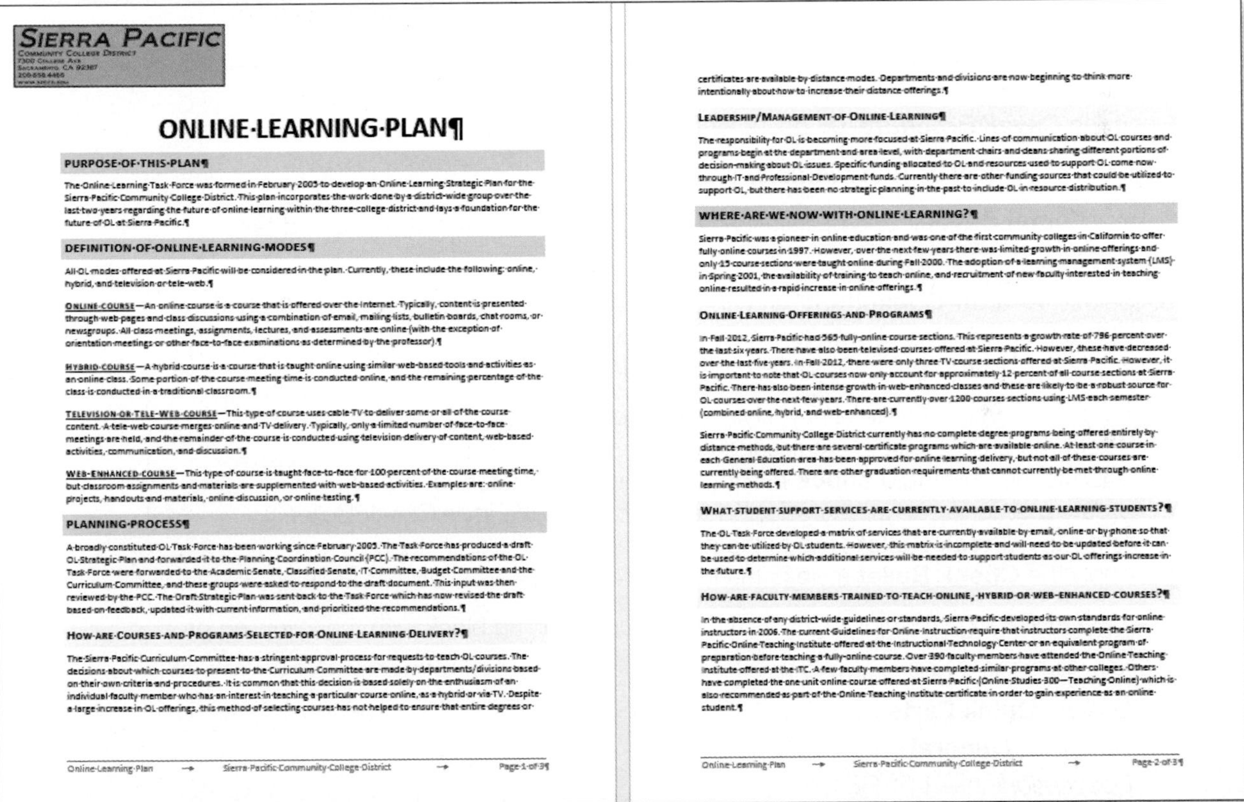

SIERRA PACIFIC
COMMUNITY COLLEGE DISTRICT

ONLINE LEARNING PLAN

PURPOSE OF THIS PLAN

The Online Learning Task Force was formed in February 2005 to develop an Online Learning Strategic Plan for the Sierra Pacific Community College District. This plan incorporates the work done by a district-wide group over the last two years regarding the future of online learning within the three-college district and lays a foundation for the future of OL at Sierra Pacific.

DEFINITION OF ONLINE LEARNING MODES

All OL modes offered at Sierra Pacific will be considered in the plan. Currently, these include the following: online, hybrid, and television or tele-web.

ONLINE COURSE—An online course is a course that is offered over the Internet. Typically, content is presented through web pages and class discussions using a combination of email, mailing lists, bulletin boards, chat rooms, or newsgroups. All class meetings, assignments, lectures, and assessments are online (with the exception of orientation meetings or other face-to-face examinations as determined by the professor).

HYBRID COURSE—A hybrid course is a course that is taught online using similar web-based tools and activities as an online class. Some portion of the course meeting time is conducted online, and the remaining percentage of the class is conducted in a traditional classroom.

TELEVISION OR TELE-WEB COURSE—This type of course uses cable TV to deliver some or all of the course content. A tele-web course merges online and TV delivery. Typically, only a limited number of face-to-face meetings are held, and the remainder of the course is conducted using television delivery of content, web-based activities, communication, and discussion.

WEB-ENHANCED COURSE—This type of course is taught face-to-face for 100 percent of the course meeting time, but classroom assignments and materials are supplemented with web-based activities. Examples are: online projects, handouts and materials, online discussion, or online testing.

PLANNING PROCESS

A broadly constituted OL Task Force has been working since February 2005. The Task Force has produced a draft OL Strategic Plan and forwarded it to the Planning Coordination Council (PCC). The recommendations of the OL Task Force were forwarded to the Academic Senate, Classified Senate, IT Committee, Budget Committee and the Curriculum Committee, and these groups were asked to respond to the draft document. This input was then reviewed by the PCC. The Draft Strategic Plan was sent back to the Task Force which has now revised the draft based on feedback, updated it with current information, and prioritized the recommendations.

HOW ARE COURSES AND PROGRAMS SELECTED FOR ONLINE LEARNING DELIVERY?

The Sierra Pacific Curriculum Committee has a stringent approval process for requests to teach OL courses. The decisions about which courses to present to the Curriculum Committee are made by departments/divisions based on their own criteria and procedures. It is common that this decision is based solely on the enthusiasm of an individual faculty member who has an interest in teaching a particular course online, as a hybrid or via TV. Despite a large increase in OL offerings, this method of selecting courses has not helped to ensure that entire degrees or

Online Learning Plan → Sierra Pacific Community College District → Page 1 of 3

certificates are available by distance modes. Departments and divisions are now beginning to think more intentionally about how to increase their distance offerings.

LEADERSHIP/MANAGEMENT OF ONLINE LEARNING

The responsibility for OL is becoming more focused at Sierra Pacific. Lines of communication about OL courses and programs begin at the department and area level, with department chairs and deans sharing different portions of decision-making about OL issues. Specific funding allocated to OL and resources used to support OL come now through IT and Professional Development funds. Currently there are other funding sources that could be utilized to support OL, but there has been no strategic planning in the past to include OL in resource distribution.

WHERE ARE WE NOW WITH ONLINE LEARNING?

Sierra Pacific was a pioneer in online education and was one of the first community colleges in California to offer fully online courses in 1997. However, over the next few years there was limited growth in online offerings and only 15 course sections were taught online during Fall 2000. The adoption of a learning management system (LMS) in Spring 2001, the availability of training to teach online, and recruitment of new faculty interested in teaching online resulted in a rapid increase in online offerings.

ONLINE LEARNING OFFERINGS AND PROGRAMS

In Fall 2012, Sierra Pacific had 565 fully-online course sections. This represents a growth rate of 796 percent over the last six years. There have also been televised courses offered at Sierra Pacific. However, these have decreased over the last five years. In Fall 2012, there were only three TV course sections offered at Sierra Pacific. However, it is important to note that OL courses now only account for approximately 12 percent of all course sections at Sierra Pacific. There has also been intense growth in web-enhanced classes and these are likely to be a robust source for OL courses over the next few years. There are currently over 1200 courses sections using LMS each semester (combined online, hybrid, and web-enhanced).

Sierra Pacific Community College District currently has no complete degree programs being offered entirely by distance methods, but there are several certificate programs which are available online. At least one course in each General Education area has been approved for online learning delivery, but not all of these courses are currently being offered. There are other graduation requirements that cannot currently be met through online learning methods.

WHAT STUDENT SUPPORT SERVICES ARE CURRENTLY AVAILABLE TO ONLINE LEARNING STUDENTS?

The OL Task Force developed a matrix of services that are currently available by email, online or by phone so that they can be utilized by OL students. However, this matrix is incomplete and will need to be updated before it can be used to determine which additional services will be needed to support students as our OL offerings increase in the future.

HOW ARE FACULTY MEMBERS TRAINED TO TEACH ONLINE, HYBRID OR WEB-ENHANCED COURSES?

In the absence of any district-wide guidelines or standards, Sierra Pacific developed its own standards for online instructors in 2006. The current Guidelines for Online Instruction require that instructors complete the Sierra Pacific Online Teaching Institute offered at the Instructional Technology Center or an equivalent program of preparation before teaching a fully-online course. Over 390 faculty members have attended the Online Teaching Institute offered at the ITC. A few faculty members have completed similar programs at other colleges. Others have completed the one unit online course offered at Sierra Pacific (Online Studies 300—Teaching Online) which is also recommended as part of the Online Teaching Institute certificate in order to gain experience as an online student.

Online Learning Plan → Sierra Pacific Community College District → Page 2 of 3

6-111 Word 6-5 completed (pages 1 and 2)

Independent Project 6-6

For this project, you revise a brochure for Emma Cavalli at Placer Hills Real Estate. You update existing styles, create new styles, apply styles, and create *Header*, *AutoText*, and *Quick Parts* building blocks. **[Student Learning Outcomes 6.1, 6.2, 6.3, 6.4, 6.5]**

File Needed: ***CavalliBrochure-06.docx***
Completed Project File Name: ***[your initials] Word 6-6.docx***

Skills Covered in This Project

- Modify text and update a style to match selected text.
- Create new styles.
- Apply styles to selected text.
- Create a *Quick Parts* building block.
- Create an *AutoText* building block.
- Create a *Header* building block.
- Create a new *Header* category.
- Assign *AutoText* building blocks to a category.
- Modify *Styles* pane options.

---

1. Open the ***CavalliBrochure-06*** document from your student data files.
2. Save the document as ***[your initials] Word 6-6***.
3. Select "**Emma Cavalli**" and update the *Heading 1* style to match the selected text.
4. Update and apply styles.
   a. Select "**Realtor Consultant**" and change the after paragraph spacing to **6 pt.**
   b. Update the *Heading 2* style to match the selected text.
   c. Apply the **Heading 2** style to the other headings in the document.
5. Modify a bulleted list, create a new style, and apply a style.
   a. Select the bulleted list in the second column.
   b. Change the bullet to a **check mark** (Wingdings, character code 252).
   c. Create a style based on the selected text and name the style Check Bullet.
   d. Apply the **Check Bullet** style to the numbered list in the first column.
   e. Apply the **Check Bullet** style to the lines of text in the "Education & Training" section.
6. Save the PHRE logo (bottom right) as a *Quick Parts* building block with the following properties:

   Name: PHRE logo bottom right
   Gallery: **Quick Parts**
   Category: **General**
   Description: Insert PHRE logo
   Save in: **Building Blocks**
   Options: **Insert content only**

7. Select the entire table in the third column and save as an *AutoText* building block with the following properties:

   Name: PHRE beliefs
   Gallery: **AutoText**
   Category: **General**

Description: Insert PHRE table
Save in: **Building Blocks**
Options: **Insert content only**

8. Select the table in the header and save it in the *Headers* gallery with the following properties:

    Name: PHRE header landscape
    Gallery: **Headers**
    Category: **PHRE** (create new category)
    Description: Insert PHRE header
    Save in: **Building Blocks**
    Options: **Insert content only**

9. Modify the *Styles* pane to display only those styles in use and sort alphabetically.
10. Save and close the document (Figure 6-112).

www.phre.com	PLACER HILLS REAL ESTATE	7100 Madrone Road • Roseville • CA • 95722 • 916.450.3300

EMMA CAVALLI

REALTOR CONSULTANT

Phone	916.450.3334
E-mail	ecavalli@phre.com
Web	www.phre.com/ecavalli

MISSION STATEMENT

I am dedicated to listening to your needs as a buyer or seller and providing you with prompt and excellent service to exceed your expectations.

BUSINESS EXPERIENCE

I have had the pleasure of working with buyers, sellers, and investors for over 15 years. Each transaction is new and exciting.

WHY I AM A REAL ESTATE AGENT

- ✓ I enjoy working with people and negotiating on their behalf.
- ✓ Communication, organization, and availability are skills I possess that make me a client-focused real estate agent.
- ✓ I am extremely conscientious of the emotions involved in both the buying and selling process.
- ✓ Customer service and satisfaction are important to me, and I pride myself in giving you the best service possible.

Putting Your Needs First!

WHAT CLIENTS ARE SAYING

Here is what others have said about me:

"It was a pleasure working with Emma Cavalli. She was very responsive and listened to all of our needs. Her marketing plan sold our home in just 3 days!"

-Rod & Luisa Ellisor, Rocklin, CA

"Emma is conscientious, personable, and professional. Her dedication and commitment to meeting our needs has been apparent from the beginning. Emma can be counted on to do what she says. I would not hesitate to refer Emma to my friends and family."

-Jon & Robin Anderson, Roseville, CA

PROFESSIONAL CREDENTIALS

- ✓ Licensed California Real Estate Salesperson
- ✓ Member of National Association of Realtors
- ✓ Member California Association of Realtors
- ✓ Member of Realtor.com
- ✓ Distinguished Realtor Award from peers
- ✓ Community Service Board position for the Roseville Unified School District
- ✓ Elected Parent/Teacher Club President for Winchester Elementary School 2004-2006

EDUCATION & TRAINING

- ✓ University of Nevada, Reno—Business Administration B.A.
- ✓ Real Estate Code of Ethics
- ✓ Certified Contract Consultant
- ✓ Certified Maximum Productivity Consultant

FAMILY & HOBBIES:

I have been a Roseville community member since 1995. I have been married since 1989 and have three children. I love to read, do crafts, travel, and watch my children play sports. I am also very involved in my church and charity work.

THE PLACER HILLS BELIEF SYSTEM	
COMMITMENT	To the needs of the client
COMMUNICATION	Seek first to listen
CREATIVITY	Ideas before results
CUSTOMERS	Always come first
INTEGRITY	Doing the right thing
SUCCESS	Results with integrity
TEAMWORK	Working together for success
TRUST	Begins with communication
WIN-WIN	Is always the goal

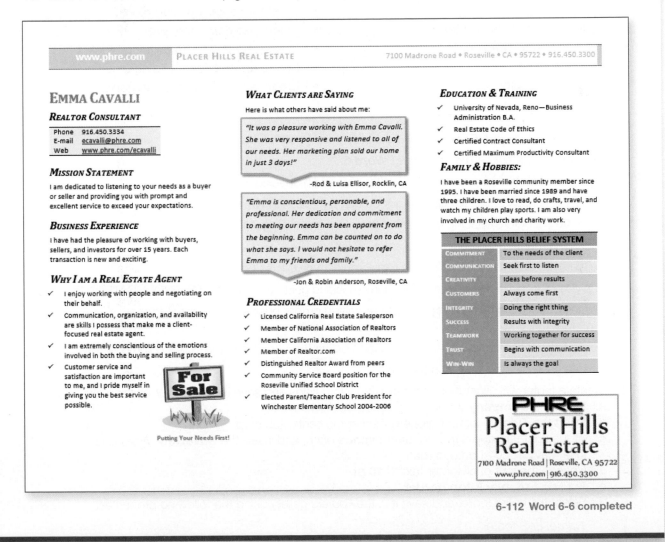

6-112 Word 6-6 completed

Improve It Project 6-7

For this project, you revise an existing weekly expense memo for Life's Animal Shelter to convert it into a form. You update an existing style, create *AutoText*, *Quick Parts*, and *Footer* building blocks, and insert document property and Word fields.
[Student Learning Outcomes 6.1, 6.3, 6.4, 6.5, 6.6]

File Needed: ***LASWeeklyExpenses-06.docx***
Completed Project File Name: ***[your initials] Word 6-7.docx***

Skills Covered in This Project

- Modify a style.
- Find all instances of a style and replace with another style.
- Apply a style to selected text.
- Modify a memo heading.
- Insert a date.
- Update Word fields.
- Create a footer and insert document property and Word fields.
- Create a *Footer* building block.
- Customize document properties.
- Create a *Quick Parts* building block.
- Create an *AutoText* building block.
- Create a new *AutoText* category.

1. Open the ***LASWeeklyExpenses-06*** document from your student data files.
2. Save the document as ***[your initials] Word 6-7***.
3. Modify the *Normal* style to have **0 pt.** after paragraph spacing.
4. Find all instances of the **No Spacing** style and replace with **Normal** style.
5. Apply **36 pt.** before spacing on the first line of the memo heading.
6. Select the memo heading lines and set a **1**" left tab.
7. Delete extra tabs so all info after the memo guide words lines up at 1".
8. Apply the **Strong** style to each of the memo heading guide words (e.g., TO, FROM, DATE, SUBJECT).
9. Delete "**[Insert Current Date]**", insert the date in proper business document format (e.g., May 31, 2014), and set it to update automatically.
10. Delete the expense values in the table. Don't delete the formulas in the *Totals* column or row.
11. Update each of the formulas in the table.
12. Create a footer with document property and Word fields and save it as a *Footer* building block.
    a. Insert the **Company** document property field on the left.
    b. Insert the **Title** document property field at the center tab stop.
    c. At the right tab stop, type Updated:, **space** once, and insert the **SaveDate** Word field (use May 31, 2014 date format).
    d. Change the font of all footer text to **10 pt.**
    e. Apply a **1 pt. black top border**.
    f. Select the entire footer and save it in the *Footers* gallery using the following properties:

       Name: LAS footer
       Gallery: **Footers**
       Category: **LAS** (create new category)

Description: Insert LAS footer
Save in: **Building Blocks**
Options: **Insert content only**

13. Use the following information to customize document properties:

    Title: Weekly Expenses
    Company: Life's Animal Shelter

14. Save the *WordArt* at the top of the document as a *Quick Parts* building block with the following properties:

    Name: LAS WordArt
    Gallery: **Quick Parts**
    Category: **General**
    Description: Insert LAS WordArt
    Save in: **Building Blocks**
    Options: **Insert content only**

15. Select the memo heading lines (include the two blank lines after) and save as an *AutoText* building block with the following properties:

    Name: LAS memo heading
    Gallery: **AutoText**
    Category: **General**
    Description: Insert memo heading
    Save in: **Building Blocks**
    Options: **Insert content only**

16. Replace "xx" at the end of the document with your initials in lower case.

17. Save and close the document (Figure 6-113).

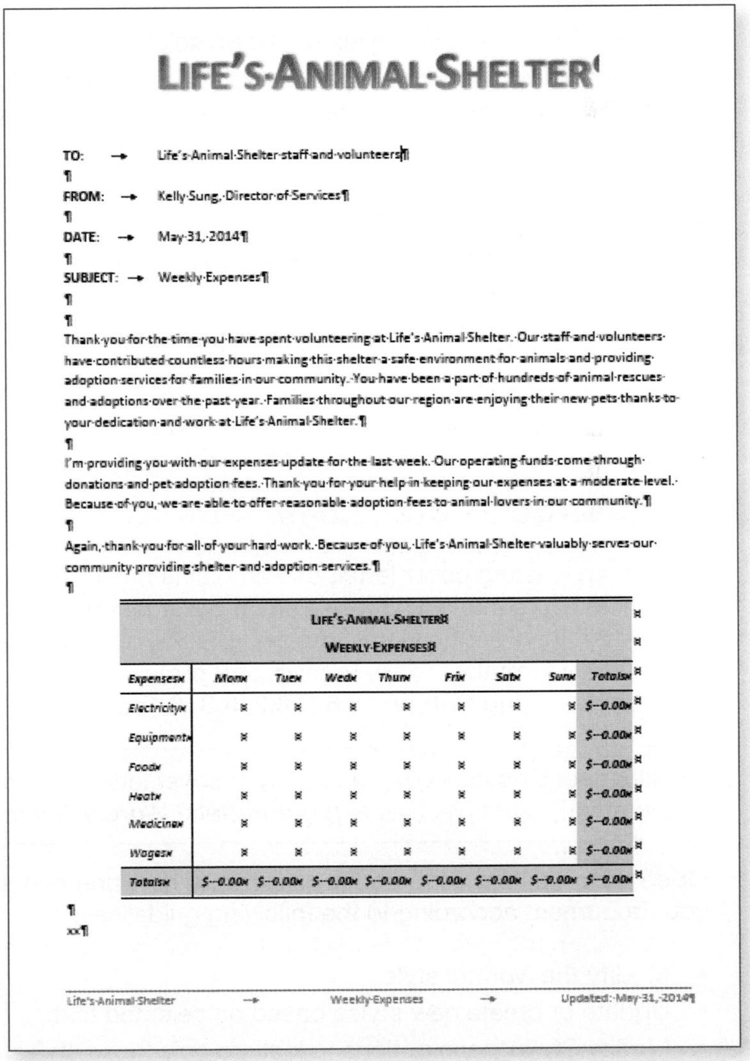

LIFE'S ANIMAL SHELTER

TO: Life's Animal Shelter staff and volunteers

FROM: Kelly Sung, Director of Services

DATE: May 31, 2014

SUBJECT: Weekly Expenses

Thank you for the time you have spent volunteering at Life's Animal Shelter. Our staff and volunteers have contributed countless hours making this shelter a safe environment for animals and providing adoption services for families in our community. You have been a part of hundreds of animal rescues and adoptions over the past year. Families throughout our region are enjoying their new pets thanks to your dedication and work at Life's Animal Shelter.

I'm providing you with our expenses update for the last week. Our operating funds come through donations and pet adoption fees. Thank you for your help in keeping our expenses at a moderate level. Because of you, we are able to offer reasonable adoption fees to animal lovers in our community.

Again, thank you for all of your hard work. Because of you, Life's Animal Shelter valuably serves our community providing shelter and adoption services.

LIFE'S ANIMAL SHELTER								
WEEKLY EXPENSES								
Expenses	*Mon*	*Tue*	*Wed*	*Thu*	*Fri*	*Sat*	*Sun*	*Totals*
Electricity								*$--0.00*
Equipment								*$--0.00*
Food								*$--0.00*
Heat								*$--0.00*
Medicine								*$--0.00*
Wages								*$--0.00*
Totals	*$--0.00*	*$--0.00*	*$--0.00*	*$--0.00*	*$--0.00*	*$--0.00*	*$--0.00*	*$--0.00*

xx

Life's Animal Shelter Weekly Expenses Updated: May 31, 2014

6-113 Word 6-7 completed

Challenge Project 6-8

Update your resume using some of the document formatting features learned in this chapter. If you don't have an existing resume, you can create a new one based on an online resume template or use a blank document to create a resume. Incorporate styles, building blocks, and document properties. Edit your resume so it is consistently formatted, easy to read, and professional looking. Do some online research on resumes to get ideas about formatting and content.
[Student Learning Outcomes 6.1, 6.2, 6.3, 6.4, 6.5, 6.6]

File Needed: Existing resume, online resume template, or new document
Completed Project File Name: ***[your initials] Word 6-8.docx***

Open your existing resume or create a new resume and save it as ***[your initials] Word 6-8***. Modify your document according to the following guidelines:

- Modify and apply existing styles to headings, subheadings, and lists to improve consistency in your resume.
- Update or create new styles based on selected text.
- Modify *Styles* pane options to include only those styles used in your resume.
- Modify the *Style* gallery to include styles used in your resume.
- Create building blocks from content in your resume.
- Create a new category to group building blocks.
- Customize document properties.
- Insert document property and Word fields.

Challenge Project 6-9

Update an existing cover letter, use an online cover letter template, or create a new one from a blank document. Do some online research on cover letters to learn about proper format for a personal business letter. Incorporate styles, building blocks, and document properties. Edit your cover letter so it is consistently formatted, easy to read, and professional looking.
[Student Learning Outcomes 6.1, 6.2, 6.3, 6.4, 6.6]

File Needed: Existing cover letter, online cover letter template, or new document
Completed Project File Name: ***[your initials] Word 6-9.docx***

Open your existing cover letter or create a new one and save it as ***[your initials] Word 6-9***. Modify your document according to the following guidelines:

- Modify the *Normal* style.
- Update or create new styles based on selected text.
- Modify *Styles* pane options to include only those styles used in your resume.

- Modify the *Style* gallery to include styles used in your resume.
- Create *AutoText* building blocks from the opening and closing lines of your cover letter.
- Save some of the paragraphs of text as *AutoText* building blocks.
- Create a new category to group the *AutoText* building blocks.
- Customize document properties.
- Insert document property fields.

Challenge Project 6-10

Create an agenda or meeting outline for an upcoming meeting for an organization you belong to, such as a club, church, volunteer organization, student group, or neighborhood association. Incorporate styles, building blocks, and document property and Word fields. Do some Internet research to learn more about the common components of successful agendas. Robert's Rules of Order is a good source of information about meetings and guidelines for meeting protocol.
[Student Learning Outcomes 6.1, 6.2, 6.3, 6.4, 6.5, 6.6]

File Needed: None
Completed Project File Name: ***[your initials] Word 6-10.docx***

Create a new document and save it as ***[your initials] Word 6-10***. Agendas or meetings can include, but are not limited to, the following items:

- Organization name as the title
- Meeting date, start time, and end time
- Meeting location
- Meeting attendees
- Topic headings
- Topic subheadings (include details for each topic heading)
- The time each topic is expected to last

Modify your document according to the following guidelines:

- Modify and apply existing styles to headings, subheadings, and lists to improve consistency in format.
- Update or create new styles based on selected text.
- Modify *Styles* pane options to include only those styles used in your document.
- Modify the *Style* gallery to include styles used in your document.
- Create building blocks from content in your document.
- Create a new category to group building blocks.
- Customize document properties.
- Insert document property and Word fields.

CHAPTER 7

Advanced Tables and Graphics

CHAPTER OVERVIEW

In Chapter 4 we covered the basics of tables, columns, and graphics. In this chapter, you are introduced to more of the advanced features that are available to you as you work with tables, columns, and graphics. The advanced topics in this chapter allow you to effectively customize table contents, layout, and styles. The final two sections in this chapter introduce you to ways you can use these advanced features when you are working with pictures and shapes.

STUDENT LEARNING OUTCOMES (SLOs)

After completing this chapter, you will be able to:

SLO 7.1 Customize table content using sorting, formulas, bullets and numbers, tabs and indents, and text direction (p. W7-381).

SLO 7.2 Customize table layouts using table properties, cell margins, the split table feature, nested tables, and a repeated header row (p. W7-390).

SLO 7.3 Enhance a table design with shading, borders, and a table style (p. W7-394).

SLO 7.4 Modify a picture using advanced layout and picture format options (p. W7-404).

SLO 7.5 Create, group, align, and modify a shape in a document (p. W7-415).

CASE STUDY

In the Pause & Practice projects, you modify a document about maximum and target heart rates for the American River Cycling Club. You use tables, columns, graphics, and shapes to effectively communicate this information.

Pause & Practice 7-1: Customize table contents by converting text to a table, sorting information in the table, adding formulas, and changing text direction.

Pause & Practice 7-2: Enhance tables in the document by customizing the table layout and applying, modifying, and creating table styles.

Pause & Practice 7-3: Insert, modify, and arrange pictures in the document.

Pause & Practice 7-4: Insert, modify, arrange, and group shapes to present information graphically in the document.

WORD

SLO 7.1

Customizing Table Content

Tables are an excellent way to succinctly and attractively present information in a document. This section reviews the basics of formatting table content and covers some of the more advanced features you can use to customize the contents of a table, such as sorting table contents, using custom formulas, adding bullets and numbering, modifying tab stops and indents, and changing text direction.

When your insertion point is in a table or when you select a table, two context-sensitive *Table Tools* tabs display on the *Ribbon:* ***Table Tools Design tab*** and ***Table Tools Layout tab***. The *Table Tools Layout* tab provides many options you can use to customize the layout and contents of tables. The *Table Tools Design* tab has options to apply and customize table styles and borders, which are covered in *SLO 7.3: Customizing Table Design*.

Convert Text to a Table

When you create a table, you can type the text into the table, or, if the text is already in the document, you can convert existing text into a table. When you convert text to a table, Word uses the existing structure of the text to create a table. You can then modify the table to meet your needs.

HOW TO: Convert Text into a Table

1. Select the text to convert to a table.
2. Click the **Table** button [*Insert* tab, *Tables* group] and select **Convert Text to Table**. The *Convert Text to Table* dialog box opens (Figure 7-1).
3. In the *Table size* area, adjust the number of columns and rows as necessary.
   - Word automatically determines the number of columns and rows based upon the structure of the text you select to convert to a table.
   - You can modify the number of columns and rows in this area.
4. In the *AutoFit behavior* area, select from the radio buttons to determine how the column widths of the table are set.
5. In the *Separate text at* area, select from the radio buttons to determine how the columns and rows are separated.
   - Word automatically selects a separation option based upon the structure of the text you select to convert to a table.
6. Click **OK** to close the dialog box and convert the text to a table.

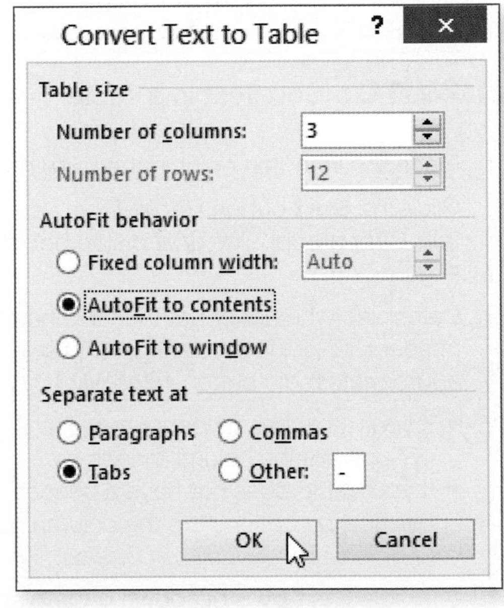

7-1 ***Convert Text to Table*** **dialog box**

Convert a Table to Text

There may also be times when you want to convert an existing table into text. The process for doing this is similar to the process for converting text to a table.

HOW TO: Convert a Table to Text

1. Select the table to convert to text.
2. Click the **Convert to Text** button [*Table Tools Layout* tab, *Data* group] (Figure 7-2). The *Convert Table to Text* dialog box opens.
3. In the *Separate text with* area, select from the radio buttons to determine how the text will be separated (Figure 7-3).
   - Word inserts paragraph marks, tabs, commas, or a custom separator to separate the text when converting a table to text.
   - Tabs are the most commonly used separator when converting a multi-column table to text.
4. Click **OK** to close the dialog box and convert the table to text.

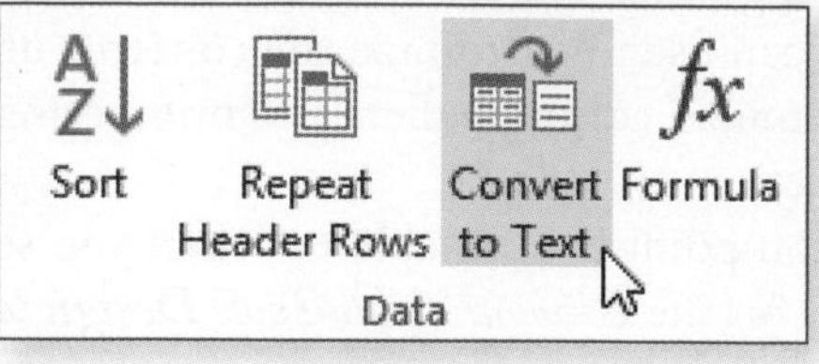

7-2 *Convert to Text* button

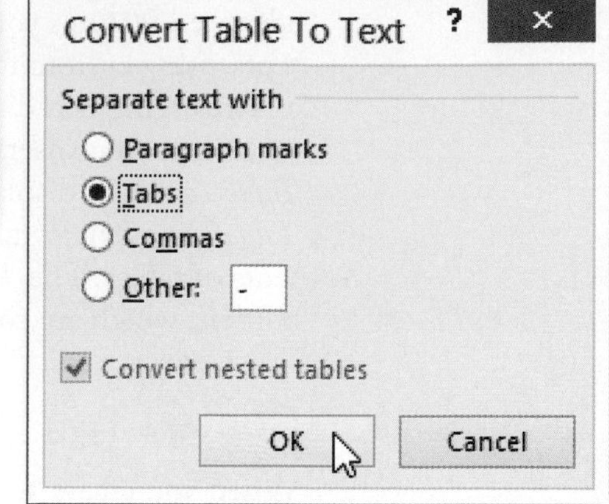

7-3 *Convert Table to Text* dialog box

Sort Text in a Table

Sorting text in a table can be useful and save you time. You can sort any of the columns in a table in ascending or descending order. Word automatically moves entire rows of information when you perform a sort. You can also perform a multi-level sort. For example, you might want to sort a table by city and then within each city sort by last name.

HOW TO: Sort Text in a Table

1. Place the insertion point in the table or select the entire table.
2. Click the **Sort** button [*Table Tools Layout* tab, *Data* group]. The *Sort* dialog box opens (Figure 7-4).
3. Determine whether or not the table has a header row (column headings) and select the appropriate radio button in the *My list has* area.
   - If your table has a header row, the *Sort by* options are the column headings.
   - If your table does not have a header row, the *Sort by* options are the column numbers (e.g., *Column 1*, *Column 2*, etc.).
4. Click the **Sort by** drop-down list and select the column heading or column to sort.
5. Click the **Type** drop-down list and select **Text**, **Number**, or **Date**.
   - When you sort text in a table, the text is sorted using paragraphs, which means entire rows are moved rather than individual cells.
6. Click the **Ascending** or **Descending** radio button to select the sort order.
7. To perform a secondary sort, click the **Then by** drop-down list, select the column heading or column to sort, and select the type and sort order.
8. Click **OK** to close the dialog box and perform the sort.

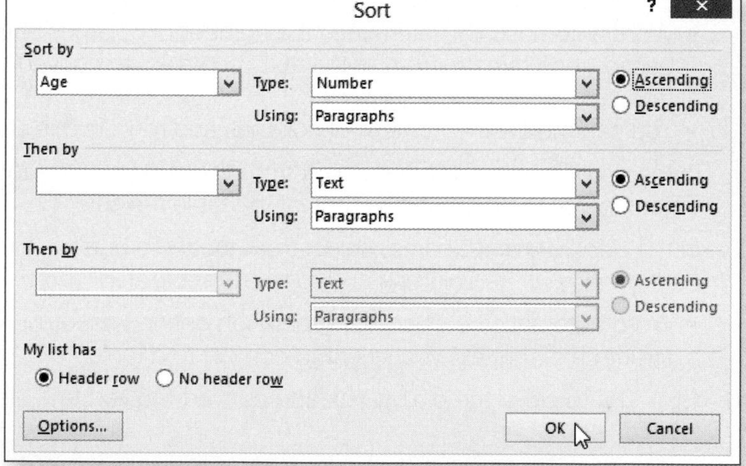

7-4 *Sort* dialog box

> **MORE INFO**
>
> The *Sort* feature is not limited to tables. You can also sort selected paragraphs of information or a bulleted list.

Formulas and Functions

In Chapter 4 you learned how to insert a simple formula into a table to add values in columns and rows. ***Formulas*** can be used in tables to perform simple or more complex mathematical calculations. You can use formulas to add, subtract, multiply, or divide values in a table. You can use ***functions***, such as *SUM* (add values) or *AVG* (average values), to calculate the sum or average of the values in a column or row.

Create a Formula

Formulas have to be constructed in a specific way, which is called ***syntax***. The formula syntax is the rule or rules that dictate how the various parts of a formula are written. For example, the equals sign (=) is always the first character you must enter when creating a formula. The other parts of a formula can include cell references, operators, and values.

Remember that tables are grouped into columns (vertical) and rows (horizontal). Columns are referenced with letters and rows are referenced with numbers. For example, the first column is A, the second column is B, the first row is 1, and the second row is 2. These column and row references are not visible in Word tables as they are in Excel.

A column and row intersect at a cell. Each cell has a ***cell address***, which is the column and row reference. In the table at the right, the cell address is displayed in each cell.

A1	B1	C1
A2	B2	C2
A3	B3	C3

When creating a formula, you refer to a cell using its cell address, which is called a ***cell reference*** in a formula.

Operators are the symbols for mathematical operations. The following table lists the mathematical operators and their order of precedence (the order they are performed in a formula):

Formula Operators

Operator	Operator Name	Order of Precedence
()	Parenthesis	First
^	Exponent	First
*	Multiplication	Second
/	Division	Second
-	Subtraction	Third
+	Addition	Third

You can also use ***values*** in formulas. For example, you can multiply a cell reference by 85% or you can subtract a cell reference from 220. The following table displays the proper syntax for formulas that use cell references, operators, and values:

Formula Syntax

Formula	Explanation
=A1+B1	Adds cells A1 and B1
=220-B3	Subtracts cell B3 from 220
=B3*85%	Multiplies cell B3 by 85% (0.85)
=(A1+A2)/2	Adds cells A1 and A2 and then divides by 2

HOW TO: Create a Formula

1. Place the insertion point in the cell where you want to insert a formula.
2. Click the **Formula** button [*Table Tools Layout* tab, *Data* group] to open the *Formula* dialog box (Figure 7-5).
3. In the *Formula* area, delete the existing formula, type = followed by the new formula.
   - Word typically inserts a function in the *Formula* area.
   - Don't include spaces between the parts of the formula.
4. Click the **Number format** drop-down list to select the format for the output of the formula.
5. Click **OK** to close the dialog box and insert the formula.

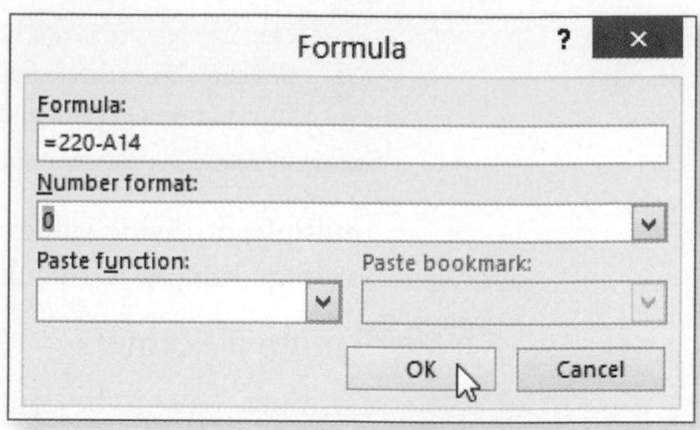

7-5 *Formula* dialog box

MORE INFO

Formulas you use in tables are similar to those used in Excel, but there are some differences. You can't select a cell to automatically insert a cell reference as you can in Excel, and formulas in Word do not update automatically when data changes.

Bookmarks can also be variables in formulas. Bookmarks were covered in *SLO 3.5: Using Bookmarks*. If you have a bookmark in your document that is a value, you can insert the bookmark into a formula. Click the **Paste bookmark** drop-down list in the *Formula* dialog box to display the available bookmarks in your document.

ANOTHER WAY

Click **Quick Parts** [*Insert* tab, *Text* group] and select **Field** to open the *Field* dialog box. Click **Formula** to open the *Formula* dialog box.

Use a Function in a Formula

Functions are built-in formulas created for common types of calculations, such as *SUM* and *AVERAGE*. Functions have a specific syntax and can save you time once you understand how to use them. Functions typically are performed on a range of values. For example, you can use a function to add the values in a column or row. The following table displays the syntax for the *SUM* and *AVERAGE* functions.

Formula Syntax

Function	Explanation
=SUM(B1:B5)	Adds values in cells B1 through B5. The colon between cell references is the syntax to represent a range of cells.
=SUM(above)	Adds all of the values in the column above. "*Above*" is the syntax used to reference all of the cells in the column above the formula.
=AVERAGE(A2:A5)	Averages the values in cells A2 through A5. The colon between cell references is the syntax to represent a range of cells.
=AVERAGE(left)	Averages all of the values in the row to the left. "*Left*" is the syntax used to reference all of the cells in the row to the left of the formula.

> **MORE INFO**
> The functions and cell references in formulas are *not* case sensitive.

HOW TO: Use a Function in a Formula

1. Place the insertion point in the cell where you want to insert a formula.
2. Click the **Formula** button [*Table Tools Layout* tab, *Data* group] to open the *Formula* dialog box (Figure 7-6).
3. In the *Formula* area, delete the existing formula and type =.
4. Click the **Paste function** drop-down list and select the function you want to use.
   - You can also type the function after the equals sign using the proper syntax.
5. Type the range in the parentheses.
   - Use a colon (:) between cell references to create a range.
   - Type "*above*" or "*left*" to use the cells above or to the left of the range.
6. Click the **Number format** drop-down list to select the format for the output of the formula.
7. Click **OK** to close the dialog box and insert the formula.

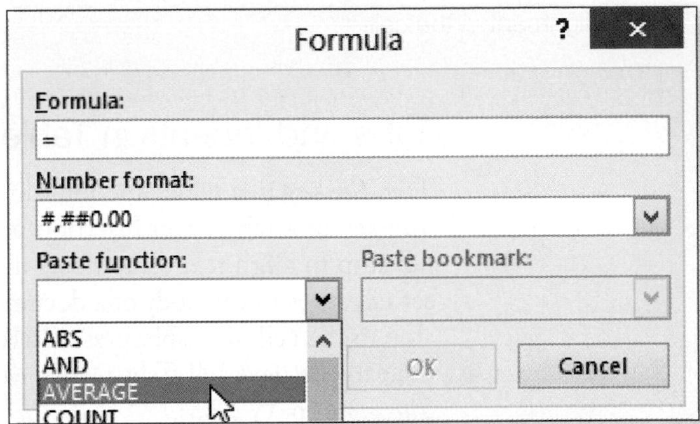

7-6 Insert *AVERAGE* function

Edit a Formula

You might need to edit a formula to change the formula or the number format. There are two ways to edit a formula.

- Select the formula and click the **Formula** button [*Table Tools Layout* tab, *Data* group] to open the *Formula* dialog box.
- Right-click the formula, select **Edit Field** from the context menu to open the *Field* dialog box, select **=(Formula)** in the *Field names* area, and click the **Formula** button to open the *Formula* dialog box.

Update a Formula

Each time you open a document, all of the Word fields in the document are automatically updated (a formula is a Word field). But when a document is open and you change the values in a table, formulas are not automatically updated; you must update the formulas manually. There are two ways to update formulas.

- Right-click the formula and select **Update Field** from the context menu.
- Select the formula and press **F9**.

Change Text Direction

You can change the direction of text in a cell of the table. For example, you might have a title column on the left side of the table and want to change the direction of the text to vertical.

HOW TO: Change Text Direction

1. Select the cell or cells to change the text direction.
2. Click the **Text Direction** button [*Table Tools Layout* tab, *Alignment* group] (Figure 7-7).
   - The *Text Direction* button cycles through the four text direction options.
   - The text on the *Text Direction* button changes to indicate the direction of the text in the cell.
3. Use the alignment buttons [*Table Tools Layout* tab, *Alignment* group] to adjust text alignment in the cell.

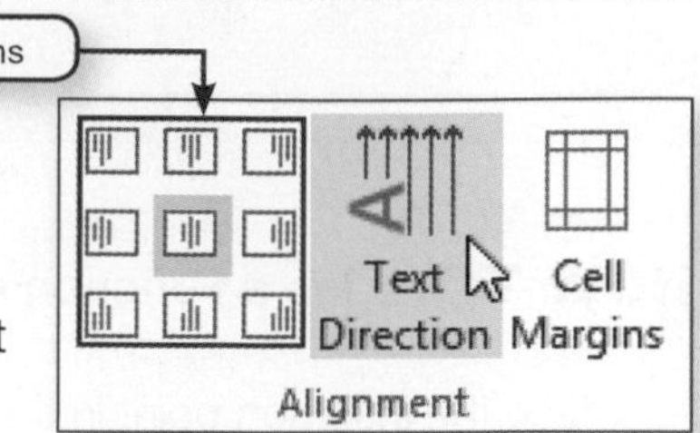

7-7 Change text direction

Tabs and Indents in Tables

The *Tab* key in a table functions differently from a tab outside of a table. When you press the *Tab* key in a table, your insertion point moves to the next cell. But what if you need to set a tab stop to align text or numbers in a cell? You can set tab stops in a table the same way you set tab stops in the body of a document; use the ruler or the *Tabs* dialog box. To move to a tab stop in the cell of a table, press **Ctrl+Tab**, which moves your cursor to the next tab stop rather than to the next cell. Tabs were covered in Chapter 2 in *SLO 2.2: Setting, Using, and Editing Tab Stops* (p. W2-66).

HOW TO: Set and Use Tab Stops in a Table

1. Select the cells in the table where you want to set a tab stop.
2. Click the **Paragraph** launcher [*Page Layout* tab, *Paragraph* group] to open the *Paragraph* dialog box.
   - You can also use the ruler to set tab stops. Select the type of tab stop from the *Tab* selector on the left side of the ruler. Click the ruler to set a tab stop.
3. Click the **Tabs** button to open the *Tabs* dialog box (Figure 7-8).
4. Type the tab stop position, select the alignment, and click **Set**.
5. Click **OK** to close the dialog box.
6. Press **Ctrl+Tab** to move to the tab stop in the cell.

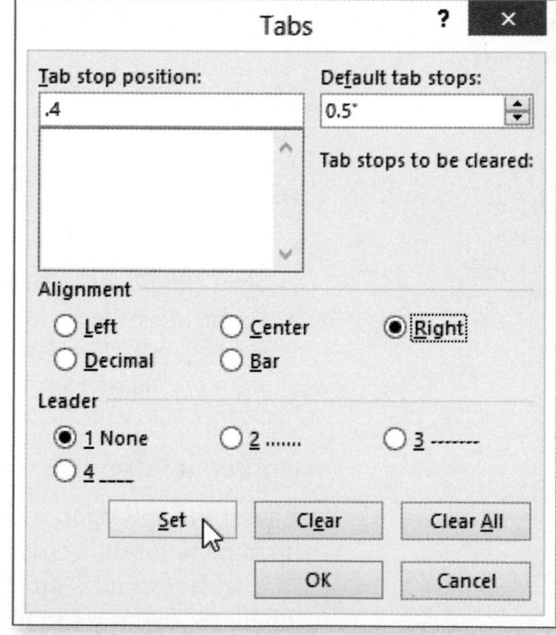

7-8 Set a tab stop in a table

You can use indents in tables to control text alignment and alignment of carryover lines the same way you use indents in the body of a document. Set or modify indents in a table using one of the following methods:

- *Paragraph* group on the *Page Layout* tab
- *Paragraph* dialog box
- *Ruler*

MORE INFO

When setting or modifying tab stops or indents in a table, be sure to select the area of the table you want to change before modifying tab stops or indents.

Bullets and Numbering in Tables

You can use bulleted and numbered lists in tables like you use them in the body of a Word document. The major difference when using lists in tables is the use of the *Tab* key. In lists that are not in a table, you use the *Tab* key to increase the level of the list. For example, in a list, if you press *Tab* before typing the text, the list is indented to the next level (*Shift+Tab* decreases the level), but in a table, pressing *Tab* moves you to the next cell and *Shift+Tab* moves you to the previous cell.

There are two ways to adjust the level of a list in a table:

- Press the **Increase Indent** or **Decrease Indent** button [*Home* tab, *Paragraph* group].
- Click the **Bullets** or **Numbering** button [*Home* tab, *Paragraph* group], select **Change List Level**, and select the level.

> **ANOTHER WAY**
>
> Options to change the list level are available from the context menu when you right-click the text in a list.

PAUSE & PRACTICE: WORD 7-1

For this Pause & Practice project, you modify a document from the American River Cycling Club about maximum and target heart rates. You convert text to a table, sort information in a table, change text direction, and create formulas.

File Needed: ***HeartRate-07.docx***
Completed Project File Name: ***[your initials] PP W7-1.docx***

---

1. Open the ***HeartRate-07*** document from your student data files.
2. Save the document as ***[your initials] PP W7-1***.
3. Convert text to a table.
   a. Select all of the text aligned with tabs beginning with the "Age" column heading and ending with "120–170" in the third column.
   b. Click the **Table** button [*Insert* tab, *Tables* group] and select **Convert Text to Table** to open the *Convert Text to Table* dialog box (Figure 7-9).
   c. In the *Table size* area, the number of columns should be **3**.
   d. Click the **AutoFit to contents** radio button in the *AutoFit behavior* area.
   e. The *Tabs* radio button in the *Separate text at* section should be selected. If it is not, select it.
   f. Click **OK** to close the dialog box and convert the text to a table.

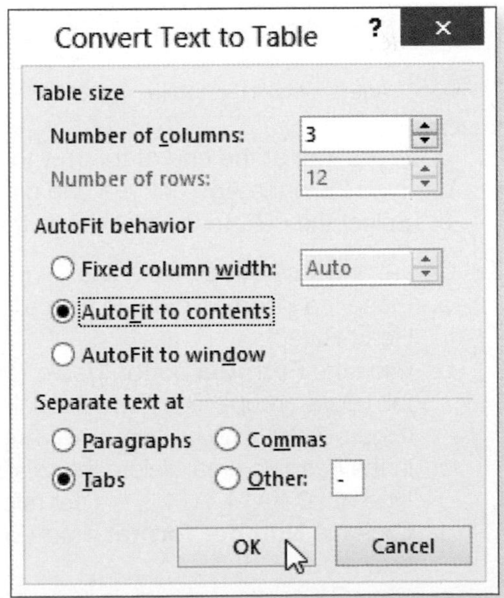

7-9 Convert selected text to a table

4. Sort the table in ascending order by age.
   a. With the table selected, click the **Sort** button [*Table Tools Layout* tab, *Data* group]. The *Sort* dialog box opens (Figure 7-10).
   b. Select the **Header row** radio button in the *My list has* area.
   c. Click the **Sort by** drop-down list and select **Age**.
   d. In the *Type* area, select **Number**.
   e. In the *Using* area, select **Paragraphs**.
   f. Click the **Ascending** radio button.
   g. Click **OK** to close the dialog box and sort the table.

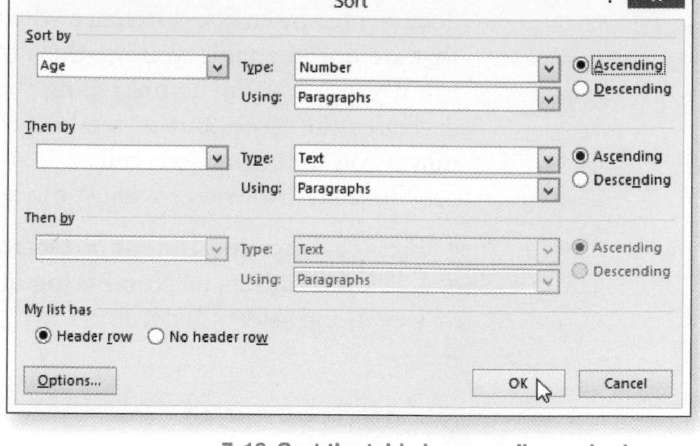

7-10 Sort the table in ascending order by age

5. Add a column, merge cells, add text, and change text direction.
   a. Place the insertion point in the first column of the table.
   b. Click the **Insert Left** button [*Table Tools Layout* tab, *Rows & Columns* group] to insert a column to the left of the first column.
   c. With the first column selected, click the **Merge Cells** button [*Table Tools Layout* tab, *Merge* group] to merge all the cells in the first column.
   d. Type Max and Target, press **Enter**, and type Heart Rates in the first column.
   e. Click the **Text Direction** button [*Table Tools Layout* tab, *Alignment* group] two times to change the text to vertical from the bottom (Figure 7-11).
   f. Click the **Align Center** button [*Table Tools Layout* tab, *Alignment* group] to align the text vertically and horizontally in the cell.
   g. Change the font size of the text in the first column to **20 pt.** and the format to **small caps**.

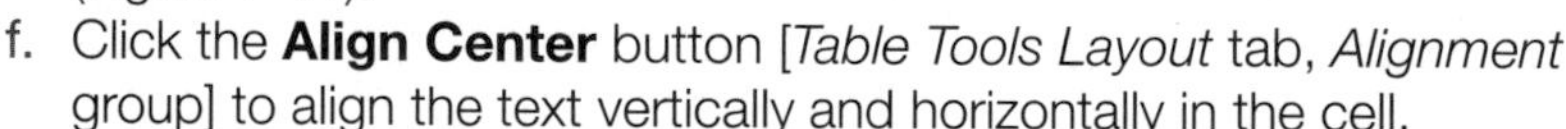

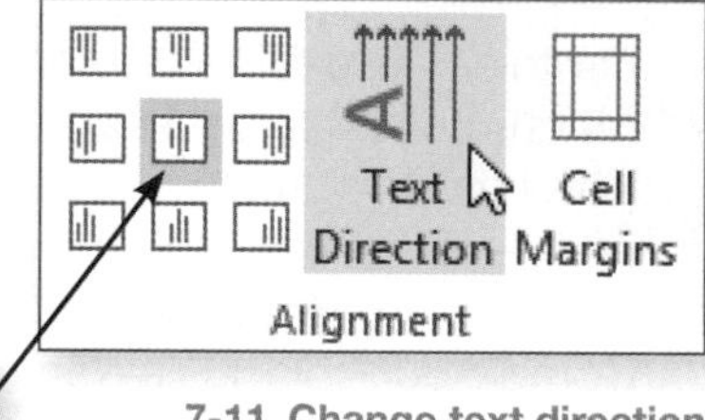

7-11 Change text direction

6. Add rows to the table and insert text.
   a. Place the insertion point in the last cell of the last row and press **Tab** to insert a new row.
   b. In the new row, type the following information:

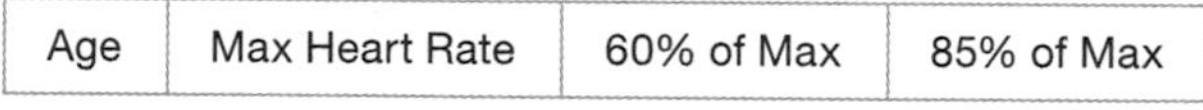

Age	Max Heart Rate	60% of Max	85% of Max

   c. Press **Tab** at the end of the row to insert a new row.
   d. Type 28 in the *Age* column and press **Tab**.
   e. Select the next to the last row in the table and make the text **bold**.

7. Create and insert three formulas.
   a. Place the insertion point in the cell below "Max Heart Rate."
   b. Click the **Formula** button [*Table Tools Layout* tab, *Data* group]. The *Formula* dialog box opens (Figure 7-12).
   c. In the *Formula* area, delete the existing formula and type =220 - A14. A14 is the cell reference for age.
   d. Click the **Number format** drop-down list and select **0**.
   e. Click **OK** to close the dialog box and insert the formula.

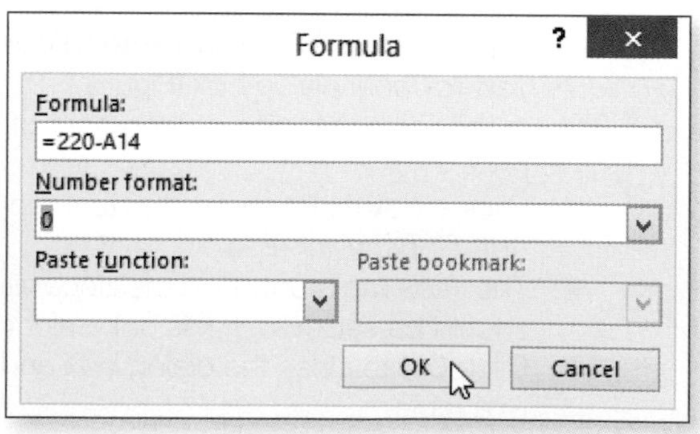

7-12 Insert a formula

f. Place the insertion point in the cell below "60% of Max" and create the following formula: =B14*60%. Use **0** as the number format.

g. Place the insertion point in the cell below "85% of Max" and create the following formula.: =B14*85%. Use **0** as the number format.

8. Edit text and update formulas.
   a. Change the age in the first cell in the last row to 33.
   b. Select the formula in the last row below "Max Heart Rate" and press **F9** to update the formula.
   c. Right-click the formula below "60% of Max" and select **Update Field** from the context menu to update the formula.
   d. Update the formula below the "85% of Max" heading using one of the update methods.

9. Add bullets to selected text and adjust indents.
   a. Select the numbers in the column below the "Predicted Max Heart Rate" column heading. Don't include the text in the last two rows.
   b. Apply a **check mark** bullet (Wingdings, character code 252).
   c. On the *Page Layout* tab [*Paragraph* group], change the left indent to **0"**.
   d. Use the **Format Painter** to apply this bullet format to the value below "Max Heart Rate" in the last row of the table.

10. Save and close the document (Figure 7-13).

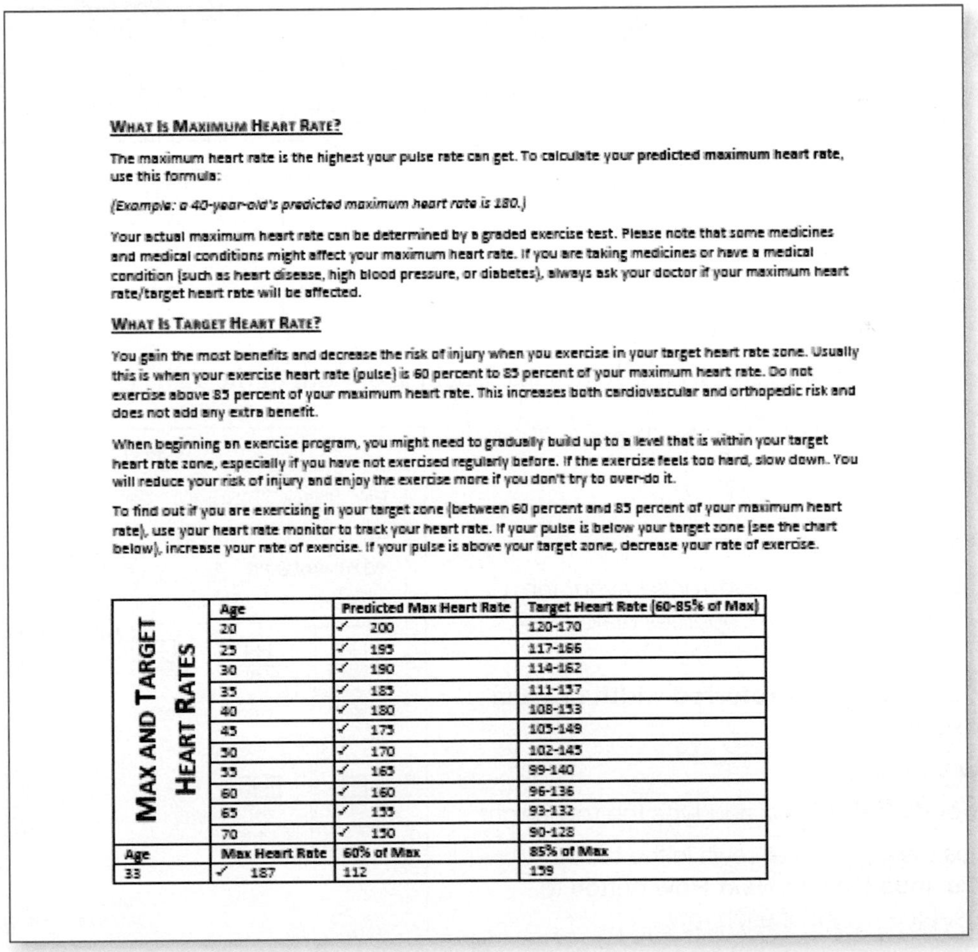

WHAT IS MAXIMUM HEART RATE?

The maximum heart rate is the highest your pulse rate can get. To calculate your **predicted maximum heart rate**, use this formula:

(Example: a 40-year-old's predicted maximum heart rate is 180.)

Your actual maximum heart rate can be determined by a graded exercise test. Please note that some medicines and medical conditions might affect your maximum heart rate. If you are taking medicines or have a medical condition (such as heart disease, high blood pressure, or diabetes), always ask your doctor if your maximum heart rate/target heart rate will be affected.

WHAT IS TARGET HEART RATE?

You gain the most benefits and decrease the risk of injury when you exercise in your target heart rate zone. Usually this is when your exercise heart rate (pulse) is 60 percent to 85 percent of your maximum heart rate. Do not exercise above 85 percent of your maximum heart rate. This increases both cardiovascular and orthopedic risk and does not add any extra benefit.

When beginning an exercise program, you might need to gradually build up to a level that is within your target heart rate zone, especially if you have not exercised regularly before. If the exercise feels too hard, slow down. You will reduce your risk of injury and enjoy the exercise more if you don't try to over-do it.

To find out if you are exercising in your target zone (between 60 percent and 85 percent of your maximum heart rate), use your heart rate monitor to track your heart rate. If your pulse is below your target zone (see the chart below), increase your rate of exercise. If your pulse is above your target zone, decrease your rate of exercise.

MAX AND TARGET HEART RATES	Age	Predicted Max Heart Rate	Target Heart Rate (60-85% of Max)
	20	✓ 200	120-170
	25	✓ 195	117-166
	30	✓ 190	114-162
	35	✓ 185	111-157
	40	✓ 180	108-153
	45	✓ 175	105-149
	50	✓ 170	102-145
	55	✓ 165	99-140
	60	✓ 160	96-136
	65	✓ 155	93-132
	70	✓ 150	90-128
Age	Max Heart Rate	60% of Max	85% of Max
33	✓ 187	112	159

7-13 PP W7-1 completed

Customizing Table Layout

SLO 7.2

After you customize the content of a table, you can customize the layout. For example, you might need to adjust the size of the table, columns, or rows. You can also modify how the table is aligned on the page and how text is aligned within the cells. Cell margins and spacing provide space around the text in cells. Tables can be split into multiple tables or you can create nested tables, which are tables within tables.

Table and Cell Size

You can modify the size of a table manually or you can use the *Table Properties* dialog box.

HOW TO: Manually Resize a Table

1. Select the entire table using one of the following methods:
   - Click the **table selector** in the upper left corner of the table (Figure 7-14).
   - Click the **Select** button [*Table Tools Layout* tab, *Table* group] and select **Table**.
2. Click and drag the **table sizing handle** in the bottom right corner of the table.
   - Your pointer becomes a diagonal sizing pointer.
   - You can increase or decrease the height and width of the table using the table sizing handle.

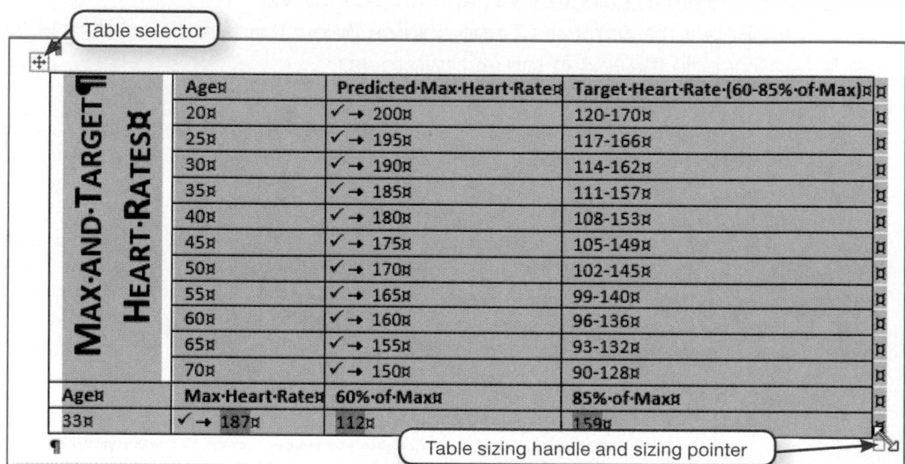

MAX·AND·TARGET HEART·RATES	Age	Predicted·Max·Heart·Rate	Target·Heart·Rate·(60-85%·of·Max)
	20	✓→ 200	120-170
	25	✓→ 195	117-166
	30	✓→ 190	114-162
	35	✓→ 185	111-157
	40	✓→ 180	108-153
	45	✓→ 175	105-149
	50	✓→ 170	102-145
	55	✓→ 165	99-140
	60	✓→ 160	96-136
	65	✓→ 155	93-132
	70	✓→ 150	90-128
Age	Max·Heart·Rate	60%·of·Max	85%·of·Max
33	✓→ 187	112	159

7-14 Resize a table using the table sizing handle

You can also set a specific table height and width in the *Table Properties* dialog box.

HOW TO: Resize a Table Using the Table Properties Dialog Box

1. Select the table.
2. Click the **Properties** button [*Table Tools Layout* tab, *Table* group] to open the *Table Properties* dialog box (Figure 7-15).
3. On the *Table* tab, check the **Preferred width** box and type the width of the table.
4. Click the **Row** tab.
5. Check the **Specify height** box and type the row height.
   - This changes the height of all rows in the table.
   - Click the **Previous Row** or **Next Row** button to individually set the height of each row.
6. Click **OK** to close the *Table Properties* dialog box.

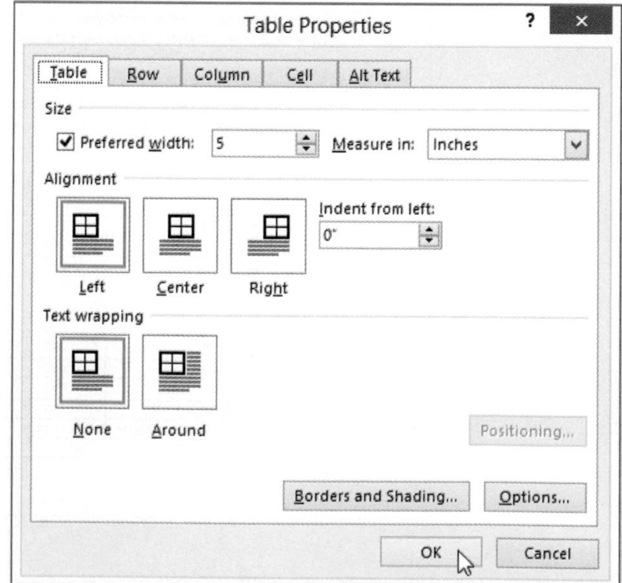

7-15 Change the width of a table

In addition to resizing the entire table, you can resize rows and columns individually using the following methods:

- Select the row or column to resize and change the size in the *Height* or *Width* area [*Table Tools Layout* tab, *Cell Size* group] (Figure 7-16).
- Use the *Row* and *Column* tabs in the *Table Properties* dialog box to change the height or width of specific columns and rows.
- Click and drag the right cell border to resize a column.
- Click and drag the bottom cell border to resize a row.

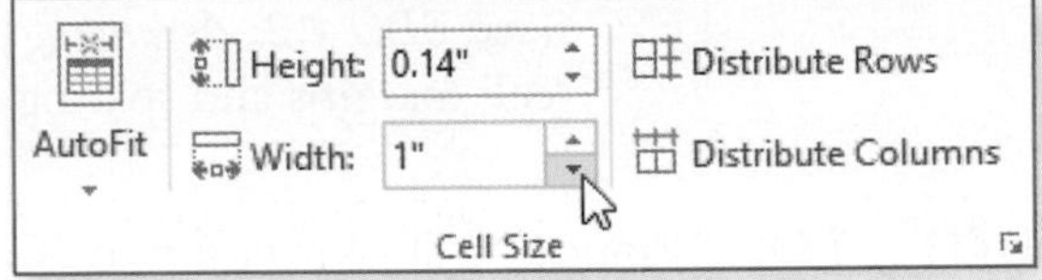

7-16 Resize columns and rows

Table Alignment and Position

You can horizontally align a table the same way you align text in a document. Select the table and select from the alignment buttons in the *Paragraph* group on the *Home* tab. You can also change the horizontal alignment of a table in the *Table Properties* dialog box on the *Table* tab.

All of the tables you have created so far have been in line with the text, which means the text has been above or below the table. However, there might be times when you want text to wrap around a table. You can position a table anywhere in a document and have text wrap around it just as you have done with graphics (see *SLO 4.5: Working with Graphics*).

HOW TO: Position a Table

1. Select the table or place the insertion point in the table.
2. Click the **Properties** button [*Table Tools Layout* tab, *Table* group] to open the *Table Properties* dialog box (Figure 7-17).
3. On the *Table* tab, click the **Around** button in the *Text wrapping* area.
   - The *Positioning* button becomes active when *Around* is selected, but it is not active if *None* is selected.
4. Click the **Positioning** button. The *Table Positioning* dialog box opens (Figure 7-18).
5. Set the **Horizontal** and **Vertical** position.
6. Set the **Distance from surrounding** text.
7. Click **OK** to close the *Table Positioning* dialog box.
8. Click **OK** to close the *Table Properties* dialog box.

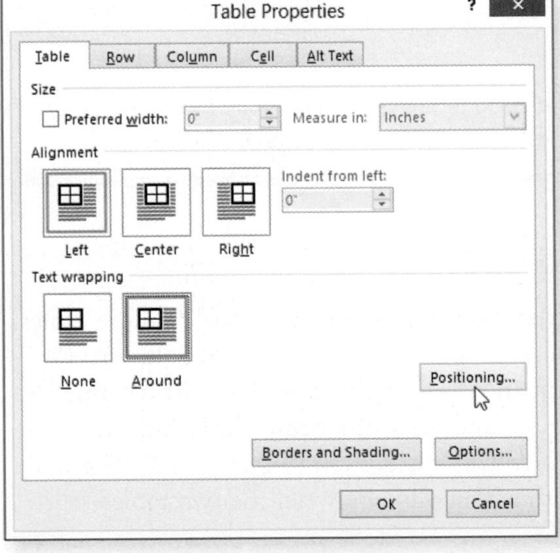

7-17 Set table to wrap around text

Table Positioning
Horizontal
Position: Left
Relative to: Column
Vertical
Position: 0"
Relative to: Paragraph
Distance from surrounding text
Top: 0"
Left: 0.13"
Bottom: 0"
Right: 0.13"
Options
Move with text
Allow overlap
OK
Cancel

7-18 *Table Positioning* dialog box

Cell Margins and Spacing

In Chapter 4 you learned about cell margins, which are the margins in a cell around the text (see *SLO 4.2: Arranging Texts in Tables*). ***Cell spacing*** refers to the space between cells. Both cell margins and spacing can be changed in the *Table Options* dialog box.

HOW TO: Change Cell Margins and Spacing

1. Select the table or place the insertion point in the table.
2. Click the **Cell Margins** button [*Table Tools Layout* tab, *Alignment* group] to open the *Table Options* dialog box (Figure 7-19).
3. In the *Default cell margins* area, set the **Top**, **Bottom**, **Left**, and **Right** cell margins.
4. Check the **Allow spacing between cells** box and set the amount of space between cells.
5. Check the **Automatically resize to fit contents** box so that the table is resized based on the new cell margins and spacing.
6. Click **OK** to close the dialog box and apply the settings.

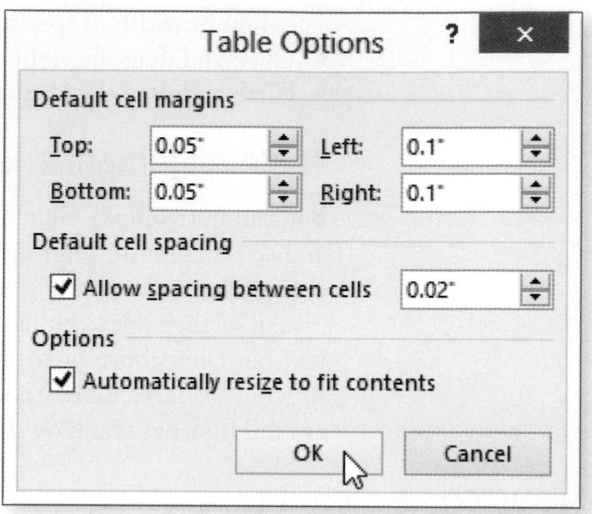

7-19 *Table Options* dialog box

> **ANOTHER WAY**
>
> Click the **Options** button on the *Table* tab in the *Table Properties* dialog box to open the *Table Options* dialog box where you can change cell margins and spacing.

Split a Table and Cells

The ***split table*** feature lets you split a table into one or more tables. When you split a table, it is split between rows, not columns. Position the insertion point in or select the row that will become the first row in the new table and click the **Split Table** button in the *Merge* group on the *Table Tools Layout* tab (Figure 7-20). The table becomes two tables with a blank line between the two tables.

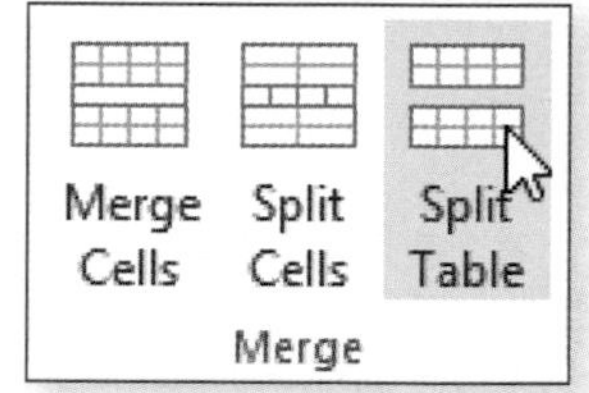

7-20 *Split Table* button

> **MORE INFO**
>
> When you split a table that has formulas with one or more cell references, formula cell reference might no longer be valid. You might need to edit those formulas and change the cell references.

You can also split cells into multiple rows or columns. You can do this on a merged cell, an individual cell that has not been merged, or a range of cells in a table.

HOW TO: Split a Cell

1. Select the cell or cells to be split.
2. Click the **Split Cells** button [*Table Tools Layout* tab, *Merge* group] to open the *Split Cells* dialog box (Figure 7-21).
3. Set the number of columns and rows.
   - If you are splitting a range of cells, the *Merge cells before split* check box is activated. Select this check box if you want to merge the cells before splitting the cells.
4. Click **OK** to close the dialog box and split the cells.

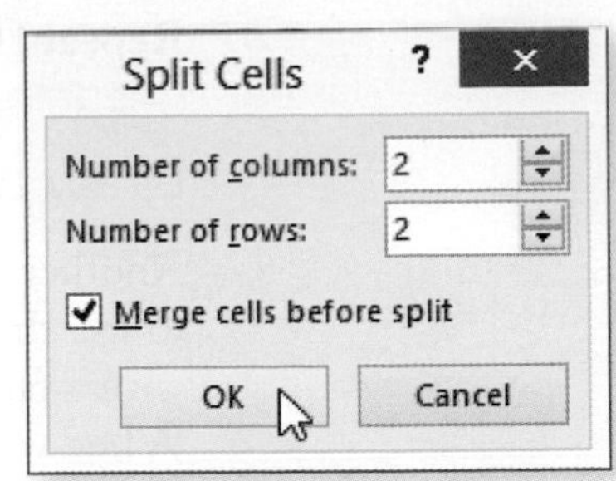

7-21 *Split Cells* dialog box

Nested Tables

Nested tables are tables within tables. You can insert a table into a cell of another table the same way you insert a table into a document. In nested tables, the main table is called the ***parent table*** and the table within the parent table is the ***child table***. You can have more than one child table in a parent table. Figure 7-22 shows an example of nested tables. The parent table has one column and two rows with only the gridlines visible. There are two child tables in the parent table.

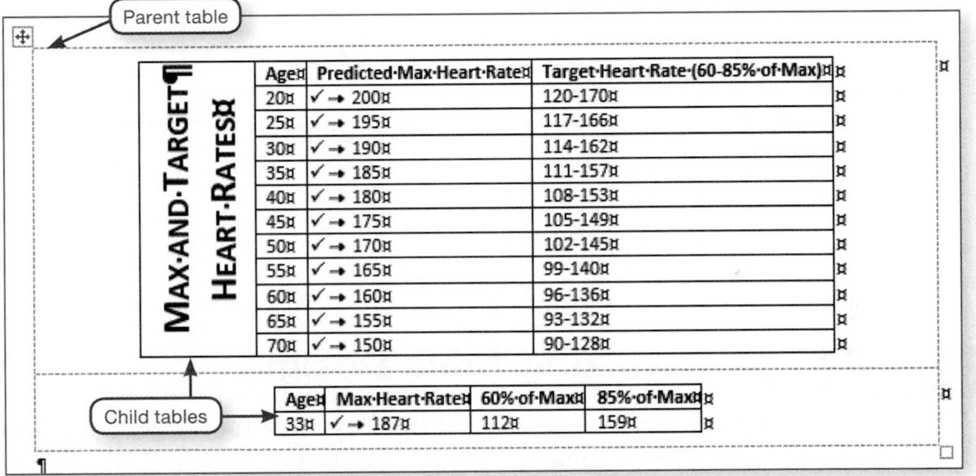

MAX·AND·TARGET HEART·RATES	Age	Predicted·Max·Heart·Rate	Target·Heart·Rate·(60-85%·of·Max)
	20	✓→ 200	120-170
	25	✓→ 195	117-166
	30	✓→ 190	114-162
	35	✓→ 185	111-157
	40	✓→ 180	108-153
	45	✓→ 175	105-149
	50	✓→ 170	102-145
	55	✓→ 165	99-140
	60	✓→ 160	96-136
	65	✓→ 155	93-132
	70	✓→ 150	90-128

Age	Max·Heart·Rate	60%·of·Max	85%·of·Max
33	✓→ 187	112	159

7-22 Nested tables

Repeat Header Rows

If you have a table that spans multiple pages, it is a good idea to have the column headings appear at the top of the second and continuing pages to improve the readability of the table. The ***repeat header rows*** feature automatically displays the header row or rows at the beginning of each page. You can choose to have one or more rows repeat as the header row or rows.

The advantage of using this feature rather than inserting a heading row at the top of each page is that the repeated header row is automatically inserted at the top of each page regardless of pagination. If information is inserted into or deleted from the table and page breaks change, the header row is repeated at the top of each page.

To use the feature, select the row or rows of the table to repeat at the top of each page and click the **Repeat Header Rows** button in the *Data* group on the *Table Tools Layout* tab

(Figure 7-23). You can turn off this feature by selecting the header row or rows and clicking the **Repeat Header Rows** button.

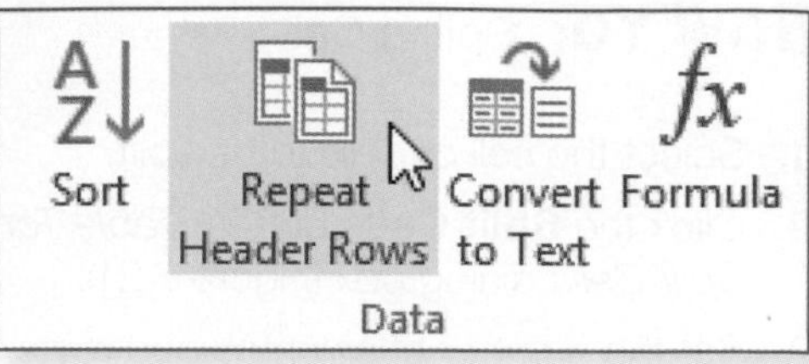

7-23 Repeat Header Rows button

Draw a Table

Another way to insert a table into a document is to use the ***draw table*** feature. Word provides you with a table drawing tool to create a table or add cells, rows, or columns to an existing table. When you draw a table, your pointer becomes a ***pen***. Using the pen, you can draw a table and split cells into rows and columns. You can also use the ***eraser*** to erase cells, rows, or columns.

HOW TO: Draw a Table

1. Click the **Table** button [*Insert* tab, *Tables* group] and select **Draw Table**. Your pointer becomes a pen.
2. Click and drag to draw the outside border of the table.
3. Draw vertical lines to create columns and horizontal lines to create rows (Figure 7-24).
   - Draw rows and columns outside the border of the table to increase the size of the table.
   - If you draw diagonally within a table, a new table is created inside the existing table.
4. Click the **Draw Table** button [*Table Tools Layout* tab, *Draw* group] to turn off the draw table feature.
5. Click the **Eraser** button [*Table Tools Layout* tab, *Draw* group] and your pointer becomes an eraser.
   - Drag the eraser to remove row or column borders.
   - Click the **Eraser** button again to turn it off.

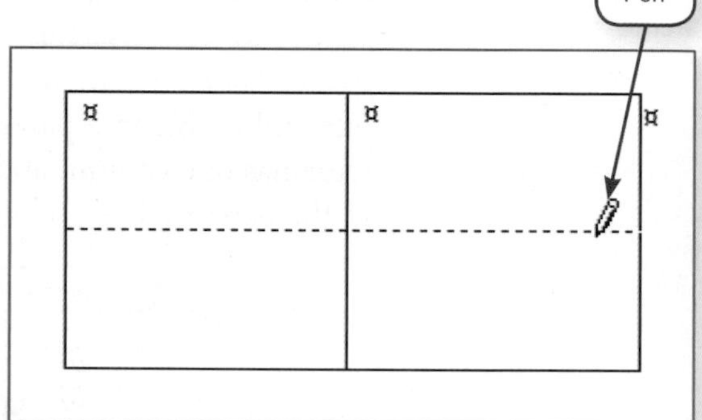

7-24 Create rows and columns using the pen

SLO 7.3

Customizing Table Design

After customizing the content and layout of your table, you can customize the table design to make it more attractive. You can use shading, borders, and table styles to improve the look and readability of your table. A ***table style*** is a collection of borders, shading, and fonts you apply to a table. You can apply table styles, modify table styles, and create your own table styles. You can also insert tables from the *Tables* building blocks gallery or add your own table to this gallery.

Custom Borders

Word 2013 has new border features to customize borders in your table. The ***Border Painter*** lets you draw borders on your table rather than selecting borders from the *Borders* drop-down list. The *Border Painter* is used similarly to how you draw a table, except it does not create new rows and columns.

HOW TO: Use the Border Painter

1. Place your insertion point somewhere in the table to activate the context-sensitive *Table Tools* tabs.
2. Select the **Table Tools Design** tab.

3. Click the **Border Painter** button [*Borders* group] (Figure 7-25).
   - When you click the *Border Painter* button, your pointer becomes a pen you use to draw borders.

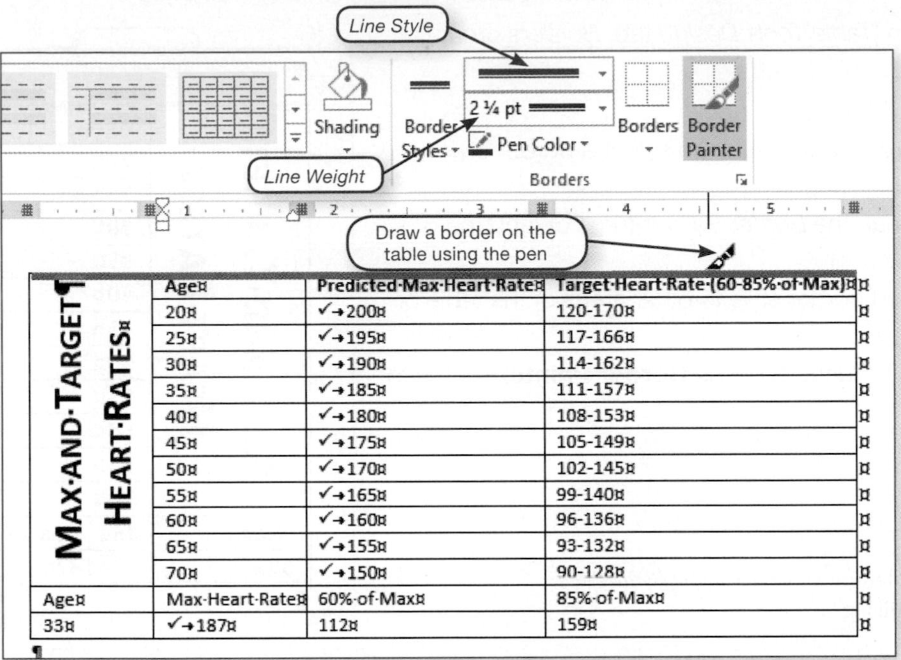

	Age	Predicted·Max·Heart·Rate	Target·Heart·Rate·(60-85%·of·Max)
	20	✓→200	120-170
	25	✓→195	117-166
	30	✓→190	114-162
	35	✓→185	111-157
	40	✓→180	108-153
	45	✓→175	105-149
	50	✓→170	102-145
	55	✓→165	99-140
	60	✓→160	96-136
	65	✓→155	93-132
	70	✓→150	90-128
Age	Max·Heart·Rate	60%·of·Max	85%·of·Max
33	✓→187	112	159

7-25 Draw a border using the *Border Painter*

4. Click the **Line Style** drop-down list and select a border line style.
5. Click the **Line Weight** drop-down list and select a border line weight.
6. Click the **Pen Color** drop-down list and select border color.
7. Place the pen on a border, press and hold the left mouse button, and drag the pen to draw a border.
8. When you are finished drawing borders, click the **Border Painter** button to turn off this feature.

The ***Border Styles*** gallery provides you with a variety of built-in border styles and colors (Figure 7-26). When you select a border style from the drop-down list, the *Border Painter* turns on so you can draw borders on your table. You can customize the border style using the *Line Style, Line Width,* and *Pen Color* drop-down lists.

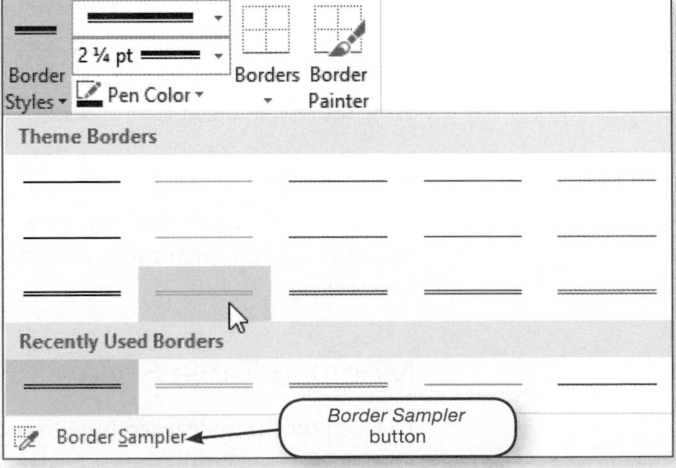

7-26 ***Border Styles*** gallery

Previously you used the *Format Painter* to copy text formatting and apply it to other text. The ***Border Sampler*** works like the *Format Painter*. The ***Border Sampler*** lets you select a border style from a table and draw it on other areas of the table or on a different table.

HOW TO: Use the Border Sampler

1. Place your insertion point somewhere in the table to activate the context-sensitive *Table Tools* tabs.
2. Click the **Border Styles** button [*Table Tools Design* tab, *Borders* group] and select **Border Sampler**.
   - Your pointer becomes an eyedropper.
3. Click the **eyedropper** on a border of your table to select a border style (Figure 7-27).
   - After you select a border format, the *Border Painter* turns on and the eyedropper becomes a pen.
4. Use the pen to draw the selected border style to other areas of the table or a different table.
5. When you are finished drawing borders, click the **Border Painter** button to turn off this feature.

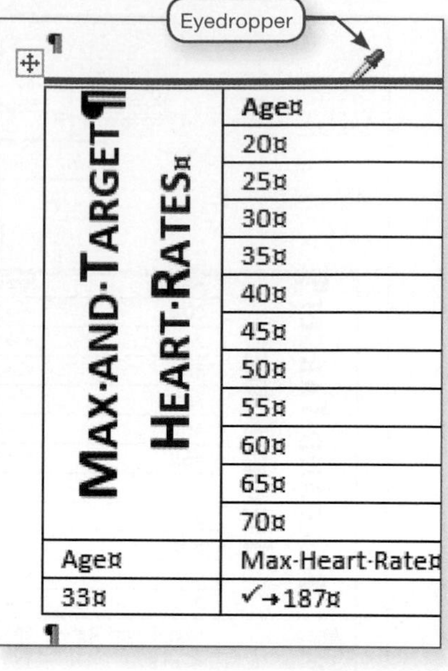

7-27 Use the eyedropper to select a border style

> **MORE INFO**
>
> The **Borders** launcher opens the *Borders and Shading* dialog box.

Table Styles

Table styles are an excellent way to enhance the appearance of your tables with borders, shading, and font formatting. The ***Table Styles gallery*** on the *Table Tools Design* tab displays the available table styles. To apply a table style to a selected table, click the **More** button to display the *Table Styles* gallery and select a style (Figure 7-28).

The ***Table Styles Options*** group offers options for special formatting in specific areas of your table, such as a first column, a header row, or banded rows. After you have applied a style and selected table style options, you can still further customize your table with borders, shading, font formatting, and paragraph formatting.

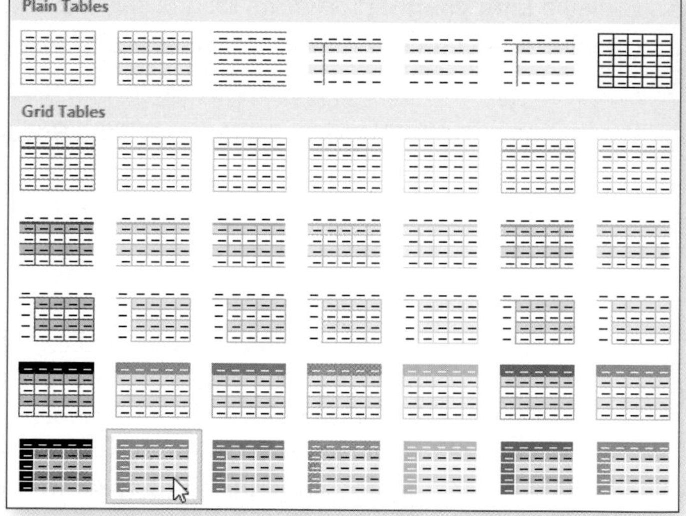

7-28 *Table Styles* gallery

Modify a Table Style

In Chapter 6, you learned how to modify and create text styles (see *SLO 6.1: Creating and Using Custom Styles*). Similarly, you can also modify and create table styles. You can modify a table style after you have applied it to a table or you can modify a table style that has not yet been applied to a table. When you modify a table style, the changes are applied to the tables that already have that style applied.

HOW TO: Modify a Table Style

1. Select your table and apply a table style from the *Table Styles* gallery [*Table Tools Design* tab, *Table Styles* group].
2. Click the **More** button in the *Table Styles* gallery and select **Modify Table Style**. The *Modify Style* dialog box opens (Figure 7-29).
   - You can also right-click a style and select **Modify Table Style**.

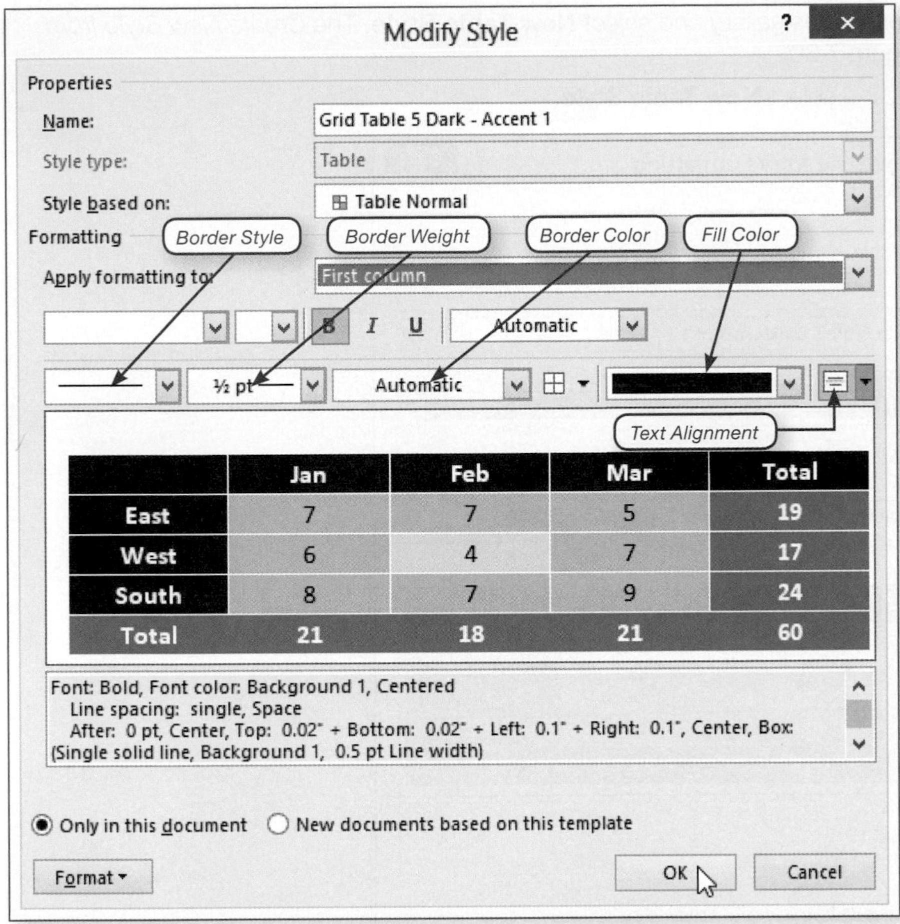

7-29 ***Modify Style* dialog box**

3. In the *Name* area, type a name for the style if you want to rename it.
4. From the *Apply formatting to* drop-down list, select an area of the table to modify formatting.
   - You can apply changes to the *Whole table* or specific parts of the table, such as *Header row* or *First column*.
   - Use the *Border Style*, *Border Weight*, *Border Color*, *Fill Color*, and *Text Alignment* drop-down lists to modify the selected part of the table.
   - The *Preview* area displays the changes you make to the table style.
5. Click the **Format** button for more formatting options.
   - You can open the following dialog boxes and make changes to the table style: *Table Properties*, *Borders and Shading*, *Banding*, *Font*, *Paragraph*, *Tabs*, and *Text Effects*.
   - Click **OK** to close any dialog box you open and return to the *Modify Style* dialog box.
6. Click **OK** to close the *Modify Style* dialog box and apply the changes to the table style.

Create a New Table Style

Creating a new table style is similar to creating a text style. Most of the table styles are based on the *Table Normal* style. When you create a new style, you can base it on any of the existing table styles and then make changes as desired.

HOW TO: Create a New Table Style

1. Click the **More** button in the *Table Styles* gallery and select **New Table Style**. The *Create New Style from Formatting* dialog box opens (Figure 7-30).
   - You can also right-click a style and select **New Table Style**.

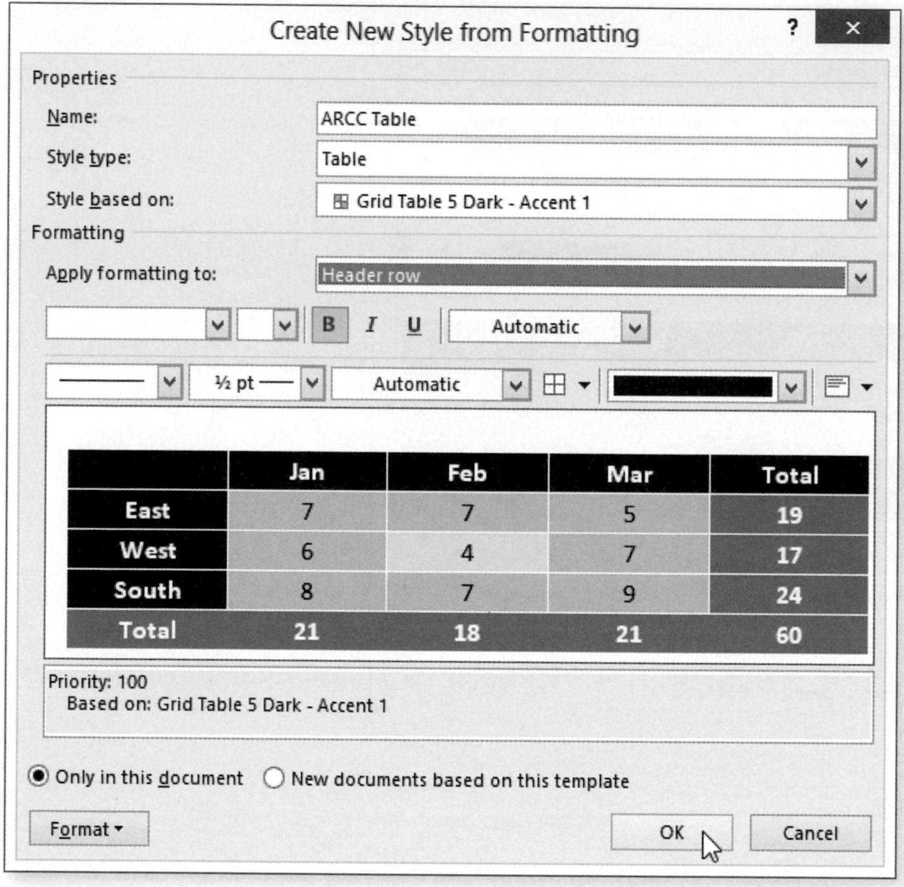

7-30 Create new table style

2. In the *Name* area, type a name for the style.
3. The *Style type* should be **Table**.
4. Click the **Style based on** drop-down list and select the table style on which to base the new style.
5. From the *Apply formatting to* drop-down list, select an area of the table to modify formatting.
   - You can apply changes to the *Whole table* or specific parts of the table, such as *Header row* or *First column*.
   - Use the *Border Style*, *Border Weight*, *Border Color*, *Fill Color*, and *Text Alignment* drop-down lists to modify the selected part of the table.
   - The *Preview* area displays the changes you make to the table style.
6. Click the **Format** button for more formatting options.
   - You can open the following dialog boxes and make changes to the table style: *Table Properties*, *Borders and Shading*, *Banding*, *Font*, *Paragraph*, *Tabs*, and *Text Effects*.
   - Click **OK** to close any dialog box you open and return to the *Create New Style from Formatting* dialog box.

7. By default, the *Only in this document* radio button is selected, which means this new style is only available in this document.
   - If you want this style available in other documents, click the **New document based on this template** radio button.
8. Click **OK** to close the *Create New Style from Formatting* dialog box and apply the changes to the table style.
   - The new style is available in the *Table Styles* gallery in the *Custom* section (Figure 7-31).

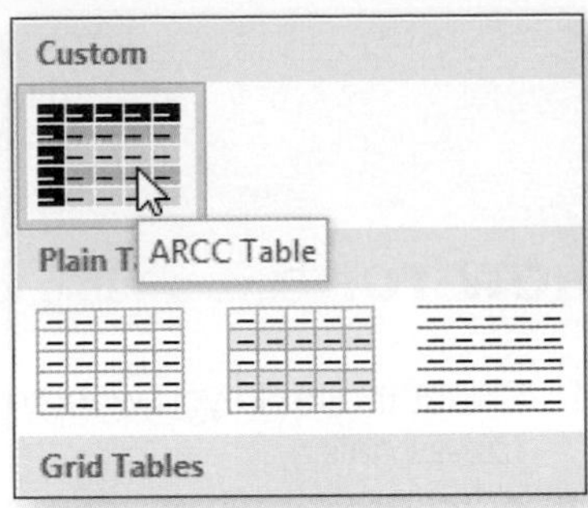

7-31 New custom style in the *Table Styles* gallery

Quick Tables Gallery

In Chapter 6, we covered building blocks (see *SLO 6.3: Understanding and Using Building Blocks*). There are ***Table building blocks*** that you can insert into your documents. *Table* building blocks are called ***Quick Tables***. You can insert a *Quick Table* into your document or you can save an existing table of yours in the *Quick Tables* gallery.

HOW TO: Insert a Table Building Block (Quick Table)

1. Place the insertion point in the document where you want the table inserted.
2. Click the **Table** button [*Insert* tab, *Tables* group].
3. Select **Quick Tables** to display the list of *Quick Tables* (Figure 7-32).

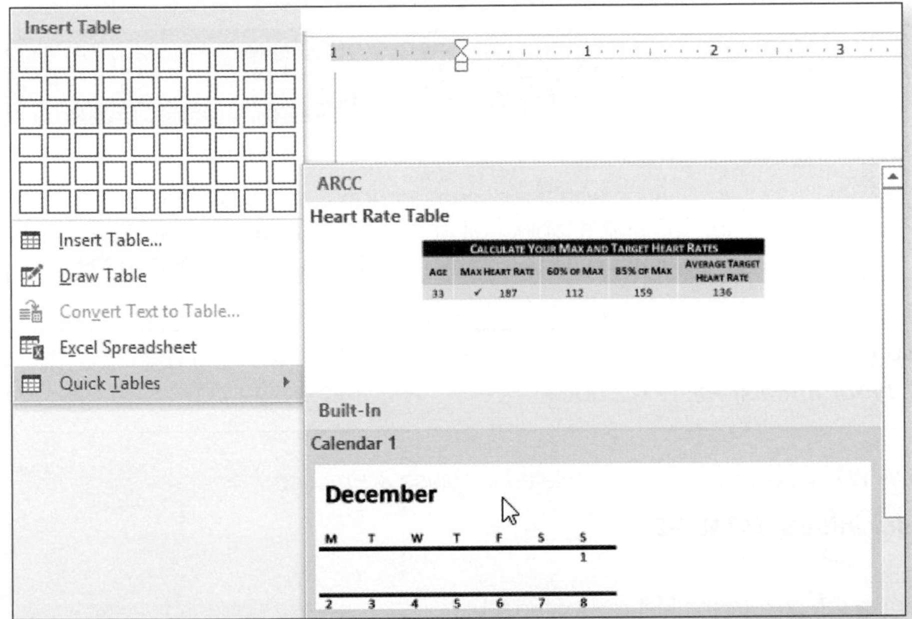

7-32 Insert *Quick Table*

4. Select a *Quick Table* to insert into your document.

ANOTHER WAY

Insert a *Quick Table* using the *Building Blocks Organizer*.

You might want to save a table you use regularly as a *Table* building block, which makes it available in the *Quick Tables* gallery. Saving a table as a building block is similar to saving a *Header, Footer, AutoText,* or *Quick Part* building block.

HOW TO: Save a Table to the Quick Tables Gallery

1. Select the table you want to save to the *Quick Tables* gallery.
2. Click the **Table** button [*Insert* tab, *Tables* group] and select **Quick Tables**.
3. Select **Save Selection to Quick Tables Gallery** at the bottom of the *Quick Tables* gallery. The *Create New Building Block* dialog box opens (Figure 7-33).
4. Fill in or select necessary *Name*, *Gallery*, *Category*, *Description*, and *Save in* information.
5. Click the **Options** drop-down list and select **Insert content in its own paragraph**.
6. Click **OK** to close the dialog box.
   - The new *Table* building block is available in the *Quick Tables* gallery and the *Building Blocks Organizer*.

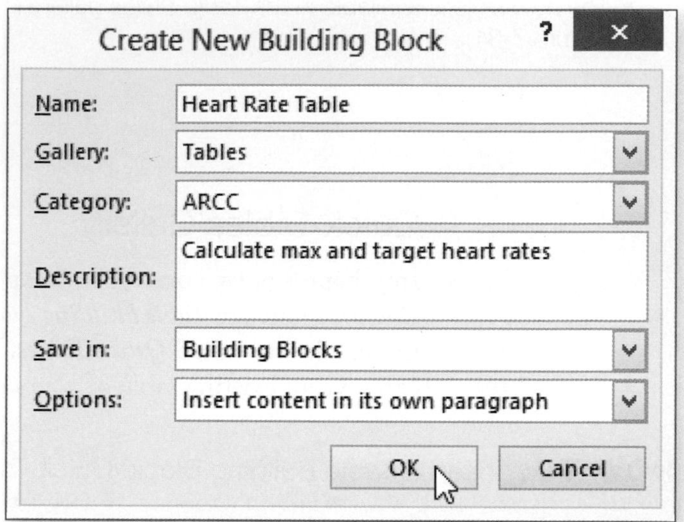

7-33 Save table as a building block in the *Quick Tables* gallery

PAUSE & PRACTICE: WORD 7-2

For this Pause & Practice project, you continue working with the document about maximum and target heart rates for the American River Cycling Club. You split a table, edit and create formulas, apply table styles, modify a table style, create a new table style, apply a custom table style, and save a table in the *Quick Tables* gallery.

File Needed: ***[your initials] PP W7-1.docx***
Completed Project File Name: ***[your initials] PP W7-2.docx***

1. Open the ***[your initials] PP W7-1*** document you completed in *Pause & Practice 7-1*.
2. Save the document as ***[your initials] PP W7-2***.
3. Split the table into two tables.
   a. Place the insertion point in the next to the last row of the table.
   b. Click the **Split Table** button [*Table Tool Layout* tab, *Merge* group]. The last two rows split into a separate table.
4. Modify the new table.
   a. In the new (second) table, add a column to the right of the last column.
   b. In the last cell in the first row, type Average Target, press **Enter**, and type Heart Rate.
   c. Add a row above the first row.

d. Merge the cells in the first row. Turn on **Show/Hide** if it is not on, and if there is a paragraph symbol in the merged row, delete it.
e. In the merged first row, type Calculate Your Max and Target Heart Rates.

5. Edit existing formulas and create a new formula.
   a. Select the maximum heart rate formula (second table, last row, second column) and click the **Formula** button [*Table Tools Layout* tab, *Data* group]. The *Formula* dialog box opens (Figure 7-34).
   b. Change the cell reference to A3 and click **OK** to close the dialog box.
   c. Edit the "60% of Max" and "85% of Max" formulas and type B3 as the cell reference.
   d. In the last cell of the last column, insert a formula to average the target heart rates. Use the following function syntax for your formula and use **0** number format.
   =AVERAGE(C3:D3)

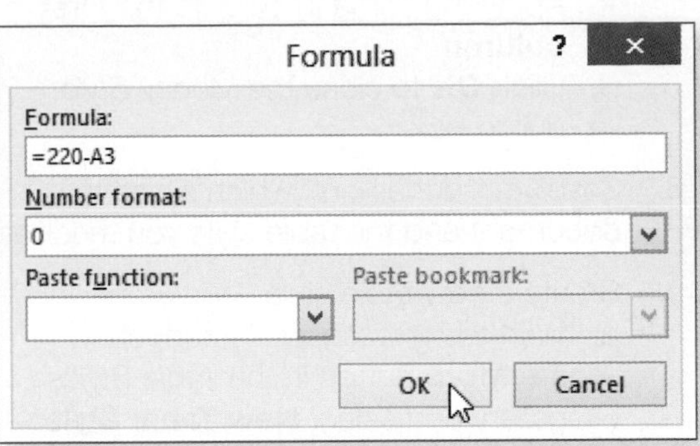

7-34 Edit existing formula

6. Modify the first table and apply a style.
   a. In the first table, place your insertion point before "Heart" (first row, third column), press **Backspace** to delete the space, and press **Enter** to make the column heading a two-line heading.
   b. In the next cell to the right, place the insertion point before "(60-85% of Max)" (first row, fourth column), press **Backspace** to delete the space, and press **Enter** to make the column heading a two-line heading.
   c. Select the first table.
   d. In the *Table Styles Options* group [*Table Tools Design* tab], check the **Header Row**, **Banded Rows**, and **First Column** boxes if they are not already checked. The other options should not be selected.
   e. Click the **More** button in the *Table Styles* gallery and select the **Grid Table 5 Dark - Accent 1** table style (Figure 7-35).

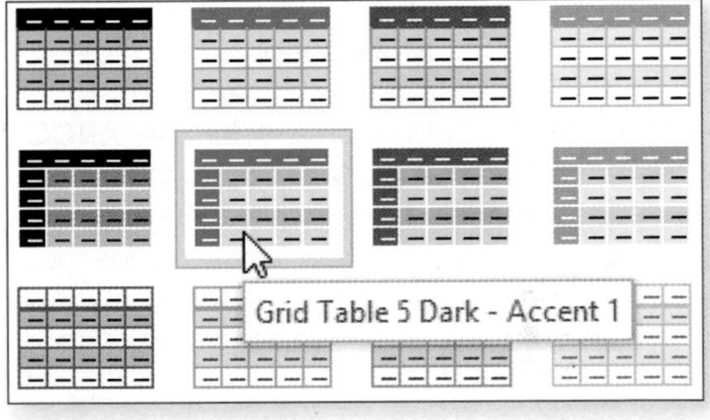

7-35 Apply a table style

7. Modify a table style.
   a. With the first table still selected, click the **More** button in the *Table Styles* gallery and select **Modify Table Style**. The *Modify Style* dialog box opens.
   b. Click the **Format** button and select **Table Properties** to open the *Table Properties* dialog box.
   c. Click the **Options** button to open the *Table Options* dialog box.
   d. Change the *Top* and *Bottom* cell margins to **0.02"** and the *Left* and *Right* cell margins to **0.1"**.
   e. Click **OK** to close the *Table Options* dialog box.
   f. On the *Table* tab in the *Alignment* area, select **Center**.
   g. Click **OK** to close the *Table Properties* dialog box.
   h. Click the **Text Alignment** drop-down list and select **Align Center** (Figure 7-36).
   i. Click the **Apply formatting to** drop-down list and select **Header row**.

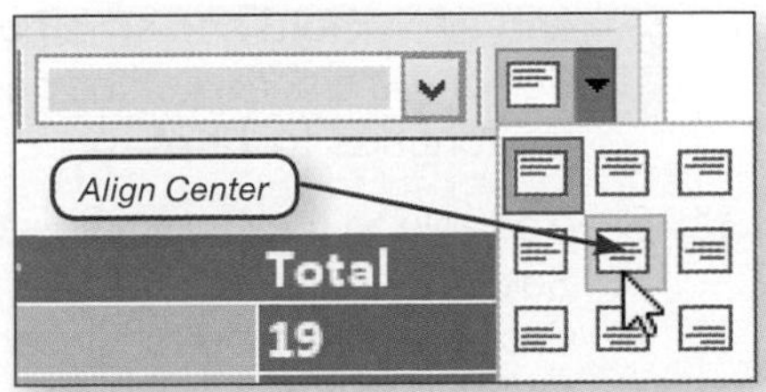

7-36 Change text alignment to *Align Center*

j. Click the **Fill Color** button and select **Dark Blue**, **Text 2**, **Darker 50%** (Figure 7-37).
k. Apply the same fill color to the **First column**.
l. Click **OK** to close the *Modify Style* dialog box.

8. Save your document, which saves the document and the table style you modified.
9. Create a new table style.
   a. With the first table selected, click the **More** button in the *Table Styles* gallery and select **New Table Style**. The *Create New Style from Formatting* dialog box opens (Figure 7-38).
   b. In the *Name* area, type ARCC Table.
   c. Click the **Style based on** drop-down list and select **Grid Table 5 Dark - Accent 1**.
   d. Click **OK** to close the dialog box and create the new table style.
10. Apply custom table style and modify tables.
    a. Select the first table.
    b. Click the **More** button in the *Table Styles* gallery.
    c. In the *Custom* area, select the **ARCC Table** to apply the custom table style to the first table (Figure 7-39).
    d. Select the first row (don't include the first column) of the first table and apply **bold** and **small caps** formatting to the text.
    e. Select the second table.
    f. Deselect the **First Column** check box [*Table Tools Design* tab, *Table Style Options* group]. *Header Row* and *Banded Rows* should be checked.
    g. Apply the **ARCC Table** custom table style.
    h. Select the first and second rows of the second table and apply **bold** and **small caps** formatting to the text.
    i. Select the first row of the second table and change the font size to **12 pt.**
11. Save a table to the *Quick Tables* gallery.
    a. Select the second table.
    b. Click the **Table** button [*Insert* tab, *Tables* group] and select **Quick Tables**.

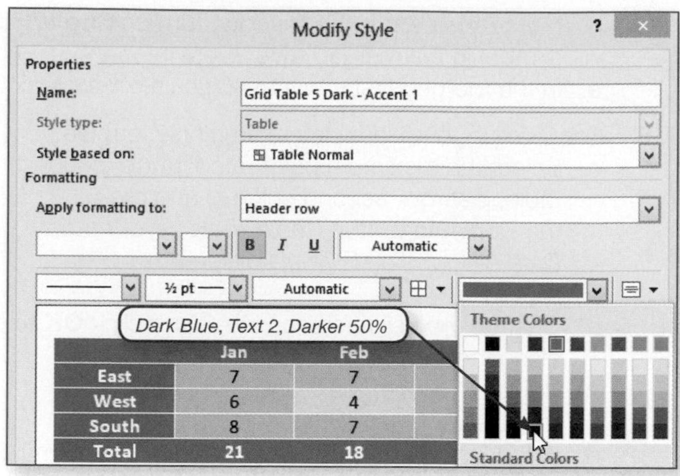

7-37 Change *Fill Color* of the header row

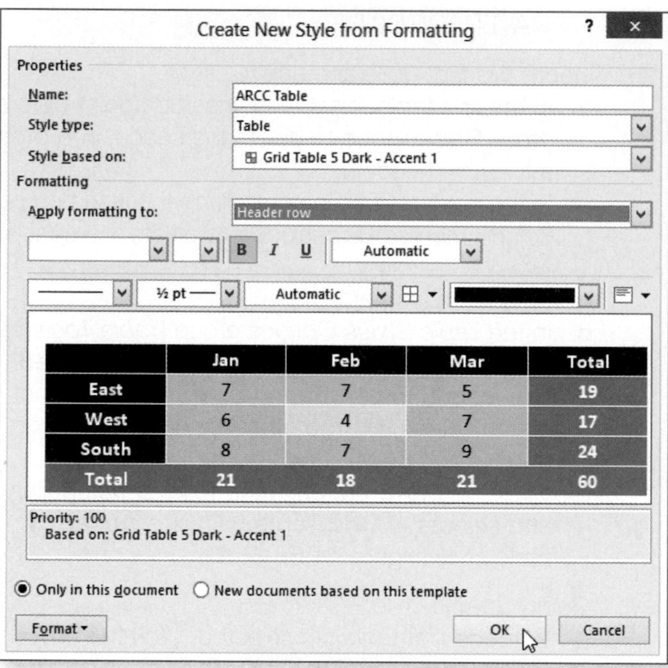

	Jan	Feb	Mar	Total
East	7	7	5	19
West	6	4	7	17
South	8	7	9	24
Total	21	18	21	60

7-38 Create new table style

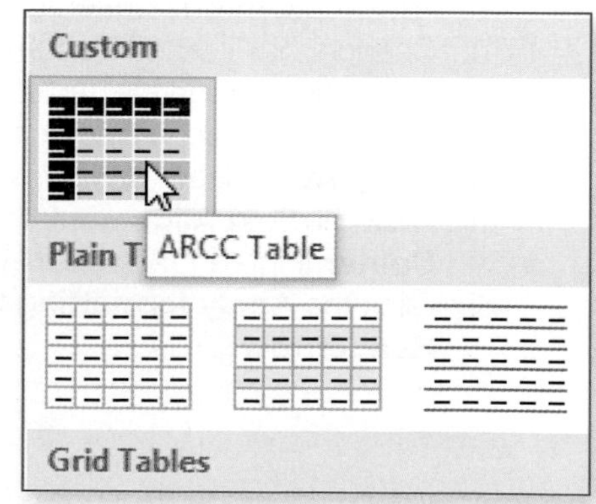

7-39 Apply custom table style

c. Select **Save Selection to Quick Tables Gallery** at the bottom of the *Quick Tables* list. The *Create New Building Block* dialog box opens (Figure 7-40).

d. Enter the following properties for the building block:

   Name: Heart Rate Table

   Gallery: **Tables**

   Category: ARCC (create new category)

   Description: Calculate max and target heart rates

   Save in: **Building Blocks**

   Options: **Insert content in its own paragraph**

e. Click **OK** to close the *Create New Building Block* dialog box.

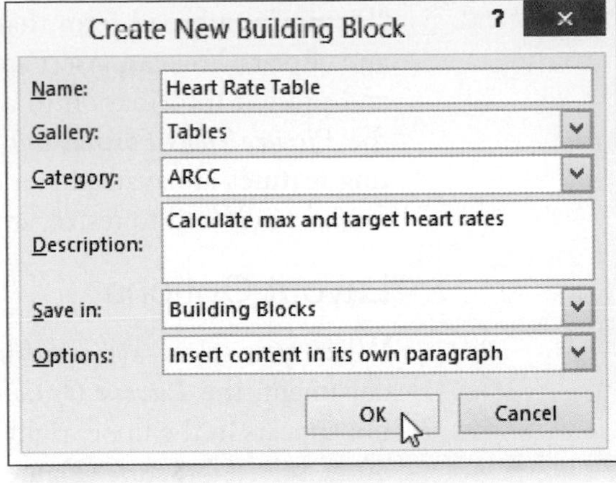

7-40 Create new table building block

12. Save and close the document (Figure 7-41).

What Is Maximum Heart Rate?

The maximum heart rate is the highest your pulse rate can get. To calculate your **predicted maximum heart rate**, use this formula:

(Example: a 40-year-old's predicted maximum heart rate is 180.)

Your actual maximum heart rate can be determined by a graded exercise test. Please note that some medicines and medical conditions might affect your maximum heart rate. If you are taking medicines or have a medical condition (such as heart disease, high blood pressure, or diabetes), always ask your doctor if your maximum heart rate/target heart rate will be affected.

What Is Target Heart Rate?

You gain the most benefits and decrease the risk of injury when you exercise in your target heart rate zone. Usually this is when your exercise heart rate (pulse) is 60 percent to 85 percent of your maximum heart rate. Do not exercise above 85 percent of your maximum heart rate. This increases both cardiovascular and orthopedic risk and does not add any extra benefit.

When beginning an exercise program, you might need to gradually build up to a level that is within your target heart rate zone, especially if you have not exercised regularly before. If the exercise feels too hard, slow down. You will reduce your risk of injury and enjoy the exercise more if you don't try to over-do it.

To find out if you are exercising in your target zone (between 60 percent and 85 percent of your maximum heart rate), use your heart rate monitor to track your heart rate. If your pulse is below your target zone (see the chart below), increase your rate of exercise. If your pulse is above your target zone, decrease your rate of exercise.

Max and Target Heart Rates	Age	Predicted Max Heart Rate	Target Heart Rate (60-85% of Max)
	20	✓ 200	120-170
	25	✓ 195	117-166
	30	✓ 190	114-162
	35	✓ 185	111-157
	40	✓ 180	108-153
	45	✓ 175	105-149
	50	✓ 170	102-145
	55	✓ 165	99-140
	60	✓ 160	96-136
	65	✓ 155	93-132
	70	✓ 150	90-128

Calculate Your Max and Target Heart Rates				
Age	Max Heart Rate	60% of Max	85% of Max	Average Target Heart Rate
33	✓ 187	112	159	136

7-41 PP W7-2 completed

SLO 7.4

Working with Pictures

"Picture" is a broad term that can refer to many types of graphical images including photos and clip art. You can insert and customize pictures in documents to enhance document layout and present information in a graphical format. When you insert a picture into a document, the ***Picture Tools Format tab*** becomes available on the *Ribbon*. Many of the picture formatting features are available on this tab. In this section, you learn some of the advanced graphic features in Word to resize, arrange, and enhance pictures in your documents.

Layout Options

When you select a picture in your document, the ***Layout Options*** button appears in the upper right corner of the selected picture (Figure 7-42). Click the **Layout Options** icon to open the *Layout Options* menu where you can select a text wrapping option. In this menu, you can also select whether the picture moves as text is rearranged (*Move with text*) or is located in a fixed position on the page (*Fix position on page*).

Click the **See more** link to open the *Layout* dialog box where you have *Position, Text Wrapping,* and *Size* tabs to further customize your picture.

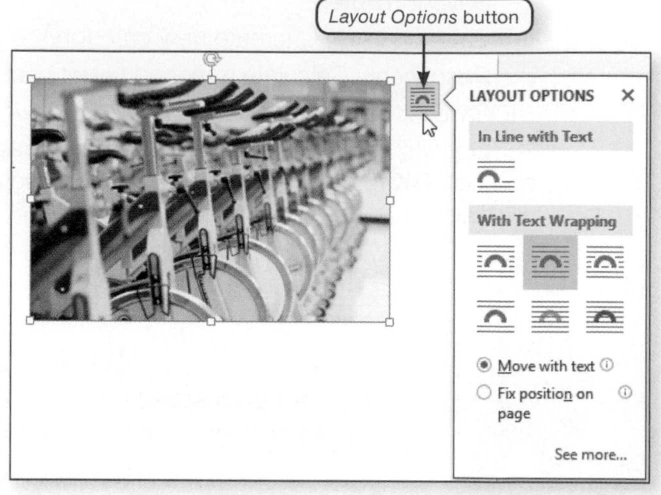

7-42 *Layout Options* menu

> **MORE INFO**
>
> *In Line with Text* is the default option when you insert a picture. To change the default wrapping option, right-click on a wrapping option in the *Layout Options* menu and select **Set as Default.**

Arrange Pictures

You can use arrangement options to control how your picture is arranged in relation to surrounding text or other pictures. For example, you can set how text wraps around the picture or you can set the picture to be placed behind the text or on top of the text. You can also anchor the picture to specific text so the picture stays with the text as the text is moved in the document.

Customize Text Wrapping

The *Wrap Text* button in the *Arrange* group on the *Picture Tools Format* tab provides a drop-down list of text wrapping options (Figure 7-43). Also in the *Arrange* group, you can use the *Bring Forward* and *Send Backward* options to further customize how your picture is arranged with text and other graphics. In the *Layout* dialog box, you have additional customization options to control text wrapping.

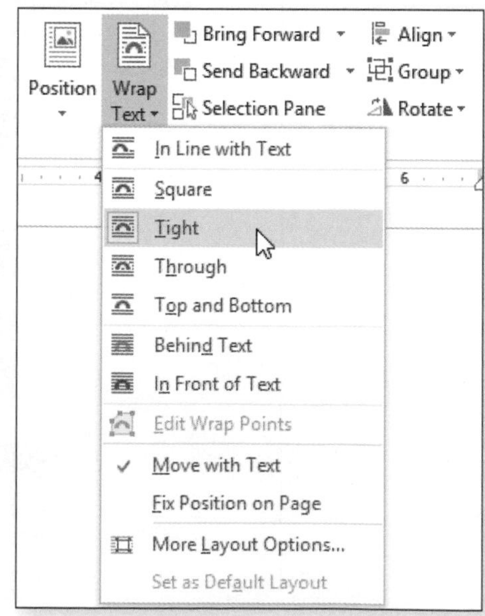

7-43 Picture arrangement options in the *Arrange* group

HOW TO: Customize Text Wrapping Options

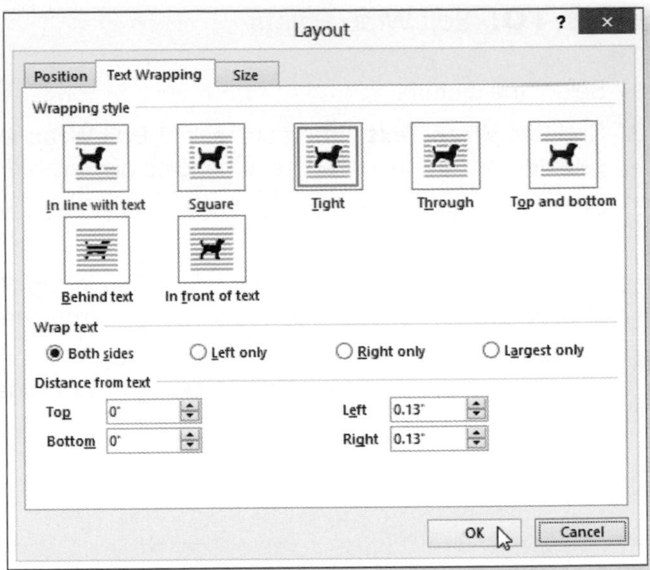

7-44 Text wrapping options

1. Select the picture.
2. Click the **Wrap Text** button [*Picture Tools Format* tab, *Arrange* group] and select **More Layout Options**. The *Layout* dialog box opens with the *Text Wrapping* tab displayed (Figure 7-44).
3. In the *Wrapping style* area, determine how the text wraps around the picture.
4. In the *Wrap text* area, select a wrapping option.
5. In the *Distance from text* area, set the specific distance for text to be placed around the graphic.
   - The *Wrapping style* option you have chosen controls which options are available in the *Distance from text* area.
6. Click **OK** to close the *Layout* dialog box.

Alignment Guides and Live Layout

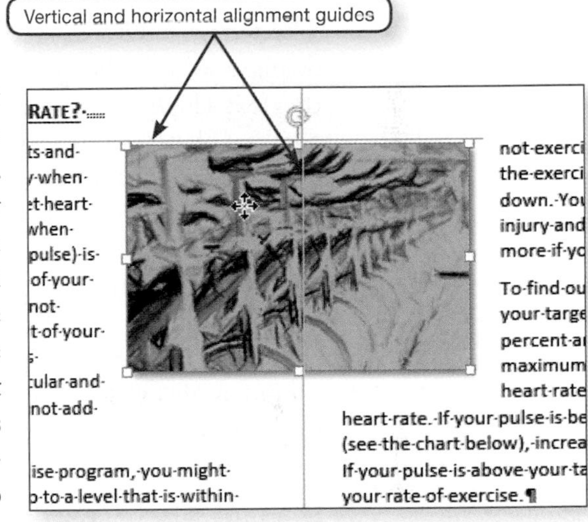

7-45 Alignment guides displayed

After you insert a picture and select a text wrapping option, you can drag the picture to the desired location in your document. Word 2013 provides you with two new features to help you accurately position pictures. ***Alignment guides*** are vertical and horizontal green lines that appear to guide alignment (Figure 7-45). As you drag the picture to a location, the vertical alignment guide appears at the left and right margins and the center of the document. The horizontal alignment guide appears at the top and bottom margins and on lines of text.

The alignment guides are on by default, but you can toggle them on or off by selecting **Use Alignment Guides** from the *Align* drop-down list in the *Arrange* group on the *Picture Tools Format* tab.

> **ANOTHER WAY**
>
> The *Align* drop-down list is also available in the *Arrange* group on the *Page Layout* tab.

Live layout automatically rearranges text and other objects in your document as you drag a picture to a new location. This allows you to instantly see how text wraps around your picture as you are dragging the picture.

Picture Wrap Points

Wrap points are the points on the picture that the text wraps around. You can edit these wrap points to more precisely customize how text wraps around the picture.

HOW TO: Edit Wrap Points

1. Select the picture.
2. Click the **Wrap Text** button and select **Edit Wrap Points**. The selected picture has wrap point handles displayed (Figure 7-46).
3. Click and drag the wrap point handle to customize how the text wraps around the picture.
4. Click the **Wrap Text** button and select **Edit Wrap Points** to accept changes and turn off the edit wrap points feature.
   - You can also click in your document away from the picture to accept changes and turn off the edit wrap points feature.

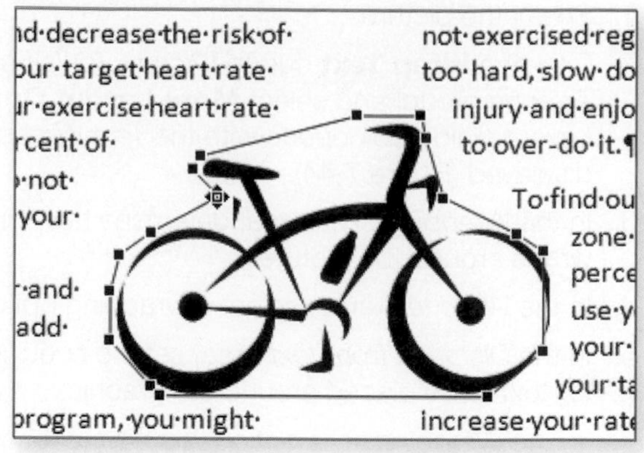

7-46 Edit wrap points

Picture Anchor

The ***picture anchor*** is a blue anchor icon and displays where the picture is anchored to the text (Figure 7-47). The picture anchor allows a picture to move with selected text if a document is modified and the text moves on the page. The picture anchor is visible when *Show/Hide* is turned on.

When you insert a picture, the picture anchor is automatically anchored to the paragraph closest to the picture. The picture anchor is always located at the beginning of a paragraph. You can move the picture anchor by clicking and dragging it to a different paragraph.

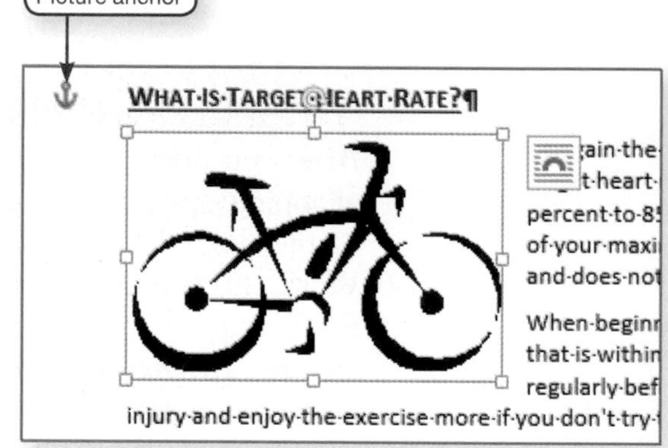

7-47 Picture anchor

Resize and Crop Pictures

The following are some of the different ways to you can resize a picture:

- ***Sizing handles***: Drag the sizing handles to increase or decrease the size of the picture.
- ***Size group***: Type a specific size in the *Height* and *Width* areas in the *Size* group on the *Picture Tools Format* tab.
- ***Layout dialog box***: Click the **Size** launcher to open the *Layout* dialog box with the *Size* tab displayed. Type in a specific height and width or scale the picture to a percentage of its original size.

When resizing a picture, it is best to keep the picture proportional to its original size, which is its ***aspect ratio***. This prevents distortion of the image. By default, when you change the size in the *Size* group or in the *Layout* dialog box, the aspect ratio is locked to keep the picture proportional to its original size. When you resize a picture using the sizing handles, the corner sizing handles resize the picture proportionally. However, the side sizing handles do *not* resize the picture proportionally.

Cropping is different from resizing a picture. While cropping does resize a picture, it does so by cutting out part of the picture. Use cropping to edit out unwanted portions of a picture.

HOW TO: Crop a Picture

1. Click the picture you want to crop to select it.
2. Click the top half of the **Crop** button [*Picture Tools Format* tab, *Size* group].
   - Cropping handles appear on your picture in the corners and on the sides (Figure 7-48).
   - When you place your pointer on a cropping handle, it becomes a cropping pointer.
   - Drag the cropping handles to edit the picture.
3. Click the **Crop** button again to accept the changes and turn off cropping.
   - You can also click outside of the picture to accept the changes and turn off cropping.

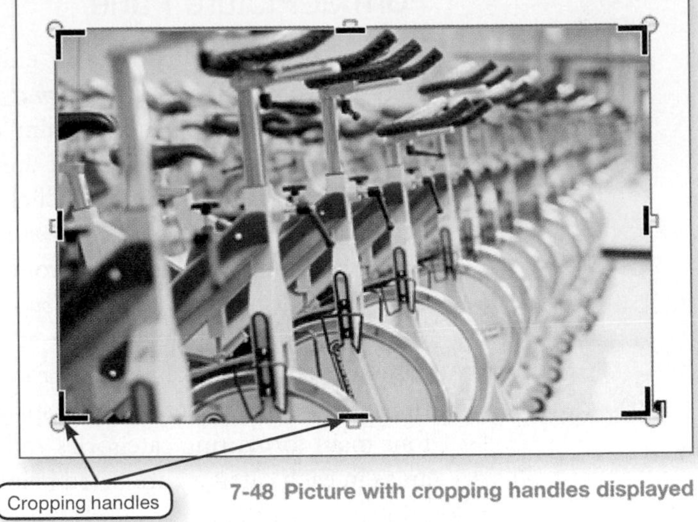

7-48 Picture with cropping handles displayed

ANOTHER WAY

To crop a picture, right-click the picture and select **Crop** from the mini toolbar.

If you click the bottom half of the **Crop** button, a drop-down list of cropping options is displayed (Figure 7-49). You can crop a picture to a specific shape or aspect ratio, or you can crop to fill or fit the picture to a specific size.

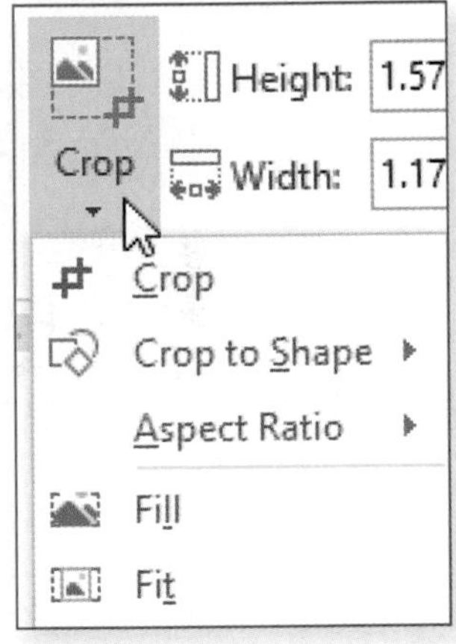

7-49 Cropping options

MORE INFO

Click the **Undo** button on the *Quick Access Toolbar* or press **Ctrl+Z** to undo changes made to a picture.

Rotate Pictures

You can rotate pictures in a document to enhance their placement. Select the picture and then use one of the following methods to rotate the picture:

- ***Rotation handle***: Click the rotation handle at the top and drag to the left or right to rotate the picture (Figure 7-50).
- ***Rotate drop-down list***: Click the **Rotate** button in the *Arrange* group on the *Picture Tools Format* tab to display the drop-down list of rotate options (Figure 7-51).
- ***Layout dialog box***: Click the **Rotate** button and select **More Rotation Options** to open the *Layout* dialog box with the *Size* tab displayed. Change the degree of rotation in the *Rotate* area.

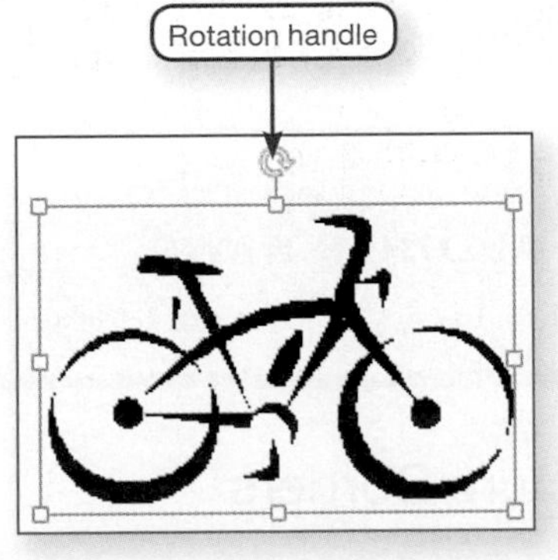

7-50 Picture with rotation handle displayed

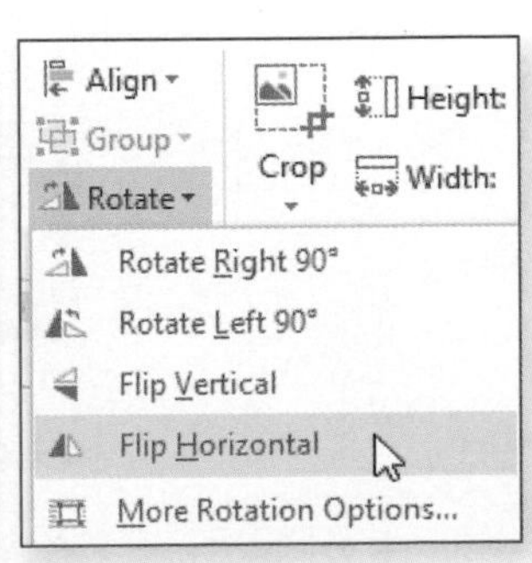

7-51 Rotation options

Format Picture Pane

As you begin modifying and enhancing your pictures, you will use the ***Format Picture pane*** (Figure 7-52). This pane contains many of the picture formatting features that are available on the *Picture Tools Format* tab. Click the **Picture Styles** launcher to open the *Format Picture* pane. You can also open this pane from many of the drop-down lists on the *Picture Tools Format* tab.

The formatting categories are at the top of this pane. When you click one of the category buttons, the options in that category display below. The four main formatting categories and the different areas in each category are listed below:

- ***Fill & Line***: *Fill* and *Line*
- ***Effects***: *Shadow, Reflection, Glow, Soft Edges, 3-D Format, 3-D Rotation,* and *Artistic Effects*
- ***Layout & Properties***: *Text Box* and *Alt Text*
- ***Picture***: *Picture Corrections, Picture Color,* and *Crop*

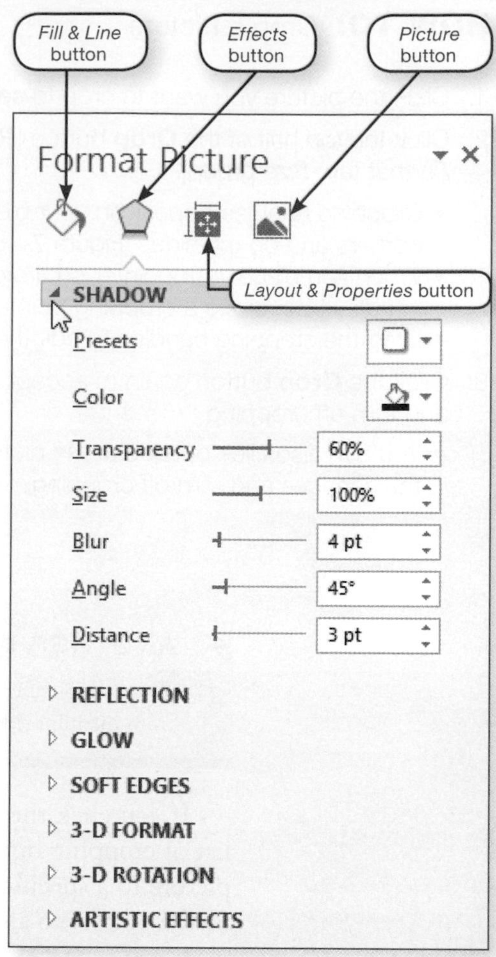

7-52 ***Format Picture*** **pane**

Picture Styles

Similar to text and table styles, ***picture styles*** apply preset borders and effects. There are many picture styles available in the ***Picture Styles gallery***. Click the **More** button in the *Picture Styles* gallery to display the entire *Picture Styles* gallery (Figure 7-53). Select a picture and click a picture style to apply it to the picture. When you place your pointer on the picture style, the picture style is temporarily applied to the picture, allowing you to preview the picture with the style applied.

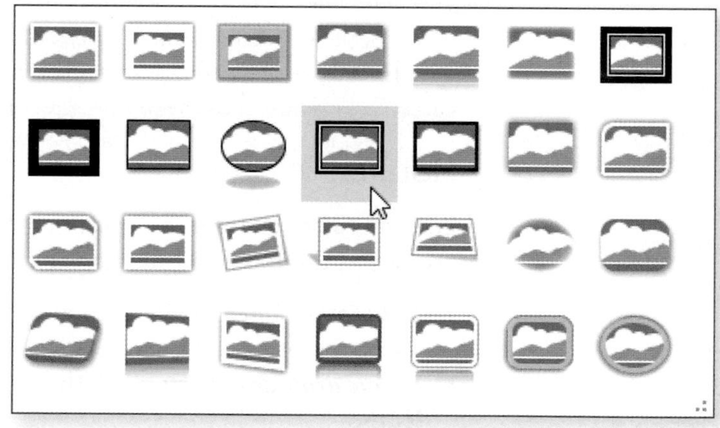

7-53 ***Picture Styles*** **gallery**

ANOTHER WAY

Right-click a picture and select a picture style from the mini toolbar.

Picture Borders

You can apply a border to your pictures. You can customize the color of the border, the border weight (size of the border), and the type of border line.

HOW TO: Apply a Border

1. Select the picture.
2. Click the **Picture Border** button [*Picture Tools Format* tab, *Picture Styles* group] to display the drop-down list of picture border options (Figure 7-54).
3. Select the border color in the *Theme Colors* or *Standard Colors* area.
   - Click **More Outline Colors** to open the *Colors* dialog box and choose from more border color options.
4. Select **Weight** to choose the thickness of the border line.
5. Select **Dashes** to choose the type of border line.
   - If you select *More Lines* from the *Weight* or *Dashes* drop-down list, the *Format Picture* pane opens and provides you with more line options.

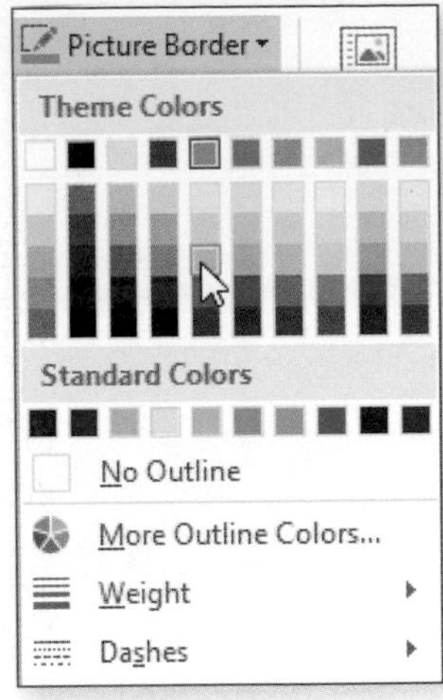

7-54 Picture border options

You can also apply a picture border from the *Format Picture* pane. Click the **Picture Styles** launcher to open the *Format Picture* pane (Figure 7-55). Click the **Fill & Line** button at the top to customize the picture border. The options for each of these categories are displayed on the right side of the dialog box.

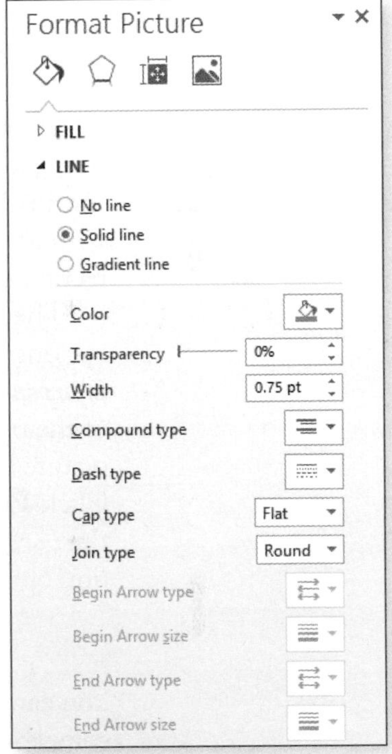

7-55 Picture border line options in the *Format Picture* pane

Picture Effects

Using ***picture effects***, you can apply *Preset, Shadow, Reflection, Glow, Soft Edges, Bevel,* or *3-D Rotation* effects to a selected picture. When you click one of the picture effect categories, a drop-down list of picture effect options displays (Figure 7-56).

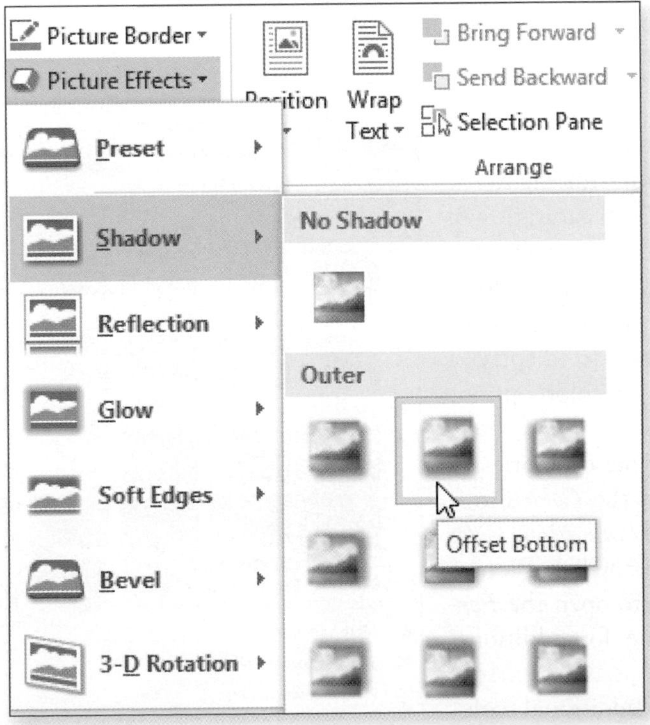

7-56 *Picture Effects* drop-down list

At the bottom of each drop-down list is an options button (e.g., *Shadow Options*). Click an options button to open the *Format Picture* pane. The *Format Picture* pane has *Shadow, Reflection, Glow, Soft Edges, 3-D Format, 3-D Rotation,* and *Artistic Effects* categories.

Picture Adjustments

You can adjust pictures to make corrections, change colors, or add artistic effects. You can also compress pictures to reduce the file size, change a picture in the document, or reset a picture to its original size and appearance. You can make all of these adjustments from the *Adjust* group on the *Picture Tools Format* tab.

> **ANOTHER WAY**
>
> You can also make each of these adjustments in the *Format Picture* pane.

Corrections

You can apply picture corrections to sharpen or soften a picture and change picture brightness and contrast. Click the **Corrections** button in the *Adjust* group on the *Picture Tools Format* tab to display a drop-down list of correction options (Figure 7-57).

There are two categories of correction options in the *Corrections* drop-down list: *Sharpen/Soften* and *Brightness/Contrast*. Each of the options in both categories changes the picture by a percentage of the original picture. Click **Picture Corrections Options** to open the *Format Picture* pane for additional correction options.

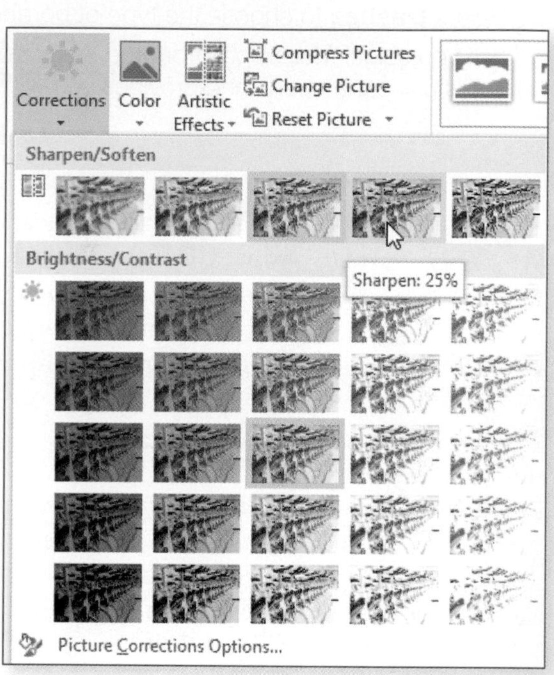

7-57 Picture correction options

Color

You can make adjustments to the color tone and color saturation of the picture or you can recolor the picture. Click the **Color** button in the *Adjust* group on the *Picture Tools Format* tab to display a drop-down list of color options (Figure 7-58).

There are three categories of color options in the *Color* drop-down list: *Color Saturation, Color Tone,* and *Recolor*. Click **Picture Color Options** to open the *Format Picture* pane for additional correction options. Click **More Variations** for additional color options.

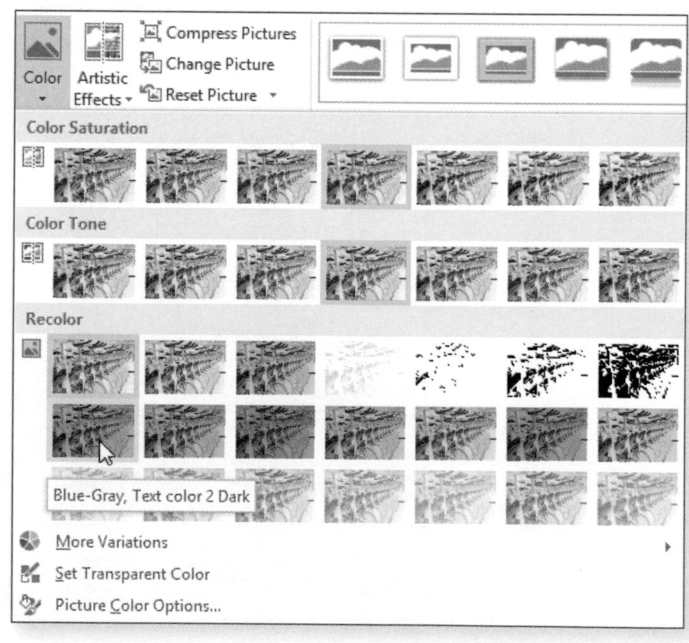

7-58 Picture color options

You can also set a color in the picture to be transparent. Click **Set Transparent Color** and select the color or colors in the picture you want to be transparent.

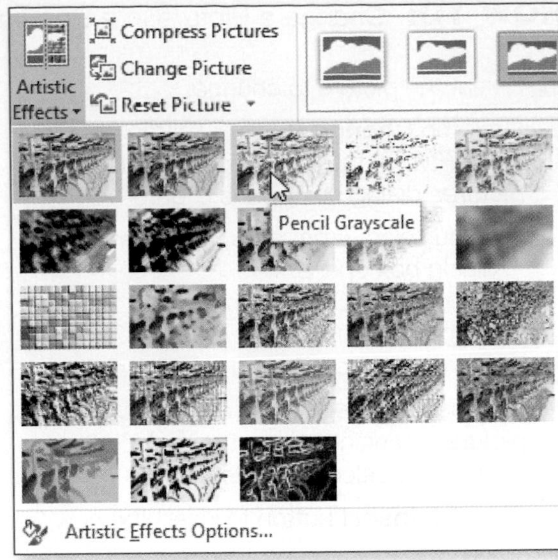

7-59 Artistic picture effects

Artistic Effects

Word provides you with a variety of artistic effects to apply to pictures. Click the **Artistic Effects** button in the *Adjust* group on the *Picture Tools Format* tab to display a drop-down list of options (Figure 7-59). Click **Artistic Effects Options** to open the *Format Picture* pane to view additional artistic effect options.

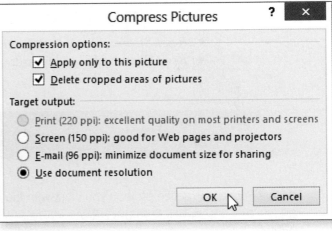

Compress Pictures

The file size of a picture can range from a few kilobytes (KB) up to a few megabytes (MB) or more. When you insert pictures into a document, this dramatically increases the file size of the document. Word provides you with options to compress the file size of pictures in your document to keep your document sizes manageable (larger files are harder to send via email, for example). When you do this, it changes the picture ***resolution***, which determines the picture quality. Compressed picture files have lower resolution and are of lesser quality.

HOW TO: Compress Pictures

1. Select the picture you want to compress.
2. Click the **Compress Pictures** button [*Picture Tools Format* tab, *Adjust* group]. The *Compress Pictures* dialog box opens (Figure 7-60).
3. In the *Compression options* area, check the **Apply only to this picture** box to apply compression only to the selected picture.
   - Deselect this check box to apply the settings to all pictures in the document.
   - The *Delete cropped areas of pictures* is checked by default. This removes the cropped area of pictures that have been cropped and reduces the file size.
4. In the *Target output* area, select one of the picture resolution radio buttons.
   - The default setting is *Use document resolution*.
   - The *Target output* options available depend on the selected picture type and its original resolution.
5. Click **OK** to close the dialog box and compress the picture or pictures.

Compress Pictures
Compression options:
Apply only to this picture
Delete cropped areas of pictures
Target output:
Print (220 ppi): excellent quality on most printers and screens
Screen (150 ppi): good for Web pages and projectors
E-mail (96 ppi): minimize document size for sharing
Use document resolution
OK Cancel

7-60 *Compress Pictures* dialog box

Change Picture

You can quickly replace a picture with another picture in a Word document. The *Change Picture* feature removes an existing picture and replaces it with a different picture while retaining the picture size and formatting.

HOW TO: Change a Picture in a Document

1. Select the picture to change.
2. Click the **Change Picture** button [*Picture Tools Format* tab, *Adjust* group]. The *Insert Pictures* dialog box opens (Figure 7-61).
   - If you select *From a file*, the *Insert Picture* dialog box opens.
   - If you select *Office.com Clip Art*, *Bing Image Search*, or *[your name's] SkyDrive*, you can search for and select a picture.
3. Browse or search to find and select the picture you want to insert to replace the picture you selected in step 1.
4. Click the **Insert** button to insert the new picture.
   - The size and formatting of the original picture are applied to the new picture.

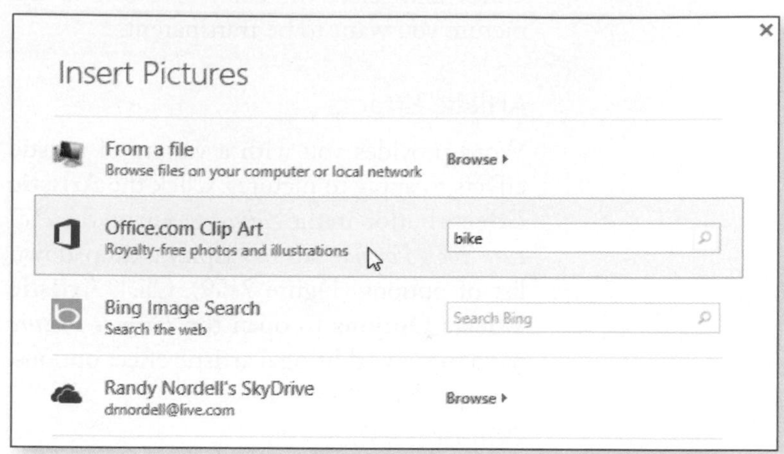

7-61 ***Insert Pictures*** **dialog box**

Reset Picture

Sometimes after making changes to a picture, you might decide to discard the changes and return to the original picture. Click the **Reset Picture** drop-down arrow in the *Adjust* group on the *Picture Tools Format* tab and select from the following options (Figure 7-62):

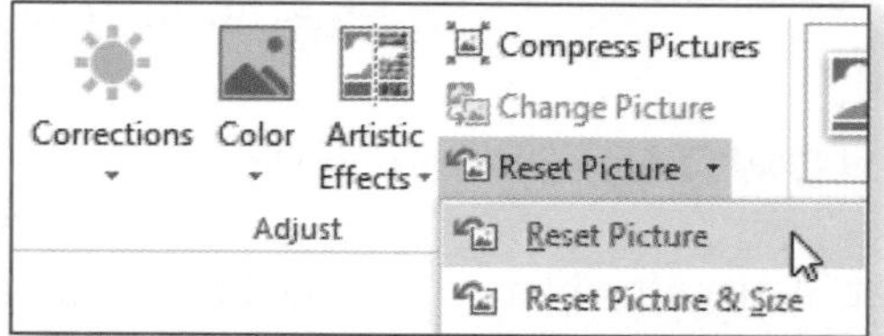

7-62 ***Reset Picture*** **options**

- ***Reset Picture*:** Discards all formatting changes
- ***Reset Picture & Size*:** Discards all formatting and sizing changes

PAUSE & PRACTICE: WORD 7-3

For this Pause & Practice project, you work with the American River Cycling Club document to insert two pictures and resize, arrange, apply a border and effects to, make adjustments to, and compress the pictures.

Files Needed: ***[your initials] PP W7-2.docx, ARCC-logo-07.png,*** and ***Bikes-07.png***
Completed Project File Name: ***[your initials] PP W7-3.docx***

1. Open the ***[your initials] PP W7-2*** document you completed in *Pause & Practice 7-2*.
2. Save the document as ***[your initials] PP W7-3***.
3. Change the top and bottom margins to **0.5"** and the left and right margins to **0.75"**.
4. Select the "**What Is Maximum Heart Rate?**" heading and change the *Before* spacing to **12 pt.**

5. Insert, resize, and arrange a picture.
   a. Place the insertion point at the beginning of the document.
   b. Insert the ***ARCC-logo-07*** picture from your student data files.
   c. Click the **Size** launcher to open the *Layout* dialog box.
   d. Use the *Size* tab in the *Layout* dialog box to scale the picture to **150%** of its original size.
   e. Click the *Text Wrapping* tab and change the text wrapping to **Top and Bottom**.
   f. Click **OK** to close the *Layout* dialog box.
   g. Drag the picture so it is positioned at the top and center of the document. Use the alignment guides to position the picture accurately (Figure 7-63)

7-63 Use the alignment guides to position the picture

6. Use the *Format Picture* pane to modify a picture.
   a. Select the logo and click the **Picture Styles** launcher to open the *Format Picture* pane.
   b. Click the **Fill & Line** button at the top of the pane and select **LINE** to open the *Line* settings (Figure 7-64).
   c. Select the **Solid line** radio button.
   d. Click the **COLOR** button and select **Dark Blue**, **Text 2**, **Darker 50%**.
   e. Change the *Width* to **1.5 pt.**
   f. Click the **Picture** button at the top of the pane and select **Picture Color** to open the *Picture Color* settings.
   g. Click the **Recolor** drop-down list and select **Blue**, **Accent color 1 Dark** (Figure 7-65).

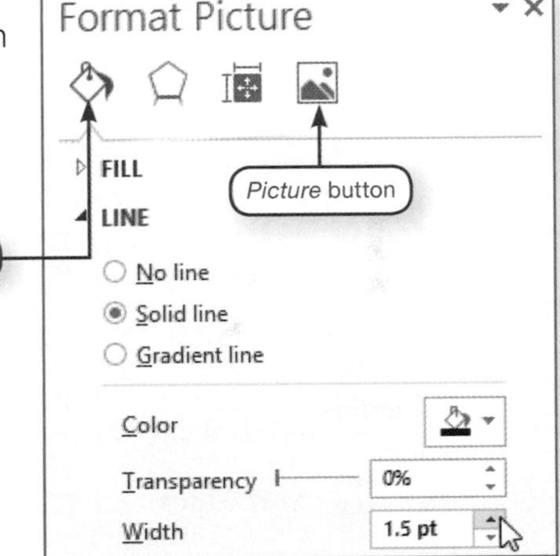

7-64 *Fill & Line* area of the *Format Picture* pane

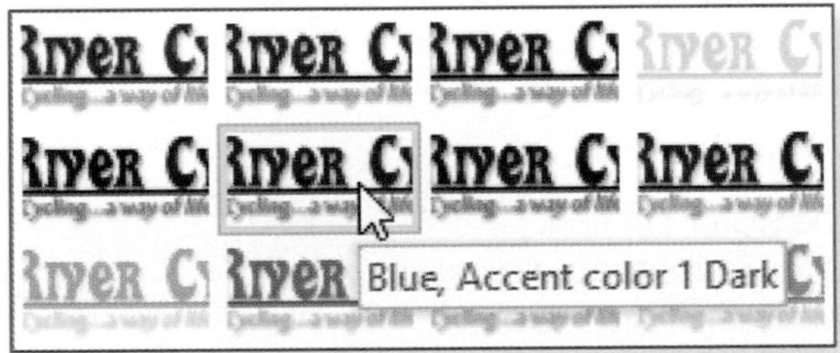

7-65 Recolor picture

   h. Click **Picture Corrections** category in the *Format Picture* pane to display the options.
   i. In the *Brightness/Contrast* area, change the *Brightness* to **20%** and the *Contrast* to **-20%**. Use the up and down arrows or type in the settings (Figure 7-66).
   j. Click the **X** in the upper right corner to close the *Format Picture* pane.

7. Insert, resize, and arrange a picture.
   a. Place the insertion point in front of "What Is Target Heart Rate?"
   b. Insert the ***Bikes-07*** picture.

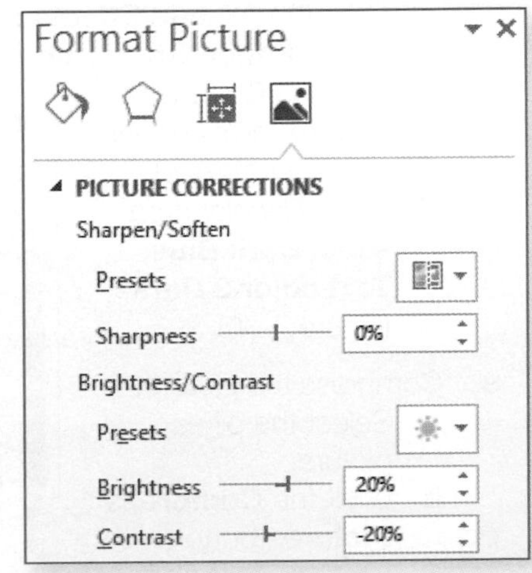

7-66 Adjust picture brightness and contrast

c. In the *Height* area [*Picture Tools Format* tab, *Size* group], type 1.5 and press **Enter**. The width is automatically adjusted to maintain the aspect ratio.
d. Click the **Wrap Text** button [*Picture Tools Format* tab, *Arrange* group] and select **Tight**.
e. Click the **Align** button [*Picture Tools Format* tab, *Arrange* group] and select **Align Right**.
f. Drag the picture anchor to the first paragraph below "What Is Target Heart Rate?" (Figure 7-67).

Picture anchor

7-67 Move picture anchor

8. Modify the picture.
   a. Click the **Picture Effects** button [*Picture Tools Format* tab, *Picture Styles* group] and select **Shadow** (Figure 7-68).

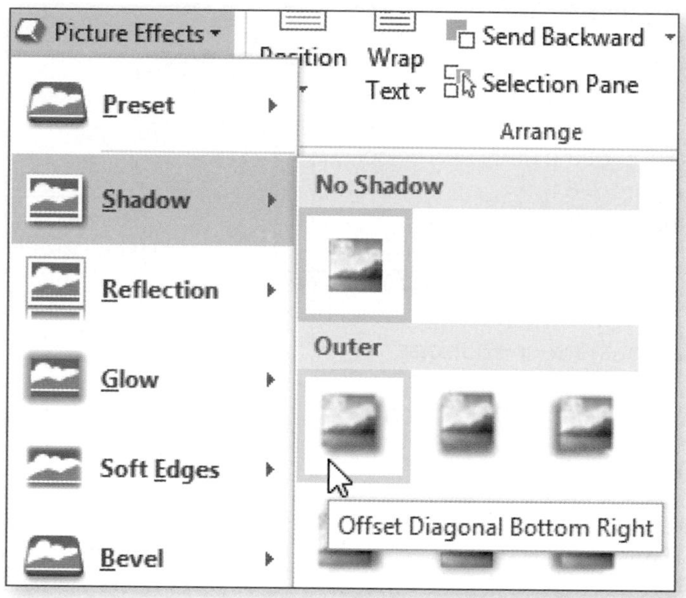

7-68 Apply shadow picture effect

   b. Select **Offset Diagonal Bottom Right** in the *Outer* section.
   c. Click the **Artistic Effects** button [*Picture Tools Format* tab, *Adjust* group].
   d. Select **Pencil Grayscale** from the drop-down list (Figure 7-69).
   e. Click the **Color** button [*Picture Tools Format* tab, *Adjust* group].
   f. In the *Recolor* area, select **Dark Blue, Text color 2 Dark** (Figure 7-70).

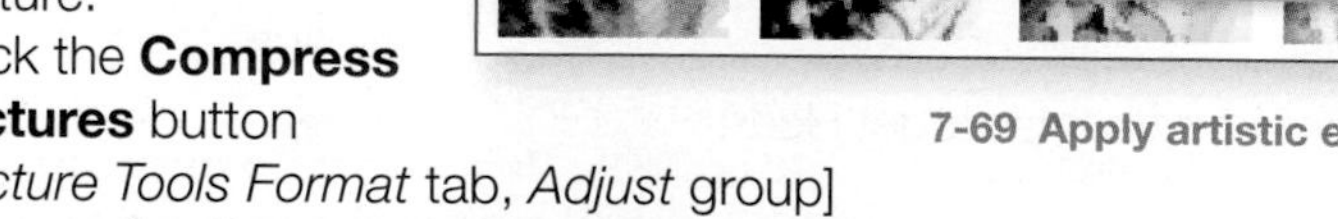

7-69 Apply artistic effect

Recolor

Dark Blue, Text color 2 Dark

7-70 Apply picture color

9. Compress the picture.
   a. Select the bikes picture.
   b. Click the **Compress Pictures** button [*Picture Tools Format* tab, *Adjust* group] to open the *Compress Pictures* dialog box.

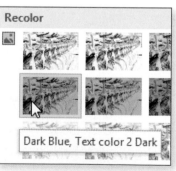

c. In the *Target output* area, select the **Screen (150 ppi)** radio button.
d. Click **OK** to close the dialog box and compress the picture.

10. Save and close the document (Figure 7-71).

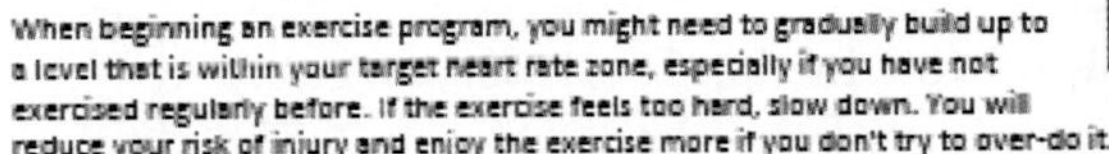

AMERICAN RIVER CYCLING CLUB

www.arcc.org Cycling...a way of life info@arcc.org

WHAT IS MAXIMUM HEART RATE?

The maximum heart rate is the highest your pulse rate can get. To calculate your predicted **maximum heart rate**, use this formula:

(Example: a 40-year-old's predicted maximum heart rate is 180.)

Your actual maximum heart rate can be determined by a graded exercise test. Please note that some medicines and medical conditions might affect your maximum heart rate. If you are taking medicines or have a medical condition (such as heart disease, high blood pressure, or diabetes), always ask your doctor if your maximum heart rate/target heart rate will be affected.

WHAT IS TARGET HEART RATE?

You gain the most benefits and decrease the risk of injury when you exercise in your target heart rate zone. Usually this is when your exercise heart rate (pulse) is 60 percent to 85 percent of your maximum heart rate. Do not exercise above 85 percent of your maximum heart rate. This increases both cardiovascular and orthopedic risk and does not add any extra benefit.

When beginning an exercise program, you might need to gradually build up to a level that is within your target heart rate zone, especially if you have not exercised regularly before. If the exercise feels too hard, slow down. You will reduce your risk of injury and enjoy the exercise more if you don't try to over-do it.

To find out if you are exercising in your target zone (between 60 percent and 85 percent of your maximum heart rate), use your heart rate monitor to track your heart rate. If your pulse is below your target zone (see the chart below), increase your rate of exercise. If your pulse is above your target zone, decrease your rate of exercise.

MAX AND TARGET HEART RATES	AGE	PREDICTED MAX HEART RATE	TARGET HEART RATE (60-85% OF MAX)
	20	✓ 200	120-170
	25	✓ 195	117-166
	30	✓ 190	114-162
	35	✓ 185	111-157
	40	✓ 180	108-153
	45	✓ 175	105-149
	50	✓ 170	102-145
	55	✓ 165	99-140
	60	✓ 160	96-136
	65	✓ 155	93-132
	70	✓ 150	90-128

CALCULATE YOUR MAX AND TARGET HEART RATES				
AGE	MAX HEART RATE	60% OF MAX	85% OF MAX	AVERAGE TARGET HEART RATE
33	✓ 187	112	159	136

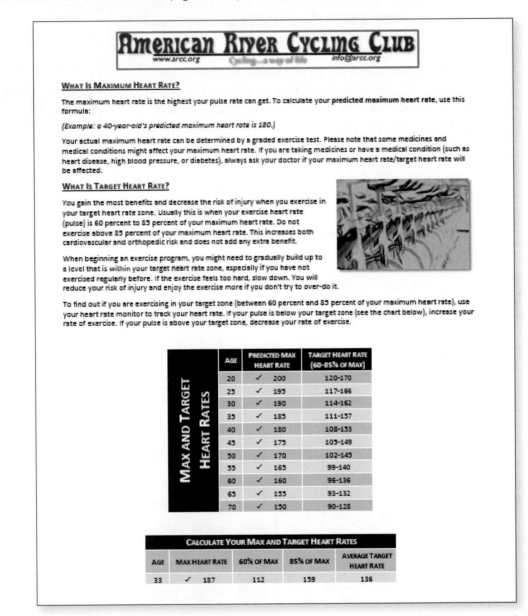

7-71 PP W7-3 completed

SLO 7.5

Working with Shapes

When you are working with shapes, you can modify their size, arrangement, style, fill color, border color, and effects. The process is similar to the way you can modify pictures, but instead of the *Picture Tools Format* tab that is available on the *Ribbon* when you are working with pictures, there is a ***Drawing Tools Format tab*** available on the *Ribbon* when you work with shapes. You can use this contextual tab to modify the shapes in your documents.

Customize Shapes

As you learned in Chapter 4, you can insert shapes by clicking on the *Shapes* button on the *Insert* tab (see *SLO 4.5: Working with Graphics*). The *Shapes* gallery includes a variety of shapes that you can draw in a document. When you select a shape from the *Shapes* gallery, your pointer becomes a crosshair (large plus sign), which is the drawing cursor.

After you have drawn a shape in your document, you can use the *Drawing Tools Format* tab or *Format Shapes* pane to customize the shape you created. You can use the *Size* and *Align* groups, the *Layout* menu, and the *Layout* dialog box to change the size, text wrapping, and position of the shapes. The size and arrangement options available to you are the same as the ones you use when you are working with a picture.

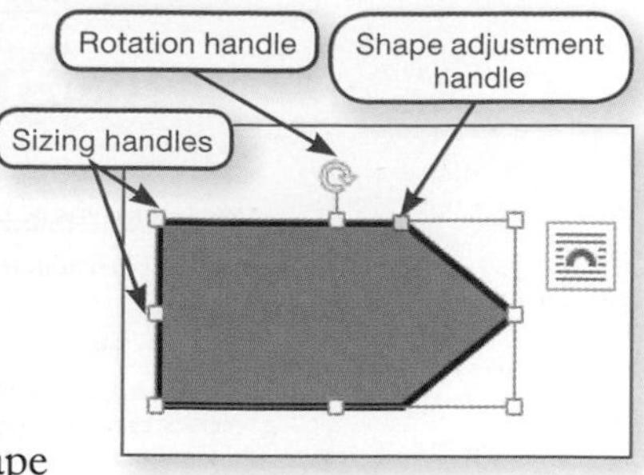

7-72 Selected shape with handles displayed

When you select a shape in your document, the shape handles appear on the shape (Figure 7-72). You can edit the shape using the sizing handles on the sides and corners. Use the shape rotation handle (circle with arrow) at the top to rotate the shape, and the shape adjustment handle (yellow square) to adjust parts of the shape.

Click the **Edit Shape** button in the *Insert Shapes* group to change a shape or edit points of the shape (Figure 7-73). When you click *Edit Points,* shape editing handles are displayed on the shape, and you can use these handles to further customize the shape.

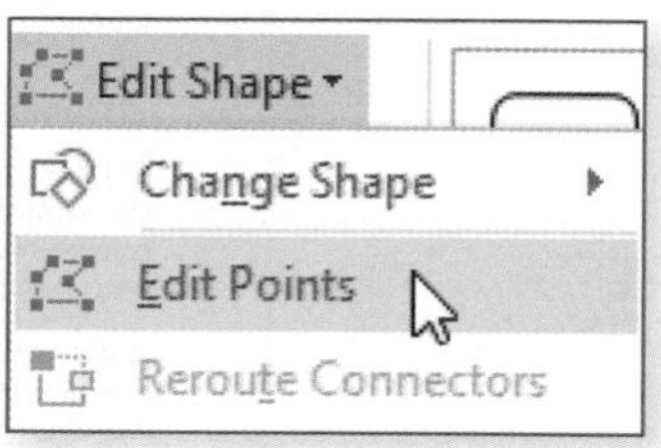

7-73 *Edit Shape* drop-down list

Shape Styles

In the *Shape Styles* group on the *Drawing Tools Format* tab, you can apply a shape style or customize the *Shape Fill, Shape Outline,* and *Shape Effects.* The *Shape Styles* gallery contains a variety of built-in styles that you can use to apply a preset outline, fill color, and effects to shapes. The document theme controls the colors of the built-in shape styles in a document. Click the **More** button in the *Shape Styles* gallery to display the available shape styles (Figure 7-74).

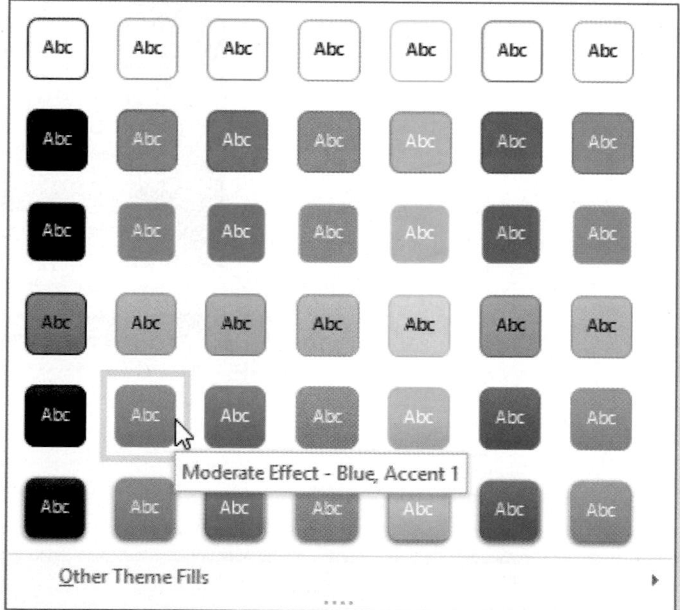

7-74 *Shape Styles* gallery

In addition to the built-in shape styles, you can customize shapes using the *Shape Fill, Shape Outline,* and *Shape Effects* drop-down lists in the *Shape Styles* group on the *Drawing Tools Format* tab. The following list details the options available in each of these areas:

- ***Shape Fill***: Customize and apply *Theme Colors, Standard Colors, No Fill, More Fill Colors, Picture, Gradient,* or *Texture* to a shape.

- ***Shape Outline***: Customize and apply *Theme Colors, Standard Colors, No Outline, More Outline Colors, Weight, Dashes,* or *Arrows* to a shape.
- ***Shape Effects***: Apply built-in *Preset, Shadow, Reflection, Glow, Soft Edges, Bevel,* or *3-D Rotation* effects to a shape.

You can also customize and apply shape fill, outline, and effects using the *Format Shape* pane. This pane is similar to the *Format Picture* pane and provides you with additional shape customization options. Click the **Shape Styles** launcher to open the *Format Shape* pane (Figure 7-75).

> **ANOTHER WAY**
>
> Right-click a shape and select a style, fill, or outline from the mini toolbar or select **Format Shape** from the context menu to open the *Format Shape* pane.

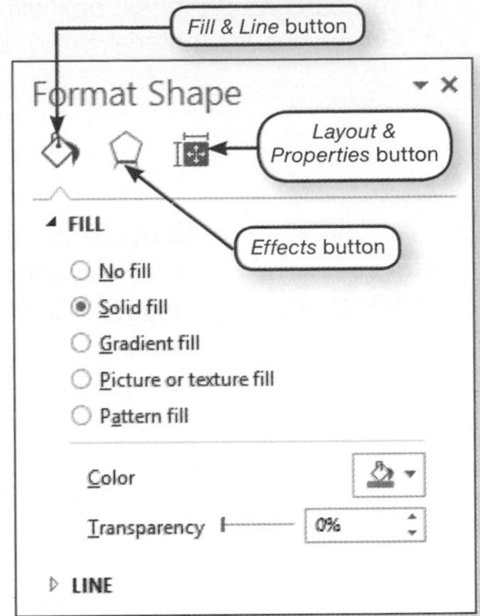

7-75 *Format Shape* pane

Add Text or a Text Box to a Shape

You can draw a shape around existing text, or you can add text to a shape. There are two different methods to add text to a shape: ***add text*** or ***draw text box***. When you add text to a shape, the text becomes part of the shape. You can format the text in a shape the same way you format any other text in your documents.

HOW TO: Add Text to a Shape

1. Select the shape where you want to add text and type the text in the shape (Figure 7-76).
   - Alternatively, right-click the shape and select **Add Text** from the context menu. The insertion point is placed in the shape.
2. Type the text.
3. Select the text and make formatting changes to font, size, styles, and effects.
   - The text added to the shape is *Normal* style text by default.
   - You might have to change line and paragraph spacing to vertically center text in the shape.
4. Click the **Align Text** button [*Drawing Tools Format* tab, *Text* group] and select **Top**, **Middle**, or **Bottom** to align the text vertically on the shape.
   - Text on a shape is centered horizontally by default.

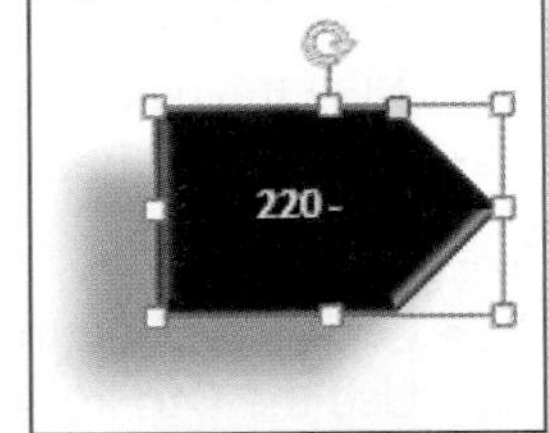

7-76 Add text to shape

You can also add text to a shape by drawing a text box and typing text in the text box. A text box is a separate object that you can modify independently of the shape.

HOW TO: Draw a Text Box

1. Click the **Draw Text Box** button [*Drawing Tools Format* tab, *Insert Shapes* group]. Your pointer becomes a drawing crosshair.
2. Draw the text box.
3. Type text in the text box (Figure 7-77).

7-77 Type text in a text box

4. Format and arrange the text box.
   - Select the text in the text box and customize the text font, size, style, and effects.
   - Select the border of the text box and customize the outline, fill, and arrangement.
   - You can group the text box with the shape so they become one object. Grouping objects is covered in the *Group Shapes* material, which is later in this section in this chapter.

When using text with shapes, you can change the text direction, change the vertical text alignment, or add a hyperlink to text using the options in the *Text* group on the *Drawing Tools Format* tab (Figure 7-78).

Text Direction
Align Text
Create Link
Text

7-78 Text group on the *Drawing Tools Format* tab

> **MORE INFO**
>
> To add a caption to a shape or picture, right-click the shape or picture and select **Insert Caption** from the context menu.

Selection Pane

When you are using shapes and pictures in your document, the ***Selection pane*** helps you view, select, and order these objects in your document. The *Selection* pane is on the right side of the Word window. It displays all of the objects in your document.

HOW TO: Use the Selection Pane

1. Click the **Selection Pane** button [*Drawing Tools Format* or *Page Layout* tab, *Arrange* group]. The *Selection* pane displays on the right side of the Word window (Figure 7-79).
   - All of the pictures and shapes in the document display.
   - Each object has a default name.
2. Click an object to select it. The object is also selected in the document.
   - Click the object name to rename the object.
   - Use the **Ctrl** key and your pointer to select multiple objects.
   - Click the **Hide** button (eye) to the right of the object name to hide the object in the document.
3. Select an object and click the **Bring Forward** (up arrow) or **Send Backward** (down arrow) button to re-order objects.
   - Ordering determines which object appears in front of or behind other objects. (Ordering is covered later in this section of the chapter.)
4. Click the **Selection Pane** button or the **X** in the upper right corner of the *Selection* pane to close it.

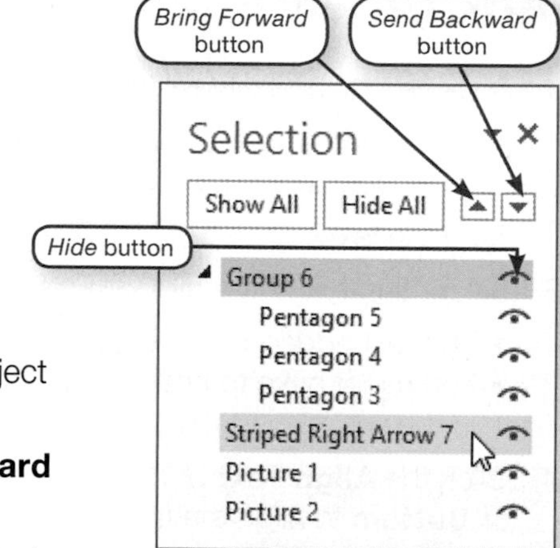

7-79 *Selection* pane

Order Shapes

Ordering is important when you are working with multiple shapes and pictures. It determines how objects are layered in front of or behind other objects. You can use the *Selection* pane to change the order of objects in your document. Alternatively, you can use the ***Bring Forward*** and ***Send Backward*** buttons in the *Arrange* group on the *Drawing Tools Format* tab.

Select the object or objects you want to reorder and click the **Bring Forward** or **Send Backward** button (Figure 7-80). The following options are available on these buttons:

- ***Bring Forward***: *Bring Forward, Bring to Front,* and *Bring in Front of Text*
- ***Send Backward***: *Send Backward, Send to Back,* and *Send Behind Text*

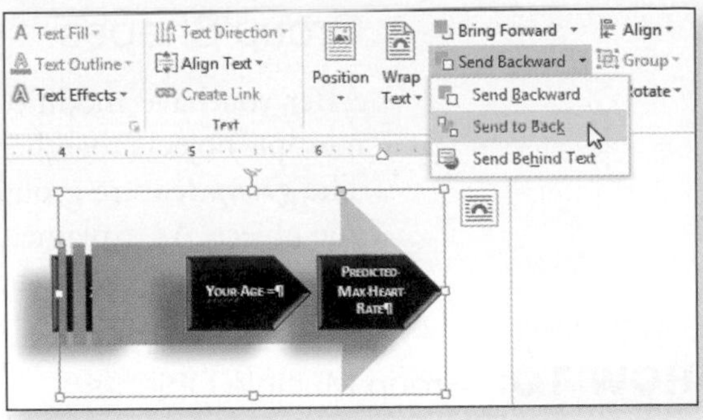

7-80 Re-order object

Align Shapes

Word provides you with a variety of options so you can accurately align shapes (or pictures) in your document. When you want to align multiple objects, use the **Shift** key and your pointer to select objects in your document or use the **Ctrl** key and your pointer to select multiple objects in the *Selection* pane. Click the **Align** button in the *Arrange* group and select from the alignment options (Figure 7-81). The following table describes each of the alignment options:

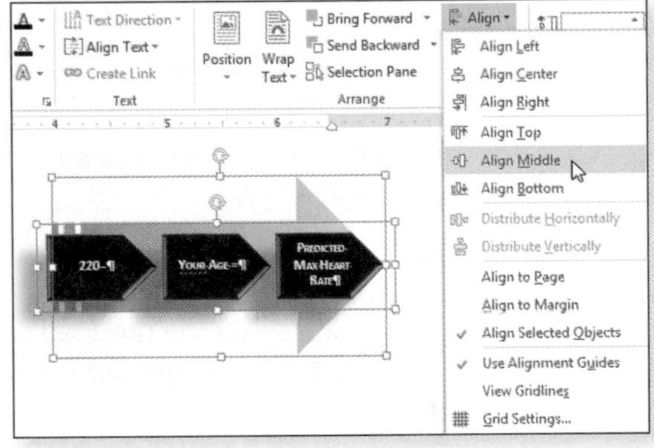

7-81 Align selected shapes

Shape Alignment Options

Alignment Option	Description
Align Left	Horizontally aligns selected objects on the left edge of objects.
Align Center	Horizontally aligns selected objects in the center of objects.
Align Right	Horizontally aligns selected objects on the right edge of objects.
Align Top	Vertically aligns selected objects on the top edge of objects.
Align Middle	Vertically aligns selected objects in the middle of objects.
Align Bottom	Vertically aligns selected objects on the bottom edge of objects.
Distribute Horizontally	Equally distributes horizontal space between selected objects.
Distribute Vertically	Equally distributes vertical space between selected objects.
Align to Page	Turn on this option to align objects in relation to the page of the document, and then select one of the horizontal or vertical alignment options.
Align to Margin	Turn on this option to align objects in relation to document margins, and then select one of the horizontal or vertical alignment options.
Align Selected Objects	This option is automatically selected when you select multiple objects to align.
Use Alignment Guides	Displays vertical and horizontal alignment guides to help you align objects when dragging an object.
View Gridlines	Displays gridlines in the document to help you accurately align objects.
Grid Settings	Opens the *Drawing Grid* dialog box where you can customize how the gridlines appear in the document.

Group Shapes

After you have modified and aligned objects in your document, you may want to combine multiple objects together so you can easily modify them as one object rather than individually. The ***group*** feature groups multiple objects so they can be resized, arranged, and modified as one object. As explained previously in this section of the chapter, you can also use the group feature to group a text box with a shape or you can group a caption with a picture.

HOW TO: Group Multiple Objects

1. Select the objects you want to group.
   - In the document, use the **Shift** key and your pointer to select the objects.
   - In the *Selection* pane, use the **Ctrl** key and your pointer to select the objects.
2. Click the **Group** button [*Drawing Tools Format* tab, *Arrange* group] (Figure 7-82).
3. Select **Group**.
   - The individual objects become one object.
   - To ungroup objects, select the grouped object, click the **Group** button, and select **Ungroup**.

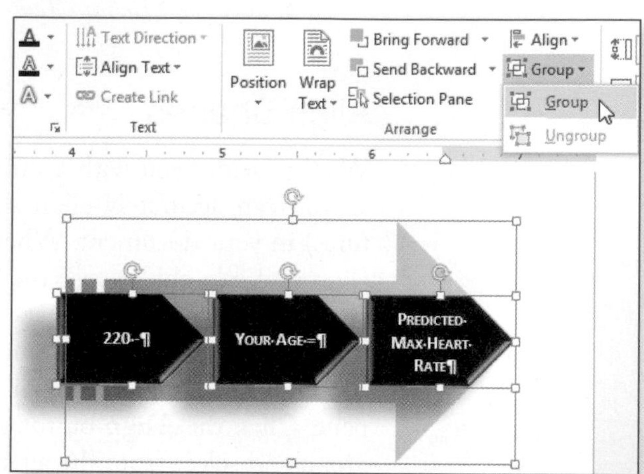

7-82 *Group* selected shapes

PAUSE & PRACTICE: WORD 7-4

For this Pause & Practice project, you finalize the heart rate document for American River Cycling Club. You insert and customize shapes, add text to shapes, align and group shapes, and arrange the grouped object.

File Needed: ***[your initials] PP W7-3.docx***
Completed Project File Name: ***[your initials] PP W7-4.docx***

1. Open the ***[your initials] PP W7-3*** document you completed in *Pause & Practice 7-3*.
2. Save the document as ***[your initials] PP W7-4***.
3. Insert, resize, and customize a shape.
   a. Click the **Shapes** button [*Insert* tab, *Illustrations* group] (Figure 7-83).
   b. Select the **Pentagon** shape in the *Block Arrows* category. Your pointer becomes a drawing crosshair.
   c. To the right of the text in the "What Is Maximum Heart Rate?" section, draw a shape approximately **1" square**. The shape will display on top of the text; you will modify text wrapping later.

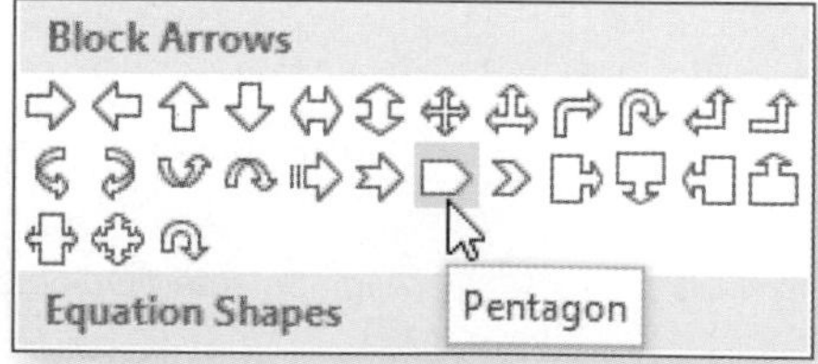

7-83 Select *Pentagon* shape

   d. Select the shape and change the *Height* to **0.6"** and the *Width* to **1"** [*Drawing Tools Format* tab, *Size* group].
   e. Click the **Shape Fill** button [*Shape Styles* group] and select **Dark Blue**, **Text 2**, **Darker 50%**.

f. Click the **Shape Outline** button [*Shape Styles* group] and select **No Outline**.
g. Click the **Shape Effects** button [*Shape Styles* group], select **Preset**, and select **Preset 5** (Figure 7-84).

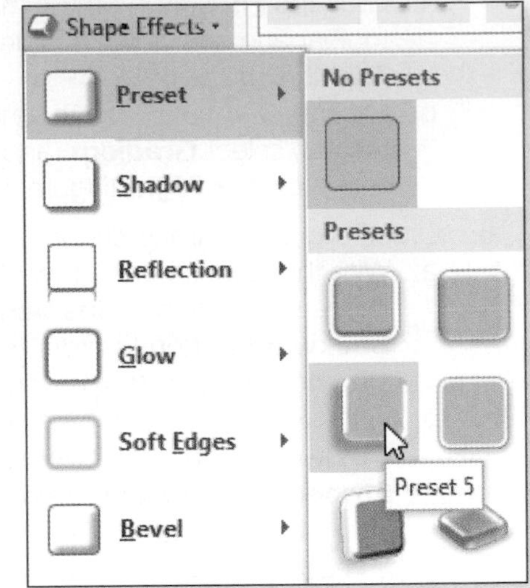

7-84 Select *Preset* shape effect

4. Add text to a shape and modify text.
   a. Right click the shape and select **Add Text** from the context menu. The insertion point is in the shape.
   b. Type 220, **space** once, and type - (hyphen).
   c. Select the text in the shape and make it **9 pt.**, **bold**, and **small caps**.
   d. Change the line spacing to **single** (**1.0**) and the after paragraph spacing to **0 pt.**
   e. Drag the shape to the left so it is approximately in the middle of the page.
5. Copy shapes and modify text in shapes.
   a. Click the edge of the shape to select it.
   b. Click **Ctrl+C** to copy the shape, and **Ctrl+V** to paste the shape.
   c. Drag copied shape so it is to the right of the first shape.
   d. Copy and paste the second shape and drag the third shape to the right of the second shape.
   e. Select the text in the second shape and type Your Age, **space** once, and type =.
   f. Select the text in the third shape and type Predicted Max Heart Rate.

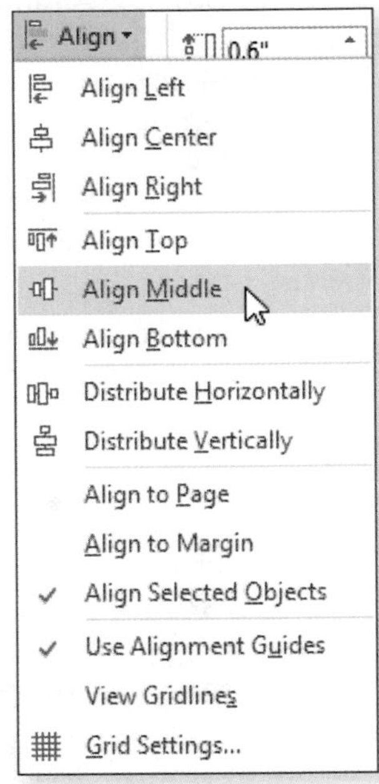

7-85 Align selected shapes

6. Align and group shapes.
   a. Manually move the shapes horizontally so they are almost touching each other, leaving only a little white space between each. Use the **Ctrl** key and **right** or **left arrows** key to move the shapes in small increments.
   b. Click the **Selection Pane** button [*Drawing Tools Format* tab, *Arrange* group] to display the *Selection* pane.
   c. Press the **Ctrl** key and select the three **Pentagon** shapes in the *Selection* pane.
   d. Click the **Align** button [*Drawing Tools Format* tab, *Arrange* group] and select **Align Selected Objects** (if it is not already checked).
   e. Click the **Align** button and select **Align Middle** to vertically center the selected shapes (Figure 7-85).
   f. Click the **Align** button and select **Distribute Horizontally** to put equal space between the selected shapes.
   g. Click the **Group** button [*Arrange* group] and select **Group** to group the selected shapes.

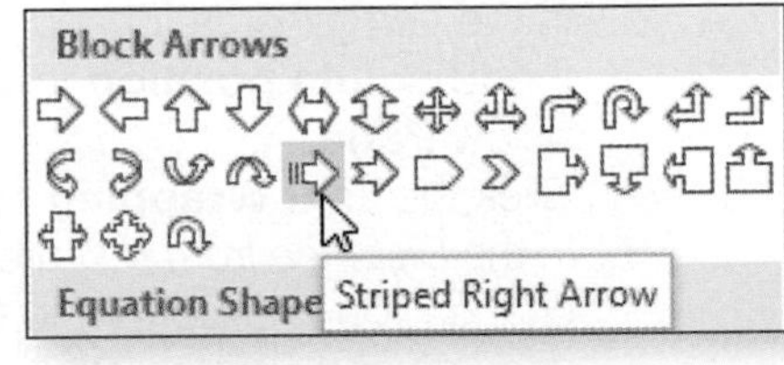

7-86 Select *Striped Right Arrow* shape

7. Draw another shape and resize and position it.
   a. Click the **Shapes** button [*Insert* tab, *Illustrations* group] (Figure 7-86).
   b. Select the **Striped Right Arrow** shape in the *Block Arrows* category. Your pointer becomes a drawing crosshair.
   c. Draw a shape approximately **3"** wide over the grouped shapes in your document.
   d. With the new shape selected, change the *Height* to **1.6"** and the *Width* to **3"** [*Drawing Tools Format* tab, *Size* group].
   e. Right-click the new shape, click the **Outline** button on the mini toolbar and select **No Outline**.

f. Click the **Fill** button on the mini toolbar and select **Dark Blue, Text 2**, **Darker 50%**.

g. Click the **Fill** button on the mini toolbar, select **Gradient**, and select **Linear Right** (Figure 7-87).

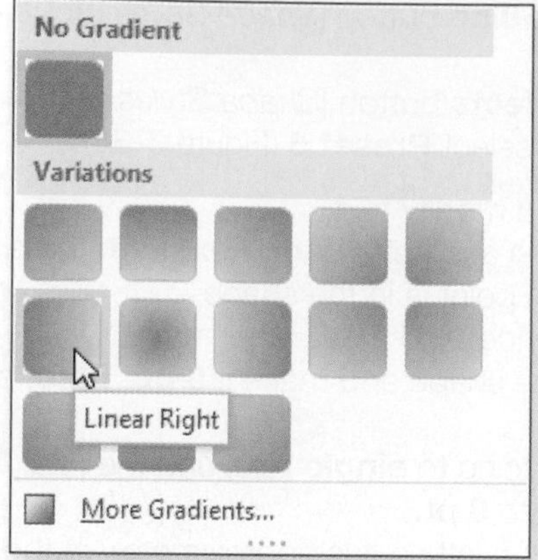

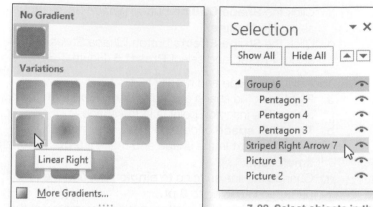

7-87 Select a *Gradient* shape fill

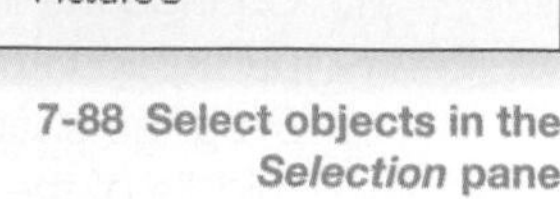

7-88 Select objects in the *Selection* pane

8. Order, align, and group shapes.
   a. With the striped right arrow shape selected, click the **Send Backward** button to order the arrow behind the grouped shapes.
   b. In the *Selection* pane, press the **Ctrl** key and click the **Group** and **Striped Right Arrow** to select both objects (Figure 7-88). The number to the right of the object name will vary.
   c. Click the **Align** button [*Arrange* group] and select **Align Middle** to vertically center the selected objects.
   d. Click the **Align** button and select **Align Right**.
   e. Click the **Group** button [*Arrange* group] and select **Group** to group the selected shapes.
   f. Click the **Selection Pane** button to close the *Selection* pane.
9. Adjust text wrapping and the position of grouped shape.
   a. With the grouped shape selected, click the **Wrap Text** button [*Drawing Tools Format* tab, *Arrange* group] and select **Tight**.
   b. Click the **Position** button [*Arrange* group] and select **More Layout Options** to open the *Layout* dialog box.
   c. In the *Horizontal* area, change the **Absolute position** to **5"** to the right of **Page**.
   d. In the *Vertical* area, change the **Absolute position** to **1.6"** below **Page**.
   e. Click the **Text Wrapping** tab.
   f. In the *Distance from text* area, change *Top* and *Bottom* to **0.2"** and *Left* and *Right* to **0"**.
   g. Click **OK** to close the *Layout* dialog box.
10. Save and close the document (Figure 7-89).

What Is Maximum Heart Rate?

The maximum heart rate is the highest your pulse rate can get. To calculate your **predicted maximum heart rate**, use this formula:

(Example: a 40-year-old's predicted maximum heart rate is 180.)

220 - Your Age = Predicted Max Heart Rate

Your actual maximum heart rate can be determined by a graded exercise test. Please note that some medicines and medical conditions might affect your maximum heart rate. If you are taking medicines or have a medical condition (such as heart disease, high blood pressure, or diabetes), always ask your doctor if your maximum heart rate/target heart rate will be affected.

What Is Target Heart Rate?

You gain the most benefits and decrease the risk of injury when you exercise in your target heart rate zone. Usually this is when your exercise heart rate (pulse) is 60 percent to 85 percent of your maximum heart rate. Do not exercise above 85 percent of your maximum heart rate. This increases both cardiovascular and orthopedic risk and does not add any extra benefit.

When beginning an exercise program, you might need to gradually build up to a level that is within your target heart rate zone, especially if you have not exercised regularly before. If the exercise feels too hard, slow down. You will reduce your risk of injury and enjoy the exercise more if you don't try to over-do it.

To find out if you are exercising in your target zone (between 60 percent and 85 percent of your maximum heart rate), use your heart rate monitor to track your heart rate. If your pulse is below your target zone (see the chart below), increase your rate of exercise. If your pulse is above your target zone, decrease your rate of exercise.

Max and Target Heart Rates	Age	Predicted Max Heart Rate	Target Heart Rate (60-85% of Max)
	20	✓ 200	120-170
	25	✓ 195	117-166
	30	✓ 190	114-162
	35	✓ 185	111-157
	40	✓ 180	108-153
	45	✓ 175	105-149
	50	✓ 170	102-145
	55	✓ 165	99-140
	60	✓ 160	96-136
	65	✓ 155	93-132
	70	✓ 150	90-128

Calculate Your Max and Target Heart Rates				
Age	Max Heart Rate	60% of Max	85% of Max	Average Target Heart Rate
33	✓ 187	112	159	136

7-89 PP W7-4 completed

Chapter Summary

7.1 Customize table content using sorting, formulas, bullets and numbers, tabs and indents, and text direction (p. W7-381).

- You can convert text to a table or convert a table to text.
- The ***Table Tools Layout tab*** has many options to customize the layout and contents of tables.
- You can ***sort*** text in a table in ascending or descending order.
- Use ***formulas*** in tables to perform calculations.
- The ***syntax*** of a formula is the structure of a formula. All formulas begin with = and can have a combination of ***cell references***, ***operators***, and ***values***.
- The ***cell address*** is the column letter and row number where a column and row intersect. A cell reference is a cell address used in a formula.
- ***Functions***, such as ***SUM*** and ***AVERAGE***, are built-in formulas used in common calculations.
- When values in a table change, you can manually ***update*** the formula.
- You can change the ***text direction*** of text in a cell of a table.
- You can use ***Tabs*** and ***indents*** in a table. Use ***Ctrl+Tab*** to move to a tab stop in the cell of a table.
- You can insert ***bulleted and numbered lists*** in a table.

7.2 Customize table layouts using table properties, cell margins, the split table feature, nested tables, and a repeated header row (p. W7-390).

- You can modify the size, alignment, and position of a table.
- Use the ***Table Properties dialog box*** to make modifications to the entire table, rows, columns, or individual cells.
- ***Cell margins*** are the amount of space around text in a cell; ***cell spacing*** is the amount of space between cells.
- You can ***split a table*** into multiple separate tables or ***split cells*** into multiple rows and columns.
- ***Nested tables*** are tables within tables. The main table is the ***parent table,*** and tables within the parent table are ***child tables***.
- You can ***repeat header rows*** to automatically display a header row or rows at the top of each page when a table spans more than one page.
- You can draw a table using the table drawing tools.

7.3 Enhance a table design with shading, borders, and a table style (p. W7-394).

- Use the ***Table Tools Design tab*** to customize table style options, ***table styles***, and borders and shading.
- Use the ***Border Painter*** to draw borders on a table.
- Use the ***Border Sampler*** to select a table border that you can then use to draw borders on the table using the *Border Painter*.
- You can modify an existing table style or you can create a new table style.
- There are built-in tables in the ***Tables gallery***. These tables are stored as building blocks, and you can create your own ***table building blocks***.

7.4 Modify a picture using advanced layout and picture format options (p. W7-404).

- You can modify pictures with the ***Picture Tools Format tab*** or the ***Format Picture pane***.
- ***Text wrapping*** controls how text wraps around a picture. You can modify a picture's ***wrap points*** to customize how text wraps around a picture.
- ***Alignment guides*** and ***live layout*** help you arrange a picture in a document.
- The ***picture anchor*** determines the text the picture is anchored to in the document. The picture anchor allows the picture to move with text when a document is modified.
- After you insert a picture into a document, you can ***resize*** the picture using the sizing handles, the *Size* group on the *Picture Tools Format* tab, or the *Layout* dialog box.
- ***Aspect ratio*** refers to the picture being proportional to its original size when it is resized.

- You can ***crop*** a picture to remove an unwanted portion, crop a picture to a shape, or crop a picture to fit a space or crop it to be a specific size.
- You can ***rotate*** a picture in a document.
- ***Picture styles*** are built-in styles that you can use to apply borders and effects to pictures.
- You can apply and customize ***picture borders*** and ***picture effects***.
- ***Adjustments*** can be made to a picture to make ***corrections***, change the ***color***, apply ***artistic effects***, ***compress*** the file size, ***change*** the picture to a different picture, or ***reset*** the picture to its original form.

7.5 Create, group, align, and modify a shape in a document (p. W7-415).

- You can draw a shape and customize its size and rotation using the ***shape handles***.
- Use ***edit points*** of the shape to further customize the shape.
- Use built-in ***shape styles*** to apply ***shape fill***, ***shape outline***, and ***shape effects*** to shapes.
- You can add text to or draw a ***text box*** on a shape.
- The ***Selection pane*** displays all objects in your document, and you can use it to reorder objects.
- The ***order*** of shapes determines which shape appears in front of or behind other shapes.
- When working with multiple shapes, you can ***align*** them vertically and horizontally in relation to each other, the page, or the margins.
- Shapes can be ***grouped*** to create one object, which you can then resize, align, position, or modify as one object. Grouped shapes can be ***ungrouped***.

Check for Understanding

In the ***Online Learning Center*** for this text (www.mhhe.com/office2013inpractice), there are a variety of resources that can be used to review the concepts covered in this chapter.

The following Online Learning Resources are available in the Online Learning Center:

- Multiple choice questions
- Short answer questions
- Matching exercises

Guided Project 7-1

For this project, you modify a document from Sierra Pacific Community College. You convert text to tables, modify tables, apply a table style, modify a style, create a new style, draw and format a shape, and insert and format a picture.
[Student Learning Outcomes 7.1, 7.2, 7.3, 7.4, 7.5]

Files Needed: ***EmergencyTelephones-07.docx*** and ***SPCCD-logo-07.png***
Completed Project File Name: ***[your initials] Word 7-1.docx***

Skills Covered in This Project

- Convert text to a table.
- Sort information in a table.
- Modify a table and change text direction.
- Apply a table style to a table.
- Modify a table style.
- Create a new table style.
- Apply a custom table style to tables.
- Draw, resize, and modify a shape.
- Insert, resize, and modify a picture.

---

1. Open the ***EmergencyTelephones-07*** document from your student data files.
2. Save the document as ***[your initials] Word 7-1***.
3. Convert text to a table and sort information in a table.
   a. Select the tabbed text in the "Emergency Phone Locations" section.
   b. Click the **Table** button [*Insert* tab, *Tables* group] and select **Convert Text to Table**. The *Convert Text to Table* dialog box opens (Figure 7-90).

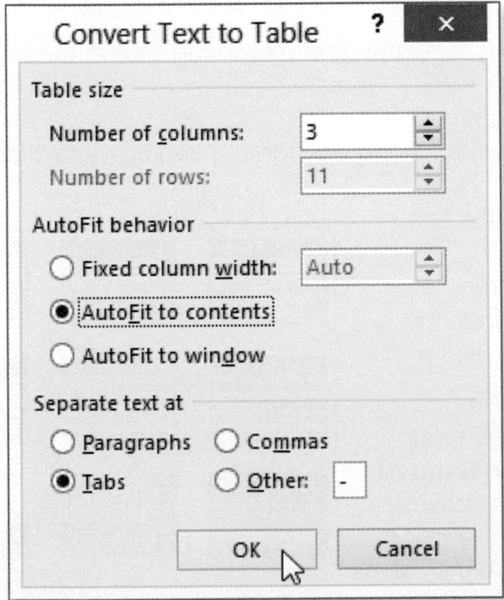

7-90 ***Convert Text to Table*** **dialog box**

c. Enter the following settings to convert the text to a table:

Number of columns: **3**
AutoFit behavior: **AutoFit to contents**
Separate text at: **Tabs**

d. Click **OK** to close the dialog box.
e. Select the table and click the **Sort** button [*Table Tools Layout* tab, *Data* group] to open the *Sort* dialog box (Figure 7-91).
f. In the *My list has* area, select the **Header row** radio button.
g. In the *Sort by* area, select **Building** in **Ascending** order, and in the *Then by* area, select **Inside/Outside** in **Ascending** order.
h. Click **OK** to close the dialog box.

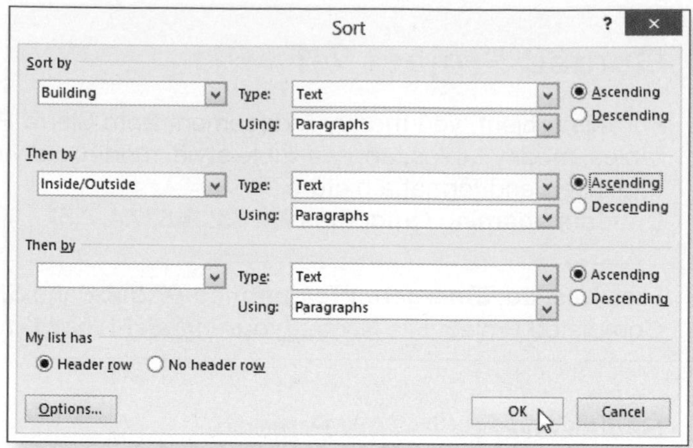

7-91 Sort information in a table

4. Convert text to a table and sort information in the table.
   a. Select the tabbed text in the "Emergency Phone Numbers" section.
   b. Click the **Table** button and select **Convert Text to Table**. The *Convert Text to Table* dialog box opens.
   c. Enter the following settings to convert the text to a table:

      Number of columns: **4**
      AutoFit behavior: **AutoFit to contents**
      Separate text at: **Tabs**

   d. Click **OK** to close the dialog box.
   e. Select the table and click the **Sort** button to open the *Sort* dialog box.
   f. In the *My list has* area, select the **Header row** radio button.
   g. In the *Sort by* area, select **Emergency Contact** in **Ascending** order.
   h. Click **OK** to close the dialog box.
5. Modify tables and change text direction.
   a. In the first table, insert a column to the left of the first column and merge the cells in the new first column.
   b. Type Emergency Phone Locations in the first column.
   c. Click the **Text Direction** button [*Table Tool Layout* tab, *Alignment* group] two times to change the text direction to vertical from bottom to top.
   d. In the second table, insert a column to the left of the first column and merge the cells in the new first column.
   e. Type Emergency Phone Numbers in the first column.
   f. Click the **Text Direction** button two times to change the text direction to vertical from bottom to top.
6. Apply a table style and modify the table.
   a. Select the first table and, in the *Table Style Options* group [*Table Tools Design* tab], check the **Header Row**, **Banded Rows**, and **First Column** boxes. The other check boxes should not be checked.
   b. Apply the **List Table 4 - Accent 1** table style from the *Table Styles* gallery (Figure 7-92).

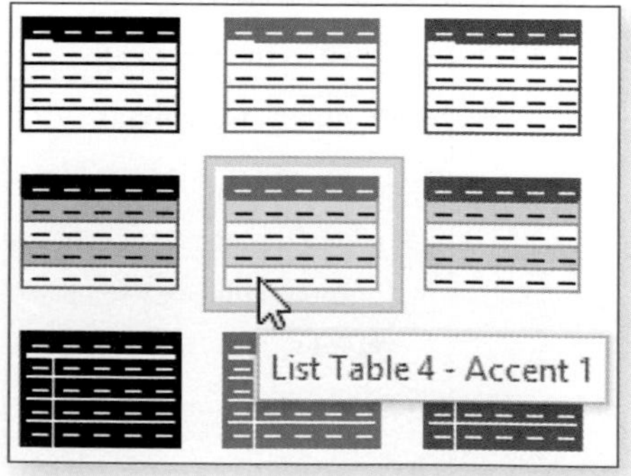

7-92 Apply a table style

c. With the table selected, click the **More** button in the *Table Styles* gallery [*Table Tools Design* tab] and select **Modify Table Style**. The *Modify Style* dialog box opens.
d. In the *Apply formatting to* area, select **Whole table**, change the font size to **10 pt.**, and change the text alignment to **Align Center Left**.
e. Click the **Format** button and select **Table Properties** to open the *Table Properties* dialog box.
f. Click the **Options** button to open the *Table Options* dialog box (Figure 7-93).
g. Set the *Top* and *Bottom* cell margins to **0.03"** and the *Left* and *Right* cell margins to **0.1"**.
h. Click **OK** to close the *Table Options* dialog box.
i. Click **OK** to close the *Table Properties* dialog box.
j. Click **OK** to close the *Modify Style* dialog box.

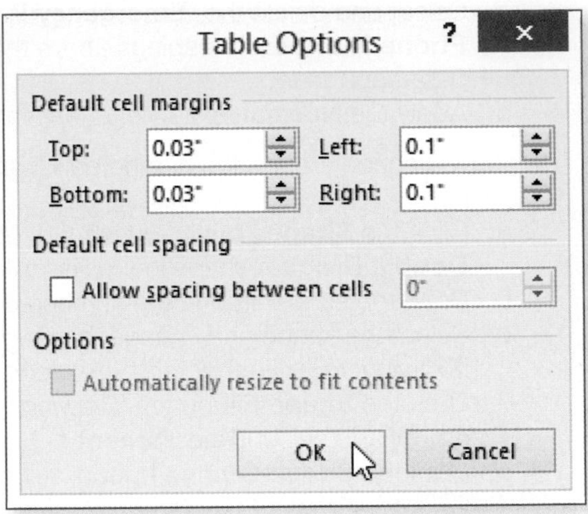

7-93 Change cell margins

7. Save the document.
8. Create a new table style.
   a. Right-click one of the table styles in the *Table Styles* gallery and select **New Table Style**. The *Create New Style from Formatting* dialog box opens (Figure 7-94).
   b. Type SPCCD table in the *Name* area.
   c. Click the **Style based on** drop-down list and select **List Table 4 - Accent 1**.
   d. Click the **Apply formatting to** drop-down list and select **First column**.
   e. Change the text alignment to **Align Center**.
   f. Click the **Format** button and select **Font** to open the *Font* dialog box.
   g. Change the font size to **11 pt.** and apply **small caps**.
   h. Click **OK** to close the *Font* dialog box.
   i. Click **OK** to close the *Create New Style from Formatting* dialog box and create the new style.

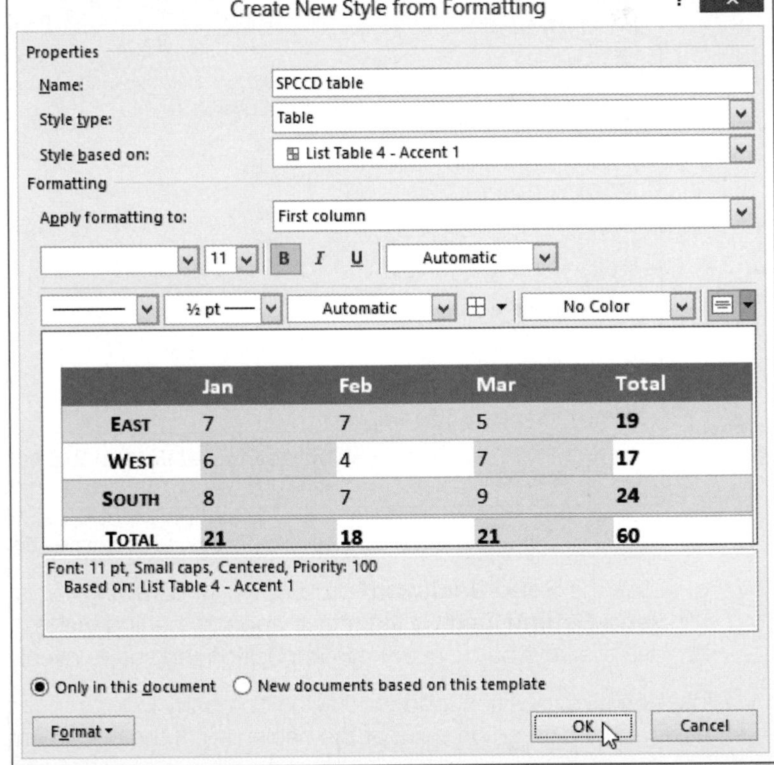

7-94 Create a new table style

9. Apply a custom table style to tables and delete text headings.
   a. Select the first table and apply the **SPCCD table** style from the *Custom* area in the *Table Styles* gallery.
   b. Select the second table and apply the **SPCCD table** style.

c. Select and delete the "**Emergency Phone Locations**" and "**Emergency Phone Numbers**" headings above the tables, but don't delete the paragraph marks.
d. Apply the **Normal** text style to the blank line above each table.

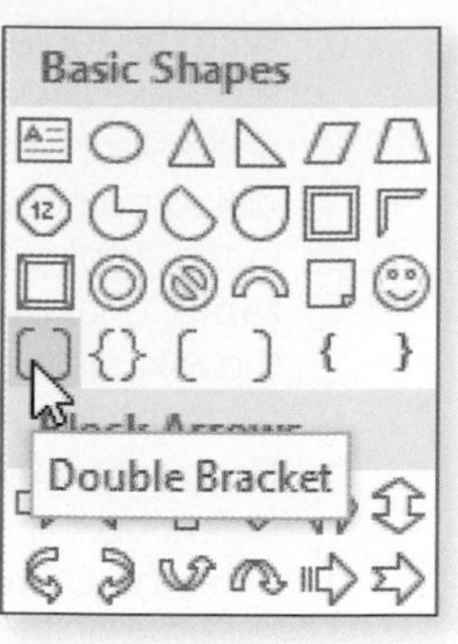

7-95 Select shape to draw

10. Draw a shape around the numbered list and resize, modify, and arrange the shape.
    a. Click the **Shapes** button [*Insert* tab, *Illustrations* group] and select the **Double Bracket** shape in the *Basic Shapes* area (Figure 7-95).
    b. Draw the shape around the numbered list.
    c. Select the shape and change the *Height* to **0.8"** and the *Width* to **4.8"** [*Drawing Tools Format* tab, *Size* group].
    d. Click the **Shape Fill** button [*Drawing Tools Format* tab, *Shape Styles* group] and select **Blue**, **Accent 1**, **Lighter 80%**.
    e. Click the **Shape Outline** button, select **Weight**, and select **2 ¼ pt.**
    f. Click the **Shape Effects** button, select **Shadow**, and select **Offset Diagonal Bottom Right** (Figure 7-96).

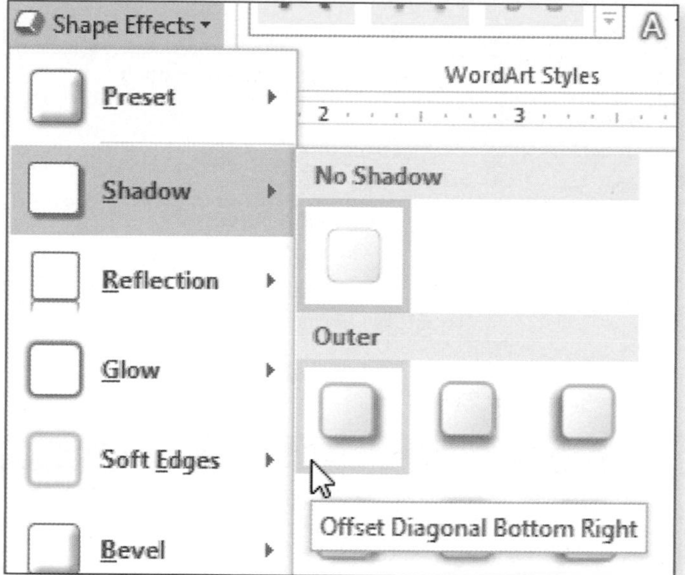

7-96 Apply a *Shadow* shape effect

    g. Click the **Send Backward** drop-down list [*Drawing Tools Format* tab, *Arrange* group] and select **Send Behind Text** so the shape appears behind the text.
    h. Use the keyboard arrow keys to position the shape evenly around the numbered list.
11. Insert, resize, position, and modify the company logo.
    a. Place the insertion point at the beginning of the document and insert the ***SPCCD-logo-07*** picture.
    b. Click the **Wrap Text** button [*Picture Tools Format* tab, *Arrange* group] and select **Tight**.
    c. Click the **Size** launcher [*Picture Tools Format* tab, *Size* group] to open the *Layout* dialog box.
    d. On the *Size* tab, change the *Scale* to **120%** of its original height and width.
    e. Click the **Position** tab.
    f. In the *Horizontal* area, set **Absolute position** to **0.3"** *to the right of* **Page**.
    g. In the *Vertical* area, set **Absolute position** to **0.3"** *below* **Page**.
    h. Click **OK** to close the *Layout* dialog box.

i. With the logo selected, click the **Corrections** button and select **Picture Corrections Options** to open the *Format Picture* pane with *Picture Corrections* area opened.
j. Change the *Brightness* to **25%** and the *Contrast* to **25%**.
k. Click the **X** in the upper right to close the *Format Picture* pane.

12. Save and close the document (Figure 7-97).

SPCCD—WEST CAMPUS EMERGENCY PROCEDURES

EMERGENCY PHONE [BLUE PHONES] PROCEDURES

1. To use, press the "Help" button. Speak when the light comes on.
2. Stay on the line. You will be connected with the college police.
3. State clearly the nature of the emergency and your location.

Emergency Phone Locations

Building	Inside/Outside	Location
Barton Hall	Inside	Second floor, west end near elevators
Barton Hall	Outside	Southwest corner
Cafeteria	Outside	Northeast entrance from parking lot B
Gymnasium	Inside	Breezeway between offices and gym entrance
Liberal Arts	Outside	North end of the C wing
Library	Inside	First floor, stairs
Library	Outside	Right side of front entrance
Math & Science	Inside	West wall of biology wing
Performing Arts	Outside	Near west entrance from Lot B
Stadium Parking Lot	Outside	Between ticket machines

Emergency Phone Numbers

Emergency Contact	Days	Hours	Phone Number
College Police	M-Su	7:00 p.m. – 7:00 p.m.	(209) 658-7777
Emergency Response System	M-Su	Available 24 hrs.	911
Evening Dean	M-Th	5:00 p.m. – 8:00 p.m.	(209) 658-7700
Health Center	M-F	7:30 a.m. – 4:00 pm.	(209) 658-2239
Information Center	M-F	8 a.m. – 5 p.m.	(209) 658-4466
Site Administrator	M-F	8:00 a.m. – 5:00 p.m.	(209) 658-8501
Weekend College Coordinator	S	8:00 a.m. – 5:00 p.m.	(209) 658-6500

Emergency Telephones   Sierra Pacific Community College District   Revised December 1, 2014

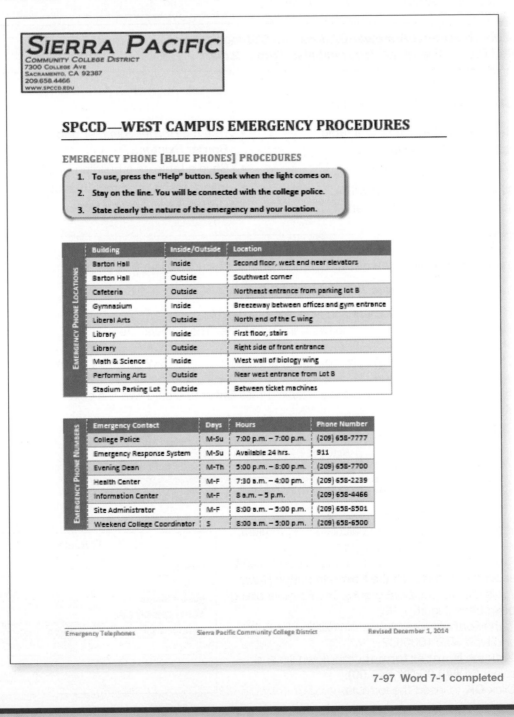

7-97 Word 7-1 completed

Guided Project 7-2

For this project, you modify an insurance renewal letter from Eva Skaar at Central Sierra Insurance. You create a table and insert text, insert formulas in the table, apply a table style, customize table borders, create a table building block, insert and format a picture, and update formulas.
[Student Learning Outcomes 7.1, 7.2, 7.3, 7.4]

Files Needed: ***InsuranceRenewal-07.docx*** and ***CSI-logo-07.png***
Completed Project File Name: ***[your initials] Word 7-2.docx***

Skills Covered in This Project

- Insert a table and add text to a table.
- Insert formulas in a table.
- Apply a table style to a table.
- Change cell margins and spacing.
- Change table and text alignment.
- Use the *Border Sampler* and *Border Painter.*
- Save a table as a building block.
- Insert, resize, and modify a picture.
- Update formulas in a table.

1. Open the ***InsuranceRenewal-07*** document from your student data files.
2. Save the document as ***[your initials] Word 7-2***.
3. Insert a table into the document and type text into the table.
   a. Place the insertion point on the blank line below the "The renewal premium is . . ." paragraph and press **Enter**.
   b. Click the **Table** button [*Insert* tab, *Tables* group] and insert a **6x2** table (six columns and two rows) using the *Insert Table* grid.
   c. Type the following information in the table. Press **Enter** to create two-line column headings as shown in the following table:

Policy Description	Premium Basis	Rate per $1,000	Premium	Discount	Discounted Premium
Construction	$325,000	$21			

4. Insert formulas in the table to calculate the premium, discount, and discounted premium.
   a. Place the insertion point in the fourth column and second row and click the **Formula** button [*Table Tools Layout* tab, *Data* group]. The *Formula* dialog box opens (Figure 7-98).
   b. In the *Formula* area, delete the existing formula and type =B2/1000*C2.
   c. Click the **Number format** drop-down list and select **$#,##0.00;($#,##0.00)**.
   d. Click **OK** to insert the formula.

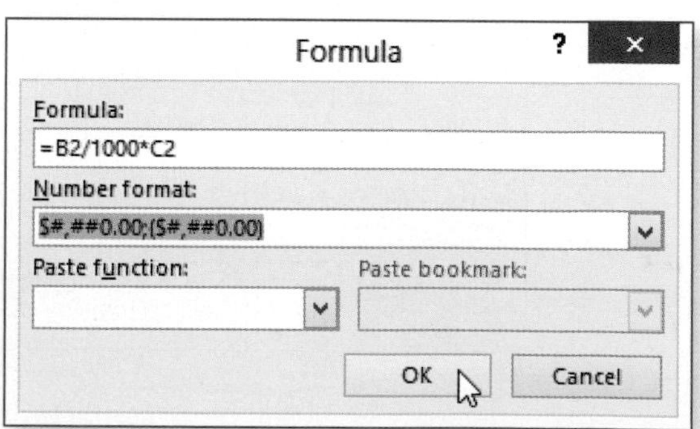

7-98 ***Formula*** **dialog box**

e. Place the insertion point in the fifth column and second row, create the following formula, and use the **$#,##0.00;($#,##0.00)** number format:

=D2*15%

f. Place the insertion point in the sixth column and second row, create the following formula, and use the **$#,##0.00;($#,##0.00)** number format:

=D2-E2

5. Apply a table style and modify the table style.
   a. Select the table and **AutoFit Contents**.
   b. In the *Table Style Option* group [*Table Tools Design* tab], check the **Header Row**, **Banded Rows**, and **Last Column** boxes. The other boxes should not be checked.
   c. Apply the **Grid Table 2** table style from the *Table Styles* gallery (Figure 7-99).
   d. Click the **Cell Margins** button [*Table Tools Layout* tab, *Alignment* group] to open the *Table Options* dialog box.
   e. Change the *Top* and *Bottom* margins to **0.05"** and the *Left* and *Right* margins to **0.15"** and click **OK** to close the dialog box.
   f. With the table selected, click the **Properties** button [*Table Tools Layout* tab, *Table* group] to open the *Table Properties* dialog box.
   g. On the *Table* tab, click the **Center** button in the *Alignment* area, and click **OK** to close the *Table Properties* dialog box.
   h. Select the first row of the table and change text alignment to **Align Bottom Center** [*Table Tools Layout* tab, *Alignment* group].
   i. Select the second row of the table and change text alignment to **Align Center**.

Grid Tables

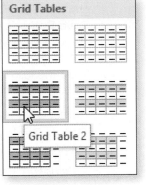

Grid Table 2

7-99 Apply a table style

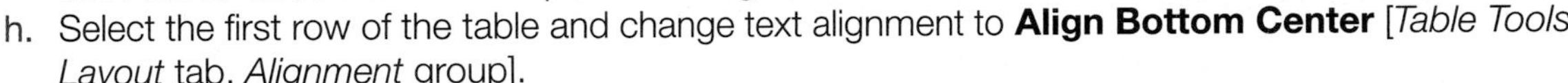

6. Use the *Border Sampler* and *Border Painter* to apply borders to the table.
   a. Click the **View Gridlines** button [*Table Tools Layout* tab, *Table* group] to display table gridlines if they are not already displayed.
   b. Click the **Border Styles** drop-down list [*Table Tools Design* tab, *Border* group] and select **Border Sampler** from the drop-down list. Your pointer becomes an eyedropper.
   c. Using the eyedropper, click the horizontal border between the first and second rows (Figure 7-100). The eyedropper copies the border style, the *Border Painter* turns on, and the eyedropper becomes a pen.
   d. Use the pen to draw a horizontal border on the table gridline above the first row (Figure 7-101).

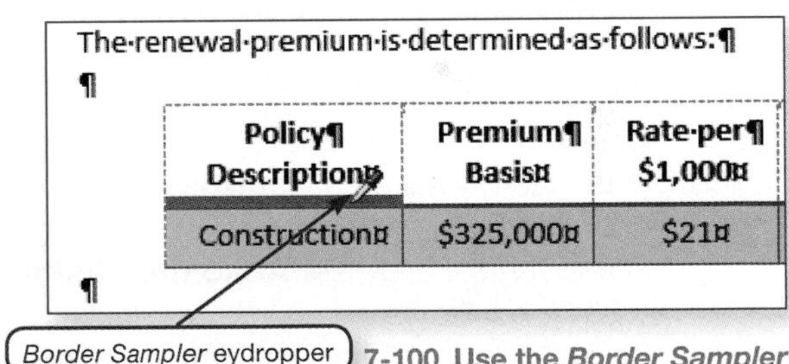

The·renewal·premium·is·determined·as·follows:¶
Policy¶ Description¤
Premium¶ Basis¤
Rate·per¶ $1,000¤
Construction¤
$325,000¤
$21¤
Border Sampler eydropper

7-100 Use the *Border Sampler*

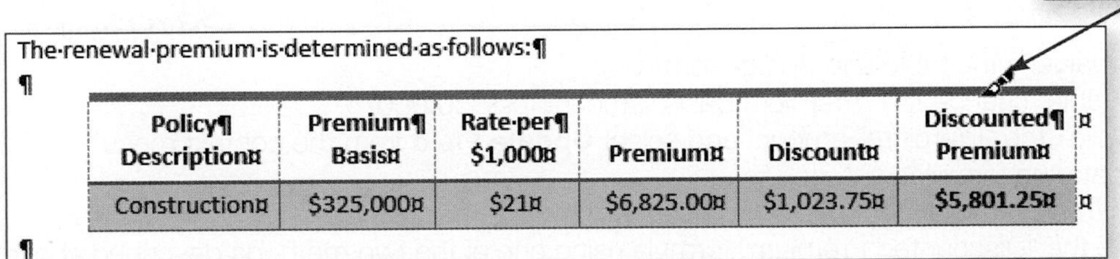

7-101 Use the *Border Painter*

   e. Use the pen to draw a horizontal border on the table gridline below the second row.

f. Click the **Border Painter** button [*Table Tools Design* tab, *Border* group] to turn off the *Border Painter*.
g. Click the **View Gridlines** button [*Table Tools Layout* tab, *Table* group] to turn off table gridlines.

7. Save the table as a building block in the *Quick Tables* gallery.
   a. Select the table.
   b. Click the **Table** button [*Insert* tab, *Tables* group], select **Quick Tables**, and then select **Save Selection to Quick Tables Gallery**. The *Create New Building Block* dialog box opens (Figure 7-102).
   c. Enter the following information to create a new table building block:

      Name: CSI Premium table
      Gallery: **Tables**
      Category: CSI (create new category)
      Description: Calculates insurance premium
      Save in: **Building Blocks**
      Options: **Insert content in its own paragraph**

7-102 Create a new building block

   d. Click **OK** to close the *Create New Building Block* dialog box.

8. Insert, resize, position, and modify company logo.
   a. Place the insertion point at the beginning of the document and insert the ***CSI-logo-07*** picture.
   b. Click the **Wrap Text** button [*Picture Tools Format* tab, *Arrange* group] and select **Square**.
   c. In the *Size* group [*Picture Tools Format* tab], change the *Width* to **4"** and press **Enter**.
   d. Drag the logo to align with the right and top margins of the document. Use the alignment guides to position the picture.
   e. Click the **Position** button [*Picture Tools Format* tab, *Arrange* group] and select **More Layout Options** to open the *Layout* dialog box.
   f. In the *Horizontal* area, set **Absolute position** to **4.2"** *to the right of* **Page**.
   g. In the *Vertical* area, set **Absolute position** to **0.3"** *below* **Page**.
   h. Click **OK** to close the *Layout* dialog box.
   i. With the logo selected, click the **Color** button [*Picture Tools Format* tab, *Adjust* group] and select **Red**, **Accent color 2 Dark** in the *Recolor* area (Figure 7-103).

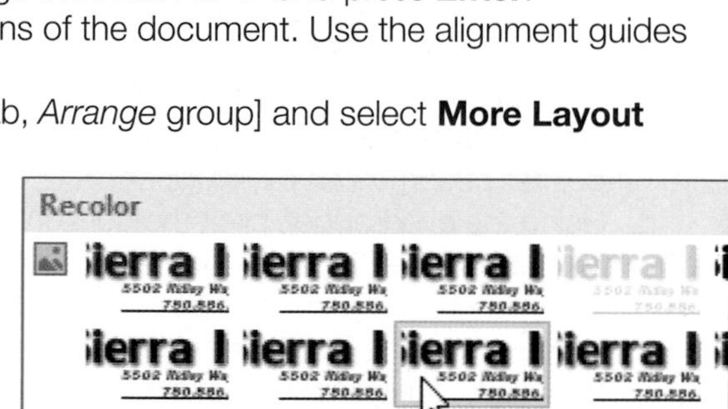
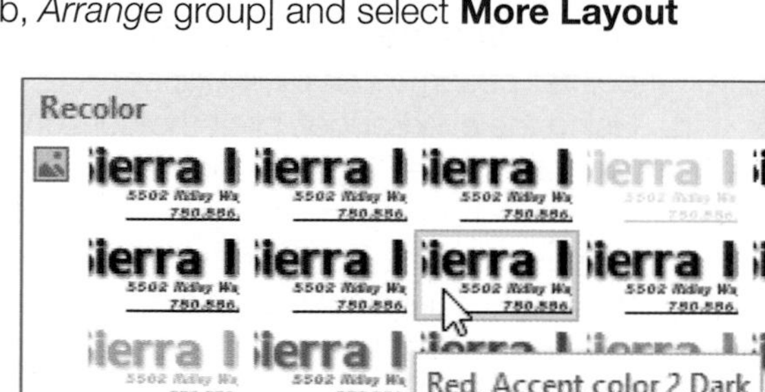

7-103 Change picture color

9. Change a value in the table and update formulas.
   a. In the table, change the "Premium Basis" amount to $350,000.
   b. Right-click the "Premium" amount and select **Update Field** from the context menu to update the formula.
   c. Select the "Discount" amount and press **F9** to update the formula.
   d. Update the "Discounted Premium" formula using one of the two methods described above.

10. Save and close the document (Figure 7-104).

Central Sierra Insurance
5502 Ridley Way | Cameron Park, CA 94663
780.886.2400 | www.centralsierra.com

March 15, 2015

Mr. Lamar Gordon
Sierra Fence Company
2405 Eureka Avenue
Fair Oaks, CA 95636

Dear Mr. Gordon:

Subject: Policy SF752284 Renewal

I am pleased to enclose your insurance renewal policy referenced above for Sierra Fence Company. Below is a summary of premium basis, premium rate, premium, discount, and discounted premium for your review and future reference.

Central Sierra Insurance prides itself in finding the insurance carrier which best meets the needs of your organization while offering a reasonably priced policy. We received quotes from four different insurance carriers. West Coast Insurance, which had very good pricing, offered the most competitive and cost-effective renewal. Due to changes in underwriting guidelines, your renewal options were limited, and this renewal is the best pricing available.

The renewal premium is determined as follows:

Policy Description	Premium Basis	Rate per $1,000	Premium	Discount	Discounted Premium
Construction	$350,000	$21	$7,350.00	$1,102.50	$6,247.50

Thank you, Lamar. As always, please do not hesitate to call or stop by the office if we may be of any assistance whatsoever.

Sincerely,

Eva Skaar, ARM, CIC, CRM
Central Sierra Insurance
eva@centralsierra.com

7-104 Word 7-2 completed

Guided Project 7-3

For this project, you modify the Tuscany cycling tour itinerary for the American River Cycling Club. You convert text to a table, modify the table, insert pictures, crop and modify pictures, and insert and modify a shape.
[Student Learning Outcomes 7.1, 7.2, 7.4, 7.5]

Files Needed: ***CyclingTuscany-07.docx, Day1-07.jpg, Day2-07.jpg, Day3-07.jpg, Day4-07.jpg, Day5-07.jpg, Day6-07.jpg, Day7-07.jpg,*** and ***Day8-07.jpg***
Completed Project File Name: ***[your initials] Word 7-3.docx***

Skills Covered in This Project

- Convert text to a table.
- Insert a column and merge cells.
- Apply a table style to a table.
- Insert and resize a picture.
- Crop a picture to a shape and apply a shadow.
- Align pictures in a table.
- *AutoFit* a table to contents.
- Draw, resize, modify, and arrange a shape.

---

1. Open the ***CyclingTuscany-07*** document from your student data files.
2. Save the document as ***[your initials] Word 7-3***.
3. Convert text to a table and modify the table.
   a. Change the top, bottom, left, and right margins to **0.5"**.
   b. Select the entire document.
   c. Click the **Table** button [*Insert* tab, *Tables* group] and select **Convert Text to Table**. The *Convert Text to Table* dialog box opens (Figure 7-105).
   d. In the *Table size* area, set *Number of columns* to **1**.
   e. In the *AutoFit behavior* area, select the **AutoFit to window** radio button.
   f. In the *Separate text at* area, select the **Paragraphs** radio button.
   g. Click **OK** to close the dialog box and convert the selected text to a table.
   h. With the table selected, click the **Borders** drop-down arrow [*Table Tools Design* tab, *Borders* group], and select **No Border** to remove all of the table borders.
   i. Click the **View Gridlines** button [*Table Tools Layout* tab, *Table* group] to display the table gridlines.

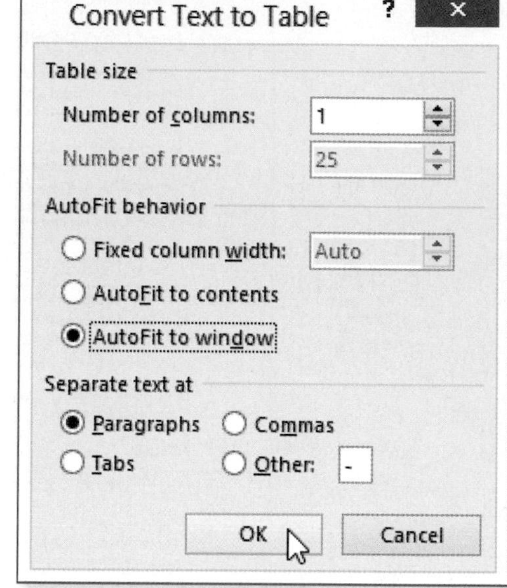

7-105 Convert text to a table

4. Insert a column and merge cells.
   a. Insert a column to the right of the existing column.
   b. Select the entire second column and apply the **Normal** text style.
   c. Select the two cells in the first row and click the **Merge Cells** button [*Table Tools Layout* tab, *Merge* group].
   d. Select the cells in the second column in rows 2–4 and click the **Merge Cells** button. This step merges the cells in the second column to the right of the "Day 1" heading, "Highlights," and description content.
   e. Repeat step 4d to merge the three cells in the second column to the right of each day, highlight, and description cell in the first column. Continue this process through the cells that contain the "Day 8" heading, highlights, and description (Figure 7-106).

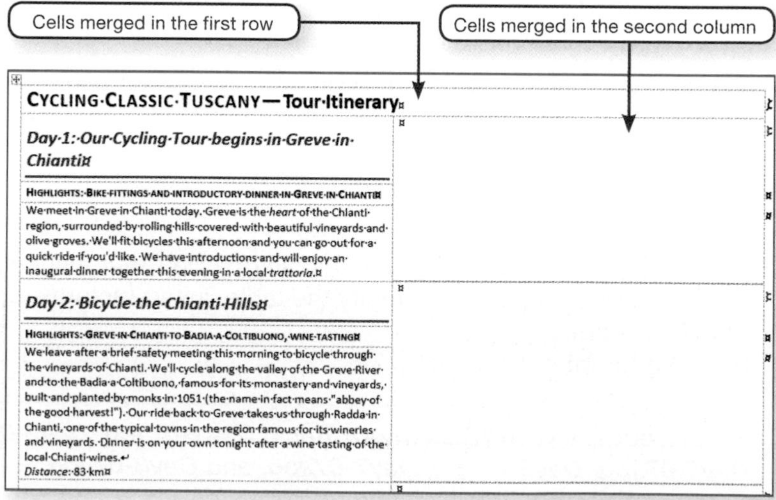

7-106 Cells merged in the first row and second column

5. Insert, resize, crop, modify, and align pictures.
   a. Place the insertion point in the cell in the second column to the right of the "Day 1" content.
   b. Insert the ***Day1-07*** picture from your student data files.
   c. In the *Size* group [*Picture Tools Format* tab], change the width of the picture to **2.5"**. The height automatically adjusts to maintain the aspect ratio.
   d. Click the **Crop** drop-down arrow [*Picture Tools Format* tab, *Size* group], select **Crop to Shape**, and then select **Rounded Rectangle** in the *Rectangles* area (Figure 7-107). The picture is cropped to the size of the shape.

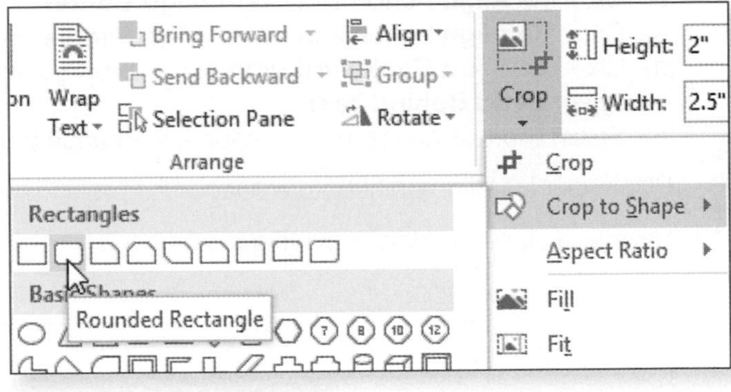

7-107 Crop picture to a shape

   e. Click the **Picture Effects** button [*Picture Tools Format* tab, *Picture Styles* group], select **Shadow**, and select **Offset Center** in the *Outer* area (Figure 7-108).
   f. With the picture selected, click the **Align Center** button [*Table Tools Layout* tab, *Alignment* group] to center the picture vertically and horizontally in the cell.
   g. Repeat steps 5b–f to insert and format the following pictures: ***Day2-07, Day3-07, Day4-07, Day5-07, Day6-07, Day7-07,*** and ***Day8-07***. Don't be concerned about pagination at this point; you address this in the next step.

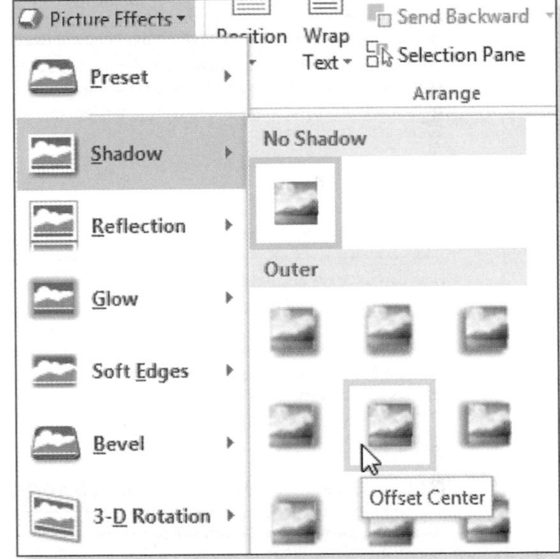

7-108 Apply a *Shadow* picture effect

6. *AutoFit* the table to contents.
   a. Select the entire table.
   b. Click the **AutoFit** button [*Table Tools Layout* tab, *Cell Size* group] and select **AutoFit Contents**.
7. Draw, resize, and modify a shape.
   a. Go to the first page of the itinerary and **center** the text in the first row.
   b. Click the **Shapes** button [*Insert* tab, *Illustrations* group] and select **Rounded Rectangle** in the *Rectangles* area.
   c. Draw a shape around the text in the first row of the table.
   d. Change the *Height* to **0.35"** and the *Width* to **5.2"** [*Drawing Tools Format* tab, *Size* group].
   e. With the shape selected, click the **Shape Fill** button [*Drawing Tools Format* tab, *Shape Styles* group] and select **Red**, **Accent 2** in the *Theme Colors* area.
   f. Click the **Shape Fill** button, select **Gradient**, and then select **Linear Up** in the *Dark Variations* area (Figure 7-109).
   g. Click the **Shape Outline** button [*Drawing Tools Format* tab, *Shape Styles* group] and select **Green** in the *Standard Colors* area.
   h. Click the **Shape Outline** button, select **Weight**, and then select **2 ¼ pt.**

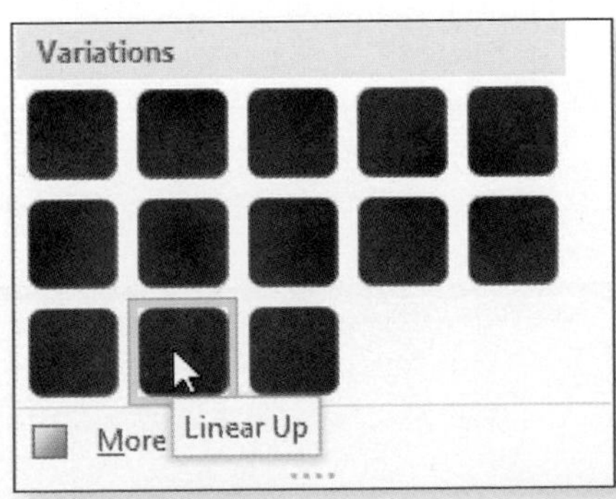

7-109 Apply a *Gradient* shape fill

8. Align and order a shape.
   a. With the shape selected, click the **Align** button [*Drawing Tools Format* tab, *Arrange* group] and select **Align to Margin**. The *Align to Margin* option should have a check to the left of it.
   b. Click the **Align** button and select **Align Center**.
   c. Click the **Align** button and select **Align Middle**.
   d. Click the **Send Backward** drop-down arrow [*Drawing Tools Format* tab, *Arrange* group] and select **Send Behind Text**.
   e. Select the text on top of the shape and change the font color to **White**, **Background 1**.
9. Place your insertion point before "Day 7" on page 2 and press **Ctrl+Enter** to insert a page break.
10. Save and close the document (Figure 7-110).

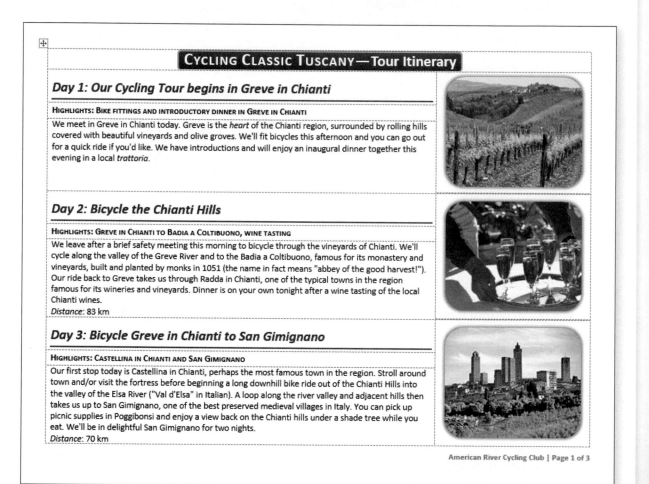

CYCLING CLASSIC TUSCANY—Tour Itinerary

Day 1: Our Cycling Tour begins in Greve in Chianti **HIGHLIGHTS: BIKE FITTINGS AND INTRODUCTORY DINNER IN GREVE IN CHIANTI** We meet in Greve in Chianti today. Greve is the *heart* of the Chianti region, surrounded by rolling hills covered with beautiful vineyards and olive groves. We'll fit bicycles this afternoon and you can go out for a quick ride if you'd like. We have introductions and will enjoy an inaugural dinner together this evening in a local *trattoria*.	
Day 2: Bicycle the Chianti Hills **HIGHLIGHTS: GREVE IN CHIANTI TO BADIA A COLTIBUONO, WINE TASTING** We leave after a brief safety meeting this morning to bicycle through the vineyards of Chianti. We'll cycle along the valley of the Greve River and to the Badia a Coltibuono, famous for its monastery and vineyards, built and planted by monks in 1051 (the name in fact means "abbey of the good harvest!"). Our ride back to Greve takes us through Radda in Chianti, one of the typical towns in the region famous for its wineries and vineyards. Dinner is on your own tonight after a wine tasting of the local Chianti wines. *Distance*: 83 km	
Day 3: Bicycle Greve in Chianti to San Gimignano **HIGHLIGHTS: CASTELLINA IN CHIANTI AND SAN GIMIGNANO** Our first stop today is Castellina in Chianti, perhaps the most famous town in the region. Stroll around town and/or visit the fortress before beginning a long downhill bike ride out of the Chianti Hills into the valley of the Elsa River ("Val d'Elsa" in Italian). A loop along the river valley and adjacent hills then takes us up to San Gimignano, one of the best preserved medieval villages in Italy. You can pick up picnic supplies in Poggibonsi and enjoy a view back on the Chianti hills under a shade tree while you eat. We'll be in delightful San Gimignano for two nights. *Distance*: 70 km	

American River Cycling Club | Page 1 of 3

7-110 Word 7-3 completed (page 1 with table gridlines visible)

Independent Project 7-4

For this project, you modify a memo detailing the weekly expenses of Life's Animal Shelter. You convert text to a table, add formulas, modify the table, insert a picture, crop and modify the picture, and insert and modify a shape.
[Student Learning Outcomes 7.1, 7.2, 7.3, 7.4, 7.5]

Files Needed: ***WeeklyExpenses-07.docx*** and ***LASfamily.jpg***
Completed Project File Name: ***[your initials] Word 7-4.docx***

Skills Covered in This Project

- Convert text to a table.
- Insert rows and columns and merge cells.
- Insert *SUM* and *AVERAGE* formulas.
- Create a new table style.
- Apply a custom table style to a table.
- Insert, crop, and resize a picture.
- Crop a picture to a shape and apply a border.
- Position a picture in the document.
- Compress a picture.
- Draw, resize, and modify a shape.
- Add text to a shape and format the text.

---

1. Open the ***WeeklyExpenses-07*** document from your student data files.
2. Save the document as ***[your initials] Word 7-4***.
3. Convert text to a table and modify the table.
   a. Select the lines of tabbed text below the body of the memo and convert the text to a table.
   b. *AutoFit* the contents of the table.
   c. Insert one column to the right of the last column.
   d. Insert two rows below the last row.
   e. In the last cell in the first row, type Totals.
   f. In the next to the last cell in the first column, type Totals.
   g. In the last cell in the first column, type Averages.
   h. Insert a row above the first row and merge the cells in this row. If there is a paragraph symbol in this row, delete it.
   i. In the new first row **center** and type Life's Animal Shelter Weekly Expenses.
4. Insert formulas to add and average expenses.
   a. In rows 3–8 in the last column, use the **SUM** function to add the numbers to the left and apply the **$#,##0.00;($#,##0.00)** number format. You can use "LEFT" as the range for the *SUM* functions (e.g., **=SUM(LEFT)**).
   b. In the next to the last row, use the **SUM** function to add the numbers above and apply the **$#,##0.00;($#,##0.00)** number format. You can use "ABOVE" as the range for the *SUM* functions.
   c. In the last row, use the **AVERAGE** function to calculate the average of the amounts in rows 3-8 above and apply the **$#,##0.00;($#,##0.00)** number format. You have to type in the cell reference range to average (e.g., **=AVERAGE(B3:B8)**). Don't include the *Totals* row in the range.
5. Create a new table style.
   a. Name the new table style LAS Expenses.
   b. Base the new table style on **Grid Table 5 Dark – Accent 3**.

c. Make the following changes to the new table style to the *Whole table:*

Change the font size to **10 pt.**
Change the top and bottom cell margins to **0.02"** and the left and right cell margins to **0.1"** (*Hint: Open the* Table Properties *dialog box from the* Format *drop-down list*).
Change the Alignment of the Table to **Center**.

d. Make the following changes to the new table style to the *Header* row:

Change the font size to **14 pt.**
Change the text alignment to **Align Center**.

6. Set the table style options and apply a custom table style.
   a. Select the table and set the *Table Style Options* to include the following: **Header Row**, **Banded Rows**, **First Column**, and **Last Column**.
   b. Apply the **LAS Expenses** custom table style to the table.
7. Modify the table format.
   a. Apply **bold** formatting to the second row and the last two rows.
   b. Change the alignment of all values and their corresponding column headings to **Align Top Right**.

7-111 Crop picture

8. Insert, crop, and modify a picture.
   a. Insert the ***LASfamily-07*** picture at the bottom of the document.
   b. Crop the picture so the edges are approximately ¼" from the individuals in the picture (Figure 7-111).
   c. Change the picture height to **2"** and maintain aspect ratio.
   d. Change the text wrapping to **Tight**.
   e. Crop the picture to the **Round Same Side Corner Rectangle** shape in the *Rectangles* area. Press **Enter** to accept the cropping changes.
   f. Apply an **Olive Green**, **Accent 3** picture border and change the picture border weight to **1 pt.**
   g. Apply the **Film Grain** *Artistic Effect* to the picture.
9. Position and compress the picture.
   a. Change the *Position* of the picture to **Position in Bottom Center with Square Text Wrapping** (Figure 7-112).
   b. Compress the picture so the target output is **Screen (150 ppi)**.
10. Draw a shape, modify the shape, and add text to the shape.
    a. Draw a **Wave** shape (*Stars and Banners* category) at the top of the document.
    b. Change the height to **1"** and the width to **4"**.
    c. Change the shape fill to **Olive Green**, **Accent 3**.
    d. Change the shape fill gradient to **From Center** (*Light Variations* category).
    e. Change the shape outline to **Olive Green**, **Accent 3** and the shape outline weight to **1 ½ pt.**
    f. Apply the **Perspective Diagonal Upper Left** (*Perspective* category) shadow shape effect.

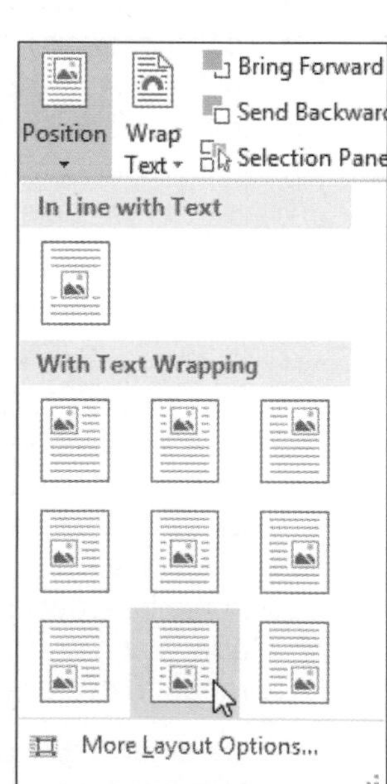

7-112 Position picture in the document

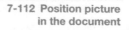

11. Position the shape and add text.
    a. Use the *Position* tab in the *Layout* dialog box to change the *Horizontal* **Alignment** to **Centered** *relative to* **Page** and change the *Vertical* **Absolute Position** to **0.2"** below the **Page**.
    b. Add text (not a text box) to the shape and type Life's Animal Shelter.
    c. Select the text on the shape and make the following changes:

       Change the text color to **Olive Green**, **Accent 3**, **Darker 50%**.
       Change the font size to **22 pt.**
       Apply **bold** and **small caps** formatting.
       Change the *After* paragraph spacing to **0 pt.**
12. Save and close the document (Figure 7-113).

LIFE'S ANIMAL SHELTER

TO: Life's Animal Shelter staff and volunteers

FROM: Kelly Sung, Director of Services

DATE: February 11, 2015

SUBJECT: Weekly Expenses

Thank you for the time you have spent volunteering at Life's Animal Shelter. Our staff and volunteers have contributed countless hours making this shelter a safe environment for animals and providing adoption services for families in our community. You have been a part of hundreds of animal rescues and adoptions over the past year. Families throughout our region are enjoying their new pets thanks to your dedication and work at Life's Animal Shelter.

I'm providing you with our expenses update for the last week. Our operating funds come through donations and pet adoption fees. Thank you for your help in keeping our expenses at a moderate level. Because of you, we are able to offer reasonable adoption fees to animal lovers in our community.

Again, thank you for all of your hard work. Because of you, Life's Animal Shelter valuably serves our community by providing shelter and adoption services.

Life's Animal Shelter Weekly Expenses							
Expenses	Mon	Tue	Wed	Thurs	Fri	Sat/Sun	Totals
Food	340.45	344.05	350.51	340.01	341.48	359.75	$2,076.25
Medicine	525.33	529.31	535.25	524.59	527.99	543.39	$3,185.86
Wages	675.21	580.91	575.88	579.55	680.81	750.05	$3,842.41
Heat	25.75	26.01	28.05	25.03	25.99	62.30	$ 193.13
Equipment	199.03	209.25	198.90	229.05	245.09	351.98	$1,433.30
Electricity	19.45	20.09	21.75	19.02	19.99	48.56	$ 148.86
Totals	$1,785.22	$1,709.62	$1,710.34	$1,717.25	$1,841.35	$2,116.03	$10,879.81
Averages	$ 297.54	$ 284.94	$ 285.06	$ 286.21	$ 306.89	$ 352.67	$1,813.30

Life's Animal Shelter — Weekly Expenses

7-113 Word 7-4 completed

Independent Project 7-5

For this project, you modify a document of Microsoft Outlook shortcuts from Courtyard Medical Plaza. You convert text to a table, include tabs and indents in the table, modify the table, modify a table style, repeat header rows, insert and modify pictures, draw and modify a shape, and align and group objects.
[Student Learning Outcomes 7.1, 7.2, 7.3, 7.4, 7.5]

Files Needed: ***OutlookShortcuts-07.docx, CMP-logo-07.png,*** and ***Email-07.png***
Completed Project File Name: ***[your initials] Word 7-5.docx***

Skills Covered in This Project

- Change margins.
- Convert text to a table.
- Customize tabs and indents in the table.
- Insert a row and merge cells.
- Apply a table style.
- Modify a table style.
- Repeat header rows.
- Insert and resize a picture.
- Align and group pictures.
- Draw, resize, and modify a shape.
- Group selected objects.
- Edit a footer.

---

1. Open the ***OutlookShortcuts-07*** document from your student data files.
2. Save the document as ***[your initials] Word 7-5***.
3. Change all margins to **0.5"**.
4. Convert text to a table.
   a. Select all of the text in the document.
   b. Separate text at **Paragraphs**.
   c. **AutoFit to window**.
   d. Change the number of columns to **2**.
5. Change tabs and indents in the table.
   a. Select the first column and set a **2.5" left tab** with a **broken line leader** (leader 3).
   b. Select the second column, set a **0.25" left indent** (*Paragraph* dialog box), and set a **2.6" left tab** with a **broken line leader**.
6. Add a row to the table and add text to the row.
   a. Add a row above the first row and type Microsoft Outlook Shortcuts in the first cell in the new row.
   b. Merge the cells in the new first row.
   c. Change the *Left* indent to **0"**.
7. Change table style options and apply a table style.
   a. Select the table and set the *Table Style Options* to include a **Header Row** and **Banded Rows**.
   b. Apply the **List Table 4 - Accent 2** table style to the table (Figure 7-114).

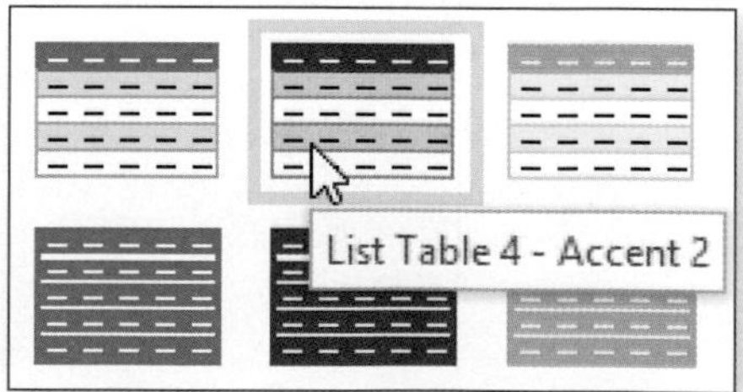

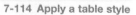

7-114 Apply a table style

8. Modify the table style.
    a. Modify the **List Table 4 - Accent 2** table style.
    b. Make the following changes to the table style to the *Whole table:*

        Change the font size to **9 pt.**
        Change the text alignment to **Align Center Left**.
        Change the top and bottom cell margins to **0.02"**. Don't change the left and right cell margins.

    c. Make the following changes to the table style to the *Header row:*

        Change the font size to **16 pt.**
        Change the text alignment to **Align Center**.

    d. Make the following change to the table style to the *Odd banded rows:*

        Change the *Fill Color* to **White**, **Background 1**, **Darker 5%**.

9. Select the first row of the table and **Repeat Header Rows**.
10. Insert and resize pictures.
    a. Place the insertion point at the end of the document and insert the ***CMP-logo-07*** picture.
    b. Change the text wrapping to **Square** and drag the picture so it is approximately one inch below the table and one inch to the right of the left side of the table.
    c. Place the insertion point at the end of the document and insert the ***Email-07*** picture.
    d. Change the height of the email picture to **1.5"** and maintain aspect ratio.
    e. Change the text wrapping to **Square** and drag the email picture so it is approximately one inch below the table and one inch to the left of the right side of the table.
11. Align and group the pictures.
    a. Select both pictures.
    b. Using the *Align* drop-down list [*Picture Tools Format* tab, *Arrange* group], select **Align to Page** and then select **Distribute Horizontally**.
    c. Select **Align Selected Objects** and then select **Align Middle**.
    d. **Group** selected objects.
12. Draw and modify a shape.
    a. Draw a **Rounded Rectangle** shape around the grouped objects.
    b. Change the height to **2"** and the width to **6"**.
    c. Use the *Selection* pane to move the grouped objects above the rounded rectangle shape.
    d. Select the shape and apply the **Subtle Effect - Black, Dark 1** from the *Shape Styles* gallery (Figure 7-115).

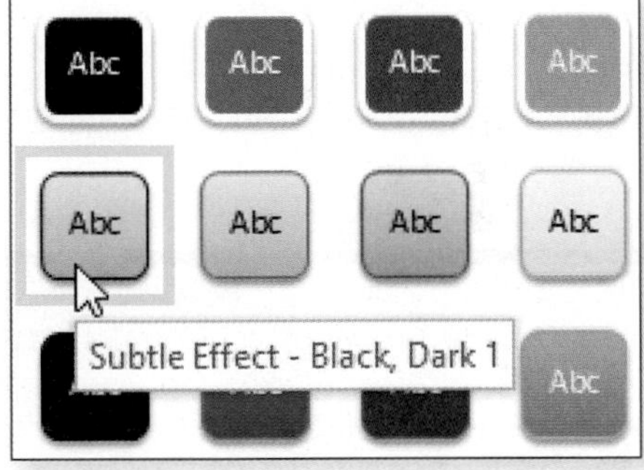

7-115 Apply a shape style

13. Align and group the objects.
    a. Use the *Selection* pane to select the shape and the grouped objects.
    b. Using the *Align* drop-down list, select **Align Selected Objects**, select **Align Center**, and then select **Align Middle**.
    c. **Group** selected objects.
    d. Select **Align to Page** and then select **Align Center**.
    e. Use the keyboard up or down arrow key to vertically position the grouped objects approximately one inch below the bottom of the table.

14. Edit the footer.
    a. In the footer, remove the existing right tab and set a **7.5" right tab**.
    b. Apply **bold** and **small caps** formatting to all of the text in the footer.
15. Save and close the document (Figure 7-116).

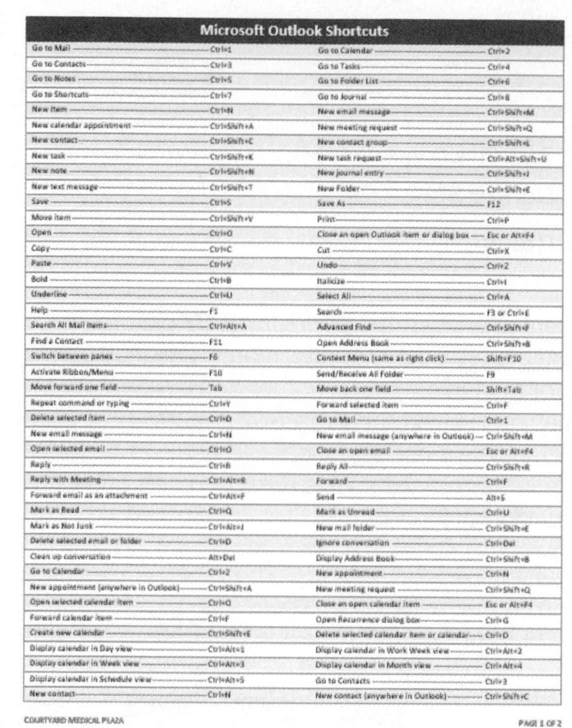

Microsoft Outlook Shortcuts			
Go to Mail	Ctrl+1	Go to Calendar	Ctrl+2
Go to Contacts	Ctrl+3	Go to Tasks	Ctrl+4
Go to Notes	Ctrl+5	Go to Folder List	Ctrl+6
Go to Shortcuts	Ctrl+7	Go to Journal	Ctrl+8
New item	Ctrl+N	New email message	Ctrl+Shift+M
New calendar appointment	Ctrl+Shift+A	New meeting request	Ctrl+Shift+Q
New contact	Ctrl+Shift+C	New contact group	Ctrl+Shift+L
New task	Ctrl+Shift+K	New task request	Ctrl+Alt+Shift+U
New note	Ctrl+Shift+N	New journal entry	Ctrl+Shift+J
New text message	Ctrl+Shift+T	New Folder	Ctrl+Shift+E
Save	Ctrl+S	Save As	F12
Move item	Ctrl+Shift+V	Print	Ctrl+P
Open	Ctrl+O	Close an open Outlook item or dialog box	Esc or Alt+F4
Copy	Ctrl+C	Cut	Ctrl+X
Paste	Ctrl+V	Undo	Ctrl+Z
Bold	Ctrl+B	Italicize	Ctrl+I
Underline	Ctrl+U	Select All	Ctrl+A
Help	F1	Search	F3 or Ctrl+E
Search All Mail Items	Ctrl+Alt+A	Advanced Find	Ctrl+Shift+F
Find a Contact	F11	Open Address Book	Ctrl+Shift+B
Switch between panes	F6	Context Menu (same as right click)	Shift+F10
Activate Ribbon/Menu	F10	Send/Receive All Folder	F9
Move forward one field	Tab	Move back one field	Shift+Tab
Repeat command or typing	Ctrl+Y	Forward selected item	Ctrl+F
Delete selected item	Ctrl+D	Go to Mail	Ctrl+1
New email message	Ctrl+N	New email message (anywhere in Outlook)	Ctrl+Shift+M
Open selected email	Ctrl+O	Close an open email	Esc or Alt+F4
Reply	Ctrl+R	Reply All	Ctrl+Shift+R
Reply with Meeting	Ctrl+Alt+R	Forward	Ctrl+F
Forward email as an attachment	Ctrl+Alt+F	Send	Alt+S
Mark as Read	Ctrl+Q	Mark as Unread	Ctrl+U
Mark as Not Junk	Ctrl+Alt+J	New mail folder	Ctrl+Shift+E
Delete selected email or folder	Ctrl+D	Ignore conversation	Ctrl+Del
Clean up conversation	Alt+Del	Display Address Book	Ctrl+Shift+B
Go to Calendar	Ctrl+2	New appointment	Ctrl+N
New appointment (anywhere in Outlook)	Ctrl+Shift+A	New meeting request	Ctrl+Shift+Q
Open selected calendar item	Ctrl+O	Close an open calendar item	Esc or Alt+F4
Forward calendar item	Ctrl+F	Open Recurrence dialog box	Ctrl+G
Create new calendar	Ctrl+Shift+E	Delete selected calendar item or calendar	Ctrl+D
Display calendar in Day view	Ctrl+Alt+1	Display calendar in Work Week view	Ctrl+Alt+2
Display calendar in Week view	Ctrl+Alt+3	Display calendar in Month view	Ctrl+Alt+4
Display calendar in Schedule view	Ctrl+Alt+5	Go to Contacts	Ctrl+3
New contact	Ctrl+N	New contact (anywhere in Outlook)	Ctrl+Shift+C

COURTYARD MEDICAL PLAZA PAGE 1 OF 2

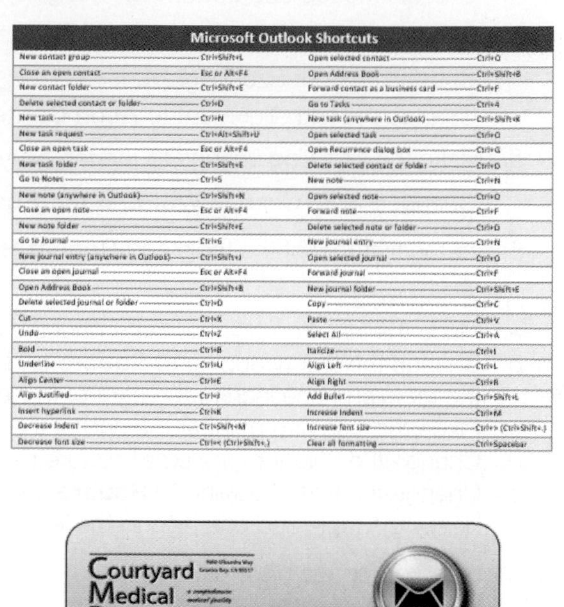

Microsoft Outlook Shortcuts			
New contact group	Ctrl+Shift+L	Open selected contact	Ctrl+O
Close an open contact	Esc or Alt+F4	Open Address Book	Ctrl+Shift+B
New contact folder	Ctrl+Shift+E	Forward contact as a business card	Ctrl+F
Delete selected contact or folder	Ctrl+D	Go to Tasks	Ctrl+4
New task	Ctrl+N	New task (anywhere in Outlook)	Ctrl+Shift+K
New task request	Ctrl+Alt+Shift+U	Open selected task	Ctrl+O
Close an open task	Esc or Alt+F4	Open Recurrence dialog box	Ctrl+G
New task folder	Ctrl+Shift+E	Delete selected contact or folder	Ctrl+D
Go to Notes	Ctrl+5	New note	Ctrl+N
New note (anywhere in Outlook)	Ctrl+Shift+N	Open selected note	Ctrl+O
Close an open note	Esc or Alt+F4	Forward note	Ctrl+F
New note folder	Ctrl+Shift+E	Delete selected note or folder	Ctrl+D
Go to Journal	Ctrl+6	New journal entry	Ctrl+N
New journal entry (anywhere in Outlook)	Ctrl+Shift+J	Open selected journal	Ctrl+O
Close an open journal	Esc or Alt+F4	Forward journal	Ctrl+F
Open Address Book	Ctrl+Shift+B	New journal folder	Ctrl+Shift+E
Delete selected journal or folder	Ctrl+D	Copy	Ctrl+C
Cut	Ctrl+X	Paste	Ctrl+V
Undo	Ctrl+Z	Select All	Ctrl+A
Bold	Ctrl+B	Italicize	Ctrl+I
Underline	Ctrl+U	Align Left	Ctrl+L
Align Center	Ctrl+E	Align Right	Ctrl+R
Align Justified	Ctrl+J	Add Bullet	Ctrl+Shift+L
Insert hyperlink	Ctrl+K	Increase Indent	Ctrl+M
Decrease Indent	Ctrl+Shift+M	Increase font size	Ctrl+> (Ctrl+Shift+.)
Decrease font size	Ctrl+< (Ctrl+Shift+,)	Clear all formatting	Ctrl+Spacebar

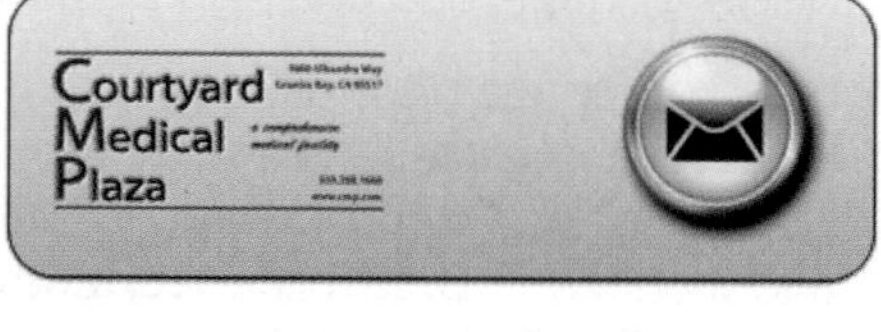

COURTYARD MEDICAL PLAZA PAGE 2 OF 2

7-116 Word 7-5 completed

Independent Project 7-6

For this project, you create a cycling event calendar for the American River Cycling Club. You insert a table, modify the table structure, apply a table style, format and align text in the table, draw and modify shapes, add text to shapes, align shapes, and insert and modify a picture.
[Student Learning Outcomes 7.2, 7.3, 7.4, 7.5]

File Needed: ***ARCC-logo-07.png***
Completed Project File Name: ***[your initials] Word 7-6.docx***

Skills Covered in This Project

- Change margins and page orientation.
- Insert a table.
- Customize row height.
- Merge cells.
- Type and align text in a table.
- Apply a table style.
- Insert and modify a shape.
- Add text to a shape and modify text.
- Align shapes.
- Insert and modify a picture.
- Position a picture in the table.

---

1. Open a new blank Word document.
2. Save the document as ***[your initials] Word 7-6***.
3. Change the page orientation to **Landscape**.
4. Change the top and bottom margins to **0.75"** and the left and right margins to **0.5"**. If you receive an error message about the margin settings, click **Ignore**.
5. Insert a table, modify table structure, and add text.
   a. Insert a **7x7** table.
   b. Change the row height to **1"** on all of the rows.
   c. Merge the cells in the first row and type June.
   d. Change the row height of the second row to **0.3"**.
   e. In the cells in the second row, type the days of the week beginning with Sunday.
   f. Beginning in the *Wednesday* column in the third row, type the day numbers beginning with 1. There are 30 days in June.
6. Set the table style options and apply table style.
   a. Select the table and set the *Table Style Options* to include a **Header Row** and **Banded Rows**.
   b. Apply the **Grid Table 4 - Accent 6** table style to the table.
7. Format text and text alignment in the table.
   a. Change the font size of the text in the first row to **72 pt.**
   b. Select the second row, change the font size to **14 pt.**, apply **bold** and **small caps** formatting, and change the text alignment to **Align Center** (center vertically and horizontally).
   c. Select rows 3–7, apply **bold** formatting, and change alignment to **Align Top Right**.
8. Add shapes to the table.
   a. Draw a **Folded Corner** shape (*Basic Shapes* category) in the *Monday*, *June 6* cell.
   b. Change the height to **0.8"** and the width to **1"**.
   c. Apply the **Subtle Effect - Green**, **Accent 6** shape style (Figure 7-117).
   d. Add text to the shape (not a text box), type Morning Ride, press **Enter**, and type 6-8 a.m. You might not be able to see all of the text you type; you format the text in the next step.
   e. Select the text in the shape (**Ctrl+A**), change the font size to **10 pt.**, apply **bold** formatting, and change the after paragraph spacing to **0 pt.**
   f. Copy and paste the shape in the three cells below. Drag the copied shapes to the cells below.
   g. Select the four shapes and, using the *Align* drop-down list, select **Align to Margin**, select **Align Left**, and select **Align Top**.

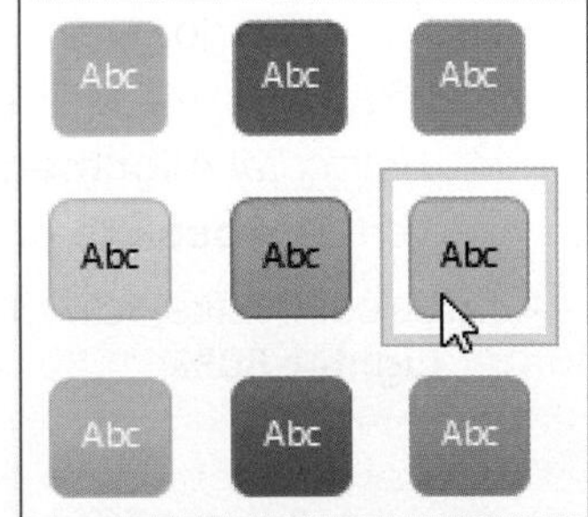

7-117 Apply a shape style

9. Add shapes to the table.
   a. Draw a **Plaque** shape (*Basic Shapes* category) in the *Wednesday*, *June 1* cell.
   b. Change the height to **0.8"** and the width to **1"**.
   c. Apply the **Subtle Effect - Blue**, **Accent 1** shape style.
   d. Add text to the shape, type River Ride, press **Enter**, and then type 6-8 p.m.
   e. Select the text in the shape (**Ctrl+A**), change the font size to **10 pt.**, apply **bold** formatting, and change the after paragraph spacing to **0 pt.**
   f. Copy and paste the shape in the four cells below.
   g. Select the five shapes, select **Align to Margin**, select **Align Left**, and then select **Align Top**.

10. Add shapes to the table.
   a. Draw a **Pentagon** shape (*Block Arrows* category) in the *Friday*, *June 3* cell.
   b. Change the height to **0.8"** and the width to **1"**.
   c. Apply the **Subtle Effect - Black**, **Dark 1** shape style.
   d. Add text to the shape, type Time Trial, press **Enter**, and then type 5-6 p.m.
   e. Select the text in the shape (**Ctrl+A**), change the font size to **10 pt.**, apply **bold** formatting, and change the after paragraph spacing to **0 pt.**
   f. Copy and paste the shape into the three cells below.
   g. Select the four shapes, select **Align to Margin**, select **Align Left**, and then select **Align Top**.

11. Add shapes to the table.
   a. Draw a **Flowchart: Document** shape (*Flowchart* category) in the *Saturday*, *June 4* cell.
   b. Change the height to **0.8"** and the width to **1"**.
   c. Apply the **Subtle Effect - Gold**, **Accent 4** shape style.
   d. Add text to the shape, type Hilly Ride, press **Enter**, and then type 8-11 a.m.
   e. Select the text in the shape (**Ctrl+A**), change the font size to **10 pt.**, apply **bold** formatting, and change the after paragraph spacing to **0 pt.**
   f. Copy and paste the shape into the three cells below.
   g. Select the four shapes, select **Align to Margin**, select **Align Left**, and then select **Align Top**.

12. Insert a picture into the table.
   a. Insert the ***ARCC-logo-07*** picture in the first row.
   b. Change the height to **0.75"** and maintain the aspect ratio.
   c. Change the text wrapping to **In Front of Text**.
   d. Use the *Picture Effect* drop-down list to apply an **Offset Top** effect (*Shadow*, *Outer* category).
   e. Use the *Layout* dialog to position the picture using the following settings:

      Horizontal **Alignment** to **Right** *relative* to **Margin**

      Vertical **Absolute position 0.3"** *below* **Margin**

   f. Select the first row of the table and change the font color to **Green**, **Accent 6**, **Lighter 80%**.

13. Save and close the document (Figure 7-118).

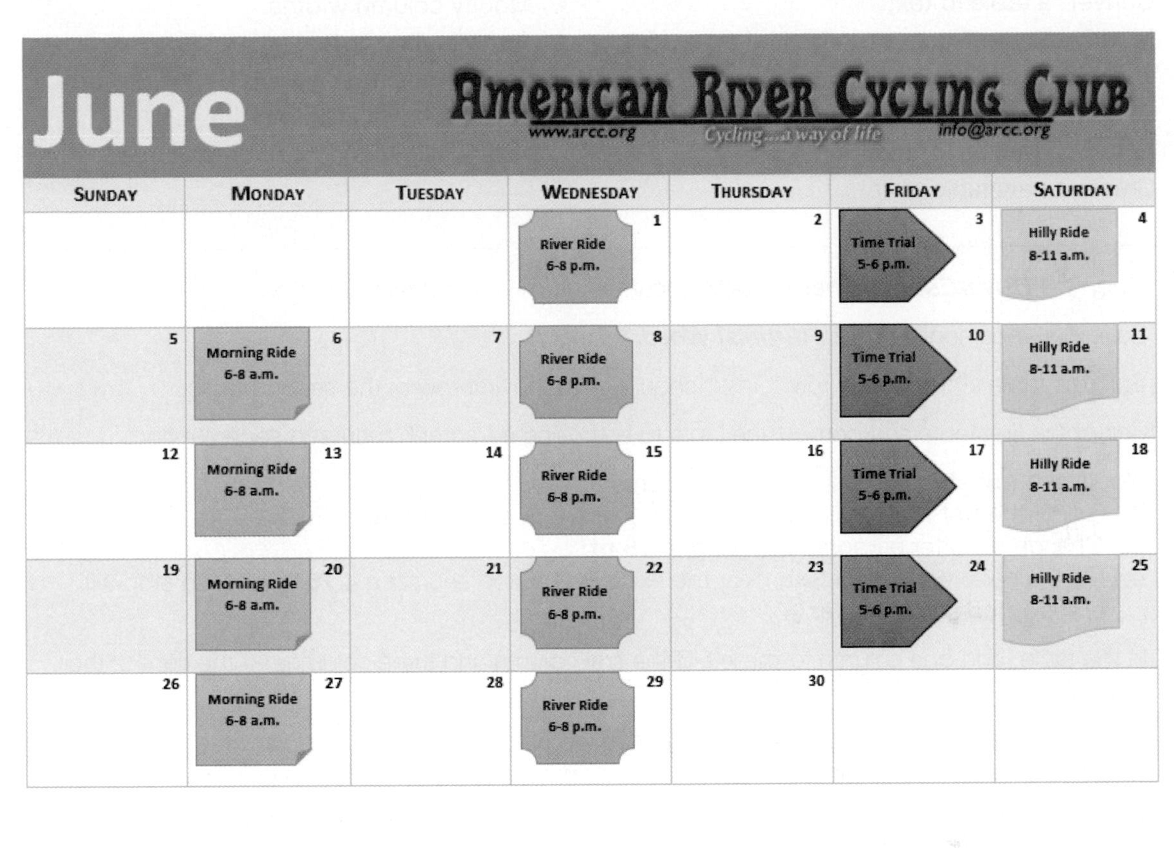

June

American River Cycling Club

www.arcc.org Cycling...a way of life info@arcc.org

Sunday	Monday	Tuesday	Wednesday	Thursday	Friday	Saturday
			1 River Ride 6-8 p.m.	2	3 Time Trial 5-6 p.m.	4 Hilly Ride 8-11 a.m.
5	6 Morning Ride 6-8 a.m.	7	8 River Ride 6-8 p.m.	9	10 Time Trial 5-6 p.m.	11 Hilly Ride 8-11 a.m.
12	13 Morning Ride 6-8 a.m.	14	15 River Ride 6-8 p.m.	16	17 Time Trial 5-6 p.m.	18 Hilly Ride 8-11 a.m.
19	20 Morning Ride 6-8 a.m.	21	22 River Ride 6-8 p.m.	23	24 Time Trial 5-6 p.m.	25 Hilly Ride 8-11 a.m.
26	27 Morning Ride 6-8 a.m.	28	29 River Ride 6-8 p.m.	30		

7-118 Word 7-6 completed

Improve It Project 7-7

For this project, you improve a buyer escrow checklist from Emma Cavalli at Placer Hills Real Estate. You split a table, convert a table to text, use bullets in the table, create a new table style, apply a custom table style, and insert and modify pictures.
[Student Learning Outcomes 7.1, 7.2, 7.3, 7.4]

Files Needed: ***BuyerEscrowChecklist-07.docx, PHRE-logo-07.png,*** and ***Checkmark-07.png***
Completed Project File Name: ***[your initials] Word 7-7.docx***

Skills Covered in This Project

- Split a table.
- Convert a table to text.
- Modify tab settings.
- Insert columns and merge cells.
- Change text direction.
- *AutoFit* a table to contents.
- Create a new table style.
- Apply a custom table style.
- Modify column widths.
- Apply bullets to text in a table.
- Modify indents in a table.
- Insert and modify a picture.
- Group, align, and position pictures.

---

1. Open the ***BuyerEscrowChecklist-07*** document from your student data files.
2. Save the document as ***[your initials] Word 7-7***.
3. Split the table at the "Task" row. "Task" should be in the first row of the second table.
4. Select the first table and convert the table to text using paragraph marks to separate text.
5. Modify the text at the beginning of the document.
   a. Select the first five lines of text and change the font size to **12 pt.**
   b. Change the after paragraph spacing to **18 pt.**
   c. On the selected lines of text, clear the existing tab stop and set a **4.75" right** tab stop with a **solid underline leader** (4).
6. In the table, add one column to the left of the first column and three columns to the right of the last column.
7. Merge cells, add text, and change text direction.
   a. Merge the cells in the first column. If there are paragraph symbols in this column, delete them.
   b. Type BUYER ESCROW CHECKLIST in the first column.
   c. Change the text direction to vertical from bottom to top.
   d. Select the first column and change the font size to **28 pt.**
8. Add text to the table and *AutoFit* the table.
   a. In the first row of the third column, type Date, press **Enter**, and then type Completed.
   b. In the first row of the fourth column, type Initials.
   c. In the first row of the fifth column, type Notes.
   d. *AutoFit* the table to contents.
9. Create a new table style.
   a. Create a new table style named PHRE that is based on the **Grid Table 5 Dark** table style.
   b. Make the following changes to the new table style to the *Whole table:*

      Change the text alignment to **Align Center Left**.

      Change the top and bottom cell margins to **0.07"**.

      Change the left and right cell margins to **0.1"**.

      Change the cell spacing to **0.04"**.

      Change the table alignment to **Center**.
10. Set table style options and apply a table style.
    a. Select the table and set the *Table Style Options* to include a **Header Row** and **First Column**.
    b. Apply the **PHRE** custom table style to the table.
11. Change the column widths in the table.

a. Change the second column width to **3"**.
b. Change the third column width to **1"**.
c. Change the fifth column width to **1.2"**.

12. Apply bullets and change indents in the text in the table.
    a. Apply an open square bullet (*Wingdings*, character code 113) to the text in the second column below the column heading.
    b. Change the left indent of the bulleted list to **0"**.
13. Change font size and text alignment in the table.
    a. Select the first column and change the text alignment of the *First column* to **Align Center**.
    b. Select the column headings in the first row (don't include the first column), change the font size to **12 pt.**, and change the text alignment to **Align Bottom Center**.
14. Delete the blank line between the tabbed text and the table.
15. Insert and modify pictures.
    a. Insert the ***PHRE-logo-07*** picture at the top of the document.
    b. Change the text wrapping to **Tight** and drag the picture to the right of the tab leaders.
    c. Apply the **Offset Diagonal Bottom Right** shadow picture effect (*Outer* category).
    d. Insert the ***Checkmark-07*** picture at the top of the document.
    e. Change the height to **1.5"** and maintain the aspect ratio.
    f. Change the text wrapping to **Tight** and drag the picture to the right of the tab leaders and below the logo picture.
    g. Apply the **Offset Diagonal Bottom Right** shadow picture effect (*Outer* category).
    h. Apply the **Pencil Grayscale** artistic effect.
16. Align and group pictures.
    a. Select both pictures.
    b. From the *Align* drop-down list, select **Align Selected Objects** and select **Align Center**.
    c. Group the two pictures.
    d. Position the grouped object using the following settings:
       Horizontal **Absolute position 6.2"** to **Right** *to the right of* **Page**
       Vertical **Absolute position 0.3"** *below* **Page**.
17. Save and close the document (Figure 7-119).

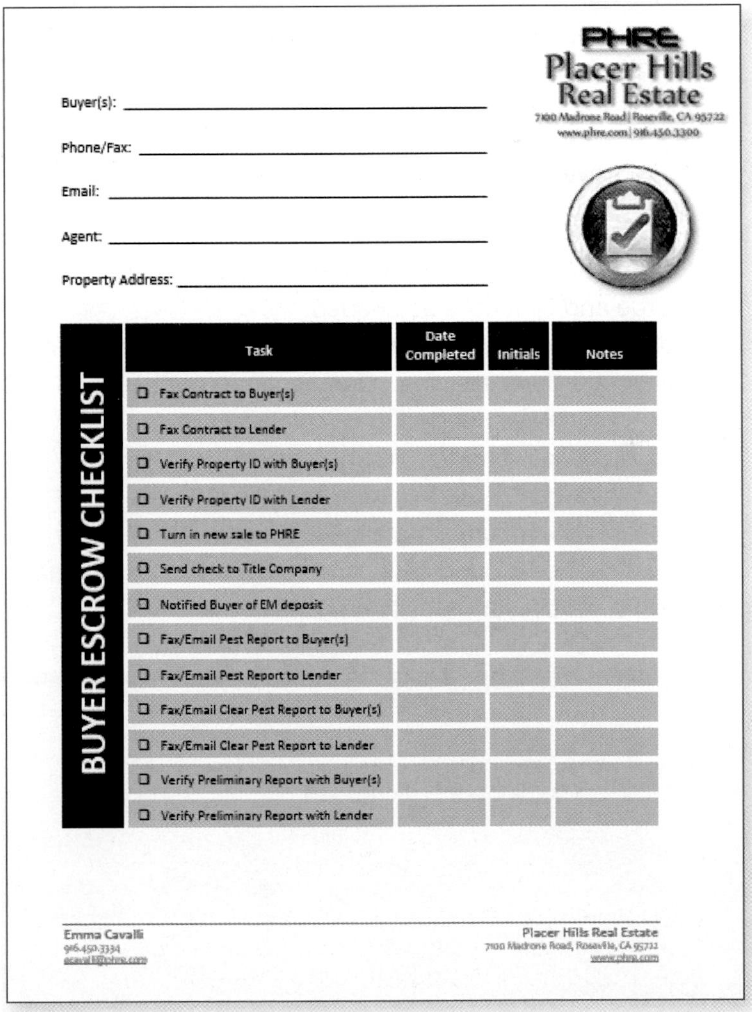

PHRE
Placer Hills Real Estate
7100 Madrone Road | Roseville, CA 95722
www.phre.com | 916.450.3300

Buyer(s): ______________________

Phone/Fax: ______________________

Email: ______________________

Agent: ______________________

Property Address: ______________________

BUYER ESCROW CHECKLIST	Task	Date Completed	Initials	Notes
	❑ Fax Contract to Buyer(s)			
	❑ Fax Contract to Lender			
	❑ Verify Property ID with Buyer(s)			
	❑ Verify Property ID with Lender			
	❑ Turn in new sale to PHRE			
	❑ Send check to Title Company			
	❑ Notified Buyer of EM deposit			
	❑ Fax/Email Pest Report to Buyer(s)			
	❑ Fax/Email Pest Report to Lender			
	❑ Fax/Email Clear Pest Report to Buyer(s)			
	❑ Fax/Email Clear Pest Report to Lender			
	❑ Verify Preliminary Report with Buyer(s)			
	❑ Verify Preliminary Report with Lender			

Emma Cavalli
916.450.3334
ecavalli@phre.com

Placer Hills Real Estate
7100 Madrone Road, Roseville, CA 95722
www.phre.com

7-119 Word 7-7 completed

Challenge Project 7-8

We all look forward to vacations, and planning a vacation builds excitement and expectations. A travel itinerary helps you make the most of your vacation and estimate a budget for your trip. Create a travel itinerary and budget for an upcoming vacation, a trip, or your dream vacation.
[Student Learning Outcomes 7.1, 7.2, 7.3, 7.4, 7.5]

File Needed: None
Completed Project File Name: ***[your initials] Word 7-8.docx***

Create a new blank document and save it as ***[your initials] Word 7-8.***

A travel itinerary and budget can include, but is not limited to, the following elements:

- Overall travel schedule
- Daily list of activities
- Description of activities
- To-do list
- Travel and accommodation information
- Pictures of destinations and hotels
- Estimated expenses

Create a travel itinerary and budget with tables, pictures, and shapes. Modify your document according to the following guidelines:

- Set up your itinerary and budget in table format.
- Merge and split cells as needed.
- Apply and modify a table style or create a new table style.
- Modify borders, shading, alignment, cell margins and spacing, and text direction.
- Use formulas as needed to calculate totals.
- Include bulleted and/or numbered lists.
- Insert pictures of destinations or places to visit.
- Crop, resize, modify, and align pictures.
- Insert shapes around objects or text, or add text to shapes.
- Resize, modify, and position shapes.

Challenge Project 7-9

Most organizations have a calendar of events, or you might keep a calendar of upcoming assignments, tests, and projects for your classes. For this project, you create a monthly or weekly calendar of upcoming events for an organization you belong to or are familiar with, such as a non-profit organization, a professional organization, a student group, a school or work project team, a religious organization, or a sports team. Or, you can create a calendar for school work that is due in the next month. **[Student Learning Outcomes 7.1, 7.2, 7.3, 7.4, 7.5]**

File Needed: None
Completed Project File Name: ***[your initials] Word 7-9.docx***

Create a new blank document and save it as ***[your initials] Word 7-9***.

Using tables, pictures, and shapes, create a calendar of events for one of your organizations or upcoming class work. Modify your document according to the following guidelines:

- Set up your events calendar in table format.
- Merge and split cells as needed.
- Resize columns and rows as needed.
- Add and align text.
- Apply and modify a table style or create a new table style.
- Modify borders, shading, alignment, cell margins and spacing, and text direction.
- Insert shapes around objects or text, or add text to shapes.
- Resize, modify, and position shapes.
- Insert an organization logo picture, picture of team members, or other appropriate pictures.
- Crop, resize, modify, and align pictures.

Challenge Project 7-10

Searching for a new car, motorcycle, bicycle, cell phone, cell phone plan, or any other expensive item can be a time-consuming task. When shopping for these high-cost items, you need to research product features and costs to make the right decision. Create a product feature and cost comparison table to organize your research about an upcoming purchase.
[Student Learning Outcomes 7.1, 7.2, 7.3, 7.4, 7.5]

File Needed: None
Completed Project File Name: ***[your initials] Word 7-10.docx***

Create a new blank document and save it as ***[your initials] Word 7-10***.

Your product feature and cost analysis can include, but is not limited to, the following elements:

- Product names
- Product features
- List of pros and cons for each product
- Cost comparison
- Cost of additional features
- Pictures of products

Create a document comparing the features and costs of different versions of a product you plan to purchase in the future. Include at least three comparable products. Modify your document according to the following guidelines:

- Set up your product comparison in table format.
- Merge and split cells as needed.
- Apply and modify a table style or create a new table style.
- Modify borders, shading, alignment, cell margins and spacing, and text direction.
- Use formulas as needed to calculate totals.
- Include bulleted and/or numbered lists.
- Insert pictures of products you plan to purchase.
- Crop, resize, modify, and align pictures.
- Insert shapes around objects or text, or add text to shapes.
- Resize, modify, and position shapes.

CHAPTER 8

Using Desktop Publishing and Graphic Features

CHAPTER OVERVIEW

In addition to being the leading word processing software on personal and business computers, Microsoft Word is also a powerful desktop publisher. You can use Word to create professional-looking newsletters, brochures, advertisements, invitations, and a variety of documents that incorporate pictures, tables, columns, charts, text boxes, and other desktop publishing features. In this chapter, you learn about some of the most useful desktop publishing features available, including text boxes, custom themes, *SmartArt*, charts, and indexes.

STUDENT LEARNING OUTCOMES (SLOs)

After completing this chapter, you will be able to:

SLO 8.1 Apply desktop publishing features to a Word document (p. W8-452).

SLO 8.2 Customize an existing theme and create a custom theme (p. W8-461).

SLO 8.3 Insert and customize a built-in text box and create a custom text box (p. W8-462).

SLO 8.4 Insert and customize a *SmartArt* graphic (p. W8-468).

SLO 8.5 Insert and customize a chart (p. W8-473).

SLO 8.6 Mark index entries and insert and customize an index page (p. W8-482).

CASE STUDY

In the Pause & Practice projects in this chapter, you use desktop publishing features to enhance a handout given to the students in a freshman composition course at Sierra Pacific Community College District.

Pause & Practice 8-1: Enhance a document using custom page settings, a drop cap, page color, a watermark, and hyphenation.

Pause & Practice 8-2: Use and customize a built-in text box, create a text box building block, draw and customize a text box, and modify an existing theme to create a custom document theme.

Pause & Practice 8-3: Insert and modify a *SmartArt* graphic and a chart.

Pause & Practice 8-4: Mark index entries in a document and create and customize an index page.

WORD

SLO 8.1

Using Desktop Publishing Features

Word's desktop publishing features allow you to create appealing documents. For example, you can apply custom page settings, insert a drop cap, use page color, insert and customize a watermark, capture and insert a screenshot, use line numbering, and apply hyphenation to text. By moderately incorporating some of these desktop publishing visual elements, you improve document readability and layout without overwhelming readers with too many formatting bells and whistles.

Custom Page Settings

In addition to changing margins, page orientation, and page size, there are a variety of custom page settings you can apply to multiple-page documents. ***Gutter margins*** and ***mirror margins*** are options for multi-page documents that you plan to print and bind on the left, right, or top. You can also change page settings to create ***2 pages per sheet*** or apply ***book fold*** to create a booklet out of a document. The following table lists and describes some popular custom page settings:

Custom Page Settings

Page Setting	Description
Gutter margins	Add extra margin space to the left or top of the document when you are planning to bind a document at the left or top. Gutter margins ensure text on bound edges is not obscured and make sure that your margin spacing is even on multiple-page bound documents.
Mirror margins	For multi-page documents that are printed on both sides and have a binding at the left or right. You can use a gutter margin with mirror margins to make sure you have additional space for binding the document.
2 pages per sheet	Used to split a page horizontally into two pages.
Book fold	Used to split a page vertically into two pages. Book fold can be used to create a booklet, menu, or invitation. When you use book fold, the page orientation of your document automatically changes to landscape.

HOW TO: Apply Custom Page Settings

1. Click the **Margins** button [*Page Layout* tab, *Page Setup* group].
2. Select **Custom Margins** to open the *Page Setup* dialog box (Figure 8-1).
3. In the *Margins* area on the *Margins* tab, change the **Gutter margin** setting and change the **Gutter position** to *Left* or *Top*.
4. In the *Pages* area, click the **Multiple pages** drop-down list and select from the options.
    - You can adjust page gutter margins after you select the *Multiple pages* option.
    - The *Preview* area displays how your document will appear.
5. In the *Apply to* area, select the part of the document where you want to apply the settings.
    - Your options are the *Whole document, This point forward*, or *Selected text*.
    - If you select *This point forward* or *Selected text*, Word inserts a section break to control page setup formatting.
6. Click **OK** to close the *Page Setup* dialog box.

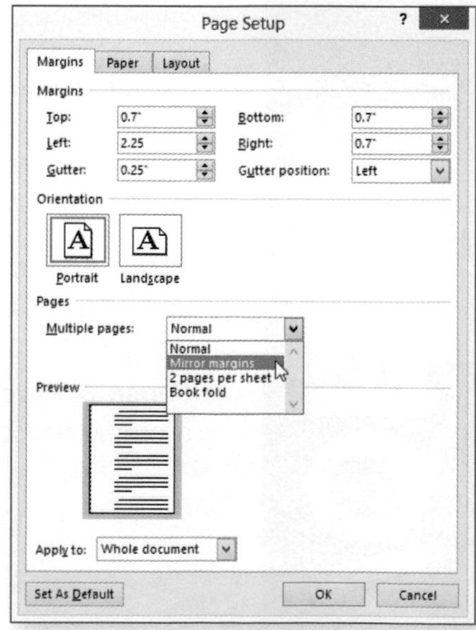

8-1 *Page Setup* dialog box

> **ANOTHER WAY**
>
> Click the **Page Setup** launcher [*Page Layout* tab] to open the *Page Setup* dialog box.

Drop Caps

A ***drop cap*** sets off and emphasizes the first letter of a paragraph (Figure 8-2). When you use this feature, the first letter of the paragraph becomes a graphic object whose appearance and placement you can customize. You can also apply the drop cap format to the entire first word (not just the first letter) at the beginning of a paragraph.

8-2 Drop cap applied to the first letter of a paragraph

HOW TO: Insert a Drop Cap

1. Place the insertion point in the paragraph where you want the drop cap to appear.
   - By default, drop cap applies to the first letter of a paragraph.
   - Alternatively, you can select the first word of the paragraph and apply drop cap formatting to the first word of the paragraph rather than just the first letter.
2. Click the **Drop Cap** button [*Insert* tab, *Text* group] to display the list of drop cap options (Figure 8-3).
3. Select the drop cap option you want to apply to the first letter of the paragraph.
   - After you have applied a drop cap, you can use the *None* option to remove the drop cap.

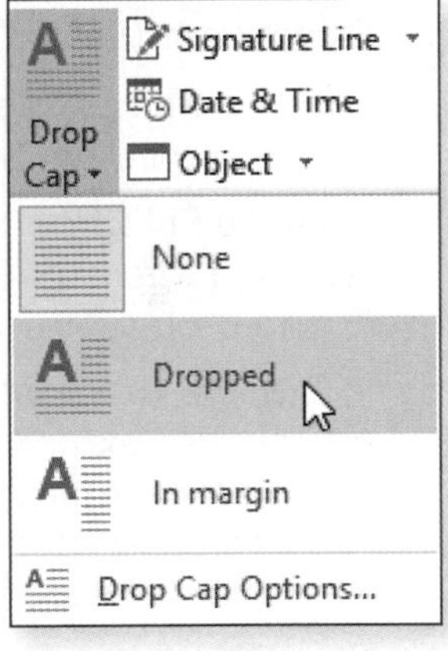

8-3 *Drop Cap* drop-down list

Drop Cap Options

After you apply drop cap formatting to a letter or word in a paragraph, you can customize its appearance. You can format the letter or word the same way you format text in your document by changing the drop cap's font, size, color, and style. You can also use the ***Drop Cap dialog box*** to customize the font and placement of the drop cap.

HOW TO: Customize a Drop Cap

1. Place the insertion point in the paragraph with the drop cap or select the drop cap.
2. Click the **Drop Cap** button [*Insert* tab, *Text* group] and select **Drop Cap Options**. The *Drop Cap* dialog box opens (Figure 8-4).
3. In the *Position* area, select the position of the drop cap.
4. Click the **Font** drop-down list to select a different font for the drop cap.
5. In the *Lines to drop* area, select the number of lines the drop cap should span.
   - The default *Lines to drop* is *3*.
6. In the *Distance from text* area, you can change the amount of space between the drop cap letter and the surrounding text.
   - The default *Distance from text* is *0"*.
7. Click **OK** to close the *Drop Cap* dialog box.

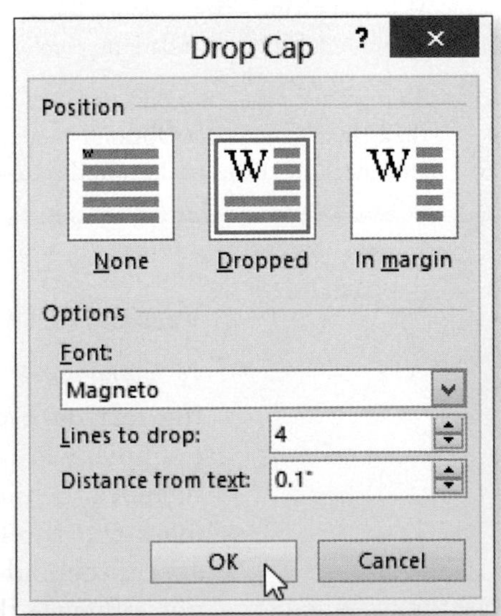

8-4 *Drop Cap* dialog box

> **MORE INFO**
>
> Some fonts display better as a drop cap than others. Standard serif and sans serif fonts work better as drop caps than script fonts.

Page Color

By default, pages are not colored in a Word document. The default page color appears white. In previous chapters, you used shading and fill colors with borders, shapes, and other graphic objects. You can similarly change the ***page color*** of a document. When you apply a page color, it applies to the entire document. You can select a page color from the theme colors or standard colors, or you can apply a gradient, texture, pattern, or picture as the background of a document.

HOW TO: Apply and Customize Page Color

1. Click the **Page Color** button [*Design* tab, *Page Background* group] to display the drop-down list of options (Figure 8-5).
2. Select from *Theme Colors* or *Standard Colors* to apply a page color.
3. Click the **More Colors** button to open the *Colors* dialog box where you can select from *Standard* or *Custom* colors.
4. Click the **Fill Effects** button to open the *Fill Effects* dialog box. Apply a *Gradient, Texture, Pattern,* or *Picture* as a page background for the document as desired (Figure 8-6).
   - Click the **Gradient** tab to select gradient *Colors, Transparency,* and *Shading* styles.
   - Click the **Texture** tab to select a *Texture* to apply as the page background.
   - Click the **Pattern** tab to select a *Pattern* and change the *Foreground* and *Background* pattern colors.
   - Click the **Picture** tab to select a picture to use as the page background.
5. Click **OK** to close the *Fill Effects* dialog box and apply the fill as the page background.
   - From the *Page Color* drop-down list, select **No Color** to remove the page color.

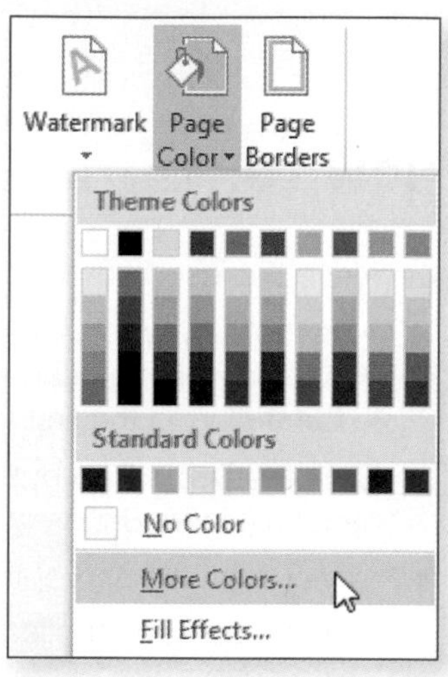

8-5 *Page Color* drop-down list

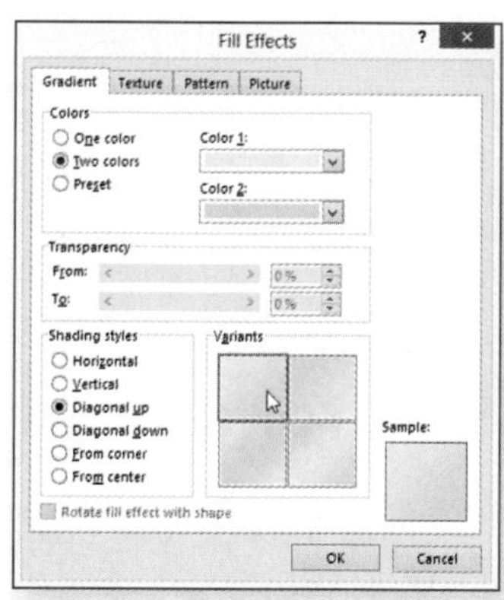

8-6 *Fill Effects* dialog box

> **MORE INFO**
>
> When applying a page color or fill, use a light color so it won't affect the readability of the document. If you use a dark page color, you can use a lighter font color for readability.
>
> To print the page color on a document, you must turn this feature on in *Word Options*. Click the **File** tab and select **Options** to open *Word Options* dialog box. Select **Display** at the left and check the **Print background colors and images** box.

Watermarks

A ***watermark*** is text or a picture that appears behind the text on every page in a document (Figure 8-7). For example, you might want the words "Draft" or "Sample" to appear behind the text as a notation for readers. Watermark text is referred to as ***ghosted text,*** which is text that appears behind the regular text in your document and does not influence the placement or wrapping of text or other objects in your document.

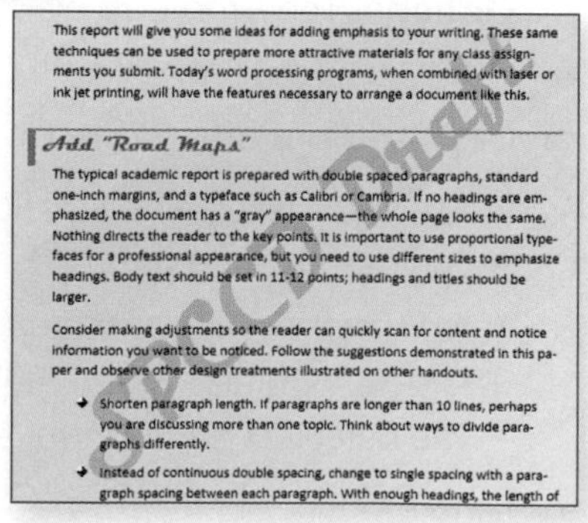

This report will give you some ideas for adding emphasis to your writing. These same techniques can be used to prepare more attractive materials for any class assignments you submit. Today's word processing programs, when combined with laser or ink jet printing, will have the features necessary to arrange a document like this.

Add "Road Maps"

The typical academic report is prepared with double spaced paragraphs, standard one-inch margins, and a typeface such as Calibri or Cambria. If no headings are emphasized, the document has a "gray" appearance—the whole page looks the same. Nothing directs the reader to the key points. It is important to use proportional typefaces for a professional appearance, but you need to use different sizes to emphasize headings. Body text should be set in 11-12 points; headings and titles should be larger.

Consider making adjustments so the reader can quickly scan for content and notice information you want to be noticed. Follow the suggestions demonstrated in this paper and observe other design treatments illustrated on other handouts.

- Shorten paragraph length. If paragraphs are longer than 10 lines, perhaps you are discussing more than one topic. Think about ways to divide paragraphs differently.
- Instead of continuous double spacing, change to single spacing with a paragraph spacing between each paragraph. With enough headings, the length of

8-7 Watermark applied to a document

You can choose built-in watermarks or you can insert a custom watermark. Watermarks are typically in a lighter color than the other text in your document and semitransparent so as not to affect the readability of the document.

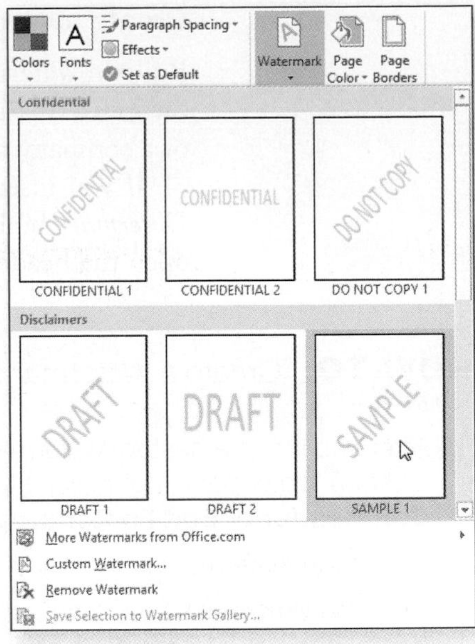

8-8 Insert a built-in watermark

Built-In Watermarks

There are a variety of built-in watermarks that you can easily and quickly insert into your documents. Built-in watermarks are grouped by categories on the *Watermark* drop-down list (Figure 8-8).

Click the **Watermark** button in the *Page Background* group on the *Design* tab and select the built-in watermark to apply to your document.

Customize a Watermark

Alternatively, you can create your own custom watermark. A custom watermark can be text or a picture. You can change the font, size, color, and layout of the custom watermark.

HOW TO: Insert a Custom Watermark

1. Click the **Watermark** button [*Design* tab, *Page Background* group] and select **Custom Watermark**. The *Printed Watermark* dialog box opens (Figure 8-9).
2. Click the **Text watermark** radio button.
   - You can also select the *Picture watermark* radio button and choose a picture to apply as a watermark.
3. In the *Text* area, select from the text options in the drop-down list or type custom text for the watermark.
4. Click the **Font** drop-down list to select the font.
5. Click the **Size** drop-down list to select the font size.
   - *Auto* is the default font size, but you can choose a specific font size.
6. Click the **Color** drop-down list to select a color.
   - By default, the *Semitransparent* check box is selected. You can deselect this check box to make the watermark darker.
7. In the *Layout* area, select the **Diagonal** or **Horizontal** radio button.
8. Click **Apply** to apply the watermark to your document.
9. Click **Close** to close the dialog box.

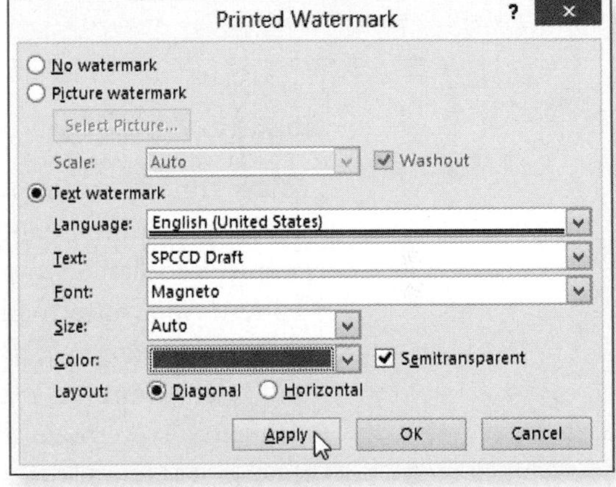

8-9 *Printed Watermark* dialog box

MORE INFO

You can also use the *Printed Watermark* dialog box to customize a built-in watermark.

Create a Watermark Building Block

Built-in watermarks are building blocks stored in the *Watermark* gallery. You can create your own watermark building block. For example, you might want to save a club or company logo or a company name as a watermark building block to use in other documents.

If you insert text or a picture as a custom watermark, you can select and save it in the *Watermark* building block gallery. In order to select a watermark in a document, you have to open the header or footer.

HOW TO: Create a Watermark Building Block

1. After you insert a custom watermark (see *How To: Insert a Custom Watermark*), right-click the header or footer and select **Edit Header** or **Edit Footer** to open the header or footer.
2. Select the watermark in the document.
3. Click the **Watermark** button [*Design* tab, *Page Background* group] and select **Save Selection to Watermark Gallery**. The *Create New Building Block* dialog box opens (Figure 8-10).
4. Type the *Name* and *Description* for your building block.
5. In the *Category* area, select from the available categories or create a new category.
6. In the *Save in* area, select the location where you want to save the building block.
7. Click **OK** to create the watermark building block.

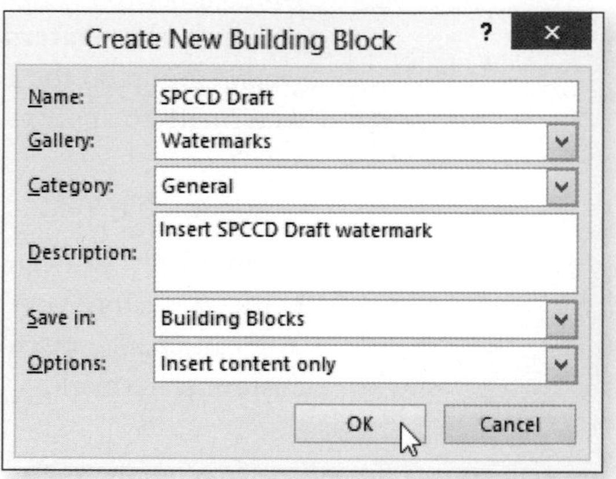

8-10 Create watermark building block

Remove a Watermark

Many times a watermark is used on a sample or draft document, and when the review process is completed, you remove the watermark. To remove a watermark, click the **Watermark** button [*Design* tab, *Page Background* group] and select **Remove Watermark** (Figure 8-11). You can also remove a watermark by selecting the **No watermark** radio button in the *Printed Watermark* dialog box (see Figure 8-9).

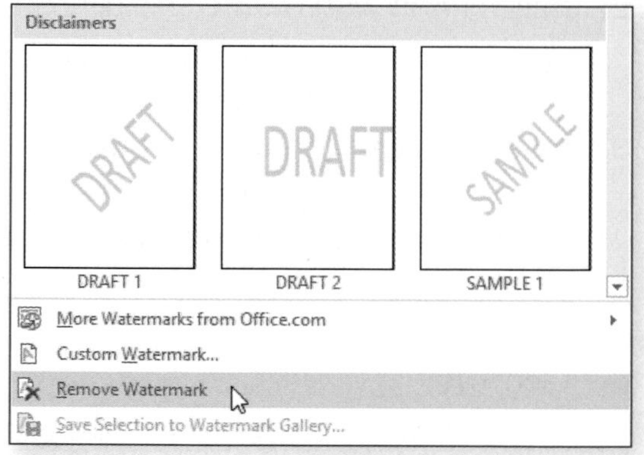

8-11 Remove a watermark

Screenshots

In Chapter 7 you inserted and customized pictures in documents. A similarly useful Word feature is ***Screenshot.*** Screenshot allows you to capture an open window on your computer such as an open document or an Internet browser window. This screenshot becomes a picture that is inserted into your document that you can resize, crop, arrange, and customize.

HOW TO: Insert a Screenshot

1. Open the file or Internet browser window that you want to use as a screenshot in your document.
2. Open the Word document and place your insertion point where you will insert a screen shot.

3. Click the **Screenshot** button [*Insert* tab, *Illustrations* group] to display the drop-down list (Figure 8-12).
4. In the *Available Windows* area, select the window you want to capture as a screenshot.
   - The screenshot is inserted in your document as a picture.
   - You can resize, move, and customize this picture as desired.

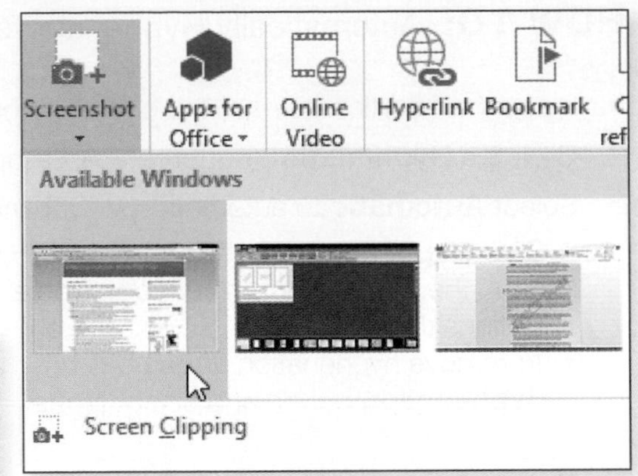

8-12 Select window to capture as a screenshot

> **MORE INFO**
>
> To save a picture inserted into your document, right-click the picture and select **Save as Picture**.

You can also capture a portion of a window, which is called a ***screen clipping.*** When you capture a screen clipping, your pointer becomes a selection crosshair to select the portion of the window to capture.

HOW TO: Insert a Screen Clipping

1. Open the window that contains the content you want to capture.
2. Open the Word document and place your insertion point where you want to insert the screen clipping.
3. Click the **Screenshot** button [*Insert* tab, *Illustrations* group] and select **Screen Clipping** from the drop-down list. The window behind the Word document opens and your pointer becomes a selection crosshair.
4. Click and drag over the region you want to capture as a screen clipping (Figure 8-13).
5. Release the pointer to capture the screen clipping.
   - The screen clipping is inserted into your document.
   - You can resize, move, and customize this picture as desired.

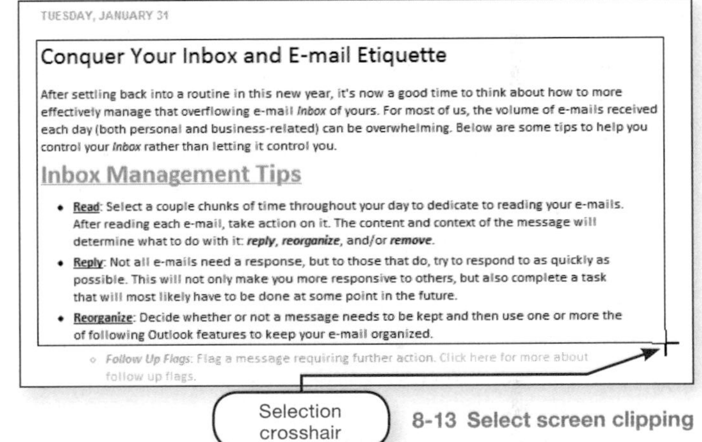

TUESDAY, JANUARY 31
Conquer Your Inbox and E-mail Etiquette
After settling back into a routine in this new year, it's now a good time to think about how to more effectively manage that overflowing e-mail Inbox of yours. For most of us, the volume of e-mails received each day (both personal and business-related) can be overwhelming. Below are some tips to help you control your Inbox rather than letting it control you.
Inbox Management Tips
Read: Select a couple chunks of time throughout your day to dedicate to reading your e-mails. After reading each e-mail, take action on it. The content and context of the message will determine what to do with it: reply, reorganize, and/or remove.
Reply: Not all e-mails need a response, but to those that do, try to respond to as quickly as possible. This will not only make you more responsive to others, but also complete a task that will most likely have to be done at some point in the future.
Reorganize: Decide whether or not a message needs to be kept and then use one or more the of following Outlook features to keep your e-mail organized.
Selection crosshair

8-13 Select screen clipping

Hyphenation

Hyphenation is another desktop publishing feature that is used to divide words at the right margin of a column or page to make line endings more even and use the space on each page more effectively. Word can automatically hyphenate your document or you can manually choose the placement of the hyphen at the end of a line of text. Hyphenation is typically used when using multiple columns in a document. The following are basic hyphenation guidelines:

- Divide words between syllables.
- Don't hyphenate one-syllable words.
- Leave at least two letters and the hyphen at the end of a line and three letters on the carryover line.
- Don't divide proper nouns or proper adjectives.

Word does a good job applying these hyphenation guidelines when you automatically hyphenate text in a document, but it is still a good idea to check your document for proper hyphenation.

HOW TO: Automatically Hyphenate Text in a Document

1. Place the insertion point at the beginning of your document.
2. Click the **Hyphenation** button [*Page Layout* tab, *Page Setup* group].
3. Select **Automatic** to automatically hyphenate the entire document.
   - Click **Hyphenation Options** from the *Hyphenation* drop-down list to open the *Hyphenation* dialog box where you customize hyphenation settings (Figure 8-14).
   - To remove hyphenation after it has been applied, click the **Hyphenation** button and select **None**.

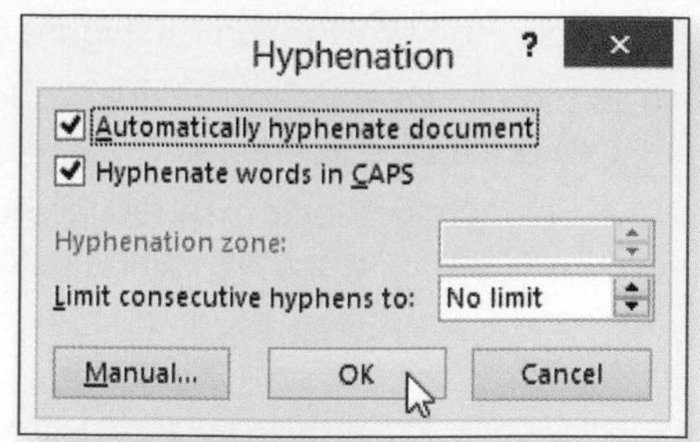

8-14 ***Hyphenation*** **dialog box**

Line Numbers

When reviewing or editing a long document with a team or in a meeting, it can be time consuming to locate specific text in the document and make sure everyone is looking at the same information. ***Line numbers*** are a helpful reference that facilitates the editing and reviewing process.

HOW TO: Turn on Line Numbering

1. Click the **Line Numbers** button [*Page Layout* tab, *Page Setup* group].
2. Select from the drop-down list of options (Figure 8-15).
   - ***Continuous:*** Numbers lines consecutively throughout the document.
   - ***Restart Each Page:*** Numbers the lines on each page beginning with 1 and restarts each page with 1.
   - ***Restart Each Section:*** Numbers the lines in each section beginning with 1 and restarts each section with 1.
   - ***Suppress for Current Paragraph:*** Turns off numbering on selected paragraph.
   - ***Line Numbering Options:*** Opens the *Page Setup* dialog box with the *Layout* tab displayed. Click the **Line Numbers** button to open the *Line Numbers* dialog box where you customize line-numbering options.
3. To turn off line numbers, click the **Line Numbers** button and select **None**.

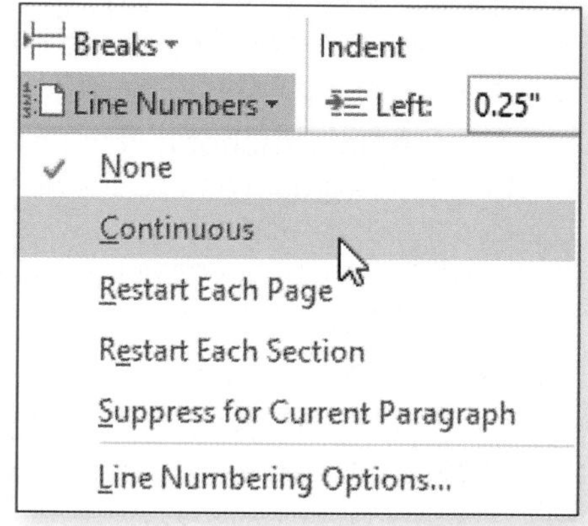

8-15 Insert line numbers

PAUSE & PRACTICE: WORD 8-1

For this Pause & Practice project, you modify a handout Sierra Pacific Community College District gives to all its freshman composition students. You change margins, add a gutter margin, apply a drop cap, apply a page color, create a custom watermark, save a watermark as a building block, and apply hyphenation.

File Needed: ***AddEmphasis-08.docx***
Completed Project File Name: ***[your initials] PP W8-1.docx***

1. Open the ***AddEmphasis-08*** document from your student data files.
2. Save the document as ***[your initials] PP W8-1***.
3. Change the margins and add a gutter margin.
   a. Change the *Top*, *Bottom*, and *Right* margins to **0.7"**.
   b. Change the *Left* margin to **2.25"**.
   c. Change the *Gutter* to **0.25"** and the *Gutter position* to **Left**.
4. Apply styles to selected text.
   a. Apply the **Heading 1** style to all bolded (but not underlined) section headings. Don't apply the *Heading 1* style to the title.
   b. Apply the **Heading 2** style to all underlined headings.
   c. Apply the **List Paragraph** style to the two bulleted lists.
5. Add a gradient page color to the document.
   a. Click the **Page Color** button [*Design* tab, *Page Background* group] and select **Fill Effects**. The *Fill Effects* dialog box opens (Figure 8-16).
   b. Click the **Two colors** radio button in the *Colors* area.
   c. Click the **Color 1** drop-down list and select **Olive Green, Accent 3, Lighter 80%**.
   d. Click the **Color 2** drop-down list and select **Olive Green, Accent 3, Lighter 60%**.
   e. In the *Shading styles* area, select the **Diagonal up** radio button.
   f. In the *Variants* area, select the upper left option.
   g. Click **OK** to close the dialog box and apply the page color.
6. Apply and customize a drop cap.
   a. Place the insertion point in the first paragraph below the title.
   b. Click the **Drop Cap** button [*Insert* tab, *Text* group] and click **Dropped**.
   c. Click the **Drop Cap** button again and select **Drop Cap Options**. The *Drop Cap* dialog box opens (Figure 8-17).
   d. Click the **Font** drop-down list and select **Magneto**.
   e. Change the *Lines to drop* to **4**.
   f. Change the *Distance from text* to **0.1"**.
   g. Click **OK** to close the *Drop Cap* dialog box.
   h. Select the drop cap in the document and change the font color to **Blue, Accent 1, Darker 50%**.
7. Create a custom watermark.
   a. Click the **Watermark** button [*Design* tab, *Page Background* group] and select **Custom Watermark**. The *Printed Watermark* dialog box opens (Figure 8-18).
   b. Click the **Text watermark** radio button.
   c. In the *Text* area, delete the existing text and type SPCCD Draft.
   d. In the *Font* area, select **Magneto**.
   e. In the *Size* area, select **Auto**.
   f. In the *Color* area, select **Red, Accent 2**.

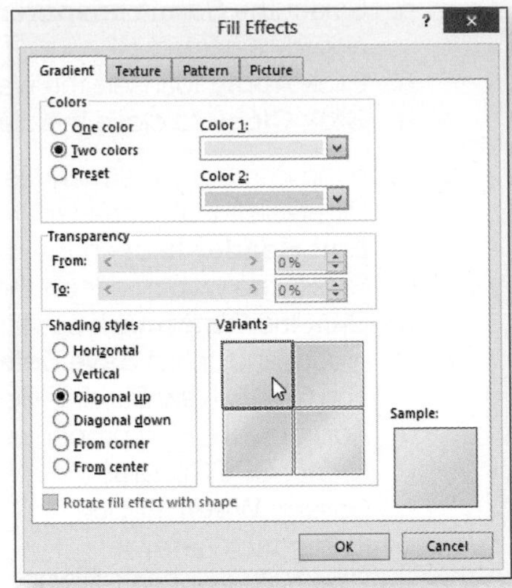

8-16 Apply gradient page color

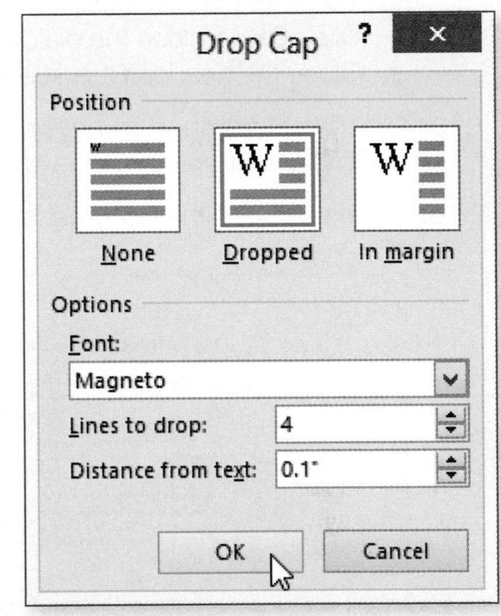

8-17 Modify drop cap options

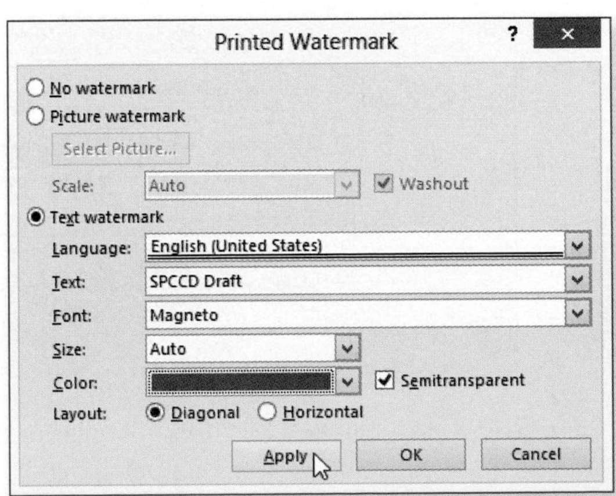

8-18 Create custom text watermark

g. Select the **Semitransparent** check box and the **Diagonal** radio button if they are not already selected.
h. Click **Apply** to insert the watermark.
i. Click **Close** to close the dialog box.

8. Save the custom watermark as a building block.
   a. Right-click in the header area on the first page and select **Edit Header** to open the header.
   b. Select the watermark on the page.
   c. Click the **Watermark** button [*Design* tab, *Page Background* group] and select **Save Selection to Watermark Gallery**. The *Create New Building Block* dialog box opens (Figure 8-19).
   d. Add the following properties for the new building block:
      Name: SPCCD Draft
      Gallery: **Watermarks**
      Category: **General**
      Description: Insert SPCCD Draft watermark
      Save in: **Building Blocks**
      Options: **Insert content only**

Create New Building Block

Name: SPCCD Draft
Gallery: Watermarks
Category: General
Description: Insert SPCCD Draft watermark
Save in: Building Blocks
Options: Insert content only
OK Cancel

8-19 Create watermark building block

   e. Click **OK** to close the dialog box and create the new building block.
   f. Close the header if it is still open.

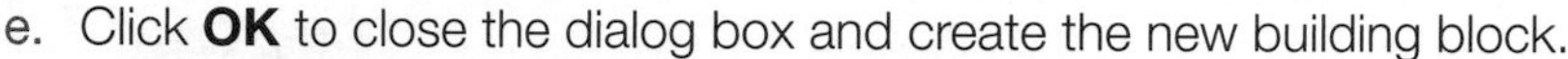

9. Click the **Hyphenation** button [*Page Layout* tab, *Page Setup* group] and select **Automatic** to automatically hyphenate the entire document.
10. Save and close the document (Figure 8-20). Click **Yes** if prompted to save changes to building blocks.

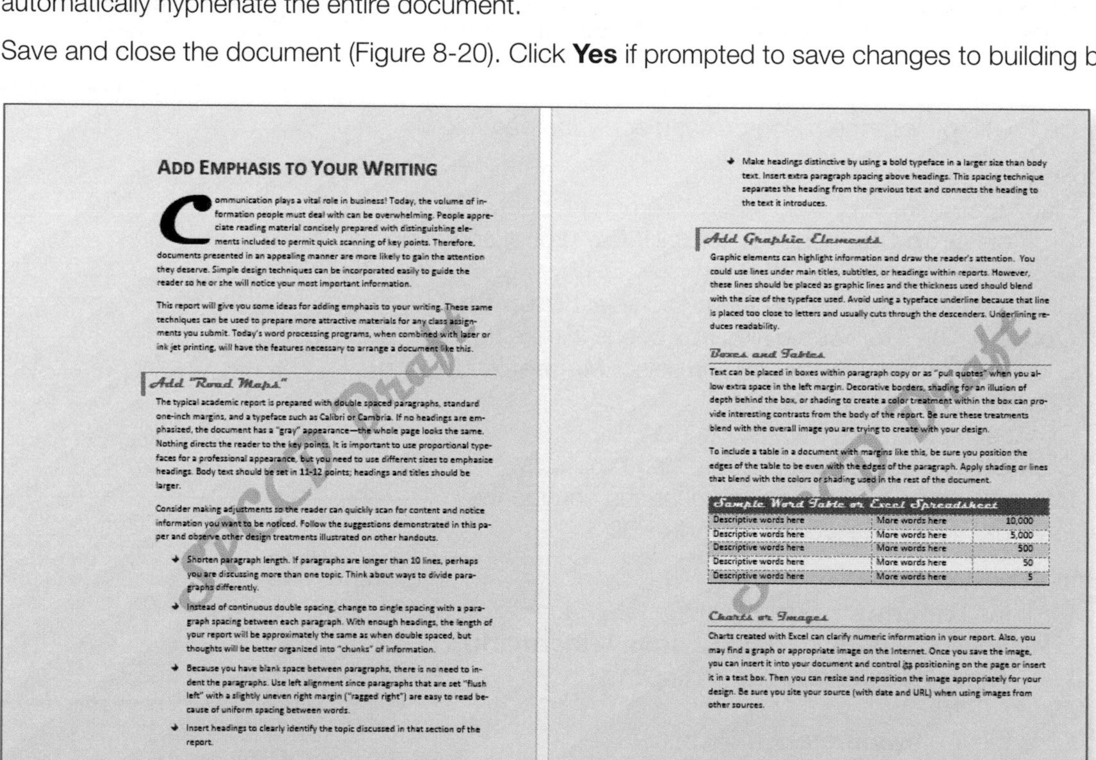

ADD EMPHASIS TO YOUR WRITING

Communication plays a vital role in business! Today, the volume of information people must deal with can be overwhelming. People appreciate reading material concisely prepared with distinguishing elements included to permit quick scanning of key points. Therefore, documents presented in an appealing manner are more likely to gain the attention they deserve. Simple design techniques can be incorporated easily to guide the reader so he or she will notice your most important information.

This report will give you some ideas for adding emphasis to your writing. These same techniques can be used to prepare more attractive materials for any class assignments you submit. Today's word processing programs, when combined with laser or ink jet printing, will have the features necessary to arrange a document like this.

Add "Road Maps"

The typical academic report is prepared with double spaced paragraphs, standard one-inch margins, and a typeface such as Calibri or Cambria. If no headings are emphasized, the document has a "gray" appearance—the whole page looks the same. Nothing directs the reader to the key points. It is important to use proportional typefaces for a professional appearance, but you need to use different sizes to emphasize headings. Body text should be set in 11-12 points; headings and titles should be larger.

Consider making adjustments so the reader can quickly scan for content and notice information you want to be noticed. Follow the suggestions demonstrated in this paper and observe other design treatments illustrated on other handouts.

- Shorten paragraph length. If paragraphs are longer than 10 lines, perhaps you are discussing more than one topic. Think about ways to divide paragraphs differently.
- Instead of continuous double spacing, change to single spacing with a paragraph spacing between each paragraph. With enough headings, the length of your report will be approximately the same as when double spaced, but thoughts will be better organized into "chunks" of information.
- Because you have blank space between paragraphs, there is no need to indent the paragraphs. Use left alignment since paragraphs that are set "flush left" with a slightly uneven right margin ("ragged right") are easy to read because of uniform spacing between words.
- Insert headings to clearly identify the topic discussed in that section of the report.

Add Emphasis to Your Writing—Page 1 of 3

- Make headings distinctive by using a bold typeface in a larger size than body text. Insert extra paragraph spacing above headings. This spacing technique separates the heading from the previous text and connects the heading to the text it introduces.

Add Graphic Elements

Graphic elements can highlight information and draw the reader's attention. You could use lines under main titles, subtitles, or headings within reports. However, these lines should be placed as graphic lines and the thickness used should blend with the size of the typeface used. Avoid using a typeface underline because that line is placed too close to letters and usually cuts through the descenders. Underlining reduces readability.

Boxes and Tables

Text can be placed in boxes within paragraph copy or as "pull quotes" when you allow extra space in the left margin. Decorative borders, shading for an illusion of depth behind the box, or shading to create a color treatment within the box can provide interesting contrasts from the body of the report. Be sure these treatments blend with the overall image you are trying to create with your design.

To include a table in a document with margins like this, be sure you position the edges of the table to be even with the edges of the paragraph. Apply shading or lines that blend with the colors or shading used in the rest of the document.

Sample Word Table or Excel Spreadsheet		
Descriptive words here	More words here	10,000
Descriptive words here	More words here	5,000
Descriptive words here	More words here	500
Descriptive words here	More words here	50
Descriptive words here	More words here	5

Charts or Images

Charts created with Excel can clarify numeric information in your report. Also, you may find a graph or appropriate image on the Internet. Once you save the image, you can insert it into your document and control its positioning on the page or insert it in a text box. Then you can resize and reposition the image appropriately for your design. Be sure you site your source (with date and URL) when using images from other sources.

Add Emphasis to Your Writing—Page 2 of 3

8-20 PP W8-1 completed (pages 1 and 2)

SLO 8.2

Customizing and Creating Themes

In *SLO 2.7: Using Styles and Themes,* you learned about themes and how a document theme controls the fonts, sizes, colors, line and paragraph spacing, and styles in a document. You can apply a theme to a document, and you can also customize an existing theme or create a custom theme.

Theme Colors, Fonts, and Effects

When you apply a theme to a document, Word automatically changes the theme *Colors, Fonts,* and *Effects* to match the selected theme. Although the theme colors, fonts, and effects are tied to the selected document theme, you still have the option to customize a document theme with different theme colors, fonts, and effects.

HOW TO: Customize a Theme

1. Click the **Themes** button [*Design* tab, *Document Formatting* group] and select a theme from the drop-down list to apply to your document.
2. Click the **Colors** button [*Design* tab, *Document Formatting* group] and select a theme color set (Figure 8-21).
3. Click the **Fonts** button [*Design* tab, *Document Formatting* group] and select a theme font set.
4. Click the **Effects** button [*Design* tab, *Document Formatting* group] and select a theme effects set.

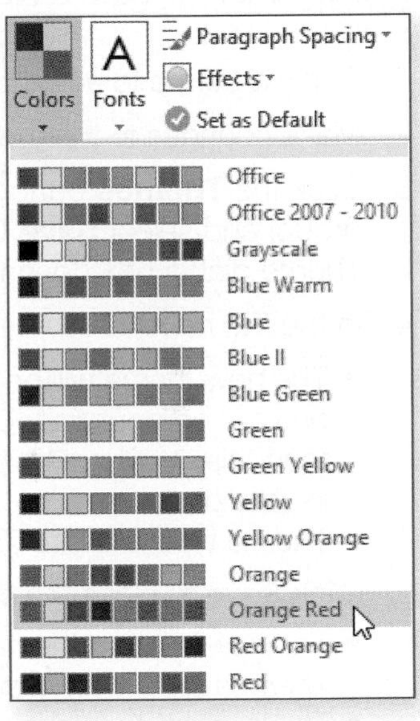

8-21 Select theme colors

Create Custom Theme Colors and Fonts

In addition to applying preset theme colors and fonts to an existing theme, you can also create your own custom theme colors and fonts that you can apply to documents. You can select specific colors and fonts and save these custom color and font sets, which you can apply to a document or document theme.

HOW TO: Create New Theme Colors

1. Click the **Colors** button [*Design* tab, *Document Formatting* group].
2. Select **Customize Colors** from the drop-down list. The *Create New Theme Colors* dialog box opens (Figure 8-22).
3. In the *Theme colors* area, select a color from the drop-down list for any of the items listed.
   - The *Sample area* displays the colors of the theme.
4. In the *Name* area, type a name for the new theme colors.
5. Click **Save** to close the dialog box.
   - The new *Theme Colors* is displayed in the *Colors* drop-down list in the *Custom* category and you can apply it to other documents or themes.

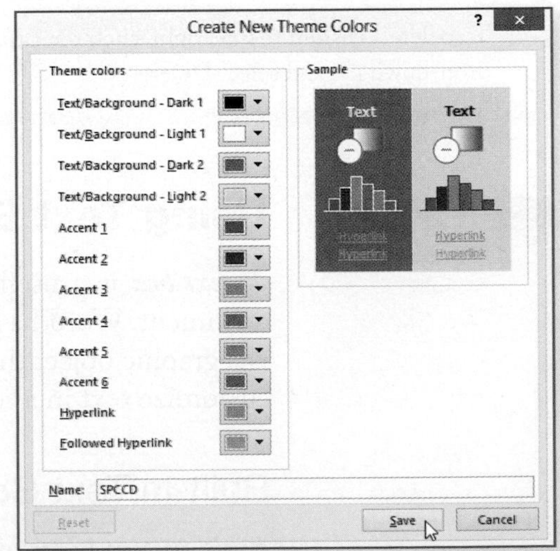

8-22 *Create New Theme Colors* dialog box

You can create new theme fonts the same way you create new theme colors. You can customize fonts that can be saved as a new set of theme fonts (Figure 8-23).

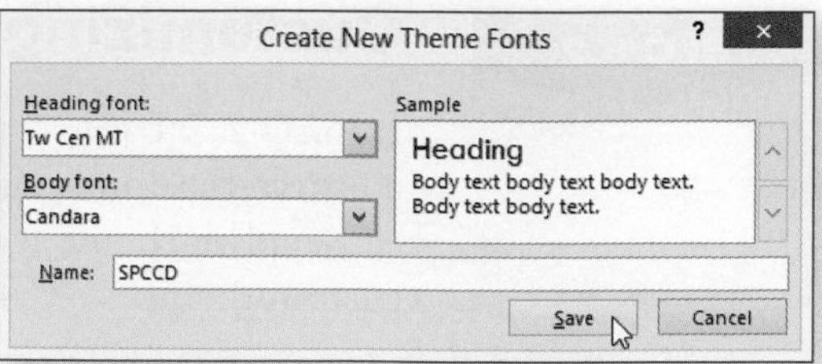

8-23 *Create New Theme Fonts* dialog box

Create a New Theme

When you modify theme fonts, colors, or effects, you can save these changes as a new document theme. You can then apply this custom document theme to other documents. Custom themes help to create consistency among documents and save you time.

HOW TO: Create a New Theme

1. Apply a theme to a document.
2. Make changes to the theme colors, fonts, and effects as desired.
3. Click the **Themes** button [*Design* tab, *Document Formatting* group] and select **Save Current Theme**. The *Save Current Theme* dialog box opens (Figure 8-24).
4. In the *File name* area, type a name for the new theme.
   - The new theme will be saved in the *Document Themes* folder on your computer. If you save the new theme in a location other than this, it will not be available in the drop-down list of themes in your documents.
   - The file type is *Office Theme*.
5. Click **Save** to close the dialog box and save your custom theme.
   - The new custom theme is available in the *Custom* category in the *Themes* drop-down list (Figure 8-25).
   - This custom theme is now available for you to apply to all your Word documents.

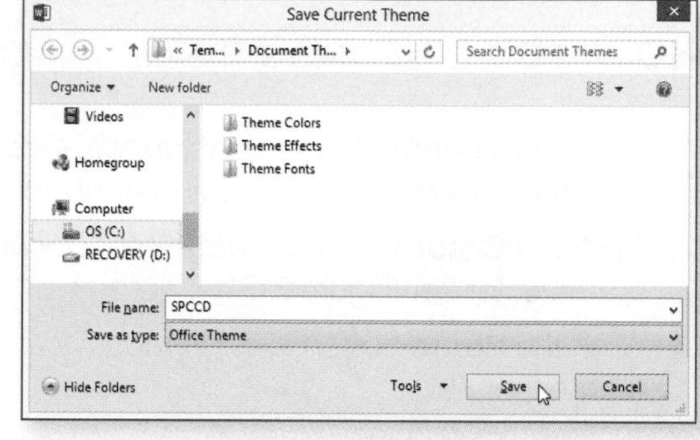

8-24 *Save Current Theme* dialog box

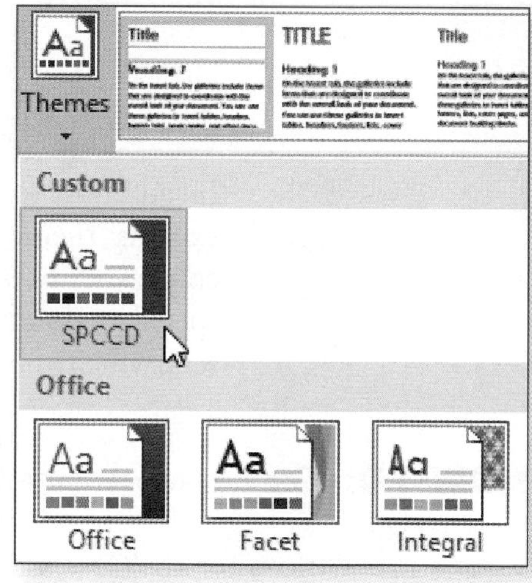

8-25 Custom theme in the *Themes* drop-down list

MORE INFO

To delete a custom theme, right-click the custom theme in the *Themes* drop-down list and select **Delete**.

SLO 8.3

Using Text Boxes

A ***text box*** is a useful desktop publishing feature that draws attention to information in a document. Word has many built-in text boxes or you can draw your own text box. A text box is a graphic object that you can resize, arrange, and customize like a shape or picture. You can customize text in a text box and create a custom text box building block.

Built-In Text Boxes

Built-in text boxes already have custom borders, fill, and effects applied. Built-in text boxes contain placeholder text in a ***content control field*** that you can replace with your own text.

A content control field is a Word field where you can insert and format custom text. After you insert a built-in text box into your document, you can customize both the text box and the text box content.

There are two main categories of built-in text boxes: ***quotes*** and ***sidebars***. You can use a quote text box to create a pull quote. A pull quote is content "pulled" from the text and placed in the text box to highlight and emphasize a point. Sidebars are typically used for additional information and are usually aligned at the left, right, top, or bottom of a page.

HOW TO: Insert a Built-In Text Box

1. Place the insertion point in your document where you want the text box inserted.
2. Click the **Text Box** button [*Insert* tab, *Text* group].
3. Select a text box to insert from the drop-down list of built-in text boxes (Figure 8-26).
   - Select **More Text Boxes from Office.com** to view more text box options.
4. Click in the content control field of the text box to replace the placeholder text with your own text.

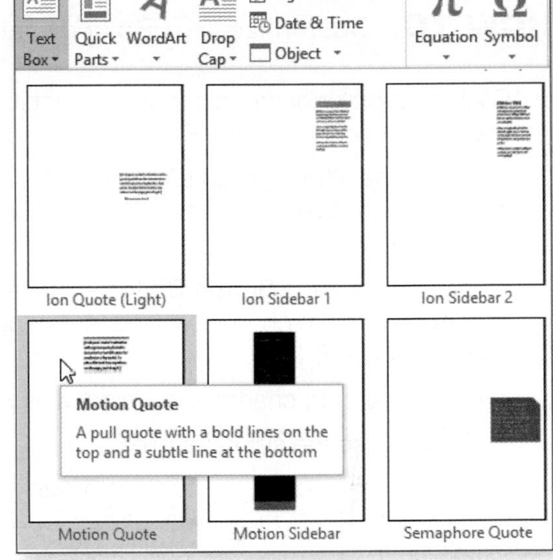

8-26 Built-in text boxes

Customize Text Box Content

After you insert a built-in text box, you replace the placeholder text with your content. You can type your information in the content control field or remove the content control field and type your text directly in the text box. You can format text in the text box the same way you format text in your documents, changing the font, size, style, color, line spacing, and paragraph spacing with the options on the *Home* tab. You can also use the text options in the *WordArt Styles* and *Text* groups on the *Drawing Tools Format* tab to customize the appearance of your text.

HOW TO: Customize Text Box Content

1. After inserting a text box, click on the placeholder text in the text box to select it (Figure 8-27).
2. Type in your custom text or copy text from a document and paste it in the content control field.
   - To remove the content control field, right-click on it and select **Remove Content Control** field from the context menu.
3. Select the text in the text box and change the font, size, style, color, line spacing, or paragraph spacing as desired.
4. In the *WordArt Styles* group [*Drawing Tools Format* tab], modify the *WordArt Style, Text Fill, Text Outline*, and *Text Effects*.
   - You can click the **Word Art Styles** launcher to open the *Format Shape* pane and customize text.
   - You can adjust the text layout and internal margins in the *Text Options* area of the *Format Shape* pane.
5. In the *Text* group, you can change the *Text Direction, Align Text*, or *Create Link* to insert a hyperlink.

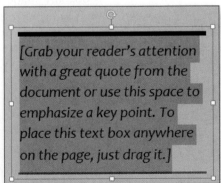

8-27 Select placeholder text in the text box

Customize Text Box Format

A text box is a shape object or group of objects that has text inserted into it. Customizing a text box shape is similar to customizing other shapes. When you insert a text box in your document, the context-sensitive *Drawing Tools Format* tab becomes available. You can customize the shape style, shape outline, shape fill, or shape effects for your text box. You can position the text box to control how text wraps around it and customize the size and position of the text box as well.

HOW TO: Customize Text Box Format

1. Click the border of the text box to select it. The *Drawing Tools Format* tab is available on the *Ribbon*.
2. In the *Shape Styles* group [*Drawing Tools Format* tab], customize the shape of your text box by modifying the *Shape Style, Shape Fill, Shape Outline*, or *Shape Effects*.
   - You can click the **Shape Styles** launcher to open the *Format Shape* pane and make changes to the format of the text box shape using this pane (Figure 8-28).
3. In the *Size* group, change the *Height* and *Width* of the text box shape.
   - You can use the sizing handles to resize the text box shape.
4. In the *Arrange* group, you can customize the text box by choosing from the *Position, Wrap Text, Align, Group*, or *Rotate* options. You can also use the *Bring Forward* or *Send Backward* options to customize the arrangement.
   - Click the **Size** launcher to open the *Layout* dialog box to customize *Position, Text Wrapping*, and *Size* of the text box.
   - You can also click the **Layout Options** button to the right of the text box and select a text wrapping option.

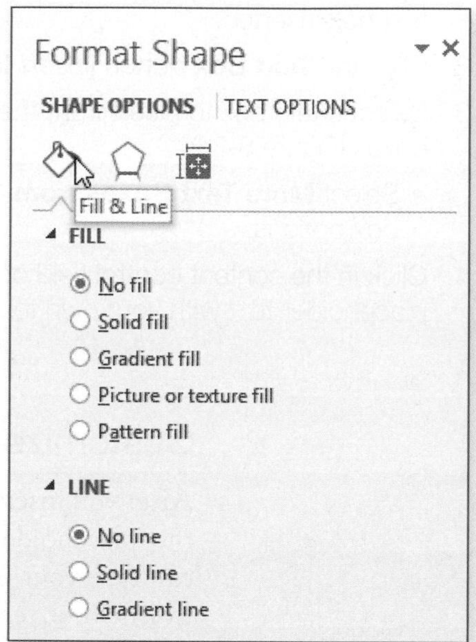

8-28 ***Format Shape*** **pane**

Draw a Text Box

Another way to insert a text box into a document is to draw a text box. You can draw a text box any shape you want anywhere in the document. After you draw a text box, you can insert and format text in the box and customize the text box shape.

HOW TO: Draw a Text Box

1. Click the **Text Box** button [*Insert* tab, *Text* group].
2. Select **Draw Text Box** from the drop-down list. Your pointer becomes a drawing crosshair pointer.
3. Draw a text box in the document (Figure 8-29). The insertion point is in the text box where you can type or paste text.
4. Type or paste text in your text box.
5. Format the text in the text box as desired.
6. Use the *Drawing Tools Format* tab to customize the text box shape, alignment, text wrapping, size, and position.

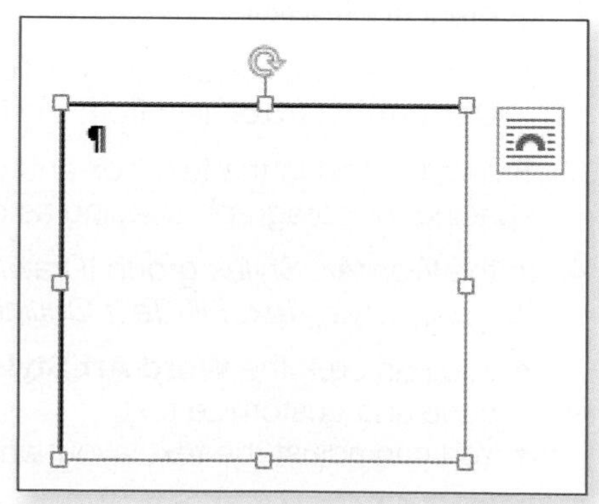

8-29 Draw a text box and type text

ANOTHER WAY

Select text in your document, click the **Text Box** button [*Insert* tab, *Text* group], and select **Draw Text Box**. A text box is inserted around the selected text.

Text Box Building Blocks

All built-in text boxes are building blocks in the *Text Box* gallery. Just like creating a watermark, header, footer, or table building block, you can create a text box building block to save a custom text box you create. Once you have stored a custom text building block, you can use it in other documents.

HOW TO: Create a Text Box Building Block

1. Create and customize a text box.
   - Alternatively, you can customize a built-in text box.
2. Select the text box.
3. Click the **Text Box** button [*Insert* tab, *Text* group] and select **Save Selection to Text Box Gallery**. The *Create New Building Block* dialog box opens (Figure 8-30).
4. Type the *Name* and *Description* for the building block.
5. In the *Category* area, select from the available categories or create a new category.
6. In the *Save in* area, select the location where you want to save the building block.
7. Click **OK** to create the text box building block.

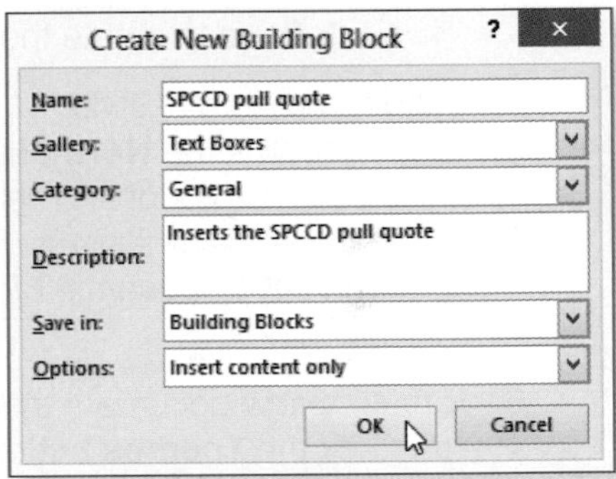

8-30 Create text box building block

PAUSE & PRACTICE: WORD 8-2

For this Pause & Practice project, you modify the document you worked with in *Pause & Practice 8-1*. You customize an existing theme, create new theme fonts, create a new theme, insert and customize a built-in text box, draw and customize a text box, and create a text box building block.

File Needed: ***[your initials] PP W8-1.docx***
Completed Project File Name: ***[your initials] PP W8-2.docx***

1. Open the ***[your initials] PP W8-1*** document you saved in *Pause & Practice 8-1*.
2. Save the document as ***[your initials] PP W8-2***.
3. Apply and customize a theme.
   a. Click the **Themes** button [*Design* tab, *Document Formatting* group] and select **Metropolitan** from the drop-down list.

b. Click the **Colors** button [*Design* tab, *Document Formatting* group] and select **Orange Red** from the drop-down list.
c. Click the **Effects** button [*Design* tab, *Document Formatting* group] and select **Subtle Solids** from the drop-down list.

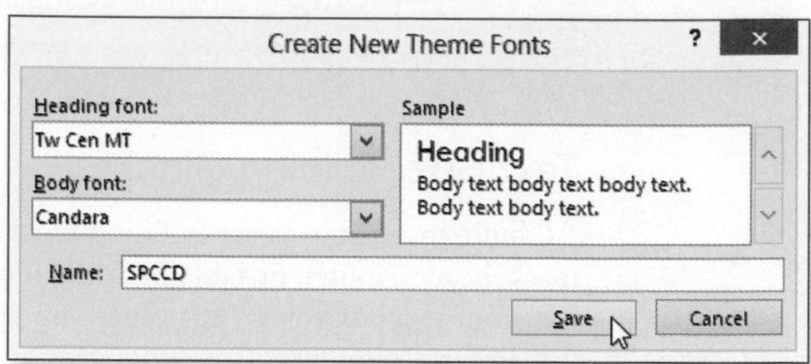

8-31 *Create New Theme Fonts* dialog box

4. Create new theme fonts.
   a. Click the **Fonts** button [*Design* tab, *Document Formatting* group].
   b. Select **Customize Fonts** from the drop-down list. The *Create New Theme Fonts* dialog box opens (Figure 8-31).
   c. Click the **Heading font** drop-down list and select **Tw Cen MT**.
   d. Click the **Body font** drop-down list and select **Candara**.
   e. In the *Name* area, type SPCCD.
   f. Click **Save** to create the new theme font and apply it to the current document theme.
5. Modify the *Normal* style.
   a. Right-click the **Normal** style [*Home* tab, *Style* group] and select **Modify**.
   b. Change the font size to **10 pt.** and click **OK** to close the *Modify Style* dialog box.
6. Create a new document theme.
   a. Click the **Themes** button [*Design* tab, *Document Formatting* group].
   b. Select **Save Current Theme** to open the *Save Current Theme* dialog box (Figure 8-32).
   c. Type SPCCD in the *File name* area. Don't change the save location.
   d. Click **Save** to close the dialog box and save the custom theme.

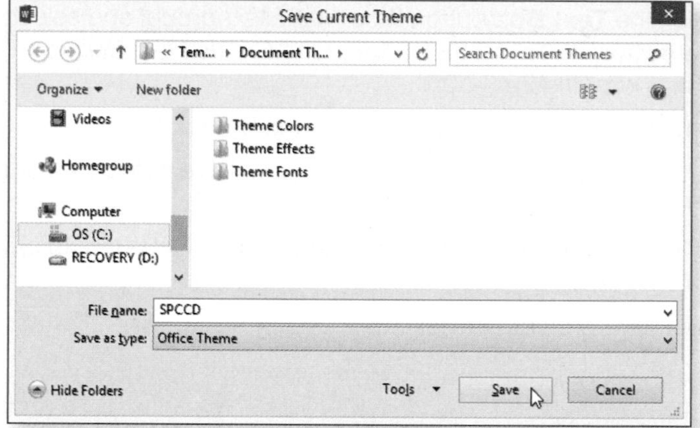

8-32 *Save Current Theme* dialog box

7. Insert and customize a built-in text box.
   a. Place the insertion point at the beginning of the first paragraph in the "Add "Road Maps"" section.
   b. Click the **Text Box** button [*Insert* tab, *Text* group] and select **Motion Quote**.
   c. Select the last sentence in the first paragraph on the first page ("Simple design techniques . . .") and copy it.
   d. Click the placeholder text in the text box to select it and press **Ctrl+V** to paste the copied text, which replaces the placeholder text.
   e. Select the text in the text box and apply **italic** formatting.
   f. Change the *Height* to **1.4"** and the *Width* to **1.8"** [*Drawing Tools Format* tab, Size group].
   g. Click the **Shape Effects** button [*Drawing Tools Format* tab, *Shape Styles* group], select **Presets**, and choose **Preset 2**.
   h. Click the **Position** button [*Drawing Tools Format* tab, *Arrange* group] and select **More Layout Options**. The *Layout* dialog box opens.
   i. Set the *Horizontal* **Absolute position** at **0.4"** to the right of **Page** and set the *Vertical* **Alignment** to **Centered** relative to **Page**.
   j. Click **OK** to close the *Layout* dialog box.

8. Create a text box building block.
   a. Select the text box from step 7 (Figure 8-33).
   b. Click the **Text Box** button [*Insert* tab, *Text* group] and select **Save Selection to Text Box Gallery**. The *Create New Building Block* dialog box opens.
   c. Add the following properties for the new building block:
      *Name:*SPCCD pull quote
      Gallery: **Text Boxes**
      Category: **General**
      Description: Inserts the SPCCD pull quote
      Save in: **Building Blocks**
      Options: **Insert content only**
   d. Click **OK** to close the dialog box and create the new building block.

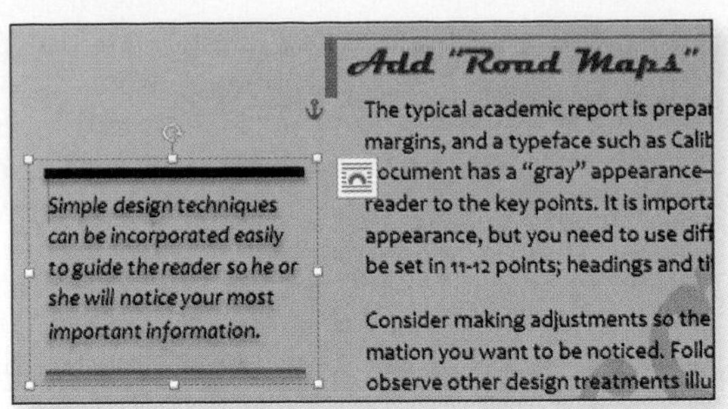

8-33 Text box aligned in the document

9. Insert and customize a text box building block.
   a. Place the insertion point at the beginning of the first paragraph on the last page.
   b. Click the **Text Box** button [*Insert* tab, *Text* group] and select **SPCCD pull quote** (Figure 8-34).
   c. Select the last sentence on the last page.
   d. Copy the text and paste it in the text box to replace the current text.
   e. Change the *Height* of the text box to **1.2"**.

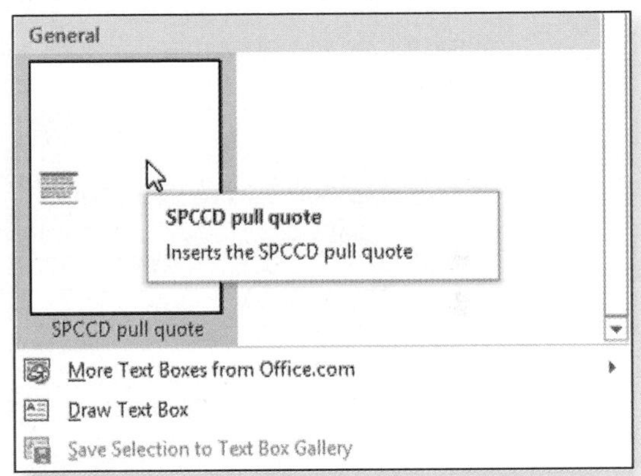

8-34 Insert text box building block

10. Draw a text box and customize the content.
   a. Place the insertion point near the middle of the second page.
   b. Click the **Text Box** button and select **Draw Text Box**. Your pointer becomes a drawing crosshair pointer.
   c. Draw a text box (approximately 1" tall and 5" wide) between the first and second paragraphs in the "Boxes and Tables" section.
   d. Change the *Height* to **0.8"** and the *Width* to **5.25"**.
   e. Type the following text in the text box:
      This is an example of a text box that was drawn between paragraphs. Remember to adjust the text box's internal margins to leave space between the text and the text box. The format of the text box has been customized.

11. Customize the text box format.
   a. Select the text box.
   b. Click the **Shape Styles** drop-down list [*Drawing Tool Format* tab, *Shape Styles* group] and select **Subtle Effect – Black, Dark 1**.
   c. Click the **Shape Styles** launcher to open the *Format Shape* pane.
   d. Click **Layout & Properties** and select **Text Box** to expand this area (Figure 8-35).
   e. Change the *Vertical alignment* to **Middle**.
   f. Set the *Left, Right, Top*, and *Bottom* internal margins to **0.1"**.
   g. Click the **X** in the upper right corner to close the *Format Shape* pane.

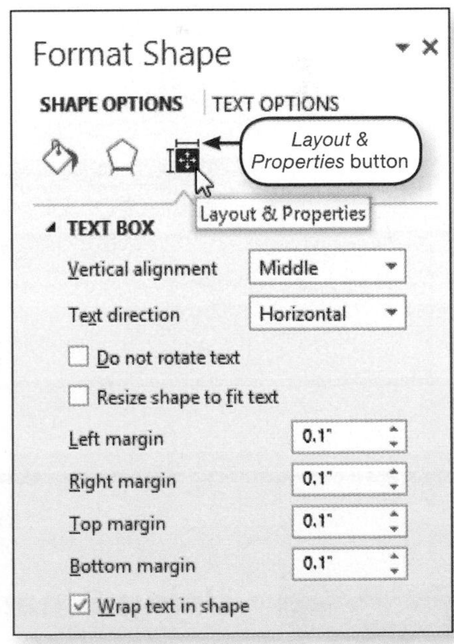

8-35 *Format Shape* pane

h. Change the text wrapping to **Tight**.
i. Drag the text box between the first and second paragraphs in the "Boxes and Tables" section.
j. Click the **Align** button [*Drawing Tools Format* tab, *Arrange* group] and select **Align to Margin**.
k. Click the **Align** button again and select **Align Left**.
l. Using the up or down keyboard arrow key, align the text box between the first and second paragraph, if necessary.

12. Click in front of the "Write Vertical Lists" heading and insert a **page break** (**Ctrl+Enter**). The text box on the third (last) page, and you will position it in the next step.
13. Position the text box on the last page.
    a. Select the text box on the last page.
    b. Click the **Position** button [*Drawing Tools Format* tab, *Arrange* group] and select **More Layout Options**. The *Layout* dialog box opens.
    c. Set the *Vertical* **Absolute position** at **0.9"** below **Margin**.
    d. Click **OK** to close the *Layout* dialog box.
14. Save and close the document (Figure 8-36).

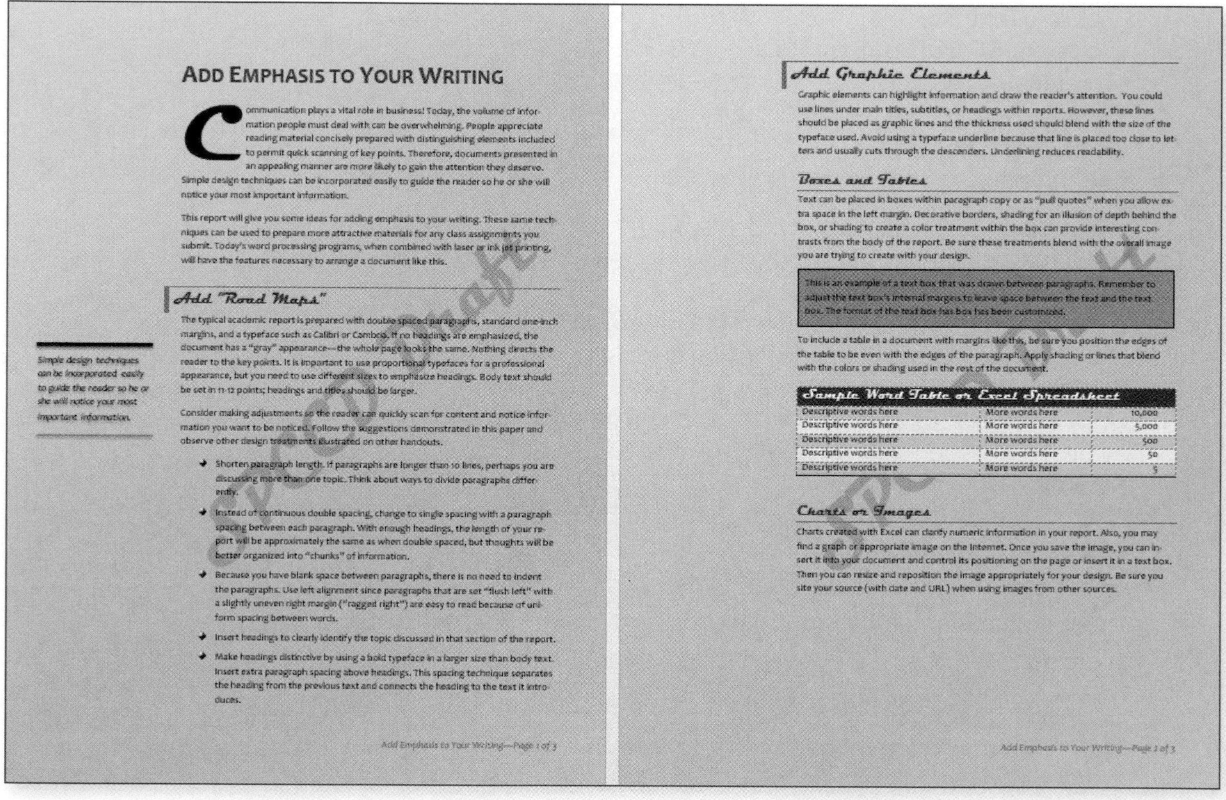

ADD EMPHASIS TO YOUR WRITING

Communication plays a vital role in business! Today, the volume of information people must deal with can be overwhelming. People appreciate reading material concisely prepared with distinguishing elements included to permit quick scanning of key points. Therefore, documents presented in an appealing manner are more likely to gain the attention they deserve. Simple design techniques can be incorporated easily to guide the reader so he or she will notice your most important information.

This report will give you some ideas for adding emphasis to your writing. These same techniques can be used to prepare more attractive materials for any class assignments you submit. Today's word processing programs, when combined with laser or ink jet printing, will have the features necessary to arrange a document like this.

Add "Road Maps"

Simple design techniques can be incorporated easily to guide the reader so he or she will notice your most important information.

The typical academic report is prepared with double spaced paragraphs, standard one-inch margins, and a typeface such as Calibri or Cambria. If no headings are emphasized, the document has a "gray" appearance—the whole page looks the same. Nothing directs the reader to the key points. It is important to use proportional typefaces for a professional appearance, but you need to use different sizes to emphasize headings. Body text should be set in 11-12 points; headings and titles should be larger.

Consider making adjustments so the reader can quickly scan for content and notice information you want to be noticed. Follow the suggestions demonstrated in this paper and observe other design treatments illustrated on other handouts.

- Shorten paragraph length. If paragraphs are longer than 10 lines, perhaps you are discussing more than one topic. Think about ways to divide paragraphs differently.
- Instead of continuous double spacing, change to single spacing with a paragraph spacing between each paragraph. With enough headings, the length of your report will be approximately the same as when double spaced, but thoughts will be better organized into "chunks" of information.
- Because you have blank space between paragraphs, there is no need to indent the paragraphs. Use left alignment since paragraphs that are set "flush left" with a slightly uneven right margin ("ragged right") are easy to read because of uniform spacing between words.
- Insert headings to clearly identify the topic discussed in that section of the report.
- Make headings distinctive by using a bold typeface in a larger size than body text. Insert extra paragraph spacing above headings. This spacing technique separates the heading from the previous text and connects the heading to the text it introduces.

Add Emphasis to Your Writing—Page 1 of 3

Add Graphic Elements

Graphic elements can highlight information and draw the reader's attention. You could use lines under main titles, subtitles, or headings within reports. However, these lines should be placed as graphic lines and the thickness used should blend with the size of the typeface used. Avoid using a typeface underline because that line is placed too close to letters and usually cuts through the descenders. Underlining reduces readability.

Boxes and Tables

Text can be placed in boxes within paragraph copy or as "pull quotes" when you allow extra space in the left margin. Decorative borders, shading for an illusion of depth behind the box, or shading to create a color treatment within the box can provide interesting contrasts from the body of the report. Be sure these treatments blend with the overall image you are trying to create with your design.

This is an example of a text box that was drawn between paragraphs. Remember to adjust the text box's internal margins to leave space between the text and the text box. The format of the text box has box has been customized.

To include a table in a document with margins like this, be sure you position the edges of the table to be even with the edges of the paragraph. Apply shading or lines that blend with the colors or shading used in the rest of the document.

Sample Word Table or Excel Spreadsheet		
Descriptive words here	More words here	10,000
Descriptive words here	More words here	5,000
Descriptive words here	More words here	500
Descriptive words here	More words here	50
Descriptive words here	More words here	5

Charts or Images

Charts created with Excel can clarify numeric information in your report. Also, you may find a graph or appropriate image on the Internet. Once you save the image, you can insert it into your document and control its positioning on the page or insert it in a text box. Then you can resize and reposition the image appropriately for your design. Be sure you site your source (with date and URL) when using images from other sources.

Add Emphasis to Your Writing—Page 2 of 3

8-36 PP W8-2 completed (pages 1 and 2)

SLO 8.4

Using SmartArt

A ***SmartArt*** graphic is an excellent way to visually display information in a document. *SmartArt* graphics are a collection of customized shapes, lines, and text. Now that you have experience working with shapes and text boxes, you can apply these methods to customize *SmartArt* graphics.

Insert a SmartArt Graphic

There are a variety of *SmartArt* categories, and each of these categories has many built-in *SmartArt* graphics that you can choose and insert in your document. Once you have selected and inserted your *SmartArt,* you can add text, customize the design, and customize the individual objects in the *SmartArt.*

HOW TO: Insert a SmartArt Graphic

1. Place your insertion point in the document where you want to insert a *SmartArt* graphic.
2. Click the **SmartArt** button [*Insert* tab, *Illustrations* group]. The *Choose a SmartArt Graphic* dialog box opens (Figure 8-37).
3. On the left, select a category of *SmartArt* graphics to view the options in that category.
4. In the middle section, select a *SmartArt* graphic.
    - A preview and description of the graphic will appear on the right.
    - The preview is the basic structure of the graphic; you can add to or remove from this structure.
5. Click **OK** to close the dialog box and insert the *SmartArt* graphic.

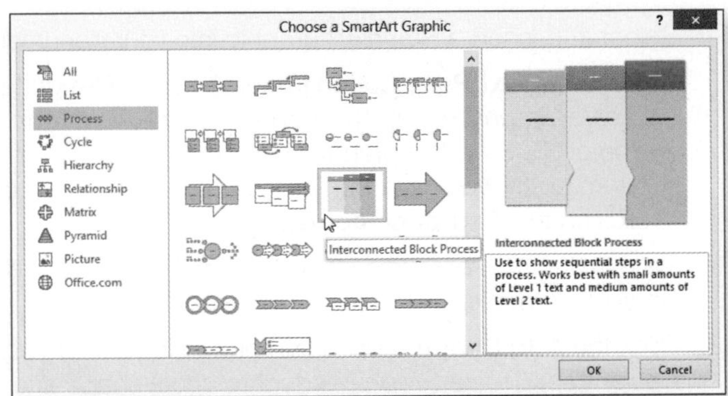

8-37 ***Choose a SmartArt Graphic*** **dialog box**

SmartArt Tools Tabs

When you insert a *SmartArt* graphic into your document, two context-sensitive *SmartArt* tabs become available: ***SmartArt Tools Design*** and ***SmartArt Tools Format.*** You can use the *SmartArt Tools Design* tab to modify the design and structure of the *SmartArt* graphic. The following groups are available on the *SmartArt Tools Design* tab:

- *Create Graphic*
- *Layouts*
- *SmartArt Styles*
- *Reset*

You can use the *SmartArt Tools Format* tab to format the shapes, text, arrangement, and size of the *SmartArt* graphic and the objects within the graphic. The following groups are available on the *SmartArt Tools Format* tab:

- *Shapes*
- *Shape Styles*
- *WordArt Styles*
- *Arrange*
- *Size*

Customize SmartArt Text

When you insert a *SmartArt* graphic into your document, you are not locked into its basic structure. You can add shapes and bulleted text or remove these items. You can type text directly in the *SmartArt* graphic or you can use the ***Text pane*** to enter and organize text.

The *Create Graphic* group on the *SmartArt Tools Design* tab includes options to add a shape or bullet, promote or demote the level of items, move items up or down, switch the layout from right to left, or modify the layout.

You can modify the text in the graphic the same way you modify any text using the *Font* and *Paragraph* groups on the *Home* tab. You can also customize the text in the *SmartArt* graphic with the *WordArt Styles, Text Fill, Text Outline,* and *Text Effects* options in the *WordArt Styles* group on the *SmartArt Tools Format* tab.

HOW TO: Customize SmartArt Text

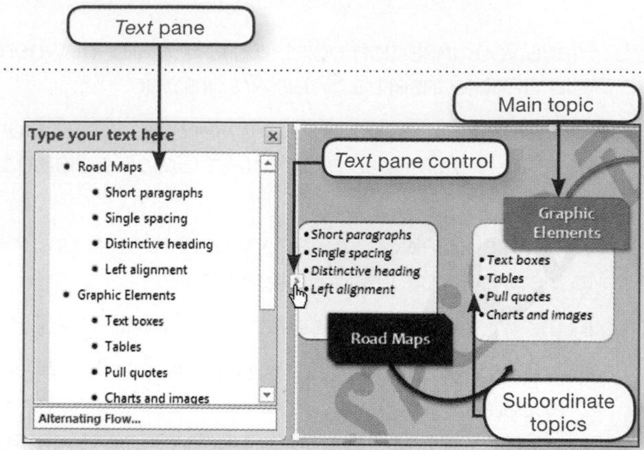

8-38 *SmartArt* graphic with *Text* pane displayed

1. Select and insert a *SmartArt* graphic into your document.
   - Click the **Text Pane** button [*SmartArt Tools Design* tab, *Create Graphic* group] to toggle on/off the *Text* pane to the side of the *SmartArt* graphic (Figure 8-38).
   - Alternatively, you can open and close the *Text* pane by clicking the **Text pane control**.
2. Type text in the *Text* pane or directly on the objects in the *SmartArt* graphic.
3. Click the **Add Shape** drop-down button [*SmartArt Tools Design* tab, *Create Graphic* group] to add a shape after, before, above, or below the selected shape in the graphic (Figure 8-39).
   - The shapes and text in the graphics automatically resize when you add shapes to the *SmartArt* graphic.
   - You can delete shapes or text by selecting them in the *Text* pane and pressing **Delete**.

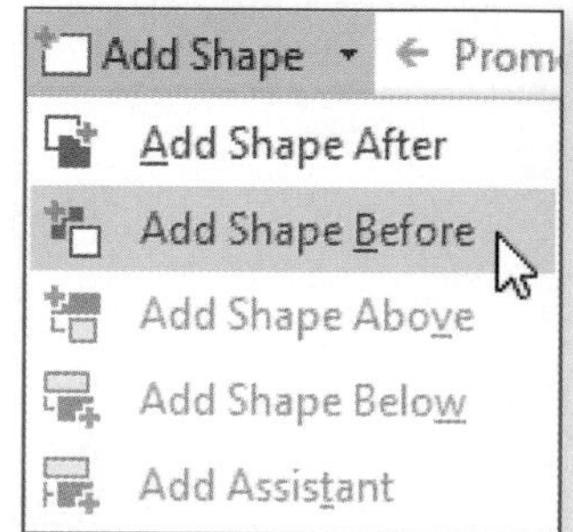

8-39 Add shape to *SmartArt* graphic

4. Click the **Add Bullet** button [*SmartArt Tools Design* tab, *Create Graphic* group] to add a subordinate topic to the list of topics.
   - Alternatively, you can press **Enter** at the end of a bulleted topic in the graphic or *Text* pane to add another bullet.
5. Click the **Promote** or **Demote** button [*SmartArt Tools Design* tab, *Create Graphic* group] to change a main topic to a subordinate topic or to change a subordinate topic to a main topic (Figure 8-40).

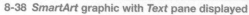

6. Click the **Move Up** or **Move Down** button [*SmartArt Tools Design* tab, *Create Graphic* group] to arrange topics in a list.
   - You can also select and drag or cut and paste topics in the *Text* pane to arrange them.

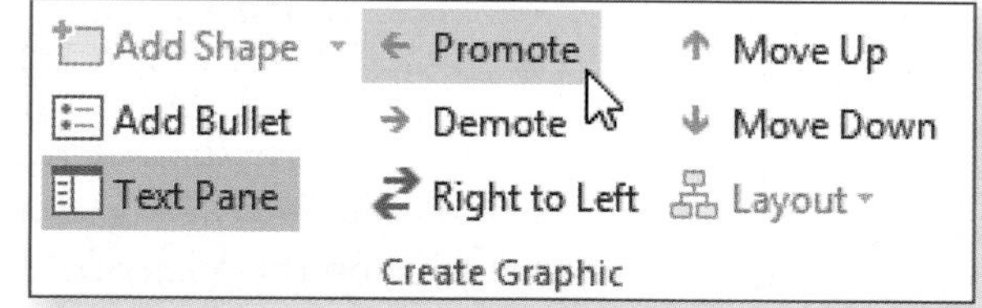

8-40 *Create Graphic* group on the *SmartArt Tools Design* tab

7. Click the **Right to Left** button [*SmartArt Tools Design* tab, *Create Graphic* group] to switch the layout of the *SmartArt* graphic from left to right or right to left.
8. Click the **WordArt Styles, Text Fill, Text Outline**, and **Text Effects** button to customize the appearance of the text [*SmartArt Tools Format* tab, *WordArt Styles* group] (Figure 8-41).
   - Be sure to select the text in the *SmartArt* graphic or in the *Text* pane before customizing the text.
9. Click the **Text Pane** button [*Table Tools Design* tab, *Create Graphic* group] or the **X** in the upper right corner of the *Text* pane to close it.

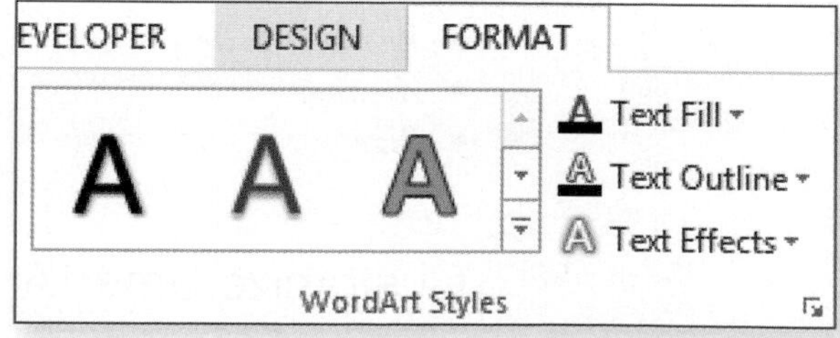

8-41 *WordArt Styles* group on the *SmartArt Tools Format* tab

ANOTHER WAY

Click the **Shape Styles** or **WordArt Styles** launcher [*SmartArt Tools Format* tab] to open the *Format Shape* pane where you can customize the *SmartArt* graphic.

Customize SmartArt Design

After typing and customizing the text in your *SmartArt* graphic, you might want to customize the overall design of the *SmartArt* graphic. For example, you might want to change the layout of the *SmartArt* graphic or modify the colors of the objects or apply a *SmartArt* style. These options are available on the *SmartArt Tools Design* tab.

HOW TO: Customize SmartArt Design

1. With the *SmartArt* graphic selected in your document, use the *Layouts* group [*SmartArt Tools Design* tab] to select a different *SmartArt* layout.
   - Click the **More** button in the *Layouts* group [*SmartArt Tools Design* tab] to display additional options in the *Layouts* gallery.
   - With the *Layouts* gallery displayed, select **More Layouts** to open the *Choose a SmartArt Graphic* dialog box where you can change the *SmartArt* layout.
2. Click the **Change Colors** button [*SmartArt Tools Design* tab, *SmartArt Styles* group] to change the color of your *SmartArt* graphic (Figure 8-42).
3. In the *SmartArt Styles* area, select a style to apply to your *SmartArt* graphic.
   - *SmartArt Styles* apply custom fill, outlines, and effects to your *SmartArt* graphic.
   - Click the **More** button [*SmartArt Tools Design* tab, *SmartArt Styles* group] to display additional style options.

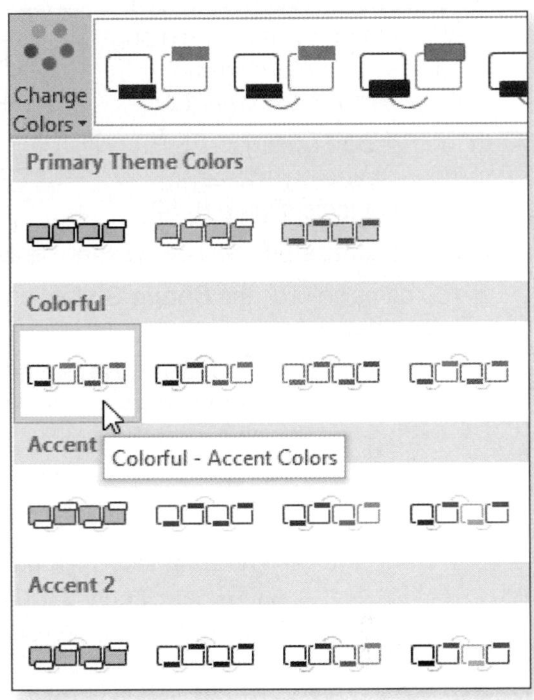

8-42 Change color of *SmartArt* graphic

MORE INFO

When you place your pointer on a layout, color, or style, Word temporarily applies the style to your *SmartArt* graphic so you can preview your graphic with the selection applied.

Customize SmartArt Objects

In addition to customizing *SmartArt* text and design, you can also customize individual objects within the *SmartArt* graphic. You can change the size or shape of individual objects in your *SmartArt* graphic. You can also apply a shape style or customize a shape fill, outline, or effects. Making changes to the individual objects in a *SmartArt* graphic is similar to customizing shapes.

HOW TO: Customize SmartArt Objects

1. Select the object to customize.
   - Use the **Ctrl** key to select multiple objects in your *SmartArt* graphic if you want to apply changes to more than one object.
   - You can also use the *Selection* pane [*SmartArt Tools Format* tab, *Arrange* group] to select objects in your *SmartArt* graphic.
2. Click the **Change Shape** button [*SmartArt Tools Format* tab, *Shapes* group] to select a different shape for the selected objects (Figure 8-43).
   - You don't have to draw a new shape; Word automatically applies the selected shape to the selected objects and adjusts the size of the text if needed.

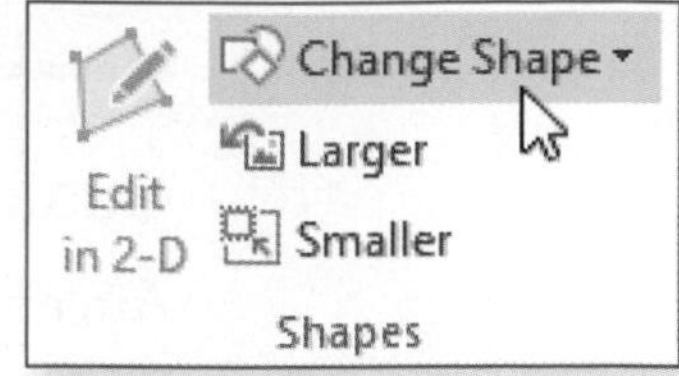

8-43 Shapes group on the *SmartArt Tools Format* tab

3. Click the **Larger** or **Smaller** button [*SmartArt Tools Format* tab, *Shapes* group] to change the size of the selected objects.
   - You can also change the size of an object by using the sizing handles or the *Size* group [*SmartArt Tools Format* tab].
4. In the *Shape Styles* gallery, select a shape style to apply selected objects (Figure 8-44).

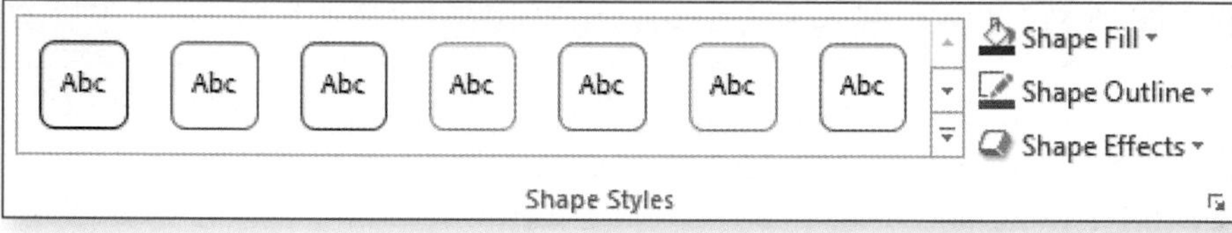

8-44 *Shape Styles* group on the *SmartArt Tools Format* tab

5. Click the **Shape Fill, Shape Outline**, or **Shape Effects** button to customize the selected shapes.
   - You can also click the **Shape Styles** launcher to open the *Format Shape* pane where you can customize selected shapes.
6. Use the **Bring Forward, Send Backward, Align, Group**, and **Rotate** buttons [*SmartArt Tool Format* tab, *Arrange* group] to arrange selected objects in your *SmartArt* graphic.

Resize, Align, and Position SmartArt

The final step in modifying your *SmartArt* graphic is to customize the size, text wrapping, alignment, and position. When you adjust the size of your *SmartArt* graphic, Word automatically resizes the objects and text in the graphic.

HOW TO: Resize, Align, and Position SmartArt

1. With the *SmartArt* graphic selected, use the *Size* group [*SmartArt Tools Format* tab] or the sizing handles to change the height and width of the graphic.
   - The sizing handles on a *SmartArt* graphic are the small squares on the sides and corners of the *SmartArt* frame.
2. Click the **Wrap Text** button [*SmartArt Tools Format* tab, *Arrange* group] to select a text wrap option.
3. Click and drag the frame of the *SmartArt* graphic to position it in your document.
   - When you place your pointer on the frame of the *SmartArt* graphic, your pointer becomes a four-pointed move pointer.
   - You can also click the **Align** or **Position** button [*SmartArt Tools Format* tab, *Arrange* group] to align your *SmartArt* graphic in relation to the page or margins.

> MORE INFO
>
> Click the **Size** launcher [*SmartArt Tools Format* tab, *Size* group] to open the *Layout* dialog box where you can modify the position, text wrapping, and size.

SLO 8.5

Using Charts

Many people use ***Charts*** in Excel worksheets and PowerPoint presentations. Charts are an excellent way to graphically display numerical data. In Word you can insert a variety of different chart types, and you can customize the data presented in the chart, the layout and elements of the chart, the chart design, and the format of the chart and specific chart elements.

Insert a Chart

There are a variety of charts that you can insert into your documents. You need to determine the type of chart that will best visually display the data you are presenting. The most common types of charts are *Column, Line, Pie,* and *Bar.* Word also offers other charts such as *Area, XY (Scatter), Stock, Surface, Doughnut, Bubble* and *Radar.*

When you insert a chart, a chart is inserted in the Word document. Also, a ***Chart in Microsoft Word worksheet*** opens in a new window and contains generic data. The information in the *Chart in Microsoft Word* worksheet is similar to a table in that it is set up in column and rows (see Figure 8-46). You can edit the data in the worksheet, and that information displays in the chart in the Word document.

HOW TO: Insert a Chart

1. Place the insertion point in your document at the location where you want to insert the chart.
2. Click the **Chart** button [*Insert* tab, *Illustrations* group]. The *Insert Chart* dialog box opens (Figure 8-45).
3. Select the chart you want to insert into your document.
   - On the left, the different categories of charts are listed.
   - On the right, a thumbnail graphic displays each chart structure.
4. Click **OK** to close the dialog box and insert the chart.
   - The chart is inserted in the document and a *Chart in Microsoft Word* worksheet window opens (Figure 8-46).

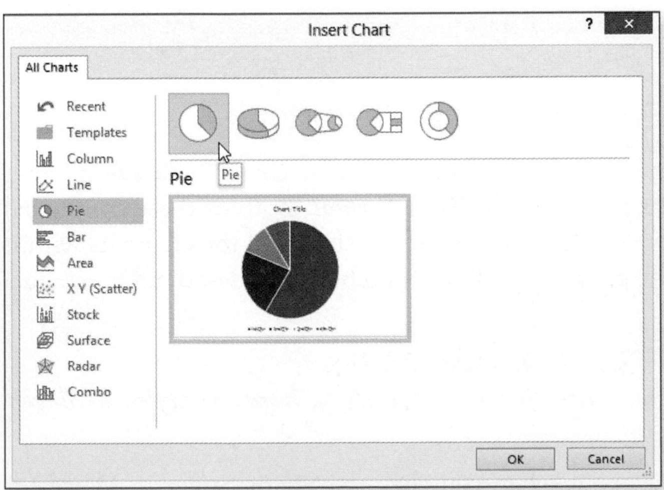

8-45 ***Insert Chart* dialog box**

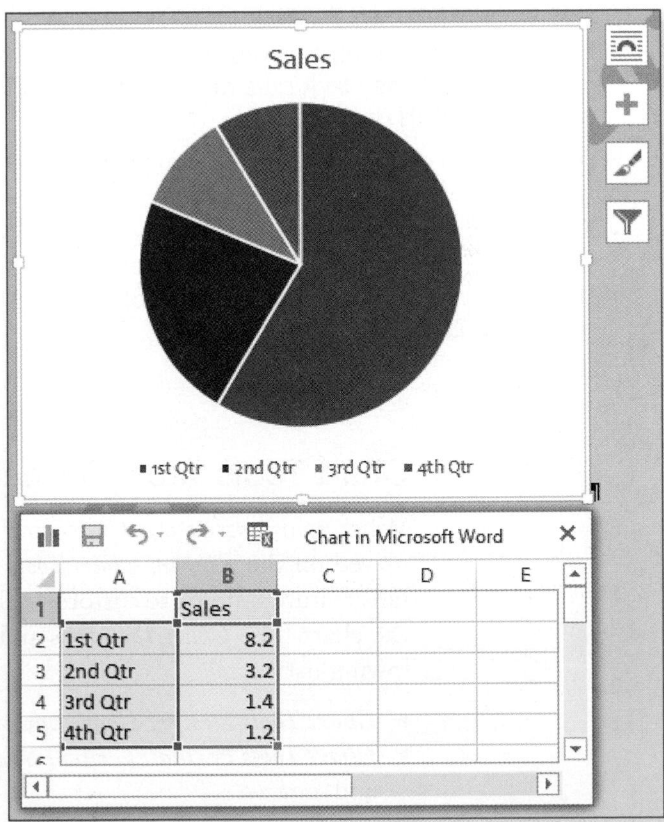

8-46 Chart inserted and *Chart in Microsoft Word* worksheet displayed

Customize Chart Data

The first thing you will do after you insert a chart is to customize the data for the chart, which is in the *Chart in Microsoft Word* worksheet. There is sample data in the worksheet when you insert the chart. You need to replace this data with your own data. Column and row headings describe the data, which you can use as axes and legend labels.

The ***chart data range*** is the information in the *Chart in Microsoft Word* worksheet that is displayed in the chart in your Word document. The chart data range is indicated with a border as shown in Figure 8-47. You customize the data in this worksheet, and you can add rows or columns of data in the worksheet and adjust the chart data range to display additional information in your chart. You can also remove data and adjust the chart data range.

HOW TO: Customize Chart Data

1. After inserting a chart in the Word document, type the chart data in the *Chart in Microsoft Word* worksheet (see Figure 8-47).
   - The data displayed in the chart is automatically updated as you edit the data in the *Chart in Microsoft Word* worksheet.
   - Be sure to include column and row headings. Column headings are typed in the first row, and row headings are typed in the first column.
   - Drag the title bar of the *Chart in Microsoft Word* worksheet to reposition the window if needed.
2. Click and drag the **chart data range** handle (bottom right corner of the chart data range) to change the chart data range.
   - Make sure there are no blank rows or columns in the chart data range or these blank data ranges will also display in the chart in the Word document.
3. When you finish editing the chart data in the *Chart in Microsoft Word* worksheet, click the **X** in the upper right corner to close the window.
   - If you need to edit the chart data after closing the Excel spreadsheet, click the **Edit Data** button [*Chart Tools Design* tab, *Data* group] to open the *Chart in Microsoft Word* window.
   - You can also edit chart data in a Microsoft Excel 2013 worksheet. Click the **Edit Data** drop-down list and select **Edit Data in Excel 2013**.

Chart in Micro

	A	B	C
1		2013 Enrollment	
2	ENGWR 101	2541	
3	ENGWR 102	2865	
4	ENGWR 201	4207	
5	ENGWR 202	3205	
6			

Chart data range handle

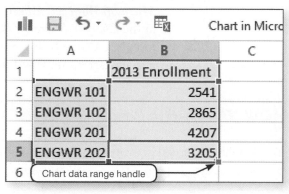

8-47 Edit chart data in the *Chart in Microsoft Word* worksheet

Chart Tools Tabs, Format Pane, and Format Buttons

When you insert a chart into your document, two context-sensitive ***Chart Tools tabs*** are displayed on the *Ribbon:* ***Chart Tools Design*** and ***Chart Tools Format.*** Both of these contextual tabs feature options to customize the design and format of the chart and the elements within the chart. The *Chart Tools* tabs and the groups available on each tab are described in the following list:

- ***Chart Tools Design:*** *Chart Layouts, Chart Styles, Data,* and *Type*
- ***Chart Tools Format:*** *Current Selection, Insert Shapes, Shape Styles, Word Art Styles, Arrange,* and *Size*

The ***Format "Chart Element" pane*** opens when you click the **Shape Styles** or **WordArt Styles** launcher on the *Chart Tools Format* tab (Figure 8-48). The *Format* pane's name changes depending on the chart element selected (e.g., *Format Chart Area, Format Chart Title*). Click the **Chart Elements** drop-down list to select a chart element. The *Format* pane provides format categories (e.g., *Fill & Line, Effects, Layout & Properties*) and options within each category. The format categories and options vary depending on the chart element selected.

Additionally, there are four format buttons on the right of a selected chart: ***Layout Options, Chart Elements, Chart Styles,*** and ***Chart Filters.*** These format buttons provide another method to customize chart design and format. Click any of these format buttons to display a list of options (Figure 8-49).

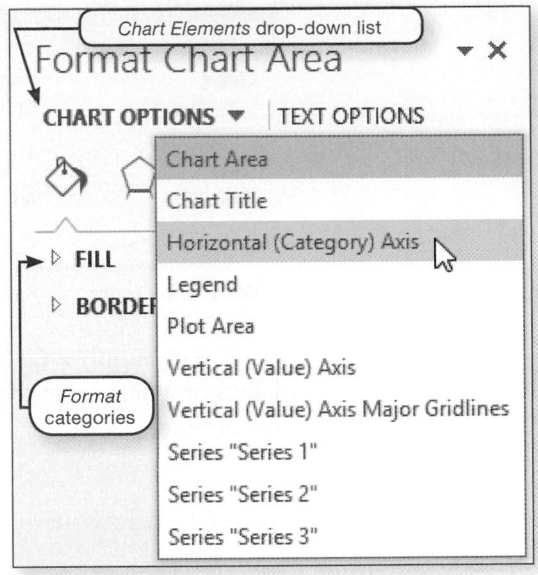

8-48 *Format "Chart Element"* pane

Customize Chart Layout

After you have inserted the chart and customized the data displayed in the chart, you add or modify the elements of the chart. For example, you can add or modify the chart title, axis titles, legend, and data labels. Depending on the type of chart you are using, different chart element options are available. Click the **Add Chart Element** button on the *Chart Tools Design* tab in the *Chart Layouts* group to display the drop-down list of chart elements. The common chart elements are listed and described in the following table:

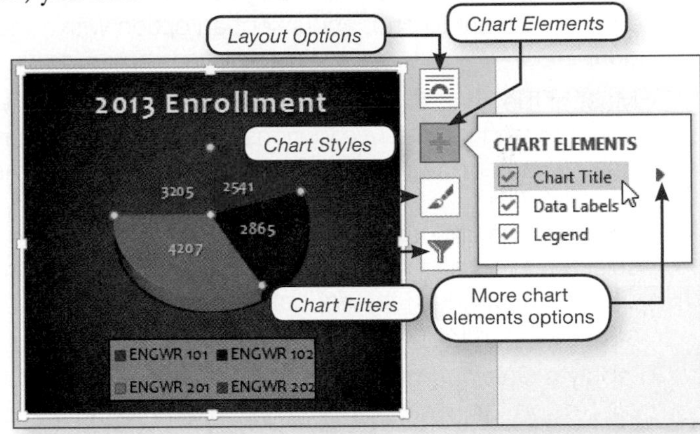

8-49 Format buttons

Chart Elements

Chart Element	Description
Axes	The horizontal axis (X-axis) and vertical axis (Y-axis) that appear on charts. You can customize the scale and format of both axes.
Axis Titles	Text displayed on the horizontal axis (X-axis) and vertical axis (Y-axis) to describe these axes.
Chart Title	Text that describes the chart's content and purpose.
Data Labels	Numerical labels on columns, bars, lines, or pie segments that display the number or percent for each value plotted on the chart.
Data Table	A table that appears below the chart that displays the data values.
Error Bars	Error bars help you see margins of error and standard deviations at a glance.
Gridlines	Vertical and horizontal lines that appear in the chart plot area to help readers distinguish values and data.
Legend	Text that describes the data represented in the chart and is typically displayed on the right or at the bottom of the chart.

continued

Chart Element	Description
Lines	Vertical lines that drop from data points to the X-axis or display vertical lines between high and low data points on line charts.
Plot Area	The area of the chart where the columns, bars, or lines display chart data.
Trendline	A line that charts the trend between data points.
Up/Down Bars	Bars that display between data points on a line chart.
Walls and Floors	Side and back walls and floors that display when using a 3-D chart.

You can apply a ***Quick Layout*** to a chart, which adds common chart elements such as data labels or a data table to a chart. You can also change the chart type after you inserted it into a document.

HOW TO: Customize Chart Layout

1. To add, remove, or modify a chart element, click the **Add Chart Element** button [*Chart Tools Design* tab, *Chart Layouts* group], select the chart element to add, and select an option within the chart element (Figure 8-50).
   - Most of the chart elements have a *More "Chart Element" Options* selection (e.g., *More Title Options*). This selection opens the *Format "Chart Element"* pane where you can further modify the chart element (Figure 8-51).
   - You can also click the **Chart Elements** button on the right of a selected chart and select or deselect a chart element (see Figure 8-49). Click the triangle on the right of each chart element in this menu to further customize each chart element.
2. To apply a *Quick Layout*, click the **Quick Layout** button [*Chart Tools Design* tab, *Chart Layouts* group] and select an option from the drop-down list.
3. To change the chart type, click the **Change Chart Type** button [*Chart Tools Design* tab, *Type* group] to open the *Change Chart Type* dialog box where you can select a different chart type.

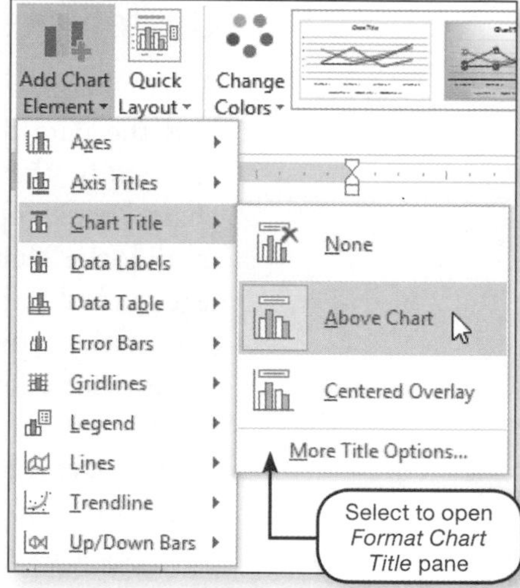

8-50 ***Add Chart Element*** **drop-down list**

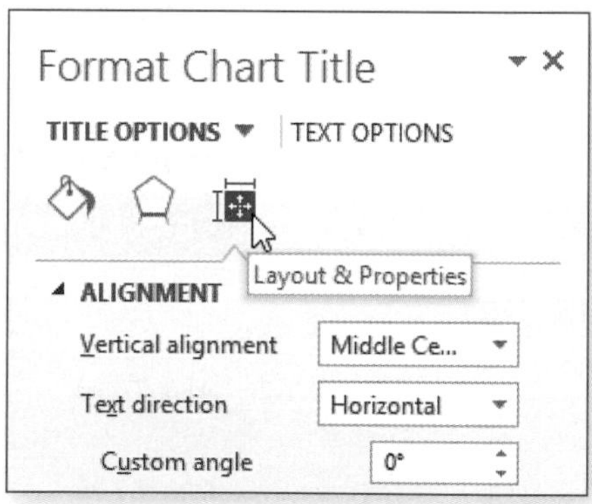

8-51 ***Format Chart Title*** **pane**

> **MORE INFO**
>
> When you place your pointer on a chart element, a tag appears with the name of the chart element.

Apply a Chart Style and Quick Color

After customizing the layout of your chart, you can apply a ***Chart Style*** and ***Quick Colors.*** A *Chart Style* is a combination of colors and chart elements that is applied to a chart with one click. *Quick Colors* are color sets that apply to the data plotted in the chart (e.g., bars, columns, lines, pie pieces). There are two different categories of *Quick Colors: Colorful* and *Monochromatic.* Both *Chart Styles* and *Quick Colors* apply to an entire chart.

HOW TO: Apply a Chart Style and Quick Color

1. Select the chart and click the **Chart Tools Design** tab.
2. Click the **More** button in the *Chart Styles* group to display the *Chart Styles* gallery (Figure 8-52).
   - When you place your pointer on a selection in the *Chart Styles* gallery, the chart style is temporarily applied to the selected chart to provide you with a live preview of the style.
3. Click the **Change Colors** button [*Chart Tools Design* tab, *Chart Styles* group] and select a *Quick Color*.
   - When you place your pointer on a selection in the *Quick Colors* drop-down list, the color set is temporarily applied to the selected chart to provide you with a live preview of the *Quick Color*.

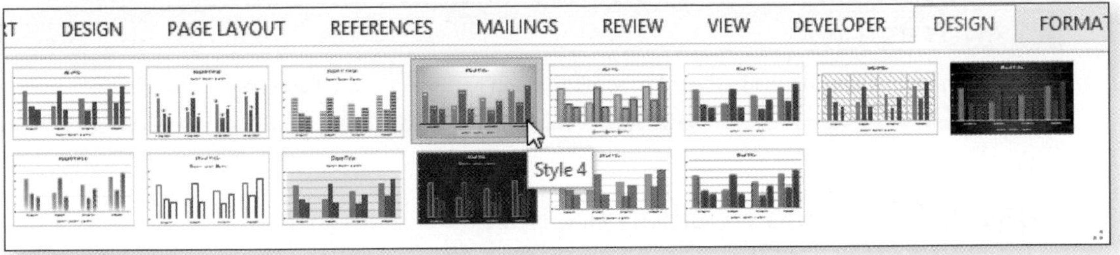

8-52 ***Chart Styles*** **gallery**

> **ANOTHER WAY**
>
> Click the **Chart Styles** button on the right of a selected chart and apply a *Chart Style* or *Quick Color*.

Format Chart Elements

After inserting a chart and customizing the data, layout, and design, you can apply styles, fills, outlines, and effects to specific chart elements. For example, you can apply a fill color to the entire chart area, change the color of a column, apply an outline to the legend, or change the font on your data labels.

HOW TO: Customize Chart Elements

1. Click the **Chart Tools Format** tab.
2. Select the chart element you want to modify.
   - You can click the specific chart element in the chart or click the **Chart Elements** drop-down list [*Chart Tools Format* tab, *Current Selection* group] and select a chart element (Figure 8-53).
3. Click the **Shape Styles** drop-down list [*Chart Tools Design* tab, *Shape Styles* group] to apply a *Shape Style* to the selected chart element (Figure 8-54).
4. Click the **Shape Fill, Shape Outline**, or **Shape Effects** button [*Shape Styles* group] to apply a fill, outline, or effect to the selected chart element.
   - Click the **Shape Styles** launcher to open the *Format* pane, which gives you more customization options. For example, if you have the chart title selected and click the *Shape Styles* launcher, the *Format Chart Title* pane opens (see Figure 8-51).

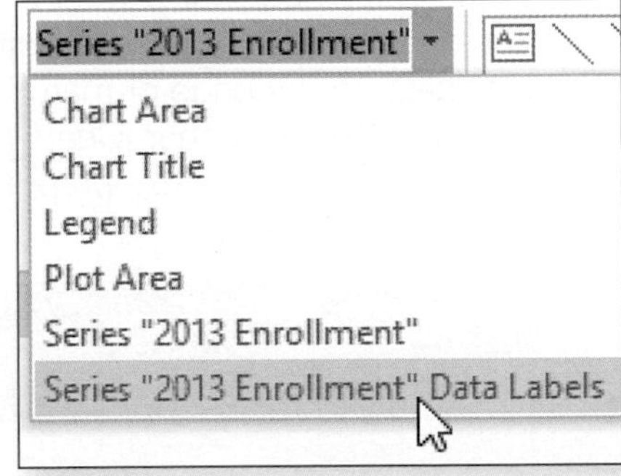

8-53 **Select chart element**

8-54 ***Shape Styles*** **group on the** ***Chart Tools Format*** **tab**

- You can also right-click a chart element and select **Format "Chart Element"** from the context menu to open the *Format "Chart Element"* pane.

5. Click the **WordArt Styles, Text Fill, Text Outline**, or **Text Effects** button [*WordArt Styles* group] to customize the selected chart element text (Figure 8-55).
   - Click the **WordArt Styles** launcher to open the *Format* pane where you can customize the selected chart element.

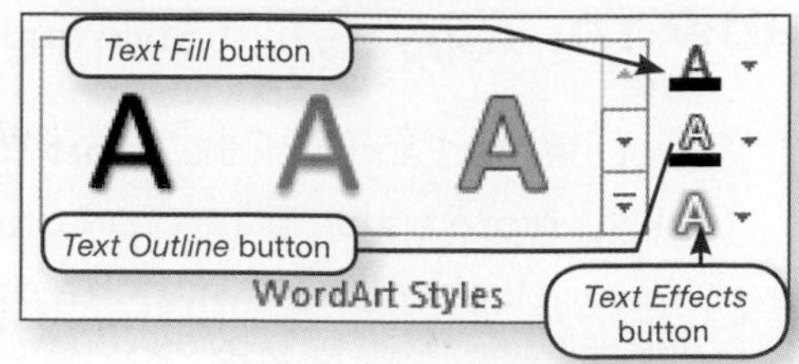

8-55 *Word Art Styles* group on the *Chart Tools Format* tab

ANOTHER WAY

Use the arrow keys on the keyboard to scroll through and select chart elements.

Resize, Align, and Position a Chart

The final step in modifying your chart is customizing the size, text wrapping, alignment, and position. Modifying the size and arrangement of the chart in your document is similar to working with *SmartArt* graphics, pictures, or shapes. Word automatically resizes chart elements when you adjust the size of your chart.

HOW TO: Resize, Align, and Position a Chart

1. With the chart selected, use the *Size* group [*Chart Tools Format* tab] or the sizing handles to change the height and width of the graphic (Figure 8-56).
2. Click the **Wrap Text** button [*Chart Tools Format* tab, *Arrange* group] to select the way the text wraps around your chart.
3. Click and drag the frame of the chart to position it in your document.
   - When you place your pointer on the frame of the chart, it becomes a four-pointed move pointer.
   - You can click the **Align** or **Position** button [*Chart Tools Format* tab, *Arrange* group] to align your chart graphic in relation to the page or margins.
   - Click the **Size** launcher [*Chart Tools Format* tab, *Size* group] to open the *Layout* dialog box where you can modify the position, text wrapping, and size of the chart.

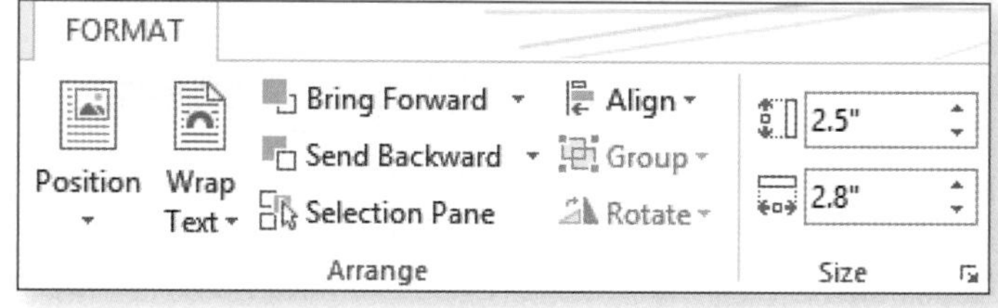

8-56 *Arrange* and *Size* groups on the *Chart Tools Format* tab

PAUSE & PRACTICE: WORD 8-3

For this Pause & Practice project, you modify the document you created in *Pause & Practice 8-2*. You insert a chart and customize the chart data, layout, design, and format, and you insert a *SmartArt* graphic and customize the *SmartArt* text, design, and objects.

File Needed: ***[your initials] PP W8-2.docx***
Completed Project File Name: ***[your initials] PP W8-3.docx***

1. Open the ***[your initials] PP W8-2*** document you saved in *Pause & Practice 8-2*.
2. Save the document as ***[your initials] PP W8-3***.
3. Insert a chart and customize the chart data.
   a. Place the insertion point at the end of the last paragraph on the second page.
   b. Click the **Chart** button [*Insert* tab, *Illustrations* group]. The *Insert Chart* dialog box opens (Figure 8-57).
   c. Click **Pie** on the left, select the **Pie** chart, and click **OK** to insert the chart and open the *Chart in Microsoft Word* worksheet window. Don't be concerned with chart placement at this point; you will modify this later.
   d. In the *Chart in Microsoft Word* worksheet, type the data shown in Figure 8-58.
   e. Click the **X** in the upper right corner of the *Chart in Microsoft Word* worksheet window to close it.
4. Modify the chart layout and design.
   a. With the chart selected, click the **Add Chart Element** button [*Chart Tools Design* tab, *Chart Layouts* group], select **Data Labels**, and select **Center**.
   b. Click the **Change Chart Type** button [*Chart Tools Design* tab, *Type* group] to open the *Change Chart Type* dialog box.
   c. Select **3-D Pie** and click **OK** to close the dialog box and change the chart type.
   d. Select **Style 7** in the *Chart Styles* gallery [*Chart Tools Design* tab, *Chart Styles* group]. You might need to click the **More** button in the *Chart Styles* group to display the *Chart Styles* gallery.
5. Customize chart elements.
   a. Click the **Chart Elements** drop-down list [*Chart Tools Format* tab, *Current Selection* group] and select **Series "2013 Enrollment" Data Labels** (Figure 8-59).
   b. Apply **bold** formatting (**Ctrl+B**) to the selected data labels.
   c. Click the **Text Effects** button [*Chart Tools Format* tab, *WordArt Styles* group], select **Shadow**, and select **Offset Diagonal Bottom Right** in the *Outer* category (Figure 8-60).
   d. Click the title of the chart to select it and apply the **Offset Diagonal Bottom Right** shadow text effect.
   e. Use the down arrow key to select the legend (rectangle box below the pie).
   f. Click the **More** button [*Shape Styles* group] to display the *Shape Styles* gallery and select **Subtle Effect – Black, Dark 1** (Figure 8-61).
   g. Click the **Shape Styles** launcher to open the *Format* pane at the right.

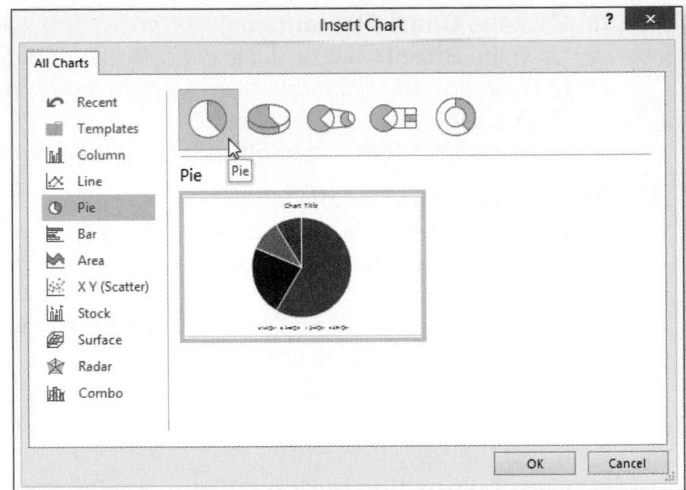

8-57 Insert pie chart

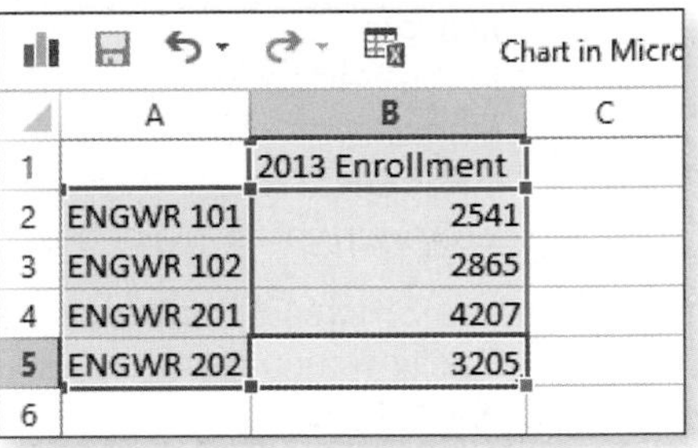

	A	B	C
1		2013 Enrollment	
2	ENGWR 101	2541	
3	ENGWR 102	2865	
4	ENGWR 201	4207	
5	ENGWR 202	3205	
6			

8-58 Edit chart data

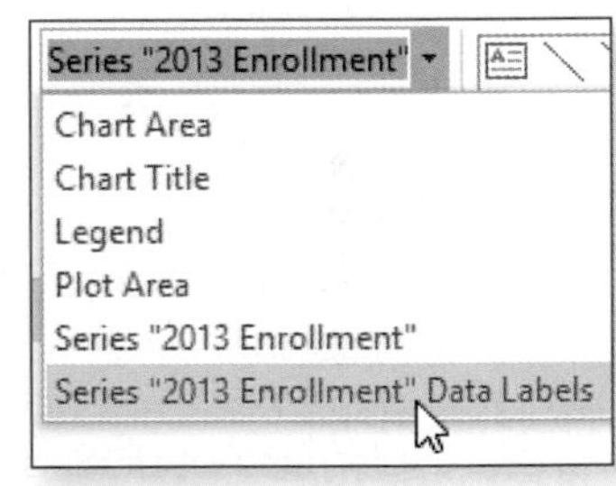

8-59 Select chart element

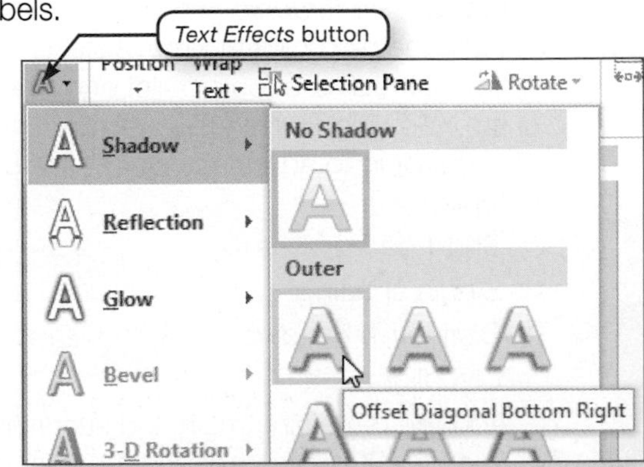

8-60 Apply a *Shadow* text effect

h. Click the **Chart Elements** drop-down list and select **Plot Area**.
i. Click the **Effects** button if it is not selected and click **3-D Rotation** to open the *3-D Rotation* options area in the *Format Plot Area* pane (Figure 8-62).
j. Change the *Y Rotation* to **50°** and close the *Format Plot Area* pane.

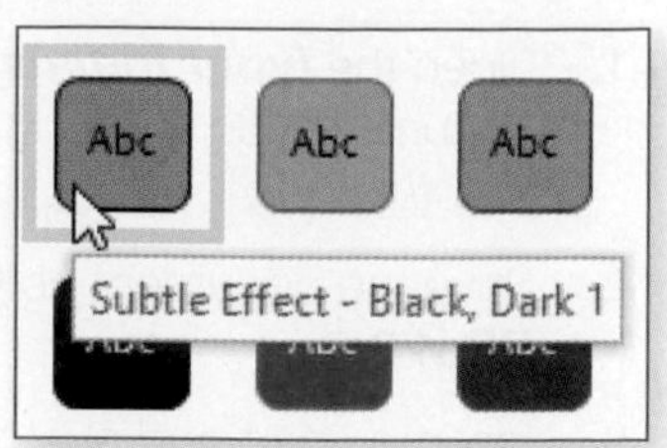

8-61 Apply a *Shape Style*

6. Resize, change text wrapping, and position the chart.
   a. Click the border of the chart to select the chart area. The tool tip displays *Chart Area* when you put your pointer on the border of the chart.
   b. In the *Size* group [*Chart Tools Format* tab], change the *Height* to **2.5"** and the *Width* to **2.8"**.
   c. Click the **Wrap Text** button [*Chart Tools Format* tab, *Arrange* group] and select **Tight**. The chart moves to the top of the second page.
   d. Click the **Position button** [*Chart Tools Format* tab, *Arrange* group] and select **More Layout Options** to open the *Layout* dialog box.
   e. In the *Horizontal* area, set **Alignment** to **Right** *relative to* **Margin**.
   f. In the *Vertical* area, set **Absolute position** at **7.4"** *below* **Page**.
   g. Click **OK** to close the dialog box. The chart is near the bottom right of the second page.

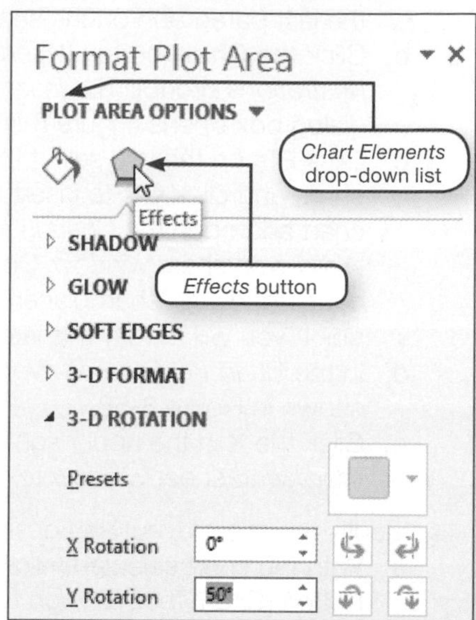

8-62 Change 3-D rotation

7. Insert a *SmartArt* graphic and add text.
   a. Position the insertion point at the end of the document (**Ctrl+End**).
   b. Click the **SmartArt** button [*Insert* tab, *Illustrations* group] to open the *Choose a SmartArt Graphic* dialog box (Figure 8-63).
   c. Click the **Process** button at the left.
   d. Select **Interconnected Block Process** and click **OK** to insert the *SmartArt* graphic.
   e. In the *Text* pane of the *SmartArt* graphic, click the first main heading bullet and type Road Maps. If the *Text* pane is not displayed, click the **Text Pane** button [*SmartArt Tools Design* tab, *Create Graphic* group].
   f. Click the next bullet to move to the first subordinate topic bullet and type the following text, pressing **Enter** after each topic to add a new subordinate topic:
      Short paragraphs
      Single spacing
      Distinctive heading
      Left alignment
   g. Add the remaining main and subordinate topics shown in Figure 8-64.
   h. Click the **X** in the upper right corner of the *Text* pane to close the *Text* pane.

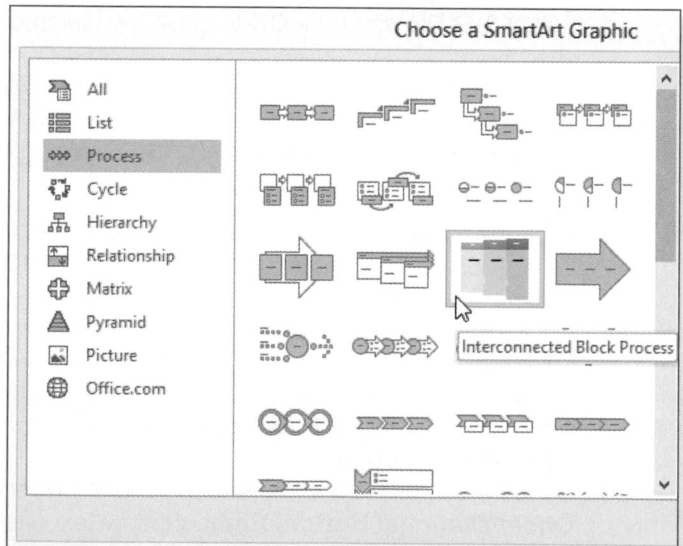

8-63 Insert a *SmartArt* graphic

8. Change *SmartArt* layout and customize design.
   a. With the *SmartArt* graphic selected, click the **More** button in the *Layouts* group [*SmartArt Tools Design* tab] to open the *Layouts* gallery.
   b. Select the **Alternating Flow** layout (Figure 8-65).
   c. Click the **Change Colors** button [*SmartArt Tools Design* tab, *SmartArt Styles* group] and select **Colorful – Accent Colors** from the *Colorful* category.
   d. Click the **More** button in the *SmartArt Styles* group [*SmartArt Tools Design* tab] to open the *SmartArt Styles* gallery and select **Intense Effect** (Figure 8-66).

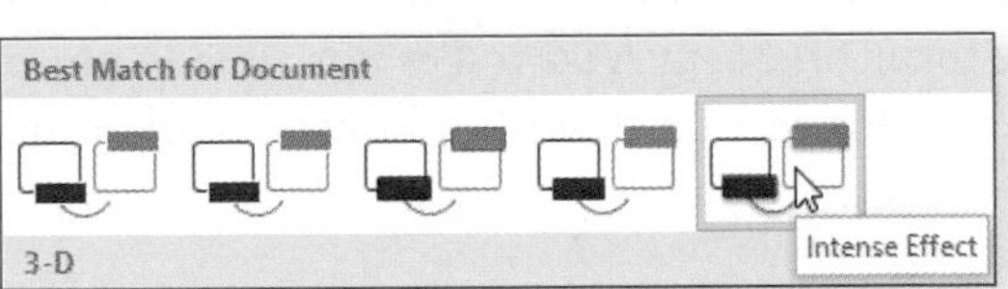

8-65 Change *SmartArt* layout

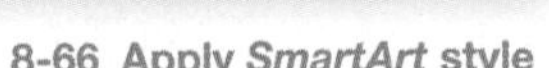

8-66 Apply *SmartArt* style

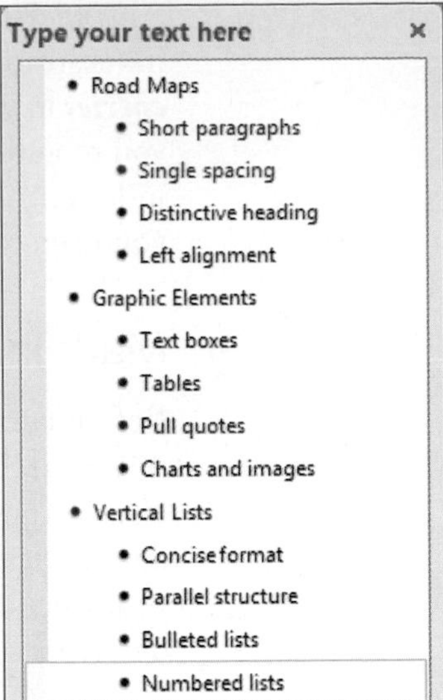

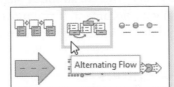

8-64 Add text using the *Text* pane

9. Modify *SmartArt* objects.
   a. Hold down the **Ctrl** key and click the border of the three main topics ("Road Maps," "Graphic Elements," and "Vertical Lists") to select all three.
   b. Click the **Change Shape** button [*SmartArt Tools Format* tab, *Shapes* group] and select the **Snip Diagonal Corner Rectangle** shape (Figure 8-67).
   c. With the three shapes still selected, apply **bold** formatting.
   d. With the three shapes still selected, click the **Text Effects** button [*SmartArt Tools Format* tab, *WordArt Styles* group], select **Shadow**, and select **Offset Diagonal Bottom Right** in the *Outer* category.
   e. Click the border of the *SmartArt* graphic to deselect the three shapes.
   f. Select the three subordinate topic shapes and apply **italic** formatting (**Ctrl+I**).

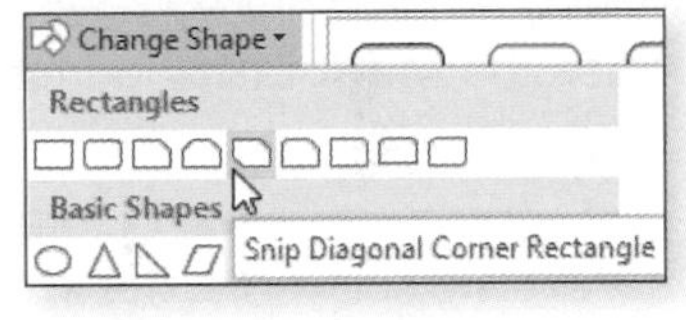

8-67 Change *SmartArt* shapes

10. Resize the *SmartArt* graphic.
    a. Click the frame of the *SmartArt* graphic to select it.
    b. In the *Size* group [*SmartArt Tools Format* tab], change the *Height* to **3"** and the *Width* to **5"**.
11. Save and close the document (Figure 8-68).

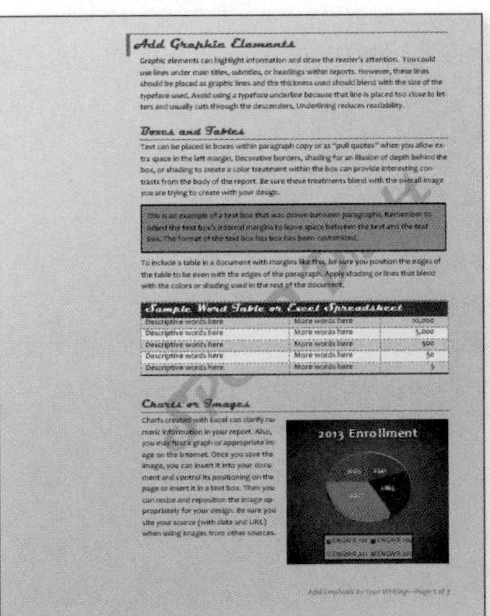

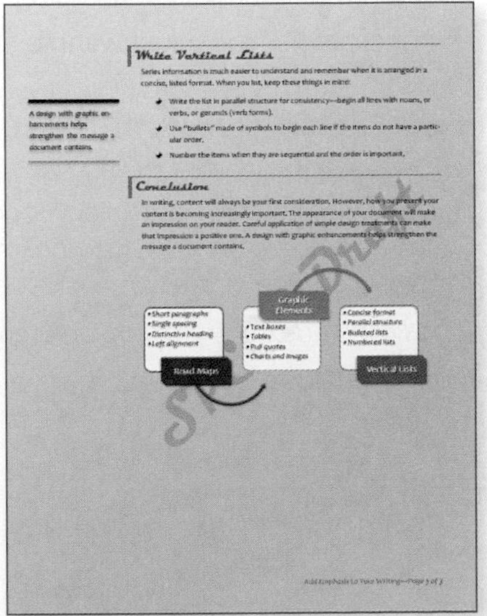

8-68 PP W8-3 completed (pages 2 and 3)

SLO 8.6

Creating an Index

An ***index page*** is a list of topic references in a long report or technical document. Using an index, readers are able to look up the location of key words in a document. You can mark ***index entries*** in your document, which you can use to create an index for the document. Word allows you to automatically generate an index page with index entries and page numbers based upon index entries in your document. If you move text in the document or make pagination changes, you need to update the index page to reflect accurate page numbers for your index entries.

Mark Index Entries

Before creating an index page, you must first mark index entries in your document. You can select specific text to mark as an index entry or you can insert an index entry at a specific location in your document. When you mark an index entry, Word inserts an ***index field code*** and automatically turns on *Show/Hide* if it is not already on so you can see the index field codes in your document. This section describes how to mark a main index entry, and the next section describes subentries.

HOW TO: Mark Index Entries

1. Select the text or place the insertion point in your document where you want to insert an index entry.
2. Click the **Mark Entry** button [*References* tab, *Index* group]. The *Mark Index Entry* dialog box opens (Figure 8-69).
   - If you selected text before clicking the *Mark Entry* button, the selected text is displayed in the *Main entry* text box.
   - If you did not select text, the *Main entry* text box is empty.
   - The text in the *Main entry* text box is the text that will be displayed on your index page.
   - You can edit the text in the *Main entry* text box.
3. Edit the text in the *Main entry* text box if necessary.
4. In the *Options* area, the *Current page* radio button is selected.
5. In the *Page number format* area, click the **Bold** or **Italic** check boxes to apply formatting to the page number that will appear on the index page.
   - For example, you might want to apply bold formatting to all main index entries.
6. Click the **Mark** or **Mark All** button.
   - *Mark* inserts an index field code on the selected text or location.
   - *Mark All* inserts an index field code on all instances of the word or words in the *Main entry* text box so you don't have to manually mark each instance of the same index entry.
7. The *Mark Index* entry dialog box remains open so you can continue marking index entries in your document.
8. Click the **Close** button when you are finished marking index entries.

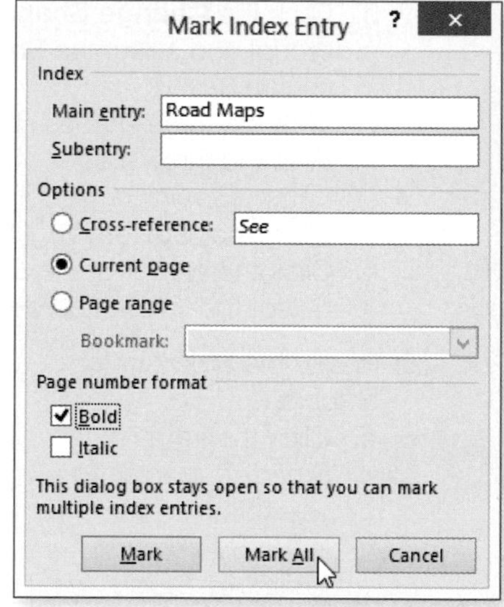

8-69 *Mark Index Entry* dialog box

MORE INFO

When you insert index entries, the index field codes affect the pagination when *Show/Hide* is turned on; don't be concerned about this. When you turn off *Show/Hide,* these hidden field codes do not affect the pagination.

Subentries

An index **subentry** is useful to index items within a main index entry. For example, you might want to mark "Boxes," "Tables," and "Pull Quotes" as subentries for the main index entry of "Graphic Elements." When you mark subentries, these entries are indented on the index page to visually indicate they are subentries to a main index entry.

HOW TO: Create an Index Subentry

1. Select the text or place the insertion point in your document where you want the index subentry inserted.
2. Click the **Mark Entry** button [*References* tab, *Index* group]. The *Mark Index Entry* dialog box opens (Figure 8-70).
3. Type the main entry in the *Main entry* text box.
   - It is very important to spell the main entry correctly as Word uses the exact spelling to index text on the index page.
4. Type the subentry in the *Subentry* text box.
5. Click **Mark** or **Mark All**.
6. Continue marking index entries or click **Close** to close the dialog box.

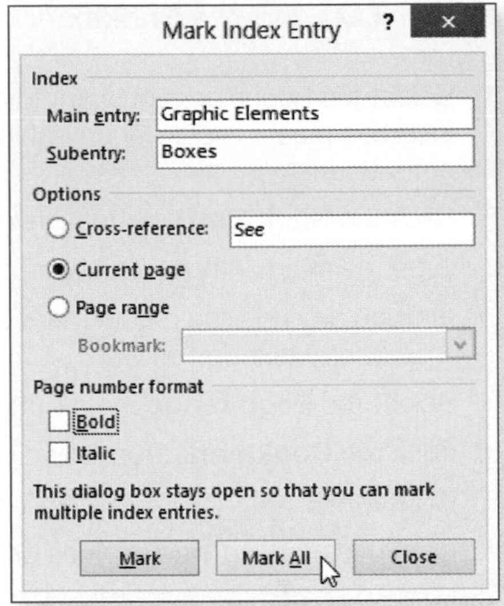

8-70 Mark an index subentry

Cross-Reference Index Entries

A ***cross-reference index entry*** references another index entry rather than a page number. You can cross-reference a main index entry or a subentry. Figure 8-71 shows an index page with a cross-reference index entry (*See* Sample SmartArt).

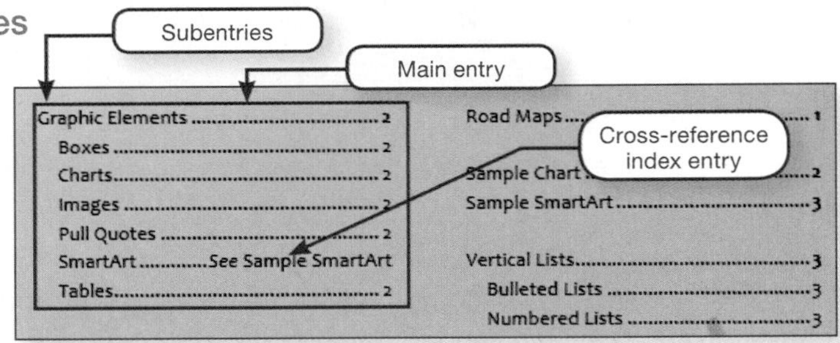

8-71 Index page with subentries and a cross-reference index entry

HOW TO: Create a Cross-Reference Index Entry

1. Select the text or place the insertion point in your document where you want to create a cross-reference index entry.
2. Click the **Mark Entry** button [*References* tab, *Index* group] (Figure 8-72).
3. Type the main entry in the *Main entry* text box.
   - If you are cross-referencing a subentry, type the subentry in the *Subentry* text box as well.
4. Select the **Cross-reference** radio button in the *Options* area.
5. Click in the *Cross-reference* text box and type the cross-reference text after "*See*," which is already inserted in the *Cross-reference* text box.
6. Click **Mark**.
7. Continue marking index entries or click **Close** to close the dialog box.

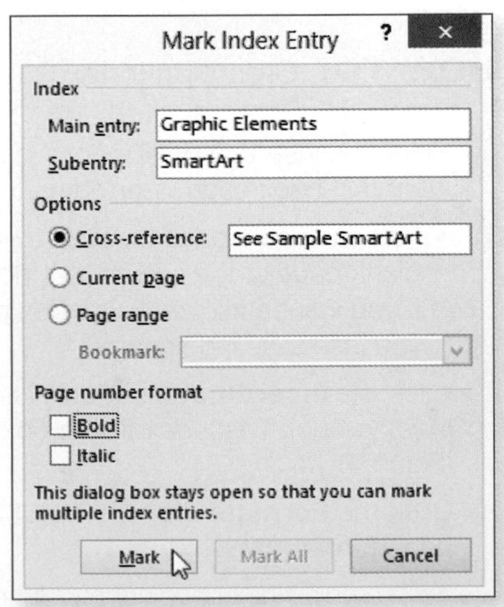

8-72 Create a cross-reference index entry

Index Bookmarks

In Chapter 3 (*SLO 3.5: Using Bookmarks*), you learned how to create and use bookmarks in your document. If you have inserted bookmarks in a document, you can index the bookmarks and have them appear on the index page. For example, you might want to index graphic objects such as a charts, pictures, or *SmartArt* graphics in your document.

HOW TO: Index a Bookmark

1. Select the bookmark you want to include in your index or place the insertion point in your document in the location where you want the index entry to refer.
2. Click the **Mark Entry** button [*References* tab, *Index* group] (Figure 8-73).
3. Type the main entry in the *Main entry* text box.
   - If you are indexing a bookmark as a subentry, type the subentry in the *Subentry* text box as well.
4. Select the **Page range** radio button in the *Options* area.
5. Click the **Bookmark** drop-down list and select the bookmark.
6. Click **Mark**.
7. Continue marking index entries or click **Close** to close the dialog box.

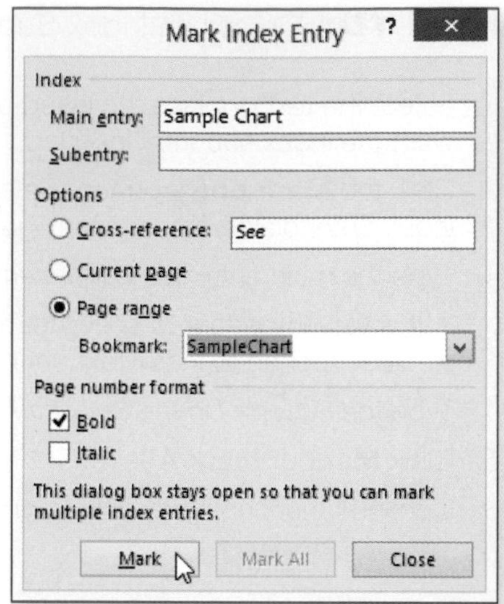

8-73 Index a bookmark

> MORE INFO
>
> To insert a bookmark, select the text or object and click **Bookmark** [*Insert* tab, *Links* group].

Insert an Index Page

After you have finished marking index entries in your document, you can insert an ***index page***. Word provides a variety of index page formats, and you can customize any of these. For example, you can change the number of columns or how page numbers are aligned. It is usually best to insert the index page on a separate page at the end of your document.

HOW TO: Create an Index Page

1. Place the insertion point in your document where you want the index page inserted.
   - You can use a page break (**Ctrl+Enter**) to insert a blank page at the end of your document.
   - If you want a title on your index page, type it before you insert the index page.
2. Click the **Insert Index** button [*References* tab, *Index* group]. The *Index* dialog box opens (Figure 8-74).
3. Click the **Formats** drop-down list and select an index page format.
   - A sample index page appears in the *Print Preview* area.

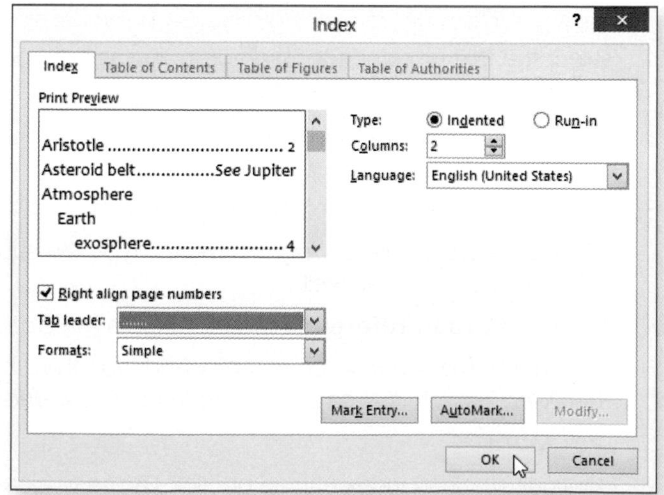

8-74 Index dialog box

4. Check the **Right align page numbers** box if you want page numbers aligned at the right.
5. Click the **Tab leader** drop-down list to select a tab leader.
6. In the *Type* area, select the **Indented** or **Run-in** radio button.
   - *Indented* places each subentry on a new line indented below the main entry. This is the default setting.
   - *Run-in* lists subentries on the same line. The document margins control how subentries wrap to the next line.
7. In the *Columns* area, select the number of columns as desired.
8. Click the **OK** button to close the dialog box and insert the index page.

Update an Index Page

After you insert an index page, you can still add or remove index entries. When you make changes to your document that affect the pagination or if you add index entries to your document, you need to update your index page to ensure index entries and page numbers are correct. Remember to turn off *Show/Hide* before you update your index page. You can update your index page in any one of the following three ways:

- Select the index page and click the **Update Index** button in the *Index* group on the *References* tab (Figure 8-75).
- Right-click the index page and **Update Field** from the context menu.
- Select the index page and press **F9**.

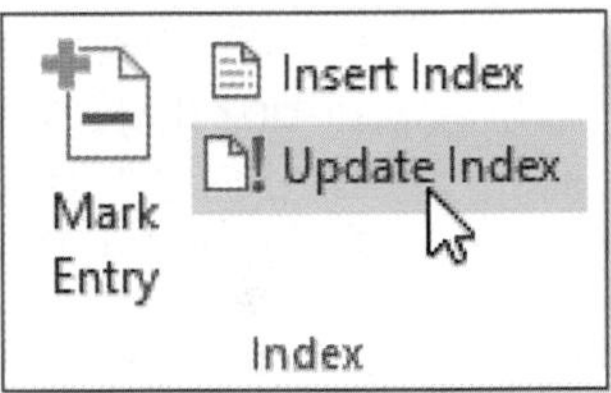

8-75 Update index page

Delete an Index Entry

If you want to remove an index entry, you need to delete the index field code.

HOW TO: Delete an Index Entry

1. Turn on **Show/Hide**.
2. Select the **index field code** and press **Delete** (Figure 8-76).

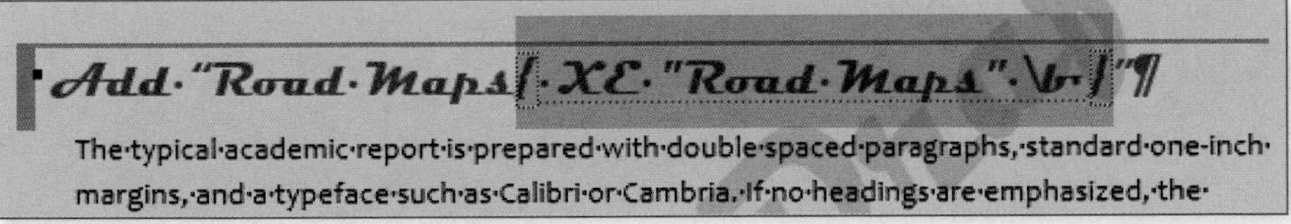

8.76 Delete index field code

   - Make sure you only select both braces and the text between them (e.g., { XE "Road Maps" \b }).
   - After you delete the index entry, check your document to make sure you did not delete any other text, spaces, or paragraph marks.
3. Turn off **Show/Hide**.
4. Update your index page.

PAUSE & PRACTICE: WORD 8-4

For this Pause & Practice project, you finalize the document for Sierra Pacific Community College District. You mark index entries including main entries, subentries, a cross-reference entry, and a bookmark index entry. You also create and customize an index page.

File Needed: ***[your initials] PP W8-3.docx***
Completed Project File Name: ***[your initials] PP W8-4.docx***

1. Open the ***[your initials] PP W8-3*** document you saved in *Pause & Practice 8-3*.
2. Save the document as ***[your initials] PP W8-4***.
3. Mark main index entries.
   a. On the first page, select "**Road Maps**" in the section heading; don't include the quotation marks.
   b. Click the **Mark Entry** button [*References* tab, *Index* group] to open the *Mark Index Entry* dialog box (Figure 8-77).
   c. The text "Road Maps" appears in the *Main entry* text box.
   d. In the *Page number format* area, check the **Bold** check box.
   e. Click **Mark All** to mark all instances of this text as a main index entry. Leave the *Mark Index Entry* dialog box open so you can mark additional index entries. You can drag the title bar of the *Mark Index Entry* dialog box to move it if needed.
   f. Select "**Graphic Elements**" in the main section heading on the second page of your document.
   g. In the *Mark Index Entry* dialog box, click in the *Main entry* text box to display the selected text, confirm the **Bold** box is checked, and click **Mark All**.
   h. Select "**Vertical Lists**" in the main section heading on the third page of your document.
   i. In the *Mark Index Entry* dialog box, click in the *Main entry* text box to display the selected text, confirm the **Bold** box is checked, and click **Mark All**.
   j. Leave the *Mark Index Entry* dialog box open to mark additional index entries. The inserted index entries affect pagination; this will be fixed later.

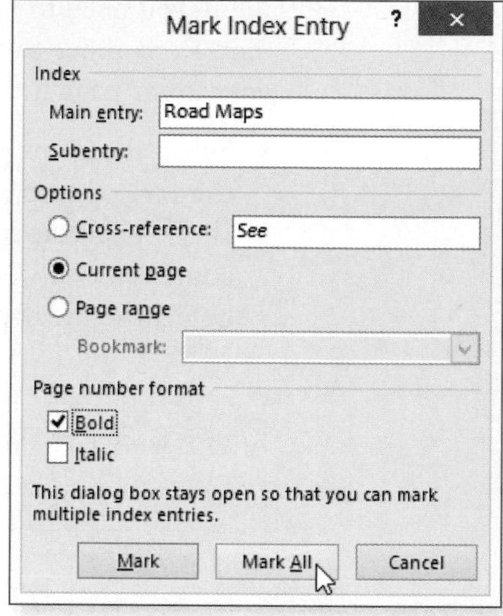

8-77 ***Mark Index Entry*** **dialog box**

4. Mark index subentries.
   a. Select "**Boxes**" in the first subheading of the "Add Graphic Elements" section.
   b. In the *Main entry* text box, delete the existing text, type Graphic Elements, and then type Boxes in the *Subentry* text box (Figure 8-78).
   c. Deselect the **Bold** check box and click **Mark All**.
   d. Repeat steps 4 a–c to mark the following index subentries in the "Add Graphic Elements" section:
   Tables ("Boxes and Tables" heading)

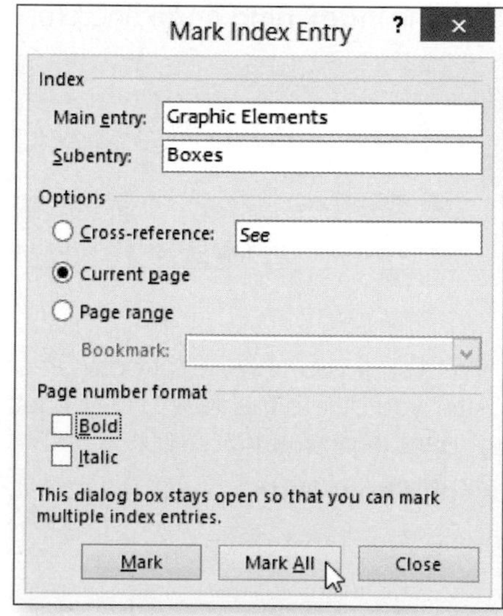

8-78 Mark index subentry

Pull Quotes (in the first sentence in the "Boxes and Tables" section)
Charts ("Charts or Images" heading)
Images ("Charts or Images" heading)

e. Place the insertion point at the end of the second bulleted item in the "Write Vertical Lists" section.
f. Type Vertical Lists in the *Main entry* text box, type Bulleted Lists in the *Subentry* text box, and click **Mark**.
g. Place the insertion point at the end of the third bulleted item in the "Write Vertical Lists" section.
h. Type Vertical Lists in the *Main entry* text box, type Numbered Lists in the *Subentry* text box, and then click **Mark**.
i. Click **Close** to close the *Mark Index Entry* dialog box.

5. Create bookmarks in the document.
   a. Select the **chart** and insert a bookmark named SampleChart (no spaces between words) [*Insert* tab, *Links* group].
   b. Select the **SmartArt graphic** and insert a bookmark named SampleSmartArt.
6. Mark bookmark as index entries.
   a. Place the insertion point at the end of the body paragraph in the "Charts or Images" section.
   b. Click the **Mark Entry** button [*References* tab, *Index* group] to open the *Mark Index Entry* dialog box (Figure 8-79).
   c. Type Sample Chart in the *Main entry* text box, click the **Page range** radio button, and select **SampleChart** from the *Bookmark* drop-down list.
   d. Select the **Bold** check box and click **Mark**.
   e. Place the insertion point at the end of the body paragraph in the "Conclusion" section.
   f. In the *Mark Index Entry* dialog box, type Sample SmartArt in the *Main entry* text box, click the **Page range** radio button, select **SampleSmartArt** from the *Bookmark* drop-down list, and then click **Mark**.
   g. Leave the *Mark Index Entry* dialog box open to mark an additional index entry.

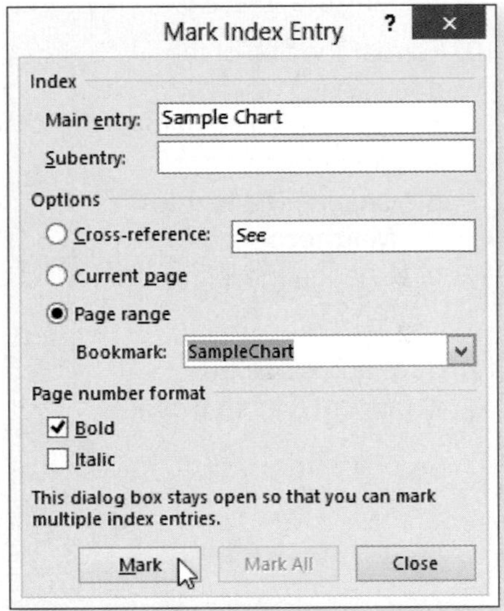

8-79 Index a bookmark

7. Create a cross-reference index entry.
   a. Select the word "**Images**" in the second subheading in the "Add Graphic Elements" section.
   b. In the *Mark Index Entry* dialog box, type Graphic Elements in the *Main entry* text box and type SmartArt in the *Subentry* text box (Figure 8-80).
   c. Select the **Cross-reference** radio button and type Sample SmartArt after the word "*See*" in the text box.
   d. Deselect the **Bold** check box and click **Mark**.
   e. Click **Close** to close the dialog box.
8. Insert and customize an index page at the end of the document.
   a. Move to the end of the document (**Ctrl+End**) and insert a **page break** (**Ctrl+Enter**).
   b. Type Index, apply the **Heading 1** style, and press **Enter**.

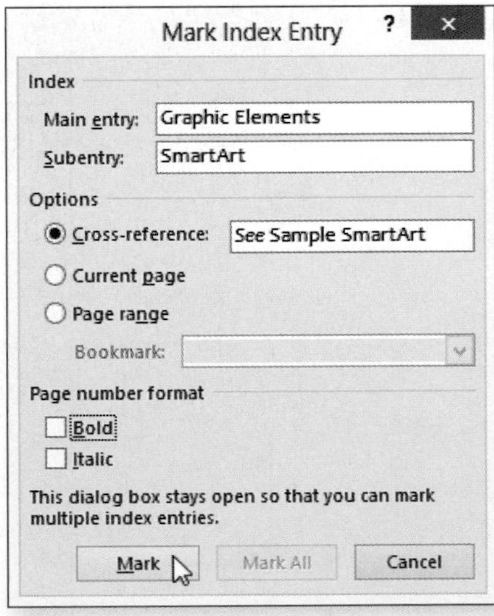

8-80 Create a cross-reference index entry

c. Click the **Insert Index** button [*References* tab, *Index* group] to open the *Index* dialog box (Figure 8-81).
d. Click the **Formats** drop-down list and select **Simple**.
e. Check the **Right align page numbers** box.
f. Click the **Tab leader** drop-down list and select the **dot leader**.
g. Confirm the *Type* is **Indented** and the number of *Columns* is **2**.
h. Click **OK** to close the dialog box and insert the index.

9. Update the index page.
   a. Click the **Show/Hide** button [*Home* tab, *Paragraph* group] to turn it off.
   b. Place the insertion point in the index and click the **Update Index** button [*References* tab, *Index* group].

8-81 ***Index*** **dialog box**

10. Format the title of the document.
    a. Select the title of the document.
    b. Change the font to **Magneto**.
    c. Change the left indent to **-2"**.
11. Save and close the document (Figure 8-82).

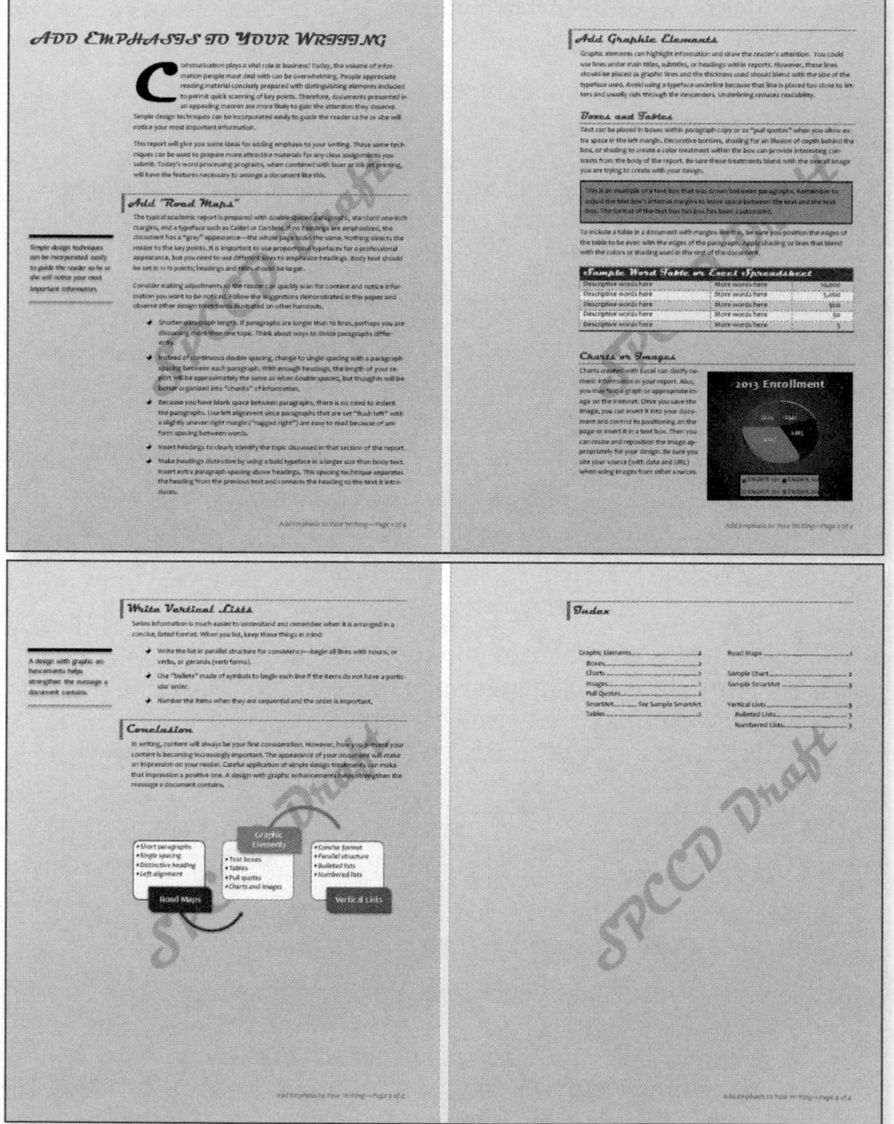

8-82 PP W8-4 completed

Chapter Summary

8.1 Apply desktop publishing features to a Word document (p. W8-452).

- ***Gutter margins, mirror margins, 2 pages per sheet***, and ***book fold*** customize page layout.
- A ***drop cap*** emphasizes the first letter or first word of a paragraph.
- You can customize a drop cap to adjust how many lines the drop cap spans and the distance from text.
- You can add ***page color*** to the document and customize page color with a fill color, gradient color, texture, pattern, or picture.
- A ***watermark*** is ***ghosted text*** that appears behind the text in the document without affecting the layout of the document. You can apply a built-in watermark, create a custom watermark, or use a picture as a watermark.
- You can create a ***watermark building block*** to save and use in other documents.
- A ***screenshot*** or ***screen clipping*** captures and inserts a window or portion of a window as a picture in your document.
- The ***hyphenation*** feature allows you to automatically or manually hyphenate an entire document.
- You can use ***Line numbering*** to insert line numbers on each line of a document. Line numbers are helpful when you are editing a long document or working with a group on document review.

8.2 Customize an existing theme and create a custom theme (p. W8-461).

- You can apply a ***theme*** and customize ***theme colors, theme fonts***, and ***theme effects***.
- You can save a custom theme, theme colors, theme fonts, and theme effects to use in other documents.

8.3 Insert and customize a built-in text box and create a custom text box (p. W8-462).

- ***Text boxes*** are shapes that have text inserted in them.
- You can use built-in text boxes or you can draw custom text boxes.
- You can customize text boxes by applying a ***shape style, fill, outline***, or ***effect***.
- You can save a text box as a ***building block***.

8.4 Insert and customize a *SmartArt* graphic (p. W8-468).

- ***SmartArt graphics*** are shapes and text that graphically present information in a document.
- Use the *SmartArt* ***Text pane*** to type information in the *SmartArt* graphic or type information directly on the graphic objects.
- You can add shapes and text in the shapes, and you can reorder or promote or demote text in the *SmartArt* graphic.
- You can customize the *SmartArt* graphic design by changing the layout, colors, or applying a *SmartArt* style using the ***SmartArt Tools Design tab***.
- You can customize the individual objects and text in a *SmartArt* graphic using the ***SmartArt Tools Layout tab***.
- Resize and arrange *SmartArt* graphics in your document in the same way you resize and arrange pictures and shapes.

8.5 Insert and customize a chart (p. W8-473).

- Charts visually present numerical data.
- When you insert a chart, a ***Chart in Microsoft Word*** window opens where you type the chart data and set the ***chart data range***.
- The contextual ***Chart Tools Design*** and ***Chart Tools Format*** tabs allow you to customize the chart and its elements.
- You can add and customize chart elements such as ***chart title, axis titles, legend, data labels, data table***, and ***gridlines*** . You can also customize chart ***axes, plot area, chart wall, chart floor***, and ***3-D rotation***.
- There are preset options for all chart elements, and you can further customize each element using the contextual ***Format "Chart Element" pane***.
- Resize and arrange charts in your document in the same way you resize and arrange *SmartArt* graphics, pictures, and shapes.

8.6 Mark index entries and insert and customize an index page (p. W8-482).

- When you mark an ***index entry*** in your document, Word inserts an ***index field code***.
- The ***Mark Entry dialog box*** lets you index a ***main entry,*** a ***subentry,*** a ***cross-reference*** entry, and a ***bookmark***. You can customize the page number format and mark an individual entry or mark all instances of specific text.
- An ***index*** lists all marked index entries with a page number.
- You can customize the layout and format of the index page.
- You can add or delete index entries and update the index when content or pagination changes.

Check for Understanding

In the ***Online Learning Center*** for this text (**www.mhhe.com/office2013inpractice**), there are a variety of resources that can be used to review the concepts covered in this chapter.

The following Online Learning Resources are available in the Online Learning Center:

- Multiple choice questions
- Short answer questions
- Matching exercises

Guided Project 8-1

For this project, you convert a document about teen substance abuse from Courtyard Medical Plaza into a booklet. You adjust page setup and margins, apply desktop publishing features, insert and customize text boxes, apply and modify a theme, insert and modify a *SmartArt* graphic, and mark index entries and create an index page.
[Student Learning Outcomes 8.1, 8.2, 8.3, 8.4, 8.6]

File Needed: ***SubstanceAbuse-08.docx***
Completed Project File Name: ***[your initials] Word 8-1.docx***

Skills Covered in This Project

- Use book fold layout and change margins.
- Apply, customize, and save a theme.
- Apply page color and hyphenation.
- Insert and customize a built-in text box.
- Insert and customize a *SmartArt* graphic.
- Use the *Find* feature.
- Mark index entries.
- Create an index page.
- Update an index.

1. Open the ***SubstanceAbuse-08*** document from your student data files.
2. Save the document as ***[your initials] Word 8-1***.
3. Change page setup and margins.
   a. Open the *Page Setup* dialog box.
   b. Click the **Multiple pages** drop-down list and select **Book fold**.
   c. In the *Sheet per booklet* area, select **All**.
   d. Change the *Top, Bottom, Inside*, and *Outside* margins to **0.5"**.
   e. Change the *Gutter* to **0.25"**.
   f. Click **OK** to close the *Page Setup* dialog box. Click **Ignore** if a dialog box opens informing you the margins are outside the printable area.
4. Apply and customize a theme.
   a. Apply the **Integral** theme [*Design* tab, *Document Formatting* group].
   b. Click the **Colors** button [*Design* tab, *Document Formatting* group] and select **Aspect**.
   c. Click the **Colors** button again and select **Customize Colors**. The *Create New Theme Colors* dialog box opens (Figure 8-83).
   d. In the *Name* area, type CMP colors.
   e. Click the **Accent 1** drop-down list and select **Red, Accent 2, Darker 25%**.
   f. Click the **Hyperlink** drop-down list and select **Red, Accent 2**.

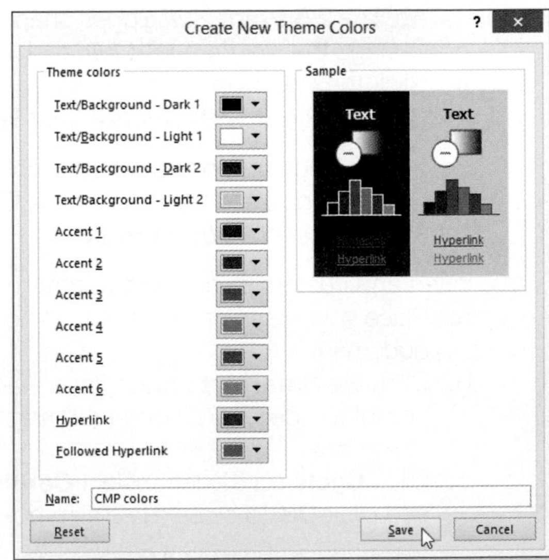

8-83 ***Create New Theme Colors*** **dialog box**

g. Click **Save** to close the dialog box and save the new theme colors.
h. Click the **Themes** button and select **Save Current Theme**. The *Save Current Theme* dialog box opens.
i. Type CMP in the *File name* area and click **Save** to save the custom theme.

5. Click the **Page Color** button [*Design* tab, *Page Background* group] and select **White, Background 1, Darker 5%**.
6. Click the **Hyphenation** button [*Page Layout* tab, *Page Setup* group] and select **Automatic** to hyphenate the entire document.
7. Insert and customize a built-in text box.
   a. Place your insertion point at the end of the first paragraph in the "Why Do Teens Abuse Drugs And Alcohol?" section.
   b. Click the **Text Box** button [*Insert* tab, *Text* group] and select **Simple Quote**.
   c. Copy the last three sentences (don't include the paragraph mark) in the first paragraph of the "What Is Teen Substance Abuse?" section.
   d. Click the placeholder text in the text box to select it and press **Ctrl+V** to paste the text in the text box.
   e. Select the text in the text box and apply **italic** formatting.
   f. Click the **Shape Effects** button [*Drawing Tools Format* tab, *Shape Styles* group], select **Soft Edges**, and select **2.5 Point**.
   g. Change the *Height* and *Width* to **1.7"** [*Drawing Tools Format* tab, *Size* group].
   h. Click the **Position** button [*Drawing Tools Format* tab, *Arrange* group] and select **Position in Middle Right with Square Text Wrapping** (Figure 8-84).
   i. If there is a blank line in the "Why Do Teens Abuse Drugs And Alcohol?" section, delete it.

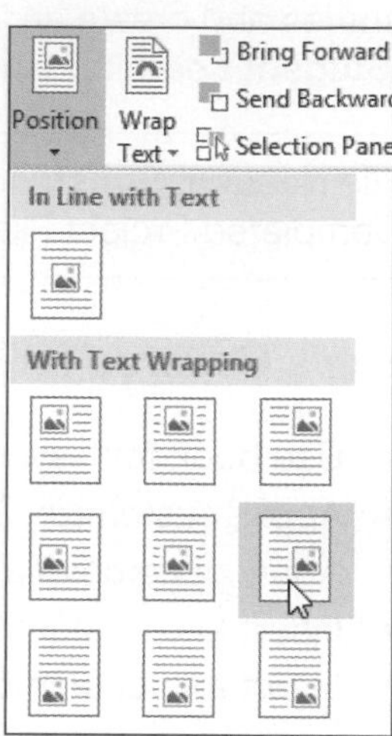

8-84 Position text box on the page

8. Insert and customize a built-in text box.
   a. On the second page, place your insertion point at the end of the last paragraph in the "What Should You Do If Your Teen Is Using?" section.
   b. Insert the **Simple Quote** built-in text box.
   c. Copy the first two sentences in the "What Should You Do If Your Teen Is Using?" section.
   d. Click the placeholder text in the text box to select it and press **Ctrl+V** to paste the text in the text box.
   e. Apply **italic** formatting to the text in the text box.
   f. Apply a **2.5 Point** *Soft Edges* shape effect.
   g. Change the *Height* and *Width* to **1.7"** [*Drawing Tools Format* tab, *Size* group].
   h. Click the **Position** button [*Drawing Tools Format* tab, *Arrange* group] and select **Position in Bottom Right with Square Text Wrapping**.
9. Place your insertion point at the beginning of the "Can Teen Substance Use and Abuse Be Prevented?" section and insert a **page break**.
10. Insert and customize a *SmartArt* graphic.
    a. Place your insertion point at the end of the document.
    b. Click the **SmartArt** button [*Insert* tab, *Illustrations* group] to open the *Choose a SmartArt Graphic* dialog box.
    c. Click **Cycle** on the left, select **Continuous Cycle**, and click **OK** to close the dialog box and insert the *SmartArt* graphic (Figure 8-85).

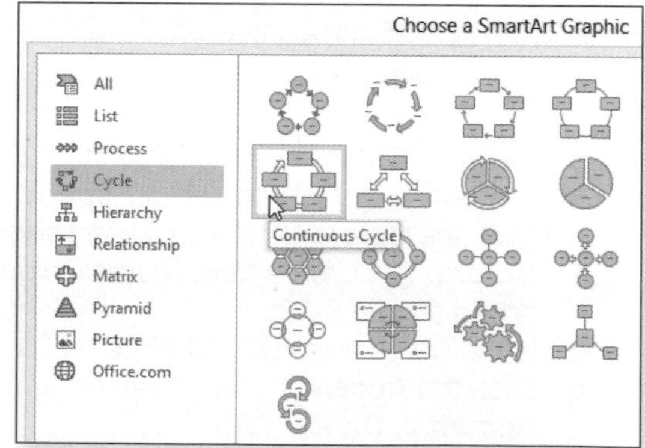

8-85 Insert a *SmartArt* graphic

d. Beginning at the top and going clockwise, type the following text in the *SmartArt* graphic boxes:

   Expectations
   Activities
   House Rules
   Communication
   Know Friends

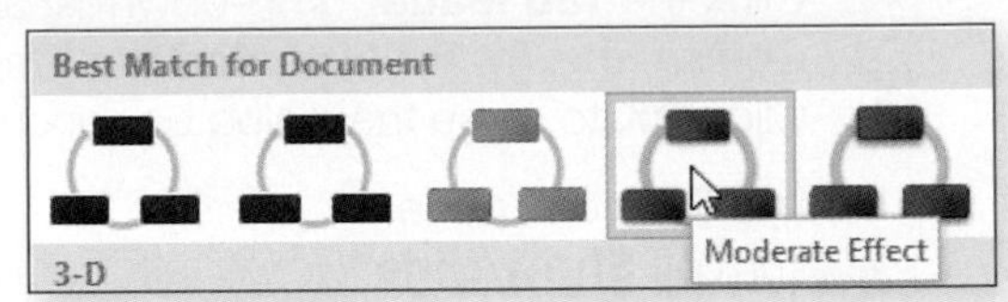

8-86 Apply *SmartArt* style

e. In the *SmartArt Styles* gallery [*SmartArt Tools Design* tab], select **Moderate Effect** (Figure 8-86).

11. Mark index entries.
   a. Click the **Find** button [*Home* tab, *Editing* group] to open the *Navigation* pane to the left of the Word window.
   b. Type alcohol in the text box at the top to find all instances of this word. Select the first occurrence of this word.
   c. Click the **Mark Entry** button [*References* tab, Index group] to open *Mark Index Entry* dialog box. The word "alcohol" appears in the *Main entry* text box (Figure 8-87).
   d. Capitalize the "A" in "alcohol" in the *Main entry* text box.
   e. Click the **Mark All** button to mark all instances of this word as an index entry.
   f. Continue this process with the following words. Capitalize the first letter of the first word in the *Main entry* text box.

      Tobacco
      Drugs
      Drug abuse
      Marijuana
      Risk
      Treatment

   g. Click **Close** to close the *Mark Index Entry* dialog box and close the *Navigation* pane.

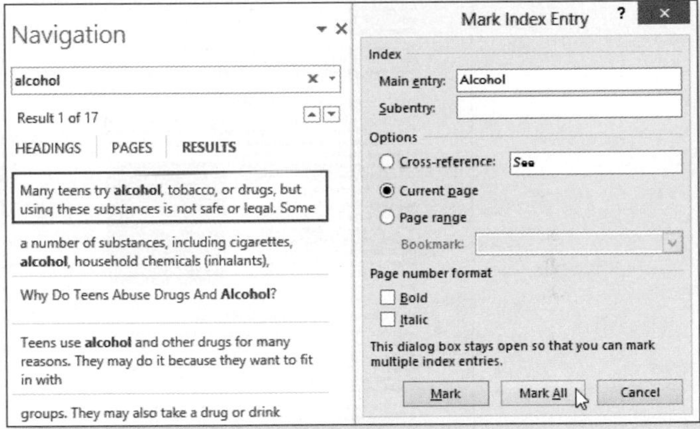

8-87 Find text and mark index entries

12. Create an index page.
   a. Place the insertion point at the end of your document (**Ctr+End**) and insert a page break (**Ctrl+Enter**).
   b. Type Index, apply the **Heading 1** style, and press **Enter**.
   c. Click the **Insert Index** button [*References* tab, *Index* group] to open the *Index* dialog box (Figure 8-88).
   d. Click the **Formats** drop-down list and select **From template**.

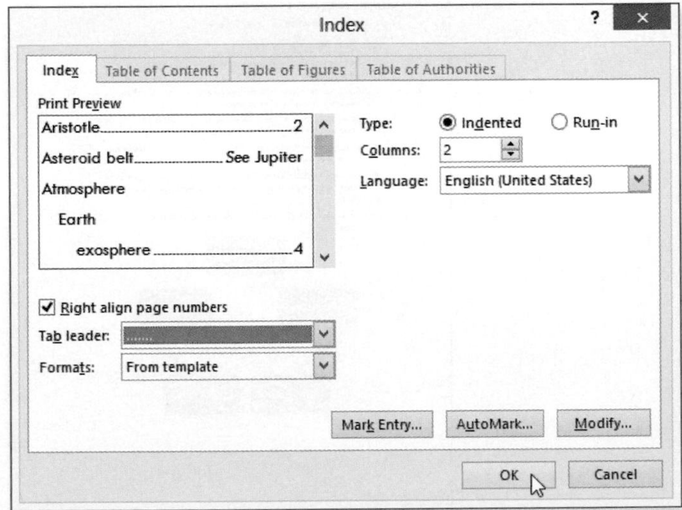

8-88 *Index* dialog box

e. Check the **Right align page numbers** box.
f. Click the **Tab leader** drop-down list and select the **dot leader**.
g. Confirm the *Type* is **Indented** and *Columns* is **2**.
h. Click **OK** to close the dialog box and insert the index.

13. Update the index page.
    a. Turn off **Show/Hide** [*Home* tab, *Paragraph* group].
    b. Place the insertion point in the index and click the **Update Index** button [*References* tab, *Index* group].
14. Save and close the document (Figure 8-89).

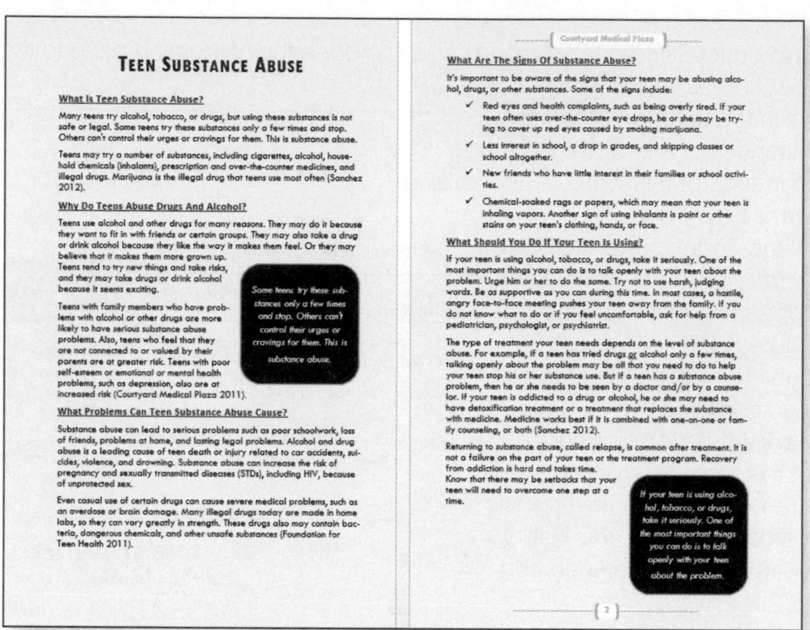

TEEN SUBSTANCE ABUSE

What Is Teen Substance Abuse?

Many teens try alcohol, tobacco, or drugs, but using these substances is not safe or legal. Some teens try these substances only a few times and stop. Others can't control their urges or cravings for them. This is substance abuse.

Teens may try a number of substances, including cigarettes, alcohol, household chemicals (inhalants), prescription and over-the-counter medicines, and illegal drugs. Marijuana is the illegal drug that teens use most often (Sanchez 2012).

Why Do Teens Abuse Drugs And Alcohol?

Teens use alcohol and other drugs for many reasons. They may do it because they want to fit in with friends or certain groups. They may also take a drug or drink alcohol because they like the way it makes them feel. Or they may believe that it makes them more grown up. Teens tend to try new things and take risks, and they may take drugs or drink alcohol because it seems exciting.

Some teens try these substances only a few times and stop. Others can't control their urges or cravings for them. This is substance abuse.

Teens with family members who have problems with alcohol or other drugs are more likely to have serious substance abuse problems. Also, teens who feel that they are not connected to or valued by their parents are at greater risk. Teens with poor self-esteem or emotional or mental health problems, such as depression, also are at increased risk (Courtyard Medical Plaza 2011).

What Problems Can Teen Substance Abuse Cause?

Substance abuse can lead to serious problems such as poor schoolwork, loss of friends, problems at home, and lasting legal problems. Alcohol and drug abuse is a leading cause of teen death or injury related to car accidents, suicides, violence, and drowning. Substance abuse can increase the risk of pregnancy and sexually transmitted diseases (STDs), including HIV, because of unprotected sex.

Even casual use of certain drugs can cause severe medical problems, such as an overdose or brain damage. Many illegal drugs today are made in home labs, so they can vary greatly in strength. These drugs also may contain bacteria, dangerous chemicals, and other unsafe substances (Foundation for Teen Health 2011).

Courtyard Medical Plaza

What Are The Signs Of Substance Abuse?

It's important to be aware of the signs that your teen may be abusing alcohol, drugs, or other substances. Some of the signs include:

- ✓ Red eyes and health complaints, such as being overly tired. If your teen often uses over-the-counter eye drops, he or she may be trying to cover up red eyes caused by smoking marijuana.
- ✓ Less interest in school, a drop in grades, and skipping classes or school altogether.
- ✓ New friends who have little interest in their families or school activities.
- ✓ Chemical-soaked rags or papers, which may mean that your teen is inhaling vapors. Another sign of using inhalants is paint or other stains on your teen's clothing, hands, or face.

What Should You Do If Your Teen Is Using?

If your teen is using alcohol, tobacco, or drugs, take it seriously. One of the most important things you can do is to talk openly with your teen about the problem. Urge him or her to do the same. Try not to use harsh, judging words. Be as supportive as you can during this time. In most cases, a hostile, angry face-to-face meeting pushes your teen away from the family. If you do not know what to do or if you feel uncomfortable, ask for help from a pediatrician, psychologist, or psychiatrist.

The type of treatment your teen needs depends on the level of substance abuse. For example, if a teen has tried drugs or alcohol only a few times, talking openly about the problem may be all that you need to do to help your teen stop his or her substance use. But if a teen has a substance abuse problem, then he or she needs to be seen by a doctor and/or by a counselor. If your teen is addicted to a drug or alcohol, he or she may need to have detoxification treatment or a treatment that replaces the substance with medicine. Medicine works best if it is combined with one-on-one or family counseling, or both (Sanchez 2012).

Returning to substance abuse, called relapse, is common after treatment. It is not a failure on the part of your teen or the treatment program. Recovery from addiction is hard and takes time. Know that there may be setbacks that your teen will need to overcome one step at a time.

If your teen is using alcohol, tobacco, or drugs, take it seriously. One of the most important things you can do is to talk openly with your teen about the problem.

2

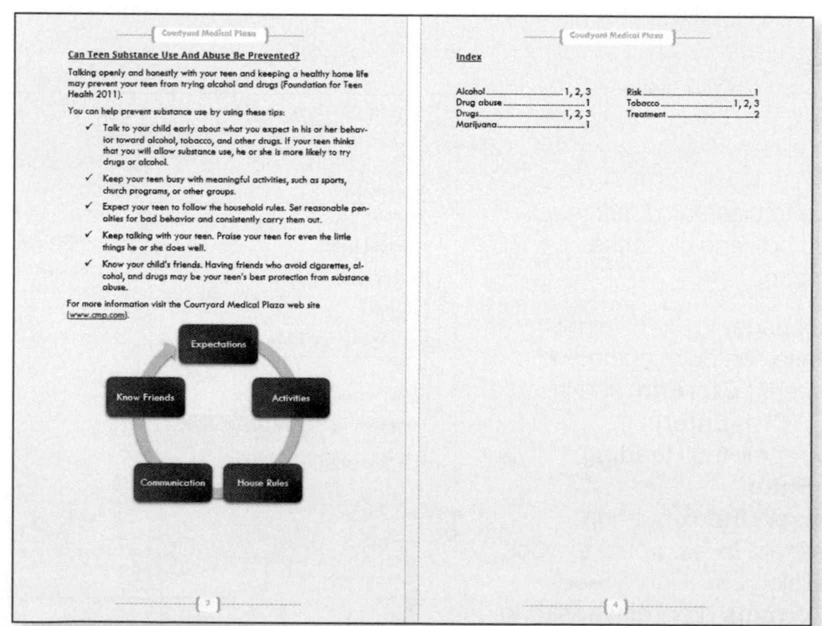

Courtyard Medical Plaza

Can Teen Substance Use And Abuse Be Prevented?

Talking openly and honestly with your teen and keeping a healthy home life may prevent your teen from trying alcohol and drugs (Foundation for Teen Health 2011).

You can help prevent substance use by using these tips:

- ✓ Talk to your child early about what you expect in his or her behavior toward alcohol, tobacco, and other drugs. If your teen thinks that you will allow substance use, he or she is more likely to try drugs or alcohol.
- ✓ Keep your teen busy with meaningful activities, such as sports, church programs, or other groups.
- ✓ Expect your teen to follow the household rules. Set reasonable penalties for bad behavior and consistently carry them out.
- ✓ Keep talking with your teen. Praise your teen for even the little things he or she does well.
- ✓ Know your child's friends. Having friends who avoid cigarettes, alcohol, and drugs may be your teen's best protection from substance abuse.

For more information visit the Courtyard Medical Plaza web site (www.cmp.com).

Expectations
Activities
House Rules
Communication
Know Friends

3

Courtyard Medical Plaza

Index

4

8-89 Word 8-1 completed

Guided Project 8-2

For this project, you modify a promotional flyer for Placer Hills Real Estate. You apply and modify a theme, apply a page color, create and customize a chart, insert and modify a *SmartArt* graphic, insert and customize a text box, and insert and position a watermark.
[Student Learning Outcomes 8.1, 8.2, 8.3, 8.4, 8.5]

File Needed: ***YourFirstHome-08.docx***
Completed Project File Name: ***[your initials] Word 8-2.docx***

Skills Covered in This Project

- Apply, customize, and save a theme.
- Apply page color.
- Insert a chart and customize chart data.
- Insert an axis title and data labels.
- Modify a vertical axis.
- Customize chart elements.
- Resize a chart.
- Insert and customize a *SmartArt* graphic.
- Resize and arrange the *SmartArt* graphic.
- Insert, customize, and align a built-in text box.

1. Open the ***YourFirstHome-08*** document from your student data files.
2. Save the document as ***[your initials] Word 8-2***.
3. Apply, customize, and save a theme.
   a. Apply the **Facet** theme [*Design* tab, *Document Formatting* group].
   b. Click the **Fonts** button [*Design* tab, *Document Formatting* group] and select **Tw Cen MT**.
   c. Click the **Colors** button [*Design* tab, *Document Formatting* group] and select **Green**.
   d. Click the **Themes** button and select **Save Current Theme**. The *Save Current Theme* dialog box opens.
   e. Type PHRE in the *File name* area and click **Save** to save the custom theme.

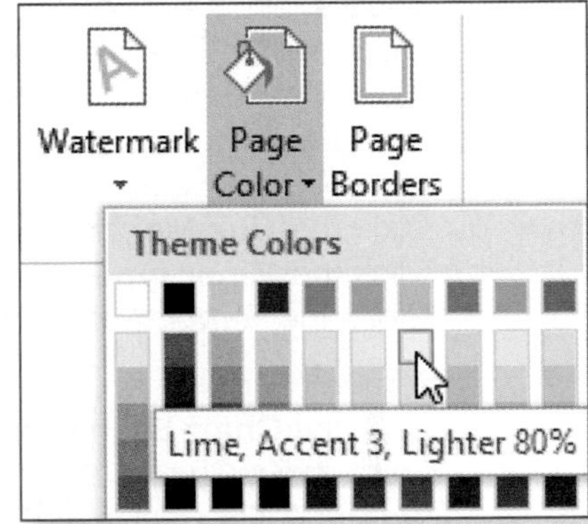

8-90 Apply a page color

4. Click the **Page Color** button [*Design* tab, *Page Background* group] and select **Lime, Accent 3, Lighter 80%** (Figure 8-90).
5. Insert a chart and customize the chart data.
   a. Position your insertion point on the blank line below the "Fixed Mortgage Rate Averages" heading.
   b. Click the **Chart** button [*Insert* tab, *Illustrations* group]. The *Insert Chart* dialog box opens (Figure 8-91).
   c. Click **Line** at the left, select **Line with Markers**, and click **OK** to insert the chart.

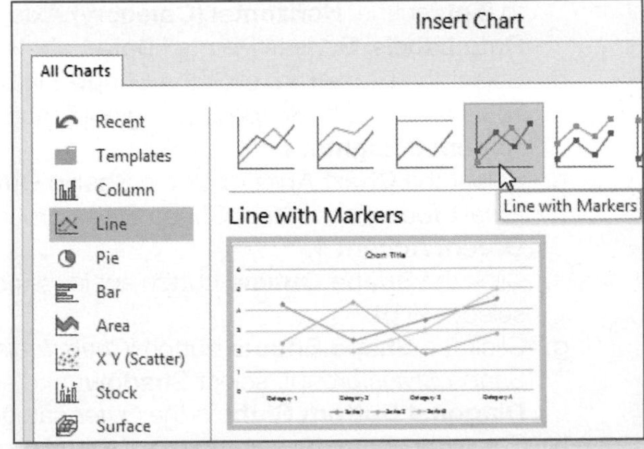

8-91 Insert a line chart

d. In the *Chart in Microsoft Word* worksheet, type the information in Figure 8-92 to replace the sample chart data. You can resize the worksheet window by clicking and dragging the bottom right corner.
e. Click and drag the **chart data range** handle so it appears around the chart data you typed. You don't have to delete the data in column D.
f. Click the **X** in the upper right corner of the *Chart in Microsoft Word* window to close it.

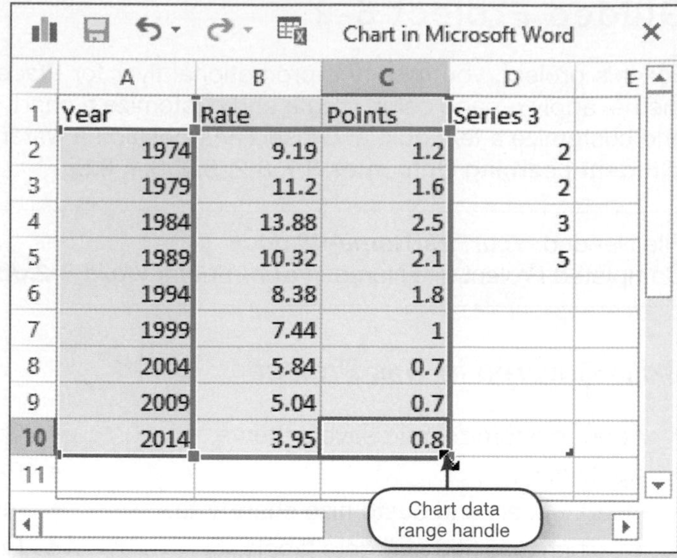

Chart in Microsoft Word
Year Rate Points Series 3
1974 9.19 1.2 2
1979 11.2 1.6 2
1984 13.88 2.5 3
1989 10.32 2.1 5
1994 8.38 1.8
1999 7.44 1
2004 5.84 0.7
2009 5.04 0.7
2014 3.95 0.8
Chart data range handle

8-92 Type chart data and select chart data range

6. Add and customize chart elements.
   a. Click the **Add Chart Element** button [*Chart Tools Design* tab, *Chart Layouts* group], select **Axis Titles**, and select **Primary Vertical**.
   b. Delete the placeholder text in the vertical axis title text box and type Percent.
   c. Click the **Add Chart Element** button, select **Data Labels**, and select **Above**.
   d. Right-click the vertical axis numbers and select **Format Axis**. The *Format Axis* pane opens (Figure 8-93).
   e. Click the **Axis Options** button if it is not already selected.
   f. In the *Minor* text box, type 1.0 in the text box.
   g. Click the **Tick Marks** heading.
   h. Click the **Minor type** drop-down list and select **Cross**.
   i. Close the *Format Axis* pane.

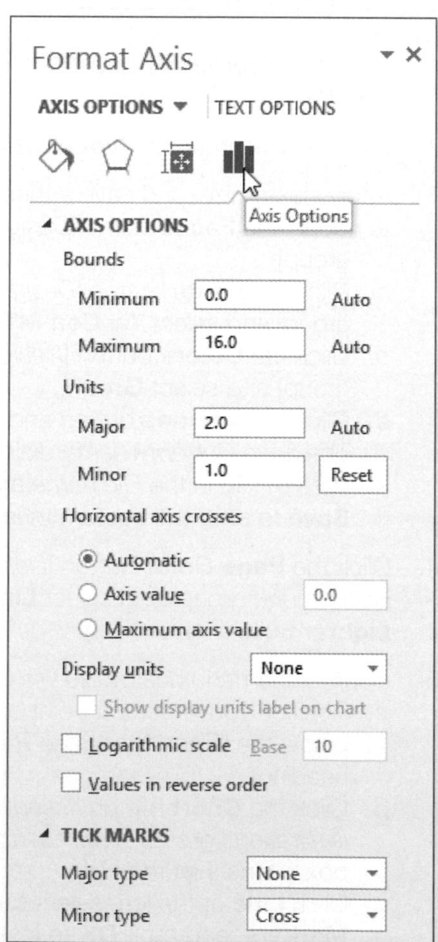

8-93 *Format Axis* pane

7. Customize chart elements.
   a. Click the **Chart Elements** drop-down list [*Chart Tools Format* tab, *Current Selection* group] and select **Vertical (Value) Axis** to select the vertical axis.
   b. Change the font size to **8 pt.** [*Home* tab, *Font* group].
   c. Select the following chart elements and change the font size to **8 pt.** on the: **Horizontal (Category) Axis, Series "Rate" Data Labels, Series "Points" Data Labels**, and **Legend**.
   d. Select the **Plot Area**, click the **Shape Fill** button [*Chart Tools Format* tab, *Shape Styles* group], and select **Lime, Accent 3, Lighter 80%**.
   e. Select the **Chart Area**, click the **Shape Outline** button [*Chart Tools Format* tab, *Shape Styles* group], and select **Green, Accent 1**.
   f. Click the **Shape Outline** button again, select **Weight**, and select **1½ pt.**
   g. Click the **Shape Effects** button [*Chart Tools Format* tab, *Shape Styles* group], select **Shadow**, and select **Offset Diagonal Bottom Right** in the *Outer* category.
   h. Select the **Chart Area** and change the *Height* to **3"** and the *Width* to **6.5"** [*Chart Tools Format* tab, *Size* group].

8. Insert and customize a *SmartArt* graphic.
   a. Place the insertion point at the end of the document (**Ctrl+End**).
   b. Click the **SmartArt** button [*Insert* tab, *Illustrations* group]. The *Choose a SmartArt Graphic* dialog box opens (Figure 8-94).
   c. Click **Process** on the left, select **Circle Process**, and then click **OK**.
   d. Click the **Add Shape** button [*SmartArt Tools Design* tab, *Create Graphic* group] three times to add three more shapes to the graphic.
   e. Beginning at the left, add the following text to the shapes:

      Be patient

      Be sure you are ready

      Determine what you can afford

      Get your credit in shape

      Save for a down payment

      Get mortgage pre-approval
   f. Click the **Change Colors** button and select **Dark 2 Fill** in the *Primary Theme Colors* category.
   g. Click the **SmartArt Styles** drop-down list and select **Inset** in the *3-D* category.
   h. Select the border of the first text box and then use **Ctrl+click** to select the other five text boxes.
   i. Apply **bold** formatting to the selected text boxes.

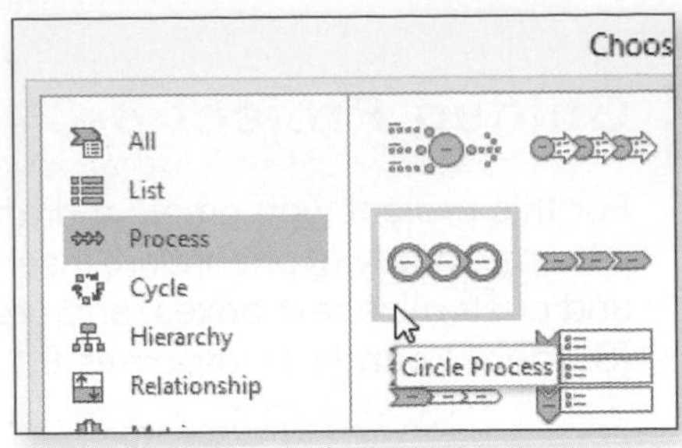

8-94 Insert *SmartArt* graphic

9. Resize and arrange the *SmartArt* graphic.
   a. Click the frame of the *SmartArt* graphic to select it and change the *Height* to **1.8"** and the *Width* to **7"** [*SmartArt Tools Format* tab, *Size* group].
   b. Click the **Wrap Text** button [*SmartArt Tools Format* tab, *Arrange* group] and select **Behind Text**.
   c. Click the **Position** button [*SmartArt Tools Format* tab, *Arrange* group] and select **More Layout Options** to open the *Layout* dialog box.
   d. In the *Horizontal* area, set **Absolute position** at **0.7"** *to the right of* **Page**.
   e. In the *Vertical* area, set **Absolute position** at **8"** *below* **Page**.
   f. Click **OK** to close the dialog box.

10. Insert and customize a built-in text box.
   a. Place your insertion point at the beginning of the document.
   b. Click the **Text Box** button [*Insert* tab, *Text* group] and select **Semaphore Quote**.
   c. Type HOME BUYING INFO FROM PLACER HILLS REAL ESTATE.
   d. Select the text, change the font size to **14 pt.**, apply **bold** formatting, and change the After paragraph spacing to **0 pt.**
   e. Change the *Height* of the text box to **0.8"** and the *Width* to **2.8"** [*Drawing Tools Format* tab, *Size* group].
   f. Click the **Align** button [*Drawing Tools Format* tab, *Arrange* group] and select **Align to Margin**. *Align to Margin* should be checked.
   g. Click the **Align** button again and select **Top**.

11. Save and close the document (Figure 8-95).

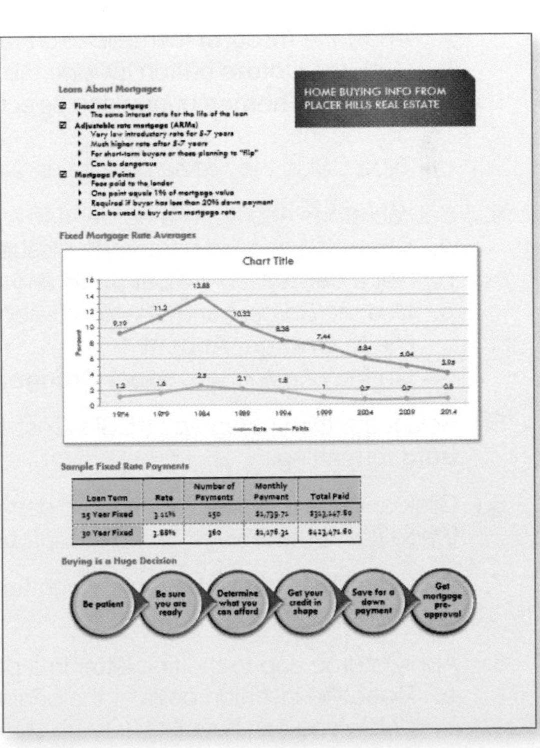

8-95 Word 8-2 completed

Guided Project 8-3

For this project, you create a draft of a newsletter for Central Sierra Insurance. You apply and modify a theme, apply hyphenation, insert a watermark, customize and apply a drop cap, use *WordArt*, insert and customize text boxes, and create and customize a chart.
[Student Learning Outcomes 8.1, 8.2, 8.3, 8.5]

File Needed: ***CSINewsletter-08.docx***
Completed Project File Name: ***[your initials] Word 8-3.docx***

Skills Covered in This Project

- Apply, customize, and save a theme.
- Set tab stops on selected text.
- Apply a border and shading to selected text.
- Apply automatic hyphenation.
- Insert a built-in watermark.
- Apply and customize a drop cap.
- Insert, resize, and arrange *WordArt*.
- Draw a text box around selected text.
- Customize text box style and arrangement.
- Insert a chart and customize chart data.
- Resize and position a chart.
- Insert a chart title and data labels.
- Modify a vertical axis.
- Customize chart elements.

1. Open the ***CSINewsletter-08*** document from your student data files.
2. Save the document as ***[your initials] Word 8-3***.
3. Apply, customize, and save a theme.
   a. Apply the **Integral** theme [*Design* tab, *Document Formatting* group].
   b. Click the **Colors** button [*Design* tab, *Document Formatting* group] and select **Yellow Orange**.
   c. Click the **Themes** button and select **Save Current Theme**. The *Save Current Theme* dialog box opens.
   d. Type CSI in the *File name* area and click **Save** to save the custom theme.
4. Set tab stops and apply a border and shading to selected text.
   a. Select the second paragraph ("Issue No. XVII . . .") and apply **bold** formatting.
   b. Set a **center** tab stop at **3.75"** and a **right** tab stop at **7.5"**.
   c. Use the *Borders and Shading* dialog box to apply a **1 pt. Box** border and change the *Color* of the line to **Orange, Accent 1**.
   d. On the *Shading* tab, select **Orange, Accent 1, Lighter 80%** as the *Fill* color.
5. Select the third paragraph ("CSI's Cost-Effective . . ."), change the font size to **22 pt.**, and apply **bold** formatting.
6. Click anywhere in the document to deselect the selected text, click the **Hyphenation** button [*Page Layout* tab, *Page Setup* group], and select **Automatic**.
7. Click the **Watermark** button [*Design* tab, *Page Background* group] and select **Draft 1** in the *Disclaimers* category.
8. Apply a drop cap to the first letter in a paragraph.
   a. Place the insertion point at the beginning of the first paragraph in the section with two columns ("Now you can have . . .").

b. Click the **Drop Cap** button [*Insert* tab, *Text* group] and select **Drop Cap Options** to open the *Drop Cap* dialog box (Figure 8-96).
c. In the *Position* area, select **Dropped**.
d. Change the *Lines to drop* to **2** and change the *Distance from text* to **0.1"**.
e. Click **OK** to close the dialog box and apply the drop cap.

9. Apply *WordArt* to the title and position the title.
   a. Select the title (first line of the document).
   b. Click the **WordArt** button [*Insert* tab, *Text* group] and select **Fill – Orange, Accent 1, Shadow** (Figure 8-97).
   c. Click the **Wrap Text** button [*Drawing Tools Format* tab, *Arrange* group] and select **Tight**.
   d. Click the **Position** button [*Drawing Tools Format* tab, *Arrange* group] and select **More Layout Options** to open the *Layout* dialog box.
   e. In the *Horizontal* area, set **Alignment** at **Centered** *relative to* **Page**.
   f. In the *Vertical* area, set **Absolute position** at **0.1"** *below* **Page**.
   g. Click **OK** to close the dialog box.

10. Draw text boxes around selected text and customize the text boxes.
   a. Select the paragraph of text beginning "**Picture mid-summer with temps** . . ."
   b. Apply bold and italic formatting to the selected text.
   c. Click the **Text Box** button [*Insert* tab, *Text* group] and select **Draw Text Box**. A text box appears around the selected text.
   d. Click the **Shape Styles** drop-down list [*Drawing Tools Format* tab, *Shape Styles* group] and select **Subtle Effect – Orange, Accent 1** (Figure 8-98).
   e. Change the *Width* of the text box to **7.5"** [*Drawing Tools Format* tab, *Size* group].
   f. Select the paragraphs of text in the second column.
   g. Click the **Text Box** button [*Insert* tab, *Text* group] and select **Draw Text Box**. A text box appears around the selected text.
   h. Click the **Shape Styles** drop-down list [*Drawing Tools Format* tab, *Shape Styles* group] and select **Subtle Effect – Orange, Accent 1**.

11. Insert a chart and customize the chart data.
   a. Place your insertion point at the end of the document (**Ctrl+End**).
   b. Click the **Chart** button [*Insert* tab, *Illustrations* group]. The *Insert Chart* dialog box opens.
   c. Click **Column** on the left, select **Clustered Column**, and click **OK** to insert the chart. A *Chart in Microsoft Word* worksheet also opens.
   d. In the worksheet, type the information in Figure 8-99 to replace the sample chart data. You can resize the column width by clicking and dragging on the right edge of a column heading.

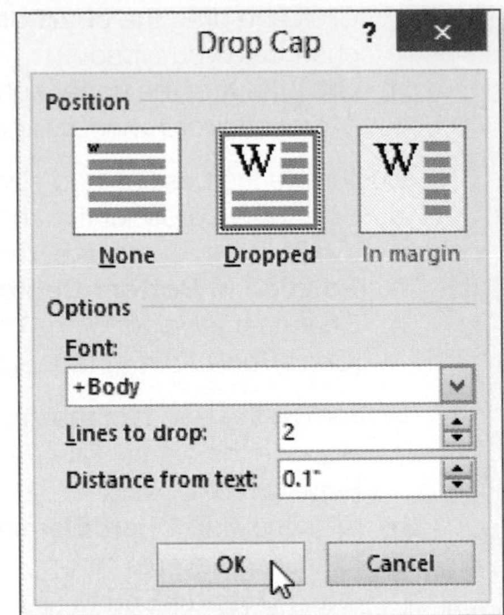

8-96 Customize and apply a drop cap

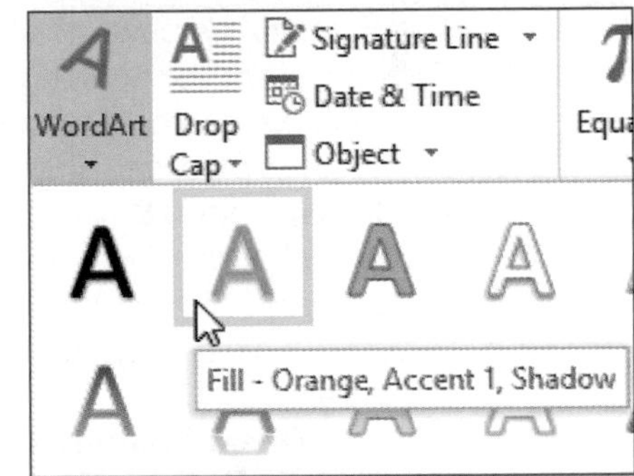

8-97 Apply *WordArt* to selected text

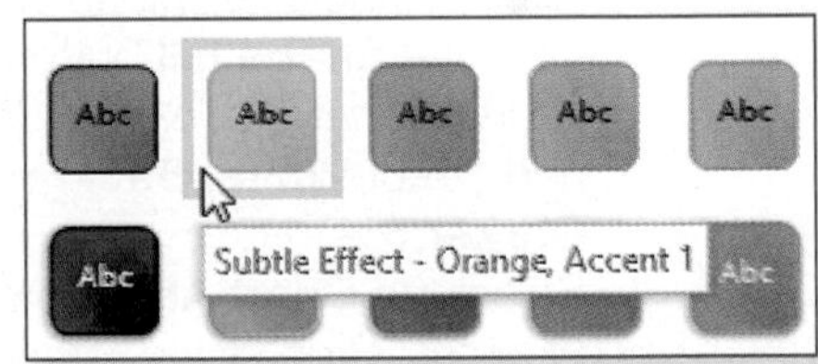

8-98 Apply shape style to text box

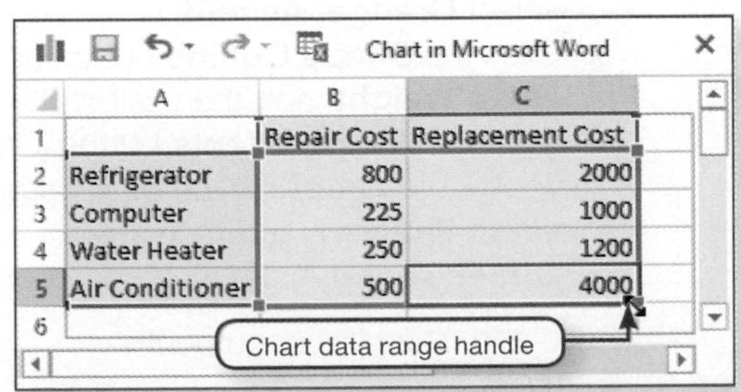

	A	B	C
1		Repair Cost	Replacement Cost
2	Refrigerator	800	2000
3	Computer	225	1000
4	Water Heater	250	1200
5	Air Conditioner	500	4000
6			

8-99 Type chart data and select chart data range

e. Click and drag the **chart data range** handle around the chart data you typed.
f. Click the **X** in the upper right corner of the *Chart in Microsoft Word* window to close it.

12. Customize the position and size of the chart.
    a. Select the border of the chart, click the **Position** button [*Chart Tools Format* tab, *Arrange* group] and select **Position in Bottom Center with Square Text Wrapping**.
    b. Change the *Height* of the chart to **2.8"** and the *Width* to **6"** [*Chart Tools Format* tab, *Size* group].
13. Customize the layout of the chart.
    a. Replace the "Chart Title" text with Estimated Repair and Replacement Costs.
    b. Click the **Add Chart Element** button [*Chart Tools Design* tab, *Chart Layouts* group], click the **Data Labels** button, and select **Outside End** to align data labels above each column.
14. Customize chart elements and design.
    a. Right-click the vertical axis numbers and select **Format Axis**. The *Format Axis* pane opens (Figure 8-100).
    b. Click the **Number** heading.
    c. In the *Category* area, select **Currency**.
    d. Set *Decimal places* to 0 and confirm that the *Symbol* is **$**.
    e. Close the *Format Axis* pane.
    f. In the *Chart Styles* gallery [*Chart Tools Design* tab, *Chart Styles* group], select **Style 14**.
    g. Click the **Chart Elements** drop-down list [*Chart Tools Format* tab, *Current Selection* group] and select **Plot Area** to select the chart plot area.
    h. Click the **Shape Fill** button [*Chart Tools Format* tab, *Shape Styles* group] and select **White, Background 1, Darker 5%**.
    i. Select the **Chart Area** from the *Chart Elements* drop-down list, click the **Shape Outline** button [*Chart Tools Format* tab, *Shape Styles* group], and select **Orange, Accent 1**.
    j. Click the **Shape Outline** button again, select **Weight**, and then select **2¼ pt.**
    k. Click the **Shape Effects** button [*Chart Tools Format* tab, *Shape Styles* group], select **Shadow**, and then select **Offset Center** in the *Outer* category.
15. Save and close the document (Figure 8-101).

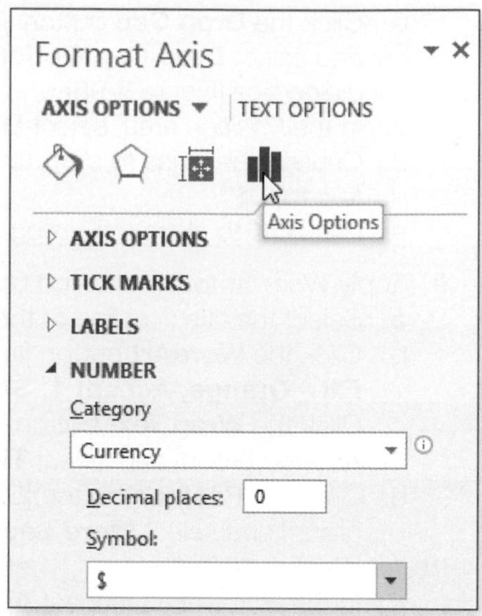

8-100 Customize vertical axis number format

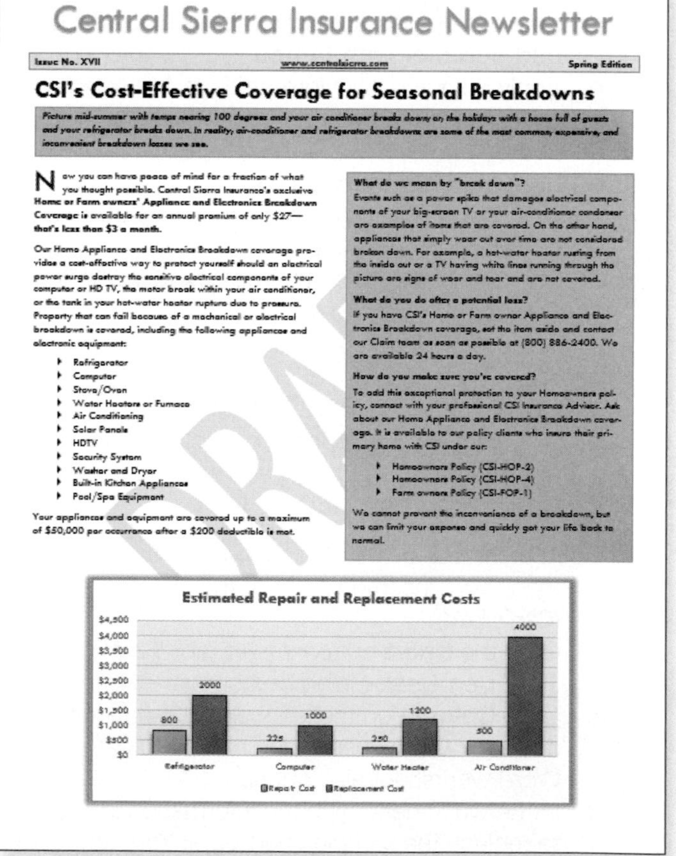

Central Sierra Insurance Newsletter

Issue No. XVII | www.centralsierra.com | Spring Edition

CSI's Cost-Effective Coverage for Seasonal Breakdowns

Picture mid-summer with temps nearing 100 degrees and your air conditioner breaks down; or, the holidays with a house full of guests and your refrigerator breaks down. In reality, air-conditioner and refrigerator breakdowns are some of the most common, expensive, and inconvenient breakdown losses we see.

Now you can have peace of mind for a fraction of what you thought possible. Central Sierra Insurance's exclusive **Home or Farm owners' Appliance and Electronics Breakdown Coverage** is available for an annual premium of only $27—**that's less than $3 a month.**

Our Home Appliance and Electronics Breakdown coverage provides a cost-effective way to protect yourself should an electrical power surge destroy the sensitive electrical components of your computer or HD TV, the motor break within your air conditioner, or the tank in your hot-water heater rupture due to pressure. Property that can fail because of a mechanical or electrical breakdown is covered, including the following appliances and electronic equipment:

- Refrigerator
- Computer
- Stove/Oven
- Water Heaters or Furnace
- Air Conditioning
- Solar Panels
- HDTV
- Security System
- Washer and Dryer
- Built-in Kitchen Appliances
- Pool/Spa Equipment

Your appliances and equipment are covered up to a maximum of $50,000 per occurrence after a $200 deductible is met.

What do we mean by "break down"?
Events such as a power spike that damages electrical components of your big-screen TV or your air-conditioner condenser are examples of items that are covered. On the other hand, appliances that simply wear out over time are not considered broken down. For example, a hot-water heater rusting from the inside out or a TV having white lines running through the picture are signs of wear and tear and are not covered.

What do you do after a potential loss?
If you have CSI's Home or Farm owner Appliance and Electronics Breakdown coverage, set the item aside and contact our Claim team as soon as possible at (800) 886-2400. We are available 24 hours a day.

How do you make sure you're covered?
To add this exceptional protection to your Homeowners policy, connect with your professional CSI Insurance Advisor. Ask about our Home Appliance and Electronics Breakdown coverage. It is available to our policy clients who insure their primary home with CSI under our:

- Homeowners Policy (CSI-HOP-2)
- Homeowners Policy (CSI-HOP-4)
- Farm owners Policy (CSI-FOP-1)

We cannot prevent the inconvenience of a breakdown, but we can limit your expense and quickly get your life back to normal.

Estimated Repair and Replacement Costs

8-101 Word 8-3 completed

Independent Project 8-4

For this project, you customize a draft of a report for Sierra Pacific Community College District. You apply desktop publishing features, apply and customize a theme, insert and customize text boxes, insert and customize a *SmartArt* graphic and a chart, mark index entries, and create an index page. **[Student Learning Outcomes 8.1, 8.2, 8.3, 8.4, 8.5, 8.6]**

File Needed: ***OnlineLearning-08.docx***
Completed Project File Name: ***[your initials] Word 8-4.docx***

Skills Covered in This Project

- Adjust document margins and gutter.
- Apply, customize, and save a theme.
- Use and customize a drop cap.
- Create and apply a custom watermark.
- Apply automatic hyphenation.
- Insert a built-in watermark.
- Insert and customize a *SmartArt* graphic.
- Insert a chart and customize chart data.
- Insert a chart title and data labels.
- Modify a vertical axis.
- Apply a shape style to a chart.
- Resize a chart.
- Insert, customize, and position built-in text boxes.
- Create a bookmark.
- Mark index main entries and subentries.
- Create a bookmark index entry.
- Create and update an index page.

1. Open the ***OnlineLearning-08*** document from your student data files.
2. Save the document as ***[your initials] Word 8-4***.
3. Adjust margins and gutter.
   a. Change the top, bottom, left, and right margins to **0.75"**.
   b. Change the gutter to **0.25"** and the gutter position to **Left**.
4. Apply and customize a theme.
   a. Apply the **Metropolitan** theme.
   b. Change the theme *Colors* to **Grayscale** and the theme *Fonts* to **Gil Sans MT**.
   c. Save the current theme as SPCCD 2.
5. Apply a **Dropped** drop cap to the first letter in the paragraph below the "PURPOSE OF THIS PLAN" heading and modify it to drop **2** lines.
6. Create and apply a custom text watermark.
   a. Type OL Draft as the text.
   b. Change the size to **120 pt.** and change the layout to **Diagonal**.
7. Insert and customize a *SmartArt* graphic.
   a. Place your insertion point at the end of the paragraph in the "PURPOSE OF THIS PLAN" section.
   b. Insert the **Horizontal Bullet List** *SmartArt* graphic.
   c. Type the information shown in Figure 8-102 in the *SmartArt* graphic.

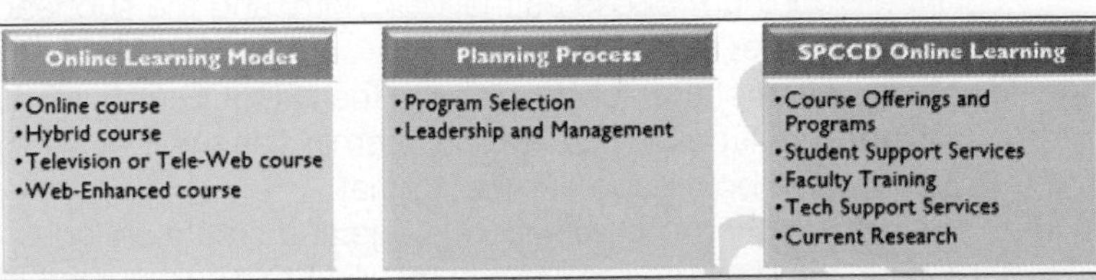

8-102 ***SmartArt*** **graphic and text**

d. Change the height of the *SmartArt* graphic to **1.5"** and the width to **6.5"**.
e. Change the *Colors* to **Colorful – Accent Colors**.
f. Apply the **Polished** *SmartArt* style.
g. **Bold** the text in the main headings.

8. Insert and customize a chart.
   a. Place your insertion point at the end of the last paragraph in the "Course Offerings and Programs" section on the second page.
   b. Insert a **Clustered Column** chart.
   c. In the worksheet, type the information in Figure 8-103 to replace the sample chart data. Adjust the chart data range as needed.
   d. Type SPCCD Course Offerings as the chart title.
   e. Apply data labels to the **Outside End** of the columns.
   f. Apply the **Style 11** chart style.
   g. Format the vertical axis and change the number format to **Number** with **0** decimal places and a **1000 separator**.
   h. Select the **Chart Area** and apply the **Subtle Effect – Gray-25%, Accent 1** shape style.
   i. Change the height of the chart to **2.5"** and the width to **6.5"**.
   j. Click at the end of the paragraph above the chart and press **Enter**.

	A	B	C
1	Year	OL Courses	Traditional Courses
2	2009	621	6900
3	2010	745	7842
4	2011	982	9352
5	2012	1106	9617
6	2013	1247	9856

8-103 Type chart data and select chart data range

9. Insert and customize text boxes.
   a. Place your insertion point at the top of the first page and insert the **Austin Quote** built-in text box.
   b. Copy the second sentence in the paragraph in the "PURPOSE OF THIS PLAN" section and paste it in the text box to replace the placeholder text.
   c. Select the text box and apply the **Subtle Effect – Black, Dark 1** shape style.
   d. Change the height of the text box to **1.25"** and the width to **3.4"**.
   e. Set the *Position* [*Drawing Tools Format* tab, *Arrange* group] as **Position in Bottom Right with Square Text Wrapping**.
   f. Place your insertion point at the top of the third page and insert the **Austin Quote** built-in text box.
   g. Copy the first and second sentences in the first paragraph in the "Tech Support Services" section and paste it in the text box to replace the placeholder text.
   h. Select the text box and apply the **Subtle Effect – Black, Dark 1** shape style.
   i. Change the height of the text box to **1.6"** and the width to **2.2"**.
   j. Set the *Position* as **Position in Middle Right with Square Text Wrapping**.

10. Select the chart on the second page and create a bookmark named CourseOfferings.

11. Mark index entries.
   a. Select and mark the four main section headings as a **Main entry**. Use **bold** page number format and click **Mark** (not *Mark All*).
   b. Select each of the types of online courses in the "ONLINE LEARNING MODES" section and mark each as **Subentry**. Type Online Learning Modes as the *Main entry* and the online course type as the *Subentry*. Do not use bold page number format.
   c. Select each of the subheadings in the "PLANNING PROCESS" section and mark as **Subentry**. Type Planning Process as the *Main entry* and the subheading as the *Subentry*. Do not use bold page number format.
   d. Select each of the subheadings in the "SPCCD ONLINE LEARNING" section and mark as **Subentry**. Type SPCCD Online Learning as the *Main entry* and the subheading as the *Subentry*. Do not use bold page number format.
   e. Select the chart on the second page and create an index entry to a bookmark. Type SPCCD Online Learning as the *Main entry* and SPCCD Course Offerings Chart as the *Subentry*. Select **CourseOfferings** as the bookmark. Do not use bold page number format.

12. Create and update an index page.
    a. At the end of the document, insert a page break, type Index, apply the **Heading 1** style, and then press **Enter**.
    b. Insert an index and use **Simple** format, **right align page** numbers, use a **dot leader**, and use **2** columns.
    c. Turn off **Show/Hide** and update the index.
13. Save and close the document (Figure 8-104).

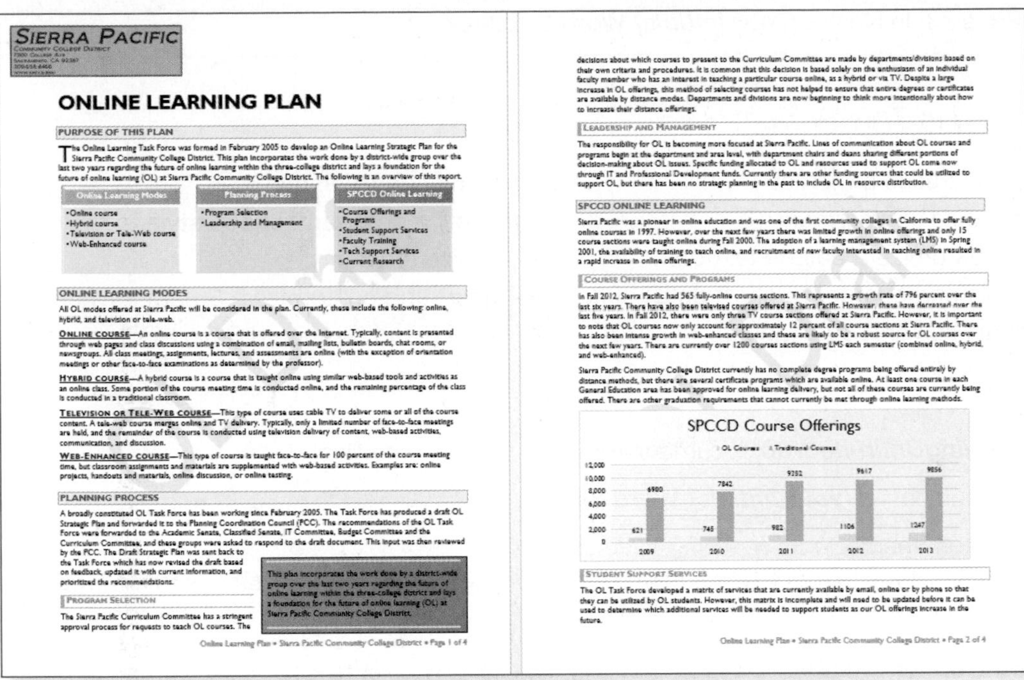

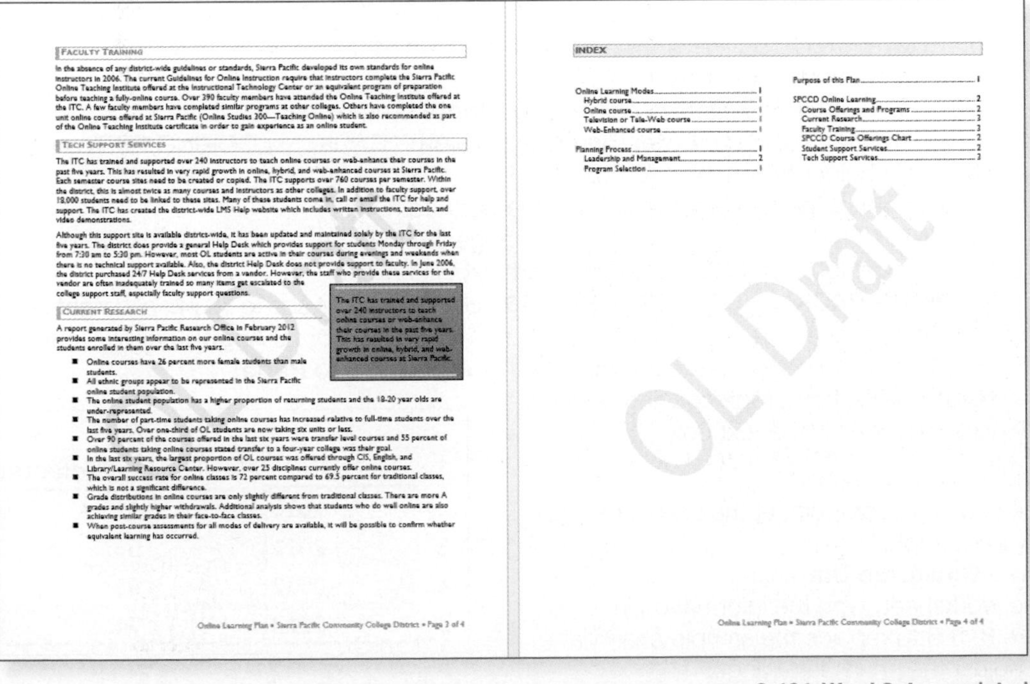

8-104 Word 8-4 completed

Independent Project 8-5

For this project, you customize an informational flyer for the Skiing Unlimited program. You apply desktop publishing features, apply and customize a theme, insert and customize a text box, and insert and customize a *SmartArt* graphic and chart.
[Student Learning Outcomes 8.1, 8.2, 8.3, 8.4, 8.5]

Files Needed: ***SkiingUnlimited-08.docx* and *Snow-08.png***
Completed Project File Name: ***[your initials] Word 8-5.docx***

Skills Covered in This Project

- Customize and save a theme.
- Use a picture as a watermark.
- Insert and customize a built-in text box.
- Insert a chart and customize chart data.
- Insert a chart title and data labels.
- Modify chart elements.
- Apply a chart and shape style to the chart.
- Resize the chart.
- Insert and customize a *SmartArt* graphic.
- Resize and arrange a *SmartArt* graphic.

1. Open the ***SkiingUnlimited-08*** document from your student data files.
2. Save the document as ***[your initials] Word 8-5***.
3. Create a custom theme.
   a. Change the theme *Colors* to **Red**, theme *Fonts* to **Candara**, and theme *Effects* to **Grunge Texture**.
   b. Save the current theme as Skiing Unlimited.
4. Apply a picture as the page color.
   a. Use the ***Snow-08*** picture from your student data files as the page color.
   b. Use *Page Color Fill Effects* and select *Picture*.
5. Insert and customize a built-in text box.
   a. At the beginning of the document, insert the **Grid Quote** built-in text box.
   b. Type SKIING UNLIMITED, press **Enter**, and type LOOKING BACK. . . LOOKING FORWARD to replace the placeholder text in the text box.
   c. Change the height of the text box to **1.5"** and the width to **8.4"**.
   d. Select "**SKIING UNLIMITED**" in the text box, change the font size to **40 pt.**, apply **bold** formatting, turn off italic formatting, and **left** align text.
   e. Select "**LOOKING BACK. . . LOOKING FORWARD,**" change the font size to **16 pt.**, and **right** align text.
   f. Using the *Position* tab in the *Layout* dialog box, change the *Horizontal* **Alignment** to **Centered** relative to **Page**, and change *Vertical* **Alignment** to **Top** relative to **Page**.
   g. Apply **10 pt.** *Before* paragraph spacing on the first body paragraph below the text box.
6. Insert and customize a chart.
   a. Place your insertion point at the end of the first body paragraph.
   b. Insert a **Clustered Bar** chart.
   c. In the worksheet, type the information in Figure 8-105 to replace the sample chart data and adjust the chart data range.

	A	B	C
1		Participants	Volunteers
2	2010	41	104
3	2011	53	138
4	2012	61	186
5	2013	74	231

8-105 Type chart data and select chart data range

d. Change the chart title to Skiing Unlimited.
e. Apply data labels to the **Outside End** of the bars.
f. Apply the **Style 12** chart style.
g. Select the **Chart Area** and apply the **Subtle Effect – Black, Dark 1** shape style.
h. Apply **bold** formatting to the data labels, vertical axis, horizontal axis, and legend.
i. Change the height of the chart to **2.5"** and the width to **6.5"**.

7. Insert and customize a *SmartArt* graphic.
   a. Place your insertion point at the end of the second body paragraph.
   b. Insert the **Circle Arrow Process** *SmartArt* graphic.
   c. Type the following information in the *SmartArt* graphic. Add shapes and use the *Text* pane as needed.

      January 18

      January 25

      February 1

      February 8

      March 1
   d. Select the text boxes in the *SmartArt* graphic and apply **bold** formatting.
   e. Change the height of the *SmartArt* graphic to **3.5"** and the width to **2"**.
   f. Change the color of the *SmartArt* graphic to **Dark 2 Fill**.
   g. Apply the **Subtle Effect** *SmartArt* style.
   h. Change the text wrapping to **Square**.
   i. Drag the *SmartArt* graphic so it is placed at the bottom right of the first page. Use the alignment guides for placement.
   j. Using the *Position* tab in the *Layout* dialog box, set the *Horizontal* **Absolute position** at **6"** *to the right of* **Page** and set the *Vertical* **Absolute position** at **7"** *below* **Page**.
8. Save and close the document (Figure 8-106).

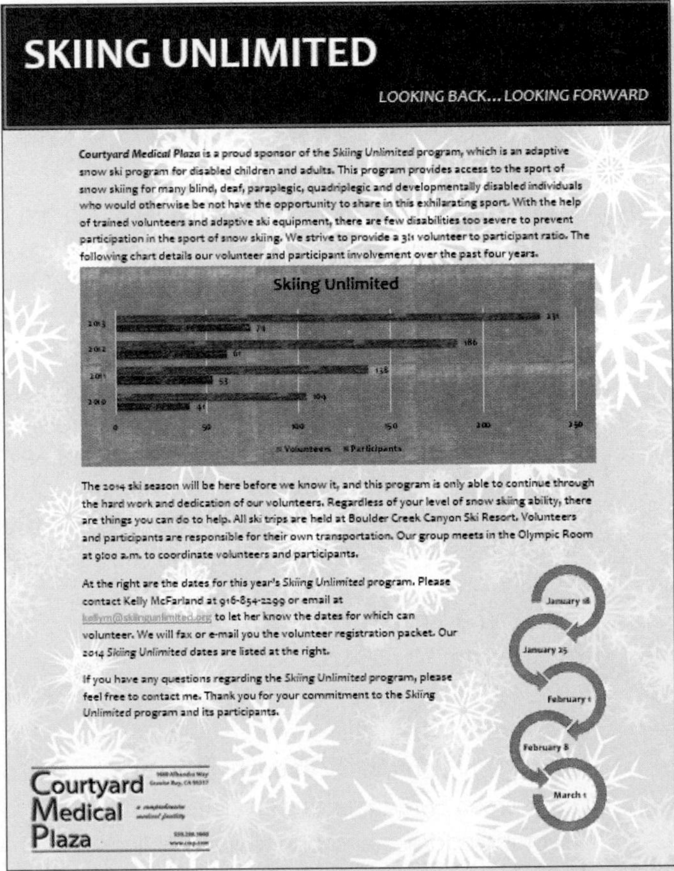

SKIING UNLIMITED

LOOKING BACK... LOOKING FORWARD

Courtyard Medical Plaza is a proud sponsor of the *Skiing Unlimited* program, which is an adaptive snow ski program for disabled children and adults. This program provides access to the sport of snow skiing for many blind, deaf, paraplegic, quadriplegic and developmentally disabled individuals who would otherwise be not have the opportunity to share in this exhilarating sport. With the help of trained volunteers and adaptive ski equipment, there are few disabilities too severe to prevent participation in the sport of snow skiing. We strive to provide a 3:1 volunteer to participant ratio. The following chart details our volunteer and participant involvement over the past four years.

The 2014 ski season will be here before we know it, and this program is only able to continue through the hard work and dedication of our volunteers. Regardless of your level of snow skiing ability, there are things you can do to help. All ski trips are held at Boulder Creek Canyon Ski Resort. Volunteers and participants are responsible for their own transportation. Our group meets in the Olympic Room at 9:00 a.m. to coordinate volunteers and participants.

At the right are the dates for this year's *Skiing Unlimited* program. Please contact Kelly McFarland at 916-854-2299 or email at kellym@skiingunlimited.org to let her know the dates for which can volunteer. We will fax or e-mail you the volunteer registration packet. Our 2014 *Skiing Unlimited* dates are listed at the right.

If you have any questions regarding the *Skiing Unlimited* program, please feel free to contact me. Thank you for your commitment to the *Skiing Unlimited* program and its participants.

8-106 Word 8-5 completed

Independent Project 8-6

For this project, you customize a weekly expense report for Life's Animal Shelter. You apply desktop publishing features, apply and customize a theme, insert and customize text boxes, and insert and customize a chart.
[Student Learning Outcomes 8.1, 8.2, 8.3, 8.5]

File Needed: ***WeeklyExpenses-08.docx***
Completed Project File Name: ***[your initials] Word 8-6.docx***

Skills Covered in This Project

- Customize and save a theme.
- Apply and customize a drop cap.
- Insert and customize built-in text boxes.
- Insert a chart and customize chart data.
- Insert a chart title and data labels.
- Modify chart elements.
- Apply a chart and shape style to the chart.
- Resize a chart.

1. Open the ***WeeklyExpenses-08*** document from your student data files.
2. Save this document as ***[your initials] Word 8-6***.
3. Change the bottom margin to **0.5"**.
4. Create a custom theme.
   a. Change the theme *Colors* to **Median**, theme *Fonts* to **Corbel**, and theme *Effects* to **Banded Edge**.
   b. Save the current theme as LAS.
5. Apply a **Dropped** drop cap to the first letter in the first body paragraph, modify it to drop **2** lines, and set the distance from text to **0.1"**.
6. Insert and customize a built-in text box.
   a. Place your insertion point at the top of the document and insert the **Grid Sidebar** built-in text box.
   b. Change the height to **11"** and the width to **2.5"**.
   c. Using the *Position* tab in the *Layout* dialog box, set the *Horizontal* **Alignment** at **Right** *relative to* **Page** and set the *Vertical* **Alignment** at **Top** *relative to* **Page**.
   d. Click in the first placeholder text and type Life's Animal Shelter.
   e. Select "**Life's Animal Shelter**" in the text box, change the font size to **28 pt.**, apply **bold** formatting, and apply the **Offset Diagonal Top Right** shadow text effect.
   f. Click in the second placeholder text and type the following, pressing **Enter** after each line except the last:

      3429 2nd Avenue North

      Park Rapids, MN 56470

      218.240.7880

      www.lifesanimalshelter.com

      "Serving our community through animal rescue and pet adoption"

      (Don't press *Enter* after this last line.)
   g. Select the address and phone number lines and change the after paragraph spacing to **0 pt.**
   h. Select the quoted text including the quotation marks ("Serving our community . . ."), and change the line spacing to **1.5** and apply **italic** formatting.

7. Insert and customize a chart.
   a. Place your insertion point at the end of the second body paragraph.
   b. Insert a **3-D Clustered Column** chart.
   c. In the worksheet, type the information in Figure 8-107 to replace the sample chart data and adjust the chart data range.
   d. Change the height of the chart to **3"** and the width to **4.5"**.
   e. Change the title to Daily Expenses.
   f. Apply the **Style 6** chart style.
   g. Select the **Chart Area** and apply the **Brown, Text 2** shape fill color.
   h. Select the **From Center** gradient in the *Dark Variations* category of the *Gradient* area on the *Shape Fill* drop-down list.
   i. Select and apply **bold** formatting to the legend and the horizontal axis labels.
   j. Place your insertion point at the end of the second body paragraph and press **Enter**.

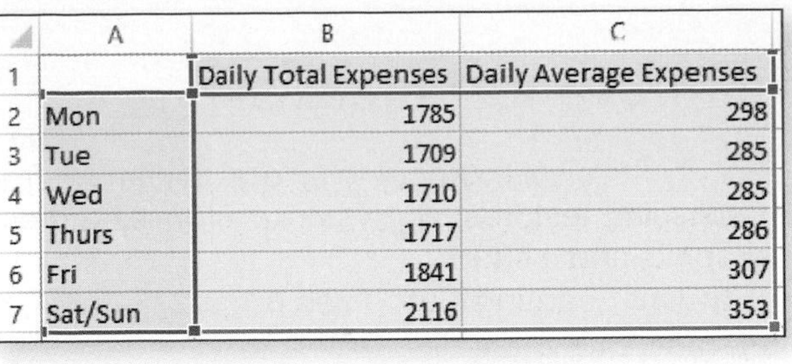

	A	B	C
1		Daily Total Expenses	Daily Average Expenses
2	Mon	1785	298
3	Tue	1709	285
4	Wed	1710	285
5	Thurs	1717	286
6	Fri	1841	307
7	Sat/Sun	2116	353

8-107 Type chart data and select chart data range

8. Insert and customize a built-in text box.
   a. Select the last body paragraph (not including the paragraph mark) and cut (**Ctrl+X**) it from the document.
   b. Insert the **Motion Quote** built-in text box and paste (**Ctrl+V**) the cut text in the text box to replace the placeholder text.
   c. Select the text and change text alignment to **Center** [*Home* tab, *Paragraph* group].
   d. Apply the **Preset 2** shape effect.
   e. Change the width of the text box to **4.5"**.
   f. Set the position as **Position in Bottom Left with Square Text Wrapping**.

9. Save and close the document (Figure 8-108).

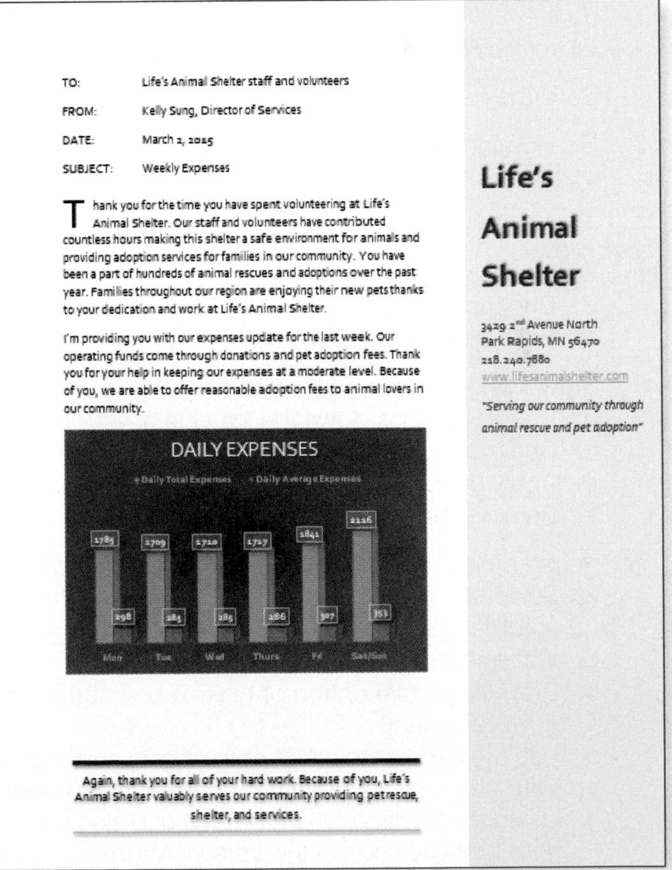

TO: Life's Animal Shelter staff and volunteers

FROM: Kelly Sung, Director of Services

DATE: March 2, 2015

SUBJECT: Weekly Expenses

Thank you for the time you have spent volunteering at Life's Animal Shelter. Our staff and volunteers have contributed countless hours making this shelter a safe environment for animals and providing adoption services for families in our community. You have been a part of hundreds of animal rescues and adoptions over the past year. Families throughout our region are enjoying their new pets thanks to your dedication and work at Life's Animal Shelter.

I'm providing you with our expenses update for the last week. Our operating funds come through donations and pet adoption fees. Thank you for your help in keeping our expenses at a moderate level. Because of you, we are able to offer reasonable adoption fees to animal lovers in our community.

Again, thank you for all of your hard work. Because of you, Life's Animal Shelter valuably serves our community providing pet rescue, shelter, and services.

Life's Animal Shelter

3429 2nd Avenue North
Park Rapids, MN 56470
218.240.7880
www.lifesanimalshelter.com

"Serving our community through animal rescue and pet adoption"

8-108 Word 8-6 completed

Improve It Project 8-7

For this project, you customize a document from American River Cycling Club. You apply desktop publishing features, apply and customize a theme, and insert and customize text boxes, a *SmartArt* graphic, and a chart.
[Student Learning Outcomes 8.1, 8.2, 8.3, 8.4, 8.5]

File Needed: ***HeartRate-08.docx***
Completed Project File Name: ***[your initials] Word 8-7.docx***

Skills Covered in This Project

- Adjust margins.
- Apply and customize a drop cap.
- Customize and save a theme.
- Draw and customize a text box.
- Align and group a picture and text box.
- Insert and customize a *SmartArt* graphic.
- Insert a chart and customize chart data.
- Resize a chart.
- Insert a chart title, axis titles, and data labels.
- Apply a chart and shape style to the chart.
- Modify chart elements.
- Insert and customize a built-in text box.

1. Open the ***HeartRate-08*** document from your student data files.
2. Save the document as ***[your initials] Word 8-7***.
3. Change the top margin to **0.75"**, the bottom margin to **0.5"**, the left margin to **1.75"**, and the right margin to **0.75"**.
4. Apply a **Dropped** drop cap to the first letter in the first body paragraph and modify it to drop **2** lines.
5. Create a custom theme.
   a. Change the theme *Colors* to **Green Yellow** and theme *Fonts* to **Gil Sans MT**.
   b. Save the current theme as ARCC.
6. Draw a text box and customize it.
   a. Draw a text box down the left side of your document.
   b. Change the height to **11"** and the width to **1.3"**.
   c. Apply the **Lime, Accent 1, Lighter 80%** shape fill.
   d. Remove the shape outline (**No Outline**).
7. Resize a picture and align and group a picture with a text box.
   a. Select the picture at the top of the document and change the width to **8.5"**. The height automatically adjusts.
   b. With the picture selected, **Rotate Left 90°**.
   c. Drag the picture on top of the text box at the left and **Bring to Front** [*Picture Tools Format* tab, *Arrange* group].
   d. Use the **Ctrl** key to select both objects and align selected object at **Align Center** and **Align Middle**.
   e. With both objects selected, **Group** the two objects.
   f. Using the *Position* tab in the *Layout* dialog box, set the *Horizontal* **Absolute position** at **0"** *to the right of* **Page** and set the *Vertical* **Alignment** at **Top** *relative to* **Page**.
8. Insert and customize a *SmartArt* graphic.
   a. Place your insertion point at the end of the second body paragraph ("Example: a 40-year-old's . . .").

b. Insert the **Equation** *SmartArt* graphic (*Process* category).
c. Type the following information in the *SmartArt* graphic:
   220
   Age
   Max Heart Rate
d. Change the height of the *SmartArt* graphic to **1"** and the width to **4"**.
e. Select the **Plus** shape and change it to a **Minus** shape [*SmartArt Tools Format* tab, *Shapes* group].
f. Apply the **Intense Effect** *SmartArt* style.
g. Change the text wrapping to **Top and Bottom**.
h. Using the *Position* tab in the *Layout* dialog box, set the *Horizontal* **Alignment** at **Centered** *relative to* **Margin** and set the *Vertical* **Alignment** at **Top** *relative to* **Line**.
i. Select the sentence below the *SmartArt* graphic and **center** it.

9. Insert and customize a chart.
   a. Select the tabbed text below the paragraphs and delete it.
   b. With your insertion point at the end of the document, insert a **Line with Markers** chart.
   c. In the worksheet, type the information in Figure 8-109 to replace the sample chart data and adjust the chart data range.
   d. Change the height of the chart to **3.3"** and the width to **6"**.
   e. Change the title to Max and Target Heart Rates.
   f. Insert a **Primary Horizontal** axis title and type Age in the text box.
   g. Insert a **Primary Vertical** axis title and type Heart Rate in the text box.

	A	B	C
1	Age	Max Heart Rate	Target Heart Rate (75%)
2	20	200	150
3	25	195	146
4	30	190	143
5	35	185	139
6	40	180	135
7	45	175	131
8	50	170	128
9	55	165	124
10	60	160	120

8-109 Type chart data and select chart data range

10. Modify chart elements.
    a. Apply the **Style 2** chart style.
    b. Select the **Chart Area** and apply the **Subtle Effect – Lime, Accent 1** shape style.
    c. Change the shape outline weight to **1½ pt.**
    d. Apply the **Offset Center** shadow shape effect (*Outer* category).

11. Insert and customize a text box.
    a. Place your insertion point at the end of the second paragraph in the "What Is Target Heart Rate?" section and insert the **Austin Quote** built-in text box.
    b. Copy the first sentence in the second paragraph in the "What Is Target Heart Rate?" section and paste it in the text box to replace the placeholder text.
    c. Select the text box and apply the **Subtle Effect – Lime, Accent 1** shape style.
    d. Change the position to **Position in Middle Right with Square Text Wrapping**.
    e. Change the height of the text box to **1.5"** and the width to **2"**.
    f. Select the text in the text box, apply **italic** formatting, and change the text alignment to **center**.

12. Save and close the document (Figure 8-110).

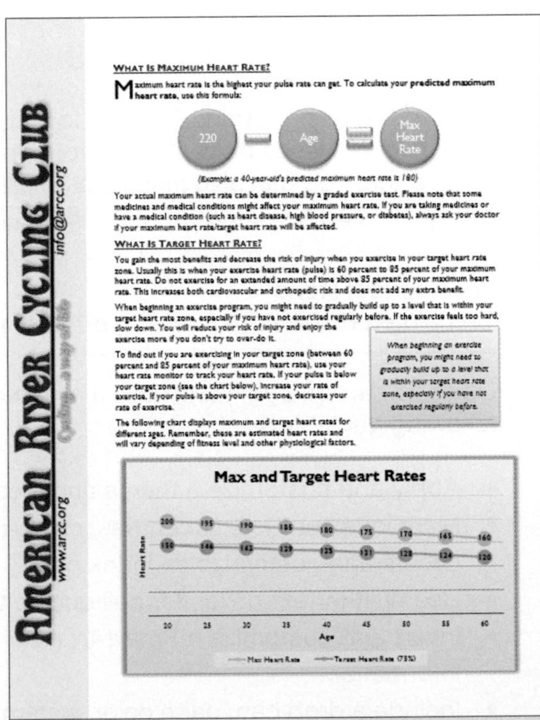
American River Cycling Club
www.arcc.org
info@arcc.org

WHAT IS MAXIMUM HEART RATE?

Maximum heart rate is the highest your pulse rate can get. To calculate your predicted maximum heart rate, use this formula:

(Example: a 40-year-old's predicted maximum heart rate is 180)

Your actual maximum heart rate can be determined by a graded exercise test. Please note that some medicines and medical conditions might affect your maximum heart rate. If you are taking medicines or have a medical condition (such as heart disease, high blood pressure, or diabetes), always ask your doctor if your maximum heart rate/target heart rate will be affected.

WHAT IS TARGET HEART RATE?

You gain the most benefits and decrease the risk of injury when you exercise in your target heart rate zone. Usually this is when your exercise heart rate (pulse) is 60 percent to 85 percent of your maximum heart rate. Do not exercise for an extended amount of time above 85 percent of your maximum heart rate. This increases both cardiovascular and orthopedic risk and does not add any extra benefit.

When beginning an exercise program, you might need to gradually build up to a level that is within your target heart rate zone, especially if you have not exercised regularly before. If the exercise feels too hard, slow down. You will reduce your risk of injury and enjoy the exercise more if you don't try to over-do it.

When beginning an exercise program, you might need to gradually build up to a level that is within your target heart rate zone, especially if you have not exercised regularly before.

To find out if you are exercising in your target zone (between 60 percent and 85 percent of your maximum heart rate), use your heart rate monitor to track your heart rate. If your pulse is below your target zone (see the chart below), increase your rate of exercise. If your pulse is above your target zone, decrease your rate of exercise.

The following chart displays maximum and target heart rates for different ages. Remember, these are estimated heart rates and will vary depending of fitness level and other physiological factors.

8-110 Word 8-7 completed

Challenge Project 8-8

It is important to plan and budget for your college education. Create an education plan and budget using some of the desktop publishing and graphics features discussed in this chapter. Use a *SmartArt* graphic to plan out your courses for your remaining semesters and use a chart to visually display your estimated expenses.
[Student Learning Outcomes 8.1, 8.2, 8.3, 8.4, 8.5]

File Needed: None
Completed Project File Name: ***[your initials] Word 8-8.docx***

Open a new document and save it as ***[your initials] Word 8-8***. Create an education plan and budget using the Word features you learned about in this chapter. Modify your document according to the following guidelines:

- Use a *SmartArt* graphic to set up your education plan.
- Use a chart to display your estimated expenses.
- Apply and customize a theme and create a custom theme.
- Customize the *SmartArt* graphic and chart layout and design.
- As appropriate, include a drop cap, page color, watermark, screenshot, and/or hyphenation.
- Insert a built-in text box or draw a text box and customize as needed.

Challenge Project 8-9

Apply desktop publishing features to improve readability and enhance the appearance of a report from one of your classes or from your job. Apply and customize a theme, mark index entries, and create an index page. You can also include a *SmartArt* graphic, a chart, and text boxes as appropriate.
[Student Learning Outcomes 8.1, 8.2, 8.3, 8.4, 8.5, 8.6]

File Needed: None
Completed Project File Name: ***[your initials] Word 8-9.docx***

Open a new document and save it as ***[your initials] Word 8-9***. Modify your document according to the following guidelines:

- Apply and customize a theme and create a custom theme.
- Mark index entries, subentries, cross-reference index entries, and a bookmark index entry.
- Create and customize an index page.
- Use built-in text boxes for pull quotes to emphasize important information in the report.
- Insert and customize a *SmartArt* graphic and/or chart as appropriate to visually display information.
- Include a drop cap, page color, watermark, screenshot, and/or hyphenation, as appropriate.

Challenge Project 8-10

Create a flyer, announcement, or invitation to an upcoming event for a student group or organization on campus, such as a blood drive, community service event, or food bank collection. Use desktop publishing and graphic features to enhance this document.
[Student Learning Outcomes 8.1, 8.2, 8.3, 8.4, 8.5]

File Needed: None
Completed Project File Name: ***[your initials] Word 8-10.docx***

Open a new document and save it as ***[your initials] Word 8-10***. Create a flyer, announcement, or invitation using Word features you learned in this chapter. Modify your document according to the following guidelines:

- Apply and customize a theme and create a custom theme.
- Appropriately include a drop cap, page color, watermark, screenshot, and/or hyphenation.
- Insert and customize text boxes to emphasize information in pull quotes.
- Insert and customize a *SmartArt* graphic and/or chart, as appropriate, to visually display information.
- Customize your *SmartArt* graphics and chart layout and design.

CHAPTER 9

Working Collaboratively and Integrating Applications

CHAPTER OVERVIEW

Microsoft Word provides tools that allow you to work collaboratively on documents with others. *Comments* and *Track Changes* are two valuable collaboration tools that you can use to edit documents. In addition to working with multiple people, you can also work with multiple applications. When preparing documents, you can use content from other Microsoft Office applications in your Word document. For example, you can include a PowerPoint slide, a chart from Excel, or a table from Access in your Word documents. You can also merge data from Outlook, Excel, and Access into a Word document.

STUDENT LEARNING OUTCOMES (SLOs)

After completing this chapter, you will be able to:

SLO 9.1 Insert, review, edit, and customize comments (p. W9-513).

SLO 9.2 Modify and review a document using *Track Changes* (p. W9-516).

SLO 9.3 Use Word collaboration features to compare, combine, protect, and share documents (p. W9-524).

SLO 9.4 Embed and link content from other Microsoft Office applications into a Word document (p. W9-535).

SLO 9.5 Use mail merge rules to customize how data is merged from other Office applications into Word documents (p. W9-543).

CASE STUDY

In the Pause & Practice projects in this chapter, you use collaboration and integration features available in Word to enhance an informational document from Hamilton Civic Center about their yoga classes.

Pause & Practice 9-1: Use *Comments* and *Track Changes* to edit a document and review a document that has comments and edits marked with tracked changes.

Pause & Practice 9-2: Prepare a document to be shared, combine changes in two documents, and protect a document.

Pause & Practice 9-3: Insert and customize content from PowerPoint and Excel into a Word document.

Pause & Practice 9-4: Merge recipients from Excel into a Word document and use rules to customize a mail merge.

WORD

SLO 9.1

Using Comments

When you are collaborating with other people on a document, you can use ***comments*** to provide feedback in the document without making changes to the text of the document. For example, you might use comments to ask a question, make a suggestion, or provide additional information. You can also use comments when working alone on a document to make notes to yourself. You can customize how comments appear in a document, review comments in a document, edit comments, and delete comments.

Insert a Comment

When you insert a comment, the comment appears in a ***balloon*** to the right of the document text in the ***Markup area***, which is the area to the right of a document that opens when a document has comments or tracked changes (we discuss tracking changes in *SLO 9.2: Using Track Changes*). Comments in a document are marked with the name of the author of the comment and time or date the comment was created. The text of the comment appears below the author's name in the balloon. You can attach a comment to a single word or a group of words.

HOW TO: Insert a Comment

1. Select the text where you want to insert a comment.
   - When you place your insertion point at the beginning of a word or within a word, the comment is attached to the entire word.
2. Click the **New Comment** button [*Review* tab, *Comments* group] (Figure 9-1).
   - The comment balloon appears in the *Markup* area on the right of the Word window.
   - The comment time or date displays as either minutes or hours ago (e.g., 4 minutes ago), or, if it was created more than 24 hours ago, the date displays.
   - The word or words in the document with the comment attached are highlighted.

9-1 ***New Comment*** **button**

3. Type comment text in the balloon (Figure 9-2).

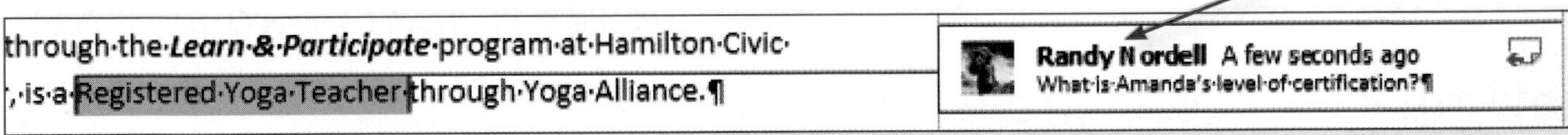

9-2 Comment in a balloon in the *Markup* area

4. Click in the document to return to the document.

> **MORE INFO**
>
> The *Display for Review* view [*Review* tab, *Tracking* group] determines how comments display in the document. *Display for Review* views are covered in the next section, *SLO 9.2: Using Track Changes.*

Change User Name

When you install Microsoft Office on your computer, you are prompted to enter your ***user name*** and ***initials,*** and Office stores this information to personalize Office on your computer. Word uses your user name as the ***author*** of each new document you create. Similarly, each comment made in Word is attributed to the username you have stored in Office. Each person editing the document is referred to as a ***reviewer***. If you are using a public computer, such as in a computer lab on your college campus, the user name is a generic name given to Office on that computer. To make sure comments you make in a document are attributed to you, you can change your user name and initials in Office.

HOW TO: Change User Name

1. Click the **Tracking** launcher [*Review* tab, *Tracking* group] to open the *Track Changes Options* dialog box.
2. Click the **Change User Name** button to open the *Word Options* dialog box (Figure 9-3).
3. Type your name in the *User name* text box.
4. Type your initials in the *Initials* text box.
5. Click **OK** to close the *Word Options* dialog box.
6. Click **OK** to close the *Track Changes Options* dialog box.

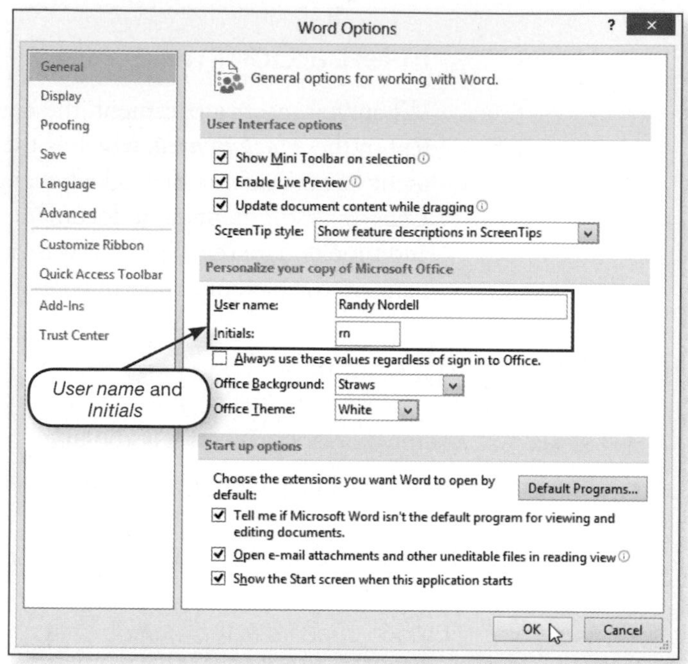

9-3 Change user name in the *Word Options* dialog box

> **ANOTHER WAY**
>
> Click the **File** tab to open the *Backstage* view and click **Options** to open the **Word Options** dialog box where you can change user name and initials.

Customize Comment Color

Comments appear in a default color when you insert a comment. If multiple reviewers are commenting on the same document, Word uses a different color for each reviewer. You can select a color to use as the color of the comment balloons in the ***Track Changes Options*** dialog box.

HOW TO: Customize Comment Color

1. Click the **Tracking** launcher [*Review* tab, *Tracking* group] to open the *Track Changes Options* dialog box.
2. Click the **Advanced Options** button to open the *Advanced Track Changes Options* dialog box (Figure 9-4).
3. Click the **Comments** drop-down list and select a color for the comments.
   - All existing and new comments change to the selected color.
   - By default, Word uses the *By author* option, which uses a different color for each author.
4. Click **OK** to close the *Advanced Track Changes Options* dialog box.
5. Click **OK** to close the *Track Changes Options* dialog box.

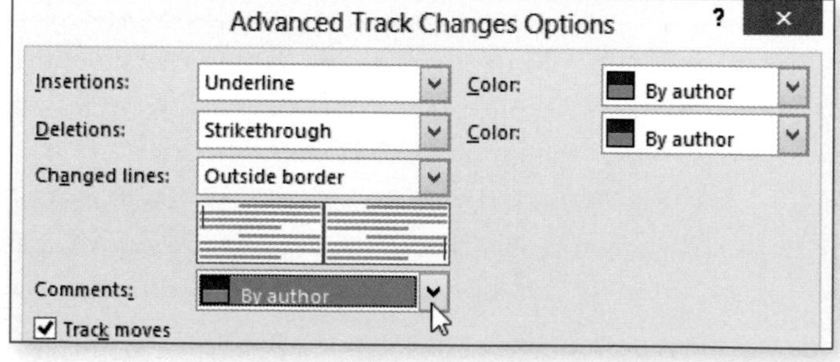

9-4 Change comment color in the *Advanced Track Changes Options* dialog box

Review Comments

Each comment in a document is attributed to the reviewer who made the comment. When you place your pointer on text in a document where a comment is attached, a tag displays with the reviewer's name, the date and time of the comment, and the comment text (Figure 9-5).

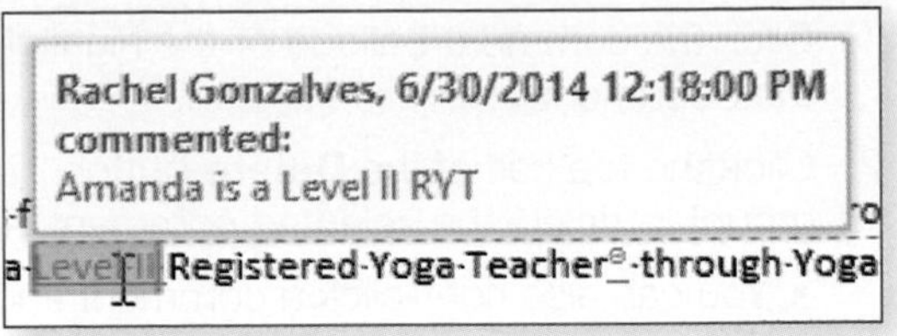

9-5 Comment details displayed in a tag

If you are working on a long document with multiple comments, Word provides navigation tools to move you to the next or previous comment in the document. Click the **Next** or **Previous** button in the *Comments* group on the *Review* tab (Figure 9-6) to move to the next or previous comment in your document.

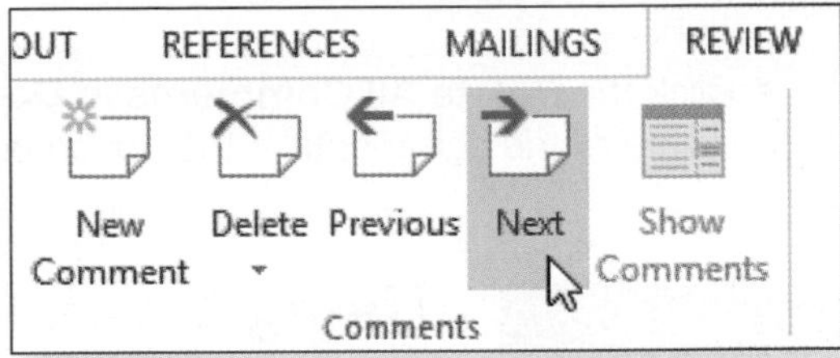

9-6 Move to the next comment

Reply to a Comment

To reply to a comment, click the **Reply** button on the right side of the comment in the *Markup* area (Figure 9-7). A reply area opens within the existing comment where you can type a reply below the original comment.

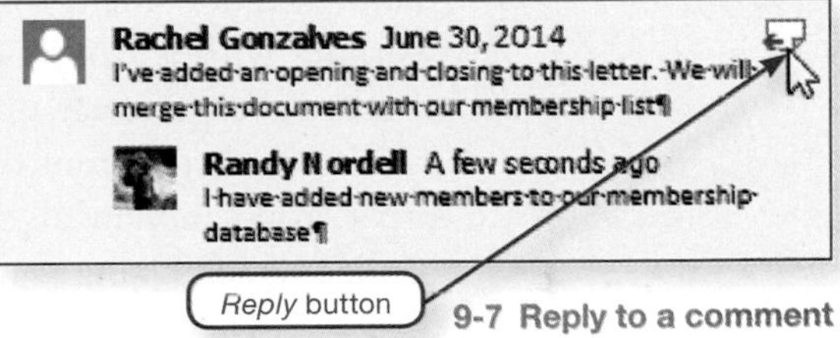

9-7 Reply to a comment

> **ANOTHER WAY**
>
> Right-click an existing comment in the *Markup* area or the highlighted text in a document with a comment attached and select **Reply To Comment** from the context menu.

Mark Comment Done

You can also mark a comment as done when you have taken action on a comment but don't want to delete the comment. When a comment is marked as done, the text of the comment changes to a light gray color, and the highlighted text in the document where the comment is attached is a lighter shade of the comment color. To mark a comment as done, right-click an existing comment in the *Markup* area or the highlighted text in a document with a comment attached, and select **Mark Comment Done** from the context menu (Figure 9-8). You can toggle off *Mark Comment Done* from the context menu to make the comment active.

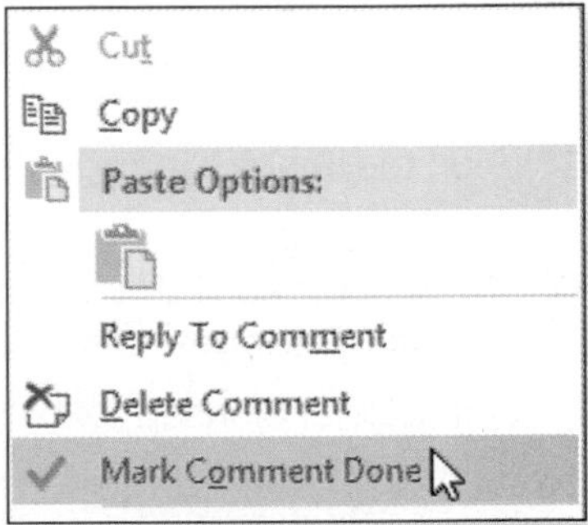

9-8 *Mark Comment Done*

Edit and Delete Comments

You can edit comments by clicking in the comment balloon and editing existing text or typing new text. You can also right-click highlighted text in your document that has a comment attached and select **Edit Comment** from the context menu.

Once you have finished reviewing comments, you can delete them. You can delete comments individually or delete all the comments in the document.

HOW TO: Delete Comments

1. Click the comment balloon or the highlighted comment text in the document.
2. Click the top half of the **Delete** button [*Review* tab, *Comments* group] to delete the selected comment (see Figure 9-6).
   - You can also right-click a comment and select **Delete Comment** from the context menu.
3. Click the bottom half of the **Delete** button for more delete options.
   - Click the **Delete All Comments in Document** button to delete all the comments in the document (Figure 9-9).

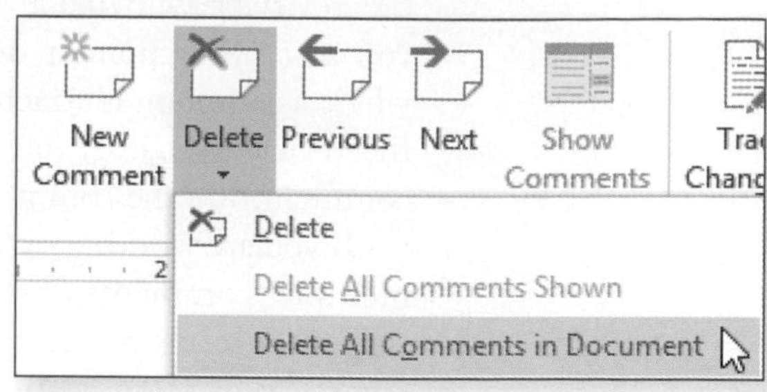

9-9 Delete all comments in the document

SLO 9.2

Using Track Changes

Track Changes is an excellent editing tool in Word that marks the changes you and others make in a document so all reviewers can see these changes. This feature is very useful when working with a group on a report or project. As you review tracked changes in a document, you can accept, reject, or skip the marked changes.

You have different options for viewing how tracked changes are displayed in the document. You can view all changes in a document in the *Reviewing* pane, and you can also customize which changes are displayed and the format of marked changes.

Track Changes

To mark editing changes in a document, you must first turn on *Track Changes.* Once you have done this, you can make additions, deletions, and changes to text and formatting in the document and these changes are tracked in the body of the document and in balloons on the right. Each line in the document that has a change is marked with a vertical gray or red line (depending on *Display for Review* view, which is covered in the next section) to the left of the line so reviewers can easily tell where changes have been made.

HOW TO: Use Track Changes

1. Click the **Track Changes** button [*Review* tab, *Tracking* group] (Figure 9-10).
   - When *Track Changes* is turned on, this button is highlighted.
   - You can also click the bottom half of the **Track Changes** button and select **Track Changes** to turn on *Track Changes*.
2. Edit, delete, or insert text in the document or make formatting changes to the document.
   - How the changes you make are displayed in the document depends on the *Display for Review* view that is selected by the document user. The *Display for Review* views are covered in the next section.
3. Click the **Track Changes** button to turn off *Track Changes*.

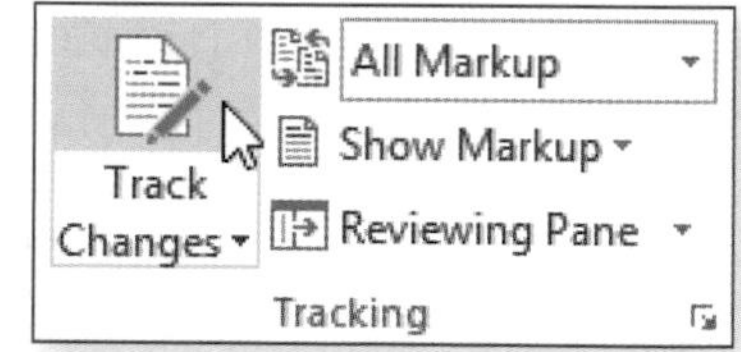

9-10 Turn on *Track Changes*

ANOTHER WAY

Ctrl+Shift+E toggles *Track* Changes on and off.

Display for Review Views

How editing changes appear when using *Track Changes* is determined by which ***Display for Review view*** is selected. The following table lists and describes each of these different views:

Display for Review Views

Display for Review View	Description
Simple Markup	Displays a final version of the document with the proposed changes incorporated. A red line to the left of a line marks changed lines in the document. Click the **Show Comments** button [*Review* tab, *Comments* group] to display or hide comments in the document.
All Markup	Displays added, deleted, and edited text in the body of the document. Formatting changes and comments are displayed in balloons on the right. A gray line to the left of a line marks changed lines in the document.
No Markup	Displays a final version of the document with the proposed changes incorporated, and all editing changes and comments are hidden.
Original	Displays the original document with proposed changes not incorporated, and all editing changes and comments are hidden.

Click the **Display for Review** drop-down list in the *Tracking* group on the *Review* tab to select a *Display for Review* view (Figure 9-11). *All Markup* is the view people typically use when reviewing a document with changes tracked (Figure 9-12).

9-11 ***Display for Review*** **views**

If you view your document in *Simple Markup*, *No Markup*, or *Original* view, the tracked changes are still in the document, but they are hidden so you can view a clean (without markup) final or original version of the document. It is important to understand and use these different views when using *Track Changes* to edit a document.

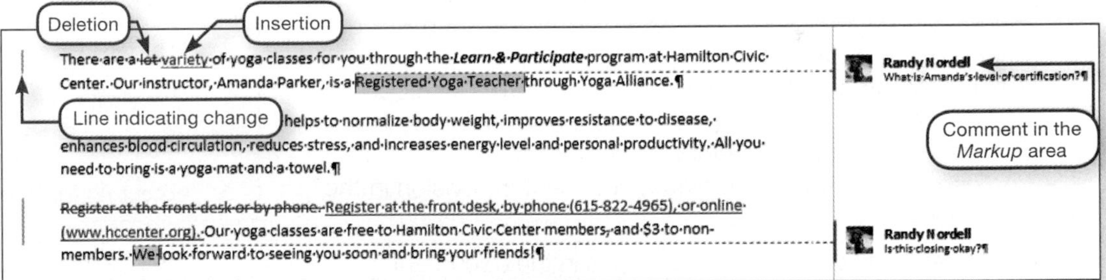

9-12 Changes tracked in a document displayed in *All Markup* view

> **MORE INFO**
>
> The **Show Comments** button [*Review* tab, *Comments* group] is only active in *Simple Markup* view. In *All Markup* view, comments are always displayed. In *No Markup* and *Original* views, comments are hidden with only balloons visible.

Accept and Reject Changes

After a document has been marked up with editing changes, you can review each proposed change and either accept or reject the change. It's best to work in *All Markup* view when reviewing a document with changes tracked. When you accept an editing or formatting change, the change is applied to the document, and the inline markup and/or balloon is removed. When you reject an editing or formatting change, the text and formatting revert back to their original form, and the inline markup and/or balloon is removed.

Similar to comments, each editing change is attributed to a reviewer. When you place your pointer on a change in the body of the text or on a balloon, a tag displays the reviewer's name, the date and time the change was made, and a description of the change (Figure 9-13).

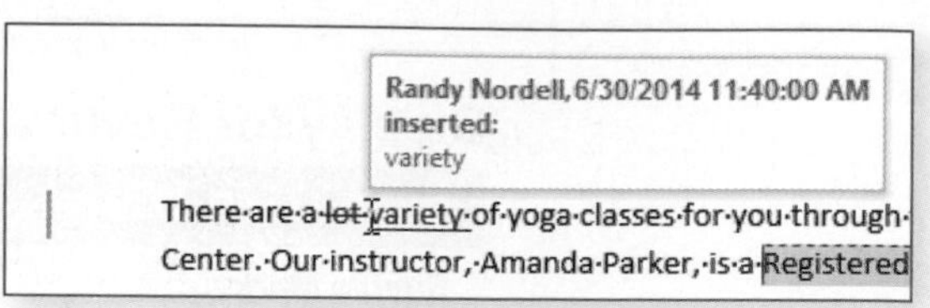

9-13 Tracked changes details displayed in a tag

HOW TO: Accept and Reject Changes

1. Place the insertion point at the beginning of the document (**Ctrl+Home**).
2. Click the **Display for Review** drop-down list [*Review* tab, *Tracking* group] and select **All Markup** if this is not the current view.
3. Click the **Next** button [*Review* tab, *Changes* group] to select the next change made to the document (Figure 9-14).
   - Click the **Previous** button to select the previous revision.
   - If you are in *No Markup* or *Original* view and press the *Next* or *Previous* button, the view automatically changes to *All Markup*.

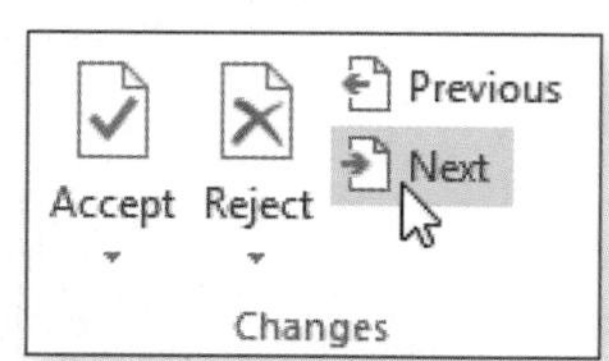

9-14 Move to next revision in the document

4. Click the **Accept** or **Reject** button [*Review* tab, *Changes* group] to accept or reject the change and move to the next revision.
   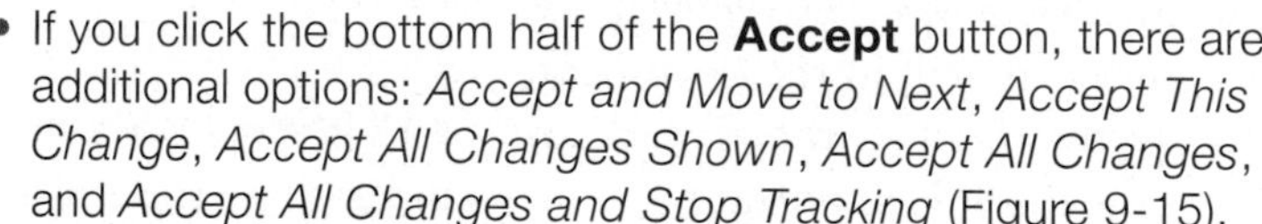
   - If you click the bottom half of the **Accept** button, there are additional options: *Accept and Move to Next*, *Accept This Change*, *Accept All Changes Shown*, *Accept All Changes*, and *Accept All Changes and Stop Tracking* (Figure 9-15).
   - If you click the bottom half of the **Reject** button, there are additional options: *Reject and Move to Next*, *Reject Change*, *Reject All Changes Shown*, *Reject All Changes*, and *Reject All Changes and Stop Tracking*.
   - When accepting and rejecting changes, Word also stops on comments. Click **Accept** to leave the comment in the document or **Reject** to delete the comment.
   - You can also click **Next** to skip a comment or revision in the document.

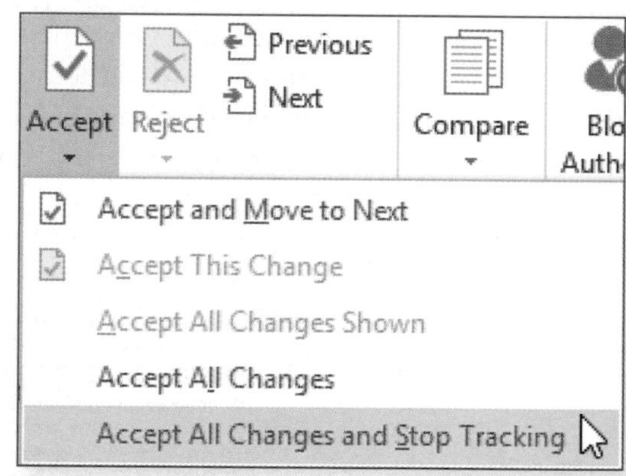

9-15 Accept all changes in the document

5. Continue accepting or rejecting changes in the document.
6. After you reach the last change in the document, a dialog box opens confirming there are no more comments or tracked changes in the document. Click **OK** (Figure 9-16).
   - When all changes have been accepted or rejected, there will be no vertical lines to the left of the text in the body of the document.

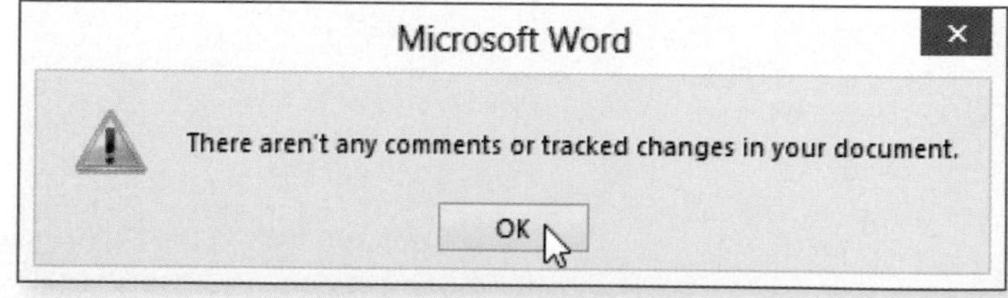

9-16 Dialog box that appears after reviewing the document

ANOTHER WAY

Right-click a change and select **Accept "description of change"** or **Reject "description of change"** from the context menu.

Reviewing Pane

If you are working with a document that has many editing changes that are marked with tracked changes, the ***Reviewing pane***, which is a separate pane that includes all the comments, is a useful tool. The *Reviewing* pane can be displayed vertically on the left side of the Word window or horizontally at the bottom of the Word window. If there are a lot of changes and comments in a document and all of the balloons cannot fit on the page, the *Reviewing* pane automatically opens.

To open the *Reviewing* pane, click the **Reviewing Pane** button in the *Tracking* group on the *Review* tab and select either **Reviewing Pane Vertical** or **Reviewing Pane Horizontal** (Figure 9-17).

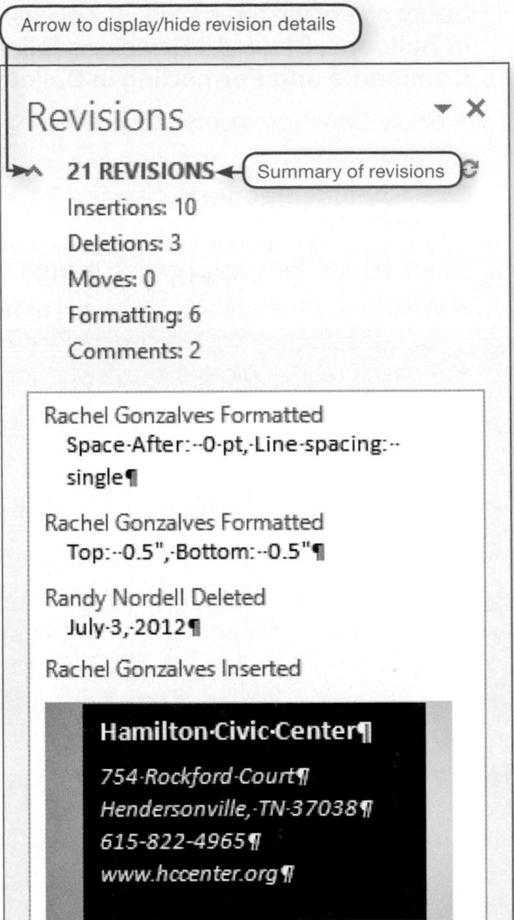

9-17 *Reviewing* pane displayed vertically

> **MORE INFO**
>
> When the *Reviewing* pane is open, the title of the pane is *Revisions*. This book refers to this pane as the *Reviewing* pane.

At the top of the *Reviewing* pane, a summary displays how many revisions are in the document. Click the arrow to the left of the revision summary to display a breakdown of how many insertions, deletions, moves, formatting changes, and comments are in the document. You can right-click any of the revisions in the *Reviewing* pane and accept or reject changes from the context menu.

Customize Show Markup Options

You can customize which markups are displayed, how they are displayed, and which reviewers' markups are displayed.

HOW TO: Customize Show Markup Options

1. Click the **Show Markup** button [*Review* tab, *Tracking* group] to display the list of markup options.
2. In the top area, select the options you want to display or hide.
   - A check mark indicates a feature is turned on.
3. Click **Balloons** to open the balloon options list (Figure 9-18).

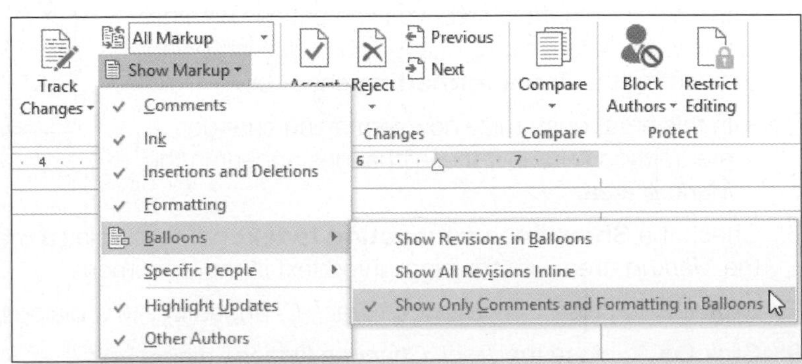

9-18 Customize *Show Markup* options

4. Select one of the three balloons options: **Show Revisions in Balloons**, **Show All Revisions Inline**, or **Show Only Comments and Formatting in Balloons**.
   - *Show Only Comments and Formatting in Balloons* is the default setting.
5. Click **Specific People** to display a list of reviewers (Figure 9-19).
6. Select or deselect reviewers as desired.
   - When you deselect a reviewer, his or her comments and revisions are not displayed in the document.
   - A check mark indicates a reviewer's comments and revisions are displayed.

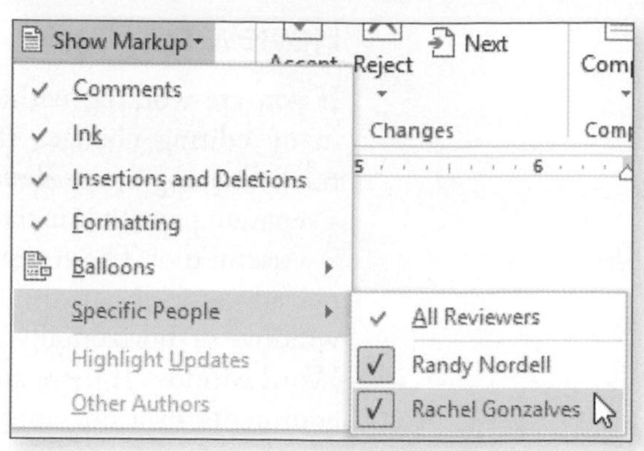

9-19 Select reviewers

Change Tracking Options

The ***Track Changes Options dialog box*** gives you additional control over how changes and comments appear in your document. You can customize how markups, moves, table cell highlighting, formatting, and balloons display in the document and the color for each of these changes. The changes you make in the *Track Changes Options* dialog box are global changes that affect all documents that use *Track Changes*.

HOW TO: Change Tracking Options

1. Click the **Tracking** launcher [*Review* tab, *Tracking* group] to open the *Track Changes Options* dialog box.
2. Click the **Advanced Options** button to open the *Advanced Track Changes Options* dialog box (Figure 9-20).
3. Click the **Insertions**, **Deletions**, **Changed lines**, **Comments**, or **Color** drop-down list and change the appearance as desired.
4. In the *Track moves* area, you can choose whether or not to track moves by selecting or deselecting the **Track moves** check box.
   - You can customize how *Moved from* and *Moved to* appear in your documents.
   - Also in this area, you can customize how *Inserted cells*, *Deleted cells*, *Merged cells*, and *Split cells* are tracked when changed.
5. In the *Track formatting* area, you can choose whether or not to track formatting changes by selecting or deselecting the **Track formatting** check box.
   - In this area, customize how formatting changes are tracked and how these changes appear in the *Markup* area.

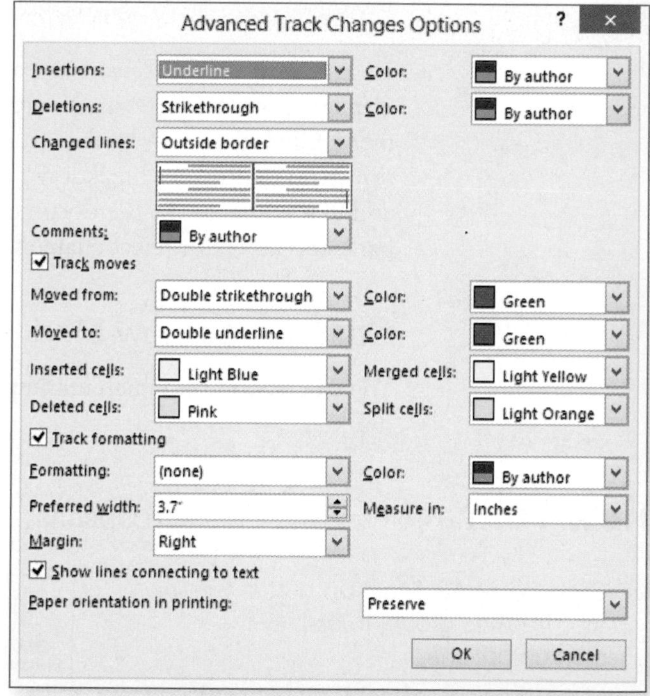

9-20 *Advanced Track Changes Options* dialog box

6. Check the **Show lines connecting to text** box to display a line connecting the formatting change displayed in the *Markup* area with the highlighted text in the document.
7. Click **OK** to close the *Advanced Track Changes Options* dialog box.
8. Click **OK** to close the *Track Changes Options* dialog box.

Lock Tracking

If you are working on a document with multiple people, you can ***Lock Tracking*** so other users cannot turn off *Track Changes* without a password. You can use this feature to ensure that all changes made to a document are tracked.

HOW TO: Lock Tracking

1. Click the bottom half of the **Track Changes** button [*Review* tab, *Tracking* group] and select **Lock Tracking**. The *Lock Tracking* dialog box opens (Figure 9-21).
2. Type a password in the *Enter password* text box.
   - If you don't type a password, users can turn off *Lock Tracking* without a password.
3. Type the same password in the *Reenter to confirm* text box.
4. Click **OK** to close the dialog box and lock tracking.

9-21 ***Lock Tracking*** **dialog box**

PAUSE & PRACTICE: WORD 9-1

For this Pause & Practice project, you work with two documents from Hamilton Civic Center. In the first document, you change user name and initials, add comments, and make revisions to the document using *Track Changes*. In the second document, you review tracked changes in the document, accept or reject them, and delete comments.

Files Needed: ***Yoga-09a.docx*** and ***Yoga-09b.docx***
Completed Project File Names: ***[your initials] PP W9-1a.docx*** and ***[your initials] PP W9-1b.docx***

1. Open the ***Yoga-09a*** document from your student data files.
2. Save the document as ***[your initials] PP W9-1a***.
3. Change user name and initials.
   a. Click the **Tracking** launcher [*Review* tab, *Tracking* group] to open the *Track Changes Options* dialog box.
   b. Click the **Change User Name** button to open the *Word Options* dialog box.
   c. In the *Personalize your copy of Microsoft Office*, type your first and last name in the *User name* text box.
   d. Type your first and last initials in lower-case letters in the *Initials* text box.
   e. Click **OK** to close the *Word Options* dialog box.
   f. Click **OK** to close the *Track Changes Options* dialog box.
4. Add comments to the document.
   a. Select "**Registered Yoga Teacher**" in the first paragraph.
   b. Click the **New Comment** button [*Review* tab, *Comments* group] to open a new comment (Figure 9-22).

through·the·*Learn·&·Participate*·program·at·Hamilton·Civic·
,·is·a·Registered·Yoga·Teacher·through·Yoga·Alliance.¶

Randy Nordell A few seconds ago
What·is·Amanda's·level·of·certification?¶

9-22 New comment inserted

c. In the new comment balloon, type What is Amanda's level of certification?
d. Select the first word in the last sentence of the last paragraph ("**We**").
e. Click the **New Comment** button and type Is this closing okay?

5. Turn on *Track Changes* and make revisions to the document.
   a. Click the top half of the **Track Changes** button [*Review* tab, *Tracking* group] to turn on track changes (or press **Ctrl+Shift+E**).
   b. Select the word "**lot**" in the first sentence of the first paragraph.
   c. Type variety to replace the selected word. Make sure there is a space after the word.
   d. Select and delete the first sentence in the last paragraph ("**Register at the front desk or by phone**").
   e. Type the following sentence as the first sentence in the last paragraph: Register at the front desk, by phone (615-822-4965), or online (www.hccenter.org). Make sure there is one space after the question mark.
   f. Delete the **comma** after "members" in the second sentence in the last paragraph.
6. Click the **Track Changes** button to turn off track changes.
7. Save and close the document (Figure 9-23).

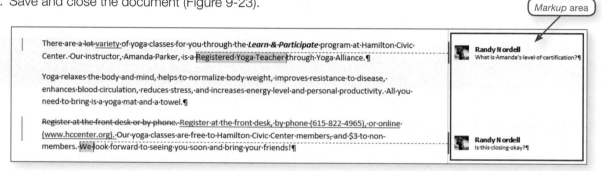

Markup area

There are a ~~lot~~ variety of yoga classes for you through the ***Learn & Participate*** program at Hamilton Civic Center. Our instructor, Amanda Parker, is a Registered Yoga Teacher through Yoga Alliance.¶

Yoga relaxes the body and mind, helps to normalize body weight, improves resistance to disease, enhances blood circulation, reduces stress, and increases energy level and personal productivity. All you need to bring is a yoga mat and a towel.¶

~~Register at the front desk or by phone.~~ Register at the front desk, by phone (615-822-4965), or online (www.hccenter.org). Our yoga classes are free to Hamilton Civic Center members~~,~~ and $3 to non-members. We look forward to seeing you soon and bring your friends!¶

Randy Nordell
What is Amanda's level of certification?¶

Randy Nordell
Is this closing okay?¶

9-23 PP W9-1a completed

8. Open the ***Yoga-09b*** document from your student data files.
9. Save the document as ***[your initials] PP W9-1b***.
10. Change *Display for Review* view.
    a. Click the **Display for Review** drop-down list [*Review* tab, *Tracking* group] and select **Original** to view the original document without changes (Figure 9-24).
    b. Click the **Display for Review** drop-down list again and select **No Markup** to view the final document with proposed changes applied.
    c. Click the **Display for Review** drop-down list again and select **Simple Markup** to view the document with proposed changes applied. A red line at the left indicates changes in the document.

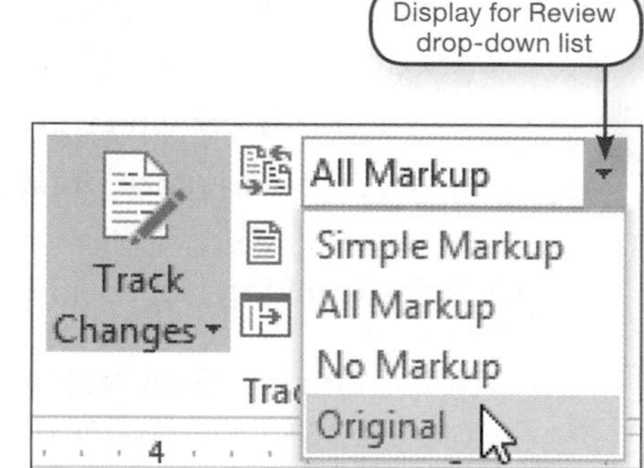

9-24 Change *Display for Review* view

    d. If the comment text displays in the balloons, click the **Show Comments** button [*Review* tab, *Comments* group] to hide comments. Only balloons display in the right margin.
    e. Click the **Display for Review** drop-down list again and select **All Markup** to view the final document with proposed changes visible inline and comments in balloons in the *Markup* area.
11. Turn on the *Reviewing* pane and reject changes.
    a. Click the **Reviewing Pane** drop-down arrow [*Review* tab, *Tracking* group] and select **Reviewing Pane Vertical**. The *Reviewing* pane is displayed on the left side of the Word window.
    b. In the *Reviewing* pane, find where "reduces stress," was inserted.

c. Right-click either "**Rachel Gonzalves Inserted**" or "**reduces stress**," and select **Reject Insertion** from the context menu (Figure 9-25).
d. In the *Reviewing* pane, find where "reduces stress," was deleted.
e. Right-click either "**Rachel Gonzalves Deleted**" or "**reduces stress**," and select **Reject Deletion** from the context menu.
f. Click the **X** in the upper right corner of the *Reviewing* pane to close it.

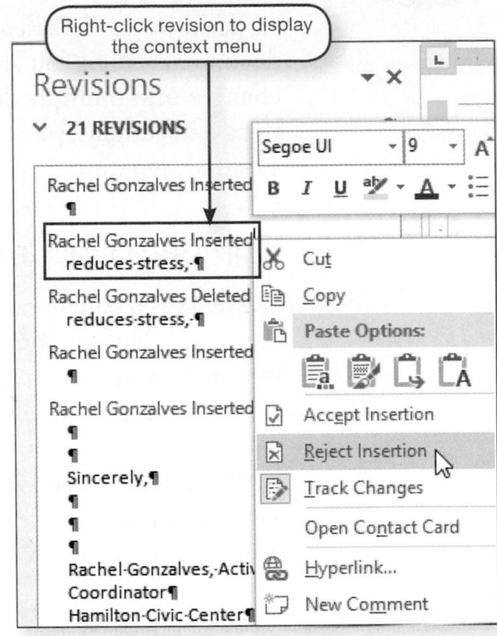

9-25 Reject an insertion in the *Reviewing* pane

12. Accept changes in the document.
    a. Move to the top of the document (**Ctrl+Home**).
    b. Click the **Next** button [*Review* tab, *Changes* group] to select the first change.
    c. Click the top half of the **Accept** button [*Review* tab, *Changes* group] to accept the change and move to the next change.
    d. Click the top half of the **Accept** button again to accept the change and move to the next change.
    e. Click the bottom half of the **Accept** button and select **Accept All Changes and Stop Tracking** from the drop-down list (Figure 9-26). All of the remaining changes in the document are accepted.

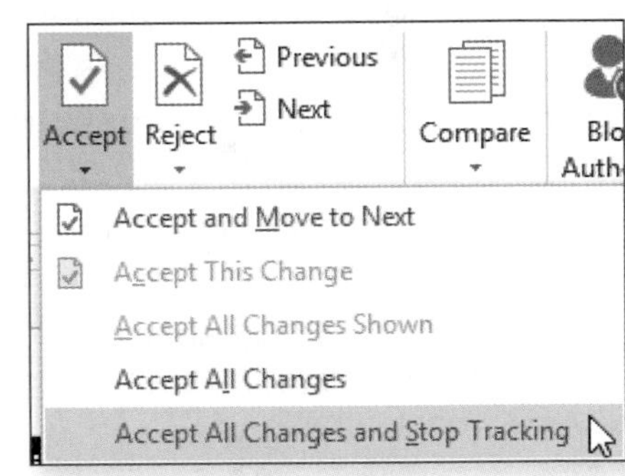

9-26 Accept all changes in the document

13. Delete comments in the document.
    a. Move to the top of the document and click the **Next** button [*Review* tab, *Comments* group] to move to the first comment.
    b. Click the top half of the **Delete** button [*Review* tab, *Comments* group] to delete the comment.
    c. Click the bottom half of the **Delete** button and select **Delete All Comments in Document** from the drop-down list to delete the remaining comments.
14. Save and close the document (Figure 9-27).

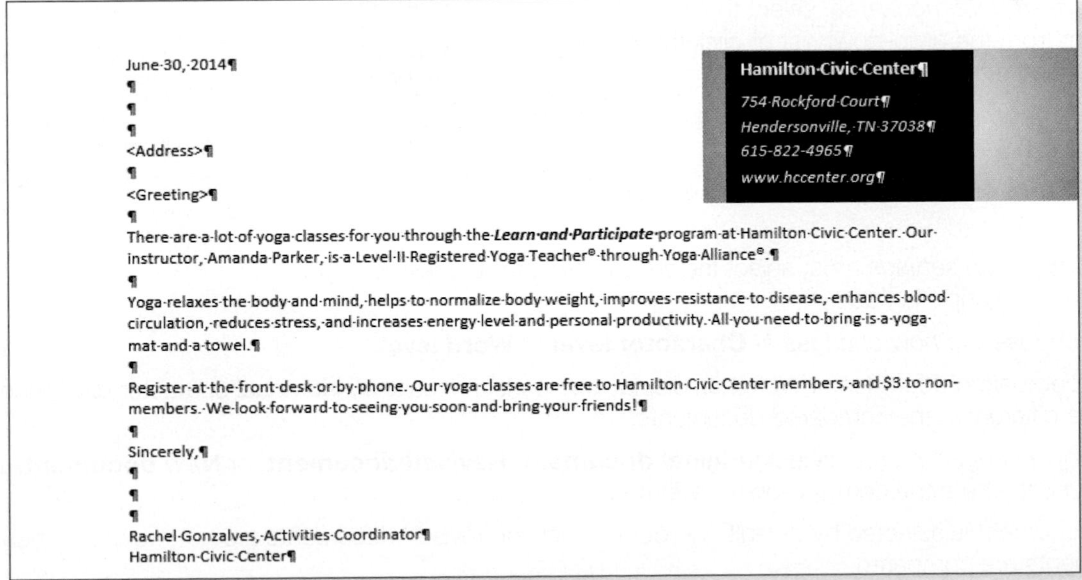

June 30, 2014

<Address>

<Greeting>

Hamilton Civic Center
754 Rockford Court
Hendersonville, TN 37038
615-822-4965
www.hccenter.org

There are a lot of yoga classes for you through the ***Learn and Participate*** program at Hamilton Civic Center. Our instructor, Amanda Parker, is a Level II Registered Yoga Teacher® through Yoga Alliance®.

Yoga relaxes the body and mind, helps to normalize body weight, improves resistance to disease, enhances blood circulation, reduces stress, and increases energy level and personal productivity. All you need to bring is a yoga mat and a towel.

Register at the front desk or by phone. Our yoga classes are free to Hamilton Civic Center members, and $3 to non-members. We look forward to seeing you soon and bring your friends!

Sincerely,

Rachel Gonzalves, Activities Coordinator
Hamilton Civic Center

9-27 PP W9-1b completed

SLO 9.3

Using Other Collaboration Features

In addition to *Comments* and *Track Changes*, Word has other features to help you manage documents when you are collaborating with others. For example, you can incorporate editing changes into multiple documents using the compare and combine features. Also, when finalizing a document, you can mark it as final, encrypt it with a password, restrict editing, and add a digital signature.

Compare Documents

Compare is a collaboration feature that compares the content of different versions of a document and displays the differences as changes that are marked with *Track Changes*. You can then review and accept or reject the tracked revisions. It is easiest to compare different versions of a document after changes have been accepted or rejected, but you can also compare documents that still have changes tracked.

When you use *Compare*, you compare an ***original document*** with a ***revised document***. You can customize which editing changes are compared, and the results of the comparison can be displayed in a new Word document, the original document, or the revised document.

HOW TO: Compare Documents

1. Click the **Compare** button [*Review* tab, *Compare* group] and select **Compare**. The *Compare Documents* dialog box opens (Figure 9-28).
   - If the documents you are comparing are open, make sure you save the documents before comparing.
2. In the *Original document* area, select the original document from the drop-down list or click the **Browse** button to locate the file.
   - When you click the **Browse** button, the *Open* dialog box opens where you can select a document.
3. In the *Revised document* area, select the revised document from the drop-down list or click the **Browse** button to locate the file.
4. In the *Label changes with* area, you can enter or change the reviewer name.
5. Click the **More** or **Less** button to display more or fewer settings.

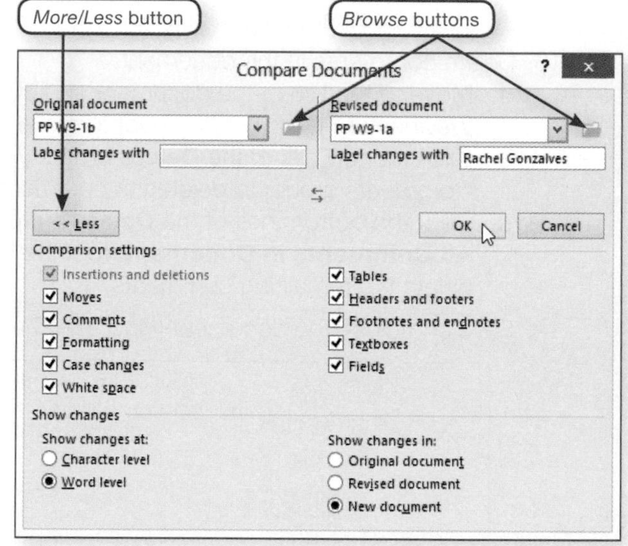

9-28 *Compare Documents* dialog box

6. In the *Comparison settings* area, select the check boxes for the revisions you want compared and marked.
7. You can choose to *Show changes at* **Character level** or **Word level**.
   - When comparing documents, Word can display comparison results by individual character differences or words that are different in the compared documents.
8. In the *Show changes in* area, select **Original document**, **Revised document**, or **New document**. This will be the document where the comparison is performed.
   - *New document* is selected by default, so your original and revised documents are not modified when documents are compared.

9. Click **OK** to close the dialog box and compare the documents.
   - If there are tracked changes in either document, a dialog box opens (Figure 9-29).

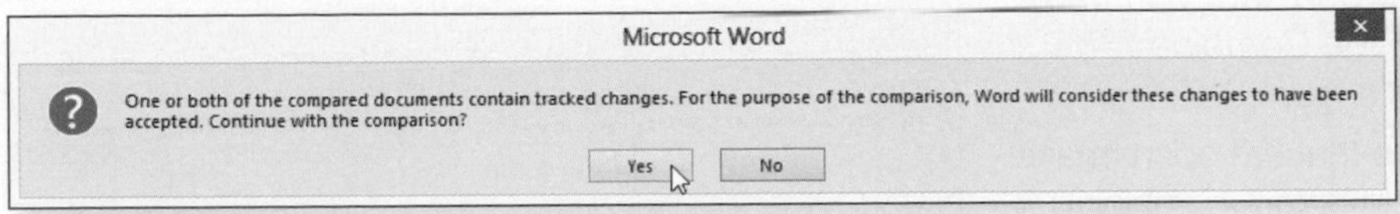

Microsoft Word
One or both of the compared documents contain tracked changes. For the purpose of the comparison, Word will consider these changes to have been accepted. Continue with the comparison?
Yes
No

9-29 Accept changes before comparing documents

   - Tracked changes in either document are accepted when the comparison is performed.
   - Click **Yes** to continue the comparison.
10. The differences between the two documents are displayed as tracked changes. You can accept or reject these proposed changes.
11. Save and close the compared document.

Show or Hide Source Documents

After comparing two documents, you can choose whether to show one or both of the source documents in the Word window or hide both source documents. If you show one or both source documents, they display to the right of the Word window. You can't edit the source documents when they are displayed in a compared document; they display for review only.

HOW TO: Show or Hide Source Documents

1. After comparing documents, the source documents may or may not display.
2. Click the **Compare** button [*Review* tab, *Compare* group].
3. Select **Show Source Documents** and select from one of the four options: **Hide Both Documents**, **Show Original**, **Show Revised**, or **Show Both** (Figure 9-30).
   - The last setting you choose applies the next time you compare documents.
   - If the source documents are displayed, click the **X** in the upper right corner to close the source document window.

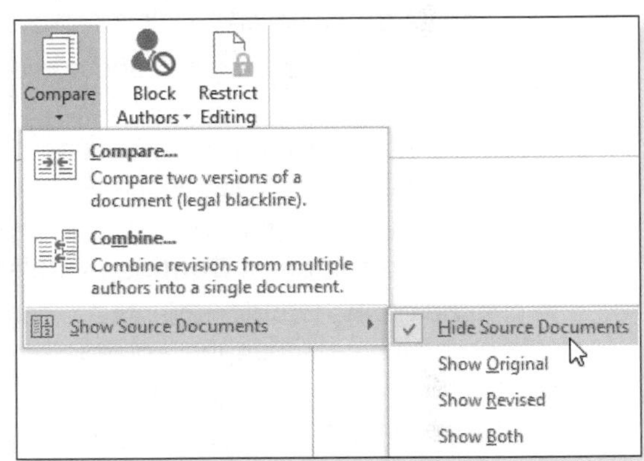

9-30 *Show Source Documents* options

> **MORE INFO**
>
> Showing or hiding source documents functions the same for both compared and combined documents.

Combine Documents

The ***Combine*** feature combines tracked changes from two documents into a single document. Whereas the *Compare* feature looks for just the *differences* between documents, the *Combine* feature incorporates *all* the changes that are tracked in both documents into one document. Once all the changes are incorporated, you can then accept or reject the changes in the combined document. You can combine all of the tracked changes in a new document, the original document, or the revised document.

HOW TO: Combine Documents

1. Click the **Compare** button [*Review* tab, *Compare* group] and select **Combine**. The *Combine Documents* dialog box opens (Figure 9-31).
   - When combining documents that are open, make sure you save the documents before combining.
2. In the *Original document* area, select the original document from the drop-down list or click the **Browse** button to locate the file.
3. In the *Revised document* area, select the revised document from the drop-down list or click the **Browse** button to locate the file.
4. In the *Label unmarked changes with* areas, you can change the reviewer name.
5. Click the **More** or **Less** button to display more or fewer settings.

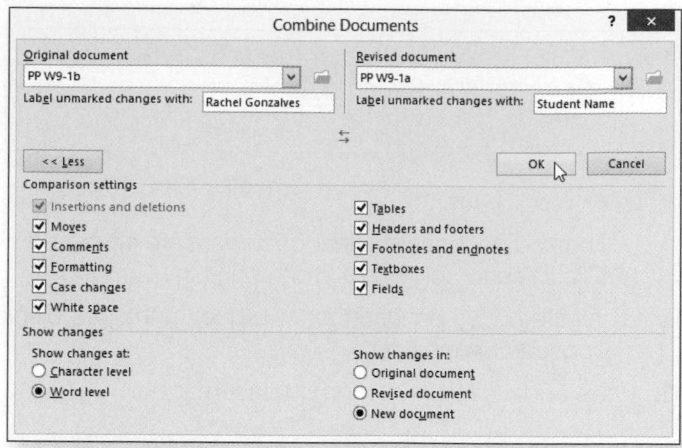

9-31 ***Combine Documents*** **dialog box**

6. In the *Comparison settings* area, select the revisions you want combined and marked.
7. You can choose to *Show changes* at **Character level** or **Word level**.
8. In the *Show changes in* area, select **Original document**, **Revised document**, or **New document**. This will be the document that will contain all the changes.
   - *New document* is selected by default, so your original and revised documents are not modified when documents are combined.
9. Click **OK** to close the dialog box and combine the documents.
   - If there are formatting changes in one or both documents, a dialog box opens asking you to select which formatting changes you want to keep (Figure 9-32).
   - Select the document that has the formatting changes you want to keep and press **Continue with Merge**.
10. The changes in the two documents are combined and displayed as tracked changes. You can accept or reject these proposed changes.
11. Save the document.

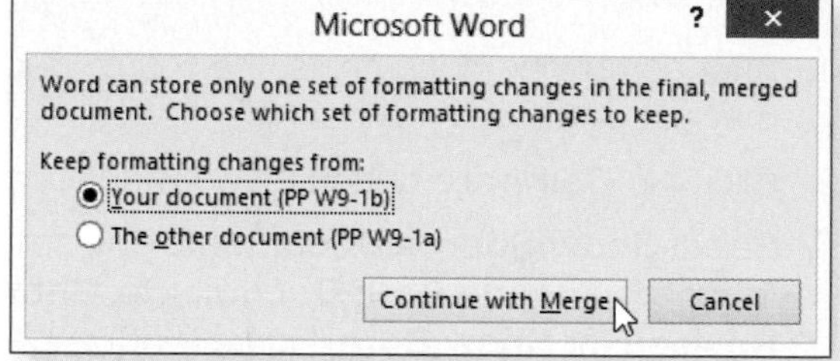

9-32 Keep formatting changes from a document

> **MORE INFO**
>
> You can compare and combine only two documents at a time. If there are multiple documents you are comparing or combining, you can perform this feature multiple times.

Check for Issues

When you are sharing a document with other users, Word provides you with tools to alert you to potential problems that might occur when the document is shared with and modified by multiple users. You can inspect your document, check accessibility, and check compatibility. All of these options are on the *Backstage* view (Figure 9-33).

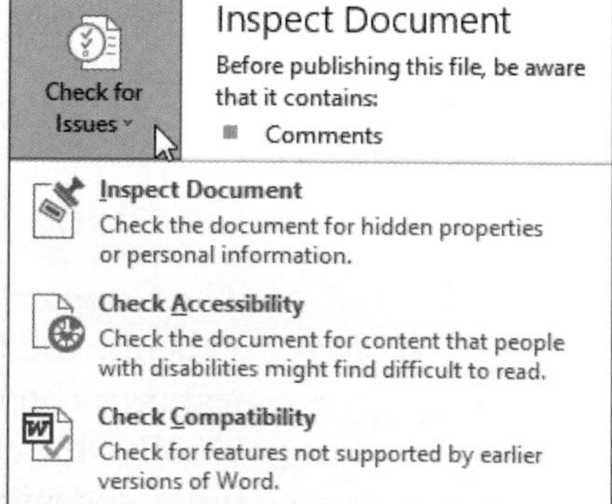

9-33 ***Check for Issues*** **on the** ***Backstage*** **view**

Inspect Document

The ***Inspect Document*** feature looks for hidden content, properties, or personal information that might create compatibility issues. When you use the *Inspect Document* feature, Word generates a report, and you can choose to remove properties or hidden information from your document before sharing with other users.

HOW TO: Inspect a Document

1. Click the **File** tab to open the *Info* area on the *Backstage* view.
2. Click the **Check for Issues** button and select **Inspect Document** from the drop-down list. The *Document Inspector* dialog box opens (Figure 9-34).
3. Select the document content you want to inspect.
   - All of the document content areas are selected by default.

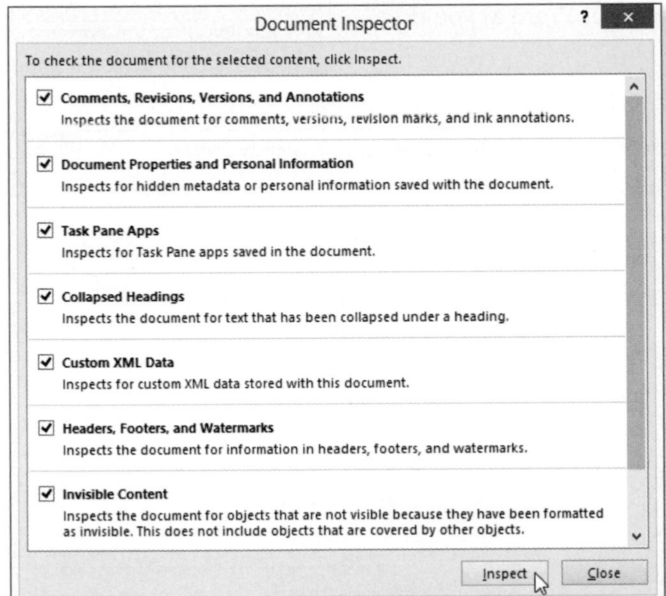

9-34 ***Document Inspector*** **dialog box**

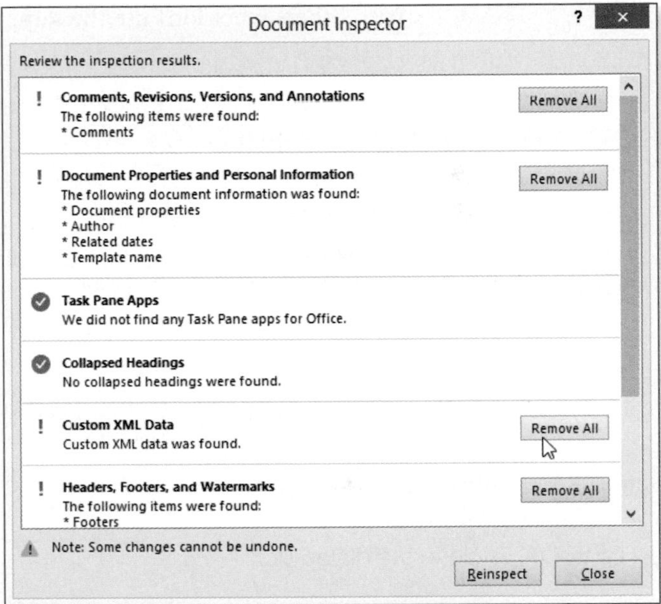

9-35 Document inspection results

4. Click **Inspect**. The inspection results appear in the *Document Inspector* dialog box (Figure 9-35).
5. Click the **Remove All** button if you want to remove information from your document.
6. Click the **Reinspect** button if you want to inspect the document again after you remove content.
7. Click the **Close** button to close the *Document Inspector* dialog box.

Check Accessibility

The ***Check Accessibility*** feature checks for potential issues that users with disabilities may have with your document. For example, users with visual impairments use document or screen readers to read the text in the document to them. Some objects in Word might cause problems for someone using a screen reader. The *Check Accessibility* feature alerts you to these potential issues and provides you with solutions in the ***Accessibility Checker pane***.

HOW TO: Check Accessibility

1. Click the **File** tab to open the *Backstage* view.
2. Click the **Check for Issues** button and select **Check Accessibility** from the drop-down list. The *Accessibility Checker* pane opens (Figure 9-36).
3. In the *Inspection Results* area, select one of the results.
   - In the *Additional Information* area, answers are provided to the questions *Why Fix* and *How to Fix*.
4. Click the **X** in the upper right corner to close the *Accessibility Checker* pane.

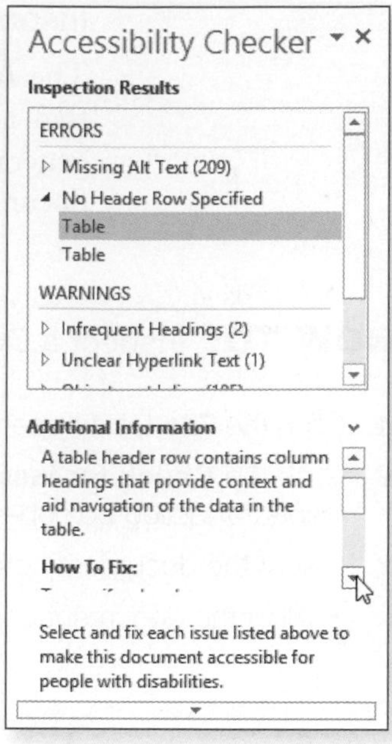

9-36 ***Accessibility Checker*** **pane**

Check Compatibility

The ***Check Compatibility*** feature looks for compatibility issues between the version of Word that you are using and older or newer versions. This feature is useful if you are sharing documents with others who don't use the same version of Word as you do.

HOW TO: Check Compatibility

1. Click the **File** tab to open the *Backstage* view.
2. Click the **Check for Issues** button and select **Check Compatibility** from the drop-down list. The *Microsoft Word Compatibility Checker* dialog box opens (Figure 9-37).
3. The *Summary* area displays potential compatibility issues.
   - Based on the summary, you can make changes in your document to deal with these potential issues.
4. Click the **Select versions to show** drop-down list to select Word versions as desired.
5. Click **OK** to close the dialog box.

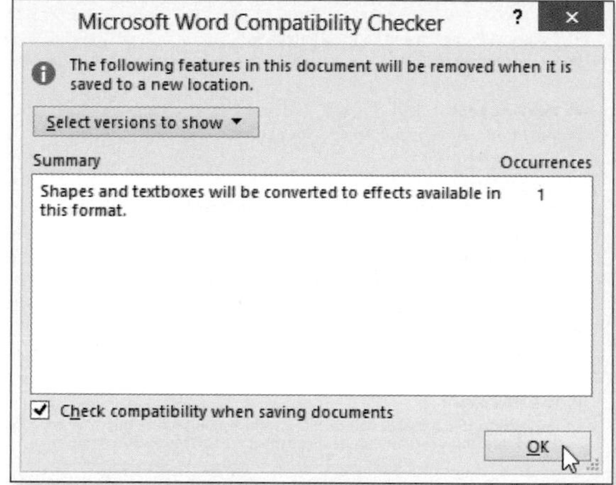

9-37 ***Microsoft Word Compatibility Checker*** **dialog box**

Protect Document

After you have shared your document and made editing changes, you might want to finalize and protect your document. You can mark a document as a final version, encrypt a document with a password, restrict editing and permissions, and add a digital signature. All of these options are available on the *Backstage* view (Figure 9-38).

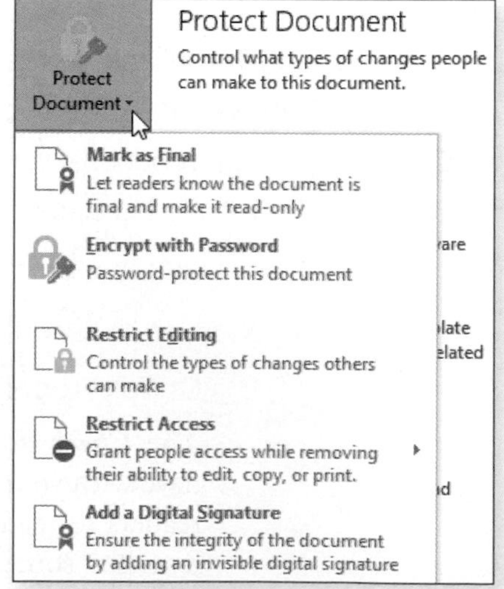

9-38 ***Protect Document*** **options**

Mark as Final

The ***Mark as Final*** feature marks a document as a final version and protects it from being edited. When a user opens a document that has been marked as final, the *Info* bar displays a message informing the user that the document has been marked as final.

HOW TO: Mark a Document as Final

1. Save the document before marking it as final.
2. Click the **File** tab to open the *Backstage* view.
3. Click the **Protect Document** button and select **Mark as Final** (see Figure 9-38).
4. Click **OK** in the dialog box that opens and informs you that the document will be marked as final and saved (Figure 9-39). Another dialog box opens.

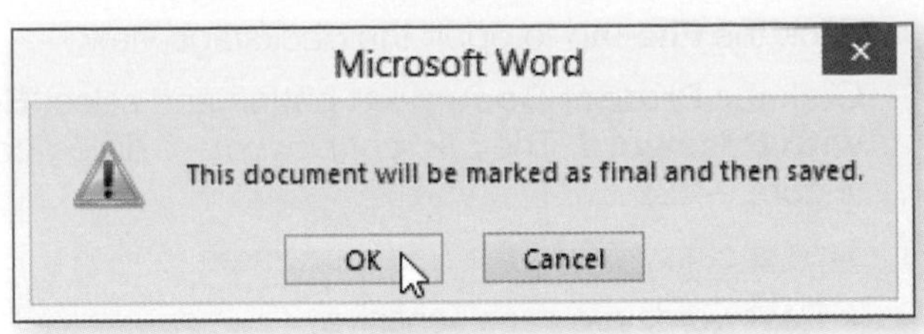

9-39 Confirm marked as final dialog box

5. Click **OK** in the dialog box that provides information about the final version (Figure 9-40).

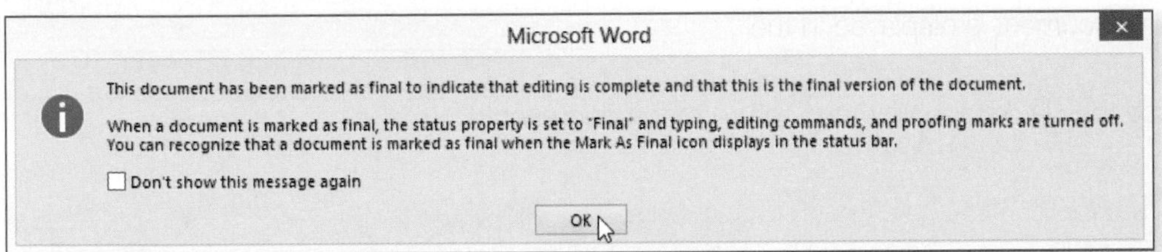

Microsoft Word
This document has been marked as final to indicate that editing is complete and that this is the final version of the document.
When a document is marked as final, the status property is set to "Final" and typing, editing commands, and proofing marks are turned off.
You can recognize that a document is marked as final when the Mark As Final icon displays in the status bar.
Don't show this message again
OK

9-40 Marked as final informational dialog box

- Select the **Don't show this message again** check box if you don't want this informational dialog box to appear again.
- On the *Backstage* view, a notation stating the document has been marked as final appears in the permissions area (Figure 9-41).

9-41 *Marked as Final* notation on the *Backstage* view

6. Click the **Back** arrow to close the *Backstage* view and return to the document.
7. The *Info* bar between the *Ribbon* and the *Ruler* displays a notation indicating that the document has been marked as final (Figure 9-42).

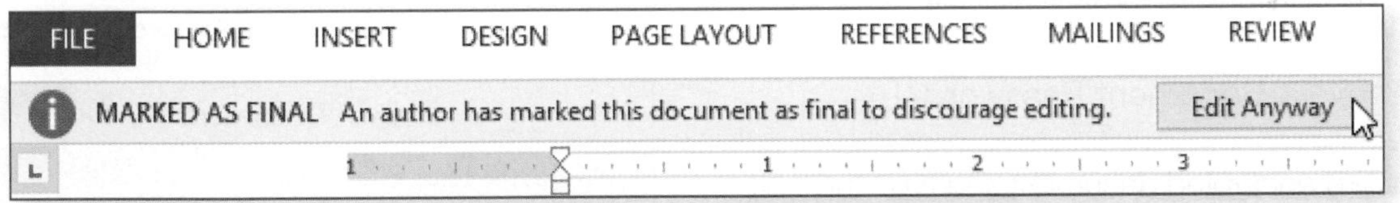

9-42 *Marked as Final* notation in the *Info* bar

- The *Ribbon* is collapsed and the document is protected from editing.

When a document is marked as final, users can still edit the document by turning off *Mark as Final*. There are two ways to turn off *Mark as Final*.

- Click the **Edit Anyway** button in the *Info* bar (see Figure 9-42).
- Click the **File** tab to open the *Backstage* view, click the **Protect Document** button, and select **Mark as Final**.

Encrypt with Password

You can protect a document from being opened and edited with the ***Encrypt with Password*** feature. When a document is encrypted with a password, a user is prompted to enter the password when opening the document.

HOW TO: Encrypt a Document with a Password

1. Click the **File** tab to open the *Backstage* view.
2. Click the **Protect Document** button and select **Encrypt with Password**. The *Encrypt Document* dialog box opens (Figure 9-43).
3. Type a password in the *Password* area.
   - Passwords are case sensitive.
4. Click **OK**. The *Confirm Password* dialog box opens.
5. Type the password in the *Reenter password* area and click **OK**.
   - On the *Backstage* view, a notation stating a password is required to open the document is displayed in the permissions area.
6. Click the **File** tab to close the *Backstage* view and return to the document.

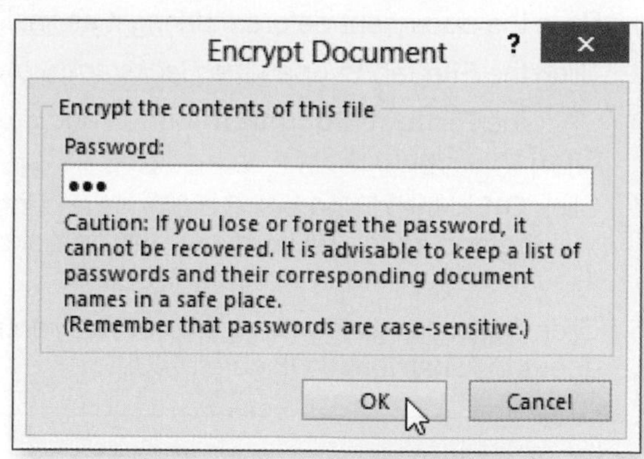

9-43 *Encrypt Document* dialog box

MORE INFO

Be sure to store document passwords in a secure location.

After you save and close the document, you are prompted to enter the password when reopening the document (Figure 9-44). Type the password in the dialog box and click **OK** to open the document.

You can remove a document password after you have opened a document that is encrypted with a password.

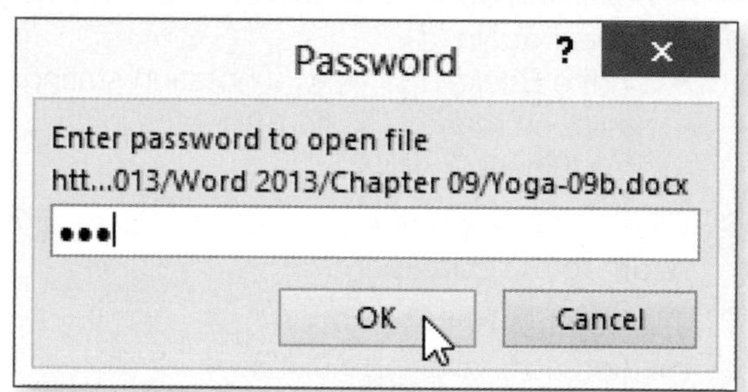

9-44 *Password* dialog box

HOW TO: Remove a Document Password

1. Open the password encrypted document and type the password to open the document.
2. Click the **File** tab to open the *Backstage* view.
3. Click the **Protect Document** button and select **Encrypt with Password**. The *Encrypt Document* dialog box opens (Figure 9-45).
4. Delete the password in the *Password* text box and leave this text box blank.
5. Click **OK** to close the dialog box and remove the password.

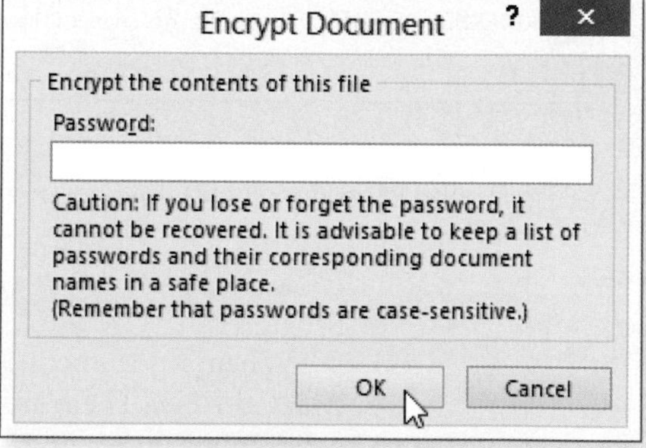

9-45 Remove a document password

Restrict Editing

Another way to protect a document is to ***restrict editing*** of a document. This feature lets you restrict what a user can do once a document is opened. Users can open the document without a password, but you control what they can and cannot change in the document. For example, you can restrict the editing of the entire document so the document becomes a read-only document, or you can allow users to add comments or use *Track Changes*.

HOW TO: Restrict Editing of a Document

1. Click the **File** tab to open the *Backstage* view.
2. Click the **Protect Document** button and select **Restrict Editing**. The *Restrict Editing* pane opens on the right side of the Word window (Figure 9-46).
3. Check the **Allow only this type of editing in the document** box in the *Editing restrictions* area.
4. Click the drop-down list and select what type of editing you wish to allow.
   - *No changes* restricts users from making any editing changes.
   - You can allow users to make *Tracked changes*, insert *Comments*, or allow *Filling in forms*.
5. Click the **Yes**, **Start Enforcing Protection** button. The *Start Enforcing Protection* dialog box opens (Figure 9-47).

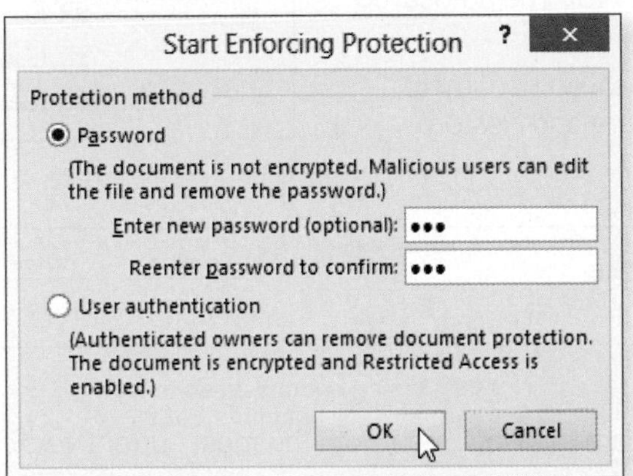

9-47 ***Start Enforcing Protection*** **dialog box**

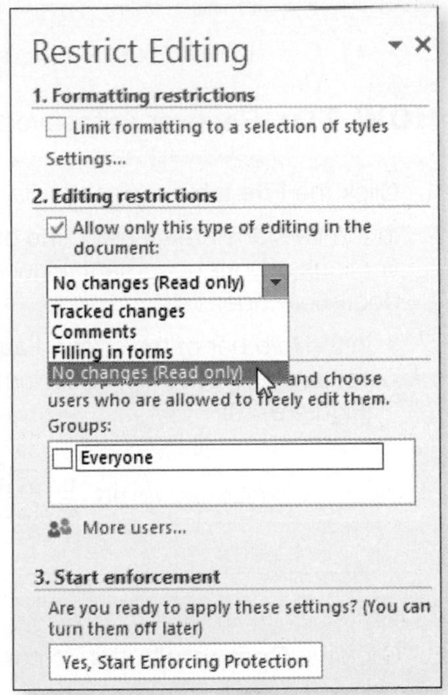

9-46 ***Restrict Editing*** **pane**

6. Select the **Password** radio button and enter and reenter the password.
   - Passwords are case sensitive.
   - Leave the password text boxes blank if you don't want a password to change restriction settings.
   - The *User authentication* option works with documents that are encrypted with a password and requires Information Rights Management (IRM) to be set up on your computer.
7. Click **OK** to close the dialog box and protect the document.
8. Click the **X** in the upper right corner of the *Restrict Editing* pane to close it.

You can remove restrictions on a document by clicking the **Stop Protection** button in the *Restrict Formatting and Editing* pane and entering the password.

Other Protect Document Settings

You also have the ability to restrict permission by people and add a digital signature to the document. Both of these features are useful when you are working with highly sensitive documents.

The ***Restrict Access*** feature lets you control users' access to a document as well as their ability to edit, copy, or print the document. To use this feature, you must set up Information Rights Management service on your computer and have a Window Live ID.

The ***Add a Digital Signature*** feature helps you ensure the integrity of a document by adding an invisible digital signature to the document. When you add a digital signature to your document, Word saves your document and marks it as final.

Manage Versions

When you are working on a document, Word automatically saves your document every 10 minutes. You can use these ***autosaved versions*** to recover previous information or a previous version of your document if your computer crashes. The different saved versions of your document are available in the *Versions* area in the *Backstage* view.

HOW TO: Recover Autosaved Versions of a Document

1. Click the **File** tab to open the *Backstage* view.
2. In the *Versions* area, select one of the autosaved versions of your document (Figure 9-48). The autosaved document opens.
   - In the *Info* bar of the opened autosaved document, you are given two options: *Compare* and *Restore* (Figure 9-49).

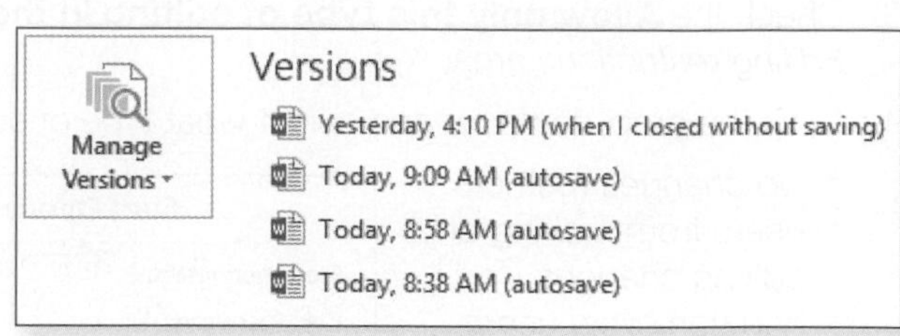

9-48 Autosaved versions of your document

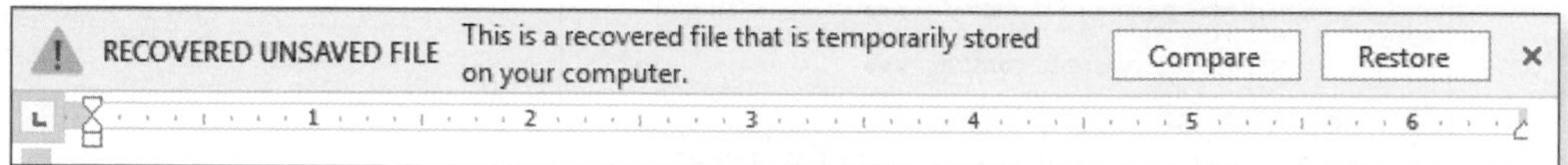

9-49 Version options on an autosaved document

3. Click the **Compare** button to compare this document with the most current version of the document.
   - A new document automatically opens with the most current version of your document so you can compare it to the previous version you have selected.
4. Click **Restore** to revert to a previous version of the document. A dialog box opens informing you that you are about to overwrite the last saved version of the document (Figure 9-50).
   - Click **OK** to overwrite the last saved version.

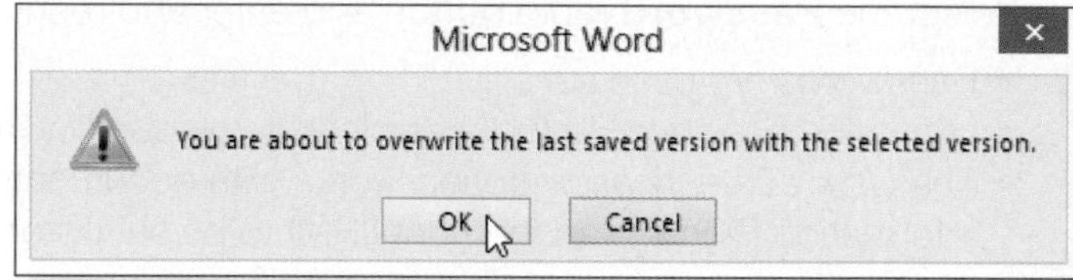

9-50 Overwrite most recent version with previous version

MORE INFO

You can customize the frequency of autosave in the *Save* area of the *Word Options* dialog box.

PAUSE & PRACTICE: WORD 9-2

For this Pause & Practice project, you combine the two documents from *Pause & Practice 9-1* into a new document. You inspect the new document, check compatibility, restrict editing, encrypt the document with a password, and mark it as final.

Files Needed: ***[your initials] PP W9-1a.docx*** and ***[your initials] PP W9-1b.docx***
Completed Project File Name: ***[your initials] PP W9-2.docx***

1. Open a new blank Word document.
2. Combine documents.
   a. Click the **Compare** button [*Review* tab, *Compare* group] and select **Combine**. The *Combine Documents* dialog box opens (Figure 9-51).
   b. In the *Original document* area, click the **Browse** button, select the ***[your initials] PP W9-1b*** document, and click **Open** to select the document.
   c. In the *Original document* area in the *Label unmarked changes with* text box, type Rachel Gonzalves.
   d. In the *Revised document* area, click the **Browse** button, select the ***[your initials] PP W9-1a*** document, and click **Open** to select the document.
   e. In the *Revised document* area in the *Label unmarked changes with* text box, type your name.
   f. Click the **More** button (if it is available) to display more settings options.
   g. In the *Comparison settings* area, make sure all check boxes are selected.
   h. In the *Show changes at* area, click the **Word level** radio button.
   i. In the *Show changes in* area, click the **New document** radio button.
   j. Click **OK** to close the dialog box and combine the documents into a new document. A dialog box opens prompting you to keep the formatting changes from one of the documents (Figure 9-52).
   k. Select the **Your document (PP W9-1b)** radio button and click **Continue with Merge**. The two documents are combined in a new Word document.

9-51 ***Combine Documents*** **dialog box**

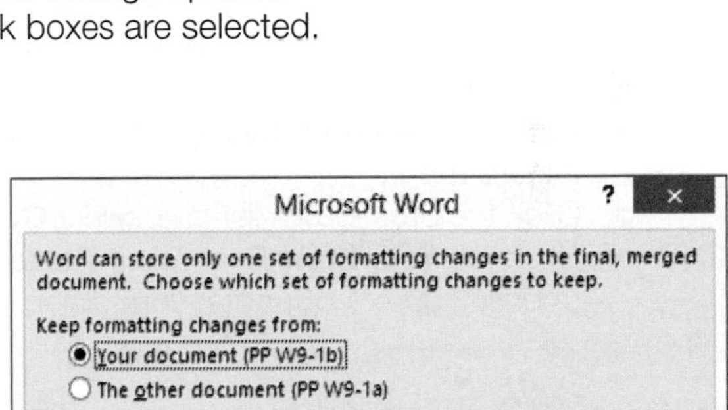

9-52 **Keep formatting changes from a document**

3. Save the combined document and hide source documents.
   a. Save this combined document as ***[your initials] PP W9-2***.
   b. If the source documents are displayed on the right, click the **Compare** button, select **Show Source Documents**, and select **Hide Source Documents**.
4. Accept changes and delete comments.
   a. Move to the top of the document (**Ctrl+Home**).
   b. Click the **Next** button [*Review* tab, *Changes* group] to move to the first tracked change in the document.
   c. Click the top half of the **Accept** button [*Review* tab, *Changes* group] to accept the change and move to the next change.
   d. Click the bottom half of the **Accept** button and select **Accept All Changes and Stop Tracking** to accept the remaining changes in the document and turn off *Track Changes*.
   e. Click the bottom half of the **Delete** button [*Review* tab, *Comments* group] and select **Delete All Comments in Document** to delete all comments.
   f. Save the document.
5. Inspect the document.
   a. Click the **File** tab to open the *Backstage* view.
   b. Click the **Check for Issues** button and select **Inspect Document** to open the *Document Inspector* dialog box.

c. Deselect the **Document Properties and Personal Information** check box.
d. Click **Inspect**. The *Document Inspector* dialog box opens with the inspection results displayed (Figure 9-53).
e. Click **Remove All** in the *Custom XML Data* area.
f. Click **Close** to close the dialog box and click the **Back** button to return to the document.
g. Save the document.

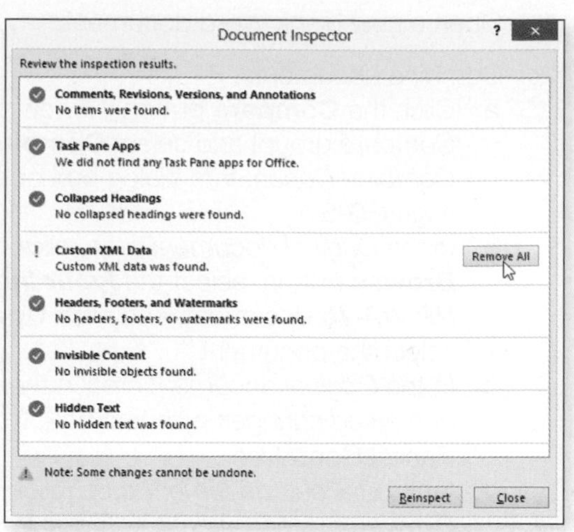

9-53 ***Document Inspector*** **with inspection results displayed**

6. Check the compatibility of the document.
   a. Click the **File** tab to open the *Backstage* view.
   b. Click the **Check for Issues** button and select **Check Compatibility**. The *Microsoft Word Compatibility Checker* dialog box opens.
   c. Review the compatibility issues.
   d. Click **OK** to close the dialog box.
7. Restrict editing of the document.
   a. Click the **File** tab to open the *Backstage* view.
   b. Click the **Protect Document** button and select **Restrict Editing**. The *Restrict Editing* pane appears on the right.
   c. Check the **Allow only this type of editing in the document** box in the *Editing restrictions* area (Figure 9-54).
   d. Click the drop-down list and select **Comments**.
   e. Click the **Yes, Start Enforcing Protection** button. The *Start Enforcing Protection* dialog box opens (Figure 9-55; note: your dialog box might appear slightly different).

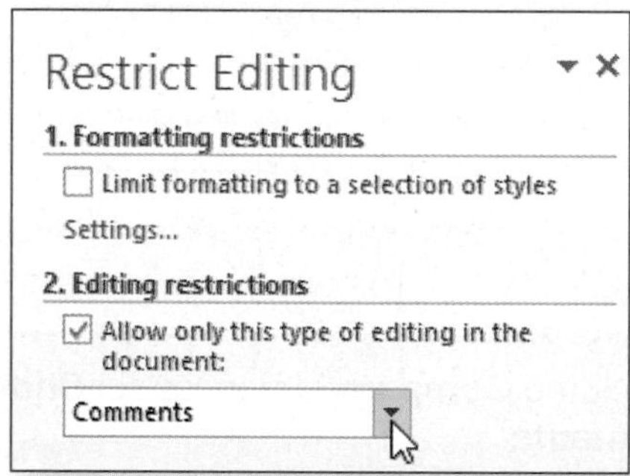

9-54 Restrict editing to only comments

9-55 Set protection password

   f. Select the **Password** radio button.
   g. In the *Enter new password* area, type HCC.
   h. In the *Reenter password to confirm* area, type HCC.
   i. Click **OK** to close the dialog box.
   j. Close the *Restrict Editing* pane.
8. Encrypt the document with a password and mark the document as final.
   a. Click the **File** tab to open the *Backstage* view.
   b. Click the **Protect Document** button and select **Encrypt with Password**. The *Encrypt Document* dialog box opens.
   c. Type HCC in the *Password* text box and click **OK**. The *Confirm Password* dialog box opens.
   d. Type HCC in the *Reenter password* text box and click **OK**.
   e. On the *Backstage* view, click the **Protect Document** button and select **Mark as Final**.

f. Click **OK** in the dialog box that informs you that the document will be marked as final and saved.
g. Click **OK** to close the next informational dialog box.
h. Click the **Back** arrow to close the *Backstage* view and return to the document.

9. Close the document (Figure 9-56).

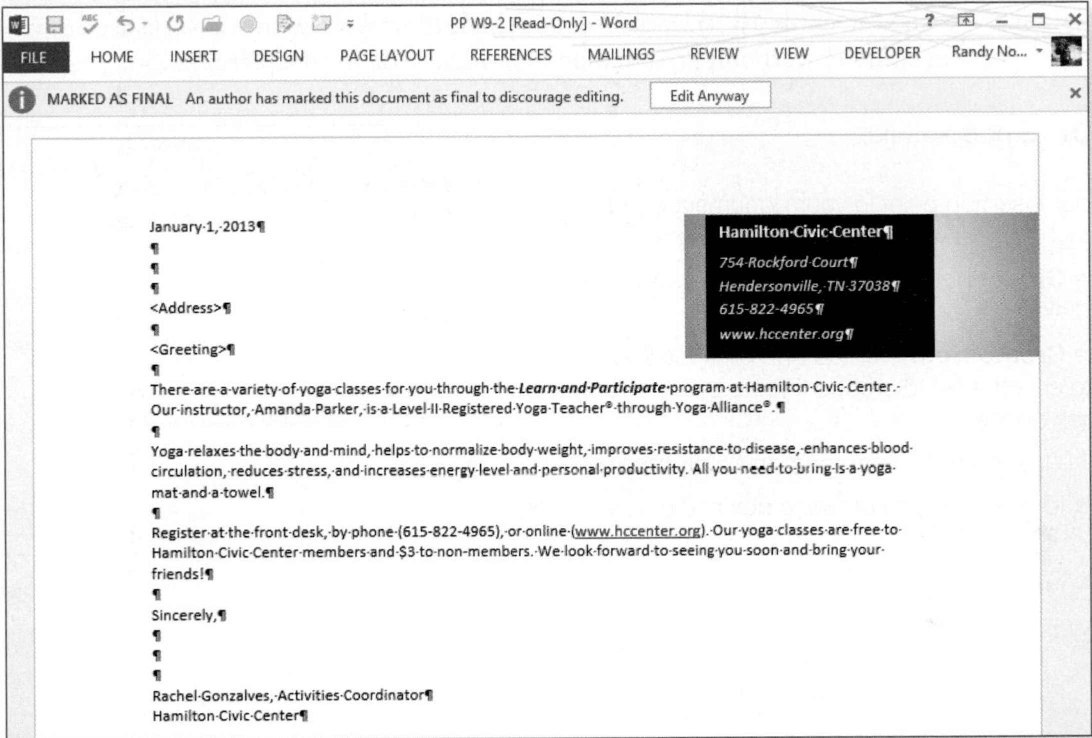

PP W9-2 [Read-Only] - Word
FILE HOME INSERT DESIGN PAGE LAYOUT REFERENCES MAILINGS REVIEW VIEW DEVELOPER Randy No...
MARKED AS FINAL An author has marked this document as final to discourage editing.
Edit Anyway
January 1, 2013
<Address>
<Greeting>
There are a variety of yoga classes for you through the Learn and Participate program at Hamilton Civic Center. Our instructor, Amanda Parker, is a Level II Registered Yoga Teacher® through Yoga Alliance®.
Yoga relaxes the body and mind, helps to normalize body weight, improves resistance to disease, enhances blood circulation, reduces stress, and increases energy level and personal productivity. All you need to bring is a yoga mat and a towel.
Register at the front desk, by phone (615-822-4965), or online (www.hccenter.org). Our yoga classes are free to Hamilton Civic Center members and $3 to non-members. We look forward to seeing you soon and bring your friends!
Sincerely,
Rachel Gonzalves, Activities Coordinator
Hamilton Civic Center
Hamilton Civic Center
754 Rockford Court
Hendersonville, TN 37038
615-822-4965
www.hccenter.org

9-56 PP W9-2 completed

SLO 9.4

Integrating Office Applications

A powerful feature of Microsoft Office 2013 is its ability to integrate information between the different applications. For example, you can use data from an Excel worksheet in a Word document or PowerPoint presentation, export data from an Access database to use in an Excel worksheet or Word document, or insert slides from a PowerPoint presentation into a Word document.

Object Linking and Embedding

Object linking and embedding, also known as ***OLE,*** refers to Microsoft Office's ability to share information between the different Microsoft Office applications. There is some terminology that is important to know when using *OLE*:

- ***Source program:*** The Office application where the content was created.
- ***Destination program:*** The Office application where the object is inserted.
- ***Source file:*** The file where the content is stored.
- ***Destination file:*** The file where the object is inserted.

When you are using *OLE* to insert content from an Office application into a Word document, you insert the content as an object and you can modify it in the Word document. There are two different ways to insert content from one application into another: ***embedding*** and ***linking***.

Embed an Object

Embedding inserts an object from one application into another. You can modify the object in the destination file independently of the source file. Use embedding when the source and destination files do not need to remain the same.

When you embed an object into a Word document, the object retains the formatting from the source program. You can embed an entire file or a portion of a file. For example, you can embed an entire Excel worksheet or a single chart from within a worksheet, or you can embed an entire PowerPoint presentation or a single slide from a presentation.

HOW TO: Embed a File

1. Place your insertion point in your document at the location where you want to insert the embedded file.
2. Click the **Object** button [*Insert* tab, *Text* group]. The *Object* dialog box opens.
3. Click the **Create from File** tab and click the **Browse** button to select a file to embed (Figure 9-57). The *Browse* dialog box opens.
4. Select the file you want to embed and click **Insert**.
5. Click **OK** to close the *Object* dialog box and embed the file.

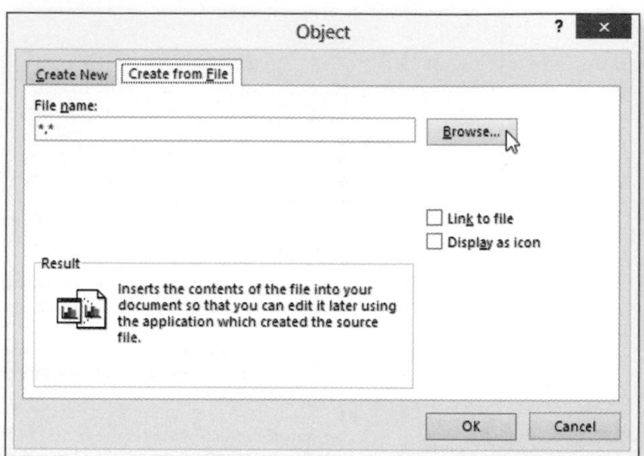

9-57 *Object* dialog box

> **MORE INFO**
>
> Be careful when embedding entire files because the destination file can become very large.

Usually when you embed an object into a Word document, you embed a portion of the document, such as a chart from an Excel worksheet or a slide from a PowerPoint presentation. When you are embedding a portion of a document, you copy the portion of the document to embed and then use the ***Paste Special dialog box*** to control how the object is inserted into the document. With this method, you can select the file format of the object you are embedding into the destination file.

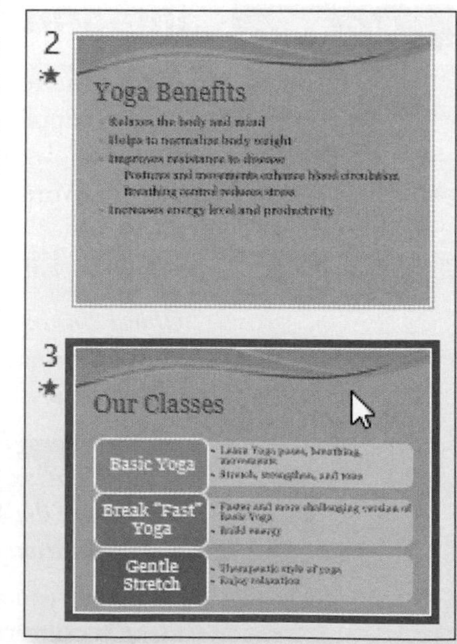

9-58 Copy object in file to embed

HOW TO: Embed an Object in a Document

1. Open the source file.
   - Use the source program to open the file or open the file from the Windows folder, which opens the source program and file.
2. Select the portion of the document you want to embed as an object (Figure 9-58).
   - If you are selecting a chart, make sure you select the chart area.
   - If you are selecting a PowerPoint slide, select the entire slide.
3. Copy the selected information.
4. Close the source file and program.

5. Place your insertion point in the destination file where you want to insert the embedded object.
6. Click the bottom half of the **Paste** button [*Home* tab, *Clipboard* group] and select **Paste Special** (Figure 9-59). The *Paste Special* dialog box opens (Figure 9-60).

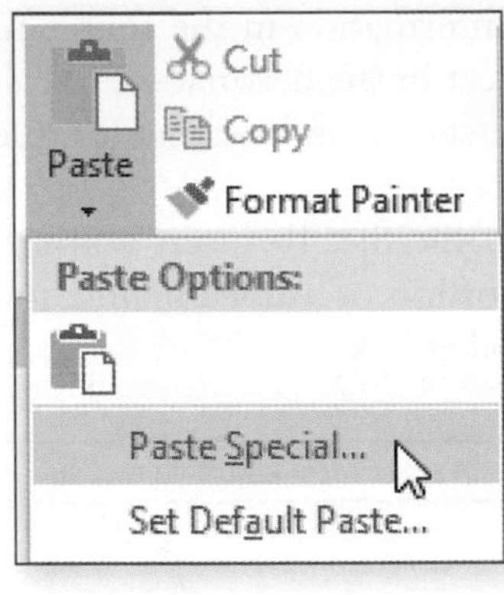

9-59 Open the *Paste Special* dialog box

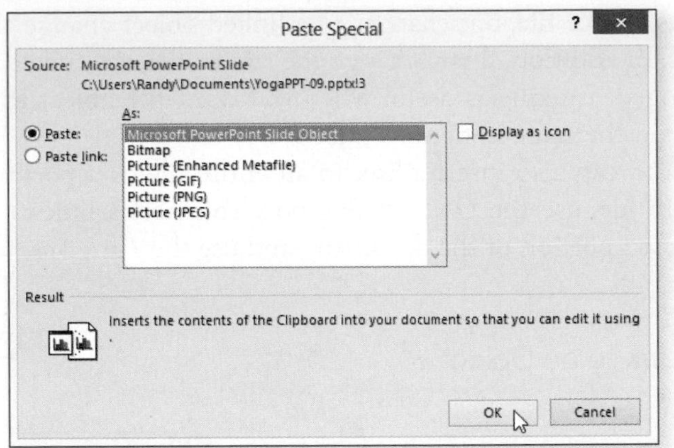

9-60 *Paste Special* dialog box

7. Select the **Paste** radio button.
8. In the *As* area, select the file type.
   - If you select the source program file type, the object retains the connection with the source program and you can edit the object. See the next section for information about modifying an embedded object.
   - If you choose a different file type, such as a *Picture* or *Microsoft Office Graphic Object*, the object does not retain connection with the source program, but rather connects to the destination program. You can edit this type of embedded object as you would a picture or graphic in Word.
9. Click **OK** to close the *Paste Special* dialog box and embed the object in the destination file.

> **ANOTHER WAY**
> **Alt+Ctrl+V** opens the *Paste Special* dialog box.

Modify an Embedded Object

You modify an embedded object similarly to how you modify other graphic objects in Word. The file type you select when you embed an object determines how the object is edited. For example, if you select the source program as the file type for the embedded object, the object retains the connection to the source program and you edit it using the *Ribbon* from the source program. When you double-click the object, the *Ribbon* and tabs from the source program open in Word. You use these to modify the embedded object.

If you select a different file type for the embedded object, such as a picture or Microsoft Office Object, you edit the object using the contextual tabs in Word associated with the object type you choose.

HOW TO: Modify an Embedded Object

1. Select the embedded object to open the contextual tab(s) associated with the object.
   - If the object is connected with the source program, double-click the object to open the *Ribbon* from the source program.
2. Modify the size, text wrapping, and arrangement of the object as desired.
   - On some objects, you can also edit the elements within the object.
3. Click outside of the object area to deselect it.

Link an Object

Linking inserts an object from one application into another and creates a link between the object in the source and destination files. An embedded object can be edited independently of its source file, but changes to a linked object change the information in the source file as well. In addition, if you change the source file, the linked object in the destination file is also changed. Linking is useful when you want the object in the source and destination files to remain the same in both locations.

You can also insert a link to an entire file or a portion of the file. To insert a link to an entire file, use the *Object* dialog box. To insert a link to a portion of a document, copy the selected portion of the document, and use the *Paste Special* dialog box.

HOW TO: Create a Link to an Object

1. Open the source file.
   - Use the source program to open the file or open the file from the Windows folder, which opens the source program and file.
2. Select the portion of the document you want to link as an object (Figure 9-61).
   - If you are selecting a chart, click the chart frame to select the *Chart Area*.
   - If you are selecting a PowerPoint slide, select the entire slide by clicking on a slide thumbnail in the *Navigation* area on the left.
3. Copy the selected information.
4. Close the source file and program.
5. Place your insertion point in the destination file at the location where you want the linked object inserted.
6. Click the bottom half of the **Paste** button [*Home* tab, *Clipboard* group] and select **Paste Special**. The *Paste Special* dialog box opens (Figure 9-62).
7. Select the **Paste link** radio button.
8. In the *As* area, select the file type.
   - All file types remain linked to the source file.
9. Click **OK** to close the *Paste Special* dialog box and insert the linked object in the destination file.

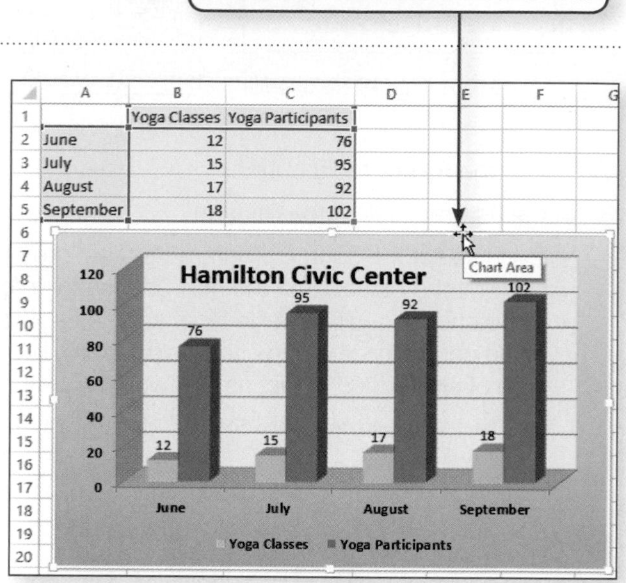

9-61 Select object to link

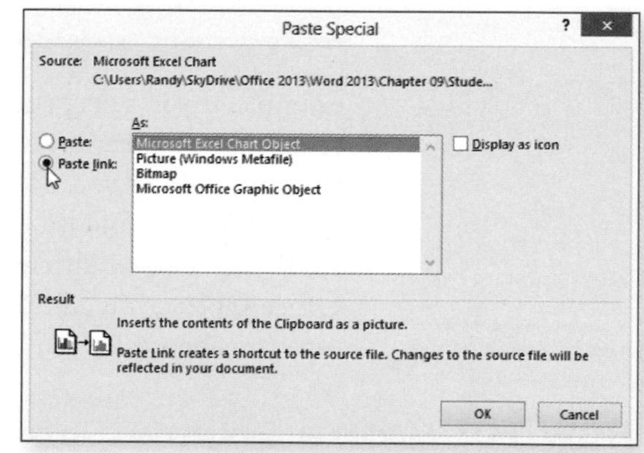

9-62 *Paste link* in the *Paste Special* dialog box

ANOTHER WAY

When embedding or linking an object, you can select from one of the *Paste Options* available in the *Paste* drop-down list or context menu.

Modify a Linked Object

When you open a document containing one or more links, you are prompted to update the links in the document. A dialog box opens informing you that there are links in the document and asking if you want to update the links (Figure 9-63). Click **Yes** to update the links.

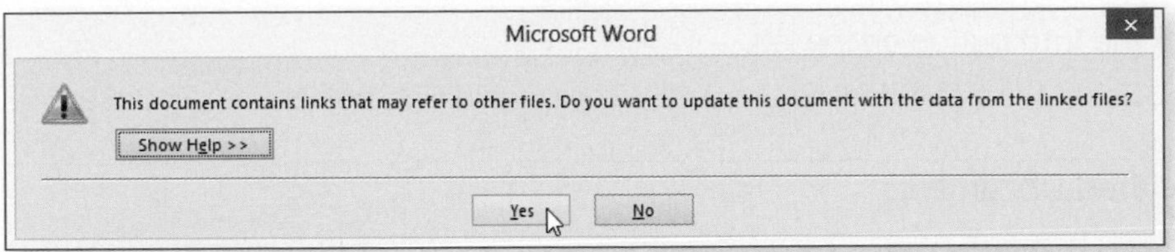

Microsoft Word
This document contains links that may refer to other files. Do you want to update this document with the data from the linked files?
Show Help >>
Yes
No

9-63 Update links in the document

You can modify the size, text wrapping, and arrangement of a linked object in the same way you modify other graphic objects. In addition, you can modify the content of the linked object, modify the links in the document, or break the link between the linked object and the source file.

Modify Linked Object Content

A linked object in a Word document is directly linked to the source file. When you edit the linked object, the source file opens where you can make changes. After you save the source file, you update the linked object to reflect the current data from the source file.

HOW TO: Modify Linked Object Content

1. Double-click the linked object to open the source program and file.
   - You can also right-click the linked object, select **Linked "object type" Object**, and select **Edit Link** or **Open Link** to open the source program and file (Figure 9-64).
2. Make changes to the source file.
3. Save and close the source file.
   - Because both files are open, the linked object is updated. If the linked object does not update, right-click the linked object and select **Update Link** from the context menu.

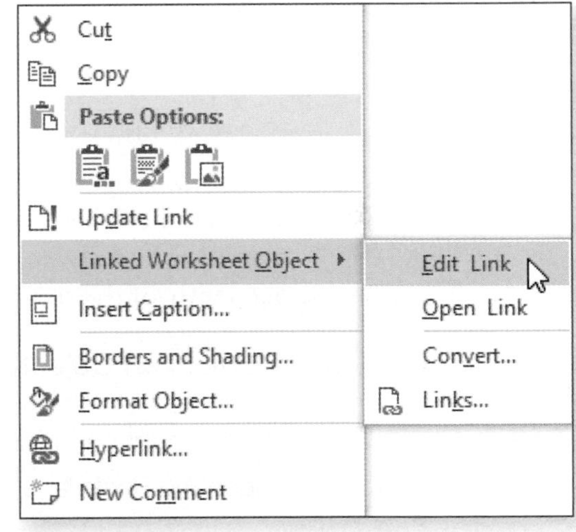

9-64 Edit a link from the context menu

You can also make changes to the source file if the destination file is not open. In that case, the next time you open the destination file with the linked object, you will be prompted to update the linked objects in the document.

Modify a Link to an Object

When you have a linked object in a document, the linked object is linked to the source file on your computer. If you change the location of the source or destination file, the link becomes corrupted and Word cannot find the source file to update the linked object in the destination file. If you want to continue to link to a file you have moved, you can edit the link to the files using the ***Links dialog box***.

HOW TO: Modify a Link

1. Open the destination file.
   - When you are prompted to update links in the document, click **Yes** to update links.
2. Click the **File** tab to open the *Backstage* view.
3. Click the **Info** button on the left.
4. Click **Edit Links to Files** (Figure 9-65). The *Links* dialog box opens (Figure 9-66).

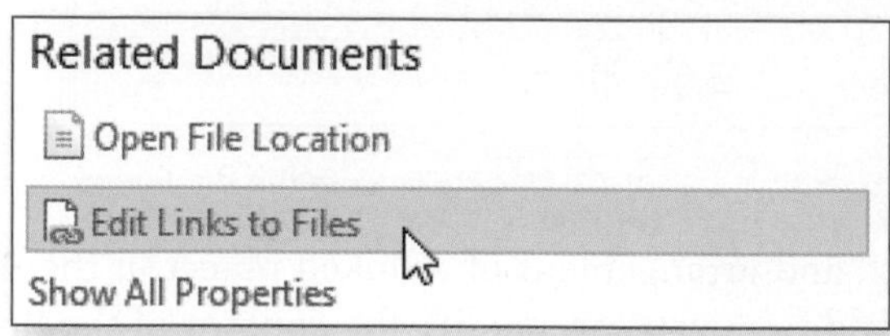

9-65 *Edit Links to Files* on the *Backstage* view

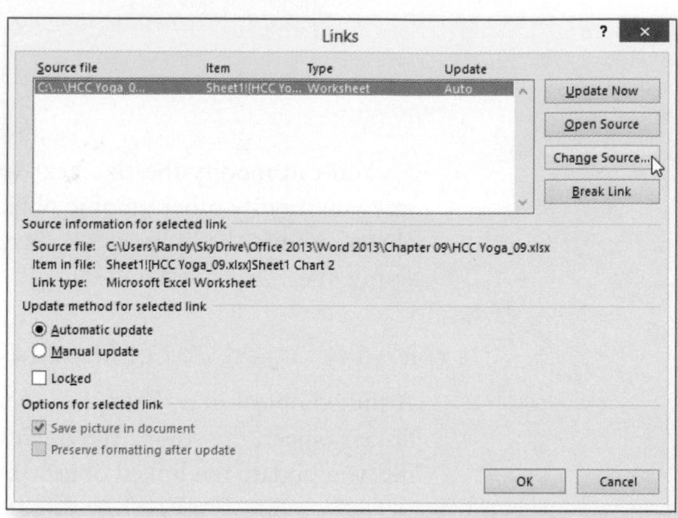

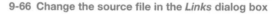

9-66 Change the source file in the *Links* dialog box

5. In the *Source file* area, select the source file of the linked object.
   - If you have multiple linked objects in a document, there will be multiple source files listed in the *Source file* area.
6. Click the **Change Source** button to open the *Change Source* dialog box.
7. Select the source file for the linked objects and click **Open** to close the *Change Source* dialog box.
8. Click **OK** to close the *Links* dialog box.
9. Click the **Back** arrow to return to the document.

Break a Link to an Object

If you no longer want a linked object connected to the source file, you can break the link between them. When you do this, the linked object is converted to an embedded object and is no longer directly linked to the source file. The embedded object can then be modified independently of the source file.

HOW TO: Break a Link to an Object

1. Open the destination file containing the linked object.
2. Click the **File** tab to open the *Backstage* view.
3. Click the **Info** button on the left.
4. Click **Edit Links to Files** (see Figure 9-65). The *Links* dialog box opens (see Figure 9-66).
5. In the *Source file* area, select the source file of the linked object.
   - If you have multiple linked objects in a document, there will be multiple source files listed in the *Source file* area.
6. Click the **Break Link** button. A dialog box opens asking if you want to break the selected link (Figure 9-67).
7. Click **Yes**. The *Links* dialog box closes automatically.
8. Click the **Back** arrow to return to the document.

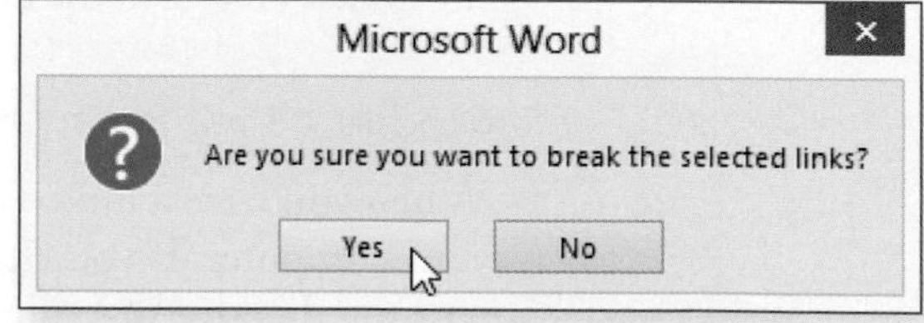

9-67 Confirm breaking links

ANOTHER WAY

Right-click a linked object, select **Linked "object type" Object**, and then select **Links** to open the *Links* dialog box.

PAUSE & PRACTICE: WORD 9-3

For this Pause & Practice project, you modify the document from *Pause & Practice 9-2*. You remove the document password and protection, insert a PowerPoint slide as an embedded object, modify the embedded object, insert an Excel chart as a linked object, and modify the linked object.

Files Needed: ***[your initials] PP W9-2.docx***, ***YogaPPT-09.pptx***, and ***HCCYoga-09.xlsx***
Completed Project File Name: ***[your initials] PP W9-3.docx***

1. Open the ***[your initials] PP W9-2*** document you saved in *Pause & Practice 9-2*.
2. Type HCC when prompted to enter a password and press **OK**. The open document is marked as final.
3. Click the **Edit Anyway** button on the *Info* bar to turn off *Mark as Final*.
4. Save the document as ***[your initials] PP W9-3***.
5. Remove the document encryption password and disable restrict editing.
   a. Click the **File** tab to open the *Backstage* view.
   b. Click the **Protect Document** button and select **Encrypt with Password** to open the *Encrypt Document* dialog box (Figure 9-68).
   c. Delete the password in the *Password* text box and click **OK**.
   d. Click the **Protect Document** button again and select **Restrict Editing**. The *Restrict Editing* pane opens at the right.
   e. Click **Stop Protection**, type HCC in the *Password* text box, and press **OK**.
   f. Close the *Restrict Editing* pane.

9-68 Remove document encryption password

6. Insert a PowerPoint slide as an embedded object.
   a. Open your student data files from the Windows folder and double-click the ***YogaPPT-09.pptx*** to open this document in PowerPoint.
   b. Select **slide 3** on the left in the *Slides* area, **copy** the slide, and close PowerPoint.
   c. Place your insertion point at the end of the third body paragraph in the ***[your initials] PP W9-3*** document.
   d. Click the bottom half of the **Paste** button [*Home* tab, *Clipboard* group] and select **Paste Special** to open the *Paste Special* dialog box (Figure 9-69).
   e. Click the **Paste** radio button.

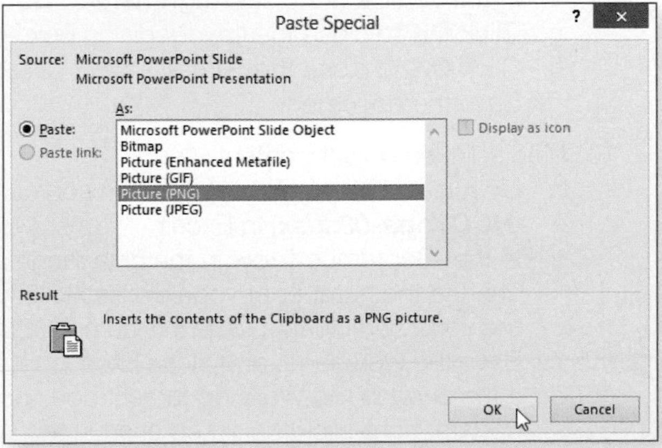

9-69 Paste embedded object

f. In the *As* area, select **Picture (PNG)**.
g. Click **OK** to close the dialog box and insert the slide as an embedded object.

7. Resize and position the embedded object.
   a. Select the picture and change the *Height* to **2.5"** [*Picture Tools Format* tab, *Size* group]. The width automatically changes.
   b. Change the *Position* to **Position in Middle Right with Square Text Wrapping**.
   c. Save the document.
8. Insert an Excel chart as a linked object.
   a. Open your student data files from the Windows folder and double-click the ***HCCYoga-09.xlsx*** to open this worksheet in Excel.
   b. Select the frame of the chart to select the *Chart Area* (Figure 9-70) and copy the chart.
   c. Place your insertion point at the end of the third body paragraph in the ***[your initials] PP W9-3*** document.
   d. Press **Alt+Ctrl+V** to open the *Paste Special* dialog box (Figure 9-71).
   e. Click the **Paste link** radio button.
   f. In the *As* area, select **Microsoft Excel Chart Object**.
   g. Click **OK** to close the dialog box and insert the chart as a linked object.
   h. Close Excel.

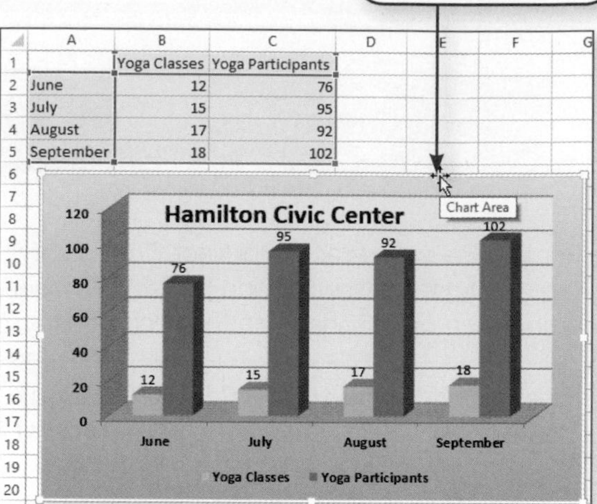

9-70 Select chart to copy

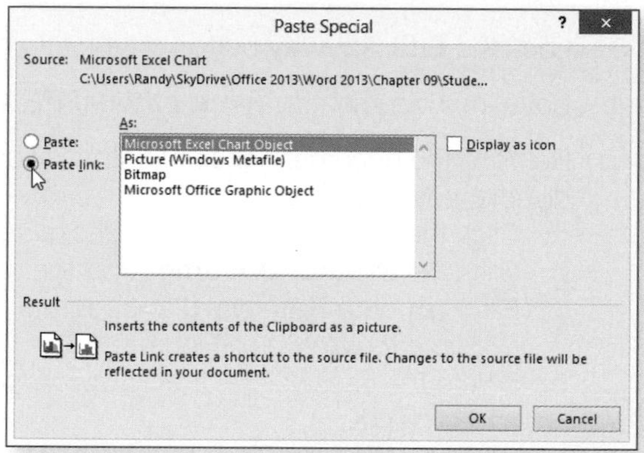

9-71 Paste link to an object

9. Modify size, text wrapping, and position of the embedded chart.
   a. Right-click the chart and select **Format Object** to open the *Format Object* dialog box.
   b. Click the **Size** tab and, in the *Height* area, change the **Absolute** size to **3"**.
   c. Click the **Layout** tab and click the **Advanced** button to open the *Layout* dialog box.
   d. On the *Text Wrapping* tab, select **Tight**.
   e. On the *Position* tab in the *Horizontal* area, set **Alignment** to **Centered** *relative to* **Margin**.
   f. In the *Vertical* area, set **Alignment** to **Bottom** *relative to* **Margin**.
   g. Click **OK** to close the *Layout* dialog box.
   h. Click **OK** to close the *Format Object* dialog box.
   i. Save the document.
10. Modify linked object content.
    a. Double-click the chart to open the source file (***HCCYoga-09.xlsx***) in Excel.
    b. In the "September" row in the data range area, change the number of yoga classes to 20 and the yoga participants to 115 (Figure 9-72).
    c. Save the worksheet and close Excel.
    d. If the chart in the Word document does not update, right-click the linked chart in the Word document and select **Update Link** from the context menu.
    The values in the chart update to reflect the changed data in the source file.

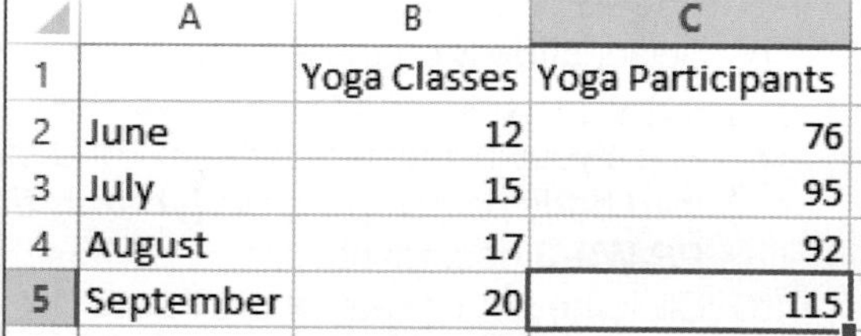

	A	B	C
1		Yoga Classes	Yoga Participants
2	June	12	76
3	July	15	95
4	August	17	92
5	September	20	115

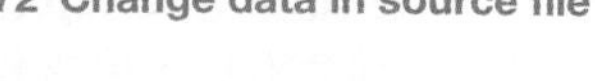
9-72 Change data in source file

11. Break the link between the linked chart and the source file.
    a. Click the **File** tab to open the *Info* area on *Backstage* view and select **Edit Links to Files** to open the *Links* dialog box (Figure 9-73).
    b. Click the **Break Link** button. A dialog box opens asking if you want to break the selected link.
    c. Click **Yes** to break the link to the source file.
    d. Click the **Back** arrow to return to the document.

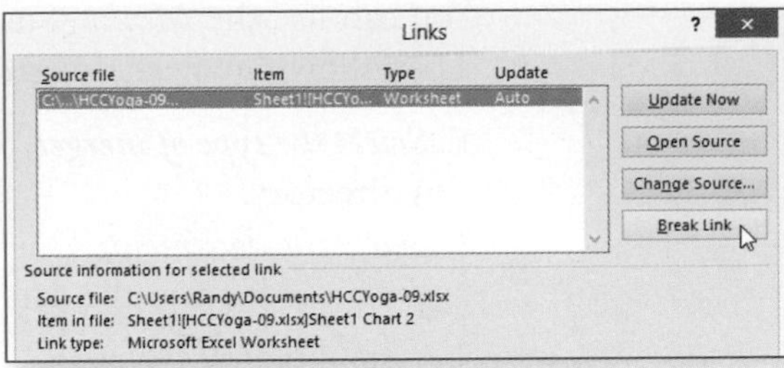

9-73 Break link to source file

12. Save and close the document (Figure 9-74).

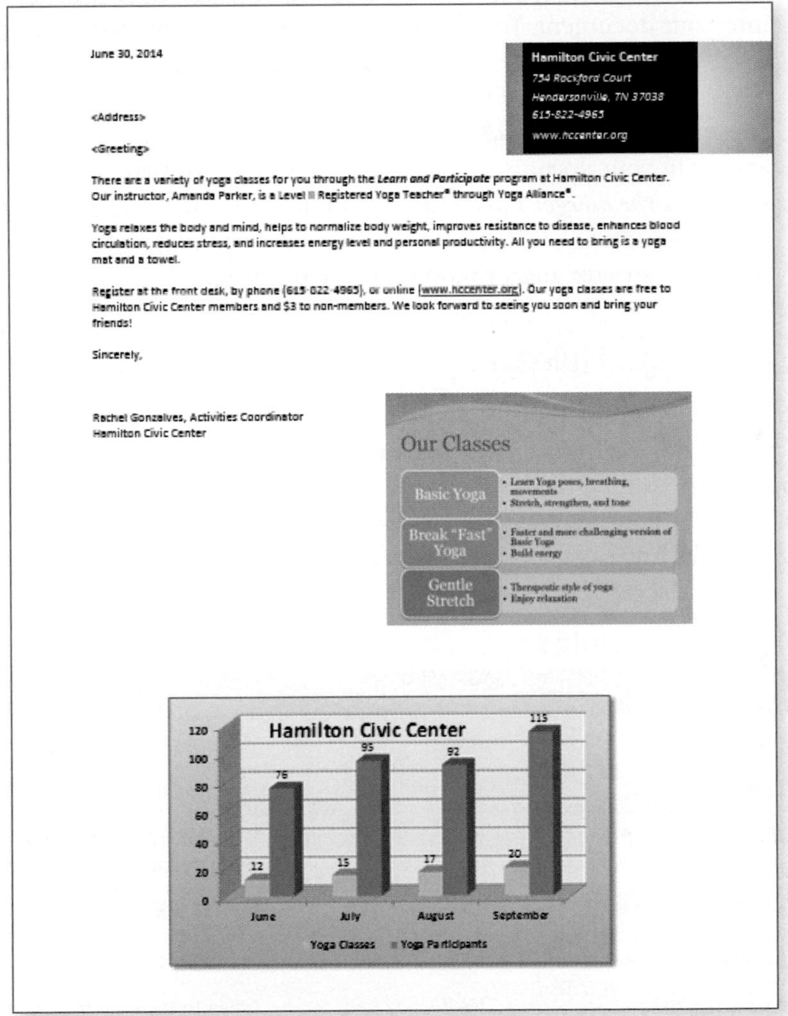

June 30, 2014

Hamilton Civic Center
734 Rockford Court
Hendersonville, TN 37038
615-822-4965
www.hccenter.org

<Address>

<Greeting>

There are a variety of yoga classes for you through the ***Learn and Participate*** program at Hamilton Civic Center. Our instructor, Amanda Parker, is a Level II Registered Yoga Teacher® through Yoga Alliance®.

Yoga relaxes the body and mind, helps to normalize body weight, improves resistance to disease, enhances blood circulation, reduces stress, and increases energy level and personal productivity. All you need to bring is a yoga mat and a towel.

Register at the front desk, by phone (615-822-4965), or online (www.hccenter.org). Our yoga classes are free to Hamilton Civic Center members and $3 to non-members. We look forward to seeing you soon and bring your friends!

Sincerely,

Rachel Gonzalves, Activities Coordinator
Hamilton Civic Center

9-74 PP W9-3 completed

SLO 9.5

Using Rules in Mail Merge

In Chapter 5, you learned about mail merge and how to merge information from other Microsoft Office applications into a Word document (*SLO 5.4*, *5.5*, and *5.6*). In Chapter 6, you learned how to insert custom content into a document using Word field codes (*SLO 6.6*). This section reviews the merge process and covers advanced merge features using rules. You can use rules, which are Word merge field codes, to customize and control the merge process.

Mail Merge Review

You can use the *Mailings* tab or the *Mail Merge Wizard* to create and customize your merge. The following are the six steps in the merge process:

1. ***Select the type of merge:*** You can create merged letters, email messages, envelopes, labels, or a directory.
2. ***Select the document:*** This is the main document where you insert merge fields and merge the records from the data source.
3. ***Select the recipients:*** You can select recipients from a data source such as an Excel worksheet, Access database, or Outlook contacts. You can also create and save a new data source.
4. ***Insert merge fields:*** These are the fields from the recipient data source that you merge into your document. You can also insert an address block or a greeting line, which combines individual field codes into one merge field code. You can customize the address block and greeting line fields to match your data source.
5. ***Preview the merge results:*** Preview how the information from your data source will appear in your document when the merge is performed.
6. ***Complete the merge:*** This final step merges information from your data source into the main document. You can send the merged document to the printer or to a new document that you can save and/or modify before printing.

Mail Merge Rules

Previously, you used Word field codes to automatically insert and update content in a document. For example, you learned how to insert the current date that updates automatically, how to insert index entries and an index page with automatic page numbering, and how to insert document properties. There are Word field codes that you can use to customize the merge process, which are called ***rules***. You can create and insert the following rules to customize the results of your merge:

Mail Merge Rules

Rule	Field Code	Description
Ask	Ask	Prompts the user for text to assign to a bookmark.
Fill-in	Fill-in	Prompts the user for text to insert into a document.
If . . . Then . . . Else	If	Displays information in a merged document based on a logical condition being true or false.
Merge Record #	MergeRec	Inserts the number of the current merge record.
Merge Sequence #	MergeSeq	Inserts the merge record sequence number.
Next Record	Next	Goes to the next record in the mail merge.
Next Record If	NextIf	Goes to the next record in the mail merge if a condition is met.
Set Bookmark	Set	Assigns new text to a bookmark.
Skip Record If	SkipIf	Skips a record in the mail merge if a condition is met.

For example, when creating a mailing, you can use the *If . . . Then . . . Else* rule to insert a specific sentence if an individual is a member of the club and insert a different sentence if the recipient is not currently a member. Or, if you are creating a targeted mailing, you can use the *Skip Record If* rule to skip all records of individuals who do not live in a specific city.

Use the *Rules* button in the *Write & Insert Fields* group on the *Mailings* tab to insert these rules into the main document that you will merge with recipients, or use the *Field* dialog box to insert these field codes.

HOW TO: Add a Rule to a Mail Merge

1. Place your insertion point in the main mail merge document at the location where you want the rule.
   - Word populates field codes sequentially in your document starting at the beginning, so it is important to place the rule in the correct location.
2. Click the **Rules** button [*Mailings* tab, *Write & Insert Fields* group] and select the rule you want to insert (Figure 9-75). The *Insert Word Field: [Rule]* dialog box opens (Figure 9-76).
3. Enter the conditions for the rule.
   - Depending on the rule you are using, you may not need to fill in all conditions of the rule.
4. Click **OK** to close the dialog box and insert the rule (field code).
   - Some field codes are hidden and not visible in your document; in the next section, you learn how to view field codes in your document.

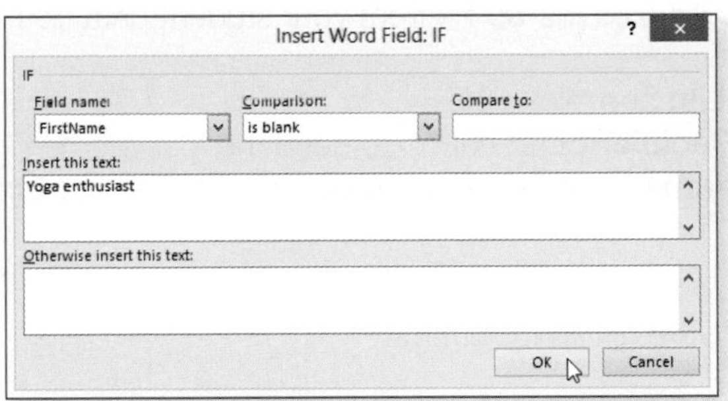

9-76 *Insert Word Field: IF* dialog box

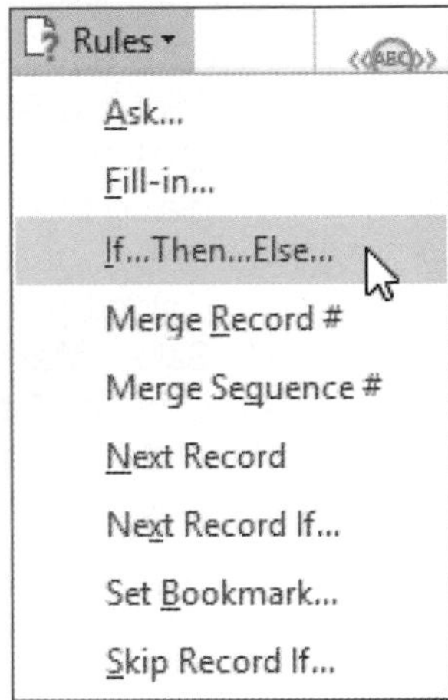

9-75 Insert rule

View Merge Field Codes

Fields codes appear differently in your document and some field codes are hidden. For example, index field codes only appear when *Show/Hide* is turned on, property field codes display the text of the document property, and an address block field code displays "<<AddressBlock>>". There are two ways to view field codes in your document:

- ***View all field codes:*** Press **Alt+F9** (Figure 9-77). **Alt+F9** toggles field code display on/off.
- ***View an individual field code:*** Right-click the field and select **Toggle Field Codes** from the context menu. Repeat to toggle off the field code.

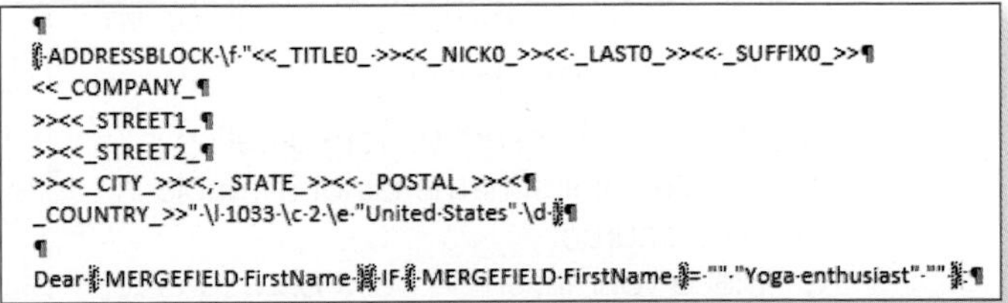

```
¶
{ADDRESSBLOCK \f "<<_TITLE0_ >><<_NICK0_>><< _LAST0_>><< _SUFFIX0_>>¶
<<_COMPANY_¶
>><<_STREET1_¶
>><<_STREET2_¶
>><<_CITY_>><<, _STATE_>><< _POSTAL_>><<¶
_COUNTRY_>>" \l 1033 \c 2 \e "United States" \d }¶
¶
Dear { MERGEFIELD FirstName }{ IF { MERGEFIELD FirstName } = "" "Yoga enthusiast" "" }.¶
```

9-77 View merge field codes

When editing a document, it is useful to be able to see where the codes are located. You can delete or move field codes the same way you delete and move text and objects in your document.

PAUSE & PRACTICE: WORD 9-4

For this Pause & Practice project, you merge the document from *Pause & Practice 9-3* with recipient data from an Excel worksheet. You select the type of merge, select recipients, insert merge fields, sort records, and create rules.

Files Needed: ***[your initials] PP W9-3.docx*** and ***HCCAddresses-09.xlsx***
Completed Project File Names: ***[your initials] PP W9-4.docx*** and ***[your initials] PP W9-4 merged.docx***

---

1. Open the ***[your initials] PP W9-3*** you saved in *Pause & Practice 9-3*.
2. Save the document as ***[your initials] PP W9-4***.
3. Start the mail merge, select recipients, and sort records.
   a. Click the **Start Mail Merge** button [*Mailings* tab, *Start Mail Merge* group] and select **Letters**.
   b. Click the **Select Recipients** button and select **Use Existing List** to open the *Select Data Source* dialog box.
   c. Select the ***HCCAddresses-09*** file from your student data files and click **Open**. The *Select Table* dialog box opens.
   d. Select **MailingList** and click **OK**.
   e. Click the **Edit Recipient List** button to open the *Mail Merge Recipients* dialog box.
   f. Click the **LastName** column heading drop-down list, select **Sort Ascending**, and click **OK** to close the dialog box.
4. Insert an address block and greeting line field codes.
   a. Turn on **Show/Hide** if it is not already on.
   b. Select **"<Address>"** and delete it. Don't delete the paragraph mark after the text.
   c. Click the **Address Block** button [*Mailings* tab, *Write & Insert Fields* group] to open the *Insert Address Block* dialog box (Figure 9-78).
   d. Select **Mr. Josh Randall Jr.** as the recipient's name format and click **OK** to close the dialog box and insert the address block.
   e. Select **"<Greeting>"** and delete it. Don't delete the paragraph mark after the text.
   f. Type Dear and **space** once.
   g. Click the **Insert Merge Field** button, select **FirstName** from the drop-down list, and type : (colon).

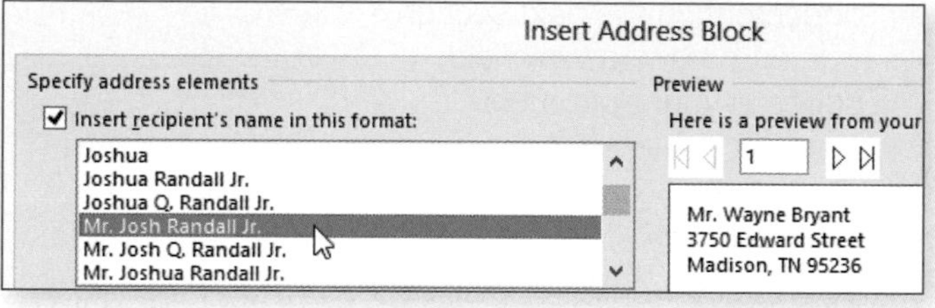

9-78 Insert *Address Block* merge field

5. Create a rule to insert custom greeting if the recipient's first name is not available in the data source.
   a. Place your insertion point between the <<*FirstName* >> field and the colon.
   b. Click the **Rules** button [*Mailings* tab, *Write & Insert Fields* group] and select **If . . . Then . . . Else** from the drop-down list. The *Insert Word Field: If* dialog box opens (Figure 9-79).

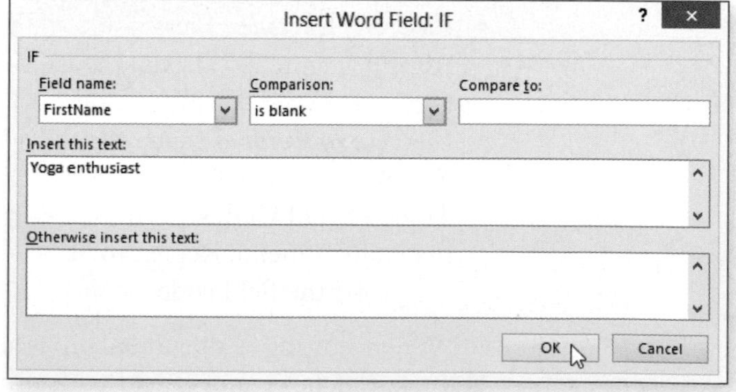

9-79 Insert *If . . . Then . . . Else* rule

c. Click the **Field name** drop-down list and select **FirstName**.
d. Click the **Comparison** drop-down list and select **is blank**.
e. In the *Insert this text* area, type Yoga enthusiast.
f. Click **OK** to close the dialog box and insert the rule. This is a hidden field code and is visible only when field codes are displayed.
g. Press **Alt+F9** to display field codes in the document and confirm that the *If* field code is between the *<<FirstName>>* field and the colon.
h. Press **Alt+F9** again to toggle off field codes.

6. Create a rule to merge only those recipients from Hendersonville.
   a. Place your insertion point in front of the *<<AddressBlock>>* field.
   b. Click the **Rules** button and select **Skip Record If** from the drop-down list. The *Insert Word Field: Skip Record If* dialog box opens (Figure 9-80).
   c. Click the **Field name** drop-down list and select **City**.
   d. Click the **Comparison** drop-down list and select **Not equal to**.
   e. In the *Compare to* area, type Hendersonville.
   f. Click **OK** to close the dialog box and insert the rule. The rule displays in front of the *<<AddressBlock>>* field code.

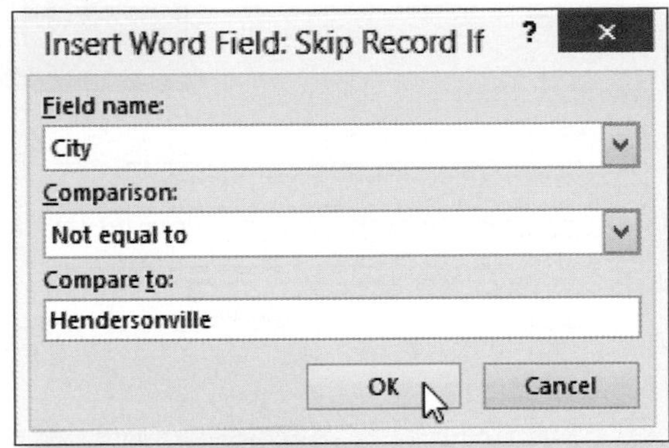

9-80 Insert *Skip Record If* rule

7. Create a rule to insert a custom sentence based on whether the recipient is a member.
   a. Delete the last sentence in the last body paragraph of the letter ("We look forward . . ."). Don't delete the paragraph mark after the sentence.
   b. Click the **Rules** button and select **If . . . Then . . . Else** from the drop-down list. The *Insert Word Field: If* dialog box opens (Figure 9-81).
   c. Click the **Field name** drop-down list and select **MembershipDate**.
   d. Click the **Comparison** drop-down list and select **is not blank**.
   e. In the *Insert this text* area, type We look forward to seeing you again in our yoga classes. Next time you come, please feel free to bring your friends who are not yet members.
   f. In the *Otherwise insert this text* area, type We hope you will try one or more of our yoga classes.
   g. Click **OK** to close the dialog box and insert the rule. If the condition is true, the sentence (see step 7e) is displayed in the document. When the document is merged, this sentence will change if the condition is false (e.g., if there is no membership date).

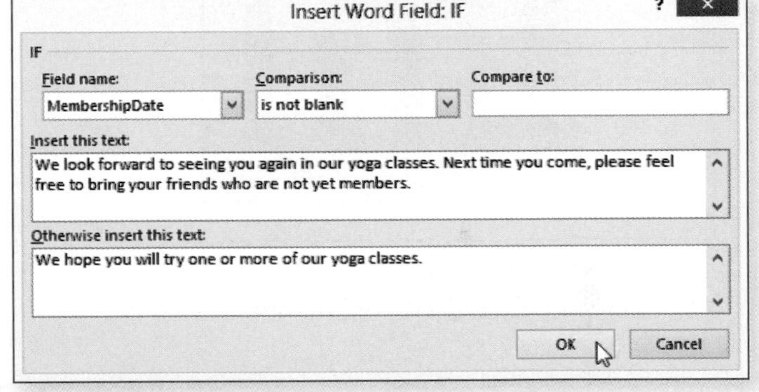

9-81 Insert *If . . . Then . . . Else* rule

8. Select date line (first line of the document) and apply **18 pt.** *Before* paragraph spacing.

9. Preview and finish the merge.
   a. Click the **Preview Results** button [*Mailings* tab, *Preview Results* group] to preview how the merged document will appear. *(Note: The* Skip Record If *rule is not applied until you finish the merge.)*
   b. Click the **Preview Results** button again to hide the recipient information and display the merge field codes.

c. Save the document.
d. Click the **Finish & Merge** button [*Mailings* tab, *Finish* group] and select **Edit Individual Documents**. The *Merge to New Document* dialog box opens.
e. Click the **All** radio button and click **OK** to finish the merge. A new document opens with the recipient information merged into the document. There should be four letters in the document.

10. Save the merged document as ***[your initials] PP 9-4 merged*** (Figure 9-82).

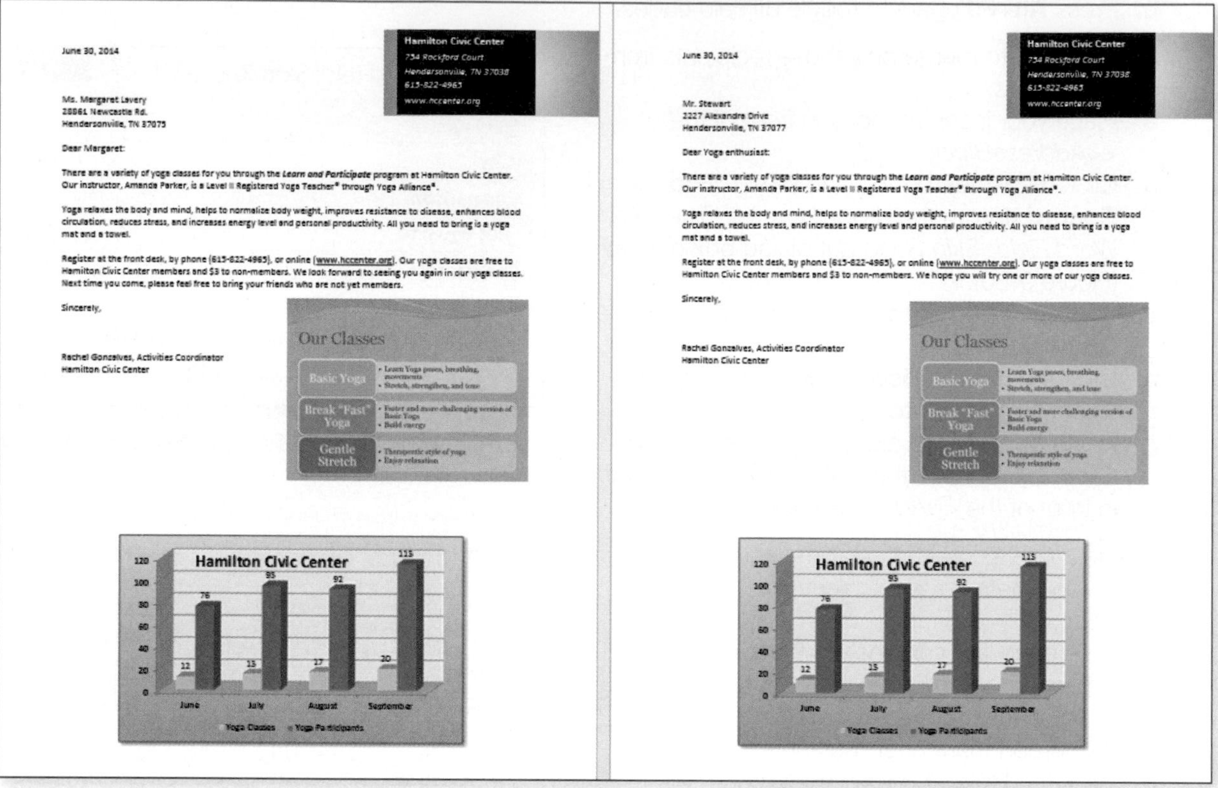

June 30, 2014

Hamilton Civic Center
734 Rockford Court
Hendersonville, TN 37038
615-822-4963
www.hccenter.org

Ms. Margaret Lavery
28861 Newcastle Rd.
Hendersonville, TN 37075

Dear Margaret:

There are a variety of yoga classes for you through the ***Learn and Participate*** program at Hamilton Civic Center. Our instructor, Amanda Parker, is a Level II Registered Yoga Teacher® through Yoga Alliance®.

Yoga relaxes the body and mind, helps to normalize body weight, improves resistance to disease, enhances blood circulation, reduces stress, and increases energy level and personal productivity. All you need to bring is a yoga mat and a towel.

Register at the front desk, by phone (615-822-4963), or online (www.hccenter.org). Our yoga classes are free to Hamilton Civic Center members and $3 to non-members. We look forward to seeing you again in our yoga classes. Next time you come, please feel free to bring your friends who are not yet members.

Sincerely,

Rachel Gonzalves, Activities Coordinator
Hamilton Civic Center

June 30, 2014

Hamilton Civic Center
734 Rockford Court
Hendersonville, TN 37038
615-822-4963
www.hccenter.org

Mr. Stewart
2227 Alexandre Drive
Hendersonville, TN 37077

Dear Yoga enthusiast:

There are a variety of yoga classes for you through the ***Learn and Participate*** program at Hamilton Civic Center. Our instructor, Amanda Parker, is a Level II Registered Yoga Teacher® through Yoga Alliance®.

Yoga relaxes the body and mind, helps to normalize body weight, improves resistance to disease, enhances blood circulation, reduces stress, and increases energy level and personal productivity. All you need to bring is a yoga mat and a towel.

Register at the front desk, by phone (615-822-4963), or online (www.hccenter.org). Our yoga classes are free to Hamilton Civic Center members and $3 to non-members. We hope you will try one or more of our yoga classes.

Sincerely,

Rachel Gonzalves, Activities Coordinator
Hamilton Civic Center

9-82 PP W9-4 merged completed (pages 1 and 2)

11. Save and close both documents.

Chapter Summary

9.1 Insert, review, edit, and customize comments (p. W9-513).

- You can use ***Comments*** to make a note or provide feedback in a document without changing the content or format of the document.
- Users can add, edit, or delete comments. They appear to the right of the document in the ***Markup area***.
- Comments are numbered sequentially in a document and are associated with a Microsoft Office ***user name*** and ***initials***, which you can customize in the *Word Options* dialog box.
- Multiple reviewers can add comments to a document.
- Use the ***Previous*** and ***Next*** buttons to review the comments in the document.
- When you place your pointer on a comment, a tag provides details about the user name and date and time the comment was made.
- You can delete comments individually or delete all comments in the document.

9.2 Modify and review a document using *Track Changes* (p. W9-516).

- ***Track Changes*** is a collaboration tool that allows reviewers to make and track changes made in a document.
- There are four different ***Display for Review views*** that you can use to review the tracked changes in a document: ***Simple Markup***, ***All Markup***, ***No Markup***, and ***Original***.
- Each change made when *Track Changes* is on is attributed to a reviewer and his or her user name.
- You can review changes using the ***Previous*** and ***Next*** buttons.
- You can accept or reject individual changes in the document, or you can accept or reject all of the changes in the document.
- The ***Reviewing pane***, which can be displayed vertically on the left side of the document or horizontally at the bottom of the document, displays all of the changes in the document.
- You can customize which markups are displayed.
- You can use the ***Track Changes Options dialog box*** to customize how tracked changes appear in your document.

9.3 Use Word collaboration features to compare, combine, protect, and share documents (p. W9-524).

- The ***Compare*** feature compares two versions of a document and displays the differences as tracked changes.
- The ***Combine*** feature combines two versions of a document.
- Word provides you with the following features to prepare your document for sharing with others: ***Inspect Document***, ***Check Accessibility***, and ***Check Compatibility***.
- ***Mark as Final*** marks the document as a final version and protects it from being edited.
- ***Encrypt with Password*** restricts a document from being opened without a password.
- When you use ***Restrict Editing***, a user can open the document but is restricted from editing it.
- When you restrict editing, you can restrict all editing or allow users to only use comments, track changes, or fill in forms.
- You can also ***Restrict Permission by People*** or ***Add a Digital Signature*** to a document.
- Word autosaves your document at set intervals. You can access previous autosaved versions of a document.

9.4 Embed and link content from other Microsoft Office applications into a Word document (p. W9-535).

- ***Object linking and embedding (OLE)*** allows users to integrate information from other Office applications into Word.
- You can copy an ***embedded object*** from the ***source file*** and paste it into the ***destination file***. You can modify the embedded object independently of the object in the source file.
- You can also copy an object from the source file and paste it into the destination file, and the linked object in the destination file retains its connection with the source file and source program.
- You can ***edit*** a linked object in the source file and ***update*** the object in the destination file to reflect the changes in the source file.
- Use the ***Paste Special dialog box*** to paste an embedded or linked object into the destination file.

- The process for resizing, arranging, or modifying embedded or linked objects in your Word document is similar to working with pictures, charts, *SmartArt,* or shapes.
- You can ***modify*** or ***break*** the link between the object in the source and destination files.

9.5 Use mail merge rules to customize how data is merged from other Office applications into Word documents (p. W9-543).

- You can use mail merge to merge recipient information from other Office applications into a Word document.
- ***Rules*** are Word field codes that you can use to customize the output of a mail merge.
- View ***Word field codes*** in your document by pressing **Alt+F9**.

Check for Understanding

In the Online Learning Center for this text (**www.mhhe.com/office2013inpractice**), there are a variety of resources that can be used to review the concepts covered in this chapter.

The following Online Learning Resources are available in the Online Learning Center:

- Multiple choice questions
- Short answer questions
- Matching exercises

Guided Project 9-1

For this project, you edit a document from Kelly Sung at Life's Animal Shelter. You review the document to accept and reject changes, review comments and make changes, link and format slides from a PowerPoint presentation, and finalize the document.
[Student Learning Outcomes 9.1, 9.2, 9.3, 9.4]

Files Needed: ***LASSupportLetter-09.docx*** and ***LASSupportPPT-09.pptx***
Completed Project File Names: ***[your initials] Word 9-1.docx*** and ***[your initials] LASSupportPPT-09.pptx***

Skills Covered in This Project

- Turn on *Track Changes* and make changes.
- Review and delete comments.
- Insert the current date.
- Change the display for *Review* view.
- Accept and reject changes in a document.
- Link slides from a PowerPoint presentation to a Word document.
- Update text in a source file.
- Update a linked object in a destination file.
- Break links in the document.
- Resize and align pictures.
- Inspect a document and remove information.
- Mark a document as final.

---

1. Open the ***LASSupportLetter-09*** document from your student data files.
2. Save the document as ***[your initials] Word 9-1***.
3. Review comments and make changes.
   a. Click the top half of the **Track Changes** button [*Review* tab, *Tracking* group] to turn on *Track Changes*.
   b. Click the **Next** button [*Review* tab, *Comments* group] to move to the first comment.
   c. Read the comment and click the **Delete** button [*Review* tab, *Comments* group] to delete the comment.
   d. Select "**[Insert Current Date]**", delete it, and insert the current date so it updates automatically. Use January 1, 2015 as the format for the date.
   e. Click the **Next** button to move to the next comment and read the comment.
   f. Click the **Delete** button to delete the comment.
4. Accept and reject tracked changes.
   a. Click the top half of the **Track Changes** button to turn off *Track Changes*.
   b. Move to the top of the document (**Ctrl+Home**).
   c. Click the **Display for Review** drop-down list [*Review* tab, *Tracking* group] and select **No Markup** to see how the final document will look with proposed changes accepted (Figure 9-83).
   d. Click the **Display for Review** drop-down list again and select **All Markup**.
   e. Click the **Next** button [*Review* tab, *Changes* group] to move to the first change in the document.

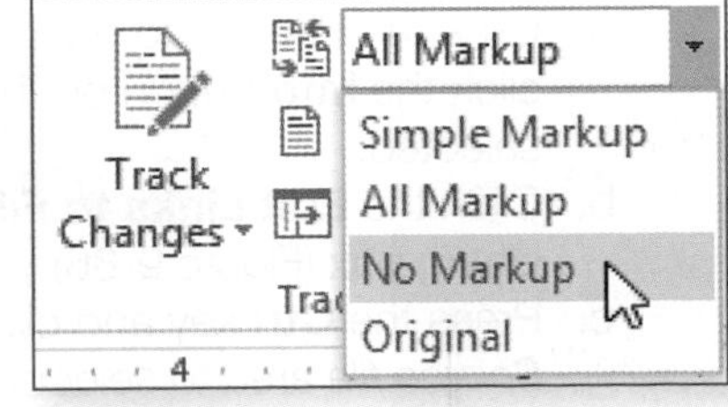

9-83 Change the *Display for Review* view to *No Markup*

12. Switch to the ***[your initials] Word 9-2b*** document and save and close the document.
13. Start and set up the document to merge with recipients from an Access database.
    a. With the ***[your initials] Word 9-2 combined*** document open, click the **Start Mail Merge** button [*Mailings* tab, *Start Mail Merge* group] and select **Letters**.
    b. Click the **Select Recipients** button [*Mailings* tab, *Start Mail Merge* group] and select **Use an Existing List**. The *Select Data Source* dialog box opens.
    c. Select the ***ARCC-09*** database from your student data file and click **Open**.
    d. Click the **Edit Recipient List** button [*Mailings* tab, *Start Mail Merge* group] to open the *Mail Merge Recipients* dialog box.
    e. Click the **Last** column heading drop-down list and select **Sort Ascending**.
    f. Deselect the **check box** next to the following names so they are not included in the merge: Roy Baxter, Rick Hermenn, and Kelsey Kroll.
    g. Click **OK** to close the dialog box.
14. Insert merge fields.
    a. Select and delete "**<Name and address>**". Don't delete the paragraph mark after these words.
    b. Click the **Address Block** button [*Mailings* tab, *Write & Insert Fields* group]. The *Insert Address Block* dialog box opens.
    c. Select **Joshua Randall Jr.** as the recipient's name format and click **OK** to close the dialog box and insert the *Address Block* merge field code.
    d. Place your insertion point after the space after "Dear".
    e. Click the **Insert Merge Field** button [*Mailings* tab, *Write & Insert Fields* group] and select **First** from the drop-down list.
    f. Place your insertion point in the first cell in the second row of the table.
    g. Click the **Insert Merge Field** button and select **Coach** from the drop-down list.
15. Create a rule to skip cyclists who are not racers.
    a. Place your insertion point in front of the <<*AddressBlock*>> merge field code.
    b. Click the **Rules** button [*Mailings* tab, *Write & Insert Fields* group] and select **Skip Record If**. The *Insert Word Field: Skip Record If* dialog box opens (Figure 9-91).
    c. Click the **Field name** drop-down list and select **Level**.
    d. Click the **Comparison** name drop-down list and select **Equal to**.
    e. In the *Compare to* text box, type Recreational.
    f. Click **OK** to close the dialog box and insert the rule.

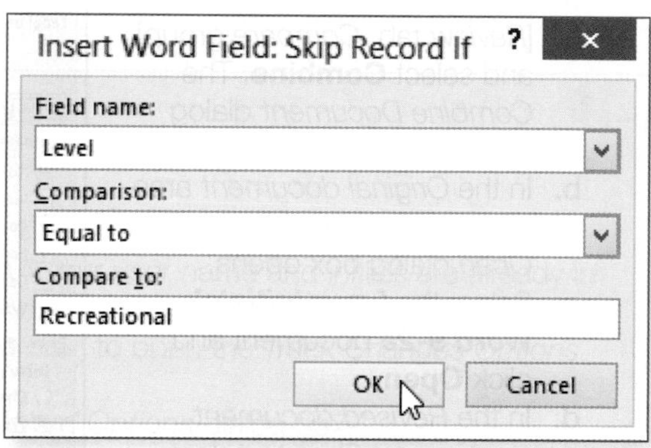

9-91 Create a *Skip Record If* rule

16. Create a rule to insert the email address of the cyclist's coach dependent upon the cyclist's gender (the men's and women's teams have different coaches).
    a. Place your insertion point in the third cell in the second row of the table.
    b. Click the **Rules** button and select **If . . . Then . . . Else**. The *Insert Word Field: If* dialog box opens (Figure 9-92).

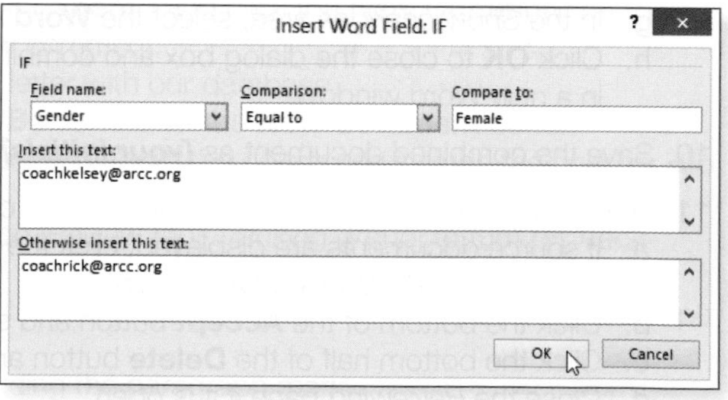

9-92 Create an *If . . . Then . . . Else* rule

c. Click the **Field name** drop-down list and select **Gender**.
d. Click the **Comparison** name drop-down list and select **Equal to**.
e. In the *Compare to* text box, type Female.
f. In the *Insert this text* text box, type coachkelsey@arcc.org.
g. In the *Otherwise insert this text* text box, type coachrick@arcc.org.
h. Click **OK** to close the dialog box and insert the rule. An email address is displayed in this cell.

17. Create a rule to insert the phone number of the cyclist's coach dependent upon the cyclist's gender.
    a. Place your insertion point in the fourth cell in the second row of the table.
    b. Click the **Rules** button and select **If . . . Then . . . Else**. The *Insert Word Field: If* dialog box opens.
    c. Click the **Field name** drop-down list and select **Gender**.
    d. Click the **Comparison** name drop-down list and select **Equal to**.
    e. In the *Compare to* text box, type Female.
    f. In the *Insert this text* text box, type 916-453-2845.
    g. In the *Otherwise insert this text* text box, type 916-451-9879.
    h. Click **OK** to close the dialog box and insert the rule. A phone number is displayed in this cell.

18. Finish the merge.
    a. Click the **Finish & Merge** button [*Mailings* tab, *Finish* group] and select **Edit Individual Documents**. The *Merge to New Document* dialog box opens.
    b. Click the **All** radio button and click **OK** to close the dialog box and finish the merge.
    c. Save the merged document as ***[your initials] Word 9-2 merged*** (Figure 9-93). There should be 13 letters.

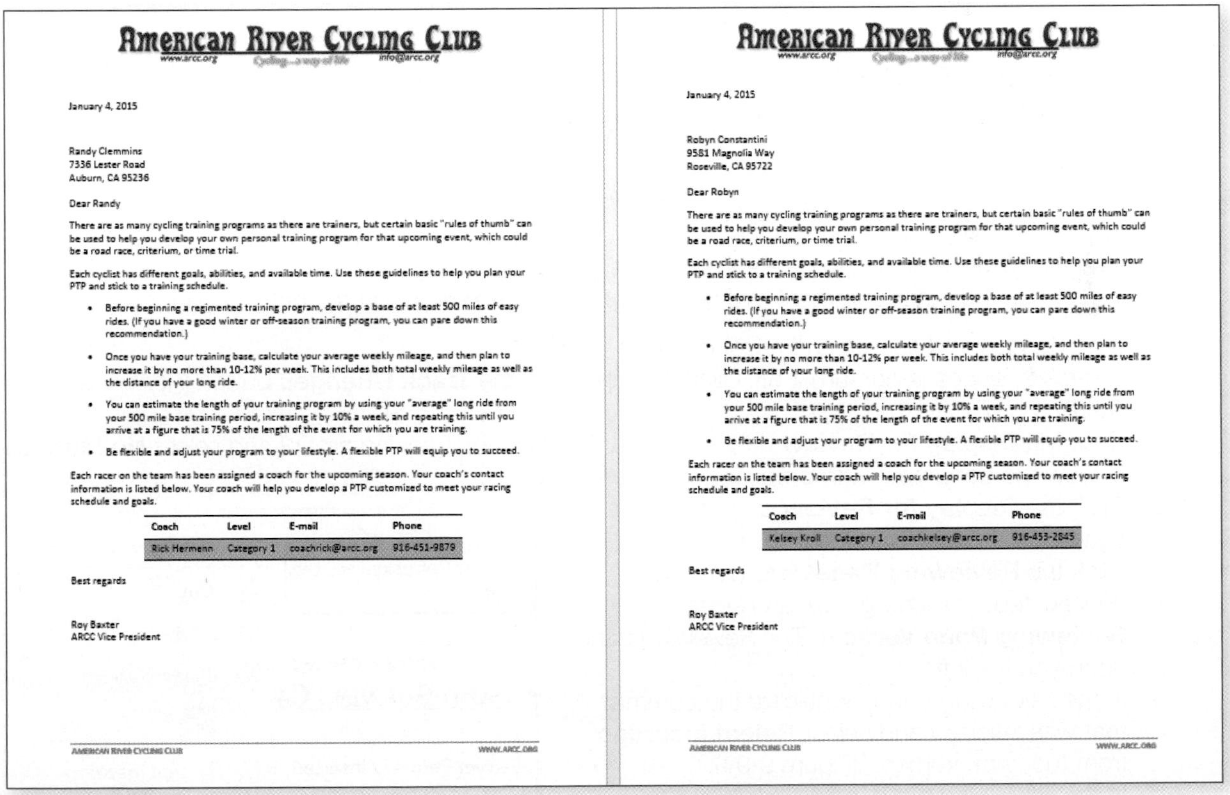

American River Cycling Club
www.arcc.org Cycling...a way of life info@arcc.org

January 4, 2015

Randy Clemmins
7336 Lester Road
Auburn, CA 95236

Dear Randy

There are as many cycling training programs as there are trainers, but certain basic "rules of thumb" can be used to help you develop your own personal training program for that upcoming event, which could be a road race, criterium, or time trial.

Each cyclist has different goals, abilities, and available time. Use these guidelines to help you plan your PTP and stick to a training schedule.

- Before beginning a regimented training program, develop a base of at least 500 miles of easy rides. (If you have a good winter or off-season training program, you can pare down this recommendation.)
- Once you have your training base, calculate your average weekly mileage, and then plan to increase it by no more than 10-12% per week. This includes both total weekly mileage as well as the distance of your long ride.
- You can estimate the length of your training program by using your "average" long ride from your 500 mile base training period, increasing it by 10% a week, and repeating this until you arrive at a figure that is 75% of the length of the event for which you are training.
- Be flexible and adjust your program to your lifestyle. A flexible PTP will equip you to succeed.

Each racer on the team has been assigned a coach for the upcoming season. Your coach's contact information is listed below. Your coach will help you develop a PTP customized to meet your racing schedule and goals.

Coach	Level	E-mail	Phone
Rick Hermenn	Category 1	coachrick@arcc.org	916-451-9879

Best regards

Roy Baxter
ARCC Vice President

AMERICAN RIVER CYCLING CLUB WWW.ARCC.ORG

American River Cycling Club
www.arcc.org Cycling...a way of life info@arcc.org

January 4, 2015

Robyn Constantini
9581 Magnolia Way
Roseville, CA 95722

Dear Robyn

There are as many cycling training programs as there are trainers, but certain basic "rules of thumb" can be used to help you develop your own personal training program for that upcoming event, which could be a road race, criterium, or time trial.

Each cyclist has different goals, abilities, and available time. Use these guidelines to help you plan your PTP and stick to a training schedule.

- Before beginning a regimented training program, develop a base of at least 500 miles of easy rides. (If you have a good winter or off-season training program, you can pare down this recommendation.)
- Once you have your training base, calculate your average weekly mileage, and then plan to increase it by no more than 10-12% per week. This includes both total weekly mileage as well as the distance of your long ride.
- You can estimate the length of your training program by using your "average" long ride from your 500 mile base training period, increasing it by 10% a week, and repeating this until you arrive at a figure that is 75% of the length of the event for which you are training.
- Be flexible and adjust your program to your lifestyle. A flexible PTP will equip you to succeed.

Each racer on the team has been assigned a coach for the upcoming season. Your coach's contact information is listed below. Your coach will help you develop a PTP customized to meet your racing schedule and goals.

Coach	Level	E-mail	Phone
Kelsey Kroll	Category 1	coachkelsey@arcc.org	916-453-2845

Best regards

Roy Baxter
ARCC Vice President

AMERICAN RIVER CYCLING CLUB WWW.ARCC.ORG

9-93 Word 9-2 merged completed (pages 1 and 2)

19. Save and close all open documents.

Guided Project 9-3

For this project, you edit a document from Sawyer Petrosky at Courtyard Medical Plaza. You review the document to accept and reject changes, review comments and make changes, link and embed objects from Excel and PowerPoint, prepare the document for sharing, and protect the document. [Student Learning Outcomes 9.1, 9.2, 9.3, 9.4]

Files Needed: ***StayingActive-09.docx***, ***EstimatedCalories-09.xlsx***, and ***CMPStayingActive-09.pptx***
Completed Project File Names: ***[your initials] Word 9-3.docx*** and ***[your initials] EstimatedCalories-09.xlsx***

Skills Covered in This Project

- Review and delete comments.
- Turn off *Track Changes* and use the *Reviewing* pane to accept and reject changes.
- Link a chart from an Excel worksheet to a Word document.
- Update data in a source file.
- Update a linked object in a destination file.
- Embed and format PowerPoint slides.
- Remove a watermark.
- Check document compatibility.
- Restrict document editing.

---

1. Open the ***StayingActive-09*** document from your student data files.
2. Save the document as ***[your initials] Word 9-3***.
3. Review and delete comments.
   a. Click the **Next** button [*Review* tab, *Comments* group] to move to the first comment.
   b. Read both of the comments in the document to know what you will do later.
   c. Click the **Delete** button to delete the comment.
   d. Right-click the other comment and select **Delete Comment** from the context menu.
4. Review changes and accept and reject changes.
   a. If *Track Changes* is on, turn it off. Click the top half of the **Track Changes** button [*Review* tab, *Tracking* group] to turn it off.
   b. Click the **Display for Review** drop-down list [*Review* tab, *Tracking* group] and select **No Markup** to view the document with proposed changes accepted.
   c. Click the **Display for Review** drop-down list again and select **Simple Markup**.
   d. Click the **Reviewing Pane** drop-down list [*Review* tab, *Tracking* group] and select **Reviewing Pane Vertical**. The *Reviewing* pane opens on the left.
   e. In the *Reviewing* pane, right-click the comma that was inserted and select **Reject Insertion** from the context menu (Figure 9-94).
   f. In the *Reviewing* pane, right-click "**Folding clothes**," which was deleted, and select **Reject Deletion** from the context menu.

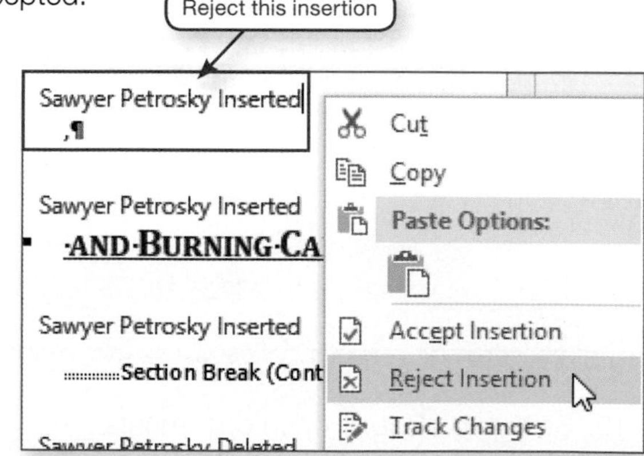

9-94 Reject an insertion

g. Click the bottom half of the **Accept** button [*Review* tab, *Changes* group] and select **Accept All Changes** to accept the remaining changes.
h. Click the **Reviewing Pane** button to close the *Reviewing* pane.

5. Paste a chart from an Excel worksheet as a link in the Word document.
   a. Using a Windows folder, browse to your student data files and open the ***EstimatedCalories-09*** Excel worksheet.
   b. Save the Excel worksheet as ***[your initials] EstimatedCalories-09***.
   c. Select the frame of the chart and copy it.
   d. Return to your Word document and place your insertion point on the blank line above the "Keep Exercise Fun and Interesting" heading.
   e. Click the bottom half of the **Paste** button [*Home* tab, *Clipboard* group] and select **Paste Special**. The *Paste Special* dialog box opens (Figure 9-95).

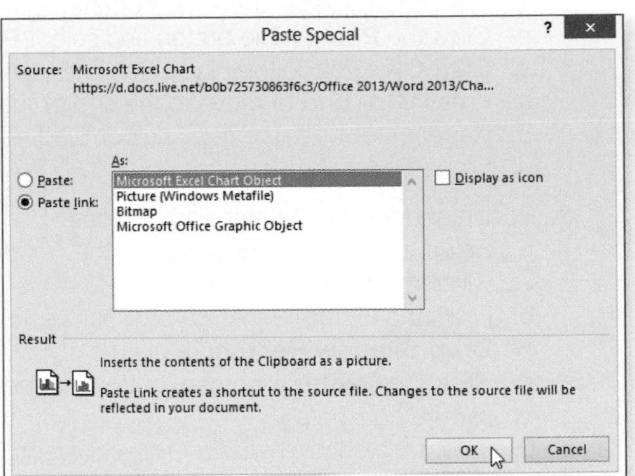

9-95 *Paste Special* dialog box

   f. Click the **Paste link** radio button and select **Microsoft Excel Chart Object** in the *As* area.
   g. Click **OK** to close the dialog box and insert the linked chart.
   h. Click the chart to select it and click the **Center** alignment button [*Home* tab, *Paragraph* group] to horizontally center the chart.

6. Edit the source file and update the linked chart.
   a. Right-click the chart, click **Linked Worksheet Object**, and select **Edit Link**. The linked Excel file opens.
   b. Click the **Moderately Active Male 31-50** cell (**C7**), type 2400, and press **Enter** (Figure 9-96).
   c. Click the **Moderately Active Male 51+** cell (**C8**), type 2300, and press **Enter**.
   d. Save the ***[your initials]* EstimatedCalories-09** worksheet and close Excel.
   e. Return to the Word document, right-click the chart in the Word document, and select **Update Link**. The data in the chart updates to match the source file.

	A	B	C	D
1	Estimated Calorie Requirements			
2		Sedentary	Moderately Active	Active
3	Female 19–30	2000	2200	2400
4	Female 31–50	1800	2000	2200
5	Female 51+	1600	1800	2100
6	Male 19–30	2400	2800	3200
7	Male 31–50	2200	2400	2900
8	Male 51+	2000	2200	2600

9-96 Make changes to the source file

7. Embed slides from a PowerPoint presentation into the Word document.
   a. Using a Windows folder, browse to your student data files and open the ***CMPStayingActive-09*** PowerPoint presentation.
   b. Select **slide 2** on the left and copy it.

c. Return to your Word document and place your insertion point on the blank line at the end of the second page.
d. Click the bottom half of the **Paste** button [*Home* tab, *Clipboard* group] and select **Paste Special**. The *Paste Special* dialog box opens.
e. Click the **Paste** radio button and select **Picture (PNG)** in the *As* area.
f. Click **OK** to close the dialog box and insert the embedded picture.
g. Press **Ctrl+End** to move to the end of the document and press **Enter**.
h. Repeat steps 7b–f to copy and embed slide 8 below slide 2. Slide 8 ends up on the third page.
i. Close PowerPoint.

8. Resize and format the embedded slides.
   a. Select the first slide and change the *Height* to **3"** [*Picture Tools Format* tab, *Size* group]. The width automatically changes.
   b. From the *Picture Styles* gallery [*Picture Tools Format* tab, *Picture Styles* group], apply the **Drop Shadow Rectangle** picture style.
   c. Click the **Center** alignment button [*Home* tab, *Paragraph* group] to center the picture horizontally.
   d. Select the second slide and repeat steps 8a–c.
9. Click the **Watermark** button [*Design* tab, *Page Background* group] and select **Remove Watermark** from the drop-down list.
10. Check document compatibility.
    a. Click the **File** tab to open the *Backstage* view.
    b. Click the **Check for Issues** button and select **Check Compatibility**. The *Microsoft Word Compatibility Checker* dialog box opens and there should be no compatibility issues found.
    c. Click **OK** to close the dialog box.
11. Restrict the document from being edited.
    a. Click the **File** tab to open the *Backstage* view.
    b. Click the **Protect Document** button and select **Restrict Editing**. The *Restrict Editing* pane opens on the right (Figure 9-97).
    c. In the *Editing Restrictions* area, check the **Allow only this type of editing in the document** box.
    d. Click the drop-down list below the check box and select **Comments**.
    e. Click the **Yes, Start Enforcing Protection** button. The *Start Enforcing Protection* dialog box opens.
    f. Click the **Password** radio button.
    g. Type CMP in the *Enter new password* text box.
    h. Type CMP in the *Reenter password to confirm* text box.
    i. Click **OK** to close the dialog box and begin enforcing protection.

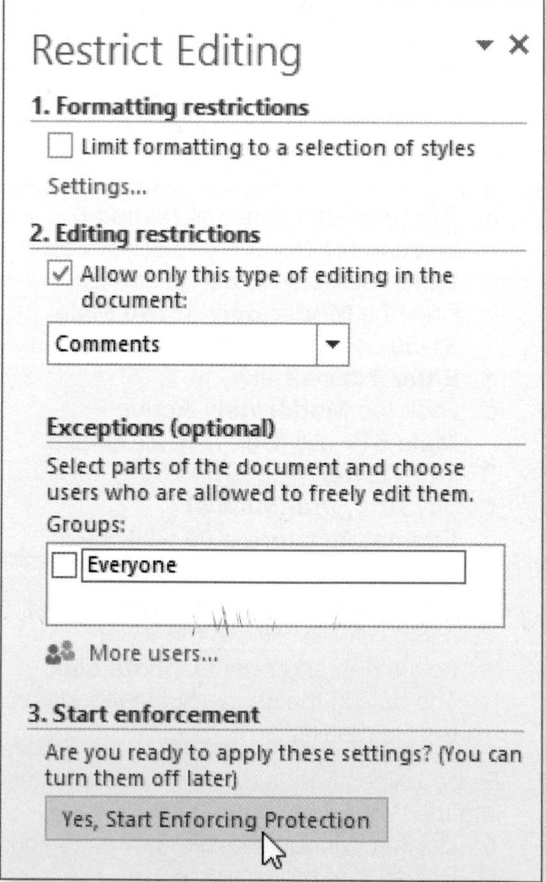

9-97 ***Restrict Editing*** **pane**

12. Save and close the document (Figure 9-98).

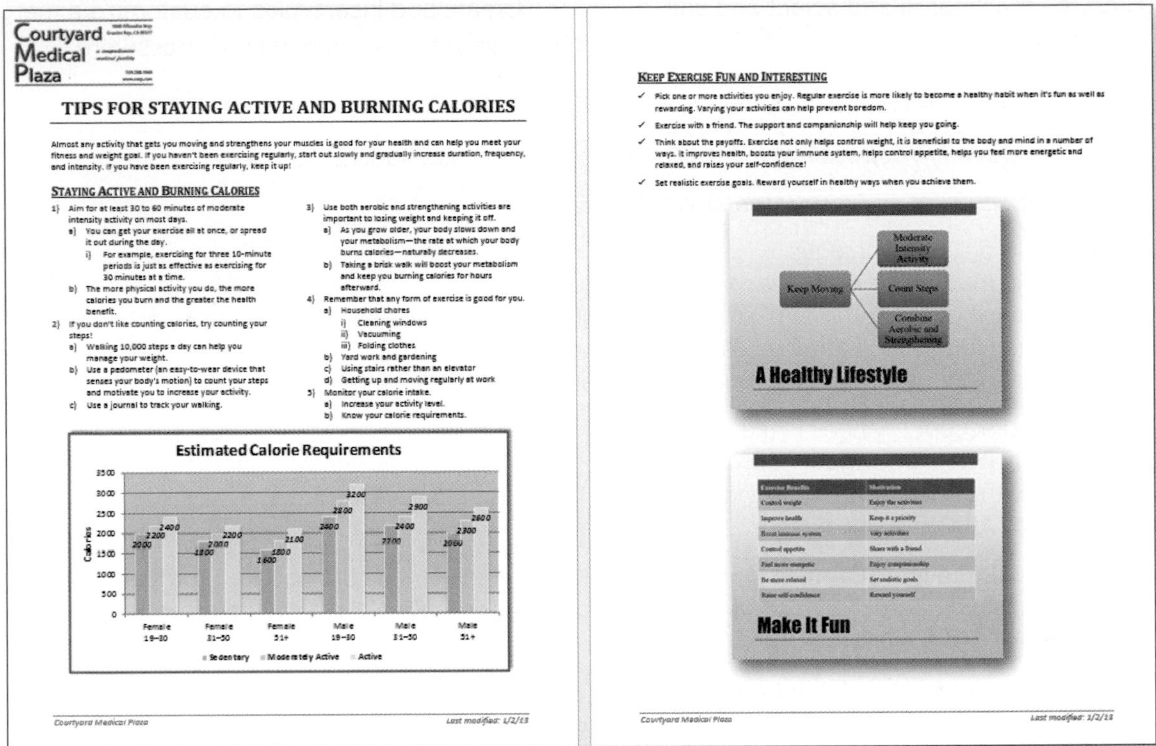

Courtyard Medical Plaza

TIPS FOR STAYING ACTIVE AND BURNING CALORIES

Almost any activity that gets you moving and strengthens your muscles is good for your health and can help you meet your fitness and weight goal. If you haven't been exercising regularly, start out slowly and gradually increase duration, frequency, and intensity. If you have been exercising regularly, keep it up!

STAYING ACTIVE AND BURNING CALORIES

1) Aim for at least 30 to 60 minutes of moderate intensity activity on most days.
    a) You can get your exercise all at once, or spread it out during the day.
        i) For example, exercising for three 10-minute periods is just as effective as exercising for 30 minutes at a time.
    b) The more physical activity you do, the more calories you burn and the greater the health benefit.
2) If you don't like counting calories, try counting your steps!
    a) Walking 10,000 steps a day can help you manage your weight.
    b) Use a pedometer (an easy-to-wear device that senses your body's motion) to count your steps and motivate you to increase your activity.
    c) Use a journal to track your walking.
3) Use both aerobic and strengthening activities are important to losing weight and keeping it off.
    a) As you grow older, your body slows down and your metabolism—the rate at which your body burns calories—naturally decreases.
    b) Taking a brisk walk will boost your metabolism and keep you burning calories for hours afterward.
4) Remember that any form of exercise is good for you.
    a) Household chores
        i) Cleaning windows
        ii) Vacuuming
        iii) Folding clothes
    b) Yard work and gardening
    c) Using stairs rather than an elevator
    d) Getting up and moving regularly at work
5) Monitor your calorie intake.
    a) Increase your activity level.
    b) Know your calorie requirements.

Courtyard Medical Plaza   Last modified: 1/2/13

KEEP EXERCISE FUN AND INTERESTING

✓ Pick one or more activities you enjoy. Regular exercise is more likely to become a healthy habit when it's fun as well as rewarding. Varying your activities can help prevent boredom.

✓ Exercise with a friend. The support and companionship will help keep you going.

✓ Think about the payoffs. Exercise not only helps control weight, it is beneficial to the body and mind in a number of ways. It improves health, boosts your immune system, helps control appetite, helps you feel more energetic and relaxed, and raises your self-confidence!

✓ Set realistic exercise goals. Reward yourself in healthy ways when you achieve them.

Courtyard Medical Plaza   Last modified: 1/2/13

9-98 Word 9-3 completed

Independent Project 9-4

For this project, you edit a prospecting letter from Emma Cavalli at Placer Hills Real Estate. You review and delete comments, review and accept changes, link a chart from Excel, merge the letter with an Access database, create rules to customize the merge, and protect the document.
[Student Learning Outcomes 9.1, 9.2, 9.3, 9.4, 9.5]

Files Needed: ***CavalliProspectingLetter-09.docx***, ***FixedMortgageRates-09.xlsx***, and ***CavalliPHRE-09.accdb***
Completed Project File Names: ***[your initials] Word 9-4.docx***, ***[your initials] FixedMortgageRates-09.xlsx***, and ***[your initials] Word 9-4 merged.docx***

Skills Covered in This Project

- Change the *Display for Review* view.
- Review and delete comments.
- Accept changes in a document.
- Link a chart from an Excel worksheet to a Word document.
- Update data in a source file.

- Update a linked object in a destination file.
- Start the mail merge and select and edit recipients.
- Insert merge field codes.
- Create and insert rules to customize a merge.
- Encrypt a document with a password.

---

1. Open the ***CavalliProspectingLetter-09*** document from your student data files.
2. Save the document as ***[your initials] Word 9-4***.
3. Review and delete comments.
   a. Change the *Display for Review* view to **All Markup**.
   b. Read each of the comments in the document to review what you will be doing in this document. Use the **Next** button to move through the comments.
   c. After reading the comments, delete all the comments in the document.
4. Review and accept changes in the document.
   a. Turn off **Track Changes**.
   b. Review the changes in *No Markup* view and then return to **All Markup**.
   c. **Accept All Changes** in the document.
5. Select and delete the "**[Current Date]**" placeholder text, insert the current date in proper business letter format (January 1, 2015), and set it to update automatically. Don't delete the paragraph mark after the placeholder text.
6. Paste an Excel worksheet chart into the Word document as a linked object.
   a. Using a Windows folder, browse to your student data files and open the ***FixedMortgageRates-09*** Excel worksheet.
   b. Save the Excel worksheet as ***[your initials] FixedMortgageRates-09***.
   c. Select the chart and copy it.
   d. In the Word document, place your insertion point on the blank line below the "Fixed Mortgage Rate Averages" heading on the second page.
   e. Paste the link as a **Microsoft Excel Chart Object**.
7. Update the source file for the linked chart.
   a. In the ***[your initials] FixedMortgageRates-09*** worksheet, change the *2014 Rate* to 3.58 and the Points to 0.6 and save the worksheet.
   b. Update the chart in the destination Word file.
   c. Close Excel.
8. Start the mail merge.
   a. Select **Letters** as the type of mail merge.
   b. Select the ***CavalliPHRE-09*** Access database as the recipients.
   c. Edit the recipient list and sort in ascending order by last name.
9. Insert merge field codes.
   a. Delete the "**<Address>**" placeholder text on the first page.
   b. Insert the **Address Block** merge field code and select the **Mr. Joshua Randall Jr.** format.
   c. Delete the "**<Greeting>**" placeholder text.
   d. After "Dear", insert the **Title** merge field code, **space** once, and insert the **Last** merge field code. Make sure there is a space after "Dear" and between the *Title* and *Last* merge field codes.
   e. Delete the "**<City>**" placeholder text in the first sentence in the first body paragraph.
   f. Insert the **City** merge field code.
   g. Check to ensure there is proper spacing around the merge field codes.

10. Insert rules to customize the merge.
    a. Place your insertion point on the blank line above the <<*AddressBlock*>> merge field code.
    b. Insert a **Skip Record If** rule to skip records where **City** is **Equal to** Roseville.
    c. Insert another **Skip Record If** rule to skip records where **City** is **Equal to** Rocklin.
    d. Insert another **Skip Record If** rule to skip records where **Status** is **Equal to** Sold.
    e. Delete "**has recently expired**" in the first sentence of the first body paragraph.
    f. **Space** once after the <<*City*>> merge field code and insert an **If . . . Then . . . Else** rule.
    g. Use the following settings for the rule: if the *Field name* **Expired** is **Equal to** True, insert has recently expired; otherwise insert will expire soon.
11. Preview the merge results to see how the records will appear in your letter. Remember, the *Skip Record If* rule is not applied until the merge is finished.
12. Save the Word document.
13. Finish the merge.
    a. Merge all the records to edit individual letters. There should be five letters (10 pages total).
    b. Save the new merged document as ***[your initials] Word 9-4 merged*** and close it (Figure 9-99).

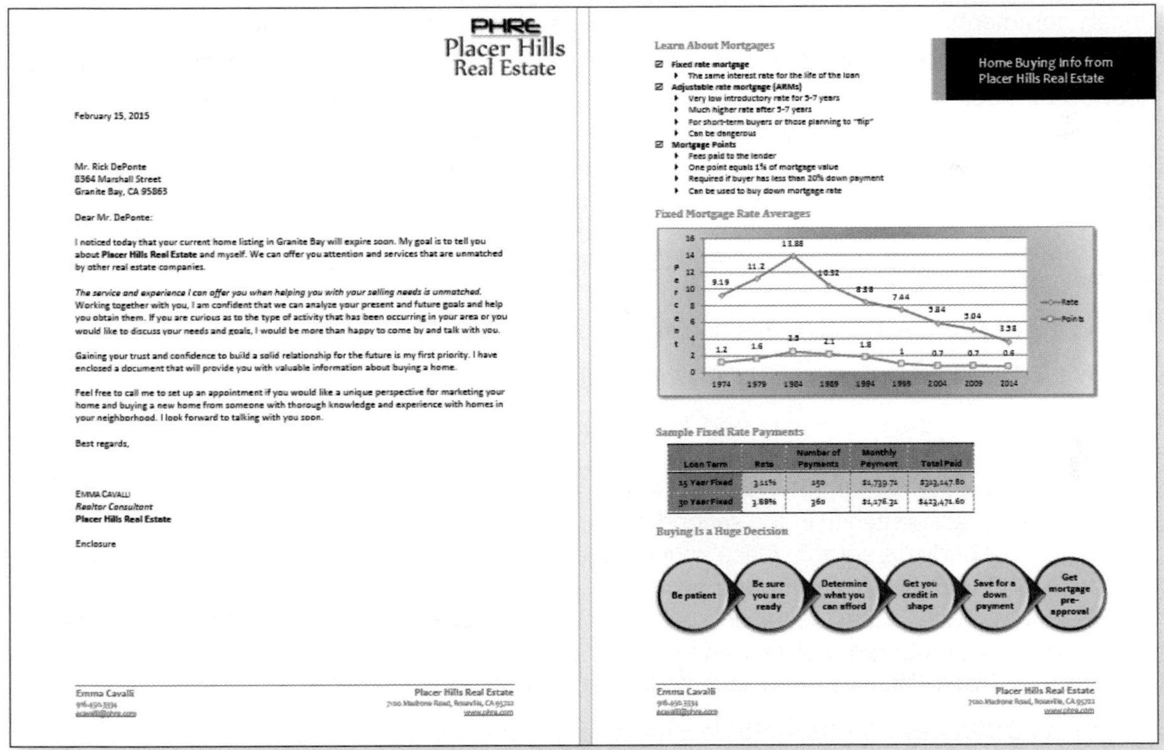

PHRE
Placer Hills
Real Estate

February 15, 2015

Mr. Rick DePonte
8364 Marshall Street
Granite Bay, CA 95863

Dear Mr. DePonte:

I noticed today that your current home listing in Granite Bay will expire soon. My goal is to tell you about **Placer Hills Real Estate** and myself. We can offer you attention and services that are unmatched by other real estate companies.

The service and experience I can offer you when helping you with your selling needs is unmatched. Working together with you, I am confident that we can analyze your present and future goals and help you obtain them. If you are curious as to the type of activity that has been occurring in your area or you would like to discuss your needs and goals, I would be more than happy to come by and talk with you.

Gaining your trust and confidence to build a solid relationship for the future is my first priority. I have enclosed a document that will provide you with valuable information about buying a home.

Feel free to call me to set up an appointment if you would like a unique perspective for marketing your home and buying a new home from someone with thorough knowledge and experience with homes in your neighborhood. I look forward to talking with you soon.

Best regards,

EMMA CAVALLI
Realtor Consultant
Placer Hills Real Estate

Enclosure

Emma Cavalli
916-450-3334
ecavalli@phre.com

Placer Hills Real Estate
7100 Madrone Road, Roseville, CA 95722
www.phre.com

Home Buying Info from Placer Hills Real Estate

Learn About Mortgages

- **Fixed rate mortgage**
  - The same interest rate for the life of the loan
- **Adjustable rate mortgage (ARMs)**
  - Very low introductory rate for 5-7 years
  - Much higher rate after 5-7 years
  - For short-term buyers or those planning to "flip"
  - Can be dangerous
- **Mortgage Points**
  - Fees paid to the lender
  - One point equals 1% of mortgage value
  - Required if buyer has less than 20% down payment
  - Can be used to buy down mortgage rate

Fixed Mortgage Rate Averages

Sample Fixed Rate Payments

Loan Term	Rate	Number of Payments	Monthly Payment	Total Paid
15 Year Fixed	3.11%	180	$1,739.71	$313,147.80
30 Year Fixed	3.68%	360	$1,176.31	$423,471.60

Buying Is a Huge Decision

Emma Cavalli
916-450-3334
ecavalli@phre.com

Placer Hills Real Estate
7100 Madrone Road, Roseville, CA 95722
www.phre.com

9-99 Word 9-4 merged completed (pages 1 and 2)

14. Encrypt the ***[your initials] Word 9-4*** document with a password. Use Cavalli as the password.
15. Save and close the document.

Independent Project 9-5

For this project, you edit an insurance renewal letter from Eva Skaar at Central Sierra Insurance. You make changes to a document, review changes and comments in another document, combine the documents into a single letter, merge the letter with an Access database, create a rule to customize the merge, and finalize the documents.
[Student Learning Outcomes 9.1, 9.2, 9.3, 9.5]

Files Needed: ***CSIRenewalLetter-09a.docx***, ***CSIRenewalLetter-09b.docx***, and ***SkaarCSIRenewals-09.accdb***
Completed Project File Names: ***[your initials] Word 9-5a.docx***, ***[your initials] Word 9-5b.docx***, ***[your initials] Word 9-5 combined.docx***, and ***[your initials] Word 9-5 merged.docx***

Skills Covered in This Project

- Turn on *Track Changes* and make changes.
- Insert comments.
- Remove a document password.
- Review and delete comments.
- Change the *Display for Review* view.
- Accept changes in the document.
- Combine documents.
- Start the mail merge and select recipients.
- Insert merge field codes.
- Create and insert rules to customize a merge.
- Inspect a document and remove *Custom XML Data*.
- Merge to a new document.
- Mark a document as final.

---

1. Open the ***CSIRenewalLetter-09a*** document from your student data files.
2. Save the document as ***[your initials] Word 9-5a***.
3. Make changes to the document using *Track Changes* and add a comment.
   a. Turn on **Track Changes** and change user name and initials to your name and initials.
   b. In the first body paragraph, change "I am" to Central Sierra Insurance is.
   c. Delete the last sentence in the second body paragraph.
   d. In the last body paragraph, place your insertion point after the space after "do not hesitate to call," type (780-886-2464), and **space** once.
   e. Select the first word in the second body paragraph ("**Central**"), insert a comment, and type Insert a table with renewal information below this paragraph.
   f. Turn off **Track Changes** and save and close this document.
4. Open the ***CSIRenewalLetter-09b*** document from your student data files.
   a. This is a password-encrypted document. Enter CSI as the password.
   b. Remove the password encryption from the document using the **Protect Document** button on the *Backstage* view.
5. Save the document as ***[your initials] Word 9-5b***.
6. Review comments and changes.
   a. Read the comments in the document and then delete them.

b. View the document with **No Markup** and then change the view back to **All Markup**.
c. Accept all the changes in the document.
d. Save the document.

7. Combine documents and review changes.
   a. Open the *Combine Documents* dialog box.
   b. Select ***[your initials] Word 9-5b*** as the *Original* document and ***[your initials] Word 9-5a*** as the *Revised* document.
   c. Combine the documents into a new document.
   d. Hide source documents if they are displayed.
   e. View the document as **Simple Markup** and then change the view back to **All Markup**.
   f. Accept all the changes in the document.
   g. Delete the comments in the document.
   h. Save the combined document as ***[your initials] Word 9-5 combined***.
   i. Save and close ***[your initials] Word 9-5b***.
   j. Leave ***[your initials] Word 9-5 combined*** open.

8. Inspect the document and **Remove All** *Custom XML Data*.

9. Start the mail merge.
   a. Select **Letters** as the type of mail merge.
   b. Select the ***SkaarCSIRenewals-09*** Access database as the recipients.
   c. Edit the recipient list and sort in ascending order by last name.

10. Insert merge field codes.
    a. Delete the "**<Address>**" placeholder text, insert the **Address Block** merge field, and use the **Mr. Joshua Randall Jr.** format.
    b. Delete the "**<Salutation>**" placeholder text, insert the **Greeting Line** merge field, and use **Dear Mr. Randall:** as the format.
    c. Delete the "**<Policy Number>**" placeholder text and insert the **Policy_Number** merge field.
    d. Delete the "**<Company>**" placeholder text and insert the **Company** merge field.
    e. Delete the "**<Insurance Company>**" placeholder text and insert the **Insurance_Company** merge field.
    f. Delete the "**<First Name>**" placeholder text and insert the **First_Name** merge field.
    g. Place your insertion point in the first cell in the second row of the table and insert the **Policy_Description** merge field.
    h. Place your insertion point after the "$" in the second cell in the second row of the table and insert the **Premium_Basis** merge field.
    i. Place your insertion point after the "$" in the third cell in the second row of the table and insert the **Rate_per_1000** merge field.
    j. Check to ensure that there is proper spacing around the merge field codes.

11. Preview the merge results to see how the records will appear in your letter.

12. Insert a rule to skip recipients who have paid online.
    a. Place your insertion point on the blank line above the *<<AddressBlock>>* merge field code.
    b. Insert a **Skip Record If** rule to skip records where **Paid_Online** is **Equal to** True.

13. Finish the merge.
    a. Merge all the records to edit individual letters. There should be five letters.
    b. Save the new merged document as ***[your initials] Word 9-5 merged*** and close it (Figure 9-100).

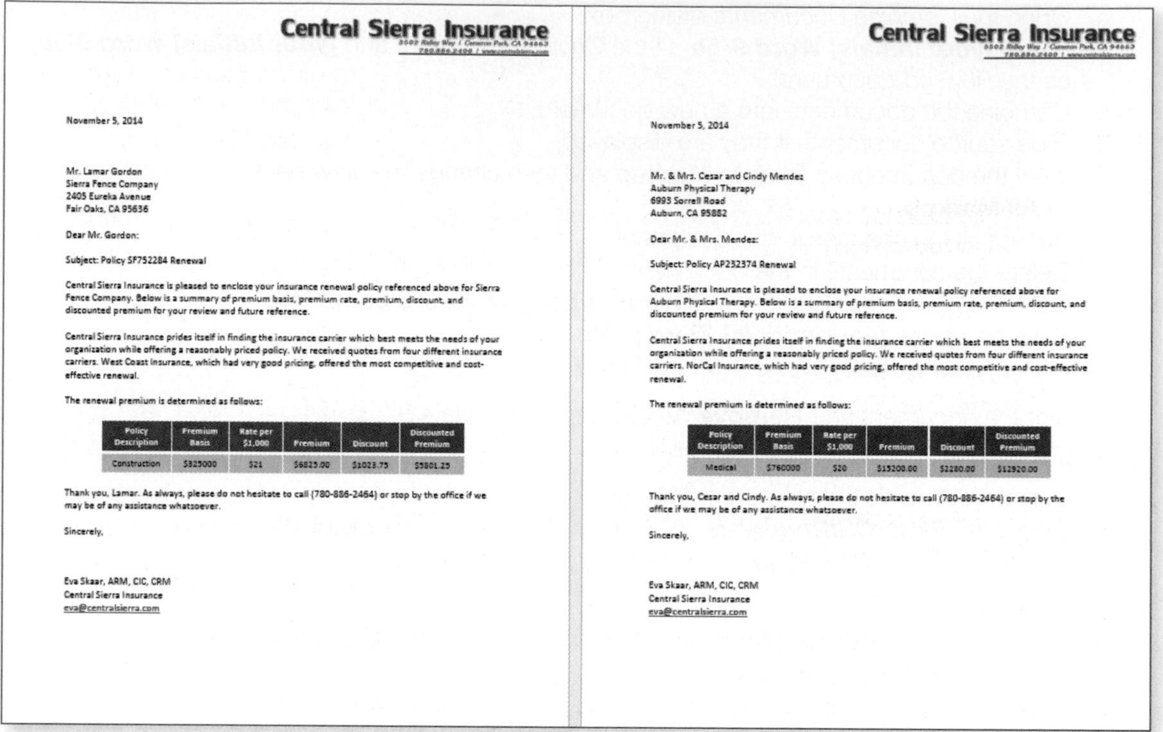

Central Sierra Insurance

November 5, 2014

Mr. Lamar Gordon
Sierra Fence Company
2405 Eureka Avenue
Fair Oaks, CA 95636

Dear Mr. Gordon:

Subject: Policy SF752284 Renewal

Central Sierra Insurance is pleased to enclose your insurance renewal policy referenced above for Sierra Fence Company. Below is a summary of premium basis, premium rate, premium, discount, and discounted premium for your review and future reference.

Central Sierra Insurance prides itself in finding the insurance carrier which best meets the needs of your organization while offering a reasonably priced policy. We received quotes from four different insurance carriers. West Coast Insurance, which had very good pricing, offered the most competitive and cost-effective renewal.

The renewal premium is determined as follows:

Policy Description	Premium Basis	Rate per $1,000	Premium	Discount	Discounted Premium
Construction	$325000	$21	$6825.00	$1023.75	$5801.25

Thank you, Lamar. As always, please do not hesitate to call (780-886-2464) or stop by the office if we may be of any assistance whatsoever.

Sincerely,

Eva Skaar, ARM, CIC, CRM
Central Sierra Insurance
eva@centralsierra.com

Central Sierra Insurance

November 5, 2014

Mr. & Mrs. Cesar and Cindy Mendez
Auburn Physical Therapy
6993 Sorrell Road
Auburn, CA 95882

Dear Mr. & Mrs. Mendez:

Subject: Policy AP232374 Renewal

Central Sierra Insurance is pleased to enclose your insurance renewal policy referenced above for Auburn Physical Therapy. Below is a summary of premium basis, premium rate, premium, discount, and discounted premium for your review and future reference.

Central Sierra Insurance prides itself in finding the insurance carrier which best meets the needs of your organization while offering a reasonably priced policy. We received quotes from four different insurance carriers. NorCal Insurance, which had very good pricing, offered the most competitive and cost-effective renewal.

The renewal premium is determined as follows:

Policy Description	Premium Basis	Rate per $1,000	Premium	Discount	Discounted Premium
Medical	$760000	$20	$15200.00	$2280.00	$12920.00

Thank you, Cesar and Cindy. As always, please do not hesitate to call (780-886-2464) or stop by the office if we may be of any assistance whatsoever.

Sincerely,

Eva Skaar, ARM, CIC, CRM
Central Sierra Insurance
eva@centralsierra.com

9-100 Word 9-5 merged completed (pages 1 and 2)

14. Mark the ***[your initials] Word 9-5 combined*** as final and then close the document.

Independent Project 9-6

For this project, you edit a fax cover sheet for Kelly McFarland, director of Skiing Unlimited. You review the document to accept and reject changes, review comments and make changes, link a chart from Excel, and protect the document.
[Student Learning Outcomes 9.1, 9.2, 9.3, 9.4]

Files Needed: ***SkiingUnlimitedFax-09.docx*** and ***SkiingUnlimitedParticipation-09.xlsx***
Completed Project File Names: ***[your initials] Word 9-6.docx*** and ***[your initials] SkiingUnlimitedParticipation-09.xlsx***

Skills Covered in This Project

- Use the *Reviewing* pane to reject and accept changes.
- Turn off *Track Changes* and make changes.
- Review and delete comments.
- Link a chart from an Excel worksheet to a Word document.
- Update data in the source file.
- Update a linked object in the destination file.
- Break links between documents.
- Encrypt a document with a password.

---

1. Open the ***SkiingUnlimitedFax-09*** document from your student data files.
2. Save the document as ***[your initials] Word 9-6***.
3. Review comments and changes.
   a. Turn off **Track Changes**.
   b. Using the *Reviewing* pane, locate where "1" was deleted from the "PAGES" area and reject this change.
   c. Accept the remaining changes in the document.
   d. Read the two comments in the document and delete them.
   e. Close the *Reviewing* pane.
4. Make changes to the document.
   a. In the "[Pick the date]" field, select the current date.
   b. After "TO:", type Seth Uribe.
   c. After "FAX:" in the first column of the second table, type 916.450.9525.
   d. After "PHONE:" in the first column of the second table, type 916.450.9515.
   e. In the "FROM:" area, type your name.
5. Paste a chart from an Excel worksheet as a linked object.
   a. Using a Windows folder, browse to your student data files and open the ***SkiingUnlimitedParticipation-09*** Excel worksheet.
   b. Save the Excel worksheet as ***[your initials] SkiingUnlimitedParticipation-09***.
   c. Select the chart and copy it.
   d. Place your insertion point on the blank line below the second table in the document.
   e. Paste the link as a **Microsoft Excel Chart Object**.
6. Edit the source file and update the chart in the destination file.
   a. In the Excel worksheet, change the 2013 participants to 74 and the volunteers to 231.
   b. Save the Excel worksheet.
   c. Update the chart in the destination file.
   d. Change the horizontal alignment of the chart in the destination file to **center**.
   e. Close the Excel worksheet.
7. Break the link between the chart in the destination file and the source file.
8. Encrypt the document with a password. Use SU as the password.

9. Save and close the document (Figure 9-101).

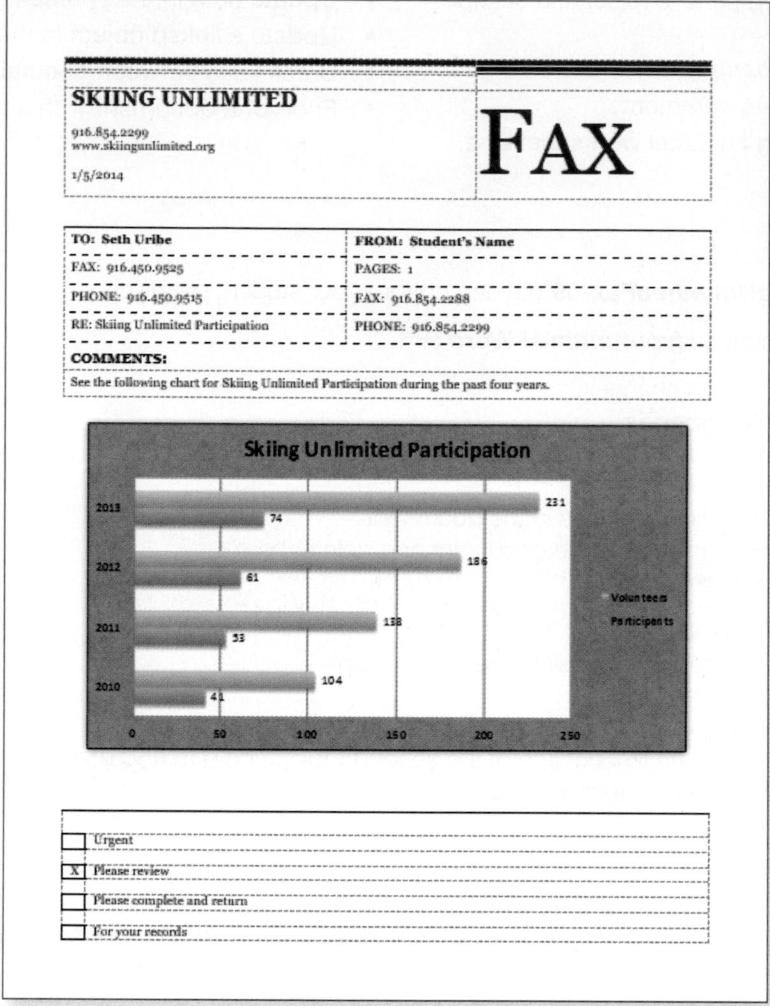

SKIING UNLIMITED

916.854.2299
www.skiingunlimited.org

1/5/2014

FAX

TO: Seth Uribe	**FROM:** Student's Name
FAX: 916.450.9525	PAGES: 1
PHONE: 916.450.9515	FAX: 916.854.2288
RE: Skiing Unlimited Participation	PHONE: 916.854.2299

COMMENTS:

See the following chart for Skiing Unlimited Participation during the past four years.

- [ ] Urgent
- [x] Please review
- [ ] Please complete and return
- [ ] For your records

9-101 Word 9-6 completed

Improve It Project 9-7

For this project, you edit an insurance newsletter for Central Sierra Insurance. You use *Track Changes*, make editing changes, accept changes, embed an Excel chart, format the chart, prepare the document for sharing, and mark the document as final.
[Student Learning Outcomes 9.1, 9.2, 9.3, 9.4]

Files Needed: ***CSINewsletter-09.docx*** and ***EstimatedCosts-09.xlsx***
Completed Project File Names: ***[your initials] Word 9-7.docx***

Skills Covered in This Project

- Open a password-encrypted document.
- Remove a document password.
- Review and delete comments.
- Turn on *Track Changes* and make changes.
- Change the *Display for Review* view.
- Accept and reject changes in a document.
- Embed and format a chart from an Excel worksheet to the Word document.
- Inspect a document.
- Mark a document as final.

---

1. Open the ***CSINewsletter-09*** document from your student data files.
   a. This document is encrypted with a password. The password is CSI.
   b. Remove the password from this document.
2. Save the document as ***[your initials] Word 9-7***.
3. Read the comments in the document and delete all comments.
4. Use *Track Changes* to make changes to the document.
   a. Turn on **Track Changes**.
   b. Change the user name and initials to your name and initials.
   c. Change the *Display for Review* view to **Simple Markup**.
   d. Select the bordered text below the title and apply **White**, **Background 1**, **Darker 5%** shading.
   e. Change hyphenation to **None**. This change will not be marked as a tracked change.
   f. Select the bulleted list and sort alphabetically in **ascending** order.
   g. In the second paragraph in the first column, select "**Home Appliance and Electronics Breakdown coverage**" and apply **bold** formatting.
   h. In the text box in the second column, apply **small caps** formatting and **0 pt.** after paragraph spacing to each of the three bolded headings.
5. Accept and reject changes.
   a. Change the *Display for Review* view to **All Markup**.
   b. Turn off **Track Changes**.
   c. Reject the three **Space After: 0 pt.** formatting changes.
   d. Accept all other changes.
6. Select the text box in the second column and change the *Height* to **4.9"**.
7. Paste a chart from an Excel worksheet as an embedded object.
   a. Using a Windows folder, browse to your student data files and open the ***EstimatedCosts-09*** Excel worksheet.
   b. Select the chart and copy it.
   c. Close the Excel worksheet.
   d. Place your insertion point on the blank line below the text box in the second column.
   e. Paste the copied chart as a **Picture (PNG)**.
8. Format the chart.
   a. Select the chart picture and change the text wrapping to **In Front of Text**.
   b. Using the *Layout* dialog box, change the *Horizontal* **Alignment** to **Centered** *relative to* **Page** and change the *Vertical* **Alignment** to **Bottom** *relative to* **Margin**.
   c. Change the *Width* of the chart picture to **7.5"**. The height adjusts automatically.
9. Inspect the document and **Remove All** *Document Properties and Personal Information*, *Custom XML Data*, and *Headers*, *Footers*, *and Watermarks*.

10. Mark the document as final and close the document (Figure 9-102).

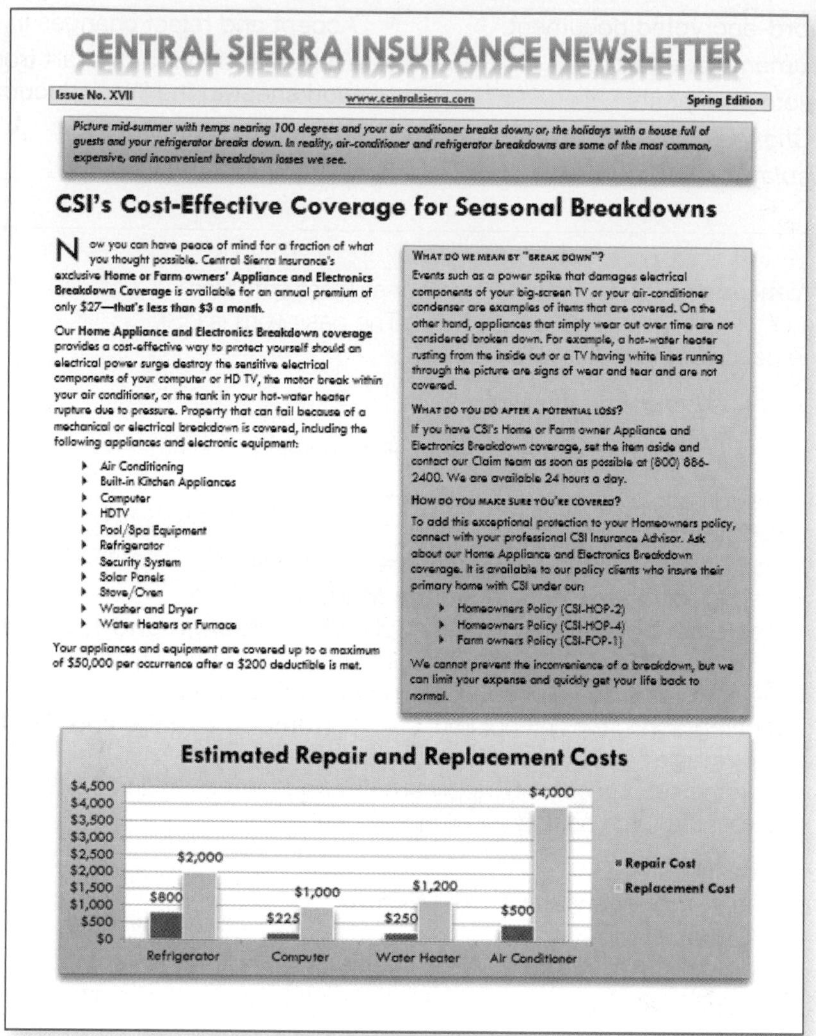

CENTRAL SIERRA INSURANCE NEWSLETTER

Issue No. XVII | www.centralsierra.com | Spring Edition

Picture mid-summer with temps nearing 100 degrees and your air conditioner breaks down; or, the holidays with a house full of guests and your refrigerator breaks down. In reality, air-conditioner and refrigerator breakdowns are some of the most common, expensive, and inconvenient breakdown losses we see.

CSI's Cost-Effective Coverage for Seasonal Breakdowns

Now you can have peace of mind for a fraction of what you thought possible. Central Sierra Insurance's exclusive **Home or Farm owners' Appliance and Electronics Breakdown Coverage** is available for an annual premium of only $27—**that's less than $3 a month.**

Our **Home Appliance and Electronics Breakdown coverage** provides a cost-effective way to protect yourself should an electrical power surge destroy the sensitive electrical components of your computer or HD TV, the motor break within your air conditioner, or the tank in your hot-water heater rupture due to pressure. Property that can fail because of a mechanical or electrical breakdown is covered, including the following appliances and electronic equipment:

- Air Conditioning
- Built-in Kitchen Appliances
- Computer
- HDTV
- Pool/Spa Equipment
- Refrigerator
- Security System
- Solar Panels
- Stove/Oven
- Washer and Dryer
- Water Heaters or Furnace

Your appliances and equipment are covered up to a maximum of $50,000 per occurrence after a $200 deductible is met.

WHAT DO WE MEAN BY "BREAK DOWN"?

Events such as a power spike that damages electrical components of your big-screen TV or your air-conditioner condenser are examples of items that are covered. On the other hand, appliances that simply wear out over time are not considered broken down. For example, a hot-water heater rusting from the inside out or a TV having white lines running through the picture are signs of wear and tear and are not covered.

WHAT DO YOU DO AFTER A POTENTIAL LOSS?

If you have CSI's Home or Farm owner Appliance and Electronics Breakdown coverage, set the item aside and contact our Claim team as soon as possible at (800) 886-2400. We are available 24 hours a day.

HOW DO YOU MAKE SURE YOU'RE COVERED?

To add this exceptional protection to your Homeowners policy, connect with your professional CSI Insurance Advisor. Ask about our Home Appliance and Electronics Breakdown coverage. It is available to our policy clients who insure their primary home with CSI under our:

- Homeowners Policy (CSI-HOP-2)
- Homeowners Policy (CSI-HOP-4)
- Farm owners Policy (CSI-FOP-1)

We cannot prevent the inconvenience of a breakdown, but we can limit your expense and quickly get your life back to normal.

9-102 Word 9-7 completed

Challenge Project 9-8

People often work collaboratively with coworkers or classmates on projects. Use the Word collaboration tools you learned in this chapter to work with others to modify a report, project, or document. **[Student Learning Outcomes 9.1, 9.2, 9.3]**

File Needed: None
Completed Project File Name: ***[your initials] Word 9-8.docx***

Open an existing document you are working on with others and save it as ***[your initials] Word 9-8***. Modify your document according to the following guidelines:

- Customize your user name and initials.
- Insert comments.
- Use *Track Changes* to mark content and formatting changes.
- View the document in different *Display for Review* views.
- Customize tracking options.
- Combine or compare documents.
- Prepare the document for sharing by inspecting the document, checking accessibility, and checking compatibility.
- Protect the document by using one or more of the protect document features. If you use a password to encrypt your document or restrict it from editing, make sure you send your instructor the password.

Challenge Project 9-9

For this project, you use the Word mail merge features to create a merged document. You can create mailing labels, a merged customized fax cover sheet, a merged letter, an invitation, or other document that you can merge with recipients from a data source. You can use an existing data source for recipients or create a new one. Use mail merge rules to customize your mail merge.
[Student Learning Outcome 9.5]

File Needed: None
Completed Project File Names: ***[your initials] Word 9-9.docx*** and ***[your initials] Word 9-9 merged.docx***

Open a new or existing document and save it as ***[your initials] Word 9-9***. Save your merged document as ***[your initials] Word 9-9 merged***. Modify your documents according to the following guidelines:

- Edit the recipient list.
- Insert the *Address Block* and/or *Greeting Line* merge field codes.
- Insert individual merge fields.
- Use rules to customize the merge.
- Preview results and finish the merge.

Challenge Project 9-10

Use object linking and embedding to modify and enhance a document. For example, link your budget from an Excel worksheet to a Word document, embed your work or school schedule into a Word document, or link or embed slides from a PowerPoint presentation to a Word document to make a notes sheet for an upcoming presentation.
[Student Learning Outcome 9.4]

File Needed: None
Completed Project File Name: ***[your initials] Word 9-10.docx***

Open a new or existing document and save it as ***[your initials] Word 9-10.*** Use the Word object linking and embedding features. Modify your document according to the following guidelines:

- Embed an object from another document in a Word document.
- Link an object from another document to a Word document.
- Resize, arrange, and format linked or embedded objects.
- Update the source file and update the linked object.
- Break the object link between the source and destination files.

CHAPTER 10

WORD

Automating Tasks Using Templates and Macros

CHAPTER OVERVIEW

Microsoft Word provides you with many tools to automate routine tasks and work more efficiently. You can use templates to store a common document structure, such as an agenda, check list, or fax cover sheet. Once you have created templates, you can use them as the structure to create new documents that you can customize and save without modifying the template structure. In addition to templates, Word gives you the option to work with macros. A macro is a set of instructions that you can save and carry out with a single command. Like templates, macros save you time and add consistency to your documents.

STUDENT LEARNING OUTCOMES (SLOs)

After completing this chapter, you will be able to:

SLO 10.1 Create, save, and use a template to generate commonly used documents (p. W10-574).

SLO 10.2 Customize template content using Word fields and shared template content (p. W10-577).

SLO 10.3 Record a set of instructions as a macro and run and delete a macro (p. W10-584).

SLO 10.4 Copy and edit an existing macro using Visual Basic and add a keyboard and button shortcut to a macro (p. W10-593).

SLO 10.5 Create and use a macro-enabled template to automate common tasks and copy a macro to another document (p. W10-600).

CASE STUDY

In the Pause & Practice projects in this chapter, you customize and use an agenda template for the student government at Sierra Pacific Community College District. You also create and use macros to automate common tasks used in Word documents.

Pause & Practice 10-1: Create and customize an agenda template and create a document based upon the template.

Pause & Practice 10-2: Create macros to store commonly used instructions and use these macros in the agenda template.

Pause & Practice 10-3: Edit existing macros, copy macros, assign a keyboard shortcut to a macro, and add macro buttons to the *Quick Access* toolbar.

Pause & Practice 10-4: Create a macro-enabled template, copy macros from another file, delete a macro, and create a document based upon the macro-enabled template.

SLO 10.1

Creating and Saving Templates

A *template* is a document with content and formatting. You can create and customize new documents from templates without modifying the structure and content of the original template file. For example, you can create an agenda template with formatting and placeholder text that you can use as the basis for a new agenda for each of your meetings. By using a template, you avoid having to recreate a new agenda from scratch each time and all of your agendas are formatted consistently.

A template file is a specific type of Word file that is different from a regular Word document. Template files have a *.dotx* extension, while regular Word document files have a *.docx* extension. You can save a new or existing file as a template or use a Word online template. Templates can store text, formatting, and objects. You can also use them to store styles, building blocks, and macros (macros are covered later in this chapter). Templates save time and help you work more efficiently and effectively. The following table lists the types and extensions of the different Word files that you will be using in this chapter:

Word Files

Word File Type	File Name Extension
Word Document	.docx
Word Template	.dotx
Word Macro-Enabled Document	.docm
Word Macro-Enabled Template	.dotm

Save a Document as a Template

When you open a new Word document, the document is by default a regular Word document (with a *.docx* extension). You can save this new document as a template (with a *dotx* extension). You can also save an existing document as a template file and use that file as a template to create new documents.

HOW TO: Save a Document as a Template

1. With a new or existing document open, press **F12** to open the *Save As* dialog box (Figure 10-1).
2. In the *File name* area, type the document name.
3. Click the **Save as type** drop-down list and select **Word Template**.
4. In the folder structure at the left, browse to the location where you want to save your file.
5. Click the **Save** button to close the dialog box and save the template.

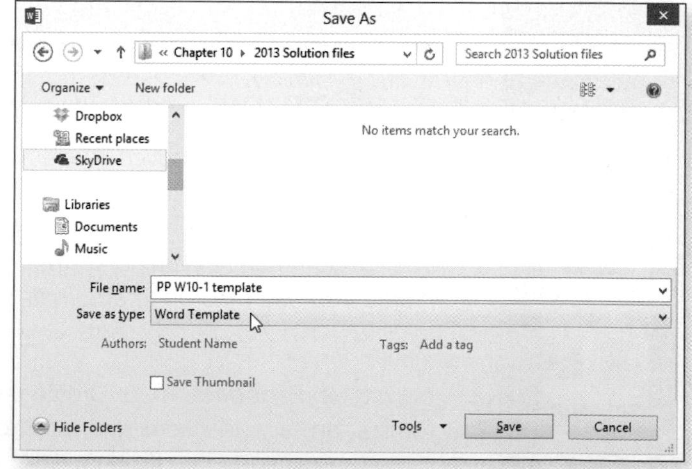

10-1 ***Save As* dialog box**

ANOTHER WAY

You can use the *Backstage* view to select a location to save a file and open the *Save As* dialog box.

You can also save templates in the *Custom Office Templates* folder, which is the default folder selected when saving a template file. When you save a template in this folder, it is available in the *Personal* templates area on the *Backstage* view. To view your personal templates, click the **File** tab to open the *Backstage* view, click **New** at the left, and select **Personal** to view templates you previously saved in the *Custom Office Templates* folder. Click a personal template to create a document based upon that template.

Online Word Templates

In addition to creating your own templates, Word provides you with a variety of online templates. These are available in the *New* area on the *Backstage* view. You can create a document based on an online template and customize it to your needs. Some common templates are pinned to the list of templates in the *New* area, and you can search for other online templates by typing in key words or clicking one of the links for suggested searches. You can unpin templates from the existing list of templates, or, when you search for templates, you can pin a template to your template list.

When you select a template, a new window opens that provides details about the template. When you create a template, it is downloaded as a regular Word document based on the template. You can save the document as a template, regular Word document, or a different file type.

HOW TO: Use an Office.com Template

1. Click the **File** tab to open the *Backstage* view.
2. Click the **New** button on the left to view the available templates (Figure 10-2).
3. Click one of the sample templates.
    - A preview window opens that provides details about the template.
4. To search for online templates, click in the **Search for online templates** text box and type key words.
    - Alternatively, you can click one of the **Suggested searches** links to display related templates.
5. Select an online template. A preview window opens that provides details about the template (Figure 10-3).
    - A preview of the template appears on the left.
    - Details about the template appear on the right.
    - Click the **Previous** or **Next** button on the left or right to scroll through other online templates in the same category.
6. Click the **Create** button.
    - The online template is created as a regular Word document and opens in a new window.
    - When you create a document based on an online template, the template is attached to the document.
7. Save the document as a template file or regular Word document.

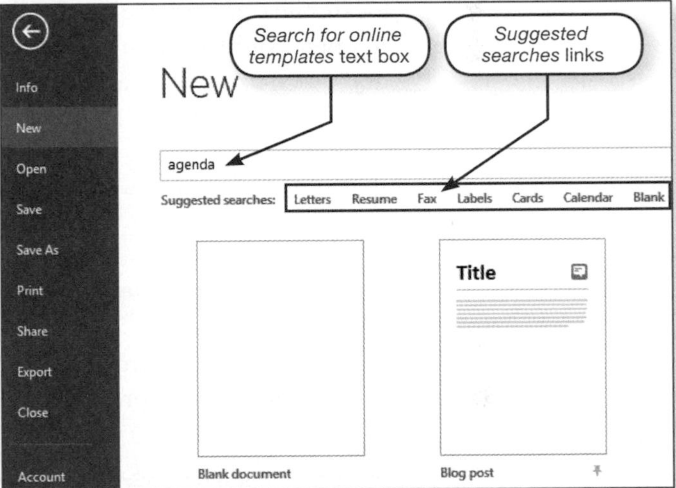

10-2 Open an Office.com template

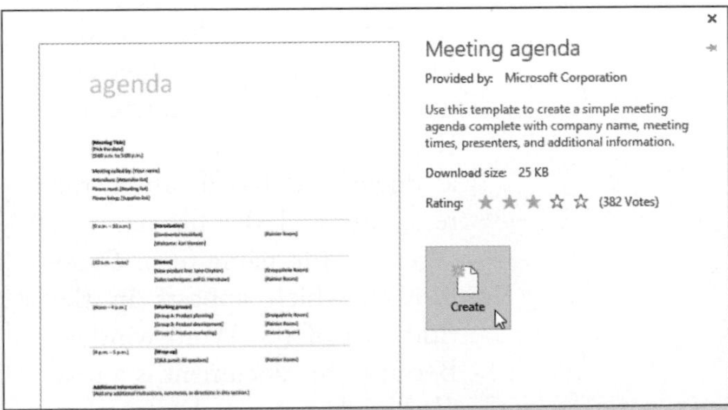

10-3 Template displayed in preview area

Open a Template

When you work with templates and documents based on templates, the way you open the file is very important. How you open the file determines whether the file opens as a template or a document based on a template. There are times when you want to customize a template file and other times when you want to create a document based on a template (see the next section, *Create a Document Based on a Template*).

The file icon for a template is different from the icon for a regular Word document. This helps you to distinguish between the two types of files (Figure 10-4). When you want to modify the content and structure of a template, there are two different ways to open a template file:

- Press **Ctrl+O** to open the *Backstage* view. Select the location of the template file or click the **Browse** button to open the *Open* dialog box (see Figure 10-4). Select the template you want to open and click the **Open** button to open the template file for editing.
- Open a **Windows folder** and locate the template file you want to open. Right-click the **template file** and select **Open** from the context menu. If you double-click a Word template file (.dotx) in a Windows folder, a Word document (.docx) based upon the template opens.

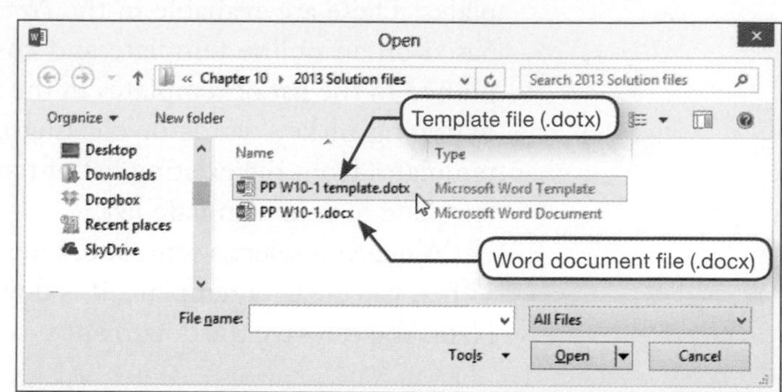

10-4 Open a template from the *Open* dialog box

> **ANOTHER WAY**
>
> Press **Ctrl+F12** to open the *Open* dialog box.

When you open a template file, the file name of the template appears in the title area at the top center of the Word window.

Create a Document Based on a Template

To open a document based on a template, always open the file from a Windows folder. Open the Windows folder and double-click the template file (Figure 10-5). Word opens a document based upon the template, and the file name is a generic file name (e.g., *Document1*), which appears in the title area of the Word window. Because this document is a new file based on a template, you are prompted to save the document before you close it.

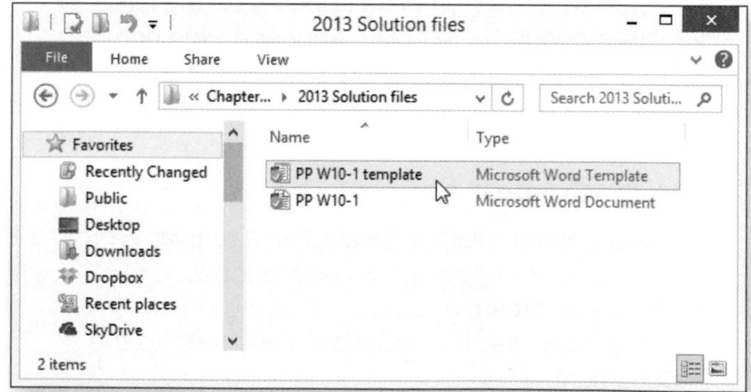

10-5 Open a document based on a template from a Windows folder

> **MORE INFO**
>
> If you have saved templates in the *Custom Office Templates* folder, these template are available when you select *Personal* in the *New* area on the *Backstage* view. Click a personal template to open a document based upon the personal template.

SLO 10.2

Customizing and Using Templates

When you create a new document from an online template, content and formatting are included in this document. You can customize the template content and format to meet your needs. Sometimes you create a document based on a template, but there are other times when you want to attach a template to an existing file so the styles and building blocks in the template are available in the document. You can also copy styles from one template to another template or document.

Customize Template Content

Some online templates provide just the basic structure and sample text in the template, while others have content control fields, Word fields, and document property fields to control the content. You can add content to or customize existing fields in a template. You can also add document properties or Word fields to a template.

Content Control Fields

Many available online templates include ***content control fields***. These fields are placeholders where users can type custom content. Some of these fields are for text. In others, users can select a date or check a check box. When you enter text in the content control field, the content control field is removed and replaced by the text you type. You can move, copy, or delete these fields.

HOW TO: Use Content Control Fields

1. Open the template or document with content control fields.
2. Click the **handle** of the content control field to select it (Figure 10-6).
3. Type your custom text in the content control field.
   - The content control field is removed from the document when you type your text.
4. You can click the content control field handle and drag the field to a new location, copy it, or delete it.
5. To deselect a content control field, use the left or right keyboard arrow key.

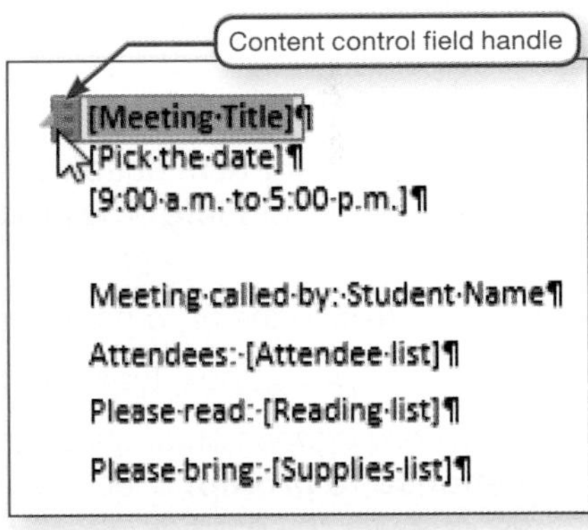

10-6 Content control field

When modifying a template with content control fields, insert text in content control fields where you do not want users to change the text and delete any unwanted content control fields. Then, when you create a document based on the template, the user can fill any remaining content control fields with custom text.

> **MORE INFO**
>
> In Chapter 11, you will learn how to insert and customize different types of content control fields.

Document Property Fields

Some online templates include ***document property fields***. You can also add document property fields to an existing template or a new template you create. Document property fields are populated with content from the document properties. If there is no content in document properties for the document property field in the template, the field displays the document property field name.

HOW TO: Customize and Insert Document Property Fields

1. Click the **handle** of the document property field to select it (Figure 10-7).
2. Type the content in the document property field.
   - The content you type populates the document property in the document.
   - You can also click the **File** tab to open the *Backstage* view and type content in the document properties. This information appears in the document property fields in the document.
3. To insert a document property field, click the **Quick Parts** button [*Insert* tab, *Text* group], click **Document Property**, and select the document property field you want to insert.

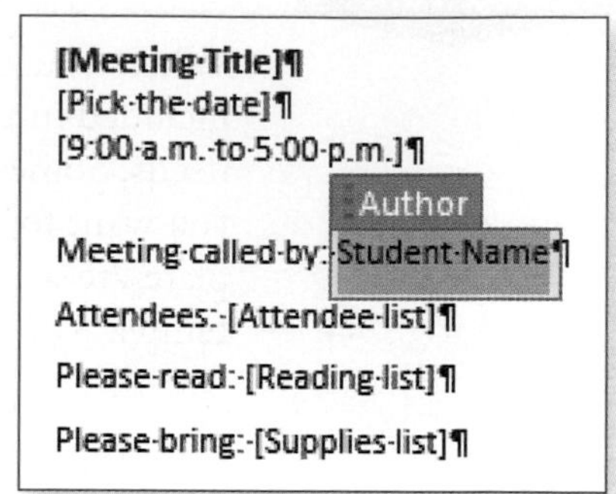

10-7 Document property field

Word Fields

Word fields in a template can automatically insert content. For example, you can insert Word fields to automatically insert the last date the document was saved (*SaveDate*), user name (*UserName*), user initials (*UserInitials*), or file name of the document (*FileName*). Another useful field for templates is the ***Fill-in*** field. The *Fill-in* field prompts a user for information when a template or document based on a template is opened.

HOW TO: Insert a Fill-In Field

1. Place your insertion point in the template where you want the *Fill-in* field inserted.
2. Click the **Quick Parts** button [*Insert* tab, *Text* group] and select **Field**. The *Field* dialog box opens (Figure 10-8).
3. Select **Fill-in** in the *Field names* area.
4. In the *Prompt* text box, type the prompt for the user.
5. In the *Field options* area, check the **Default response to prompt** check box and type a default response for the prompt.
   - The default response is the text that is inserted if the user does not type a response to the fill-in prompt.
6. Click **OK** to close the dialog box and insert the field. A prompt dialog box opens (Figure 10-9).

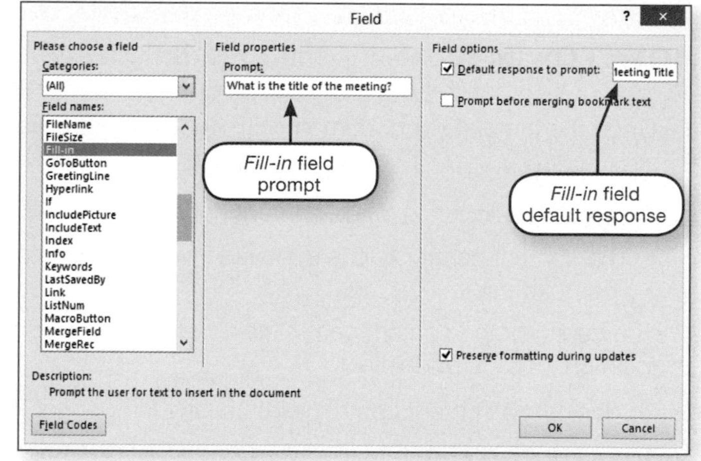

10-8 Insert a *Fill-in* field

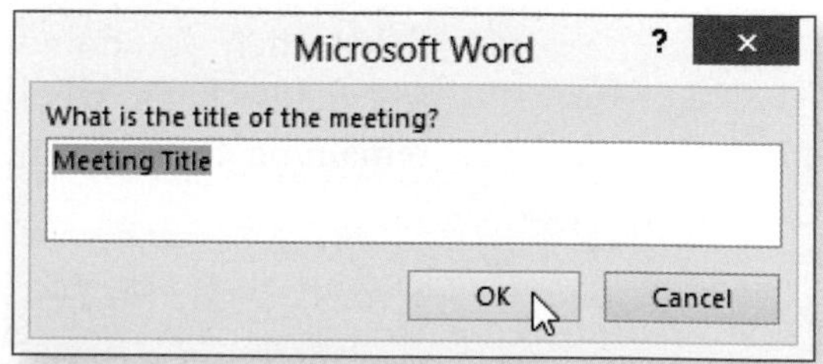

10-9 *Fill-in* field prompt dialog box

7. Click **OK** to close the prompt dialog box and insert the default text.
   - The default text is inserted in the *Fill-in* field (Figure 10-10). When creating or modifying a template, it is best to include the default response to the prompt for this field.
   - When you create a document based on this template, the prompt dialog box opens, and the user types in the text to replace the default response and populate the *Fill-in* field (see Figure 10-9).

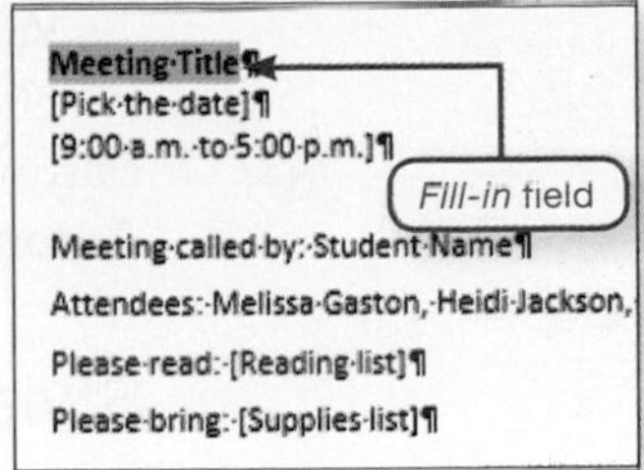

10-10 ***Fill-in* field in the template**

MORE INFO

You can use multiple *Fill-in* fields in a document. An individual dialog box opens for each *Fill-in* field prompting the user to enter information.

Attach a Template to a Document

When you create a document based on a template, the template is automatically attached to the document. Another way to connect a template to a document is to attach the template to the document. When you attach a template to a document, the styles, building blocks, and macros stored in the template are available in the document. In addition, you can set the document to automatically update whenever changes are made in the template file.

HOW TO: Attach a Template to a Document

1. Open the document that you want to attach to a template.
2. Click the **Document Template** button [*Developer* tab, *Templates* group]. The *Templates and Add-ins* dialog box opens (Figure 10-11).
   - If the *Developer* tab is not available on your *Ribbon*, click the **File** tab to open the *Backstage* view, select the **Options** to open the *Word Options* dialog box, click **Customize Ribbon**, and check the **Developer** check box at the right.
3. Click the **Attach** button in the *Document template* area. The *Attach Template* dialog box opens.
4. Browse and select the template you want to attach.
5. Click **Open** to close the *Attach Template* dialog box.
6. Check the **Automatically update document styles** box.
   - If this box is checked, the styles in the document are updated each time styles are modified in the template.
   - If this box is not checked, the styles in the document are not updated when the styles in the template are modified.
7. Click **OK** to close the *Templates and Add-ins* dialog box and attach the template to the document.

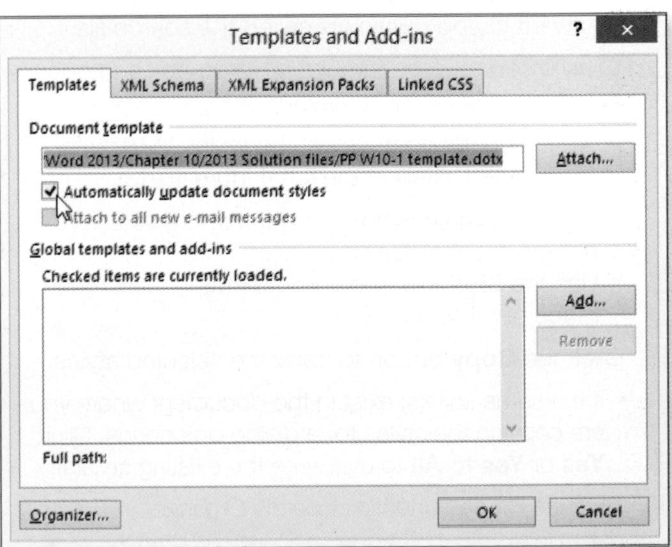

10-11 Attach a template to a document

When you create a document based on a template, the template file is automatically attached to the document, but by default the document is not set to update styles automatically when the styles in the template are modified. You can change this setting by checking the **Automatically update document styles** check box in the *Templates and Add-ins* dialog box.

Styles Organizer

> **MORE INFO**
>
> You cannot attach a template to a template file.

Another way to automate tasks and create consistency in documents is to copy styles from one document to another. For example, you might not want to attach a template to a document or create a document based on a template, but you want to use styles that already exist in a template or other document. In cases like this, you can use the *Organizer* dialog box to copy styles from a template or document to another template or document. This process saves you the time of recreating these styles.

HOW TO: Copy Styles into a Document

1. Open the document or template into which you want to copy styles.
2. Click the **Document Template** button [*Developer* tab, *Templates* group] to open the *Templates and Add-ins* dialog box.
3. Click the **Organizer** button to open the *Organizer* dialog box (Figure 10-12).
   - The document you have open is listed on the left and the styles in the document are displayed in the list.
   - The template the document is based on is listed on the right. By default, new blank Word documents are based on the *Normal* template.
4. Click the **Close File** button below the styles in the document on the right.
   - This closes the template the document is based on and the *Close File* button becomes the *Open File* button.
5. Click the **Open File** button. The *Open* dialog box opens.
6. Browse and select the file that contains the styles you want to copy, which is called the source file.
7. Click **Open** to close the *Open* dialog box and open the source file for the styles.
8. In the list on the right, select the styles to copy to the document listed at the left (Figure 10-13).
   - Use the **Ctrl** key and your pointer to select non-adjacent styles.
   - Use the **Shift** key and your pointer to select a range of adjacent styles.
9. Click the **Copy** button to copy the selected styles.
   - If the same style(s) exist in the document where you are copying the styles to, a dialog box opens. Click **Yes** or **Yes to All** to overwrite the existing style(s).
10. Click the **Close** button to close the *Organizer* dialog box.
    - The copied styles are listed in the *Styles* gallery and *Styles* pane.

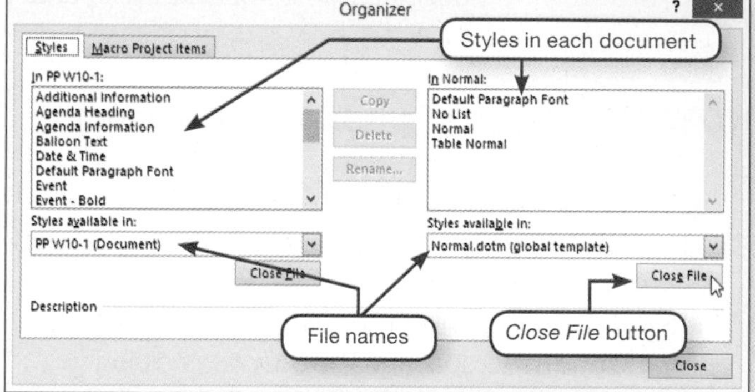

10-12 *Organizer* dialog box

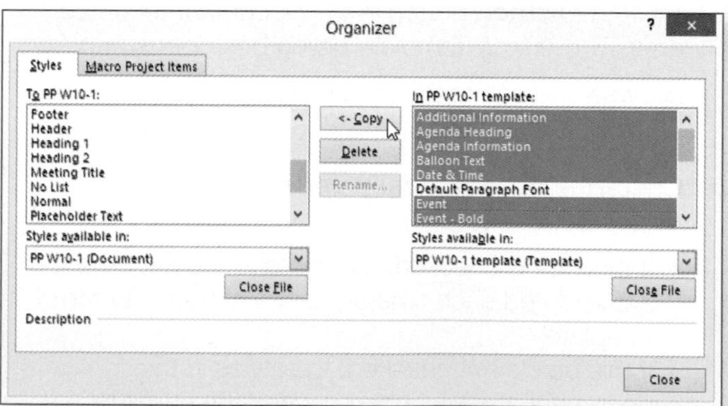

10-13 Copy selected styles

MORE INFO

The *Organizer* dialog box can also be used to delete styles from a document.

PAUSE & PRACTICE: WORD 10-1

For this Pause & Practice project, you create and modify a template for Sierra Pacific Community College student government meeting agendas. You save a document as a template, customize document property and content control fields, insert *Fill-in* fields, and create a document based on the template.

File Needed: ***SPCCDAgenda-10.docx***
Completed Project File Names: ***[your initials] PP W10-1 template.dotx*** and ***[your initials] PP W10-1. docx***

1. Open the ***SPCCDAgenda_10*** document from your student data files.
2. Save the document as a template named ***[your initials] PP W10-1 template***.
   a. Open the *Save As* dialog box (Figure 10-14).
   b. In the **File name** area, type [your initials] PP W10-1 template.
   c. Click the **Save as type** drop-down list and select **Word Template**.
   d. In the folder structure on the left, browse to the location where you want to save your file.
   e. Click **Save** to close the dialog box and the save the template.

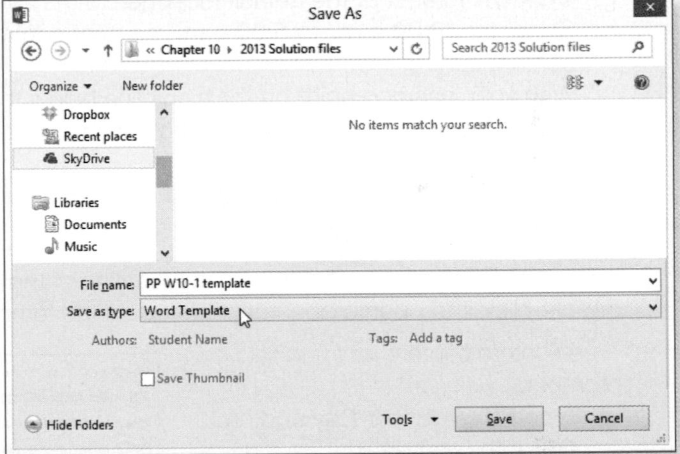

10-14 Save document as a Word template file

3. Customize the title.
   a. Select "**agenda**" and delete it. Don't delete the paragraph mark.
   b. Type SPCCD Student Government Agenda.
4. Update document property and content control fields.
   a. Click the "**Author**" (Student Name) document property field handle to select the field (Figure 10-15).
   b. Type your first and last name to replace the existing document property.
   c. Select the "**Attendee list**" content control field and replace the placeholder text with the following text: Melissa Gaston, Heidi Jackson, Rachel Sanchez, Peter Zanko, Ron Costa, Roietta Molden, and Ravi Kumar.
   d. In the table, select the "**Introduction**" content control field and type Welcome and Meeting Overview to replace the placeholder text.
   e. Select the "**Wrap-up**" content control field and type Wrap-up and Adjourn to replace the placeholder text.

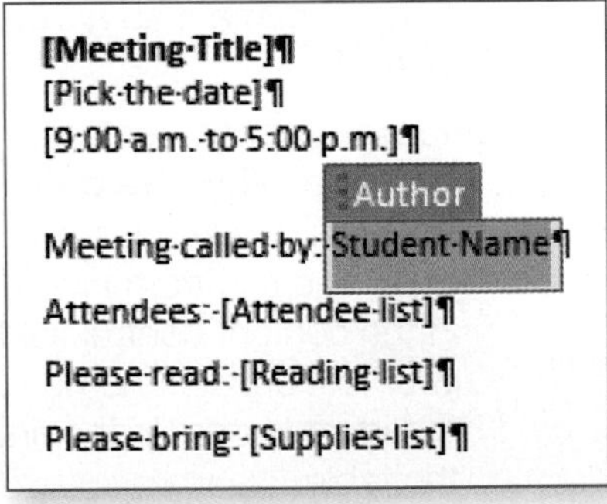

10-15 Update document property field

5. Customize the table content.
    a. Place your insertion point on the blank line above the content control field in the third cell in the first row of the table.
    b. Type Location.
    c. Select "**Location**" and apply the **Event–Bold** style [*Home* tab, *Styles* group].
6. Insert *Fill-in* fields.
    a. Select the "**Meeting Title**" content control field handle to select it and press **Delete** to remove the content control field.
    b. With your insertion point on the blank line above the "Pick the date" field, click the **Quick Parts** button [*Insert* tab, *Text* group] and select **Field** to open the *Field* dialog box (Figure 10-16).
    c. In the *Field names* area, select **Fill-in**.
    d. In the *Prompt* area, type What is the title of the meeting?
    e. Check the **Default response to prompt** check box and type Meeting Title in the text box.
    f. Click **OK** to close the *Field* dialog box and insert the *Fill-in* field. The prompt dialog box opens.
    g. Click **OK** to accept the default response to the *Fill-in* prompt.
    h. Select the "**9:00 a.m. to 5:00 p.m.**" content control field handle and press **Delete** to remove the content control field.
    i. With your insertion point on the blank line below the "Pick the date" field, insert another *Fill-in* field.
    j. Type What is the time of the meeting? as the prompt and Meeting Time as the default response to the prompt.
    k. Click **OK** in the *Field* dialog box and click **OK** to accept the default response to the *Fill-in* prompt.

10-16 Insert *Fill-in* field

7. Save and close the template.
8. Using a Windows folder, browse to the location of the ***[your initials] PP W10-1 template*** file and double-click it to open a document based on the template.
9. Type custom content for *Fill-in* field prompts.
    a. Type Fall Welcome Day and click **OK** at the first prompt.
    b. Type 3 to 5 p.m. and click **OK** at the second prompt.
10. Save the document as ***[your initials] PP W10-1***.
11. Customize agenda content.
    a. Click the "**Pick the date**" field and select next Tuesday.
    b. Insert the text from Figure 10-17 in the content control fields. Type your first and last name to replace "Student Name" in the first row of the table.
12. Change the document so styles are updated automatically if the template is modified.
    a. Click the **Document Template** button [*Developer* tab, *Templates* group] to open the *Templates and Add-ins* dialog box.
    b. Check the **Automatically update document styles** box and click **OK** to close the dialog box.

Meeting·called·by:·Student·Name¶
Attendees:·Melissa·Gaston,·Heidi·Jackson,·Rachel·Sanchez,·Peter·Zanko,·Ron·Costa,·Roietta·Molden,·and·Ravi·Kumar¶
Please·read:·Fall·Welcome·Day·Flyer·and·Welcome·Day·Guidelines¶
Please·bring:·Same·as·above¶

3:00-3:15¤	**Welcome·and·Meeting·Overview¶** Student·Name¤	**Location¶** Sequoia·Room¤
3:15-4:00¤	**Breakout·Groups¶** Club·Presidents:·Melissa·Gaston¶ Marketing:·Peter·Zanko¶ Facilities:·Rachel·Sanchez¤	¶ Sequoia·Room¶ Redwood·Room¶ Oak·Room¤
4:00-4:45¤	**Fall·Welcome·Day·Planning¶** To-do·lists·and·needs·from·each·group¤	¶ Sequoia·Room¤
4:45-5:00¤	**Wrap-up·and·Adjourn¶** Old·business¤	¶ Sequoia·Room¤

Additional·Information:¶
Our·next·meeting·is·next·Tuesday·from·3·to·5·p.m.¶

10-17 Type text in content control fields

MORE INFO

If the *Developer* tab is not available on your *Ribbon,* click the **File** tab to open the *Backstage* view, select the **Options** to open the *Word Options* dialog box, click **Customize Ribbon**, and then check the **Developer** check box on the right.

13. Save and close the document.
14. Modify styles in the template file.
    a. From within Word, open the ***[your initials] PP W10-1 template*** file.
    b. Select the title and change the font size to **28 pt.**, apply **bold** and **small caps** formatting, change line spacing to **1**, and change the before paragraph spacing to **12 pt.** and the after paragraph spacing to **0 pt.**
    c. With the text selected, update the **Agenda Heading** style to match the selection.
    d. Modify the **Event – Bold** style to apply **small caps** formatting. Each of the headings in the table changes to small caps.
15. Save and close the template.
16. From within Word, open the ***[your initials] PP W10-1*** file. The style changes in the template are reflected in this document based on the template (Figure 10-18).
17. Save and close the document.

SPCCD STUDENT GOVERNMENT AGENDA

Fall Welcome Day
9/9/2014
3 to 5 p.m.

Meeting called by: Student Name
Attendees: Melissa Gaston, Heidi Jackson, Rachel Sanchez, Peter Zanko, Ron Costa, Roietta Molden, and Ravi Kumar
Please read: Fall Welcome Day Flyer and Welcome Day Guidelines
Please bring: Same as above

3:00-3:15	**WELCOME AND MEETING OVERVIEW** Student Name	**LOCATION** Sequoia Room
3:15-4:00	**BREAKOUT GROUPS** Club Presidents: Melissa Gaston Marketing: Peter Zanko Facilities: Rachel Sanchez	 Sequoia Room Redwood Room Oak Room
4:00-4:45	**FALL WELCOME DAY PLANNING** To-do lists and needs from each group	Sequoia Room
4:45-5:00	**WRAP-UP AND ADJOURN** Old business	Sequoia Room

Additional Information:
Our next meeting is next Tuesday from 3 to 5 p.m.

10-18 PP W10-1 completed

3. In the *Macro name* area, type a name for the macro.
   - You cannot use spaces between words in a macro name. If needed, use an underscore to separate words.
4. Click the ***Store macro in*** drop-down list and select the document or template where the macro is stored.
5. In the *Description* area, type a brief description for the macro.
6. Click the **Button** button. The *Word Options* dialog box opens (Figure 10-24).

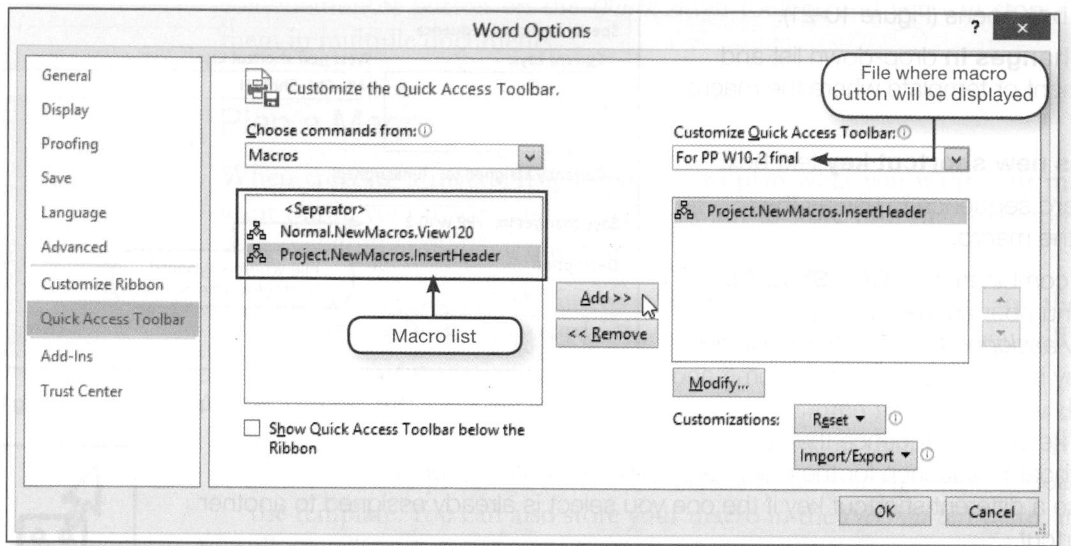

10-24 **Add a macro to the *Quick Access* toolbar**

7. Click the **Customize Quick Access Toolbar** drop-down list and select the document where you want the macro button.
8. Select the **macro** in the list on the left and click the **Add** button.
9. Click the **Modify** button. The *Modify Button* dialog box opens (Figure 10-25).
10. In the *Display name* area, type a name for the button.
11. Select the icon to use as the button. Word provides you with a variety of button icon options.
12. Click **OK** to close the *Modify Button* dialog box.
13. Click the **OK** button to close the *Word Options* dialog box and begin recording your macro. Your pointer changes to a macro-recording pointer.
14. Perform the actions to record as a macro.
15. Click the **Stop Recording** button [*Developer* tab, *Code* group] to stop recording the macro.
    - The macro button appears on the *Quick Access* toolbar (Figure 10-26).

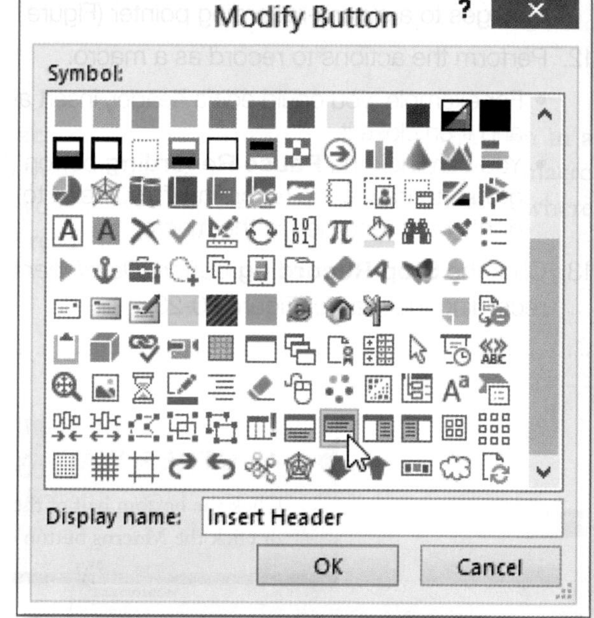

10-25 ***Modify Button* dialog box**

10-26 **Macro button on the *Quick Access* toolbar**

Save a Macro-Enabled Document

When you create a macro in a document, you have to save the document as a macro-enabled document in order for the macro to be stored in the document. When you save the document, you will be prompted to either save the document as a Word macro-enabled document or remove the macros from the document. A Word macro-enabled document has a ***.docm*** file extension.

> **MORE INFO**
>
> If a document contains macros and you don't save it as a macro-enabled document, the macros in the document are removed.

HOW TO: Save as a Macro-Enabled Document

1. When you save a document that contains a macro, a dialog box opens informing you that there are macros in the document (Figure 10-27).

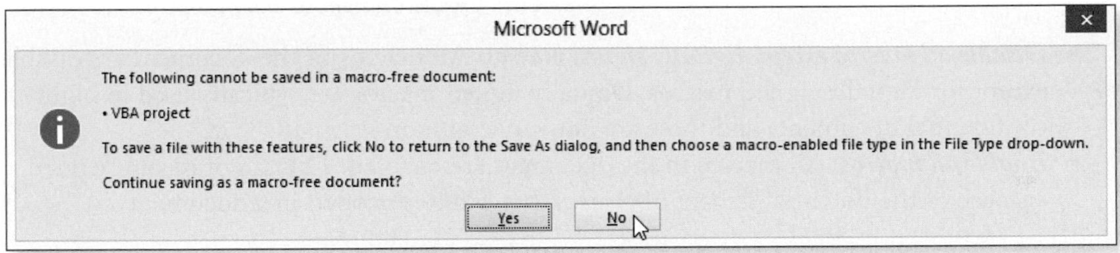

10-27 Dialog box prompting you to save as a macro-enabled document

2. Click **No** to open the *Save As* dialog box (Figure 10-28).
   - If you click *Yes*, the document is saved and the macros are removed from the document.
3. Type the name of the file in the *File name* area.
4. Click the **Save as type** drop-down list and select **Word Macro-Enabled Document**.
   - Be sure to save as a *Word Macro-Enabled Document*. Saving a document as a macro-enabled template is covered in *SLO 10.5: Using Macro-Enabled Templates*.
5. Click the **Save** button.

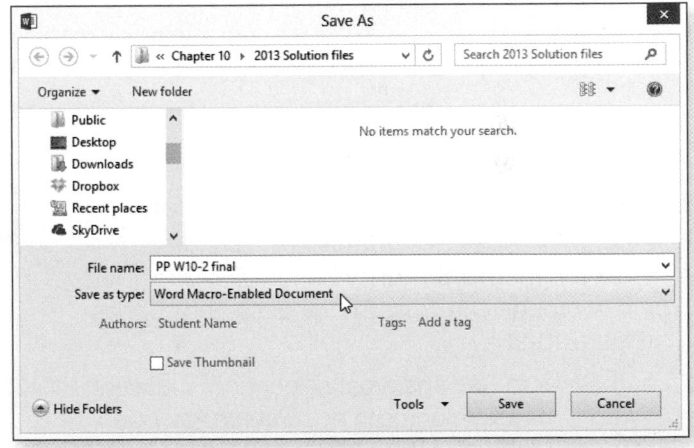

10-28 Save as a Word macro-enabled document

If you are creating a document that will contain macros, save the document as a macro-enabled document when you first save the document.

> **MORE INFO**
>
> The file icon for a macro-enabled document is different from the icon for a regular Word document.

Macro Security Settings

Because a macro is actually a program that runs within your document, Word provides security settings to control how macros are handled when you open a document containing macros. There are four different macro settings:

- ***Disable all macros without notification:*** All macros in the document are disabled without notifying you.
- ***Disable all macros with notification:*** All macros in the document will be disabled and a security warning appears in the *Info* bar when you open the document (Figure 10-29). Click the **Enable Content** button to enable macros in the document. This is the default setting and the best setting to use.

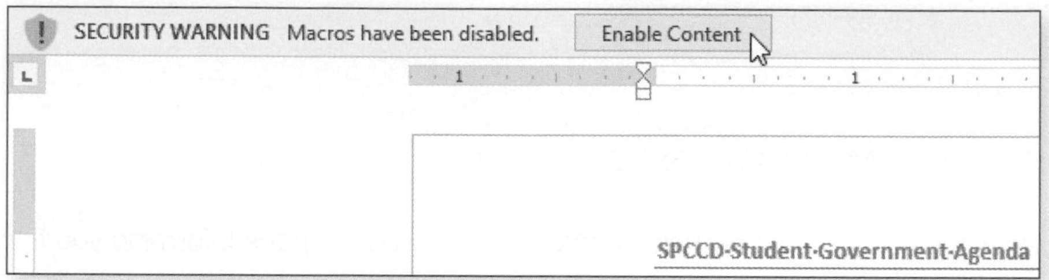

10-29 Click *Enable Content* to enable macros

- ***Disable all macros except digitally signed macros:*** All macros in the document are disabled except for digitally signed macros. Digitally signed macros are typically used in highly confidential documents and these are not very common.
- ***Enable all macros:*** All macros in the document are enabled. This is not recommended because of the potential danger of viruses that can be encoded in a document.

> MORE INFO
>
> When you open a document containing macros, you are usually prompted to enable the macros. Click the **Enable Content** button in the Info bar (see Figure 10-29).

HOW TO: Change Macro Security Settings

1. Click the **Macro Security** button [*Developer* tab, *Code* group]. The *Trust Center* dialog box opens (Figure 10-30).
2. In the *Macro Settings* area, select how you want Word to handle macros in documents you open.
3. Click **OK** to close the *Trust Center* dialog box.

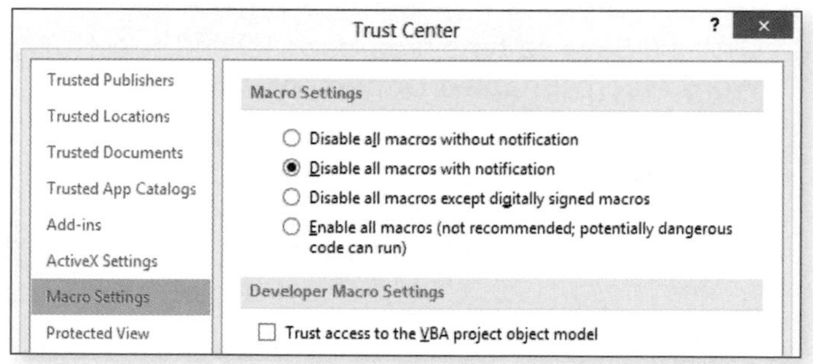

10-30 Macro settings in the *Trust Center* dialog box

Run a Macro

When you run a macro, you insert what is recorded in the macro into a document. Depending on how a macro is recorded and saved in a document, you can run a macro in a variety of ways. You run a keyboard-activated macro by pressing the shortcut key. You run a button-activated macro by clicking the macro button on the *Quick Access* toolbar. You can also run a macro from the ***Macros dialog box.***

HOW TO: Run a Macro from the Macros Dialog Box

1. Click the **Macro** button [*Developer* tab, *Code* group] to open the *Macros* dialog box (Figure 10-31).
2. In the *Macro name* area, select the macro you want to run.
3. Click the **Run** button.
   - The *Macros* dialog box automatically closes when you run a macro.

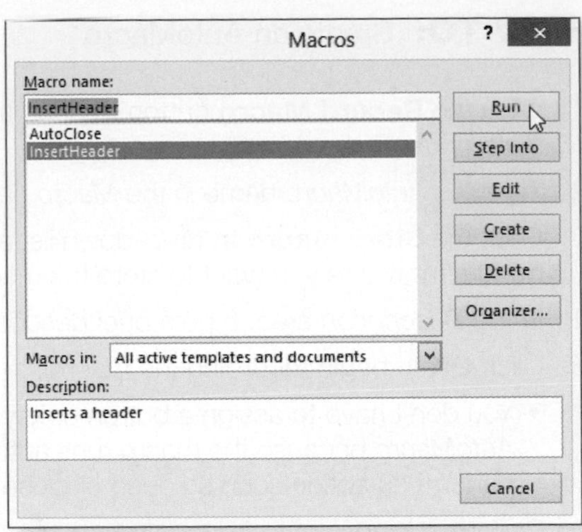

10-31 ***Macros* dialog box**

> **ANOTHER WAY**
>
> **Alt+F8** opens the *Macros* dialog box.

Delete a Macro

If you make a mistake when you record a macro or if you want to delete a macro from a document, delete it using the *Macros* dialog box.

HOW TO: Delete a Macro

1. Click the **Macros** button [*Developer* tab, *Code* group] to open the *Macros* dialog box.
2. In the *Macro name* area, select the macro you want to delete.
3. Click the **Delete** button. A dialog box opens asking if you want to delete the macro (Figure 10-32).
4. Click **Yes** to delete the macro.

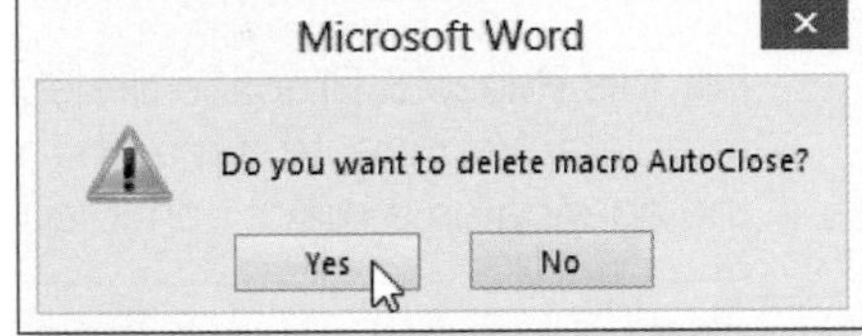

10-32 Delete a macro

Create an AutoMacro

Word provides you with a set of macros that automatically runs when you perform a specific action. For example, you can create an ***AutoMacro*** to insert the current date each time you open a document or remove a watermark when you save and close a document. Each of these macros uses a specific name that Word recognizes as an *AutoMacro* name. Because *AutoMacros* run automatically when you perform an action, you don't have to assign the macro to a button or keyboard sequence. The following table lists each of the *AutoMacros* and a description:

Types of AutoMacros

AutoMacro	Description
AutoExec	Runs when you open Word.
AutoOpen	Runs each time you open a Word document.
AutoNew	Runs each time you create a new Word document.
AutoClose	Runs each time you close a Word document.
AutoExit	Runs when you exit Word.

HOW TO: Create an AutoMacro

1. Click the **Record Macro** button to open the *Record Macro* dialog box (Figure 10-33).
2. Type the *AutoMacro* name in the *Macro* name area.
3. Click the **Store macro in** drop-down list and select the document where you want to store the macro.
4. In the *Description* area, type a brief description of the macro.
5. Click **OK** to begin recording the macro.
   - You don't have to assign a button or keyboard sequence to an *AutoMacro* because the macro runs automatically when you perform an action such as open or close a document.
6. Perform the actions to be recorded in the *AutoMacro*.
7. Click the **Stop Recording** button [*Developer* tab, *Code* group].
   - The *AutoMacro* runs the next time you perform the specified action.
   - The *AutoMacro* is listed in the *Macros* dialog box.

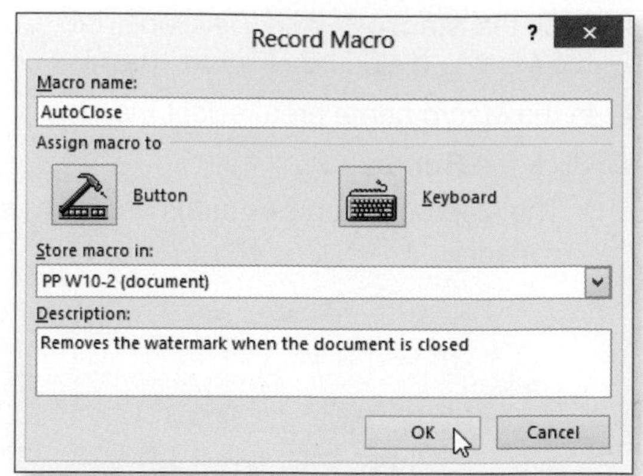

10-33 Record an *AutoMacro*

PAUSE & PRACTICE: WORD 10-2

For this Pause & Practice project, you modify the agenda document you created based on the agenda template. You create a macro to insert a header, create an *AutoMacro* to remove a watermark, save the agenda as a macro-enabled document, and delete a macro.

File Needed: ***[your initials] PP W10-1.docx***
Completed Project File Names: ***[your initials] PP W10-2.docx*** and ***[your initials] PP W10-2 final.docm***

1. Open the ***[your initials] PP W10-1*** document you created in *Pause & Practice 10-1*.
2. Save the document as **[your initials] PP W10-2** (regular Word document).
3. Create a keyboard-activated macro.
   a. Click the **Record Macro** button [*Developer* tab, *Code* group] to open the *Record Macro* dialog box (Figure 10-34).
   b. In the *Macro name* area, type InsertHeader (no spaces between words).
   c. Click the **Store macro in** drop-down list and select **[your initials] PP W10-2 (document)**.
   d. In the *Description* area, type Inserts a header.
   e. Click the **Keyboard** button to open the *Customize Keyboard* dialog box (Figure 10-35).

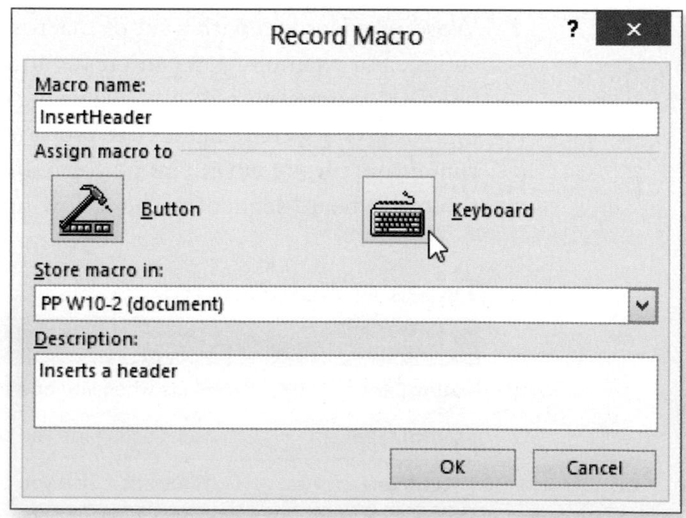

10-34 Record a keyboard-activated macro

f. Click the **Save changes in** drop-down list and select **[your initials] PP W10-2**.
g. Place your insertion point in the **Press new shortcut key** text box and press **Alt+Ctrl+Shift+H**.
h. Click the **Assign** button to assign the keyboard shortcut to the macro.
i. Click the **Close** button to close the *Customize Keyboard* dialog box and begin recording the macro.

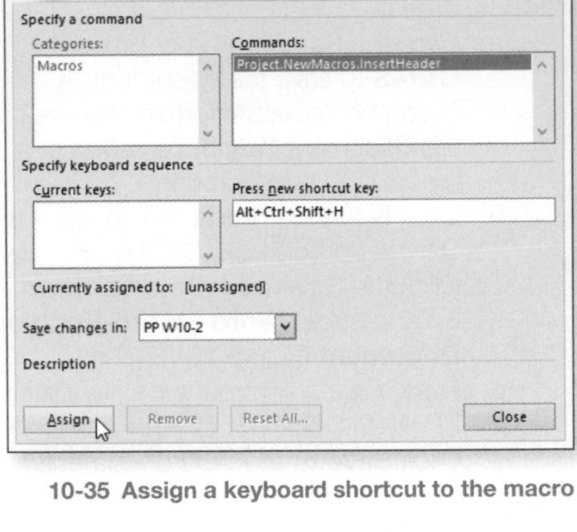

10-35 Assign a keyboard shortcut to the macro

4. Record a macro to insert a header in the agenda.
   a. Click the **Header** button [*Insert* tab, *Header & Footer* group] and select **Edit Header** from the drop-down list to open the header.
   b. Click the **Bold** button [*Home* tab, *Font* group].
   c. Type SPCCD Student Government Agenda and press **Tab** two times to move the insertion point to the right margin.
   d. Type Last updated: and **space** once.
   e. Click the **Date & Time** button [*Insert* tab, *Text* group] to open the *Date and Time* dialog box.
   f. Select the first date format (1/1/2013), check the **Update automatically** box, and click **OK** to close the dialog box and insert the date.
   g. Click the **Borders** drop-down button [*Home* tab, *Paragraph* group] and select **Bottom Border**.
   h. Click the **Close Header and Footer** button [*Header & Footer Tools Design* tab, *Close* group] to close the header.
   i. Click the **Stop Recording** button [*Developer* tab, *Code* group].
5. Test the macro.
   a. Open the header, delete all of the information in the header, and close the header.
   b. Press **Alt+Ctrl+Shift+H** to run the macro. The header is inserted in the document.
6. Click the **Watermark** button [*Design* tab, *Page Background* group] and select the **Draft 1** watermark.
7. Create an *AutoClose* macro that runs each time you close the document.
   a. Click the **Record Macro** button [*Developer* tab, *Code* group] to open the *Record Macro* dialog box (Figure 10-36).
   b. In the *Macro name* area, type AutoClose (no spaces between words).
   c. Click the **Store macro in** drop-down list and select **[your initials] PP W10-2 (document)**.
   d. In the *Description* area, type Removes the watermark when the document is closed.
   e. Click the **OK** button to close the *Record Macro* dialog box and begin recording the macro.

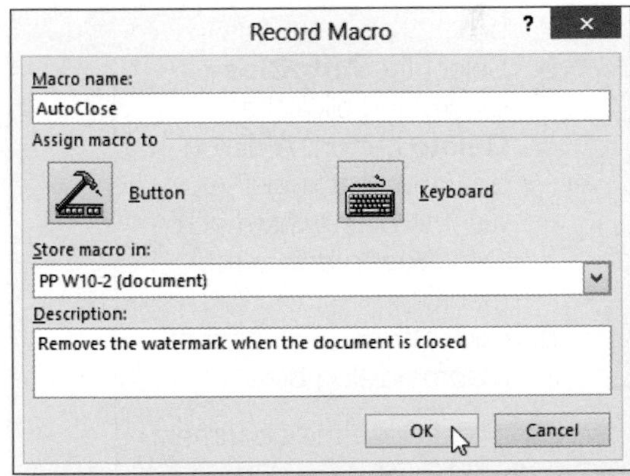

10-36 Record an *AutoClose* macro

8. Record a macro to remove a watermark.
   a. Click the **Watermark** button [*Design* tab, *Page Background* group] and select **Remove Watermark** from the drop-down list.
   b. Click the **Stop Recording** button [*Developer* tab, *Code* group].
9. Click the **Watermark** button and select the **Draft 1** watermark to insert it.

10. Save the document as a macro-enabled document.
    a. Click the **Save** button or press **Ctrl+S** to save the document. A dialog box opens informing you that the document cannot be saved in a macro-free environment.
    b. Click **No** in the dialog box to open the *Save As* dialog box.
    c. Click the **Save as type** drop-down list and select **Word Macro-Enabled Document** (Figure 10-37).
    d. In the *File name* area, type [your initials] PP W10-2 final.
    e. Click **Save** to save the document.

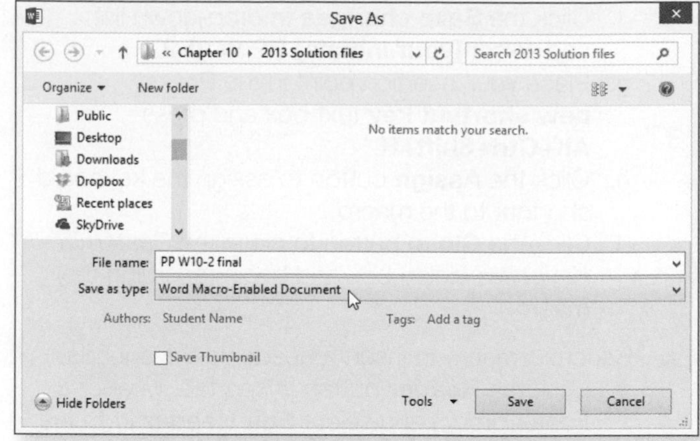

10-37 Save the agenda as a macro-enabled document

11. Close the document.
    a. The watermark is removed and you are prompted to save the document.
    b. Click **Save** to save and close the document.

12. Open a macro-enabled document and enable the macro content.
    a. Open the ***[your initials] PP W10-2 final*** document. If this document is not listed in the location where you saved the file, click the file type drop-down list in the *Open* dialog box (above the *Open* button) and select **All Files**.
    b. A security warning may appear in the *Info* bar (Figure 10-38). If so, click **Enable Content** in the *Info* bar to enable the macros in the document. Notice that the watermark has been removed.

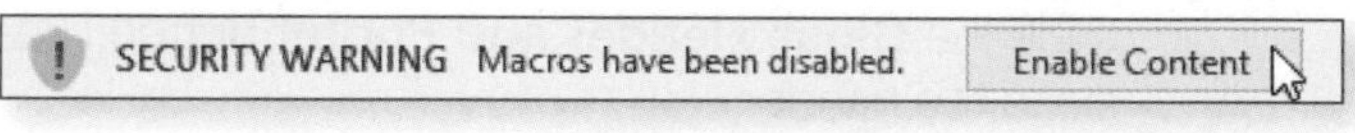

10-38 Enable macros in the document

13. Delete the *AutoClose* macro.
    a. Click the **Macros** button to open the *Macros* dialog box.
    b. Select the **AutoClose** macro and click the **Delete** button. A dialog box opens asking if you want to delete the macro.
    c. Click **Yes** to delete the macro.
    d. Click **Close** to close the *Macros* dialog box.

14. Save and close the document (Figure 10-39).

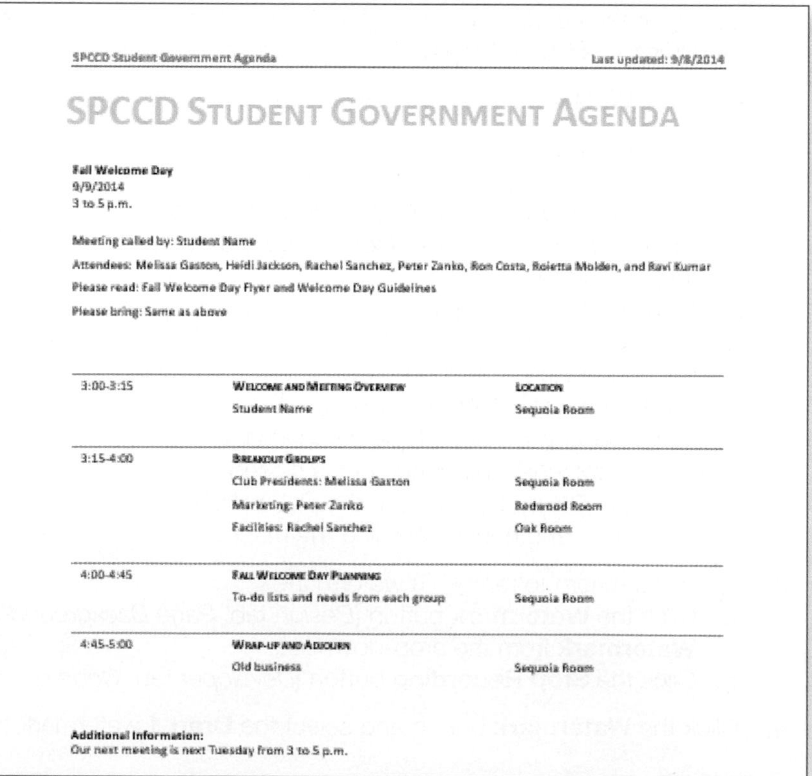

SPCCD Student Government Agenda — Last updated: 9/8/2014

SPCCD STUDENT GOVERNMENT AGENDA

Fall Welcome Day
9/9/2014
3 to 5 p.m.

Meeting called by: Student Name

Attendees: Melissa Gaston, Heidi Jackson, Rachel Sanchez, Peter Zanko, Ron Costa, Roietta Molden, and Ravi Kumar

Please read: Fall Welcome Day Flyer and Welcome Day Guidelines

Please bring: Same as above

3:00-3:15	WELCOME AND MEETING OVERVIEW	LOCATION
	Student Name	Sequoia Room
3:15-4:00	BREAKOUT GROUPS	
	Club Presidents: Melissa Gaston	Sequoia Room
	Marketing: Peter Zanko	Redwood Room
	Facilities: Rachel Sanchez	Oak Room
4:00-4:45	FALL WELCOME DAY PLANNING	
	To-do lists and needs from each group	Sequoia Room
4:45-5:00	WRAP-UP AND ADJOURN	
	Old business	Sequoia Room

Additional Information:
Our next meeting is next Tuesday from 3 to 5 p.m.

10-39 PP W10-2 final completed

SLO 10.4 Editing Macros

Macros are programs that run within Word, and they are coded in a programming language called ***Visual Basic***. When you record a macro, the Visual Basic code is created and stored in the macro. There might be times when you want to copy a macro and make changes to it rather than recreate the macro. The ***Microsoft Visual Basic editor*** is the program that you use to edit or copy a macro. You don't need knowledge of Visual Basic to copy a macro and do simple editing.

Copy a Macro

Copying a macro can save you time if the macro you are copying is similar to the one you want to create. For example, you can copy a macro that inserts a header and edit it so it inserts a footer instead. This section explains how to copy a macro and the next section explains how to edit a macro. Copy a macro when you want to create a macro that is similar to the original macro. If you are creating a macro that is very different from an existing macro, it is easier to record a new macro.

HOW TO: Copy a Macro

1. Click the **Macros** button [*Developer* tab, *Code* group] to open the *Macros* dialog box.
2. Select the macro to copy and click the **Edit** button. The *Microsoft Visual Basic* editor opens.
3. Select the Visual Basic code for the macro and click the **Copy** button or press **Ctrl+C** to copy it (Figure 10-40).
   - A macro begins with "Sub" and the name of the macro.
   - A macro ends with "End Sub."
   - The green text near the top is the description of the macro.
   - The coding in the middle describes the actions the macro performs.
4. Place your insertion point on the blank line below "End Sub."
5. Click the **Paste** button or press **Ctrl+V** to paste the copied macro.
   - The copied macro appears below the original macro. A horizontal line separates the two.

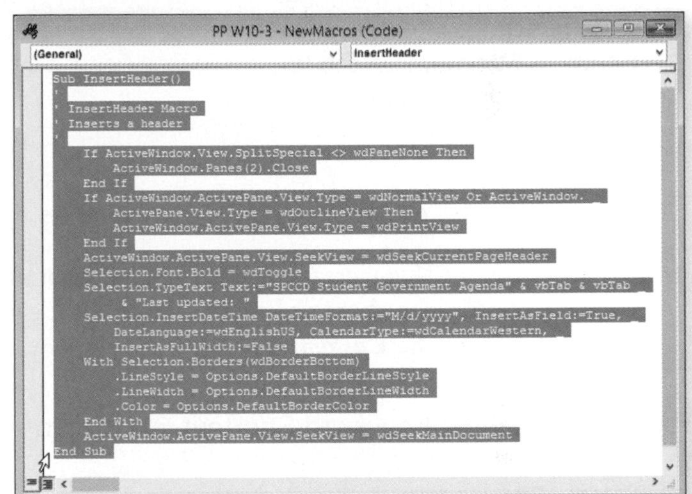
PP W10-3 - NewMacros (Code)
(General)
InsertHeader
Sub InsertHeader()
'
' InsertHeader Macro
' Inserts a header
'
If ActiveWindow.View.SplitSpecial <> wdPaneNone Then
ActiveWindow.Panes(2).Close
End If
If ActiveWindow.ActivePane.View.Type = wdNormalView Or ActiveWindow.
ActivePane.View.Type = wdOutlineView Then
ActiveWindow.ActivePane.View.Type = wdPrintView
End If
ActiveWindow.ActivePane.View.SeekView = wdSeekCurrentPageHeader
Selection.Font.Bold = wdToggle
Selection.TypeText Text:="SPCCD Student Government Agenda" & vbTab & vbTab
& "Last updated: "
Selection.InsertDateTime DateTimeFormat:="M/d/yyyy", InsertAsField:=True,
DateLanguage:=wdEnglishUS, CalendarType:=wdCalendarWestern,
InsertAsFullWidth:=False
With Selection.Borders(wdBorderBottom)
.LineStyle = Options.DefaultBorderLineStyle
.LineWidth = Options.DefaultBorderLineWidth
.Color = Options.DefaultBorderColor
End With
ActiveWindow.ActivePane.View.SeekView = wdSeekMainDocument
End Sub

10-40 Copy a macro in the Microsoft Visual Basic editor

6. On the copied macro, change the name of the macro after "Sub" (Figure 10-41).
   - Don't delete the beginning and ending parentheses () after the macro name.
   - The name of the macro is the macro name that appears in the *Macros* dialog box.

End Sub
Sub InsertFooter()
'

10-41 Change the macro name

7. Press **Ctrl+S** or click the **Save** button to save the macros.
8. Click the **File** menu in the upper left corner and select **Close and Return to Microsoft Word** to return to your document.

Edit a Macro

After copying a macro, you can edit the macro using the Microsoft Visual Basic editor. You can also edit an existing macro. For example, you can change text in a macro, change the macro name or description, change a header to a footer, or change a border.

HOW TO: Edit a Macro

1. Click the **Macros** button [*Developer* tab, *Code* group] to open the *Macros* dialog box.
2. Select the macro you want to edit and click the **Edit** button. The Microsoft Visual Basic editor opens (Figure 10-42).
3. Edit the existing code to customize the macro.
   - Figure 10-42 shows highlighted changes made to a macro to make it easier to see the edits in the figure.
   - When you actually edit a macro, changes are not highlighted.
4. Press **Ctrl+S** or click the **Save** button to save the macros.
5. Click the **File** menu in the upper left corner and select **Close and Return to Microsoft Word** to return to your document.

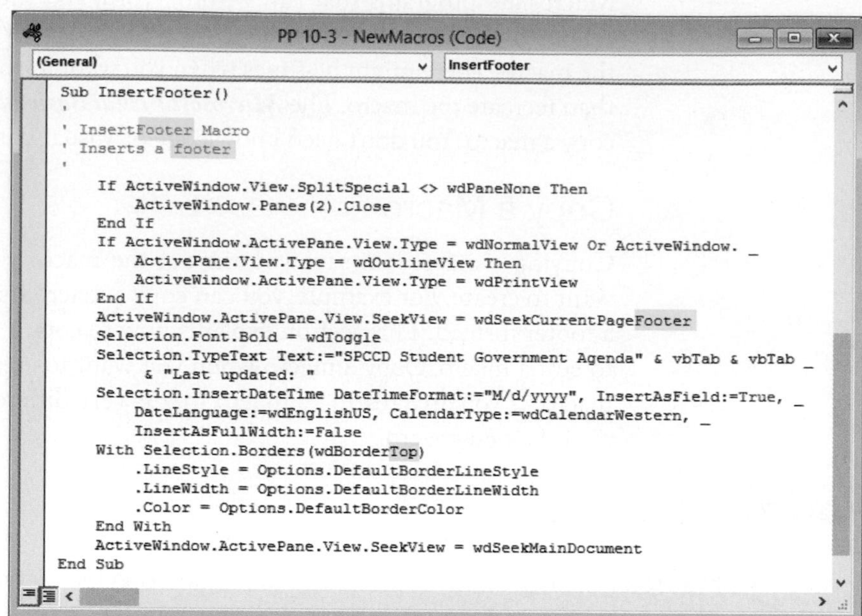

PP 10-3 - NewMacros (Code)
(General)
InsertFooter
```
Sub InsertFooter()
'
' InsertFooter Macro
' Inserts a footer
'
    If ActiveWindow.View.SplitSpecial <> wdPaneNone Then
        ActiveWindow.Panes(2).Close
    End If
    If ActiveWindow.ActivePane.View.Type = wdNormalView Or ActiveWindow. _
        ActivePane.View.Type = wdOutlineView Then
        ActiveWindow.ActivePane.View.Type = wdPrintView
    End If
    ActiveWindow.ActivePane.View.SeekView = wdSeekCurrentPageFooter
    Selection.Font.Bold = wdToggle
    Selection.TypeText Text:="SPCCD Student Government Agenda" & vbTab & vbTab _
         & "Last updated: "
    Selection.InsertDateTime DateTimeFormat:="M/d/yyyy", InsertAsField:=True, _
        DateLanguage:=wdEnglishUS, CalendarType:=wdCalendarWestern, _
        InsertAsFullWidth:=False
    With Selection.Borders(wdBorderTop)
        .LineStyle = Options.DefaultBorderLineStyle
        .LineWidth = Options.DefaultBorderLineWidth
        .Color = Options.DefaultBorderColor
    End With
    ActiveWindow.ActivePane.View.SeekView = wdSeekMainDocument
End Sub
```

10-42 Edit the macro

Add a Shortcut Key to a Macro

If you created a macro and did not assign a shortcut key to the macro, or if you want to change the shortcut key on a macro, you can add or change the shortcut keys for your macros using the ***Customize Keyboard dialog box.***

HOW TO: Add a Keyboard Shortcut to a Macro

1. Click the **File** tab to open the *Backstage* view.
2. Select **Options** at the left to open the *Word Options* dialog box.
3. Click **Customize Ribbon** at the left.
4. Click the **Customize** button in the *Keyboard shortcuts* area. The *Customize Keyboard* dialog box opens (Figure 10-43).
5. In the *Categories* area, scroll down and select **Macros**.
6. Click the **Save changes in** drop-down list and select the document where the macro is stored.
7. In the *Macros* list, select the macro that you want to add a shortcut key to.
8. Place your insertion point in the *Press new shortcut key* text box.
9. Press the shortcut key (e.g., **Alt+Ctrl+Shift+F**) you want to assign to the selected macro.

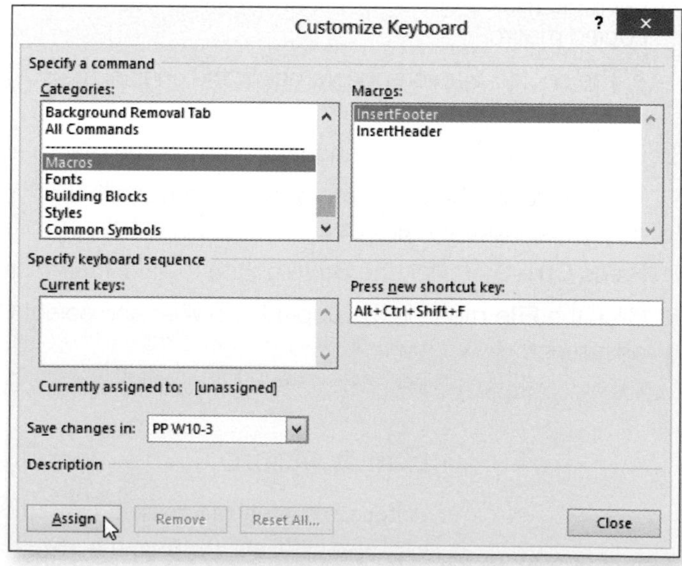

Customize Keyboard
Specify a command
Categories:
Background Removal Tab
All Commands
Macros
Fonts
Building Blocks
Styles
Common Symbols
Macros:
InsertFooter
InsertHeader
Specify keyboard sequence
Current keys:
Press new shortcut key:
Alt+Ctrl+Shift+F
Currently assigned to: [unassigned]
Save changes in: PP W10-3
Description
Assign
Remove
Reset All...
Close

10-43 Add a keyboard shortcut to a macro

10. Click the **Assign** button.
    - After you click the **Assign** button, the shortcut key appears in the *Current keys* area.
    - If a selected macro already has a shortcut key, it is displayed in the *Current keys* area.
    - You can remove a shortcut key by selecting it in the *Current keys* area and clicking the **Remove** button. After removing an existing shortcut key from a macro, you can add a new one.
11. Click **Close** to close the *Customize Keyboard* dialog box.
12. Click **OK** to close the *Word Options* dialog box.

Add a Macro Button to the Quick Access Toolbar

Recall that you can also run a macro using a button on the *Quick Access* toolbar. If you didn't create a button-activated macro when you originally recorded the macro, you can add a macro button to the *Quick Access* toolbar to run an existing macro, or you can edit an existing macro button to change the icon or display name.

HOW TO: Add a Macro Button to the Quick Access Toolbar

1. Click the **File** tab to open the *Backstage* view.
2. Select **Options** at the left to open the *Word Options* dialog box.
3. Click **Quick Access Toolbar** on the left to display the *Customize the Quick Access Toolbar* area (Figure 10-44).

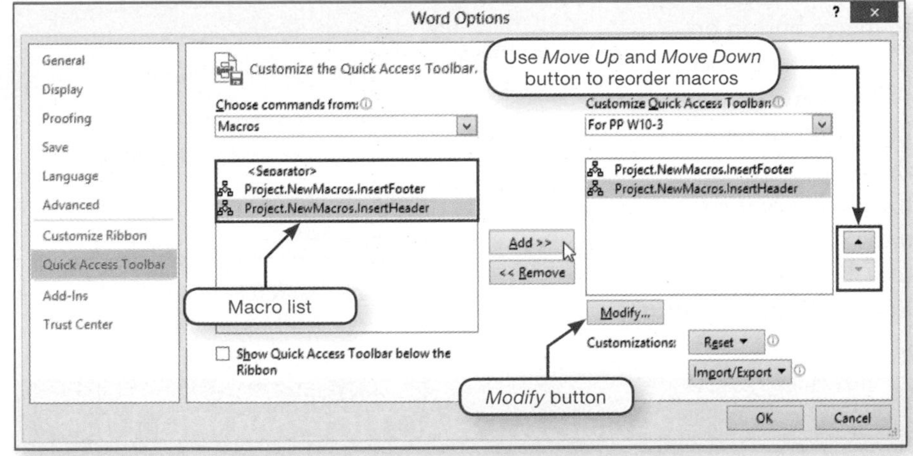

10-44 Add a macro to the *Quick Access* toolbar

4. Click the **Choose commands from** drop-down list and select **Macros**.
5. Click the **Customize Quick Access Toolbar** drop-down list and select the document where the macro is stored.
6. In the list of macros at the left, select the macro that you want to add to the *Quick Access* toolbar and click the **Add** button.
    - After adding macros to the *Quick Access* toolbar, you can reorder macros using the *Move Up* and *Move Down* buttons to the right of *Customize Quick Access* toolbar area.
7. Click the **Modify** button to open the *Modify Button* dialog box (Figure 10-45).
    - If a macro already has a *Quick Access* toolbar button assigned to it, you can modify the display name or button icon.
8. In the *Display name* area, type the display name for the macro.
    - The display name is the tag that appears when you put your pointer on the button on the *Quick Access* toolbar.

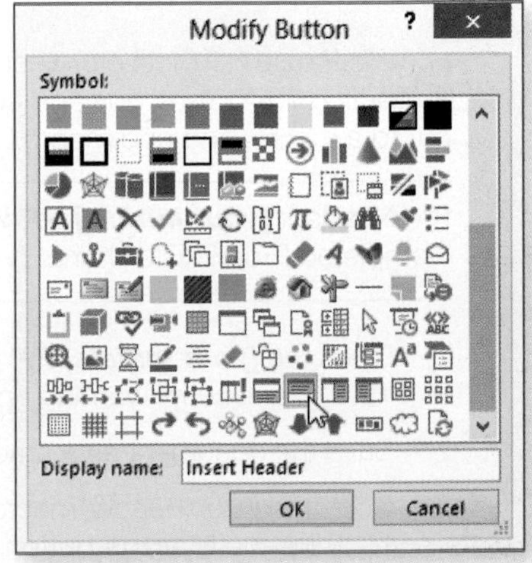

10-45 Modify the macro button and display name

9. Select the icon you want to use as the button on the *Quick Access* toolbar.
10. Click **OK** to close the *Modify Button* dialog box.
11. Click **OK** to close the *Word Options* dialog box.
    - The macro button appears on the *Quick Access* toolbar.

ANOTHER WAY

Click the **Quick Access toolbar** drop-down list and select **More Commands** to open the *Customize the Quick Access Toolbar* area in the *Word Options* dialog box. You can also right-click the *Ribbon* and select **Customize Quick Access Toolbar** or **Customize the Ribbon** to open the *Word Options* dialog box.

Remove a Macro Button from the Quick Access Toolbar

If you delete a macro that has a button assigned to it on the *Quick Access* toolbar, the button assigned to the macro on the *Quick Access* toolbar is not deleted. You receive an error message if you click the button after the macro has been deleted. It is best to remove the button assigned to the macro if you have deleted the macro. You can also remove a macro button from the *Quick Access* toolbar even if the macro has not been deleted.

There are two different ways to remove a macro button from the *Quick Access* toolbar:

- Right-click the macro button on the *Quick Access* toolbar and select **Remove from Quick Access Toolbar** from the context menu (Figure 10-46).
- In the *Customize the Quick Access Toolbar* area in the *Word Options* dialog box, select the macro button to remove and click the **Remove** button.

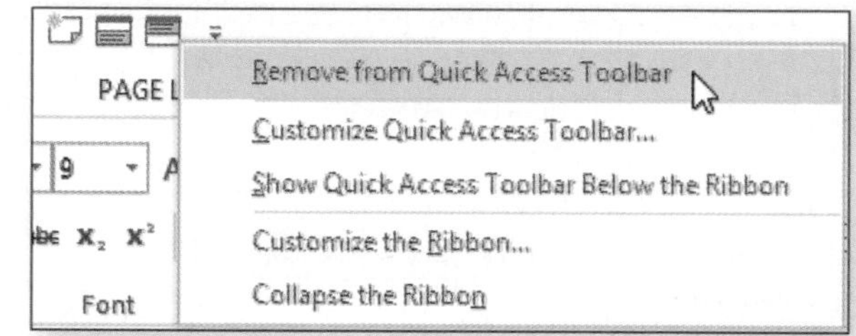

10-46 Remove a macro button from the *Quick Access* toolbar

PAUSE & PRACTICE: WORD 10-3

For this Pause & Practice project, you modify the macro-enabled agenda document you created in *Pause & Practice 10-2*. You copy and edit a macro using the Microsoft Visual Basic editor, add a keyboard shortcut to a macro, and add macro buttons to the *Quick Access* toolbar.

File Needed: ***[your initials] PP W10-2 final.docm***
Completed Project File Name: ***[your initials] PP W10-3.docm***

1. Open the ***[your initials] PP W10-2 final*** macro-enabled document you created in *Pause & Practice 10-2*. If a security warning appears in the *Info* bar, click **Enable Content**.
2. Save the document as a macro-enabled document named ***[your initials] PP W10-3***.
3. Copy the *InsertHeader* macro using the Microsoft Visual Basic editor.
    a. Click the **Macros** button [*Developer* tab, *Code* group] to open the *Macros* dialog box.
    b. Click the **Macros in** drop-down list and select **[your initials] PP W10-3 (document)**.

c. Select the **InsertHeader** macro and click the **Edit** button. The *Microsoft Visual Basic* editor opens.
d. Select the Visual Basic code for the macro beginning with "**Sub InsertHeader ()**" and ending with "**End Sub**" (Figure 10-47).
e. Click the **Copy** button or press **Ctrl+C** to copy the code for the macro.
f. Place your insertion point on the blank line after "End Sub."
g. Press **Ctrl+V** to paste the copied macro. The copied macro appears below the original macro, and a horizontal line separates the two.
h. On the copied macro, change the name of the macro after "Sub" to InsertFooter (Figure 10-48).
i. Press **Ctrl+S** or click the **Save** button to save the macros.
j. Click the **File** menu in the upper left corner and select **Close and Return to Microsoft Word** to return to your document.

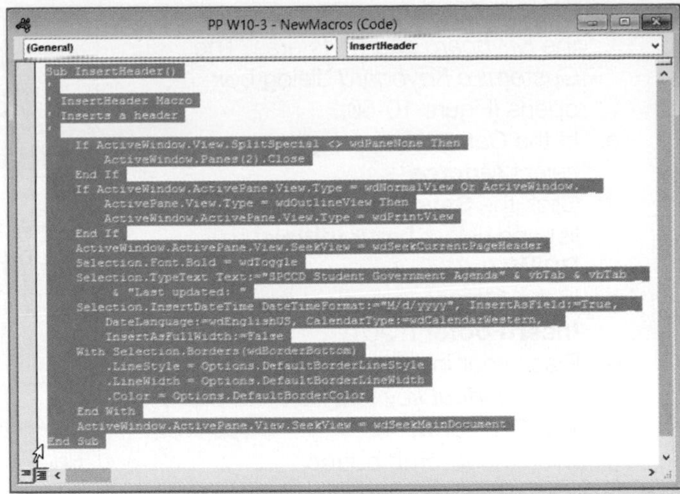
PP W10-3 - NewMacros (Code)
(General)
InsertHeader
Sub InsertHeader()
'
' InsertHeader Macro
' Inserts a header
'
If ActiveWindow.View.SplitSpecial <> wdPaneNone Then
ActiveWindow.Panes(2).Close
End If
If ActiveWindow.ActivePane.View.Type = wdNormalView Or ActiveWindow.
ActivePane.View.Type = wdOutlineView Then
ActiveWindow.ActivePane.View.Type = wdPrintView
End If
ActiveWindow.ActivePane.View.SeekView = wdSeekCurrentPageHeader
Selection.Font.Bold = wdToggle
Selection.TypeText Text:="SPCCD Student Government Agenda" & vbTab & vbTab
& "Last updated: "
Selection.InsertDateTime DateTimeFormat:="M/d/yyyy", InsertAsField:=True,
DateLanguage:=wdEnglishUS, CalendarType:=wdCalendarWestern,
InsertAsFullWidth:=False
With Selection.Borders(wdBorderBottom)
.LineStyle = Options.DefaultBorderLineStyle
.LineWidth = Options.DefaultBorderLineWidth
.Color = Options.DefaultBorderColor
End With
ActiveWindow.ActivePane.View.SeekView = wdSeekMainDocument
End Sub
10-47 Select and copy macro Visual Basic code

End Sub
Sub InsertFooter()
'
10-48 Change the macro name

4. Edit the *InsertFooter* macro.
   a. Click the **Macros** button to open the *Macros* dialog box.
   b. Click the **Macros in** drop-down list and select **[your initials] PP W10-3 (document)**.
   c. Select the **InsertFooter** macro and click the **Edit** button. The *Microsoft Visual Basic* editor opens.
   d. Make the four changes that are highlighted in Figure 10-49.
   e. Press **Ctrl+S** or click the **Save** button to save the macros.
   f. Click the **File** menu and select **Close and Return to Microsoft Word** to return to your document.

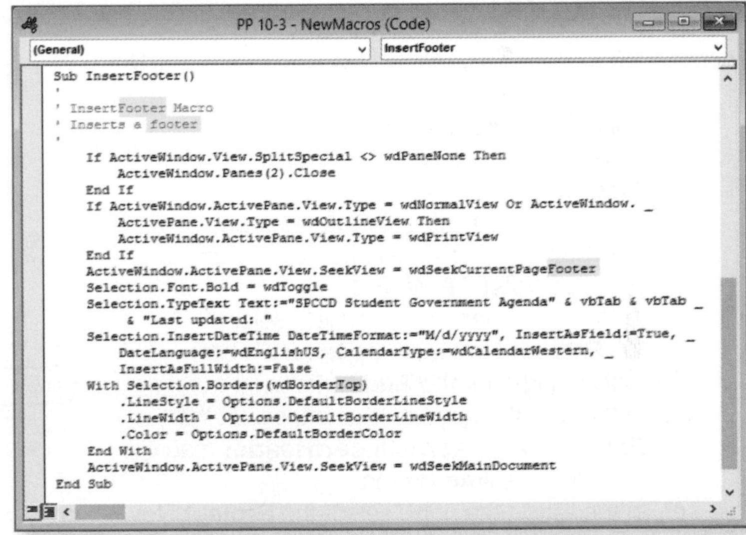
PP 10-3 - NewMacros (Code)
(General)
InsertFooter
Sub InsertFooter()
'
' InsertFooter Macro
' Inserts a footer
'
If ActiveWindow.View.SplitSpecial <> wdPaneNone Then
ActiveWindow.Panes(2).Close
End If
If ActiveWindow.ActivePane.View.Type = wdNormalView Or ActiveWindow. _
ActivePane.View.Type = wdOutlineView Then
ActiveWindow.ActivePane.View.Type = wdPrintView
End If
ActiveWindow.ActivePane.View.SeekView = wdSeekCurrentPageFooter
Selection.Font.Bold = wdToggle
Selection.TypeText Text:="SPCCD Student Government Agenda" & vbTab & vbTab _
& "Last updated: "
Selection.InsertDateTime DateTimeFormat:="M/d/yyyy", InsertAsField:=True, _
DateLanguage:=wdEnglishUS, CalendarType:=wdCalendarWestern, _
InsertAsFullWidth:=False
With Selection.Borders(wdBorderTop)
.LineStyle = Options.DefaultBorderLineStyle
.LineWidth = Options.DefaultBorderLineWidth
.Color = Options.DefaultBorderColor
End With
ActiveWindow.ActivePane.View.SeekView = wdSeekMainDocument
End Sub
10-49 Edit the *InsertFooter* macro Visual Basic code

5. Test the *InsertFooter* macro.
   a. Click the **Macros** button to open the *Macros* dialog box.
   b. Select the **InsertFooter** macro and click the **Run** button. A footer with a top border is inserted in the document.
   c. Select and delete the header and footer content in the document, and close the header and footer area.
6. Add a keyboard shortcut to the *InsertFooter* macro.
   a. Click the **File** tab to open the *Backstage* view.
   b. Select **Options** on the left to open the *Word Options* dialog box.
   c. Click **Customize Ribbon** on the left.

d. Click the **Customize** button in the *Keyboard shortcuts* area. The *Customize Keyboard* dialog box opens (Figure 10-50).
e. In the *Categories* area, scroll down and select **Macros**.
f. Click the **Save changes in** drop-down list and select **[your initials] PP W10-3**.
g. In the *Macros* list, select the **InsertFooter** macro.
h. Place your insertion point in the *Press new shortcut key* text box and press **Alt+Ctrl+Shift+F**.
i. Click the **Assign** button.
j. Click **Close** to close the *Customize Keyboard* dialog box and click **OK** to close the *Word Options* dialog box.

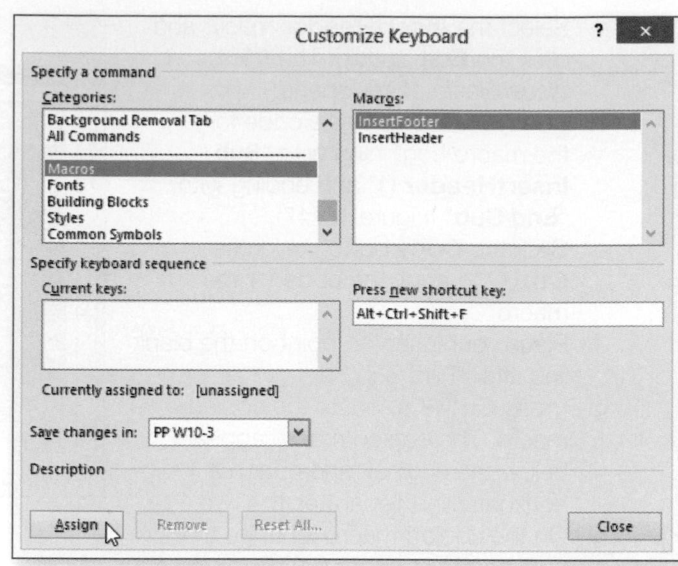
10-50 Add a keyboard shortcut to the *InsertFooter* macro

7. Add macro buttons to the *Quick Access* toolbar.
   a. Click the **File** tab to open the *Backstage* view and select **Options** on the left to open the *Word Options* dialog box.
   b. Select **Quick Access Toolbar** on the left to display the *Customize the Quick Access Toolbar* area (Figure 10-51).
   c. Click the **Choose commands from** drop-down list and select **Macros**.
   d. Click the **Customize Quick Access Toolbar** drop-down list and select **For [your initials] PP W10-3**.
   e. In the list of macros on the left, select the **Project.NewMacros.InsertFooter** macro and click the **Add** button.
   f. In the list of macros on the left, select the **Project.NewMacros.InsertHeader** macro and click the **Add** button.
   g. In the list on the right, select the **Project.NewMacros.InsertHeader** macro and click the **Modify** button to open the *Modify Button* dialog box (Figure 10-52).
   h. In the *Display name* area, type Insert Header, select the icon shown in Figure 10-52, and click **OK** to close the *Modify Button* dialog box.
   i. In the list on the right, select the **Project.NewMacros.InsertFooter** macro and click the **Modify** button.
   j. In the *Display name* area, type Insert Footer, select the icon shown in Figure 10-52, and click **OK** to close the *Modify Button* dialog box.
   k. Click **OK** to close the *Word Options* dialog box.

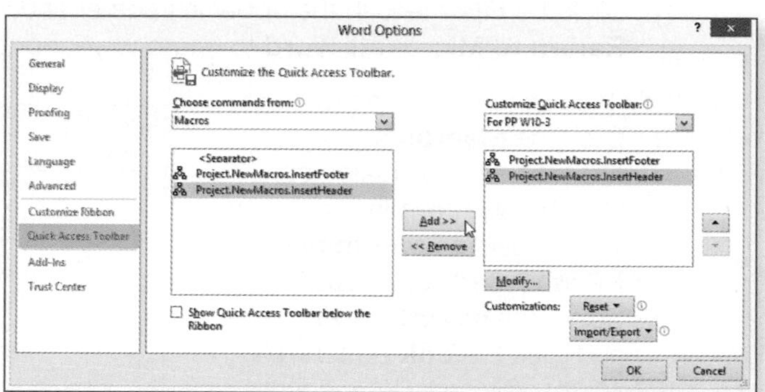
10-51 Add macros to the *Quick Access* toolbar

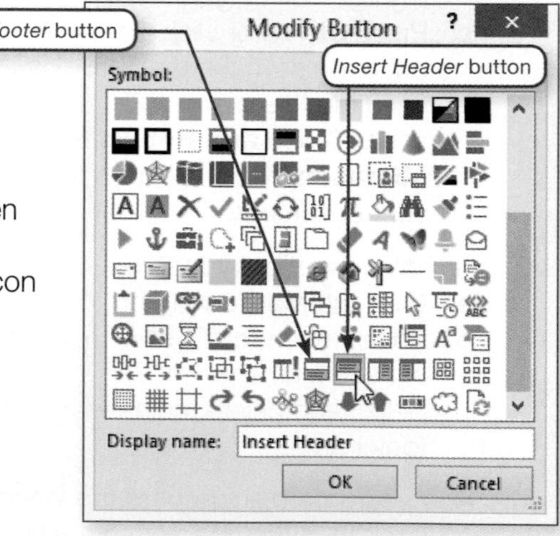

10-52 Modify the macro button and display name

8. Test a macro button and macro keyboard shortcut.
   a. Click the **Insert Header** button on the *Quick Access* toolbar to insert the header in the document (Figure 10-53).
   b. Press **Alt+Ctrl+Shift+F** to insert the footer.
   c. Delete the header content from the document.
9. Save and close the document (Figure 10-54).

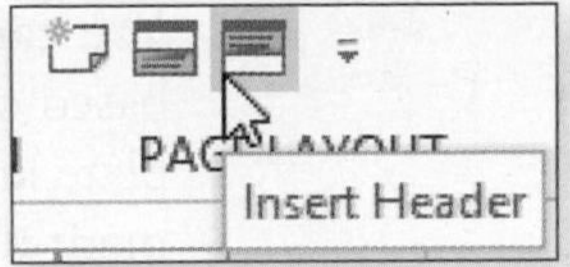

10-53 ***Insert Header*** **button on the** ***Quick Access*** **toolbar**

SPCCD STUDENT GOVERNMENT AGENDA

Fall Welcome Day
9/9/2014
3 to 5 p.m.

Meeting called by: Student Name

Attendees: Melissa Gaston, Heidi Jackson, Rachel Sanchez, Peter Zanko, Ron Costa, Roietta Molden, and Ravi Kumar

Please read: Fall Welcome Day Flyer and Welcome Day Guidelines

Please bring: Same as above

3:00-3:15	**WELCOME AND MEETING OVERVIEW**	**LOCATION**
	Student Name	Sequoia Room
3:15-4:00	**BREAKOUT GROUPS**	
	Club Presidents: Melissa Gaston	Sequoia Room
	Marketing: Peter Zanko	Redwood Room
	Facilities: Rachel Sanchez	Oak Room
4:00-4:45	**FALL WELCOME DAY PLANNING**	
	To-do lists and needs from each group	Sequoia Room
4:45-5:00	**WRAP-UP AND ADJOURN**	
	Old business	Sequoia Room

Additional Information:
Our next meeting is next Tuesday from 3 to 5 p.m.

SPCCD Student Government Agenda   Last updated: 9/8/2014

10-54 PP W10-3 completed

SLO 10.5 Using Macro-Enabled Templates

You can store macros in templates to further automate tasks. When you create a document based on a template or a template is attached to a document, the macros stored in the template are available in those documents. You can also copy macros from a template or document to another template or document so you don't have to recreate macros that already exist in another file.

Save a Macro-Enabled Template

Similar to a Word document containing macros (macro-enabled document), a template that contains macros must be saved as a ***macro-enabled template*** (*.dotm*) in order for the macros to function in the template and in documents that you create based on the template.

HOW TO: Save a Macro-Enabled Template

1. Open the template you want to save as a macro-enabled template.
2. Press **F12** to open the *Save As* dialog box (Figure 10-55).
3. Type the name of the template in the *File name* area.
4. Click the **Save as type** drop-down list and select **Word Macro-Enabled Template**.
5. Browse to the location on your computer where you want to save the template.
   - Be specific when selecting the save location for templates because Word, by default, selects the default template location when you save a template file.
6. Click **Save** to close the dialog box and save the macro-enabled template.

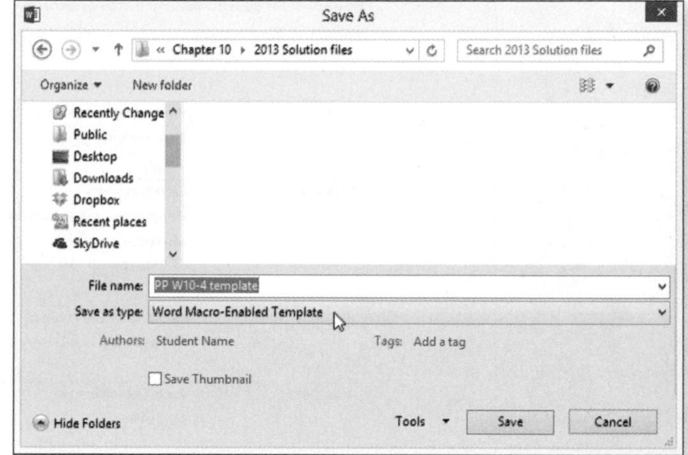

10-55 Save as a macro-enabled template

If you create macros in a template and then save the template, a dialog box opens informing you that the document cannot be saved in a macro-free environment. In this dialog box, click **No** to open the *Save As* dialog box and save the document as a macro-enabled template so the macros are available in the document.

Copy a Macro to Another File

A time-saving feature in Word is the ability to copy macros from one document or template to another. Copying macros is similar to copying styles. You use the *Organizer* dialog box to select the file you want to copy the macros to and the file from which you will copy the macros. When you copy macros from one file to another, you copy the entire ***macro project item,*** which are all of the macros contained in the file. After you have copied macros into a document, you can delete unwanted macros using the *Macros* dialog box.

HOW TO: Copy Macros to Another Document

1. Open the document or template where you want to copy the macros.
2. Click the **Macros** button [*Developer* tab, *Code* group] to open the *Macros* dialog box.
3. Click the **Organizer** button. The *Organizer* dialog box opens.
   - Your document is listed on the left and the *Normal* template is listed on the right.
4. Click the **Close File** button on the right to close the *Normal* template.
5. Click the **Open File** button to open the *Open* dialog box (Figure 10-56).
6. Click the **File type** drop-down list to the right of the *File name* text box and select **All Word Documents**.

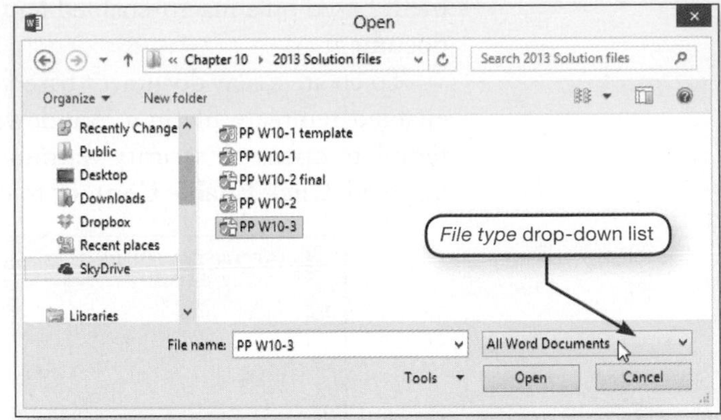

10-56 Open the document containing the macros

7. Browse to locate and select the file containing the macros and click **Open** to close the dialog box.
   - The opened file appears on the right in the *Organizer* dialog box.
8. Select the macro project item (on the right) to copy to your open document (on the left) (Figure 10-57) and click the **Copy** button.
   - The macro project item is copied to your document.

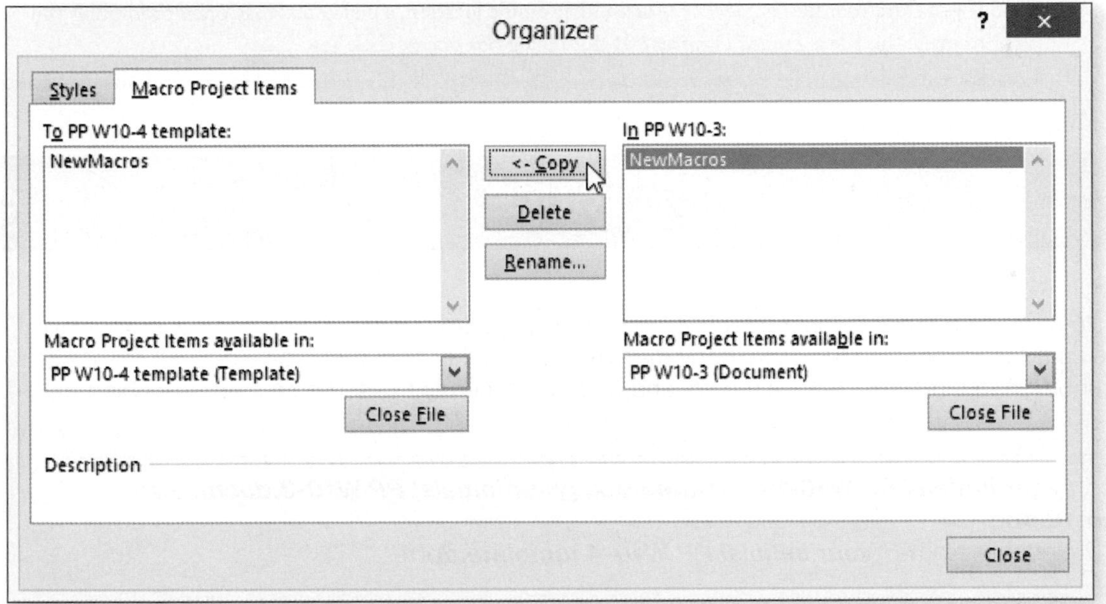

10-57 Copy macros from one file to another

9. Click the **Close** button to close the *Organizer* dialog box.
10. In your document, click the **Macros** button to open the *Macros* dialog box where the copied macros are displayed.

> **MORE INFO**
>
> You can also use the *Organizer* dialog box to delete and rename macro project items.

Use a Macro-Enabled Template

Using a macro-enabled template is similar to using a template. When you create a new document based on a macro-enabled template, the macros in the template are available in the new document.

To create a new document based on the macro-enabled template, double-click the macro-enabled template file in a Windows folder. A new document based on the macro-enabled template opens. A security warning appears in the *Info* bar informing you that macros are disabled. Click **Enable Content** to enable the macros in the new document (Figure 10-58).

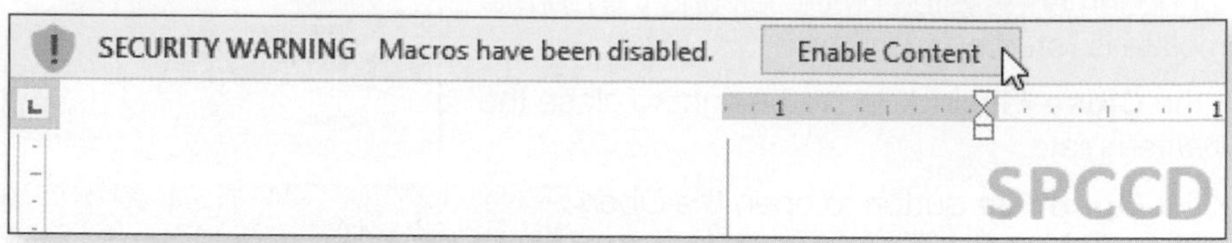

10-58 Enable macros in the document

You can edit a macro-enabled template by opening it from within Word. Because the macro-enabled template contains macros, a security warning appears in the *Info* bar. Click **Enable Content** to enable the macros in the macro-enabled template.

MORE INFO

If you store your files on *SkyDrive* or another online location, a dialog box may open prompting you to make this file a *Trusted Document*. If this dialog box opens, click **Yes**.

PAUSE & PRACTICE: WORD 10-4

For this Pause & Practice project, you modify the agenda template from *Pause & Practice 10-1*. You save the template as a macro-enabled template, copy macros from another document, delete a macro, assign a keyboard shortcut to a macro, create a macro, and create a document based on a macro-enabled template.

Files Needed: ***[your initials] PP W10-1 template.dotx, [your initials] PP W10-3.docm***, and ***SPCCDlogo-10.png***
Completed Project File Name: ***[your initials] PP W10-4 template.dotm***

1. From within Word, open the ***[your initials] PP W10-1 template*** Word template you created in *Pause & Practice 10-1*.
2. Save the template as a macro-enabled template.
   a. Press **F12** to open the *Save As* dialog box.
   b. In the *File name area*, type [your initials] PP W10-4 template.
   c. Click the **Save as type** drop-down list and select **Word Macro-Enabled Template**.
   d. Browse to the location on your computer where you want to save the macro-enabled template.
   e. Click **Save** to close the dialog box and save the macro-enabled template.

3. Copy macros from a macro-enabled document into your macro-enabled template.
   a. Click the **Macros** button [*Developer* tab, *Code* group] to open the *Macros* dialog box.
   b. Click the **Organizer** button to open the *Organizer* dialog box.
   c. Click the **Close File** button on the right to close the *Normal* template.
   d. Click the **Open File** button on the right to open the *Open* dialog box.
   e. Click the **File type** drop-down list to the right of the *File name* text box and select **All Word Documents**.
   f. Browse to locate and select the ***[your initials] PP W10-3*** macro-enabled document and click **Open** to close the dialog box and return to the *Organizer* dialog box.
   g. Select the **NewMacros** macro project item (on the right) and click the **Copy** button (Figure 10-59).
   h. Click the **Close** button to close the *Organizer* dialog box.

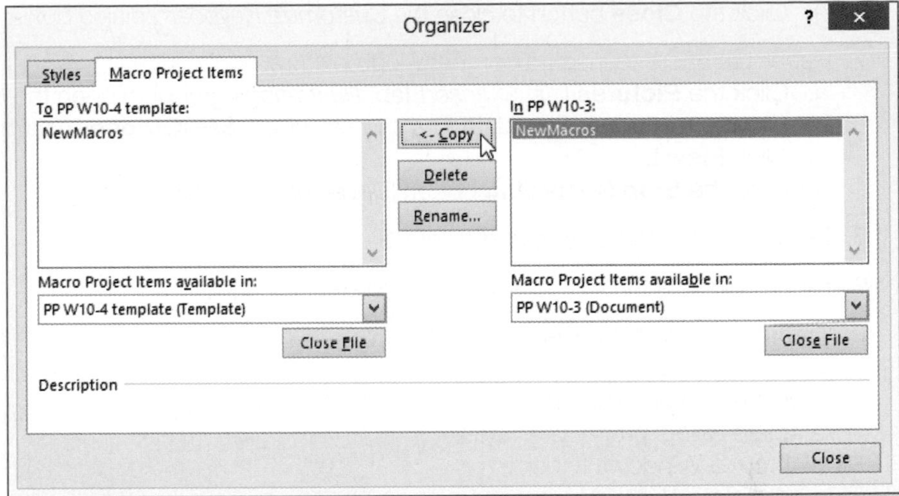

10-59 Copy macros from a macro-enabled document to a macro-enabled template

4. Delete the *InsertHeader* macro.
   a. Click the **Macros** button [*Developer* tab, *Code* group] to open the *Macros* dialog box.
   b. Click the **Macros in** drop-down list and select **PP W10-4 template (template)**.
   c. Select the **InsertHeader** macro and click the **Delete** button.
   d. Click **Yes** in the dialog box that opens, confirming the deletion of the macro.
   e. Click **Close** to close the *Macros* dialog box.

5. Add a keyboard shortcut to the *InsertFooter* macro.
   a. Click the **File** tab to open the *Backstage* view.
   b. Select **Options** on the left to open the *Word Options* dialog box.
   c. Click **Customize Ribbon** on the left.
   d. Click the **Customize** button in the *Keyboard shortcuts* area. The *Customize Keyboard* dialog box opens.
   e. In the *Categories* area, scroll down and select **Macros**.
   f. Click the **Save changes in** area and select **[your initials] PP W10-4 template**.
   g. In the *Macros* list, select the **InsertFooter** macro.
   h. Place your insertion point in the *Press new shortcut key* text box and press **Alt+Ctrl+Shift+F**.
   i. Click the **Assign** button.
   j. Click **Close** to close the *Customize Keyboard* dialog box, and click **OK** to close the *Word Options* dialog box.

6. Create a keyboard-activated macro.
   a. Place your insertion point after the content control field in the "Additional Information" section and press **Enter** two times.
   b. Click the **Record Macro** button [*Developer* tab, *Code* group] to open the *Record Macro* dialog box.
   c. In the *Macro name* area, type InsertPicture (no spaces between words).

   d. Click the **Store macro in** drop-down list and select **Documents Based On [your initials] PP W10-4 template**.
   e. In the *Description* area, type Inserts a picture.
   f. Click the **Keyboard** button to open the *Customize Keyboard* dialog box.
   g. Click the **Save changes in** drop-down list and select **[your initials] PP W10-4 template**.
   h. Place your insertion point in the *Press new shortcut key* text box and press **Alt+Ctrl+Shift+P**.
   i. Click the **Assign** button to assign the keyboard shortcut to the macro.
   j. Click the **Close** button to close the *Customize Keyboard* dialog box and begin recording the macro.

7. Record a macro to insert a company logo picture.
   a. Click the **Pictures** button [*Insert* tab, *Illustrations* group] to open the *Insert Picture* dialog box.
   b. Browse to your student data files and select the ***SPCCDlogo-10*** picture.
   c. Click **Insert**.
   d. Click the **Stop Recording** button [*Developer* tab, *Code* group].

8. Select the inserted picture and delete it.

9. Save and close the macro-enabled template.

10. Create a document based on the macro-enabled template to make sure the template works properly.
    a. From a Windows folder, double click the ***[your initials] PP W10-4 template*** macro-enabled template to create a new document based on the template.
    b. Click **OK** to accept the default responses to the two *Fill-in* field prompt dialog boxes.
    c. Click **Enable Content** on the security warning to enable the macros in the new document.
    d. Press **Alt+Ctrl+Shift+F** to run the *InsertFooter* macro.
    e. Press **Ctrl+End** to move to the end of the document.
    f. Press **Alt+Ctrl+Shift+P** to run the *InsertPicture* macro.
    g. Examine the document to make sure both macros are inserted (Figure 10-60).

11. Close the document without saving.

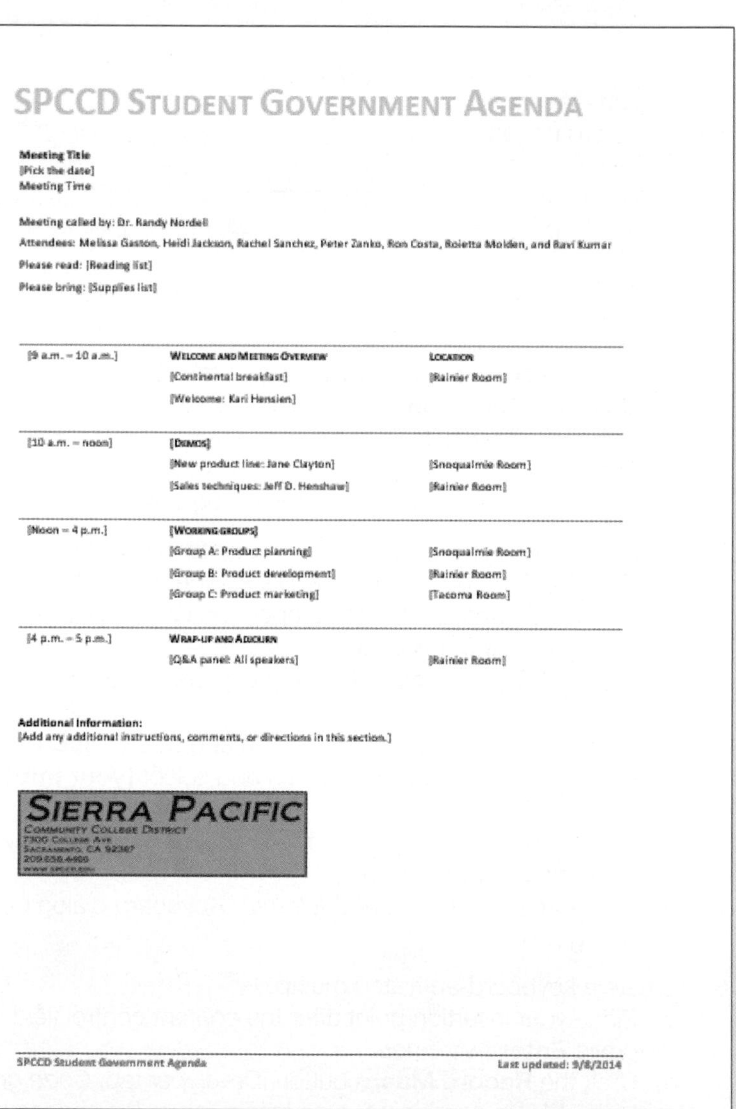

SPCCD STUDENT GOVERNMENT AGENDA

Meeting Title
[Pick the date]
Meeting Time

Meeting called by: Dr. Randy Nordell

Attendees: Melissa Gaston, Heidi Jackson, Rachel Sanchez, Peter Zanko, Ron Costa, Roietta Molden, and Ravi Kumar

Please read: [Reading list]

Please bring: [Supplies list]

[9 a.m. – 10 a.m.]	**WELCOME AND MEETING OVERVIEW**	**LOCATION**
	[Continental breakfast]	[Rainier Room]
	[Welcome: Kari Hensien]	
[10 a.m. – noon]	**[DEMOS]**	
	[New product line: Jane Clayton]	[Snoqualmie Room]
	[Sales techniques: Jeff D. Henshaw]	[Rainier Room]
[Noon – 4 p.m.]	**[WORKING GROUPS]**	
	[Group A: Product planning]	[Snoqualmie Room]
	[Group B: Product development]	[Rainier Room]
	[Group C: Product marketing]	[Tacoma Room]
[4 p.m. – 5 p.m.]	**WRAP-UP AND ADJOURN**	
	[Q&A panel: All speakers]	[Rainier Room]

Additional Information:
[Add any additional instructions, comments, or directions in this section.]

SPCCD Student Government Agenda — Last updated: 9/8/2014

10-60 New document based on PP 10-4 template

Chapter Summary

10.1 Create, save, and use a template to generate commonly used documents (p. W10-574).

- A ***template*** is a type of Word file that you can use to store content and formatting; you can create other documents from a template.
- A template file has a ***.dotx*** file name extension.
- You can save an existing or new document as a template.
- There are a variety of online templates available in Word in the *New* area on the *Backstage* view. Search for templates using key words.
- To edit a template, open the template file from within Word.
- To create a document based on a template, double-click the template file in a Windows folder.
- A new document based on a template has a generic file name such as "*Document1*."

10.2 Customize template content using Word fields and shared template content (p. W10-577).

- A document based on an online template includes a combination of ***Word fields, content control fields***, and ***document property fields***.
- You can customize the content in the fields or copy, move, or delete these fields.
- Templates also use formatting and styles that you can modify and apply to other areas of the template or document based on the template.
- When you attach a template to a document, the styles included in the template are available in the document.
- When you attach a template to a document, you can set the document to update each time styles are changed in the template.
- Use the ***Organizer dialog box*** to copy styles from one template to another template or document.

10.3 Record a set of instructions as a macro and run and delete a macro (p. W10-584).

- A ***macro*** is a combination of instructions and keystrokes that you can store and run in a document.
- Before creating and recording a macro, plan what the macro will do, where you will store the macro, and how you will run the macro.
- Use the ***Record Macro dialog box*** to create the macro and name it.
- You can create a ***button-activated macro*** or a ***keyboard-activated macro***. A button-activated macro runs when you click the macro button on the *Quick Access* toolbar. A keyboard-activated macro runs when you press a shortcut key.
- You must save a document that contains macros as a ***macro-enabled document*** in order for the macros to be stored in the document. A macro-enabled document has a ***.docm*** file name extension.
- When you open a document containing macros, a security warning appears in the *Info* bar. Click the ***Enable Content*** button to enable macros in the document.
- Use the ***Macros dialog box*** to run a macro or delete a macro.
- ***AutoMacros*** are macros that run automatically when you perform a specific action such as open or close a document.

10.4 Copy and edit an existing macro using Visual Basic and add a keyboard and button shortcut to a macro (p. W10-593).

- Macros are recorded in ***Visual Basic***, which is a programming language.
- To duplicate an existing macro in a document, you can copy a macro using the ***Microsoft Visual Basic editor***.
- You can edit the macro code in the Microsoft Visual Basic editor to change an existing macro or make changes to a copied macro.
- You can edit the shortcut key assigned to a macro or add a shortcut key to a macro in the ***Customize Keyboard dialog box***.
- You can add to, change, or delete a macro button from the *Quick Access* toolbar in the ***Word Options dialog box***.

10.5 Create and use a macro-enabled template to automate common tasks and copy a macro to another document (p. W10-600).

- When you use a macro in a template, you must save the template as a macro-enabled template.
- A macro-enabled template has a ***.dotm*** file name extension.
- You can copy a macro from one file to another using the ***Organizer dialog box***.

- When you copy macros from one file to another, you copy the ***macro project item***, which is the set of macros stored in a file.
- A security warning appears in the *Info* bar when you open a template containing macros or a document based on a macro-enabled template.

Check for Understanding

In the ***Online Learning Center*** for this text (www.mhhe.com/office2013inpractice), there are a variety of resources that can be used to review the concepts covered in this chapter.

The following Online Learning Resources are available in the Online Learning Center:

- Multiple choice questions
- Short answer questions
- Matching exercises

Guided Project 10-1

For this project, you create a macro-enabled template from an existing Courtyard Medical Plaza document. You insert *Fill-in* fields, record a macro, assign a button to the macro, and create a document based on the template.
[Student Learning Outcomes 10.1, 10.2, 10.3, 10.4, 10.5]

File Needed: ***PrivacyNotice-10.docx***
Completed Project File Names: ***[your initials] Word 10-1 template.dotm*** and ***[your initials] Word 10-1.docx***

Skills Covered in This Project

- Save a document as a macro-enabled template.
- Insert a *Fill-in* field.
- Create a keyboard-activated macro.
- Add a macro button to the *Quick Access* toolbar.
- Create a new document based on a macro-enabled template.
- Insert information in a *Fill-in* field prompt dialog box.
- Enable the macro content in the document.
- Run a macro using the macro button on the *Quick Access* toolbar.

1. Open the ***PrivacyNotice-10*** document from your student data files.
2. Save the document as a macro-enabled template.
   a. Press **F12** to open the *Save As* dialog box.
   b. In the *File name* area, type [your initials] Word 10-1 template.
   c. Click the **Save as type** drop-down list and select **Word Macro-Enabled Template**.
   d. Browse to the location on your computer where you want to save the file.
   e. Click **Save** to close the dialog box and save the macro-enabled template.
3. In the shaded heading area, delete the information to the right of the tab on each line (Figure 10-61).
4. Insert *Fill-in* fields to prompt user for information when a document is created based on the template.
   a. Place your insertion point after the tab and before the paragraph mark in the first line of the heading ("Name:").
   b. Click the **Quick Parts** button [*Insert* tab, *Text* group] and select **Field** from the drop-down list to open the *Field* dialog box (Figure 10-62).
   c. Select **Fill-in** in the *Field names* list.
   d. In the *Prompt* area, type What is the employee's name?

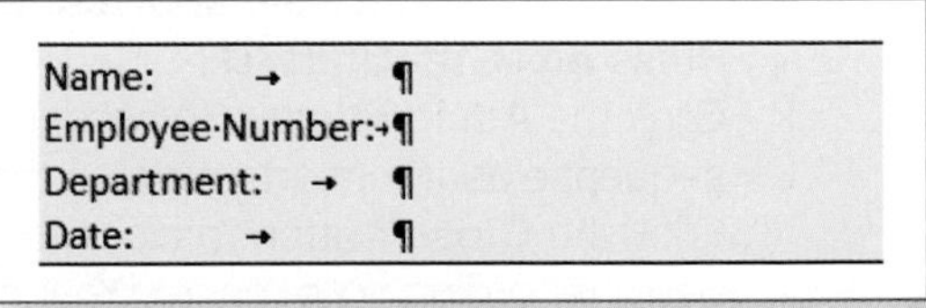

10-61 Remove text in the heading

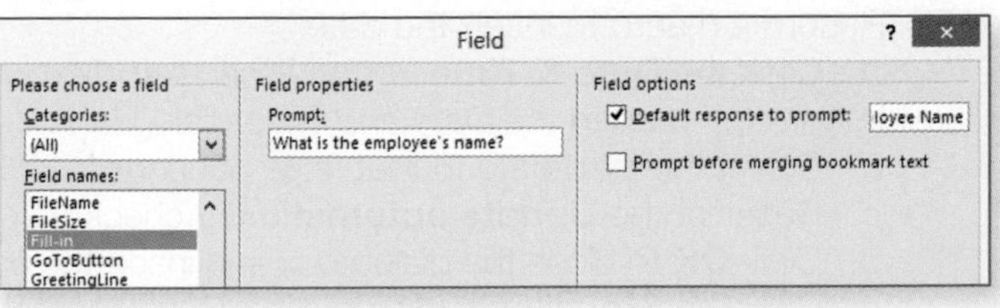

10-62 Insert *Fill-in* field

e. Check the **Default response to prompt** box and type Employee Name in the text box.
f. Click **OK** to close the *Field* dialog box and insert the *Fill-in* field. A dialog box opens prompting you for the employee's name.
g. Click **OK** to accept the default response to the prompt (Figure 10-63).
h. Place your insertion point after the tab on the second line and insert another *Fill-in* field.
i. Type What is the employee's number? as the prompt and type Employee Number as the default response to the prompt.
j. Click **OK** to close the *Field* dialog box and **OK** to accept the default response at the prompt.
k. Place your insertion point after the tab on the third line and insert another *Fill-in* field.
l. Type What is the employee's department? as the prompt and type Employee Department as the default response to the prompt.
m. Click **OK** to close the *Field* dialog box and **OK** to accept the default response at the prompt (Figure 10-64).

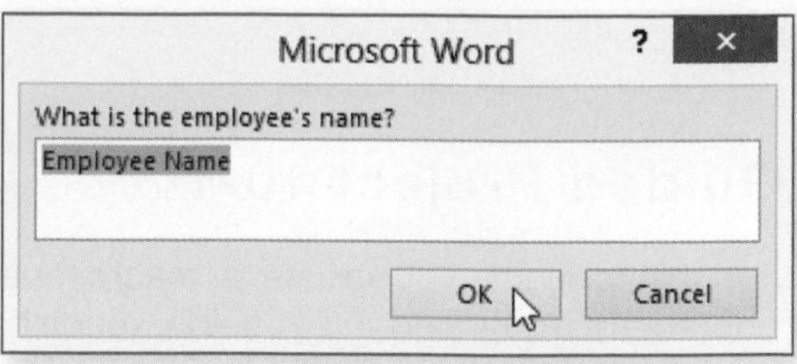

10-63 *Fill-in* field prompt dialog box

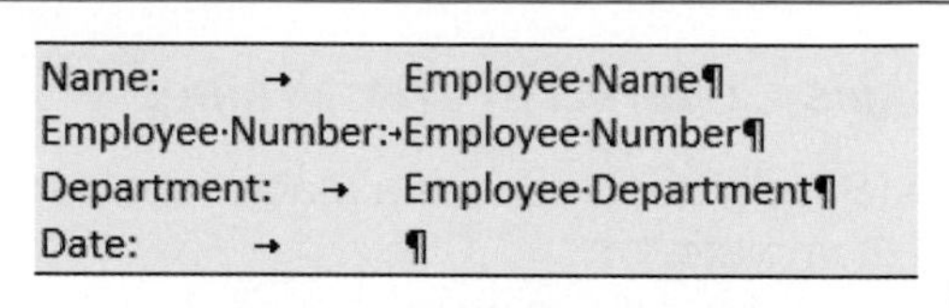

10-64 *Fill-in* fields inserted in the document

5. Create a keyboard-activated macro.
   a. Place your insertion point after the tab on the fourth line in the heading ("Date:").
   b. Click the **Record Macro** button [*Developer* tab, *Code* group]. The *Record Macro* dialog box opens (Figure 10-65).
   c. In the *Macro name* area, type InsertDate.
   d. Click the **Store macro in** drop-down list and select **Documents Based On [your initials] Word 10-1 template**.
   e. In the *Description* area, type Inserts the date.
   f. Click the **Keyboard** button. The *Customize Keyboard* dialog box opens (Figure 10-66).
   h. Click the **Save changes in** drop-down list and select **[your initials] Word 10-1 template**.
   i. Click in the **Press new shortcut key** text box.
   j. Press **Alt+Ctrl+Shift+D**.
   k. Click the **Assign** button to assign the keyboard sequence as the shortcut to run the macro.
   l. Click the **Close** button to close the dialog box and begin recording your macro. Your pointer changes to a macro-recording pointer.
6. Record a macro to insert the date.
   a. Click the **Date & Time** button [*Insert* tab, *Text* group] to open the *Date and Time* dialog box.
   b. Select the third date format (e.g., January 1, 2014).
   c. Deselect the **Update automatically** check box.
   d. Click **OK** to close the dialog box and insert the date.
   e. Click the **Stop Recording** button [*Developer* tab, *Code* group] to stop recording the macro.

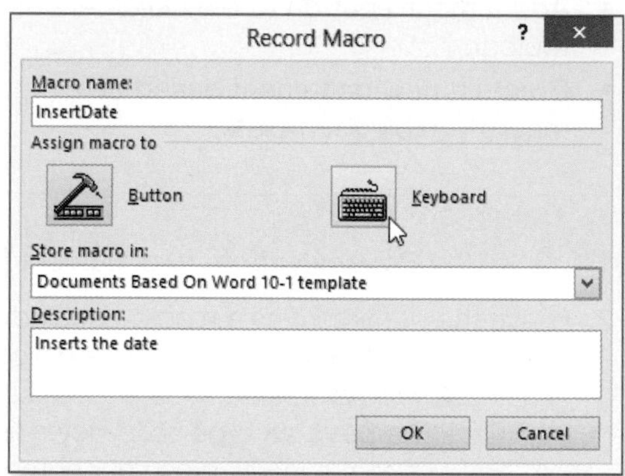

10-65 Create a keyboard-activated macro

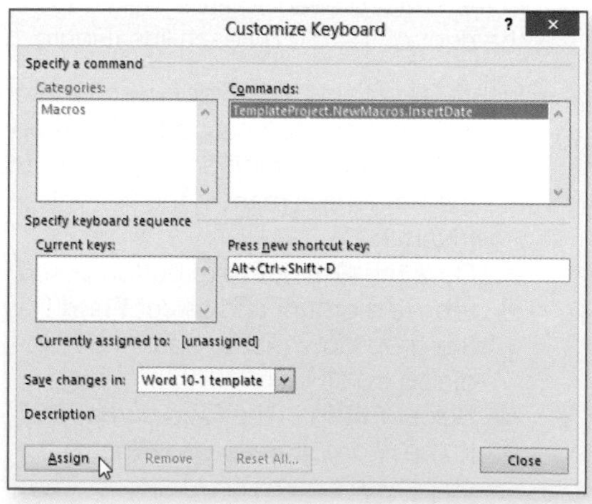

10-66 Assign a keyboard shortcut to the macro

7. Test the macro to make sure it works properly.
   a. Place your insertion point after the tab on the fourth line in the heading.
   b. Delete the date that was inserted in the heading.
   c. Press **Alt+Ctrl+Shift+D** to run the macro.
   d. Delete the date you just inserted.
8. Add a macro button to the *Quick Access* toolbar.
   a. Click the **File** tab to open the *Backstage* view.
   b. Select **Options** on the left to open the *Word Options* dialog box.
   c. Click **Quick Access Toolbar** at the left to display the *Customize the Quick Access Toolbar* area (Figure 10-67).

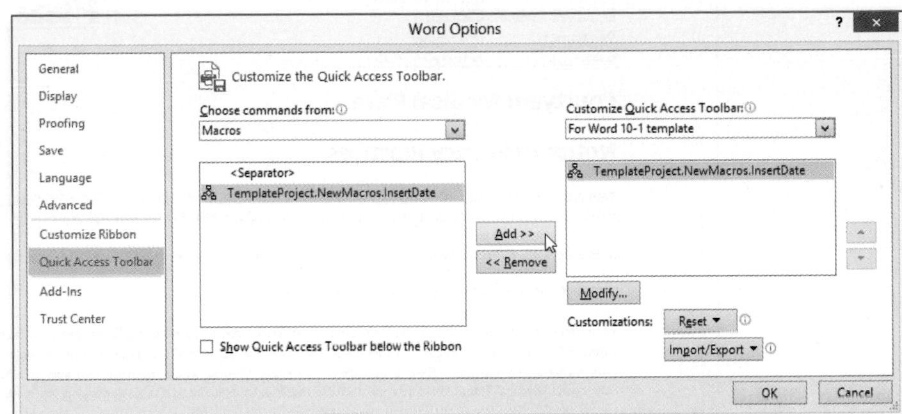

10-67 Add macro to the *Quick Access* toolbar

   d. Click the **Choose commands from** drop-down list and select **Macros**.
   e. Click the **Customize Quick Access Toolbar** drop-down list and select **For [your initials] Word 10-1 template**.
   f. In the list of macros on the left, select **TemplateProject. NewMacros.InsertDate** and click the **Add** button.
   g. Click the **Modify** button to open the *Modify Button* dialog box (Figure 10-68).
   h. In the *Display name* area, type Insert Date.
   i. Select the icon shown in Figure 10-68 to use as the button on the *Quick Access* toolbar.
   j. Click **OK** to close the *Modify Button* dialog box.
   k. Click **OK** to close the *Word Options* dialog box.

10-68 Modify the macro button and display name

9. Save and close the macro-enabled template.
10. Create a new document based on ***[your initials] Word 10-1 template***.
    a. Open a Windows folder and browse to locate the ***[your initials] Word 10-1 template*** file.
    b. Double-click the file to open a new document based on the template.
    c. In the first prompt dialog box, type Mrs. Karen Draper and click **OK**.
    d. In the second prompt dialog box, type 0001484 and click **OK**.
    e. In the third prompt dialog box, type Marketing and click **OK**.
    f. Click the **Enable Content** button in the security warning in the *Info* bar to enable the macro in the document.
11. Save the document as a *Word Document* named ***[your initials] Word 10-1***.
12. Run the macro to insert the date.
    a. Place your insertion point after the tab on the fourth line of the heading ("Date:").
    b. Click the **Insert Date** macro button on the *Quick Access* toolbar to insert the date.

13. Save and close the document (Figure 10-69).

Name:	Mrs. Karen Draper
Employee Number:	0001484
Department:	Marketing
Date:	January 14, 2015

Courtyard Medical Plaza

Notice of Privacy Practices

THIS NOTICE DESCRIBES HOW MEDICAL INFORMATION ABOUT YOU MAY BE USED AND DISCLOSED AND HOW YOU CAN GET ACCESS TO THIS INFORMATION. ***PLEASE REVIEW IT CAREFULLY.***

In this notice we use the terms "we," "us," and "our" to describe Courtyard Medical Plaza (CMP).

WHAT IS "PROTECTED HEALTH INFORMATION (PHI)?"

Your PHI is health information that contains identifiers, such as your name, Social Security number, or other information that reveals who you are. For example, your medical record is PHI because it includes your name and other identifiers. If you are a Courtyard Medical Plaza member and also an employee of Courtyard Medical Plaza, PHI does not include the health information in your employment records.

ABOUT OUR RESPONSIBILITY TO PROTECT YOUR PROTECTED HEALTH INFORMATION

By law, we must:

1. protect the privacy of your PHI,
2. tell you about your rights and our legal duties with respect to your PHI, and
3. tell you about our privacy practices and follow our notice currently in effect.

We take these responsibilities seriously and, as in the past, we will continue to take appropriate steps to safeguard the privacy of your PHI.

YOUR RIGHTS REGARDING YOUR PROTECTED HEALTH INFORMATION

This section tells you about your rights regarding your PHI—for example, your medical and billing records. It also describes how you can exercise these rights.

YOUR RIGHT TO SEE AND RECEIVE COPIES OF YOUR PROTECTED HEALTH INFORMATION

In general, you have a right to see and receive copies of your PHI in designated record sets such as your medical record or billing records. If you would like to see or receive a copy of such a record, please write us. When you know the facility or medical office where you received your care, please write to us at that address. If you need that address please call **1-559-288-1660**. However, if you don't know where the record that you want is located, please write to us at the **Office of Privacy & Compliance, 1660 Alhandra Way, Granite Bay, CA 95517**.

Courtyard Medical Plaza Page 1 of 2 Notice of Privacy Practices

10-69 Word 10-1 completed (page 1 of 2)

Guided Project 10-2

For this project, you open an online Word template and create a letter template for Emma Cavalli at Placer Hills Real Estate. You customize content control fields, delete content control fields, insert text from another file, create a document based on the template, and customize that document.
[Student Learning Outcomes 10.1, 10.2]

Files Needed: ***Business Letter*** **online Word template** and ***CavalliLetter-10.docx***
Completed Project File Names: ***[your initials] Word 10-2 template.dotx*** and ***[your initials] Word 10-2.docx***

Skills Covered in This Project

- Create a document based on an online Word template.
- Save a document as a template.
- Customize a content control field.
- Delete a content control field.
- Copy text from a document to paste into a template.
- Create a new document based on a template.
- Customize a document based on a template.

1. Open an online Word template.
   a. Click the **File** button to open the *Backstage* view.
   b. Click the **New** button to display the Word templates.
   c. Click the **Letters** link in the *Suggested searches* area to display the available online letter templates.
   d. Select **Business letter (Apothecary design)**. A preview window opens (Figure 10-70). You can also search for a specific template using the *Search for online templates* text box.
   e. Click the **Create** button to create a document based on this template.
   f. *Note: If this template is not available in Word, open the* ***BusinessLetter-10*** *file from your student data files*.

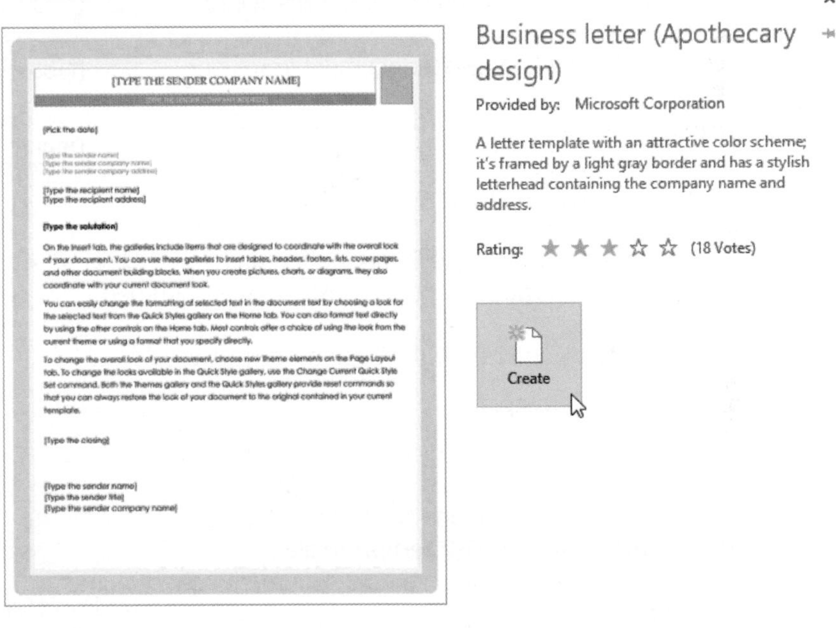

10-70 Create a document based on an online template

2. Save this document as a template.
   a. Press **F12** to open the **Save As** dialog box.
   b. Type [your initials] Word 10-2 template as the file name.
   c. Click the **Save as type** drop-down list and select **Word Template**.
   d. Browse to the location on your computer where you want to save the template and click the **Save** button.
   e. A dialog box might open informing you that you are saving the document in the most current version of Word. Click **OK** if this dialog box appears.
3. Customize content control fields.
   a. Click in the "**TYPE THE SENDER COMPANY NAME**" content control field at the top and type in all caps PLACER HILLS REAL ESTATE.
   b. Click in the "**TYPE THE SENDER COMPANY ADDRESS**" content control field at the top and type in all caps 7100 MADRONE ROAD, ROSEVILLE, CA 95722.

c. Click in the "**Type the salutation**" content control field above the body and type Dear and **space** once.
d. Click in the "**Type the closing**" content control field at the bottom and type Best regards.
e. In the author name content control field below "Best regards", type Emma Cavalli to replace the existing author name if there is one.
f. Click in the "**Type the sender title**" content control field at the bottom and type Realtor Consultant.

4. Add text to the document.
   a. Place your insertion point after the company name at the bottom and press **Enter**.
   b. Type ecavalli@phre.com and press **Enter**.
   c. Type 916.450.3334.

5. Delete content control fields.
   a. Below the date, select the three content control fields and the paragraph mark at the end of each line, and press **Delete** (Figure 10-71).
   b. Right-click the body content control field (below "Dear") and select **Remove Content Control** from the context menu.

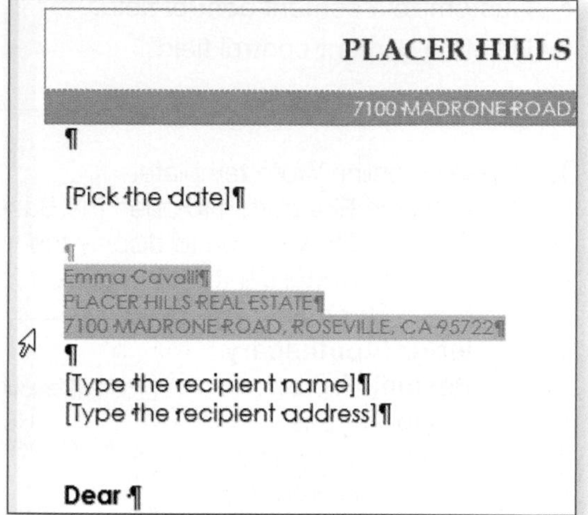

10-71 Delete content control fields

6. Copy text from another document and paste it into the template.
   a. Open the ***CavalliLetter-10*** document from your student data files.
   b. Select and copy the text in the document and close the document.
   c. Place your insertion point on the blank line below "Dear."
   d. Click the bottom half of the **Paste** button and select **Use Destination Theme** to paste the text into the document (Figure 10-72).
   e. Delete the blank line below the pasted body text.

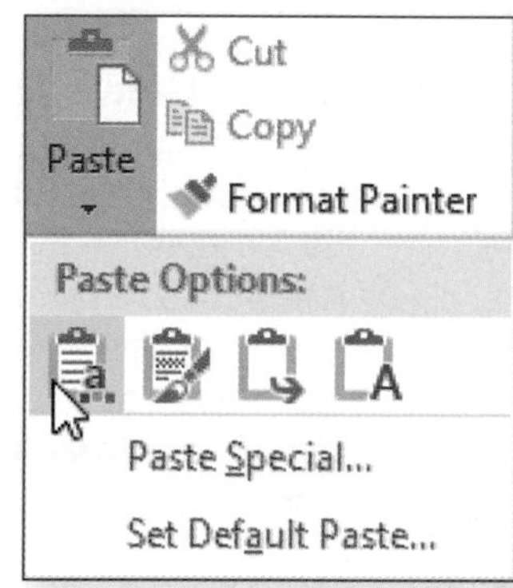

10-72 Paste text using the destination theme

7. Save and close the template.
8. Create a new document based on ***[your initials] Word 10-2 template***.
   a. Open a Windows folder and browse to locate the ***[your initials] Word 10-2 template*** file.
   b. Double-click the file to open a new document based on the template.
9. Save the file as a Word document named ***[your initials] Word 10-2***.
10. Customize the document based on the template.
    a. Click the "**Pick the date**" content control field and select the current date.
    b. Click the "**Type the recipient name**" content control field and type Mr. & Mrs. Robert and Lanita McCartney.
    c. Click the "**Type the recipient address**" content control field and type 7105 High Street, press **Enter**, and type Folsom, CA 93714.
    d. Place your insertion point after the space after "Dear" and type Robert and Lanita.
    e. Confirm that "Emma Cavalli" is the author name that appears in the content control field at the bottom. If it is not, change it to Emma Cavalli.

11. Save and close the document (Figure 10-73).

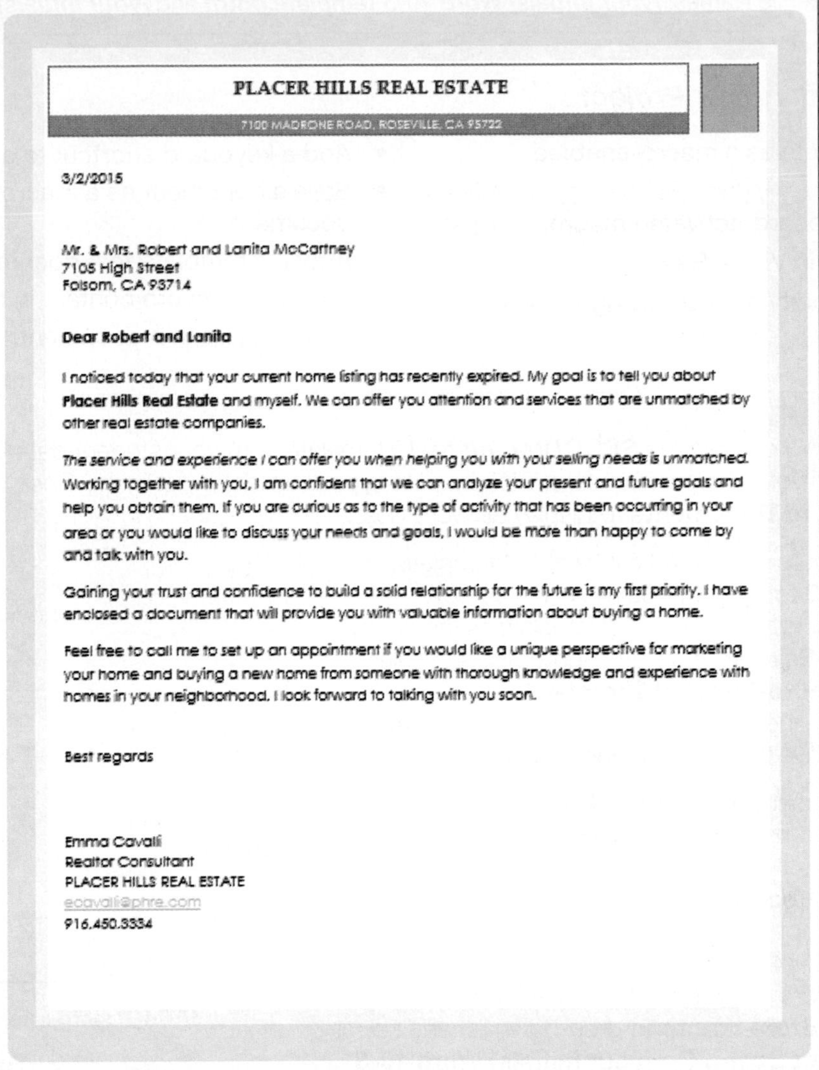

PLACER HILLS REAL ESTATE

7100 MADRONE ROAD, ROSEVILLE, CA 95722

3/2/2015

Mr. & Mrs. Robert and Lanita McCartney
7105 High Street
Folsom, CA 93714

Dear Robert and Lanita

I noticed today that your current home listing has recently expired. My goal is to tell you about **Placer Hills Real Estate** and myself. We can offer you attention and services that are unmatched by other real estate companies.

The service and experience I can offer you when helping you with your selling needs is unmatched. Working together with you, I am confident that we can analyze your present and future goals and help you obtain them. If you are curious as to the type of activity that has been occurring in your area or you would like to discuss your needs and goals, I would be more than happy to come by and talk with you.

Gaining your trust and confidence to build a solid relationship for the future is my first priority. I have enclosed a document that will provide you with valuable information about buying a home.

Feel free to call me to set up an appointment if you would like a unique perspective for marketing your home and buying a new home from someone with thorough knowledge and experience with homes in your neighborhood. I look forward to talking with you soon.

Best regards

Emma Cavalli
Realtor Consultant
PLACER HILLS REAL ESTATE
ecavalli@phre.com
916.450.3334

10-73 Word 10-2 completed

Guided Project 10-3

For this project, you modify a template and document for Sierra Pacific Community College District. You save a template as a macro-enabled template, record and edit a macro, copy and modify a macro, and attach a template to a document.
[Student Learning Outcomes 10.1, 10.2, 10.3, 10.4, 10.5]

Files Needed: ***SPCCDtemplate-10.dotx*** and ***SPCCDValues-10.docx***
Completed Project File Names: ***[your initials] Word 10-3 template.dotm*** and ***[your initials] Word 10-3.docm***

Skills Covered in This Project

- Save a template as a macro-enabled template.
- Create a keyboard-activated macro.
- Edit a macro in Visual Basic.
- Copy and modify a macro using the Visual Basic Editor.
- Add a keyboard shortcut to a macro.
- Save a document as a macro-enabled document.
- Attach a template to a document.
- Enable the macro content in the document.
- Run a macro in a document.

1. From within Word, open the ***SPCCDtemplate-10*** template from your student data files. If you don't find this file in your student data files, click the **File type** drop-down list in the *Open* dialog box and select **All Word Documents** to display all Word files.
2. Save the document as a macro-enabled template.
   a. Press **F12** to open the **Save As** dialog box.
   b. Type [your initials] Word 10-3 template as the file name.
   c. Click the **Save as type** drop-down list and select **Word Macro-Enabled Template**.
   d. Browse to the location on your computer where you want to save the template and click the **Save** button.
3. Create a keyboard-activated macro.
   a. Place your insertion point anywhere in "*Two Columns*".
   b. Click the **Record Macro** button [*Developer* tab, *Code* group] to open the *Record Macro* dialog box (Figure 10-74).
   c. In the *Macro name* area, type TwoColumns.
   d. Click the **Store macro in** drop-down list and select **Document Based On [your initials] Word 10-3 template**.
   e. In the *Description* area, type Change to two columns.
   f. Click the **Keyboard** button to open the *Customize Keyboard* dialog box (Figure 10-75).
   g. Click the **Save changes in** drop-down list and select **[your initials] Word 10-3 template**.
   h. Place your insertion point in the *Press new shortcut key* area and press **Alt+Shift+Ctrl+2** (the keyboard shortcut is displayed as *Alt+Ctrl+@*).
   i. Click the **Assign** button and click **Close** to begin recording the macro.
4. Record a macro to change the number of columns to two.
   a. Click the **Columns** button [*Page Layout* tab, *Page Setup* group] and select **Two** from the drop-down list.
   b. Click the **Stop Recording** button [*Developer* tab, *Code* group].

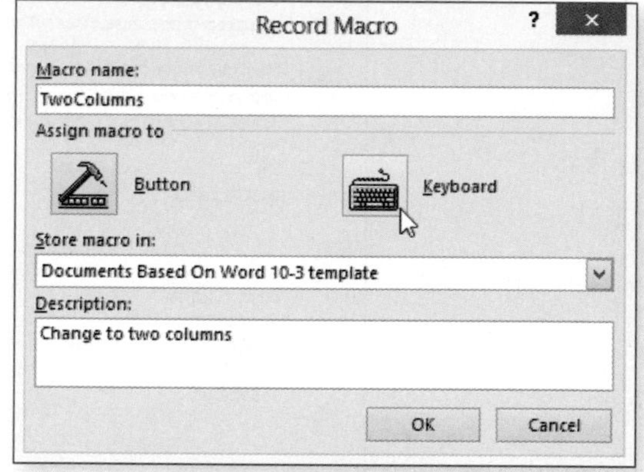

10-74 Record a keyboard-activated macro

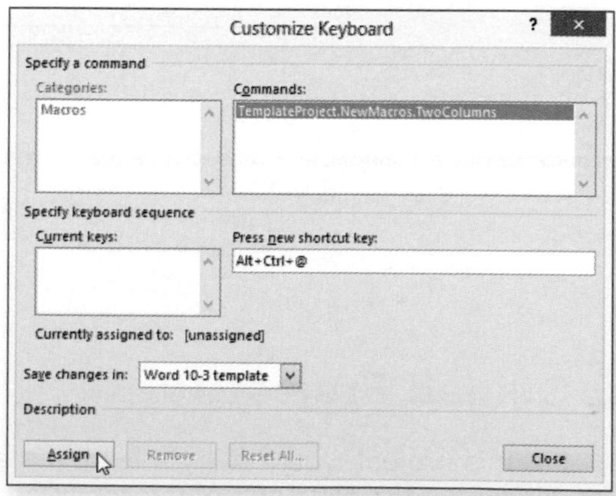

10-75 Assign a keyboard shortcut to the macro

5. Edit a macro so it will work on documents with different margins and page layout.
   a. Click the **Macros** button to open the *Macros* dialog box.
   b. Select the **TwoColumns** macro and click the **Edit** button. The Microsoft Visual Basic editor opens.
   c. Select **".Width = InchesToPoints(6.5)"** and **delete** it. It is okay if there is a blank line where you deleted the code (Figure 10-76).
   d. Press **Ctrl+S** to save the macro code and leave the Microsoft Visual Basic editor open.
6. Copy the macro and modify it to change to three columns.
   a. Select the *TwoColumns* macro code beginning with "**Sub TwoColumns ()**" and ending with "**End Sub**" and press **Ctrl+C** to copy the code.
   b. Place your insertion point below "End Sub" and press **Ctrl+V** to paste the copied macro code.
   c. Make the highlighted changes in Figure 10-77 to the copied macro code.
   d. Press **Ctrl+S** to save the macro code.
   e. Click the **File** menu and select **Close and Return to Microsoft Word**.
7. Assign a keyboard shortcut to a macro.
   a. Click the **File** tab to open the *Backstage* view.
   b. Select **Options** on the left to open the *Word Options* dialog box.
   c. Click **Customize Ribbon** on the left.
   d. Click the **Customize** button in the *Keyboard shortcuts* area. The *Customize Keyboard* dialog box opens (Figure 10-78).
   e. In the *Categories* area, scroll down and select **Macros**.
   f. Click the **Save changes in** drop-down list and select **[your initials] Word 10-3 template**.
   g. In the *Macros* list, select the **ThreeColumns** macro.
   h. Place your insertion point in the *Press new shortcut key* text box and press **Alt+Ctrl+Shift+3** (*Alt+Ctrl+#* is displayed as the keyboard shortcut).
   i. Click the **Assign** button.
   j. Click **Close** to close the *Customize Keyboard* dialog box and click **OK** to close the *Word Options* dialog box.

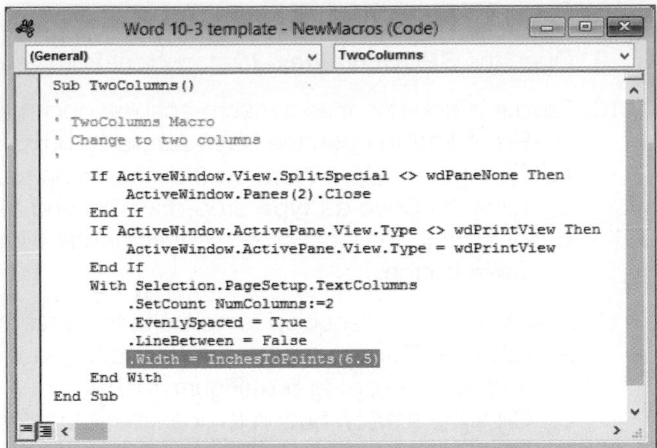

Word 10-3 template - NewMacros (Code)
(General)
TwoColumns
Sub TwoColumns()
'
' TwoColumns Macro
' Change to two columns
'
If ActiveWindow.View.SplitSpecial <> wdPaneNone Then
ActiveWindow.Panes(2).Close
End If
If ActiveWindow.ActivePane.View.Type <> wdPrintView Then
ActiveWindow.ActivePane.View.Type = wdPrintView
End If
With Selection.PageSetup.TextColumns
.SetCount NumColumns:=2
.EvenlySpaced = True
.LineBetween = False
.Width = InchesToPoints(6.5)
End With
End Sub

10-76 Delete macro code

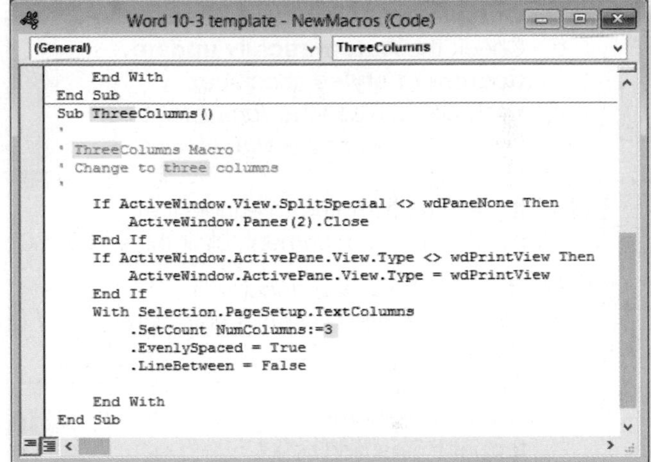

Word 10-3 template - NewMacros (Code)
(General)
ThreeColumns
End With
End Sub
Sub ThreeColumns()
'
' ThreeColumns Macro
' Change to three columns
'
If ActiveWindow.View.SplitSpecial <> wdPaneNone Then
ActiveWindow.Panes(2).Close
End If
If ActiveWindow.ActivePane.View.Type <> wdPrintView Then
ActiveWindow.ActivePane.View.Type = wdPrintView
End If
With Selection.PageSetup.TextColumns
.SetCount NumColumns:=3
.EvenlySpaced = True
.LineBetween = False
End With
End Sub

10-77 Modify the macro code

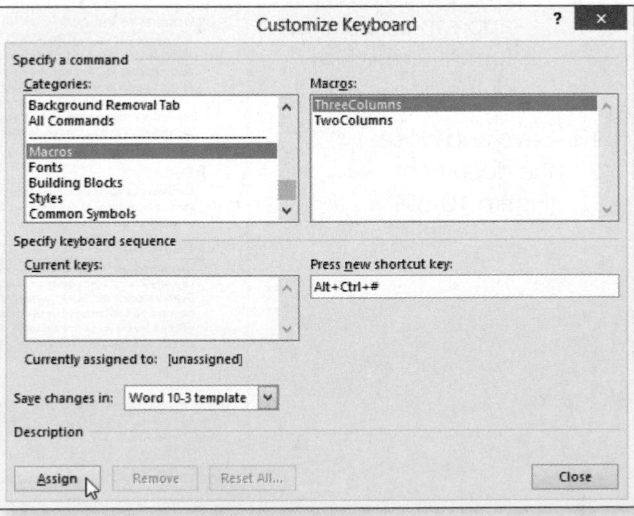

10-78 Add a keyboard shortcut to a macro

8. Save and close the macro-enabled template.
9. Open the ***SPCCDValues-10*** document from your student data files.
10. Save this document as a macro-enabled document.
    a. Press **F12** to open the **Save As** dialog box.
    b. Type [your initials] Word 10-3 as the file name.
    c. Click the **Save as type** drop-down list and select **Word Macro-Enabled Document**.
    d. Browse to the location on your computer where you want to save the document and click the **Save** button.
11. Attach the macro-enabled template to the document.
    a. Click the **Document Template** button [*Developer* tab, *Templates* group] to open the *Templates and Add-ins* dialog box (Figure 10-79).
    b. Click the **Attach** button to open the *Attach Template* dialog box.
    c. Browse to locate and select the ***[your initials] Word 10-3 template*** macro-enabled template and click the **Open** button.
    d. Check the **Automatically update document styles** check box.
    e. Click **OK** to close the *Templates and Add-ins* dialog box and attach the template.
    f. If you are prompted to enable the macros in the document, click the **Enable Content** button.

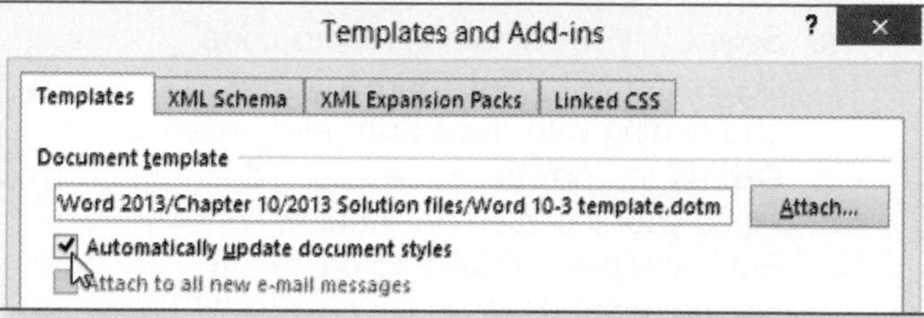

10-79 Attach a template to a document

12. Run the macros in the document.
    a. Place your insertion point anywhere in the body of the document below the title.
    b. Press **Alt+Ctrl+Shift+2** to apply two-column format to the body of the document.
    c. Press **Alt+Ctrl+Shift+3** to apply three-column format to the body of the document.
13. Save and close the document (Figure 10-80).

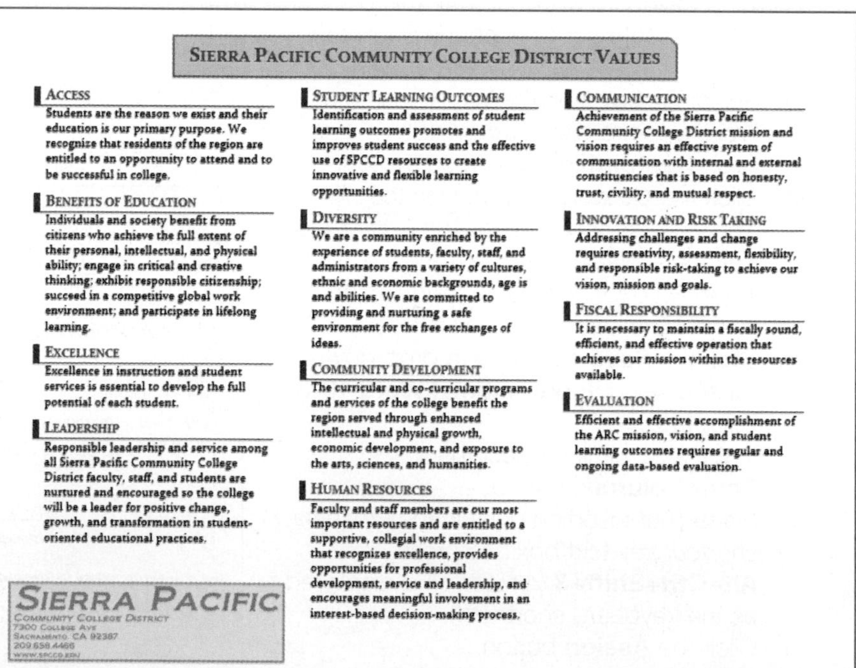

SIERRA PACIFIC COMMUNITY COLLEGE DISTRICT VALUES

ACCESS
Students are the reason we exist and their education is our primary purpose. We recognize that residents of the region are entitled to an opportunity to attend and to be successful in college.

BENEFITS OF EDUCATION
Individuals and society benefit from citizens who achieve the full extent of their personal, intellectual, and physical ability; engage in critical and creative thinking; exhibit responsible citizenship; succeed in a competitive global work environment; and participate in lifelong learning.

EXCELLENCE
Excellence in instruction and student services is essential to develop the full potential of each student.

LEADERSHIP
Responsible leadership and service among all Sierra Pacific Community College District faculty, staff, and students are nurtured and encouraged so the college will be a leader for positive change, growth, and transformation in student-oriented educational practices.

STUDENT LEARNING OUTCOMES
Identification and assessment of student learning outcomes promotes and improves student success and the effective use of SPCCD resources to create innovative and flexible learning opportunities.

DIVERSITY
We are a community enriched by the experience of students, faculty, staff, and administrators from a variety of cultures, ethnic and economic backgrounds, age is and abilities. We are committed to providing and nurturing a safe environment for the free exchanges of ideas.

COMMUNITY DEVELOPMENT
The curricular and co-curricular programs and services of the college benefit the region served through enhanced intellectual and physical growth, economic development, and exposure to the arts, sciences, and humanities.

HUMAN RESOURCES
Faculty and staff members are our most important resources and are entitled to a supportive, collegial work environment that recognizes excellence, provides opportunities for professional development, service and leadership, and encourages meaningful involvement in an interest-based decision-making process.

COMMUNICATION
Achievement of the Sierra Pacific Community College District mission and vision requires an effective system of communication with internal and external constituencies that is based on honesty, trust, civility, and mutual respect.

INNOVATION AND RISK TAKING
Addressing challenges and change requires creativity, assessment, flexibility, and responsible risk-taking to achieve our vision, mission and goals.

FISCAL RESPONSIBILITY
It is necessary to maintain a fiscally sound, efficient, and effective operation that achieves our mission within the resources available.

EVALUATION
Efficient and effective accomplishment of the ARC mission, vision, and student learning outcomes requires regular and ongoing data-based evaluation.

SIERRA PACIFIC
COMMUNITY COLLEGE DISTRICT

10-80 Word 10-3 completed

Independent Project 10-4

For this project, you create a fax template for American River Cycling Club from an online Word template. You save the template as a macro-enabled template, modify the template format and structure, customize the template content, insert *Fill-in* fields, record and copy macros in the template, and create a macro-enabled document based on the template.
[Student Learning Outcomes 10.1, 10.2, 10.3, 10.5]

Files Needed: ***Fax cover sheet (rust)* online Word template** and ***ARCClogo-10.png***
Completed Project File Names: ***[your initials] Word 10-4 template.dotm*** and ***[your initials] Word 10-4.docm***

Skills Covered in This Project

- Create a document based on an online Word template.
- Save a document as a macro-enabled template.
- Insert and resize a picture.
- Delete and customize a content control field.
- Modify the structure and format of a table in a template.
- Insert a *Fill-in* field.
- Record a button-activated macro.
- Copy and modify a macro.
- Add a macro button to the *Quick Access* toolbar.
- Create a document based on a template.
- Respond to a *Fill-in* field prompt.
- Enable the macro content in the document.
- Save a document as a macro-enabled document.
- Run a macro in the document.

---

1. Create a document from an online Word template.
   a. Click the **File** tab to open the *Backstage* view and select **New** to display templates.
   b. Click the **Fax** link in the *Suggested searches* area.
   c. Select the **Fax cover sheet (Rust design)** online Word template and click **Create** to create a document based on this online template. You can also search for a specific template using the *Search for online templates* text box.
   d. *Note: If this online template is not available in Word, open the* ***FaxCoverSheet-10*** *file from your student data files.*
2. Save the document as a macro-enabled template named ***[your initials] Word 10-4 template***. Be sure to select the specific location to save the template.
3. Replace the picture in the content control field and resize the picture.
   a. Select the picture in the "Picture" content control field and replace it with the ***ARCClogo-10*** picture from your student data files.
   b. Select the picture and change the width to **4"**. The height automatically adjusts.
4. Delete the "**Your company slogan**" and "**Comments**" content control fields.
5. Modify the tables in the template.
   a. Turn on **View Gridlines** so you can see the tables in the template (there are four tables).
   b. Select the first table and change the bottom border color to **Olive Green, Accent 3**.
   c. Select the second table and change the font color to **Black, Text 1**.
   d. Select the third table and change the color of all borders to **Olive Green, Accent 3**.

e. With the third table selected, change the font color to **Black, Text 1**.
f. Delete the last two rows of the third table.
g. In the third table, delete **FROM:** and type DATE:.
h. Select the fourth table and change the color of all borders to **Olive Green, Accent 3**.
i. Select the first row of the fourth table and change the shading color to **Olive Green, Accent 3**.

6. Use the following information to customize the fax template content control fields.
Your Company Name: Kelly Weatherby
Street Address: P.O. Box 4472
City, ST ZIP Code: Sacramento, CA 95841
Phone: 916-450-3320
Fax: 916-450-3301
Email: kelly@arcc.org

7. In the third table, insert the date in the cell to the right of "DATE:". Use the third date format (e.g., January 1, 2015) and set it to update automatically.

8. Insert *Fill-in* fields in the third table.
   a. In the cell to the right of "TO:", insert a *Fill-in* field. Type Who is the fax recipient? as the prompt and Fax Recipient as the default response to the prompt. When prompted, click **OK** to accept the default response.
   b. In the cell to the right of "FAX:", insert a *Fill-in* field. Type What is the recipient's fax number? as the prompt and Fax Number as the default response to the prompt. When prompted, click **OK** to accept the default response.
   c. In the cell to the right of "PAGES:", insert a *Fill-in* field. Type How many pages? as the prompt and Pages as the default response to the prompt. When prompted, click **OK** to accept the default response.

9. Record a button-activated macro to insert text.
   a. Place your insertion point in the second row of the fourth table.
   b. Create a macro name MembershipReceipt and store it in **Documents Based On [your initials] Word 10-4 template**.
   c. Type Membership receipt text as the *Description*.
   d. Click **Button** to assign a button to this macro.
   e. Add the *MembershipReceipt* macro to the **[your initials] Word 10-4 template**.
   f. Modify the macro button to use Membership Receipt as the display name and the **green square** as the icon for the button.
   g. Begin recording the macro. With your insertion point in the second row of the fourth table, type Your membership receipt is included with this fax.
   h. Stop recording the macro, delete the text you just typed, and test the macro by clicking the **Membership Receipt** macro button on the *Quick Access* toolbar.
   i. Delete the text inserted by the macro.

10. Copy and modify a macro.
    a. From the *Macros* dialog box, edit the **MembershipReceipt** macro.
    b. Copy the macro code and paste it below the existing macro.
    c. Make the highlighted changes shown in Figure 10-81.
    d. Save the macro code, and close and return to the Word document.

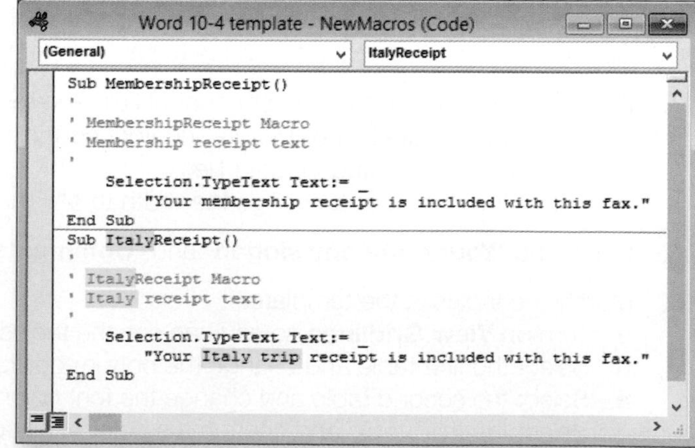

10-81 Modify the macro code

11. Customize the *Quick Access* toolbar for the Word 10-4 template to add a macro button for the *ItalyReceipt* macro.
    a. Use Italy Receipt as the display name.
    b. Select the **blue square** as the icon for the button.
    c. Place your insertion point in the second row of the fourth table and run the *ItalyReceipt* macro using the macro button on the *Quick Access* toolbar.
    d. Delete the text inserted by the macro.
12. Save and close the macro-enabled template.
13. Open a document based on the **[your initials] Word 10-4 template**.
14. Use the following information for the three *Fill-in* prompt dialog boxes.
    Recipient name: Rick Hermenn
    Recipient fax number: 916-452-9226
    Number of pages: 3
15. Enable the macro content in the document.
16. Save the document as a macro-enabled document named ***[your initials] Word 10-4***.
17. Run the *ItalyReceipt* macro using the button on the *Quick Access* toolbar in the second row of the fourth table.
18. Save and close the document (Figure 10-82).

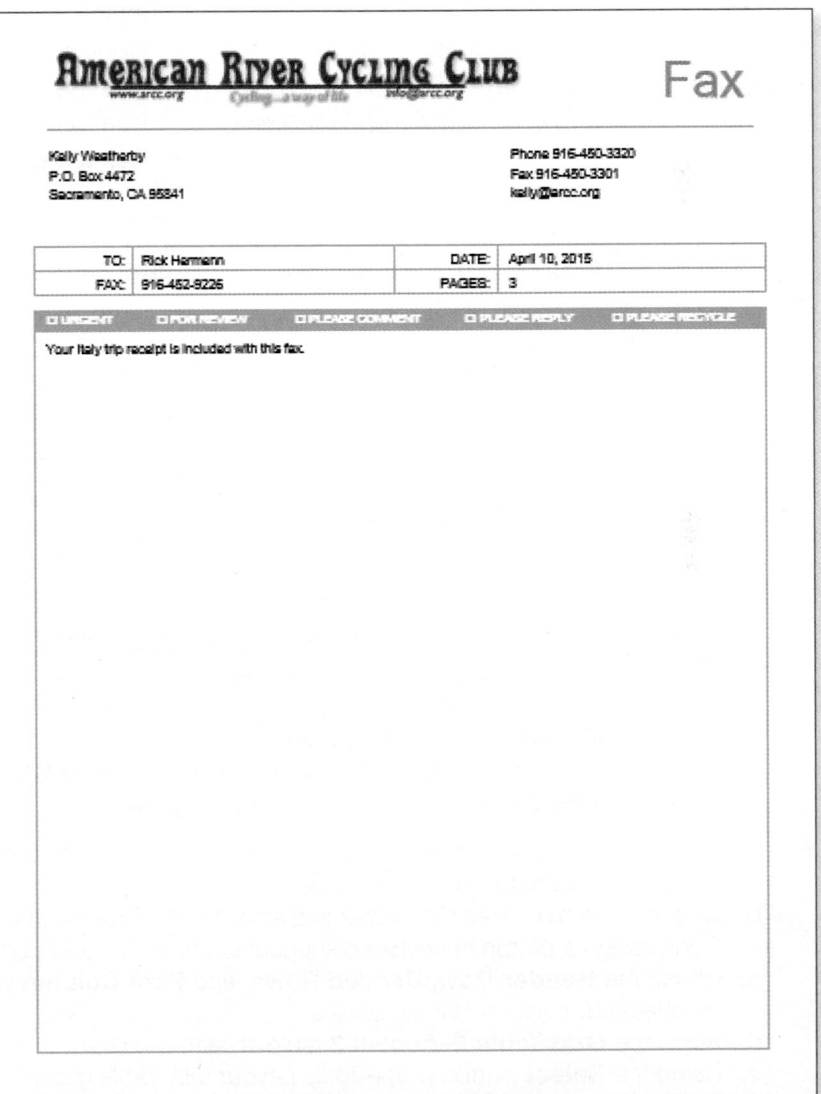

American River Cycling Club
www.arcc.org
Cycling...a way of life
info@arcc.org
Fax
Kelly Weatherby
P.O. Box 4472
Sacramento, CA 95841
Phone 916-450-3320
Fax 916-450-3301
kelly@arcc.org
TO: Rick Hermenn
DATE: April 10, 2015
FAX: 916-452-9226
PAGES: 3
☐ URGENT ☐ FOR REVIEW ☐ PLEASE COMMENT ☐ PLEASE REPLY ☐ PLEASE RECYCLE
Your Italy trip receipt is included with this fax.

10-82 Word 10-4 completed

Independent Project 10-5

For this project, you modify a document from Courtyard Medical Plaza using macros you create in another document. You create macros in a document, copy and modify a macro, and copy macros to another document.
[Student Learning Outcomes 10.3, 10.4, 10.5]

Files Needed: ***CMPmacros-10.docx, VaccinationSchedule-10.docx,*** and ***CMPlogo-10.png***
Completed Project File Names: ***[your initials] Word 10-5 macros.docm*** and ***[your initials] Word 10-5.docm***

Skills Covered in This Project

- Save a document as a macro-enabled document.
- Insert and arrange a picture.
- Save a picture as an *AutoText* building block.
- Create a macro to insert an *AutoText* building block.
- Create a macro to apply and modify a table style.
- Copy and modify a macro.
- Use the *Organizer* dialog box to copy a macro from one file to another.
- Run a macro in a document.

1. Open the ***CMPmacros-10*** document from your student data files.
2. Save the document as a macro-enabled document named ***[your initials] Word 10-5 macros***.
3. Insert a picture and save it as an *AutoText* building block.
   a. On the blank line below the table, insert the ***CMPlogo-10*** picture.
   b. Change the text wrapping to **Tight**.
   c. Change the *Horizontal* **Absolute position** to **0.3"** *to the right of* **Page**.
   d. Change the *Vertical* **Absolute position** to **9.6"** *below* **Page**.
   e. Select the picture and **Save Selection to AutoText Gallery**.
   f. Use Insert CMP logo as the name and save in the **Normal** template.
   g. Delete the picture from your document.
4. Create and record a macro to insert the *AutoText* building block into the footer of the document.
   a. Place your insertion point on the blank line below the table.
   b. Create a macro named InsertLogoFooter and save it in the **[your initials] Word 10-5 macros (document)**. Don't assign a button or keyboard shortcut to the macro and don't include a description.
   c. When recording the macro, **Edit Footer**, insert the **Insert CMP logo** *AutoText* building block, **Close Header and Footer**, and stop recording the macro.
5. Create and record a macro to apply and modify a table style to the table.
   a. Place your insertion point in the table.
   b. Create a macro named GridTable2 and save it in the **[your initials] Word 10-5 macros (document)**. Don't assign a button or keyboard shortcut to the macro and don't include a description.
   c. Check the **Header Row, Banded Rows**, and **First Column** boxes. The other boxes should not be checked.
   d. Apply the **Grid Table 2–Accent 2** table style to the table.
   e. Using the **Select** button [*Table Tools Layout* tab, *Table* group], select the entire table.
   f. Open the *Table Properties* dialog box [*Table Tools Layout* tab, *Table* group], click the **Cell** tab, and change the vertical alignment to **Center**.
   g. Click **OK** to close the *Table Properties* dialog box and stop recording the macro.

6. Copy and modify a macro.
   a. From the *Macros* dialog box, edit the **GridTable2** macro.
   b. Copy the *GridTable2* macro code and paste it below the existing macro.
   c. Make the highlighted changes from Figure 10-83.

```
Sub GridTable5()
'
' GridTable5 Macro
'
'
    Selection.Tables(1).ApplyStyleHeadingRows = Not Selection.Tables(1). _
        ApplyStyleHeadingRows
    Selection.Tables(1).ApplyStyleRowBands = Not Selection.Tables(1). _
        ApplyStyleRowBands
    Selection.Tables(1).ApplyStyleFirstColumn = Not Selection.Tables(1). _
        ApplyStyleFirstColumn
    Selection.Tables(1).Style = "Grid Table 5 Dark - Accent 2"
    Selection.Tables(1).Select
    Selection.Cells.VerticalAlignment = wdCellAlignVerticalCenter
End Sub
```

10-83 Modify the macro code

   d. Save the macro code and close and return to the Word document.

7. Place your insertion point in the table and using the *Macros* dialog box, run the **GridTable5** macro.
8. Save and close the macro-enabled document.
9. Open the ***VaccinationSchedule-10*** document from your student data files.
10. Save this document as a macro-enabled document named ***[your initials] Word 10-5***.
11. Copy the macros from the ***[your initials] Word 10-5 macros*** document to ***[your initials] Word 10-5***.
   a. From the *Macros* dialog box, open the *Organizer* dialog box (Figure 10-84).

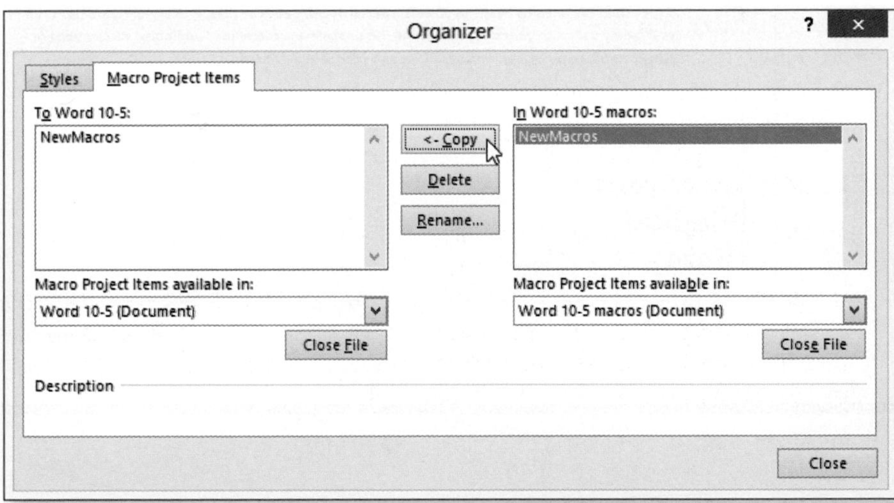

10-84 Copy macros from one file to another

   b. Close the file on the right and open the ***[your initials] Word 10-5 macros*** document. Make sure you select **All Word Documents** in the type of file drop-down list.
   c. Select the **NewMacros** macro project item from ***[your initials] Word 10-5 macros*** (on the right) and copy to ***[your initials] Word 10-5*** (on the left).
   d. Close the *Organizer* dialog box.

12. From the *Macros* dialog box, run the **InsertLogoFooter** macro to insert the footer into the document.

13. Place your insertion point in the table and run the **GridTable5** macro.
14. With your insertion point in the table, run the **GridTable2** macro.
15. Save and close the document (Figure 10-85).

VACCINATION SCHEDULE

Think of vaccines as a coat of armor for your child. To keep it shiny and strong, you have to make sure your child's immunizations are up to date. Timely vaccinations help to prevent disease and keep your family and the community healthy. Some immunizations are given in a single shot, while others require a series of shots over a period of time.

Don't neglect you vaccinations!

Vaccines for children and teenagers are listed alphabetically below with their routinely recommended ages. Missed doses will be assessed by your child's physician and given if necessary. Keep a personal record of all immunizations and bring it with you to each office visit.

RECOMMENED VACCINATION SCHEDULE

Name of Vaccine	*When It's Recommended*	*Total Doses*
Chickenpox (varicella)	At 12 months and 4-6 years	2
Diphtheria, tetanus, and pertussis (DTaP)	At 2, 4, 6 and 12-15 months, and 4-6 years	5
Haemophilus influenzae type b (Hib)	At 2, 4, 6, and 12 months	4
Hepatitis A (HepA)	At 12 and 18 months	3
Hepatitis B (HepB)	At birth, 1-2 months, and 6 months	3
Human papillomavirus (HPV)	3-dose series for girls at age 11-12 years	3
Inactivated influenza (flu shot)	Annually starting at age 6 months	Annually
Inactivated poliovirus (IPV)	At 2, 4, 6 months, and 4-6 years	4
Live intranasal influenza	Annually starting at age 2 years	Annually
Measles, mumps, and rubella (MMR)	At 12 months and 4-6 years	2
Meningococcal conjugate (MCV)	At 11-12 years	1
Pneumococcal conjugate (PCV)	At 2, 4, 6, and 12 months	4
Pneumococcal polysaccharide (PPSV)	At 2, 4, 6, and 12 months	4
Rotavirus (RV)	At 2, 4, and 6 months	3
Tetanus and diphtheria (Td)	At 11-12 years	1

These recommendations are for generally healthy children and teenagers and are for information only. If your child has ongoing health problems, special health needs or risks, or if certain conditions run in your family, talk with your child's physician. He or she may recommend additional vaccinations or schedules based on earlier immunizations and special health needs.

10-85 Word 10-5 completed

Independent Project 10-6

For this project, you create an insurance renewal letter template for Central Sierra Insurance. You create a macro-enabled template, insert *Fill-in* fields, record a macro, copy and modify a macro, and create a document based on the template.
[Student Learning Outcomes 10.1, 10.2, 10.3, 10.4, 10.5]

File Needed: ***CSIPolicyRenewal-10.docx***
Completed Project File Names: ***[your initials] Word 10-6 template.dotm*** and ***[your initials] Word 10-6.docm***

Skills Covered in This Project

- Save a document as a macro-enabled template.
- Insert a *Fill-in* field.
- Create a keyboard-activated macro to insert the closing lines of a letter.
- Copy and modify a macro.
- Assign a keyboard shortcut to a macro.
- Create a document based on a macro-enabled template.
- Respond to a *Fill-in* field prompt.
- Enable the macro content in the document.
- Save a document as a macro-enabled document.
- Update formulas in a table.
- Run a macro in a document.

1. Open the ***CSIPolicyRenewal-10*** document from your student data files.
2. Save the document as a macro-enabled template named ***[your initials] Word 10-6 template***.
3. Insert *Fill-in* fields to replace each of the bracketed placeholder text.
   a. Use the following information for the five *Fill-in* fields.
   b. Accept the default response as you create each *Fill-in* field.

	Prompt	Default Response to Prompt
Name and Address	Type name, company, and address.	Name/Company/Address
First Name	Type client's first name.	First Name
Insurance Company	Type name of insurance company.	Insurance Company
Premium Basis	What is the premium basis?	Premium Basis
Rate per $1000	What is the rate per $1000?	Rate per $1000

4. Create and record a macro to insert the closing lines of the letter.
   a. Place your insertion point on the last blank line in the document.
   b. Create a macro named GretchenClosing and store the macro in **Document Based On [your initials] Word 10-6 template**.
   c. Type Inserts Gretchen Souza closing lines as the description.
   d. Assign **Alt+Ctrl+Shift+G** as the keyboard shortcut and save it in the ***[your initials] Word 10-6 template***.
   e. Record the following lines of text as the macro:
   Sincerely and press **Enter** four times
   Gretchen Souza, ARM, CIC, CRM
   Central Sierra Insurance
   gretchen@centralsierra.com
   f. Stop recording the macro and delete the text you just typed. Make sure there are two blank lines below the last paragraph in the letter.

5. Copy and modify a macro.
   a. Use the Microsoft Visual Basic editor to copy the *GretchenClosing* macro and paste it below the last line of macro code.
   b. Make the highlighted changes in Figure 10-86 to the copied macro.
   c. Save and close the macro and return to Microsoft Word.
6. Assign a keyboard shortcut to the *JuanClosing* macro using the *Customize Keyboard* dialog box.
   a. Save changes in the **[your initials] Word 10-6 template**.
   b. Use **Alt+Ctrl+Shift+J** as the keyboard shortcut.

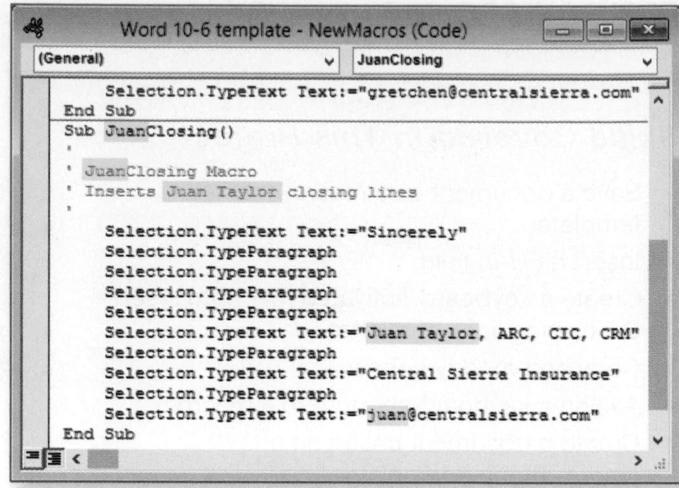

10-86 Modify the macro code

7. Test the macro and finalize the template.
   a. Use the keyboard shortcut to test the *JuanClosing* macro.
   b. Delete the inserted macro text. There should be two blank lines below the last body paragraph in the letter.
8. Check the spacing in the document around the *Fill-in* fields to ensure proper spacing.
9. Save and close the template.
10. From a Windows folder, create a new document based on the ***[your initials] Word 10-6 template***.
11. Use the following information for the *Fill-in* field prompts:
    Name/Company/Address:
    Mr. Lamar Gordon
    Sierra Fence Company
    2405 Eureka Avenue
    Fair Oaks, CA 95636
    First Name: Lamar
    Insurance Company: West Coast Insurance
    Premium Basis: $325,000
    Rate per $1000: $21
12. Enable the macro content in the document.
13. Save the document as a macro-enabled document named ***[your initials] Word 10-6***.
14. Update the formulas in the last three cells in the second row of the table.
15. On the second blank line below the body, run the *JuanClosing* macro.
16. Save and close the document (Figure 10-87).

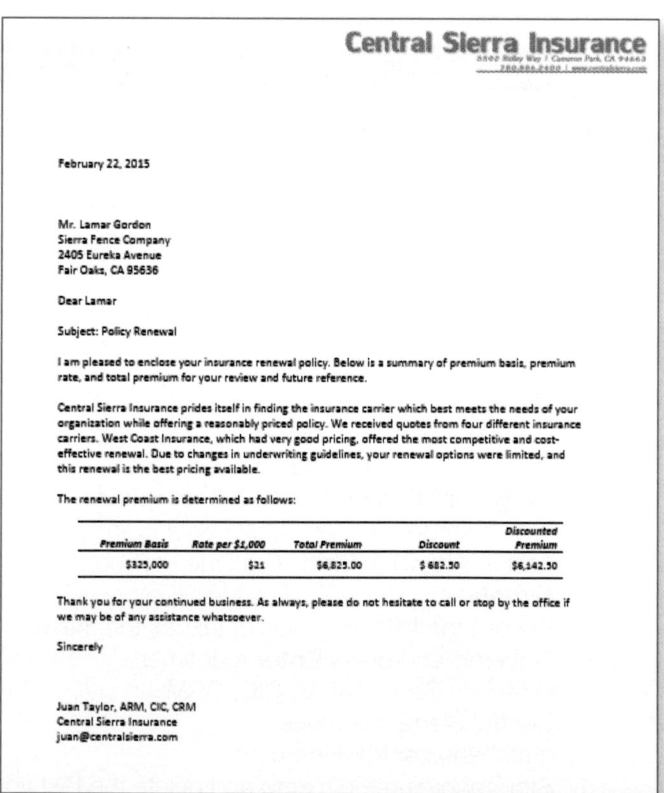

Central Sierra Insurance

February 22, 2015

Mr. Lamar Gordon
Sierra Fence Company
2405 Eureka Avenue
Fair Oaks, CA 95636

Dear Lamar

Subject: Policy Renewal

I am pleased to enclose your insurance renewal policy. Below is a summary of premium basis, premium rate, and total premium for your review and future reference.

Central Sierra Insurance prides itself in finding the insurance carrier which best meets the needs of your organization while offering a reasonably priced policy. We received quotes from four different insurance carriers. West Coast Insurance, which had very good pricing, offered the most competitive and cost-effective renewal. Due to changes in underwriting guidelines, your renewal options were limited, and this renewal is the best pricing available.

The renewal premium is determined as follows:

Premium Basis	*Rate per $1,000*	*Total Premium*	*Discount*	*Discounted Premium*
$325,000	$21	$6,825.00	$ 682.50	$6,142.50

Thank you for your continued business. As always, please do not hesitate to call or stop by the office if we may be of any assistance whatsoever.

Sincerely

Juan Taylor, ARM, CIC, CRM
Central Sierra Insurance
juan@centralsierra.com

10-87 Word 10-6 completed

Improve It Project 10-7

For this project, you create an invoice template for Eller Software Services from an online Word template. You save the template as a macro-enabled template, customize the template content, insert a *Fill-in* field, record macros in the template, and create a macro-enabled document based on the template. [Student Learning Outcomes 10.1, 10.2, 10.3, 10.5]

Files Needed: ***Invoice* online Word template** and ***ESSlogo-10.png***
Completed Project File Names: ***[your initials] Word 10-7 template.dotm*** and ***[your initials] Word 10-7.docm***

Skills Covered in This Project

- Create a document based on a Word online template.
- Save a document as a macro-enabled template.
- Insert, resize, and arrange a picture.
- Customize a content control field.
- Delete a row from a table.
- Insert a *Fill-in* field.
- Insert a formula in a table.
- Record a button-activated macro.
- Create a document based on a template.
- Respond to a *Fill-in* field prompt.
- Enable the macro content in the document.
- Save a document as a macro-enabled document.
- Run a macro in a document.

---

1. Create a document from an online Word template.
   a. In the *New* area on the *Backstage* view, search for online templates and use invoice as the keyword.
   b. Select the **Invoice (Red design)** online Word template and create a document based on this template.
   c. *Note: If this template is not available in Word, open the* ***Invoice-10*** *file from your student data files*.
2. Save the document as a macro-enabled template named ***[your initials] Word 10-7 template***.
3. Replace the existing logo picture and resize and arrange the picture.
   a. Change the sample logo picture and replace it with ***ESSlogo-10*** from your student data files.
   b. Change the height to **0.6"** while maintaining the aspect ratio.
   c. Change the text wrapping to **In Front of Text** and change the alignment to **Top** and **Right** relative to the margin.
4. Customize the content of the template.
   a. In the "Company" content control field, type Eller Software Services.
   b. In the "Street Address, City, ST ZIP Code" content control field, type 3421 East Avenue, Saint Cloud, MN 56301.
   c. In the "Add additional instructions" content control field, type Payment is due within 30 days after the invoice date.
   d. In the footer, type the following information in the content control fields:
      Telephone: 320.675.4100
      Fax: 320.675.4101
      Email: info@ellerss.com
      Web: www.ellerss.com
   e. In the bottom table in the body of the document, delete the next to the last row ("Shipping & Handling").

5. Insert a *Fill-in* field.
   a. Delete the content control field below "To" and insert a *Fill-in* field.
   b. Type What is the client's name, company, and address? as the prompt and Client info as the default response to the prompt.
   c. Accept the default response to the prompt.

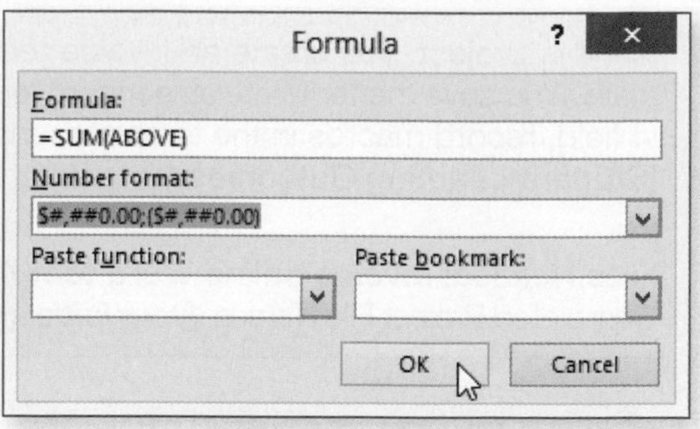

10-88 Insert formula to add the cells above

6. Insert formulas in the table.
   a. Insert a formula in the cell to the right of "Subtotal" to **SUM** the cells **ABOVE** (Figure 10-88). Use the number format shown.
   b. Insert a formula in the cell to the right of "Sales Tax" to multiply cell **D13** by **7.5%** and use the same number format.
   c. Insert a formula in the cell to the right of "Total Due By [Date]" to add cells **D13** and **D14** and use the same number format.

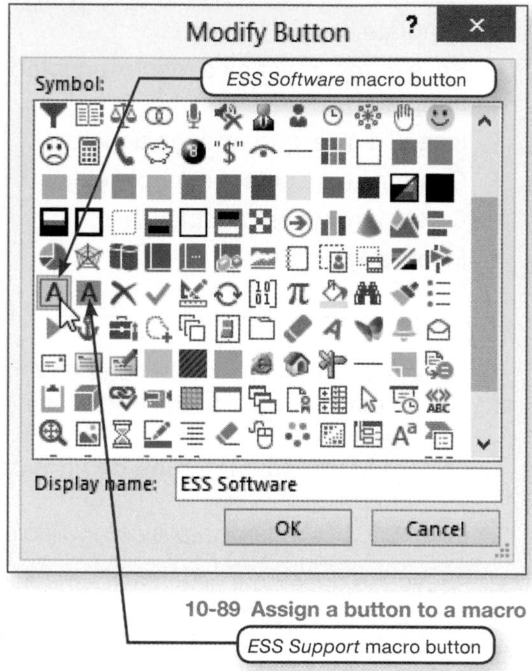

10-89 Assign a button to a macro

7. Create a button-activated macro to insert a product into the invoice.
   a. Place your insertion point in the cell below "Quantity."
   b. Create a macro named ESS_Software and store it in **Documents Based On [your initials] Word 10-7 template**.
   c. For the description, type Inserts ESS Accounting Software package.
   d. Assign the macro to a button and add the macro to the *Quick Access* tool bar for the **[your initials] Word 10-7 template**.
   e. Modify the button to use ESS Software as the display name, and select the button icon shown in Figure 10-89.
8. Record the macro.
   a. Type the following information in the first row of the table, pressing **Tab** to move from cell to cell:
      1 ESS Accounting Software $875.00 $875.00
   b. Stop recording the macro.
   c. Delete the text you typed in the table.
9. Create another button-activated macro to insert a product into the invoice.
   a. Place your insertion point in the cell below "Quantity".
   b. Create a macro named ESS_Support and store it in **Documents Based On [your initials] Word 10-7 template**.
   c. For the description, type Inserts ESS Accounting Software **Support package**.
   d. Assign the macro to a button and add the macro to the *Quick Access* tool bar for the **[your initials] Word 10-7 template**.
   e. Modify the button to use ESS Support as the display name, and select the button icon to the right of the button icon selected in Figure 10-89.
10. Record the macro.
    a. Type the following information in the first row of the table, pressing **Tab** to move from cell to cell:
       8 hrs ESS Accounting Software Support $75.00 $600.00
    b. Stop recording the macro.
    c. Delete the text you typed in the table.

11. Save and close the macro-enabled template.
12. From a Windows folder, create a new document based on the ***[your initials] Word 10-7 template***.
13. Use the following information for the *Fill-in* field prompt:
    Ms. Amanda Mendez
    Paradise Lakes Resort
    1256 Raymond Drive
    Cass Lake, MN 56633
14. Enable macro content in the document.
15. Save the document as a macro-enabled document named ***[your initials] Word 10-7***.
16. Customize content control fields.
    a. Type ESS2305 in the invoice number content control field.
    b. In the "Click to select date" content control field, select the current date.
    c. In the "Date" content control field ("Total Due By [Date]"), select the date one month from today.
17. Run macros.
    a. Place your insertion point in the cell below "Quantity" and run the *ESS_Software* macro using the button on the *Quick Access* toolbar.
    b. Place your insertion point in the first cell in the next row and run the *ESS_Support* macro.
18. Update the formulas in the table.
19. Save and close the document (Figure 10-90).

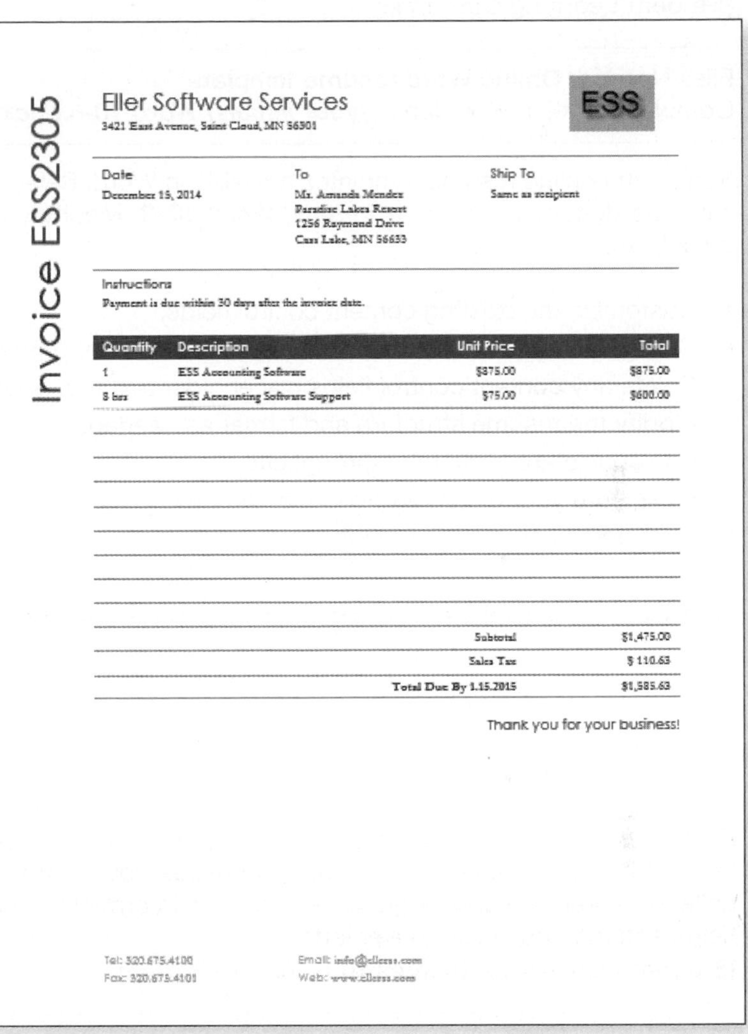
Invoice ESS2305

Eller Software Services
3421 East Avenue, Saint Cloud, MN 56301

ESS

Date
December 15, 2014

To
Ms. Amanda Mendez
Paradise Lakes Resort
1256 Raymond Drive
Cass Lake, MN 56633

Ship To
Same as recipient

Instructions
Payment is due within 30 days after the invoice date.

Quantity	Description	Unit Price	Total
1	ESS Accounting Software	$875.00	$875.00
8 hrs	ESS Accounting Software Support	$75.00	$600.00
		Subtotal	$1,475.00
		Sales Tax	$ 110.63
		Total Due By 1.15.2015	$1,585.63

Thank you for your business!

Tel: 320.675.4100
Fax: 320.675.4101
Email: info@elless.com
Web: www.elless.com

10-90 Word 10-7 completed

Challenge Project 10-8

For this project, you create a résumé based on an online Word template. You can use content from a previous résumé to customize the new résumé. Your college career center is a good resource for information about an effective résumé.
[Student Learning Outcomes 10.1, 10.2]

Files Needed: **Online Word résumé template**
Completed Project File Name: ***[your initials] Word 10-8.docx***

Search the online résumé templates available in Word. Select the résumé template of your choice and save the document as ***[your initials] Word 10-8***. Modify your document according to the following guidelines:

- Customize the existing content control fields.
- Customize document properties and add document property fields as needed.
- Delete any content control fields placeholder text that is not needed.
- Modify the résumé structure and format as needed.
- Use consistent formatting throughout.
- Make sure your résumé is no longer than two pages.
- Save and close the document.

Challenge Project 10-9

For this project, you create a cover letter (job application letter) template based on an online Word template. You can use content from a previous cover letter to customize the new cover letter. Your college career center is a good resource for information about an effective cover letter. Use *Fill-in* fields and macros in your cover letter.
[Student Learning Outcomes 10.1, 10.2, 10.3, 10.5]

Files Needed: **Online Word cover letter template**
Completed Project File Name: ***[your initials] Word 10-9 template.dotm*** and ***[your initials] Word 10-9.docm***

Search for online cover letter templates available in Word. Select the cover letter template of your choice and save it as a macro-enabled template named ***[your initials] Word 10-9 template***. Modify your template according to the following guidelines:

- Customize the existing content and control fields.
- Customize document properties and add document property fields as needed.
- Delete any content control fields placeholder text that is not needed.
- Use *Fill-in* fields for the recipient's name and address and the salutation.

- Record macros for paragraphs of information in the body of the letter. Store these macros in the template so you can customize future cover letters with information from the macros.
- Modify the cover letter structure and format as needed.
- Use consistent formatting throughout and fit the cover letter on one page.
- Save and close the template.

Create a document based on your cover letter template. Customize information in the *Fill-in* field prompts and enable macro content. Insert content from macros as needed. Save the document as a macro-enabled document named ***[your initials] Word 10-9***.

Challenge Project 10-10

Most of your classes have homework assignments, and your professors usually want you to turn in these assignments in a specific format. For example, you might have to include a header with your name, your professor's name, and the name of the assignment. In this project, create a macro-enabled template that you can use for your homework assignments.
[Student Learning Outcomes 10.2, 10.3, 10.4, 10.5]

Files Needed: None
Completed Project File Name: ***[your initials] Word 10-10 template.dotm***

Create a new document and save it as a macro-enabled template named ***[your initials] Word 10-10 template***. Modify your template according to the following guidelines:

- Plan the macros you want included in this document.
- Create and record macros for content to insert into your homework assignment document.
- If some macros are similar, copy and edit them to create new macros.
- Assign the macros to a button or keyboard shortcut.
- Include *Fill-in* fields as needed.
- Run macros to make sure they work properly.
- Include a heading to label each macro content in the document.

CHAPTER 11

Working with Forms and Master Documents

CHAPTER OVERVIEW

In previous chapters, you used content control fields in templates and cover pages. In this chapter, you learn how to insert and customize a variety of content control fields. You can use content control fields and templates together to create fillable forms. You can also group or protect forms so that users can only edit the content control fields. This step helps you to preserve the formatting of your fillable forms.

In Chapter 3, *Working with Reports and Multipage Documents*, you worked with reports and long documents. In this chapter, you will learn how to manage long documents using a master document and subdocuments. *Outline* view and heading styles are useful tools when you are working with a master document and subdocuments.

STUDENT LEARNING OUTCOMES (SLOs)

After completing this chapter, you will be able to:

SLO 11.1 Insert, customize, and arrange a variety of content control fields (p. W11-631).

SLO 11.2 Insert and customize content control fields where a user selects from a list of choices (p. W11-639).

SLO 11.3 Edit a content control field to change the format and lock content, and use *Design* mode to edit placeholder text (p. W11-641).

SLO 11.4 Group content control fields, protect and edit a form, create a form based on a template, fill in a form, and save a form based on a template (p. W11-647).

SLO 11.5 Manage a long document using a master document and subdocuments (p. W11-651).

CASE STUDY

In the first three Pause & Practice projects in this chapter, you create a registration form for Central Sierra Insurance using content control fields. In Pause & Practice 11-4, you manage a long report using a master document and subdocuments.

Pause & Practice 11-1: Customize a registration form using basic content control fields.

Pause & Practice 11-2: Insert and customize content control fields where users select from options.

Pause & Practice 11-3: Group content control fields, save a form as a template, and create a new form based on the template.

Pause & Practice 11-4: Use a master document and subdocuments to manage a long report.

WORD

SLO 11.1

Using Content Control Fields

You are familiar with customizing information in content control fields from *SLO 3.4: Inserting a Cover Page* and *SLO 10.2: Customizing and Using Templates.* In this section, you learn how to insert and customize basic content control fields where users can enter information such as their name and company, check a check box, pick a date, or insert a picture. Each content control field has a title and properties associated with it and you can arrange fields in a document using a variety of formatting methods.

Content Control Fields

Recall that ***content control fields*** are containers for information or objects. Each content control field is designed to contain a specific type of information. The following table lists some of the basic content control fields and how you can use each type:

Content Control Fields

Content Control Field	Use
Rich Text	User can type in text and the text can be formatted.
Plain Text	User can type in text and all the text is formatted the same way.
Check Box	User can select or deselect a check box.
Date Picker	User can select a date from a calendar thumbnail. You can set the format of the date that is inserted.
Picture	User can insert a picture into the content control field.

The size of *Rich Text* and *Plain Text* content control fields adjust as a user types text in the fields. These content control fields can contain a few words or paragraphs of text. *Check Box* content control fields can be checked or unchecked by a user and do not change in size. *Date Picker* content control fields automatically adjust in size to fit the date format you select. *Picture* content control fields automatically resize to fit the pictures the users insert.

Control Content Control Field Arrangement

When you use content control fields in a document or form, you need to plan where you will place these fields in the document and how you will arrange the fields. You can use ***tab stops*** and ***indents*** to control the location of these fields in the document and to control how the text wraps to the next line when you are using *Rich Text* or *Plain Text* content control fields.

Tables are also an effective way to arrange content control fields in a document. You can insert one or more content control fields in a cell and use horizontal and vertical alignment to align them in a cell. You can also use tab stops and indents to arrange content control fields in the cells of a table.

Insert a Rich Text Content Control Field

For an open-ended response from the user, use a ***Rich Text content control field.*** The user who is filling out the form can enter a single word, a sentence, or paragraphs of text. The user can also copy text and paste it in the *Rich Text* content control field. Users can apply formatting to individual words in a *Rich Text* content control field. In other words, not all text has to be formatted the same. For example, you can apply bold and italic formatting to a specific word or to all of the text entered into the field.

Check Box Content Control Field

A ***Check Box content control field*** lets users select an option by clicking a check box. A *Check Box* content control field limits users to only two options: checked or unchecked. By default, an unchecked *Check Box* content control field is an open box, and when the user checks the box, it appears as a box with an X in it. You can customize how the unchecked and checked box appears. For example, you might use the square with a check mark symbol for the checked *Check Box* content control field.

HOW TO: Insert and Customize a Check Box Content Control Field

1. Place your insertion point in the document where you want to insert the content control field.
2. Click the **Check Box Content Control** button [*Developer* tab, *Controls* group] to insert a *Check Box* content control field (Figure 11-7).
3. Select the content control field and click the **Properties** button [*Developer* tab, *Control* field] to open the *Content Control Properties* dialog box.
4. In the *Title* text box, type the title of the content control field.
5. To change the checked or unchecked symbol, click the **Change** button (Figure 11-8). The *Symbol* dialog box opens (Figure 11-9).

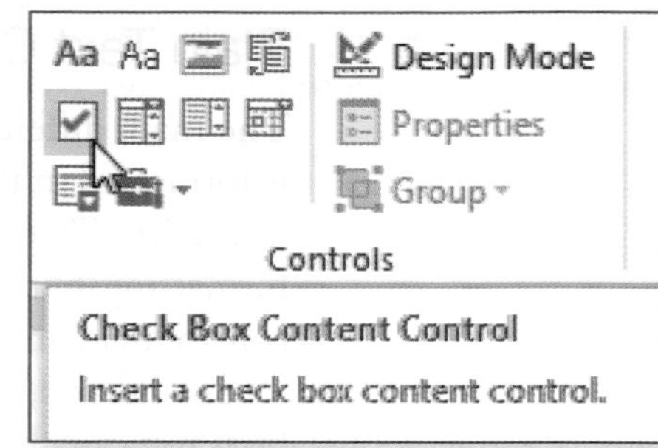

11-7 Insert *Check Box* content control field

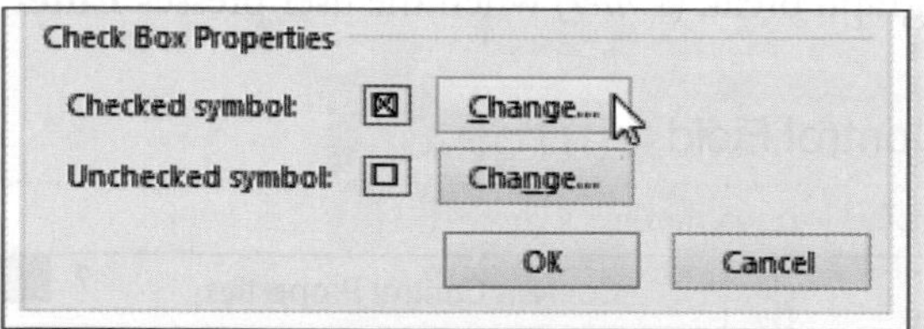

11-8 Change symbol for checked and unchecked

6. Click the **Font** drop-down list and select a font set.
7. Select a symbol to use.
   - Alternatively, you can select a symbol from the *Recently used symbols* area.
8. Click **OK** to close the *Symbols* dialog box.
9. Click **OK** to close the *Content Control Properties* dialog box.
   - A *Check Box* content control field is, by default, unchecked.

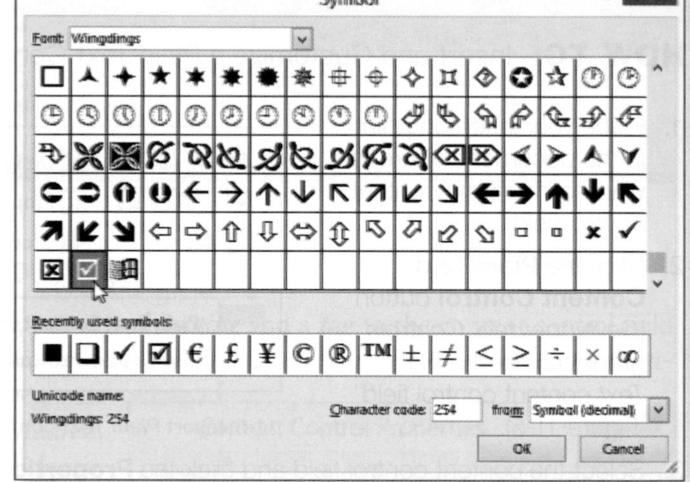

11-9 *Symbol* dialog box

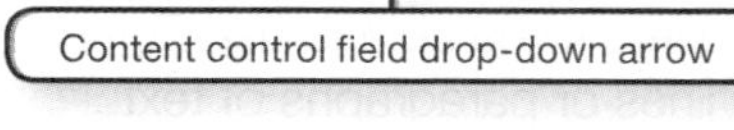

Date Picker Content Control Field

The ***Date Picker content control field*** lets the user pick a date from a calendar thumbnail rather than typing in a date (Figure 11-10). This ensures consistency in how dates are displayed in the document. You can control the format of the date in the *Content Control Properties* dialog box.

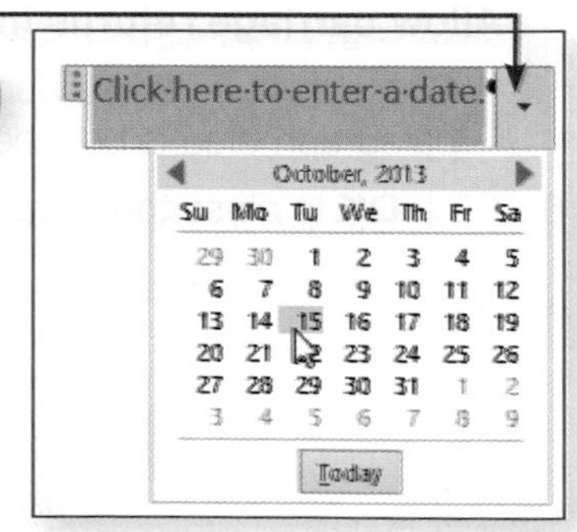

11-10 *Date Picker* content control field

HOW TO: Insert and Customize a Date Picker Content Control Field

1. Place your insertion point in the document where you want to insert the content control field.
2. Click the **Date Picker Content Control** button [*Developer* tab, *Controls* group] to insert a *Date Picker* content control field (Figure 11-11).

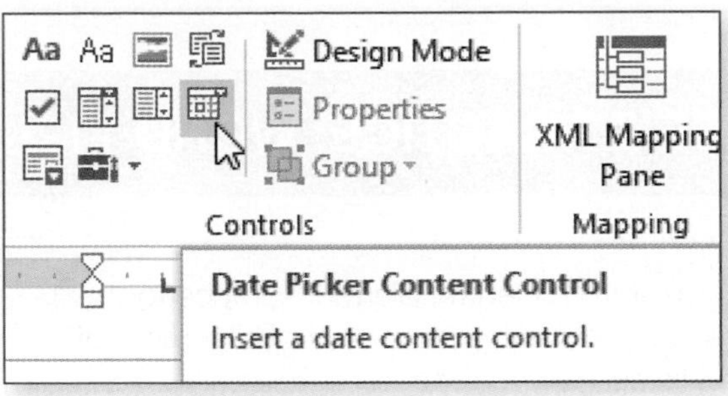

11-11 Insert *Date Picker* content control field

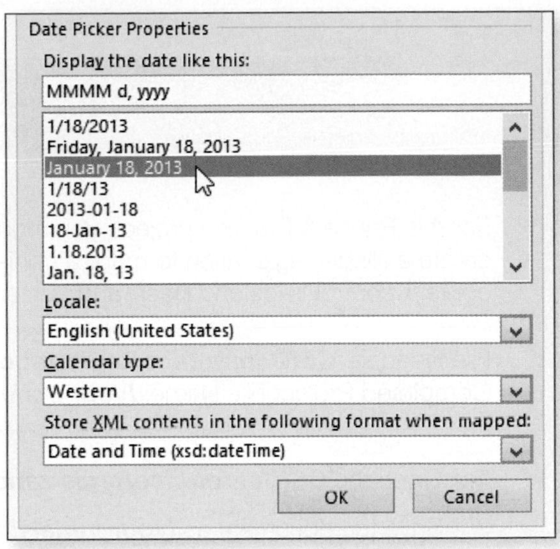

11-12 Select the date format

3. Select the content control field and click the **Properties** button [*Developer* tab, *Control* group] to open the *Content Control Properties* dialog box.
4. In the *Title* text box, type a title for the content control field.
5. Select the date format from the list in the *Date Picker Properties* area in the *Content Control Properties* dialog box (Figure 11-12).
6. Click **OK** to close the *Content Control Properties* dialog box.

Picture Content Control Field

A ***Picture content control field*** allows the user to insert a picture at a specific location in the document (Figure 11-13). For example, you might use this type of content control field in a real estate listing template where a picture of the home is inserted in a specific location in the template. A *Picture* content control field automatically resizes to fit the selected picture. You can arrange a *Picture* content control field in a document the same way you arrange a picture with text wrapping and alignment.

When you use a *Picture* content control field, it is important to consider how the inserted picture will affect the formatting of the document. Make sure you arrange the *Picture* content control field in a location that does not negatively affect other text and fields in the document.

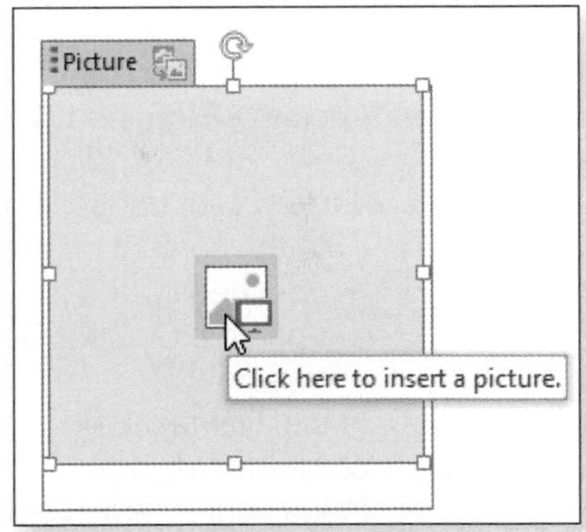

11-13 *Picture* content control field

HOW TO: Insert and Customize a Picture Content Control Field

1. Place your insertion point in the document where you want to insert the content control field.
2. Click the **Picture Content Control** button [*Developer* tab, *Controls* group] to insert a *Picture* content control field (Figure 11-14).

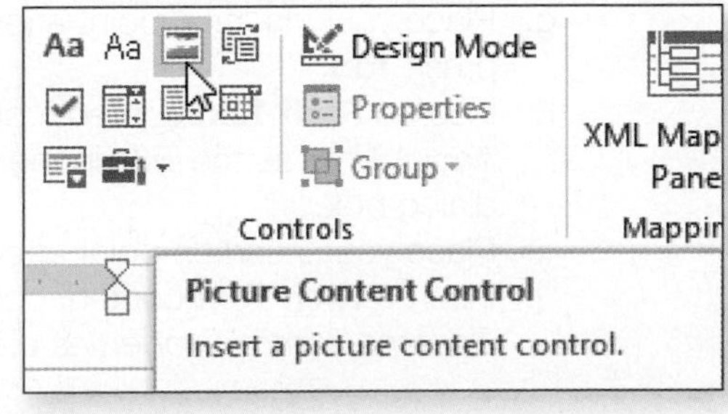

11-14 Insert *Picture* content control field

3. Select the content control field and click the **Properties** button [*Developer* tab, *Control* group] to open the *Content Control Properties* dialog box.
4. In the *Title* text box, type a title for the content control field.
5. Click **OK** to close the *Content Control Properties* dialog box.

PAUSE & PRACTICE: WORD 11-1

For this Pause & Practice project, you modify an existing document from Central Sierra Insurance to create a fillable registration form for a conference. You set a tab stop and indents to control alignment of content control fields and insert and customize content control fields.

File Needed: ***CSIConferenceRegistration-11.docx***
Completed Project File Name: ***[your initials] PP W11-1.docx***

1. Open the ***CSIConferenceRegistration-11*** document from your student data files.
2. Save the document as ***[your initials] PP W11-1***.
3. Add a tab stop and set a hanging indent.
   a. If the ruler is not displayed, turn it on [*View* tab, *Show* group].
   b. Select the "**Name:**" and "**Agency Name:**" paragraphs and set a **1" left** tab.
   c. Select the next two paragraphs of text ("Yes, . . ." and "No, . . ."), set a **0.25" left** tab, and set a **0.25" hanging** indent.
4. Insert and customize *Rich Text* content control fields.
   a. Place your insertion point after "Name:" and press **Tab**.
   b. Click the **Rich Text Content Control** button [*Developer* tab, *Controls* group] to insert a *Rich Text* content control field.
   c. With the content control field selected, click the **Properties** button [*Developer* tab, *Controls* group] to open the *Content Control Properties* dialog box (Figure 11-15).
   d. In the *Title* text box, type Name and click **OK** to close the text box.
   e. Place your insertion point after "Agency Name:" and press **Tab**.
   f. Insert a **Rich Text** content control field, and type Agency Name as the *Title* in the *Content Control Properties* dialog box.
   g. Place your insertion point after "Arrival Time:" and press **Tab**.
   h. Insert a **Rich Text** content control field, and type Arrival Time as the *Title* in the *Content Control Properties* dialog box.
   i. Place your insertion point after "Departure Time:" and press **Tab**.
   j. Insert a **Rich Text** content control field, and type Departure Time as the *Title* in the *Content Control Properties* dialog box.

11-15 Add a title to the content control field

5. Insert *Check Box* content control fields, customize the properties, and change the symbol.
   a. Place your insertion point before "Yes, . . ."
   b. Click the **Check Box Content Control** button [*Developer* tab, *Controls* group] to insert a *Check Box* content control field.
   c. Open the *Content Control Properties* dialog box and type Attending as the *Title* (Figure 11-16).
   d. Click the **Change** button to the right of *Checked symbol*. The *Symbol* dialog box opens (Figure 11-17).

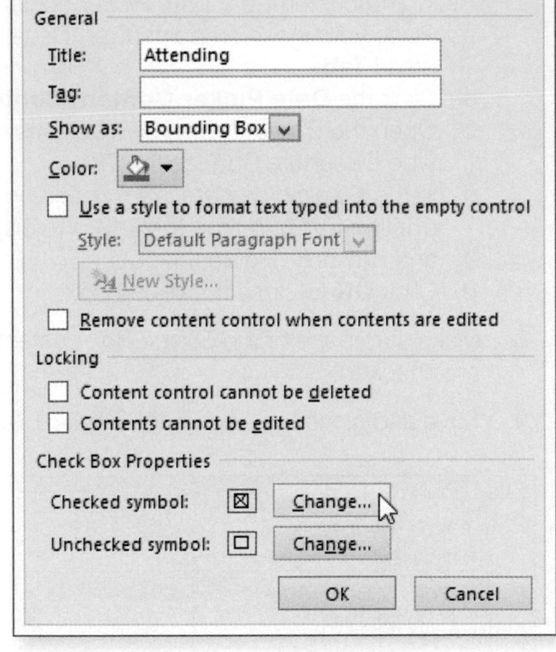

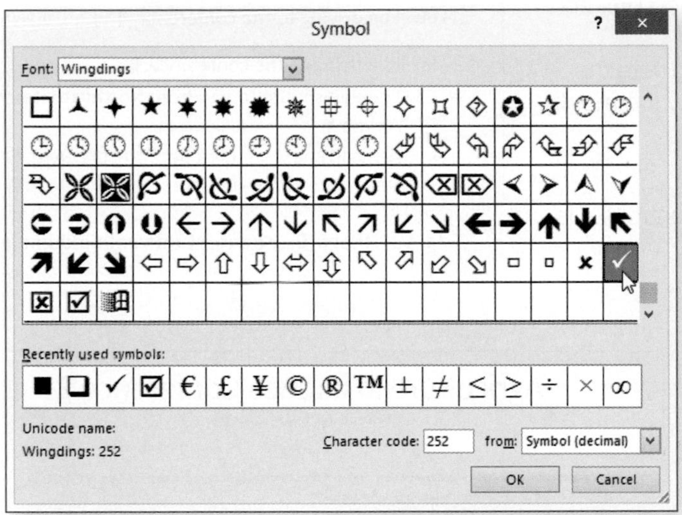
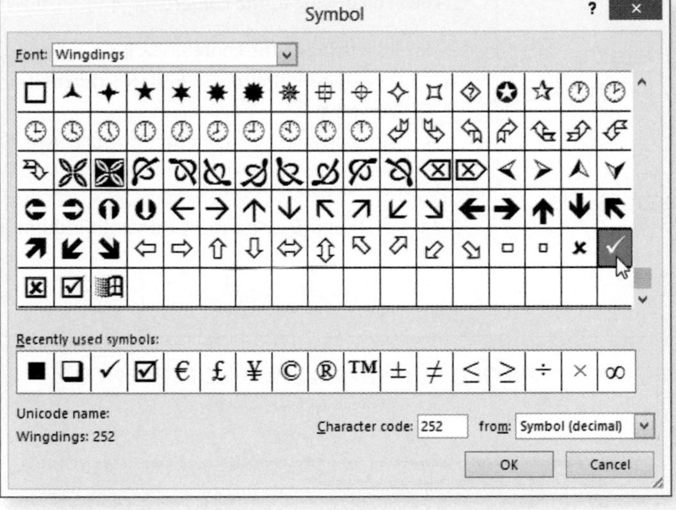

11-17 Select symbol for checked

11-16 Change checked symbol

   e. Click the **Font** drop-down list and select **Wingdings**.
   f. Select the **check mark** symbol (character code 252).
   g. Click **OK** to close the *Symbol* dialog box.
   h. Click **OK** to close the *Content Control Properties* dialog box.
   i. Press the **right** arrow key two times to deselect the *Check Box* content control field and position the insertion point between the content control field and the text.
   j. Press **Tab**.
   k. Place your insertion point before "No, . . ."
   l. Repeat steps 5b–j to insert another *Check Box* content control field. Type Not Attending as the *Title*.

6. Insert and customize *Check Box* content control fields. For all of the *Check Box* content control fields in this step, *don't* change the *Checked symbol* as you did in step 5.
   a. Place your insertion point before "I will be staying . . .", insert a **Check Box** content control field, and type Staying at Northgate as the *Title* in the *Content Control Properties* dialog box.
   b. Use the **right** arrow key to deselect the content control field and position the insertion point between the content control field and the text, and press **Tab**.
   c. Place your insertion point before "I will not be staying . . .", insert a **Check Box** content control field, and type Not Staying at Northgate as the *Title*.
   d. **Tab** between the content control field and the text.
   e. Place your insertion point before "I will be driving . . .", insert a **Check Box** content control field, and type Driving as the *Title*.
   f. **Tab** between the content control field and the text.
   g. Place your insertion point before "I will be flying . . .", insert a **Check Box** content control field, and type Flying as the *Title*.
   h. **Tab** between the content control field and the text.

   i. Place your insertion point between the tab and "I need a shuttle . . .", insert a **Check Box** content control field, and type Shuttle as the *Title*.
   j. **Tab** between the content control field and the text (Figure 11-18).

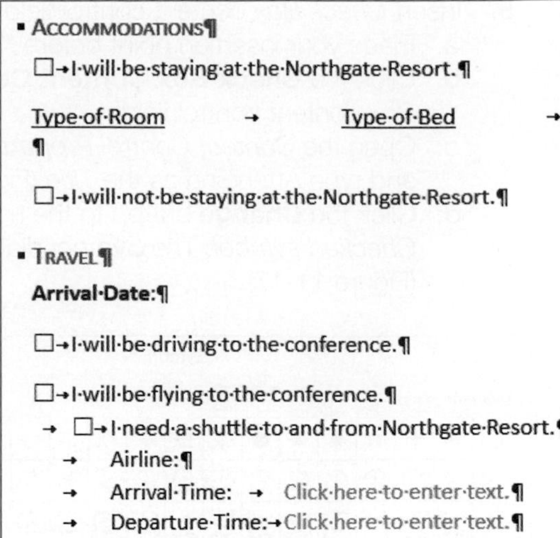

11-18 *Check Box* content control fields inserted

7. Insert and customize a *Date Picker* content control field.
   a. Place your insertion point after "Departure Date:" and press **Tab**.
   b. Click the **Date Picker Content Control** button.
   c. Open the *Content Control Properties* dialog box and type Departure Date as the *Title*.
   d. In the *Display the date like this* text box, delete the existing text and type MMMM d to display the month and day only (Figure 11-19).
   e. Click **OK** to close the dialog box.
8. Make sure none of the *Check Box* content control fields are checked.
9. Save and close the document (Figure 11-20).

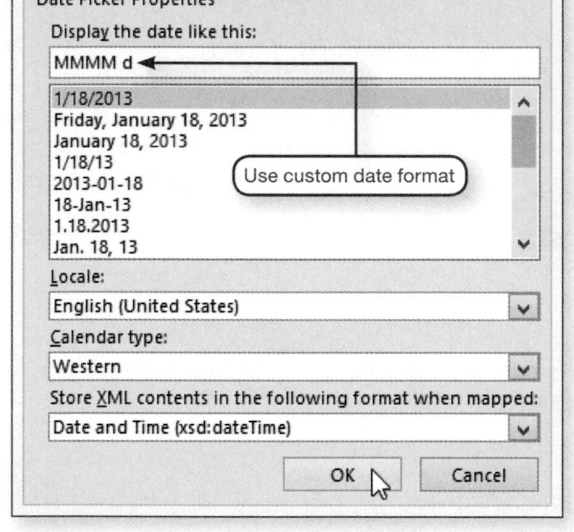

11-19 Select date format

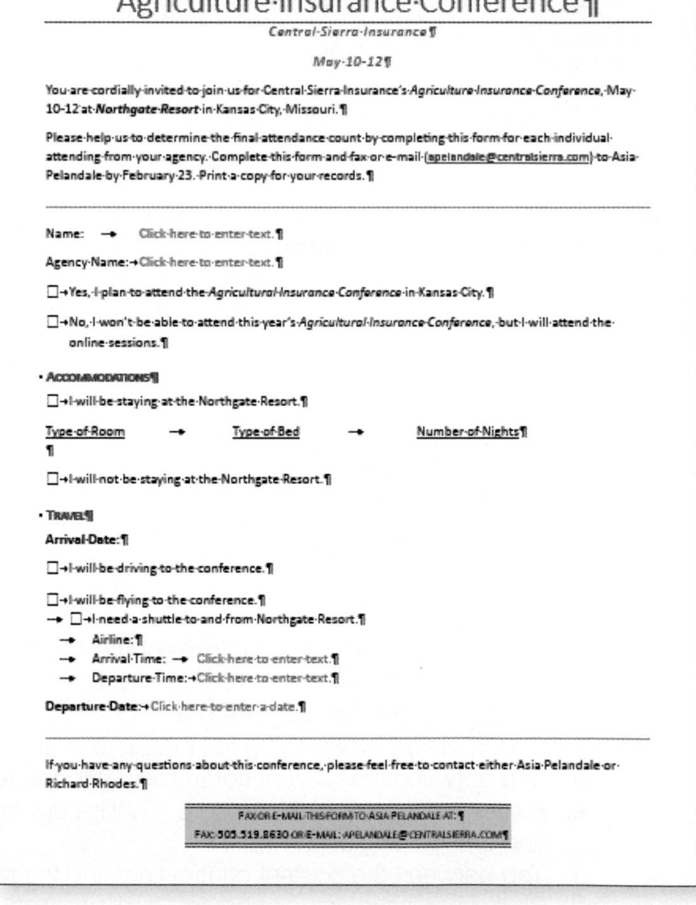

Agriculture·Insurance·Conference¶

Central·Sierra·Insurance¶

May·10-12¶

You·are·cordially·invited·to·join·us·for·Central·Sierra·Insurance's·*Agriculture·Insurance·Conference*,·May·10-12·at·***Northgate·Resort***·in·Kansas·City,·Missouri.¶

Please·help·us·to·determine·the·final·attendance·count·by·completing·this·form·for·each·individual·attending·from·your·agency.·Complete·this·form·and·fax·or·e-mail·(apelandale@centralsierra.com)·to·Asia·Pelandale·by·February·23.·Print·a·copy·for·your·records.¶

Name: → Click·here·to·enter·text.¶

Agency·Name:→Click·here·to·enter·text.¶

☐→Yes,·I·plan·to·attend·the·*Agricultural·Insurance·Conference*·in·Kansas·City.¶

☐→No,·I·won't·be·able·to·attend·this·year's·*Agricultural·Insurance·Conference*,·but·I·will·attend·the·online·sessions.¶

▪ ACCOMMODATIONS¶

☐→I·will·be·staying·at·the·Northgate·Resort.¶

Type·of·Room → Type·of·Bed → Number·of·Nights¶
¶

☐→I·will·not·be·staying·at·the·Northgate·Resort.¶

▪ TRAVEL¶

Arrival·Date:¶

☐→I·will·be·driving·to·the·conference.¶

☐→I·will·be·flying·to·the·conference.¶
→ ☐→I·need·a·shuttle·to·and·from·Northgate·Resort.¶
→ Airline:¶
→ Arrival·Time: → Click·here·to·enter·text.¶
→ Departure·Time:→Click·here·to·enter·text.¶

Departure·Date:→Click·here·to·enter·a·date.¶

If·you·have·any·questions·about·this·conference,·please·feel·free·to·contact·either·Asia·Pelandale·or·Richard·Rhodes.¶

FAX·OR·E-MAIL·THIS·FORM·TO·ASIA·PELANDALE·AT:¶
FAX:·505.519.8630·OR·E-MAIL:·APELANDALE@CENTRALSIERRA.COM¶

11-20 PP W11-1 completed

SLO 11.2

Using Advanced Content Control Fields

In addition to the content control fields you learned about in *SLO 11.1*, there are also content control fields that allow users to select from pre-defined options. The *Combo Box* and *Drop-Down List* content control fields allow users to choose from a list of choices that you create. These content control fields limit the responses of users and save users time by allowing them to select an option from the list rather than typing a response. The *Building Block Gallery* content control field lets users insert a building block. *Legacy Tools* are form fields that are available in older versions of Word.

Combo Box Content Control Field

A ***Combo Box content control field*** lists user options in the form of a drop-down list (Figure 11-21). When you insert a *Combo Box* content control field, you create the list of options in the *Content Control Properties* dialog box. This type of content control field also allows users the option of typing in their own responses in the field. For example, you set up a list of dates from which users can choose, but they also have the option of typing in a different date instead.

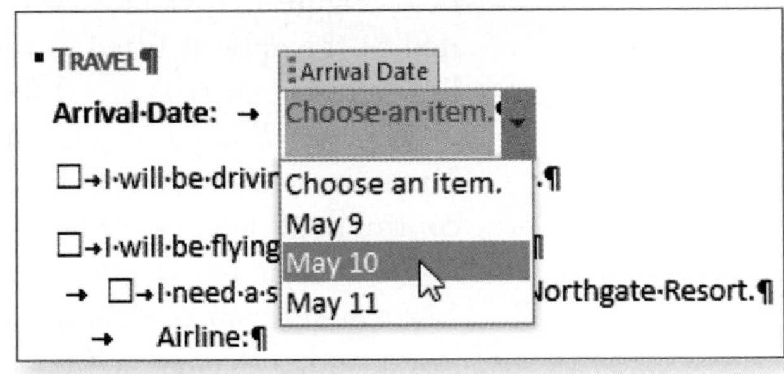

11-21 *Combo Box* content control field

HOW TO: Insert and Customize a Combo Box Content Control Field

1. Place your insertion point in the document where you want to insert the content control field.
2. Click the **Combo Box Content Control** button [*Developer* tab, *Controls* group] to insert a *Combo Box* content control field (Figure 11-22).
3. Select the content control field and click the **Properties** button [*Developer* tab, *Controls* group] to open the *Content Control Properties* dialog box.
4. In the *Title* text box, type a title for the content control field.
5. Click the **Add** button in the *Drop-Down List Properties* area (Figure 11-23). The *Add Choice* dialog box opens (Figure 11-24).
6. In the *Display Name* area, type a choice.
   - The *Value* field is automatically filled in with the same text that is in the *Display Name* area.
   - You can change the *Value* to something different from the *Display Name*, but normally these two fields are the same.
7. Click **OK** (or press **Enter**) to close the *Add Choice* dialog box.
   - Continue to **Add** choices to populate the *Combo Box* drop-down list as desired.
8. You can modify the drop-down list.
   - Select an item in the list and click **Modify** to change an option in the list.
   - Select an item in the list and click **Remove** to remove an option from the list.

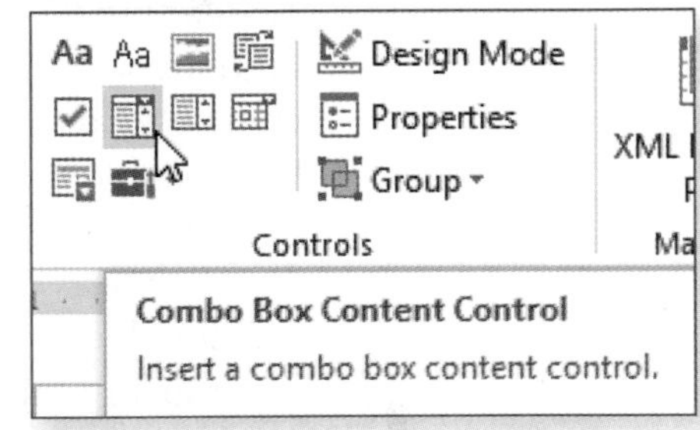

11-22 Insert *Combo Box* content control field

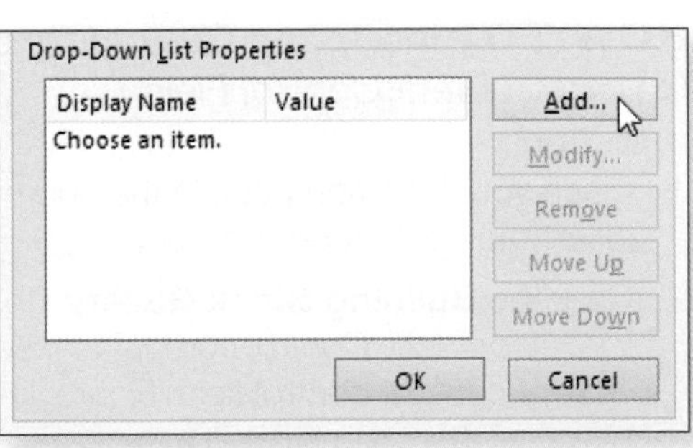

11-23 *Drop-Down List Properties*

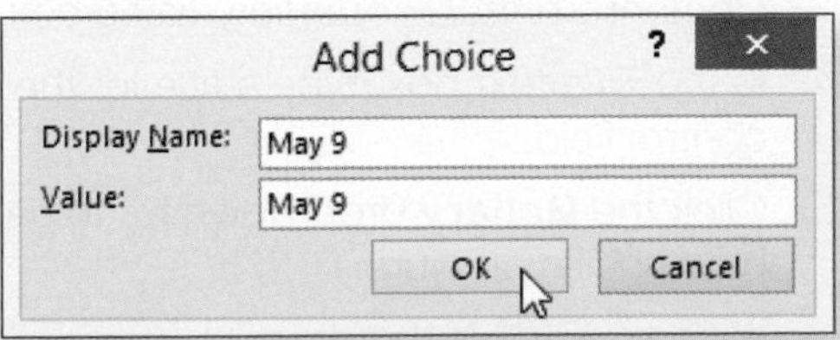

11-24 *Add Choice* dialog box

- Select an item in the list and click **Move Up** or **Move Down** to reorder the list.
- The first item in the list is the default choice visible to users when the *Combo Box* drop-down list is collapsed. You can remove the instructions "Choose an item" or modify the instructions to display different text.

9. Click **OK** to close the *Content Control Properties* dialog box.

Drop-Down List Content Control Field

A ***Drop-Down List content control field*** is very similar to a *Combo Box* content control field (Figure 11-25). However, users are limited to the options listed in the drop-down list; they cannot type in a different response in the *Drop-Down List* content control field. *Drop-Down List* and *Combo Box* content control fields look the same in a document.

You insert and customize a *Drop-Down List* content control field the same way you insert and customize a *Combo Box* content control field. See *How To: Insert and Customize a Combo Box Content Control Field* above.

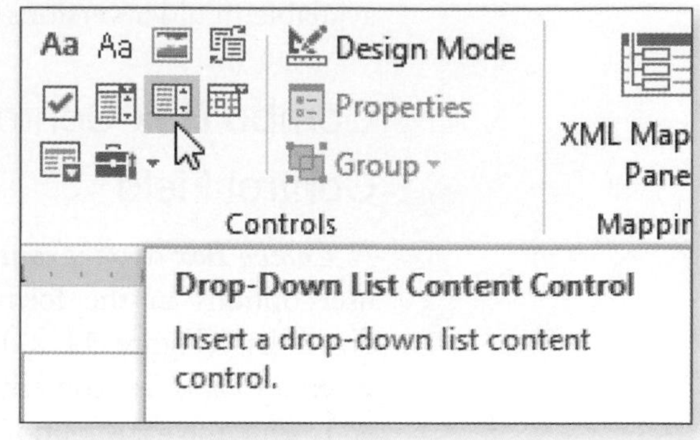

11-25 Insert *Drop-Down List* content control field

Building Block Gallery Content Control Field

A ***Building Block Gallery content control field*** allows users to insert a building block from the building block gallery you specify. The advantage of using a *Building Block Gallery* content control field rather than just inserting a building block is that you can control where the building block is inserted. For example, if you create a form letter, you could save paragraphs of text as individual building blocks in *the AutoText* building block gallery and then insert a *Building Block Gallery* content control field. Users would then select the appropriate *AutoText* building block from the *Building Block Gallery* content control field to insert into the document in a specific location.

HOW TO: Insert and Customize a Building Block Gallery Content Control Field

1. Place your insertion point in the document where you want to insert the content control field.
2. Click the **Building Block Gallery Content Control** button [*Developer* tab, *Controls* group] to insert a *Building Block Gallery* content control field (Figure 11-26).
3. Select the content control field and click the **Properties** button [*Developer* tab, *Controls* group] to open the *Content Control Properties* dialog box.
4. In the *Title* text box, type a title for the content control field.
5. Click the **Gallery** drop-down list to select a building block gallery (Figure 11-27).
   - *Quick Parts* is the default building block category when you insert a *Building Block Gallery* content control field.

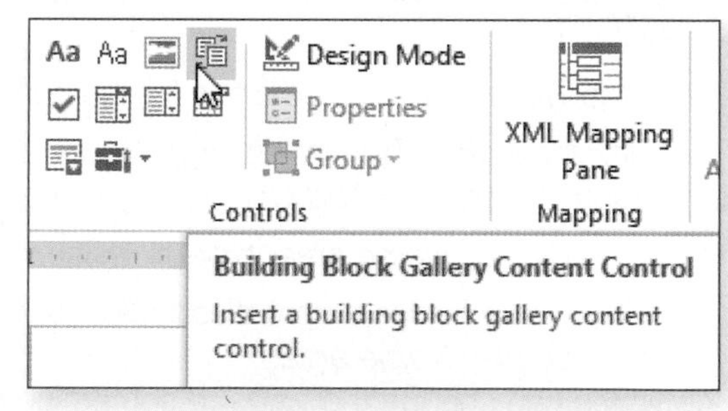

11-26 Insert *Building Block Gallery* content control field

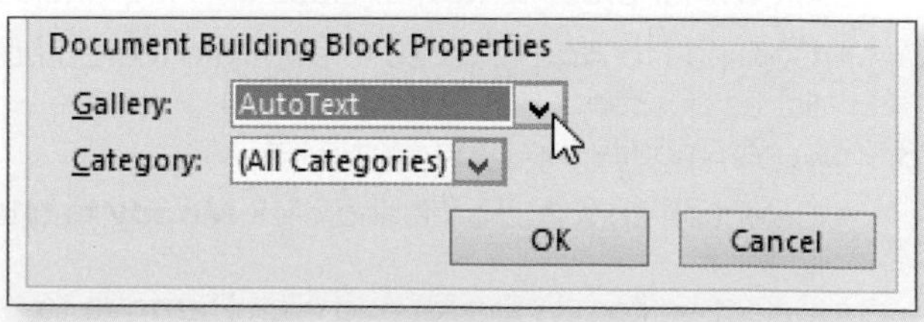

11-27 Select the *Building Block* gallery and category

6. Click the **Category** drop-down list to select a category, which limits the user's choice to building blocks in the selected category.
7. Click **OK** to close the *Content Control Properties* dialog box.
   - Users click the drop-down list in the *Building Block Gallery* content control field to select a building block to insert (Figure 11-28).

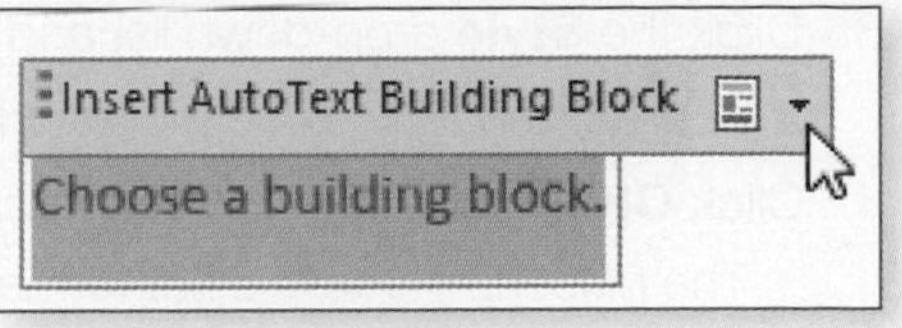

11-28 *Building Block Gallery* drop-down list

Legacy Tools

Legacy tools are a set of form fields from previous versions of Word that can still be used in current versions (Figure 11-29). Whereas content control fields function in both documents and templates even if the document or template is not protected, legacy tools function only in protected templates.

Legacy tools include ***legacy form fields*** and ***ActiveX control fields***. You can insert legacy form fields into forms and they are very similar to content control fields (but they only function in a protected template). *ActiveX* control fields require macros to function and are usually used in web pages.

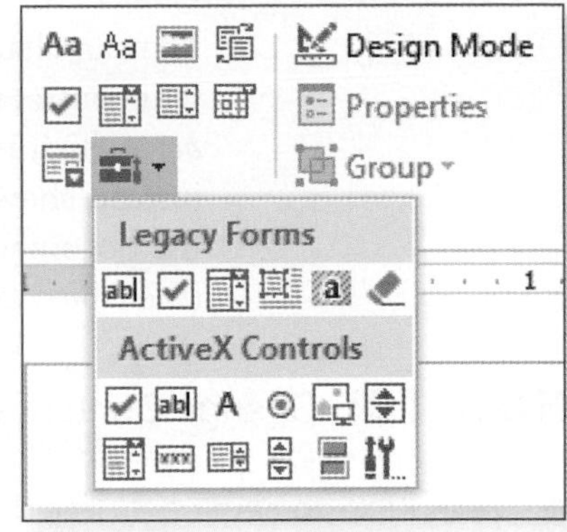

11-29 *Legacy* tools

SLO 11.3

Editing Content Control Fields

After you have created your form and inserted content control fields, you might want to change the color of the content control fields, change how the fields are displayed in the document, or change what content control fields do when users enter information. You also have the option of locking content control fields and the content in these fields. You use *Design* mode to change the placeholder text for some content control fields.

Use Styles with Content Control Fields

When you insert content control fields where users type text (*Rich Text* or *Plain Text*) or select an item from a list (*Combo Box*, *Drop-Down List*, or *Date Picker*), the typed or selected text is formatted with the style of the paragraph where the content control field is located. For example, if you insert a *Rich Text* or *Plain Text* content control field in a paragraph that is formatted with the *Normal* style, the text you type or select is formatted in *Normal* style. You can select a style that is applied to the text typed in a content control field.

11-30 Apply a style to content control field contents

HOW TO: Change Text Style in a Content Control Field

1. Select the content control field to modify and click the **Properties** button [*Developer* tab, *Controls* group] to open the *Content Control Properties* dialog box (Figure 11-30).
2. Check the **Use a style to format text typed into the empty control** box.

3. Click the **Style** drop-down list and select a style to apply to the contents of the content control field.
   - Alternatively, you can click **New Style** to create a new style to apply.
4. Click **OK** to close the *Content Control Properties* dialog box.
   - The placeholder text is not formatted with the style applied; only the inserted or selected text is formatted with the style.

Change Content Control Display and Color

You can change how content control fields display in your document and the color of the content control field. When you insert a content control field, it is, by default, shown as a ***bounding box***, which is a border and handle. You can change the settings so the content control field is instead shown with ***start and end tags***, which make the content control fields more visible in the document. Content control fields can also be shown with no border or start and end tags (the *None* option). The *None* option displays the content control field with only shading.

HOW TO: Change Content Control Display and Color

1. Select the content control field you want to modify and click the **Properties** button [*Developer* tab, *Controls* group] to open the *Content Control Properties* dialog box (Figure 11-31).
2. Click the **Show as** drop down list and select from the three options: *Bounding Box* (Figure 11-32), *Start/End Tag* (Figure 11-33), or *None* (Figure 11-34).

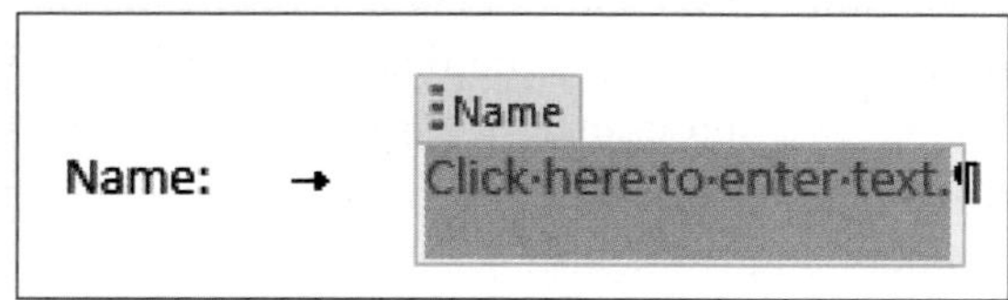

11-32 Content control field shown as a *Bounding Box* and a color applied

11-31 Modify content control field display and color

11-33 Content control field shown as *Start/End Tags* and a color applied

11-34 Content control field shown as *None* and a color applied

3. Click the **Color** drop-down list and select a color for the content control field.
   - By default, the color of the content control field is based on the theme of the document.
   - To change the content control field back to the theme color after you have changed it, click the **Color** drop-down list and select **Automatic**.
4. Click **OK** to close the *Content Control Properties* dialog box.

> **MORE INFO**
>
> When a content control field is shown as *None*, no color is applied to the content control field even if you select a color. The color of the field remains gray.

User Interaction with Content Control Fields

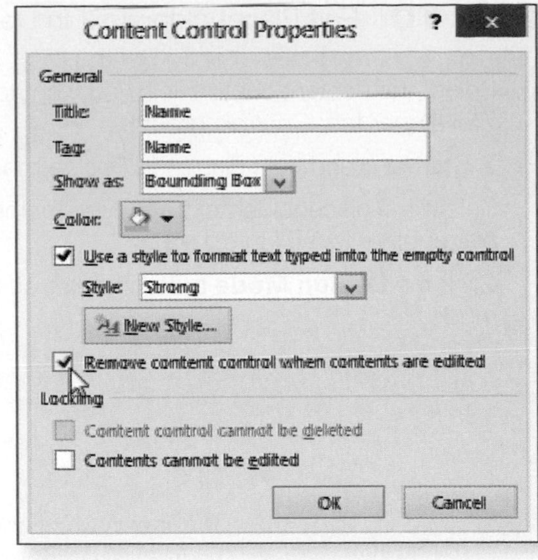

11-35 Remove content control when contents are edited

Previously when you worked with online templates or cover pages that included content control fields, the content control fields were set to be removed when you typed text in the content control field. In other words, when you typed in a content control field, the text replaced the field. When you insert a content control field, by default, the content control field is not removed when a user types text. You can select what happens to the content control field when a user interacts with it.

If you check the **Remove content control when contents are edited** box, the content control field is removed when a user types or selects information in the content control field (Figure 11-35). When this happens, only the text or selection remains. If this check box is not checked, the content control field remains in the document after the user makes his or her entry.

Lock a Content Control Field

When using content control fields in a document, you have the ability to lock a field so it cannot be deleted and/or edited by a user. Locking a content control field so it cannot be deleted prevents users from inadvertently deleting a content control field. If a content control field is locked so it cannot be deleted, the user can still edit the contents of the content control field. If you lock a content control field so it cannot be edited, users cannot edit the content of the field.

HOW TO: Lock Content Control Fields

1. Select the content control field you want to modify and click the **Properties** button [*Developer* tab, *Controls* group] to open the *Content Control Properties* dialog box (Figure 11-36).
2. In the *Locking* area, check the **Content control cannot be deleted** box to prevent the content control field from being deleted.
3. Check the **Contents cannot be edited** box to prevent users from editing the content control field.
4. Click **OK** to close the *Content Control Properties* dialog box.

11-36 Lock a content control field

Design Mode

You can use ***Design mode*** to view and edit content control fields in your document. When you insert a content control field in a document, Word automatically inserts placeholder text (e.g., "Click here to enter text.") in the field (with the exception of *Picture* and *Check Box* content controls). In *Design* mode, you can customize the placeholder text and easily view the content control fields in your document.

HOW TO: Edit Placeholder Text in Design Mode

1. Select the content control field you want to modify and click the **Design Mode** button [*Developer* tab, *Controls* group].
   - Start and end tags display in *Design* mode.
2. Select the placeholder text and type the new placeholder text (Figure 11-37).
3. Click the **Design Mode** button to turn off *Design* mode.

11-37 Modify placeholder text in a content control field

> **MORE INFO**
>
> When you use *Design* mode, the formatting of your document may appear distorted. It will look normal again when you turn off *Design* mode.

Delete a Content Control Field

When customizing a document or form that contains content control fields, you might need to delete an existing content control field. There are two different ways to remove a content control field.

- Click the handle of the content control field to select it and press **Delete**.
- Right-click the content control field and select **Remove Content Control** from the context menu.

If you have already edited the contents of the content control field and you use the context menu to remove the field, the content control field is deleted, but the contents of the field remain in the document.

PAUSE & PRACTICE: WORD 11-2

For this Pause & Practice project, you work with the form from *Pause & Practice 11-1*. You insert content control fields, modify the properties of the content control fields, and use *Design* mode to change the placeholder text.

File Needed: ***[your initials] PP W11-1.docx***
Completed Project File Name: ***[your initials] PP W11-2.docx***

1. Open the ***[your initials] PP W11-1*** you modified in *Pause & Practice 11-1*.
2. Save the document as ***[your initials] PP W11-2***.
3. Insert and customize a *Drop-Down List* content control field.
   a. Place your insertion point on the blank line below "Type of Room."
   b. Click the **Drop-Down List Content Control** button [*Developer* tab, *Controls* group] to insert a *Drop-Down List* content control field.

c. With the content control field selected, click the **Properties** button [*Developer* tab, *Controls* group] to open the *Content Control Properties* dialog box (Figure 11-38).
d. Type Room Type in the *Title* area.
e. Check the **Content control cannot be deleted** box.
f. Click the **Add** button to open the *Add Choice* dialog box.
g. In the *Display Name* area, type Non-Smoking and press **Enter** (or click **OK**) to close the *Add Choice* dialog box.
h. Press **Enter** again (or click **Add**) to open the *Add Choice* dialog box.
i. Type Smoking in the *Display Name* area and press **Enter** to close the *Add Choice* dialog box.
j. Select **Choose an item** in the *Drop-Down List Properties* area and click the **Remove** button to remove this option from the list.
k. Click **OK** to close the *Content Control Properties* dialog box.
l. Use the right arrow key to deselect the *Drop-Down List* content control field and press **Tab** to position your insertion point below "Type of Bed."

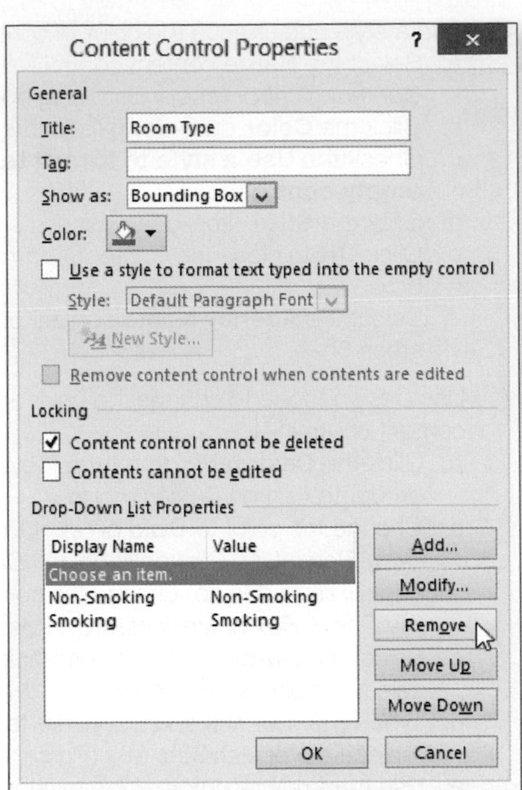

11-38 Insert and customize a *Drop-Down List* content control field

4. Insert another *Drop-Down List* content control field.
   a. With your insertion point below "Type of Bed," insert a **Drop-Down List** content control field.
   b. In the *Content Control Properties* dialog box, type Bed Type as the title and check the **Content control cannot be deleted** box.
   c. Add the following choices: King, Queen, Two Doubles.
   d. Remove **Choose an item** from the list of choices and click **OK** to close the dialog box.
   e. Use the right arrow key to deselect the *Drop-Down List* content control field and press **Tab** to position your insertion point below "Number of Nights".

5. Insert *Combo Box* content control fields.
   a. With your insertion point below "Number of Nights", insert a **Combo Box** content control field.
   b. In the *Content Control Properties* dialog box, type Number of Nights as the title and check the **Content control cannot be deleted** box.
   c. Add the following choices: 1, 2, 3, 4.
   d. Remove **Choose an item** from the list of choices and click **OK** to close the dialog box.
   e. Place your insertion point after "Arrival Date:", press **Tab**, and insert a **Combo Box** content control field.
   f. In the *Content Control Properties* dialog box, type Arrival Date as the title and check the **Content control cannot be deleted** box.
   g. Add the following choices: May 9, May 10, May 11.
   h. Remove **Choose an item** from the list of choices and click **OK** to close the dialog box.
   i. Place your insertion point after "Airline:", press **Tab**, and insert a **Combo Box** content control field.
   j. In the *Content Control Properties* dialog box, type Airline as the title and check the **Content control cannot be deleted** box.
   k. Add the following choices: American, Delta, Southwest, United.
   l. Remove **Choose an item** from the list of choices and click **OK** to close the dialog box.

6. Add a style and change the color of content control fields.
   a. Select the **Name** content control field and open the *Content Control Properties* dialog box (Figure 11-39).
   b. Click the **Color** drop-down list and select **Gold**.
   c. Check the **Use a style to format text typed into the empty control** box.
   d. Click the **Style** drop-down list and select **Strong**.
   e. Click **OK** to close the *Content Control Properties* dialog box.
   f. Select the **Agency Name** content control field and repeat steps 6b–e.

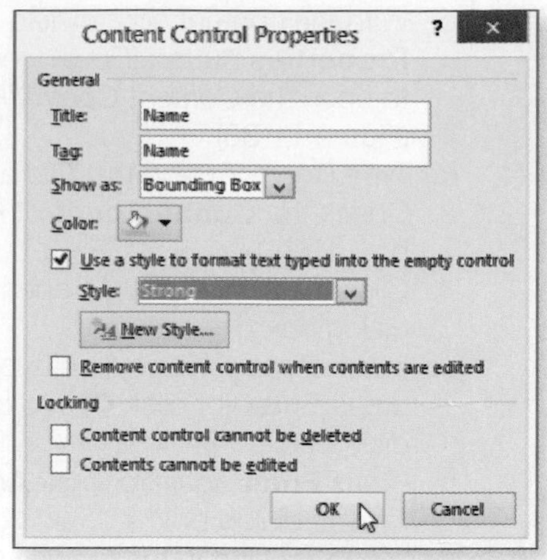

11-39 Change the color and add a style to a content control field

7. Use *Design* mode to change the color and placeholder text on content control fields.
   a. Click the **Design Mode** button [*Developer* tab, *Controls* group] to turn on *Design* mode.
   b. Change the color to **Gold** on all of the remaining *Rich Text*, *Drop-Down List*, *Combo Box*, and *Date Picker* content control fields. Do not change the color on the *Check Box* content control fields.
   c. Select the **Name** content control field and select the placeholder text.
   d. Type Type your first and last name to replace the placeholder text (Figure 11-40).
   e. Use the following information to change the placeholder text on other content control fields.

      Agency Name: Type your agency name
      Room Type: Select room type
      Bed Type: Select bed type
      Number of Nights: Select or type # of nights
      Arrival Date: Select or type arrival date
      Airline: Select or type airline
      Arrival Time: Type arrival time
      Departure Time: Type departure time
      Departure Date: Select departure date

   f. Click the **Design Mode** button to turn off *Design* mode.
8. Save and close the document (Figure 11-41).

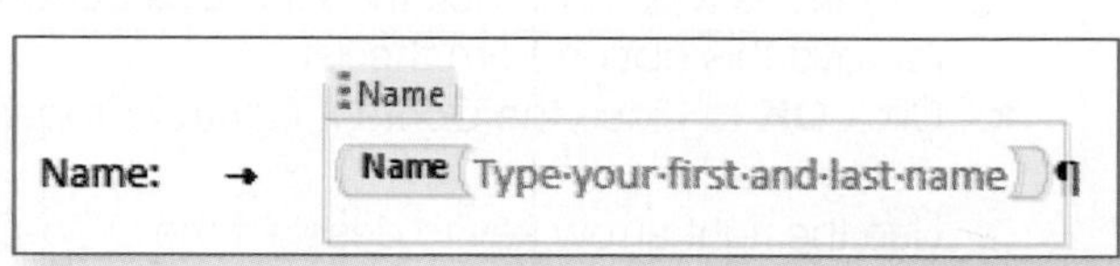

11-40 Customize placeholder text using *Design* mode

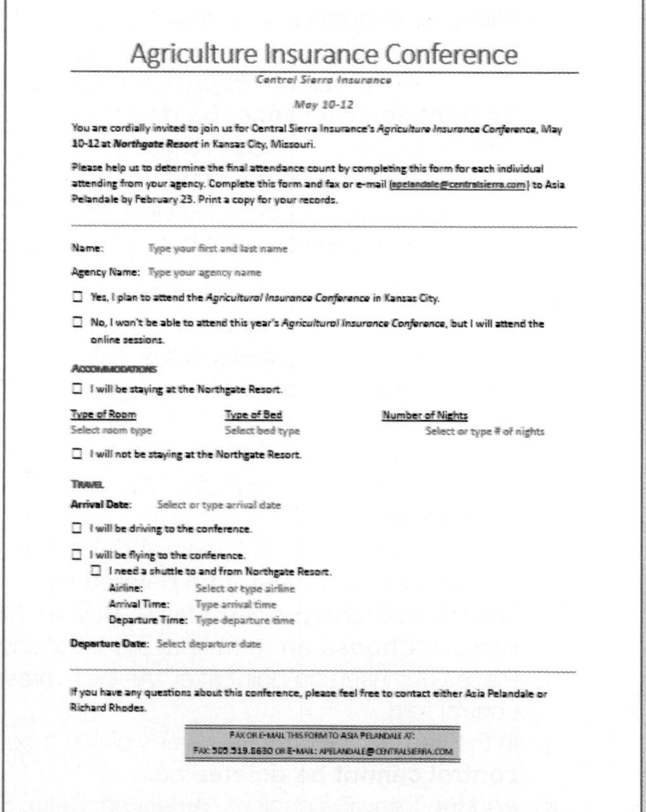

Agriculture Insurance Conference

Central Sierra Insurance

May 10-12

You are cordially invited to join us for Central Sierra Insurance's *Agriculture Insurance Conference*, May 10-12 at *Northgate Resort* in Kansas City, Missouri.

Please help us to determine the final attendance count by completing this form for each individual attending from your agency. Complete this form and fax or e-mail (apelandale@centralsierra.com) to Asia Pelandale by February 23. Print a copy for your records.

Name: Type your first and last name

Agency Name: Type your agency name

☐ Yes, I plan to attend the *Agricultural Insurance Conference* in Kansas City.

☐ No, I won't be able to attend this year's *Agricultural Insurance Conference*, but I will attend the online sessions.

ACCOMMODATIONS

☐ I will be staying at the Northgate Resort.

Type of Room	Type of Bed	Number of Nights
Select room type	Select bed type	Select or type # of nights

☐ I will not be staying at the Northgate Resort.

TRAVEL

Arrival Date: Select or type arrival date

☐ I will be driving to the conference.

☐ I will be flying to the conference.

☐ I need a shuttle to and from Northgate Resort.

Airline: Select or type airline
Arrival Time: Type arrival time
Departure Time: Type departure time

Departure Date: Select departure date

If you have any questions about this conference, please feel free to contact either Asia Pelandale or Richard Rhodes.

FAX OR E-MAIL THIS FORM TO ASIA PELANDALE AT:
FAX: 505.519.8630 OR E-MAIL: APELANDALE@CENTRALSIERRA.COM

11-41 PP W11-2 completed

SLO 11.4

Using Forms

After you insert and customize content control fields to create a form, you need to determine how to set up your form so others can use it. In Chapters 5 and 10, you learned how to create and use a template, which is an excellent way to set up a form. To begin this process, you use a form template to create a new form (document) based on the form template.

When you create a form, usually you want the users to fill in only the contents of the form fields without modifying the structure of the form. Grouping form fields keeps the form from being modified while allowing editing of content control fields. You can also use the protect feature to allow editing of content control fields while protecting other parts of the form.

Group Content Control Fields

The ***Group*** feature lets you protect the contents and format of a document containing content control fields but still allows users to edit the contents of content control fields. The *Group* feature locks all parts of a document except content control fields. An advantage of using the *Group* feature with content control fields in a document is that users can fill in these fields, and you do not need to save a document as a template. For example, you can create a fillable registration form, save it as a document, and group the content control fields. You can then email this registration form to users, who can edit the contents of the form fields and save and return the form.

HOW TO: Group Content Control Fields

1. Open the document where you want to group the content control fields.
2. Select the entire document (**Ctrl+A**).
3. Click the **Group** button [*Developer* tab, *Controls* group] and select **Group** from the drop-down list (Figure 11-42).
   - Grouping protects the text and formatting in the document but still allows users to edit the contents of content control fields.
   - To turn off grouping, select the entire document, click the **Group** button, and select **Ungroup**.

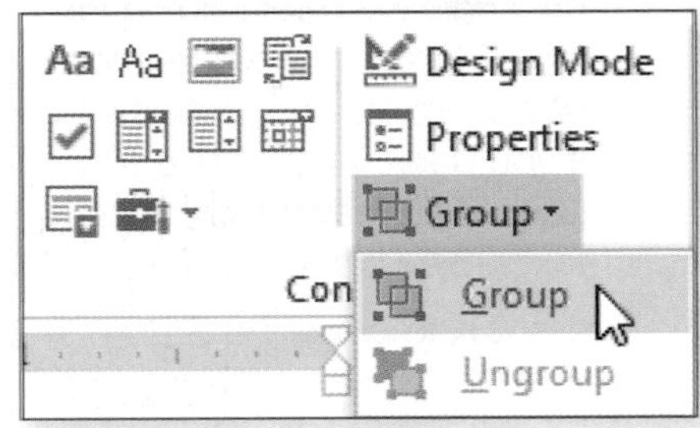

11-42 Group content control fields

Save a Form as a Template

Grouping content control fields is useful when the form is not going to be used again by the same person so it is not important that the original file remains unchanged. Saving a form as a ***template*** is a good idea if the form is going to be reused. For example, a business might want to create a weekly expense form that users will fill out each week to report expenses. In this case, it is best to save the form as a template so the form can be used repeatedly and users can create a new expense report document each week from the template. This preserves the original template.

HOW TO: Save a Form as a Template

1. Open the form you want to save as a template.
2. Open the *Save As* dialog box (**F12**).
3. In the *File name* area, type a file name for the template.
4. Click the **Save as type** drop-down list and select **Word Template**.
5. Browse to the location on your computer or *SkyDrive* where you want to save the document.
6. Click **Save** to close the dialog box and save the template.

Protect a Form

Like grouping, ***restrict editing*** is another way to protect a form. *Restrict Editing* is commonly used with forms that are saved as templates and lets you control what areas of the template can be edited. You can use *Restrict Editing* to let users fill in forms while protecting the rest of the contents and the format of the document.

HOW TO: Protect a Form

1. Open the form you want to protect.
2. Click the **Restrict Editing** button [*Developer* tab, *Protect* group]. The *Restrict Editing* pane opens to the right (Figure 11-43).
3. Check the **Allow only this type of editing in the document** box.
4. Click the drop-down list and select **Filling in forms**.
5. Click the **Yes, Start Enforcing Protection** button. The *Start Enforcing Protection* dialog box opens (Figure 11-44).
    - Protecting the document with a password is optional.
    - If you want to use a password, type a password in the *Enter new password* text box and type it again in the *Reenter password to confirm* text box.
    - If you don't want to use a password, leave both of the text boxes blank.
6. Press **OK** to close the *Start Enforcing Protection* dialog box.

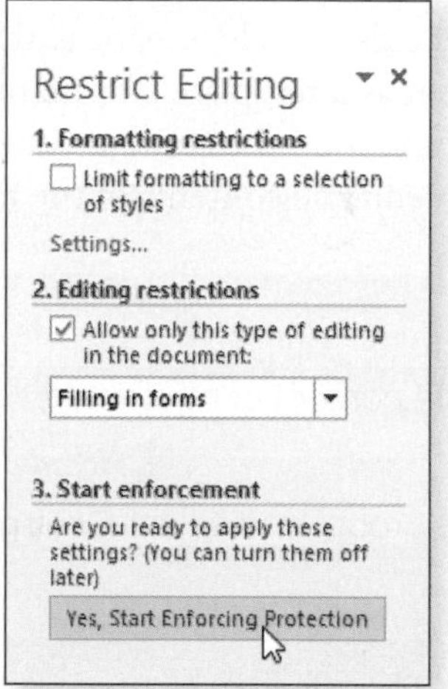

11-43 ***Restrict Editing*** **pane**

11-44 ***Start Enforcing Protection*** **dialog box**

To turn off restrict editing, click the **Stop Protection** button in the *Restrict Editing* pane (Figure 11-45). If you used a password to restrict editing, you are prompted to type the password in the *Unprotect Document* dialog box to turn off restrict editing.

11-45 Stop protecting a document

> **MORE INFO**
>
> When using grouping or protection on forms, do not check the *Remove content control when contents are edited* box in the *Content Control Properties* dialog box. Checking the box prevents users from typing information in these fields.

Open and Fill in a Form

After you finish creating your form, inserting and customizing content control fields, and grouping content control fields or protecting the form, you are ready to fill out the form by editing the contents of content control fields.

HOW TO: Open and Fill in a Form

1. Open the form you want to fill in.
   - If the form is a document, open from within Word.
   - If the form is a template, double-click the template file in a Windows folder to create a document based on the template.
2. Select a content control field and type information, check a box, or select from a drop-down list.
3. Press the **Tab** key to move from field to field or click the next field.
   - Don't press *Tab* after typing information in a *Rich Text* or *Plain Text* content control field, which would insert a tab after the text you typed. Instead, click the next field to fill in information.
   - On *Check Box* content control fields, click the box or press the **spacebar** to select or deselect the check box.
   - On *Combo Box*, *Drop-Down List*, *Date Picker*, and *Building Block Gallery* content control fields, click the **drop-down arrow** on the right to view selections (Figure 11-46).
   - On *Picture* content control fields, click the **icon** in the middle to select a picture to insert.
4. When you finish filling in the form, save and close the document.

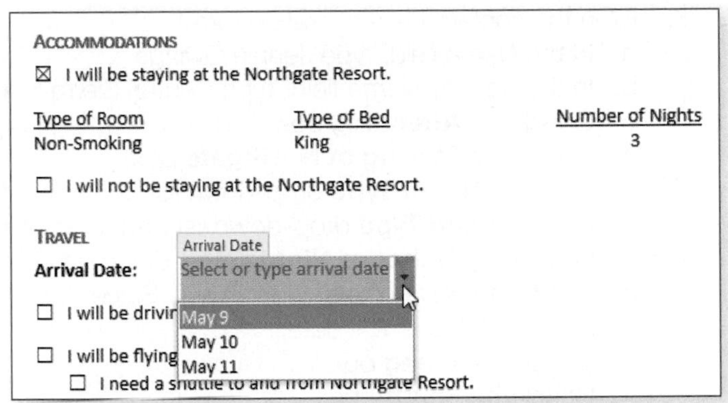

11-46 Filling in a form

Edit and Save a Form

You open a form template or document to edit it. You can add, copy, or move content control fields. You can customize the properties of each content control field or use *Design* mode to change the placeholder text. To edit a template, make sure you open the template from within Word, so you open the template file rather than creating a document based on the template. If you have grouped content control fields or restricted editing of the document, you need to ungroup content control fields or stop protecting the document to edit the content control fields in the document. After editing your form, you can group content control fields or restrict editing of the document, and then save the document.

PAUSE & PRACTICE: WORD 11-3

For this Pause & Practice project, you finalize the form you modified in *Pause & Practice 11-2*. You save the form as a template, group content control fields, create a document based on the form template, and fill in content control fields.

File Needed: ***[your initials] PP W11-2.docx***
Completed Project File Names: ***[your initials] PP W11-3 form.dotx*** and ***[your initials] PP W11-3.docx***

1. Open the ***[your initials] PP W11-2*** file that you modified in *Pause & Practice 11-2*.
2. Save the document as a **Word Template** named ***[your initials] PP W11-3 form***.

3. Group content control fields.
   a. Select the entire document (**Ctrl+A**).
   b. Click the **Group** button [*Developer* tab, *Controls* group] and select **Group** from the drop-down list.
4. Save and close the template.
5. From a Windows folder, create a document based on the ***[your initials] PP W11-3 form***.
6. Save the document as ***[your initials] PP W11-3***.
7. Fill in the conference registration form.
   a. In the *Name* field, type Jennie Owings.
   b. In the *Agency Name* field, type Central Sierra Insurance.
   c. Check the **Attending** box.
   d. Check the **Staying at Northgate** box.
   e. Click the **Room Type** drop-down list and select **Non-Smoking**.
   f. Click the **Bed Type** drop-down list and select **King**.
   g. Click the **Number of Nights** drop-down list and select **4**.
   h. In the *Arrival Date* field, type May 8. Since "May 8" is not a selection in the drop-down list, you must type the arrival date.
   i. Check the **Flying** box.
   j. Check the **Shuttle** box.
   k. Click the **Airline** drop-down list and select **United**.
   l. In the *Arrival Time* field, type 9:45 a.m.
   m. In the *Departure Time* field, type 6:20 p.m.
   n. Click the **Departure Date** date picker and select **May 12**.
8. Save and close the document (Figure 11-47).

Agriculture Insurance Conference

Central Sierra Insurance

May 10-12

You are cordially invited to join us for Central Sierra Insurance's ***Agriculture Insurance Conference***, May 10-12 at ***Northgate Resort*** in Kansas City, Missouri.

Please help us to determine the final attendance count by completing this form for each individual attending from your agency. Complete this form and fax or e-mail (apelandale@centralsierra.com) to Asia Pelandale by February 23. Print a copy for your records.

Name: **Jennie Owings**

Agency Name: **Central Sierra Insurance**

✓ Yes, I plan to attend the *Agricultural Insurance Conference* in Kansas City.

☐ No, I won't be able to attend this year's *Agricultural Insurance Conference*, but I will attend the online sessions.

ACCOMMODATIONS

☒ I will be staying at the Northgate Resort.

Type of Room	Type of Bed	Number of Nights
Non-Smoking	King	4

☐ I will not be staying at the Northgate Resort.

TRAVEL

Arrival Date: May 8

☐ I will be driving to the conference.

☒ I will be flying to the conference.

☒ I need a shuttle to and from Northgate Resort.

Airline: United
Arrival Time: 9:45 a.m.
Departure Time: 6:20 p.m.

Departure Date: May 12

If you have any questions about this conference, please feel free to contact either Asia Pelandale or Richard Rhodes.

FAX OR E-MAIL THIS FORM TO ASIA PELANDALE AT:
FAX: 505.519.8630 OR E-MAIL: APELANDALE@CENTRALSIERRA.COM

11-47 PP W11-3 completed

SLO 11.5

Working with a Master Document

When you are working with a long document, you may want to combine multiple documents into one ***master document***. A master document consists of text in that document and text from ***subdocuments***. Subdocuments are other files that you insert and link to a master document. For example, you might work on a report with others where each person is responsible for writing a section of the report. You can insert and link each person's contributions as subdocuments in the master document.

An advantage of using a master document and subdocuments is that once the files are all linked, you can modify and save each file (subdocument) independently of the master document, and then when you update a subdocument those changes are reflected in the master document. Similarly, you can also make changes in the master document, and those updates are included in the subdocument files.

Use Outline View

You have worked extensively with heading styles in previous chapters. Recall that in Chapters 2 and 6, you applied styles to headings, such as *Heading 1* and *Heading 2*, to organize long documents and to create a table of contents based on the document headings. You can also use headings styles to show the outline structure of your document. ***Outline view*** allows you the ability to view your document as an outline and easily rearrange sections of your document. For example, you can change a heading level by promoting it to a higher-level heading or demoting it to a lower-level heading. You can also add, delete, or edit text in *Outline* view. When you use *Outline* view, the ***Outlining tab*** is displayed. When working with master and subdocuments, use *Outline view.*

HOW TO: Use Outline View

1. Click the **Outline** button [*View* tab, *Views* group] to display the document in *Outline* view and open the *Outlining* tab (Figure 11-48).
    - Text with a heading style applied has a ***section selector*** (plus icon) to the left.
    - Text with *Normal* style (*Body* style) or other styles applied has an open circle bullet to the left of the first line.
2. Click the **Promote** or **Demote** button to change a heading level.
    - Alternatively, you can click the **Outline Level** drop-down list and select a heading level to apply or use the **Promote to Heading 1** or **Demote to Body Text** buttons.
3. Click the **Move Up** or **Move Down** button to move selected text up or down in the outline.
4. Click the **Expand** or **Collapse** button to expand or collapse a section.
    - Alternatively, you can double-click the **section selector** to the left of a heading to expand or collapse a section.
5. Click the **Show Level** drop-down list to select which levels are displayed in the outline.
    - By default, all levels are displayed.

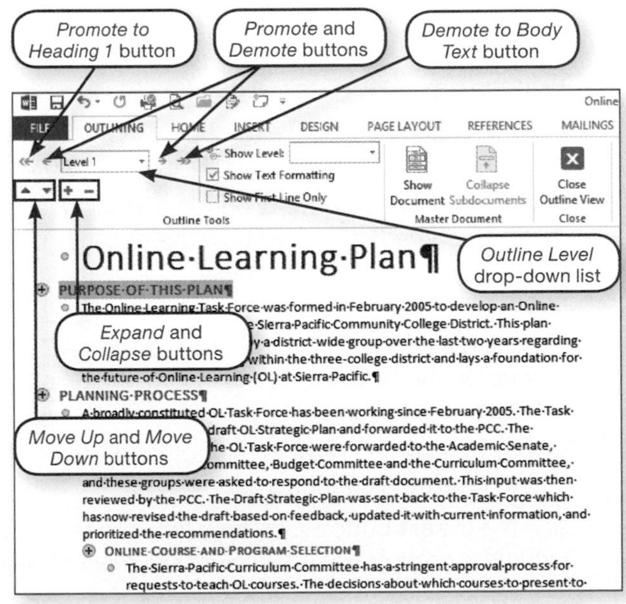

11-48 Using *Outline* view and the *Outlining* tab

6. Check the **Show Text Formatting** check box to display the style formatting.
    - If this check box is not selected, text in the outline is displayed without styles applied.
7. Check the **Show First Line Only** box to display only one line of text for each heading in the outline.
8. Click the **Close Outline View** button to close *Outline* view.

> **ANOTHER WAY**
>
> Press **Alt+Shift+Left** to promote to a higher level.
> Press **Alt+Shift+Right** to demote to a lower level.
> Press **Alt+Shift+Up** to move selected text up.
> Press **Alt+Shift+Down** to move selected text down.

Insert a Subdocument into a Master Document

You can use any document as a master document. When you insert subdocuments into a document, the document you insert the subdocuments into becomes the master document. When you are working with master and subdocuments, you use ***Outline view***. An advantage of working with a master document and subdocuments is that you can impose consistent formatting and use of styles across documents. When a subdocument is inserted, the styles from the master document are applied to the subdocument even if the styles in the original subdocument are different.

When you insert a subdocument into a master document, the two documents become linked. Changes made in either the master document or subdocument are updated in the linked file. Word inserts section breaks before and after an inserted subdocument.

HOW TO: Insert a Subdocument into a Master Document

1. Open the document that will become the master document.
2. Click the **Outline** button [*View* tab, *Views* group] to display the document in *Outline* view and open the *Outlining* tab.
3. Click the **Show Document** button [*Outlining* tab, *Master Document* group] to view the options available for working with a master document and subdocuments (Figure 11-49).
    - You use the options in the *Master Document* group on the *Outlining* tab to insert, create, and manage subdocuments.
4. Place your insertion point in the outline where you want to insert the subdocument.
5. Click the **Insert** button [*Outlining* tab, *Master Document* group]. The *Insert Subdocument* dialog box opens.
6. Select the subdocument to insert and click **Open**. The subdocument is inserted into the master document (Figure 11-50).
    - If the subdocument has heading styles applied, a dialog box opens asking if you want to rename

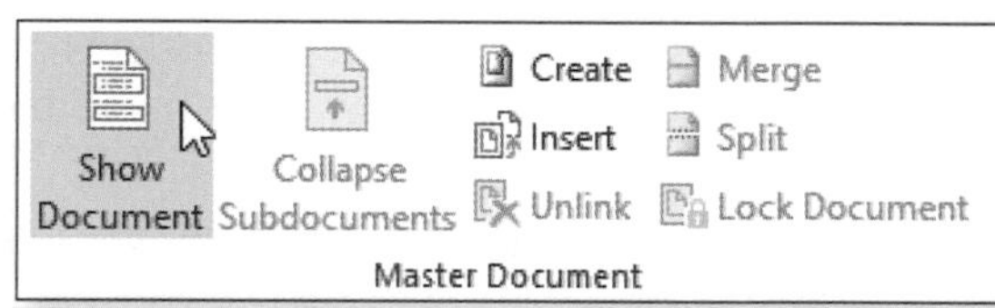

11-49 *Master Document* group on the *Outlining* tab

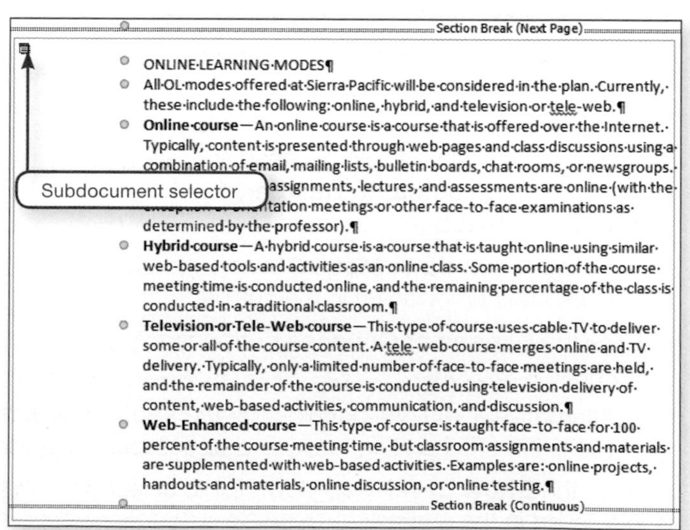

Section Break (Next Page)

- ONLINE·LEARNING·MODES¶
- All·OL·modes·offered·at·Sierra·Pacific·will·be·considered·in·the·plan.·Currently,·these·include·the·following:·online,·hybrid,·and·television·or·tele-web.¶
- **Online·course**—An·online·course·is·a·course·that·is·offered·over·the·Internet.·Typically,·content·is·presented·through·web·pages·and·class·discussions·using·a·combination·of·email,·mailing·lists,·bulletin·boards,·chat·rooms,·or·newsgroups.· assignments,·lectures,·and·assessments·are·online·(with·the· tation·meetings·or·other·face-to-face·examinations·as·determined·by·the·professor).¶
- **Hybrid·course**—A·hybrid·course·is·a·course·that·is·taught·online·using·similar·web-based·tools·and·activities·as·an·online·class.·Some·portion·of·the·course·meeting·time·is·conducted·online,·and·the·remaining·percentage·of·the·class·is·conducted·in·a·traditional·classroom.¶
- **Television·or·Tele-Web·course**—This·type·of·course·uses·cable·TV·to·deliver·some·or·all·of·the·course·content.·A·tele-web·course·merges·online·and·TV·delivery.·Typically,·only·a·limited·number·of·face-to-face·meetings·are·held,·and·the·remainder·of·the·course·is·conducted·using·television·delivery·of·content,·web-based·activities,·communication,·and·discussion.¶
- **Web-Enhanced·course**—This·type·of·course·is·taught·face-to-face·for·100·percent·of·the·course·meeting·time,·but·classroom·assignments·and·materials·are·supplemented·with·web-based·activities.·Examples·are:·online·projects,·handouts·and·materials,·online·discussion,·or·online·testing.¶

Section Break (Continuous)

11-50 Subdocument inserted into a master document

the style(s) in the subdocument. Click **Yes** or **Yes to All** to rename the styles in the subdocument to match the styles in the master document. Click **No** or **No to All** if you do not want the styles in the subdocument to be renamed.
- A next page section break is inserted before and a continuous section break is inserted after the subdocument.
- You can remove these section breaks in *Outline* view or in *Print Layout* view.
- A border is placed around the subdocument in the outline. This border is not displayed in *Print Layout* view.
- A ***subdocument selector*** is displayed to the left of the first line of the subdocument. Click this icon to select the entire subdocument.

7. Click the **Insert** button to insert another subdocument into the master document.
8. Click the **Close Outline View** button to close *Outline* view.

Create a Subdocument

In addition to inserting an existing subdocument file into a master document, you can create a subdocument in the master document in *Outline* view. When you create a subdocument, Word actually creates a separate subdocument file that is saved in the same location as the master document. You can type the subdocument text in the master document or open the subdocument file and modify it.

HOW TO: Create a Subdocument

1. Place your insertion point in the outline where you want to create the subdocument.
   - You can only create a subdocument in the master document at a heading level (e.g., *Heading 1*, *Heading 2*), not at the body level. You receive an error message if you try to create a subdocument at the body level.
2. Click the **Create** button [*Outlining* tab, *Master Document* group] to create a new subdocument (Figure 11-51).
   - The new subdocument is blank.
   - There are section breaks before and after the new subdocument and there is a border around the subdocument in *Outline* view.
3. Type content in the subdocument.
   - You can use the **Promote** or **Demote** button to change heading levels.
4. Save the master document.
   - When you save the master document, all subdocuments are also saved.

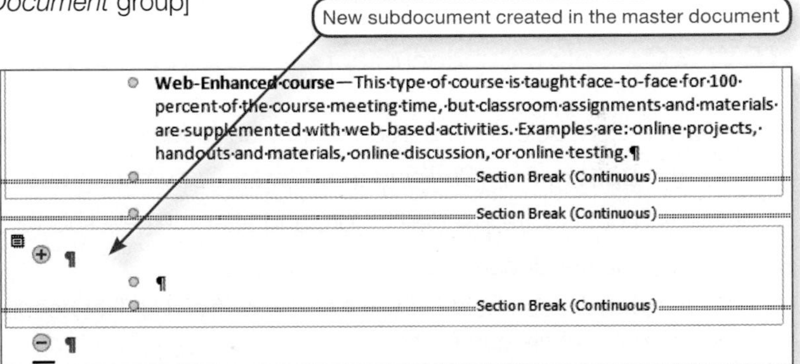

11-51 Create a new subdocument in the master document

Merge Subdocuments

After you have inserted subdocuments into your master document, you have the option of merging two or more adjacent subdocuments into one subdocument. For example, if you are working on two smaller adjacent subdocuments, you can merge them into one subdocument. The new merged subdocument is saved with the file name of the first subdocument. The other subdocument files remain on your computer, but they are no longer linked to the master document.

HOW TO: Merge Subdocuments

1. In *Outline* view, select the subdocuments you want to merge together.
   - Press the **Shift** key and click the **subdocument selectors** to select multiple subdocuments (Figure 11-52). You can also click and drag to select subdocuments.
2. Click the **Merge** button [*Outlining* tab, *Master Document* group].
   - The section breaks between subdocuments are not removed.
3. Save the master document.
   - The contents of the merged subdocument are saved in the first subdocument file.
   - The other subdocument files are no longer linked to the master document, but the files remain in their original location.

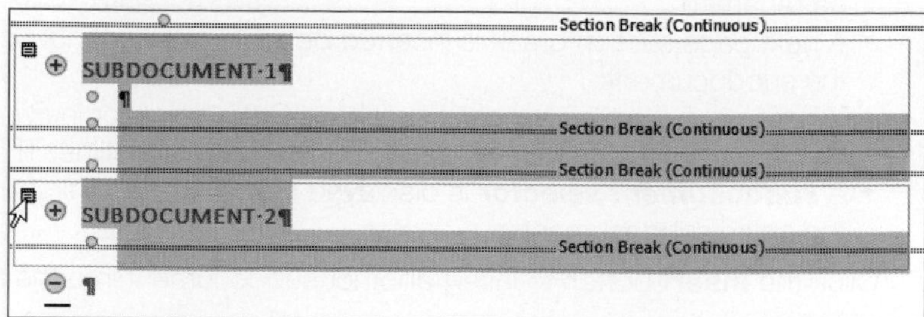

11-52 Select subdocuments to merge

MORE INFO

You cannot merge a subdocument with text in the master document, and you cannot merge non-adjacent subdocuments.

Split a Subdocument

If you have a large subdocument in your master document, you can select a portion of the subdocument and split it into a separate subdocument. When you split a subdocument, a new subdocument file is created and the selected text is removed from the original subdocument.

HOW TO: Split a Subdocument

1. In *Outline* view, select the portion of the subdocument you want to split into a new subdocument.
2. Click the **Split** button [*Outlining* tab, *Master Document* group] to split the selected text into a new subdocument.
   - Section breaks are inserted before and after the new subdocument.
3. Save the master document.
   - The new subdocument is saved as a new file. The first heading of the new subdocument is used as the subdocument file name.

MORE INFO

You cannot split a part of the master document to create a new subdocument.

Unlink a Subdocument

You can ***unlink*** a subdocument from the master document to break the connection between the two documents. When you unlink a subdocument, the text of the subdocument remains in the master document, but since the documents are no longer linked, changes made in the subdocument file are not updated in the master document. The text from the unlinked subdocument becomes part of the master document.

HOW TO: Unlink a Subdocument

1. In *Outline* view, click the **Show Document** button [*Outlining* tab, *Master Document* group] to display the borders around the subdocuments.
2. Select or place your insertion point within a subdocument.
3. Click the **Unlink** button [*Outlining* tab, *Master Document* group] to unlink the subdocument from the master document.
   - When you unlink a subdocument, it becomes part of the master document.
   - After you have unlinked a subdocument from the master document, you cannot merge or split the text that was previously a subdocument.

Arrange Text in an Outline

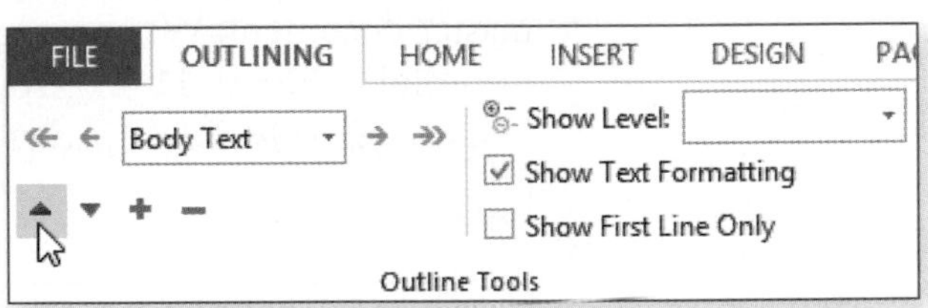

11-53 Use the *Move Up* or *Move Down* button to arrange sections of subdocuments

After you have inserted, merged, and split subdocuments, you can easily move subdocuments or sections within a subdocument or the master document in *Outline* view. Use the **Move Up (Alt+Shift+Up)** or **Move Down (Alt+Shift+Down)** button to move a selected subdocument or section up or down in the outline (Figure 11-53). You can also drag selected text to a different location in the outline.

> **MORE INFO**
>
> When you move the contents of a subdocument into the master document text, the link between the subdocument and the master document is removed.

If you are working on a long document, you can collapse sections of the document so the text below a heading is not displayed in *Outline* view. This makes it easier to rearrange subdocuments and selected sections. You can also check the **Show First Line Only** box to display only the first line of text on each heading and body level. This can make the document less cluttered and easier to edit. Click the **Show Document** button to view borders around the subdocuments.

Lock a Subdocument

You can lock a subdocument so that changes cannot be made to the subdocument in *Outline* view or *Print Layout* view. After a subdocument is locked, you can still make changes to the original subdocument file, and those changes are updated in the master document.

HOW TO: Lock a Subdocument

1. In *Outline* view, click the **Show Document** button [*Outlining* tab, *Master Document* group] to display the borders around the subdocuments.
2. Select or place your insertion point within a subdocument.
3. Click the **Lock Document** button [*Outlining* tab, *Master Document* group] to lock the subdocument in the master document.
   - A lock icon appears below the subdocument icon (Figure 11-54).

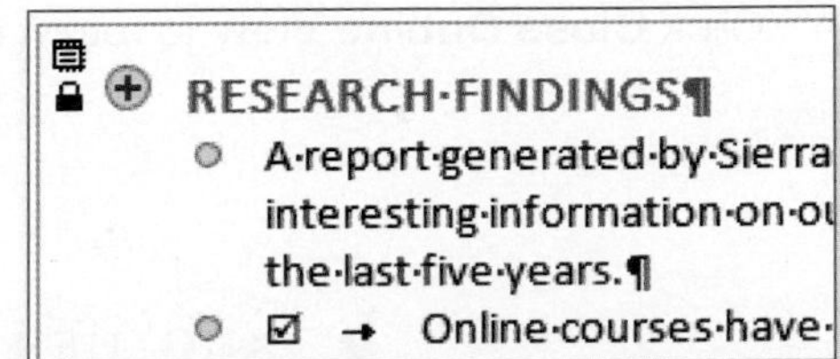

11-54 Locked subdocument

When you have a master document and a subdocument open, the subdocument is automatically locked in the master document, and changes can only be made in the subdocument. When you close the subdocument file, the subdocument in the master document is unlocked.

Save and Reopen a Master Document

When you save a master document, all of the subdocuments are also saved. If you made changes to text in any of the subdocuments in the master document, those changed are included in the subdocument files. This ensures that your linked subdocument files are consistent with the subdocument text in the master document.

You can modify subdocument files when the master document is closed, and when you open the master document, the updated content from the subdocument files will be available in the master document. When you reopen a master document, the subdocuments are displayed as hyperlinks (Figure 11-55). You can click a subdocument link to open the subdocument file. You can *Expand Subdocuments* in *Outline* view to display the text of the subdocuments.

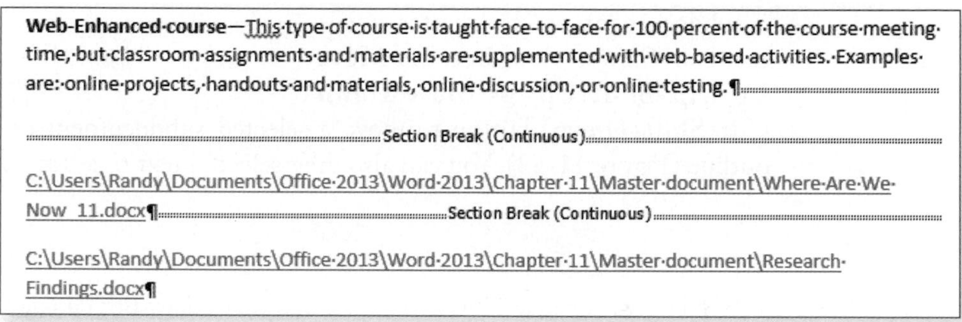

11-55 Subdocuments displayed as hyperlinks in the master document

HOW TO: Reopen a Master Document and Display Subdocuments

1. Open the master document and click the **Outline** button [*View* tab, *Views* group] to display the document in *Outline* view.
2. Click the **Show Document** button [*Outlining* tab, *Master Document* group].
3. Click the **Expand Subdocuments** button [*Outlining* tab, *Master Document* group] to display the contents of the subdocuments (Figure 11-56).

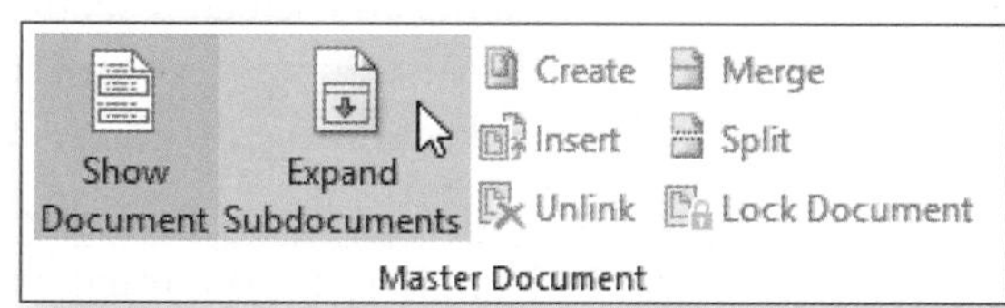

11-56 Expand subdocuments to display subdocument text in the master document

   - This button toggles between **Expand Subdocuments** and **Collapse Subdocuments**.
   - When subdocuments are expanded, the options in the *Master Document* group become active.
   - Click **Collapse Subdocuments** to display hyperlinks to subdocuments.
   - Click a subdocument hyperlink to open the subdocument file.
4. Click **Close Outline View** to return to your document.

ANOTHER WAY

Ctrl+ toggles between expanding documents and collapsing documents in any view.

PAUSE & PRACTICE: WORD 11-4

For this Pause & Practice project, you work with a master document and subdocuments. You insert subdocuments into a master document, split a subdocument, arrange subdocuments, modify subdocuments, reopen a master document, and unlink documents.

Files Needed: ***OnlineLearning-11.docx***, ***LearningModes-11.docx***, and ***WhereAreWeNow-11.docx***
Completed Project File Name: ***[your initials] PP W11-4.docx***

---

1. Open the ***OnlineLearning-11*** file from your student data files.
2. Save the document as ***[your initials] PP W11-4***.
3. In a Windows folder, locate the ***LearningModes-11*** and ***WhereAreWeNow-11*** files from your student data files and copy these to the same location as your ***[your initials] PP W11-4*** file.
4. Use *Outline* view to change heading level and arrange sections.
   a. With ***[your initials] PP W11-4*** open, click the **Outline** button [*View* tab, *Views* group] to display the document in *Outline* view.
   b. Click the **section selector** (plus icon) to the left of the "ONLINE COURSE AND PROGRAM SELECTION" heading to select the heading and body text.
   c. Click the **Demote** button [*Outlining* tab, *Outline Tools* group] to demote the heading to *Level 2* (Figure 11-57).
   d. Click the **section selector** to the left of the "Leadership and Management of Online Learning" heading to select the heading and body text.
   e. Click the **Move Down** button twice [*Outlining* tab, *Outline Tools* group] to move this section below the "Online Course and Program Selection" heading and body text in the outline.

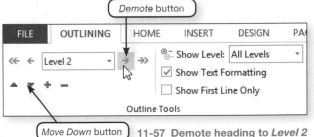

11-57 Demote heading to *Level 2*

5. Insert subdocuments into the master document.
   a. Place your insertion point on the blank line below the last body paragraph in the outline.
   b. Click the **Show Document** button [*Outlining* tab, *Master Document* group].
   c. Click the **Insert** button [*Outlining* tab, *Master Document* group] to open the *Insert Subdocument* dialog box.
   d. Browse to the location where your master document and subdocuments are saved.
   e. Select the ***LearningModes-11*** file and click **Open** to insert the subdocument.
   f. Select the "**Online Learning Modes**" line in the subdocument.
   g. Click the **Outline Level** drop-down list [*Outlining* tab, *Outline Tools* group] and select **Level 1** (Figure 11-58).

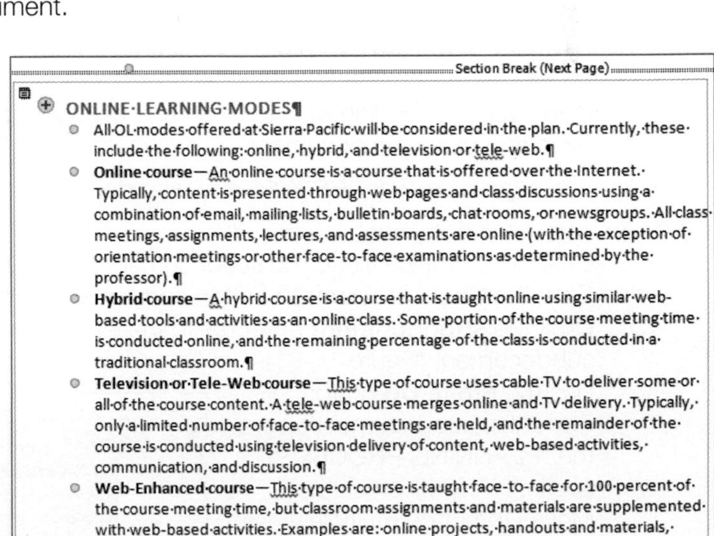
Section Break (Next Page)

ONLINE·LEARNING·MODES¶

All·OL·modes·offered·at·Sierra·Pacific·will·be·considered·in·the·plan.·Currently,·these·include·the·following:·online,·hybrid,·and·television·or·tele-web.¶

Online·course—An·online·course·is·a·course·that·is·offered·over·the·Internet.·Typically,·content·is·presented·through·web·pages·and·class·discussions·using·a·combination·of·email,·mailing·lists,·bulletin·boards,·chat·rooms,·or·newsgroups.·All·class·meetings,·assignments,·lectures,·and·assessments·are·online·(with·the·exception·of·orientation·meetings·or·other·face-to-face·examinations·as·determined·by·the·professor).¶

Hybrid·course—A·hybrid·course·is·a·course·that·is·taught·online·using·similar·web-based·tools·and·activities·as·an·online·class.·Some·portion·of·the·course·meeting·time·is·conducted·online,·and·the·remaining·percentage·of·the·class·is·conducted·in·a·traditional·classroom.¶

Television·or·Tele-Web·course—This·type·of·course·uses·cable·TV·to·deliver·some·or·all·of·the·course·content.·A·tele-web·course·merges·online·and·TV·delivery.·Typically,·only·a·limited·number·of·face-to-face·meetings·are·held,·and·the·remainder·of·the·course·is·conducted·using·television·delivery·of·content,·web-based·activities,·communication,·and·discussion.¶

Web-Enhanced·course—This·type·of·course·is·taught·face-to-face·for·100·percent·of·the·course·meeting·time,·but·classroom·assignments·and·materials·are·supplemented·with·web-based·activities.·Examples·are:·online·projects,·handouts·and·materials,·online·discussion,·or·online·testing.¶

Section Break (Continuous)

11-58 Subdocument inserted into the master document

h. Place your insertion point on the last blank line in the outline.
i. Insert the **WhereAreWeNow-11** file as a subdocument.
j. Click **Yes to All** in the dialog box asking if you want to rename styles in the subdocument (Figure 11-59).

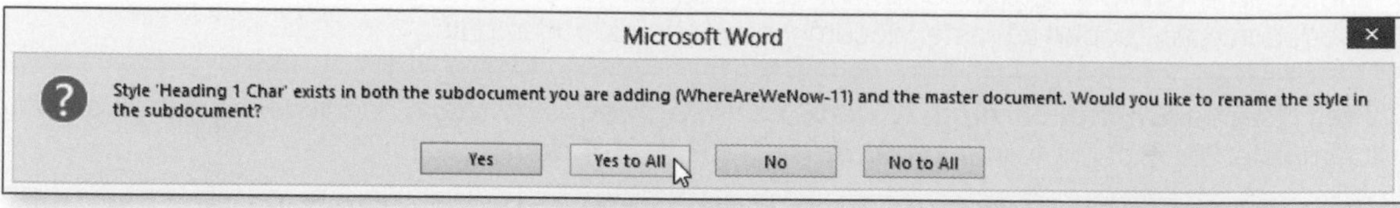

Microsoft Word
Style 'Heading 1 Char' exists in both the subdocument you are adding (WhereAreWeNow-11) and the master document. Would you like to rename the style in the subdocument?
Yes
Yes to All
No
No to All

11-59 Rename styles in the subdocument file

6. Split a subdocument.
   a. Check the **Show First Line Only** box [*Outlining* tab, *Outline* Tools group] to display only the first line of text at each level.
   b. Click the **section selector** to the left of the "Research Findings" section in the second subdocument.
   c. Click the **Split** button [*Outlining* tab, *Master Document* group] to split the section into a new subdocument.
   d. With the section still selected, click the **Promote** button once. The "Research Findings" heading changes to *Level 1*.
   e. Place your insertion point before "RESEARCH FINDINGS," type SPCCD, and **space** once (Figure 11-60).
   f. Click the **Close Outline View** button and change to **Print Layout** view.

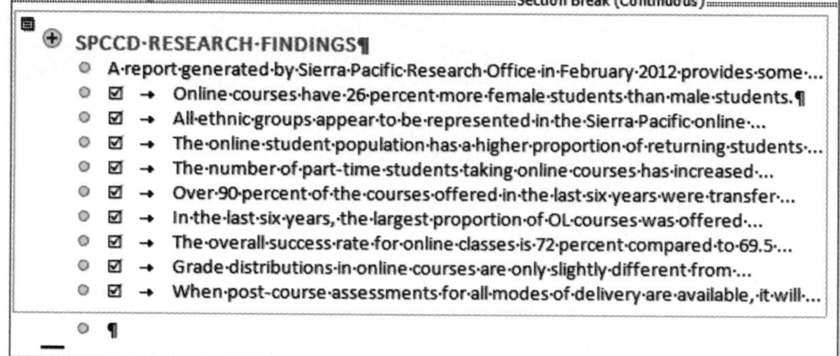

11-60 Split subdocument and promote heading

7. Save and close the master document (***[your initials] PP W11-4***).
8. Modify a subdocument.
   a. Open the ***WhereAreWeNow-11*** document from the location where your master document and subdocuments are located.
   b. In the last subheading of this document, change "Tech" to Instructor.
   c. Save and close the document.
9. Open the ***[your initials] PP W11-4*** master document.
10. Arrange a subdocument.
    a. Change to *Outline* view. The subdocuments display as hyperlinks.
    b. Click the **Show Document** button and the **Expand Subdocuments** button.
    c. Click the **subdocument selector** to the left of "ONLINE LEARNING MODES" to select the entire subdocument (Figure 11-61).
    d. Use the **Move Up** button to move this subdocument above the "PLANNING PROCESS" section. You will press the *Move Up* button multiple times. The moved subdocument becomes part of the master document and is no longer linked to the subdocument file.

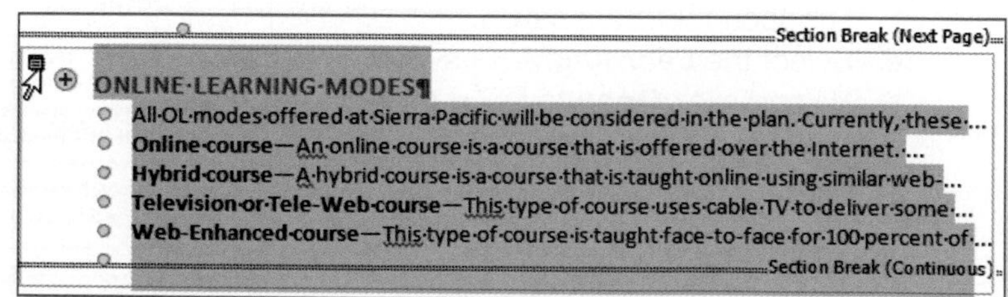

11-61 Select subdocument

11. Unlink subdocuments from the master document.
    a. Click the **subdocument selector** to the left of "WHERE ARE WE NOW WITH ONLINE LEARNING" to select the entire subdocument.
    b. Click the **Unlink** button [*Outlining* tab, *Master Document* group] to unlink this document from the subdocument file.
    c. Unlink the last subdocument ("SPCCD RESEARCH FINDINGS").
12. Remove section breaks from the document.
    a. Deselect the **Show First Line Only** check box [*Outlining* tab, *Outline Tools* group] to display the entire outline.
    b. Place your insertion point on each of the section break indicators and press **Delete** to remove each of the section breaks in the document. Be careful not to delete any text.
    c. Make sure there are no blank lines between sections.
    d. Close *Outline* view and return to *Print Layout* view.
13. Insert **page breaks** before the "Online Course and Program Selection" and "Student Support Services" headings to keep the headings with the text that follows.
14. Save and close the document (Figure 11-62).

Online Learning Plan

PURPOSE OF THIS PLAN

The Online Learning Task Force was formed in February 2005 to develop an Online Learning Strategic Plan for the Sierra Pacific Community College District. This plan incorporates the work done by a district-wide group over the last two years regarding the future of online learning within the three-college district and lays a foundation for the future of Online Learning (OL) at Sierra Pacific.

ONLINE LEARNING MODES

All OL modes offered at Sierra Pacific will be considered in the plan. Currently, these include the following: online, hybrid, and television or tele-web.

Online course—An online course is a course that is offered over the Internet. Typically, content is presented through web pages and class discussions using a combination of email, mailing lists, bulletin boards, chat rooms, or newsgroups. All class meetings, assignments, lectures, and assessments are online (with the exception of orientation meetings or other face-to-face examinations as determined by the professor).

Hybrid course—A hybrid course is a course that is taught online using similar web-based tools and activities as an online class. Some portion of the course meeting time is conducted online, and the remaining percentage of the class is conducted in a traditional classroom.

Television or Tele-Web course—This type of course uses cable TV to deliver some or all of the course content. A tele-web course merges online and TV delivery. Typically, only a limited number of face-to-face meetings are held, and the remainder of the course is conducted using television delivery of content, web-based activities, communication, and discussion.

Web-Enhanced course—This type of course is taught face-to-face for 100 percent of the course meeting time, but classroom assignments and materials are supplemented with web-based activities. Examples are: online projects, handouts and materials, online discussion, or online testing.

PLANNING PROCESS

A broadly constituted OL Task Force has been working since February 2005. The Task Force has produced a draft OL Strategic Plan and forwarded it to the PCC. The recommendations of the OL Task Force were forwarded to the Academic Senate, Classified Senate, IT Committee, Budget Committee and the Curriculum Committee, and these groups were asked to respond to the draft document. This input was then reviewed by the PCC. The Draft Strategic Plan was sent back to the Task Force which has now revised the draft based on feedback, updated it with current information, and prioritized the recommendations.

Page 3 of 4

ONLINE COURSE AND PROGRAM SELECTION

The Sierra Pacific Curriculum Committee has a stringent approval process for requests to teach OL .courses. The decisions about which courses to present to the Curriculum Committee are made by departments/divisions based on their own criteria and procedures. It is common that this decision is based solely on the enthusiasm of an individual faculty member who has an interest in teaching a particular course online, as a hybrid or via TV. Despite a large increase in OL offerings, this method of selecting courses has not helped to ensure that entire degrees or certificates are available by distance modes. Departments and divisions are now beginning to think more intentionally about how to increase their distance offerings.

LEADERSHIP AND MANAGEMENT OF ONLINE LEARNING

The responsibility for OL is becoming more focused at Sierra Pacific. Lines of communication about OL courses and programs begin at the department and area level, with department chairs and deans sharing different portions of decision-making about OL issues. Specific funding allocated to OL and resources used to support OL come now through IT and Professional Development funds. Currently there are other funding sources that could be utilized to support OL, but there has been no strategic planning in the past to include OL in resource distribution.

WHERE ARE WE NOW WITH ONLINE LEARNING?

Sierra Pacific was a pioneer in online education and was one of the first community colleges in California to offer fully online courses in 1997. However, over the next few years there was limited growth in online offerings and only 15 course sections were taught online during Fall 2000. The adoption of a learning management system (LMS) in Spring 2001, the availability of training to teach online, and recruitment of new faculty interested in teaching online resulted in a rapid increase in online offerings.

ONLINE LEARNING OFFERINGS AND PROGRAMS

In Fall 2012, Sierra Pacific had 565 fully-online course sections. This represents a growth rate of 796 percent over the last six years. There have also been televised courses offered at Sierra Pacific. However, these have decreased over the last five years. In Fall 2012, there were only three TV course sections offered at Sierra Pacific. However, it is important to note that OL courses now only account for approximately 12 percent of all course sections at Sierra Pacific. There has also been intense growth in web-enhanced classes and these are likely to be a robust source for OL courses over the next few years. There are currently over 1200 courses sections using LMS each semester (combined online, hybrid, and web-enhanced).

Sierra Pacific Community College District currently has no complete degree programs being offered entirely by distance methods, but there are several certificate programs which are available online. At least one course in each General Education area has been approved for online learning delivery, but not all of these courses are currently being offered. There are other graduation requirements that cannot currently be met through online learning methods.

Sierra Pacific Community College District—Online Learning Plan   Last updated: January 19, 2015

11-62 PP W11-4 completed (pages 1 and 2 of 4)

Chapter Summary

11.1 Insert, customize, and arrange a variety of content control fields (p. W11-631).

- ***Content control fields*** are containers you can include in your documents for users to enter text or objects.
- Use ***tab stops***, ***indents***, and ***tables*** to align and arrange content control fields in a document.
- Use ***Rich Text*** and ***Plain Text*** content control fields for open-ended responses from users.
- In a ***Rich Text*** content control field, users can apply formatting to specific text.
- A ***Check Box*** content control field lets a user select or deselect a check box.
- Users select (or enter) a date in a ***Date Picker*** content control field.
- A ***Picture*** content control field prompts a user to insert a picture into a document.
- You can add a ***title*** and modify the properties of a content control field using the ***Content Control Properties*** dialog box.

11.2 Insert and customize content control fields where a user selects from a list of choices (p. W11-639).

- A ***Combo Box*** content control field lets users select from a list of choices or type their own responses.
- A ***Drop-Down List*** content control field lets users select from a list of choices. In a *Drop-Down List*, users cannot type in their own responses.
- You can add, remove, and modify the users' choices in both *Combo Box* and *Drop-Down List* content control fields.
- A ***Building Block Gallery*** content control field lets users select a building block to insert into a document.
- You can specify which building block gallery and category that users can select.
- ***Legacy form fields*** and ***ActiveX*** control fields are other available form fields you can use in your Word documents.

11.3 Edit a content control field to change the format and lock content, and use *Design* mode to edit placeholder text (p. W11-641).

- You can set up a content control field to ***apply a style*** to the contents a user enters. You can select from an existing style or create a new style.
- You can also change the ***color*** of content control fields. By default, the content control field color is controlled by the theme of the document.
- A content control field can be displayed in the document as a ***bounding box***, with ***start and end tags***, or not shown at all (the ***None*** option). By default, content control fields are displayed as bounding boxes.
- You can set up a content control field so the field is left in the document when a user enters information, or you can set it so the field is removed when a user enters information.
- You can ***lock*** content control fields so the field cannot be deleted and you can lock a field so it cannot be edited by users.
- You can copy, move, or delete content control fields or modify placeholder text in ***Design mode***.

11.4 Group content control fields, protect and edit a form, create a form based on a template, fill in a form, and save a form based on a template (p. W11-647).

- You can ***group*** content control fields so users can enter or select information in content control fields but cannot edit the content or format of the other parts of the document.
- You can save a form as a ***template***, so you can base a new document on the template without modifying the structure or content of the template.
- You can ***restrict editing*** of forms so users can only fill in content control fields.

11.5 Manage a long document using a master document and subdocuments. (p. W11-651)

- A ***master document*** is useful when you are working with long documents.
- A ***subdocument*** is a Word document that you insert and link to a master document.
- ***Outline view*** is a good tool to use when you are working with a master document and subdocuments.
- You can ***expand*** or ***collapse*** and ***promote*** or ***demote*** headings using the ***Outlining tab*** in *Outline* view.

- You can ***merge*** subdocuments to combine multiple subdocuments into one subdocument file.
- You can ***split*** a portion of a subdocument to create a new subdocument.
- After you ***unlink*** a subdocument from a master document, the changes made in the subdocument are not updated in the master document.
- You can move subdocuments and sections of text in subdocuments and the master document in the outline in *Outline* view.
- You can ***lock*** a subdocument to prevent subdocument text from being edited in the master document.

Check for Understanding

In the ***Online Learning Center*** for this text (**www.mhhe.com/office2013inpractice**), there are a variety of resources that can be used to review the concepts covered in this chapter.

The following Online Learning Resources are available in the Online Learning Center:

- Multiple choice questions
- Short answer questions
- Matching exercises

Guided Project 11-1

For this project, you create form template for Emma Cavalli at Placer Hills Real Estate. You set up the form using content control fields, customize content control fields, protect the form, and create a new document based on the form template.
[Student Learning Outcomes 11.1, 11.2, 11.3, 11.4]

Files Needed: ***PHREAuthorizationLetter-11.docx*** and ***BurgessHome-11.jpg***
Completed Project File Names: ***[your initials] Word 11-1 form.dotx*** and ***[your initials] Word 11-1.docx***

Skills Covered in This Project

- Save a document as a template.
- Set a tab stop to align text and content control fields.
- Insert and customize *Date Picker*, *Combo Box*, *Rich Text*, and *Plain Text* content control fields.
- Use *Design* mode to customize placeholder text.
- Protect a form.
- Create a document based on a template.
- Fill in a content control field.

1. Open the ***PHREAuthorizationLetter-11*** document from your student data files.
2. Save the document as a Word template named ***[your initials] Word 11-1 form***.
3. Set tab stops to align text and content control fields.
   a. Select the lines of text beginning with "**Loan Application Date**" and ending with "**Street Address**" and set a **1.5" left** tab.
   b. Select the line of text beginning with "**City**" and set the following **left** tab stops: **0.4"**, **1.5"**, and **1.8"**.
   c. Place your insertion point after "City:", press **Tab** twice, and type Zip:.
   d. Select the line of text beginning with "**Sincerely,**" and set a **center** tab at **5.25"**.
4. Insert and customize a *Date Picker* content control field.
   a. Place your insertion point after "Loan Application Date:" and press **Tab**.
   b. Click the **Date Picker Content Control** button [*Developer* tab, *Controls* group] to insert a *Date Picker* content control field.
   c. Click the **Properties** button [*Developer* tab, *Controls* group] to open the *Content Control Properties* dialog box.
   d. In the *Title* text box, type Application Date.
   e. In the *Date Picker Properties* area, select the third date format.
   f. Click **OK** to close the *Content Control Properties* dialog box.
5. Insert and customize *Combo Box* content control fields.
   a. Place your insertion point after "Financial Institution:" and press **Tab**.
   b. Click the **Combo Box Content Control** button [*Developer* tab, *Controls* group] to insert a *Combo Box* content control field.
   c. Click the **Properties** button to open the *Content Control Properties* dialog box.
   d. In the *Title* text box, type Financial Institution.
   e. Click the **Add** button in the *Drop-Down List Properties* area to open the *Add Choice* dialog box.

f. Type Bank of America in the *Display Name* area and press **OK** to close the dialog box and add the choice.
g. Add two more choices: Chase Bank and Wells Fargo Bank.
h. Select **Choose an item** and click the **Remove** button (Figure 11-63).
i. Click **OK** to close the *Content Control Properties* dialog box.
j. Place your insertion point after the first tab after "City:" and insert a **Combo Box** content control field.
k. Open the *Content Control Properties* dialog box and type City as the *Title*.
l. Add Lincoln, Loomis, Rocklin, and Roseville as the choices, remove **Choose an item**, and click **OK** to close the dialog box.

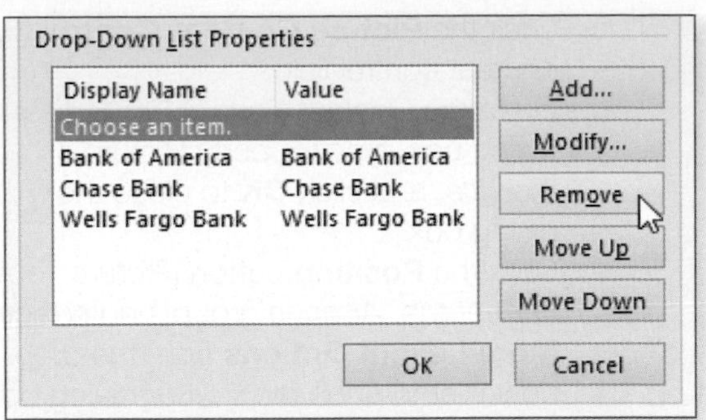

11-63 Add choices to the *Combo Box* and remove a choice

6. Insert and customize *Rich Text* content control fields.
   a. Place your insertion point after "Loan Number:" and press **Tab**.
   b. Click the **Rich Text Content Control** button [*Developer* tab, *Controls* group] to insert a *Rich Text* content control field.
   c. Open the *Content Control Properties* dialog box and type Loan Number as the *Title* (Figure 11-64).
   d. Click the **Show as** drop-down list and select **None**.
   e. Check the **Use a style to format text typed into the empty control** box.
   f. Click the **Style** drop-down list and select **Book Title**.
   g. Click **OK** to close the dialog box.
   h. Place your insertion point after "Borrower Name(s):" and press **Tab**.

11-64 Customize *Rich Text* content control field

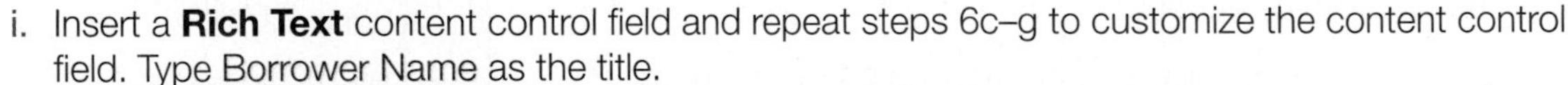

   i. Insert a **Rich Text** content control field and repeat steps 6c–g to customize the content control field. Type Borrower Name as the title.

7. Insert and customize *Plain Text* content control fields.
   a. Place your insertion point after "Street Address:" and press **Tab**.
   b. Click the **Plain Text Content Control** button [*Developer* tab, *Controls* group].
   c. Open the *Content Control Properties* dialog box and type the Street Address as the *Title*.
   d. Click the **Show as** drop-down list and select **None**.
   e. Click **OK** to close the dialog box.
   f. Place your insertion point after "Zip:" and press **Tab**.
   g. Insert a **Plain Text** content control field.
   h. Open the *Content Control Properties* dialog box, type the Zip Code as the *Title*, click the **Show as** drop-down list, and select **None**.
   i. Click **OK** to close the dialog box.
8. Insert and customize a *Picture* content control field.
   a. Place your insertion point after "Sincerely," press **Tab**, and type Picture of the Property.
   b. Place your insertion point on the blank line below the phone number at the end of the document.

c. Click the **Picture Content Control** button [*Developer* tab, *Controls* group] to insert a *Picture* content control field.

d. Open the *Content Control Properties* dialog box, type Property Picture as the *Title*, and click **OK** to close the dialog box.

e. Click the **Position** button [*Picture Tools Format* tab, *Arrange* group] and select **More Layout Options** from the drop-down list to open the *Layout* dialog box.

f. Click the **Size** tab and change the *Height* and *Width* to **2.5"**.

g. Click the **Text Wrapping** tab and select **Tight**.

h. Click the **Position** tab and set the *Horizontal* **Alignment** to **Right** relative to **Margin** and the *Vertical* **Absolute** position at **5.7"** below **Page** (Figure 11-65).

i. Click **OK** to close the *Layout* dialog box.

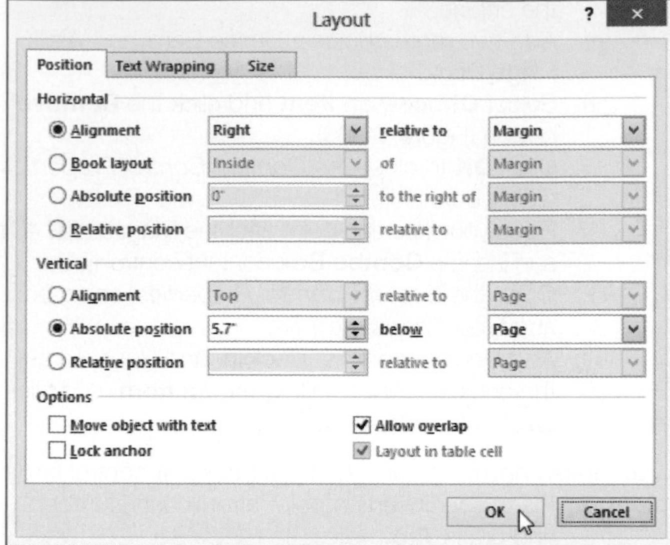

11-65 Customize the layout of the *Picture* content control field

9. Use *Design* mode to customize placeholder text.
   a. Place your insertion point at the beginning of the document.
   b. Click the **Design Mode** button [*Developer* tab, *Controls* group] to turn on *Design* mode.
   c. Use the following information to customize the placeholder text:

      Application Date: Select date of loan application
      Financial Institution: Select or type financial institution
      Loan Number: Type loan number
      Borrower Name: Type borrower name(s)
      Street Address: Type street address
      City: Select or type city
      Zip Code: Type zip code

   d. Click the **Design Mode** button to turn off *Design* mode.

10. Protect the form template.
   a. Click the **Restrict Editing** button [*Developer* tab, *Protect* group] to display the *Restrict Editing* pane at the right (Figure 11-66).
   b. In the *Editing restrictions* area, check the **Allow only this type of editing in the document** box.
   c. Click the drop-down list and select **Filling in Forms**.
   d. Click **Yes, Start Enforcing Protection**. The *Start Enforcing Protection* dialog box opens.
   e. Click **OK** to protect the document without a password.
   f. Click the **Restrict Editing** button to close the *Restrict Editing* pane.

11. Save and close the form template.

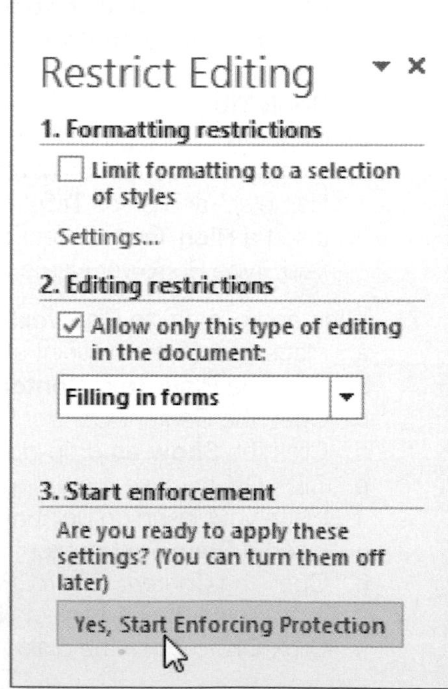

11-66 Restrict editing to *Filling in forms*

12. From a Windows folder, create a new document based on the ***[your initials] Word 11-1 form*** template.
13. Save the document as ***[your initials] Word 11-1***.
14. Use the following information to fill in the content control fields:

    Application Date: Select the previous Monday
    Financial Institution: **Chase Bank**
    Loan Number: CB2003476
    Borrower Name: John and Robyn Burgess
    Street Address: 85741 Auberry Road
    City: **Roseville**
    Zip Code: 95722

15. Insert a picture in the *Picture* content control field.
    a. Click the **icon** in the center of the *Picture* content control field to open the *Insert Pictures* dialog box.
    b. Select **From a file** to open the *Insert Picture* dialog box.
    c. Locate the ***BurgessHome-11*** picture from your student data files and click **Insert**.
16. Save and close the document (Figure 11-67).

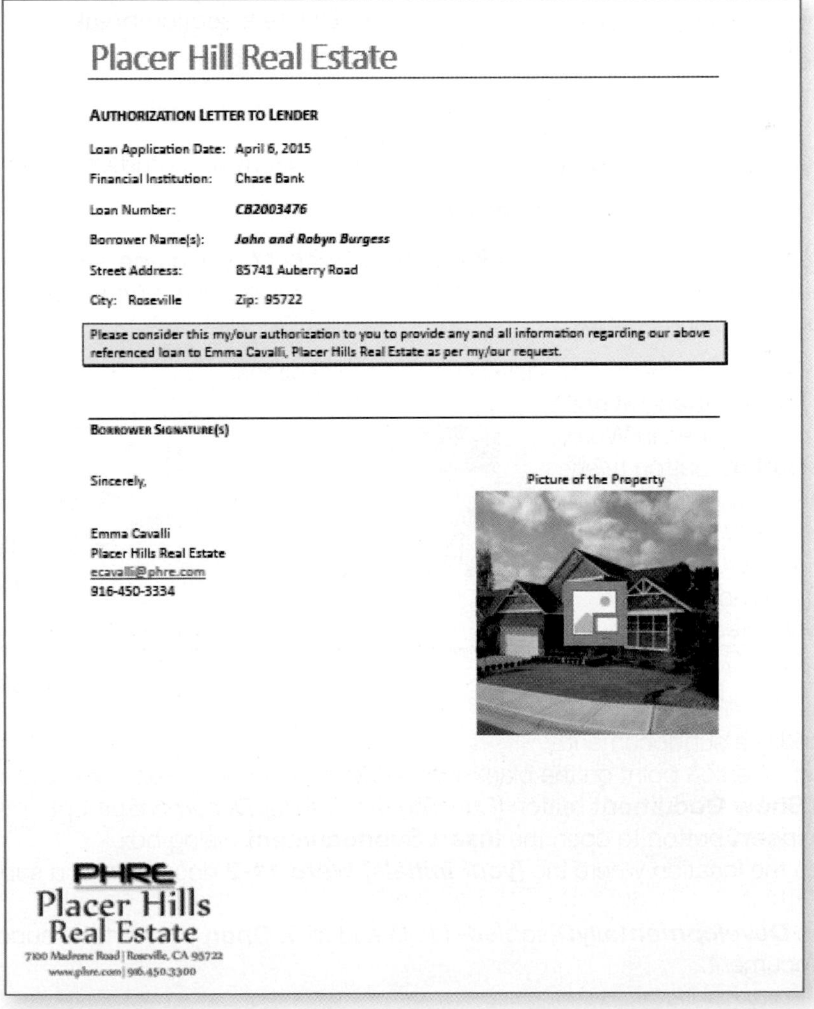

Placer Hill Real Estate

AUTHORIZATION LETTER TO LENDER

Loan Application Date: April 6, 2015

Financial Institution: Chase Bank

Loan Number: *CB2003476*

Borrower Name(s): ***John and Robyn Burgess***

Street Address: 85741 Auberry Road

City: Roseville Zip: 95722

Please consider this my/our authorization to you to provide any and all information regarding our above referenced loan to Emma Cavalli, Placer Hills Real Estate as per my/our request.

BORROWER SIGNATURE(S)

Sincerely,

Emma Cavalli
Placer Hills Real Estate
ecavalli@phre.com
916-450-3334

Picture of the Property

PHRE
Placer Hills
Real Estate
7100 Madrone Road | Roseville, CA 95722
www.phre.com | 916.450.3300

11-67 Word 11-1 completed

Guided Project 11-2

For this project, you use a master document and subdocuments to create a training guide for the Skiing Unlimited program. You insert subdocuments into a master document, split and merge subdocuments, change heading levels, and arrange sections of a subdocument.
[Student Learning Outcomes 11.5]

Files Needed: ***SkiingUnlimitedTrainingGuide-11.docx***, ***FourTrackandThreeTrack-11.docx***, ***DevelopmentallyDisabled-11.docx***, and ***VisuallyImpaired-11.docx***
Completed Project File Name: ***[your initials] Word 11-2.docx***

Skills Covered in This Project

- Use *Outline* view.
- Insert subdocuments into a master document.
- Promote and demote headings.
- Arrange sections in a subdocument.
- View different levels in *Outline* view.
- Modify subdocument text.
- Merge two subdocuments.
- Split a subdocument into two subdocuments.
- Unlink subdocuments.
- Delete a section break.
- Insert a page break.

---

1. Open the ***SkiingUnlimitedTrainingGuide-11*** document from your student data files.
2. Save the document as ***[your initials] Word 11-2***.
3. In a Windows folder, locate the ***FourTrackandThreeTrack-11***, ***DevelopmentallyDisabled-11***, and ***VisuallyImpaired-11*** files and copy these to the same location as your ***[your initials] Word 11-2*** file. These are your subdocument files.
4. Use *Outline* view to change heading level and arrange sections.
   a. With the ***[your initials] Word 11-2*** document open in Word, click the **Outline** button [*View* tab, *Views* group] to display the document in *Outline* view.
   b. Place your insertion point in "Introduction" and click the **Promote to Heading 1** button [*Outlining* tab, *Outline Tools* group] (Figure 11-68).

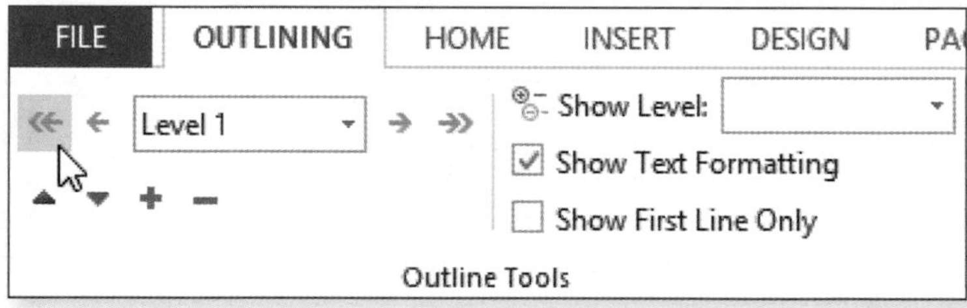

11-68 Promote selected text

5. Insert and modify a subdocument.
   a. Place your insertion point on the blank line below the last line of text in the outline.
   b. Click the **Show Document** button [*Outlining* tab, *Master Document* group].
   c. Click the **Insert** button to open the **Insert Subdocument** dialog box.
   d. Browse to the location where the ***[your initials] Word 11-2*** document and subdocuments are located.
   e. Select the ***DevelopmentallyDisabled-11*** file and click **Open** to insert the subdocument into the master document.

f. Click **Yes to All** in the dialog box that opens and asks if you want to rename styles in the subdocument (Figure 11-69).

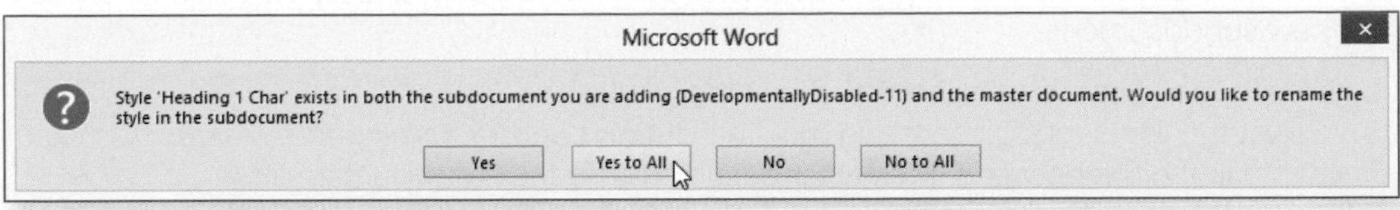

11-69 Rename styles in the subdocument file

g. Click the **heading selector** to the left of "Disabilities" to select the heading and the text below the heading.
h. Click the **Demote** button [*Outlining* tab, *Outline Tools* group] to change the selected heading to *Level 2*.
i. **Demote** to *Level 2* each of the next three headings in the subdocument.

6. Insert and modify another subdocument.
   a. Place your insertion point on the last blank line in the outline.
   b. **Insert** the ***VisuallyImpaired-11*** file and click **Yes to All** in the dialog box that opens and asks if you want to rename styles in the subdocument.
   c. Click the **Show Level** drop-down list and select **Level 2** to display two levels of headings in the outline (Figure 11-70).

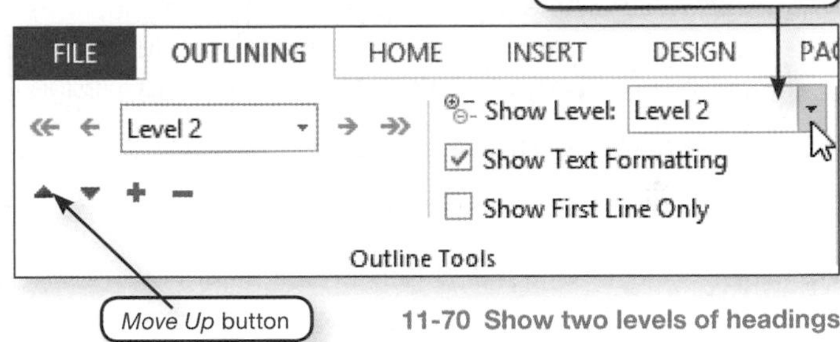

11-70 Show two levels of headings

   d. Select the "**Disabilities**" section in the second subdocument and click the **Move Up** [*Outlining* tab, *Outline Tools* group] button to move this section above the "Physical Evaluation" section.
7. Insert and modify another subdocument.
   a. Click the **Show Level** drop-down list and select **All Levels** to display all the text in the outline.
   b. Place your insertion point on the last blank line in the outline.
   c. **Insert** the ***FourTrackandThreeTrack-11*** file and click **Yes to All** in the dialog box that opens and asks if you want to rename styles in the subdocument.
   d. Select the "**Four-Track and Three-Track**" section and **promote** to *Level 1*.
   e. Select the "**Bi-Ski and Mono-Ski**" section and **promote** to *Level 1*.
8. Modify subdocuments.
   a. Click the **Show Level** drop-down list and select **Level 2**.
   b. In the first subdocument ("Developmentally Disabled (DD)"), place your insertion point before "Disabilities," type Common, and then **space** once.
   c. Repeat step 8b in the second subdocument.
9. Merge subdocuments.
   a. Click the **subdocument selector** for the first subdocument, hold down the **Shift** key, and click the **subdocument selector** for the second subdocument to select both subdocuments (Figure 11-71).
   b. Click the **Merge** button [*Outlining* tab, *Master Document* group] to merge the two subdocuments.

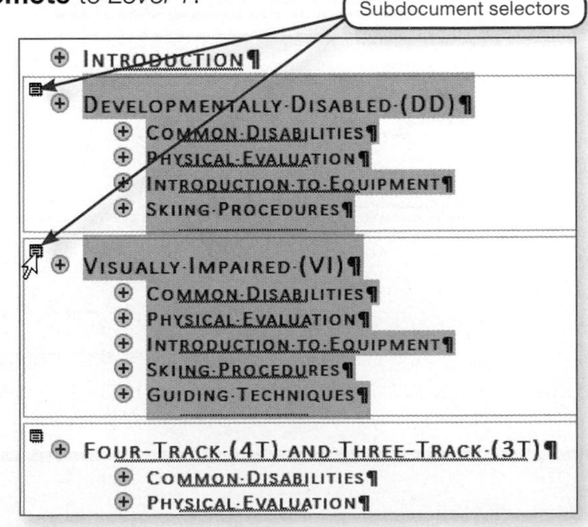

11-71 Select subdocument to merge

10. Split a section of a subdocument to create a new subdocument.
    a. Select the "**Bi-Ski and Mono-Ski**" section.
    b. Click the **Split** button [*Outlining* tab, *Master Document* group] to split the selected section into a new subdocument.
11. Unlink subdocuments and remove section breaks.
    a. Select the first subdocument and click the **Unlink** button [*Outlining* tab, *Master Document* group] to break the link between the master document and the subdocument file.
    b. **Unlink** the other two subdocuments.
    c. Click the **Show Level** drop-down list and select **All Levels**.
    d. Click the first section break and press **Delete**.
    e. Delete the remaining section breaks in the document.
    f. Delete any blank lines between sections and at the end of the document.
12. Click the **Close Outline View** button [*Outlining* tab, *Close* group] and view the document in *Print Layout* view.
13. Insert page breaks to keep text with headings.
    a. Insert a **page break** before the "Introduction to Equipment" section at the bottom of page 4.
    b. Insert a **page break** before the "Gliding Wedge Turns" section at the bottom of page 5.
14. Save and close the document (Figure 11-72).

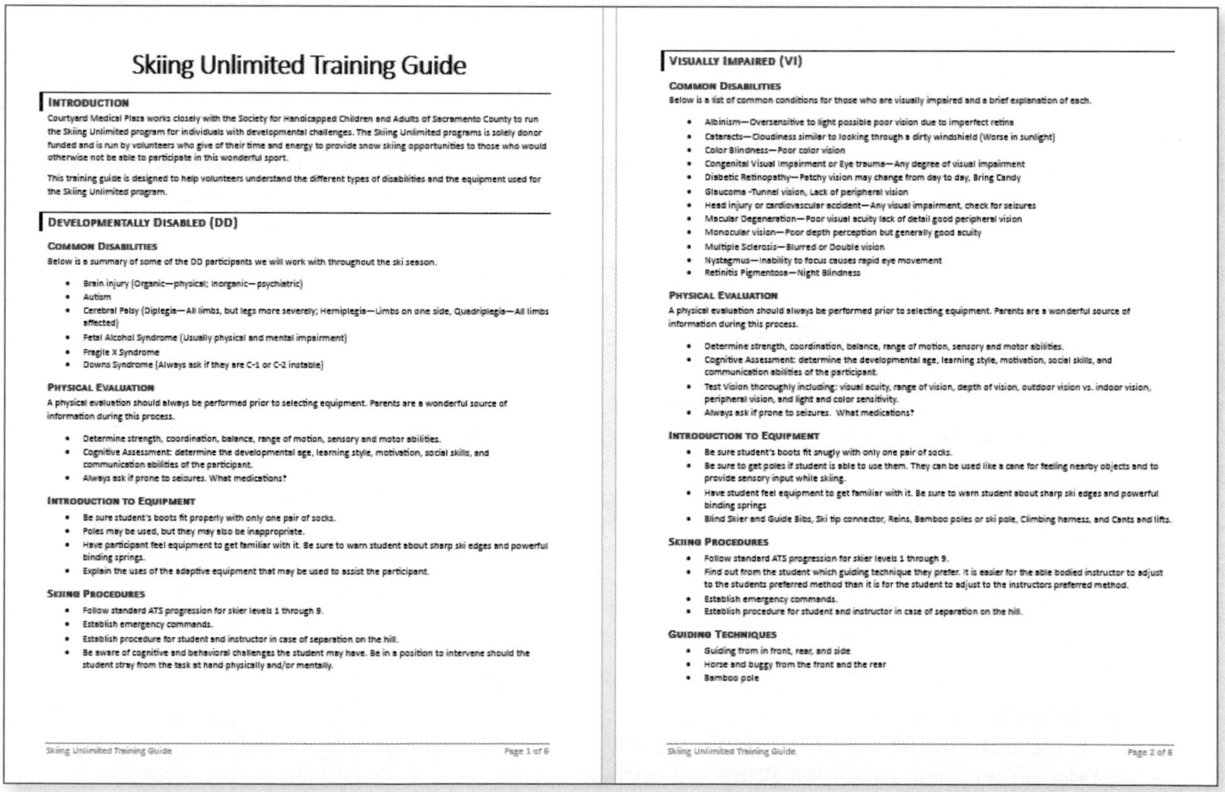

Skiing Unlimited Training Guide

Introduction

Courtyard Medical Plaza works closely with the Society for Handicapped Children and Adults of Sacramento County to run the Skiing Unlimited program for individuals with developmental challenges. The Skiing Unlimited programs is solely donor funded and is run by volunteers who give of their time and energy to provide snow skiing opportunities to those who would otherwise not be able to participate in this wonderful sport.

This training guide is designed to help volunteers understand the different types of disabilities and the equipment used for the Skiing Unlimited program.

Developmentally Disabled (DD)

Common Disabilities

Below is a summary of some of the DD participants we will work with throughout the ski season.

- Brain injury (Organic—physical; Inorganic—psychiatric)
- Autism
- Cerebral Palsy (Diplegia—All limbs, but legs more severely; Hemiplegia—Limbs on one side, Quadriplegia—All limbs affected)
- Fetal Alcohol Syndrome (Usually physical and mental impairment)
- Fragile X Syndrome
- Downs Syndrome (Always ask if they are C-1 or C-2 instable)

Physical Evaluation

A physical evaluation should always be performed prior to selecting equipment. Parents are a wonderful source of information during this process.

- Determine strength, coordination, balance, range of motion, sensory and motor abilities.
- Cognitive Assessment: determine the developmental age, learning style, motivation, social skills, and communication abilities of the participant.
- Always ask if prone to seizures. What medications?

Introduction to Equipment

- Be sure student's boots fit properly with only one pair of socks.
- Poles may be used, but they may also be inappropriate.
- Have participant feel equipment to get familiar with it. Be sure to warn student about sharp ski edges and powerful binding springs.
- Explain the uses of the adaptive equipment that may be used to assist the participant.

Skiing Procedures

- Follow standard ATS progression for skier levels 1 through 9.
- Establish emergency commands.
- Establish procedure for student and instructor in case of separation on the hill.
- Be aware of cognitive and behavioral challenges the student may have. Be in a position to intervene should the student stray from the task at hand physically and/or mentally.

Skiing Unlimited Training Guide Page 1 of 6

Visually Impaired (VI)

Common Disabilities

Below is a list of common conditions for those who are visually impaired and a brief explanation of each.

- Albinism—Oversensitive to light possible poor vision due to imperfect retina
- Cataracts—Cloudiness similar to looking through a dirty windshield (Worse in sunlight)
- Color Blindness—Poor color vision
- Congenital Visual Impairment or Eye trauma—Any degree of visual impairment
- Diabetic Retinopathy—Patchy vision may change from day to day, Bring Candy
- Glaucoma -Tunnel vision, Lack of peripheral vision
- Head injury or cardiovascular accident—Any visual impairment, check for seizures
- Macular Degeneration—Poor visual acuity lack of detail good peripheral vision
- Monocular vision—Poor depth perception but generally good acuity
- Multiple Sclerosis—Blurred or Double vision
- Nystagmus—Inability to focus causes rapid eye movement
- Retinitis Pigmentosa—Night Blindness

Physical Evaluation

A physical evaluation should always be performed prior to selecting equipment. Parents are a wonderful source of information during this process.

- Determine strength, coordination, balance, range of motion, sensory and motor abilities.
- Cognitive Assessment: determine the developmental age, learning style, motivation, social skills, and communication abilities of the participant.
- Test Vision thoroughly including: visual acuity, range of vision, depth of vision, outdoor vision vs. indoor vision, peripheral vision, and light and color sensitivity.
- Always ask if prone to seizures. What medications?

Introduction to Equipment

- Be sure student's boots fit snugly with only one pair of socks.
- Be sure to get poles if student is able to use them. They can be used like a cane for feeling nearby objects and to provide sensory input while skiing.
- Have student feel equipment to get familiar with it. Be sure to warn student about sharp ski edges and powerful binding springs
- Blind Skier and Guide Bibs, Ski tip connector, Reins, Bamboo poles or ski pole, Climbing harness, and Cants and lifts.

Skiing Procedures

- Follow standard ATS progression for skier levels 1 through 9.
- Find out from the student which guiding technique they prefer. It is easier for the able bodied instructor to adjust to the students preferred method than it is for the student to adjust to the instructors preferred method.
- Establish emergency commands.
- Establish procedure for student and instructor in case of separation on the hill.

Guiding Techniques

- Guiding from in front, rear, and side
- Horse and buggy from the front and the rear
- Bamboo pole

Skiing Unlimited Training Guide Page 2 of 6

11-72 Word 11-2 completed (pages 1 and 2 of 6)

Guided Project 11-3

For this project, you create a volunteer form for Life's Animal Shelter. You set up the form using content control fields, customize content control fields, group content control fields, and create a new document based on the form template.
[Student Learning Outcomes 11.1, 11.2, 11.3, 11.4]

File Needed: ***LASVolunteerForm-11.docx***
Completed Project File Names: ***[your initials] Word 11-3 form.docx*** and ***[your initials] Word 11-3.docx***

Skills Covered in This Project

- Set a tab stop to align text and content control fields.
- Change table row height and text alignment.
- Insert and customize *Rich Text*, *Plain Text*, *Check Box*, *Drop-Down List*, and *Combo Box* content control fields.
- Copy and customize a content control field.
- Use *Design* mode to customize placeholder text.
- Group content control fields.
- Fill in a content control field.

1. Open the ***LASVolunteerForm-11*** document from your student data files.
2. Save the document as ***[your initials] Word 11-3 form***.
3. Set a tab stop to align text and content control fields and modify the table.
   a. Select the last four rows of the table and set a **0.25" left** tab stop.
   b. Place your insertion point before the text in the fourth row of the table ("Yes, I can volunteer . . .") and press **Ctrl+Tab** to insert a tab before the text.
   c. Use **Ctrl+Tab** to insert a tab before the text in the last three rows of the table.
   d. Select the table, change the row height to **0.3"**, and change the text alignment to **Align Center Left**.
4. Insert and customize a *Rich Text* content control field.
   a. Place your insertion point in the second cell in the first row.
   b. Click the **Rich Text Content Control** button [*Developer* tab, *Controls* group] to insert a *Rich Text* content control field.
   c. Click the **Properties** button to open the *Content Control Properties* dialog box (Figure 11-73).
   d. Type Name as the *Title*.
   e. Click the **Color** drop-down list and select **Indigo**.
   f. Check the **Use a style to format text typed into the empty control** box.

11-73 Customize a *Rich Text* content control field

g. Click the **Style** drop-down list and select **Strong**.
h. Check the **Content control cannot be deleted** box in the *Locking* area.
i. Click **OK** to close the dialog box.

5. Insert and customize *Plain Text* content control fields.
   a. Place your insertion point in the second cell in the second row.
   b. Click the **Plain Text Content Control** button [*Developer* tab, *Controls* group] to insert a *Plain Text* content control field.
   c. Open the *Content Control Properties* dialog box and type Email Address as the *Title*.
   d. Click the **Color** drop-down list and select **Indigo**.
   e. Check the **Content control cannot be deleted** box in the *Locking* area.
   f. Click **OK** to close the dialog box.
   g. Place your insertion point in the second cell in the third row.
   h. Repeat steps 5b–f to insert and customize another *Plain Text* content control field. Type Phone Number as the title.

6. Insert and customize a *Check Box* content control field.
   a. Place your insertion point before the tab in front of "Yes, I can volunteer . . ."
   b. Click the **Check Box Content Control** button [*Developer* tab, *Controls* group] to insert a *Check Box* content control field.
   c. Open the *Content Control Properties* dialog box and type Volunteer as the *Title* (Figure 11-74).
   d. Click the **Color** drop-down list and select **Indigo**.
   e. In the *Checked symbol* area, click the **Change** button to open the *Symbol* dialog box.
   f. Click the **Font** drop-down list and select **Wingdings**.
   g. Select the **smiley face** icon (character code 74) and click **OK** to close the *Symbol* dialog box.
   h. Click **OK** to close the *Content Control Properties* dialog box.

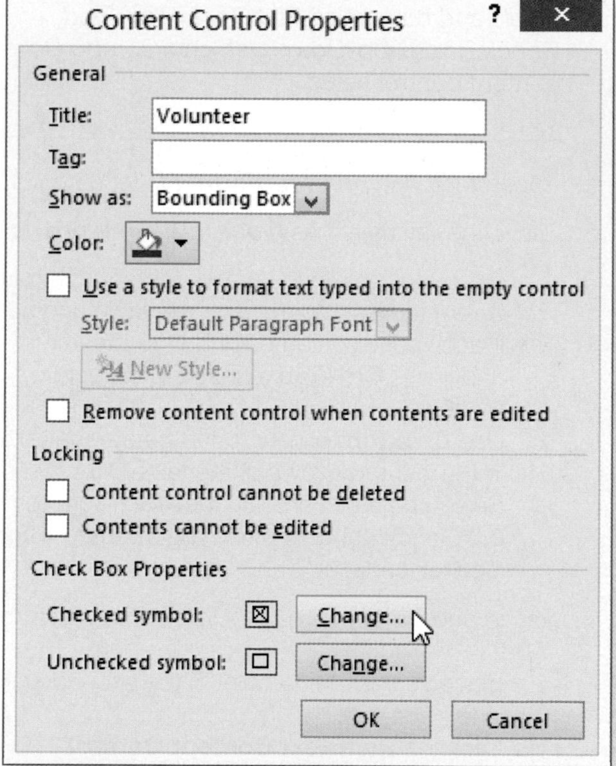

11-74 Customize a *Check Box* content control field

7. Copy and modify a *Check Box* content control field.
   a. Select the **Volunteer** *Check Box* content control field and **copy** it.
   b. Place your insertion point before the tab in front of "Yes, I would like to donate . . ."
   c. Paste the copied content control field.
   d. Select the pasted *Check Box* content control field and open the *Content Control Properties* dialog box. Don't check the box so the icon changes to a smiley face.
   e. Type Donate as the *Title*, delete the text in the *Tag* area, and click **OK** to close the dialog box.

8. Insert and customize a *Drop-Down List* content control field.
   a. Place your insertion point after "Hours per week I can volunteer:" and **space** once.
   b. Click the **Drop-Down List Content Control** button [*Developer* tab, *Controls* group] to insert a *Drop-Down List* content control field.

c. Open the *Content Control Properties* dialog box and type Volunteer Hours as the *Title*.
d. Click the **Color** drop-down list and select **Indigo**.
e. Apply the **Strong** style to format the contents of the content control field.
f. Check the **Content control cannot be deleted** box in the *Locking* area.
g. Click the **Add** button in the *Drop-Down List Properties* area to open the *Add Choice* dialog box.
h. Type 1-5 hours in the *Display Name* area and press **OK** to close the dialog box and add the choice.
i. Add three more choices: 6-10 hours, 11-15 hours, and 16-20 hours.
j. Select **Choose an item** and click the **Remove** button (Figure 11-75).
k. Click **OK** to close the *Content Control Properties* dialog box.

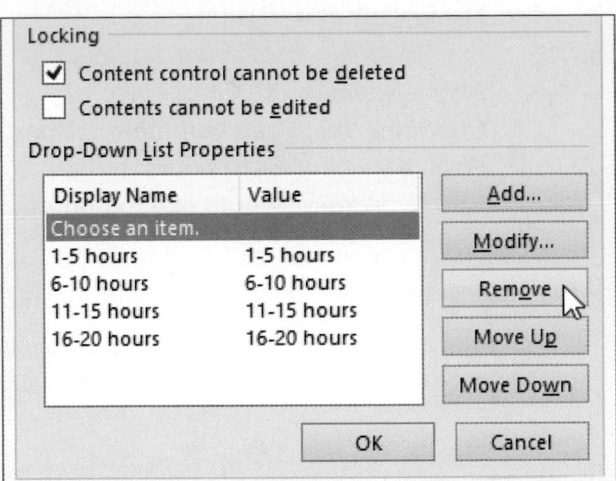

11-75 Add and remove choices from a *Drop-Down List* content control field

9. Insert and customize a *Combo Box* content control field.
   a. Place your insertion point after "Amount:" and **space** once.
   b. Click the **Combo Box Content Control** button [*Developer* tab, *Controls* group] to insert a *Combo Box* content control field.
   c. Open the *Content Control Properties* dialog box and type Donation Amount as the *Title*.
   d. Click the **Color** drop-down list and select **Indigo**.
   e. Apply the **Strong** style to format the contents of the content control field.
   f. Check the **Content control cannot be deleted** box in the *Locking* area.
   g. Add the following choices: $10, $25, $50, and $100.
   h. Select **Choose an item** and click the **Remove** button.
   i. Click **OK** to close the *Content Control Properties* dialog box.

10. Use *Design* mode to customize placeholder text.
    a. Place your insertion point at the beginning of the table.
    b. Click the **Design Mode** button [*Developer* tab, *Controls* group] to turn on *Design* mode.
    c. Use the following information to customize the placeholder text:

       Name: Type first and last name
       Email Address: Type email address
       Phone Number: Type phone number
       Volunteer Hours: Select hours
       Donation Amount: Select or type donation amount

    d. Click the **Design Mode** button to turn off *Design* mode.

11. Group content control fields to lock the text in the document.
    a. Select the entire document (**Ctrl+A**).
    b. Click the **Group** button [*Developer* tab, *Controls* group] and select **Group** from the drop-down list.
    c. Click anywhere in the document to deselect the selected text.

12. Save the document, but do not close it.

13. Save the document as ***[your initials] Word 11-3***.

14. Use the following information to fill in the content control fields in the table:
   Name: Cammi Acevedo
   Email Address: cammia@live.com
   Phone Number: 218.285.3776
   Check the **Yes, I can volunteer . . .** box.
   Volunteer Hours: **6–10 hours**
   Check the **Yes, I would like to donate . . .** box.
   Donation Amount: $25
15. Save and close the document (Figure 11-76).

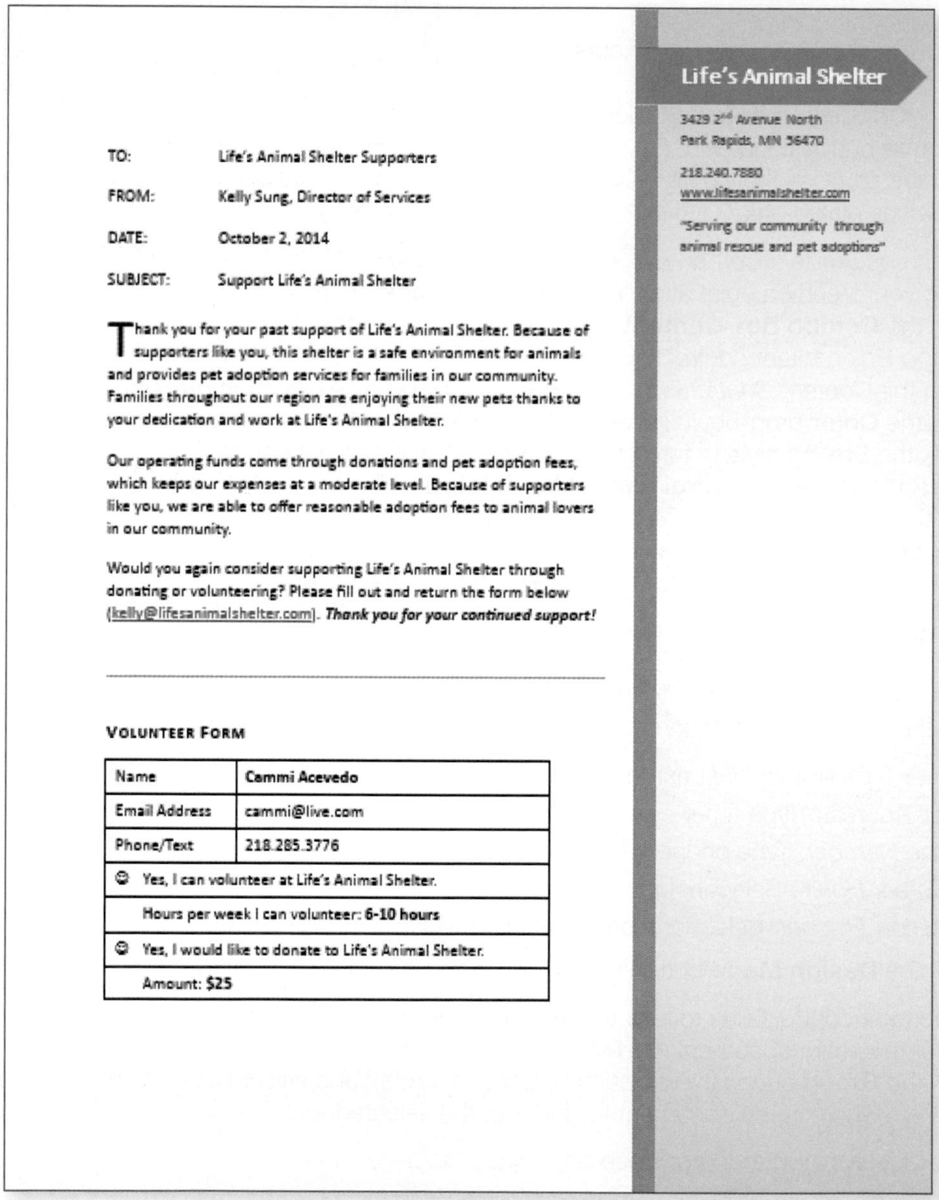

Life's Animal Shelter

3429 2nd Avenue North
Park Rapids, MN 56470

218.240.7880
www.lifesanimalshelter.com

"Serving our community through animal rescue and pet adoptions"

TO: Life's Animal Shelter Supporters

FROM: Kelly Sung, Director of Services

DATE: October 2, 2014

SUBJECT: Support Life's Animal Shelter

Thank you for your past support of Life's Animal Shelter. Because of supporters like you, this shelter is a safe environment for animals and provides pet adoption services for families in our community. Families throughout our region are enjoying their new pets thanks to your dedication and work at Life's Animal Shelter.

Our operating funds come through donations and pet adoption fees, which keeps our expenses at a moderate level. Because of supporters like you, we are able to offer reasonable adoption fees to animal lovers in our community.

Would you again consider supporting Life's Animal Shelter through donating or volunteering? Please fill out and return the form below (kelly@lifesanimalshelter.com). ***Thank you for your continued support!***

VOLUNTEER FORM

Name	**Cammi Acevedo**
Email Address	cammi@live.com
Phone/Text	218.285.3776
☺ Yes, I can volunteer at Life's Animal Shelter.	
Hours per week I can volunteer: **6-10 hours**	
☺ Yes, I would like to donate to Life's Animal Shelter.	
Amount: **$25**	

11-76 Word 11-3 completed

Independent Project 11-4

For this project, you create a training log form for American River Cycling Club and then insert the form into a master document. You will insert and customize content control fields, copy and paste content control fields, insert a subdocument into a master document, and modify the contents of the master document. **[Student Learning Outcomes 11.1, 11.2, 11.3, 11.4, 11.5]**

Files Needed: ***TrainingLogForm-11.docx*** and ***TrainingLog-11.docx***
Completed Project File Names: ***[your initials] Word 11-4 form.docx*** and ***[your initials] Word 11-4.docx***

Skills Covered in This Project

- Insert and customize *Date Picker*, *Rich Text*, and *Drop-Down List* content control fields.
- Copy, paste, and modify a content control field.
- Use *Outline* view.
- Insert a subdocument into a master document.
- Promote a heading level.
- Remove a section break in an outline.
- Unlink a subdocument.
- Group content control fields.

---

1. Open the ***TrainingLogForm-11*** document from your student data files.
2. Save the document as ***[your initials] Word 11-4 form***.
3. Insert and customize a *Date Picker* content control field.
   a. Place your insertion point after the text in the first row of the table and **space** once.
   b. Insert a *Date Picker* content control field.
   c. Change the title to Training Week.
   d. Change the color to **Yellow**.
   e. Apply the **Table Title** style to format the contents of the content control field.
   f. Select the third date format.
4. Insert and customize a *Rich Text* content control field.
   a. Place your insertion point in the first cell in the third row and insert a *Rich Text* content control field.
   b. Change the title to Miles and the color to **Yellow**.
5. Copy, paste, and modify *Rich Text* content control fields.
   a. Copy the *Rich Text* content control field and paste it in the second cell in the third row ("Duration" column).
   b. Change the title to Duration and remove the text in the *Tag* area.
   c. Paste the *Rich Text* content control field in the third cell in the third row and change the title to Average Speed and remove the text in the *Tag* area.
   d. Paste the *Rich Text* content control field in the fourth cell in the third row and change the title to Average HR and remove the text in the *Tag* area.
6. Insert and customize a *Drop-Down List* content control field.
   a. Place your insertion point in the last cell in the third row and insert a *Drop-Down List* content control field.
   b. Change the title to How I Felt and the color to **Yellow**.
   c. **Add** the following choices: Like a Pro, Strong, Average, and Tired.
   d. Remove **Choose an item**.

7. Use *Design* mode to change the placeholder text with the following information:

   Miles: Enter miles
   Duration: Enter hours
   Average Speed: Enter avg. speed
   Average HR: Enter avg. HR
   How I Felt: Select how I felt

8. Turn off *Design* mode.
9. Copy and paste content control fields.
   a. Select and copy the **Miles** content control field.
   b. Paste the content control field in each of the six cells that are below its current location.
   c. Repeat the above steps for the remaining content control fields in the other columns (Figure 11-77).

TRAINING LOG FOR THE WEEK OF Click here to enter a date.				
MILES	DURATION	AVERAGE SPEED	AVERAGE HR	HOW I FELT
Enter miles	Enter hours	Enter avg. speed	Enter avg. HR	Select how I felt
Enter miles	Enter hours	Enter avg. speed	Enter avg. HR	Select how I felt
Enter miles	Enter hours	Enter avg. speed	Enter avg. HR	Select how I felt
Enter miles	Enter hours	Enter avg. speed	Enter avg. HR	Select how I felt
Enter miles	Enter hours	Enter avg. speed	Enter avg. HR	Select how I felt
Enter miles	Enter hours	Enter avg. speed	Enter avg. HR	Select how I felt
Enter miles	Enter hours	Enter avg. speed	Enter avg. HR	Select how I felt

11-77 Copy and paste content control fields

10. Save and close the document.
11. Open the ***TrainingLog-11*** document from your student data files.
12. Save the document as ***[your initials] Word 11-4***.
13. Insert a subdocument into this master document.
    a. Change to *Outline* view.
    b. Place your insertion point on the blank line at the end of the outline.
    c. **Insert** the ***[your initials] Word 11-4 form*** as a subdocument. Click **Yes to All** when prompted to rename styles in the subdocument.
14. Select and **Unlink** the subdocument from the master document.
15. Delete the section breaks in the outline.
16. Change the "Training Intensity and Heart Rate" heading to **Level 1**.
17. Close the *Outline* view and return to *Print Layout* view.
18. Select the entire document and **Group** the content controls fields.
19. Save and close the document (Figure 11-78).

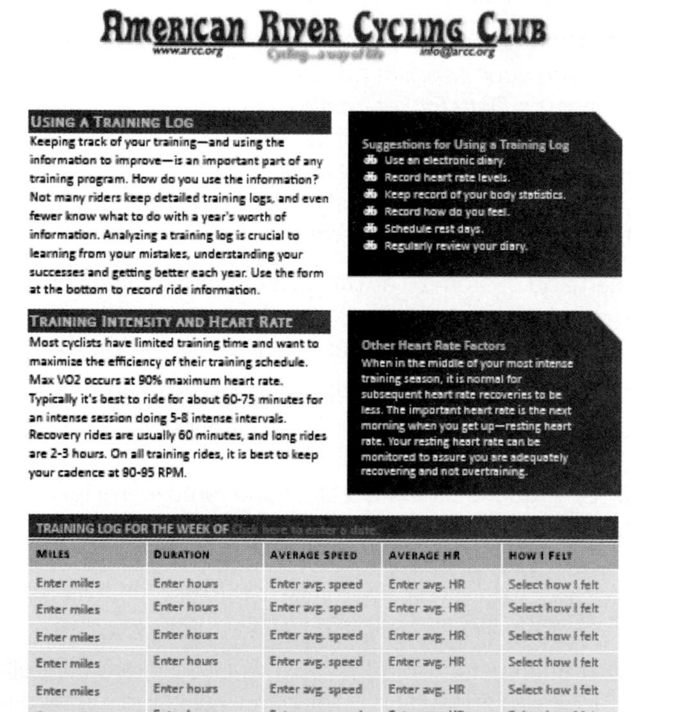

AMERICAN RIVER CYCLING CLUB
www.arcc.org Cycling...a way of life info@arcc.org

USING A TRAINING LOG
Keeping track of your training—and using the information to improve—is an important part of any training program. How do you use the information? Not many riders keep detailed training logs, and even fewer know what to do with a year's worth of information. Analyzing a training log is crucial to learning from your mistakes, understanding your successes and getting better each year. Use the form at the bottom to record ride information.

Suggestions for Using a Training Log
- Use an electronic diary.
- Record heart rate levels.
- Keep record of your body statistics.
- Record how do you feel.
- Schedule rest days.
- Regularly review your diary.

TRAINING INTENSITY AND HEART RATE
Most cyclists have limited training time and want to maximize the efficiency of their training schedule. Max VO2 occurs at 90% maximum heart rate. Typically it's best to ride for about 60-75 minutes for an intense session doing 5-8 intense intervals. Recovery rides are usually 60 minutes, and long rides are 2-3 hours. On all training rides, it is best to keep your cadence at 90-95 RPM.

Other Heart Rate Factors
When in the middle of your most intense training season, it is normal for subsequent heart rate recoveries to be less. The important heart rate is the next morning when you get up—resting heart rate. Your resting heart rate can be monitored to assure you are adequately recovering and not overtraining.

TRAINING LOG FOR THE WEEK OF Click here to enter a date.				
MILES	DURATION	AVERAGE SPEED	AVERAGE HR	HOW I FELT
Enter miles	Enter hours	Enter avg. speed	Enter avg. HR	Select how I felt
Enter miles	Enter hours	Enter avg. speed	Enter avg. HR	Select how I felt
Enter miles	Enter hours	Enter avg. speed	Enter avg. HR	Select how I felt
Enter miles	Enter hours	Enter avg. speed	Enter avg. HR	Select how I felt
Enter miles	Enter hours	Enter avg. speed	Enter avg. HR	Select how I felt
Enter miles	Enter hours	Enter avg. speed	Enter avg. HR	Select how I felt
Enter miles	Enter hours	Enter avg. speed	Enter avg. HR	Select how I felt

11-78 Word 11-4 completed

Independent Project 11-5

For this project, you create an insurance questionnaire for Central Sierra Insurance. You insert and customize content control fields, copy and modify content control fields, protect the document, create a new document based on the questionnaire, and fill in content control fields.
[Student Learning Outcomes 11.1, 11.2, 11.3, 11.4]

File Needed: ***InsuranceQuestionnaire-11.docx***
Completed Project File Names: ***[your initials] Word 11-5 form.docx*** and ***[your initials] Word 11-5.docx***

Skills Covered in This Project

- Insert and customize *Rich Text*, *Drop-Down List*, *Combo Box*, and *Date Picker* content control fields.
- Change the display for a content control field.
- Apply a style to a content control field.
- Copy, paste, and customize a content control field.
- Use *Design* mode to customize placeholder text.
- Restrict editing to filling in forms.
- Fill in a content control field.

1. Open the ***InsuranceQuestionnaire-11*** document from your student data files.
2. Save the document as ***[your initials] Word 11-5 form***.
3. Insert and customize a *Rich Text* content control field.
   a. Place your insertion point in the second cell in the first row and insert a *Rich Text* content control field.
   b. Change the title to Question 1 and change *Show as* to **None**.
4. Copy, paste, and modify *Rich Text* content control fields.
   a. Copy the "Question 1" content control field and paste it in the second column for questions 2–5.
   b. Change the title to the question number (e.g., *Question 2*, *Question 3*) and remove the text from the *Tag* area.
5. Insert and customize a *Drop-Down List* content control field.
   a. Place your insertion point in the second column on *Question 6* and insert a *Drop-Down List* content control field.
   b. Change the title to Question 6.
   c. **Add** Yes and No as the choices and remove **Choose an item**.
   d. Use *Design* mode to change the placeholder text to Select Yes or No.
6. Copy, paste, and modify *Drop-Down List* content control fields.
   a. Copy the "Question 6" content control field and paste it in the second column for questions 7–10. Don't copy the content control field to 7a, 8a, 9a, 10a, and 10b.
   b. Change the title to the question number and remove the text from the *Tag* area.
7. Insert and customize a *Combo Box* content control field.
   a. Place your insertion point in the second column on *Question 7a* and insert a *Combo Box* content control field.
   b. Change the title to Question 7a.
   c. Apply the **Emphasis** style to format the contents of the content control field.
   d. **Add** N/A as the choice and remove **Choose an item**.
   e. Use *Design* mode to change the placeholder text to Type a response or select N/A.

8. Copy, paste, and modify *Combo Box* content control fields.
   a. Copy the "Question 7a" content control field and paste it in the second column for *Questions 8a*, *9a*, *10a*, and *10b*.
   b. Change the title to the question number (e.g., *Question 8a*, *Question 9a*) and remove the text from the *Tag* area.
9. Insert and customize a *Date Picker* content control field.
   a. Place your insertion point after "Date of Application:", **space** once, and insert a *Date Picker* content control field.
   b. Change the title to Application Date and select the third date format.
   c. Use *Design* mode to change the placeholder text to Select date of application.
10. Turn off *Design* mode if it is still on.
11. Restrict editing of the questionnaire.
   a. Allow only **Filling in forms**.
   b. Start enforcing protection and don't use a password.
12. Save the document.
13. Save the document as a different file name. Save it as ***[your initials] Word 11-5***.
14. Use the information in the following table to fill in the questionnaire:

Question 1	Tish Waterson
Question 2	95002 North Avenue, Loomis, CA 96885
Question 3	916-528-6861
Question 4	CA3775409
Question 5	18
Question 6	**Yes**
Question 7	**Yes**
Question 7a	15%
Question 8	**No**
Question 8a	**N/A**
Question 9	**No**
Question 9a	**N/A**
Question 10	**No**
Question 10a	**N/A**
Question 10b	**N/A**
Application Date	**Select current date**

15. Save and close the document (Figure 11-79).

Central Sierra Insurance

Contractor's Insurance Questionnaire

PLEASE CAREFULLY READ AND UNDERSTAND ALL QUESTIONS.

Applicant's Instructions

Please type or select a response to ALL questions. Questionnaire must be signed and dated by owner, partner, or officer.

1) Applicant:	Tish Waterson
2) Street, City, State, Zip	95002 North Avenue, Loomis, CA 96885
3) Telephone Number:	916-528-6861
4) Contractor License #:	CA3775409
5) Years in business:	18
6) Are written contracts required from sub-contractors?	Yes
7) In the past five years, have you worked on any condominium or townhouse projects?	Yes
a) If "yes," what percentage of receipts did the condos and townhouses represent?	*15%*
8) Has any licensing authority taken any action against you?	No
a) If "yes," explain outcome:	*N/A*
9) Are you or your subcontractors involved in any removal hazardous materials?	No
a) If "yes," what type of hazardous materials?	*N/A*
10) Do you have operations other than contracting?	No
a) If "yes," what type of operation?	*N/A*
b) If "yes," are these operations to be covered by this insurance?	*N/A*

Insurance Application Disclaimer

The undersigned applicant warrants that the above statements and particulars, together with any attached or appended documents or materials (this supplemental application), are true and completed and do not misrepresent, misstate or omit any material facts. Furthermore, the applicant authorizes the company, as administrative and servicing manager, to make any investigations and inquiry in connection with the supplemental application, as it may deem necessary.

The applicant agrees to notify the company of any material changes in the answers to the questions on this supplemental application which may arise prior to the effective date of any policy issued pursuant to this supplemental application and applicant understands that any outstanding quotations may be modified or withdrawn based upon such changes at the sole discretion of the company.

Date of Application: April 20, 2015

Signature of Insured: ______________________________

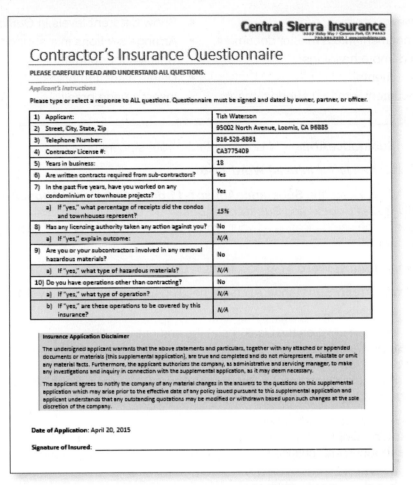

11-79 Word 11-5 completed

Independent Project 11-6

For this project, you use a master document and subdocuments to create a report for Courtyard Medical Plaza. You insert subdocuments into a master document, split and merge subdocuments, change heading levels, and arrange sections of a subdocument.
[Student Learning Outcomes 11.5]

Files Needed: ***TeenSubstanceAbuse-11.docx***, ***SubstanceAbuse1-11.docx***, ***SubstanceAbuse2-11.docx***, ***SubstanceAbuse3-11.docx***, and ***SubstanceAbuse4-11.docx***
Completed Project File Name: ***[your initials] Word 11-6.docx***

Skills Covered in This Project

- Use *Outline* view.
- Insert a subdocument into a master document.
- Promote and demote headings.
- Merge subdocuments.
- Split a subdocument into two subdocuments.
- Show different levels in *Outline* view.
- Arrange sections in a subdocument.
- Unlink subdocuments.
- Delete a section break.
- Insert a page break.

---

1. Open the ***TeenSubstanceAbuse-11*** document from your student data files.
2. Save the document as ***[your initials] Word 11-6***.
3. In a Windows folder, locate the ***SubstanceAbuse1-11.docx***, ***SubstanceAbuse2-11.docx***, ***SubstanceAbuse3-11.docx***, and ***SubstanceAbuse4-11.docx*** files from your student data files and copy these to the same location as your ***[your initials] Word 11-6*** file. These are your subdocument files.
4. Display the ***[your initials] Word 11-6*** document in *Outline* view.
5. Select the "**What is Teen Substance Abuse?**" heading and change it to **Level 1**.
6. Insert subdocuments into the master document.
   a. Place your insertion point on the blank line at the end of the outline.
   b. Insert the ***SubstanceAbuse1-11*** file. This file should be located in the same folder as ***[your initials] Word 11-6***.
   c. Insert the following subdocuments: ***SubstanceAbuse2-11.docx***, ***SubstanceAbuse3-11.docx***, and ***SubstanceAbuse4-11.docx***.
7. Change heading levels in the subdocuments.
   a. **Show First Line Only** in the outline.
   b. In the first subdocument, change the "What Problems Can Teen Substance Abuse Cause?" heading to **Level 2**.
   c. In the second subdocument, change the "What are the Signs of Substance Abuse?" heading to **Level 2**.
   d. In the third subdocument, change the "Why do Teens Abuse Drugs and Alcohol?" heading to **Level 1**.
   e. In the fourth subdocument, change the "What Should You do if Your Teen is Using?" and "Bibliography" headings to **Level 1**.
   f. In the fourth subdocument, change the "Can Teen Substance Use and Abuse be Prevented?" and "What are the Treatment Options?" headings to **Level 2**.
8. Merge and split subdocuments.
   a. Select the first three subdocuments and **merge** them into one subdocument.
   b. Select the "**Bibliography**" section and **split** it into a separate subdocument.
9. Arrange sections in subdocuments.
   a. Change the outline display to show **Level 2**, which displays *Levels 1* and *2* in the outline.
   b. In the first subdocument, move the *Level 1* heading above the *Level 2* headings.
   c. In the second subdocument, move the second *Level 2* heading ("What are the Treatment Options?") above the first *Level 2* heading in that subdocument.
10. Save the document.

11. **Unlink** the three subdocuments from the master document.
12. Close *Outline* view and display the document in *Print Layout* view.
13. Remove section breaks from the document and insert page breaks.
    a. Delete all of the section breaks and blank lines in the document.
    b. Place your insertion point in front of "Bibliography" and insert a **page break**.
    c. Place your insertion point in front of "Can Teen Substance Use and Abuse be Prevented?" and insert a **page break**.
14. Save and close the document (Figure 11-80).

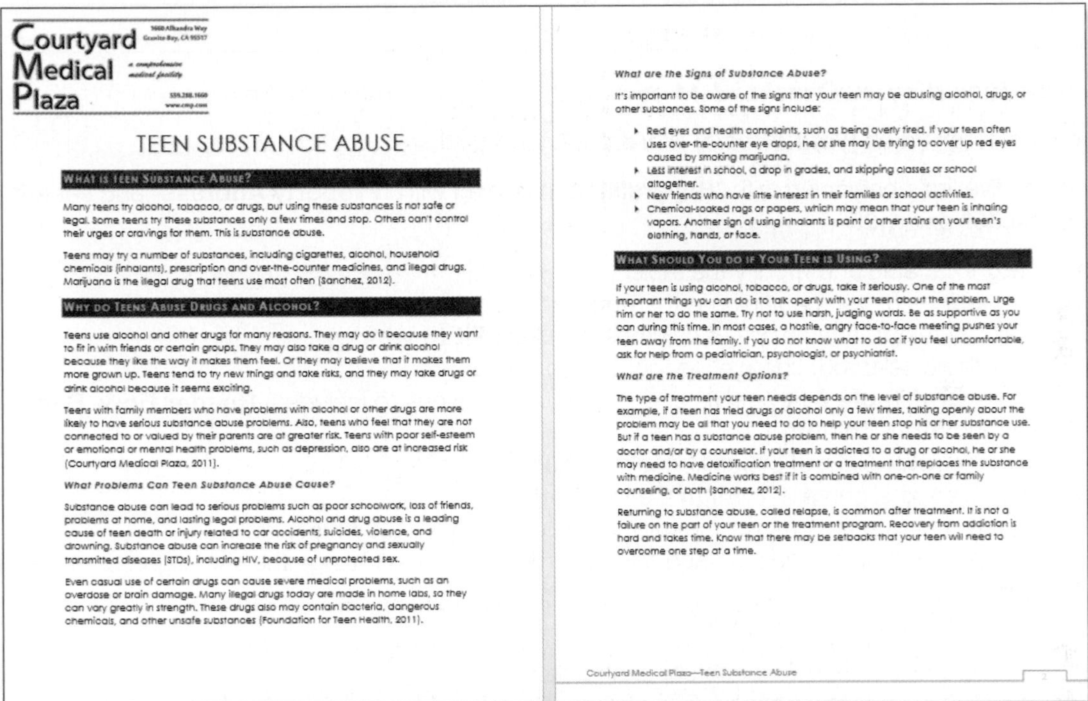

Courtyard Medical Plaza

TEEN SUBSTANCE ABUSE

WHAT IS TEEN SUBSTANCE ABUSE?

Many teens try alcohol, tobacco, or drugs, but using these substances is not safe or legal. Some teens try these substances only a few times and stop. Others can't control their urges or cravings for them. This is substance abuse.

Teens may try a number of substances, including cigarettes, alcohol, household chemicals (inhalants), prescription and over-the-counter medicines, and illegal drugs. Marijuana is the illegal drug that teens use most often (Sanchez, 2012).

WHY DO TEENS ABUSE DRUGS AND ALCOHOL?

Teens use alcohol and other drugs for many reasons. They may do it because they want to fit in with friends or certain groups. They may also take a drug or drink alcohol because they like the way it makes them feel. Or they may believe that it makes them more grown up. Teens tend to try new things and take risks, and they may take drugs or drink alcohol because it seems exciting.

Teens with family members who have problems with alcohol or other drugs are more likely to have serious substance abuse problems. Also, teens who feel that they are not connected to or valued by their parents are at greater risk. Teens with poor self-esteem or emotional or mental health problems, such as depression, also are at increased risk (Courtyard Medical Plaza, 2011).

What Problems Can Teen Substance Abuse Cause?

Substance abuse can lead to serious problems such as poor schoolwork, loss of friends, problems at home, and lasting legal problems. Alcohol and drug abuse is a leading cause of teen death or injury related to car accidents, suicides, violence, and drowning. Substance abuse can increase the risk of pregnancy and sexually transmitted diseases (STDs), including HIV, because of unprotected sex.

Even casual use of certain drugs can cause severe medical problems, such as an overdose or brain damage. Many illegal drugs today are made in home labs, so they can vary greatly in strength. These drugs also may contain bacteria, dangerous chemicals, and other unsafe substances (Foundation for Teen Health, 2011).

What are the Signs of Substance Abuse?

It's important to be aware of the signs that your teen may be abusing alcohol, drugs, or other substances. Some of the signs include:

- Red eyes and health complaints, such as being overly tired. If your teen often uses over-the-counter eye drops, he or she may be trying to cover up red eyes caused by smoking marijuana.
- Less interest in school, a drop in grades, and skipping classes or school altogether.
- New friends who have little interest in their families or school activities.
- Chemical-soaked rags or papers, which may mean that your teen is inhaling vapors. Another sign of using inhalants is paint or other stains on your teen's clothing, hands, or face.

WHAT SHOULD YOU DO IF YOUR TEEN IS USING?

If your teen is using alcohol, tobacco, or drugs, take it seriously. One of the most important things you can do is to talk openly with your teen about the problem. Urge him or her to do the same. Try not to use harsh, judging words. Be as supportive as you can during this time. In most cases, a hostile, angry face-to-face meeting pushes your teen away from the family. If you do not know what to do or if you feel uncomfortable, ask for help from a pediatrician, psychologist, or psychiatrist.

What are the Treatment Options?

The type of treatment your teen needs depends on the level of substance abuse. For example, if a teen has tried drugs or alcohol only a few times, talking openly about the problem may be all that you need to do to help your teen stop his or her substance use. But if a teen has a substance abuse problem, then he or she needs to be seen by a doctor and/or by a counselor. If your teen is addicted to a drug or alcohol, he or she may need to have detoxification treatment or a treatment that replaces the substance with medicine. Medicine works best if it is combined with one-on-one or family counseling, or both (Sanchez, 2012).

Returning to substance abuse, called relapse, is common after treatment. It is not a failure on the part of your teen or the treatment program. Recovery from addiction is hard and takes time. Know that there may be setbacks that your teen will need to overcome one step at a time.

Courtyard Medical Plaza—Teen Substance Abuse 2

11-80 Word 11-6 completed (pages 1 and 2 of 4)

Improve It Project 11-7

For this project, you create a buyer escrow checklist form for Placer Hills Real Estate. You convert text to a table, modify the table, insert and customize content control fields, copy and modify content control fields, and group content control fields.
[Student Learning Outcomes 11.1, 11.2, 11.3, 11.4]

File Needed: ***BuyerEscrowCheckList-11.docx***
Completed Project File Name: ***[your initials] Word 11-7.docx***

Skills Covered in This Project

- Set tab stops to align text.
- Convert text to a table.
- Apply a table style.
- Modify row height and column width and change text alignment.
- Insert and customize *Rich Text*, *Plain Text*, *Combo Box*, and *Date Picker* content control fields.
- Change color and apply a style to a content control field.
- Copy, paste, and customize a content control field.
- Use *Design* mode to customize placeholder text.
- Group content control fields.

---

1. Open the ***BuyerEscrowCheckList-11*** document from your student data files.
2. Save the document as ***[your initials] Word 11-7***.
3. Select the five lines beginning with "**Buyers(s)**" and ending with "**Property Address**" and set **left** tab stops at **0.75"** and **1.25"**.
4. Convert text to a table and modify the table.
   a. Select the lines of text beginning with "**Task**" through the last line of the document.
   b. Convert the text to a table with **4** columns and **AutoFit to window**.
   c. With the table selected, change the font size to **10 pt.**
   d. Apply the **Grid Table 2** table style and set the table options to include a **Header Row**, **Banded Rows**, and **First Column**.
   e. Change the row height of the entire table to **0.3"**.
   f. Change the text alignment to **Align Center Left**.
   g. Select the first column, change the width to **2.8"**, and set a **0.25" left** tab.
   h. Change the width of the second and third columns to **1"** and change the text alignment to **Align Center**.
   i. Change the width of the fourth column to **1.6"**.
5. Insert and customize a *Rich Text* content control field.
   a. Insert a *Rich Text* content control field after the tab after "Buyer(s):".
   b. Change the title to Buyer, change the color to **Green**, and apply the **Book Title** style.
6. Insert and customize a *Plain Text* content control field.
   a. Insert a *Plain Text* content control field after the tab after "Phone:".
   b. Change the title to Phone and change the color to **Green**.
7. Copy and modify *Plain Text* content control fields.
   a. Copy the *Plain Text* content control field and paste it after the tab after "Email" and "Property Address."
   b. Change the titles to Email and Address respectively and remove the text from the *Tag* field.
   c. Copy and paste the *Plain Text* content control field in the cells below "Initials" and "Notes" in the table.
   d. Change the titles to Initials and Notes respectively and remove the text from the *Tag* field.
8. Insert and customize a *Combo Box* content control field.
   a. Insert a *Combo Box* content control field after the tab after "Agent:".
   b. Change the title to Agent and change the color to **Green**.
   c. Add Emma Cavalli, Ames Bellah, Hudson Alves, and Simon Bidou as the choices and remove **Choose an item**.

9. Insert and customize a *Date Picker* content control field.
   a. Insert a *Date Picker* content control field in the cell below "Date Completed" in the table.
   b. Change the title to Date Completed, change the color to **Green**, and select the first date format.
10. Insert *Check Box* content control fields.
    a. Insert a *Check Box* content control field before "Fax Contract to Buyer(s)."
    b. Deselect the content control field and use **Ctrl+Tab** to insert a tab between the *Check Box* content control field and the text.
    c. Repeat steps 10a and b above on each of the remaining cells in the first column.
11. Use *Design* mode to change the placeholder text.
    a. Turn on *Design* mode and enter the following information:

       Buyer: Type buyer's name(s)
       Phone: Type phone number
       Email: Type email address
       Agent: Select or type agent's name
       Property Address: Type property address
       Date Completed: Select date
       Initials: Type initials
       Notes: Type notes

    b. Turn off *Design* mode.
12. Copy each of the content control fields in the second, third, and fourth columns of the table to the cells below to fill the table with content control fields.
13. Select the entire document and **group** the content control fields.
14. Save and close the document (Figure 11-81).

PHRE
Placer Hills
Real Estate

Buyer Escrow Checklist

Buyer(s): Type buyer's name(s)
Phone: Type phone number
Email: Type email address
Agent: Select or type agent's name
Property Address: Type property address

Task	Date Completed	Initials	Notes
☐ Fax Contract to Buyer(s)	Select date	Type initials	Type notes
☐ Fax Contract to Lender	Select date	Type initials	Type notes
☐ Verify Property ID with Buyer(s)	Select date	Type initials	Type notes
☐ Verify Property ID with Lender	Select date	Type initials	Type notes
☐ Turn in new sale to PHRE	Select date	Type initials	Type notes
☐ Send check to Title Company	Select date	Type initials	Type notes
☐ Notified Buyer of EM deposit	Select date	Type initials	Type notes
☐ Fax/Email Pest Report to Buyer(s)	Select date	Type initials	Type notes
☐ Fax/Email Pest Report to Lender	Select date	Type initials	Type notes
☐ Fax/Email Clear Pest Report to Buyer(s)	Select date	Type initials	Type notes
☐ Fax/Email Clear Pest Report to Lender	Select date	Type initials	Type notes
☐ Verify Preliminary Report with Buyer(s)	Select date	Type initials	Type notes
☐ Verify Preliminary Report with Lender	Select date	Type initials	Type notes

Emma Cavalli
916-450-3334
ecavalli@phre.com

Placer Hills Real Estate
7100 Madrone Road, Roseville, CA 95722
www.phre.com

11-81 Word 11-7 completed

Challenge Project 11-8

Before each semester begins, you have a variety of tasks to accomplish so that you are ready when classes begin. For example, you may need to register and pay for classes, complete financial aid paperwork, buy books and supplies, download and read your course syllabi, check professors' web sites, or log into learning management systems.

For this project, you create a form using content control fields to keep track of the things you need to accomplish before the semester begins.
[Student Learning Outcomes 11.1, 11.2, 11.3, 11.4]

File Needed: None
Completed Project File Names: ***[your initials] Word 11-8 check list.dotx*** and ***[your initials] Word 11-8.docx***

Create a new document and save it as a template named ***[your initials] Word 11-8 checklist***. Modify your document according to the following guidelines:

- List the text and content control fields you will need in this checklist based on the tasks you need to complete before the semester begins.
- Use tab stops, indents, and/or a table to control alignment of text and content control fields.
- Insert text and content control fields for the tasks you need to complete before the semester begins.
- Customize content control fields to include titles. Change the color and how the field is displayed, apply a style, and add choices to *Combo Box* and *Drop-Down List* content control fields.
- Copy and modify content control fields as needed.
- Use *Design* mode to customize placeholder text.
- Group the content control fields.

Create a new document based on the checklist template and save it as ***[your initials] Word 11-8***.

- Fill in the content control fields.
- Save and close the document.

Challenge Project 11-9

For this project, you create a form you can use for an upcoming conference or workshop or a membership form for a club or organization. Use a variety of text and content control fields in this form.
[Student Learning Outcomes 11.1, 11.2, 11.3, 11.4]

File Needed: None
Completed Project File Name: ***[your initials] Word 11-9.docx***

Create a new document and save it as a template named ***[your initials] Word 11-9***. Modify your document according to the following guidelines:

- List the text and content control fields you will need in this form.
- Use tab stops and indents to control alignment of text and content control fields.
- Insert text and content control fields for your form.
- Customize content control fields to include a title. Change the color and how the field is displayed, apply a style, and add choices to *Combo Box* and *Drop-Down List* content control fields.
- Copy and modify content control fields as needed.
- Use *Design* mode to customize placeholder text.
- Restrict editing of the document and protect with a password.

Challenge Project 11-10

It is important to create a budget and live within it. You need to track what you're spending in order to create an accurate budget and effectively control your spending. For this project, you create an expenditure template to track your weekly spending, and then create a document based upon the expenditure template.
[Student Learning Outcomes 11.1, 11.2, 11.3, 11.4]

File Needed: None
Completed Project File Names: ***[your initials] Word 11-10 template.dotx*** and ***[your initials] Word 11-10.docx***

Create a new document and save it as a template named ***[your initials] Word 11-10 template***. Modify your template according to the following guidelines:

- List the text and content control fields you need in your weekly expenditure template.
- Use a table to control alignment of text and content control fields.
- Insert text and content control fields for expenses.
- Customize content control fields to include a title. Change the color and how the field is displayed, apply a style, and add choices to *Combo Box* and *Drop-Down List* content control fields.
- Copy and modify content control fields as needed.
- Use *Design* mode to customize placeholder text.
- Insert a formula at the bottom of the table to total your expenditures for the week.
- Group the content control fields.

Create a new document based on the expenditure template and save it as ***[your initials] Word 11-10***.

- Fill in your weekly spending in the content control fields.
- Update the formula in the table to total expenses.
- Save and close the document.

CHAPTER 12

Customizing Word and Using SkyDrive and Office Web Apps

CHAPTER OVERVIEW

Now that you have learned how to use the many features of Word 2013, you can customize Word settings to personalize your working environment. As an added convenience, in addition to being fully customizable, Office 2013 also integrates "cloud" technology, which allows you to use your Office files in *SkyDrive*, *SkyDrive* groups, and Office Web Apps. These different cloud services let your files and Office settings roam with you. With these features, you are not locked into using Office on only one computer and you don't have to save your files on a USB drive or portable hard drive to have access to your files.

STUDENT LEARNING OUTCOMES (SLOs)

After completing this chapter, you will be able to:

SLO 12.1 Customize Word options, the *Ribbon*, and the *Quick Access* toolbar to personalize your working environment (p. W12-685).

SLO 12.2 View and modify Office account settings and add an Office app (p. W12-695).

SLO 12.3 Create a folder, add a file, move and copy a file, and share a file in *SkyDrive* (p. W12-701).

SLO 12.4 Create a group in *SkyDrive*, invite a member, and change group options (p. W12-708).

SLO 12.5 Open, create, edit, print, share, use comments, and collaborate on a document in Office Web Apps (p. W12-714).

CASE STUDY

For the Pause & Practice projects in this chapter, you customize your Word settings and use Microsoft cloud services to save, edit, and share documents for Courtyard Medical Plaza.

Pause & Practice 12-1: Customize Word 2013 working environment and Office accounts settings and add an app.

Pause & Practice 12-2: Use *SkyDrive* and a *SkyDrive* group to save, create, edit, and share documents.

Pause & Practice 12-3: Create, save, edit, and share documents using Office Web Apps.

WORD

SLO 12.1

Customizing Word 2013

In this book, you have used many Word features to customize a variety of documents. There is another set of customization options that doesn't just affect single documents or templates but that alters Word settings globally. Once implemented, these options apply to all the documents you create and edit in Word. You can customize these Word settings in the ***Word Options dialog box***, which you open from the *Backstage* view.

Word Options

In the *Word Options* dialog box, the settings are grouped into different option categories. Within each of these categories, you can change many individual settings. In some of the areas, you can open a dialog box to see additional customization settings. The following list includes the different categories in the *Word Options* dialog box. Each category is discussed further in the sections that follow.

- *General*
- *Display*
- *Proofing*
- *Save*
- *Language*
- *Advanced*
- *Customize Ribbon*
- *Quick Access Toolbar*
- *Add-Ins*
- *Trust Center*

HOW TO: Customize Word Options

1. Click the **File** tab to open the *Backstage* view.
2. Click the **Options** button on the left to open the *Word Options* dialog box (Figure 12-1).
3. Click the options category on the left to display the available customization options on the right.
4. Change your options using check boxes, text boxes, drop-down lists, or buttons.
   - When you click a button, a dialog box with additional option settings opens.
5. Click **OK** to close the *Word Options* dialog box and apply the settings.

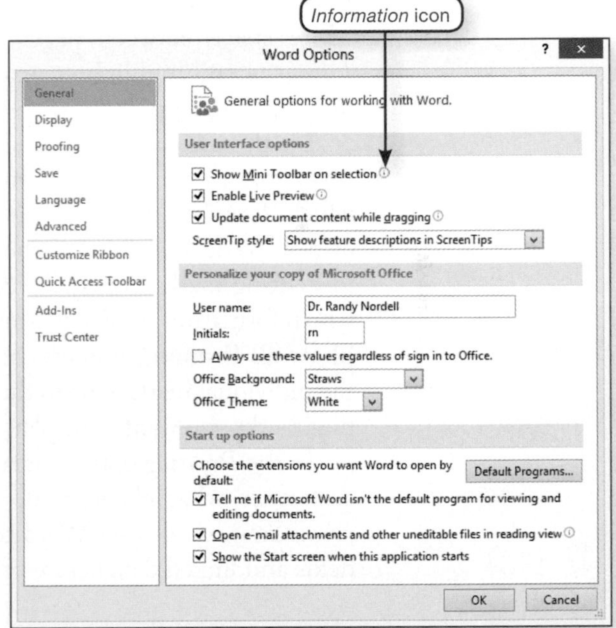

12-1 ***Word Options*** **dialog box**

General

The *General* category includes the following areas: *User Interface options*, *Personalize your copy of Microsoft Office*, and *Start up options* (see Figure 12-1).

In the *User Interface options* area, you can show/hide the mini toolbar display, enable/disable live preview, and turn on/off document content while dragging. You can also customize the ScreenTip style.

> **MORE INFO**
>
> Put your pointer on the *Information* icon at the end of a selection to display information about that selection.

In the *Personalize your copy of Microsoft Office* area, you can change your user name and initials, make it so your Word settings are imposed for all users on the current computer, and change the Office background.

In the *Start up options* area, you can set the default program, choose how email attachments are displayed, and determine whether or not the *Start* screen displays when Word opens. The *Start* screen displays your recent documents and Word templates.

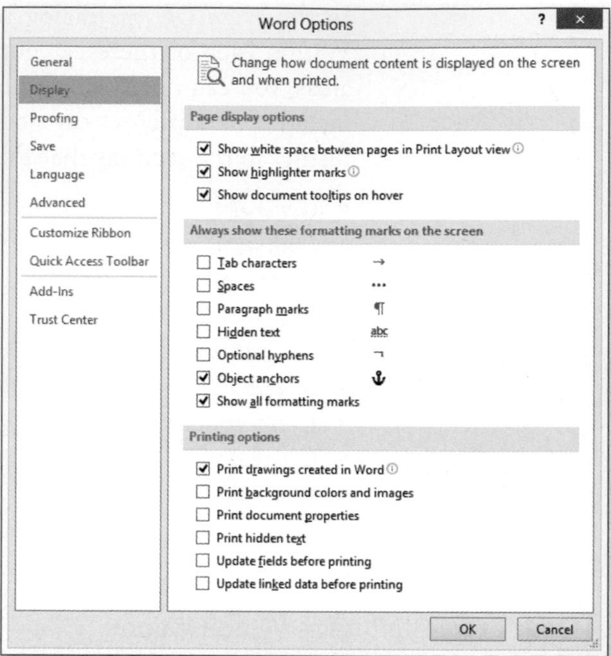

12-2 *Display* options in the *Word Options* dialog box

Display

In the *Display* options category, you can change how document content is displayed on the screen and when it is printed (Figure 12-2). In the *Page display options* area, you can show/hide white space between pages in *Print Layout* view, highlighter marks, and document tooltips.

In the *Always show these formatting marks on the screen* area, you can set which formatting marks you want to display. By default, object anchors and all formatting marks display. To customize which formatting marks display, deselect **Show all formatting marks** and check the individual marks next to the formatting marks you want to display.

In the *Printing* options area, you can customize what elements do or don't print. You can also set Word to update fields and linked data before printing.

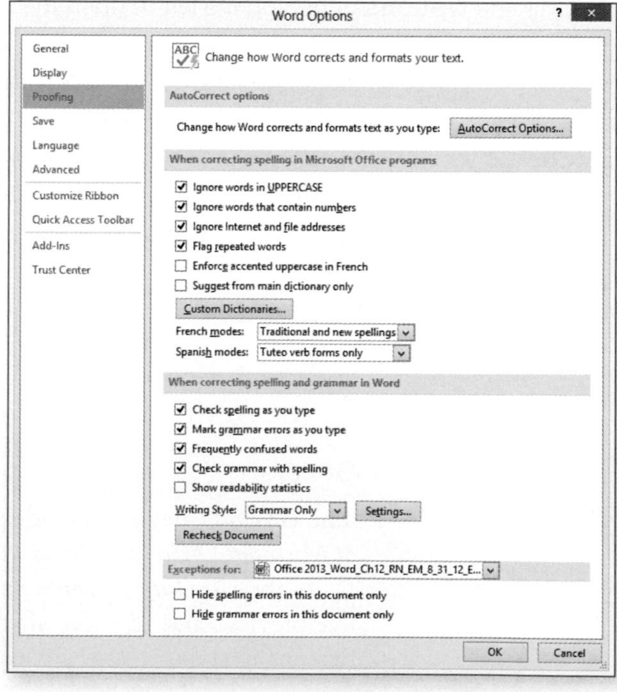

12-3 *Proofing* options in the *Word Options* dialog box

Proofing

In the *Proofing* category of the Word options dialog box, you can change how Word corrects and formats your text (Figure 12-3). Click the **AutoCorrect options** button to open the *AutoCorrect* dialog box and change *AutoCorrect*, *Math AutoCorrect*, *AutoFormat As You Type*, *AutoFormat*, and *Actions*.

In the *When correcting spelling in Microsoft Office programs* area, Word is by default set to ignore words in uppercase, words that contain numbers, and Internet and file addresses. Click the **Custom Dictionaries** button to open the *Custom Dictionaries* and add, edit, or delete words from the custom dictionary.

In the *When correcting spelling and grammar in Word* area, you can control how and when the spelling and grammar check functions. You can also turn on ***readability statistics*** to display statistics about your document when you finish checking spelling and grammar.

By default, Word checks spelling and grammar, but not style. You can have Word check grammar and style. Click the **Settings** button to customize grammar and style settings.

In the *Exceptions for* area, you can hide spelling and grammatical errors in a selected document or in all new Word documents (which is probably not a good idea since you want to be able to see your errors so you can correct them).

> **MORE INFO**
>
> Many changes you make in the *Proofing* category are applied in all Office applications and files.

Save

In the *Save* category, you can control how and where documents are saved (Figure 12-4). In the *Save documents* area, you can set the default file format to save documents, establish the frequency that *AutoRecover* saves your open documents, and determine where these files are stored. By default, when you press **Ctrl+O** or **Ctrl+S** to open or save a document, the *Backstage* view is displayed, but you can turn this off. You also set the default save location for documents and templates. Click the **Browse** button to select a different default save location, such as *SkyDrive*.

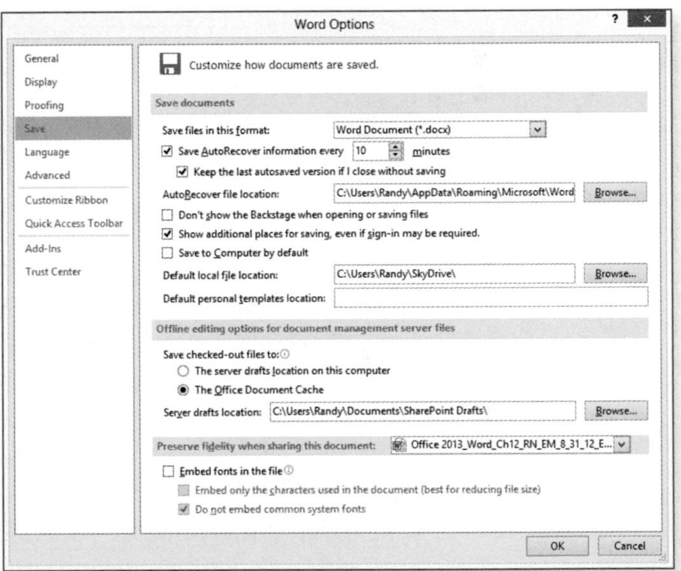

12-4 ***Save*** **options in the** ***Word Options*** **dialog box**

The *Offline editing options for document management server files* area pertains to documents shared in Microsoft SharePoint, which is a server that facilitates storage and sharing of files. *Preserve fidelity when sharing this document* controls how fonts are stored when sharing a document between users who may not all have the same fonts installed on their computers. Neither of these customization options is common.

Language

The *Language* category controls the language preferences in Word and the other Office programs you use (Figure 12-5). In the *Choose Editing Languages* area, you can select the language to use for spelling, grammar, dictionaries, and sorting. You can add a new language, set a language as the default, or remove a language.

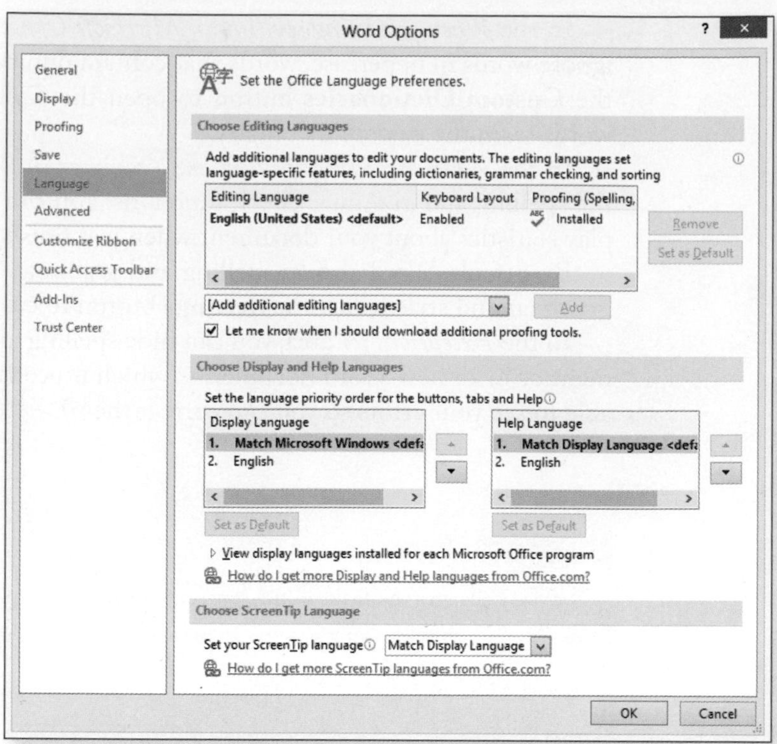

12-5 ***Language*** **options in the** ***Word Options*** **dialog box**

In the *Choose Display and Help Languages* area, you can set the language for display tabs, buttons, and *Help*. In the *Choose ScreenTip Language* area, you can change the language of the ScreenTips.

> **MORE INFO**
>
> The language settings in Office are determined by the default language you selected when you installed Windows.

Advanced

The *Advanced* category provides you with a variety of customization options (Figure 12-6). The following is a list of the different options in the *Advanced* category. Scroll through each of these areas to familiarize yourself with the different customization options available.

- *Editing options*
- *Cut, copy, and paste*
- *Image Size and Quality*
- *Chart*
- *Show document control*
- *Display*
- *Print*

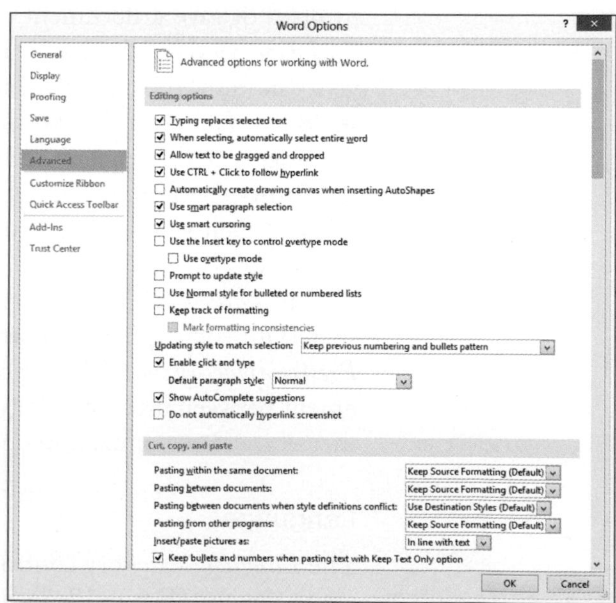

12-6 ***Advanced*** **options in the** ***Word Options*** **dialog box**

- *When printing this document*
- *Save*
- *Preserve fidelity when sharing this document*
- *General*
- *Layout options*
- *Compatibility options*

MORE INFO

The *Customize Ribbon* and *Quick Access Toolbar* options are covered later in this section.

Add-Ins

Add-ins are programs that add functionality to your Office programs. Some programs you install on your computer are recognized by Office as add-in programs such as Google Desktop or Snag-It.

In the *Add-Ins* category in the *Word Options* dialog box, you can view the add-in programs that interact with Office (Figure 12-7). You can manage add-ins and make them active or inactive. Click the **Manage** drop-down list to select a category and click **Go**. A dialog box opens and lets you turn on or off add-ins.

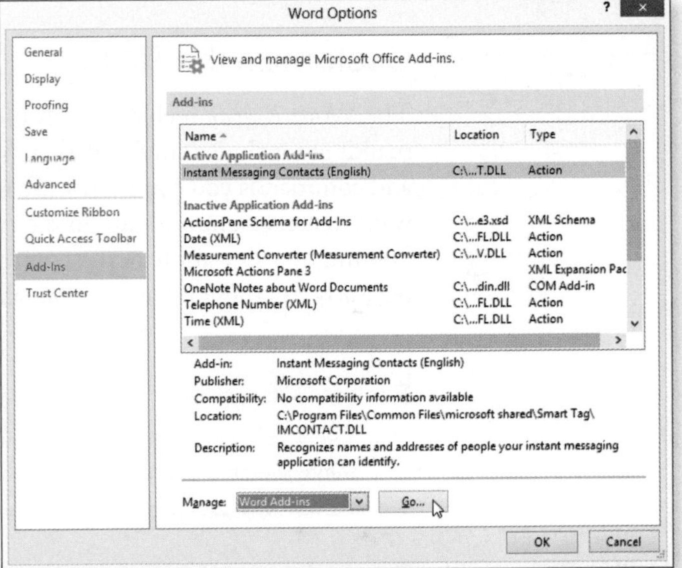

12-7 *Add-In* options in the *Word Options* dialog box

Trust Center

The *Trust Center* helps keep your documents safe and prevents your documents and computer from becoming infected with viruses. There are many different areas that you can customize in the *Trust Center* dialog box. It is generally recommended that you keep the default settings in the *Trust Center* to keep your documents and computer safe.

MORE INFO

For more information on macros and the *Trust Center*, see *SLO 10.3: Creating and Running Macros*.

HOW TO: Customize Trust Center Settings

1. Click the **File** tab to open the *Backstage* view.
2. Click the **Options** button on the left to open the *Word Options* dialog box.
3. Click the **Trust Center** button on the right.

4. Click the **Trust Center Settings** button to open the *Trust Center* dialog box (Figure 12-8).
5. Click the different categories on the left to view the available options. Make changes only as needed.
6. Click **OK** to close the *Trust Center* dialog box.
7. Click **OK** to close the *Word Options* dialog box.

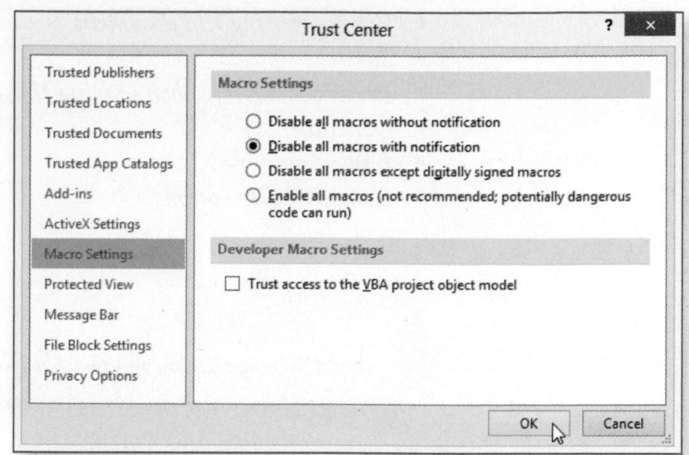

12-8 *Trust Center* dialog box

Customize the Ribbon

The Word *Ribbon* includes many of the common commands you use, but not all available commands are included on the *Ribbon*. You can customize the *Ribbon* to add a new group to a tab or add commands you commonly use that are not included on the *Ribbon*. For example, you might want to create a new group on the *Home* tab that includes a button to open the *Tabs* dialog box. You might also want to add a button to add a comment and turn on *Track Changes* because you regularly use these items. You can also create a custom tab with groups and commands.

> **MORE INFO**
>
> You can add commands to custom groups, but you cannot add new commands to, or remove existing commands from, existing groups.

HOW TO: Add a Tab, Group, and Commands to the Ribbon

1. Right-click anywhere on the **Ribbon** and select **Customize the Ribbon** from the context menu. The *Word Options* dialog box opens with *Customize Ribbon* displayed (Figure 12-9).
   - You can also click the **File** tab to open the *Backstage* view, click the **Options** button to open the *Word Options* dialog box, and select **Customize Ribbon**.
   - The left side lists the different commands and groups available, and the right side lists the existing tabs and groups displayed on the *Ribbon*.
   - The drop-down lists at the top of each of the lists provide you with other commands and tabs to display in these lists.

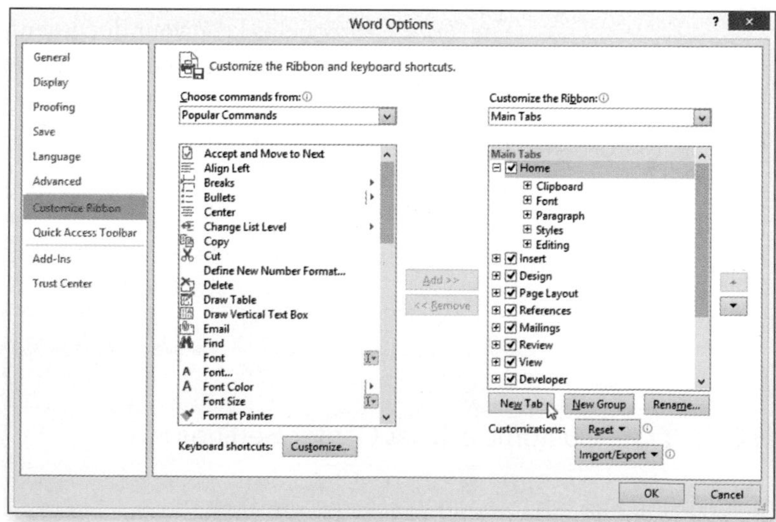

12-9 ***Customize Ribbon*** **area of the** ***Word Options*** **dialog box**

2. On the right, click the tab where you want to insert a new tab after.
3. Click the **New Tab** button. A new custom tab and group are inserted below the selected tab.

4. Select the new tab and click **Rename** to open the *Rename* dialog box (Figure 12-10).
5. Type the name of the new tab and click **OK** to close the *Rename* dialog box.
6. Select the new group and click **Rename** to open the *Rename* dialog box (Figure 12-11).
7. Select a symbol (optional), type the new group name in the *Display name* area, and click **OK** to close the *Rename* dialog box.

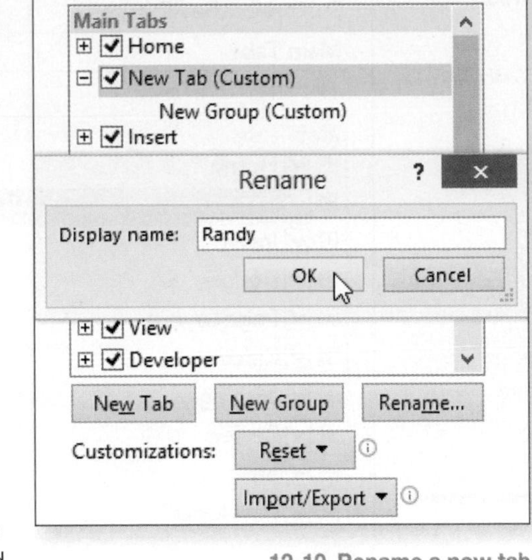

12-10 Rename a new tab

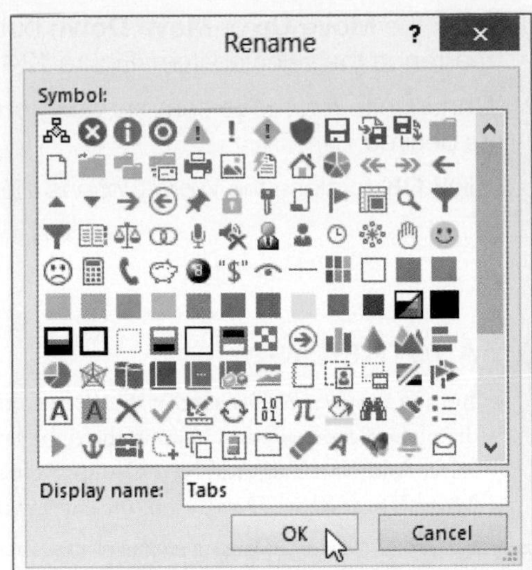

12-11 Rename a new group

8. On the right, select the group where you want to add a command.
   - Click the plus or minus sign by a tab or group to expand or collapse it.
9. Click the **Choose commands from** drop-down list on the left side and select **All Commands** to display all the available commands.
10. Select the command to add to the group and click the **Add** button between the two lists to add the command to the group (Figure 12-12).

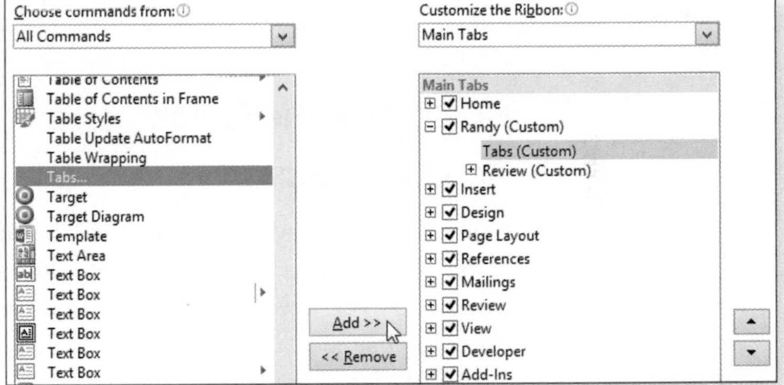

12-12 Add a command to a custom group

11. Continue to add and rename groups and add commands to groups as desired.
12. Click **OK** to close the *Word Options* dialog box.
    - The new tab and group display on the *Ribbon* (Figure 12-13).

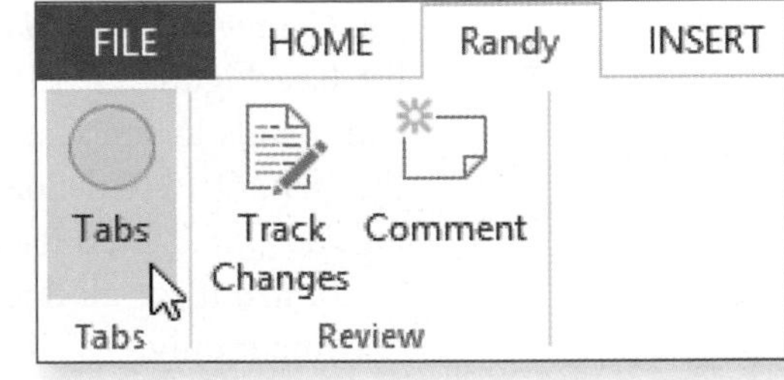

12-13 Custom tab, group, and commands on the *Ribbon*

> **MORE INFO**
>
> You can also rearrange groups on tabs and rearrange tabs on the *Ribbon*. You cannot rearrange existing commands within existing groups, but you can rearrange commands in custom groups.

HOW TO: Rearrange Tabs, Groups, and Commands on the Ribbon

1. Right-click anywhere on the **Ribbon** and select **Customize the Ribbon** from the context menu. The *Word Options* dialog box opens with *Customize Ribbon* displayed.
2. Select the command, group, or tab you want to rearrange.

3. Click the **Move Up** or **Move Down** button to rearrange the selected item (Figure 12-14).
4. Continue to rearrange commands, groups, and tabs as desired.
5. Click **OK** to close the *Word Options* dialog box.

> **ANOTHER WAY**
>
> In the *Customize Ribbon* area of the *Word Options* dialog box, right-click an item on the right side and select **Add New Tab, Add New Group, Rename, Move Up**, or **Move Down** from the context menu.

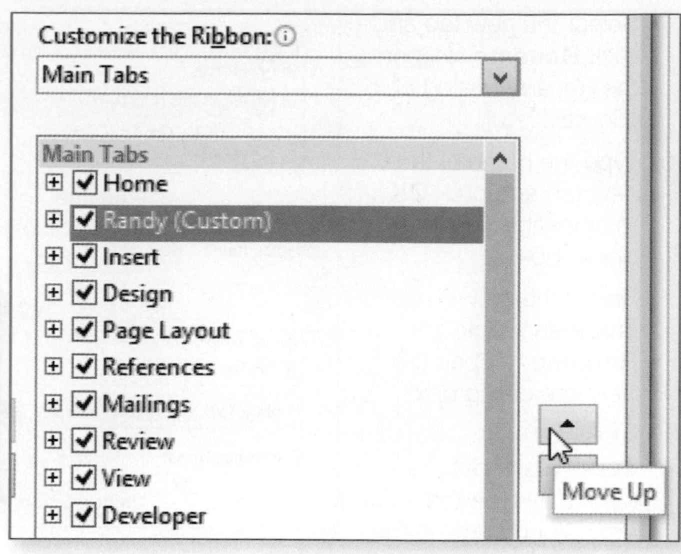

12-14 Rearrange a tab on the *Ribbon*

Customize the Quick Access Toolbar

Similarly to the way you added macro buttons to the *Quick Access* toolbar, you can also add commands you frequently use to the *Quick Access* toolbar so you can quickly access them. The *Save*, *Undo*, and *Redo* commands are by default displayed on the *Quick Access* toolbar. You can add commonly used commands from the *Customize Quick Access Toolbar* drop-down list (see Figure 12-15) or you can add other commands in the *Quick Access Toolbar* area in the *Word Options* dialog box. When customizing the *Quick Access* toolbar, you can choose to customize it for all documents or the current document only.

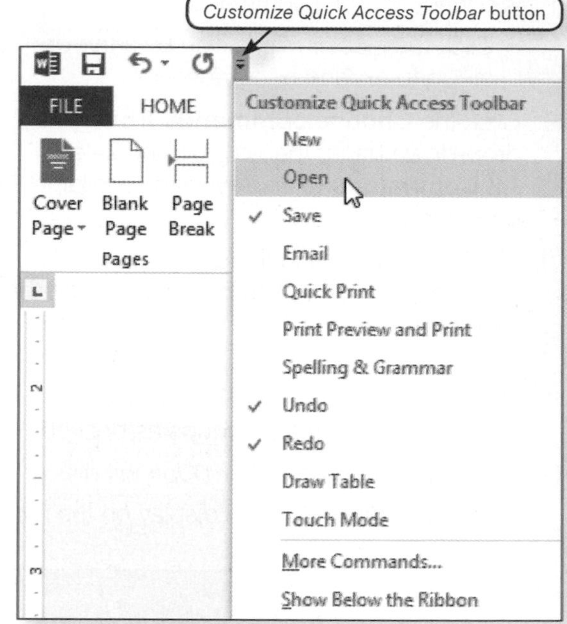

12-15 Add a command to the *Quick Access* toolbar

HOW TO: Customize the Quick Access Toolbar

1. Click the **Customize Quick Access Toolbar** drop-down list on the right edge of the *Quick Access* toolbar (Figure 12-15).
2. Select a command to add to the *Quick Access* toolbar. The command is placed on the *Quick Access* toolbar.
   - Items on the *Customize Quick Access Toolbar* drop-down list with a check mark are commands that are displayed on the *Quick Access* toolbar.
3. To add a command that is not listed on the *Customize Quick Access Toolbar*, click the **Customize Quick Access Toolbar** drop-down list and select **More Commands**. The *Word Options* dialog box opens with the *Quick Access Toolbar* area displayed (Figure 12-16).

4. Click the **Customize Quick Access Toolbar** drop-down list on the right and select **For all documents** or the current document.
   - If you select *For all documents*, the change is made to the *Quick Access* toolbar for all documents you open in Word.
   - If you select the current document, the change is made to the *Quick Access* toolbar in that document only.
5. On the left, select the command you want to add.
   - If you can't find the command you're looking for, click the **Choose commands from** drop-down list and select **All Commands**.
6. Click the **Add** button.
7. Add other commands as desired.
8. To rearrange commands on the *Quick Access* toolbar, select the command to move and click the **Move Up** or **Move Down** button.
9. Click **OK** to close the *Word Options* dialog box.

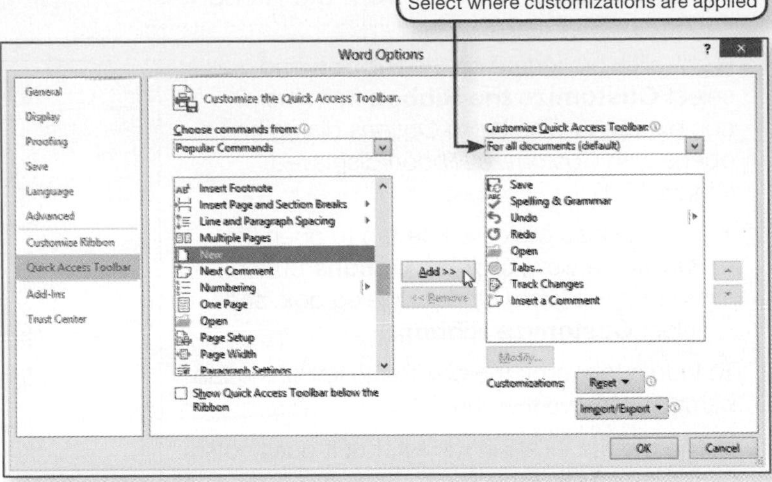

12-16 Customize the *Quick Access* toolbar

> **MORE INFO**
>
> To display the *Quick Access* toolbar below the *Ribbon*, click the **Customize Quick Access Toolbar** drop-down list and select **Show Below the Ribbon**.

Reset the Ribbon and the Quick Access Toolbar

After you customize your *Ribbon* and your *Quick Access* toolbar, you may want to remove commands, groups, or tabs. There are two different ways to get your *Ribbon* and your *Quick Access* toolbar back to their original settings:

- ***Remove:*** You can remove commands from the *Quick Access* toolbar or custom groups, and you can remove custom tabs and groups from the *Ribbon*.
- ***Reset:*** You can reset your *Ribbon* and your *Quick Access* toolbar to their original settings.

HOW TO: Remove Commands from the Quick Access Toolbar

1. Right-click the item you want to remove in the *Quick Access* toolbar.
2. Select **Remove from Quick Access Toolbar** from the context menu.
   - You can also remove commands from the *Quick Access* toolbar in the *Quick Access Toolbar* area of the *Word Options* dialog box by selecting the command you want to remove and clicking the **Remove** button.

To remove custom tabs, groups, or commands from the *Ribbon*, use the *Customize Ribbon* area of the *Word Options* dialog box. You cannot remove existing default tabs, but you can deselect one or more in the *Customize the Ribbon* area so they are hidden and do not display on the *Ribbon*. Also, you cannot delete individual commands from an existing default group.

HOW TO: Remove Items from the Ribbon

1. Right-click anywhere on the **Ribbon** and select **Customize the Ribbon** from the context menu. The *Word Options* dialog box opens with *Customize Ribbon* displayed (Figure 12-17).
   - You can also click the **File** tab to open the *Backstage* view, click the **Options** button to open the *Word Options* dialog box, and select **Customize Ribbon**.
2. To hide a tab, click the box to the left of the tab name to remove the check.
   - The tab still exists in the list, but it does not display on the *Ribbon*.
3. On the right, select the custom tab, group, or command you want to remove from the *Ribbon*.
   - Click the plus or minus sign to the left of a tab or group to expand or collapse the tab and group.
4. Click the **Remove** button.
   - You can also right-click on a tab or group and select **Remove** from the context menu.
5. Click **OK** to close the *Word Options* dialog box.

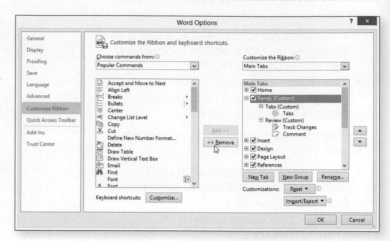

12-17 Remove items from the *Ribbon*

You can also reset the *Ribbon* or the *Quick Access* toolbar to its original settings. When you do this, you reset both the *Quick Access* toolbar and the *Ribbon* in the *Word Options* dialog box. When resetting the *Ribbon*, you can reset a specific tab or all *Ribbon* customizations.

HOW TO: Reset the Ribbon or the Quick Access Toolbar

1. Open the *Word Options* dialog box and select either **Customize Ribbon** or **Quick Access Toolbar**.
2. If you are resetting a specific tab, select the tab to reset.
3. At the bottom of the right list, click the **Reset** button.
4. Select from the available options (Figures 12-18 and 12-19).

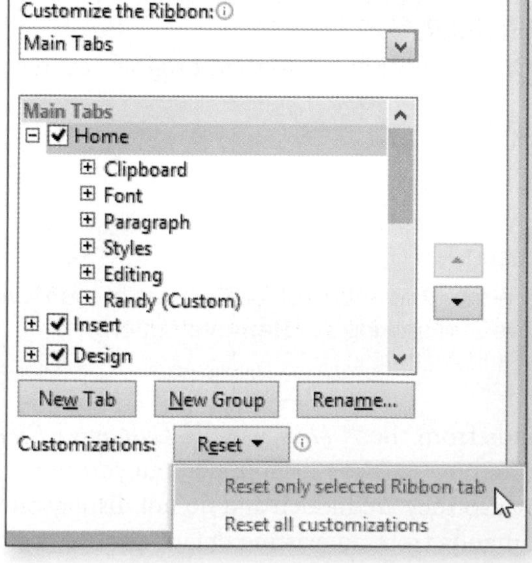

12-18 Reset the *Ribbon*

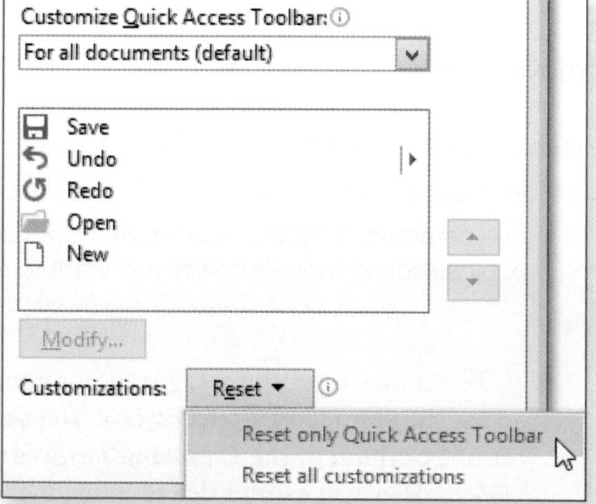

12-19 Reset the *Quick Access* toolbar

- If you are resetting the *Ribbon*, you can **Reset only selected Ribbon tab** or **Reset all customizations**.
- If you are resetting the *Quick Access* toolbar, you can **Reset only Quick Access Toolbar** or **Reset all customizations**.
- If you select **Reset all customizations** for either the *Ribbon* or *Quick Access* toolbar, Word resets both the *Ribbon* and the *Quick Access* toolbar.

5. Depending on your selection, a dialog box may open asking you to confirm that you want to reset customizations (Figure 12-20). Click **Yes** to delete the customization.

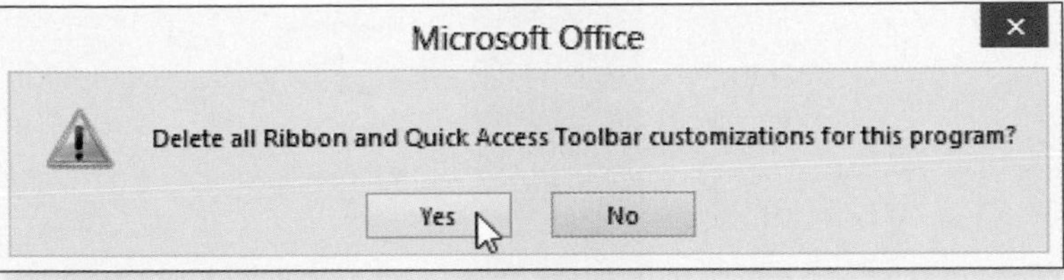

12-20 Confirm to delete all customizations

6. Click **OK** to close the *Word Options* dialog box.

SLO 12.2

Customizing Office Account Options

When you purchase and install Office 2013, you set up your account options. For example, you establish your Microsoft user name and password and choose the Office background. If you upgrade from Office 2010 to Office 2013, many of your settings are automatically transferred for you. You can view and customize your Office account settings in the *Backstage* view.

Microsoft Account Information

One of the features that is new in Office 2013 is the portability of your documents and account settings. Your Office settings and files can travel with you, which means that you are not restricted to using just a single computer. For example, you can now log in to Office 2013 on a public computer at a computer lab on your college campus or at a public library or on a friend's computer, and your Office 2013 settings are available on that computer.

When you sign in to your computer using Windows 8, you can log in with a Microsoft user name (Live, Hotmail, MSN, Messenger, or other Microsoft service account) and password. Microsoft Office uses this information to transfer your Office 2013 settings to the computer you are using. Your account settings display in the upper right corner of the Word window.

> **MORE INFO**
>
> If you are using an older version of Windows and Office 2013, you are prompted to sign in to your Microsoft account when you open an Office 2013 application or file.

Your Microsoft account not only signs you in to Windows and Office but also signs you in to other free Microsoft online services, such as ***SkyDrive***, ***SkyDrive groups***, and ***Office Web Apps***. If you don't have a Microsoft account, you can create a free account at www.live.com. For more info on these online Microsoft services, see *SLO 12-3: Using SkyDrive*, *SLO 12.4: Using SkyDrive Groups*, and *SLO 12.5: Using Office Web Apps*.

HOW TO: Use Your Microsoft Account in Office

1. Click your name or the log on area in the upper right corner of the Word window (Figure 12-21).
2. Click the **Account settings** link to open the *Account* area on the *Backstage* view (Figure 12-22).
   - You can also click the **File** tab and select **Account** on the left.
   - Your account information is displayed in this area.

12-21 Microsoft account information

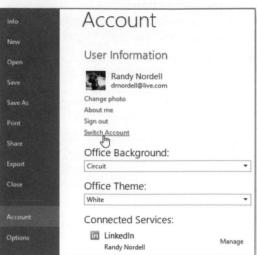

12-22 Office account information and settings

3. If you are not logged in to Office 2013, click the **Switch Account** link to switch accounts. The *Sign In* dialog box opens.
4. Type your Microsoft account email address and click **Sign in**. Another *Sign in* dialog box opens (Figure 12-23).
5. Type your password and click **Sign in**.
   - If you don't have a Microsoft account, click the **Sign up now** link to take you to a web page where you create a free Microsoft account.
   - You also use your Microsoft account to log in to *SkyDrive* where you can create store and share files, use Office Web Apps, and create *SkyDrive* groups.
6. Click the **Back** arrow to return to Word.

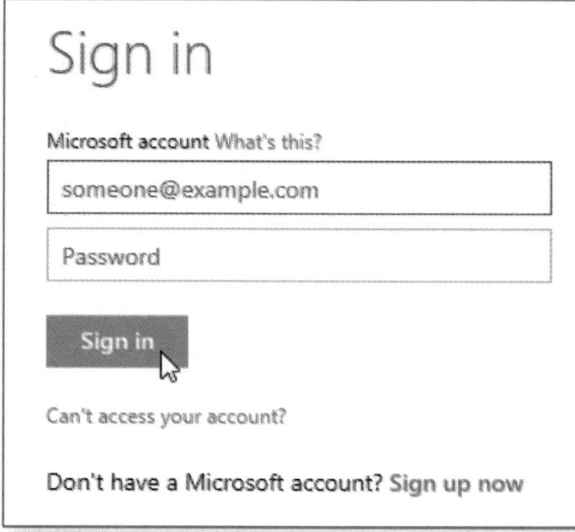

12-23 Sign in to Office using a Microsoft account

> **MORE INFO**
>
> If you are using a public computer, be sure to click the **Sign out** link in the *Account* area on the *Backstage* view to log out of your Office account.

Office Background and Theme

You can change the Office background and theme in the *General* category in the *Word Options* dialog box, and you can also change the background in the *Account* area on the *Backstage* view. Click the **Office Background** or Office Theme drop-down list and select a background or theme (Figure 12-24). The background displays a graphic pattern in the upper right corner of the Word window. The theme controls the colors of the working *Ribbon*, the *Backstage* view, and dialog boxes. The background and theme you select apply to all Office applications you use.

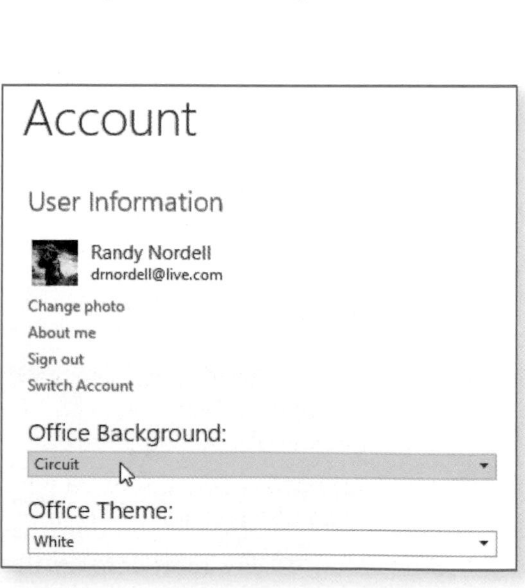

12-24 Change *Office Background* or *Office Theme*

Connected Services

Office 2013 has added many features to allow you to connect to online services. In the *Account* area on the *Backstage* view, add online services you regularly use by clicking the **Add a service** drop-down list and selecting a service (Figure 12-25). When you add a service, you are usually prompted to enter your user name and password to connect to the online service. The services you are currently connected to are listed in the ***Connected Service*** area.

All of the connected services in your account travel with you when you log in to Office on another computer. The following services are available in the different service categories listed:

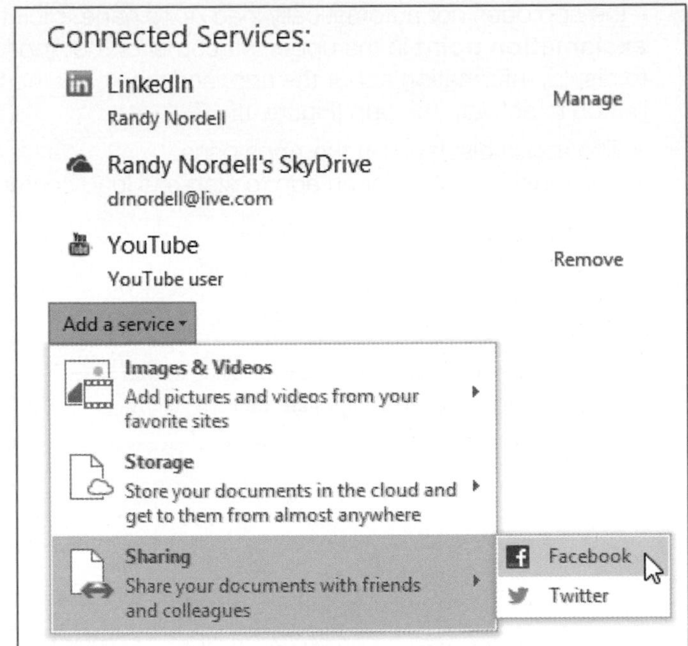

12-25 Add an online service to your Office account

- ***Images & Video:*** Facebook for Office, Flickr, and YouTube
- ***Storage:*** Office365 SharePoint and *SkyDrive*
- ***Sharing:*** Facebook and LinkedIn

Add and Manage Apps for Office

Another feature new to Office 2013 is the ability to add ***apps*** (applications) to your Office 2013 program. Just like the apps on your smart phone, apps for Office are programs that add functionality to your Office software. For example, you can add a dictionary, encyclopedia, a news feed, or maps.

HOW TO: Add Apps to Office

1. Click the top half of the **Apps for Office** button [*Insert* tab, *Apps* group] to open the *Apps for Office* dialog box (Figure 12-26).
   - The *Apps for Office* button is a split button. Click the bottom half of the button to see your recently used apps or select See All to open the *Apps for Office* dialog box.
   - Click **My Apps** to display Office apps you previously installed.
   - Click **Featured Apps** to display available apps. Use the search text box to type keywords and search for matching apps.
2. Select an app and click the **Add** button to install an app. The *Apps* pane opens on the right.
   - Depending on the app you select, you may be taken to a web site to add the app.

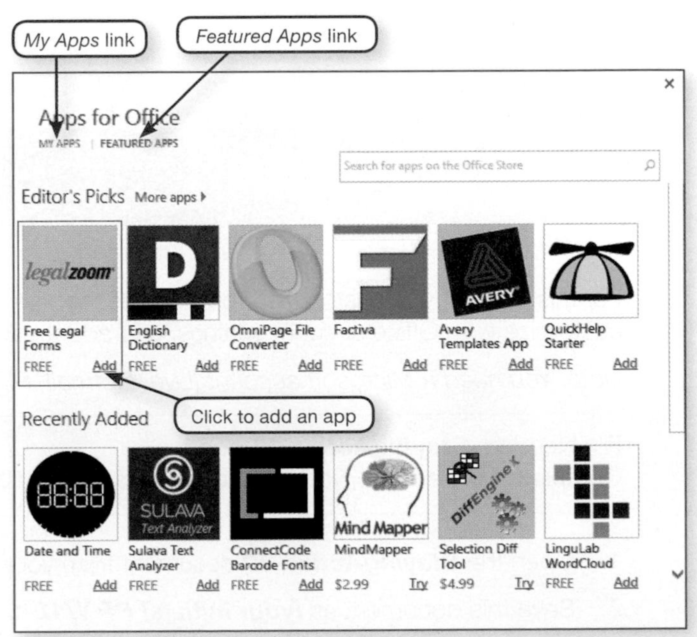

12-26 *Apps for Office* dialog box

3. If the app does not automatically load *Apps* pane, click the **exclamation point** in the upper left corner of the *Apps* pane to display information about the app, and then click the **Start** button to activate the app (Figure 12-27).
   - The app is displayed in the *Apps* pane.
   - You must be online for an app to start and load content.

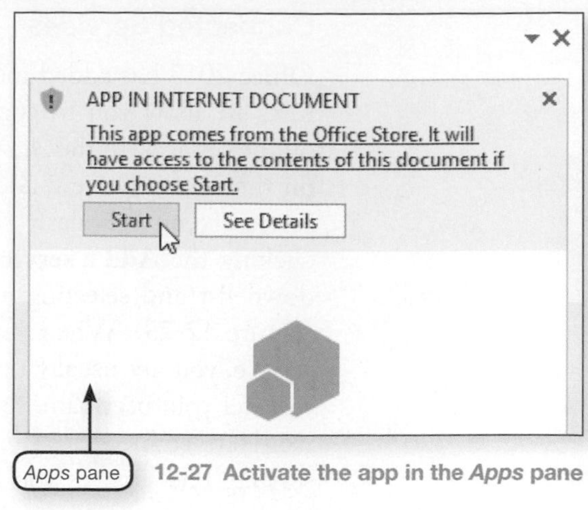

12-27 Activate the app in the *Apps* pane

> **MORE INFO**
>
> Regularly check the *Apps for Office* dialog box for new and featured apps. New apps are added regularly.

After installing apps in Office, you can manage your apps by clicking the **Manage My Apps** link in the *My Apps* area in *Apps for Office* dialog box. You are taken to *My Apps for Office and SharePoint* web page where you can view your apps, hide apps, and search for other apps to install (Figure 12-28).

12-28 Manage your apps online

PAUSE & PRACTICE: WORD 12-1

For this project, you customize Word options, add items to the *Ribbon* and the *Quick Access* toolbar, customize your Office account settings, and add an app.

Note: You need a Microsoft account (Live, Hotmail, MSN) to complete this project.

File Needed: ***StayingActive-12.docx***
Completed Project File Name: ***[your initials] PP W12-1.docx***

1. Open the ***StayingActive-12*** document from your student data files.
2. Save this document as ***[your initials] PP W12-1***.

3. Log in to Office using your Microsoft account. Skip this step if you are already logged in with your Microsoft account.
   a. In the upper right corner of the Word window, log in to Office using your Microsoft account.
   b. If you don't have a Microsoft account, go to www.live.com and follow the instructions to create a free Microsoft account.
4. Customize Word options.
   a. Click the **File** tab to open the *Backstage* view and select **Options** to open the *Word Options* dialog box.
   b. Select **General** on the left and type your name and initials in the *User name* and *Initials* area if they are not already there.
   c. Uncheck the **Show the Start screen when this application starts** box.
   d. Select **Display** on the left and check the **Update fields before printing** and **Update linked data before printing** boxes in the *Printing options* area.
   e. Select **Save** on the left and check the **Don't show the Backstage when opening or saving files** box in the *Save documents* area.
   f. Select **Advanced** on the left and check the **Show bookmarks** box in the *Show document content* area if it is not already checked.
   g. Click **OK** to close the *Word Options* dialog box and apply the changes.
5. Add a tab, a group, and commands to the *Ribbon*.
   a. Right-click anywhere on the **Ribbon** and select **Customize the Ribbon** from the context menu to open the *Word Options* dialog box with the *Customize Ribbon* area displayed.
   b. On the right, click the **Home** tab (under *Main Tabs*) and click the **New Tab** button. A new tab and group are inserted below the *Home* tab.
   c. Select **New Tab (Custom)** and click the **Rename** button to open the *Rename* dialog box.
   d. Type your first name in all caps and click **OK** to close the *Rename* dialog box.
   e. Select **New Group (Custom)** and click the **Rename** button to open the *Rename* dialog box (Figure 12-29).
   f. Select the smiley face symbol, type Common Commands as the group name in the *Display name* area, and click **OK** to close the *Rename* dialog box.
   g. On the right, select the **Common Commands** group.
   h. Click the **Choose commands from** drop-down list on the left side and select **All Commands** to display all the available commands in the list on the left.
   i. Scroll down and select the **Borders and Shading** command (the first one listed) and click the **Add** button between the two lists to add the command to the group (Figure 12-30).

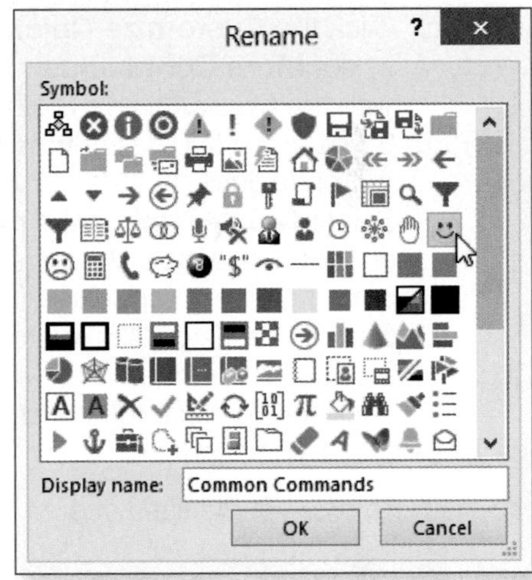

12-29 Rename new custom group

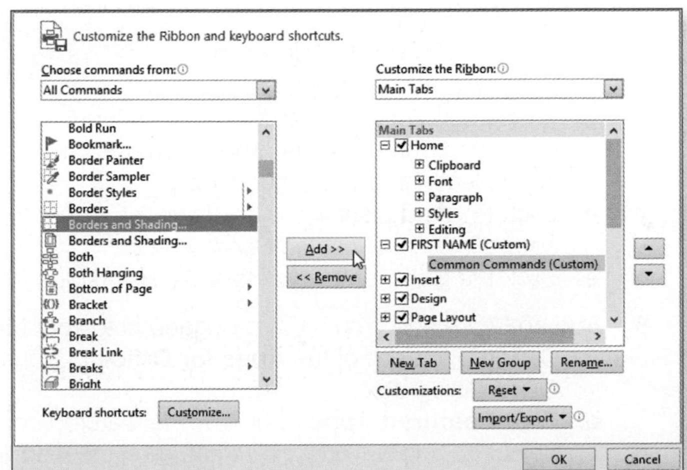

12-30 Add command to custom group

j. Select and add the **Tabs** and **Custom Margins** commands to the *Common Commands* group.
k. Click **OK** to close the *Word Options* dialog box.
l. Click the **[your first name]** tab on the *Ribbon* (Figure 12-31).

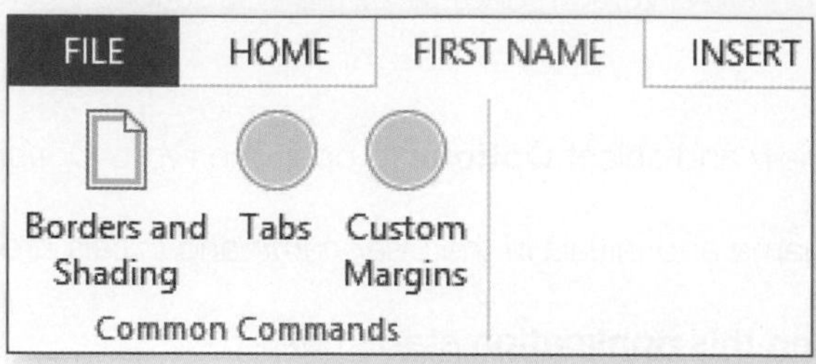

12-31 New tab and group

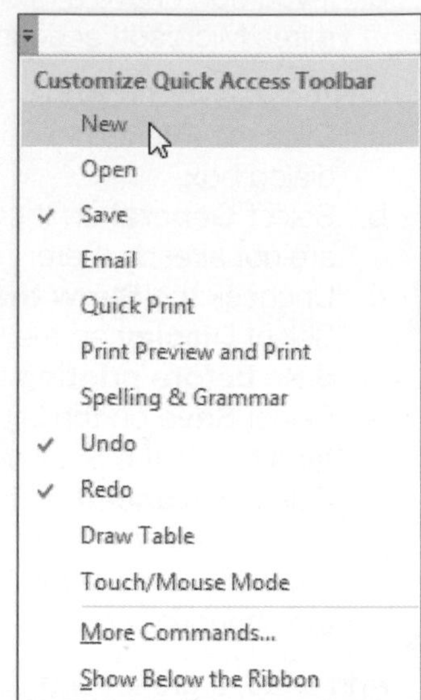

12-32 Add a command to the *Quick Access* toolbar

6. Add commands to the *Quick Access* toolbar.
   a. Click the **Customize Quick Access Toolbar** drop-down list and select **New** (Figure 12-32).
   b. Add **Open** and **Quick Print** to the *Quick Access* toolbar from the *Customize Quick Access Toolbar* drop-down list.
   c. Click the **Customize Quick Access Toolbar** drop-down list and select **More Commands** to open the *Word Options* dialog box with the *Quick Access Toolbar* area displayed.
   d. Scroll down and select **Insert a Comment** and click the **Add** button (Figure 12-33).
   e. Select **Quick Print** on the right and use the **Move Up** button to rearrange it so it appears after *Save* in the *Quick Access* toolbar list of commands.
   f. Click **OK** to close the *Word Options* dialog box.

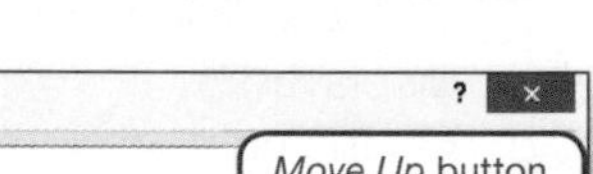

12-33 Add a command to the *Quick Access* toolbar

7. Customize your Office account settings.
   a. Click the **File** tab and select **Account** to display your account information on the *Backstage* view.
   b. Click the **Office Background** drop-down list and select a background of your choice.
   c. Click the **Office Theme** drop-down list and select a theme of your choice.
   d. Click the **Add** a service drop-down list, select **Images & Videos**, and click **YouTube**. YouTube is added in the *Connected Services* area.
   e. Click the **Back** button to close the *Backstage* view.
8. Add an Office app. You must be logged in to your Microsoft account to add an app.
   a. Click the top half of the **Apps for Office** button [*Insert* tab, *Apps* group] to open the *Apps for Office* dialog box.
   b. Click **Featured Apps** to display the featured apps.
   c. Select an app of your choice and click the **Add** link. The *Apps* pane opens on the right.

d. If the app does not automatically load in the *Apps* pane, click the **exclamation point** in the upper left corner of the *Apps* pane to display information about the app, and then click the **Start** button to activate the app (Figure 12-34).
e. Close the *Apps* pane.

9. Save and close the document (Figure 12-35).

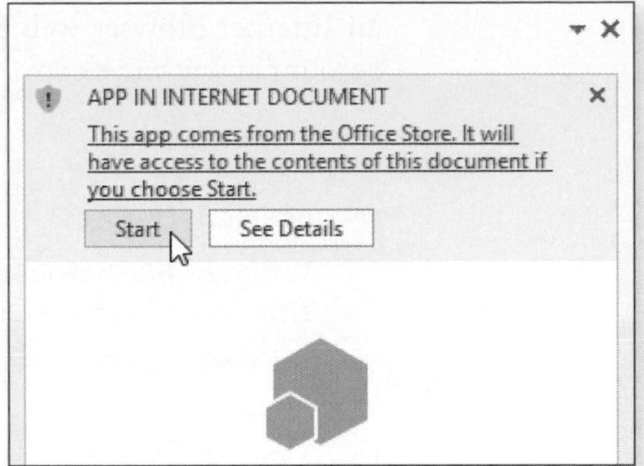

12-34 *Apps* pane

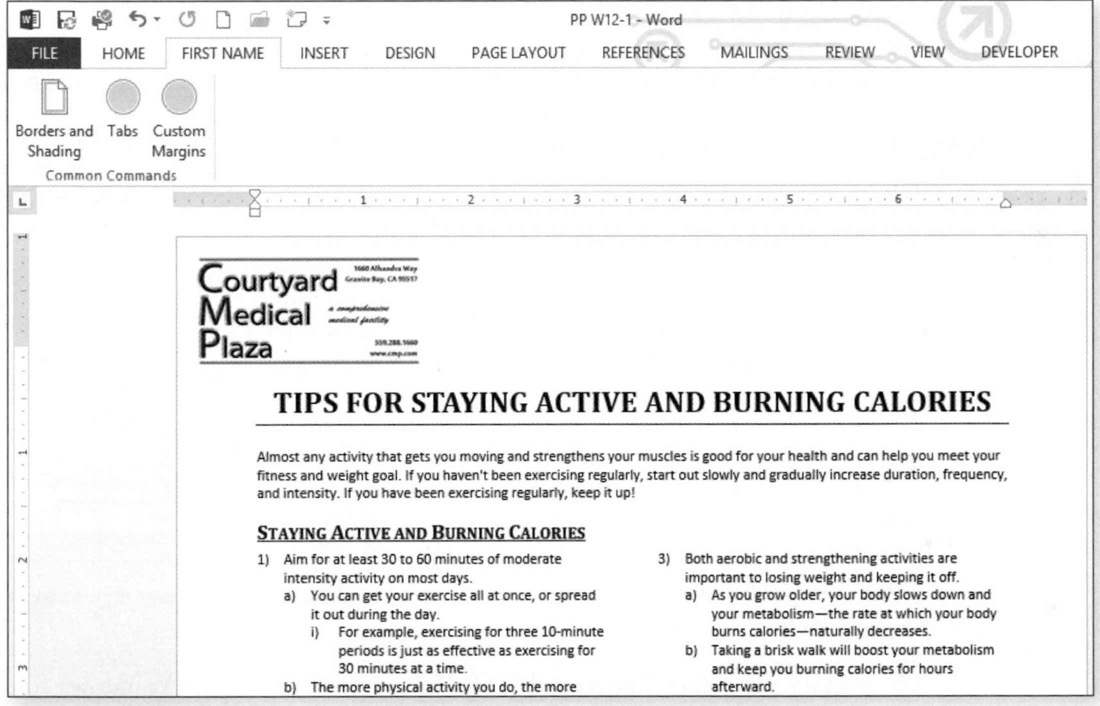

12-35 PP W12-1 completed (page 1 and customized *Ribbon* and *Quick Access* toolbar displayed)

SLO 12.3

Using SkyDrive

Microsoft Office 2013 works in conjunction with ***Microsoft SkyDrive*** to provide access to your files from any computer. *SkyDrive* is a "cloud" storage area where you can store files in an online location and access them from any computer. Cloud storage means you don't have to be tied to one computer and you don't have to take your files with you on a portable storage device.

When you have a Microsoft account (Live, Hotmail, MSN, Messenger, or other Microsoft service account), you also have a *SkyDrive* account. Your *SkyDrive* account is a private and secure online location. You can use *SkyDrive* to store files, create folders to organize stored files, share files with others, and create *SkyDrive* groups where you invite people to become members and store and share files. Using Windows 8, you can access your *SkyDrive* files from a Windows folder, or you can access *SkyDrive* online from any computer using an Internet browser web page. If you don't have a Microsoft account, you can create a free account at www.live.com.

> **MORE INFO**
>
> While *SkyDrive* is secure and does require a username and password to log in, no online accounts are 100% secure. Highly sensitive documents should not be stored online.

Use SkyDrive in a Windows Folder

With Windows 8, *SkyDrive* is one of your storage location folders, similar to your *Document* or *Pictures* folders (Figure 12-36). You can save, open, and edit your *SkyDrive* files from a Windows folder. Your ***SkyDrive folder*** looks and functions similarly to other Windows folders.

> **MORE INFO**
>
> If you are using Windows 7 or a previous version of Windows, you need to download and install the free ***SkyDrive desktop app for Windows*** on your computer. After you do this, the *SkyDrive* folder is available when you open Windows Explorer or a Windows folder. Use an Internet search engine to find, download, and install this program.

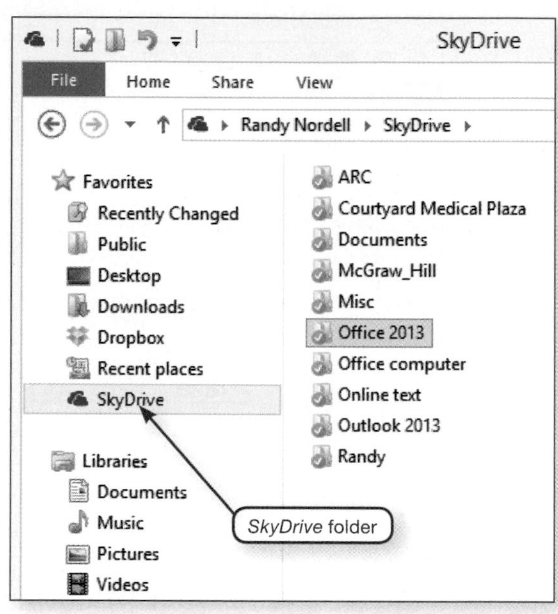

12-36 ***SkyDrive*** **folder displayed in a Windows Explorer folder**

The primary difference between the *SkyDrive* folder and other Windows folders is the physical location where the files are stored. If you save a document in your *Documents* folder, the file is stored on the hard drive on your computer, and you have access to this file only when you are working on your computer. When you save a document in your *SkyDrive* folder, the file is stored on the *SkyDrive* cloud, and you have access to the file from your computer *and* any other computer with Internet access.

> **MORE INFO**
>
> To access your *SkyDrive* folder from Windows, you must be logged in to your Microsoft account.

When you open the *Save As* or *Open* dialog box in Word, *SkyDrive* is one of the available folders. You can save, open, and edit documents from the *SkyDrive* folder. You can also create folders and rename, move, or delete files from your *SkyDrive* folder. In Word Options, you can set *SkyDrive* as the default save location.

Use SkyDrive Online

The main benefit of using *SkyDrive* to store your files is the freedom it gives you to access your files from any computer with Internet access. In addition to accessing your *SkyDrive* files from a Windows folder on your computer, you can access your *SkyDrive* files from a web page using an Internet browser. You sign in to the *SkyDrive* web page using your Microsoft account.

HOW TO: Use SkyDrive Online

1. Open an Internet browser Window and go to the *SkyDrive* web site (www.skydrive.com), which takes you to the *SkyDrive* sign in page (Figure 12-37).
   - You can use any Internet browser to access *SkyDrive* (e.g., Internet Explorer, Google Chrome, Mozilla Firefox).
2. Type in your Microsoft account email address and password.
   - If you are on your own computer, check the **Keep me signed in** check box to stay signed in to *SkyDrive* when you return to the page.
3. Click the **Sign In** button to go to your *SkyDrive* web page (Figure 12-38).
   - The different areas of *SkyDrive* are displayed under the *SkyDrive* button in the upper left corner (e.g., *Files, Recent docs, Groups*).
4. On the *SkyDrive* page, there are sort and view options available in the upper right corner of the window (Figure 12-39).
   - Click the **Sort by** drop-down list to select a sort option.
   - Click the **Details view** or **Thumbnails view** buttons to change how files and folders are displayed. Figure 12-39 shows *SkyDrive* displayed in *Details view*.
5. Click the **Files** button on the left to display your folders and files in the *Files* area on the right.
6. Click a file or folder check box on the left to select it.
   - At the top, there are buttons and drop-down menus you use to perform actions on selected files and folders.
   - If you click a folder, the folder opens.
   - If you click an Office file, the file opens in Office Web Apps (see *SLO 12.5: Using Office Web Apps*).
7. Click the **SkyDrive** drop-down list to navigate between the different areas of your Microsoft Account: *Mail*, *People* (contacts), *Calendar*, and *SkyDrive*.
8. Click your name in the upper right corner and select **Sign out** to sign out of *SkyDrive*.

12-37 Sign in to *SkyDrive* (www.skydrive.com)

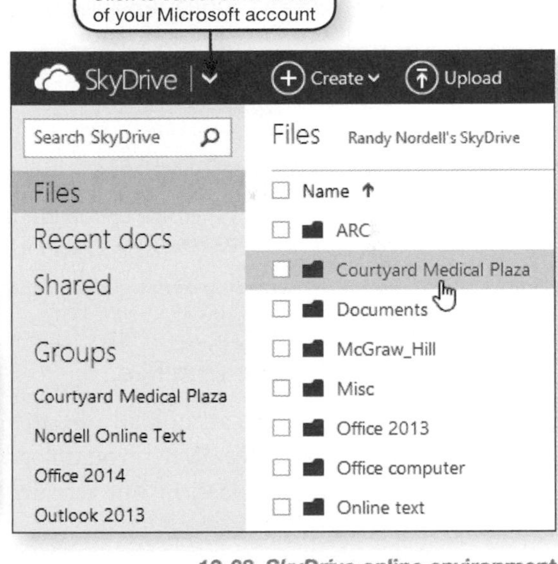

12-38 *SkyDrive* online environment

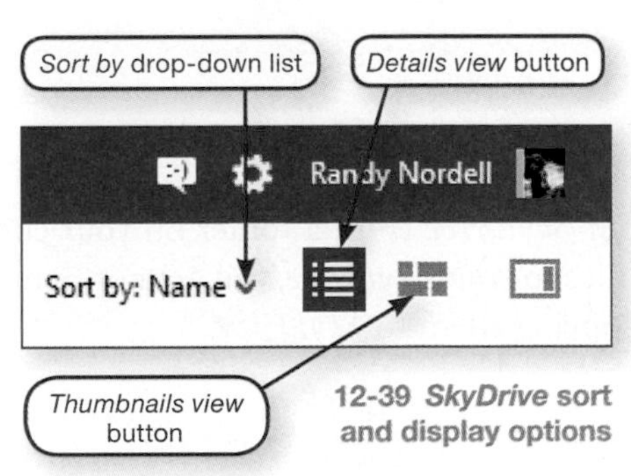

12-39 *SkyDrive* sort and display options

MORE INFO

If you're using a public computer, do not check the *Keep me signed in* check box. You do not want your *SkyDrive* files available to the next person who uses the computer.

Create a Folder

In *SkyDrive*, you can create folders to organize your files in a way that is similar to how you organize Windows folders.

HOW TO: Create SkyDrive Folders

1. Click the **Files** button on the left to display the contents of your *SkyDrive* folder in the *Files* area on the right.
2. Click the **Create** button and select **Folder** from the drop-down list. A new folder is created (Figure 12-40).
3. Type the name of the new folder and press **Enter**.
4. Click a folder to open the folder.
    - You can create a new folder inside an existing folder, or you can upload files to the folder (see the following *Upload a File* section).
    - Click ***[your name's]*** **SkyDrive** link above the folder area to return to the main *SkyDrive* folder.

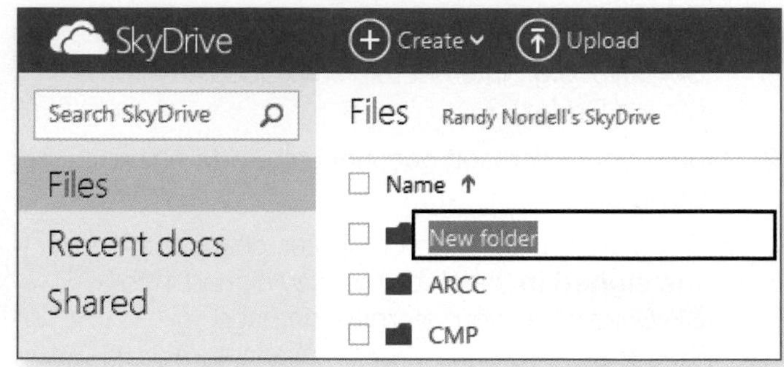

12-40 Add a new *SkyDrive* folder

MORE INFO

When you upload files or create folders online in *SkyDrive*, these changes are reflected in your Windows *SkyDrive* folder on your computer.

Upload a File

You can upload files to your *SkyDrive* from a folder on your computer or a portable storage device. When you upload files to your *SkyDrive*, you are not removing the files from the original location, but actually copying them to *SkyDrive*.

HOW TO: Upload Files to SkyDrive

1. Click **Files** on the left to display your files and folders in the *Files* area on the right.
    - If you are uploading a file to a folder, click the folder to open it.
2. Click the **Upload** button (Figure 12-41). An upload dialog box opens (Figure 12-42), and the name of this dialog box varies depending on the browser you use.

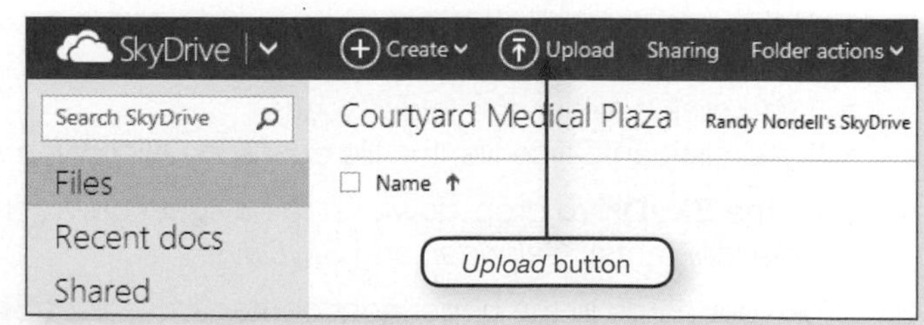

12-41 Upload a file to *SkyDrive*

- Google Chrome: *Open* dialog box.
- Microsoft Internet Explorer: *Choose File to Upload* dialog box.
- Mozilla Firefox: *File Upload* dialog box.
- The figures in the book use Google Chrome.

3. Select the file or files you want to upload to your *SkyDrive* and click **Open**.
   - You can select more than one file. Use the **Ctrl** key to select non-adjacent files, the **Shift** key to select a range of files, or **Ctrl+A** to select all files in a folder.
   - You can only upload files, not a folder.
4. An upload status window appears in the bottom right corner when you are uploading files.
5. The files you upload appear in the files and folders area of *SkyDrive*.

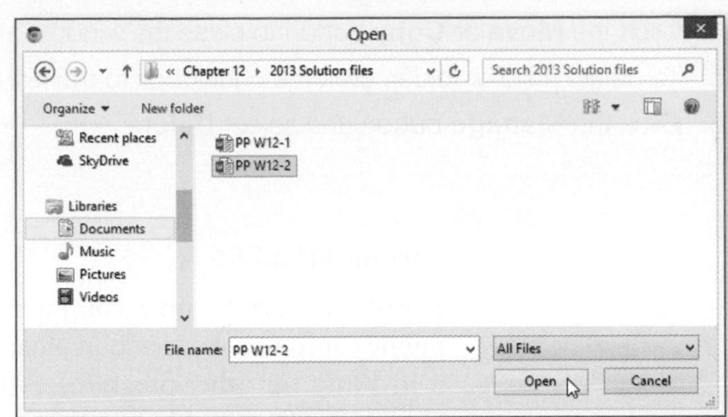

12-42 Select files to upload to your *SkyDrive*

Move, Copy, and Delete Files and Folders

You can also move, copy, and delete files and folders online in *SkyDrive*. When you move a file or folder, it is removed from its location and placed in the new location you select. When you copy a file or folder, it is copied to the new location you select, and the file or folder also remains in its original location.

HOW TO: Move, Copy, and Delete SkyDrive Files

1. Click the **check box** to the left of the file or folder you want to move or copy.
   - You can move multiple items by selecting the check boxes of all of the items you want to move.
2. Click the **Manage** button and at the top select **Move to** or **Copy to** from the drop-down list (Figure 12-43). A move or copy window opens (Figure 12-44).
   - You can select and move multiple files at the same time.
   - You can copy only one file at a time.

12-43 Move a *SkyDrive* file

3. Select the folder where you want to move or copy the selected items.
   - You can place selected items in an existing folder or create a new folder for moved or copied items.
   - Press **Esc** on the keyboard or click away from the move or copy window to cancel the move or copy process and close the window.

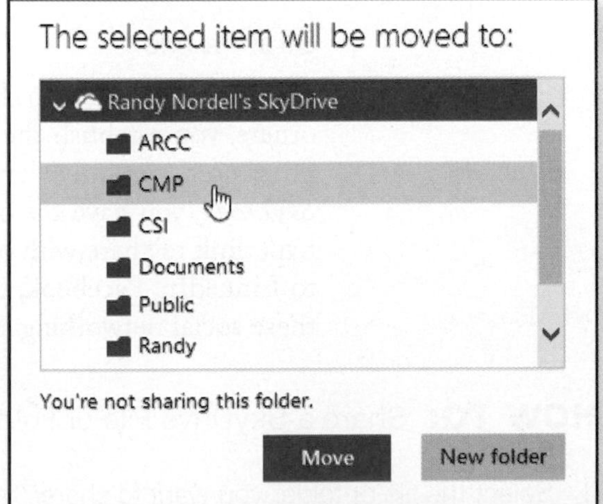

12-44 Select folder where you will move or copy selected items

4. Click the **Move** or **Copy** button to close the window and move or copy the selected items.
5. To delete a file or folder, click the check box to the left of the items to delete.
6. Click the **Manage** button and select **Delete**.

Download a File

If you are working on a computer in a computer lab on your college campus or any other public computer, you can download a file or folder from your *SkyDrive* folder so you can open it in Word (or other program). After you finish modifying the document, you can upload it to your *SkyDrive* folder so the most recent version of your document is in *SkyDrive*. When you download items from *SkyDrive*, the items are not removed from *SkyDrive*. A copy of the items is downloaded.

HOW TO: Download Files from SkyDrive

1. Click the **check box** to the left of the file or folder you want to download.
   - If you select more than one file or a folder to download, a compressed (zipped) folder downloads with the files/folders you selected.
   - If you select a single file, *SkyDrive* downloads the file.
2. Click the **Download** button at the top. The *Save As* dialog box opens (Figure 12-45).
3. Select the location where you want to save the downloaded items.
4. If you want to rename the file, type a file name in the *File name* area.
5. Click the **Save** button to close the *Save As* dialog box and download the selected items.

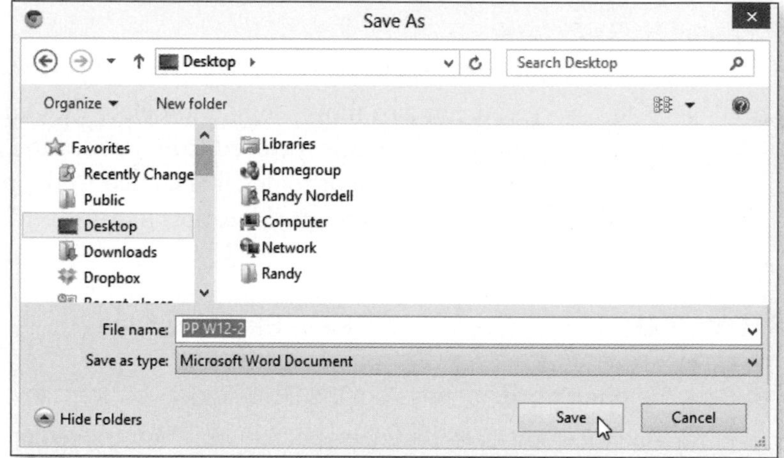

12-45 Save downloaded items from *SkyDrive*

Share a File

SkyDrive allows you to share files or folders with others. When you share files or folders with others, you establish the access they have to the items you share. You can choose whether other users can only view files or view and edit files. When you share a file or folder in your *SkyDrive*, you have the option to send an email with a link to the shared item or generate a hyperlink to share with others that gives them access. If your Windows account is connected to LinkedIn, Facebook, or Twitter, you can also post a link to a shared file in one or more of these social networking sites.

HOW TO: Share a SkyDrive File or Folder

1. Select the file or folder you want to share.
   - You can select only one file or folder at a time. You can share as many files or folders as you want, but you have to select and share them one at a time.
   - If you share a folder, shared users have access to all of the files in the folder.

2. Click the **Sharing** button at the top. A sharing window opens with different sharing options (Figure 12-46).
3. To send an email, click **Send email**, type the email address, and type a brief message.
   - Press **Tab** after typing an email address to add another recipient.
   - You can click **Get a link** to generate a link that you can send to recipients using your own email account, or you can post a link to the shared file on Facebook, Twitter, or LinkedIn.

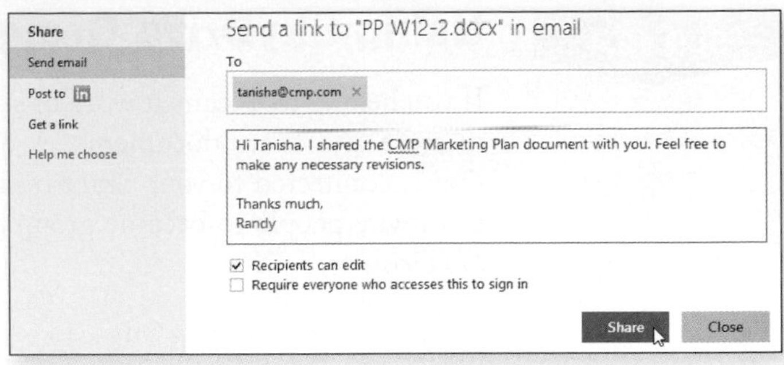

12-46 Send a sharing email

4. Check the **Recipients can edit** box if you want the recipient to be able to edit the file.
   - Deselect this check box if you want recipients only to be able to view the file.
   - You can also require recipients to sign in to *SkyDrive* in order to view or edit the file by checking the **Require everyone who accesses this to sign in** box.
5. Click the **Share** button to send the sharing invitation email.
   - The people you have chosen receive an email containing a link to the shared file or folder.
6. Click **Close** in the confirmation window that opens.

You can change the sharing permission or remove sharing on a file or folder. The ***Details pane*** on the right displays properties of the selected file or folder.

HOW TO: Change or Remove SkyDrive Sharing

1. Select the shared file or folder.
2. Click the **Details** button in the upper right corner. The *Details* pane opens on the right (Figure 12-47).
   - The *Sharing* area lists those who have permission to view or edit the selected item.
3. Click the **Can view** or **Can edit** link to open the *Share* window (Figure 12-48).
   - The display name of this link changes (*Can view* or *Can edit*) depending on the sharing permission of the file.

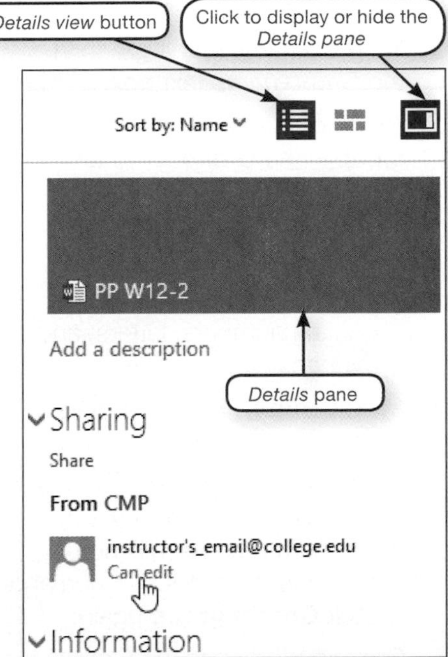

12-47 Change or remove sharing permission in the *Details* pane

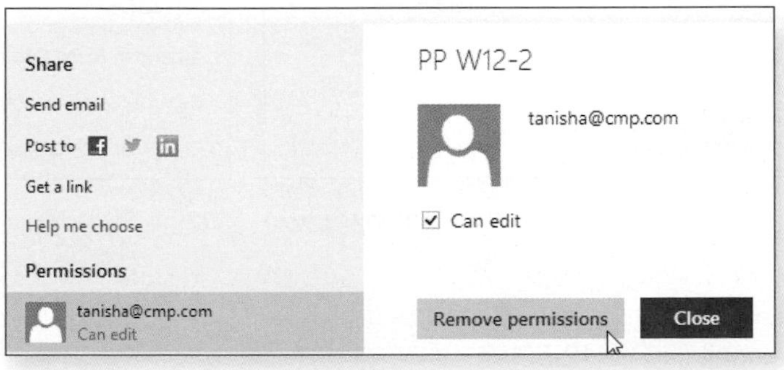

12-48 Change or remove sharing permissions

4. Select or deselect the **Can edit** check box to change this permission.
5. Click the **Remove permissions** button to remove all sharing permissions.
6. Click the **Close** button to close the *Share* window.
7. Click the **Details** button again to close the *Details* pane.

SLO 12.4 Using SkyDrive Groups

If you belong to a team at work or school or an organization, you can create a ***SkyDrive group*** to store and share documents. A *SkyDrive* group is another free Microsoft online service that is connected to your *SkyDrive* account and available from your *SkyDrive* web page. You can invite people to become group members. Members can also access the group from their *SkyDrive* web page.

MORE INFO

If *Groups* are not available on your *SkyDrive* page, you need to activate this feature. Using an Internet browser, search for "create SkyDrive groups". On the "How do I create a group?" Windows page, click the **Go to Groups** button to create a *SkyDrive* group.

Create a SkyDrive Group

When you create a *SkyDrive* group, your group has a name, web address, and group email address. After you create a group, you can invite members and establish a role for each member. Members you invite to your group must have a Microsoft account to access the group. Members can store and share documents in this group on *SkyDrive*.

HOW TO: Create a SkyDrive Group

1. On your *SkyDrive* web page, click **Groups** on the left to open the area where you create a new group (Figure 12-49).
2. Type the name of the group in the *Group name* text box.
3. Type an email address for the group in the *Group email* text box.
   - *SkyDrive* group email addresses are limited to 24 characters and can only contain numbers, letters, and hyphens.
4. Click **Create group** to create your group.
   - The new group is listed in the *Groups* area on the left.
   - If the email address is not available, try a different one and click **Create group** again.

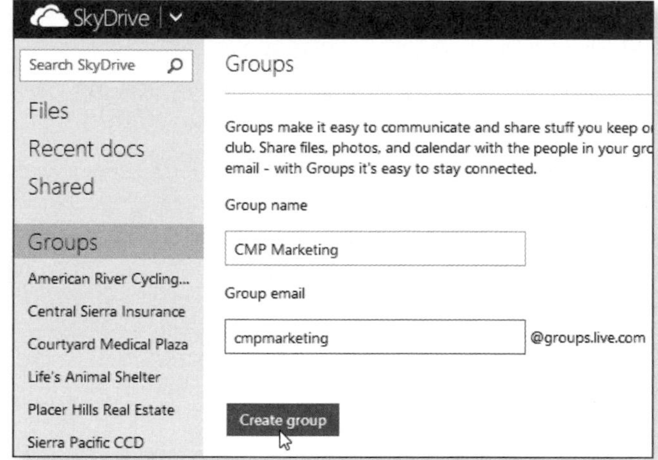

12-49 Create a *SkyDrive* group

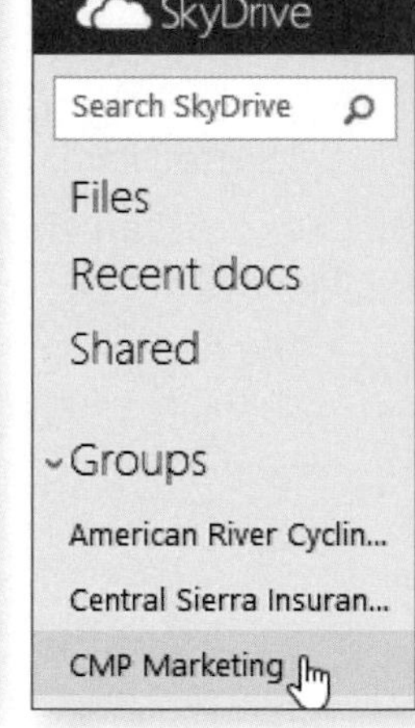

12-50 *SkyDrive* group

5. Click your group in the *Groups* area on the left to select it (Figure 12-50).
   - You can upload files and create folders in your group.

People you invite as members receive an email that invites them to join the group. When they accept the invitation, they are listed in the *Group membership* area of the group.

> **MORE INFO**
>
> You can upload files to your group the same way you upload files to your *SkyDrive* folder.

Invite and Manage SkyDrive Group Members

After you create your group and invite members, you can add new members, remove members, and change roles of members. You can set members' ***roles*** as *Owner*, *Co-Owner*, and *Member*. Roles control the permission level assigned to a group member. *Owners* and *Co-Owners* have full access to create, edit, and delete files and folders in the group, and to customize group options. *Members* can create files and folders, edit them, and view others' files and folders.

HOW TO: Invite and Manage SkyDrive Group Members

1. On your *SkyDrive* web page, select your group.
2. Click the **Group actions** button at the top and select **Invite people** to open an area where you can invite members (Figure 12-51).
3. Type email addresses for those you want to invite to the group.
   - Press **Tab** after typing an email address to enter another one.
4. Click **Invite** to send the group invitation.
   - Invitees receive an email message inviting them to the group.
   - They have to accept the invitation to join the group.
   - When you invite people to become a member of a *SkyDrive* group, their role (permission level), by default, is *Member*. You can change members' roles.
5. Click the **Group Actions** button and select **View membership** to view group membership, change group members' roles, or remove members. The *Membership* area displays.
6. Select a member, click the **Change role** button, and select a membership role (Figure 12-52).
7. To delete a member, select the **Member** and click the **Remove** button.

12-51 Invite *SkyDrive* group members

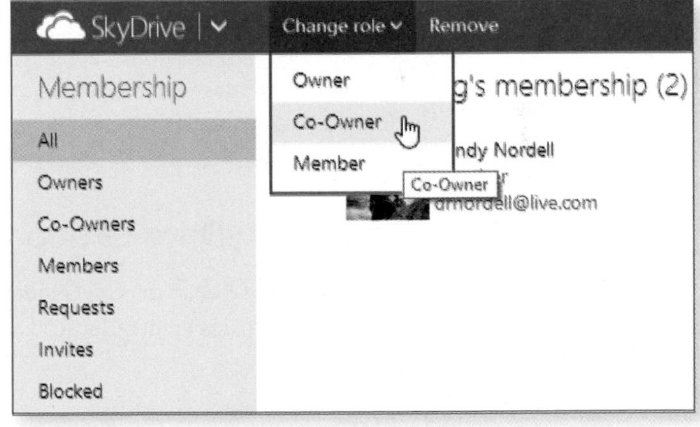

12-52 Change a group member's role

Email SkyDrive Group Members

When you create a group, you choose an email address for the group. You can send an email to the group using this *SkyDrive* group email address. When you send the email, it is sent to each of the group members.

HOW TO: Email SkyDrive Group Members

1. On your *SkyDrive* web page, select your group.
2. Click the **Group Actions** button at the top and select **Send an email message**. A new message opens in your Microsoft account email (Figure 12-53).
   - This window might vary depending on the type of Microsoft email address you have (e.g., Live.com, Hotmail, or Outlook.com).
   - The *SkyDrive* group email address is in the *To* area. You can add recipients.
3. Type a subject and a message.
4. Click **Send** to send the email message.

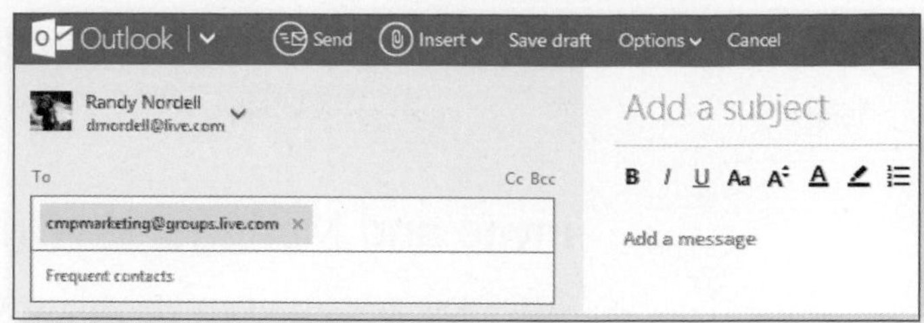

12-53 Send an email to *SkyDrive* group members

> **MORE INFO**
>
> You can view the group email history by selecting **Show email messages** from the *Group actions* drop-down list.

You can also create a group email or view email history by clicking on a link in the *Details* pane (Figure 12-54). Click the **Details** button to open the *Details* pane. Click the **group email address** link to create a new group email. Click the **View** link to the left of *Group email history* to view group emails.

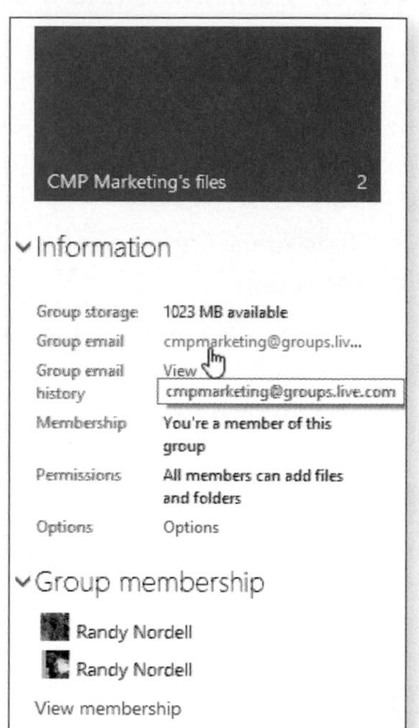

12-54 *Details* pane

> **ANOTHER WAY**
>
> Select **Properties** from the *Group actions* drop-down list to display the *Details* pane.

Change SkyDrive Group Options

If you are the *Owner* or *Co-Owner* of a group, you can customize the group options. The following categories are available:

- *General*
- *Email*
- *Group conversations*
- *Personal*
- *Leave group*
- *Delete group*

Select a group and click the **Group options** button at the top to display the *Options* page (Figure 12-55). Click one of the categories on the left to display the customization options for that category. When you finish

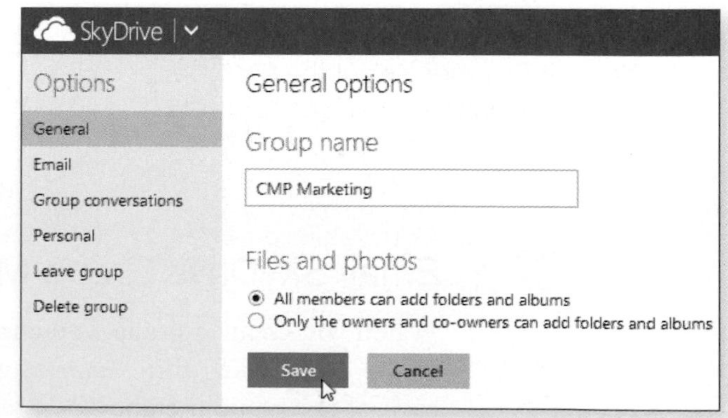

12-55 *SkyDrive* group options

making changes, click the **Save** button at the bottom to save and apply the changes. The *Options* area is where you can leave a group or delete a group.

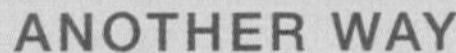

ANOTHER WAY

Click the **Options** link in the *Details* pane to open the *Options* area for the select group.

PAUSE & PRACTICE: WORD 12-2

For this project, you upload files to and create folders in your *SkyDrive* folder, move files, share a file, create and modify a *SkyDrive* group, and invite members.

Note to Instructor and Students:

General Information: *For this project, you use the* SkyDrive *Windows folder and* SkyDrive *groups. If these are not available on your computer, refer to the instructions in the* More Info *boxes on pages 702 (second* More Info *box) and 708.*
Students: *For this project, you share* SkyDrive *files with your instructor and invite your instructor to become a member of your* SkyDrive *group.*
Instructor: *In order to complete this project, your students need your Microsoft email address. You can create a new Live or Hotmail account for projects in this chapter.*

Files Needed: ***[your initials] PP W12-1.docx***, ***SkiingUnlimited-12.docx***, ***TeenSubstanceAbuse-12.docx***, and ***StayingActive-12.docx***
Completed Project File Name: ***[your initials] PP W12-2.docx***

---

1. Open the ***[your initials] PP W12-1*** document.
2. Save this document as ***[your initials] PP W12-2***.
3. Create a folder in your *SkyDrive* folder and save this document in the new folder.
    a. Open the *Save As* dialog box and select the **SkyDrive** folder on the left.
    b. Click the **New Folder** button (Figure 12-56).
    c. Type your first name and press **Enter**.
    d. Double-click **your folder** to open it and click **Save** to save the ***[your initials] PP W12-2*** document in your folder in *SkyDrive*.
4. Close the document and exit Word.
5. Log in to *SkyDrive* online, create a new folder, and upload files.
    a. Open an Internet browser window, type www.skydrive.com in the address bar at the top, and press **Enter** to go to the *SkyDrive* log in page.
    b. Type your Microsoft email address and password to log in to *SkyDrive*.

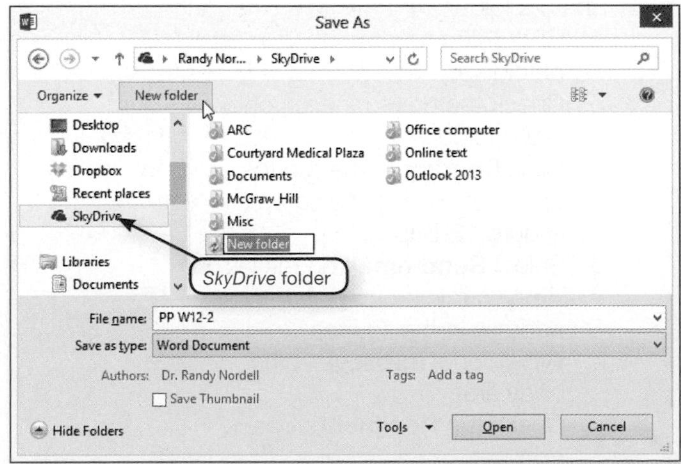

12-56 Create a new folder in your *SkyDrive* folder

c. Click **Files** on the left to display the contents of your *SkyDrive* folder. The new folder you created is displayed in *SkyDrive* (there might be other folders listed as well).
d. Click the **Create** button at the top and select **Folder** from the drop-down list (Figure 12-57).
e. Type CMP as the name for the new folder and press **Enter**.
f. Click the **CMP** folder (not the check box) to open it.
g. Click the **Upload** button at the top to open an upload dialog box. Remember, the name of this dialog box varies depending on the Internet browser you are using.
h. Select the ***SkiingUnlimited-12*** and ***TeenSubstanceAbuse-12*** files from your student data files (use the **Ctrl** key to select non-adjacent files) and click **Open**. The two files are added to the *CMP* folder.

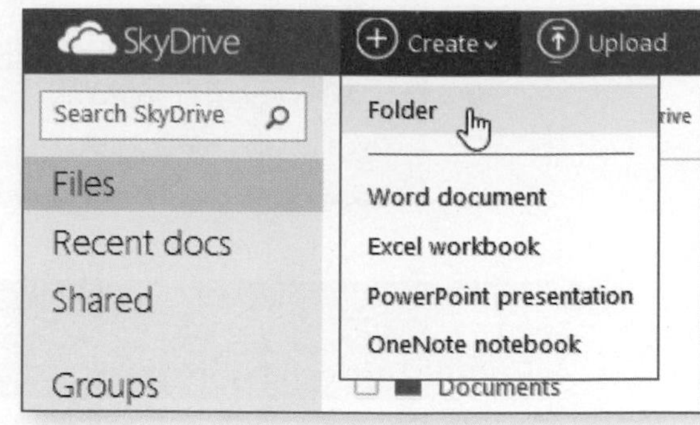

12-57 Create a new folder in *SkyDrive*

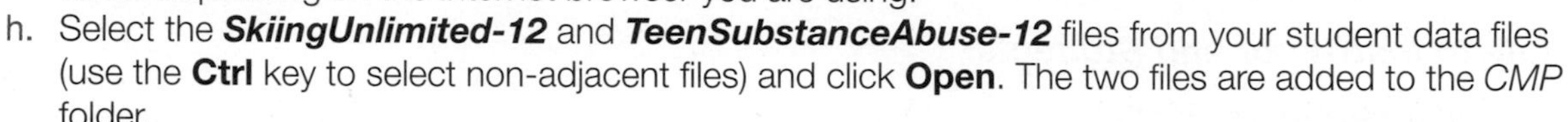

6. Move a file.
   a. Click **Files** on the left to return to your list of folders.
   b. Click the **Details view** button at the right to display folders and files in a list.
   c. Click the **[your first name]** folder to open it. The ***[your initials] PP W12-2*** file is in this folder. If it is not, add the file.
   d. Check the box to the left of the ***[your initials] PP W12-2*** file to select it.
   e. Click the **Manage** button and select **Move to** from the drop-down list. A dialog box opens (Figure 12-58).
   f. Select the **CMP** folder and click **Move**.
   g. Click **Files** to return to your list of folders.
   h. Click the **CMP** folder to open it and confirm that the file moved.

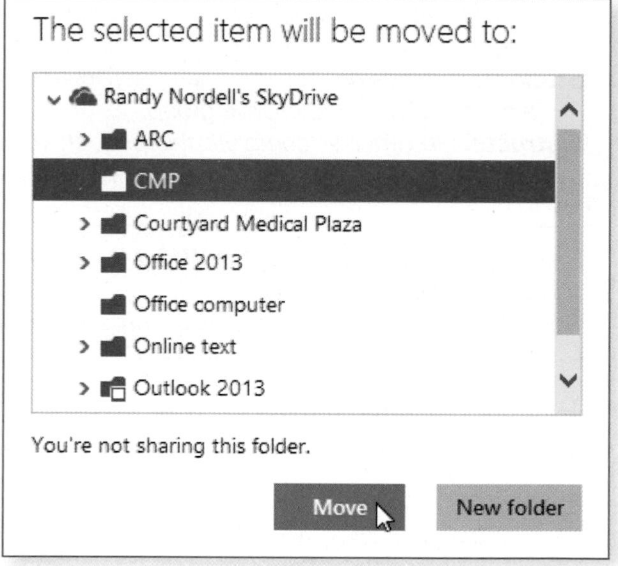

12-58 Move a file to a folder

7. Share a folder.
   a. Click **Files** to return to your list of folders.
   b. Check the box to the left of the **CMP** folder.
   c. Click **Sharing** at the top to open the sharing dialog box (Figure 12-59).
   d. Select **Send email** on the left.
   e. Type your instructor's email address in the *To* area.
   f. Type a brief message in the body area.
   g. Check the **Recipients can edit** box.
   h. Click **Share** to send the sharing email to your instructor.
   i. Click **Close** in the *Share* window that opens.

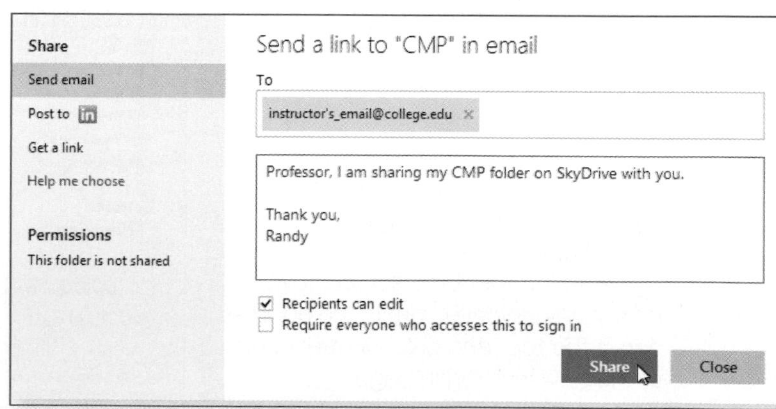

12-59 Share a folder and send an email

8. Create a *SkyDrive* group and invite a member.
    a. Click **Groups** on the left to open the *Groups* page (Figure 12-60).
    b. Type Courtyard Medical Plaza in the *Group name* text box.
    c. Type your last name, first initial, and -CMP in the email area (e.g., NordellR-CMP).
    d. Click **Create group** to create your group. If the email address was already taken, type a different one. After the group is created, you are taken back to *SkyDrive* with the *Courtyard Medical Plaza* group selected.

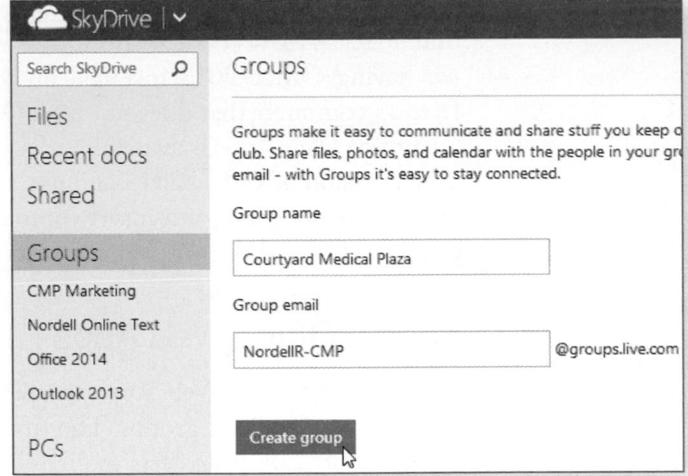

12-60 Create a *SkyDrive* group

9. Invite a member to your group.
    a. Confirm that the *Courtyard Medical Plaza* group is selected in the *Groups* area on the left. If it is not, select it.
    b. Click the **Group actions** button at the top and select **Invite people**. An *Invite* window opens.
    c. Type your instructor's email address and click **Invite**.
10. Upload files to your group.
    a. Confirm that the *Courtyard Medical Plaza* group is selected in the *Groups* area on the left. If it is not, select it.
    b. Click the **Upload** button to open an upload dialog box.
    c. Select the ***SkiingUnlimited-12***, ***StayingActive-12***, and ***TeenSubstanceAbuse-12*** files from your student data files and click **Open**. The files are added to your group. (You may need to refresh your browser window to display the files.)
11. Change group options.
    a. With your group selected on the left, click the **Group options** button at the top. The *Options* page opens.
    b. Select **Email** on the left if it is not already selected.
    c. In the *Link to group website* area, click the **Only group members can view the group using this link** radio button.
    d. Click the **Save** button. The *Options* page closes and you return to your group.
    e. Click the **Group options** button again to reopen the *Options* page.
    f. Click **Group conversations** on the left.
    g. Click **Turn off group conversations**. The *Options* area closes and you return to your group.
    h. Confirm the three files are in your Courtyard Medical Plaza group folder (Figure 12-61).
12. Click **[your name]** in the upper right corner and select **Sign out** from the *Account* drop-down list.

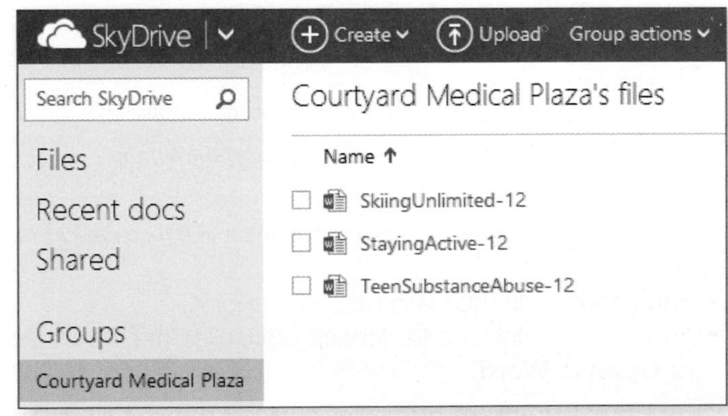

12-61 PP W12-2 completed (*SkyDrive* group displayed)

SLO 12.5

Using Office Web Apps

Office Web Apps is free online software from Microsoft that works in conjunction with your online *SkyDrive* account. With Office Web Apps, you can work with Office files online *without* having Office 2013 installed on the computer you are using, such as when you use a friend's computer that does not have Office 2013 installed.

Office Web Apps is available from your *SkyDrive* web page. Office Web Apps is a scaled-down version of Office 2013 and not as robust in terms of features, but you can use it to create, edit, print, share, and insert comments on files. If you need more advanced features, you can open Office Web Apps documents in Office 2013.

Edit an Office Web Apps File

You can use Office Web Apps to open and edit many Office files you have stored in your *SkyDrive* or *SkyDrive* groups. The working environment in Office Web Apps is very similar to Microsoft Office and has the familiar *Ribbon*, tabs, and groups. However, there are not as many tabs and features available in Office Web Apps.

When you initially open an Office file from either *SkyDrive* or a *SkyDrive* group, the file is displayed in ***read-only mode*** in the browser window where you view the document. When you edit the file in the browser window, Office Web Apps opens your file in ***edit mode*** in the appropriate program. For example, if you edit a Word document in *SkyDrive*, your document opens in ***Word Web App***.

HOW TO: Edit an Office Web Apps File

1. Log in to your *SkyDrive* account in an Internet browser window.
2. Click an Office file to open from *SkyDrive* or a *SkyDrive* group (Figure 12-62). The file is displayed in *read-only* mode in an Office Web Apps window (Figure 12-63).

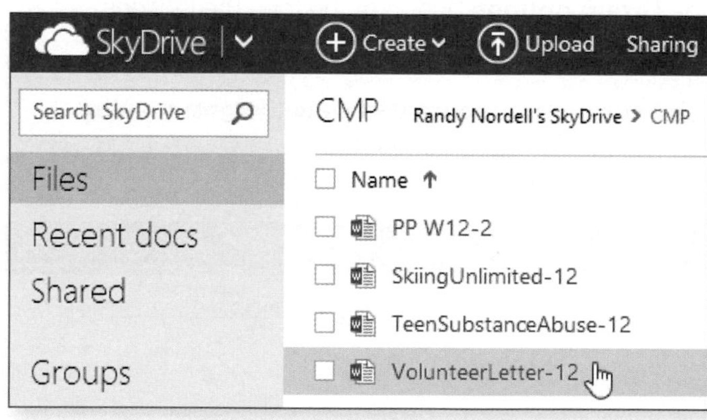

12-62 Open a document in Office Web Apps

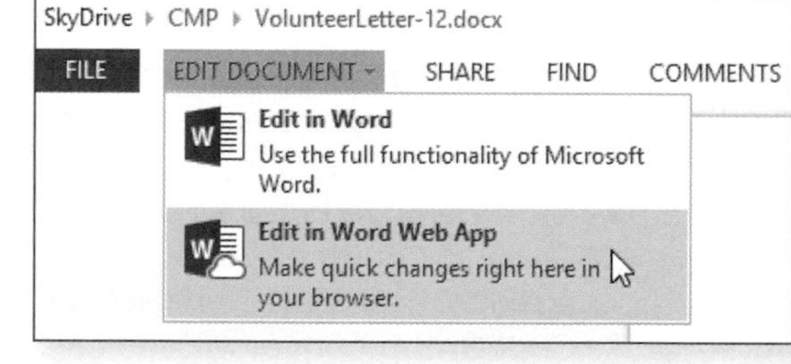

12-63 Change from *read-only* mode to *edit* mode in Word Web App

- You cannot edit the file in *read-only* mode.
- You can also select a file (check box), click the **Open** drop-down list, and select **Open in Word Web App** or **Open in Word**.

3. Click **Edit Document** and select **Edit in [Office Web App]** from the drop-down list (e.g., *Edit in Word Web App*) to edit the file in Office Web Apps.
   - You can also open an Office Web Apps file in Microsoft Office. To do this, you must have Microsoft Office installed on the computer you are using.
   - Click **Edit in [Office application]** (e.g., *Edit in Word*) to launch Office and open the file in the appropriate Office application.

4. Make desired editing and formatting changes in Office Web Apps (Figure 12-64).

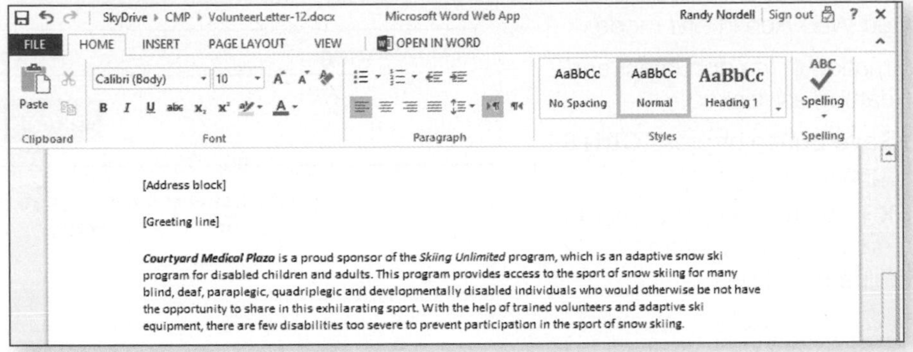

12-64 Edit a document in Word Web App

- The *File*, *Home*, *Insert*, *Page Layout*, and *View* tabs are on the *Ribbon*.
- Click **Open in [Office application]** (e.g., *Open in Word*) to open the document in Office.
- You can make editing and formatting changes, apply styles, and cut, copy and paste selected text.
- When using Office Web Apps, some advanced formatting such as text boxes, pictures, charts, and *SmartArt* might not be arranged and aligned as they are when you open the document in Word 2013.

5. Click the **Save** button or press **Ctrl+S** to save changes to the file.
6. Click the **X** in the upper right corner to close the document and return to your *SkyDrive* folders and files.
   - Alternatively, click the **SkyDrive** link at the top to return to your *SkyDrive* folders and files.

MORE INFO

When you are in *read-only* mode in Word Web App, the *Ribbon* does not display. In *edit* mode, the Word Web App *Ribbon* displays.

Create an Office Web Apps File

You are not limited to editing existing documents in Office Web Apps; you can create new Word documents, Excel workbooks, PowerPoint presentations, and OneNote notebooks. When you create an Office Web Apps file, the document is saved in your *SkyDrive* or *SkyDrive* group.

MORE INFO

OneNote is a note-taking application that is a part of Microsoft Office. You can use OneNote to create, gather, organize, and share notes.

HOW TO: Create an Office Web Apps File

1. In *SkyDrive* or a *SkyDrive* group, select the location where you want to create a new file.
2. Click the **Create** button and select the type of file to create (**Word document**, **Excel workbook**, **PowerPoint presentation**, **OneNote notebook**, or **Excel survey**) (Figure 12-65). The *New Microsoft Word document* dialog box opens (Figure 12-66).

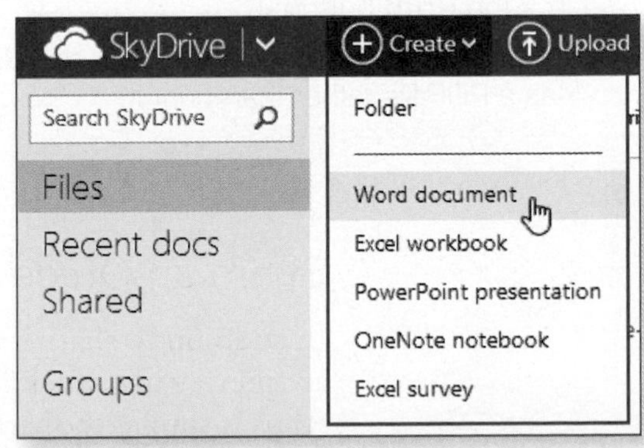

12-65 Create a Word Web App document

3. Type the name of the document and click the **Create** button. The file opens in the selected Web App in *edit* mode.
4. Type information in the document and apply formatting as desired.
5. Click the **Save** button or press **Ctrl+S** to save changes to the file.
6. Click the **X** in the upper right corner to close the document and return to your *SkyDrive* folders and files.

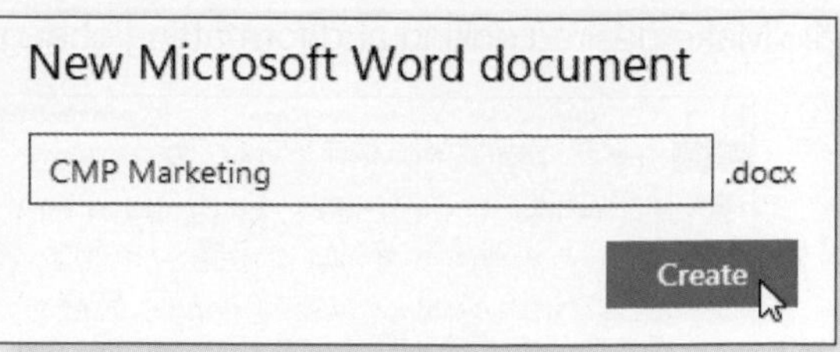

12-66 Create and name a new Word document in Word Web App

Print an Office Web Apps File

You can print files from Office Web Apps similarly to how you print files in Office. The difference when printing in Office Web Apps is that the program creates a PDF (portable document format) file when you print a document so the document retains its original format. You can print from either *read-only* or *edit* mode.

HOW TO: Print an Office Web Apps File

1. Click a file to open from *SkyDrive* or a *SkyDrive* group.
2. In either *read-only* or *edit* mode, click the **File** tab.
3. Select **Print** and click the **Print to PDF** button (Figure 12-67).
4. Click the **Click here to view the PDF of your document** link to open the printable PDF file (Figure 12-68).
   - The printable PDF file opens in a *Print* window with a preview of the document on the right.

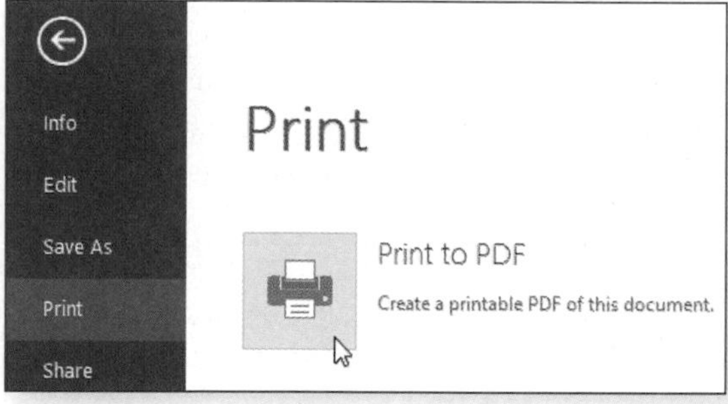

12-67 Print to PDF

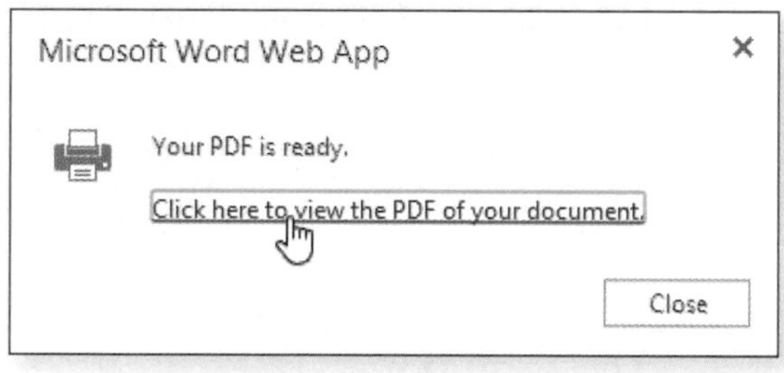

12-68 Click to view printable PDF file

5. Click the **Print** button.
   - From the *Print* area, you can click the **Change** button and select **Save as PDF** to save the document as a PDF file rather than print it.

Share an Office Web Apps File

In addition to sharing a file from *SkyDrive* or a *SkyDrive* group, you can also share a file you are previewing or editing in Office Web Apps. The process for sharing a file in Office Web Apps is similar to sharing a file or folder in *SkyDrive*.

HOW TO: Share an Office Web Apps File

1. Open a file in Office Web Apps.
2. In *read-only* mode, click the **Share** button above the document. The *Share* window opens with different options (Figure 12-69).
   - In either *read-only* or *edit* mode, click the **File** tab and select **Share** on the left.
3. To send an email, click **Send email**, type the desired recipient's email address, and type a brief message.
   - Press **Tab** after typing an email address to add another recipient.
   - You can also click **Get a link** to generate a link that you can send to recipients.

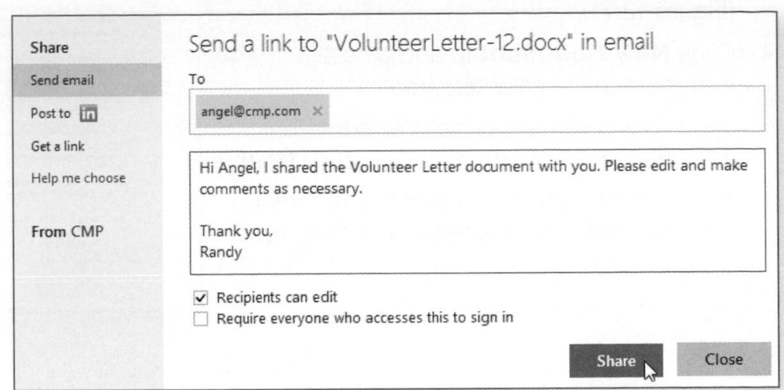

12-69 Share an Office Web Apps file

4. Check the **Recipients can edit** box if you want the recipient to be able to edit the file.
   - Deselect this check box if you want recipients only to be able to view the file.
   - You can also require recipients to sign in to *SkyDrive* in order to view or edit the file by checking the **Require everyone who accesses this to sign in** box.
5. Click the **Share** button.
   - Recipients receive an email containing a link to the shared file or folder.
6. Click **Close** to close the *Share* window and return to the Office Web Apps document.

Collaborate in Office Web Apps

Office Web Apps let you synchronously or asynchronously collaborate on an Office file with others who have access to the shared file. If two or more users are working on the same file in Office Web Apps, collaboration information is displayed in the *Status bar* in the bottom right corner of the Office Web Apps window (Figure 12-70). You are alerted of available updates and told how many people are editing the file.

Click **Updates Available** in the *Status bar* to apply updates to your document. Click **People Editing** to view the names of users who are currently editing the file.

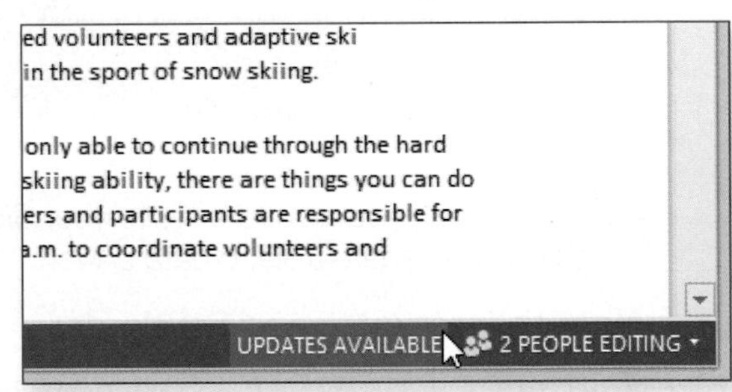

12-70 Collaboration information displayed in the *Status bar*

Use Comments in Office Web Apps

In Office Web Apps, you can add comments to a file, review comments from others, reply to comments, mark comments as done, and delete comments. When reviewing a document in Word Web App, you can only make comments in *read-only* mode.

HOW TO: Add Comments in Office Web Apps

1. Open a file in Office Web Apps in *read-only* mode.
2. Select an area of the file where you want to make a comment.

3. Click the **Comments** button at the top to open the *Comments* pane on the right (Figure 12-71).
4. Click **New Comment** to add a new comment to the selected area.
5. Type your comment in the new comment area in the *Comments* pane and click **Post**.
    - A comment balloon displays to the right of the area you selected in the document.

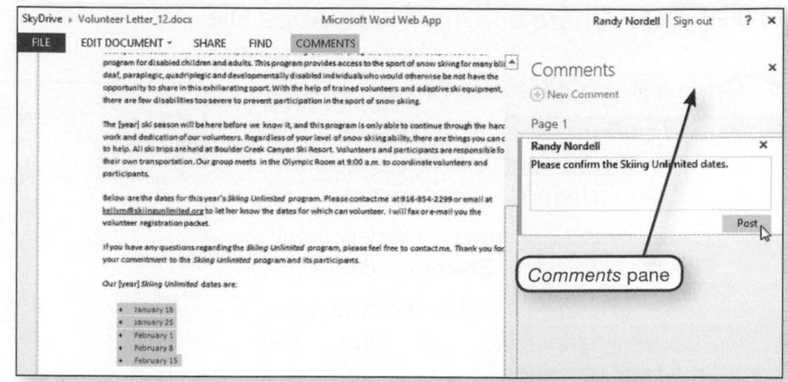

12-71 Using comments in Office Web Apps

When reviewing your own comments or comments from others, click a comment balloon in the document to open the *Comments* pane on the right (Figure 12-72). You can take the following actions on existing comments:

- Click the **Reply** button to reply to a comment.
- Click the **Mark as Done** button to mark a comment as done after you have acted on the comment or when it is no longer relevant.
- Click the **Delete** button to delete a comment.

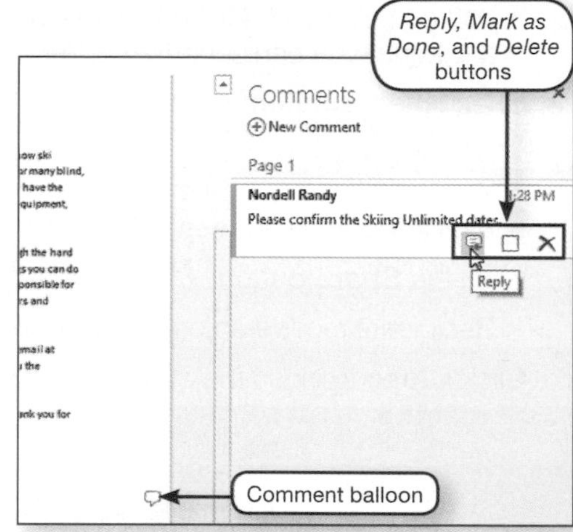

12-72 Review comments

PAUSE & PRACTICE: WORD 12-3

For this project, you upload a file to your *SkyDrive*, edit a document in Word Web App, add comments to the document, share a file, create a Word Web App document, and copy and rename files.

Note to Instructor and Students:

Students: *For this project, you share a* SkyDrive *file with your instructor.*
Instructor: *In order to complete this project, your students need your Microsoft email address. You can create a new Live or Hotmail account for the projects in this chapter.*

File Needed: ***VolunteerLetter-12.docx***
Completed Project File Names: ***[your initials] PP W12-3a.docx*** and ***[your initials] PP W12-3b.docx***

1. Open an Internet browser page and log in to your *SkyDrive* account (www.skydrive.com).
2. Upload a file to a folder in your *SkyDrive*.
    a. Click the **CMP** folder to open it.
    b. Click the **Upload** button to open an upload dialog box.
    c. Select the ***VolunteerLetter-12*** from your student data files and click **Open** to add this file to the *CMP* folder.

3. Edit a file in Word Web App.
   a. Click the ***VolunteerLetter-12*** file in the *CMP* folder to open it in Word Web App in *read-only* mode. When you open a document in Word Web App, by default it opens in *read-only* mode.
   b. Click the **Edit Document** button at the top and select **Edit in Word Web App** from the drop-down list.
   c. In the second and fifth paragraphs, select "**[year]**" and the space following it and delete both instances. Make sure there is proper spacing between words.
   d. Replace the placeholder text in the bulleted list with the following dates:

      January 18
      January 25
      February 1
      February 8
      February 15

   e. Click the **Save** button or press **Ctrl+S** to save the document.
   f. Click the **SkyDrive** link at the top or the **X** (*Exit*) in the upper right of the Word Web App window to close the document and return to your *SkyDrive* folders. Don't click the *X* in the upper right corner of the Internet browser window, which closes the Internet browser window.
4. Add a comment to the document.
   a. Click the **CMP** folder to open it.
   b. Click the ***VolunteerLetter-12*** file in the *CMP* folder to open it in Word Web App in *read-only* mode.
   c. Select the bulleted list.
   d. Click **Comments** at the top to open the *Comments* pane at the right.
   e. Click **New Comment** in the *Comments* pane to create a comment on the selected text (Figure 12-73).
   f. Type Confirm these dates with Angel in the new comment area and click **Post**.

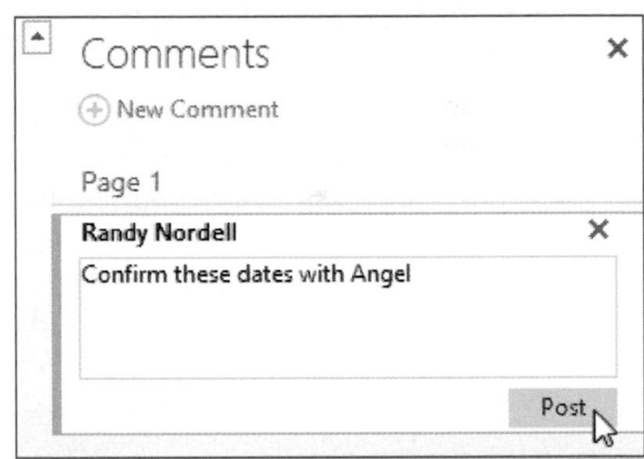

12-73 Add comment

5. Share the document with your instructor.
   a. Click **Sharing** at the top to open the *Share* window (Figure 12-74).
   b. Select **Send email** on the left.
   c. Type your instructor's email address in the *To* area.
   d. Type a brief message in the body area.
   e. Check the **Recipients can edit** check box.
   f. Click **Share** to send the sharing email to your instructor.
   g. Click **Close** to close the *Share* window.
   h. Click the **SkyDrive** link at the top to return to your *SkyDrive* folders.

12-74 Share a document

6. Create a new Word document in Word Web App.
   a. Click the **CMP** folder to open it.
   b. Click the **Create** button and select **Word document**. The *New Microsoft Word document* window opens.
   c. Type CMP Marketing as the title of the new document and click **Create**. The new document opens in Word Web App in *edit* mode.

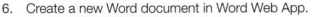

d. Type CMP Marketing on the first line and press **Enter**.
e. Click the **Bullets** button to turn on bullets and type the following three bulleted items:

   Skiing Unlimited (January and February)
   Healthy Lifestyle Workshops (April and October)
   Substance Abuse Prevention Conference (June)

f. Select "**CMP Marketing**," apply the **Heading 1** style, and apply **bold** formatting.
g. Click the **Save** button or press **Ctrl+S** to save the document.
h. Close the document and return to your *SkyDrive* folders.

7. Copy and rename files.
   a. Click the **CMP** folder to open it.
   b. Click the ***VolunteerLetter-12*** check box to select it.
   c. Click the **Manage** button and select **Copy to** from the drop-down list to open the *Copy* dialog box (Figure 12-75).
   d. Click the **[your first name]** folder and click **Copy** to close the dialog box and copy the document.
   e. Deselect (uncheck) the ***VolunteerLetter-12*** document and select (check) the ***CMP Marketing*** document.
   f. Copy the ***CMP Marketing*** document to the **[your first name]** folder.
   g. Open the **[your first name]** folder and click the ***VolunteerLetter-12*** check box to select it.
   h. Click the **Manage** button and select **Rename** from the drop-down list.
   i. Type [your initials] PP W12-3a and press **Enter**.
   j. Deselect the ***[your initials] PP W12-3a*** check box.
   k. Rename the ***CMP Marketing*** document to [your initials] PP W12-3b (Figure 12-76).

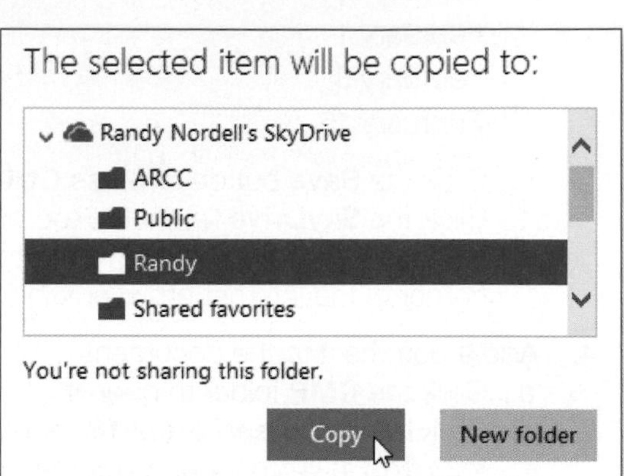

12-75 Copy a file to a folder

8. Select **[your name]** in the upper right corner and select **Sign out** from the *Account* drop-down list.

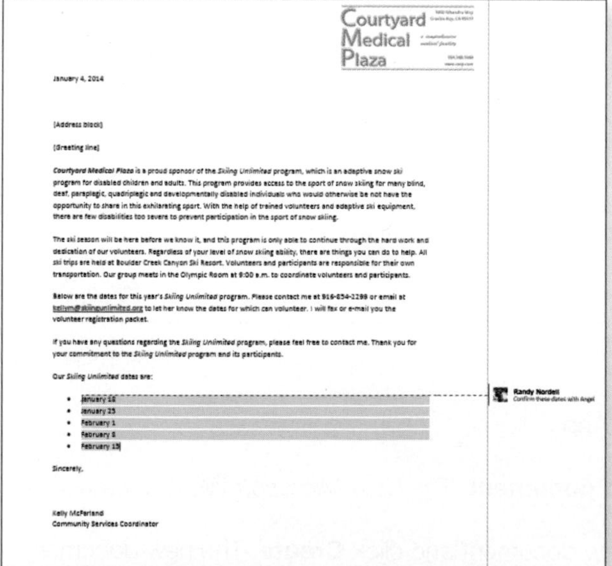

Courtyard Medical Plaza

January 4, 2014

[Address block]

[Greeting line]

Courtyard Medical Plaza is a proud sponsor of the *Skiing Unlimited* program, which is an adaptive snow ski program for disabled children and adults. This program provides access to the sport of snow skiing for many blind, deaf, paraplegic, quadriplegic and developmentally disabled individuals who would otherwise be not have the opportunity to share in this exhilarating sport. With the help of trained volunteers and adaptive ski equipment, there are few disabilities too severe to prevent participation in the sport of snow skiing.

The ski season will be here before we know it, and this program is only able to continue through the hard work and dedication of our volunteers. Regardless of your level of snow skiing ability, there are things you can do to help. All ski trips are held at Boulder Creek Canyon Ski Resort. Volunteers and participants are responsible for their own transportation. Our group meets in the Olympic Room at 9:00 a.m. to coordinate volunteers and participants.

Below are the dates for this year's *Skiing Unlimited* program. Please contact me at 916-854-2299 or email at kellym@skiingunlimited.org to let her know the dates for which can volunteer. I will fax or e-mail you the volunteer registration packet.

If you have any questions regarding the *Skiing Unlimited* program, please feel free to contact me. Thank you for your commitment to the *Skiing Unlimited* program and its participants.

Our *Skiing Unlimited* dates are:

- January 18
- January 25
- February 1
- February 8
- February 15

Sincerely,

Kelly McFarland
Community Services Coordinator

Randy Nordell
Confirm these dates with Angel

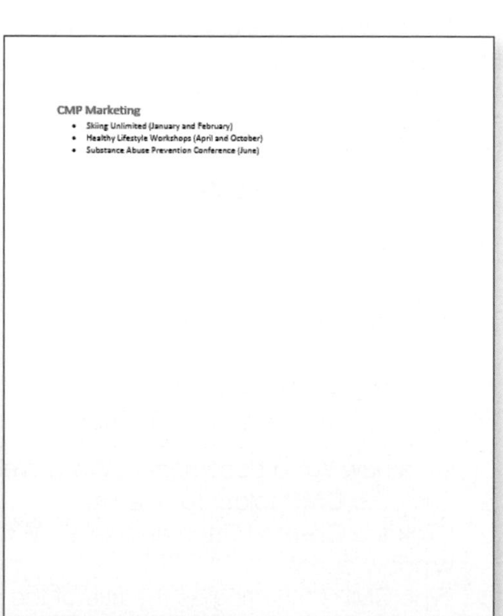

CMP Marketing

- Skiing Unlimited (January and February)
- Healthy Lifestyle Workshops (April and October)
- Substance Abuse Prevention Conference (June)

12-76 PP W12-3a and PP W12-3b completed

Chapter Summary

12.1 Customize Word options, the *Ribbon*, and the *Quick Access* toolbar to personalize your working environment (p. W12-685).

- The ***Word Options dialog box*** allows you to customize global settings in Word. Some settings apply to all Office programs.
- The *Word Options* dialog box features the following categories: ***General***, ***Display***, ***Proofing***, ***Save***, ***Language***, ***Advanced***, ***Customize Ribbon***, ***Quick Access Toolbar***, ***Add-Ins***, and ***Trust Center***.
- Use the *Word Options* dialog box to customize the ***Ribbon***. Create a new tab or group, add commands to custom groups, rearrange existing tabs and groups, and rename existing and custom tabs and group.
- You can quickly customize and add commands to the ***Quick Access toolbar*** from the *Customize Quick Access Toolbar* drop-down list, or you can add other commands using the *Word Options* dialog box.
- Both the *Ribbon* and the *Quick Access* toolbar can be reset to return them to their original settings. You can reset the *Ribbon* or the *Quick Access* toolbar individually or reset all customizations, which resets both the *Ribbon* and the *Quick Access* toolbar.

12.2 View and modify Office account settings and add an Office app (p. W12-695).

- The ***Account area*** on the *Backstage* view provides you with information and account customization options.
- Your ***Office account information and settings*** are available whenever you log in to Word (or any Office application) using your ***Microsoft account***. You can obtain your own free Microsoft account through Live, Hotmail, Messenger, or MSN.
- You can change the ***Office background*** in the *Account* area on the *Backstage* view.
- *You can add* ***connected services*** to your account to access online services for ***Images & Videos***, ***Storage***, and ***Sharing***.
- ***Apps*** (applications) provide additional functionality to Office. The ***Apps for Office*** window lists available apps for Office.

12.3 Create a folder, add a file, move and copy a file, and share a file in SkyDrive (p. W12-701).

- ***SkyDrive*** is a ***cloud storage*** area that provides you with online storage space for your files. If you have a Microsoft account (Live, Hotmail, MSN, Messenger, or other Microsoft service account), you have access to *SkyDrive*.
- You can access your *SkyDrive* files from any computer that has Internet access.
- Log in to *SkyDrive* using your Microsoft account.
- If you use Windows 8, *SkyDrive* is one of your storage options. You can save and edit *SkyDrive* files using a Windows folder or online using an Internet browser.
- In *SkyDrive*, you can add files, create folders, and move, copy, delete, and download files.
- You can share *SkyDrive* files with others. You determine the access other users have to view and/or edit your *SkyDrive* files.

12.4 Create a group in *SkyDrive*, invite a member, and change group options (p. W12-708).

- A ***SkyDrive group*** is an online workspace you can use to store and share documents with other group members.
- *SkyDrive* groups are connected to *SkyDrive*, and you can create groups if you have a Microsoft account.
- You can access groups you create or are a member of from your *SkyDrive* page.
- You can invite a person to become a ***member*** of your *SkyDrive* group. You can determine each member's role. A member can be an ***owner***, a ***co-owner***, or a ***member***.
- Each *SkyDrive* group has a ***web address*** and ***group email account***. You can send email to all group members using the group email address.
- You can add and edit files and create folders in groups.

12.5 Open, create, edit, print, share, use comments, and collaborate on documents in Office Web Apps (p. W11-714).

- ***Office Web Apps*** is free online software that works in conjunction with your *SkyDrive* account and is available from your *SkyDrive* web page.

- Office Web Apps is similar to Microsoft Office 2013 but less robust in available features.
- Office 2013 does not have to be installed on your computer when using Office Web Apps.
- You can edit existing files from your *SkyDrive* account in Office Web Apps and create new Office files using Office Web Apps.
- You can share Office Web Apps files with others.
- More than one user can edit an Office Web Apps file at the same time, which allows real-time collaboration on documents.
- You can add comments, reply to comments, mark a comment as done, or delete comments on Office Web Apps files.

Check for Understanding

In the ***Online Learning Center*** for this text (www.mhhe.com/office2013inpractice), there are a variety of resources that can be used to review the concepts covered in this chapter.

The following Online Learning Resources are available in the Online Learning Center:

- Multiple choice questions
- Short answer questions
- Matching exercises

Note to Instructor and Students: *For most of these projects, you use the* SkyDrive *Windows folder and* SkyDrive *groups. If these are not available on your computer, refer to the instructions in the* More Info *boxes on pages 702 (second* More Info *box) and 708.*

Guided Project 12-1

For this project, you work on documents from American River Cycling Club using *SkyDrive*, Office Web Apps, and *SkyDrive* groups.
[Student Learning Outcomes 12.1, 12.3, 12.4, 12.5]

Note to Students and Instructor:

Students: *For this project, you share a* SkyDrive *file with your instructor and invite your instructor to a* SkyDrive *group.*
Instructor: *In order to complete this project, your students need your Microsoft email address.*

Files Needed: ***TrainingLog-12.docx***, ***ARCCCyclingCalendar-12.docx***, ***FlexibilityExercises-12.docx***, and ***HeartRate-12.docx***
Completed Project File Name: ***[your initials] Word 12-1.docx***

Skills Covered in This Project

- Reset customizations to the *Ribbon* and *Quick Access* toolbar.
- Customize the *Quick Access* toolbar for the current document.
- Log in to *SkyDrive* and create a folder.
- Upload a file to your *SkyDrive* folder.
- Share a *SkyDrive* file.
- Create a *SkyDrive* group and invite a member.
- Upload a file to your group.
- Customize group options.

---

1. Open the ***TrainingLog-12*** document from your student data files.
2. Save this document as ***[your initials] Word 12-1***.
3. Reset the *Ribbon* and *Quick Access* toolbar.
   a. Click the **Customize Quick Access Toolbar** drop-down list and select **More Commands** to open the *Word Options* dialog box with the *Quick Access Toolbar* area displayed (Figure 12-77).
   b. Click the **Reset** button and select **Reset all customizations**. A confirmation dialog box opens.
   c. Click **Yes** to delete all *Ribbon* and *Quick Access* toolbar customizations.
4. Add commands to the *Quick Access* toolbar for this document only.
   a. With the *Word Options* dialog box still open and the *Quick Access Toolbar* area displayed, click the

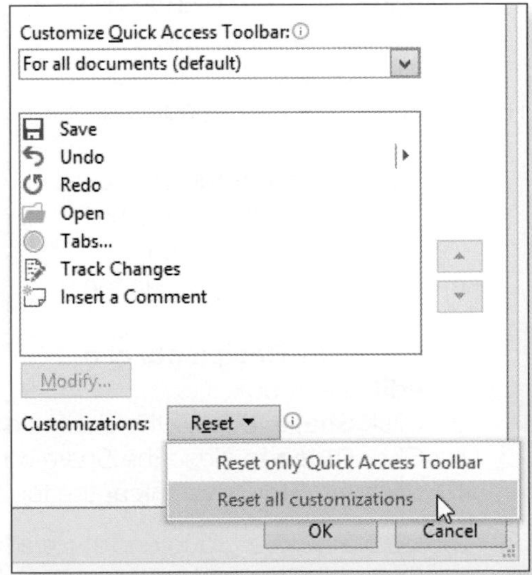

12-77 Reset *Ribbon* and *Quick Access* toolbar customizations

Customize Quick Access Toolbar drop-down list on the right and select **For [your initials] Word 12-1** (Figure 12-78).

b. In the list on the left, select **Quick Print** and select **Add**.
c. Add **Spelling & Grammar** and **Open** to the *Quick Access* toolbar.
d. Click **OK** to close the *Word Options* dialog box.

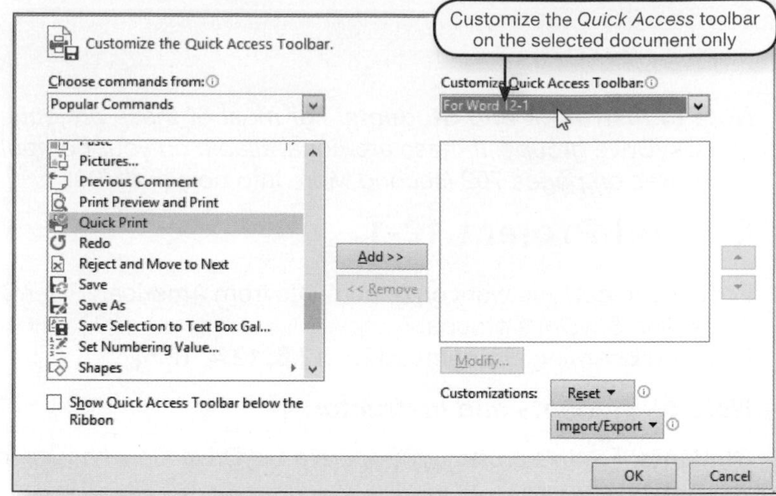

12-78 Add commands to the *Quick Access* toolbar on this document only

5. Save and close the document and exit Word.
6. Open an Internet browser page and log in to your *SkyDrive* account (www.skydrive.com).
7. Create a folder and upload files to your *SkyDrive*.
   a. Click the **Files** button on the left to display your *SkyDrive* folders and files.
   b. Click the **Create** button and select **Folder** from the drop-down list.
   c. Type ARCC as the name of the new folder and press **Enter**.
   d. Click the **ARCC** folder to open it.
   e. Click the **Upload** button to open an upload dialog box.
   f. Select ***[your initials] Word 12-1*** from your solutions files and click **Open** to add this file to the *ARCC* folder.
   g. Upload the following files to the *ARCC* folder from your student data files: ***ARCCCyclingCalendar-12***, ***FlexibilityExercises-12***, and ***HeartRate-12***.
8. Share a file on *SkyDrive* with your instructor.
   a. Click the ***[your initials] Word 12-1*** file in the *ARCC* folder to open it in Word Web App in *read-only* mode.
   b. Click **Share** at the top to open the *Share* window (Figure 12-79).
   c. Select **Send email** on the left.
   d. Type your instructor's email address in the *To* area.
   e. Type a brief message in the body area.
   f. Check the **Recipients can edit** check box.

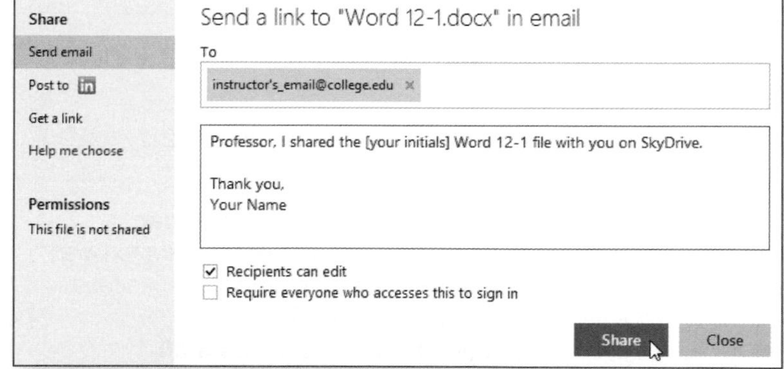

12-79 Share a document

   g. Click **Share** to send the sharing email to your instructor.
   h. Click **Close** to close the *Share* window.
   i. Click the **SkyDrive** link at the top to return to your *SkyDrive* folders.
9. Create a *SkyDrive* group and invite a member.
   a. Click the **Groups** button on the left to open the *Groups* area.
   b. Type American River Cycling Club in the *Group name* text box.

c. Type your last name, first initial, and -ARCC in the *Group email* text box (e.g., NordellR-ARCC).
d. Click **Create group** to create your group. If the email address is not available, type a different one.

10. Invite a member to your group.
    a. Click the **Group actions** button at the top and select **Invite people**.
    b. Type your instructor's email address in the *Add people* area.
    c. Click **Invite**.
11. Upload files to your group.
    a. Select **American River Cycling Club** in the *Groups* area on the left if it is not already selected.
    b. Click the **Upload** button to open an upload dialog box.
    c. Select the ***ARCCCyclingCalendar-12***, ***FlexibilityExercises-12***, ***HeartRate-12***, and ***TrainingLog-12*** files from your student data files and click **Open** to add the files to your group.
12. Change group options.
    a. With your group selected, click the **Group options** button at the top. The *Options* page opens.
    b. Select **Email** on the left to display email options.
    c. In the *Link to group website* area, select the **Only group members can view the group using this link** radio button.
    d. Click **Save** at the bottom to save and apply the changes. The *Options* page closes.
    e. Click the **Group options** button again to reopen the *Options* page.
    f. Select **Group conversations** on the left to display group conversation options.
    g. Select **Turn off group conversations**. You are taken back to your *SkyDrive* group.
    h. Click **SkyDrive** at the top to return to your *SkyDrive* folders and groups.
13. Select **[your name]** in the upper right corner and select **Sign out** from the *Account* drop-down list (Figure 12-80).

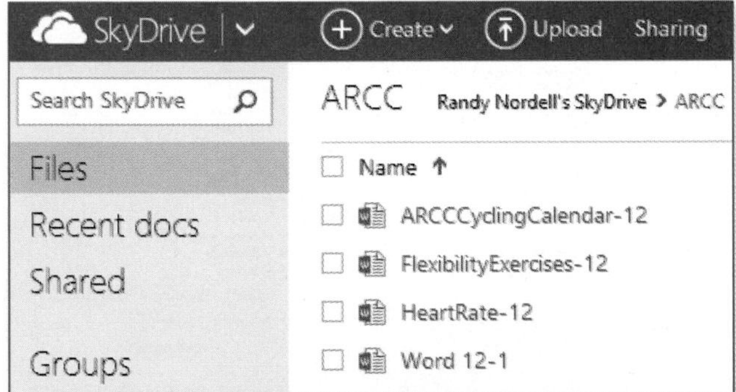

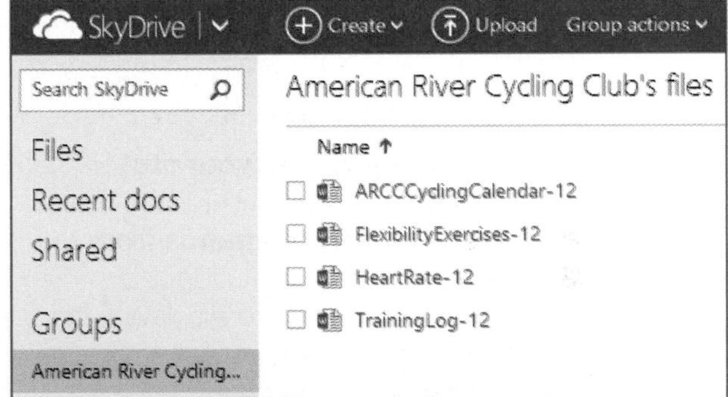

12-80 Word 12-1 completed (*ARCC* folder in *SkyDrive* and *American River Cycling Club* group)

Guided Project 12-2

For this project, you use *SkyDrive* and Word Web App to customize a document for Hamilton Civic Center.
[Student Learning Outcomes 12.1, 12.3, 12.5]

Note to Students and Instructor:

Students*: In this project, you share a* SkyDrive *folder with your instructor.*
Instructor*: In order to complete this project, your students need your Microsoft email address.*

File Needed: ***YogaClasses-12.docx***
Completed Project File Name: ***[your initials] Word 12-2.docx***

Skills Covered in This Project

- Create a new group on the *Home* tab.
- Add and arrange commands in the custom group.
- Arrange a group on a tab.
- Save a file to your *SkyDrive* folder.
- Log in to *SkyDrive* and create a folder.
- Copy a file to a *SkyDrive* folder.
- Edit a document in Word Web App.
- Add a comment to a document in Word Web App.
- Share a *SkyDrive* folder.

1. Open the ***YogaClasses-12*** document from your student data files.
2. Save this document as ***[your initials] Word 12-2***.
3. Customize the *Ribbon* to add a group and commands.
   a. Right-click anywhere on the **Ribbon** and select **Customize the Ribbon** from the context menu to open the *Word Options* dialog box with the *Customize Ribbon* area displayed.
   b. On the right, click the **Home** tab and click the **New Group** button. A new group is inserted below the existing groups on the *Home* tab.
   c. Select **New Group (Custom)** and click **Rename** to open the *Rename* dialog box.
   d. Select a symbol of your choice, type your first name as the group name in the *Display name* area, and click **OK** to close the *Rename* dialog box.
   e. On the right, select the **[your first name]** group.
   f. Click the **Choose commands from** drop-down list on the left side and select **All Commands** to display all the available commands in the list on the left (Figure 12-81).
   g. Select the **New Comment** command and click the **Add** button between the two lists to add the command to the group.
   h. Add the **Tabs**, **Custom Margins**, and **Borders and Shading** (first one) commands to the *[your first name]* group.
   i. Use the **Move Up** and **Move Down** buttons to arrange the commands in alphabetical order.
   j. Select the **[your first name] (Custom)** group and click the **Move Up** button so it appears between the *Styles* and *Editing* groups.
   k. Click **OK** to close the *Word Options* dialog box.
   l. Click the **Home** tab to view your custom group (Figure 12-82).

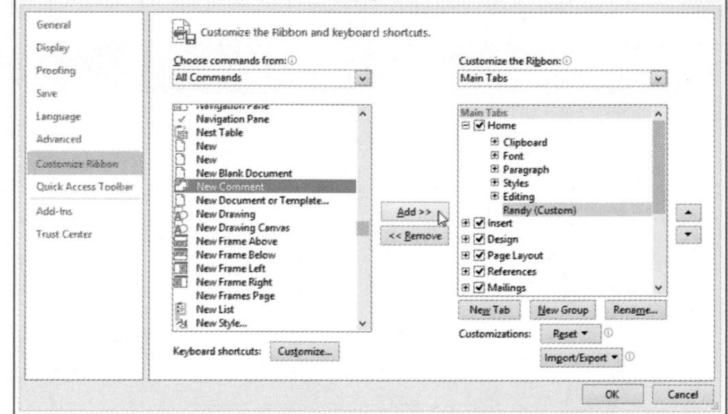

12-81 Add a custom group and commands to the *Home* tab

12-82 Custom group displayed on the *Home* tab

4. Save the file to a *SkyDrive* folder.
   a. Open the *Save As* dialog box and select **SkyDrive** on the left.
   b. Double-click the **[your first name]** folder to open it and click **Save**. If you don't have a *[your first name]* folder in your *SkyDrive*, create it.
5. Close the document and exit Word.
6. Open an Internet browser page and log in to your *SkyDrive* account (www.skydrive.com).
7. Create a folder and copy a file.
   a. Select **Files** on the left if it is not already selected.
   b. Click the **Create** button and select **Folder** from the drop-down list.
   c. Type HCC as the name of the new folder and press **Enter**.
   d. Click the **[your first name]** folder to open it.
   e. Click the ***[your initials] Word 12-2*** check box to select this file.
   f. Click the **Manage** button and select **Copy to** from the drop-down list to open the copy to dialog box.
   g. Click the **HCC** folder and click **Copy** to close the dialog box and copy the file to the selected folder.
8. Edit a document in Word Web App.
   a. Click **Files** on the left to return to your *SkyDrive* folders.
   b. Click the **HCC** folder to open it.
   c. Click the ***[your initials] Word 12-2*** file to open it in Word Web App.
   d. Click the **Edit Document** button and select **Edit in Word Web App**. The text box that was in the upper right corner is not displayed correctly, and text wrapping around the picture might not display correctly. Don't try to fix these in Word Web App.
   e. Place your insertion point at the end of the second body paragraph (" . . . yoga mat and towel.") and press **Enter** two times.
   f. Type Our yoga classes are taught on the following days and times: and press **Enter** two times.
   g. Click the **Bullets** button and type the following bulleted lines:

      Monday, Wednesday, and Friday at 6 and 8 a.m.
      Tuesday and Thursday at 7 a.m. and 12:30 p.m.
      Saturday and Sunday at 9 a.m.

   h. Click the **Save** button or press **Ctrl+S** to save the document.
9. Add a comment to a document in Word Web App.
   a. Click the **SkyDrive** link at the top to return to your *SkyDrive* folders.
   b. Click the **HCC** folder to open it.
   c. Click the ***[your initials] Word 12-2*** file to open it in Word Web App.
   d. Select the sentence before the bulleted list.
   e. Click the **Comments** button to open the *Comments* pane on the right.
   f. Click the **New Comment** button in the *Comments* pane to create a new comment (Figure 12-83).
   g. In the new comment area, type Rachel, please confirm with Amanda the days/times of the yoga classes and click **Post**.

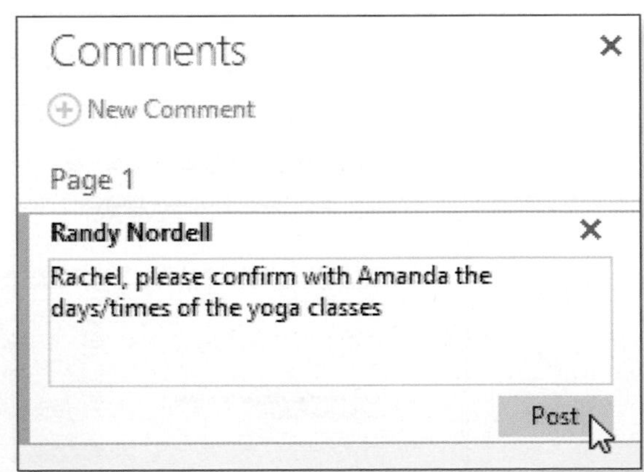

12-83 Create and post a new comment in Word Web App

10. Share a folder on *SkyDrive* with your instructor.
    a. Click the **SkyDrive** link at the top to return to your *SkyDrive* folders.
    b. Click the **HCC** folder check box to select it.

c. Click the **Sharing** link at the top to open the sharing dialog box (Figure 12-84).
d. Select **Send email** on the left.
e. Type your instructor's email address in the *To* area.
f. Type a brief message in the body area.
g. Check the **Recipients can edit** check box.
h. Click **Share** to send the sharing email to your instructor.
i. Click **Close** to close the sharing dialog box.

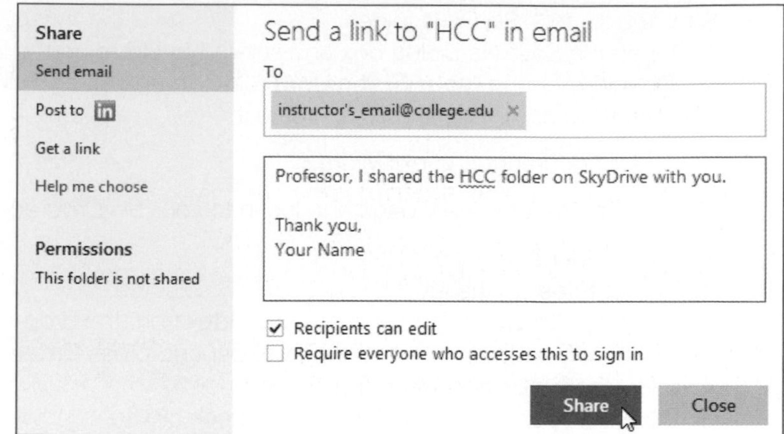

12-84 Share a folder

11. Select **[your name]** in the upper right corner and select **Sign out** from the *Account* drop-down list.
12. Open a document in Word.
    a. Open Word and open the *Open* dialog box.
    b. Select **SkyDrive** on the left, double-click the **HCC** folder to open it, and open the ***[your initials] Word 12-2*** document.
    c. The comment you created in Word Web App is visible on the right (Figure 12-85).
13. Save this document where you store your completed files and close the document. If you are prompted, select **Replace existing file** and click **OK**.

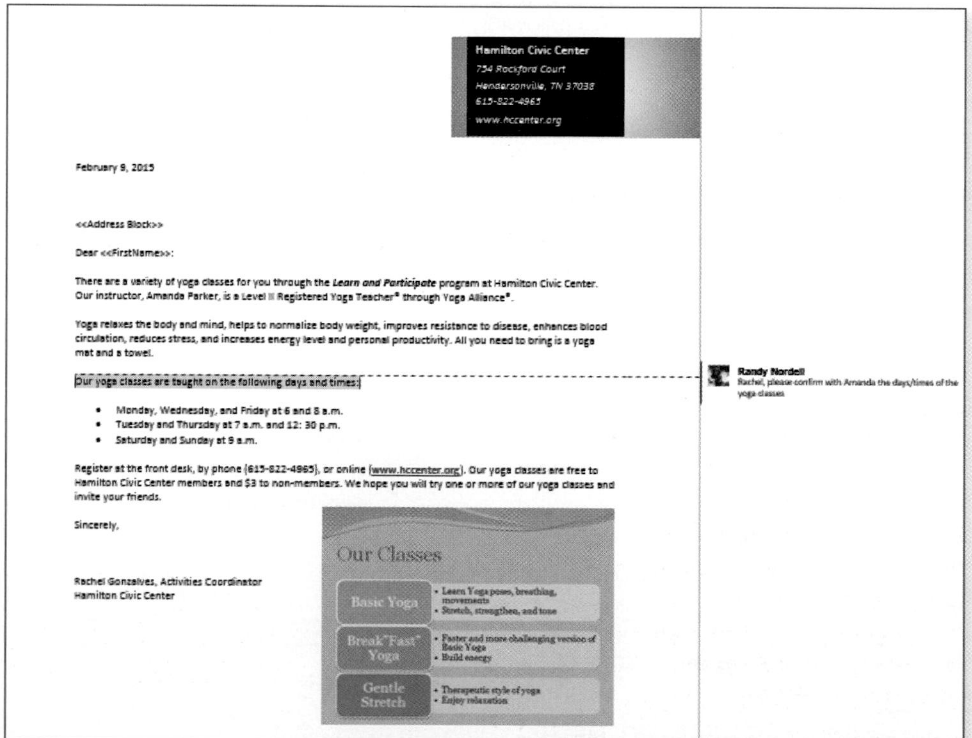

Hamilton Civic Center
754 Rockford Court
Hendersonville, TN 37038
615-822-4965
www.hccenter.org

February 9, 2015

<<Address Block>>

Dear <<FirstName>>:

There are a variety of yoga classes for you through the ***Learn and Participate*** program at Hamilton Civic Center. Our instructor, Amanda Parker, is a Level II Registered Yoga Teacher® through Yoga Alliance®.

Yoga relaxes the body and mind, helps to normalize body weight, improves resistance to disease, enhances blood circulation, reduces stress, and increases energy level and personal productivity. All you need to bring is a yoga mat and a towel.

Our yoga classes are taught on the following days and times:

- Monday, Wednesday, and Friday at 6 and 8 a.m.
- Tuesday and Thursday at 7 a.m. and 12: 30 p.m.
- Saturday and Sunday at 9 a.m.

Register at the front desk, by phone (615-822-4965), or online (www.hccenter.org). Our yoga classes are free to Hamilton Civic Center members and $3 to non-members. We hope you will try one or more of our yoga classes and invite your friends.

Sincerely,

Rachel Gonzalves, Activities Coordinator
Hamilton Civic Center

Our Classes
Basic Yoga: Learn Yoga poses, breathing, movements; Stretch, strengthen, and tone
Break"Fast" Yoga: Faster and more challenging version of Basic Yoga; Build energy
Gentle Stretch: Therapeutic style of yoga; Enjoy relaxation

Randy Nordell
Rachel, please confirm with Amanda the days/times of the yoga classes

12-85 Word 12-2 completed

Guided Project 12-3

For this project, you customize your working environment in Word and create a *SkyDrive* group and modify files for Placer Hills Real Estate.
[Student Learning Outcomes 12.1, 12.3, 12.4, 12.5]

Note to Students and Instructor:

Students: *For this project, you create a* SkyDrive *group and invite your instructor to become a member.*
Instructor: *In order to complete this project, your students need your Microsoft email address.*

Files Needed: ***ExpirationLetter-12.docx***, ***EscrowChecklist-12.docx***, and ***HomeBuying-12.docx***
Completed Project File Name: ***[your initials] Word 12-3.docx***

Skills Covered in This Project

- Change default save location in Word.
- Reset the *Quick Access* toolbar.
- Add and rearrange commands on the *Quick Access* toolbar.
- Save a file to a *SkyDrive* folder.
- Create a *SkyDrive* group and invite a member.
- Upload a file to your group.
- Create a folder and copy a file in a *SkyDrive* group.
- Edit a document in Word Web App.
- Rename a *SkyDrive* file.

---

1. Open the ***ExpirationLetter-12*** document from your student data files.
2. Change default save location.
   a. Click the **File** tab to open the *Backstage* view and click **Options** to open the *Word Options* dialog box.
   b. Select **Save** to display save options (Figure 12-86).
   c. Click the **Browse** button to the right of *Default local file location*. The *Modify Location* dialog box opens.
   d. Select the **SkyDrive** folder on the left and click **OK** to close *the Modify Location* dialog box and change the default save location. Leave the *Word Options* dialog box open.

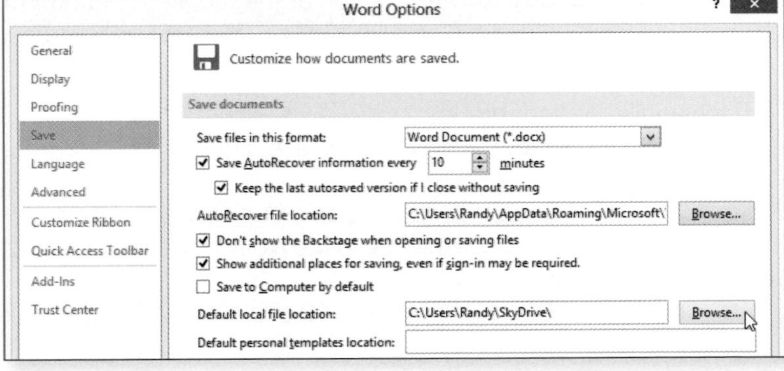

12-86 Change default save location

3. Reset and modify the *Quick Access* toolbar.
   a. In the *Word Options* dialog box, select **Quick Access Toolbar** on the left.
   b. Click the **Reset** button and select **Reset only Quick Access Toolbar**. Note: if your *Quick Access* toolbar is already at its original settings, the *Reset only Quick Access Toolbar* option is not active and you can skip both this step and 9c.
   c. Click **Yes** in the dialog box that opens to confirm the reset.

d. In the list of commands on the left, select **Email** and click the **Add** button to add it to the *Quick Access* toolbar (Figure 12-87).
e. Add **Insert a Comment**, **Quick Print**, and **Open** to the *Quick Access* toolbar.
f. Use the **Move Up** button to move *Open* up so it appears after *Save*.
g. Click **OK** to close the *Word Options* dialog box.

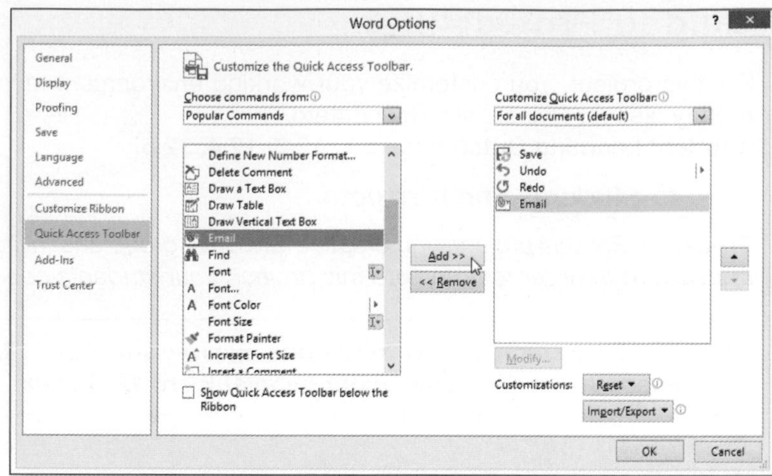

12-87 Add commands to the *Quick Access* toolbar

4. Use the *Save As* dialog box to save this document as ***ExpirationLetter-12*** in the *[your first name]* folder in the *SkyDrive* folder (don't rename the file).
5. Close the document and exit Word.
6. Create a *SkyDrive* group and invite a member.
   a. Open an Internet browser page and log in to your *SkyDrive* account (www.skydrive.com).
   b. Click the **Groups** button on the left to open the *Groups* area.
   c. Type Placer Hills Real Estate in the *Group name* text box.
   d. Type your last name, first initial, and -PHRE in the *Group email* text box (e.g., NordellR-PHRE).
   e. Click **Create group** to create your group. If the email address is not available, type a different one.
7. Invite a member to your group.
   a. Click the **Group actions** button at the top and select **Invite people**.
   b. Type your instructor's email address in the *Add people* area.
   c. Click **Invite**.
8. Upload files to your group.
   a. Select the **Placer Hills Real Estate** group in the *Groups* area on the left if it is not already selected.
   b. Click the **Upload** button to open an upload dialog box.
   c. Select ***ExpirationLetter-12*** in the *[your first name]* folder in the *SkyDrive* folder and click **Open** to add the file to your group.
   d. Upload the **EscrowChecklist-12** and **HomeBuying-12** files to your group from your student data files.
9. Create a folder and copy a file.
   a. In the *Placer Hills Real Estate* group, click the **Create** button and select **Folder** from the drop-down list.
   b. Type Expiration Letters and press **Enter**.
   c. Click the ***ExpirationLetter-12*** check box (make sure this is the only check box selected).
   d. Click the **Manage** button and select **Copy to** from the drop-down list to open the copy to dialog box.
   e. Select the **Expiration Letters** folder and click **Copy**.
10. Edit a document in Word Web App.
   a. Click the **Expiration Letters** folder to open it.
   b. Click the ***ExpirationLetter-12*** file to open it in Word Web App.

c. Click the **Edit Document** button at the top and select **Edit in Word Web App**.
d. Replace the "*<Address Block>*" placeholder text with the following recipient address:

   Mr. Rick DePonte
   8364 Marshall Street
   Granite Bay, CA 95863

e. Replace the "*<Salutation>*" placeholder text with Mr. DePonte.
f. Click the **Save** button (Figure 12-88).
g. Click the **SkyDrive** link at the top to return to your *SkyDrive* folders.

PHRE
Placer Hills
Real Estate

October 9, 2014

Mr. Rick DePonte
8364 Marshall Street
Granite Bay, CA 95863

Dear Mr. DePonte:

I noticed today that your current home listing in Granite Bay will expire soon. My goal is to tell you about **Placer Hills Real Estate** and myself. We can offer you attention and services that are unmatched by other real estate companies.

The service and experience I can offer you when helping you with your selling needs is unmatched. Working together with you, I am confident that we can analyze your present and future goals and help you obtain them. If you are curious as to the type of activity that has been occurring in your area or you would like to discuss your needs and goals, I would be more than happy to come by and talk with you.

Gaining your trust and confidence to build a solid relationship for the future is my first priority. I have enclosed a document that will provide you with valuable information about buying a home.

Feel free to call me to set up an appointment if you would like a unique perspective for marketing your home and buying a new home from someone with thorough knowledge and experience with homes in your neighborhood. I look forward to talking with you soon.

Best regards,

EMMA CAVALLI
Realtor Consultant
Placer Hills Real Estate

Enclosure

Emma Cavalli | Placer Hills Real Estate

12-88 Word 12-3 completed

11. Rename a file in *SkyDrive*.
    a. Select the **Placer Hills Real Estate** group on the left and click the **Expiration Letters** folder.
    b. Click the ***Expiration Letter_12*** check box to select it.
    c. Click the **Manage** button and select **Rename** from the drop-down list.
    d. Type [your initials] Word 12-3 as the file name and press **Enter**.
12. Select **[your name]** in the upper right corner and select **Sign out** from the *Account* drop-down list.

Independent Project 12-4

For this project, you customize the working environment in Word and use *SkyDrive*, Word Web App, and a *SkyDrive* group to customize, store, edit, and share documents for Sierra Pacific Community College District.
[Student Learning Outcomes 12.1, 12.2, 12.3, 12.4, 12.5]

Note to Students and Instructor:

Students*: For this project, you share a* SkyDrive *file with your instructor and invite your instructor to become a member of a* SkyDrive *group.*
Instructor*: In order to complete this project, your students need your Microsoft email address.*

Files Needed: ***OnlineLearning-12.docx***, ***EmergencyProcedures-12.docx***, and ***WritingTips-12.docx***
Completed Project File Name: ***[your initials] Word 12-4.docx***

Skills Covered in This Project

- Create a *SkyDrive* folder.
- Reset the *Ribbon* and the *Quick Access* toolbar.
- Create a new tab and group on the *Ribbon*.
- Add and arrange commands in a custom group.
- Add commands to the *Quick Access* toolbar.
- Log in to *SkyDrive* and upload a file.
- Create a document in Word Web App and apply formatting.
- Add a comment to a document and share a document in Word Web App.
- Create a *SkyDrive* group and invite a member.
- Upload a file to a group.
- Customize group options.

---

1. Create a *SkyDrive* folder and open and save a document.
   a. Open Windows Explorer or a Windows folder, open your **SkyDrive** folder, and create a new folder named SPCCD.
   b. Open Word and open the ***OnlineLearning-12*** document from your student data files.
   c. Save this file as ***OnlineLearning-12*** in the *SPCCD* folder in your *SkyDrive* folder.
2. Reset and customize the *Ribbon* and the *Quick Access* toolbar.
   a. Reset all customizations to the *Ribbon* and the *Quick Access* toolbar.
   b. Create a new tab after the *Home* tab.
   c. Rename the new tab to SPCCD.
   d. Create a new group in the *SPCCD* tab.
   e. Rename the new custom group to Frequent Commands and select a symbol of your choice.
   f. Add the following commands (in *Popular Commands*) to the *Frequent Commands* group: **Save As**, **Spelling & Grammar**, **New Comment**, **Page Setup**, **Paragraph**, and **Pictures**.
   g. Arrange these commands in alphabetical order.
   h. Add **Open** and **Quick Print** to the *Quick Access* toolbar.
3. Customize Word options.
   a. Open the *Word Options* dialog box and select the **General** tab.
   b. Confirm that your *User name* and *Initials* are correct.
   c. Select an *Office Background* and *Office Theme* of your choice.
   d. Select the **Advanced** category on the left and check the **Expand all headings when opening a document** check box in the *Show document content* area.

4. Save and close the document and exit Word (don't rename the document).
5. Upload files to your *SkyDrive* folder.
   a. Open an Internet browser page and log in to your *SkyDrive* account (www.skydrive.com).
   b. Open the **SPCCD** folder and add the following files from your student data files: ***EmergencyProcedures-12*** and ***WritingTips-12***. The ***OnlineLearning-12*** document is already in this folder. If it is not, add it.
6. Create a new document in Word Web App.
   a. In the *SPCCD* folder, create a new **Word document** using Word Web App and name it [your initials] Word 12-4.
   b. Refer to Figure 12-89 and enter the information in the new document.
   c. Apply **Heading 1** style and **bold** format to the first line.
   d. Apply **Bullets** and **6 pt. after** paragraph spacing to the bulleted list.
   e. Save the document and return to your *SPCCD* folder in *SkyDrive*.

SPCCD Fall Semester Important Dates

- August 22: Classes Begin
- August 30: Last Day to Register
- October 1: Apply for Fall Graduation
- November 8: Last Day to Drop
- December 14-18: Final Exams

12-89 Data for document in Word Web App

7. Add a comment and share the file.
   a. Open the ***[your initials] Word 12-4*** document in *read-only* mode in Word Web App.
   b. Add and post the following comment to the bulleted list in the document: Please confirm these dates are correct.
   c. Share this file with your instructor, include a brief message, and allow him or her to edit the document.
8. Create a new group, invite a member, and upload files.
   a. Create a new group named Sierra Pacific CCD.
   b. Type your last name, first initial, and -SPCCD in the email area (e.g., NordellR-SPCCD).
   c. Use your instructor's email address to invite him or her as a member.
   d. Upload the following files from your *SPCCD* folder in *SkyDrive* to the *Sierra Pacific CCD* group: ***[your initials] Word 12-4***, ***EmergencyProcedures-12***, ***OnlineLearning-12***, and ***WritingTips-12***.
9. Sign out of *SkyDrive* (Figure 12-90).

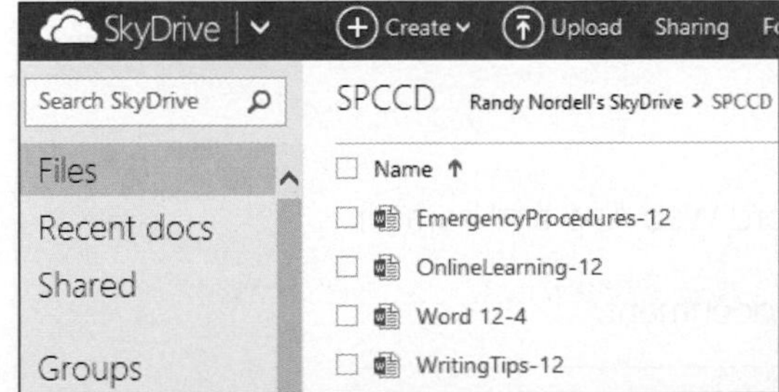

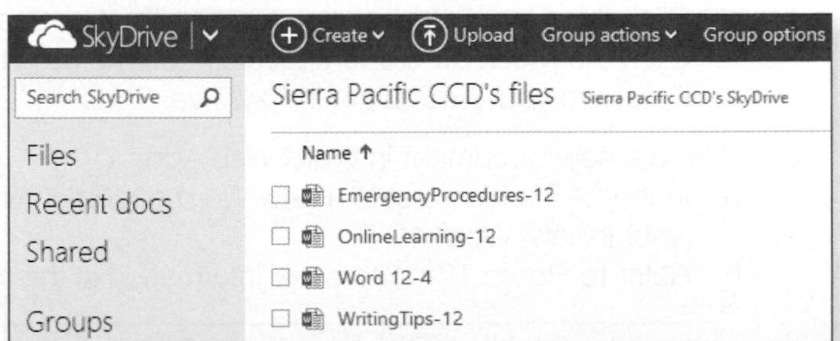

12-90 Word 12-4 completed (*SPCCD* folder in *SkyDrive* and *Sierra Pacific CCD* group)

Independent Project 12-5

For this project, you use *SkyDrive*, Word Web App, and a *SkyDrive* group to customize, store, edit, and share documents for Life's Animal Shelter.
[Student Learning Outcomes 12.3, 12.4, 12.5]

Note to Students and Instructor:

***Students**: For this project, you share a* SkyDrive *folder with your instructor and invite your instructor to become a member of a* SkyDrive *group.*
***Instructor**: In order to complete this project, your students need your Microsoft email address.*

Files Needed: ***LASExpenses-12.docx*** and ***LASSupportForm-12.docx***
Completed Project File Name: ***[your initials] Word 12-5.docx***

Skills Covered in This Project

- Create a *SkyDrive* folder.
- Upload a file to a *SkyDrive* folder.
- Edit a document in Word Web App.
- Mark a comment as done.
- Create a document in Word Web App and apply formatting.
- Share a *SkyDrive* folder.
- Create a *SkyDrive* group and invite a member.
- Upload a file to a group.
- Customize group options.

---

1. Create a *SkyDrive* folder and upload files to the *SkyDrive* folder.
   a. Open an Internet browser page and log in to your *SkyDrive* account (www.skydrive.com).
   b. Create a new folder name LAS in the *Files* area.
   c. Upload the following files from your student data files to the *LAS* folder: ***LASExpenses-12*** and ***LASSupportForm-12***.
2. Edit a document and a comment.
   a. Open the ***LASExpenses-12*** document in *SkyDrive* and edit in Word Web App.
   b. Change the day in the "DATE" line to 22. It should be March 22, 2015.
   c. Save and close the document and open it in *read-only* mode in Word Web App.
   d. Click the **comment balloon** to open the *Comments* pane.
   e. Click the **Mark as Done** check box on the comment.
   f. Return to your *LAS* folder in *SkyDrive*.
3. Create a new document in Word Web App.
   a. In the *LAS* folder, create a new Word document in Word Web App and name it [your initials] Word 12-5.
   b. Refer to Figure 12-91 to enter information in the new document.

New LAS Supporters

Name	Email	Phone
Jennie Solara	jennies@live.com	208-773-2519
Ramon and Mary Clifton	cliftonrm@gmail.com	208-836-9914
Trevor Andrews	tandrews@outlook.com	208-228-3498

12-91 Data for document in Word Web App

c. Insert a table for the body information.
d. Apply **Heading 2** style and **bold** formatting to the first line.
e. Apply **Heading 3** style and **bold** formatting to the column headings.
f. Save the document and return to your *LAS* folder.

4. Share the *LAS* folder with your instructor, include a brief message, and allow him or her to edit the document.
5. Create a new group, invite a member, and add files.
   a. Create a new group named Life's Animal Shelter.
   b. Type your last name, first initial, and -LAS in the email area (e.g., NordellR-LAS).
   c. Use your instructor's email address to invite him or her as a member.
   d. Upload all of the files from your *LAS* folder in *SkyDrive* to the *Life's Animal Shelter* group.
6. Customize the group options to turn off group conversations.
7. Sign out of *SkyDrive* (Figure 12-92).

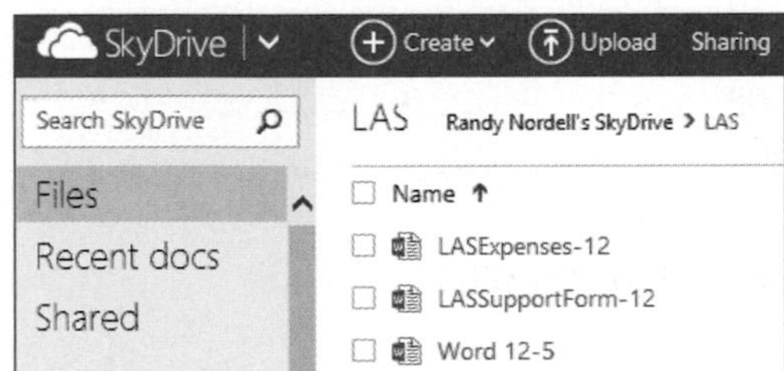

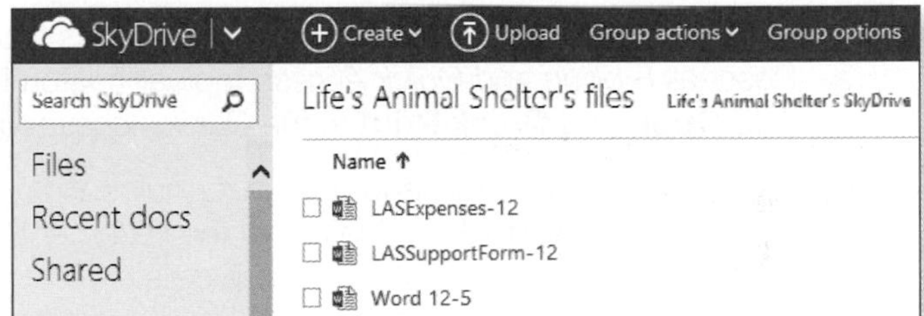

12-92 Word 12-5 completed (*LAS* folder in *SkyDrive* and *Life's Animal Shelter* group)

Independent Project 12-6

For this project, you use *SkyDrive*, Word Web App, and a *SkyDrive* group to customize, store, edit, and share documents for Central Sierra Insurance.
[Student Learning Outcomes 12.1, 12.3, 12.4, 12.5]

Note to Students and Instructor:

Students: *For this project, you share a* SkyDrive *file with your instructor and invite your instructor to become a member of a* SkyDrive *group.*
Instructor: *In order to complete this project, your students need your Microsoft email address.*

Files Needed: ***RenewalLetter-12.docx*** and ***ConferenceRegistrationForm-12.docx***
Completed Project File Name: ***[your initials] Word 12-6.docx***

Skills Covered in This Project

- Reset the *Ribbon* and the *Quick Access* toolbar.
- Edit a document and update formulas.
- Log in to *SkyDrive* and create a folder.
- Move a file and upload a file to a *SkyDrive* folder.
- Delete a comment from a document and share a document in Word Web App.
- Add a comment to a document and share a document in Word Web App.
- Create a *SkyDrive* group and invite a member.
- Upload a file to a group.

---

1. In Word, open the ***RenewalLetter-12*** document from your student data files.
2. Save this file as ***[your initials] Word 12-6*** in the *[your first name]* folder in your *SkyDrive* folder.
3. Reset and customize the *Ribbon* and *Quick Access* toolbar.
   a. Reset all *Ribbon* and *Quick Access* toolbar customizations.
   b. Add **Open** and **Quick Print** to the *Quick Access* toolbar.
4. Edit information in the table and update formulas.
   a. In the table, change the value below the *Rate per $1,000* column heading to $19.50.
   b. Update the formulas in the next three cells.
5. Save and close the document and exit Word.
6. Create a *SkyDrive* folder, move a file, and upload a file to your *SkyDrive*.
   a. Open an Internet browser page and log in to your *SkyDrive* account (www.skydrive.com).
   b. Create a new folder named CSI.
   c. Move the ***[your initials] Word 12-6*** file to the *CSI* folder.
   d. Open the **CSI** folder and upload the ***ConferenceRegistrationForm-12*** file from your student data files.
7. Delete a comment and share a document.
   a. Open the ***[your initials] Word 12-6*** document (in the *CSI* folder) in Word Web App in *read-only* mode and delete the comment.
   b. Share this document with your instructor, include a brief message, and allow him or her to edit the document.
8. Add a comment to a document and share the document.
   a. Open the ***ConferenceRegistrationForm-12*** file from your *CSI* folder in Word Web App in *read-only* view.
   b. Add and post the following comment on the first line of the document: Please email this conference registration form to all CSI sales staff.
9. Create a new group, invite a member, and upload files.
   a. Create a new group named Central Sierra Insurance.
   b. Type your last name, first initial, and -CSI in the email area (e.g., NordellR-CSI).
   c. Use your instructor's email address to invite him or her as a member.
   d. Upload both of the files from your *CSI* folder in *SkyDrive* to the *Central Sierra Insurance* group.

10. Sign out of *SkyDrive* (Figure 12-93).

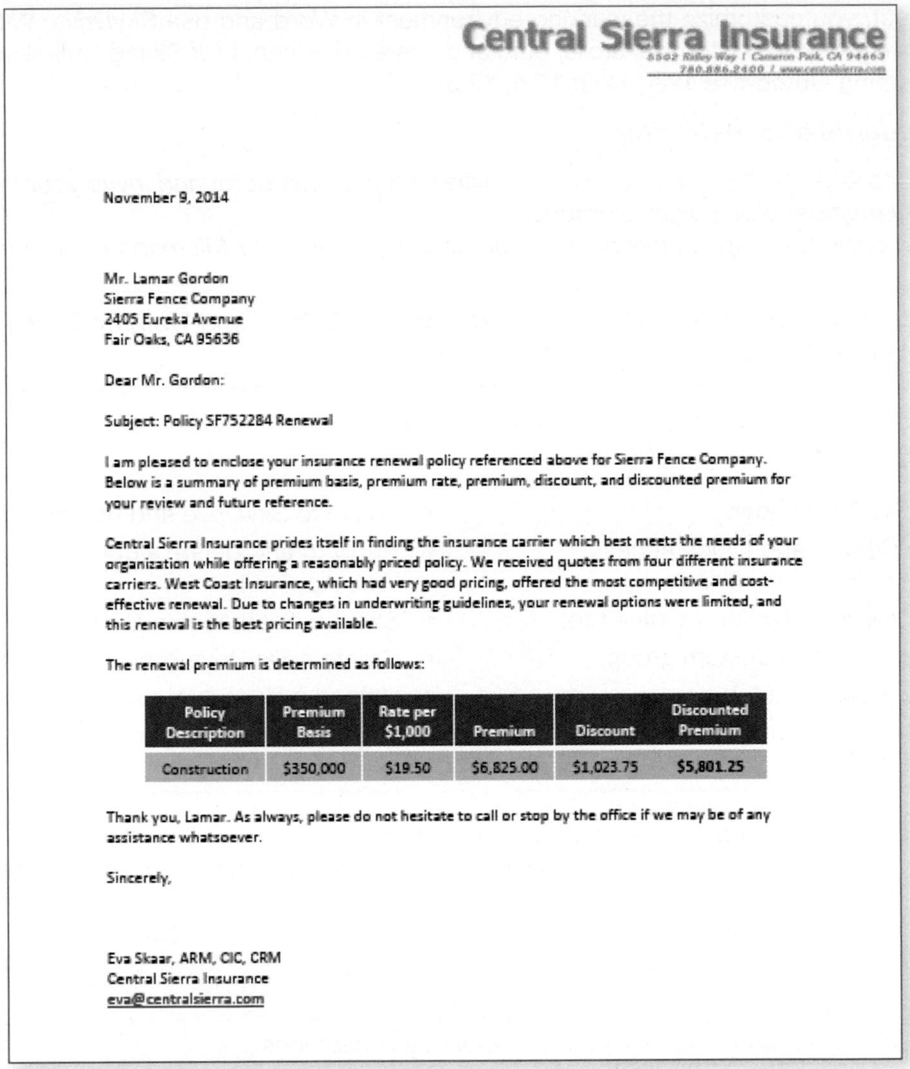

Central Sierra Insurance
6502 Ridley Way | Cameron Park, CA 94663
780.886.2400 | www.centralsierra.com

November 9, 2014

Mr. Lamar Gordon
Sierra Fence Company
2405 Eureka Avenue
Fair Oaks, CA 95636

Dear Mr. Gordon:

Subject: Policy SF752284 Renewal

I am pleased to enclose your insurance renewal policy referenced above for Sierra Fence Company. Below is a summary of premium basis, premium rate, premium, discount, and discounted premium for your review and future reference.

Central Sierra Insurance prides itself in finding the insurance carrier which best meets the needs of your organization while offering a reasonably priced policy. We received quotes from four different insurance carriers. West Coast Insurance, which had very good pricing, offered the most competitive and cost-effective renewal. Due to changes in underwriting guidelines, your renewal options were limited, and this renewal is the best pricing available.

The renewal premium is determined as follows:

Policy Description	Premium Basis	Rate per $1,000	Premium	Discount	Discounted Premium
Construction	$350,000	$19.50	$6,825.00	$1,023.75	**$5,801.25**

Thank you, Lamar. As always, please do not hesitate to call or stop by the office if we may be of any assistance whatsoever.

Sincerely,

Eva Skaar, ARM, CIC, CRM
Central Sierra Insurance
eva@centralsierra.com

12-93 Word 12-6 completed

Improve It Project 12-7

For this project, you customize the working environment in Word and use *SkyDrive*, Word Web App, and a *SkyDrive* group to customize, store, edit, and share documents for Skiing Unlimited. [Student Learning Outcomes 12.1, 12.3, 12.4, 12.5]

Note to Students and Instructor:

Students: *For this project, you share a* SkyDrive *file with your instructor and invite your instructor to become a member of a* SkyDrive *group.*

Instructor: *In order to complete this project, your students need your Microsoft email address.*

Files Needed: ***VolunteerLetter-12.docx***, ***SkiingUnlimited-12.docx***, and ***TrainingGuide-12.docx***
Completed Project File Name: ***[your initials] Word 12-7.docx***

Skills Covered in This Project

- Create a *SkyDrive* folder.
- Reset the *Ribbon* and *Quick Access* toolbar.
- Create a new group on an existing tab.
- Add commands to a custom group.
- Arrange a group on a tab.
- Add commands to the *Quick Access* toolbar.
- Log in to *SkyDrive* and upload a file.
- Reply to and delete a comment in Word Web App.
- Share a document in *SkyDrive*.
- Create a *SkyDrive* group and invite a member.
- Upload a file to a group.
- Customize group options.

---

1. Create a *SkyDrive* folder and open and save a document.
   a. Open Windows Explorer or a Windows folder, open your **SkyDrive** folder, and create a new folder named Skiing Unlimited.
   b. In Word, open the ***VolunteerLetter-12*** document from your student data files.
   c. Save this file as ***[your initials] Word 12-7*** in the *Skiing Unlimited* folder in your *SkyDrive* folder.
2. Reset and customize the *Ribbon* and the *Quick Access* toolbar.
   a. Reset all *Ribbon* and the *Quick Access* toolbar customizations.
   b. Create a new group on the *Home* tab.
   c. Rename the new custom group as Skiing Unlimited and select a symbol of your choice.
   d. Add the following commands to the *Skiing Unlimited* group: **Date & Time**, **New Comment**, **Page Setup**, **Paragraph**, and **Tabs**.
   e. Move this group up so it appears between the *Paragraph* and *Styles* groups.
   f. Add **Open**, **Quick Print**, **Save As**, and **Track Changes** to the *Quick Access* toolbar.
3. Edit the document.
   a. Replace the "[year]" placeholder text (second and fifth body paragraphs) with 2015.
   b. Replace the placeholder text in the bulleted list with the following dates:

      January 18
      January 25
      February 1
      February 8
      February 15

4. Save the document and exit Word.
5. Upload files to your *SkyDrive*.
   a. Open an Internet browser page and log in to your *SkyDrive* account (www.skydrive.com).
   b. Open the **Skiing Unlimited** folder and upload the following files from your student data files: ***SkiingUnlimited-12*** and ***TrainingGuide-12***. The ***[your initials] Word 12-7*** document is already in this folder. If it is not, add it.
6. Edit comments in Word Web App.
   a. Open the ***SkiingUnlimited-12*** document in *read-only* mode in Word Web App.
   b. Reply to the existing comment and post the following comment: The dates are correct.
   c. Return to your *Skiing Unlimited* folder in *SkyDrive* and open the ***TrainingGuide-12*** document in *read-only* mode in Word Web App.
   d. Delete the existing comment.
   e. Share this file with your instructor, include a brief message, and allow him or her to edit the document.
7. Create a new group, invite a member, and add files.
   a. Create a new group named Skiing Unlimited.
   b. Type your last name, first initial, and -SU in the email area (e.g., NordellR-SU).
   c. Use your instructor's email address to invite him or her as a member.
   d. Upload the following files from your *Skiing Unlimited* folder in *SkyDrive* to the *Skiing Unlimited* group: ***[your initials] Word 12-7***, ***SkiingUnlimited-12***, and ***TrainingGuide-12***.
8. Sign out of *SkyDrive* (Figure 12-94).

Courtyard Medical Plaza

December 5, 2014

[Address block]

[Greeting line]

Courtyard Medical Plaza is a proud sponsor of the *Skiing Unlimited* program, which is an adaptive snow ski program for disabled children and adults. This program provides access to the sport of snow skiing for many blind, deaf, paraplegic, quadriplegic and developmentally disabled individuals who would otherwise be not have the opportunity to share in this exhilarating sport. With the help of trained volunteers and adaptive ski equipment, there are few disabilities too severe to prevent participation in the sport of snow skiing.

The 2015 ski season will be here before we know it, and this program is only able to continue through the hard work and dedication of our volunteers. Regardless of your level of snow skiing ability, there are things you can do to help. All ski trips are held at Boulder Creek Canyon Ski Resort. Volunteers and participants are responsible for their own transportation. Our group meets in the Olympic Room at 9:00 a.m. to coordinate volunteers and participants.

Below are the dates for this year's *Skiing Unlimited* program. Please contact me at 916-854-2299 or email at kellym@skiingunlimited.org to let her know the dates for which can volunteer. I will fax or e-mail you the volunteer registration packet.

If you have any questions regarding the *Skiing Unlimited* program, please feel free to contact me. Thank you for your commitment to the *Skiing Unlimited* program and its participants.

Our 2015 *Skiing Unlimited* dates are:

- January 18
- January 25
- February 1
- February 8
- February 15

Sincerely,

Kelly McFarland
Community Services Coordinator

12-94 Word 12-7 completed

Chall

SkyDrive
and subf
ber, it is
[Student

Note to

Student
Instructo

File Need
Complete

Create a
to the fol

- Create
- Create
  "Club
- Uploa
- Share

Challe

Now that
tomize th
Quick Ac
[Student

File Need
Complete

Create a
you have
and the *Q*

- Create
- Apply
  docum
- Modify

glossary

2 pages per sheet Custom page setting that splits a page horizontally into two pages.

A

Add Text Inserts text on a shape object.

Address Block Single merge field that groups individual merge fields to make a complete mailing address in mail merge.

alignment guides Vertical and horizontal green lines that appear when you drag a graphic object; help to align the object to margins, text, or other objects.

alternative text (alt text) Information tag that appears when a reader places the pointer on a table or graphic object; also used with screen readers to accommodate those with visual impairments.

app Short for application; software program or Windows 8 application or accessory.

Apps for Office Third-party applications users can add to Office application programs to provide enhanced functionality.

Artistic Effects Built-in formatting that can be applied to a picture.

ascending order Sort order that arranges data from lowest to highest for a numeric field or from A to Z for a text field.

aspect ratio Proportional size of an object that remains consistent when you resize an object; prevents object distortion.

AutoComplete Feature that fills in the complete day, month, or date as you type.

AutoCorrect Feature that corrects commonly misspelled words.

***AutoCorrect Options* smart tag** Tag that appears by a word that has been automatically corrected.

AutoFit Formatting option that automatically adjusts column width to adjust the width of a table.

AutoFormat Feature that controls the formatting of items such as numbered and bulleted lists, fractions, ordinal numbers, hyphens and dashes, quotes, indents, and hyperlinks.

AutoMacro A macro that automatically runs when an action, such as opening or closing a document, occurs.

AutoText Building block gallery where you store information; you can insert *AutoText* building blocks in a document.

axis (pl. axes) Vertical or horizontal boundary on the plot area of line, column, and bar charts.

axis title Chart element that names the horizontal and vertical axes using placeholders or textboxes.

B

***Backstage* view** Area of an Office application where you perform common actions, such as *Save*, *Open*, *Print*, and *Share*, and change application options; document properties are displayed here.

balloons Objects in the markup area that contain comments and changes.

Banded Columns *Table Style* option featuring columns that have alternating colors.

Banded Rows *Table Style* option featuring rows that have alternating colors.

bar chart Chart type that is similar to a column chart with bars shown horizontally.

bar tab stop Tab that inserts a vertical line at the tab stop.

bibliography List of the sources used in a report.

bibliography style Style that determines the formatting of sources and citations in a report.

Book fold Custom page setting that splits a page vertically into two pages.

bookmark Location in a document that is electronically marked and can be linked to a hyperlink or cross-reference.

border Line around text, paragraph, page, cell, table, or graphic object.

Border Painter Pointer used to draw borders on a table.

Border Sampler Tool that applies an existing border style on a table to other areas of a table; similar to the *Format Painter*.

Border Style Built-in border color, weight, and format applied to selected boundaries of a table.

building block Text, formatting, and/or object that is saved and can be inserted into a document; there are a variety of different building block galleries (e.g., *Quick Parts*, *AutoText*, *Header*, *Footer*, or *Tables*).

***Building Block Gallery* content control field** Word field in which users insert a building block into the content control field.

bulleted list Unordered list of items; a bullet symbol precedes each item, and a left and hanging indent controls left alignment.

button-activated macro A macro that runs when a button on the *Quick Access* toolbar or *Ribbon* is pressed.

C

caption Descriptive text that appears above or below a graphic.

cell Intersection of a column and a row.

cell address Letter of the column and number of the row that represents the location of a cell; also referred to as a cell reference.

cell margins Space around the top, bottom, left, and right of the text inside a table cell.

cell reference Column letter and row number that represents the location of the cell; also referred to as a cell address.

cell spacing Amount of space between cells in a table.

center tab stop Tab that centers text at the tab stop.

Change Case Button used to change text from the case shown to a different case such as uppercase to lowercase.

Change Colors Gallery that lists different color combinations for *SmartArt* layouts that are based on theme colors.

character spacing Space between letters and words.

***Character* style** Style that applies to selected text.

chart Object that displays numeric data in the form of a graph to compare data values or display data trends.

Chart Area One of several chart background elements; background area where the entire chart is displayed in a frame.

chart element One of the components that make up a chart, such as chart floor, chart area, data series, chart wall, etc.

chart floor Horizontal bottom area of a 3-D chart.

chart label A title, legend, or data table used to organize chart data.

chart object An object that represents a chart in a workbook.

Chart Styles Gallery that lists preset effects for chart elements.

chart title Chart element that names the chart using placeholders or text boxes.

chart type Category of charts that represent data using various shapes and subtypes.

chart walls Vertical side and back areas of a 3-D chart.

Check Accessibility Examines a document for potential issues that users with disabilities might have when using a screen reader or other adaptive resources.

check box Box that allows you to choose one or more from a group of options.

***Check Box* content control field** Word field in which users select or deselect a check box.

Check Compatibility Examines a document for potential version compatibility issues.

child table Table inside parent table.

citation Abbreviated source information in the body of a report that credits the source of information referred to in the document.

Clear Formatting Command that removes formatting from selected text and formats the text in *Normal* style.

clip art Electronic graphical image.

Clipboard Location where multiple copied items from an Office file or other source such as a web page are stored.

***Clipboard* pane** Pane that displays the contents of the *Clipboard*.

column Vertical grouping of cells in a table or a vertical area of text in a document.

Column Break Formatting option that ends a column and pushes subsequent text to the next column.

column selector Pointer that selects a column of a table.

Combine Tool that merges an original document and a revised document and displays differences between the two documents as marked changes.

***Combo Box* content control field** Word field in which users select from a list of options or type in their own response.

Comment Word collaboration feature that allows users to add notations to a document without affecting text or objects in the document.

Compare Tool that reviews an original document and a revised document and displays differences between the two documents as marked changes.

Compress Picture Feature that reduces the resolution and file size of a picture or all pictures in a document.

connected services Third-party services users can add to Office application programs, such as Facebook, LinkedIn, and YouTube.

Content Control Display Options that control how content control fields are shown in the document; there are three display (*Show as*) options: *Bounding Box*, *Start/End Tag*, and *None*.

content control field Word field in which you type custom information such as the date or year.

Content Control Field Properties Unique identifiers, content, and format of a content control field.

context menu Menu of commands that appears when you right-click text or an object.

context-sensitive Describes menu options that change depending on what you have selected.

Continuous Section Break Formatting option that divides a document into different sections on the same page so sections can be formatted independently of each other; can also be used at the end of columns to balance column length.

copy Duplicate text or other information.

crop Trim unwanted areas of a selected picture.

crosshair Large plus sign tool used to draw a shape.

cross-reference Note in a document that directs readers to another location in a document.

cross-reference index entry Index entry that references another index entry rather than a page number.

custom dictionary Location in Office where words that you add to the dictionary are stored.

cut Remove text or other information.

D

data label Numerical value on data plotted in a chart.

database An organized collection of integrated and related tables.

***Date Picker* content control field** Word field in which users select a date from a calendar

decimal tab stop Tab that aligns text at the decimal point at the tab stop.

default Setting that is automatically applied by an application unless you make specific changes.

descending order Sort order that arranges data from highest to lowest for a numeric field or from Z to A for a text field.

***Design* mode** Setting that allows users to edit placeholder text in content control fields.

destination file File where an object is inserted.

destination program Office application where an object is inserted.

dialog box Window that opens and displays additional features.

Different First Page Formatting option that imposes first-page header or footer content that differs from the other headers and footers in a document.

Different Odd & Even Pages Formatting option that imposes headers and/or footers that differ on odd and even pages.

Display for Review View options that show tracked changes and comments in a document; there are four *Display for Review* views: *Simple Markup*, *All Markup*, *No Markup*, and *Original*.

Distribute Columns Table option that evenly distributes column width.

Distribute Rows Table option that evenly distributes row height.

document property Information about a file such as title, author name, subject, etc.

document property field Word field that displays the document property contents in the body, header, or footer of a document.

Drop Cap Feature that changes the first letter or word of a paragraph to a larger font, graphic object.

***Drop-Down List* content control field** Word field in which users select from a list of options and are limited to those selections; users cannot type in their own response as they can in a *Combo Box* content control field.

drop-down list List of options that displays when you click a button.

E

edit mode Office Web Apps view where users can edit and save a file.

effect Formatting feature such as shadow, glow, or soft edges added to an element.

embed Insert an object from an Office application into another file; an embedded object is no longer connected to the original file and can be modified independently without affecting the original object.

Enable Content Button that activates content blocked by Word macro security settings.

Encrypt with Password Protects a document from being opened and edited; a password is required to open the document.

endnote Reference, citation, or other text that appears at the end of a document.

eraser Pointer used to erase parts of a table.

error bars Bars that display margin of error and standard deviation of data plotted in a chart.

extract Create a regular folder from a zipped folder.

F

field handle Area to select a document property of content control field.

field name Label associated with each field in a database or recipient list in mail merge.

File Explorer Window where you browse for, open, and manage files and folders (formerly called Windows Explorer).

file name extension A series of letters automatically added to a file name that identifies the type of file (e.g., *.docx*, *.dotx*, *.docm*, and *.dotm*).

Filter Feature used to select records in a recipients list that match specific criteria.

Find Feature that searches a file to locate specific text and/or formatting.

first line indent Horizontal space between the first line of a paragraph and the left margin.

footer Displays content at the bottom of a document page or object.

footnote Reference, citation, or other text that appears at the bottom of a page.

Format Painter Tool that duplicates formatting choices, such as font, font size, line spacing, indents, bullets, numbering, styles, etc., from one selection to another selection.

formula Mathematical syntax in a cell that calculates and updates results.

function Predefined formula that performs a specific task (e.g., *SUM* or *AVERAGE*).

G

gallery Group of options on a tab.

Gradient Option that blends two or more colors or light and dark variations of the current fill color in different directions.

graphics Visual objects such as pictures, clip art, shapes, *SmartArt*, charts, and *WordArt*.

grayscale A range of shades of black in a display or printout.

Greeting Line Single merge field that groups individual merge fields to make a complete salutation in a business letter in mail merge.

gridlines Lines that visually frame rows and columns in a table.

Group/Ungroup *Group* combines multiple graphic objects; *Ungroup* separates previously grouped objects into separate objects; also used with content control fields to restrict editing of a document and allow editing only of content control fields.

group Area on a tab that contains related commands and options.

***Gutter* margins** Custom page settings that add extra margin space at the top or left of a document to accommodate binding.

H

hanging indent Additional horizontal space between second and carry-over lines of a paragraph and the left margin.

header Displays content at the top of each page of a document.

header row First row of a table.

Highlight Merge Fields Feature used in mail merge to shade all merge fields in a document to visually identify the location of the merge fields.

horizontal alignment Content positioning option that aligns material in relation to the left, center, right, or middle (justified) of the margins, column, or cell; can also refer to the position of objects in relation to each other.

hyperlink Text or an object that a reader can click to be taken to another location in the document, to a web page, or to a different file.

Hyphenation Feature that automatically hyphenates text in a document; facilitates tighter text wrapping at the right margin.

I

Import/Export Styles Tool that copies styles from one document to another.

index Alphabetical list of key words with page number references for where they can be found in a document, typically found at the end of a document; also called an index page.

index entry Text, bookmark, or location in a document that is marked with a field code and is used to generate an index page.

index field code Word field code that marks an index entry.

insert control Button that allows you to quickly insert a row or column into a table.

Inspect Document Examines a document for hidden content, properties, or personal information that might create document compatibility issues.

J

justified alignment Content positioning option that aligns material with both the left and right margins.

K

kerning Space between letters in a proportional font.

keyboard shortcut Key or combination of keys that you press to apply a command.

keyboard-activated macro A macro that runs when a keystroke combination is pressed.

L

Labels Pre-defined table format used to arrange information so it prints correctly on a sheet of labels; can be used to create individual labels, a full sheet of the same label, or in mail merge.

landscape orientation Page layout option in which the page is oriented so it is wider than it is tall.

leader Series of dots or characters that fills the blank space between text and a tab stop.

left indent Horizontal space between a paragraph and the left margin.

left tab stop Tab that aligns text at the left of the tab stop.

Legacy Tools Content control fields available in previous versions of Word.

legend Descriptive text in a table that describes a data series.

line break Formatting option that controls where lines begin and end; can be used to keep lines together in a bulleted or numbered list.

Line Numbers Feature that automatically numbers lines in a document; facilitates collaborative editing and reviewing process.

line spacing Amount of space between lines of text within a paragraph.

link Insert an object from an Office application file into another file; linking maintains a connection between the source file and the destination file, and when the original object is modified, the linked object updates automatically.

***Linked* style** Style that applies to selected text or an entire paragraph.

***List* style** Style that applies a numbered or bulleted list style to selected paragraphs.

***Live* layout** Feature that automatically and instantly rearranges text and other objects when you drag a graphic object to a different location.

live preview Display option that allows you to temporarily apply and view a style or formatting feature.

lock a subdocument Protect a subdocument from being modified within a master document; users can edit the original subdocument file, and changes are reflected in the master document.

Lock Tracking Keeps *Track Changes* turned on so all changes reviewers make are marked.

M

macro Recorded combination of instructions and keystrokes that are saved and can be inserted in other documents.

Macro Security Settings Options that control how macros are handled when a user opens a document.

macro-enabled document Word document that contains macros.

macro-enabled template Word template that contains macros; a document based on a macro-enabled template contains the macros that are stored in the template.

Mail Merge Feature that combines information from a recipient list into a main document, such as a letter or labels.

mail merge rule Controls the results of a mail merge by applying a condition and action to the merge.

Mail Merge Wizard Step-by-step instructions to guide a user to create a mail merge.

main document Document where a mail merge is performed, such as a letter or labels.

Manage Versions Allows users to recover a previous version of a document.

margin Blank space at the top, bottom, left, or right of a document; in a text box, the space between the outside of the box and the text within the box; in a table, the space between a cell border and the cell text.

Mark as Final Saves a document and prevents it from being edited.

markup area Area outside the right margin of a document where comments and tracked changes display.

master document File containing links to one or more subdocuments.

Match Fields Feature used in mail merge to select fields from a recipient list to match corresponding fields in an address block or greeting line.

mathematical order of operations Set of rules that establishes the sequence that operations are performed in multiple-operation expressions and formulas.

maximize Increase the size of the window of an open Office file so it fills the entire computer monitor.

Merge Completes a mail merge by inserting information from the recipient list into the merge fields in the main document.

Merge Cells Command that combines two or more cells in a row or column.

merge field An individual piece of information from a recipient list, such as first name, last name, or company name, that is inserted in the main document during a mail merge.

merge subdocuments Combine two or more subdocuments in a master document.

Microsoft Account User profile used to log in to Windows 8 and Microsoft Office 2013; this free account also provides access to *SkyDrive*, *SkyDrive* group, and Office Web Apps.

Microsoft Visual Basic editor Program used to edit macro code.

mini toolbar Toolbar listing formatting options that appears when you select text or right-click.

minimize Place an open Office file on the *Taskbar* so it is not displayed on the desktop.

***Mirror* margins** Margin settings for multi-page documents that are printed on both sides; ensures consistent margin space when the document is bound on the left.

multilevel list Customized list that includes a combination of numbers, letters, or bullets.

N

nested table A table inside another table; the main table is the parent table, and tables inside the parent table are child tables.

non-breaking space Formatting option that keeps words together so they are not separated by word wrap at the end of a line.

***Normal* template** Predesigned and ready-to-use document that includes default fonts, font sizes, line and paragraph spacing, styles, and margins; new blank document (*Normal.dotx*).

numbered list List that arranges items in order; a number or letter precedes each item, and a left and hanging indent controls left alignment.

***NumPages* field** Word field that lists the number of pages in a document.

O

Object Linking and Embedding (OLE) Integration feature to insert content from other Office application files into a Word document.

Office Background Color of the working environment in Word.

Office Theme Graphic image display in the working environment of Word.

Office Web Apps Free online Microsoft Office software applications that allow users to create, save, and edit Office files; Office Web Apps are accessed from online *SkyDrive* accounts.

online Word template Preset template available on Office.com that users can use to create documents and customize content.

operating system Software that makes a computer function and controls the working environment.

operator Mathematical symbol used in formulas.

outdent Negative indent that lines up information outside the left or right margins.

outline Border around selected element.

***Outline* view** View option used to arrange and edit subdocuments in a master document.

P

Page Break Formatting option that controls where text on a page ends.

Page Color Fill color, color gradient, picture, or texture applied to the entire page(s) of a document.

***Page* number field** Word field that lists the page number.

paragraph alignment Formatting option that determines how a paragraph is positioned horizontally on the page.

Paragraph Break Formatting option that you insert when you press *Enter* at the end of a word, line, or paragraph.

paragraph spacing Amount of spacing before and after a paragraph.

***Paragraph* style** Style that applies to an entire paragraph.

paragraph symbol Icon that indicates a paragraph break.

parent table The main table that has child tables inside of it.

paste Place text or other objects that have been stored on the *Clipboard* in a new location.

Paste Special Dialog box that allows users to choose how a copied object or text is inserted into a document.

PDF (portable document format) File format used to convert a file into a static image.

pen Pointer used to draw a table or add columns, rows, or cells.

picture anchor Location in a document where an object connects to text.

***Picture* content control field** Word field in which users insert a picture into the field.

Picture Correction Options Feature that sharpens, softens, or changes the brightness or contrast of a picture by a percentage of its original resolution.

Picture Fill *Shape Fill* option that fills the *WordArt* or shape with a picture from a file or from the Office.com clip art collection.

placeholder Text that temporarily marks a spot in a document where a citation is missing and needs to be completed.

***Plain Text* content control field** Word field in which users can type text; all of the text in the field is formatted the same way.

plot area Area of a chart that displays chart data.

pointer Small icon, such as a block plus sign, thin black plus sign, or white arrow, that appears and moves when you move your mouse or touch your touchpad.

portrait orientation Page layout option in which the page is oriented so it is taller than it is wide.

position A character-spacing option that raises or lowers text by a designated number of points.

Preview Mail Merge Displays information from the recipient list in the merge fields in a main document in mail merge.

program options Area in each Office application where you can make changes to the program settings.

protection Layer of security you can apply to a document for form fields that allows various areas to be accessible while others are not.

Q

***Quick Access* toolbar** Area located above the *Ribbon* with buttons you use to perform commonly used commands.

Quick Parts Building block gallery where you store information; you can insert *Quick Parts* building blocks in a document.

Quick Tables Gallery of built-in and custom table building blocks.

R

radio button Round button you click to choose one option from a list.

range Group of cells.

read-only mode Office Web Apps view where users can view and add comments to a file.

recipients Data that can be merged into a main document from an external source, such as an Excel worksheet, Access database, or text file, used in mail merge.

record Collection of related data fields used in mail merge.

Recycle Bin Location where deleted files and folders are stored.

Redo Repeat an action.

reference marker Number, letter, or symbol that marks a footnote or endnote in the body of a document.

Replace Feature that searches a file to locate specific text and/or formatting and replace it with specified replacement text and/or formatting.

Reset Picture Command used to restore a picture's original characteristics and dimensions.

resizing pointer Pointer that resizes a graphic object or a table column or row.

restore down Decrease the size of the window of an open Office file so it does not fill the entire computer monitor.

Restrict Editing Protects an entire document or portions of a document; a user can customize to allow comments or tracked changes.

reviewer User who inserts comments and changes in a document; a document can have multiple reviewers.

***Reviewing* pane** Area to the left of the Word window where tracked changes and comments display.

Ribbon Bar that appears at the top of an Office file window and displays available commands.

***Rich Text* content control field** Word field in which users can type and format some or all of the text.

right indent Horizontal space between a paragraph and the right margin.

right tab stop Tab that aligns text at the right of the tab stop.

roles Settings in *SkyDrive* groups that control members' ability to view, edit, create, and delete folders and files in the group.

rotation handle Green circle that rotates a graphic object.

row Horizontal grouping of cells.

row selector Pointer that selects a row of a table.

Ruler Vertical or horizontal guide that displays measurements within the margins of a document.

S

sans serif font One of several font typefaces with letters that do not include structural details (flair).

scale Character-spacing option that changes spacing by a designated percentage.

screen clipping A capture of a portion of an open window on your computer as a graphic object.

screenshot A capture of an open window on your computer as a graphic object.

ScreenTip Descriptive information about a button, drop-down list, launcher, or gallery selection that appears when you place your pointer on the item.

section break Formatting option used to break a document into different sections so sections can be formatted independently of each other.

Select Recipients Feature used in mail merge to choose the recipients that will be merged into the main document.

***Selection* pane** Window that displays graphic objects in a document; used to select, rearrange, group, or hide objects.

selection/move pointer Four-pointed arrow that selects and moves objects.

serif font One of several font typefaces with letters that feature structural details (flair).

shading Fill color applied to text, paragraph, page, cell, table, or graphic object.

Shadow Style effect option that provides dimension by inserting a shadow behind or below text or an object.

shape Graphic object that can be drawn, such as a line, arrow, circle, or rectangle.

shape adjustment handle Yellow diamond that changes the contour of a shape.

shape effect Format feature, such as *Shadow*, *Reflection*, or *Glow*, applied to a graphic object.

Shape Fill Color, gradient color, picture, or texture applied to a graphic object.

Shape Outline Border, border color, and border weight applied to a graphic object.

Shape Style Set of built-in formats for shapes that include borders, fill colors, and effect components.

share Allow other users access to a *Skydrive* folder or file.

Show/Hide Button that displays or hides paragraph breaks, line breaks, spaces, tabs, and other formatting symbols in a document.

sizing handles Squares on the corners and sides of an object that resize the object.

SkyDrive Online (cloud) storage area that is a part of your Microsoft account where you can store and access documents from any computer with an Internet connection.

***SkyDrive* folder** Windows folder that displays folders and files stored on a user's *SkyDrive* account; synchronizes folders and files stored in the *SkyDrive* folder with *SkyDrive* cloud storage.

***SkyDrive* group** Free Microsoft online service where folders and files can be stored and users can be invited to become members; group members have access to folders and files stored in the *SkyDrive* group.

SmartArt Object that presents information in graphical format.

SmartArt Styles Gallery that lists different effects for emphasizing shapes within a layout.

Soft Edges Style effect option that creates a feathered edge, which gradually blends into the background color.

soft page break Formatting option that allows text to flow to the next page when it reaches the bottom margin of a page.

Sort Feature that arranges text, table rows, or records in alphabetical or numerical order.

source Complete bibliographic reference for a book, journal article, or web page.

source documents The two documents (original and revised) used when comparing and combining documents.

source file File where content is stored.

source program Office application where content is created.

split a subdocument Create a new subdocument from a portion of a subdocument.

split cells Divide a single cell into two or more cells.

split table Divides an existing table into two tables.

style Set of built-in formats, which include a variety of borders, shading, alignment, and other options.

***Style* gallery** Collection of preset effects for text, shapes, pictures, or other objects.

Style Set Group of styles and formatting applied to an entire document.

style template Word template used to store styles; a new document based upon a style template contains the styles in the styles template; a style template can be attached to a document so styles are available and update automatically.

Styles Organizer Dialog box that allows users to copy styles from one document or template to another document or template; also referred to as the *Organizer* dialog box.

***Styles* pane** Window that opens on the right and displays styles in a document where you can insert or modify styles.

subdocument File inserted into and linked to a master document.

subentry Index entry that is subordinate to a main index entry.

syntax Rules that dictate how the various parts of a formula must be written.

T

tab Area on the *Ribbon* that lists groups of related commands and options.

tab selector Button at the top of the vertical *Ruler* where you select the type of tab stop you want to set on the *Ruler*.

tab stop Marker that controls where the insertion point stops when *Tab* is pressed.

table Information arranged in columns and rows.

***Table* building block** An entire table saved as a building block that can be inserted in a document; table building blocks are stored in the *Quick Tables* gallery.

table of contents List of topics in a document; lists headings in the document and related page numbers.

***Table* properties** Alignment, text wrapping, size, and position options for an entire table.

table selector handle Handle that appears at the upper left of a table when the pointer is on a table.

***Table* style** Built-in formats for tables, which include a variety of borders, shading, alignment, and other options.

Table Style Options Tool that applies table style formatting to specific areas of a table, such as header row, first column, or banded rows.

target frame Window where a reader is directed when a hyperlink document or web site opens.

task pane Area at the left or right of an Office application window where you can perform tasks.

Taskbar Horizontal area at the bottom of the Windows desktop where you can launch programs or open folders.

template Predesigned and ready-to-use file upon which other Word documents can be created and modified; a Word template has a *.dotx* file name extension.

text box Graphic object where you can type text.

***Text* pane** Area where you enter text for *SmartArt* shapes.

text wrapping Formatting option that controls how text wraps around a graphic.

theme Collection of fonts, colors, and effects that you can apply to an entire document, workbook, or presentation.

theme colors Set of background and accent colors.

theme fonts Pair of fonts used in headings and body text.

Thesaurus Resource tool that lists synonyms for a selected word.

thumbnail Small picture of an image or layout.

tick marks Symbols that identify the categories, values, or series on an axis.

Track Changes Word feature that marks text and formatting changes in a document.

Track Changes Options Settings that customize how changes and comments are tracked and displayed in a document.

U

Undo Reverse an action.

unlink a subdocument Break the links between the master document and the subdocument file.

up/down bars Bars that display between data points on a line chart.

Update Labels Feature used in mail merge to insert merge fields that were inserted into the first label into the remaining labels.

V

value Number that you type in a cell for numbers, currency, dates, and percentages.

value axis (Y axis) Vertical border in the plot area that measures charted data.

vertical alignment Content positioning option that aligns material in relation to the top, bottom, or middle of the page; can also refer to the position of objects in relation to each other.

Visual Basic Programming language used to record and store macros.

W

watermark Background text or image that appears on every page of a document.

***Watermark* building block** Saved watermark object that you can insert from the *Watermark* gallery.

weight Thickness of an outline measured in points.

white space Blank space around text and objects in a document; improves the readability of a document and prevents the document from appearing cluttered.

Windows desktop Working area in Windows.

Windows *Start* page Opening area of Windows where you select and open programs or apps.

Word field Code inserted in a document that controls content display (e.g., a document property field, formula field, or page number field).

Word Options Dialog box that allows users to customize global Word settings.

word wrap Formatting option that ensures that text automatically continues to the next line when a line ends at the right margin.

WordArt Graphic object that visually enhances text.

worksheet Individual sheet within an Excel workbook; also referred to as a sheet; comparable to a page in a book.

wrap points Locations on a graphic object that function as boundaries for an object and determine where text wraps around the object; you can adjust wrap points for precise text wrapping.

Wrap Text Formatting tool that enables you to display the contents of a cell on multiple lines.

X axis Axis displayed horizontally, usually on the bottom of a chart; also called the category axis.

Y axis Axis displayed vertically, usually on the left of a chart; also called the value axis.

Z

zipped (compressed) folder Folder that has a reduced file size and can be attached to an email.

Zoom Change file display size.

appendices

APPENDIX A

Common Office 2013 Keyboard Shortcuts

Action	Keyboard Shortcut
Save	Ctrl+S
Copy	Ctrl+C
Cut	Ctrl+X
Paste	Ctrl+V
Select All	Ctrl+A
Bold	Ctrl+B
Italic	Ctrl+I
Underline	Ctrl+U
Close *Start* page or *Backstage* view	Esc
Open *Help* dialog box	F1
Switch windows	Alt+Tab

Word 2013 Keyboard Shortcuts

Action	Keyboard Shortcut
File Management	
Save	Ctrl+S
Open *Save As* dialog box	F12
Open a new blank Word document	Ctrl+N
Open an existing document from the *Backstage* view	Ctrl+O
Open an existing document from the *Open* dialog box	Ctrl+F12
Close a document	Ctrl+W
Editing	
Toggle on/off *Show/Hide*	Ctrl+Shift+8
Copy	Ctrl+C
Cut	Ctrl+X
Paste	Ctrl+V
Bold	Ctrl+B
Italic	Ctrl+I
Underline	Ctrl+U
Left align text	Ctrl+L
Center text	Ctrl+E
Right align text	Ctrl+R
Justify text	Ctrl+J
Single line spacing	Ctrl+1

Action	Keyboard Shortcut
Double line spacing	Ctrl+2
1.5 line spacing	Ctrl+5
Undo	Ctrl+Z
Repeat/Redo	Ctrl+Y
Insert line break	Shift+Enter
Insert page break	Ctrl+Enter
Insert column break	Ctrl+Shift+Enter
Insert non-breaking space	Ctrl+Shift+spacebar
Copy formatting	Ctrl+Shift+C
Paste formatting	Ctrl+Shift+V
Increase font size	Ctrl+Shift+. (Ctrl+>)
Decrease font size	Ctrl+Shift+, (Ctrl+<)
Insert an endnote	Alt+Ctrl+D
Insert a footnote	Alt+Ctrl+F
Update field	F9
Toggle on/off *View all field codes*	Alt+F9
Toggle on/off *Track Changes*	Ctrl+Shift+E
Promote to a higher level in *Outline* view	Alt+Shift+left arrow
Demote to a lower level in *Outline* view	Alt+Shift+right arrow
Move selected text up in *Outline* view	Alt+Shift+up arrow
Move selected text down in *Outline* view	Alt+Shift+down arrow
Expand/Collapse subdocuments	Ctrl+\
Open Panes and Dialog Boxes	
Print area on the *Backstage* view	Ctrl+P
Open *Apply Styles* pane	Ctrl+Shift+S
Open *Navigation* pane	Ctrl+F
Open *Spelling and Grammar* pane	F7
Open *Styles* pane	Alt+Ctrl+Shift+S
Open *Thesaurus* pane	Shift+F7
Open *Find and Replace* dialog box with the *Go To* tab selected	Ctrl+G or F5
Open *Find and Replace* dialog box with the *Replace* tab selected	Ctrl+H
Open *Font* dialog box	Ctrl+D
Open *Insert Hyperlink* dialog box	Ctrl+K
Open *Macros* dialog box	Alt+F8
Open *Mark Index Entry* dialog box	Alt+Shift+X
Open *Paste Special* dialog box	Alt+Ctrl+V
Open Visual Basic editor	Alt+F11
Open *Word Help* dialog box	F1

Action	Keyboard Shortcut
Selection and Navigation	
Select all	Ctrl+A
Turn selection on (continue to press F8 to select word, sentence, paragraph, or document)	F8
Move the insertion point to the beginning of the document	Ctrl+Home
Move the insertion point to the end of the document	Ctrl+End
Move the insertion point to the beginning of a line	Ctrl+left arrow
Move the insertion point to the end of a line	Ctrl+right arrow
Switch window	Alt+Tab

index

Symbols

Numbers

A

B

C

E

F

G

H

I

J

K

L

M

N

P

Q

R

S

T

U

V

W